Best Jobs™ for the 21st Century

Fourth Edition

Part of JIST's Best Jobs™ Series

Michael Farr

With Database Work by Laurence Shatkin, Ph.D.

Also in JIST's *Best Jobs* Series

- *300 Best Jobs Without a Four-Year Degree*
- *200 Best Jobs for College Graduates*
- *250 Best Jobs Through Apprenticeships*
- *50 Best Jobs for Your Personality*
- *40 Best Fields for Your Career*
- *225 Best Jobs for Baby Boomers*

jist Works
America's Career Publisher

Best Jobs for the 21st Century, Fourth Edition

© 2006 by JIST Publishing, Inc.

Published by JIST Works, an imprint of JIST Publishing, Inc.
8902 Otis Avenue
Indianapolis, IN 46216-1033

Phone: 1-800-648-JIST   Fax: 1-800-JIST-FAX
E-mail: info@jist.com   Web site: www.jist.com

Best Jobs for the 21st Century was chosen as one of the top three career books of the year at the Publishers Marketing Association's Benjamin Franklin awards.

Some Other Books by the Authors

Michael Farr

Seven-Step Job Search

The Quick Resume & Cover Letter Book

Getting the Job You Really Want

The Very Quick Job Search

Laurence Shatkin

Quick Guide to College Majors and Careers

Quick Guide to Career Training in Two Years
or Less

Quantity discounts are available for JIST products. Please call 1-800-648-JIST or visit www.jist.com for a free catalog and more information.

Visit www.jist.com for information on JIST, free job search information, book excerpts, and ordering information on our many products. For free information on 14,000 job titles, visit www.careeroink.com.

Acquisitions Editor: Susan Pines
Development Editor: Stephanie Koutek
Cover and Interior Designer: Aleata Howard
Interior Layout: Carolyn J. Newland
Proofreader: Linda Seifert
Indexer: Jeanne Clark

Printed in the United States of America

10 09 08 07 06 05   9 8 7 6 5 4 3 2 1

Library of Congress Cataloging-in-Publication data is on file with the Library of Congress.

ISBN 1-59357-240-9

This Is a Big Book, But It Is Very Easy to Use

This book is designed to help you explore career options in a variety of interesting ways. The nice thing about it is that you don't have to read it all. Instead, we designed it to allow you to browse and find information that most interests you.

The table of contents will give you a good idea of what's inside and how to use the book, so we suggest you start there. Part I of the book is made up of interesting lists that will help you explore jobs based on pay, interests, education level, personality type, and many other criteria. Part II provides descriptions for each job included in the book. Just find a job that interests you in one of the lists in Part I and look up its description in Part II. Simple.

How We Selected the Best Jobs for the 21st Century

Deciding on the "best" job is a choice that only you can make, but objective criteria can help you identify jobs that are, for example, better paying than other jobs with similar duties. Here is an explanation of the process we used to determine which jobs to include in this book.

We sorted 905 major jobs in terms of earnings, growth rate through 2012, and number of annual openings. We then assigned a number to their relative position on each list, with 1 being the best. The job position numbers on the three lists were then combined, and the jobs were ranked by total score. We included the top 500 jobs in the book. The first list in Part I is called "The 500 Best Jobs Overall," and it contains the 500 best jobs in order of their combined scores on all three measures (earnings, growth rate, and openings).

Of the 905 major jobs, one was a job called Postsecondary Teachers, which is actually a composite that we created from 36 specialized postsecondary teaching jobs that are described by Department of Labor databases. A list of these specialized job titles is provided in the introduction to Part I.

You can find descriptions for all 500 best jobs in Part II, along with descriptions of the various specialized postsecondary teaching jobs, for a total of 535 descriptions in all.

(continued)

(continued)

We are not suggesting that the 500 jobs with the best overall scores for earnings, growth, and number of openings are all good ones for you to consider—some will not be. But the 500 jobs that met our criteria present such a wide range of jobs that you are likely to find one or more that will interest you. The jobs that met our "best jobs" criteria are also more likely than average to have higher pay, faster projected growth, and a larger number of openings than other jobs at similar levels of education and training.

Some Things You Can Do with This Book

- Identify more-interesting or better-paying jobs that don't require additional training or education.
- Develop long-term plans that may require additional training, education, or experience.
- Explore and select a college major or a training or educational program that relates to a career objective.
- Find reliable earnings information to negotiate pay.
- Prepare for interviews and the job search.

These are a few of the many ways you can use this book. We hope you find it as interesting to browse as we did to put together. We have tried to make it easy to use and as interesting as occupational information can be.

When you are done with this book, pass it along or tell someone else about it. We wish you well in your career and in your life.

Credits and Acknowledgments: While the authors created this book, it is based on the work of many others. The occupational information is based on data obtained from the U.S. Department of Labor and the U.S. Census Bureau. These sources provide the most authoritative occupational information available. The job titles and their related descriptions are from the O*NET database, which was developed by researchers and developers under the direction of the U.S. Department of Labor. They, in turn, were assisted by thousands of employers who provided details on the nature of work in the many thousands of job samplings used in the database's development. We used the most recent version of the O*NET database, release 8.0. We appreciate and thank the staff of the U.S. Department of Labor for their efforts and expertise in providing such a rich source of data.

Table of Contents

Summary of Major Sections

Introduction. A short overview to help you better understand and use the book. *Starts on page 1.*

Part I—The Best Jobs Lists. Very useful for exploring career options! Lists are arranged into easy-to-use groups. The first group of lists presents the best overall jobs–jobs with the highest earnings, projected growth, and number of openings. More-specialized lists follow, presenting the best jobs for workers age 16–24, workers 55 and over, part-time workers, self-employed workers, women, and men. Other lists present the best jobs at various levels of education, by interest, and by personality type. The column starting at right presents all the list titles within the groups. *Starts on page 13.*

Part II—The Job Descriptions. Provides complete descriptions of the 500 jobs that met our criteria for high pay, fast growth, or large number of openings plus the more-specialized jobs included in the Teachers, Postsecondary, job title. Each description contains information on earnings, projected growth, job duties, skills, related job titles, education and training required, related knowledge and courses, and many other details. *Starts on page 141.*

Detailed Table of Contents

Table of Contents

Introduction

We kept this introduction short to encourage you to actually read it. For this reason, we don't provide many details on the technical issues involved in creating the job lists or descriptions. Instead, we give you short explanations to help you understand and use the information the book provides for career exploration or planning. We think this brief and user-oriented approach makes sense for most people who will use this book.

Who This Book Is For and What It Covers

We created this book to help students and adults explore their career, education, training, and life options. Employers, educators, program planners, career counselors, and others will also find this book to be of value.

To create it, we started with more than 900 major jobs at all levels of training and education. From these, we selected those with the highest earnings, projected growth rate, and number of job openings. Part I contains lists that rank the jobs according to many criteria, including earnings, growth, openings, education level, and interest area. Part II contains job descriptions for all of the jobs.

We think you will find many of the job lists in Part I interesting and useful for identifying career options to consider. The job descriptions are also packed with useful information.

Where the Information Comes From

The information we used in creating this book comes from three major government sources:

⊙ **The U.S. Department of Labor:** We used a variety of data sources to construct the information we used in this book. We started with the jobs included in the U.S. Department of Labor's O*NET database. The O*NET includes information on more than 1,000 occupations and is now the primary source of detailed information on occupations. The Labor Department updates the O*NET on a regular basis, and we used the most recent one available, version 8.

◎ **The U.S. Census Bureau:** Because we wanted to include earnings, growth, number of openings, and other data not included in the O*NET, we used information on earnings from the U.S. Department of Labor's Bureau of Labor Statistics (BLS). Some of this data came from the Current Population Survey, conducted by the U.S. Census Bureau, and other data came from the BLS's own Occupational Employment Statistics survey. The information on earnings is the most reliable information we could obtain. The BLS uses a slightly different system of job titles than the O*NET does, but we were able to link the BLS data to most of the O*NET job titles we used to develop this book. The Current Population Survey also provided information about the proportion of workers in each job who are self employed or work part time.

◎ **The U.S. Department of Education:** We used the Classification of Instructional Programs, a system developed by the U.S. Department of Education, to cross-reference the education or training programs related to each job.

Data Complexities

For those of you who like details, we present some of the complexities inherent in our sources of information and what we did to make sense of them here. You don't need to know this to use the book, so jump to the next section of the introduction if you are bored with details.

Earnings, Growth, and Number of Openings

We include information on earnings, projected growth, and number of job openings for each job throughout this book. We think this information is important to most people, but getting it for each job is not a simple task.

Earnings

The employment security agency of each state gathers information on earnings for various jobs and forwards it to the U.S. Bureau of Labor Statistics. This information is organized in standardized ways by a BLS program called the Occupational Employment Statistics, or OES. To keep the earnings for the various jobs and regions comparable, the OES screens out certain types of earnings and includes others, so the OES earnings we use in this book represent straight-time gross pay, exclusive of premium pay. More specifically, the OES earnings include the job's base rate; cost-of-living allowances; guaranteed pay; hazardous-duty pay; incentive pay, including commissions and production bonuses; on-call pay; and tips, but they do not include back pay, jury duty pay, overtime pay, severance pay, shift differentials, non-production bonuses, or tuition reimbursements. Also, self-employed workers are not included in the earnings estimates, and they can be a significant segment in certain occupations. The average earnings for all workers in all occupations was $28,770 in May 2004.

The OES earnings data uses a system of job titles called the Standard Occupational Classification system, or SOC. Most of these jobs can be cross-referenced to the O*NET job titles we use in this book, so we can attach earnings information to most job titles and descriptions. But a small number of the O*NET jobs simply do not have earnings data available for them from the sources we used and therefore were not included. In some other cases, an SOC title cross-references to more than one O*NET job title. For example, the O*NET has separate information for Accountants and for Auditors, but the SOC reports earnings for a single occupation called Accountants and Auditors. Therefore you may notice that the salary we report for Accountants ($50,770) is identical to the salary we report for Auditors. In reality there probably is a difference, but this is the best information that is available.

Projected Growth and Number of Job Openings

This information comes from the Office of Occupational Statistics and Employment Projections, a program within the Bureau of Labor Statistics that develops information about projected trends in the nation's labor market for the next ten years. The most recent projections available cover the years from 2002 to 2012. The projections are based on information about people moving into and out of occupations. The BLS uses data from various sources in projecting the growth and number of openings for each job title—some data comes from the Census Bureau's Current Population Survey and some comes from an OES survey. The projections assume that there will be no major war, depression, or other economic upheaval.

Like the earnings figures, the figures on projected growth and job openings are reported according to the SOC classification, so again we had to exclude a few jobs from this book because this information is not available for them. As with earnings, some of the SOC jobs crosswalk to more than one O*NET job. To continue the example we used above, SOC reports growth (19.5%) and openings (119,000) for one occupation called Accountants and Auditors, but in this book we report these figures separately for the occupation Accountants and for the occupation Auditors. When you see that Accountants has a 19.5% projected growth rate and 119,000 projected job openings and Auditors has the same two numbers, you should realize that the 19.5% rate of projected growth represents the average of these two occupations—one may actually experience higher growth than the other—and that these two occupations will share the 119,000 projected openings.

While salary figures are fairly straightforward, you may not know what to make of job-growth figures. For example, is projected growth of 15.0% good or bad? You should keep in mind that the average (mean) growth projected for all occupations in the OES survey is 14.8%. One quarter of the occupations have a growth projection of 4.7% or lower. Growth of 12.6% is the median, meaning that half of the occupations have more, half less. Only one quarter of the occupations have growth projected at more than 19.4%.

Remember, however, that the jobs in this book are a distinguished set—they were selected as "best" partly on the basis of high growth, so their mean growth is a lofty 18.2%. Among these 500 high-powered jobs, the job ranked 125th by projected growth has a figure of 23.0%, the job ranked 250th (the median) has a projected growth of 17.0%, and the job ranked 375th has a projected growth of 11.4%.

Information in the Job Descriptions

We used a variety of government and other sources to compile the job descriptions we provide in Part II. Details on these various sources are mentioned later in this introduction in the section "Part II: The Job Descriptions."

How the 500 Best Jobs Were Selected

The "This Is a Big Book" section at the beginning of this book gives a brief description of how we selected the jobs we include in this book. Here are a few more details:

1. We began by creating our own database of information from the O*NET, the Census Bureau, and other sources to include the information we wanted. This database covered 1,167 job titles at all levels of education and training.

2. We eliminated 212 O*NET jobs for which we lacked useful information, plus an additional eight jobs that are expected to employ fewer than 500 workers per year and to shrink rather than grow in workforce size. We also combined 36 very similar college teaching jobs into one job.

3. We created three lists that ranked the remaining 905 jobs based on three major criteria: median annual earnings, projected growth through 2012, and number of job openings projected per year. Each of these lists was then sorted from highest to lowest and assigned a score based on its position on each list, from 1 to 905.

4. We then added the number scores for all three lists. The higher a job landed on each list, the lower its score was, so we sorted the total scores from lowest to highest total score. We then assigned a position number from 1 to 905 to each job. Job titles with lower total scores were listed first. For example, the job of Computer Software Engineers, Applications, has the lowest total combined score, so Computer Software Engineers, Applications, is listed first in our 500 Best Jobs Overall list, even though this job is not the highest-paying job (which is a tie between Anesthesiologists; Internists, General; Obstetricians and Gynecologists; Oral and Maxillofacial Surgeons; Orthodontists; Prosthodontists; Psychiatrists; and Surgeons), the fastest-growing job (which is Medical Assistants), or the job with the most openings (which is Cashiers). Only those 500 jobs with the lowest or "best" total scores were selected to be included in this book.

Why This Book Has More Than 500 Jobs

We didn't think you would mind that this book actually provides information on more than 500 jobs. Among the jobs it includes are 36 specialized postsecondary education jobs that we combined into one job called Teachers, Postsecondary. We use this one job title throughout the lists but provide descriptions for all 36 specialized postsecondary jobs in Part II. This means that we used 500 job titles to construct the lists, but we have a total of 535 job descriptions in Part II. You can find a list of the 36 specialized postsecondary teaching jobs in the "Some Details on the Lists" section at the beginning of Part I.

The Data in This Book Can Be Misleading

We use the most reliable data we can obtain for the earnings, projected growth, number of openings, and other information to create this book, but keep in mind that this information may or may not be accurate for your situation. This is because the information is true on the average. But just as there is no precisely average person, there is no such thing as a statistically average example of a particular job. We say this because data, while helpful, can also be misleading.

Take, for example, the yearly earnings information in this book. This is highly reliable data obtained from a very large U.S. working population sample by the Bureau of Labor Statistics. It tells us the median annual pay received by people in various job titles. This sounds very useful until you consider that half of all people in that occupation earned less than that amount and half earn more. (We often use "average" instead of "median" elsewhere in this book for ease of explanation.)

For example, people just entering the occupation or people with few years of work experience will often earn much less than the average. People who live in rural areas or who work for smaller employers typically earn less than those who do similar work in cities, where the cost of living is higher, or for larger employers.

So, in reviewing the information in this book, please understand the limitations of the data it presents. You need to use common sense in career decision-making as in most other things in life. Even so, we hope that you find the information helpful and interesting.

Part I: The Best Jobs Lists

There are 67 separate lists in Part I of this book—look in the table of contents for a complete list of them. The lists are not difficult to understand because they have clear titles and are organized into groupings of related lists.

Depending on your situation, some of the jobs lists in Part I will interest you more than others. For example, if you are young, you may be interested to learn the highest-paying jobs that employ high percentages of workers age 16–24. Other lists show jobs within interest groupings, by personality type, by level of education, and in other ways that you might find helpful in exploring your career options.

Whatever your situation, we suggest that you use the lists that make sense for you to help explore career options. Following are the names of each group of lists along with short comments on each group. You will find additional information in a brief introduction provided at the beginning of each group of lists in Part I.

Here is an overview of each major group of lists you will find in Part I.

Best Jobs Overall: Lists of Jobs with the Highest Pay, Fastest Growth, and Most Openings

Four lists are in this group, and they are the ones that most people want to see first. The first list presents all 500 job titles in order of their combined scores for earnings, growth, and number of job openings. Three more lists in this group present the 100 jobs with the highest earnings, the 100 jobs projected to grow most rapidly, and the 100 jobs with the most openings.

Best Jobs Lists with High Percentages of Workers Age 16–24, Workers Age 55 and Over, Part-Time Workers, Self-Employed Workers, Women, and Men

This group of lists presents interesting information for a variety of types of people based on data from the U.S. Census Bureau. The lists are arranged into groups for workers age 16–24, workers age 55 and older, part-time workers, self-employed workers, women, and men. We created five lists for each group, basing the last four on the information in the first list:

◉ The jobs having the highest percentage of people of each type

◉ The 25 jobs with the best combined scores for earnings, growth, and number of openings

◉ The 25 jobs with the highest earnings

◉ The 25 jobs with the highest growth rates

◉ The 25 jobs with the largest number of openings

Best Jobs Lists Based on Levels of Education and Experience

We created separate lists for each level of education and training as defined by the U.S. Department of Labor. We put each of the 500 job titles into one of the lists based on the education and training required for entry. Jobs within these lists are presented in order of their total combined scores for earnings, growth, and number of openings. The lists include jobs in these groupings:

- Short-term on-the-job training
- Moderate-term on-the-job training
- Long-term on-the-job training
- Work experience in a related job
- Postsecondary vocational training
- Associate degree
- Bachelor's degree
- Work experience plus degree
- Master's degree
- Doctoral degree
- First professional degree

Best Jobs Lists Based on Interests

These lists organize the 500 jobs into groups based on interests. Within each list, jobs are presented in order of their total scores for earnings, growth, and number of openings. Here are the 16 interest areas used in these lists: Agriculture and Natural Resources; Architecture and Construction; Arts and Communication; Business and Administration; Education and Training; Finance and Insurance; Government and Public Administration; Health Science; Hospitality, Tourism, and Recreation; Human Service; Information Technology; Law and Public Safety; Manufacturing; Retail and Wholesale Sales and Service; Scientific Research, Engineering, and Mathematics; Transportation, Distribution, and Logistics.

Best Jobs Lists Based on Personality Types

These lists organize the 500 jobs into six personality types, which are described in the introduction to the lists: Realistic, Investigative, Artistic, Social, Enterprising, and Conventional. The jobs within each list are presented in order of their total scores for earnings, growth, and number of openings.

Part II: The Job Descriptions

This part of the book provides a brief but information-packed description for each of the 537 jobs that met our criteria for this book. The descriptions in Part II are presented in alphabetical order. This makes it easy to look up any job you identify in a list from Part I that you want to learn more about.

We used the most current information from a variety of government sources to create the descriptions. We designed the descriptions to be easy to understand, and the sample that follows—with an explanation of each of its component parts—will help you better understand and use the descriptions.

Job Title

Biophysicists

Data Elements

- Education/Training Required: Doctoral degree
- Annual Earnings: $68,950
- Growth: 22.9%
- Annual Job Openings: 2,000
- Self-Employed: 2.6%
- Part-Time: 7.1%

Summary Description and Tasks

Research or study physical principles of living cells and organisms, their electrical and mechanical energy, and related phenomena. Studies physical principles of living cells and organisms and their electrical and mechanical energy. Investigates transmission of electrical impulses along nerves and muscles. Studies absorption of light by chlorophyll in photosynthesis or by pigments of eye involved in vision. Researches cancer treatment, using radiation and nuclear particles. Analyzes functions of electronic and human brains, such as learning, thinking, and memory. Investigates dynamics of seeing and hearing. Studies spatial configuration of submicroscopic molecules, such as proteins, using X-ray and electron microscope. Researches manner in which characteristics of plants and animals are carried through successive generations. Investigates damage to cells and tissues caused by X rays and nuclear particles. Researches transformation of substances in cells, using atomic isotopes. **SKILLS—Science:** Using scientific rules and methods to solve problems. **Reading Comprehension:** Understanding written sentences and paragraphs in work-related documents. **Writing:** Communicating effectively in writing as appropriate for the needs of the audience. **Mathematics:** Using mathematics to solve problems. **Active Learning:** Understanding the implications of new information for both current and future problem-solving and decision-making. **Critical Thinking:**

Skills

Using logic and reasoning to identify the strengths and weaknesses of alternative solutions, conclusions, or approaches to problems. **Complex Problem Solving:** Identifying complex problems and reviewing related information to develop and evaluate options and implement solutions. **Programming:** Writing computer programs for various purposes. **GOE—Interest Area:** 15. Scientific Research, Engineering, and Mathematics. **Work Group:** 15.03. Life Sciences. **Other Jobs in This Work Group:** Biochemists; Biologists; Environmental Scientists and Specialists, Including Health; Epidemiologists; Medical Scientists, Except Epidemiologists; Microbiologists. **PERSONALITY TYPE:** Investigative.

GOE Information

Personality Type

EDUCATION/TRAINING PROGRAM(S)—Biochemistry; Biochemistry/Biophysics and Molecular Biology; Biophysics; Cell/Cellular Biology and Anatomical Sciences, Other; Molecular Biochemistry; Molecular Biophysics; Soil Chemistry and Physics; Soil Microbiology. **RELATED KNOWLEDGE/COURSES—Biology:** Knowledge of plant and animal organisms and their tissues, cells, functions, interdependencies, and interactions with each other and the environment. **Physics:** Knowledge and prediction of physical principles and laws and their interrelationships and applications to understanding fluid, material, and atmospheric dynamics and mechanical, electrical, atomic, and subatomic structures and processes. **Mathematics:** Knowledge of arithmetic, algebra, geometry, calculus, and statistics and their applications. **Chemistry:** Knowledge of the chemical composition, structure, and properties of substances and of the chemical processes and transformations that they undergo. This includes uses of chemicals and their danger signs, production techniques, and disposal methods.

Education/Training Program(s)

Related Knowledge/Courses

- **Job Title:** This is the job title for the job as defined by the U.S. Department of Labor and used in its O*NET database.
- **Data Elements:** The information on education, earnings, growth, annual openings, percentage of self-employed workers, and percentage of part-time workers comes from various government databases, as we explain earlier in this introduction.
- **Summary Description and Tasks:** The first part of each job description provides a summary of the occupation in bold type. It is followed by a listing of tasks that are generally performed by people who work in the job. This information comes from the O*NET database.

- **Skills:** The O*NET database provides data on 35 skills, so we decided to list only those that were most important for each job rather than list pages of unhelpful details. For each job, we identified any skill with a rating that was higher than the average rating for this skill for all jobs. We order the skills by the amount by which their ratings exceed the average rating for all occupations, from highest to lowest. If there are more than eight such skills, we include only those eight with the highest ratings. We include up to 10 skills if scores were tied for eighth place. If no skill has a rating higher than the average for all jobs, we say "None met the criteria." Each listed skill is followed by a brief description of that skill.

- **GOE Information:** This information cross-references the Guide for Occupational Exploration (or the GOE), a system developed by the U.S. Department of Labor that organizes jobs based on interests. We use the groups from the fourth edition of the *New Guide for Occupational Exploration*, as published by JIST. This edition uses a set of interest fields based on the 16 career clusters developed by the U.S. Department of Education and used in a variety of career information systems. The description includes the major Interest Area the job fits into, its more-specific Work Group, and a list of related O*NET job titles that are in this same GOE Work Group. This information will help you identify other job titles that have similar interests or require similar skills. You can find more information on the GOE and its Interest Areas in the introduction to the lists of jobs based on interests in Part I.

- **Personality Type:** The O*NET database assigns each job to its most closely related personality type. Our job descriptions include the name of the related personality type. You can find more information on the personality types as well as a brief definition of each type in the introduction to the lists of jobs based on personality types in Part I.

- **Education/Training Program(s):** This part of the job description provides the name of the educational or training program or programs for the job. It will help you identify sources of formal or informal training for a job that interests you. To get this information, we used a crosswalk created by the National Crosswalk Service Center to connect information in the Classification of Instructional Programs (CIP) to the O*NET job titles we use in this book. We made various changes to connect the O*NET job titles to the education or training programs related to them and also modified the names of some education and training programs so they would be more easily understood.

- **Related Knowledge/Courses:** This entry in the job description will help you understand the most important knowledge areas that are required for the job and the types of courses or programs you will likely need to take to prepare for it. We used information in the Department of Labor's O*NET database for this entry. We went through a process similar to the one described for the skills (noted earlier) to end up with entries that are most important for each job.

Getting all the information we used in the job descriptions was not a simple process, and it is not always perfect. Even so, we used the best and most recent sources of data we could find, and we think that our efforts will be helpful to many people.

Sources of Additional Information

Hundreds of sources of career information exist, so here are a few we consider most helpful in getting additional information on the jobs listed in this book.

Print References

◎ *O*NET Dictionary of Occupational Titles*: Revised on a regular basis, this book provides good descriptions for all jobs listed in the U.S. Department of Labor's O*NET database. There are more than 1,100 job descriptions at all levels of education and training, plus lists of related job titles in other major career information sources, educational programs, and other information. Published by JIST.

◎ *New Guide for Occupational Exploration,* **Fourth Edition:** The new edition of the *GOE* is cross-referenced in the descriptions in Part II. The *New GOE* provides helpful information to consider about each of the Interest Areas and Work Groups, descriptions of all O*NET jobs within each *GOE* group, and many other features useful for exploring career options. This most recent edition is published by JIST.

◎ *Enhanced Occupational Outlook Handbook*: Updated regularly, this book provides thorough descriptions for more than 270 major jobs in the current *Occupational Outlook Handbook,* brief descriptions for the O*NET jobs that are related to each, brief descriptions of thousands of more-specialized jobs from the *Dictionary of Occupational Titles,* and other information. Published by JIST.

Internet Resources

◎ **The U.S. Department of Labor Bureau of Labor Statistics Web site:** The Department of Labor Bureau of Labor Statistics Web site (http://www.bls.gov) provides a lot of career information, including links to other Web pages that provide information on the jobs covered in this book. This Web site is a bit formal and, well, confusing, but it will take you to the major sources of government career information if you explore its options.

◎ **O*NET site:** Go to http://www.onetcenter.org for a variety of information on the O*NET database, including links to sites that provide detailed information on the O*NET job titles presented in Part II of this book.

◎ **CareerOINK.com:** This site (http://www.careeroink.com) is operated by JIST and includes free information on thousands of jobs (including all O*NET jobs included in *Best Jobs for the 21st Century*), easy-to-use crosswalks between major career information systems, links from military to civilian jobs, sample resumes, and many other features. A link at http://www.jist.com will also take you to the CareerOINK Web site.

Thanks

Thanks for reading this introduction. You are surely a more thorough person than those who jumped into the book without reading it, and you will probably get more out of the book as a result. We wish you a satisfying career and, more importantly, a good life.

PART I

The Best Jobs Lists

Tips on Using These Lists

We've tried to make the Best Jobs lists in this section both fun to use and informative. You can use the table of contents at the front of the book to find a complete listing of all the list titles in this section. You can then review the lists that most interest you or simply browse the lists in this section. Most, such as the list of highest-paying jobs, are easy to understand and require little explanation. We provide comments on each group of related lists to inform you of the selection criteria or other details we think you may want to know.

As you review the lists, mark job titles that appeal to you (or, if someone else will be using this book, write them on a separate sheet of paper) so that you can look up their descriptions later in Part II.

Understand the Limitations of the Information

Many of the lists emphasize jobs with high pay, high growth, or large numbers of openings. Most people consider these factors important in selecting a desirable job, and they are also easily quantifiable. While these measures are important, we believe that you should also think about other factors in considering your career options. For example, location, liking the people you work with, having an opportunity to serve others, and enjoying your work are just a few of the many factors that may define the ideal job for you. These measures are difficult or impossible to objectively quantify and are not, therefore, presented in this book. For this reason, we suggest that you consider the importance of these issues yourself and that you thoroughly research any job before making a firm decision.

For example, of the 500 jobs in our Best Jobs Overall list, the last job is Letterpress Setters and Set-Up Operators. It has annual earnings of $29,900, a 4.6 percent growth rate, and 30,000 job openings per year. Is this a "bad" job, one you should avoid? No, of course not. It all depends on what you like or want to do. Another example is the job that had the very best overall score for earnings, growth, and number of openings, Computer Software Engineers, Applications. Is this job a great job to consider? Many people (the authors included) would not want to work in this job or may not have the skills or interest needed to do it well. It would be a great job for someone who was good at it and who would enjoy doing it, but it would simply not be right for someone else. On the other hand, the perfect job for some people would be Letterpress Setters and Set-Up Operators because they enjoy it and are good at it.

So, as you look at the lists that follow, keep in mind that earnings, growth, and number of openings are just some things to consider. Also consider that half of all people in a given job earn more than the earnings you will see in this book—and half earn less. If a job really appeals to you, you should consider it even if it is not among the highest pay-ing. And you should also consider jobs not among the fastest growing and jobs with few openings for similar reasons, because openings are always available, even for jobs with slow or negative growth projections or with small numbers of openings.

Some Details on the Lists

The sources of the information we used in constructing these lists are presented in this book's introduction. Here are some additional details on how we created the lists:

- **We excluded some jobs for which very little information is available.** In the full list of 1,167 jobs that are described in the U.S. Department of Labor's O*NET database, 212 have no information beyond a definition and, in some cases, a list of tasks. These are either catch-all titles (such as "Financial Specialists, All Other") that make the O*NET as comprehensive as possible or dummy occupations that help the O*NET match up better with occupational information from other government agencies. Census Bureau data is available for some of them, but no O*NET data is available for them, so we dropped them from consideration. We also reluctantly excluded seven jobs because no wage information is available for them: Actors; Biologists; Dancers; Human Resources Managers; Hunters and Trappers; Musicians, Instrumental; and Singers.

- **We excluded some jobs that are shrinking or that offer very few opportunities.** Among the 948 jobs for which we have both O*NET and wage information, nine are expected to have fewer than 500 openings per year and to shrink rather than grow in workforce size: Bridge and Lock Tenders; Fabric Menders, Except Garment; Marine Architects; Marine Engineers; Marine Engineers and Naval Architects (this job was also one of those with limited information); Mathematicians; Mining and Geological Engineers, Including Mining Safety Engineers; Nuclear Power Reactor Operators; and Radio Operators. These jobs can't be considered "best jobs," so we excluded them from con-sideration for this book.

◎ **We collapsed a number of specialized postsecondary education jobs into one title.** The government database we used for the job titles and descriptions included 38 job titles for postsecondary educators, yet the data source we used for growth and number of openings provided data only for the more general job of Teachers, Postsecondary. To make our lists more useful, we included only one listing—Teachers, Postsecondary— rather than separate listings for each specialized postsecondary education job. We did, however, include descriptions for all the specific postsecondary teaching jobs in Part II (except two for which no detailed information is available). Should you wonder, here are the more specialized titles: Agricultural Sciences Teachers, Postsecondary; Anthropology and Archeology Teachers, Postsecondary; Architecture Teachers, Postsecondary; Area, Ethnic, and Cultural Studies Teachers, Postsecondary; Art, Drama, and Music Teachers, Postsecondary; Atmospheric, Earth, Marine, and Space Sciences Teachers, Post- secondary; Biological Science Teachers, Postsecondary; Business Teachers, Postsecondary; Chemistry Teachers, Postsecondary; Communications Teachers, Postsecondary; Computer Science Teachers, Postsecondary; Criminal Justice and Law Enforcement Teachers, Postsecondary; Economics Teachers, Postsecondary; Education Teachers, Postsecondary; Engineering Teachers, Postsecondary; English Language and Literature Teachers, Postsecondary; Environmental Science Teachers, Postsecondary; Foreign Language and Literature Teachers, Postsecondary; Forestry and Conservation Science Teachers, Postsecondary; Geography Teachers, Postsecondary; Graduate Teaching Assistants; Health Specialties Teachers, Postsecondary; History Teachers, Postsecondary; Home Economics Teachers, Postsecondary; Law Teachers, Postsecondary; Library Science Teachers, Postsecondary; Mathematical Science Teachers, Postsecondary; Nursing Instructors and Teachers, Postsecondary; Philosophy and Religion Teachers, Postsecondary; Physics Teachers, Postsecondary; Political Science Teachers, Postsecondary; Psychology Teachers, Postsecondary; Recreation and Fitness Studies Teachers, Postsecondary; Social Work Teachers, Postsecondary; Sociology Teachers, Postsecondary; Vocational Education Teachers, Postsecondary.

◎ **Some jobs have the same scores for one or more data elements.** For example, in the category of jobs with the most openings, three jobs (Middle School Teachers, Except Special and Vocational Education; Packaging and Filling Machine Operators and Tenders; and Painters, Construction and Maintenance) are expected to have the same number of job openings per year, 69,000. Therefore we ordered these three jobs alpha- betically, and their order has no other significance. There was no way to avoid these ties, so simply understand that the difference of several positions on a list may not mean as much as it seems.

Best Jobs Overall: Lists of Jobs with the Highest Pay, Fastest Growth, and Most Openings

The four lists that follow are this book's premier lists. They are the lists that are most often mentioned in the media and the ones that most readers want to see.

To create these lists, we ranked 905 major jobs according to a combination of their earnings, growth, and openings. We then selected the 500 jobs with the best total scores for use in this book. (The process for ranking the jobs is explained in more detail in the introduction.)

The first list presents all 500 best jobs according to these combined rankings for pay, growth, and number of openings. Three additional lists present the 100 jobs with the top scores in each of three measures: annual earnings, projected percentage growth through 2012, and number of annual openings. Descriptions for all the jobs in these lists are included in Part II.

The 500 Best Jobs Overall—Jobs with the Best Combination of Pay, Growth, and Openings

This list arranges all 500 jobs that were selected for this book in order of their overall scores for pay, growth, and number of openings. To obtain this list, we sorted 905 jobs into three lists based on pay, growth, and number of openings. We sorted each of these lists from highest to lowest and then assigned a number to each entry. For example, the job with the highest pay was given a score of 1, the one with the next highest pay was given a score of 2, and so on. This scoring process was continued for each job on each of the three lists. We then combined the three scores for each job and sorted the new list based on the total score for all three measures.

The job with the best overall score was Computer Software Engineers, Applications. Other jobs follow in order of their total scores for pay, growth, and openings. These 500 jobs are the ones we use throughout this book in the other lists in Part I and in the descriptions found in Part II.

As you look over the list, remember that jobs near the top of the list are not necessarily "good" jobs—nor are jobs toward the end of the list necessarily "bad" ones for you to consider. Their position in the list is simply a result of their total scores based on pay, growth, and number of openings. This means, for example, that some jobs with low pay, modest growth, but a high number of openings appear higher on the list, while some jobs with higher pay, modest growth, but a low number of openings appear toward the end of the list. The "right" job for you could be anywhere on this list.

The 500 Best Jobs Overall

Job	Annual Earnings	Percent Growth	Annual Openings
1. Computer Software Engineers, Applications	$74,980	45.5%	55,000
2. Computer Systems Analysts	$66,460	39.4%	68,000
3. Computer Software Engineers, Systems Software	$79,740	45.5%	39,000
4. Teachers, Postsecondary	$51,614	38.1%	216,000
5. Management Analysts	$63,450	30.4%	78,000

The 500 Best Jobs Overall

Job	Annual Earnings	Percent Growth	Annual Openings
6. Sales Managers	$84,220	30.5%	54,000
7. Computer and Information Systems Managers	$92,570	36.1%	39,000
8. Logisticians	$57,110	27.5%	162,000
9. Registered Nurses	$52,330	27.3%	215,000
10. General and Operations Managers	$77,420	18.4%	260,000
11. Network Systems and Data Communications Analysts	$60,600	57.0%	29,000
12. Medical and Health Services Managers	$67,430	29.3%	33,000
13. Computer Security Specialists	$58,190	37.4%	35,000
14. Network and Computer Systems Administrators	$58,190	37.4%	35,000
15. Pharmacists	$84,900	30.1%	23,000
16. Anesthesiologists	more than $145,600	19.5%	38,000
17. Financial Managers, Branch or Department	$81,880	18.3%	71,000
18. Internists, General	more than $145,600	19.5%	38,000
19. Obstetricians and Gynecologists	more than $145,600	19.5%	38,000
20. Psychiatrists	more than $145,600	19.5%	38,000
21. Surgeons	more than $145,600	19.5%	38,000
22. Treasurers, Controllers, and Chief Financial Officers	$81,880	18.3%	71,000
23. Family and General Practitioners	$137,090	19.5%	38,000
24. Pediatricians, General	$135,730	19.5%	38,000
25. Marketing Managers	$87,640	21.3%	30,000
26. Special Education Teachers, Secondary School	$45,700	30.0%	59,000
27. Chief Executives	$140,350	16.7%	63,000
28. Government Service Executives	$140,350	16.7%	63,000
29. Private Sector Executives	$140,350	16.7%	63,000
30. Accountants	$50,770	19.5%	119,000
31. Auditors	$50,770	19.5%	119,000
32. Education Administrators, Elementary and Secondary School	$74,190	20.7%	31,000
33. Lawyers	$94,930	17.0%	53,000
34. Personal Financial Advisors	$62,700	34.6%	18,000
35. Administrative Services Managers	$60,290	19.8%	40,000
36. Special Education Teachers, Middle School	$44,160	30.0%	59,000
37. Highway Patrol Pilots	$45,210	24.7%	67,000
38. Police Patrol Officers	$45,210	24.7%	67,000
39. Sheriffs and Deputy Sheriffs	$45,210	24.7%	67,000
40. Database Administrators	$60,650	44.2%	16,000

(continued)

(continued)

The 500 Best Jobs Overall

Job	Annual Earnings	Percent Growth	Annual Openings
41. Education Administrators, Postsecondary	$68,340	25.9%	19,000
42. Sales Representatives, Agricultural	$58,580	19.3%	44,000
43. Sales Representatives, Chemical and Pharmaceutical	$58,580	19.3%	44,000
44. Sales Representatives, Electrical/Electronic	$58,580	19.3%	44,000
45. Sales Representatives, Instruments	$58,580	19.3%	44,000
46. Sales Representatives, Mechanical Equipment and Supplies	$58,580	19.3%	44,000
47. Sales Representatives, Medical	$58,580	19.3%	44,000
48. Special Education Teachers, Preschool, Kindergarten, and Elementary School	$43,570	30.0%	59,000
49. Computer Support Specialists	$40,430	30.3%	71,000
50. Physical Therapists	$60,180	35.3%	16,000
51. Sales Representatives, Wholesale and Manufacturing, Except Technical and Scientific Products	$45,400	19.1%	160,000
52. Training and Development Specialists	$44,570	27.9%	35,000
53. Electricians	$42,300	23.4%	65,000
54. Secondary School Teachers, Except Special and Vocational Education	$45,650	18.2%	118,000
55. Training and Development Managers	$67,460	19.4%	21,000
56. Compensation and Benefits Managers	$66,530	19.4%	21,000
57. Public Relations Specialists	$43,830	32.9%	28,000
58. Market Research Analysts	$56,140	23.4%	18,000
59. Advertising and Promotions Managers	$63,610	25.0%	13,000
60. Clinical Psychologists	$54,950	24.4%	17,000
61. Counseling Psychologists	$54,950	24.4%	17,000
62. School Psychologists	$54,950	24.4%	17,000
63. Physician Assistants	$69,410	48.9%	7,000
64. Computer Programmers	$62,890	14.6%	45,000
65. Dental Hygienists	$58,350	43.1%	9,000
66. Kindergarten Teachers, Except Special Education	$41,400	27.2%	34,000
67. Occupational Therapists	$54,660	35.2%	10,000
68. Financial Analysts	$61,910	18.7%	22,000
69. Social and Community Service Managers	$46,810	27.7%	19,000
70. Public Relations Managers	$70,000	23.4%	10,000
71. Instructional Coordinators	$48,790	25.4%	18,000
72. Sales Agents, Financial Services	$69,200	13.0%	39,000
73. Sales Agents, Securities and Commodities	$69,200	13.0%	39,000
74. Construction Managers	$69,870	12.0%	47,000

The 500 Best Jobs Overall

Job	Annual Earnings	Percent Growth	Annual Openings
75. Employment Interviewers, Private or Public Employment Service	$41,190	27.3%	29,000
76. Personnel Recruiters	$41,190	27.3%	29,000
77. Environmental Engineers	$66,480	38.2%	6,000
78. Heating and Air Conditioning Mechanics	$36,260	31.8%	35,000
79. Refrigeration Mechanics	$36,260	31.8%	35,000
80. Compensation, Benefits, and Job Analysis Specialists	$47,490	28.0%	15,000
81. Paralegals and Legal Assistants	$39,130	28.7%	29,000
82. Storage and Distribution Managers	$66,600	19.7%	13,000
83. Transportation Managers	$66,600	19.7%	13,000
84. Loan Officers	$48,830	18.8%	30,000
85. First-Line Supervisors and Manager/Supervisors—Construction Trades Workers	$50,450	14.1%	67,000
86. First-Line Supervisors and Manager/Supervisors—Extractive Workers	$50,450	14.1%	67,000
87. Speech-Language Pathologists	$52,410	27.2%	10,000
88. Pipe Fitters	$41,290	18.7%	56,000
89. Pipelaying Fitters	$41,290	18.7%	56,000
90. Plumbers	$41,290	18.7%	56,000
91. Elementary School Teachers, Except Special Education	$43,160	15.2%	183,000
92. First-Line Supervisors/Managers of Mechanics, Installers, and Repairers	$50,340	15.4%	42,000
93. Cost Estimators	$49,940	18.6%	25,000
94. Child Support, Missing Persons, and Unemployment Insurance Fraud Investigators	$53,990	22.4%	11,000
95. Criminal Investigators and Special Agents	$53,990	22.4%	11,000
96. Immigration and Customs Inspectors	$53,990	22.4%	11,000
97. Police Detectives	$53,990	22.4%	11,000
98. Police Identification and Records Officers	$53,990	22.4%	11,000
99. Tractor-Trailer Truck Drivers	$33,520	19.0%	299,000
100. Truck Drivers, Heavy	$33,520	19.0%	299,000
101. Licensed Practical and Licensed Vocational Nurses	$33,970	20.2%	105,000
102. Medical Scientists, Except Epidemiologists	$61,320	26.9%	6,000
103. Child, Family, and School Social Workers	$34,820	23.2%	45,000
104. Medical and Public Health Social Workers	$40,080	28.6%	18,000
105. Radiologic Technicians	$43,350	22.9%	21,000
106. Radiologic Technologists	$43,350	22.9%	21,000

(continued)

(continued)

The 500 Best Jobs Overall

Job	Annual Earnings	Percent Growth	Annual Openings
107. Correctional Officers and Jailers	$33,600	24.2%	49,000
108. Medical and Clinical Laboratory Technologists	$45,730	19.3%	21,000
109. Refractory Materials Repairers, Except Brickmasons	$37,640	16.3%	155,000
110. Self-Enrichment Education Teachers	$30,880	40.1%	39,000
111. Sales Engineers	$70,620	19.9%	7,000
112. Graphic Designers	$38,030	21.9%	29,000
113. Forest Fire Fighters	$38,330	20.7%	29,000
114. Municipal Fire Fighters	$38,330	20.7%	29,000
115. Technical Writers	$53,490	27.1%	6,000
116. Respiratory Therapists	$43,140	34.8%	10,000
117. Legal Secretaries	$36,720	18.8%	39,000
118. First-Line Supervisors/Managers of Police and Detectives	$64,430	15.3%	14,000
119. First-Line Supervisors/Managers of Non-Retail Sales Workers	$59,300	6.8%	72,000
120. Airline Pilots, Copilots, and Flight Engineers	$129,250	18.5%	6,000
121. Educational, Vocational, and School Counselors	$45,570	15.0%	32,000
122. Adjustment Clerks	$27,020	24.3%	419,000
123. Customer Service Representatives, Utilities	$27,020	24.3%	419,000
124. Sheet Metal Workers	$35,560	19.8%	30,000
125. Veterinarians	$66,590	25.1%	4,000
126. Physical Therapist Assistants	$37,890	44.6%	10,000
127. Directors—Stage, Motion Pictures, Television, and Radio	$52,840	18.3%	10,000
128. Producers	$52,840	18.3%	10,000
129. Program Directors	$52,840	18.3%	10,000
130. Talent Directors	$52,840	18.3%	10,000
131. Technical Directors/Managers	$52,840	18.3%	10,000
132. Forest Fire Fighting and Prevention Supervisors	$58,920	18.7%	8,000
133. Municipal Fire Fighting and Prevention Supervisors	$58,920	18.7%	8,000
134. Medical Assistants	$24,610	58.9%	78,000
135. Environmental Scientists and Specialists, Including Health	$51,080	23.7%	6,000
136. Mental Health and Substance Abuse Social Workers	$33,920	34.5%	17,000
137. Caption Writers	$44,350	16.1%	23,000
138. Copy Writers	$44,350	16.1%	23,000
139. Creative Writers	$44,350	16.1%	23,000
140. Poets and Lyricists	$44,350	16.1%	23,000
141. Dental Assistants	$28,330	42.5%	35,000

The 500 Best Jobs Overall

Job	Annual Earnings	Percent Growth	Annual Openings
142. Claims Examiners, Property and Casualty Insurance	$44,220	14.2%	31,000
143. Insurance Adjusters, Examiners, and Investigators	$44,220	14.2%	31,000
144. Architects, Except Landscape and Naval	$60,300	17.3%	8,000
145. Bill and Account Collectors	$27,450	24.5%	76,000
146. Massage Therapists	$31,960	27.1%	24,000
147. Chiropractors	$69,910	23.3%	3,000
148. First-Line Supervisors/Managers of Production and Operating Workers	$44,740	9.5%	66,000
149. Social and Human Service Assistants	$24,270	48.7%	63,000
150. Flight Attendants	$43,440	15.9%	23,000
151. Engineering Managers	$97,630	9.2%	16,000
152. Cement Masons and Concrete Finishers	$31,400	26.1%	24,000
153. Adult Literacy, Remedial Education, and GED Teachers and Instructors	$38,980	20.4%	14,000
154. First-Line Supervisors and Manager/Supervisors— Landscaping Workers	$35,340	21.6%	18,000
155. Lawn Service Managers	$35,340	21.6%	18,000
156. Receptionists and Information Clerks	$21,830	29.5%	296,000
157. Maintenance and Repair Workers, General	$30,710	16.3%	155,000
158. Truck Drivers, Light or Delivery Services	$24,540	23.2%	219,000
159. Industrial Engineers	$65,020	10.6%	16,000
160. Purchasing Agents, Except Wholesale, Retail, and Farm Products	$47,680	11.2%	29,000
161. Diagnostic Medical Sonographers	$52,490	24.0%	4,000
162. Production, Planning, and Expediting Clerks	$36,340	14.1%	51,000
163. Fitness Trainers and Aerobics Instructors	$25,470	44.5%	38,000
164. Multi-Media Artists and Animators	$50,360	15.8%	12,000
165. Surgical Technologists	$34,010	27.9%	13,000
166. Education Administrators, Preschool and Child Care Center/Program	$35,730	32.0%	9,000
167. Food Service Managers	$39,610	11.5%	58,000
168. Credit Analysts	$47,260	18.7%	9,000
169. Middle School Teachers, Except Special and Vocational Education	$43,670	9.0%	69,000
170. Security Guards	$20,320	31.9%	228,000
171. Brazers	$30,620	17.0%	71,000
172. Costume Attendants	$25,050	27.8%	66,000

(continued)

(continued)

The 500 Best Jobs Overall

Job	Annual Earnings	Percent Growth	Annual Openings
173. Solderers	$30,620	17.0%	71,000
174. Welder-Fitters	$30,620	17.0%	71,000
175. Welders and Cutters	$30,620	17.0%	71,000
176. Welders, Production	$30,620	17.0%	71,000
177. Clergy	$36,690	15.5%	34,000
178. Human Resources Assistants, Except Payroll and Timekeeping	$31,750	19.3%	36,000
179. Industrial Production Managers	$73,000	7.9%	18,000
180. Cardiovascular Technologists and Technicians	$38,690	33.5%	6,000
181. Preschool Teachers, Except Special Education	$20,980	36.2%	88,000
182. Property, Real Estate, and Community Association Managers	$39,980	12.8%	35,000
183. Telecommunications Line Installers and Repairers	$40,330	18.8%	13,000
184. Biochemists	$68,950	22.9%	2,000
185. Biophysicists	$68,950	22.9%	2,000
186. Nursing Aides, Orderlies, and Attendants	$20,980	24.9%	302,000
187. First-Line Supervisors/Managers of Transportation and Material-Moving Machine and Vehicle Operators	$44,810	12.1%	23,000
188. Home Health Aides	$18,330	48.1%	141,000
189. Agents and Business Managers of Artists, Performers, and Athletes	$55,080	27.8%	2,000
190. Ceiling Tile Installers	$34,030	21.4%	17,000
191. Drywall Installers	$34,030	21.4%	17,000
192. Boat Builders and Shipwrights	$34,900	10.1%	193,000
193. Brattice Builders	$34,900	10.1%	193,000
194. Carpenter Assemblers and Repairers	$34,900	10.1%	193,000
195. Construction Carpenters	$34,900	10.1%	193,000
196. Rough Carpenters	$34,900	10.1%	193,000
197. Ship Carpenters and Joiners	$34,900	10.1%	193,000
198. Roofers	$30,840	18.6%	38,000
199. Mental Health Counselors	$32,960	26.7%	13,000
200. Electronics Engineers, Except Computer	$75,770	9.4%	11,000
201. Appraisers, Real Estate	$43,390	17.6%	11,000
202. Assessors	$43,390	17.6%	11,000
203. Brickmasons and Blockmasons	$41,740	14.2%	21,000
204. Interior Designers	$40,670	21.7%	8,000
205. Personal and Home Care Aides	$16,900	40.5%	154,000

The 500 Best Jobs Overall

Job	Annual Earnings	Percent Growth	Annual Openings
206. Automotive Master Mechanics	$32,450	12.4%	100,000
207. Automotive Specialty Technicians	$32,450	12.4%	100,000
208. Civil Engineers	$64,230	8.0%	17,000
209. Emergency Medical Technicians and Paramedics	$25,310	33.1%	32,000
210. Calibration and Instrumentation Technicians	$46,310	10.0%	24,000
211. Electrical Engineering Technicians	$46,310	10.0%	24,000
212. Electronics Engineering Technicians	$46,310	10.0%	24,000
213. Hazardous Materials Removal Workers	$33,320	43.1%	8,000
214. Irradiated-Fuel Handlers	$33,320	43.1%	8,000
215. Interviewers, Except Eligibility and Loan	$23,670	28.0%	46,000
216. Advertising Sales Agents	$40,300	13.4%	24,000
217. First-Line Supervisors, Administrative Support	$41,030	6.6%	140,000
218. First-Line Supervisors, Customer Service	$41,030	6.6%	140,000
219. Medical Records and Health Information Technicians	$25,590	46.8%	24,000
220. Radiation Therapists	$57,700	31.6%	1,000
221. Rehabilitation Counselors	$27,870	33.8%	19,000
222. Nuclear Medicine Technologists	$56,450	23.6%	2,000
223. Budget Analysts	$56,040	14.0%	8,000
224. Pharmacy Technicians	$23,650	28.8%	39,000
225. Health Educators	$38,480	21.9%	8,000
226. Insurance Sales Agents	$41,720	8.4%	52,000
227. Coroners	$47,390	9.8%	20,000
228. Environmental Compliance Inspectors	$47,390	9.8%	20,000
229. Equal Opportunity Representatives and Officers	$47,390	9.8%	20,000
230. Executive Secretaries and Administrative Assistants	$34,970	8.7%	210,000
231. Government Property Inspectors and Investigators	$47,390	9.8%	20,000
232. Licensing Examiners and Inspectors	$47,390	9.8%	20,000
233. Pressure Vessel Inspectors	$47,390	9.8%	20,000
234. Directors, Religious Activities and Education	$30,700	24.1%	16,000
235. Bus and Truck Mechanics and Diesel Engine Specialists	$35,780	14.2%	28,000
236. Meeting and Convention Planners	$39,620	21.3%	7,000
237. Art Directors	$63,840	11.4%	8,000
238. Landscaping and Groundskeeping Workers	$20,420	22.0%	203,000
239. Respiratory Therapy Technicians	$36,740	34.2%	5,000
240. Teacher Assistants	$19,410	23.0%	259,000
241. City and Regional Planning Aides	$34,360	17.5%	18,000

(continued)

(continued)

The 500 Best Jobs Overall

Job	Annual Earnings	Percent Growth	Annual Openings
242. Social Science Research Assistants	$34,360	17.5%	18,000
243. Counter and Rental Clerks	$18,280	26.3%	144,000
244. Medical and Clinical Laboratory Technicians	$30,840	19.4%	21,000
245. Commercial and Industrial Designers	$52,310	14.7%	7,000
246. Dietitians and Nutritionists	$43,630	17.8%	8,000
247. First-Line Supervisors/Managers of Retail Sales Workers	$32,720	9.1%	251,000
248. Grader, Bulldozer, and Scraper Operators	$35,360	10.4%	45,000
249. Operating Engineers	$35,360	10.4%	45,000
250. Landscape Architects	$53,120	22.2%	2,000
251. Audiologists	$51,470	29.0%	1,000
252. Chemists	$56,060	12.7%	7,000
253. Optometrists	$88,410	17.1%	2,000
254. Probation Officers and Correctional Treatment Specialists	$39,600	14.7%	15,000
255. Emergency Management Specialists	$45,390	28.2%	2,000
256. Elevator Installers and Repairers	$58,710	17.1%	3,000
257. Film and Video Editors	$43,590	26.4%	3,000
258. Combined Food Preparation and Serving Workers, Including Fast Food	$14,690	22.8%	734,000
259. Occupational Therapist Assistants	$38,430	39.2%	3,000
260. Substance Abuse and Behavioral Disorder Counselors	$32,130	23.3%	10,000
261. Biomedical Engineers	$67,690	26.1%	fewer than 500
262. Automatic Teller Machine Servicers	$35,150	15.1%	19,000
263. Data Processing Equipment Repairers	$35,150	15.1%	19,000
264. Office Machine and Cash Register Servicers	$35,150	15.1%	19,000
265. Editors	$43,890	11.8%	14,000
266. Chefs and Head Cooks	$30,680	15.8%	33,000
267. Private Detectives and Investigators	$32,110	25.3%	9,000
268. Librarians	$45,900	10.1%	15,000
269. Locker Room, Coatroom, and Dressing Room Attendants	$17,550	27.8%	66,000
270. Packaging and Filling Machine Operators and Tenders	$22,200	21.1%	69,000
271. Hydrologists	$61,510	21.0%	1,000
272. Natural Sciences Managers	$88,660	11.3%	5,000
273. Environmental Science and Protection Technicians, Including Health	$35,340	36.8%	4,000
274. Epidemiologists	$54,800	32.5%	fewer than 500
275. Medical Transcriptionists	$28,380	22.6%	18,000

The 500 Best Jobs Overall

Job	Annual Earnings	Percent Growth	Annual Openings
276. First-Line Supervisors/Managers of Helpers, Laborers, and Material Movers, Hand	$38,280	14.0%	16,000
277. Structural Iron and Steel Workers	$42,430	15.9%	9,000
278. Agricultural Crop Farm Managers	$50,700	5.1%	25,000
279. Fish Hatchery Managers	$50,700	5.1%	25,000
280. Nursery and Greenhouse Managers	$50,700	5.1%	25,000
281. Occupational Health and Safety Specialists	$51,570	13.2%	6,000
282. Construction and Building Inspectors	$43,670	13.8%	10,000
283. Insurance Underwriters	$48,550	10.0%	12,000
284. First-Line Supervisors/Managers of Correctional Officers	$44,720	19.0%	4,000
285. Aircraft Body and Bonded Structure Repairers	$45,290	11.0%	12,000
286. Aircraft Engine Specialists	$45,290	11.0%	12,000
287. Airframe-and-Power-Plant Mechanics	$45,290	11.0%	12,000
288. Medical Secretaries	$26,540	17.2%	50,000
289. Athletes and Sports Competitors	$48,310	19.2%	3,000
290. Environmental Engineering Technicians	$38,550	28.4%	3,000
291. Amusement and Recreation Attendants	$15,550	27.8%	66,000
292. Painters, Construction and Maintenance	$30,260	11.6%	69,000
293. First-Line Supervisors/Managers of Food Preparation and Serving Workers	$25,410	15.5%	154,000
294. Automotive Body and Related Repairers	$34,690	13.2%	23,000
295. Food Preparation Workers	$16,710	20.2%	267,000
296. Mechanical Engineers	$66,320	4.8%	14,000
297. Tapers	$39,070	20.8%	5,000
298. Mapping Technicians	$30,380	23.1%	10,000
299. Surveying Technicians	$30,380	23.1%	10,000
300. Janitors and Cleaners, Except Maids and Housekeeping Cleaners	$18,790	18.3%	454,000
301. Security and Fire Alarm Systems Installers	$33,410	30.2%	5,000
302. Bus Drivers, Transit and Intercity	$29,730	15.2%	33,000
303. Refuse and Recyclable Material Collectors	$25,760	17.6%	42,000
304. Microbiologists	$54,840	20.0%	1,000
305. Actuaries	$76,340	14.9%	2,000
306. Tile and Marble Setters	$35,410	26.5%	4,000
307. Housekeeping Supervisors	$29,510	16.2%	28,000
308. Janitorial Supervisors	$29,510	16.2%	28,000
309. Construction Laborers	$25,160	14.2%	166,000

(continued)

(continued)

The 500 Best Jobs Overall

Job	Annual Earnings	Percent Growth	Annual Openings
310. Dispatchers, Except Police, Fire, and Ambulance	$30,920	14.4%	28,000
311. Hotel, Motel, and Resort Desk Clerks	$17,700	23.9%	46,000
312. Vocational Education Teachers, Secondary School	$45,920	9.0%	12,000
313. Painters, Transportation Equipment	$35,120	17.5%	9,000
314. Bus Drivers, School	$23,250	16.7%	76,000
315. Veterinary Technologists and Technicians	$24,940	44.1%	11,000
316. Carpet Installers	$34,090	16.8%	10,000
317. Marriage and Family Therapists	$38,980	22.4%	3,000
318. Recreation Workers	$19,320	20.5%	56,000
319. Audio and Video Equipment Technicians	$32,570	26.7%	5,000
320. Air Traffic Controllers	$102,030	12.6%	2,000
321. Atmospheric and Space Scientists	$70,100	16.2%	1,000
322. Economists	$72,780	13.4%	2,000
323. Purchasing Managers	$72,450	4.8%	9,000
324. Gaming Supervisors	$40,840	15.7%	6,000
325. Podiatrists	$94,400	15.0%	1,000
326. Coaches and Scouts	$26,350	18.3%	26,000
327. Biological Technicians	$33,210	19.4%	7,000
328. Desktop Publishers	$32,340	29.2%	4,000
329. Waiters and Waitresses	$14,050	17.5%	721,000
330. Geographers	$58,970	19.5%	fewer than 500
331. Tax Preparers	$27,730	23.2%	11,000
332. Electrical Engineers	$71,610	2.5%	11,000
333. Helpers—Installation, Maintenance, and Repair Workers	$21,310	20.3%	33,000
334. Computer Hardware Engineers	$81,150	6.1%	6,000
335. Cooks, Restaurant	$19,520	15.9%	211,000
336. Sound Engineering Technicians	$38,110	25.5%	2,000
337. Water and Liquid Waste Treatment Plant and System Operators	$34,960	16.0%	9,000
338. Urban and Regional Planners	$53,450	10.7%	5,000
339. Electrical and Electronics Repairers, Commercial and Industrial Equipment	$42,600	10.3%	10,000
340. Oral and Maxillofacial Surgeons	more than $145,600	4.1%	7,000
341. Orthodontists	more than $145,600	4.1%	7,000
342. Prosthodontists	more than $145,600	4.1%	7,000
343. Industrial Truck and Tractor Operators	$26,580	11.1%	94,000
344. Machinists	$33,960	8.2%	30,000

The 500 Best Jobs Overall

Job	Annual Earnings	Percent Growth	Annual Openings
345. Retail Salespersons	$18,680	14.6%	1,014,000
346. Orthotists and Prosthetists	$50,260	18.9%	1,000
347. Commercial Pilots	$53,870	14.9%	2,000
348. Dentists, General	$123,060	4.1%	7,000
349. Library Assistants, Clerical	$20,720	21.5%	27,000
350. Counter Attendants, Cafeteria, Food Concession, and Coffee Shop	$15,660	16.7%	190,000
351. Interpreters and Translators	$33,860	22.1%	4,000
352. Nonfarm Animal Caretakers	$17,460	22.2%	32,000
353. Real Estate Sales Agents	$35,670	5.7%	34,000
354. Residential Advisors	$21,430	33.6%	12,000
355. Geologists	$68,730	11.5%	2,000
356. Real Estate Brokers	$58,720	2.4%	11,000
357. Operations Research Analysts	$60,190	6.2%	6,000
358. Insulation Workers, Mechanical	$33,330	15.8%	9,000
359. Taxi Drivers and Chauffeurs	$19,570	21.7%	28,000
360. Athletic Trainers	$33,940	29.9%	2,000
361. Mobile Heavy Equipment Mechanics, Except Engines	$38,150	9.6%	12,000
362. Central Office and PBX Installers and Repairers	$49,840	−0.6%	23,000
363. Communication Equipment Mechanics, Installers, and Repairers	$49,840	−0.6%	23,000
364. Frame Wirers, Central Office	$49,840	−0.6%	23,000
365. Station Installers and Repairers, Telephone	$49,840	−0.6%	23,000
366. Telecommunications Facility Examiners	$49,840	−0.6%	23,000
367. Cargo and Freight Agents	$34,250	15.5%	8,000
368. Reservation and Transportation Ticket Agents	$27,750	12.2%	35,000
369. Travel Clerks	$27,750	12.2%	35,000
370. Office Clerks, General	$22,770	10.4%	550,000
371. Glaziers	$32,650	17.2%	7,000
372. Industrial-Organizational Psychologists	$71,400	16.0%	fewer than 500
373. Wholesale and Retail Buyers, Except Farm Products	$42,230	4.3%	24,000
374. Fire-Prevention and Protection Engineers	$63,730	7.9%	4,000
375. Industrial Safety and Health Engineers	$63,730	7.9%	4,000
376. Product Safety Engineers	$63,730	7.9%	4,000
377. Gaming Dealers	$14,340	24.7%	26,000
378. Demonstrators and Product Promoters	$20,700	17.0%	38,000

(continued)

(continued)

The 500 Best Jobs Overall

Job	Annual Earnings	Percent Growth	Annual Openings
379. Hosts and Hostesses, Restaurant, Lounge, and Coffee Shop	$15,630	16.4%	95,000
380. Mechanical Engineering Technicians	$43,400	11.0%	6,000
381. Cartoonists	$38,060	16.5%	4,000
382. Painters and Illustrators	$38,060	16.5%	4,000
383. Sculptors	$38,060	16.5%	4,000
384. Sketch Artists	$38,060	16.5%	4,000
385. Packers and Packagers, Hand	$17,150	14.4%	198,000
386. Farmers and Ranchers	$40,440	–20.6%	118,000
387. Industrial Machinery Mechanics	$39,060	5.5%	19,000
388. Library Technicians	$24,940	16.8%	22,000
389. Cashiers	$16,240	13.2%	1,221,000
390. Electric Meter Installers and Repairers	$43,710	12.0%	5,000
391. Meter Mechanics	$43,710	12.0%	5,000
392. Valve and Regulator Repairers	$43,710	12.0%	5,000
393. Forensic Science Technicians	$44,010	18.9%	1,000
394. Curators	$43,620	17.0%	2,000
395. Financial Examiners	$60,310	8.9%	3,000
396. Exhibit Designers	$35,800	20.9%	2,000
397. Hairdressers, Hairstylists, and Cosmetologists	$19,800	14.7%	68,000
398. Set Designers	$35,800	20.9%	2,000
399. Billing, Cost, and Rate Clerks	$27,040	7.9%	78,000
400. Billing, Posting, and Calculating Machine Operators	$27,040	7.9%	78,000
401. First-Line Supervisors/Managers of Personal Service Workers	$30,350	9.4%	26,000
402. Judges, Magistrate Judges, and Magistrates	$93,070	8.7%	2,000
403. Physical Therapist Aides	$21,380	46.4%	8,000
404. Statement Clerks	$27,040	7.9%	78,000
405. Composers	$34,570	13.5%	8,000
406. Music Arrangers and Orchestrators	$34,570	13.5%	8,000
407. Music Directors	$34,570	13.5%	8,000
408. Highway Maintenance Workers	$29,550	10.4%	25,000
409. Dining Room and Cafeteria Attendants and Bartender Helpers	$14,770	14.9%	143,000
410. Opticians, Dispensing	$27,950	18.2%	10,000
411. Gaming Managers	$58,580	12.4%	1,000
412. Loan Counselors	$33,970	17.8%	4,000

The 500 Best Jobs Overall

Job	Annual Earnings	Percent Growth	Annual Openings
413. Fashion Designers	$55,840	10.6%	2,000
414. Postal Service Mail Carriers	$44,450	–0.5%	20,000
415. Gaming Change Persons and Booth Cashiers	$20,530	24.1%	12,000
416. Insulation Workers, Floor, Ceiling, and Wall	$30,310	15.8%	9,000
417. Subway and Streetcar Operators	$49,290	13.2%	2,000
418. Industrial Engineering Technicians	$43,590	8.7%	7,000
419. Tree Trimmers and Pruners	$26,150	18.6%	11,000
420. Aviation Inspectors	$50,380	7.7%	5,000
421. Freight Inspectors	$50,380	7.7%	5,000
422. Marine Cargo Inspectors	$50,380	7.7%	5,000
423. Motor Vehicle Inspectors	$50,380	7.7%	5,000
424. Public Transportation Inspectors	$50,380	7.7%	5,000
425. Railroad Inspectors	$50,380	7.7%	5,000
426. Slaughterers and Meat Packers	$20,860	18.1%	23,000
427. Child Care Workers	$16,760	11.7%	406,000
428. Nannies	$16,760	11.7%	406,000
429. Medical Equipment Repairers	$37,220	14.8%	4,000
430. Bookkeeping, Accounting, and Auditing Clerks	$28,570	3.0%	274,000
431. Civil Engineering Technicians	$38,480	7.6%	10,000
432. Electrical and Electronic Inspectors and Testers	$28,410	4.7%	87,000
433. Helpers—Electricians	$23,420	17.9%	17,000
434. Materials Inspectors	$28,410	4.7%	87,000
435. Mechanical Inspectors	$28,410	4.7%	87,000
436. Plasterers and Stucco Masons	$32,440	13.5%	8,000
437. Police, Fire, and Ambulance Dispatchers	$28,930	12.7%	15,000
438. Precision Devices Inspectors and Testers	$28,410	4.7%	87,000
439. Production Inspectors, Testers, Graders, Sorters, Samplers, Weighers	$28,410	4.7%	87,000
440. Transit and Railroad Police	$45,430	15.9%	1,000
441. Loading Machine Operators, Underground Mining	$33,250	8.9%	14,000
442. Veterinary Assistants and Laboratory Animal Caretakers	$18,660	26.2%	11,000
443. Pest Control Workers	$26,220	17.0%	11,000
444. Cartographers and Photogrammetrists	$46,080	15.1%	1,000
445. First-Line Supervisors and Manager/Supervisors—Agricultural Crop Workers	$35,490	11.4%	6,000
446. First-Line Supervisors and Manager/Supervisors—Animal Care Workers, Except Livestock	$35,490	11.4%	6,000

(continued)

(continued)

The 500 Best Jobs Overall

Job	Annual Earnings	Percent Growth	Annual Openings
447. First-Line Supervisors and Manager/Supervisors—Animal Husbandry Workers	$35,490	11.4%	6,000
448. First-Line Supervisors and Manager/Supervisors—Fishery Workers	$35,490	11.4%	6,000
449. First-Line Supervisors and Manager/Supervisors—Horticultural Workers	$35,490	11.4%	6,000
450. First-Line Supervisors and Manager/Supervisors—Logging Workers	$35,490	11.4%	6,000
451. Electro-Mechanical Technicians	$41,440	11.5%	4,000
452. Recreational Vehicle Service Technicians	$28,980	21.8%	4,000
453. Tellers	$21,120	9.4%	127,000
454. Camera Operators, Television, Video, and Motion Picture	$37,610	13.4%	4,000
455. Lifeguards, Ski Patrol, and Other Recreational Protective Service Workers	$16,540	14.3%	60,000
456. Court Clerks	$28,430	12.3%	14,000
457. License Clerks	$28,430	12.3%	14,000
458. Municipal Clerks	$28,430	12.3%	14,000
459. Production Laborers	$20,180	11.3%	67,000
460. New Accounts Clerks	$26,860	11.2%	24,000
461. Locksmiths and Safe Repairers	$30,360	21.0%	3,000
462. Lodging Managers	$37,660	6.6%	10,000
463. Photographers, Scientific	$26,080	13.6%	18,000
464. Professional Photographers	$26,080	13.6%	18,000
465. Architectural Drafters	$39,190	4.2%	14,000
466. Civil Drafters	$39,190	4.2%	14,000
467. Dragline Operators	$31,970	8.9%	14,000
468. Excavating and Loading Machine Operators	$31,970	8.9%	14,000
469. Survey Researchers	$26,490	33.6%	3,000
470. Archivists	$36,470	17.0%	2,000
471. Sociologists	$57,870	13.4%	fewer than 500
472. Materials Scientists	$72,390	8.5%	1,000
473. Parking Lot Attendants	$16,800	19.2%	19,000
474. Insurance Appraisers, Auto Damage	$45,330	11.7%	2,000
475. Arbitrators, Mediators, and Conciliators	$54,760	13.7%	fewer than 500
476. Electrical Power-Line Installers and Repairers	$49,100	1.6%	9,000
477. Meat, Poultry, and Fish Cutters and Trimmers	$18,900	16.4%	27,000
478. Tax Examiners, Collectors, and Revenue Agents	$43,490	5.0%	9,000

The 500 Best Jobs Overall

Job	Annual Earnings	Percent Growth	Annual Openings
479. Maids and Housekeeping Cleaners	$16,900	9.2%	352,000
480. Plant Scientists	$51,200	9.1%	2,000
481. Soil Scientists	$51,200	9.1%	2,000
482. Physicists	$87,450	6.9%	1,000
483. Food Scientists and Technologists	$50,840	9.1%	2,000
484. Model Makers, Metal and Plastic	$44,250	14.6%	1,000
485. Weighers, Measurers, Checkers, and Samplers, Recordkeeping	$24,570	14.6%	16,000
486. Crane and Tower Operators	$37,410	10.8%	5,000
487. Freight, Stock, and Material Movers, Hand	$20,120	6.6%	525,000
488. Grips and Set-Up Workers, Motion Picture Sets, Studios, and Stages	$20,120	6.6%	525,000
489. Stevedores, Except Equipment Operators	$20,120	6.6%	525,000
490. Millwrights	$43,720	5.3%	7,000
491. Septic Tank Servicers and Sewer Pipe Cleaners	$28,870	21.2%	3,000
492. Laundry and Drycleaning Machine Operators and Tenders, Except Pressing	$17,220	12.3%	47,000
493. Precision Dyers	$17,220	12.3%	47,000
494. Reinforcing Iron and Rebar Workers	$35,160	16.7%	2,000
495. Spotters, Dry Cleaning	$17,220	12.3%	47,000
496. Court Reporters	$42,920	12.7%	2,000
497. Design Printing Machine Setters and Set-Up Operators	$29,900	4.6%	30,000
498. Embossing Machine Set-Up Operators	$29,900	4.6%	30,000
499. Engraver Set-Up Operators	$29,900	4.6%	30,000
500. Letterpress Setters and Set-Up Operators	$29,900	4.6%	30,000

The 100 Best-Paying Jobs

We sorted all 500 jobs based on their annual median earnings from highest to lowest. *Median earnings* means that half of all workers in these jobs earn more than that amount and half earn less. We then selected the 100 jobs with the highest earnings to create the list that follows.

It shouldn't be a big surprise that most of the highest-paying jobs require advanced levels of education, training, and experience. For example, most of the 20 jobs with the highest earnings require a doctoral or professional degree, and others, such as Chief Executives and Engineering Managers, require extensive training and experience. Although the top 20 jobs may not appeal to you for a variety of reasons, you are likely to find others that will among the top 100 jobs with the highest earnings. Keep in mind that the earnings reflect the national average for all workers in the occupation. This is an important consideration, because starting pay in the job is usually a lot less than the pay that workers can earn with several years of experience. Earnings also vary significantly by region of the country, so actual pay in your area could be substantially different.

The 100 Best-Paying Jobs

Job	Annual Earnings
1. Anesthesiologists	more than $145,600
2. Internists, General	more than $145,600
3. Obstetricians and Gynecologists	more than $145,600
4. Oral and Maxillofacial Surgeons	more than $145,600
5. Orthodontists	more than $145,600
6. Prosthodontists	more than $145,600
7. Psychiatrists	more than $145,600
8. Surgeons	more than $145,600
9. Chief Executives	$140,350
10. Government Service Executives	$140,350
11. Private Sector Executives	$140,350
12. Family and General Practitioners	$137,090
13. Pediatricians, General	$135,730
14. Airline Pilots, Copilots, and Flight Engineers	$129,250
15. Dentists, General	$123,060
16. Air Traffic Controllers	$102,030
17. Engineering Managers	$97,630
18. Lawyers	$94,930
19. Podiatrists	$94,400
20. Judges, Magistrate Judges, and Magistrates	$93,070
21. Computer and Information Systems Managers	$92,570
22. Natural Sciences Managers	$88,660
23. Optometrists	$88,410
24. Marketing Managers	$87,640
25. Physicists	$87,450
26. Pharmacists	$84,900
27. Sales Managers	$84,220
28. Financial Managers, Branch or Department	$81,880
29. Treasurers, Controllers, and Chief Financial Officers	$81,880
30. Computer Hardware Engineers	$81,150

The 100 Best-Paying Jobs

Job	Annual Earnings
31. Computer Software Engineers, Systems Software	$79,740
32. General and Operations Managers	$77,420
33. Actuaries	$76,340
34. Electronics Engineers, Except Computer	$75,770
35. Computer Software Engineers, Applications	$74,980
36. Education Administrators, Elementary and Secondary School	$74,190
37. Industrial Production Managers	$73,000
38. Economists	$72,780
39. Purchasing Managers	$72,450
40. Materials Scientists	$72,390
41. Electrical Engineers	$71,610
42. Industrial-Organizational Psychologists	$71,400
43. Sales Engineers	$70,620
44. Atmospheric and Space Scientists	$70,100
45. Public Relations Managers	$70,000
46. Chiropractors	$69,910
47. Construction Managers	$69,870
48. Physician Assistants	$69,410
49. Sales Agents, Financial Services	$69,200
50. Sales Agents, Securities and Commodities	$69,200
51. Biochemists	$68,950
52. Biophysicists	$68,950
53. Geologists	$68,730
54. Education Administrators, Postsecondary	$68,340
55. Biomedical Engineers	$67,690
56. Training and Development Managers	$67,460
57. Medical and Health Services Managers	$67,430
58. Storage and Distribution Managers	$66,600
59. Transportation Managers	$66,600
60. Veterinarians	$66,590
61. Compensation and Benefits Managers	$66,530
62. Environmental Engineers	$66,480
63. Computer Systems Analysts	$66,460
64. Mechanical Engineers	$66,320
65. Industrial Engineers	$65,020
66. First-Line Supervisors/Managers of Police and Detectives	$64,430

(continued)

(continued)

The 100 Best-Paying Jobs

Job	Annual Earnings
67. Civil Engineers	$64,230
68. Art Directors	$63,840
69. Fire-Prevention and Protection Engineers	$63,730
70. Industrial Safety and Health Engineers	$63,730
71. Product Safety Engineers	$63,730
72. Advertising and Promotions Managers	$63,610
73. Management Analysts	$63,450
74. Computer Programmers	$62,890
75. Personal Financial Advisors	$62,700
76. Financial Analysts	$61,910
77. Hydrologists	$61,510
78. Medical Scientists, Except Epidemiologists	$61,320
79. Database Administrators	$60,650
80. Network Systems and Data Communications Analysts	$60,600
81. Financial Examiners	$60,310
82. Architects, Except Landscape and Naval	$60,300
83. Administrative Services Managers	$60,290
84. Operations Research Analysts	$60,190
85. Physical Therapists	$60,180
86. First-Line Supervisors/Managers of Non-Retail Sales Workers	$59,300
87. Geographers	$58,970
88. Forest Fire Fighting and Prevention Supervisors	$58,920
89. Municipal Fire Fighting and Prevention Supervisors	$58,920
90. Real Estate Brokers	$58,720
91. Elevator Installers and Repairers	$58,710
92. Gaming Managers	$58,580
93. Sales Representatives, Agricultural	$58,580
94. Sales Representatives, Chemical and Pharmaceutical	$58,580
95. Sales Representatives, Electrical/Electronic	$58,580
96. Sales Representatives, Instruments	$58,580
97. Sales Representatives, Mechanical Equipment and Supplies	$58,580
98. Sales Representatives, Medical	$58,580
99. Dental Hygienists	$58,350
100. Computer Security Specialists	$58,190

The 100 Fastest-Growing Jobs

We created this list by sorting all 500 best jobs by their projected growth over the ten-year period from 2002 to 2012. Growth rates are one measure to consider in exploring career options, as jobs with higher growth rates tend to provide more job opportunities.

Jobs in the computer and medical fields dominate the 20 fastest-growing jobs. Medical Assistants is the job with the highest growth rate—the number employed is projected to better than double during this time. You can find a wide range of rapidly growing jobs in a variety of fields and at different levels of training and education among the jobs in this list.

The 100 Fastest-Growing Jobs

Job	Percent Growth
1. Medical Assistants	58.9%
2. Network Systems and Data Communications Analysts	57.0%
3. Physician Assistants	48.9%
4. Social and Human Service Assistants	48.7%
5. Home Health Aides	48.1%
6. Medical Records and Health Information Technicians	46.8%
7. Physical Therapist Aides	46.4%
8. Computer Software Engineers, Applications	45.5%
9. Computer Software Engineers, Systems Software	45.5%
10. Physical Therapist Assistants	44.6%
11. Fitness Trainers and Aerobics Instructors	44.5%
12. Database Administrators	44.2%
13. Veterinary Technologists and Technicians	44.1%
14. Dental Hygienists	43.1%
15. Hazardous Materials Removal Workers	43.1%
16. Irradiated-Fuel Handlers	43.1%
17. Dental Assistants	42.5%
18. Personal and Home Care Aides	40.5%
19. Self-Enrichment Education Teachers	40.1%
20. Computer Systems Analysts	39.4%
21. Occupational Therapist Assistants	39.2%
22. Environmental Engineers	38.2%
23. Teachers, Postsecondary	38.1%
24. Computer Security Specialists	37.4%
25. Network and Computer Systems Administrators	37.4%
26. Environmental Science and Protection Technicians, Including Health	36.8%
27. Preschool Teachers, Except Special Education	36.2%

(continued)

(continued)

The 100 Fastest-Growing Jobs

Job	Percent Growth
28. Computer and Information Systems Managers	36.1%
29. Physical Therapists	35.3%
30. Occupational Therapists	35.2%
31. Respiratory Therapists	34.8%
32. Personal Financial Advisors	34.6%
33. Mental Health and Substance Abuse Social Workers	34.5%
34. Respiratory Therapy Technicians	34.2%
35. Rehabilitation Counselors	33.8%
36. Residential Advisors	33.6%
37. Survey Researchers	33.6%
38. Cardiovascular Technologists and Technicians	33.5%
39. Emergency Medical Technicians and Paramedics	33.1%
40. Public Relations Specialists	32.9%
41. Epidemiologists	32.5%
42. Education Administrators, Preschool and Child Care Center/Program	32.0%
43. Security Guards	31.9%
44. Heating and Air Conditioning Mechanics	31.8%
45. Refrigeration Mechanics	31.8%
46. Radiation Therapists	31.6%
47. Sales Managers	30.5%
48. Management Analysts	30.4%
49. Computer Support Specialists	30.3%
50. Security and Fire Alarm Systems Installers	30.2%
51. Pharmacists	30.1%
52. Special Education Teachers, Middle School	30.0%
53. Special Education Teachers, Preschool, Kindergarten, and Elementary School	30.0%
54. Special Education Teachers, Secondary School	30.0%
55. Athletic Trainers	29.9%
56. Receptionists and Information Clerks	29.5%
57. Medical and Health Services Managers	29.3%
58. Desktop Publishers	29.2%
59. Audiologists	29.0%
60. Pharmacy Technicians	28.8%
61. Paralegals and Legal Assistants	28.7%
62. Medical and Public Health Social Workers	28.6%
63. Environmental Engineering Technicians	28.4%
64. Emergency Management Specialists	28.2%

The 100 Fastest-Growing Jobs

Job	Percent Growth
65. Compensation, Benefits, and Job Analysis Specialists	28.0%
66. Interviewers, Except Eligibility and Loan	28.0%
67. Surgical Technologists	27.9%
68. Training and Development Specialists	27.9%
69. Agents and Business Managers of Artists, Performers, and Athletes	27.8%
70. Amusement and Recreation Attendants	27.8%
71. Costume Attendants	27.8%
72. Locker Room, Coatroom, and Dressing Room Attendants	27.8%
73. Social and Community Service Managers	27.7%
74. Logisticians	27.5%
75. Employment Interviewers, Private or Public Employment Service	27.3%
76. Personnel Recruiters	27.3%
77. Registered Nurses	27.3%
78. Kindergarten Teachers, Except Special Education	27.2%
79. Speech-Language Pathologists	27.2%
80. Massage Therapists	27.1%
81. Technical Writers	27.1%
82. Medical Scientists, Except Epidemiologists	26.9%
83. Audio and Video Equipment Technicians	26.7%
84. Mental Health Counselors	26.7%
85. Tile and Marble Setters	26.5%
86. Film and Video Editors	26.4%
87. Counter and Rental Clerks	26.3%
88. Veterinary Assistants and Laboratory Animal Caretakers	26.2%
89. Biomedical Engineers	26.1%
90. Cement Masons and Concrete Finishers	26.1%
91. Education Administrators, Postsecondary	25.9%
92. Sound Engineering Technicians	25.5%
93. Instructional Coordinators	25.4%
94. Private Detectives and Investigators	25.3%
95. Veterinarians	25.1%
96. Advertising and Promotions Managers	25.0%
97. Nursing Aides, Orderlies, and Attendants	24.9%
98. Gaming Dealers	24.7%
99. Highway Patrol Pilots	24.7%
100. Police Patrol Officers	24.7%

The 100 Jobs with the Most Openings

We created this list by sorting all 500 best jobs by the number of job openings that each is expected to have per year. Jobs that employ lots of people are also likely to have more job openings in a given year. Many of these occupations, such as Cashiers, are not among the highest-paying jobs. But jobs with large numbers of openings often provide easier entry for new workers, make it easier to move from one position to another, or are attractive for other reasons. Some of these jobs may also appeal to people re-entering the labor market, part-time workers, and workers who want to move from one employer to another. And some of these jobs pay quite well, offer good benefits, or have other advantages.

The 100 Jobs with the Most Openings

Job	Annual Openings
1. Cashiers	1,221,000
2. Retail Salespersons	1,014,000
3. Combined Food Preparation and Serving Workers, Including Fast Food	734,000
4. Waiters and Waitresses	721,000
5. Office Clerks, General	550,000
6. Freight, Stock, and Material Movers, Hand	525,000
7. Grips and Set-Up Workers, Motion Picture Sets, Studios, and Stages	525,000
8. Stevedores, Except Equipment Operators	525,000
9. Janitors and Cleaners, Except Maids and Housekeeping Cleaners	454,000
10. Adjustment Clerks	419,000
11. Customer Service Representatives, Utilities	419,000
12. Child Care Workers	406,000
13. Nannies	406,000
14. Maids and Housekeeping Cleaners	352,000
15. Nursing Aides, Orderlies, and Attendants	302,000
16. Tractor-Trailer Truck Drivers	299,000
17. Truck Drivers, Heavy	299,000
18. Receptionists and Information Clerks	296,000
19. Bookkeeping, Accounting, and Auditing Clerks	274,000
20. Food Preparation Workers	267,000
21. General and Operations Managers	260,000
22. Teacher Assistants	259,000
23. First-Line Supervisors/Managers of Retail Sales Workers	251,000
24. Security Guards	228,000
25. Truck Drivers, Light or Delivery Services	219,000
26. Teachers, Postsecondary	216,000
27. Registered Nurses	215,000

The 100 Jobs with the Most Openings

Job	Annual Openings
28. Cooks, Restaurant	211,000
29. Executive Secretaries and Administrative Assistants	210,000
30. Landscaping and Groundskeeping Workers	203,000
31. Packers and Packagers, Hand	198,000
32. Boat Builders and Shipwrights	193,000
33. Brattice Builders	193,000
34. Carpenter Assemblers and Repairers	193,000
35. Construction Carpenters	193,000
36. Rough Carpenters	193,000
37. Ship Carpenters and Joiners	193,000
38. Counter Attendants, Cafeteria, Food Concession, and Coffee Shop	190,000
39. Elementary School Teachers, Except Special Education	183,000
40. Construction Laborers	166,000
41. Logisticians	162,000
42. Sales Representatives, Wholesale and Manufacturing, Except Technical and Scientific Products	160,000
43. Maintenance and Repair Workers, General	155,000
44. Refractory Materials Repairers, Except Brickmasons	155,000
45. First-Line Supervisors/Managers of Food Preparation and Serving Workers	154,000
46. Personal and Home Care Aides	154,000
47. Counter and Rental Clerks	144,000
48. Dining Room and Cafeteria Attendants and Bartender Helpers	143,000
49. Home Health Aides	141,000
50. First-Line Supervisors, Administrative Support	140,000
51. First-Line Supervisors, Customer Service	140,000
52. Tellers	127,000
53. Accountants	119,000
54. Auditors	119,000
55. Farmers and Ranchers	118,000
56. Secondary School Teachers, Except Special and Vocational Education	118,000
57. Licensed Practical and Licensed Vocational Nurses	105,000
58. Automotive Master Mechanics	100,000
59. Automotive Specialty Technicians	100,000
60. Hosts and Hostesses, Restaurant, Lounge, and Coffee Shop	95,000
61. Industrial Truck and Tractor Operators	94,000
62. Preschool Teachers, Except Special Education	88,000

(continued)

(continued)

The 100 Jobs with the Most Openings

Job	Annual Openings
63. Electrical and Electronic Inspectors and Testers	87,000
64. Materials Inspectors	87,000
65. Mechanical Inspectors	87,000
66. Precision Devices Inspectors and Testers	87,000
67. Production Inspectors, Testers, Graders, Sorters, Samplers, Weighers	87,000
68. Billing, Cost, and Rate Clerks	78,000
69. Billing, Posting, and Calculating Machine Operators	78,000
70. Management Analysts	78,000
71. Medical Assistants	78,000
72. Statement Clerks	78,000
73. Bill and Account Collectors	76,000
74. Bus Drivers, School	76,000
75. First-Line Supervisors/Managers of Non-Retail Sales Workers	72,000
76. Brazers	71,000
77. Computer Support Specialists	71,000
78. Financial Managers, Branch or Department	71,000
79. Solderers	71,000
80. Treasurers, Controllers, and Chief Financial Officers	71,000
81. Welder-Fitters	71,000
82. Welders and Cutters	71,000
83. Welders, Production	71,000
84. Middle School Teachers, Except Special and Vocational Education	69,000
85. Packaging and Filling Machine Operators and Tenders	69,000
86. Painters, Construction and Maintenance	69,000
87. Computer Systems Analysts	68,000
88. Hairdressers, Hairstylists, and Cosmetologists	68,000
89. First-Line Supervisors and Manager/Supervisors—Construction Trades Workers	67,000
90. First-Line Supervisors and Manager/Supervisors—Extractive Workers	67,000
91. Highway Patrol Pilots	67,000
92. Police Patrol Officers	67,000
93. Production Laborers	67,000
94. Sheriffs and Deputy Sheriffs	67,000
95. Amusement and Recreation Attendants	66,000
96. Costume Attendants	66,000
97. First-Line Supervisors/Managers of Production and Operating Workers	66,000
98. Locker Room, Coatroom, and Dressing Room Attendants	66,000
99. Electricians	65,000
100. Chief Executives	63,000

Best Jobs Lists with High Percentages of Workers Age 16–24, Workers Age 55 and Over, Part-Time Workers, Self-Employed Workers, Women, and Men

We decided that it would be interesting to include lists in this section that show what sorts of jobs different types of people are most likely to have. For example, what jobs have the highest percentage of men or younger workers? We're not saying that men or younger workers should consider these jobs over others, but it is interesting information to know.

In some cases, the lists can give you ideas for jobs to consider that you might otherwise overlook. For example, perhaps women should consider some jobs that traditionally have high percentages of men in them. Older workers might consider some jobs typically held by younger ones. Although these are not obvious ways of using these lists, the lists may give you some good ideas on jobs to consider. The lists may also help you identify jobs that work well for others in your situation (for example, jobs with plentiful opportunities for part-time work, if that is something you want to do).

All of the lists in this section were created by using a similar process. We began with all 500 best jobs and sorted those jobs in order of the primary criterion for each set of lists. Then, we selected the jobs with the highest percentage of workers fitting the primary criterion and listed them along with their earnings, growth, and number of openings data. (For example, we sorted all 500 jobs based on the percentage of workers age 16 to 24 and then selected the jobs with more than 20 percent of these workers for inclusion in the first list for this group.)

From the list of jobs with a high percentage of each type of worker, we created four more-specialized lists:

- ☺ 25 Best Jobs Overall (jobs with the best total score for earnings, growth rate, and number of openings)
- ☺ 25 Best-Paying Jobs
- ☺ 25 Fastest-Growing Jobs
- ☺ 25 Jobs with the Most Openings

Again, each of these four lists includes only jobs from among those with the highest percentages of different types of workers. The same basic process was used to create all the lists in this section. The lists are interesting, and we hope you find them helpful.

Note that when we list the jobs that pay best, are growing fastest, and have the most openings, we use the figures for **all** people working in the occupation. It would be nice if, for example, we could based the list of Best-Paying Jobs for Part-Time Workers on the earnings of part-timers, especially since we know that in some occupations part-timers average a higher or lower hourly wage than full-timers. But because data on these groups is limited, we have to base our lists on the averages for all workers.

Best Jobs with the Highest Percentage of Workers Age 16–24

From our list of 500 jobs used in this book, this list contains jobs with the highest percentage (more than 20 percent) of workers age 16 to 24, presented in order of the percentage of these young workers in each job. Younger workers are found in all jobs, but jobs with higher percentages of younger workers may present more opportunities for initial entry or upward mobility. Many jobs with the highest percentages of younger workers are those that don't require extensive training or education, and there is a wide variety of jobs in different fields among these jobs.

Best Jobs with the Highest Percentage of Workers Age 16–24

Job	Percent Age 16–24	Annual Earnings	Percent Growth	Annual Openings
1. Hosts and Hostesses, Restaurant, Lounge, and Coffee Shop	77.8%	$15,630	16.4%	95,000
2. Counter Attendants, Cafeteria, Food Concession, and Coffee Shop	75.4%	$15,660	16.7%	190,000
3. Lifeguards, Ski Patrol, and Other Recreational Protective Service Workers	71.6%	$16,540	14.3%	60,000
4. Waiters and Waitresses	53.1%	$14,050	17.5%	721,000
5. Amusement and Recreation Attendants	52.3%	$15,550	27.8%	66,000
6. Costume Attendants	52.3%	$25,050	27.8%	66,000
7. Locker Room, Coatroom, and Dressing Room Attendants	52.3%	$17,550	27.8%	66,000
8. Cashiers	49.1%	$16,240	13.2%	1,221,000
9. Gaming Change Persons and Booth Cashiers	49.1%	$20,530	24.1%	12,000
10. Combined Food Preparation and Serving Workers, Including Fast Food	49.0%	$14,690	22.8%	734,000
11. Hotel, Motel, and Resort Desk Clerks	46.0%	$17,700	23.9%	46,000
12. Helpers—Electricians	44.7%	$23,420	17.9%	17,000
13. Dining Room and Cafeteria Attendants and Bartender Helpers	43.6%	$14,770	14.9%	143,000
14. Library Technicians	43.5%	$24,940	16.8%	22,000
15. Counter and Rental Clerks	42.2%	$18,280	26.3%	144,000
16. Food Preparation Workers	41.3%	$16,710	20.2%	267,000
17. Tellers	40.3%	$21,120	9.4%	127,000
18. Parking Lot Attendants	36.5%	$16,800	19.2%	19,000
19. Athletes and Sports Competitors	35.3%	$48,310	19.2%	3,000
20. Coaches and Scouts	35.3%	$26,350	18.3%	26,000
21. Residential Advisors	34.1%	$21,430	33.6%	12,000

Best Jobs with the Highest Percentage of Workers Age 16–24

Job	Percent Age 16–24	Annual Earnings	Percent Growth	Annual Openings
22. Cooks, Restaurant	33.6%	$19,520	15.9%	211,000
23. Nonfarm Animal Caretakers	32.5%	$17,460	22.2%	32,000
24. Freight, Stock, and Material Movers, Hand	31.9%	$20,120	6.6%	525,000
25. Grips and Set-Up Workers, Motion Picture Sets, Studios, and Stages	31.9%	$20,120	6.6%	525,000
26. Stevedores, Except Equipment Operators	31.9%	$20,120	6.6%	525,000
27. City and Regional Planning Aides	30.8%	$34,360	17.5%	18,000
28. Environmental Science and Protection Technicians, Including Health	30.8%	$35,340	36.8%	4,000
29. Forensic Science Technicians	30.8%	$44,010	18.9%	1,000
30. Social Science Research Assistants	30.8%	$34,360	17.5%	18,000
31. Retail Salespersons	30.4%	$18,680	14.6%	1,014,000
32. Fitness Trainers and Aerobics Instructors	29.1%	$25,470	44.5%	38,000
33. Recreation Workers	29.1%	$19,320	20.5%	56,000
34. Child Care Workers	27.9%	$16,760	11.7%	406,000
35. Nannies	27.9%	$16,760	11.7%	406,000
36. Receptionists and Information Clerks	27.6%	$21,830	29.5%	296,000
37. Recreational Vehicle Service Technicians	26.7%	$28,980	21.8%	4,000
38. Library Assistants, Clerical	26.7%	$20,720	21.5%	27,000
39. Landscaping and Groundskeeping Workers	26.6%	$20,420	22.0%	203,000
40. Tree Trimmers and Pruners	26.6%	$26,150	18.6%	11,000
41. Helpers—Installation, Maintenance, and Repair Workers	25.8%	$21,310	20.3%	33,000
42. Pharmacy Technicians	24.7%	$23,650	28.8%	39,000
43. Respiratory Therapy Technicians	24.7%	$36,740	34.2%	5,000
44. Surgical Technologists	24.7%	$34,010	27.9%	13,000
45. Veterinary Technologists and Technicians	24.7%	$24,940	44.1%	11,000
46. First-Line Supervisors/Managers of Food Preparation and Serving Workers	24.3%	$25,410	15.5%	154,000
47. Construction Laborers	23.7%	$25,160	14.2%	166,000
48. Office Clerks, General	23.3%	$22,770	10.4%	550,000
49. Roofers	22.7%	$30,840	18.6%	38,000
50. Medical Assistants	21.5%	$24,610	58.9%	78,000
51. Medical Transcriptionists	21.5%	$28,380	22.6%	18,000
52. Veterinary Assistants and Laboratory Animal Caretakers	21.5%	$18,660	26.2%	11,000
53. Security Guards	20.6%	$20,320	31.9%	228,000

(continued)

(continued)

Best Jobs with the Highest Percentage of Workers Age 16–24

Job	Percent Age 16–24	Annual Earnings	Percent Growth	Annual Openings
54. Interviewers, Except Eligibility and Loan	20.6%	$23,670	28.0%	46,000
55. Medical Records and Health Information Technicians	20.6%	$25,590	46.8%	24,000
56. Adjustment Clerks	20.5%	$27,020	24.3%	419,000
57. Customer Service Representatives, Utilities	20.5%	$27,020	24.3%	419,000
58. Insulation Workers, Floor, Ceiling, and Wall	20.4%	$30,310	15.8%	9,000
59. Insulation Workers, Mechanical	20.4%	$33,330	15.8%	9,000

The jobs in the following four lists are derived from the preceding list of the jobs with the highest percentage of workers age 16–24.

Best Jobs Overall with a High Percentage of Workers Age 16–24

Job	Percent Age 16–24	Annual Earnings	Percent Growth	Annual Openings
1. Adjustment Clerks	20.5%	$27,020	24.3%	419,000
2. Customer Service Representatives, Utilities	20.5%	$27,020	24.3%	419,000
3. Medical Assistants	21.5%	$24,610	58.9%	78,000
4. Receptionists and Information Clerks	27.6%	$21,830	29.5%	296,000
5. Fitness Trainers and Aerobics Instructors	29.1%	$25,470	44.5%	38,000
6. Surgical Technologists	24.7%	$34,010	27.9%	13,000
7. Security Guards	20.6%	$20,320	31.9%	228,000
8. Costume Attendants	52.4%	$25,050	27.8%	66,000
9. Roofers	22.7%	$30,840	18.6%	38,000
10. Interviewers, Except Eligibility and Loan	20.6%	$23,670	28.0%	46,000
11. Medical Records and Health Information Technicians	20.6%	$25,590	46.8%	24,000
12. Pharmacy Technicians	24.7%	$23,650	28.8%	39,000
13. Landscaping and Groundskeeping Workers	26.6%	$20,420	22.0%	203,000
14. Respiratory Therapy Technicians	24.7%	$36,740	34.2%	5,000
15. City and Regional Planning Aides	30.8%	$34,360	17.5%	18,000
16. Social Science Research Assistants	30.8%	$34,360	17.5%	18,000
17. Counter and Rental Clerks	42.2%	$18,280	26.3%	144,000
18. Combined Food Preparation and Serving Workers, Including Fast Food	49.0%	$14,690	22.8%	734,000

Best Jobs Overall with a High Percentage of Workers Age 16–24

Job	Percent Age 16–24	Annual Earnings	Percent Growth	Annual Openings
19. Locker Room, Coatroom, and Dressing Room Attendants	52.4%	$17,550	27.8%	66,000
20. Environmental Science and Protection Technicians, Including Health	30.8%	$35,340	36.8%	4,000
21. Medical Transcriptionists	21.5%	$28,380	22.6%	18,000
22. Athletes and Sports Competitors	35.3%	$48,310	19.2%	3,000
23. Amusement and Recreation Attendants	52.4%	$15,550	27.8%	66,000
24. First-Line Supervisors/Managers of Food Preparation and Serving Workers	24.3%	$25,410	15.5%	154,000
25. Food Preparation Workers	41.3%	$16,710	20.2%	267,000

Best-Paying Jobs with a High Percentage of Workers Age 16–24

Job	Percent Age 16–24	Annual Earnings	Percent Growth	Annual Openings
1. Athletes and Sports Competitors	35.3%	$48,310	19.2%	3,000
2. Forensic Science Technicians	30.8%	$44,010	18.9%	1,000
3. Respiratory Therapy Technicians	24.7%	$36,740	34.2%	5,000
4. Environmental Science and Protection Technicians, Including Health	30.8%	$35,340	36.8%	4,000
5. City and Regional Planning Aides	30.8%	$34,360	17.5%	18,000
6. Social Science Research Assistants	30.8%	$34,360	17.5%	18,000
7. Surgical Technologists	24.7%	$34,010	27.9%	13,000
8. Insulation Workers, Mechanical	20.5%	$33,330	15.8%	9,000
9. Roofers	22.7%	$30,840	18.6%	38,000
10. Insulation Workers, Floor, Ceiling, and Wall	20.5%	$30,310	15.8%	9,000
11. Recreational Vehicle Service Technicians	26.7%	$28,980	21.8%	4,000
12. Medical Transcriptionists	21.5%	$28,380	22.6%	18,000
13. Adjustment Clerks	20.5%	$27,020	24.3%	419,000
14. Customer Service Representatives, Utilities	20.5%	$27,020	24.3%	419,000
15. Coaches and Scouts	35.3%	$26,350	18.3%	26,000
16. Tree Trimmers and Pruners	26.6%	$26,150	18.6%	11,000
17. Medical Records and Health Information Technicians	20.6%	$25,590	46.8%	24,000
18. Fitness Trainers and Aerobics Instructors	29.1%	$25,470	44.5%	38,000

(continued)

(continued)

Best-Paying Jobs with a High Percentage of Workers Age 16–24

Job	Percent Age 16–24	Annual Earnings	Percent Growth	Annual Openings
19. First-Line Supervisors/Managers of Food Preparation and Serving Workers	24.3%	$25,410	15.5%	154,000
20. Construction Laborers	23.7%	$25,160	14.2%	166,000
21. Costume Attendants	52.4%	$25,050	27.8%	66,000
22. Library Technicians	43.5%	$24,940	16.8%	22,000
23. Veterinary Technologists and Technicians	24.7%	$24,940	44.1%	11,000
24. Medical Assistants	21.5%	$24,610	58.9%	78,000
25. Interviewers, Except Eligibility and Loan	20.6%	$23,670	28.0%	46,000

Fastest-Growing Jobs with a High Percentage of Workers Age 16–24

Job	Percent Age 16–24	Annual Earnings	Percent Growth	Annual Openings
1. Medical Assistants	21.5%	$24,610	58.9%	78,000
2. Medical Records and Health Information Technicians	20.6%	$25,590	46.8%	24,000
3. Fitness Trainers and Aerobics Instructors	29.1%	$25,470	44.5%	38,000
4. Veterinary Technologists and Technicians	24.7%	$24,940	44.1%	11,000
5. Environmental Science and Protection Technicians, Including Health	30.8%	$35,340	36.8%	4,000
6. Respiratory Therapy Technicians	24.7%	$36,740	34.2%	5,000
7. Residential Advisors	34.1%	$21,430	33.6%	12,000
8. Security Guards	20.6%	$20,320	31.9%	228,000
9. Receptionists and Information Clerks	27.6%	$21,830	29.5%	296,000
10. Pharmacy Technicians	24.7%	$23,650	28.8%	39,000
11. Interviewers, Except Eligibility and Loan	20.6%	$23,670	28.0%	46,000
12. Surgical Technologists	24.7%	$34,010	27.9%	13,000
13. Amusement and Recreation Attendants	52.4%	$15,550	27.8%	66,000
14. Costume Attendants	52.4%	$25,050	27.8%	66,000
15. Locker Room, Coatroom, and Dressing Room Attendants	52.4%	$17,550	27.8%	66,000
16. Counter and Rental Clerks	42.2%	$18,280	26.3%	144,000
17. Veterinary Assistants and Laboratory Animal Caretakers	21.5%	$18,660	26.2%	11,000
18. Adjustment Clerks	20.5%	$27,020	24.3%	419,000
19. Customer Service Representatives, Utilities	20.5%	$27,020	24.3%	419,000

Fastest-Growing Jobs with a High Percentage of Workers Age 16–24

Job	Percent Age 16–24	Annual Earnings	Percent Growth	Annual Openings
20. Gaming Change Persons and Booth Cashiers	49.1%	$20,530	24.1%	12,000
21. Hotel, Motel, and Resort Desk Clerks	46.0%	$17,700	23.9%	46,000
22. Combined Food Preparation and Serving Workers, Including Fast Food	49.0%	$14,690	22.8%	734,000
23. Medical Transcriptionists	21.5%	$28,380	22.6%	18,000
24. Nonfarm Animal Caretakers	32.5%	$17,460	22.2%	32,000
25. Landscaping and Groundskeeping Workers	26.6%	$20,420	22.0%	203,000

Jobs with the Most Openings with a High Percentage of Workers Age 16–24

Job	Percent Age 16–24	Annual Earnings	Percent Growth	Annual Openings
1. Cashiers	49.1%	$16,240	13.2%	1,221,000
2. Retail Salespersons	30.5%	$18,680	14.6%	1,014,000
3. Combined Food Preparation and Serving Workers, Including Fast Food	49.0%	$14,690	22.8%	734,000
4. Waiters and Waitresses	53.1%	$14,050	17.5%	721,000
5. Office Clerks, General	23.3%	$22,770	10.4%	550,000
6. Freight, Stock, and Material Movers, Hand	31.9%	$20,120	6.6%	525,000
7. Grips and Set-Up Workers, Motion Picture Sets, Studios, and Stages	31.9%	$20,120	6.6%	525,000
8. Stevedores, Except Equipment Operators	31.9%	$20,120	6.6%	525,000
9. Adjustment Clerks	20.5%	$27,020	24.3%	419,000
10. Customer Service Representatives, Utilities	20.5%	$27,020	24.3%	419,000
11. Child Care Workers	27.9%	$16,760	11.7%	406,000
12. Nannies	27.9%	$16,760	11.7%	406,000
13. Receptionists and Information Clerks	27.6%	$21,830	29.5%	296,000
14. Food Preparation Workers	41.3%	$16,710	20.2%	267,000
15. Security Guards	20.6%	$20,320	31.9%	228,000
16. Cooks, Restaurant	33.6%	$19,520	15.9%	211,000
17. Landscaping and Groundskeeping Workers	26.6%	$20,420	22.0%	203,000
18. Counter Attendants, Cafeteria, Food Concession, and Coffee Shop	75.4%	$15,660	16.7%	190,000
19. Construction Laborers	23.7%	$25,160	14.2%	166,000

(continued)

(continued)

Jobs with the Most Openings with a High Percentage of Workers Age 16–24

Job	Percent Age 16–24	Annual Earnings	Percent Growth	Annual Openings
20. First-Line Supervisors/Managers of Food Preparation and Serving Workers	24.3%	$25,410	15.5%	154,000
21. Counter and Rental Clerks	42.2%	$18,280	26.3%	144,000
22. Dining Room and Cafeteria Attendants and Bartender Helpers	43.6%	$14,770	14.9%	143,000
23. Tellers	40.3%	$21,120	9.4%	127,000
24. Hosts and Hostesses, Restaurant, Lounge, and Coffee Shop	77.8%	$15,630	16.4%	95,000
25. Medical Assistants	21.5%	$24,610	58.9%	78,000

Best Jobs with a High Percentage of Workers Age 55 and Over

Older workers don't change careers as often as younger ones do, and on the average, they tend to have been in their jobs for quite some time. Many of the jobs with the highest percentages of workers age 55 and over—and those with the highest earnings—require considerable preparation, either through experience or through education and training. These are not the sort of jobs most younger workers could easily get. That should not come as a big surprise, as many of these folks have been in the workforce for a long time and therefore have lots of experience.

But go down the list of the jobs with the highest percentage (more than 20 percent) of older workers and you will find a variety of jobs that many older workers could more easily enter if they were changing careers. Some would make good "retirement" jobs, particularly if they allowed for part-time work or self-employment.

Best Jobs with the Highest Percentage of Workers Age 55 and Over

Job	Percent Age 55 and Over	Annual Earnings	Percent Growth	Annual Openings
1. Farmers and Ranchers	48.7%	$40,440	–20.6%	118,000
2. Physicists	44.4%	$87,450	6.9%	1,000
3. Arbitrators, Mediators, and Conciliators	42.4%	$54,760	13.7%	fewer than 500
4. Judges, Magistrate Judges, and Magistrates	42.4%	$93,070	8.7%	2,000

Best Jobs with the Highest Percentage of Workers Age 55 and Over

Job	Percent Age 55 and Over	Annual Earnings	Percent Growth	Annual Openings
5. Tax Preparers	35.2%	$27,730	23.2%	11,000
6. Demonstrators and Product Promoters	34.2%	$20,700	17.0%	38,000
7. Real Estate Brokers	33.4%	$58,720	2.4%	11,000
8. Real Estate Sales Agents	33.4%	$35,670	5.7%	34,000
9. Model Makers, Metal and Plastic	33.3%	$44,250	14.6%	1,000
10. Clergy	32.7%	$36,690	15.5%	34,000
11. Property, Real Estate, and Community Association Managers	32.0%	$39,980	12.8%	35,000
12. Clinical Psychologists	31.4%	$54,950	24.4%	17,000
13. Counseling Psychologists	31.4%	$54,950	24.4%	17,000
14. Industrial-Organizational Psychologists	31.4%	$71,400	16.0%	fewer than 500
15. School Psychologists	31.4%	$54,950	24.4%	17,000
16. Taxi Drivers and Chauffeurs	31.1%	$19,570	21.7%	28,000
17. Agricultural Crop Farm Managers	30.1%	$50,700	5.1%	25,000
18. Fish Hatchery Managers	30.1%	$50,700	5.1%	25,000
19. Nursery and Greenhouse Managers	30.1%	$50,700	5.1%	25,000
20. Bus Drivers, School	29.6%	$23,250	16.7%	76,000
21. Bus Drivers, Transit and Intercity	29.6%	$29,730	15.2%	33,000
22. Librarians	28.9%	$45,900	10.1%	15,000
23. Management Analysts	27.4%	$63,450	30.4%	78,000
24. Lodging Managers	26.9%	$37,660	6.6%	10,000
25. Dentists, General	26.1%	$123,060	4.1%	7,000
26. Oral and Maxillofacial Surgeons	26.1%	more than $145,600	4.1%	7,000
27. Orthodontists	26.1%	more than $145,600	4.1%	7,000
28. Prosthodontists	26.1%	more than $145,600	4.1%	7,000
29. Education Administrators, Elementary and Secondary School	25.9%	$74,190	20.7%	31,000
30. Education Administrators, Postsecondary	25.9%	$68,340	25.9%	19,000
31. Education Administrators, Preschool and Child Care Center/Program	25.9%	$35,730	32.0%	9,000
32. Chief Executives	25.5%	$140,350	16.7%	63,000
33. Government Service Executives	25.5%	$140,350	16.7%	63,000
34. Private Sector Executives	25.5%	$140,350	16.7%	63,000
35. Personal and Home Care Aides	25.4%	$16,900	40.5%	154,000
36. Desktop Publishers	25.0%	$32,340	29.2%	4,000
37. Reinforcing Iron and Rebar Workers	25.0%	$35,160	16.7%	2,000
38. Teachers, Postsecondary	24.5%	$51,614	38.1%	216,000

(continued)

(continued)

Best Jobs with the Highest Percentage of Workers Age 55 and Over

Job	Percent Age 55 and Over	Annual Earnings	Percent Growth	Annual Openings
39. Appraisers, Real Estate	24.4%	$43,390	17.6%	11,000
40. Assessors	24.4%	$43,390	17.6%	11,000
41. Security Guards	24.3%	$20,320	31.9%	228,000
42. Construction and Building Inspectors	24.2%	$43,670	13.8%	10,000
43. Directors, Religious Activities and Education	24.1%	$30,700	24.1%	16,000
44. Social and Community Service Managers	23.8%	$46,810	27.7%	19,000
45. Caption Writers	23.7%	$44,350	16.1%	23,000
46. Copy Writers	23.7%	$44,350	16.1%	23,000
47. Creative Writers	23.7%	$44,350	16.1%	23,000
48. Poets and Lyricists	23.7%	$44,350	16.1%	23,000
49. Private Detectives and Investigators	23.4%	$32,110	25.3%	9,000
50. Bookkeeping, Accounting, and Auditing Clerks	23.2%	$28,570	3.0%	274,000
51. Audiologists	23.1%	$51,470	29.0%	1,000
52. Meeting and Convention Planners	23.1%	$39,620	21.3%	7,000
53. Urban and Regional Planners	22.7%	$53,450	10.7%	5,000
54. Art Directors	22.6%	$63,840	11.4%	8,000
55. Cartoonists	22.6%	$38,060	16.5%	4,000
56. Multi-Media Artists and Animators	22.6%	$50,360	15.8%	12,000
57. Painters and Illustrators	22.6%	$38,060	16.5%	4,000
58. Sculptors	22.6%	$38,060	16.5%	4,000
59. Sketch Artists	22.6%	$38,060	16.5%	4,000
60. Helpers—Installation, Maintenance, and Repair Workers	22.6%	$21,310	20.3%	33,000
61. Pharmacists	22.4%	$84,900	30.1%	23,000
62. Janitors and Cleaners, Except Maids and Housekeeping Cleaners	22.3%	$18,790	18.3%	454,000
63. Laundry and Drycleaning Machine Operators and Tenders, Except Pressing	22.3%	$17,220	12.3%	47,000
64. Precision Dyers	22.3%	$17,220	12.3%	47,000
65. Spotters, Dry Cleaning	22.3%	$17,220	12.3%	47,000
66. Veterinarians	22.0%	$66,590	25.1%	4,000
67. Lawyers	21.8%	$94,930	17.0%	53,000
68. Composers	21.8%	$34,570	13.5%	8,000
69. Music Arrangers and Orchestrators	21.8%	$34,570	13.5%	8,000
70. Music Directors	21.8%	$34,570	13.5%	8,000
71. First-Line Supervisors and Manager/Supervisors —Agricultural Crop Workers	21.5%	$35,490	11.4%	6,000

Best Jobs with the Highest Percentage of Workers Age 55 and Over

Job	Percent Age 55 and Over	Annual Earnings	Percent Growth	Annual Openings
72. First-Line Supervisors and Manager/Supervisors—Animal Care Workers, Except Livestock	21.5%	$35,490	11.4%	6,000
73. First-Line Supervisors and Manager/Supervisors—Animal Husbandry Workers	21.5%	$35,490	11.4%	6,000
74. First-Line Supervisors and Manager/Supervisors—Fishery Workers	21.5%	$35,490	11.4%	6,000
75. First-Line Supervisors and Manager/Supervisors—Horticultural Workers	21.5%	$35,490	11.4%	6,000
76. First-Line Supervisors and Manager/Supervisors—Logging Workers	21.5%	$35,490	11.4%	6,000
77. Insurance Sales Agents	21.4%	$41,720	8.4%	52,000
78. Cost Estimators	21.0%	$49,940	18.6%	25,000
79. First-Line Supervisors/Managers of Personal Service Workers	21.0%	$30,350	9.4%	26,000
80. Instructional Coordinators	20.9%	$48,790	25.4%	18,000
81. Economists	20.6%	$72,780	13.4%	2,000

The jobs in the following four lists are derived from the preceding list of the jobs with the highest percentage of workers age 55 and over.

Best Jobs Overall with a High Percentage of Workers Age 55 and Over

Job	Percent Age 55 and Over	Annual Earnings	Percent Growth	Annual Openings
1. Teachers, Postsecondary	24.5%	$51,614	38.1%	216,000
2. Management Analysts	27.4%	$63,450	30.4%	78,000
3. Pharmacists	22.4%	$84,900	30.1%	23,000
4. Chief Executives	25.5%	$140,350	16.7%	63,000
5. Government Service Executives	25.5%	$140,350	16.7%	63,000
6. Private Sector Executives	25.5%	$140,350	16.7%	63,000
7. Education Administrators, Elementary and Secondary School	25.9%	$74,190	20.7%	31,000
8. Lawyers	21.8%	$94,930	17.0%	53,000
9. Education Administrators, Postsecondary	25.9%	$68,340	25.9%	19,000
10. Clinical Psychologists	31.4%	$54,950	24.4%	17,000
11. Counseling Psychologists	31.4%	$54,950	24.4%	17,000

(continued)

(continued)

Best Jobs Overall with a High Percentage of Workers Age 55 and Over

Job	Percent Age 55 and Over	Annual Earnings	Percent Growth	Annual Openings
12. School Psychologists	31.4%	$54,950	24.4%	17,000
13. Social and Community Service Managers	23.8%	$46,810	27.7%	19,000
14. Instructional Coordinators	20.9%	$48,790	25.4%	18,000
15. Cost Estimators	21.0%	$49,940	18.6%	25,000
16. Veterinarians	22.0%	$66,590	25.1%	4,000
17. Caption Writers	23.7%	$44,350	16.1%	23,000
18. Copy Writers	23.7%	$44,350	16.1%	23,000
19. Creative Writers	23.7%	$44,350	16.1%	23,000
20. Poets and Lyricists	23.7%	$44,350	16.1%	23,000
21. Multi-Media Artists and Animators	22.6%	$50,360	15.8%	12,000
22. Education Administrators, Preschool and Child Care Center/Program	25.9%	$35,730	32.0%	9,000
23. Security Guards	24.3%	$20,320	31.9%	228,000
24. Clergy	32.7%	$36,690	15.5%	34,000
25. Property, Real Estate, and Community Association Managers	32.0%	$39,980	12.8%	35,000

Best-Paying Jobs with a High Percentage of Workers Age 55 and Over

Job	Percent Age 55 and Over	Annual Earnings	Percent Growth	Annual Openings
1. Oral and Maxillofacial Surgeons	26.1% more than	$145,600	4.1%	7,000
2. Orthodontists	26.1% more than	$145,600	4.1%	7,000
3. Prosthodontists	26.1% more than	$145,600	4.1%	7,000
4. Chief Executives	25.5%	$140,350	16.7%	63,000
5. Government Service Executives	25.5%	$140,350	16.7%	63,000
6. Private Sector Executives	25.5%	$140,350	16.7%	63,000
7. Dentists, General	26.1%	$123,060	4.1%	7,000
8. Lawyers	21.8%	$94,930	17.0%	53,000
9. Judges, Magistrate Judges, and Magistrates	42.4%	$93,070	8.7%	2,000
10. Physicists	44.4%	$87,450	6.9%	1,000
11. Pharmacists	22.4%	$84,900	30.1%	23,000
12. Education Administrators, Elementary and Secondary School	25.9%	$74,190	20.7%	31,000
13. Economists	20.6%	$72,780	13.4%	2,000
14. Industrial-Organizational Psychologists	31.4%	$71,400	16.0%	fewer than 500

Best-Paying Jobs with a High Percentage of Workers Age 55 and Over

Job	Percent Age 55 and Over	Annual Earnings	Percent Growth	Annual Openings
15. Education Administrators, Postsecondary	25.9%	$68,340	25.9%	19,000
16. Veterinarians	22.0%	$66,590	25.1%	4,000
17. Art Directors	22.6%	$63,840	11.4%	8,000
18. Management Analysts	27.4%	$63,450	30.4%	78,000
19. Real Estate Brokers	33.4%	$58,720	2.4%	11,000
20. Clinical Psychologists	31.4%	$54,950	24.4%	17,000
21. Counseling Psychologists	31.4%	$54,950	24.4%	17,000
22. School Psychologists	31.4%	$54,950	24.4%	17,000
23. Arbitrators, Mediators, and Conciliators	42.4%	$54,760	13.7%	fewer than 500
24. Urban and Regional Planners	22.7%	$53,450	10.7%	5,000
25. Teachers, Postsecondary	24.5%	$51,614	38.1%	216,000

Fastest-Growing Jobs with a High Percentage of Workers Age 55 and Over

Job	Percent Age 55 and Over	Annual Earnings	Percent Growth	Annual Openings
1. Personal and Home Care Aides	25.4%	$16,900	40.5%	154,000
2. Teachers, Postsecondary	24.5%	$51,614	38.1%	216,000
3. Education Administrators, Preschool and Child Care Center/Program	25.9%	$35,730	32.0%	9,000
4. Security Guards	24.3%	$20,320	31.9%	228,000
5. Management Analysts	27.4%	$63,450	30.4%	78,000
6. Pharmacists	22.4%	$84,900	30.1%	23,000
7. Desktop Publishers	25.0%	$32,340	29.2%	4,000
8. Audiologists	23.1%	$51,470	29.0%	1,000
9. Social and Community Service Managers	23.8%	$46,810	27.7%	19,000
10. Education Administrators, Postsecondary	25.9%	$68,340	25.9%	19,000
11. Instructional Coordinators	20.9%	$48,790	25.4%	18,000
12. Private Detectives and Investigators	23.4%	$32,110	25.3%	9,000
13. Veterinarians	22.0%	$66,590	25.1%	4,000
14. Clinical Psychologists	31.4%	$54,950	24.4%	17,000
15. Counseling Psychologists	31.4%	$54,950	24.4%	17,000
16. School Psychologists	31.4%	$54,950	24.4%	17,000
17. Directors, Religious Activities and Education	24.1%	$30,700	24.1%	16,000

(continued)

(continued)

Fastest-Growing Jobs with a High Percentage of Workers Age 55 and Over

Job	Percent Age 55 and Over	Annual Earnings	Percent Growth	Annual Openings
18. Tax Preparers	35.2%	$27,730	23.2%	11,000
19. Taxi Drivers and Chauffeurs	31.1%	$19,570	21.7%	28,000
20. Meeting and Convention Planners	23.1%	$39,620	21.3%	7,000
21. Education Administrators, Elementary and Secondary School	25.9%	$74,190	20.7%	31,000
22. Helpers—Installation, Maintenance, and Repair Workers	22.6%	$21,310	20.3%	33,000
23. Cost Estimators	21.0%	$49,940	18.6%	25,000
24. Janitors and Cleaners, Except Maids and Housekeeping Cleaners	22.3%	$18,790	18.3%	454,000
25. Appraisers, Real Estate	24.4%	$43,390	17.6%	11,000

Jobs with the Most Openings with a High Percentage of Workers Age 55 and Over

Job	Percent Age 55 and Over	Annual Earnings	Percent Growth	Annual Openings
1. Janitors and Cleaners, Except Maids and Housekeeping Cleaners	22.3%	$18,790	18.3%	454,000
2. Bookkeeping, Accounting, and Auditing Clerks	23.2%	$28,570	3.0%	274,000
3. Security Guards	24.3%	$20,320	31.9%	228,000
4. Teachers, Postsecondary	24.5%	$51,614	38.1%	216,000
5. Personal and Home Care Aides	25.4%	$16,900	40.5%	154,000
6. Farmers and Ranchers	48.7%	$40,440	–20.6%	118,000
7. Management Analysts	27.4%	$63,450	30.4%	78,000
8. Bus Drivers, School	29.6%	$23,250	16.7%	76,000
9. Chief Executives	25.5%	$140,350	16.7%	63,000
10. Government Service Executives	25.5%	$140,350	16.7%	63,000
11. Private Sector Executives	25.5%	$140,350	16.7%	63,000
12. Lawyers	21.8%	$94,930	17.0%	53,000
13. Insurance Sales Agents	21.4%	$41,720	8.4%	52,000
14. Laundry and Drycleaning Machine Operators and Tenders, Except Pressing	22.3%	$17,220	12.3%	47,000
15. Precision Dyers	22.3%	$17,220	12.3%	47,000
16. Spotters, Dry Cleaning	22.3%	$17,220	12.3%	47,000

Jobs with the Most Openings with a High Percentage of Workers Age 55 and Over

Job	Percent Age 55 and Over	Annual Earnings	Percent Growth	Annual Openings
17. Demonstrators and Product Promoters	34.2%	$20,700	17.0%	38,000
18. Property, Real Estate, and Community Association Managers	32.0%	$39,980	12.8%	35,000
19. Clergy	32.7%	$36,690	15.5%	34,000
20. Real Estate Sales Agents	33.4%	$35,670	5.7%	34,000
21. Bus Drivers, Transit and Intercity	29.6%	$29,730	15.2%	33,000
22. Helpers—Installation, Maintenance, and Repair Workers	22.6%	$21,310	20.3%	33,000
23. Education Administrators, Elementary and Secondary School	25.9%	$74,190	20.7%	31,000
24. Taxi Drivers and Chauffeurs	31.1%	$19,570	21.7%	28,000
25. First-Line Supervisors/Managers of Personal Service Workers	21.0%	$30,350	9.4%	26,000

Best Jobs with a High Percentage of Part-Time Workers

Look over the list of the jobs with high percentages (more than 25 percent) of part-time workers and you will find some interesting things. For example, six of the top twenty involve food and beverage preparation and service, which leads one to think that many people working in this industry do so less than full time. In some cases, people work part time in these jobs because they want the freedom of time this arrangement can provide, but others may do so because they can't find full-time employment in these areas. These folks may work in other full- or part-time jobs to make ends meet. If you want to work part time now or in the future, these lists will help you identify jobs that are more likely to provide that opportunity. If you want full-time work, the lists may also help you identify jobs for which such opportunities are more difficult to find. In either case, it's good information to know in advance.

Best Jobs with the Highest Percentage of Part-Time Workers

Job	Percent Part-Time Workers	Annual Earnings	Percent Growth	Annual Openings
1. Hosts and Hostesses, Restaurant, Lounge, and Coffee Shop	66.9%	$15,630	16.4%	95,000

(continued)

(continued)

Best Jobs with the Highest Percentage of Part-Time Workers

Job	Percent Part-Time Workers	Annual Earnings	Percent Growth	Annual Openings
2. Counter Attendants, Cafeteria, Food Concession, and Coffee Shop	65.8%	$15,660	16.7%	190,000
3. Dental Hygienists	57.8%	$58,350	43.1%	9,000
4. Lifeguards, Ski Patrol, and Other Recreational Protective Service Workers	57.1%	$16,540	14.3%	60,000
5. Dining Room and Cafeteria Attendants and Bartender Helpers	54.0%	$14,770	14.9%	143,000
6. Library Technicians	53.4%	$24,940	16.8%	22,000
7. Demonstrators and Product Promoters	52.5%	$20,700	17.0%	38,000
8. Amusement and Recreation Attendants	51.9%	$15,550	27.8%	66,000
9. Costume Attendants	51.9%	$25,050	27.8%	66,000
10. Locker Room, Coatroom, and Dressing Room Attendants	51.9%	$17,550	27.8%	66,000
11. Library Assistants, Clerical	50.4%	$20,720	21.5%	27,000
12. Waiters and Waitresses	49.9%	$14,050	17.5%	721,000
13. Cashiers	44.8%	$16,240	13.2%	1,221,000
14. Gaming Change Persons and Booth Cashiers	44.8%	$20,530	24.1%	12,000
15. Food Preparation Workers	41.9%	$16,710	20.2%	267,000
16. Massage Therapists	41.2%	$31,960	27.1%	24,000
17. Teacher Assistants	41.1%	$19,410	23.0%	259,000
18. Self-Enrichment Education Teachers	41.0%	$30,880	40.1%	39,000
19. Adult Literacy, Remedial Education, and GED Teachers and Instructors	41.0%	$38,980	20.4%	14,000
20. Combined Food Preparation and Serving Workers, Including Fast Food	40.4%	$14,690	22.8%	734,000
21. Composers	39.5%	$34,570	13.5%	8,000
22. Music Arrangers and Orchestrators	39.5%	$34,570	13.5%	8,000
23. Music Directors	39.5%	$34,570	13.5%	8,000
24. Athletes and Sports Competitors	36.3%	$48,310	19.2%	3,000
25. Coaches and Scouts	36.3%	$26,350	18.3%	26,000
26. Counter and Rental Clerks	35.9%	$18,280	26.3%	144,000
27. Fitness Trainers and Aerobics Instructors	35.6%	$25,470	44.5%	38,000
28. Recreation Workers	35.6%	$19,320	20.5%	56,000
29. Dental Assistants	35.6%	$28,330	42.5%	35,000
30. Bus Drivers, Transit and Intercity	35.6%	$29,730	15.2%	33,000
31. Bus Drivers, School	35.6%	$23,250	16.7%	76,000
32. Child Care Workers	35.2%	$16,760	11.7%	406,000

Best Jobs with the Highest Percentage of Part-Time Workers

Job	Percent Part-Time Workers	Annual Earnings	Percent Growth	Annual Openings
33. Nannies	35.2%	$16,760	11.7%	406,000
34. Personal and Home Care Aides	34.0%	$16,900	40.5%	154,000
35. Retail Salespersons	32.6%	$18,680	14.6%	1,014,000
36. Maids and Housekeeping Cleaners	31.9%	$16,900	9.2%	352,000
37. Nonfarm Animal Caretakers	31.7%	$17,460	22.2%	32,000
38. Parking Lot Attendants	31.6%	$16,800	19.2%	19,000
39. Cooks, Restaurant	31.6%	$19,520	15.9%	211,000
40. Receptionists and Information Clerks	31.5%	$21,830	29.5%	296,000
41. Occupational Therapists	31.1%	$54,660	35.2%	10,000
42. Hairdressers, Hairstylists, and Cosmetologists	31.1%	$19,800	14.7%	68,000
43. Tellers	30.9%	$21,120	9.4%	127,000
44. Interviewers, Except Eligibility and Loan	30.4%	$23,670	28.0%	46,000
45. Flight Attendants	29.9%	$43,440	15.9%	23,000
46. Directors, Religious Activities and Education	28.2%	$30,700	24.1%	16,000
47. Speech-Language Pathologists	28.1%	$52,410	27.2%	10,000
48. Clinical Psychologists	27.2%	$54,950	24.4%	17,000
49. Counseling Psychologists	27.2%	$54,950	24.4%	17,000
50. Industrial-Organizational Psychologists	27.2%	$71,400	16.0%	fewer than 500
51. School Psychologists	27.2%	$54,950	24.4%	17,000
52. Hotel, Motel, and Resort Desk Clerks	27.2%	$17,700	23.9%	46,000
53. Interpreters and Translators	26.3%	$33,860	22.1%	4,000
54. Office Clerks, General	25.7%	$22,770	10.4%	550,000
55. Occupational Therapist Assistants	25.5%	$38,430	39.2%	3,000
56. Medical Assistants	25.3%	$24,610	58.9%	78,000
57. Medical Transcriptionists	25.3%	$28,380	22.6%	18,000
58. Veterinary Assistants and Laboratory Animal Caretakers	25.3%	$18,660	26.2%	11,000
59. Optometrists	25.1%	$88,410	17.1%	2,000

The jobs in the following four lists are derived from the preceding list of the jobs with the highest percentage of part-time workers.

Best Jobs Overall with a High Percentage of Part-Time Workers

Job	Percent Part-Time Workers	Annual Earnings	Percent Growth	Annual Openings
1. Clinical Psychologists	27.2%	$54,950	24.4%	17,000
2. Counseling Psychologists	27.2%	$54,950	24.4%	17,000
3. School Psychologists	27.2%	$54,950	24.4%	17,000
4. Dental Hygienists	57.8%	$58,350	43.1%	9,000
5. Occupational Therapists	31.1%	$54,660	35.2%	10,000
6. Speech-Language Pathologists	28.1%	$52,410	27.2%	10,000
7. Self-Enrichment Education Teachers	41.0%	$30,880	40.1%	39,000
8. Medical Assistants	25.3%	$24,610	58.9%	78,000
9. Dental Assistants	35.6%	$28,330	42.5%	35,000
10. Massage Therapists	41.2%	$31,960	27.1%	24,000
11. Flight Attendants	29.9%	$43,440	15.9%	23,000
12. Adult Literacy, Remedial Education, and GED Teachers and Instructors	41.0%	$38,980	20.4%	14,000
13. Receptionists and Information Clerks	31.5%	$21,830	29.5%	296,000
14. Fitness Trainers and Aerobics Instructors	35.6%	$25,470	44.5%	38,000
15. Costume Attendants	51.9%	$25,050	27.8%	66,000
16. Personal and Home Care Aides	34.0%	$16,900	40.5%	154,000
17. Interviewers, Except Eligibility and Loan	30.4%	$23,670	28.0%	46,000
18. Directors, Religious Activities and Education	28.2%	$30,700	24.1%	16,000
19. Teacher Assistants	41.1%	$19,410	23.0%	259,000
20. Counter and Rental Clerks	35.9%	$18,280	26.3%	144,000
21. Optometrists	25.1%	$88,410	17.1%	2,000
22. Combined Food Preparation and Serving Workers, Including Fast Food	40.4%	$14,690	22.8%	734,000
23. Occupational Therapist Assistants	25.5%	$38,430	39.2%	3,000
24. Locker Room, Coatroom, and Dressing Room Attendants	51.9%	$17,550	27.8%	66,000
25. Medical Transcriptionists	25.3%	$28,380	22.6%	18,000

Best-Paying Jobs with a High Percentage of Part-Time Workers

Job	Percent Part-Time Workers	Annual Earnings	Percent Growth	Annual Openings
1. Optometrists	25.1%	$88,410	17.1%	2,000
2. Industrial-Organizational Psychologists	27.2%	$71,400	16.0%	fewer than 500
3. Dental Hygienists	57.8%	$58,350	43.1%	9,000
4. Clinical Psychologists	27.2%	$54,950	24.4%	17,000
5. Counseling Psychologists	27.2%	$54,950	24.4%	17,000
6. School Psychologists	27.2%	$54,950	24.4%	17,000
7. Occupational Therapists	31.1%	$54,660	35.2%	10,000
8. Speech-Language Pathologists	28.1%	$52,410	27.2%	10,000
9. Athletes and Sports Competitors	36.3%	$48,310	19.2%	3,000
10. Flight Attendants	29.9%	$43,440	15.9%	23,000
11. Adult Literacy, Remedial Education, and GED Teachers and Instructors	41.0%	$38,980	20.4%	14,000
12. Occupational Therapist Assistants	25.5%	$38,430	39.2%	3,000
13. Composers	39.5%	$34,570	13.5%	8,000
14. Music Arrangers and Orchestrators	39.5%	$34,570	13.5%	8,000
15. Music Directors	39.5%	$34,570	13.5%	8,000
16. Interpreters and Translators	26.3%	$33,860	22.1%	4,000
17. Massage Therapists	41.2%	$31,960	27.1%	24,000
18. Self-Enrichment Education Teachers	41.0%	$30,880	40.1%	39,000
19. Directors, Religious Activities and Education	28.2%	$30,700	24.1%	16,000
20. Bus Drivers, Transit and Intercity	35.6%	$29,730	15.2%	33,000
21. Medical Transcriptionists	25.3%	$28,380	22.6%	18,000
22. Dental Assistants	35.6%	$28,330	42.5%	35,000
23. Coaches and Scouts	36.3%	$26,350	18.3%	26,000
24. Fitness Trainers and Aerobics Instructors	35.6%	$25,470	44.5%	38,000
25. Costume Attendants	51.9%	$25,050	27.8%	66,000

Fastest-Growing Jobs with a High Percentage of Part-Time Workers

Job	Percent Part-Time Workers	Annual Earnings	Percent Growth	Annual Openings
1. Medical Assistants	25.3%	$24,610	58.9%	78,000
2. Fitness Trainers and Aerobics Instructors	35.6%	$25,470	44.5%	38,000
3. Dental Hygienists	57.8%	$58,350	43.1%	9,000
4. Dental Assistants	35.6%	$28,330	42.5%	35,000

(continued)

(continued)

Fastest-Growing Jobs with a High Percentage of Part-Time Workers

Job	Percent Part-Time Workers	Annual Earnings	Percent Growth	Annual Openings
5. Personal and Home Care Aides	34.0%	$16,900	40.5%	154,000
6. Self-Enrichment Education Teachers	41.0%	$30,880	40.1%	39,000
7. Occupational Therapist Assistants	25.5%	$38,430	39.2%	3,000
8. Occupational Therapists	31.1%	$54,660	35.2%	10,000
9. Receptionists and Information Clerks	31.5%	$21,830	29.5%	296,000
10. Interviewers, Except Eligibility and Loan	30.4%	$23,670	28.0%	46,000
11. Amusement and Recreation Attendants	51.9%	$15,550	27.8%	66,000
12. Costume Attendants	51.9%	$25,050	27.8%	66,000
13. Locker Room, Coatroom, and Dressing Room Attendants	51.9%	$17,550	27.8%	66,000
14. Speech-Language Pathologists	28.1%	$52,410	27.2%	10,000
15. Massage Therapists	41.2%	$31,960	27.1%	24,000
16. Counter and Rental Clerks	35.9%	$18,280	26.3%	144,000
17. Veterinary Assistants and Laboratory Animal Caretakers	25.3%	$18,660	26.2%	11,000
18. Clinical Psychologists	27.2%	$54,950	24.4%	17,000
19. Counseling Psychologists	27.2%	$54,950	24.4%	17,000
20. School Psychologists	27.2%	$54,950	24.4%	17,000
21. Directors, Religious Activities and Education	28.2%	$30,700	24.1%	16,000
22. Gaming Change Persons and Booth Cashiers	44.8%	$20,530	24.1%	12,000
23. Hotel, Motel, and Resort Desk Clerks	27.2%	$17,700	23.9%	46,000
24. Teacher Assistants	41.1%	$19,410	23.0%	259,000
25. Combined Food Preparation and Serving Workers, Including Fast Food	40.4%	$14,690	22.8%	734,000

Jobs with the Most Openings with a High Percentage of Part-Time Workers

Job	Percent Part-Time Workers	Annual Earnings	Percent Growth	Annual Openings
1. Cashiers	44.8%	$16,240	13.2%	1,221,000
2. Retail Salespersons	32.6%	$18,680	14.6%	1,014,000
3. Combined Food Preparation and Serving Workers, Including Fast Food	40.4%	$14,690	22.8%	734,000
4. Waiters and Waitresses	49.9%	$14,050	17.5%	721,000
5. Office Clerks, General	25.7%	$22,770	10.4%	550,000

Jobs with the Most Openings with a High Percentage of Part-Time Workers

Job	Percent Part-Time Workers	Annual Earnings	Percent Growth	Annual Openings
6. Child Care Workers	35.2%	$16,760	11.7%	406,000
7. Nannies	35.2%	$16,760	11.7%	406,000
8. Maids and Housekeeping Cleaners	31.9%	$16,900	9.2%	352,000
9. Receptionists and Information Clerks	31.5%	$21,830	29.5%	296,000
10. Food Preparation Workers	41.9%	$16,710	20.2%	267,000
11. Teacher Assistants	41.1%	$19,410	23.0%	259,000
12. Cooks, Restaurant	31.6%	$19,520	15.9%	211,000
13. Counter Attendants, Cafeteria, Food Concession, and Coffee Shop	65.8%	$15,660	16.7%	190,000
14. Personal and Home Care Aides	34.0%	$16,900	40.5%	154,000
15. Counter and Rental Clerks	35.9%	$18,280	26.3%	144,000
16. Dining Room and Cafeteria Attendants and Bartender Helpers	54.0%	$14,770	14.9%	143,000
17. Tellers	30.9%	$21,120	9.4%	127,000
18. Hosts and Hostesses, Restaurant, Lounge, and Coffee Shop	66.9%	$15,630	16.4%	95,000
19. Medical Assistants	25.3%	$24,610	58.9%	78,000
20. Bus Drivers, School	35.6%	$23,250	16.7%	76,000
21. Hairdressers, Hairstylists, and Cosmetologists	31.1%	$19,800	14.7%	68,000
22. Amusement and Recreation Attendants	51.9%	$15,550	27.8%	66,000
23. Costume Attendants	51.9%	$25,050	27.8%	66,000
24. Locker Room, Coatroom, and Dressing Room Attendants	51.9%	$17,550	27.8%	66,000
25. Lifeguards, Ski Patrol, and Other Recreational Protective Service Workers	57.1%	$16,540	14.3%	60,000

Best Jobs with a High Percentage of Self-Employed Workers

More than 10 percent of the workforce is self-employed. Although you may think of the self-employed as having similar jobs, they actually work in an enormous range of situations, fields, and work environments that you may not have considered.

Among the self-employed are people who own small or large businesses; professionals such as lawyers, psychologists, and medical doctors; part-time workers; people working on a contract basis for one or more employers; people running home consulting companies or other home-based businesses; and people in many other situations. They may go to the same office every day, like an attorney might; visit multiple employers during the course of a week; or do most of their work from home. Some work part time, others full time, some as a way to have fun, some so they can spend time with their kids or go to school.

The point is that there is an enormous range of situations, and one of them could make sense for you now or in the future.

The following list contains jobs in which more than 30 percent of the workers are self-employed.

Best Jobs with the Highest Percentage of Self-Employed Workers

Job	Percent Self-Employed Workers	Annual Earnings	Percent Growth	Annual Openings
1. Farmers and Ranchers	99.3%	$40,440	–20.6%	118,000
2. Massage Therapists	70.1%	$31,960	27.1%	24,000
3. Caption Writers	67.9%	$44,350	16.1%	23,000
4. Copy Writers	67.9%	$44,350	16.1%	23,000
5. Creative Writers	67.9%	$44,350	16.1%	23,000
6. Poets and Lyricists	67.9%	$44,350	16.1%	23,000
7. Real Estate Brokers	59.1%	$58,720	2.4%	11,000
8. Real Estate Sales Agents	59.0%	$35,670	5.7%	34,000
9. Chiropractors	58.5%	$69,910	23.3%	3,000
10. Cartoonists	55.5%	$38,060	16.5%	4,000
11. Painters and Illustrators	55.5%	$38,060	16.5%	4,000
12. Sculptors	55.5%	$38,060	16.5%	4,000
13. Sketch Artists	55.5%	$38,060	16.5%	4,000
14. Art Directors	53.6%	$63,840	11.4%	8,000
15. Carpet Installers	53.5%	$34,090	16.8%	10,000
16. Multi-Media Artists and Animators	53.5%	$50,360	15.8%	12,000
17. Photographers, Scientific	52.5%	$26,080	13.6%	18,000
18. Professional Photographers	52.5%	$26,080	13.6%	18,000
19. Lodging Managers	50.3%	$37,660	6.6%	10,000
20. First-Line Supervisors/Managers of Personal Service Workers	49.4%	$30,350	9.4%	26,000
21. Construction Managers	46.9%	$69,870	12.0%	47,000
22. Property, Real Estate, and Community Association Managers	46.0%	$39,980	12.8%	35,000
23. First-Line Supervisors/Managers of Non-Retail Sales Workers	44.7%	$59,300	6.8%	72,000
24. Podiatrists	44.4%	$94,400	15.0%	1,000
25. Hairdressers, Hairstylists, and Cosmetologists	44.3%	$19,800	14.7%	68,000

Best Jobs with the Highest Percentage of Self-Employed Workers

Job	Percent Self-Employed Workers	Annual Earnings	Percent Growth	Annual Openings
26. Child Care Workers	43.4%	$16,760	11.7%	406,000
27. Nannies	43.4%	$16,760	11.7%	406,000
28. Demonstrators and Product Promoters	42.1%	$20,700	17.0%	38,000
29. Painters, Construction and Maintenance	41.7%	$30,260	11.6%	69,000
30. Dentists, General	39.9%	$123,060	4.1%	7,000
31. Oral and Maxillofacial Surgeons	39.9%	more than $145,600	4.1%	7,000
32. Orthodontists	39.9%	more than $145,600	4.1%	7,000
33. Prosthodontists	39.9%	more than $145,600	4.1%	7,000
34. Composers	39.3%	$34,570	13.5%	8,000
35. Music Arrangers and Orchestrators	39.3%	$34,570	13.5%	8,000
36. Music Directors	39.3%	$34,570	13.5%	8,000
37. Gaming Managers	38.6%	$58,580	12.4%	1,000
38. Personal Financial Advisors	37.7%	$62,700	34.6%	18,000
39. Appraisers, Real Estate	34.8%	$43,390	17.6%	11,000
40. Assessors	34.8%	$43,390	17.6%	11,000
41. First-Line Supervisors and Manager/Supervisors—Landscaping Workers	34.7%	$35,340	21.6%	18,000
42. Food Service Managers	34.7%	$39,610	11.5%	58,000
43. Lawn Service Managers	34.7%	$35,340	21.6%	18,000
44. Private Detectives and Investigators	34.7%	$32,110	25.3%	9,000
45. Gaming Supervisors	33.8%	$40,840	15.7%	6,000
46. First-Line Supervisors/Managers of Retail Sales Workers	33.0%	$32,720	9.1%	251,000
47. Directors—Stage, Motion Pictures, Television, and Radio	32.8%	$52,840	18.3%	10,000
48. Producers	32.8%	$52,840	18.3%	10,000
49. Program Directors	32.8%	$52,840	18.3%	10,000
50. Talent Directors	32.8%	$52,840	18.3%	10,000
51. Technical Directors/Managers	32.8%	$52,840	18.3%	10,000
52. Exhibit Designers	32.2%	$35,800	20.9%	2,000
53. Interior Designers	32.2%	$40,670	21.7%	8,000
54. Set Designers	32.2%	$35,800	20.9%	2,000
55. Roofers	31.9%	$30,840	18.6%	38,000
56. Graphic Designers	31.8%	$38,030	21.9%	29,000
57. Athletes and Sports Competitors	31.5%	$48,310	19.2%	3,000
58. Commercial and Industrial Designers	31.0%	$52,310	14.7%	7,000

The jobs in the following four lists are derived from the preceding list of the jobs with the highest percentage of self-employed workers.

Best Jobs Overall with a High Percentage of Self-Employed Workers

Job	Percent Self-Employed Workers	Annual Earnings	Percent Growth	Annual Openings
1. Personal Financial Advisors	37.7%	$62,700	34.6%	18,000
2. Construction Managers	46.9%	$69,870	12.0%	47,000
3. Graphic Designers	31.8%	$38,030	21.9%	29,000
4. First-Line Supervisors/Managers of Non-Retail Sales Workers	44.7%	$59,300	6.8%	72,000
5. Directors—Stage, Motion Pictures, Television, and Radio	32.8%	$52,840	18.3%	10,000
6. Producers	32.8%	$52,840	18.3%	10,000
7. Program Directors	32.8%	$52,840	18.3%	10,000
8. Talent Directors	32.8%	$52,840	18.3%	10,000
9. Technical Directors/Managers	32.8%	$52,840	18.3%	10,000
10. Caption Writers	67.9%	$44,350	16.1%	23,000
11. Copy Writers	67.9%	$44,350	16.1%	23,000
12. Creative Writers	67.9%	$44,350	16.1%	23,000
13. Poets and Lyricists	67.9%	$44,350	16.1%	23,000
14. Massage Therapists	70.1%	$31,960	27.1%	24,000
15. Chiropractors	58.5%	$69,910	23.3%	3,000
16. First-Line Supervisors and Manager/Supervisors—Landscaping Workers	34.7%	$35,340	21.6%	18,000
17. Lawn Service Managers	34.7%	$35,340	21.6%	18,000
18. Multi-Media Artists and Animators	53.5%	$50,360	15.8%	12,000
19. Food Service Managers	34.7%	$39,610	11.5%	58,000
20. Property, Real Estate, and Community Association Managers	46.0%	$39,980	12.8%	35,000
21. Roofers	31.9%	$30,840	18.6%	38,000
22. Appraisers, Real Estate	34.8%	$43,390	17.6%	11,000
23. Assessors	34.8%	$43,390	17.6%	11,000
24. Interior Designers	32.2%	$40,670	21.7%	8,000
25. Art Directors	53.6%	$63,840	11.4%	8,000

Best-Paying Jobs with a High Percentage of Self-Employed Workers

Job	Percent Self-Employed Workers	Annual Earnings	Percent Growth	Annual Openings
1. Oral and Maxillofacial Surgeons	39.9% ..more than	$145,600	4.1%	7,000
2. Orthodontists	39.9% ..more than	$145,600	4.1%	7,000
3. Prosthodontists	39.9% ..more than	$145,600	4.1%	7,000
4. Dentists, General	39.9%	$123,060	4.1%	7,000
5. Podiatrists	44.4%	$94,400	15.0%	1,000
6. Chiropractors	58.5%	$69,910	23.3%	3,000
7. Construction Managers	46.9%	$69,870	12.0%	47,000
8. Art Directors	53.6%	$63,840	11.4%	8,000
9. Personal Financial Advisors	37.7%	$62,700	34.6%	18,000
10. First-Line Supervisors/Managers of Non-Retail Sales Workers	44.7%	$59,300	6.8%	72,000
11. Real Estate Brokers	59.1%	$58,720	2.4%	11,000
12. Gaming Managers	38.6%	$58,580	12.4%	1,000
13. Directors—Stage, Motion Pictures, Television, and Radio	32.8%	$52,840	18.3%	10,000
14. Producers	32.8%	$52,840	18.3%	10,000
15. Program Directors	32.8%	$52,840	18.3%	10,000
16. Talent Directors	32.8%	$52,840	18.3%	10,000
17. Technical Directors/Managers	32.8%	$52,840	18.3%	10,000
18. Commercial and Industrial Designers	31.0%	$52,310	14.7%	7,000
19. Multi-Media Artists and Animators	53.5%	$50,360	15.8%	12,000
20. Athletes and Sports Competitors	31.5%	$48,310	19.2%	3,000
21. Caption Writers	67.9%	$44,350	16.1%	23,000
22. Copy Writers	67.9%	$44,350	16.1%	23,000
23. Creative Writers	67.9%	$44,350	16.1%	23,000
24. Poets and Lyricists	67.9%	$44,350	16.1%	23,000
25. Appraisers, Real Estate	34.8%	$43,390	17.6%	11,000

Fastest-Growing Jobs with a High Percentage of Self-Employed Workers

Job	Percent Self-Employed Workers	Annual Earnings	Percent Growth	Annual Openings
1. Personal Financial Advisors	37.7%	$62,700	34.6%	18,000
2. Massage Therapists	70.1%	$31,960	27.1%	24,000
3. Private Detectives and Investigators	34.7%	$32,110	25.3%	9,000
4. Chiropractors	58.5%	$69,910	23.3%	3,000
5. Graphic Designers	31.8%	$38,030	21.9%	29,000
6. Interior Designers	32.2%	$40,670	21.7%	8,000
7. First-Line Supervisors and Manager/Supervisors—Landscaping Workers	34.7%	$35,340	21.6%	18,000
8. Lawn Service Managers	34.7%	$35,340	21.6%	18,000
9. Exhibit Designers	32.2%	$35,800	20.9%	2,000
10. Set Designers	32.2%	$35,800	20.9%	2,000
11. Athletes and Sports Competitors	31.5%	$48,310	19.2%	3,000
12. Roofers	31.9%	$30,840	18.6%	38,000
13. Directors—Stage, Motion Pictures, Television, and Radio	32.8%	$52,840	18.3%	10,000
14. Producers	32.8%	$52,840	18.3%	10,000
15. Program Directors	32.8%	$52,840	18.3%	10,000
16. Talent Directors	32.8%	$52,840	18.3%	10,000
17. Technical Directors/Managers	32.8%	$52,840	18.3%	10,000
18. Appraisers, Real Estate	34.8%	$43,390	17.6%	11,000
19. Assessors	34.8%	$43,390	17.6%	11,000
20. Demonstrators and Product Promoters	42.1%	$20,700	17.0%	38,000
21. Carpet Installers	53.5%	$34,090	16.8%	10,000
22. Cartoonists	55.5%	$38,060	16.5%	4,000
23. Painters and Illustrators	55.5%	$38,060	16.5%	4,000
24. Sculptors	55.5%	$38,060	16.5%	4,000
25. Sketch Artists	55.5%	$38,060	16.5%	4,000

Jobs with the Most Openings
with a High Percentage of Self-Employed Workers

Job	Percent Self-Employed Workers	Annual Earnings	Percent Growth	Annual Openings
1. Child Care Workers	43.4%	$16,760	11.7%	406,000
2. Nannies	43.4%	$16,760	11.7%	406,000
3. First-Line Supervisors/Managers of Retail Sales Workers	33.0%	$32,720	9.1%	251,000
4. Farmers and Ranchers	99.3%	$40,440	–20.6%	118,000
5. First-Line Supervisors/Managers of Non-Retail Sales Workers	44.7%	$59,300	6.8%	72,000
6. Painters, Construction and Maintenance	41.7%	$30,260	11.6%	69,000
7. Hairdressers, Hairstylists, and Cosmetologists	44.3%	$19,800	14.7%	68,000
8. Food Service Managers	34.7%	$39,610	11.5%	58,000
9. Construction Managers	46.9%	$69,870	12.0%	47,000
10. Demonstrators and Product Promoters	42.1%	$20,700	17.0%	38,000
11. Roofers	31.9%	$30,840	18.6%	38,000
12. Property, Real Estate, and Community Association Managers	46.0%	$39,980	12.8%	35,000
13. Real Estate Sales Agents	59.0%	$35,670	5.7%	34,000
14. Graphic Designers	31.8%	$38,030	21.9%	29,000
15. First-Line Supervisors/Managers of Personal Service Workers	49.4%	$30,350	9.4%	26,000
16. Massage Therapists	70.1%	$31,960	27.1%	24,000
17. Caption Writers	67.9%	$44,350	16.1%	23,000
18. Copy Writers	67.9%	$44,350	16.1%	23,000
19. Creative Writers	67.9%	$44,350	16.1%	23,000
20. Poets and Lyricists	67.9%	$44,350	16.1%	23,000
21. First-Line Supervisors and Manager/Supervisors—Landscaping Workers	34.7%	$35,340	21.6%	18,000
22. Lawn Service Managers	34.7%	$35,340	21.6%	18,000
23. Personal Financial Advisors	37.7%	$62,700	34.6%	18,000
24. Photographers, Scientific	52.5%	$26,080	13.6%	18,000
25. Professional Photographers	52.5%	$26,080	13.6%	18,000

Best Jobs Employing a High Percentage of Women

To create the four lists that follow, we sorted the 500 best jobs according to the percentages of women and men in the workforce. These are our most controversial lists, and we knew we would create some controversy when we first included the best jobs lists with high percentages (more than 70 percent) of men and women in earlier editions. But these lists are not meant to restrict women or men from considering job options—our reason for including these lists is exactly the opposite. We hope the lists help people see possibilities that they might not otherwise have considered.

The fact is that jobs with high percentages of women or high percentages of men offer good opportunities for both men and women if they want to do one of these jobs. So we suggest that women browse the lists of jobs that employ high percentages of men and that men browse the lists of jobs with high percentages of women. There are jobs among both lists that pay well, and women or men who are interested in them and who have or can obtain the necessary education and training should consider them.

An interesting and unfortunate tidbit to bring up at your next party is that the jobs with the highest percentage of women have average earnings of $32,563, compared to average earnings of $51,002 for the jobs with the highest percentage of men. But earnings don't tell the whole story. We computed the average growth and job openings of the jobs with the highest percentage of women and found statistics of 23.9% growth and 102,453 openings, compared to 15.6% growth and 44,335 openings for the jobs with the highest percentage of men college grads. This discrepancy reinforces the idea that men have had more problems than women in adapting to an economy dominated by service and information-based jobs. Many women may simply be better prepared for these jobs, possessing more appropriate skills for the jobs that are now growing rapidly and have more job openings.

Best Jobs Employing the Highest Percentage of Women				
Job	Percent Women	Annual Earnings	Percent Growth	Annual Openings
1. Kindergarten Teachers, Except Special Education	97.8%	$41,400	27.2%	34,000
2. Preschool Teachers, Except Special Education	97.8%	$20,980	36.2%	88,000
3. Dental Hygienists	97.7%	$58,350	43.1%	9,000
4. Dental Assistants	97.1%	$28,330	42.5%	35,000
5. Executive Secretaries and Administrative Assistants	96.5%	$34,970	8.7%	210,000
6. Legal Secretaries	96.5%	$36,720	18.8%	39,000
7. Medical Secretaries	96.5%	$26,540	17.2%	50,000
8. Speech-Language Pathologists	95.1%	$52,410	27.2%	10,000
9. Child Care Workers	94.7%	$16,760	11.7%	406,000
10. Nannies	94.7%	$16,760	11.7%	406,000

Best Jobs Employing the Highest Percentage of Women

Job	Percent Women	Annual Earnings	Percent Growth	Annual Openings
11. Licensed Practical and Licensed Vocational Nurses	93.0%	$33,970	20.2%	105,000
12. Receptionists and Information Clerks	92.7%	$21,830	29.5%	296,000
13. Registered Nurses	92.4%	$52,330	27.3%	215,000
14. Teacher Assistants	91.6%	$19,410	23.0%	259,000
15. Medical Records and Health Information Technicians	91.0%	$25,590	46.8%	24,000
16. Dietitians and Nutritionists	90.5%	$43,630	17.8%	8,000
17. Hairdressers, Hairstylists, and Cosmetologists	90.3%	$19,800	14.7%	68,000
18. Occupational Therapists	90.0%	$54,660	35.2%	10,000
19. Tellers	89.7%	$21,120	9.4%	127,000
20. Bookkeeping, Accounting, and Auditing Clerks	89.4%	$28,570	3.0%	274,000
21. Billing, Cost, and Rate Clerks	88.5%	$27,040	7.9%	78,000
22. Billing, Posting, and Calculating Machine Operators	88.5%	$27,040	7.9%	78,000
23. Statement Clerks	88.5%	$27,040	7.9%	78,000
24. Medical Assistants	88.0%	$24,610	58.9%	78,000
25. Medical Transcriptionists	88.0%	$28,380	22.6%	18,000
26. Veterinary Assistants and Laboratory Animal Caretakers	88.0%	$18,660	26.2%	11,000
27. Home Health Aides	87.8%	$18,330	48.1%	141,000
28. Nursing Aides, Orderlies, and Attendants	87.8%	$20,980	24.9%	302,000
29. Maids and Housekeeping Cleaners	87.6%	$16,900	9.2%	352,000
30. Hosts and Hostesses, Restaurant, Lounge, and Coffee Shop	87.3%	$15,630	16.4%	95,000
31. Personal and Home Care Aides	87.3%	$16,900	40.5%	154,000
32. Occupational Therapist Assistants	87.2%	$38,430	39.2%	3,000
33. Special Education Teachers, Middle School	86.6%	$44,160	30.0%	59,000
34. Special Education Teachers, Preschool, Kindergarten, and Elementary School	86.6%	$43,570	30.0%	59,000
35. Special Education Teachers, Secondary School	86.6%	$45,700	30.0%	59,000
36. Paralegals and Legal Assistants	86.1%	$39,130	28.7%	29,000
37. New Accounts Clerks	85.0%	$26,860	11.2%	24,000
38. Office Clerks, General	83.9%	$22,770	10.4%	550,000
39. Librarians	82.6%	$45,900	10.1%	15,000
40. Library Assistants, Clerical	81.9%	$20,720	21.5%	27,000
41. Massage Therapists	81.2%	$31,960	27.1%	24,000

(continued)

(continued)

Best Jobs Employing the Highest Percentage of Women

Job	Percent Women	Annual Earnings	Percent Growth	Annual Openings
42. Human Resources Assistants, Except Payroll and Timekeeping	81.1%	$31,750	19.3%	36,000
43. Pharmacy Technicians	80.7%	$23,650	28.8%	39,000
44. Respiratory Therapy Technicians	80.7%	$36,740	34.2%	5,000
45. Surgical Technologists	80.7%	$34,010	27.9%	13,000
46. Veterinary Technologists and Technicians	80.7%	$24,940	44.1%	11,000
47. Elementary School Teachers, Except Special Education	79.0%	$43,160	15.2%	183,000
48. Middle School Teachers, Except Special and Vocational Education	79.0%	$43,670	9.0%	69,000
49. Flight Attendants	78.7%	$43,440	15.9%	23,000
50. Child, Family, and School Social Workers	78.5%	$34,820	23.2%	45,000
51. Medical and Public Health Social Workers	78.5%	$40,080	28.6%	18,000
52. Mental Health and Substance Abuse Social Workers	78.5%	$33,920	34.5%	17,000
53. Court Clerks	78.2%	$28,430	12.3%	14,000
54. License Clerks	78.2%	$28,430	12.3%	14,000
55. Municipal Clerks	78.2%	$28,430	12.3%	14,000
56. Demonstrators and Product Promoters	77.4%	$20,700	17.0%	38,000
57. Audiologists	76.7%	$51,470	29.0%	1,000
58. Cashiers	76.0%	$16,240	13.2%	1,221,000
59. Gaming Change Persons and Booth Cashiers	76.0%	$20,530	24.1%	12,000
60. Physical Therapist Aides	76.0%	$21,380	46.4%	8,000
61. Physical Therapist Assistants	76.0%	$37,890	44.6%	10,000
62. Meeting and Convention Planners	75.4%	$39,620	21.3%	7,000
63. Library Technicians	74.2%	$24,940	16.8%	22,000
64. Waiters and Waitresses	74.2%	$14,050	17.5%	721,000
65. Medical and Clinical Laboratory Technicians	73.9%	$30,840	19.4%	21,000
66. Medical and Clinical Laboratory Technologists	73.9%	$45,730	19.3%	21,000
67. Court Reporters	73.3%	$42,920	12.7%	2,000
68. Cardiovascular Technologists and Technicians	71.7%	$38,690	33.5%	6,000
69. Diagnostic Medical Sonographers	71.7%	$52,490	24.0%	4,000
70. Nuclear Medicine Technologists	71.7%	$56,450	23.6%	2,000
71. Radiologic Technicians	71.7%	$43,350	22.9%	21,000
72. Radiologic Technologists	71.7%	$43,350	22.9%	21,000
73. Interviewers, Except Eligibility and Loan	71.4%	$23,670	28.0%	46,000
74. Bill and Account Collectors	71.0%	$27,450	24.5%	76,000
75. Physical Therapists	70.4%	$60,180	35.3%	16,000

The jobs in the following four lists are derived from the preceding list of the jobs employing the highest percentage of women.

Best Jobs Overall Employing a High Percentage of Women

Job	Percent Women	Annual Earnings	Percent Growth	Annual Openings
1. Registered Nurses	92.4%	$52,330	27.3%	215,000
2. Special Education Teachers, Secondary School	86.6%	$45,700	30.0%	59,000
3. Special Education Teachers, Middle School	86.6%	$44,160	30.0%	59,000
4. Special Education Teachers, Preschool, Kindergarten, and Elementary School	86.6%	$43,570	30.0%	59,000
5. Physical Therapists	70.4%	$60,180	35.3%	16,000
6. Dental Hygienists	97.7%	$58,350	43.1%	9,000
7. Kindergarten Teachers, Except Special Education	97.8%	$41,400	27.2%	34,000
8. Occupational Therapists	90.0%	$54,660	35.2%	10,000
9. Paralegals and Legal Assistants	86.1%	$39,130	28.7%	29,000
10. Speech-Language Pathologists	95.1%	$52,410	27.2%	10,000
11. Elementary School Teachers, Except Special Education	79.0%	$43,160	15.2%	183,000
12. Licensed Practical and Licensed Vocational Nurses	93.0%	$33,970	20.2%	105,000
13. Child, Family, and School Social Workers	78.5%	$34,820	23.2%	45,000
14. Medical and Public Health Social Workers	78.5%	$40,080	28.6%	18,000
15. Radiologic Technicians	71.7%	$43,350	22.9%	21,000
16. Radiologic Technologists	71.7%	$43,350	22.9%	21,000
17. Medical and Clinical Laboratory Technologists	73.9%	$45,730	19.3%	21,000
18. Legal Secretaries	96.5%	$36,720	18.8%	39,000
19. Physical Therapist Assistants	76.0%	$37,890	44.6%	10,000
20. Medical Assistants	88.0%	$24,610	58.9%	78,000
21. Mental Health and Substance Abuse Social Workers	78.5%	$33,920	34.5%	17,000
22. Dental Assistants	97.1%	$28,330	42.5%	35,000
23. Bill and Account Collectors	71.0%	$27,450	24.5%	76,000
24. Massage Therapists	81.2%	$31,960	27.1%	24,000
25. Flight Attendants	78.7%	$43,440	15.9%	23,000

Best-Paying Jobs Employing a High Percentage of Women

Job	Percent Women	Annual Earnings	Percent Growth	Annual Openings
1. Physical Therapists	70.4%	$60,180	35.3%	16,000
2. Dental Hygienists	97.7%	$58,350	43.1%	9,000
3. Nuclear Medicine Technologists	71.7%	$56,450	23.6%	2,000
4. Occupational Therapists	90.0%	$54,660	35.2%	10,000
5. Diagnostic Medical Sonographers	71.7%	$52,490	24.0%	4,000
6. Speech-Language Pathologists	95.1%	$52,410	27.2%	10,000
7. Registered Nurses	92.4%	$52,330	27.3%	215,000
8. Audiologists	76.7%	$51,470	29.0%	1,000
9. Librarians	82.6%	$45,900	10.1%	15,000
10. Medical and Clinical Laboratory Technologists	73.9%	$45,730	19.3%	21,000
11. Special Education Teachers, Secondary School	86.6%	$45,700	30.0%	59,000
12. Special Education Teachers, Middle School	86.6%	$44,160	30.0%	59,000
13. Middle School Teachers, Except Special and Vocational Education	79.0%	$43,670	9.0%	69,000
14. Dietitians and Nutritionists	90.5%	$43,630	17.8%	8,000
15. Special Education Teachers, Preschool, Kindergarten, and Elementary School	86.6%	$43,570	30.0%	59,000
16. Flight Attendants	78.7%	$43,440	15.9%	23,000
17. Radiologic Technicians	71.7%	$43,350	22.9%	21,000
18. Radiologic Technologists	71.7%	$43,350	22.9%	21,000
19. Elementary School Teachers, Except Special Education	79.0%	$43,160	15.2%	183,000
20. Court Reporters	73.3%	$42,920	12.7%	2,000
21. Kindergarten Teachers, Except Special Education	97.8%	$41,400	27.2%	34,000
22. Medical and Public Health Social Workers	78.5%	$40,080	28.6%	18,000
23. Meeting and Convention Planners	75.4%	$39,620	21.3%	7,000
24. Paralegals and Legal Assistants	86.1%	$39,130	28.7%	29,000
25. Cardiovascular Technologists and Technicians	71.7%	$38,690	33.5%	6,000

Fastest-Growing Jobs Employing a High Percentage of Women

Job	Percent Women	Annual Earnings	Percent Growth	Annual Openings
1. Medical Assistants	88.0%	$24,610	58.9%	78,000
2. Home Health Aides	87.8%	$18,330	48.1%	141,000
3. Medical Records and Health Information Technicians	91.0%	$25,590	46.8%	24,000

Fastest-Growing Jobs Employing a High Percentage of Women

Job	Percent Women	Annual Earnings	Percent Growth	Annual Openings
4. Physical Therapist Aides	76.0%	$21,380	46.4%	8,000
5. Physical Therapist Assistants	76.0%	$37,890	44.6%	10,000
6. Veterinary Technologists and Technicians	80.7%	$24,940	44.1%	11,000
7. Dental Hygienists	97.7%	$58,350	43.1%	9,000
8. Dental Assistants	97.1%	$28,330	42.5%	35,000
9. Personal and Home Care Aides	87.3%	$16,900	40.5%	154,000
10. Occupational Therapist Assistants	87.2%	$38,430	39.2%	3,000
11. Preschool Teachers, Except Special Education	97.8%	$20,980	36.2%	88,000
12. Physical Therapists	70.4%	$60,180	35.3%	16,000
13. Occupational Therapists	90.0%	$54,660	35.2%	10,000
14. Mental Health and Substance Abuse Social Workers	78.5%	$33,920	34.5%	17,000
15. Respiratory Therapy Technicians	80.7%	$36,740	34.2%	5,000
16. Cardiovascular Technologists and Technicians	71.7%	$38,690	33.5%	6,000
17. Special Education Teachers, Middle School	86.6%	$44,160	30.0%	59,000
18. Special Education Teachers, Preschool, Kindergarten, and Elementary School	86.6%	$43,570	30.0%	59,000
19. Special Education Teachers, Secondary School	86.6%	$45,700	30.0%	59,000
20. Receptionists and Information Clerks	92.7%	$21,830	29.5%	296,000
21. Audiologists	76.7%	$51,470	29.0%	1,000
22. Pharmacy Technicians	80.7%	$23,650	28.8%	39,000
23. Paralegals and Legal Assistants	86.1%	$39,130	28.7%	29,000
24. Medical and Public Health Social Workers	78.5%	$40,080	28.6%	18,000
25. Interviewers, Except Eligibility and Loan	71.4%	$23,670	28.0%	46,000

Jobs with the Most Openings Employing a High Percentage of Women

Job	Percent Women	Annual Earnings	Percent Growth	Annual Openings
1. Cashiers	76.0%	$16,240	13.2%	1,221,000
2. Waiters and Waitresses	74.2%	$14,050	17.5%	721,000
3. Office Clerks, General	83.9%	$22,770	10.4%	550,000
4. Child Care Workers	94.7%	$16,760	11.7%	406,000
5. Nannies	94.7%	$16,760	11.7%	406,000
6. Maids and Housekeeping Cleaners	87.6%	$16,900	9.2%	352,000

(continued)

(continued)

Jobs with the Most Openings Employing a High Percentage of Women

Job	Percent Women	Annual Earnings	Percent Growth	Annual Openings
7. Nursing Aides, Orderlies, and Attendants	87.8%	$20,980	24.9%	302,000
8. Receptionists and Information Clerks	92.7%	$21,830	29.5%	296,000
9. Bookkeeping, Accounting, and Auditing Clerks	89.4%	$28,570	3.0%	274,000
10. Teacher Assistants	91.6%	$19,410	23.0%	259,000
11. Registered Nurses	92.4%	$52,330	27.3%	215,000
12. Executive Secretaries and Administrative Assistants	96.5%	$34,970	8.7%	210,000
13. Elementary School Teachers, Except Special Education	79.0%	$43,160	15.2%	183,000
14. Personal and Home Care Aides	87.3%	$16,900	40.5%	154,000
15. Home Health Aides	87.8%	$18,330	48.1%	141,000
16. Tellers	89.7%	$21,120	9.4%	127,000
17. Licensed Practical and Licensed Vocational Nurses	93.0%	$33,970	20.2%	105,000
18. Hosts and Hostesses, Restaurant, Lounge, and Coffee Shop	87.3%	$15,630	16.4%	95,000
19. Preschool Teachers, Except Special Education	97.8%	$20,980	36.2%	88,000
20. Billing, Cost, and Rate Clerks	88.5%	$27,040	7.9%	78,000
21. Billing, Posting, and Calculating Machine Operators	88.5%	$27,040	7.9%	78,000
22. Medical Assistants	88.0%	$24,610	58.9%	78,000
23. Statement Clerks	88.5%	$27,040	7.9%	78,000
24. Bill and Account Collectors	71.0%	$27,450	24.5%	76,000
25. Middle School Teachers, Except Special and Vocational Education	79.0%	$43,670	9.0%	69,000

Best Jobs Employing a High Percentage of Men

If you have not already read the intro to the previous group of lists, jobs with high percentages of women, consider doing so. Much of the content there applies to these lists as well.

We did not include these groups of lists with the assumption that men should consider jobs with high percentages of men or that women should consider jobs with high percentages of women. Instead, these lists are here because we think they are interesting and perhaps helpful in considering nontraditional career options. For example, some men would do very well in and enjoy some of the jobs with high percentages of women but may not have considered them seriously. In a similar way, some women would very much enjoy and do well in some jobs that traditionally have been held by high percentages of men. We hope that these lists help you consider options that you simply did not seriously consider because of gender stereotypes.

In the jobs on the following lists, more than 70 percent of the workers are men.

Best Jobs Employing the Highest Percentage of Men

Job	Percent Men	Annual Earnings	Percent Growth	Annual Openings
1. Mobile Heavy Equipment Mechanics, Except Engines	99.0%	$38,150	9.6%	12,000
2. Brickmasons and Blockmasons	98.9%	$41,740	14.2%	21,000
3. Bus and Truck Mechanics and Diesel Engine Specialists	98.8%	$35,780	14.2%	28,000
4. Plasterers and Stucco Masons	98.7%	$32,440	13.5%	8,000
5. Cement Masons and Concrete Finishers	98.6%	$31,400	26.1%	24,000
6. Elevator Installers and Repairers	98.6%	$58,710	17.1%	3,000
7. Recreational Vehicle Service Technicians	98.4%	$28,980	21.8%	4,000
8. Roofers	98.4%	$30,840	18.6%	38,000
9. Pipe Fitters	98.3%	$41,290	18.7%	56,000
10. Pipelaying Fitters	98.3%	$41,290	18.7%	56,000
11. Plumbers	98.3%	$41,290	18.7%	56,000
12. Dragline Operators	98.2%	$31,970	8.9%	14,000
13. Excavating and Loading Machine Operators	98.2%	$31,970	8.9%	14,000
14. Heating and Air Conditioning Mechanics	98.2%	$36,260	31.8%	35,000
15. Loading Machine Operators, Underground Mining	98.2%	$33,250	8.9%	14,000
16. Refrigeration Mechanics	98.2%	$36,260	31.8%	35,000
17. Automotive Master Mechanics	98.1%	$32,450	12.4%	100,000
18. Automotive Specialty Technicians	98.1%	$32,450	12.4%	100,000
19. Boat Builders and Shipwrights	98.1%	$34,900	10.1%	193,000
20. Brattice Builders	98.1%	$34,900	10.1%	193,000
21. Carpenter Assemblers and Repairers	98.1%	$34,900	10.1%	193,000
22. Construction Carpenters	98.1%	$34,900	10.1%	193,000
23. Rough Carpenters	98.1%	$34,900	10.1%	193,000
24. Ship Carpenters and Joiners	98.1%	$34,900	10.1%	193,000
25. Automotive Body and Related Repairers	97.9%	$34,690	13.2%	23,000
26. Grader, Bulldozer, and Scraper Operators	97.8%	$35,360	10.4%	45,000
27. Millwrights	97.8%	$43,720	5.3%	7,000
28. Operating Engineers	97.8%	$35,360	10.4%	45,000
29. Reinforcing Iron and Rebar Workers	97.6%	$35,160	16.7%	2,000

(continued)

(continued)

Best Jobs Employing the Highest Percentage of Men

Job	Percent Men	Annual Earnings	Percent Growth	Annual Openings
30. Structural Iron and Steel Workers	97.6%	$42,430	15.9%	9,000
31. Carpet Installers	97.5%	$34,090	16.8%	10,000
32. Tile and Marble Setters	97.5%	$35,410	26.5%	4,000
33. Electricians	97.4%	$42,300	23.4%	65,000
34. Ceiling Tile Installers	97.3%	$34,030	21.4%	17,000
35. Drywall Installers	97.3%	$34,030	21.4%	17,000
36. Electrical Power-Line Installers and Repairers	97.3%	$49,100	1.6%	9,000
37. Tapers	97.3%	$39,070	20.8%	5,000
38. First-Line Supervisors and Manager/Supervisors —Construction Trades Workers	97.2%	$50,450	14.1%	67,000
39. First-Line Supervisors and Manager/Supervisors —Extractive Workers	97.2%	$50,450	14.1%	67,000
40. Forest Fire Fighting and Prevention Supervisors	97.1%	$58,920	18.7%	8,000
41. Municipal Fire Fighting and Prevention Supervisors	97.1%	$58,920	18.7%	8,000
42. Security and Fire Alarm Systems Installers	96.9%	$33,410	30.2%	5,000
43. Septic Tank Servicers and Sewer Pipe Cleaners	96.9%	$28,870	21.2%	3,000
44. Crane and Tower Operators	96.6%	$37,410	10.8%	5,000
45. Construction Laborers	96.5%	$25,160	14.2%	166,000
46. Forest Fire Fighters	96.4%	$38,330	20.7%	29,000
47. Municipal Fire Fighters	96.4%	$38,330	20.7%	29,000
48. Industrial Machinery Mechanics	96.2%	$39,060	5.5%	19,000
49. Refractory Materials Repairers, Except Brickmasons	96.2%	$37,640	16.3%	155,000
50. Airline Pilots, Copilots, and Flight Engineers	96.0%	$129,250	18.5%	6,000
51. Commercial Pilots	96.0%	$53,870	14.9%	2,000
52. Highway Maintenance Workers	96.0%	$29,550	10.4%	25,000
53. Insulation Workers, Floor, Ceiling, and Wall	95.9%	$30,310	15.8%	9,000
54. Insulation Workers, Mechanical	95.9%	$33,330	15.8%	9,000
55. Maintenance and Repair Workers, General	95.9%	$30,710	16.3%	155,000
56. Sheet Metal Workers	95.9%	$35,560	19.8%	30,000
57. Glaziers	95.6%	$32,650	17.2%	7,000
58. Electric Meter Installers and Repairers	95.2%	$43,710	12.0%	5,000
59. Meter Mechanics	95.2%	$43,710	12.0%	5,000
60. Valve and Regulator Repairers	95.2%	$43,710	12.0%	5,000
61. Aircraft Body and Bonded Structure Repairers	95.1%	$45,290	11.0%	12,000
62. Aircraft Engine Specialists	95.1%	$45,290	11.0%	12,000
63. Airframe-and-Power-Plant Mechanics	95.1%	$45,290	11.0%	12,000

Best Jobs for the 21st Century, Fourth Edition © JIST Works

Best Jobs Employing the Highest Percentage of Men

Job	Percent Men	Annual Earnings	Percent Growth	Annual Openings
64. Helpers—Electricians	94.8%	$23,420	17.9%	17,000
65. Machinists	94.7%	$33,960	8.2%	30,000
66. Water and Liquid Waste Treatment Plant and System Operators	94.6%	$34,960	16.0%	9,000
67. Electrical and Electronics Repairers, Commercial and Industrial Equipment	94.1%	$42,600	10.3%	10,000
68. Tractor-Trailer Truck Drivers	94.1%	$33,520	19.0%	299,000
69. Truck Drivers, Heavy	94.1%	$33,520	19.0%	299,000
70. Truck Drivers, Light or Delivery Services	94.1%	$24,540	23.2%	219,000
71. Sales Engineers	94.0%	$70,620	19.9%	7,000
72. Pest Control Workers	93.7%	$26,220	17.0%	11,000
73. Mechanical Engineers	93.5%	$66,320	4.8%	14,000
74. Telecommunications Line Installers and Repairers	93.5%	$40,330	18.8%	13,000
75. Engineering Managers	93.4%	$97,630	9.2%	16,000
76. First-Line Supervisors and Manager/Supervisors —Landscaping Workers	93.3%	$35,340	21.6%	18,000
77. Lawn Service Managers	93.3%	$35,340	21.6%	18,000
78. Construction Managers	93.2%	$69,870	12.0%	47,000
79. Locksmiths and Safe Repairers	93.0%	$30,360	21.0%	3,000
80. Brazers	92.6%	$30,620	17.0%	71,000
81. Painters, Construction and Maintenance	92.6%	$30,260	11.6%	69,000
82. Solderers	92.6%	$30,620	17.0%	71,000
83. Welder-Fitters	92.6%	$30,620	17.0%	71,000
84. Welders and Cutters	92.6%	$30,620	17.0%	71,000
85. Welders, Production	92.6%	$30,620	17.0%	71,000
86. Industrial Truck and Tractor Operators	92.4%	$26,580	11.1%	94,000
87. Landscaping and Groundskeeping Workers	92.4%	$20,420	22.0%	203,000
88. Tree Trimmers and Pruners	92.4%	$26,150	18.6%	11,000
89. First-Line Supervisors/Managers of Mechanics, Installers, and Repairers	91.8%	$50,340	15.4%	42,000
90. Electrical Engineers	91.3%	$71,610	2.5%	11,000
91. Electronics Engineers, Except Computer	91.3%	$75,770	9.4%	11,000
92. Mapping Technicians	91.1%	$30,380	23.1%	10,000
93. Subway and Streetcar Operators	91.1%	$49,290	13.2%	2,000
94. Surveying Technicians	91.1%	$30,380	23.1%	10,000
95. Hazardous Materials Removal Workers	90.8%	$33,320	43.1%	8,000
96. Irradiated-Fuel Handlers	90.8%	$33,320	43.1%	8,000

(continued)

Best Jobs Employing the Highest Percentage of Men

Job	Percent Men	Annual Earnings	Percent Growth	Annual Openings
97. Refuse and Recyclable Material Collectors	90.8%	$25,760	17.6%	42,000
98. Helpers—Installation, Maintenance, and Repair Workers	90.7%	$21,310	20.3%	33,000
99. Construction and Building Inspectors	90.2%	$43,670	13.8%	10,000
100. Civil Engineers	89.9%	$64,230	8.0%	17,000
101. Biomedical Engineers	89.6%	$67,690	26.1%	fewer than 500
102. Cost Estimators	88.0%	$49,940	18.6%	25,000
103. Medical Equipment Repairers	87.9%	$37,220	14.8%	4,000
104. First-Line Supervisors/Managers of Police and Detectives	87.2%	$64,430	15.3%	14,000
105. Atmospheric and Space Scientists	87.1%	$70,100	16.2%	1,000
106. Central Office and PBX Installers and Repairers	87.0%	$49,840	–0.6%	23,000
107. Communication Equipment Mechanics, Installers, and Repairers	87.0%	$49,840	–0.6%	23,000
108. Frame Wirers, Central Office	87.0%	$49,840	–0.6%	23,000
109. Parking Lot Attendants	87.0%	$16,800	19.2%	19,000
110. Station Installers and Repairers, Telephone	87.0%	$49,840	–0.6%	23,000
111. Telecommunications Facility Examiners	87.0%	$49,840	–0.6%	23,000
112. Highway Patrol Pilots	86.9%	$45,210	24.7%	67,000
113. Police Patrol Officers	86.9%	$45,210	24.7%	67,000
114. Sheriffs and Deputy Sheriffs	86.9%	$45,210	24.7%	67,000
115. Transit and Railroad Police	86.9%	$45,430	15.9%	1,000
116. Taxi Drivers and Chauffeurs	86.7%	$19,570	21.7%	28,000
117. Automatic Teller Machine Servicers	86.5%	$35,150	15.1%	19,000
118. Data Processing Equipment Repairers	86.5%	$35,150	15.1%	19,000
119. Office Machine and Cash Register Servicers	86.5%	$35,150	15.1%	19,000
120. Physicists	86.1%	$87,450	6.9%	1,000
121. Audio and Video Equipment Technicians	85.8%	$32,570	26.7%	5,000
122. Sound Engineering Technicians	85.8%	$38,110	25.5%	2,000
123. Clergy	85.7%	$36,690	15.5%	34,000
124. Agricultural Crop Farm Managers	85.5%	$50,700	5.1%	25,000
125. Fish Hatchery Managers	85.5%	$50,700	5.1%	25,000
126. Nursery and Greenhouse Managers	85.5%	$50,700	5.1%	25,000
127. Farmers and Ranchers	85.4%	$40,440	–20.6%	118,000
128. Model Makers, Metal and Plastic	85.2%	$44,250	14.6%	1,000
129. First-Line Supervisors and Manager/Supervisors —Agricultural Crop Workers	84.4%	$35,490	11.4%	6,000

Best Jobs Employing the Highest Percentage of Men

Job	Percent Men	Annual Earnings	Percent Growth	Annual Openings
130. First-Line Supervisors and Manager/Supervisors —Animal Care Workers, Except Livestock	84.4%	$35,490	11.4%	6,000
131. First-Line Supervisors and Manager/Supervisors —Animal Husbandry Workers	84.4%	$35,490	11.4%	6,000
132. First-Line Supervisors and Manager/Supervisors —Fishery Workers	84.4%	$35,490	11.4%	6,000
133. First-Line Supervisors and Manager/Supervisors —Horticultural Workers	84.4%	$35,490	11.4%	6,000
134. First-Line Supervisors and Manager/Supervisors —Logging Workers	84.4%	$35,490	11.4%	6,000
135. Podiatrists	84.3%	$94,400	15.0%	1,000
136. Aviation Inspectors	83.8%	$50,380	7.7%	5,000
137. Freight Inspectors	83.8%	$50,380	7.7%	5,000
138. Marine Cargo Inspectors	83.8%	$50,380	7.7%	5,000
139. Motor Vehicle Inspectors	83.8%	$50,380	7.7%	5,000
140. Public Transportation Inspectors	83.8%	$50,380	7.7%	5,000
141. Railroad Inspectors	83.8%	$50,380	7.7%	5,000
142. Computer Hardware Engineers	83.7%	$81,150	6.1%	6,000
143. Fire-Prevention and Protection Engineers	83.4%	$63,730	7.9%	4,000
144. Industrial Engineers	83.4%	$65,020	10.6%	16,000
145. Industrial Production Managers	83.4%	$73,000	7.9%	18,000
146. Industrial Safety and Health Engineers	83.4%	$63,730	7.9%	4,000
147. Product Safety Engineers	83.4%	$63,730	7.9%	4,000
148. Painters, Transportation Equipment	83.2%	$35,120	17.5%	9,000
149. Storage and Distribution Managers	82.9%	$66,600	19.7%	13,000
150. Transportation Managers	82.9%	$66,600	19.7%	13,000
151. Design Printing Machine Setters and Set-Up Operators	82.2%	$29,900	4.6%	30,000
152. Embossing Machine Set-Up Operators	82.2%	$29,900	4.6%	30,000
153. Engraver Set-Up Operators	82.2%	$29,900	4.6%	30,000
154. Letterpress Setters and Set-Up Operators	82.2%	$29,900	4.6%	30,000
155. Dentists, General	82.1%	$123,060	4.1%	7,000
156. Oral and Maxillofacial Surgeons	82.1% more than	$145,600	4.1%	7,000
157. Orthodontists	82.1% more than	$145,600	4.1%	7,000
158. Prosthodontists	82.1% more than	$145,600	4.1%	7,000
159. Cartographers and Photogrammetrists	82.0%	$46,080	15.1%	1,000
160. Air Traffic Controllers	81.6%	$102,030	12.6%	2,000

(continued)

(continued)

Best Jobs Employing the Highest Percentage of Men

Job	Percent Men	Annual Earnings	Percent Growth	Annual Openings
161. Chief Executives	81.2%	$140,350	16.7%	63,000
162. First-Line Supervisors/Managers of Helpers, Laborers, and Material Movers, Hand	81.2%	$38,280	14.0%	16,000
163. First-Line Supervisors/Managers of Transportation and Material-Moving Machine and Vehicle Operators	81.2%	$44,810	12.1%	23,000
164. Freight, Stock, and Material Movers, Hand	81.2%	$20,120	6.6%	525,000
165. Government Service Executives	81.2%	$140,350	16.7%	63,000
166. Grips and Set-Up Workers, Motion Picture Sets, Studios, and Stages	81.2%	$20,120	6.6%	525,000
167. Private Sector Executives	81.2%	$140,350	16.7%	63,000
168. Stevedores, Except Equipment Operators	81.2%	$20,120	6.6%	525,000
169. Camera Operators, Television, Video, and Motion Picture	81.1%	$37,610	13.4%	4,000
170. Film and Video Editors	81.1%	$43,590	26.4%	3,000
171. Calibration and Instrumentation Technicians	80.9%	$46,310	10.0%	24,000
172. Civil Engineering Technicians	80.9%	$38,480	7.6%	10,000
173. Electrical Engineering Technicians	80.9%	$46,310	10.0%	24,000
174. Electro-Mechanical Technicians	80.9%	$41,440	11.5%	4,000
175. Electronics Engineering Technicians	80.9%	$46,310	10.0%	24,000
176. Environmental Engineering Technicians	80.9%	$38,550	28.4%	3,000
177. Industrial Engineering Technicians	80.9%	$43,590	8.7%	7,000
178. Mechanical Engineering Technicians	80.9%	$43,400	11.0%	6,000
179. Chefs and Head Cooks	80.8%	$30,680	15.8%	33,000
180. Architectural Drafters	80.1%	$39,190	4.2%	14,000
181. Civil Drafters	80.1%	$39,190	4.2%	14,000
182. Architects, Except Landscape and Naval	79.7%	$60,300	17.3%	8,000
183. Landscape Architects	79.7%	$53,120	22.2%	2,000
184. First-Line Supervisors/Managers of Production and Operating Workers	79.1%	$44,740	9.5%	66,000
185. Child Support, Missing Persons, and Unemployment Insurance Fraud Investigators	79.0%	$53,990	22.4%	11,000
186. Criminal Investigators and Special Agents	79.0%	$53,990	22.4%	11,000
187. Immigration and Customs Inspectors	79.0%	$53,990	22.4%	11,000
188. Police Detectives	79.0%	$53,990	22.4%	11,000
189. Police Identification and Records Officers	79.0%	$53,990	22.4%	11,000
190. Security Guards	79.0%	$20,320	31.9%	228,000

Best Jobs Employing the Highest Percentage of Men

Job	Percent Men	Annual Earnings	Percent Growth	Annual Openings
191. Chiropractors	77.8%	$69,910	23.3%	3,000
192. Environmental Engineers	77.8%	$66,480	38.2%	6,000
193. Computer Security Specialists	76.7%	$58,190	37.4%	35,000
194. Network and Computer Systems Administrators	76.7%	$58,190	37.4%	35,000
195. Meat, Poultry, and Fish Cutters and Trimmers	76.3%	$18,900	16.4%	27,000
196. Slaughterers and Meat Packers	76.3%	$20,860	18.1%	23,000
197. Environmental Scientists and Specialists, Including Health	75.9%	$51,080	23.7%	6,000
198. Geologists	75.9%	$68,730	11.5%	2,000
199. Hydrologists	75.9%	$61,510	21.0%	1,000
200. Computer Software Engineers, Applications	75.3%	$74,980	45.5%	55,000
201. Computer Software Engineers, Systems Software	75.3%	$79,740	45.5%	39,000
202. First-Line Supervisors/Managers of Correctional Officers	74.3%	$44,720	19.0%	4,000
203. Correctional Officers and Jailers	74.0%	$33,600	24.2%	49,000
204. Food Scientists and Technologists	73.9%	$50,840	9.1%	2,000
205. Plant Scientists	73.9%	$51,200	9.1%	2,000
206. Sales Representatives, Agricultural	73.9%	$58,580	19.3%	44,000
207. Sales Representatives, Chemical and Pharmaceutical	73.9%	$58,580	19.3%	44,000
208. Sales Representatives, Electrical/Electronic	73.9%	$58,580	19.3%	44,000
209. Sales Representatives, Instruments	73.9%	$58,580	19.3%	44,000
210. Sales Representatives, Mechanical Equipment and Supplies	73.9%	$58,580	19.3%	44,000
211. Sales Representatives, Medical	73.9%	$58,580	19.3%	44,000
212. Sales Representatives, Wholesale and Manufacturing, Except Technical and Scientific Products	73.9%	$45,400	19.1%	160,000
213. Soil Scientists	73.9%	$51,200	9.1%	2,000
214. General and Operations Managers	73.7%	$77,420	18.4%	260,000
215. Network Systems and Data Communications Analysts	73.5%	$60,600	57.0%	29,000
216. Anesthesiologists	73.2%	$145,600	19.5%	38,000
217. Family and General Practitioners	73.2%	$137,090	19.5%	38,000
218. Internists, General	73.2%	more than $145,600	19.5%	38,000
219. Obstetricians and Gynecologists	73.2%	more than $145,600	19.5%	38,000
220. Pediatricians, General	73.2%	$135,730	19.5%	38,000

(continued)

(continued)

Best Jobs Employing the Highest Percentage of Men

Job	Percent Men	Annual Earnings	Percent Growth	Annual Openings
221. Psychiatrists	73.2% ..more than	$145,600	19.5%	38,000
222. Surgeons	73.2% ..more than	$145,600	19.5%	38,000
223. Cargo and Freight Agents	73.1%	$34,250	15.5%	8,000
224. Computer Programmers	72.5%	$62,890	14.6%	45,000
225. Optometrists	72.4%	$88,410	17.1%	2,000
226. Lawyers	71.3%	$94,930	17.0%	53,000
227. Computer and Information Systems Managers	70.3%	$92,570	36.1%	39,000
228. Janitors and Cleaners, Except Maids and Housekeeping Cleaners	70.1%	$18,790	18.3%	454,000

The jobs in the following four lists are derived from the preceding list of the jobs employing the highest percentage of men.

Best Jobs Overall Employing a High Percentage of Men

Job	Percent Men	Annual Earnings	Percent Growth	Annual Openings
1. Computer Software Engineers, Applications	75.3%	$74,980	45.5%	55,000
2. Computer Software Engineers, Systems Software	75.3%	$79,740	45.5%	39,000
3. Computer and Information Systems Managers	70.3%	$92,570	36.1%	39,000
4. General and Operations Managers	73.7%	$77,420	18.4%	260,000
5. Network Systems and Data Communications Analysts	73.5%	$60,600	57.0%	29,000
6. Computer Security Specialists	76.7%	$58,190	37.4%	35,000
7. Network and Computer Systems Administrators	76.7%	$58,190	37.4%	35,000
8. Anesthesiologists	73.2% ..more than	$145,600	19.5%	38,000
9. Internists, General	73.2% ..more than	$145,600	19.5%	38,000
10. Obstetricians and Gynecologists	73.2% ..more than	$145,600	19.5%	38,000
11. Psychiatrists	73.2% ..more than	$145,600	19.5%	38,000
12. Surgeons	73.2% ..more than	$145,600	19.5%	38,000
13. Family and General Practitioners	73.2%	$137,090	19.5%	38,000
14. Pediatricians, General	73.2%	$135,730	19.5%	38,000
15. Chief Executives	81.2%	$140,350	16.7%	63,000
16. Government Service Executives	81.2%	$140,350	16.7%	63,000
17. Private Sector Executives	81.2%	$140,350	16.7%	63,000

Best Jobs Overall Employing a High Percentage of Men

Job	Percent Men	Annual Earnings	Percent Growth	Annual Openings
18. Lawyers	71.3%	$94,930	17.0%	53,000
19. Highway Patrol Pilots	86.9%	$45,210	24.7%	67,000
20. Police Patrol Officers	86.9%	$45,210	24.7%	67,000
21. Sheriffs and Deputy Sheriffs	86.9%	$45,210	24.7%	67,000
22. Sales Representatives, Agricultural	73.9%	$58,580	19.3%	44,000
23. Sales Representatives, Chemical and Pharmaceutical	73.9%	$58,580	19.3%	44,000
24. Sales Representatives, Electrical/Electronic	73.9%	$58,580	19.3%	44,000
25. Sales Representatives, Instruments	73.9%	$58,580	19.3%	44,000

Best-Paying Jobs Employing a High Percentage of Men

Job	Percent Men	Annual Earnings	Percent Growth	Annual Openings
1. Anesthesiologists	73.2% more than	$145,600	19.5%	38,000
2. Internists, General	73.2% more than	$145,600	19.5%	38,000
3. Obstetricians and Gynecologists	73.2% more than	$145,600	19.5%	38,000
4. Oral and Maxillofacial Surgeons	82.1% more than	$145,600	4.1%	7,000
5. Orthodontists	82.1% more than	$145,600	4.1%	7,000
6. Prosthodontists	82.1% more than	$145,600	4.1%	7,000
7. Psychiatrists	73.2% more than	$145,600	19.5%	38,000
8. Surgeons	73.2% more than	$145,600	19.5%	38,000
9. Chief Executives	81.2%	$140,350	16.7%	63,000
10. Government Service Executives	81.2%	$140,350	16.7%	63,000
11. Private Sector Executives	81.2%	$140,350	16.7%	63,000
12. Family and General Practitioners	73.2%	$137,090	19.5%	38,000
13. Pediatricians, General	73.2%	$135,730	19.5%	38,000
14. Airline Pilots, Copilots, and Flight Engineers	96.0%	$129,250	18.5%	6,000
15. Dentists, General	82.1%	$123,060	4.1%	7,000
16. Air Traffic Controllers	81.6%	$102,030	12.6%	2,000
17. Engineering Managers	93.4%	$97,630	9.2%	16,000
18. Lawyers	71.3%	$94,930	17.0%	53,000
19. Podiatrists	84.3%	$94,400	15.0%	1,000
20. Computer and Information Systems Managers	70.3%	$92,570	36.1%	39,000
21. Optometrists	72.4%	$88,410	17.1%	2,000
22. Physicists	86.1%	$87,450	6.9%	1,000

(continued)

(continued)

Best-Paying Jobs Employing a High Percentage of Men

Job	Percent Men	Annual Earnings	Percent Growth	Annual Openings
23. Computer Hardware Engineers	83.7%	$81,150	6.1%	6,000
24. Computer Software Engineers, Systems Software	75.3%	$79,740	45.5%	39,000
25. General and Operations Managers	73.7%	$77,420	18.4%	260,000

Fastest-Growing Jobs Employing a High Percentage of Men

Job	Percent Men	Annual Earnings	Percent Growth	Annual Openings
1. Network Systems and Data Communications Analysts	73.5%	$60,600	57.0%	29,000
2. Computer Software Engineers, Applications	75.3%	$74,980	45.5%	55,000
3. Computer Software Engineers, Systems Software	75.3%	$79,740	45.5%	39,000
4. Hazardous Materials Removal Workers	90.8%	$33,320	43.1%	8,000
5. Irradiated-Fuel Handlers	90.8%	$33,320	43.1%	8,000
6. Environmental Engineers	77.8%	$66,480	38.2%	6,000
7. Computer Security Specialists	76.7%	$58,190	37.4%	35,000
8. Network and Computer Systems Administrators	76.7%	$58,190	37.4%	35,000
9. Computer and Information Systems Managers	70.3%	$92,570	36.1%	39,000
10. Security Guards	79.0%	$20,320	31.9%	228,000
11. Heating and Air Conditioning Mechanics	98.2%	$36,260	31.8%	35,000
12. Refrigeration Mechanics	98.2%	$36,260	31.8%	35,000
13. Security and Fire Alarm Systems Installers	96.9%	$33,410	30.2%	5,000
14. Environmental Engineering Technicians	80.9%	$38,550	28.4%	3,000
15. Audio and Video Equipment Technicians	85.8%	$32,570	26.7%	5,000
16. Tile and Marble Setters	97.5%	$35,410	26.5%	4,000
17. Film and Video Editors	81.1%	$43,590	26.4%	3,000
18. Biomedical Engineers	89.6%	$67,690	26.1%	fewer than 500
19. Cement Masons and Concrete Finishers	98.6%	$31,400	26.1%	24,000
20. Sound Engineering Technicians	85.8%	$38,110	25.5%	2,000
21. Highway Patrol Pilots	86.9%	$45,210	24.7%	67,000
22. Police Patrol Officers	86.9%	$45,210	24.7%	67,000
23. Sheriffs and Deputy Sheriffs	86.9%	$45,210	24.7%	67,000
24. Correctional Officers and Jailers	74.0%	$33,600	24.2%	49,000
25. Environmental Scientists and Specialists, Including Health	75.9%	$51,080	23.7%	6,000

Jobs with the Most Openings Employing a High Percentage of Men

Job	Percent Men	Annual Earnings	Percent Growth	Annual Openings
1. Freight, Stock, and Material Movers, Hand	81.2%	$20,120	6.6%	525,000
2. Grips and Set-Up Workers, Motion Picture Sets, Studios, and Stages	81.2%	$20,120	6.6%	525,000
3. Stevedores, Except Equipment Operators	81.2%	$20,120	6.6%	525,000
4. Janitors and Cleaners, Except Maids and Housekeeping Cleaners	70.1%	$18,790	18.3%	454,000
5. Tractor-Trailer Truck Drivers	94.1%	$33,520	19.0%	299,000
6. Truck Drivers, Heavy	94.1%	$33,520	19.0%	299,000
7. General and Operations Managers	73.7%	$77,420	18.4%	260,000
8. Security Guards	79.0%	$20,320	31.9%	228,000
9. Truck Drivers, Light or Delivery Services	94.1%	$24,540	23.2%	219,000
10. Landscaping and Groundskeeping Workers	92.4%	$20,420	22.0%	203,000
11. Boat Builders and Shipwrights	98.1%	$34,900	10.1%	193,000
12. Brattice Builders	98.1%	$34,900	10.1%	193,000
13. Carpenter Assemblers and Repairers	98.1%	$34,900	10.1%	193,000
14. Construction Carpenters	98.1%	$34,900	10.1%	193,000
15. Rough Carpenters	98.1%	$34,900	10.1%	193,000
16. Ship Carpenters and Joiners	98.1%	$34,900	10.1%	193,000
17. Construction Laborers	96.5%	$25,160	14.2%	166,000
18. Sales Representatives, Wholesale and Manufacturing, Except Technical and Scientific Products	73.9%	$45,400	19.1%	160,000
19. Maintenance and Repair Workers, General	95.9%	$30,710	16.3%	155,000
20. Refractory Materials Repairers, Except Brickmasons	96.2%	$37,640	16.3%	155,000
21. Farmers and Ranchers	85.4%	$40,440	–20.6%	118,000
22. Automotive Master Mechanics	98.1%	$32,450	12.4%	100,000
23. Automotive Specialty Technicians	98.1%	$32,450	12.4%	100,000
24. Industrial Truck and Tractor Operators	92.4%	$26,580	11.1%	94,000
25. Brazers	92.6%	$30,620	17.0%	71,000

Best Jobs Lists Based on Levels of Education and Experience

The lists in this section organize the 500 best jobs into groups based on the education or training typically required for entry. Unlike many of the previous sections, here we do not include separate lists for highest pay, growth, or number of openings. Instead, we provide one list that includes all the occupations in our database that fit into each of the education levels and ranks them by their total combined score for earnings, growth, and number of openings.

These lists can help you identify a job with higher earnings or upward mobility but with a similar level of education to the job you now hold. For example, you will find jobs within the same level of education that require similar skills, yet one pays significantly better than the other, is projected to grow more rapidly, or has significantly more job openings per year. This information can help you leverage your present skills and experience into jobs that might provide better long-term career opportunities.

You can also use these lists to explore possible job options if you were to get additional training, education, or work experience. For example, you can use these lists to identify occupations that offer high potential and then look into the education or training required to get the jobs that interest you most.

The lists can also help you when you plan your education. For example, you might be thinking about a particular training program or college major because the pay is very good, but the lists may help you identify a job that interests you more and offers even better potential for the same general educational requirements.

The Education Levels

A clear relationship exists between education and earnings—the more education or training you have, the more you are likely to earn. The lists that follow arrange all the jobs that met our criteria for inclusion in this book (see the introduction) by level of education, training, and work experience. These are the levels typically required for a new entrant to begin work in the occupation.

We included on each list all the occupations in our database that fit into each of the education levels. We then arranged these occupations based on their total scores for earnings, growth, and number of openings.

Once again, our lists use the same categories used by the U.S. Department of Labor for entry into various occupations.

Use the Lists to Locate Better Job Opportunities

Considering jobs with similar requirements can be very helpful because it will tell you how to leverage your present skills and experience into better-paying or more interesting opportunities. As we mentioned in the introduction to the book, doing this could, with just a bit of effort, result in big advances in pay for doing similar work.

You can also use these lists to explore career options if you were to get additional training, education, or work experience. For example, maybe you are a high school graduate interested in the field of medicine. You will find jobs related to medicine at most levels of training and education, and you can consider what jobs you might be qualified for if you were to get, say, a year or so of training. You could then work in that field and, later, get more training for an even better-paying job in the medical area. Or maybe you are enrolled in college or considering a four-year college degree. Looking over the lists in this section can help you identify a possible area of study or eliminate one you were considering.

The list of jobs by education should also help you when planning your education. For example, a job as restaurant cook requires long-term, on-the-job training, but its pay is quite modest. A flight attendant requires the same level of education, but the job pays considerably more. This looks like a good reason to be a flight attendant until you note that there are relatively few job openings per year for flight attendants, while there are many more openings for restaurant cooks. These are also very different types of jobs, and a person who would enjoy and be good at one job would not be likely to enjoy and do well in the other.

The following definitions are used by the federal government to classify jobs based on the minimum level of education or training typically required for entry into a job. We use these definitions to construct the lists in this section. Use the training and education level descriptions as guidelines that can help you understand what is generally required, but understand that you will need to learn more about specific requirements before you make a decision on one career over another.

- **Short-term on-the-job training:** It is possible to work in these occupations and achieve an average level of performance within a few days or weeks through on-the-job training.
- **Moderate-term on-the-job training:** Occupations that require this type of training can be performed adequately after a 1- to 12-month period of combined on-the-job and informal training. Typically, untrained workers begin by observing experienced workers performing tasks and are gradually moved into progressively more difficult assignments.
- **Long-term on-the-job training:** This type of training requires more than 12 months of on-the-job training or combined work experience and formal classroom instruction. This includes occupations that use formal apprenticeships for training workers that may take up to four years. It also includes intensive occupation-specific employer-sponsored training like police academies. Furthermore, it includes occupations that require natural talent that must be developed over many years.

◎ **Work experience in a related occupation:** This type of job requires a worker to have experience—usually several years of experience—in a related occupation (such as police detectives, who are selected based on their experience as police patrol officers).

◎ **Postsecondary vocational training:** This training requirement can vary in length; training usually lasts from a few months up to one year. In a few instances, there may be as many as four years of training.

◎ **Associate degree:** The associate degree usually requires 60 to 63 semester hours to complete. A normal course load for a full-time student each semester is 15 hours. This means that it typically takes two years to complete an associate degree.

◎ **Bachelor's degree:** A bachelor's degree usually requires 120 to 130 semester hours to complete. A full-time student usually takes four to five years to complete a bachelor's degree, depending on the complexity of courses. Traditionally, people have thought of the bachelor's degree as a four-year degree. There are some bachelor's degrees—like the Bachelor of Architecture—that are considered a first professional degree and take five or more years to complete.

◎ **Work experience plus degree:** Some jobs require work experience in a related job in addition to a degree. For example, almost all managers have worked in a related job before being promoted into a management position. Most of the jobs in this group require a four-year bachelor's degree, although some require an associate degree or a master's degree.

◎ **Master's degree:** This degree usually requires 33 to 60 semester hours beyond the bachelor's degree. The academic master's degrees—like a Master of Arts in Political Science—usually require 33 to 36 hours. A first professional degree at the master's level—like a Master of Social Work—requires almost two years of full-time work.

◎ **Doctoral degree:** The doctoral degree prepares students for careers that consist primarily of theory development, research, and/or college teaching. This type of degree is typically the Doctor of Philosophy (Ph.D.) or Doctor of Education (Ed.D.). Normally, a requirement for a doctoral degree is the completion of a master's degree plus an additional two to three years of full-time coursework and a one- to two-semester research project and paper called the dissertation. It usually takes four to five years beyond the bachelor's degree to complete a doctoral degree.

◎ **First professional degree:** Some professional degrees require three or more years of full-time academic study beyond the bachelor's degree. A professional degree prepares students for a specific profession. It uses theory and research to teach practical applications in a professional occupation. Examples of this type of degree are Doctor of Medicine (M.D.) for physicians, Doctor of Ministry (D.Min.) for clergy, and Juris Doctor (J.D.) for attorneys.

Another Warning About the Data

We warned you in the introduction to use caution in interpreting the data we use, and we want to do it again here. The occupational data we use is the most accurate available anywhere, but it has limitations. For example, a four-year degree in accounting, finance, or a related area is typically required for entry into the accounting profession. But some people working as accountants don't have such a degree, and others have much more education than the "minimum" required for entry.

In a similar way, people with a graduate degree will typically earn considerably more than someone with an associate or bachelor's degree. However, some people with an associate degree earn considerably more than the average for those with higher levels of education. In a similar way, new entrants to any job will typically earn less than the average, and some areas of the country have lower wages overall (but may also have lower costs of living).

So as you browse the lists that follow, please use them as a way to be encouraged rather than discouraged. Education and training are very important for success in the labor market, but so are ability, drive, initiative, and, yes, luck.

Having said this, we encourage you to get as much education and training as you can. It used to be that you got your schooling and never went back, but this is not a good attitude to have now. You will probably need to continue learning new things throughout your working life. This can be done by going to school, which is a good thing for many people to do. But there are also many other ways to learn, such as workshops, adult education programs, certification programs, employer training, professional conferences, Internet training, reading related books and magazines, and many others. Upgrading your computer skills—and other technical skills—is particularly important in our rapidly changing workplace, and you avoid doing so at your peril.

Best Jobs Requiring Short-Term On-the-Job Training

Job	Annual Earnings	Percent Growth	Annual Openings
1. Truck Drivers, Heavy	$33,520	19.0%	299,000
2. Refractory Materials Repairers, Except Brickmasons	$37,640	16.3%	155,000
3. Bill and Account Collectors	$27,450	24.5%	76,000
4. Receptionists and Information Clerks	$21,830	29.5%	296,000
5. Truck Drivers, Light or Delivery Services	$24,540	23.2%	219,000
6. Production, Planning, and Expediting Clerks	$36,340	14.1%	51,000
7. Security Guards	$20,320	31.9%	228,000
8. Brazers	$30,620	17.0%	71,000
9. Solderers	$30,620	17.0%	71,000
10. Welders, Production	$30,620	17.0%	71,000
11. Human Resources Assistants, Except Payroll and Timekeeping	$31,750	19.3%	36,000
12. Nursing Aides, Orderlies, and Attendants	$20,980	24.9%	302,000
13. Home Health Aides	$18,330	48.1%	141,000
14. Personal and Home Care Aides	$16,900	40.5%	154,000

(continued)

(continued)

Best Jobs Requiring Short-Term On-the-Job Training

Job	Annual Earnings	Percent Growth	Annual Openings
15. Interviewers, Except Eligibility and Loan	$23,670	28.0%	46,000
16. Landscaping and Groundskeeping Workers	$20,420	22.0%	203,000
17. Teacher Assistants	$19,410	23.0%	259,000
18. Counter and Rental Clerks	$18,280	26.3%	144,000
19. Combined Food Preparation and Serving Workers, Including Fast Food	$14,690	22.8%	734,000
20. Locker Room, Coatroom, and Dressing Room Attendants	$17,550	27.8%	66,000
21. Packaging and Filling Machine Operators and Tenders	$22,200	21.1%	69,000
22. Amusement and Recreation Attendants	$15,550	27.8%	66,000
23. Food Preparation Workers	$16,710	20.2%	267,000
24. Janitors and Cleaners, Except Maids and Housekeeping Cleaners	$18,790	18.3%	454,000
25. Refuse and Recyclable Material Collectors	$25,760	17.6%	42,000
26. Hotel, Motel, and Resort Desk Clerks	$17,700	23.9%	46,000
27. Bus Drivers, School	$23,250	16.7%	76,000
28. Waiters and Waitresses	$14,050	17.5%	721,000
29. Helpers—Installation, Maintenance, and Repair Workers	$21,310	20.3%	33,000
30. Industrial Truck and Tractor Operators	$26,580	11.1%	94,000
31. Retail Salespersons	$18,680	14.6%	1,014,000
32. Library Assistants, Clerical	$20,720	21.5%	27,000
33. Counter Attendants, Cafeteria, Food Concession, and Coffee Shop	$15,660	16.7%	190,000
34. Nonfarm Animal Caretakers	$17,460	22.2%	32,000
35. Taxi Drivers and Chauffeurs	$19,570	21.7%	28,000
36. Reservation and Transportation Ticket Agents	$27,750	12.2%	35,000
37. Travel Clerks	$27,750	12.2%	35,000
38. Office Clerks, General	$22,770	10.4%	550,000
39. Hosts and Hostesses, Restaurant, Lounge, and Coffee Shop	$15,630	16.4%	95,000
40. Packers and Packagers, Hand	$17,150	14.4%	198,000
41. Library Technicians	$24,940	16.8%	22,000
42. Cashiers	$16,240	13.2%	1,221,000
43. Billing, Cost, and Rate Clerks	$27,040	7.9%	78,000
44. Billing, Posting, and Calculating Machine Operators	$27,040	7.9%	78,000
45. Statement Clerks	$27,040	7.9%	78,000
46. Dining Room and Cafeteria Attendants and Bartender Helpers	$14,770	14.9%	143,000
47. Postal Service Mail Carriers	$44,450	−0.5%	20,000
48. Gaming Change Persons and Booth Cashiers	$20,530	24.1%	12,000

Best Jobs Requiring Short-Term On-the-Job Training

Job	Annual Earnings	Percent Growth	Annual Openings
49. Tree Trimmers and Pruners	$26,150	18.6%	11,000
50. Child Care Workers	$16,760	11.7%	406,000
51. Nannies	$16,760	11.7%	406,000
52. Helpers—Electricians	$23,420	17.9%	17,000
53. Production Inspectors, Testers, Graders, Sorters, Samplers, Weighers	$28,410	4.7%	87,000
54. Veterinary Assistants and Laboratory Animal Caretakers	$18,660	26.2%	11,000
55. Tellers	$21,120	9.4%	127,000
56. Lifeguards, Ski Patrol, and Other Recreational Protective Service Workers	$16,540	14.3%	60,000
57. Court Clerks	$28,430	12.3%	14,000
58. License Clerks	$28,430	12.3%	14,000
59. Municipal Clerks	$28,430	12.3%	14,000
60. Production Laborers	$20,180	11.3%	67,000
61. Parking Lot Attendants	$16,800	19.2%	19,000
62. Meat, Poultry, and Fish Cutters and Trimmers	$18,900	16.4%	27,000
63. Maids and Housekeeping Cleaners	$16,900	9.2%	352,000
64. Weighers, Measurers, Checkers, and Samplers, Recordkeeping	$24,570	14.6%	16,000
65. Freight, Stock, and Material Movers, Hand	$20,120	6.6%	525,000
66. Grips and Set-Up Workers, Motion Picture Sets, Studios, and Stages	$20,120	6.6%	525,000
67. Stevedores, Except Equipment Operators	$20,120	6.6%	525,000
68. Spotters, Dry Cleaning	$17,220	12.3%	47,000

Best Jobs Requiring Moderate-Term On-the-Job Training

Job	Annual Earnings	Percent Growth	Annual Openings
1. Sales Representatives, Agricultural	$58,580	19.3%	44,000
2. Sales Representatives, Chemical and Pharmaceutical	$58,580	19.3%	44,000
3. Sales Representatives, Electrical/Electronic	$58,580	19.3%	44,000
4. Sales Representatives, Instruments	$58,580	19.3%	44,000
5. Sales Representatives, Mechanical Equipment and Supplies	$58,580	19.3%	44,000
6. Sales Representatives, Medical	$58,580	19.3%	44,000
7. Sales Representatives, Wholesale and Manufacturing, Except Technical and Scientific Products	$45,400	19.1%	160,000

(continued)

(continued)

Best Jobs Requiring Moderate-Term On-the-Job Training

Job	Annual Earnings	Percent Growth	Annual Openings
8. Pipelaying Fitters	$41,290	18.7%	56,000
9. Tractor-Trailer Truck Drivers	$33,520	19.0%	299,000
10. Correctional Officers and Jailers	$33,600	24.2%	49,000
11. Adjustment Clerks	$27,020	24.3%	419,000
12. Customer Service Representatives, Utilities	$27,020	24.3%	419,000
13. Sheet Metal Workers	$35,560	19.8%	30,000
14. Medical Assistants	$24,610	58.9%	78,000
15. Caption Writers	$44,350	16.1%	23,000
16. Dental Assistants	$28,330	42.5%	35,000
17. Social and Human Service Assistants	$24,270	48.7%	63,000
18. Costume Attendants	$25,050	27.8%	66,000
19. Ceiling Tile Installers	$34,030	21.4%	17,000
20. Drywall Installers	$34,030	21.4%	17,000
21. Brattice Builders	$34,900	10.1%	193,000
22. Carpenter Assemblers and Repairers	$34,900	10.1%	193,000
23. Rough Carpenters	$34,900	10.1%	193,000
24. Ship Carpenters and Joiners	$34,900	10.1%	193,000
25. Roofers	$30,840	18.6%	38,000
26. Hazardous Materials Removal Workers	$33,320	43.1%	8,000
27. Irradiated-Fuel Handlers	$33,320	43.1%	8,000
28. Advertising Sales Agents	$40,300	13.4%	24,000
29. Pharmacy Technicians	$23,650	28.8%	39,000
30. Executive Secretaries and Administrative Assistants	$34,970	8.7%	210,000
31. Grader, Bulldozer, and Scraper Operators	$35,360	10.4%	45,000
32. Operating Engineers	$35,360	10.4%	45,000
33. Painters, Construction and Maintenance	$30,260	11.6%	69,000
34. Tapers	$39,070	20.8%	5,000
35. Mapping Technicians	$30,380	23.1%	10,000
36. Bus Drivers, Transit and Intercity	$29,730	15.2%	33,000
37. Construction Laborers	$25,160	14.2%	166,000
38. Dispatchers, Except Police, Fire, and Ambulance	$30,920	14.4%	28,000
39. Painters, Transportation Equipment	$35,120	17.5%	9,000
40. Carpet Installers	$34,090	16.8%	10,000
41. Tax Preparers	$27,730	23.2%	11,000
42. Residential Advisors	$21,430	33.6%	12,000
43. Insulation Workers, Mechanical	$33,330	15.8%	9,000

Best Jobs Requiring Moderate-Term On-the-Job Training

Job	Annual Earnings	Percent Growth	Annual Openings
44. Cargo and Freight Agents	$34,250	15.5%	8,000
45. Demonstrators and Product Promoters	$20,700	17.0%	38,000
46. Electric Meter Installers and Repairers	$43,710	12.0%	5,000
47. Meter Mechanics	$43,710	12.0%	5,000
48. Valve and Regulator Repairers	$43,710	12.0%	5,000
49. Highway Maintenance Workers	$29,550	10.4%	25,000
50. Insulation Workers, Floor, Ceiling, and Wall	$30,310	15.8%	9,000
51. Subway and Streetcar Operators	$49,290	13.2%	2,000
52. Slaughterers and Meat Packers	$20,860	18.1%	23,000
53. Medical Equipment Repairers	$37,220	14.8%	4,000
54. Bookkeeping, Accounting, and Auditing Clerks	$28,570	3.0%	274,000
55. Electrical and Electronic Inspectors and Testers	$28,410	4.7%	87,000
56. Materials Inspectors	$28,410	4.7%	87,000
57. Police, Fire, and Ambulance Dispatchers	$28,930	12.7%	15,000
58. Precision Devices Inspectors and Testers	$28,410	4.7%	87,000
59. Loading Machine Operators, Underground Mining	$33,250	8.9%	14,000
60. Pest Control Workers	$26,220	17.0%	11,000
61. Camera Operators, Television, Video, and Motion Picture	$37,610	13.4%	4,000
62. Locksmiths and Safe Repairers	$30,360	21.0%	3,000
63. Dragline Operators	$31,970	8.9%	14,000
64. Excavating and Loading Machine Operators	$31,970	8.9%	14,000
65. Model Makers, Metal and Plastic	$44,250	14.6%	1,000
66. Crane and Tower Operators	$37,410	10.8%	5,000
67. Septic Tank Servicers and Sewer Pipe Cleaners	$28,870	21.2%	3,000
68. Laundry and Drycleaning Machine Operators and Tenders, Except Pressing	$17,220	12.3%	47,000
69. Letterpress Setters and Set-Up Operators	$29,900	4.6%	30,000

Best Jobs Requiring Long-Term On-the-Job Training

Job	Annual Earnings	Percent Growth	Annual Openings
1. Highway Patrol Pilots	$45,210	24.7%	67,000
2. Police Patrol Officers	$45,210	24.7%	67,000
3. Sheriffs and Deputy Sheriffs	$45,210	24.7%	67,000
4. Electricians	$42,300	23.4%	65,000

(continued)

(continued)

Best Jobs Requiring Long-Term On-the-Job Training

Job	Annual Earnings	Percent Growth	Annual Openings
5. Heating and Air Conditioning Mechanics	$36,260	31.8%	35,000
6. Refrigeration Mechanics	$36,260	31.8%	35,000
7. Pipe Fitters	$41,290	18.7%	56,000
8. Plumbers	$41,290	18.7%	56,000
9. Forest Fire Fighters	$38,330	20.7%	29,000
10. Municipal Fire Fighters	$38,330	20.7%	29,000
11. Talent Directors	$52,840	18.3%	10,000
12. Technical Directors/Managers	$52,840	18.3%	10,000
13. Claims Examiners, Property and Casualty Insurance	$44,220	14.2%	31,000
14. Insurance Adjusters, Examiners, and Investigators	$44,220	14.2%	31,000
15. Flight Attendants	$43,440	15.9%	23,000
16. Cement Masons and Concrete Finishers	$31,400	26.1%	24,000
17. Maintenance and Repair Workers, General	$30,710	16.3%	155,000
18. Welder-Fitters	$30,620	17.0%	71,000
19. Welders and Cutters	$30,620	17.0%	71,000
20. Telecommunications Line Installers and Repairers	$40,330	18.8%	13,000
21. Boat Builders and Shipwrights	$34,900	10.1%	193,000
22. Construction Carpenters	$34,900	10.1%	193,000
23. Brickmasons and Blockmasons	$41,740	14.2%	21,000
24. Environmental Compliance Inspectors	$47,390	9.8%	20,000
25. Equal Opportunity Representatives and Officers	$47,390	9.8%	20,000
26. Government Property Inspectors and Investigators	$47,390	9.8%	20,000
27. Licensing Examiners and Inspectors	$47,390	9.8%	20,000
28. Pressure Vessel Inspectors	$47,390	9.8%	20,000
29. Elevator Installers and Repairers	$58,710	17.1%	3,000
30. Automatic Teller Machine Servicers	$35,150	15.1%	19,000
31. Office Machine and Cash Register Servicers	$35,150	15.1%	19,000
32. Structural Iron and Steel Workers	$42,430	15.9%	9,000
33. Athletes and Sports Competitors	$48,310	19.2%	3,000
34. Automotive Body and Related Repairers	$34,690	13.2%	23,000
35. Surveying Technicians	$30,380	23.1%	10,000
36. Tile and Marble Setters	$35,410	26.5%	4,000
37. Audio and Video Equipment Technicians	$32,570	26.7%	5,000
38. Air Traffic Controllers	$102,030	12.6%	2,000
39. Coaches and Scouts	$26,350	18.3%	26,000
40. Cooks, Restaurant	$19,520	15.9%	211,000

Best Jobs Requiring Long-Term On-the-Job Training

Job	Annual Earnings	Percent Growth	Annual Openings
41. Water and Liquid Waste Treatment Plant and System Operators	$34,960	16.0%	9,000
42. Machinists	$33,960	8.2%	30,000
43. Interpreters and Translators	$33,860	22.1%	4,000
44. Telecommunications Facility Examiners	$49,840	–0.6%	23,000
45. Glaziers	$32,650	17.2%	7,000
46. Cartoonists	$38,060	16.5%	4,000
47. Painters and Illustrators	$38,060	16.5%	4,000
48. Sculptors	$38,060	16.5%	4,000
49. Sketch Artists	$38,060	16.5%	4,000
50. Farmers and Ranchers	$40,440	–20.6%	118,000
51. Industrial Machinery Mechanics	$39,060	5.5%	19,000
52. Opticians, Dispensing	$27,950	18.2%	10,000
53. Mechanical Inspectors	$28,410	4.7%	87,000
54. Plasterers and Stucco Masons	$32,440	13.5%	8,000
55. Transit and Railroad Police	$45,430	15.9%	1,000
56. Recreational Vehicle Service Technicians	$28,980	21.8%	4,000
57. Photographers, Scientific	$26,080	13.6%	18,000
58. Professional Photographers	$26,080	13.6%	18,000
59. Insurance Appraisers, Auto Damage	$45,330	11.7%	2,000
60. Electrical Power-Line Installers and Repairers	$49,100	1.6%	9,000
61. Millwrights	$43,720	5.3%	7,000
62. Reinforcing Iron and Rebar Workers	$35,160	16.7%	2,000
63. Engraver Set-Up Operators	$29,900	4.6%	30,000

Best Jobs Requiring Work Experience in a Related Occupation

Job	Annual Earnings	Percent Growth	Annual Openings
1. Storage and Distribution Managers	$66,600	19.7%	13,000
2. Transportation Managers	$66,600	19.7%	13,000
3. First-Line Supervisors and Manager/Supervisors—Construction Trades Workers	$50,450	14.1%	67,000
4. First-Line Supervisors and Manager/Supervisors—Extractive Workers	$50,450	14.1%	67,000
5. First-Line Supervisors/Managers of Mechanics, Installers, and Repairers	$50,340	15.4%	42,000

(continued)

(continued)

Best Jobs Requiring Work Experience in a Related Occupation

Job	Annual Earnings	Percent Growth	Annual Openings
6. Child Support, Missing Persons, and Unemployment Insurance Fraud Investigators	$53,990	22.4%	11,000
7. Criminal Investigators and Special Agents	$53,990	22.4%	11,000
8. Immigration and Customs Inspectors	$53,990	22.4%	11,000
9. Police Detectives	$53,990	22.4%	11,000
10. Police Identification and Records Officers	$53,990	22.4%	11,000
11. Self-Enrichment Education Teachers	$30,880	40.1%	39,000
12. First-Line Supervisors/Managers of Police and Detectives	$64,430	15.3%	14,000
13. First-Line Supervisors/Managers of Non-Retail Sales Workers	$59,300	6.8%	72,000
14. Forest Fire Fighting and Prevention Supervisors	$58,920	18.7%	8,000
15. Municipal Fire Fighting and Prevention Supervisors	$58,920	18.7%	8,000
16. First-Line Supervisors/Managers of Production and Operating Workers	$44,740	9.5%	66,000
17. First-Line Supervisors and Manager/Supervisors— Landscaping Workers	$35,340	21.6%	18,000
18. Lawn Service Managers	$35,340	21.6%	18,000
19. Food Service Managers	$39,610	11.5%	58,000
20. First-Line Supervisors/Managers of Transportation and Material-Moving Machine and Vehicle Operators	$44,810	12.1%	23,000
21. First-Line Supervisors, Administrative Support	$41,030	6.6%	140,000
22. First-Line Supervisors, Customer Service	$41,030	6.6%	140,000
23. Coroners	$47,390	9.8%	20,000
24. First-Line Supervisors/Managers of Retail Sales Workers	$32,720	9.1%	251,000
25. Emergency Management Specialists	$45,390	28.2%	2,000
26. Private Detectives and Investigators	$32,110	25.3%	9,000
27. First-Line Supervisors/Managers of Helpers, Laborers, and Material Movers, Hand	$38,280	14.0%	16,000
28. Agricultural Crop Farm Managers	$50,700	5.1%	25,000
29. Fish Hatchery Managers	$50,700	5.1%	25,000
30. Nursery and Greenhouse Managers	$50,700	5.1%	25,000
31. Construction and Building Inspectors	$43,670	13.8%	10,000
32. First-Line Supervisors/Managers of Correctional Officers	$44,720	19.0%	4,000
33. First-Line Supervisors/Managers of Food Preparation and Serving Workers	$25,410	15.5%	154,000
34. Housekeeping Supervisors	$29,510	16.2%	28,000
35. Janitorial Supervisors	$29,510	16.2%	28,000
36. Real Estate Brokers	$58,720	2.4%	11,000

Best Jobs Requiring Work Experience in a Related Occupation

Job	Annual Earnings	Percent Growth	Annual Openings
37. First-Line Supervisors/Managers of Personal Service Workers	$30,350	9.4%	26,000
38. Aviation Inspectors	$50,380	7.7%	5,000
39. Freight Inspectors	$50,380	7.7%	5,000
40. Marine Cargo Inspectors	$50,380	7.7%	5,000
41. Motor Vehicle Inspectors	$50,380	7.7%	5,000
42. Public Transportation Inspectors	$50,380	7.7%	5,000
43. Railroad Inspectors	$50,380	7.7%	5,000
44. New Accounts Clerks	$26,860	11.2%	24,000
45. Lodging Managers	$37,660	6.6%	10,000

Best Jobs Requiring Postsecondary Vocational Training

Job	Annual Earnings	Percent Growth	Annual Openings
1. Licensed Practical and Licensed Vocational Nurses	$33,970	20.2%	105,000
2. Legal Secretaries	$36,720	18.8%	39,000
3. Massage Therapists	$31,960	27.1%	24,000
4. Fitness Trainers and Aerobics Instructors	$25,470	44.5%	38,000
5. Surgical Technologists	$34,010	27.9%	13,000
6. Appraisers, Real Estate	$43,390	17.6%	11,000
7. Assessors	$43,390	17.6%	11,000
8. Automotive Master Mechanics	$32,450	12.4%	100,000
9. Automotive Specialty Technicians	$32,450	12.4%	100,000
10. Emergency Medical Technicians and Paramedics	$25,310	33.1%	32,000
11. Bus and Truck Mechanics and Diesel Engine Specialists	$35,780	14.2%	28,000
12. Respiratory Therapy Technicians	$36,740	34.2%	5,000
13. Data Processing Equipment Repairers	$35,150	15.1%	19,000
14. Chefs and Head Cooks	$30,680	15.8%	33,000
15. Aircraft Body and Bonded Structure Repairers	$45,290	11.0%	12,000
16. Aircraft Engine Specialists	$45,290	11.0%	12,000
17. Airframe-and-Power-Plant Mechanics	$45,290	11.0%	12,000
18. Medical Secretaries	$26,540	17.2%	50,000
19. Security and Fire Alarm Systems Installers	$33,410	30.2%	5,000
20. Gaming Supervisors	$40,840	15.7%	6,000
21. Desktop Publishers	$32,340	29.2%	4,000

(continued)

(continued)

Best Jobs Requiring Postsecondary Vocational Training

Job	Annual Earnings	Percent Growth	Annual Openings
22. Sound Engineering Technicians	$38,110	25.5%	2,000
23. Electrical and Electronics Repairers, Commercial and Industrial Equipment	$42,600	10.3%	10,000
24. Commercial Pilots	$53,870	14.9%	2,000
25. Real Estate Sales Agents	$35,670	5.7%	34,000
26. Mobile Heavy Equipment Mechanics, Except Engines	$38,150	9.6%	12,000
27. Central Office and PBX Installers and Repairers	$49,840	–0.6%	23,000
28. Communication Equipment Mechanics, Installers, and Repairers	$49,840	–0.6%	23,000
29. Frame Wirers, Central Office	$49,840	–0.6%	23,000
30. Station Installers and Repairers, Telephone	$49,840	–0.6%	23,000
31. Gaming Dealers	$14,340	24.7%	26,000
32. Hairdressers, Hairstylists, and Cosmetologists	$19,800	14.7%	68,000
33. Civil Drafters	$39,190	4.2%	14,000
34. Precision Dyers	$17,220	12.3%	47,000
35. Court Reporters	$42,920	12.7%	2,000
36. Design Printing Machine Setters and Set-Up Operators	$29,900	4.6%	30,000
37. Embossing Machine Set-Up Operators	$29,900	4.6%	30,000

Best Jobs Requiring an Associate Degree

Job	Annual Earnings	Percent Growth	Annual Openings
1. Registered Nurses	$52,330	27.3%	215,000
2. Computer Support Specialists	$40,430	30.3%	71,000
3. Dental Hygienists	$58,350	43.1%	9,000
4. Paralegals and Legal Assistants	$39,130	28.7%	29,000
5. Radiologic Technicians	$43,350	22.9%	21,000
6. Radiologic Technologists	$43,350	22.9%	21,000
7. Respiratory Therapists	$43,140	34.8%	10,000
8. Physical Therapist Assistants	$37,890	44.6%	10,000
9. Diagnostic Medical Sonographers	$52,490	24.0%	4,000
10. Cardiovascular Technologists and Technicians	$38,690	33.5%	6,000
11. Calibration and Instrumentation Technicians	$46,310	10.0%	24,000
12. Electrical Engineering Technicians	$46,310	10.0%	24,000
13. Electronics Engineering Technicians	$46,310	10.0%	24,000

Best Jobs for the 21st Century, Fourth Edition © JIST Works

Best Jobs Requiring an Associate Degree

Job	Annual Earnings	Percent Growth	Annual Openings
14. Medical Records and Health Information Technicians	$25,590	46.8%	24,000
15. Radiation Therapists	$57,700	31.6%	1,000
16. Nuclear Medicine Technologists	$56,450	23.6%	2,000
17. City and Regional Planning Aides	$34,360	17.5%	18,000
18. Social Science Research Assistants	$34,360	17.5%	18,000
19. Medical and Clinical Laboratory Technicians	$30,840	19.4%	21,000
20. Occupational Therapist Assistants	$38,430	39.2%	3,000
21. Environmental Science and Protection Technicians, Including Health	$35,340	36.8%	4,000
22. Medical Transcriptionists	$28,380	22.6%	18,000
23. Environmental Engineering Technicians	$38,550	28.4%	3,000
24. Veterinary Technologists and Technicians	$24,940	44.1%	11,000
25. Biological Technicians	$33,210	19.4%	7,000
26. Mechanical Engineering Technicians	$43,400	11.0%	6,000
27. Forensic Science Technicians	$44,010	18.9%	1,000
28. Physical Therapist Aides	$21,380	46.4%	8,000
29. Industrial Engineering Technicians	$43,590	8.7%	7,000
30. Civil Engineering Technicians	$38,480	7.6%	10,000
31. First-Line Supervisors and Manager/Supervisors— Agricultural Crop Workers	$35,490	11.4%	6,000
32. First-Line Supervisors and Manager/Supervisors— Animal Care Workers, Except Livestock	$35,490	11.4%	6,000
33. First-Line Supervisors and Manager/Supervisors— Animal Husbandry Workers	$35,490	11.4%	6,000
34. First-Line Supervisors and Manager/Supervisors— Fishery Workers	$35,490	11.4%	6,000
35. First-Line Supervisors and Manager/Supervisors— Horticultural Workers	$35,490	11.4%	6,000
36. Electro-Mechanical Technicians	$41,440	11.5%	4,000
37. Architectural Drafters	$39,190	4.2%	14,000

Best Jobs Requiring a Bachelor's Degree

Job	Annual Earnings	Percent Growth	Annual Openings
1. Computer Software Engineers, Applications	$74,980	45.5%	55,000
2. Computer Systems Analysts	$66,460	39.4%	68,000
3. Computer Software Engineers, Systems Software	$79,740	45.5%	39,000
4. Logisticians	$57,110	27.5%	162,000
5. Network Systems and Data Communications Analysts	$60,600	57.0%	29,000
6. Computer Security Specialists	$58,190	37.4%	35,000
7. Network and Computer Systems Administrators	$58,190	37.4%	35,000
8. Special Education Teachers, Secondary School	$45,700	30.0%	59,000
9. Accountants	$50,770	19.5%	119,000
10. Auditors	$50,770	19.5%	119,000
11. Personal Financial Advisors	$62,700	34.6%	18,000
12. Special Education Teachers, Middle School	$44,160	30.0%	59,000
13. Database Administrators	$60,650	44.2%	16,000
14. Special Education Teachers, Preschool, Kindergarten, and Elementary School	$43,570	30.0%	59,000
15. Training and Development Specialists	$44,570	27.9%	35,000
16. Secondary School Teachers, Except Special and Vocational Education	$45,650	18.2%	118,000
17. Public Relations Specialists	$43,830	32.9%	28,000
18. Market Research Analysts	$56,140	23.4%	18,000
19. Physician Assistants	$69,410	48.9%	7,000
20. Computer Programmers	$62,890	14.6%	45,000
21. Kindergarten Teachers, Except Special Education	$41,400	27.2%	34,000
22. Occupational Therapists	$54,660	35.2%	10,000
23. Financial Analysts	$61,910	18.7%	22,000
24. Social and Community Service Managers	$46,810	27.7%	19,000
25. Sales Agents, Financial Services	$69,200	13.0%	39,000
26. Sales Agents, Securities and Commodities	$69,200	13.0%	39,000
27. Construction Managers	$69,870	12.0%	47,000
28. Employment Interviewers, Private or Public Employment Service	$41,190	27.3%	29,000
29. Personnel Recruiters	$41,190	27.3%	29,000
30. Environmental Engineers	$66,480	38.2%	6,000
31. Compensation, Benefits, and Job Analysis Specialists	$47,490	28.0%	15,000
32. Loan Officers	$48,830	18.8%	30,000
33. Elementary School Teachers, Except Special Education	$43,160	15.2%	183,000
34. Cost Estimators	$49,940	18.6%	25,000
35. Child, Family, and School Social Workers	$34,820	23.2%	45,000

Best Jobs Requiring a Bachelor's Degree

Job	Annual Earnings	Percent Growth	Annual Openings
36. Medical and Public Health Social Workers	$40,080	28.6%	18,000
37. Medical and Clinical Laboratory Technologists	$45,730	19.3%	21,000
38. Sales Engineers	$70,620	19.9%	7,000
39. Graphic Designers	$38,030	21.9%	29,000
40. Technical Writers	$53,490	27.1%	6,000
41. Airline Pilots, Copilots, and Flight Engineers	$129,250	18.5%	6,000
42. Environmental Scientists and Specialists, Including Health	$51,080	23.7%	6,000
43. Copy Writers	$44,350	16.1%	23,000
44. Creative Writers	$44,350	16.1%	23,000
45. Poets and Lyricists	$44,350	16.1%	23,000
46. Architects, Except Landscape and Naval	$60,300	17.3%	8,000
47. Adult Literacy, Remedial Education, and GED Teachers and Instructors	$38,980	20.4%	14,000
48. Industrial Engineers	$65,020	10.6%	16,000
49. Purchasing Agents, Except Wholesale, Retail, and Farm Products	$47,680	11.2%	29,000
50. Multi-Media Artists and Animators	$50,360	15.8%	12,000
51. Credit Analysts	$47,260	18.7%	9,000
52. Middle School Teachers, Except Special and Vocational Education	$43,670	9.0%	69,000
53. Industrial Production Managers	$73,000	7.9%	18,000
54. Preschool Teachers, Except Special Education	$20,980	36.2%	88,000
55. Property, Real Estate, and Community Association Managers	$39,980	12.8%	35,000
56. Electronics Engineers, Except Computer	$75,770	9.4%	11,000
57. Interior Designers	$40,670	21.7%	8,000
58. Civil Engineers	$64,230	8.0%	17,000
59. Rehabilitation Counselors	$27,870	33.8%	19,000
60. Budget Analysts	$56,040	14.0%	8,000
61. Insurance Sales Agents	$41,720	8.4%	52,000
62. Directors, Religious Activities and Education	$30,700	24.1%	16,000
63. Meeting and Convention Planners	$39,620	21.3%	7,000
64. Commercial and Industrial Designers	$52,310	14.7%	7,000
65. Dietitians and Nutritionists	$43,630	17.8%	8,000
66. Landscape Architects	$53,120	22.2%	2,000
67. Chemists	$56,060	12.7%	7,000
68. Probation Officers and Correctional Treatment Specialists	$39,600	14.7%	15,000
69. Film and Video Editors	$43,590	26.4%	3,000

(continued)

(continued)

Best Jobs Requiring a Bachelor's Degree

Job	Annual Earnings	Percent Growth	Annual Openings
70. Biomedical Engineers	$67,690	26.1%	fewer than 500
71. Editors	$43,890	11.8%	14,000
72. Hydrologists	$61,510	21.0%	1,000
73. Insurance Underwriters	$48,550	10.0%	12,000
74. Mechanical Engineers	$66,320	4.8%	14,000
75. Vocational Education Teachers, Secondary School	$45,920	9.0%	12,000
76. Recreation Workers	$19,320	20.5%	56,000
77. Atmospheric and Space Scientists	$70,100	16.2%	1,000
78. Economists	$72,780	13.4%	2,000
79. Geographers	$58,970	19.5%	fewer than 500
80. Electrical Engineers	$71,610	2.5%	11,000
81. Computer Hardware Engineers	$81,150	6.1%	6,000
82. Orthotists and Prosthetists	$50,260	18.9%	1,000
83. Geologists	$68,730	11.5%	2,000
84. Athletic Trainers	$33,940	29.9%	2,000
85. Wholesale and Retail Buyers, Except Farm Products	$42,230	4.3%	24,000
86. Fire-Prevention and Protection Engineers	$63,730	7.9%	4,000
87. Industrial Safety and Health Engineers	$63,730	7.9%	4,000
88. Product Safety Engineers	$63,730	7.9%	4,000
89. Financial Examiners	$60,310	8.9%	3,000
90. Exhibit Designers	$35,800	20.9%	2,000
91. Set Designers	$35,800	20.9%	2,000
92. Music Arrangers and Orchestrators	$34,570	13.5%	8,000
93. Loan Counselors	$33,970	17.8%	4,000
94. Fashion Designers	$55,840	10.6%	2,000
95. Cartographers and Photogrammetrists	$46,080	15.1%	1,000
96. First-Line Supervisors and Manager/Supervisors—Logging Workers	$35,490	11.4%	6,000
97. Survey Researchers	$26,490	33.6%	3,000
98. Materials Scientists	$72,390	8.5%	1,000
99. Tax Examiners, Collectors, and Revenue Agents	$43,490	5.0%	9,000
100. Plant Scientists	$51,200	9.1%	2,000
101. Soil Scientists	$51,200	9.1%	2,000
102. Food Scientists and Technologists	$50,840	9.1%	2,000

Best Jobs Requiring Work Experience Plus Degree

Job	Annual Earnings	Percent Growth	Annual Openings
1. Management Analysts	$63,450	30.4%	78,000
2. Sales Managers	$84,220	30.5%	54,000
3. Computer and Information Systems Managers	$92,570	36.1%	39,000
4. General and Operations Managers	$77,420	18.4%	260,000
5. Medical and Health Services Managers	$67,430	29.3%	33,000
6. Financial Managers, Branch or Department	$81,880	18.3%	71,000
7. Treasurers, Controllers, and Chief Financial Officers	$81,880	18.3%	71,000
8. Marketing Managers	$87,640	21.3%	30,000
9. Chief Executives	$140,350	16.7%	63,000
10. Government Service Executives	$140,350	16.7%	63,000
11. Private Sector Executives	$140,350	16.7%	63,000
12. Education Administrators, Elementary and Secondary School	$74,190	20.7%	31,000
13. Administrative Services Managers	$60,290	19.8%	40,000
14. Education Administrators, Postsecondary	$68,340	25.9%	19,000
15. Training and Development Managers	$67,460	19.4%	21,000
16. Compensation and Benefits Managers	$66,530	19.4%	21,000
17. Advertising and Promotions Managers	$63,610	25.0%	13,000
18. Public Relations Managers	$70,000	23.4%	10,000
19. Directors—Stage, Motion Pictures, Television, and Radio	$52,840	18.3%	10,000
20. Producers	$52,840	18.3%	10,000
21. Program Directors	$52,840	18.3%	10,000
22. Engineering Managers	$97,630	9.2%	16,000
23. Education Administrators, Preschool and Child Care Center/Program	$35,730	32.0%	9,000
24. Agents and Business Managers of Artists, Performers, and Athletes	$55,080	27.8%	2,000
25. Art Directors	$63,840	11.4%	8,000
26. Natural Sciences Managers	$88,660	11.3%	5,000
27. Actuaries	$76,340	14.9%	2,000
28. Purchasing Managers	$72,450	4.8%	9,000
29. Judges, Magistrate Judges, and Magistrates	$93,070	8.7%	2,000
30. Gaming Managers	$58,580	12.4%	1,000
31. Arbitrators, Mediators, and Conciliators	$54,760	13.7%	fewer than 500

Best Jobs Requiring a Master's Degree

Job	Annual Earnings	Percent Growth	Annual Openings
1. Physical Therapists	$60,180	35.3%	16,000
2. Clinical Psychologists	$54,950	24.4%	17,000
3. Counseling Psychologists	$54,950	24.4%	17,000
4. School Psychologists	$54,950	24.4%	17,000
5. Instructional Coordinators	$48,790	25.4%	18,000
6. Speech-Language Pathologists	$52,410	27.2%	10,000
7. Educational, Vocational, and School Counselors	$45,570	15.0%	32,000
8. Mental Health and Substance Abuse Social Workers	$33,920	34.5%	17,000
9. Mental Health Counselors	$32,960	26.7%	13,000
10. Health Educators	$38,480	21.9%	8,000
11. Audiologists	$51,470	29.0%	1,000
12. Substance Abuse and Behavioral Disorder Counselors	$32,130	23.3%	10,000
13. Librarians	$45,900	10.1%	15,000
14. Occupational Health and Safety Specialists	$51,570	13.2%	6,000
15. Marriage and Family Therapists	$38,980	22.4%	3,000
16. Urban and Regional Planners	$53,450	10.7%	5,000
17. Operations Research Analysts	$60,190	6.2%	6,000
18. Industrial-Organizational Psychologists	$71,400	16.0%	fewer than 500
19. Curators	$43,620	17.0%	2,000
20. Composers	$34,570	13.5%	8,000
21. Music Directors	$34,570	13.5%	8,000
22. Archivists	$36,470	17.0%	2,000
23. Sociologists	$57,870	13.4%	fewer than 500

Best Jobs Requiring a Doctoral Degree

Job	Annual Earnings	Percent Growth	Annual Openings
1. Medical Scientists, Except Epidemiologists	$61,320	26.9%	6,000
2. Biochemists	$68,950	22.9%	2,000
3. Biophysicists	$68,950	22.9%	2,000
4. Epidemiologists	$54,800	32.5%	fewer than 500
5. Microbiologists	$54,840	20.0%	1,000
6. Physicists	$87,450	6.9%	1,000

Best Jobs Requiring a First Professional Degree

Job	Annual Earnings	Percent Growth	Annual Openings
1. Pharmacists	$84,900	30.1%	23,000
2. Anesthesiologists	more than $145,600	19.5%	38,000
3. Internists, General	more than $145,600	19.5%	38,000
4. Obstetricians and Gynecologists	more than $145,600	19.5%	38,000
5. Psychiatrists	more than $145,600	19.5%	38,000
6. Surgeons	more than $145,600	19.5%	38,000
7. Family and General Practitioners	$137,090	19.5%	38,000
8. Pediatricians, General	$135,730	19.5%	38,000
9. Lawyers	$94,930	17.0%	53,000
10. Veterinarians	$66,590	25.1%	4,000
11. Chiropractors	$69,910	23.3%	3,000
12. Clergy	$36,690	15.5%	34,000
13. Optometrists	$88,410	17.1%	2,000
14. Podiatrists	$94,400	15.0%	1,000
15. Oral and Maxillofacial Surgeons	more than $145,600	4.1%	7,000
16. Orthodontists	more than $145,600	4.1%	7,000
17. Prosthodontists	more than $145,600	4.1%	7,000
18. Dentists, General	$123,060	4.1%	7,000

Best Jobs Lists Based on Interests

This group of lists organizes the 500 best jobs into 16 interest areas. You can use these lists to quickly identify jobs based on your interests.

Find the interest area or areas that interest you most. Then review the jobs in those areas to identify jobs you want to explore in more detail and look up their descriptions in Part II. You can also review interest areas where you have had past experience, education, or training to see if other jobs in those areas would meet your current requirements.

Within each interest area, jobs are listed in order of their total combined scores based on earnings, growth, and number of openings.

Note: The 16 interest areas used in these lists are those used in the *New Guide for Occupational Exploration,* Fourth Edition, published by JIST. The original GOE was developed by the U.S. Department of Labor as an intuitive way to assist in career exploration. The 16 interest areas used in the *New GOE* are based on the 16 career clusters that were developed by the U.S. Department of Education's Office of Vocational and Adult Education around 1999 and that presently are being used by many states to organize their career-oriented programs and career information.

Descriptions for the 16 Interest Areas

Brief descriptions for the 16 interest areas we use in the lists follow. The descriptions are from the *New Guide for Occupational Exploration,* Fourth Edition.

Also note that we put each of the 500 best jobs into only one interest area list, the one it fit into best. However, many jobs could be included in more than one list, so consider reviewing a variety of these interest areas to find jobs that you might otherwise overlook.

- **Agriculture and Natural Resources:** *An interest in working with plants, animals, forests, or mineral resources for agriculture, horticulture, conservation, extraction, and other purposes.* You can satisfy this interest by working in farming, landscaping, forestry, fishing, mining, and related fields. You may like doing physical work outdoors, such as on a farm or ranch, in a forest, or on a drilling rig. If you have scientific curiosity, you could study plants and animals or analyze biological or rock samples in a lab. If you have management ability, you could own, operate, or manage a fish hatchery, a landscaping business, or a greenhouse.

- **Architecture and Construction:** *An interest in designing, assembling, and maintaining components of buildings and other structures.* You may want to be part of the team of architects, drafters, and others who design buildings and render the plans. If construction interests you, you can find fulfillment in the many building projects that are being undertaken at all times. If you like to organize and plan, you can find careers in managing these projects. Or you can play a more direct role in putting up and finishing buildings by doing jobs such as plumbing, carpentry, masonry, painting, or roofing, either as a skilled craftsworker or as a helper. You can prepare the building site by operating heavy equipment or install, maintain, and repair vital building equipment and systems such as electricity and heating.

- **Arts and Communication:** *An interest in creatively expressing feelings or ideas, in communicating news or information, or in performing.* You can satisfy this interest in creative, verbal, or performing activities. For example, if you enjoy literature, perhaps writing or editing would appeal to you. Journalism and public relations are other fields for people who like to use their writing or speaking skills. Do you prefer to work in the performing arts? If so, you could direct or perform in drama, music, or dance. If you especially enjoy the visual arts, you could create paintings, sculpture, or ceramics or design products or visual displays. A flair for technology might lead you to specialize in photography, broadcast production, or dispatching.

- **Business and Administration:** *An interest in making a business organization or function run smoothly.* You can satisfy this interest by working in a position of leadership or by specializing in a function that contributes to the overall effort in a business, a nonprofit organization, or a government agency. If you especially enjoy working with people, you may find fulfillment from working in human resources. An interest in numbers may lead you to consider accounting, finance, budgeting, billing, or financial record-keeping. A job as an administrative assistant may interest you if you like a variety of work in a busy environment. If you are good with details and word processing, you may enjoy a job as a secretary or data entry keyer. Or perhaps you would do well as the manager of a business.

⦿ **Education and Training:** *An interest in helping people learn.* You can satisfy this interest by teaching students, who may be preschoolers, retirees, or any age in between. You may specialize in a particular academic field or work with learners of a particular age, with a particular interest, or with a particular learning problem. Working in a library or museum may give you an opportunity to expand people's understanding of the world.

⦿ **Finance and Insurance:** *An interest in helping businesses and people be assured of a financially secure future.* You can satisfy this interest by working in a financial or insurance business in a leadership or support role. If you like gathering and analyzing information, you may find fulfillment as an insurance adjuster or financial analyst. Or you may deal with information at the clerical level as a banking or insurance clerk or in person-to-person situations providing customer service. Another way to interact with people is to sell financial or insurance services that will meet their needs.

⦿ **Government and Public Administration:** *An interest in helping a government agency serve the needs of the public.* You can satisfy this interest by working in a position of leadership or by specializing in a function that contributes to the role of government. You may help protect the public by working as an inspector or examiner to enforce standards. If you enjoy using clerical skills, you may work as a clerk in a law court or government office. Or perhaps you prefer the top-down perspective of a government executive or urban planner.

⦿ **Health Science:** *An interest in helping people and animals be healthy.* You can satisfy this interest by working in a health care team as a doctor, therapist, or nurse. You might specialize in one of the many different parts of the body (such as the teeth or eyes) or in one of the many different types of care. Or you may wish to be a generalist who deals with the whole patient. If you like technology, you might find satisfaction working with X rays or new methods of diagnosis. You might work with healthy people, helping them eat right. If you enjoy working with animals, you might care for them and keep them healthy.

⦿ **Hospitality, Tourism, and Recreation:** *An interest in catering to the personal wishes and needs of others so that they may enjoy a clean environment, good food and drink, comfortable lodging away from home, and recreation.* You can satisfy this interest by providing services for the convenience, care, and pampering of others in hotels, restaurants, airplanes, beauty parlors, and so on. You may wish to use your love of cooking as a chef. If you like working with people, you may wish to provide personal services by being a travel guide, a flight attendant, a concierge, a hairdresser, or a waiter. You may wish to work in cleaning and building services if you like a clean environment. If you enjoy sports or games, you may work for an athletic team or casino.

⦿ **Human Service:** *An interest in improving people's social, mental, emotional, or spiritual well-being.* You can satisfy this interest as a counselor, social worker, or religious worker who helps people sort out their complicated lives or solve personal problems. You may work as a caretaker for very young people or the elderly. Or you may interview people to help identify the social services they need.

⦿ **Information Technology:** *An interest in designing, developing, managing, and supporting information systems.* You can satisfy this interest by working with hardware, software, multimedia, or integrated systems. If you like to use your organizational skills, you might work as an administrator of a system or database. Or you can solve complex problems as a software engineer or systems analyst. If you enjoy getting your hands on the hardware, you might find work servicing computers, peripherals, and information-intense machines such as cash registers and ATMs.

- **Law and Public Safety:** *An interest in upholding people's rights or in protecting people and property by using authority, inspecting, or investigating.* You can satisfy this interest by working in law, law enforcement, fire fighting, the military, and related fields. For example, if you enjoy mental challenge and intrigue, you could investigate crimes or fires for a living. If you enjoy working with verbal skills and research skills, you may want to defend citizens in court or research deeds, wills, and other legal documents. If you want to help people in critical situations, you may want to fight fires, work as a police officer, or become a paramedic. Or, if you want more routine work in public safety, perhaps a job in guarding, patrolling, or inspecting would appeal to you. If you have management ability, you could seek a leadership position in law enforcement and the protective services. Work in the military gives you a chance to use technical and leadership skills while serving your country.

- **Manufacturing:** *An interest in processing materials into intermediate or final products or maintaining and repairing products by using machines or hand tools.* You can satisfy this interest by working in one of many industries that mass-produce goods or by working for a utility that distributes electric power or other resources. You may enjoy manual work, using your hands or hand tools in highly skilled jobs such as assembling engines or electronic equipment. If you enjoy making machines run efficiently or fixing them when they break down, you could seek a job installing or repairing such devices as copiers, aircraft engines, cars, or watches. Perhaps you prefer to set up or operate machines that are used to manufacture products made of food, glass, or paper. You may enjoy cutting and grinding metal and plastic parts to desired shapes and measurements. Or you may wish to operate equipment in systems that provide water and process wastewater. You may like inspecting, sorting, counting, or weighing products. Another option is to work with your hands and machinery to move boxes and freight in a warehouse. If leadership appeals to you, you could manage people engaged in production and repair.

- **Retail and Wholesale Sales and Service:** *An interest in bringing others to a particular point of view by personal persuasion and by sales and promotional techniques.* You can satisfy this interest in a variety of jobs that involve persuasion and selling. If you like using knowledge of science, you may enjoy selling pharmaceutical, medical, or electronic products or services. Real estate offers several kinds of sales jobs as well. If you like speaking on the phone, you could work as a telemarketer. Or you may enjoy selling apparel and other merchandise in a retail setting. If you prefer to help people, you may want a job in customer service.

- **Scientific Research, Engineering, and Mathematics:** *An interest in discovering, collecting, and analyzing information about the natural world; in applying scientific research findings to problems in medicine, the life sciences, human behavior, and the natural sciences; in imagining and manipulating quantitative data; and in applying technology to manufacturing, transportation, and other economic activities.* You can satisfy this interest by working with the knowledge and processes of the sciences. You may enjoy researching and developing new knowledge in mathematics, or perhaps solving problems in the physical, life, or social sciences would appeal to you. You may wish to study engineering and help create new machines, processes, and structures. If you want to work with scientific equipment and procedures, you could seek a job in a research or testing laboratory.

◉ **Transportation, Distribution, and Logistics:** *An interest in operations that move people or materials.* You can satisfy this interest by managing a transportation service, by helping vehicles keep on their assigned schedules and routes, or by driving or piloting a vehicle. If you enjoy taking responsibility, perhaps managing a rail line would appeal to you. If you work well with details and can take pressure on the job, you might consider being an air traffic controller. Or would you rather get out on the highway, on the water, or up in the air? If so, then you could drive a truck from state to state, be employed on a ship, or fly a crop duster over a cornfield. If you prefer to stay closer to home, you could drive a delivery van, taxi, or school bus. You can use your physical strength to load freight and arrange it so it gets to its destination in one piece.

Best Jobs for People Interested in Agriculture and Natural Resources

Job	Annual Earnings	Percent Growth	Annual Openings
1. Environmental Engineers	$66,480	38.2%	6,000
2. First-Line Supervisors and Manager/Supervisors—Extractive Workers	$50,450	14.1%	67,000
3. First-Line Supervisors and Manager/Supervisors—Landscaping Workers	$35,340	21.6%	18,000
4. Lawn Service Managers	$35,340	21.6%	18,000
5. Landscaping and Groundskeeping Workers	$20,420	22.0%	203,000
6. Environmental Science and Protection Technicians, Including Health	$35,340	36.8%	4,000
7. Agricultural Crop Farm Managers	$50,700	5.1%	25,000
8. Fish Hatchery Managers	$50,700	5.1%	25,000
9. Nursery and Greenhouse Managers	$50,700	5.1%	25,000
10. Farmers and Ranchers	$40,440	−20.6%	118,000
11. Tree Trimmers and Pruners	$26,150	18.6%	11,000
12. Loading Machine Operators, Underground Mining	$33,250	8.9%	14,000
13. Pest Control Workers	$26,220	17.0%	11,000
14. First-Line Supervisors and Manager/Supervisors—Agricultural Crop Workers	$35,490	11.4%	6,000
15. First-Line Supervisors and Manager/Supervisors—Animal Husbandry Workers	$35,490	11.4%	6,000
16. First-Line Supervisors and Manager/Supervisors—Fishery Workers	$35,490	11.4%	6,000

(continued)

(continued)

Best Jobs for People Interested in Agriculture and Natural Resources

Job	Annual Earnings	Percent Growth	Annual Openings
17. First-Line Supervisors and Manager/Supervisors—Horticultural Workers	$35,490	11.4%	6,000
18. First-Line Supervisors and Manager/Supervisors—Logging Workers	$35,490	11.4%	6,000
19. Excavating and Loading Machine Operators	$31,970	8.9%	14,000
20. Plant Scientists	$51,200	9.1%	2,000
21. Soil Scientists	$51,200	9.1%	2,000
22. Food Scientists and Technologists	$50,840	9.1%	2,000

Best Jobs for People Interested in Architecture and Construction

Job	Annual Earnings	Percent Growth	Annual Openings
1. Electricians	$42,300	23.4%	65,000
2. Construction Managers	$69,870	12.0%	47,000
3. Heating and Air Conditioning Mechanics	$36,260	31.8%	35,000
4. Refrigeration Mechanics	$36,260	31.8%	35,000
5. First-Line Supervisors and Manager/Supervisors—Construction Trades Workers	$50,450	14.1%	67,000
6. Pipe Fitters	$41,290	18.7%	56,000
7. Pipelaying Fitters	$41,290	18.7%	56,000
8. Plumbers	$41,290	18.7%	56,000
9. Refractory Materials Repairers, Except Brickmasons	$37,640	16.3%	155,000
10. Sheet Metal Workers	$35,560	19.8%	30,000
11. Architects, Except Landscape and Naval	$60,300	17.3%	8,000
12. Cement Masons and Concrete Finishers	$31,400	26.1%	24,000
13. Maintenance and Repair Workers, General	$30,710	16.3%	155,000
14. Telecommunications Line Installers and Repairers	$40,330	18.8%	13,000
15. Ceiling Tile Installers	$34,030	21.4%	17,000
16. Drywall Installers	$34,030	21.4%	17,000
17. Boat Builders and Shipwrights	$34,900	10.1%	193,000
18. Brattice Builders	$34,900	10.1%	193,000
19. Carpenter Assemblers and Repairers	$34,900	10.1%	193,000
20. Construction Carpenters	$34,900	10.1%	193,000
21. Rough Carpenters	$34,900	10.1%	193,000
22. Ship Carpenters and Joiners	$34,900	10.1%	193,000

Best Jobs for People Interested in Architecture and Construction

Job	Annual Earnings	Percent Growth	Annual Openings
23. Roofers	$30,840	18.6%	38,000
24. Brickmasons and Blockmasons	$41,740	14.2%	21,000
25. Hazardous Materials Removal Workers	$33,320	43.1%	8,000
26. Grader, Bulldozer, and Scraper Operators	$35,360	10.4%	45,000
27. Operating Engineers	$35,360	10.4%	45,000
28. Landscape Architects	$53,120	22.2%	2,000
29. Elevator Installers and Repairers	$58,710	17.1%	3,000
30. Structural Iron and Steel Workers	$42,430	15.9%	9,000
31. Construction and Building Inspectors	$43,670	13.8%	10,000
32. Painters, Construction and Maintenance	$30,260	11.6%	69,000
33. Tapers	$39,070	20.8%	5,000
34. Security and Fire Alarm Systems Installers	$33,410	30.2%	5,000
35. Tile and Marble Setters	$35,410	26.5%	4,000
36. Construction Laborers	$25,160	14.2%	166,000
37. Carpet Installers	$34,090	16.8%	10,000
38. Helpers—Installation, Maintenance, and Repair Workers	$21,310	20.3%	33,000
39. Insulation Workers, Mechanical	$33,330	15.8%	9,000
40. Central Office and PBX Installers and Repairers	$49,840	−0.6%	23,000
41. Communication Equipment Mechanics, Installers, and Repairers	$49,840	−0.6%	23,000
42. Frame Wirers, Central Office	$49,840	−0.6%	23,000
43. Station Installers and Repairers, Telephone	$49,840	−0.6%	23,000
44. Telecommunications Facility Examiners	$49,840	−0.6%	23,000
45. Glaziers	$32,650	17.2%	7,000
46. Electric Meter Installers and Repairers	$43,710	12.0%	5,000
47. Meter Mechanics	$43,710	12.0%	5,000
48. Highway Maintenance Workers	$29,550	10.4%	25,000
49. Insulation Workers, Floor, Ceiling, and Wall	$30,310	15.8%	9,000
50. Helpers—Electricians	$23,420	17.9%	17,000
51. Plasterers and Stucco Masons	$32,440	13.5%	8,000
52. Architectural Drafters	$39,190	4.2%	14,000
53. Civil Drafters	$39,190	4.2%	14,000
54. Dragline Operators	$31,970	8.9%	14,000
55. Electrical Power-Line Installers and Repairers	$49,100	1.6%	9,000
56. Crane and Tower Operators	$37,410	10.8%	5,000
57. Grips and Set-Up Workers, Motion Picture Sets, Studios, and Stages	$20,120	6.6%	525,000
58. Septic Tank Servicers and Sewer Pipe Cleaners	$28,870	21.2%	3,000
59. Reinforcing Iron and Rebar Workers	$35,160	16.7%	2,000

Best Jobs for People Interested in Arts and Communication

Job	Annual Earnings	Percent Growth	Annual Openings
1. Public Relations Specialists	$43,830	32.9%	28,000
2. Public Relations Managers	$70,000	23.4%	10,000
3. Graphic Designers	$38,030	21.9%	29,000
4. Technical Writers	$53,490	27.1%	6,000
5. Directors—Stage, Motion Pictures, Television, and Radio	$52,840	18.3%	10,000
6. Producers	$52,840	18.3%	10,000
7. Program Directors	$52,840	18.3%	10,000
8. Talent Directors	$52,840	18.3%	10,000
9. Technical Directors/Managers	$52,840	18.3%	10,000
10. Caption Writers	$44,350	16.1%	23,000
11. Copy Writers	$44,350	16.1%	23,000
12. Creative Writers	$44,350	16.1%	23,000
13. Poets and Lyricists	$44,350	16.1%	23,000
14. Multi-Media Artists and Animators	$50,360	15.8%	12,000
15. Costume Attendants	$25,050	27.8%	66,000
16. Agents and Business Managers of Artists, Performers, and Athletes	$55,080	27.8%	2,000
17. Interior Designers	$40,670	21.7%	8,000
18. Art Directors	$63,840	11.4%	8,000
19. Commercial and Industrial Designers	$52,310	14.7%	7,000
20. Film and Video Editors	$43,590	26.4%	3,000
21. Editors	$43,890	11.8%	14,000
22. Dispatchers, Except Police, Fire, and Ambulance	$30,920	14.4%	28,000
23. Audio and Video Equipment Technicians	$32,570	26.7%	5,000
24. Air Traffic Controllers	$102,030	12.6%	2,000
25. Sound Engineering Technicians	$38,110	25.5%	2,000
26. Interpreters and Translators	$33,860	22.1%	4,000
27. Cartoonists	$38,060	16.5%	4,000
28. Painters and Illustrators	$38,060	16.5%	4,000
29. Sculptors	$38,060	16.5%	4,000
30. Sketch Artists	$38,060	16.5%	4,000
31. Exhibit Designers	$35,800	20.9%	2,000
32. Set Designers	$35,800	20.9%	2,000
33. Composers	$34,570	13.5%	8,000
34. Music Arrangers and Orchestrators	$34,570	13.5%	8,000
35. Music Directors	$34,570	13.5%	8,000
36. Fashion Designers	$55,840	10.6%	2,000
37. Police, Fire, and Ambulance Dispatchers	$28,930	12.7%	15,000
38. Camera Operators, Television, Video, and Motion Picture	$37,610	13.4%	4,000
39. Professional Photographers	$26,080	13.6%	18,000

Best Jobs for People Interested in Business and Administration

Job	Annual Earnings	Percent Growth	Annual Openings
1. Management Analysts	$63,450	30.4%	78,000
2. Logisticians	$57,110	27.5%	162,000
3. General and Operations Managers	$77,420	18.4%	260,000
4. Chief Executives	$140,350	16.7%	63,000
5. Private Sector Executives	$140,350	16.7%	63,000
6. Accountants	$50,770	19.5%	119,000
7. Auditors	$50,770	19.5%	119,000
8. Administrative Services Managers	$60,290	19.8%	40,000
9. Training and Development Specialists	$44,570	27.9%	35,000
10. Training and Development Managers	$67,460	19.4%	21,000
11. Compensation and Benefits Managers	$66,530	19.4%	21,000
12. Employment Interviewers, Private or Public Employment Service	$41,190	27.3%	29,000
13. Personnel Recruiters	$41,190	27.3%	29,000
14. Compensation, Benefits, and Job Analysis Specialists	$47,490	28.0%	15,000
15. Legal Secretaries	$36,720	18.8%	39,000
16. Production, Planning, and Expediting Clerks	$36,340	14.1%	51,000
17. Human Resources Assistants, Except Payroll and Timekeeping	$31,750	19.3%	36,000
18. First-Line Supervisors, Administrative Support	$41,030	6.6%	140,000
19. First-Line Supervisors, Customer Service	$41,030	6.6%	140,000
20. Budget Analysts	$56,040	14.0%	8,000
21. Executive Secretaries and Administrative Assistants	$34,970	8.7%	210,000
22. Meeting and Convention Planners	$39,620	21.3%	7,000
23. Medical Secretaries	$26,540	17.2%	50,000
24. Housekeeping Supervisors	$29,510	16.2%	28,000
25. Janitorial Supervisors	$29,510	16.2%	28,000
26. Tax Preparers	$27,730	23.2%	11,000
27. Operations Research Analysts	$60,190	6.2%	6,000
28. Office Clerks, General	$22,770	10.4%	550,000
29. Billing, Cost, and Rate Clerks	$27,040	7.9%	78,000
30. Billing, Posting, and Calculating Machine Operators	$27,040	7.9%	78,000
31. Statement Clerks	$27,040	7.9%	78,000
32. Industrial Engineering Technicians	$43,590	8.7%	7,000
33. Bookkeeping, Accounting, and Auditing Clerks	$28,570	3.0%	274,000
34. Weighers, Measurers, Checkers, and Samplers, Recordkeeping	$24,570	14.6%	16,000

Best Jobs for People Interested in Education and Training

Job	Annual Earnings	Percent Growth	Annual Openings
1. Teachers, Postsecondary	$51,614	38.1%	216,000
2. Special Education Teachers, Secondary School	$45,700	30.0%	59,000
3. Education Administrators, Elementary and Secondary School	$74,190	20.7%	31,000
4. Special Education Teachers, Middle School	$44,160	30.0%	59,000
5. Education Administrators, Postsecondary	$68,340	25.9%	19,000
6. Special Education Teachers, Preschool, Kindergarten, and Elementary School	$43,570	30.0%	59,000
7. Secondary School Teachers, Except Special and Vocational Education	$45,650	18.2%	118,000
8. Kindergarten Teachers, Except Special Education	$41,400	27.2%	34,000
9. Instructional Coordinators	$48,790	25.4%	18,000
10. Elementary School Teachers, Except Special Education	$43,160	15.2%	183,000
11. Self-Enrichment Education Teachers	$30,880	40.1%	39,000
12. Educational, Vocational, and School Counselors	$45,570	15.0%	32,000
13. Adult Literacy, Remedial Education, and GED Teachers and Instructors	$38,980	20.4%	14,000
14. Fitness Trainers and Aerobics Instructors	$25,470	44.5%	38,000
15. Education Administrators, Preschool and Child Care Center/Program	$35,730	32.0%	9,000
16. Middle School Teachers, Except Special and Vocational Education	$43,670	9.0%	69,000
17. Preschool Teachers, Except Special Education	$20,980	36.2%	88,000
18. Health Educators	$38,480	21.9%	8,000
19. Teacher Assistants	$19,410	23.0%	259,000
20. Librarians	$45,900	10.1%	15,000
21. Vocational Education Teachers, Secondary School	$45,920	9.0%	12,000
22. Library Assistants, Clerical	$20,720	21.5%	27,000
23. Library Technicians	$24,940	16.8%	22,000
24. Curators	$43,620	17.0%	2,000
25. Archivists	$36,470	17.0%	2,000

Best Jobs for People Interested in Finance and Insurance

Job	Annual Earnings	Percent Growth	Annual Openings
1. Financial Managers, Branch or Department	$81,880	18.3%	71,000
2. Treasurers, Controllers, and Chief Financial Officers	$81,880	18.3%	71,000
3. Personal Financial Advisors	$62,700	34.6%	18,000
4. Market Research Analysts	$56,140	23.4%	18,000
5. Financial Analysts	$61,910	18.7%	22,000
6. Sales Agents, Financial Services	$69,200	13.0%	39,000
7. Sales Agents, Securities and Commodities	$69,200	13.0%	39,000
8. Loan Officers	$48,830	18.8%	30,000
9. Cost Estimators	$49,940	18.6%	25,000
10. Claims Examiners, Property and Casualty Insurance	$44,220	14.2%	31,000
11. Insurance Adjusters, Examiners, and Investigators	$44,220	14.2%	31,000
12. Bill and Account Collectors	$27,450	24.5%	76,000
13. Credit Analysts	$47,260	18.7%	9,000
14. Appraisers, Real Estate	$43,390	17.6%	11,000
15. Assessors	$43,390	17.6%	11,000
16. Advertising Sales Agents	$40,300	13.4%	24,000
17. Insurance Sales Agents	$41,720	8.4%	52,000
18. Insurance Underwriters	$48,550	10.0%	12,000
19. Loan Counselors	$33,970	17.8%	4,000
20. Tellers	$21,120	9.4%	127,000
21. New Accounts Clerks	$26,860	11.2%	24,000
22. Survey Researchers	$26,490	33.6%	3,000
23. Insurance Appraisers, Auto Damage	$45,330	11.7%	2,000

Best Jobs for People Interested in Government and Public Administration

Job	Annual Earnings	Percent Growth	Annual Openings
1. Government Service Executives	$140,350	16.7%	63,000
2. Social and Community Service Managers	$46,810	27.7%	19,000
3. Child Support, Missing Persons, and Unemployment Insurance Fraud Investigators	$53,990	22.4%	11,000
4. Immigration and Customs Inspectors	$53,990	22.4%	11,000
5. Environmental Compliance Inspectors	$47,390	9.8%	20,000
6. Equal Opportunity Representatives and Officers	$47,390	9.8%	20,000
7. Government Property Inspectors and Investigators	$47,390	9.8%	20,000

(continued)

(continued)

Best Jobs for People Interested in Government and Public Administration

Job	Annual Earnings	Percent Growth	Annual Openings
8. Licensing Examiners and Inspectors	$47,390	9.8%	20,000
9. Pressure Vessel Inspectors	$47,390	9.8%	20,000
10. City and Regional Planning Aides	$34,360	17.5%	18,000
11. Occupational Health and Safety Specialists	$51,570	13.2%	6,000
12. Urban and Regional Planners	$53,450	10.7%	5,000
13. Financial Examiners	$60,310	8.9%	3,000
14. Aviation Inspectors	$50,380	7.7%	5,000
15. Marine Cargo Inspectors	$50,380	7.7%	5,000
16. Motor Vehicle Inspectors	$50,380	7.7%	5,000
17. Railroad Inspectors	$50,380	7.7%	5,000
18. Mechanical Inspectors	$28,410	4.7%	87,000
19. Court Clerks	$28,430	12.3%	14,000
20. License Clerks	$28,430	12.3%	14,000
21. Municipal Clerks	$28,430	12.3%	14,000
22. Tax Examiners, Collectors, and Revenue Agents	$43,490	5.0%	9,000
23. Court Reporters	$42,920	12.7%	2,000

Best Jobs for People Interested in Health Science

Job	Annual Earnings	Percent Growth	Annual Openings
1. Registered Nurses	$52,330	27.3%	215,000
2. Medical and Health Services Managers	$67,430	29.3%	33,000
3. Pharmacists	$84,900	30.1%	23,000
4. Anesthesiologists	more than $145,600	19.5%	38,000
5. Internists, General	more than $145,600	19.5%	38,000
6. Obstetricians and Gynecologists	more than $145,600	19.5%	38,000
7. Psychiatrists	more than $145,600	19.5%	38,000
8. Surgeons	more than $145,600	19.5%	38,000
9. Family and General Practitioners	$137,090	19.5%	38,000
10. Pediatricians, General	$135,730	19.5%	38,000
11. Physical Therapists	$60,180	35.3%	16,000
12. Physician Assistants	$69,410	48.9%	7,000
13. Dental Hygienists	$58,350	43.1%	9,000
14. Occupational Therapists	$54,660	35.2%	10,000
15. Speech-Language Pathologists	$52,410	27.2%	10,000

Best Jobs for People Interested in Health Science

Job	Annual Earnings	Percent Growth	Annual Openings
16. Licensed Practical and Licensed Vocational Nurses	$33,970	20.2%	105,000
17. Radiologic Technicians	$43,350	22.9%	21,000
18. Radiologic Technologists	$43,350	22.9%	21,000
19. Medical and Clinical Laboratory Technologists	$45,730	19.3%	21,000
20. Respiratory Therapists	$43,140	34.8%	10,000
21. Veterinarians	$66,590	25.1%	4,000
22. Physical Therapist Assistants	$37,890	44.6%	10,000
23. Medical Assistants	$24,610	58.9%	78,000
24. Dental Assistants	$28,330	42.5%	35,000
25. Massage Therapists	$31,960	27.1%	24,000
26. Chiropractors	$69,910	23.3%	3,000
27. Diagnostic Medical Sonographers	$52,490	24.0%	4,000
28. Surgical Technologists	$34,010	27.9%	13,000
29. Cardiovascular Technologists and Technicians	$38,690	33.5%	6,000
30. Nursing Aides, Orderlies, and Attendants	$20,980	24.9%	302,000
31. Home Health Aides	$18,330	48.1%	141,000
32. Medical Records and Health Information Technicians	$25,590	46.8%	24,000
33. Radiation Therapists	$57,700	31.6%	1,000
34. Nuclear Medicine Technologists	$56,450	23.6%	2,000
35. Pharmacy Technicians	$23,650	28.8%	39,000
36. Coroners	$47,390	9.8%	20,000
37. Respiratory Therapy Technicians	$36,740	34.2%	5,000
38. Medical and Clinical Laboratory Technicians	$30,840	19.4%	21,000
39. Dietitians and Nutritionists	$43,630	17.8%	8,000
40. Audiologists	$51,470	29.0%	1,000
41. Optometrists	$88,410	17.1%	2,000
42. Occupational Therapist Assistants	$38,430	39.2%	3,000
43. Medical Transcriptionists	$28,380	22.6%	18,000
44. Veterinary Technologists and Technicians	$24,940	44.1%	11,000
45. Podiatrists	$94,400	15.0%	1,000
46. Biological Technicians	$33,210	19.4%	7,000
47. Oral and Maxillofacial Surgeons	more than $145,600	4.1%	7,000
48. Orthodontists	more than $145,600	4.1%	7,000
49. Prosthodontists	more than $145,600	4.1%	7,000
50. Orthotists and Prosthetists	$50,260	18.9%	1,000
51. Dentists, General	$123,060	4.1%	7,000
52. Nonfarm Animal Caretakers	$17,460	22.2%	32,000

(continued)

(continued)

Best Jobs for People Interested in Health Science

Job	Annual Earnings	Percent Growth	Annual Openings
53. Athletic Trainers	$33,940	29.9%	2,000
54. Physical Therapist Aides	$21,380	46.4%	8,000
55. Opticians, Dispensing	$27,950	18.2%	10,000
56. Veterinary Assistants and Laboratory Animal Caretakers	$18,660	26.2%	11,000
57. First-Line Supervisors and Manager/Supervisors—Animal Care Workers, Except Livestock	$35,490	11.4%	6,000

Best Jobs for People Interested in Hospitality, Tourism, and Recreation

Job	Annual Earnings	Percent Growth	Annual Openings
1. Flight Attendants	$43,440	15.9%	23,000
2. Food Service Managers	$39,610	11.5%	58,000
3. Combined Food Preparation and Serving Workers, Including Fast Food	$14,690	22.8%	734,000
4. Chefs and Head Cooks	$30,680	15.8%	33,000
5. Locker Room, Coatroom, and Dressing Room Attendants	$17,550	27.8%	66,000
6. Athletes and Sports Competitors	$48,310	19.2%	3,000
7. Amusement and Recreation Attendants	$15,550	27.8%	66,000
8. First-Line Supervisors/Managers of Food Preparation and Serving Workers	$25,410	15.5%	154,000
9. Food Preparation Workers	$16,710	20.2%	267,000
10. Janitors and Cleaners, Except Maids and Housekeeping Cleaners	$18,790	18.3%	454,000
11. Hotel, Motel, and Resort Desk Clerks	$17,700	23.9%	46,000
12. Recreation Workers	$19,320	20.5%	56,000
13. Gaming Supervisors	$40,840	15.7%	6,000
14. Coaches and Scouts	$26,350	18.3%	26,000
15. Waiters and Waitresses	$14,050	17.5%	721,000
16. Cooks, Restaurant	$19,520	15.9%	211,000
17. Counter Attendants, Cafeteria, Food Concession, and Coffee Shop	$15,660	16.7%	190,000
18. Reservation and Transportation Ticket Agents	$27,750	12.2%	35,000
19. Travel Clerks	$27,750	12.2%	35,000
20. Gaming Dealers	$14,340	24.7%	26,000
21. Hosts and Hostesses, Restaurant, Lounge, and Coffee Shop	$15,630	16.4%	95,000

Best Jobs for People Interested in Hospitality, Tourism, and Recreation

Job	Annual Earnings	Percent Growth	Annual Openings
22. Hairdressers, Hairstylists, and Cosmetologists	$19,800	14.7%	68,000
23. First-Line Supervisors/Managers of Personal Service Workers	$30,350	9.4%	26,000
24. Dining Room and Cafeteria Attendants and Bartender Helpers	$14,770	14.9%	143,000
25. Gaming Managers	$58,580	12.4%	1,000
26. Lodging Managers	$37,660	6.6%	10,000
27. Maids and Housekeeping Cleaners	$16,900	9.2%	352,000

Best Jobs for People Interested in Human Service

Job	Annual Earnings	Percent Growth	Annual Openings
1. Clinical Psychologists	$54,950	24.4%	17,000
2. Counseling Psychologists	$54,950	24.4%	17,000
3. Child, Family, and School Social Workers	$34,820	23.2%	45,000
4. Medical and Public Health Social Workers	$40,080	28.6%	18,000
5. Mental Health and Substance Abuse Social Workers	$33,920	34.5%	17,000
6. Social and Human Service Assistants	$24,270	48.7%	63,000
7. Clergy	$36,690	15.5%	34,000
8. Mental Health Counselors	$32,960	26.7%	13,000
9. Personal and Home Care Aides	$16,900	40.5%	154,000
10. Interviewers, Except Eligibility and Loan	$23,670	28.0%	46,000
11. Rehabilitation Counselors	$27,870	33.8%	19,000
12. Directors, Religious Activities and Education	$30,700	24.1%	16,000
13. Probation Officers and Correctional Treatment Specialists	$39,600	14.7%	15,000
14. Substance Abuse and Behavioral Disorder Counselors	$32,130	23.3%	10,000
15. Marriage and Family Therapists	$38,980	22.4%	3,000
16. Residential Advisors	$21,430	33.6%	12,000
17. Child Care Workers	$16,760	11.7%	406,000
18. Nannies	$16,760	11.7%	406,000

Best Jobs for People Interested in Information Technology

Job	Annual Earnings	Percent Growth	Annual Openings
1. Computer Software Engineers, Applications	$74,980	45.5%	55,000
2. Computer Systems Analysts	$66,460	39.4%	68,000
3. Computer Software Engineers, Systems Software	$79,740	45.5%	39,000
4. Computer and Information Systems Managers	$92,570	36.1%	39,000
5. Network Systems and Data Communications Analysts	$60,600	57.0%	29,000
6. Computer Security Specialists	$58,190	37.4%	35,000
7. Network and Computer Systems Administrators	$58,190	37.4%	35,000
8. Database Administrators	$60,650	44.2%	16,000
9. Computer Support Specialists	$40,430	30.3%	71,000
10. Computer Programmers	$62,890	14.6%	45,000
11. Automatic Teller Machine Servicers	$35,150	15.1%	19,000
12. Data Processing Equipment Repairers	$35,150	15.1%	19,000
13. Office Machine and Cash Register Servicers	$35,150	15.1%	19,000

Best Jobs for People Interested in Law and Public Safety

Job	Annual Earnings	Percent Growth	Annual Openings
1. Lawyers	$94,930	17.0%	53,000
2. Highway Patrol Pilots	$45,210	24.7%	67,000
3. Police Patrol Officers	$45,210	24.7%	67,000
4. Sheriffs and Deputy Sheriffs	$45,210	24.7%	67,000
5. Paralegals and Legal Assistants	$39,130	28.7%	29,000
6. Criminal Investigators and Special Agents	$53,990	22.4%	11,000
7. Police Detectives	$53,990	22.4%	11,000
8. Police Identification and Records Officers	$53,990	22.4%	11,000
9. Correctional Officers and Jailers	$33,600	24.2%	49,000
10. Forest Fire Fighters	$38,330	20.7%	29,000
11. Municipal Fire Fighters	$38,330	20.7%	29,000
12. First-Line Supervisors/Managers of Police and Detectives	$64,430	15.3%	14,000
13. Forest Fire Fighting and Prevention Supervisors	$58,920	18.7%	8,000
14. Municipal Fire Fighting and Prevention Supervisors	$58,920	18.7%	8,000
15. Security Guards	$20,320	31.9%	228,000
16. Emergency Medical Technicians and Paramedics	$25,310	33.1%	32,000
17. Emergency Management Specialists	$45,390	28.2%	2,000

Best Jobs for People Interested in Law and Public Safety

Job	Annual Earnings	Percent Growth	Annual Openings
18. Private Detectives and Investigators	$32,110	25.3%	9,000
19. First-Line Supervisors/Managers of Correctional Officers	$44,720	19.0%	4,000
20. Forensic Science Technicians	$44,010	18.9%	1,000
21. Judges, Magistrate Judges, and Magistrates	$93,070	8.7%	2,000
22. Transit and Railroad Police	$45,430	15.9%	1,000
23. Lifeguards, Ski Patrol, and Other Recreational Protective Service Workers	$16,540	14.3%	60,000
24. Arbitrators, Mediators, and Conciliators	$54,760	13.7%	fewer than 500

Best Jobs for People Interested in Manufacturing

Job	Annual Earnings	Percent Growth	Annual Openings
1. First-Line Supervisors/Managers of Mechanics, Installers, and Repairers	$50,340	15.4%	42,000
2. First-Line Supervisors/Managers of Production and Operating Workers	$44,740	9.5%	66,000
3. Brazers	$30,620	17.0%	71,000
4. Solderers	$30,620	17.0%	71,000
5. Welder-Fitters	$30,620	17.0%	71,000
6. Welders and Cutters	$30,620	17.0%	71,000
7. Welders, Production	$30,620	17.0%	71,000
8. Industrial Production Managers	$73,000	7.9%	18,000
9. Automotive Master Mechanics	$32,450	12.4%	100,000
10. Automotive Specialty Technicians	$32,450	12.4%	100,000
11. Irradiated-Fuel Handlers	$33,320	43.1%	8,000
12. Bus and Truck Mechanics and Diesel Engine Specialists	$35,780	14.2%	28,000
13. Packaging and Filling Machine Operators and Tenders	$22,200	21.1%	69,000
14. First-Line Supervisors/Managers of Helpers, Laborers, and Material Movers, Hand	$38,280	14.0%	16,000
15. Aircraft Body and Bonded Structure Repairers	$45,290	11.0%	12,000
16. Aircraft Engine Specialists	$45,290	11.0%	12,000
17. Airframe-and-Power-Plant Mechanics	$45,290	11.0%	12,000
18. Automotive Body and Related Repairers	$34,690	13.2%	23,000
19. Refuse and Recyclable Material Collectors	$25,760	17.6%	42,000
20. Painters, Transportation Equipment	$35,120	17.5%	9,000

(continued)

(continued)

Best Jobs for People Interested in Manufacturing

Job	Annual Earnings	Percent Growth	Annual Openings
21. Desktop Publishers	$32,340	29.2%	4,000
22. Water and Liquid Waste Treatment Plant and System Operators	$34,960	16.0%	9,000
23. Electrical and Electronics Repairers, Commercial and Industrial Equipment	$42,600	10.3%	10,000
24. Industrial Truck and Tractor Operators	$26,580	11.1%	94,000
25. Machinists	$33,960	8.2%	30,000
26. Mobile Heavy Equipment Mechanics, Except Engines	$38,150	9.6%	12,000
27. Packers and Packagers, Hand	$17,150	14.4%	198,000
28. Industrial Machinery Mechanics	$39,060	5.5%	19,000
29. Valve and Regulator Repairers	$43,710	12.0%	5,000
30. Slaughterers and Meat Packers	$20,860	18.1%	23,000
31. Medical Equipment Repairers	$37,220	14.8%	4,000
32. Electrical and Electronic Inspectors and Testers	$28,410	4.7%	87,000
33. Materials Inspectors	$28,410	4.7%	87,000
34. Precision Devices Inspectors and Testers	$28,410	4.7%	87,000
35. Production Inspectors, Testers, Graders, Sorters, Samplers, Weighers	$28,410	4.7%	87,000
36. Recreational Vehicle Service Technicians	$28,980	21.8%	4,000
37. Production Laborers	$20,180	11.3%	67,000
38. Locksmiths and Safe Repairers	$30,360	21.0%	3,000
39. Meat, Poultry, and Fish Cutters and Trimmers	$18,900	16.4%	27,000
40. Model Makers, Metal and Plastic	$44,250	14.6%	1,000
41. Freight, Stock, and Material Movers, Hand	$20,120	6.6%	525,000
42. Millwrights	$43,720	5.3%	7,000
43. Laundry and Drycleaning Machine Operators and Tenders, Except Pressing	$17,220	12.3%	47,000
44. Precision Dyers	$17,220	12.3%	47,000
45. Spotters, Dry Cleaning	$17,220	12.3%	47,000
46. Design Printing Machine Setters and Set-Up Operators	$29,900	4.6%	30,000
47. Embossing Machine Set-Up Operators	$29,900	4.6%	30,000
48. Engraver Set-Up Operators	$29,900	4.6%	30,000
49. Letterpress Setters and Set-Up Operators	$29,900	4.6%	30,000

Best Jobs for People Interested in Retail and Wholesale Sales and Service

Job	Annual Earnings	Percent Growth	Annual Openings
1. Sales Managers	$84,220	30.5%	54,000
2. Marketing Managers	$87,640	21.3%	30,000
3. Sales Representatives, Agricultural	$58,580	19.3%	44,000
4. Sales Representatives, Chemical and Pharmaceutical	$58,580	19.3%	44,000
5. Sales Representatives, Electrical/Electronic	$58,580	19.3%	44,000
6. Sales Representatives, Instruments	$58,580	19.3%	44,000
7. Sales Representatives, Mechanical Equipment and Supplies	$58,580	19.3%	44,000
8. Sales Representatives, Medical	$58,580	19.3%	44,000
9. Sales Representatives, Wholesale and Manufacturing, Except Technical and Scientific Products	$45,400	19.1%	160,000
10. Advertising and Promotions Managers	$63,610	25.0%	13,000
11. Sales Engineers	$70,620	19.9%	7,000
12. First-Line Supervisors/Managers of Non-Retail Sales Workers	$59,300	6.8%	72,000
13. Adjustment Clerks	$27,020	24.3%	419,000
14. Customer Service Representatives, Utilities	$27,020	24.3%	419,000
15. Receptionists and Information Clerks	$21,830	29.5%	296,000
16. Purchasing Agents, Except Wholesale, Retail, and Farm Products	$47,680	11.2%	29,000
17. Property, Real Estate, and Community Association Managers	$39,980	12.8%	35,000
18. Counter and Rental Clerks	$18,280	26.3%	144,000
19. First-Line Supervisors/Managers of Retail Sales Workers	$32,720	9.1%	251,000
20. Purchasing Managers	$72,450	4.8%	9,000
21. Retail Salespersons	$18,680	14.6%	1,014,000
22. Real Estate Sales Agents	$35,670	5.7%	34,000
23. Real Estate Brokers	$58,720	2.4%	11,000
24. Wholesale and Retail Buyers, Except Farm Products	$42,230	4.3%	24,000
25. Demonstrators and Product Promoters	$20,700	17.0%	38,000
26. Cashiers	$16,240	13.2%	1,221,000
27. Gaming Change Persons and Booth Cashiers	$20,530	24.1%	12,000

Best Jobs for People Interested in
Scientific Research, Engineering, and Mathematics

Job	Annual Earnings	Percent Growth	Annual Openings
1. School Psychologists	$54,950	24.4%	17,000
2. Medical Scientists, Except Epidemiologists	$61,320	26.9%	6,000
3. Environmental Scientists and Specialists, Including Health	$51,080	23.7%	6,000
4. Engineering Managers	$97,630	9.2%	16,000
5. Industrial Engineers	$65,020	10.6%	16,000
6. Biochemists	$68,950	22.9%	2,000
7. Biophysicists	$68,950	22.9%	2,000
8. Electronics Engineers, Except Computer	$75,770	9.4%	11,000
9. Civil Engineers	$64,230	8.0%	17,000
10. Calibration and Instrumentation Technicians	$46,310	10.0%	24,000
11. Electrical Engineering Technicians	$46,310	10.0%	24,000
12. Electronics Engineering Technicians	$46,310	10.0%	24,000
13. Social Science Research Assistants	$34,360	17.5%	18,000
14. Chemists	$56,060	12.7%	7,000
15. Biomedical Engineers	$67,690	26.1%	fewer than 500
16. Hydrologists	$61,510	21.0%	1,000
17. Natural Sciences Managers	$88,660	11.3%	5,000
18. Epidemiologists	$54,800	32.5%	fewer than 500
19. Environmental Engineering Technicians	$38,550	28.4%	3,000
20. Mechanical Engineers	$66,320	4.8%	14,000
21. Mapping Technicians	$30,380	23.1%	10,000
22. Surveying Technicians	$30,380	23.1%	10,000
23. Microbiologists	$54,840	20.0%	1,000
24. Actuaries	$76,340	14.9%	2,000
25. Atmospheric and Space Scientists	$70,100	16.2%	1,000
26. Economists	$72,780	13.4%	2,000
27. Geographers	$58,970	19.5%	fewer than 500
28. Electrical Engineers	$71,610	2.5%	11,000
29. Computer Hardware Engineers	$81,150	6.1%	6,000
30. Geologists	$68,730	11.5%	2,000
31. Industrial-Organizational Psychologists	$71,400	16.0%	fewer than 500
32. Fire-Prevention and Protection Engineers	$63,730	7.9%	4,000
33. Industrial Safety and Health Engineers	$63,730	7.9%	4,000
34. Product Safety Engineers	$63,730	7.9%	4,000
35. Mechanical Engineering Technicians	$43,400	11.0%	6,000

Best Jobs for People Interested in Scientific Research, Engineering, and Mathematics

Job	Annual Earnings	Percent Growth	Annual Openings
36. Civil Engineering Technicians	$38,480	7.6%	10,000
37. Cartographers and Photogrammetrists	$46,080	15.1%	1,000
38. Electro-Mechanical Technicians	$41,440	11.5%	4,000
39. Photographers, Scientific	$26,080	13.6%	18,000
40. Sociologists	$57,870	13.4%	fewer than 500
41. Materials Scientists	$72,390	8.5%	1,000
42. Physicists	$87,450	6.9%	1,000

Best Jobs for People Interested in Transportation, Distribution, and Logistics

Job	Annual Earnings	Percent Growth	Annual Openings
1. Storage and Distribution Managers	$66,600	19.7%	13,000
2. Transportation Managers	$66,600	19.7%	13,000
3. Tractor-Trailer Truck Drivers	$33,520	19.0%	299,000
4. Truck Drivers, Heavy	$33,520	19.0%	299,000
5. Airline Pilots, Copilots, and Flight Engineers	$129,250	18.5%	6,000
6. Truck Drivers, Light or Delivery Services	$24,540	23.2%	219,000
7. First-Line Supervisors/Managers of Transportation and Material-Moving Machine and Vehicle Operators	$44,810	12.1%	23,000
8. Bus Drivers, Transit and Intercity	$29,730	15.2%	33,000
9. Bus Drivers, School	$23,250	16.7%	76,000
10. Commercial Pilots	$53,870	14.9%	2,000
11. Taxi Drivers and Chauffeurs	$19,570	21.7%	28,000
12. Cargo and Freight Agents	$34,250	15.5%	8,000
13. Postal Service Mail Carriers	$44,450	−0.5%	20,000
14. Subway and Streetcar Operators	$49,290	13.2%	2,000
15. Freight Inspectors	$50,380	7.7%	5,000
16. Public Transportation Inspectors	$50,380	7.7%	5,000
17. Parking Lot Attendants	$16,800	19.2%	19,000
18. Stevedores, Except Equipment Operators	$20,120	6.6%	525,000

Best Jobs Lists Based on Personality Types

These lists organize the 500 best jobs into groups matching six personality types. The personality types are Realistic, Investigative, Artistic, Social, Enterprising, and Conventional. This system was developed by John Holland and is used in the *Self Directed Search (SDS)* and other career assessment inventories and information systems.

If you have used one of these career inventories or systems, the lists will help you identify jobs that most closely match these personality types. Even if you have not used one of these systems, the concept of personality types and the jobs that are related to them can help you identify jobs that most closely match the type of person you are.

We've ranked the jobs within each personality type based on their total combined scores for earnings, growth, and annual job openings. Like the job lists for education levels, there is only one list for each personality type. Note that each job is listed in the one personality type it most closely matches, even though it might also fit into others. (The only exception is Teachers, Postsecondary, which is included in several lists because the various postsecondary teaching occupations fall into several personality types. A footnote lists the specific postsecondary teaching occupations for each personality type.) Consider reviewing the jobs for more than one personality type so you don't overlook possible jobs that would interest you. Also, note that we did not have data to crosswalk 40 of the 500 best jobs to their related personality type, so some of the best jobs do not appear on the lists in this section.

Following are brief descriptions for each of the six personality types used in the lists. Select the two or three descriptions that most closely describe you and then use the lists to identify jobs that best fit these personality types.

Descriptions of the Six Personality Types

- **Realistic:** These occupations frequently involve work activities that include practical, hands-on problems and solutions. They often deal with plants, animals, and real-world materials like wood, tools, and machinery. Many of the occupations require working outside and do not involve a lot of paperwork or working closely with others.

- **Investigative:** These occupations frequently involve working with ideas and require an extensive amount of thinking. These occupations can involve searching for facts and figuring out problems mentally.

- **Artistic:** These occupations frequently involve working with forms, designs, and patterns. They often require self-expression, and the work can be done without following a clear set of rules.

- **Social:** These occupations frequently involve working with, communicating with, and teaching people. These occupations often involve helping or providing service to others.

☞ **Enterprising:** These occupations frequently involve starting up and carrying out projects. These occupations can involve leading people and making many decisions. They sometimes require risk taking and often deal with business.

☞ **Conventional:** These occupations frequently involve following set procedures and routines. These occupations can include working with data and details more than with ideas. Usually there is a clear line of authority to follow.

Best Jobs for People with a Realistic Personality Type

Job	Annual Earnings	Percent Growth	Annual Openings
1. Highway Patrol Pilots	$45,210	24.7%	67,000
2. Electricians	$42,300	23.4%	65,000
3. Heating and Air Conditioning Mechanics	$36,260	31.8%	35,000
4. Refrigeration Mechanics	$36,260	31.8%	35,000
5. Pipe Fitters	$41,290	18.7%	56,000
6. Pipelaying Fitters	$41,290	18.7%	56,000
7. Plumbers	$41,290	18.7%	56,000
8. Tractor-Trailer Truck Drivers	$33,520	19.0%	299,000
9. Truck Drivers, Heavy	$33,520	19.0%	299,000
10. Radiologic Technicians	$43,350	22.9%	21,000
11. Radiologic Technologists	$43,350	22.9%	21,000
12. Correctional Officers and Jailers	$33,600	24.2%	49,000
13. Refractory Materials Repairers, Except Brickmasons	$37,640	16.3%	155,000
14. Forest Fire Fighters	$38,330	20.7%	29,000
15. Municipal Fire Fighters	$38,330	20.7%	29,000
16. Airline Pilots, Copilots, and Flight Engineers	$129,250	18.5%	6,000
17. Sheet Metal Workers	$35,560	19.8%	30,000
18. Technical Directors/Managers	$52,840	18.3%	10,000
19. Forest Fire Fighting and Prevention Supervisors	$58,920	18.7%	8,000
20. Municipal Fire Fighting and Prevention Supervisors	$58,920	18.7%	8,000
21. Cement Masons and Concrete Finishers	$31,400	26.1%	24,000
22. First-Line Supervisors and Manager/Supervisors— Landscaping Workers	$35,340	21.6%	18,000
23. Maintenance and Repair Workers, General	$30,710	16.3%	155,000
24. Truck Drivers, Light or Delivery Services	$24,540	23.2%	219,000
25. Surgical Technologists	$34,010	27.9%	13,000
26. Brazers	$30,620	17.0%	71,000
27. Solderers	$30,620	17.0%	71,000
28. Welder-Fitters	$30,620	17.0%	71,000
29. Welders and Cutters	$30,620	17.0%	71,000

(continued)

Best Jobs for People with a Realistic Personality Type

Job	Annual Earnings	Percent Growth	Annual Openings
30. Welders, Production	$30,620	17.0%	71,000
31. Telecommunications Line Installers and Repairers	$40,330	18.8%	13,000
32. Ceiling Tile Installers	$34,030	21.4%	17,000
33. Drywall Installers	$34,030	21.4%	17,000
34. Boat Builders and Shipwrights	$34,900	10.1%	193,000
35. Brattice Builders	$34,900	10.1%	193,000
36. Carpenter Assemblers and Repairers	$34,900	10.1%	193,000
37. Construction Carpenters	$34,900	10.1%	193,000
38. Rough Carpenters	$34,900	10.1%	193,000
39. Ship Carpenters and Joiners	$34,900	10.1%	193,000
40. Roofers	$30,840	18.6%	38,000
41. Brickmasons and Blockmasons	$41,740	14.2%	21,000
42. Automotive Master Mechanics	$32,450	12.4%	100,000
43. Automotive Specialty Technicians	$32,450	12.4%	100,000
44. Civil Engineers	$64,230	8.0%	17,000
45. Calibration and Instrumentation Technicians	$46,310	10.0%	24,000
46. Electrical Engineering Technicians	$46,310	10.0%	24,000
47. Electronics Engineering Technicians	$46,310	10.0%	24,000
48. Irradiated-Fuel Handlers	$33,320	43.1%	8,000
49. Pressure Vessel Inspectors	$47,390	9.8%	20,000
50. Bus and Truck Mechanics and Diesel Engine Specialists	$35,780	14.2%	28,000
51. Landscaping and Groundskeeping Workers	$20,420	22.0%	203,000
52. Medical and Clinical Laboratory Technicians	$30,840	19.4%	21,000
53. Grader, Bulldozer, and Scraper Operators	$35,360	10.4%	45,000
54. Operating Engineers	$35,360	10.4%	45,000
55. Elevator Installers and Repairers	$58,710	17.1%	3,000
56. Combined Food Preparation and Serving Workers, Including Fast Food	$14,690	22.8%	734,000
57. Automatic Teller Machine Servicers	$35,150	15.1%	19,000
58. Data Processing Equipment Repairers	$35,150	15.1%	19,000
59. Office Machine and Cash Register Servicers	$35,150	15.1%	19,000
60. Packaging and Filling Machine Operators and Tenders	$22,200	21.1%	69,000
61. Structural Iron and Steel Workers	$42,430	15.9%	9,000
62. Aircraft Body and Bonded Structure Repairers	$45,290	11.0%	12,000
63. Aircraft Engine Specialists	$45,290	11.0%	12,000
64. Airframe-and-Power-Plant Mechanics	$45,290	11.0%	12,000

Best Jobs for People with a Realistic Personality Type

Job	Annual Earnings	Percent Growth	Annual Openings
65. Amusement and Recreation Attendants	$15,550	27.8%	66,000
66. Painters, Construction and Maintenance	$30,260	11.6%	69,000
67. Automotive Body and Related Repairers	$34,690	13.2%	23,000
68. Food Preparation Workers	$16,710	20.2%	267,000
69. Mechanical Engineers	$66,320	4.8%	14,000
70. Tapers	$39,070	20.8%	5,000
71. Surveying Technicians	$30,380	23.1%	10,000
72. Janitors and Cleaners, Except Maids and Housekeeping Cleaners	$18,790	18.3%	454,000
73. Bus Drivers, Transit and Intercity	$29,730	15.2%	33,000
74. Refuse and Recyclable Material Collectors	$25,760	17.6%	42,000
75. Tile and Marble Setters	$35,410	26.5%	4,000
76. Construction Laborers	$25,160	14.2%	166,000
77. Painters, Transportation Equipment	$35,120	17.5%	9,000
78. Bus Drivers, School	$23,250	16.7%	76,000
79. Carpet Installers	$34,090	16.8%	10,000
80. Biological Technicians	$33,210	19.4%	7,000
81. Desktop Publishers	$32,340	29.2%	4,000
82. Helpers—Installation, Maintenance, and Repair Workers	$21,310	20.3%	33,000
83. Cooks, Restaurant	$19,520	15.9%	211,000
84. Sound Engineering Technicians	$38,110	25.5%	2,000
85. Water and Liquid Waste Treatment Plant and System Operators	$34,960	16.0%	9,000
86. Electrical and Electronics Repairers, Commercial and Industrial Equipment	$42,600	10.3%	10,000
87. Industrial Truck and Tractor Operators	$26,580	11.1%	94,000
88. Machinists	$33,960	8.2%	30,000
89. Commercial Pilots	$53,870	14.9%	2,000
90. Nonfarm Animal Caretakers	$17,460	22.2%	32,000
91. Insulation Workers, Mechanical	$33,330	15.8%	9,000
92. Taxi Drivers and Chauffeurs	$19,570	21.7%	28,000
93. Mobile Heavy Equipment Mechanics, Except Engines	$38,150	9.6%	12,000
94. Central Office and PBX Installers and Repairers	$49,840	–0.6%	23,000
95. Communication Equipment Mechanics, Installers, and Repairers	$49,840	–0.6%	23,000
96. Frame Wirers, Central Office	$49,840	–0.6%	23,000
97. Station Installers and Repairers, Telephone	$49,840	–0.6%	23,000
98. Telecommunications Facility Examiners	$49,840	–0.6%	23,000

(continued)

(continued)

Best Jobs for People with a Realistic Personality Type

Job	Annual Earnings	Percent Growth	Annual Openings
99. Glaziers	$32,650	17.2%	7,000
100. Mechanical Engineering Technicians	$43,400	11.0%	6,000
101. Packers and Packagers, Hand	$17,150	14.4%	198,000
102. Farmers and Ranchers	$40,440	–20.6%	118,000
103. Industrial Machinery Mechanics	$39,060	5.5%	19,000
104. Electric Meter Installers and Repairers	$43,710	12.0%	5,000
105. Meter Mechanics	$43,710	12.0%	5,000
106. Valve and Regulator Repairers	$43,710	12.0%	5,000
107. Highway Maintenance Workers	$29,550	10.4%	25,000
108. Dining Room and Cafeteria Attendants and Bartender Helpers	$14,770	14.9%	143,000
109. Insulation Workers, Floor, Ceiling, and Wall	$30,310	15.8%	9,000
110. Subway and Streetcar Operators	$49,290	13.2%	2,000
111. Tree Trimmers and Pruners	$26,150	18.6%	11,000
112. Aviation Inspectors	$50,380	7.7%	5,000
113. Motor Vehicle Inspectors	$50,380	7.7%	5,000
114. Railroad Inspectors	$50,380	7.7%	5,000
115. Slaughterers and Meat Packers	$20,860	18.1%	23,000
116. Medical Equipment Repairers	$37,220	14.8%	4,000
117. Civil Engineering Technicians	$38,480	7.6%	10,000
118. Electrical and Electronic Inspectors and Testers	$28,410	4.7%	87,000
119. Helpers—Electricians	$23,420	17.9%	17,000
120. Materials Inspectors	$28,410	4.7%	87,000
121. Mechanical Inspectors	$28,410	4.7%	87,000
122. Plasterers and Stucco Masons	$32,440	13.5%	8,000
123. Precision Devices Inspectors and Testers	$28,410	4.7%	87,000
124. Production Inspectors, Testers, Graders, Sorters, Samplers, Weighers	$28,410	4.7%	87,000
125. Loading Machine Operators, Underground Mining	$33,250	8.9%	14,000
126. Veterinary Assistants and Laboratory Animal Caretakers	$18,660	26.2%	11,000
127. Pest Control Workers	$26,220	17.0%	11,000
128. First-Line Supervisors and Manager/Supervisors—Animal Care Workers, Except Livestock	$35,490	11.4%	6,000
129. First-Line Supervisors and Manager/Supervisors— Fishery Workers	$35,490	11.4%	6,000
130. First-Line Supervisors and Manager/Supervisors— Horticultural Workers	$35,490	11.4%	6,000

Best Jobs for People with a Realistic Personality Type

Job	Annual Earnings	Percent Growth	Annual Openings
131. First-Line Supervisors and Manager/Supervisors— Logging Workers	$35,490	11.4%	6,000
132. Electro-Mechanical Technicians	$41,440	11.5%	4,000
133. Recreational Vehicle Service Technicians	$28,980	21.8%	4,000
134. Lifeguards, Ski Patrol, and Other Recreational Protective Service Workers	$16,540	14.3%	60,000
135. Production Laborers	$20,180	11.3%	67,000
136. Locksmiths and Safe Repairers	$30,360	21.0%	3,000
137. Architectural Drafters	$39,190	4.2%	14,000
138. Civil Drafters	$39,190	4.2%	14,000
139. Dragline Operators	$31,970	8.9%	14,000
140. Excavating and Loading Machine Operators	$31,970	8.9%	14,000
141. Parking Lot Attendants	$16,800	19.2%	19,000
142. Electrical Power-Line Installers and Repairers	$49,100	1.6%	9,000
143. Meat, Poultry, and Fish Cutters and Trimmers	$18,900	16.4%	27,000
144. Maids and Housekeeping Cleaners	$16,900	9.2%	352,000
145. Model Makers, Metal and Plastic	$44,250	14.6%	1,000
146. Crane and Tower Operators	$37,410	10.8%	5,000
147. Freight, Stock, and Material Movers, Hand	$20,120	6.6%	525,000
148. Grips and Set-Up Workers, Motion Picture Sets, Studios, and Stages	$20,120	6.6%	525,000
149. Stevedores, Except Equipment Operators	$20,120	6.6%	525,000
150. Millwrights	$43,720	5.3%	7,000
151. Septic Tank Servicers and Sewer Pipe Cleaners	$28,870	21.2%	3,000
152. Laundry and Drycleaning Machine Operators and Tenders, Except Pressing	$17,220	12.3%	47,000
153. Precision Dyers	$17,220	12.3%	47,000
154. Reinforcing Iron and Rebar Workers	$35,160	16.7%	2,000
155. Spotters, Dry Cleaning	$17,220	12.3%	47,000
156. Design Printing Machine Setters and Set-Up Operators	$29,900	4.6%	30,000
157. Embossing Machine Set-Up Operators	$29,900	4.6%	30,000
158. Engraver Set-Up Operators	$29,900	4.6%	30,000
159. Letterpress Setters and Set-Up Operators	$29,900	4.6%	30,000

Best Jobs for People with an Investigative Personality Type

Job	Annual Earnings	Percent Growth	Annual Openings
1. Computer Software Engineers, Applications	$74,980	45.5%	55,000
2. Computer Systems Analysts	$66,460	39.4%	68,000
3. Computer Software Engineers, Systems Software	$79,740	45.5%	39,000
4. Teachers, Postsecondary	$51,614	38.1%	216,000
5. Network Systems and Data Communications Analysts	$60,600	57.0%	29,000
6. Computer Security Specialists	$58,190	37.4%	35,000
7. Pharmacists	$84,900	30.1%	23,000
8. Anesthesiologists	more than $145,600	19.5%	38,000
9. Internists, General	more than $145,600	19.5%	38,000
10. Obstetricians and Gynecologists	more than $145,600	19.5%	38,000
11. Psychiatrists	more than $145,600	19.5%	38,000
12. Surgeons	more than $145,600	19.5%	38,000
13. Family and General Practitioners	$137,090	19.5%	38,000
14. Pediatricians, General	$135,730	19.5%	38,000
15. Database Administrators	$60,650	44.2%	16,000
16. Computer Support Specialists	$40,430	30.3%	71,000
17. Market Research Analysts	$56,140	23.4%	18,000
18. Clinical Psychologists	$54,950	24.4%	17,000
19. School Psychologists	$54,950	24.4%	17,000
20. Physician Assistants	$69,410	48.9%	7,000
21. Computer Programmers	$62,890	14.6%	45,000
22. Financial Analysts	$61,910	18.7%	22,000
23. Compensation, Benefits, and Job Analysis Specialists	$47,490	28.0%	15,000
24. Medical Scientists, Except Epidemiologists	$61,320	26.9%	6,000
25. Medical and Clinical Laboratory Technologists	$45,730	19.3%	21,000
26. Respiratory Therapists	$43,140	34.8%	10,000
27. Veterinarians	$66,590	25.1%	4,000
28. Environmental Scientists and Specialists, Including Health	$51,080	23.7%	6,000
29. Chiropractors	$69,910	23.3%	3,000
30. Cardiovascular Technologists and Technicians	$38,690	33.5%	6,000
31. Biochemists	$68,950	22.9%	2,000
32. Biophysicists	$68,950	22.9%	2,000
33. Electronics Engineers, Except Computer	$75,770	9.4%	11,000
34. Nuclear Medicine Technologists	$56,450	23.6%	2,000
35. Coroners	$47,390	9.8%	20,000
36. Environmental Compliance Inspectors	$47,390	9.8%	20,000

Best Jobs for People with an Investigative Personality Type

Job	Annual Earnings	Percent Growth	Annual Openings
37. Dietitians and Nutritionists	$43,630	17.8%	8,000
38. Chemists	$56,060	12.7%	7,000
39. Optometrists	$88,410	17.1%	2,000
40. Hydrologists	$61,510	21.0%	1,000
41. Natural Sciences Managers	$88,660	11.3%	5,000
42. Environmental Science and Protection Technicians, Including Health	$35,340	36.8%	4,000
43. Epidemiologists	$54,800	32.5%	fewer than 500
44. Microbiologists	$54,840	20.0%	1,000
45. Atmospheric and Space Scientists	$70,100	16.2%	1,000
46. Economists	$72,780	13.4%	2,000
47. Geographers	$58,970	19.5%	fewer than 500
48. Electrical Engineers	$71,610	2.5%	11,000
49. Computer Hardware Engineers	$81,150	6.1%	6,000
50. Urban and Regional Planners	$53,450	10.7%	5,000
51. Oral and Maxillofacial Surgeons	more than $145,600	4.1%	7,000
52. Orthodontists	more than $145,600	4.1%	7,000
53. Prosthodontists	more than $145,600	4.1%	7,000
54. Dentists, General	$123,060	4.1%	7,000
55. Geologists	$68,730	11.5%	2,000
56. Operations Research Analysts	$60,190	6.2%	6,000
57. Industrial-Organizational Psychologists	$71,400	16.0%	fewer than 500
58. Fire-Prevention and Protection Engineers	$63,730	7.9%	4,000
59. Industrial Safety and Health Engineers	$63,730	7.9%	4,000
60. Product Safety Engineers	$63,730	7.9%	4,000
61. Forensic Science Technicians	$44,010	18.9%	1,000
62. Industrial Engineering Technicians	$43,590	8.7%	7,000
63. Archivists	$36,470	17.0%	2,000
64. Sociologists	$57,870	13.4%	fewer than 500
65. Materials Scientists	$72,390	8.5%	1,000
66. Plant Scientists	$51,200	9.1%	2,000
67. Soil Scientists	$51,200	9.1%	2,000
68. Physicists	$87,450	6.9%	1,000
69. Food Scientists and Technologists	$50,840	9.1%	2,000

Teachers, Postsecondary, is listed here because the following jobs are associated with the Investigative personality type: Agricultural Sciences Teachers, Postsecondary; Biological Science Teachers, Postsecondary; Chemistry Teachers, Postsecondary; Computer Science Teachers, Postsecondary; Engineering Teachers, Postsecondary; Forestry and Conservation Science Teachers, Postsecondary; Health Specialties Teachers, Postsecondary; Mathematical Science Teachers, Postsecondary; and Physics Teachers, Postsecondary.

Best Jobs for People with an Artistic Personality Type

Job	Annual Earnings	Percent Growth	Annual Openings
1. Teachers, Postsecondary	$51,614	38.1%	216,000
2. Advertising and Promotions Managers	$63,610	25.0%	13,000
3. Graphic Designers	$38,030	21.9%	29,000
4. Technical Writers	$53,490	27.1%	6,000
5. Directors—Stage, Motion Pictures, Television, and Radio	$52,840	18.3%	10,000
6. Producers	$52,840	18.3%	10,000
7. Talent Directors	$52,840	18.3%	10,000
8. Caption Writers	$44,350	16.1%	23,000
9. Copy Writers	$44,350	16.1%	23,000
10. Creative Writers	$44,350	16.1%	23,000
11. Poets and Lyricists	$44,350	16.1%	23,000
12. Architects, Except Landscape and Naval	$60,300	17.3%	8,000
13. Costume Attendants	$25,050	27.8%	66,000
14. Interior Designers	$40,670	21.7%	8,000
15. Art Directors	$63,840	11.4%	8,000
16. Commercial and Industrial Designers	$52,310	14.7%	7,000
17. Landscape Architects	$53,120	22.2%	2,000
18. Film and Video Editors	$43,590	26.4%	3,000
19. Editors	$43,890	11.8%	14,000
20. Librarians	$45,900	10.1%	15,000
21. Interpreters and Translators	$33,860	22.1%	4,000
22. Cartoonists	$38,060	16.5%	4,000
23. Painters and Illustrators	$38,060	16.5%	4,000
24. Sculptors	$38,060	16.5%	4,000
25. Sketch Artists	$38,060	16.5%	4,000
26. Curators	$43,620	17.0%	2,000
27. Exhibit Designers	$35,800	20.9%	2,000
28. Set Designers	$35,800	20.9%	2,000
29. Composers	$34,570	13.5%	8,000
30. Music Arrangers and Orchestrators	$34,570	13.5%	8,000
31. Music Directors	$34,570	13.5%	8,000
32. Fashion Designers	$55,840	10.6%	2,000
33. Camera Operators, Television, Video, and Motion Picture	$37,610	13.4%	4,000
34. Photographers, Scientific	$26,080	13.6%	18,000
35. Professional Photographers	$26,080	13.6%	18,000

Teachers, Postsecondary, is listed here because the following jobs are associated with the Artistic personality type: Art, Drama, and Music Teachers, Postsecondary; English Language and Literature Teachers, Postsecondary; and Foreign Language and Literature Teachers, Postsecondary.

Best Jobs for People with a Social Personality Type

Job	Annual Earnings	Percent Growth	Annual Openings
1. Teachers, Postsecondary	$51,614	38.1%	216,000
2. Registered Nurses	$52,330	27.3%	215,000
3. Special Education Teachers, Secondary School	$45,700	30.0%	59,000
4. Education Administrators, Elementary and Secondary School	$74,190	20.7%	31,000
5. Personal Financial Advisors	$62,700	34.6%	18,000
6. Special Education Teachers, Middle School	$44,160	30.0%	59,000
7. Police Patrol Officers	$45,210	24.7%	67,000
8. Sheriffs and Deputy Sheriffs	$45,210	24.7%	67,000
9. Special Education Teachers, Preschool, Kindergarten, and Elementary School	$43,570	30.0%	59,000
10. Physical Therapists	$60,180	35.3%	16,000
11. Training and Development Specialists	$44,570	27.9%	35,000
12. Secondary School Teachers, Except Special and Vocational Education	$45,650	18.2%	118,000
13. Counseling Psychologists	$54,950	24.4%	17,000
14. Dental Hygienists	$58,350	43.1%	9,000
15. Kindergarten Teachers, Except Special Education	$41,400	27.2%	34,000
16. Occupational Therapists	$54,660	35.2%	10,000
17. Social and Community Service Managers	$46,810	27.7%	19,000
18. Instructional Coordinators	$48,790	25.4%	18,000
19. Employment Interviewers, Private or Public Employment Service	$41,190	27.3%	29,000
20. Speech-Language Pathologists	$52,410	27.2%	10,000
21. Elementary School Teachers, Except Special Education	$43,160	15.2%	183,000
22. Licensed Practical and Licensed Vocational Nurses	$33,970	20.2%	105,000
23. Child, Family, and School Social Workers	$34,820	23.2%	45,000
24. Medical and Public Health Social Workers	$40,080	28.6%	18,000
25. Self-Enrichment Education Teachers	$30,880	40.1%	39,000
26. Educational, Vocational, and School Counselors	$45,570	15.0%	32,000
27. Physical Therapist Assistants	$37,890	44.6%	10,000
28. Medical Assistants	$24,610	58.9%	78,000
29. Mental Health and Substance Abuse Social Workers	$33,920	34.5%	17,000
30. Dental Assistants	$28,330	42.5%	35,000
31. Social and Human Service Assistants	$24,270	48.7%	63,000
32. Adult Literacy, Remedial Education, and GED Teachers and Instructors	$38,980	20.4%	14,000
33. Fitness Trainers and Aerobics Instructors	$25,470	44.5%	38,000

(continued)

(continued)

Best Jobs for People with a Social Personality Type

Job	Annual Earnings	Percent Growth	Annual Openings
34. Education Administrators, Preschool and Child Care Center/Program	$35,730	32.0%	9,000
35. Middle School Teachers, Except Special and Vocational Education	$43,670	9.0%	69,000
36. Security Guards	$20,320	31.9%	228,000
37. Clergy	$36,690	15.5%	34,000
38. Preschool Teachers, Except Special Education	$20,980	36.2%	88,000
39. Nursing Aides, Orderlies, and Attendants	$20,980	24.9%	302,000
40. Home Health Aides	$18,330	48.1%	141,000
41. Mental Health Counselors	$32,960	26.7%	13,000
42. Personal and Home Care Aides	$16,900	40.5%	154,000
43. Emergency Medical Technicians and Paramedics	$25,310	33.1%	32,000
44. Radiation Therapists	$57,700	31.6%	1,000
45. Health Educators	$38,480	21.9%	8,000
46. Equal Opportunity Representatives and Officers	$47,390	9.8%	20,000
47. Directors, Religious Activities and Education	$30,700	24.1%	16,000
48. Teacher Assistants	$19,410	23.0%	259,000
49. Audiologists	$51,470	29.0%	1,000
50. Probation Officers and Correctional Treatment Specialists	$39,600	14.7%	15,000
51. Occupational Therapist Assistants	$38,430	39.2%	3,000
52. Substance Abuse and Behavioral Disorder Counselors	$32,130	23.3%	10,000
53. Locker Room, Coatroom, and Dressing Room Attendants	$17,550	27.8%	66,000
54. Occupational Health and Safety Specialists	$51,570	13.2%	6,000
55. Vocational Education Teachers, Secondary School	$45,920	9.0%	12,000
56. Recreation Workers	$19,320	20.5%	56,000
57. Podiatrists	$94,400	15.0%	1,000
58. Waiters and Waitresses	$14,050	17.5%	721,000
59. Orthotists and Prosthetists	$50,260	18.9%	1,000
60. Counter Attendants, Cafeteria, Food Concession, and Coffee Shop	$15,660	16.7%	190,000
61. Residential Advisors	$21,430	33.6%	12,000
62. Athletic Trainers	$33,940	29.9%	2,000
63. Physical Therapist Aides	$21,380	46.4%	8,000
64. Child Care Workers	$16,760	11.7%	406,000
65. Police, Fire, and Ambulance Dispatchers	$28,930	12.7%	15,000

Teachers, Postsecondary, is listed here because the following jobs are associated with the Social personality type: Anthropology and Archeology Teachers, Postsecondary; Area, Ethnic, and Cultural Studies Teachers, Postsecondary; Economics Teachers, Postsecondary; History Teachers, Postsecondary; Nursing Instructors and Teachers, Postsecondary; Political Science Teachers, Postsecondary; Psychology Teachers, Postsecondary; and Sociology Teachers, Postsecondary.

Best Jobs for People with an Enterprising Personality Type

Job	Annual Earnings	Percent Growth	Annual Openings
1. Management Analysts	$63,450	30.4%	78,000
2. Sales Managers	$84,220	30.5%	54,000
3. Computer and Information Systems Managers	$92,570	36.1%	39,000
4. Medical and Health Services Managers	$67,430	29.3%	33,000
5. Financial Managers, Branch or Department	$81,880	18.3%	71,000
6. Treasurers, Controllers, and Chief Financial Officers	$81,880	18.3%	71,000
7. Marketing Managers	$87,640	21.3%	30,000
8. Government Service Executives	$140,350	16.7%	63,000
9. Private Sector Executives	$140,350	16.7%	63,000
10. Lawyers	$94,930	17.0%	53,000
11. Administrative Services Managers	$60,290	19.8%	40,000
12. Education Administrators, Postsecondary	$68,340	25.9%	19,000
13. Sales Representatives, Agricultural	$58,580	19.3%	44,000
14. Sales Representatives, Chemical and Pharmaceutical	$58,580	19.3%	44,000
15. Sales Representatives, Electrical/Electronic	$58,580	19.3%	44,000
16. Sales Representatives, Instruments	$58,580	19.3%	44,000
17. Sales Representatives, Mechanical Equipment and Supplies	$58,580	19.3%	44,000
18. Sales Representatives, Medical	$58,580	19.3%	44,000
19. Sales Representatives, Wholesale and Manufacturing, Except Technical and Scientific Products	$45,400	19.1%	160,000
20. Training and Development Managers	$67,460	19.4%	21,000
21. Compensation and Benefits Managers	$66,530	19.4%	21,000
22. Public Relations Specialists	$43,830	32.9%	28,000
23. Sales Agents, Financial Services	$69,200	13.0%	39,000
24. Sales Agents, Securities and Commodities	$69,200	13.0%	39,000
25. Construction Managers	$69,870	12.0%	47,000
26. Personnel Recruiters	$41,190	27.3%	29,000
27. Paralegals and Legal Assistants	$39,130	28.7%	29,000
28. Storage and Distribution Managers	$66,600	19.7%	13,000
29. Transportation Managers	$66,600	19.7%	13,000
30. Loan Officers	$48,830	18.8%	30,000
31. First-Line Supervisors and Manager/Supervisors—Construction Trades Workers	$50,450	14.1%	67,000
32. First-Line Supervisors and Manager/Supervisors—Extractive Workers	$50,450	14.1%	67,000
33. First-Line Supervisors/Managers of Mechanics, Installers, and Repairers	$50,340	15.4%	42,000

(continued)

(continued)

Best Jobs for People with an Enterprising Personality Type

Job	Annual Earnings	Percent Growth	Annual Openings
34. Child Support, Missing Persons, and Unemployment Insurance Fraud Investigators	$53,990	22.4%	11,000
35. Criminal Investigators and Special Agents	$53,990	22.4%	11,000
36. Police Detectives	$53,990	22.4%	11,000
37. Sales Engineers	$70,620	19.9%	7,000
38. First-Line Supervisors/Managers of Police and Detectives	$64,430	15.3%	14,000
39. First-Line Supervisors/Managers of Non-Retail Sales Workers	$59,300	6.8%	72,000
40. Program Directors	$52,840	18.3%	10,000
41. Insurance Adjusters, Examiners, and Investigators	$44,220	14.2%	31,000
42. First-Line Supervisors/Managers of Production and Operating Workers	$44,740	9.5%	66,000
43. Flight Attendants	$43,440	15.9%	23,000
44. Engineering Managers	$97,630	9.2%	16,000
45. Lawn Service Managers	$35,340	21.6%	18,000
46. Industrial Engineers	$65,020	10.6%	16,000
47. Purchasing Agents, Except Wholesale, Retail, and Farm Products	$47,680	11.2%	29,000
48. Food Service Managers	$39,610	11.5%	58,000
49. Industrial Production Managers	$73,000	7.9%	18,000
50. Property, Real Estate, and Community Association Managers	$39,980	12.8%	35,000
51. First-Line Supervisors/Managers of Transportation and Material-Moving Machine and Vehicle Operators	$44,810	12.1%	23,000
52. Agents and Business Managers of Artists, Performers, and Athletes	$55,080	27.8%	2,000
53. Appraisers, Real Estate	$43,390	17.6%	11,000
54. Advertising Sales Agents	$40,300	13.4%	24,000
55. First-Line Supervisors, Administrative Support	$41,030	6.6%	140,000
56. First-Line Supervisors, Customer Service	$41,030	6.6%	140,000
57. Insurance Sales Agents	$41,720	8.4%	52,000
58. Government Property Inspectors and Investigators	$47,390	9.8%	20,000
59. Meeting and Convention Planners	$39,620	21.3%	7,000
60. First-Line Supervisors/Managers of Retail Sales Workers	$32,720	9.1%	251,000
61. Chefs and Head Cooks	$30,680	15.8%	33,000
62. Private Detectives and Investigators	$32,110	25.3%	9,000
63. First-Line Supervisors/Managers of Helpers, Laborers, and Material Movers, Hand	$38,280	14.0%	16,000
64. Agricultural Crop Farm Managers	$50,700	5.1%	25,000
65. Fish Hatchery Managers	$50,700	5.1%	25,000

Best Jobs for People with an Enterprising Personality Type

Job	Annual Earnings	Percent Growth	Annual Openings
66. Nursery and Greenhouse Managers	$50,700	5.1%	25,000
67. Athletes and Sports Competitors	$48,310	19.2%	3,000
68. First-Line Supervisors/Managers of Food Preparation and Serving Workers	$25,410	15.5%	154,000
69. Housekeeping Supervisors	$29,510	16.2%	28,000
70. Janitorial Supervisors	$29,510	16.2%	28,000
71. Purchasing Managers	$72,450	4.8%	9,000
72. Gaming Supervisors	$40,840	15.7%	6,000
73. Coaches and Scouts	$26,350	18.3%	26,000
74. Retail Salespersons	$18,680	14.6%	1,014,000
75. Real Estate Sales Agents	$35,670	5.7%	34,000
76. Wholesale and Retail Buyers, Except Farm Products	$42,230	4.3%	24,000
77. Gaming Dealers	$14,340	24.7%	26,000
78. Demonstrators and Product Promoters	$20,700	17.0%	38,000
79. Hosts and Hostesses, Restaurant, Lounge, and Coffee Shop	$15,630	16.4%	95,000
80. Financial Examiners	$60,310	8.9%	3,000
81. Hairdressers, Hairstylists, and Cosmetologists	$19,800	14.7%	68,000
82. First-Line Supervisors/Managers of Personal Service Workers	$30,350	9.4%	26,000
83. Judges, Magistrate Judges, and Magistrates	$93,070	8.7%	2,000
84. Opticians, Dispensing	$27,950	18.2%	10,000
85. Gaming Managers	$58,580	12.4%	1,000
86. Loan Counselors	$33,970	17.8%	4,000
87. Public Transportation Inspectors	$50,380	7.7%	5,000
88. Transit and Railroad Police	$45,430	15.9%	1,000
89. First-Line Supervisors and Manager/Supervisors—Agricultural Crop Workers	$35,490	11.4%	6,000
90. First-Line Supervisors and Manager/Supervisors—Animal Husbandry Workers	$35,490	11.4%	6,000
91. Lodging Managers	$37,660	6.6%	10,000
92. Arbitrators, Mediators, and Conciliators	$54,760	13.7%	fewer than 500

Best Jobs for People with a Conventional Personality Type

Job	Annual Earnings	Percent Growth	Annual Openings
1. Accountants	$50,770	19.5%	119,000
2. Auditors	$50,770	19.5%	119,000
3. Cost Estimators	$49,940	18.6%	25,000
4. Immigration and Customs Inspectors	$53,990	22.4%	11,000
5. Police Identification and Records Officers	$53,990	22.4%	11,000
6. Legal Secretaries	$36,720	18.8%	39,000
7. Adjustment Clerks	$27,020	24.3%	419,000
8. Customer Service Representatives, Utilities	$27,020	24.3%	419,000
9. Claims Examiners, Property and Casualty Insurance	$44,220	14.2%	31,000
10. Bill and Account Collectors	$27,450	24.5%	76,000
11. Receptionists and Information Clerks	$21,830	29.5%	296,000
12. Production, Planning, and Expediting Clerks	$36,340	14.1%	51,000
13. Credit Analysts	$47,260	18.7%	9,000
14. Human Resources Assistants, Except Payroll and Timekeeping	$31,750	19.3%	36,000
15. Assessors	$43,390	17.6%	11,000
16. Interviewers, Except Eligibility and Loan	$23,670	28.0%	46,000
17. Medical Records and Health Information Technicians	$25,590	46.8%	24,000
18. Budget Analysts	$56,040	14.0%	8,000
19. Pharmacy Technicians	$23,650	28.8%	39,000
20. Executive Secretaries and Administrative Assistants	$34,970	8.7%	210,000
21. Licensing Examiners and Inspectors	$47,390	9.8%	20,000
22. City and Regional Planning Aides	$34,360	17.5%	18,000
23. Counter and Rental Clerks	$18,280	26.3%	144,000
24. Construction and Building Inspectors	$43,670	13.8%	10,000
25. Insurance Underwriters	$48,550	10.0%	12,000
26. Medical Secretaries	$26,540	17.2%	50,000
27. Mapping Technicians	$30,380	23.1%	10,000
28. Actuaries	$76,340	14.9%	2,000
29. Dispatchers, Except Police, Fire, and Ambulance	$30,920	14.4%	28,000
30. Hotel, Motel, and Resort Desk Clerks	$17,700	23.9%	46,000
31. Audio and Video Equipment Technicians	$32,570	26.7%	5,000
32. Air Traffic Controllers	$102,030	12.6%	2,000
33. Tax Preparers	$27,730	23.2%	11,000
34. Library Assistants, Clerical	$20,720	21.5%	27,000
35. Cargo and Freight Agents	$34,250	15.5%	8,000
36. Reservation and Transportation Ticket Agents	$27,750	12.2%	35,000
37. Travel Clerks	$27,750	12.2%	35,000

Best Jobs for People with a Conventional Personality Type

Job	Annual Earnings	Percent Growth	Annual Openings
38. Office Clerks, General	$22,770	10.4%	550,000
39. Library Technicians	$24,940	16.8%	22,000
40. Cashiers	$16,240	13.2%	1,221,000
41. Billing, Cost, and Rate Clerks	$27,040	7.9%	78,000
42. Billing, Posting, and Calculating Machine Operators	$27,040	7.9%	78,000
43. Statement Clerks	$27,040	7.9%	78,000
44. Postal Service Mail Carriers	$44,450	–0.5%	20,000
45. Freight Inspectors	$50,380	7.7%	5,000
46. Marine Cargo Inspectors	$50,380	7.7%	5,000
47. Bookkeeping, Accounting, and Auditing Clerks	$28,570	3.0%	274,000
48. Cartographers and Photogrammetrists	$46,080	15.1%	1,000
49. Tellers	$21,120	9.4%	127,000
50. Court Clerks	$28,430	12.3%	14,000
51. License Clerks	$28,430	12.3%	14,000
52. Municipal Clerks	$28,430	12.3%	14,000
53. New Accounts Clerks	$26,860	11.2%	24,000
54. Insurance Appraisers, Auto Damage	$45,330	11.7%	2,000
55. Tax Examiners, Collectors, and Revenue Agents	$43,490	5.0%	9,000
56. Weighers, Measurers, Checkers, and Samplers, Recordkeeping	$24,570	14.6%	16,000

PART II

The Job Descriptions

This part of the book provides descriptions for all the jobs included in one or more of the lists in Part I. The introduction gives more details on how to use and interpret the job descriptions, but here is some additional information:

- ◉ Job descriptions are arranged in alphabetical order by job title. This approach allows you to quickly find a description if you know its correct title from one of the lists in Part I.

- ◉ If you are using this section to browse for interesting options, we suggest you begin with the table of contents. Part I features many interesting lists that will help you identify job titles to explore in more detail. If you have not browsed the lists in Part I, consider spending some time there. The lists are interesting and will help you identify job titles you can find described in the material that follows. The job titles in Part II are also listed in the table of contents.

- ◉ We include descriptions for the many specific jobs that we included under the single job title of Teachers, Postsecondary used in the lists in Part I. Here are the titles of the jobs included in the Teachers, Postsecondary title: Agricultural Sciences Teachers, Postsecondary; Anthropology and Archeology Teachers, Postsecondary; Architecture Teachers, Postsecondary; Area, Ethnic, and Cultural Studies Teachers, Postsecondary; Art, Drama, and Music Teachers, Postsecondary; Atmospheric, Earth, Marine, and Space Sciences Teachers, Postsecondary; Biological Science Teachers, Postsecondary; Business Teachers, Postsecondary; Chemistry Teachers, Postsecondary; Communications Teachers, Postsecondary; Computer Science Teachers, Postsecondary; Criminal Justice and Law Enforcement Teachers, Postsecondary; Economics Teachers, Postsecondary; Education Teachers, Postsecondary; Engineering Teachers, Postsecondary; English Language and Literature Teachers, Postsecondary; Environmental Science Teachers, Postsecondary; Foreign Language and Literature Teachers, Postsecondary; Forestry and Conservation Science Teachers, Postsecondary; Geography Teachers, Postsecondary; Graduate Teaching Assistants; Health Specialties Teachers, Postsecondary; History Teachers, Postsecondary; Home Economics Teachers, Postsecondary; Law Teachers, Postsecondary; Library Science Teachers, Postsecondary;

Mathematical Science Teachers, Postsecondary; Nursing Instructors and Teachers, Postsecondary; Philosophy and Religion Teachers, Postsecondary; Physics Teachers, Postsecondary; Political Science Teachers, Postsecondary; Psychology Teachers, Postsecondary; Recreation and Fitness Studies Teachers, Postsecondary; Social Work Teachers, Postsecondary; Sociology Teachers, Postsecondary; Vocational Education Teachers, Postsecondary.

Accountants

- ◎ Education/Training Required: Bachelor's degree
- ◎ Annual Earnings: $50,770
- ◎ Growth: 19.5%
- ◎ Annual Job Openings: 119,000
- ◎ Self-Employed: 10.6%
- ◎ Part-Time: 8.8%

Analyze financial information and prepare financial reports to determine or maintain record of assets, liabilities, profit and loss, tax liability, or other financial activities within an organization. Prepare, examine, and analyze accounting records, financial statements, and other financial reports to assess accuracy, completeness, and conformance to reporting and procedural standards. Compute taxes owed and prepare tax returns, ensuring compliance with payment, reporting, and other tax requirements. Analyze business operations, trends, costs, revenues, financial commitments, and obligations to project future revenues and expenses or to provide advice. Report to management regarding the finances of establishment. Establish tables of accounts and assign entries to proper accounts. Develop, maintain, and analyze budgets, preparing periodic reports that compare budgeted costs to actual costs. Develop, implement, modify, and document record-keeping and accounting systems, making use of current computer technology. Prepare forms and manuals for accounting and bookkeeping personnel and direct their work activities. Survey operations to ascertain accounting needs and to recommend, develop, and maintain solutions to business and financial problems. Work as Internal Revenue Service agents. Advise management about issues such as resource utilization, tax strategies, and the assumptions underlying budget forecasts. Provide internal and external auditing services for businesses and individuals. Advise clients in areas such as compensation, employee health care benefits, the design of accounting and data processing systems, and long-range tax and estate plans. Investigate bankruptcies and other complex financial transactions and prepare reports summarizing the findings. Represent clients before taxing authorities and provide support during litigation involving financial issues. Appraise, evaluate, and inventory real property and equipment, recording information such as the property's description, value, and location. Maintain and examine the records of government agencies. **SKILLS—Management of Financial Resources:** Determining how money will be spent to get the work done and accounting for these expenditures. **Systems Analysis:** Determining how a system should work and how changes in conditions, operations, and the environment will affect outcomes. **Systems Evaluation:** Identifying measures or indicators of system performance and the actions needed to improve or correct performance relative to the goals of the system. **Operations Analysis:** Analyzing needs and product requirements to create a design. **Judgment and Decision Making:** Considering the relative costs and benefits of potential actions to choose the most appropriate one. **Time Management:** Managing one's own time and the time of others. **Monitoring:** Monitoring or assessing your performance or that of other individuals or organizations to make improvements or take corrective action. **Negotiation:** Bringing others together and trying to reconcile differences. **GOE—Interest Area:** 04. Business and Administration. **Work Group:** 04.05. Accounting, Auditing, and Analytical Support. **Other Jobs in This Work Group:** Auditors; Budget Analysts; Industrial Engineering Technicians; Logisticians; Management Analysts; Operations Research Analysts. **PERSONALITY TYPE:** Conventional.

EDUCATION/TRAINING PROGRAM(S)— Accounting; Accounting and Business/Management; Accounting and Computer Science; Accounting and Finance; Auditing; Taxation. **RELATED KNOWLEDGE/COURSES—Economics and Accounting:** Knowledge of economic and accounting principles and practices, the financial markets, banking, and the analysis and reporting of financial data. **Clerical Practices:** Knowledge of administrative and clerical procedures and systems such as word processing, managing files and records, stenography and transcription, designing forms, and other office procedures and terminology. **Mathematics:** Knowledge of arithmetic, algebra, geometry, calculus, and statistics and their applications. **Law and Government:** Knowledge of laws, legal codes, court procedures, precedents, government regulations, executive orders, agency rules, and the democratic political process. **Customer and Personal Service:** Knowledge of principles and processes for providing customer and personal services. This includes customer needs assessment, meeting quality standards for services, and evaluation of customer satisfaction. **Computers and Electronics:** Knowledge of circuit boards, processors, chips, electronic equipment, and computer hardware and software, including applications and programming.

Actuaries

- ◎ Education/Training Required: Work experience plus degree
- ◎ Annual Earnings: $76,340
- ◎ Growth: 14.9%
- ◎ Annual Job Openings: 2,000
- ◎ Self-Employed: 1.4%
- ◎ Part-Time: 6.4%

Analyze statistical data, such as mortality, accident, sickness, disability, and retirement rates, and construct probability tables to forecast risk and liability for payment of future benefits. May ascertain premium rates required and cash reserves necessary to ensure payment of future benefits. Ascertain premium rates required and cash reserves and liabilities necessary to ensure payment of future benefits. Analyze statistical information to estimate mortality, accident, sickness, disability, and retirement rates. Design, review, and help administer insurance, annuity, and pension plans, determining financial soundness and calculating premiums. Collaborate with programmers, underwriters, accounts, claims experts, and senior management to help companies develop plans for new lines of business or improving existing business. Determine or help determine company policy and explain complex technical matters to company executives, government officials, shareholders, policyholders, and/or the public. Testify before public agencies on proposed legislation affecting businesses. Provide advice to clients on a contract basis, working as a consultant. Testify in court as expert witness or to provide legal evidence on matters such as the value of potential lifetime earnings of a person who is disabled or killed in an accident. Construct probability tables for events such as fires, natural disasters, and unemployment, based on analysis of statistical data and other pertinent information. Determine policy contract provisions for each type of insurance. **SKILLS—Programming:** Writing computer programs for various purposes. **Mathematics:** Using mathematics to solve problems. **Active Learning:** Understanding the implications of new information for both current and future problem-

solving and decision-making. **Complex Problem Solving:** Identifying complex problems and reviewing related information to develop and evaluate options and implement solutions. **Critical Thinking:** Using logic and reasoning to identify the strengths and weaknesses of alternative solutions, conclusions, or approaches to problems. **Operations Analysis:** Analyzing needs and product requirements to create a design. **Monitoring:** Monitoring or assessing your performance or that of other individuals or organizations to make improvements or take corrective action. **Instructing:** Teaching others how to do something. **Troubleshooting:** Determining causes of operating errors and deciding what to do about them. **GOE— Interest Area:** 15. Scientific Research, Engineering, and Mathematics. **Work Group:** 15.06. Mathematics and Data Analysis. **Other Jobs in This Work Group:** Mathematical Technicians; Mathematicians; Social Science Research Assistants; Statistical Assistants; Statisticians. **PERSONALITY TYPE:** Conventional.

EDUCATION/TRAINING PROGRAM(S)—Actuarial Science. **RELATED KNOWLEDGE/COURSES—Mathematics:** Knowledge of arithmetic, algebra, geometry, calculus, and statistics and their applications. **Economics and Accounting:** Knowledge of economic and accounting principles and practices, the financial markets, banking, and the analysis and reporting of financial data. **Computers and Electronics:** Knowledge of circuit boards, processors, chips, electronic equipment, and computer hardware and software, including applications and programming. **Sales and Marketing:** Knowledge of principles and methods for showing, promoting, and selling products or services. This includes marketing strategy and tactics, product demonstrations, sales techniques, and sales control systems. **English Language:** Knowledge of the structure and content of the English language, including the meaning and spelling of words, rules of composition, and grammar. **Administration and Management:** Knowledge of business and management principles involved in strategic planning, resource allocation, human resources modeling, leadership technique, production methods, and coordination of people and resources. **Personnel and Human Resources:** Knowledge of principles and procedures for personnel recruitment, selection, training, compensation and benefits, labor relations and negotiation, and personnel information systems.

Adjustment Clerks

- Education/Training Required: Moderate-term on-the-job training
- Annual Earnings: $27,020
- Growth: 24.3%
- Annual Job Openings: 419,000
- Self-Employed: 0.5%
- Part-Time: 14.8%

Investigate and resolve customers' inquiries concerning merchandise, service, billing, or credit rating. Examine pertinent information to determine accuracy of customers' complaints and responsibility for errors. Notify customers and appropriate personnel of findings, adjustments, and recommendations, such as exchange of merchandise, refund of money, credit to customers' accounts, or adjustment to customers' bills. Notifies customer and designated personnel of findings and recommendations, such as exchanging merchandise, refunding money, or adjustment of bill. Examines weather conditions, calculates number of days in billing period, and reviews meter accounts for errors which might explain high utility charges. Writes work order. Prepares reports showing volume, types, and disposition of claims handled. Compares merchandise with original requisition and information on invoice and prepares invoice for returned goods. Orders tests to detect product malfunction and determines if defect resulted from faulty construction. Trains dealers or service personnel in construction of products, service operations, and customer service. Reviews claims adjustments with dealer, examines parts claimed to be defective, and approves or disapproves of dealer's claim. **SKILLS—Instructing:** Teaching others how to do something. **Speaking:** Talking to others to convey information effectively. **Writing:** Communicating effectively in writing as appropriate for the needs of the audience. **Active Listening:** Giving full attention to what other people are saying, taking time to understand the points being made, asking questions as appropriate, and not interrupting at inappropriate times. **Service Orientation:** Actively looking for ways to help people. **Persuasion:** Persuading others to change their minds or behavior. **Negotiation:** Bringing others together and trying to reconcile differences. **GOE—Interest Area:** 14. Retail and Wholesale Sales and Service. **Work Group:** 14.06. Customer Service. **Other Jobs in This Work Group:** Cashiers; Counter and Rental Clerks; Customer Service Representatives, Utilities; Gaming Change Persons and Booth Cashiers; Order Clerks; Receptionists and Information Clerks. **PERSONALITY TYPE:** Conventional.

EDUCATION/TRAINING PROGRAM(S)—Customer Service Support/Call Center/Teleservice Operation; Receptionist. **RELATED KNOWLEDGE/ COURSES—Economics and Accounting:** Knowledge of economic and accounting principles and practices, the financial markets, banking, and the analysis and reporting of financial data. **Clerical Practices:** Knowledge of administrative and clerical procedures and systems such as word processing, managing files and records, stenography and transcription, designing forms, and other office procedures and terminology. **Education and Training:** Knowledge of principles and methods for curriculum and training design, teaching and instruction for individuals and groups, and the measurement of training effects.

Administrative Services Managers

- Education/Training Required: Work experience plus degree
- Annual Earnings: $60,290
- Growth: 19.8%
- Annual Job Openings: 40,000
- Self-Employed: 0.2%
- Part-Time: 4.6%

Plan, direct, or coordinate supportive services of an organization, such as record keeping, mail distribution, telephone operator/receptionist, and other office support services. May oversee facilities planning and maintenance and custodial operations. Monitor the facility to ensure that it remains safe, secure, and well maintained. Direct or coordinate the supportive services department of a business, agency, or organization. Set goals and deadlines for the department. Prepare and review operational reports and schedules to ensure accuracy and efficiency. Analyze internal processes and recommend and implement procedural or policy changes to improve operations, such as supply changes or the disposal of records. Acquire, distribute, and store supplies. Plan, administer, and control budgets for contracts, equipment, and supplies. Oversee construction and renovation projects to improve efficiency and to ensure that facilities meet environmental, health, and security standards and comply with government regulations. Hire and terminate clerical and administrative personnel. Oversee the maintenance and repair of machinery, equipment, and electrical and mechanical systems. Manage leasing of facility space. **SKILLS—Management of Personnel Resources:** Motivating, developing, and directing people as they work, identifying the best people for the job. **Service Orientation:** Actively looking for ways to help people. **Coordination:** Adjusting actions in relation to others' actions. **Management of Financial Resources:** Determining how money will be spent to get the work done and accounting for these expenditures. **Monitoring:** Monitoring or assessing your performance or that of other individuals or organizations to make improvements or take corrective action. **Social Perceptiveness:** Being aware of others' reactions and understanding why they react as they do. **Speaking:** Talking to others to convey information effectively. **Programming:** Writing computer programs for various purposes. **GOE—Interest Area:** 04. Business and Administration. **Work Group:** 04.02. Managerial Work in Business Detail. **Other Jobs in This Work Group:** First-Line Supervisors, Administrative Support; First-Line Supervisors, Customer Service; Housekeeping Supervisors; Janitorial Supervisors; Meeting and Convention Planners. **PERSONALITY TYPE:** Enterprising.

EDUCATION/TRAINING PROGRAM(S)—Business Administration and Management, General; Business/Commerce, General; Medical/Health Management and Clinical Assistant/Specialist; Public Administration; Purchasing, Procurement/Acquisitions and Contracts Management. **RELATED KNOWLEDGE/COURSES—Personnel and Human Resources:** Knowledge of principles and procedures for personnel recruitment, selection, training, compensation and benefits, labor relations and negotiation, and personnel information systems. **Clerical Practices:** Knowledge of administrative and clerical procedures and systems such as word processing, managing files and records, stenography and transcription, designing forms, and other office procedures and terminology. **Customer and Personal Service:** Knowledge of principles and processes for providing customer and personal services. This includes customer needs assessment, meeting quality standards for services, and evaluation of customer satisfaction. **Eco-**nomics and Accounting: Knowledge of economic and accounting principles and practices, the financial markets, banking, and the analysis and reporting of financial data. **Administration and Management:** Knowledge of business and management principles involved in strategic planning, resource allocation, human resources modeling, leadership technique, production methods, and coordination of people and resources. **Public Safety and Security:** Knowledge of relevant equipment, policies, procedures, and strategies to promote effective local, state, or national security operations for the protection of people, data, property, and institutions.

Adult Literacy, Remedial Education, and GED Teachers and Instructors

- ◎ Education/Training Required: Bachelor's degree
- ◎ Annual Earnings: $38,980
- ◎ Growth: 20.4%
- ◎ Annual Job Openings: 14,000
- ◎ Self-Employed: 19.5%
- ◎ Part-Time: 41.0%

Teach or instruct out-of-school youths and adults in remedial education classes, preparatory classes for the General Educational Development test, literacy, or English as a Second Language. Teaching may or may not take place in a traditional educational institution. Adapt teaching methods and instructional materials to meet students' varying needs, abilities, and interests. Observe and evaluate students' work to determine progress and make suggestions for improvement. Plan and conduct activities for a balanced program of instruction, demonstration, and work time that provides students with opportunities to observe, question, and investigate. Instruct students individually and in groups, using various teaching methods such as lectures, discussions, and demonstrations. Maintain accurate and complete student records as required by laws or administrative policies. Prepare materials and classrooms for class activities. Establish clear objectives for all lessons, units, and projects and communicate those objectives to students. Conduct classes, workshops, and demonstrations to teach principles, techniques, or methods in subjects such as basic English language skills, life skills, and workforce entry skills. Prepare students for further education by encouraging them to explore learning opportunities and to persevere with challenging tasks. Establish and enforce rules for behavior and procedures for maintaining order among the students for whom they are responsible. Provide information, guidance, and preparation for the General Equivalency Diploma (GED) examination. Assign and grade class work and homework. Observe students to determine qualifications, limitations, abilities, interests, and other individual characteristics. Register, orient, and assess new students according to standards and procedures. Prepare and implement remedial programs for students requiring extra help. Prepare and administer written, oral, and performance tests and issue grades in accordance with performance. Use computers, audiovisual aids, and other equipment and materials to supplement presentations. Prepare objectives and outlines for courses of study, following curriculum guidelines or requirements of states and schools. Guide and counsel students with adjustment and/or academic problems or special academic interests. Enforce administration policies and rules governing students. **SKILLS—Instructing:** Teaching others how to do something. **Learning Strategies:** Selecting and using training/instructional methods and procedures appropriate for the situation when learning or teaching new things. **Social Perceptiveness:** Being aware of others' reactions and understanding why they react as they do. **Service Orientation:** Actively looking for ways to help people. **Persuasion:** Persuading others to change their minds or behavior. **Speaking:** Talking to others to convey information effectively. **Monitoring:** Monitoring or assessing your performance or that of other individuals or organizations to make improvements or take corrective action. **Active Listening:** Giving full attention to what other people are saying, taking time to understand the points being made, asking questions as appropriate, and not interrupting at inappropriate times. **GOE—Interest Area:** 05. Education and Training. **Work Group:** 05.03. Postsecondary and Adult Teaching and Instructing. **Other Jobs in This Work Group:** Agricultural Sciences Teachers, Postsecondary; Anthropology and Archeology Teachers, Postsecondary; Architecture Teachers, Postsecondary; Area, Ethnic, and Cultural Studies Teachers, Postsecondary; Art, Drama, and Music Teachers, Postsecondary; Atmospheric, Earth, Marine, and Space Sciences Teachers, Postsecondary; Biological Science Teachers, Postsecondary; Business Teachers, Postsec-

ondary; Chemistry Teachers, Postsecondary; Communications Teachers, Postsecondary; Computer Science Teachers, Postsecondary; Criminal Justice and Law Enforcement Teachers, Postsecondary; Economics Teachers, Postsecondary; Education Teachers, Postsecondary; Engineering Teachers, Postsecondary; English Language and Literature Teachers, Postsecondary; Environmental Science Teachers, Postsecondary; Farm and Home Management Advisors; Foreign Language and Literature Teachers, Postsecondary; Forestry and Conservation Science Teachers, Postsecondary; Geography Teachers, Postsecondary; Graduate Teaching Assistants; Health Specialties Teachers, Postsecondary; History Teachers, Postsecondary; Home Economics Teachers, Postsecondary; Law Teachers, Postsecondary; Library Science Teachers, Postsecondary; Mathematical Science Teachers, Postsecondary; Nursing Instructors and Teachers, Postsecondary; Philosophy and Religion Teachers, Postsecondary; Physics Teachers, Postsecondary; Political Science Teachers, Postsecondary; Psychology Teachers, Postsecondary; Recreation and Fitness Studies Teachers, Postsecondary; Self-Enrichment Education Teachers; Social Work Teachers, Postsecondary; Sociology Teachers, Postsecondary; Vocational Education Teachers, Postsecondary. **PERSONALITY TYPE:** Social.

EDUCATION/TRAINING PROGRAM(S)—Adult and Continuing Education and Teaching; Adult Literacy Tutor/Instructor; Bilingual and Multilingual Education; Multicultural Education; Teaching English as a Second or Foreign Language/ESL Language Instructor. **RELATED KNOWLEDGE/COURSES—Education and Training:** Knowledge of principles and methods for curriculum and training design, teaching and instruction for individuals and groups, and the measurement of training effects. **English Language:** Knowledge of the structure and content of the English language, including the meaning and spelling of words, rules of composition, and grammar. **Psychology:** Knowledge of human behavior and performance; individual differences in ability, personality, and interests; learning and motivation; psychological research methods; and the assessment and treatment of behavioral and affective disorders. **Sociology and Anthropology:** Knowledge of group behavior and dynamics, societal trends and influences, human migrations, ethnicity, and cultures and their history and origins. **Geography:** Knowledge of principles and methods for describing the features of land, sea, and air masses, including their physical characteristics; locations;

interrelationships; and distribution of plant, animal, and human life. **History and Archeology:** Knowledge of historical events and their causes, indicators, and effects on civilizations and cultures.

Advertising and Promotions Managers

- ◎ Education/Training Required: Work experience plus degree
- ◎ Annual Earnings: $63,610
- ◎ Growth: 25.0%
- ◎ Annual Job Openings: 13,000
- ◎ Self-Employed: 2.4%
- ◎ Part-Time: 7.5%

Plan and direct advertising policies and programs or produce collateral materials, such as posters, contests, coupons, or giveaways, to create extra interest in the purchase of a product or service for a departmentor an entire organization or on an account basis. Prepare budgets and submit estimates for program costs as part of campaign plan development. Plan and prepare advertising and promotional material to increase sales of products or services, working with customers, company officials, sales departments, and advertising agencies. Assist with annual budget development. Inspect layouts and advertising copy and edit scripts, audiotapes, videotapes, and other promotional material for adherence to specifications. Coordinate activities of departments, such as sales, graphic arts, media, finance, and research. Prepare and negotiate advertising and sales contracts. Identify and develop contacts for promotional campaigns and industry programs that meet identified buyer targets such as dealers, distributors, or consumers. Gather and organize information to plan advertising campaigns. Confer with department heads and/or staff to discuss topics such as contracts, selection of advertising media, or product to be advertised. Confer with clients to provide marketing or technical advice. Monitor and analyze sales promotion results to determine cost-effectiveness of promotion campaigns. Read trade journals and professional literature to stay informed on trends, innovations, and changes that affect media planning. Formulate plans to extend business with established accounts and to transact business as agent for advertising accounts. Provide presentation and product demonstration support during the introduction of new products and services to field staff and customers. Direct, motivate, and monitor the mobilization of a campaign team to advance campaign goals. Plan and execute advertising policies and strategies for organizations. Track program budgets and expenses and campaign response rates to evaluate each campaign based on program objectives and industry norms. Assemble and communicate with a strong, diverse coalition of organizations and/or public figures, securing their cooperation, support, and action to further campaign goals. Train and direct workers engaged in developing and producing advertisements. Coordinate with the media to disseminate advertising. **SKILLS—Service Orientation:** Actively looking for ways to help people. **Management of Financial Resources:** Determining how money will be spent to get the work done and accounting for these expenditures. **Persuasion:** Persuading others to change their minds or behavior. **Negotiation:** Bringing others together and trying to reconcile differences. **Time Management:** Managing one's own time and the time of others. **Coordination:** Adjusting actions in relation to others' actions. **Management of Personnel Resources:** Motivating, developing, and directing people as they work, identifying the best people for the job. **Monitoring:** Monitoring or assessing your performance or that of other individuals or organizations to make improvements or take corrective action. **GOE—Interest Area:** 14. Retail and Wholesale Sales and Service. **Work Group:** 14.01. Managerial Work in Retail/Wholesale Sales and Service. **Other Jobs in This Work Group:** First-Line Supervisors/Managers of Non-Retail Sales Workers; First-Line Supervisors/Managers of Retail Sales Workers; Funeral Directors; Marketing Managers; Property, Real Estate, and Community Association Managers; Purchasing Managers; Sales Managers. **PERSONALITY TYPE:** Artistic.

EDUCATION/TRAINING PROGRAM(S)— Advertising; Marketing/Marketing Management, General; Public Relations/Image Management. **RELATED KNOWLEDGE/COURSES—Sales and Marketing:** Knowledge of principles and methods for showing, promoting, and selling products or services. This includes marketing strategy and tactics, product demonstrations, sales techniques, and sales control systems. **Customer and Personal Service:** Knowledge of principles and processes for providing customer and personal services. This includes customer needs assessment, meeting quality standards for services, and evaluation of customer satisfaction. **Communications and Media:** Knowledge of media production, communication, and dissemination techniques and methods. This includes alternative ways to inform and entertain via written, oral, and visual media. **Production and Processing:** Knowledge of raw materials, production processes, quality control, costs, and other techniques for maximizing the effective manufacture and distribution of goods. **Design:** Knowledge of design techniques, tools, and principles involved in production of precision technical plans, blueprints, drawings, and models. **Clerical Practices:** Knowledge of administrative and clerical procedures and systems such as word processing, managing files and records, stenography and transcription, designing forms, and other office procedures and terminology.

Advertising Sales Agents

◎ Education/Training Required: Moderate-term on-the-job training
◎ Annual Earnings: $40,300
◎ Growth: 13.4%
◎ Annual Job Openings: 24,000
◎ Self-Employed: 9.5%
◎ Part-Time: 11.2%

Sell or solicit advertising, including graphic art, advertising space in publications, custom-made signs, or TV and radio advertising time. May obtain leases for outdoor advertising sites or persuade retailer to use sales promotion display items. Prepare and deliver sales presentations to new and existing customers in order to sell new advertising programs and to protect and increase existing advertising. Explain to customers how specific types of advertising will help promote their products or services in the most effective way possible. Maintain assigned account bases while developing new accounts. Process all correspondence and paperwork related to accounts. Deliver advertising or illustration proofs to customers for approval. Draw up contracts for advertising work and collect payments due. Locate and contact potential clients in order to offer advertising services. Provide clients with estimates of the costs of advertising products or services. Recommend appropriate sizes and formats for advertising, depending on medium being used. Inform customers of available options for advertisement artwork and provide samples. Obtain and study information about clients' products, needs, problems, advertising history, and business practices in order to offer effective sales presentations and appropriate product assistance. Determine advertising medium to be used and prepare sample advertisements within the selected medium for presentation to customers. Consult with company officials, sales departments, and advertising agencies in order to develop promotional plans. Prepare promotional plans, sales literature, media kits, and sales contracts, using computer. Identify new advertising markets and propose products to serve them. Write copy as part of layout. Attend sales meetings, industry trade shows, and training seminars to gather information, promote products, expand network of contacts, and increase knowledge. Gather all relevant material for bid processes and coordinate bidding and contract approval. **SKILLS—Negotiation:** Bringing others together and trying to reconcile differences. **Social Perceptiveness:** Being aware of others' reactions and understanding why they react as they do. **Persuasion:** Persuading others to change their minds or behavior. **Service Orientation:** Actively looking for ways to help people. **Management of Financial Resources:** Determining how money will be spent to get the work done and accounting for these expenditures. **Speaking:** Talking to others to convey information effectively. **Instructing:** Teaching others how to do something. **Learning Strategies:** Selecting and using training/instructional methods and procedures appropriate for the situation when learning or teaching new things. **Complex Problem Solving:** Identifying complex problems and reviewing related information to develop and evaluate options and implement solutions. **GOE—Interest Area:** 06. Finance and Insurance. **Work Group:** 06.05. Finance/Insurance Sales and Support. **Other Jobs in This Work Group:** Insurance Sales Agents; Personal Financial Advisors; Sales Agents, Financial Services; Sales Agents, Securities and Commodities. **PERSONALITY TYPE:** Enterprising.

EDUCATION/TRAINING PROGRAM(S)—Advertising. RELATED KNOWLEDGE/COURSES—**Sales and Marketing:** Knowledge of principles and methods for showing, promoting, and selling products or services. This includes marketing strategy and tactics, product demonstrations, sales techniques, and sales control systems. **Customer and Personal Service:** Knowledge of principles and processes for providing customer and personal services. This includes customer needs assessment, meeting quality standards for services, and evaluation of customer satisfaction.

Economics and Accounting: Knowledge of economic and accounting principles and practices, the financial markets, banking, and the analysis and reporting of financial data. **Communications and Media:** Knowledge of media production, communication, and dissemination techniques and methods. This includes alternative ways to inform and entertain via written, oral, and visual media. **English Language:** Knowledge of the structure and content of the English language, including the meaning and spelling of words, rules of composition, and grammar. **Administration and Management:** Knowledge of business and management principles involved in strategic planning, resource allocation, human resources modeling, leadership technique, production methods, and coordination of people and resources.

Agents and Business Managers of Artists, Performers, and Athletes

◎ Education/Training Required: Work experience plus degree

◎ Annual Earnings: $55,080

◎ Growth: 27.8%

◎ Annual Job Openings: 2,000

◎ Self-Employed: 27.0%

◎ Part-Time: 15.2%

Represent and promote artists, performers, and athletes to prospective employers. May handle contract negotiation and other business matters for clients. Arrange meetings concerning issues involving their clients. Collect fees, commissions, or other payments according to contract terms. Conduct auditions or interviews in order to evaluate potential clients. Confer with clients to develop strategies for their careers and to explain actions taken on their behalf. Develop contacts with individuals and organizations and apply effective strategies and techniques to ensure their clients' success. Keep informed of industry trends and deals. Manage business and financial affairs for clients, such as arranging travel and lodging, selling tickets, and directing marketing and advertising activities. Negotiate with managers, promoters, union officials, and other persons regarding clients' contractual rights and obligations. Obtain information about and/or inspect performance facilities, equipment, and accommodations to ensure that they meet specifications. Schedule promotional or performance engagements for clients. Advise clients on financial and legal matters such as investments and taxes. Hire trainers or coaches to advise clients on performance matters such as training techniques or performance presentations. Prepare periodic accounting statements for clients. **SKILLS— Negotiation:** Bringing others together and trying to reconcile differences. **Management of Financial Resources:** Determining how money will be spent to get the work done and accounting for these expenditures. **Management of Personnel Resources:** Motivating, developing, and directing people as they work, identifying the best people for the job. **Time Management:** Managing one's own time and the time of others. **Service Orientation:** Actively looking for ways to help people. **Speaking:** Talking to others to convey information effectively. **Systems Evaluation:** Identifying measures or indicators of system performance and the actions needed to improve or correct performance relative to the goals of the system. **Coordination:** Adjusting actions in relation to others' actions. **Systems Analysis:** Determining how a system should work and how changes in conditions, operations, and the environment will affect outcomes. **GOE—Interest Area:** 03. Arts and Communication. **Work Group:** 03.01. Managerial Work in Arts and Communication. **Other Jobs in This Work Group:** Art Directors; Producers; Program Directors; Public Relations Managers; Technical Directors/Managers. **PERSONALITY TYPE:** Enterprising.

EDUCATION/TRAINING PROGRAM(S)—Arts Management; Purchasing, Procurement/Acquisitions, and Contracts Management. **RELATED KNOWLEDGE/COURSES—Economics and Accounting:** Knowledge of economic and accounting principles and practices, the financial markets, banking, and the analysis and reporting of financial data. **Sales and Marketing:** Knowledge of principles and methods for showing, promoting, and selling products or services. This includes marketing strategy and tactics, product demonstrations, sales techniques, and sales control systems. **Personnel and Human Resources:** Knowledge of principles and procedures for personnel recruitment, selection, training, compensation and benefits, labor relations and negotiation, and personnel information systems. **Administration and Management:** Knowledge of business and management principles involved in strategic planning, resource allocation, human resources modeling, leadership technique, production methods, and coordination of people and resources. **Fine Arts:** Knowledge of the theory and techniques required to compose, produce, and perform works of music, dance, the visual arts, drama, and sculpture. **Law and Government:** Knowledge of laws, legal codes, court procedures, precedents, government regulations, executive orders, agency rules, and the democratic political process.

Agricultural Crop Farm Managers

◎ Education/Training Required: Work experience in a related occupation
◎ Annual Earnings: $50,700
◎ Growth: 5.1%
◎ Annual Job Openings: 25,000
◎ Self-Employed: 0.9%
◎ Part-Time: 9.2%

Direct and coordinate, through subordinate supervisory personnel, activities of workers engaged in agricultural crop production for corporations, cooperatives, or other owners. Directs and coordinates worker activities, such as planting, irrigation, chemical application, harvesting, grading, payroll, and record-keeping. Contracts with farmers or independent owners for raising of crops or for management of crop production. Coordinates growing activities with those of engineering, equipment maintenance, packing houses, and other related departments. Analyzes market conditions to determine acreage allocations. Confers with purchasers and arranges for sale of crops. Records information such as production, farm management practices, and parent stock and prepares financial and operational reports. Determines procedural changes in drying, grading, storage, and shipment for greater efficiency and accuracy. Analyzes soil to determine type and quantity of fertilizer required for maximum production. Inspects equipment to ensure proper functioning. Inspects orchards and fields to determine maturity dates of crops or to estimate potential crop damage from weather. Plans and directs development and production of hybrid plant varieties with high yield or disease- and insect-resistant characteristics. Purchases machinery, equipment, and supplies, such as tractors, seed, fertilizer, and chemicals.

Hires, discharges, transfers, and promotes workers; enforces safety regulations; and interprets policies. Negotiates with bank officials to obtain credit from bank. Evaluates financial statements and makes budget proposals. **SKILLS—Management of Financial Resources:** Determining how money will be spent to get the work done and accounting for these expenditures. **Management of Personnel Resources:** Motivating, developing, and directing people as they work, identifying the best people for the job. **Negotiation:** Bringing others together and trying to reconcile differences. **Management of Material Resources:** Obtaining and seeing to the appropriate use of equipment, facilities, and materials needed to do certain work. **Coordination:** Adjusting actions in relation to others' actions. **Systems Analysis:** Determining how a system should work and how changes in conditions, operations, and the environment will affect outcomes. **Writing:** Communicating effectively in writing as appropriate for the needs of the audience. **Speaking:** Talking to others to convey information effectively. **Systems Evaluation:** Identifying measures or indicators of system performance and the actions needed to improve or correct performance relative to the goals of the system. **GOE—Interest Area:** 01. Agriculture and Natural Resources. **Work Group:** 01.01. Managerial Work in Agriculture and Natural Resources. **Other Jobs in This Work Group:** Farmers and Ranchers; First-Line Supervisors and Manager/Supervisors—Agricultural Crop Workers; First-Line Supervisors and Manager/Supervisors—Animal Husbandry Workers; First-Line Supervisors and Manager/Supervisors—Extractive Workers; First-Line Supervisors and Manager/Supervisors—Fishery Workers; First-Line Supervisors and Manager/Supervisors—Horticultural Workers; First-Line Supervisors and Manager/Supervisors—Landscaping Workers; First-Line Supervisors and Manager/Supervisors—Logging Workers; Fish Hatchery Managers; Lawn Service Managers; Nursery and Greenhouse Managers; Park Naturalists; Purchasing Agents and Buyers, Farm Products. **PERSONALITY TYPE:** Enterprising.

EDUCATION/TRAINING PROGRAM(S)— Agribusiness/Agricultural Business Operations; Agricultural Business and Management, General; Agricultural Business and Management, Other; Agricultural Production Operations, General; Agricultural Production Operations, Other; Agronomy and Crop Science; Crop Production; Dairy Husbandry and Production; Farm/Farm and Ranch Management; Greenhouse Operations and Management; Horticultural Science; Ornamental Horticulture; Plant Nursery Operations and Management; Plant Protection and Integrated Pest Management; Plant Sciences, General; Range Science and Management. **RELATED KNOWLEDGE/COURSES—Food Production:** Knowledge of techniques and equipment for planting, growing, and harvesting food products (both plant and animal) for consumption, including storage/handling techniques. **Economics and Accounting:** Knowledge of economic and accounting principles and practices, the financial markets, banking, and the analysis and reporting of financial data. **Administration and Management:** Knowledge of business and management principles involved in strategic planning, resource allocation, human resources modeling, leadership technique, production methods, and coordination of people and resources. **Production and Processing:** Knowledge of raw materials, production processes, quality control, costs, and other techniques for maximizing the effective manufacture and distribution of goods. **Personnel and Human Resources:** Knowledge of principles and procedures for personnel recruitment, selection, training, compensation and benefits, labor relations and negotiation, and personnel information systems. **Mathematics:** Knowledge of arithmetic, algebra, geometry, calculus, and statistics and their applications.

Agricultural Sciences Teachers, Postsecondary

- Education/Training Required: Master's degree
- Annual Earnings: $65,190
- Growth: 38.1%
- Annual Job Openings: 216,000
- Self-Employed: 0.3%
- Part-Time: 27.7%

Teach courses in the agricultural sciences. Includes teachers of agronomy, dairy sciences, fisheries management, horticultural sciences, poultry sciences, range management, and agricultural soil conservation. Prepare course materials such as syllabi, homework assignments, and handouts. Evaluate and grade students' class work, laboratory work, assignments, and papers. Keep abreast of developments in their field by reading current literature, talking with colleagues,

and participating in professional conferences. Prepare and deliver lectures to undergraduate and/or graduate students on topics such as crop production, plant genetics, and soil chemistry. Initiate, facilitate, and moderate classroom discussions. Conduct research in a particular field of knowledge and publish findings in professional journals, books, and/or electronic media. Supervise laboratory sessions and field work and coordinate laboratory operations. Supervise undergraduate and/or graduate teaching, internship, and research work. Compile, administer, and grade examinations or assign this work to others. Advise students on academic and vocational curricula and on career issues. Plan, evaluate, and revise curricula, course content, and course materials and methods of instruction. Maintain student attendance records, grades, and other required records. Write grant proposals to procure external research funding. Collaborate with colleagues to address teaching and research issues. Maintain regularly scheduled office hours in order to advise and assist students. Participate in student recruitment, registration, and placement activities. Select and obtain materials and supplies such as textbooks and laboratory equipment. Act as advisers to student organizations. Participate in campus and community events. Serve on academic or administrative committees that deal with institutional policies, departmental matters, and academic issues. Provide professional consulting services to government and/or industry. Perform administrative duties such as serving as department head. **SKILLS—Science:** Using scientific rules and methods to solve problems. **Instructing:** Teaching others how to do something. **Writing:** Communicating effectively in writing as appropriate for the needs of the audience. **Management of Financial Resources:** Determining how money will be spent to get the work done and accounting for these expenditures. **Reading Comprehension:** Understanding written sentences and paragraphs in work-related documents. **Learning Strategies:** Selecting and using training/instructional methods and procedures appropriate for the situation when learning or teaching new things. **Active Learning:** Understanding the implications of new information for both current and future problem-solving and decision-making. **Persuasion:** Persuading others to change their minds or behavior. **GOE—Interest Area:** 05. Education and Training. **Work Group:** 05.03. Postsecondary and Adult Teaching and Instructing. **Other Jobs in This Work Group:** Adult Literacy, Remedial Education, and GED Teachers and Instructors; Anthropology and Archeology Teachers, Postsecondary; Architecture Teachers, Postsecondary; Area, Ethnic, and Cultural Studies Teachers, Postsecondary; Art, Drama, and Music Teachers, Postsecondary; Atmospheric, Earth, Marine, and Space Sciences Teachers, Postsecondary; Biological Science Teachers, Postsecondary; Business Teachers, Postsecondary; Chemistry Teachers, Postsecondary; Communications Teachers, Postsecondary; Computer Science Teachers, Postsecondary; Criminal Justice and Law Enforcement Teachers, Postsecondary; Economics Teachers, Postsecondary; Education Teachers, Postsecondary; Engineering Teachers, Postsecondary; English Language and Literature Teachers, Postsecondary; Environmental Science Teachers, Postsecondary; Farm and Home Management Advisors; Foreign Language and Literature Teachers, Postsecondary; Forestry and Conservation Science Teachers, Postsecondary; Geography Teachers, Postsecondary; Graduate Teaching Assistants; Health Specialties Teachers, Postsecondary; History Teachers, Postsecondary; Home Economics Teachers, Postsecondary; Law Teachers, Postsecondary; Library Science Teachers, Postsecondary; Mathematical Science Teachers, Postsecondary; Nursing Instructors and Teachers, Postsecondary; Philosophy and Religion Teachers, Postsecondary; Physics Teachers, Postsecondary; Political Science Teachers, Postsecondary; Psychology Teachers, Postsecondary; Recreation and Fitness Studies Teachers, Postsecondary; Self-Enrichment Education Teachers; Social Work Teachers, Postsecondary; Sociology Teachers, Postsecondary; Vocational Education Teachers, Postsecondary. **PERSONALITY TYPE:** Investigative.

EDUCATION/TRAINING PROGRAM(S)— Agribusiness/Agricultural Business Operations; Agricultural and Domestic Animal Services, Other; Agricultural and Food Products Processing; Agricultural and Horticultural Plant Breeding; Agricultural Animal Breeding; Agricultural Business and Management, General; Agricultural Business and Management, Other; Agricultural Economics; Agricultural Mechanization, General; Agricultural Mechanization, Other; Agricultural Power Machinery Operation; Agricultural Production Operations, General; Agricultural Production Operations, Other; Agricultural Teacher Education; Agricultural/Farm Supplies Retailing and Wholesaling; Agriculture, Agriculture Operations, and Related Sciences, Other; Agriculture, General; Agronomy and Crop Science; Animal Health; Animal Nutrition; Animal Sciences, General; Animal Sciences, Other; Animal Training; Animal/Livestock Husbandry

and Production; Applied Horticulture/Horticultural Business Services, Other; Applied Horticulture/Horticultural Operations, General; Aquaculture; Crop Production; Dairy Science; Equestrian/Equine Studies; Farm/Farm and Ranch Management; Food Science; Greenhouse Operations and Management; Horticultural Science; International Agriculture; Landscaping and Groundskeeping; Livestock Management; Ornamental Horticulture; Plant Nursery Operations and Management; Plant Protection and Integrated Pest Management; Plant Sciences, General; Plant Sciences, Other; Poultry Science; Range Science and Management; Soil Science and Agronomy, General; Turf and Turfgrass Management. **RELATED KNOWLEDGE/COURSES—Biology:** Knowledge of plant and animal organisms and their tissues, cells, functions, interdependencies, and interactions with each other and the environment. **Education and Training:** Knowledge of principles and methods for curriculum and training design, teaching and instruction for individuals and groups, and the measurement of training effects. **Food Production:** Knowledge of techniques and equipment for planting, growing, and harvesting food products (both plant and animal) for consumption, including storage/handling techniques. **English Language:** Knowledge of the structure and content of the English language, including the meaning and spelling of words, rules of composition, and grammar. **Chemistry:** Knowledge of the chemical composition, structure, and properties of substances and of the chemical processes and transformations that they undergo. This includes uses of chemicals and their danger signs, production techniques, and disposal methods. **Geography:** Knowledge of principles and methods for describing the features of land, sea, and air masses, including their physical characteristics; locations; interrelationships; and distribution of plant, animal, and human life.

Air Traffic Controllers

- Education/Training Required: Long-term on-the-job training
- Annual Earnings: $102,030
- Growth: 12.6%
- Annual Job Openings: 2,000
- Self-Employed: 0%
- Part-Time: 3.6%

Control air traffic on and within vicinity of airport and movement of air traffic between altitude sectors and control centers according to established procedures and policies. Authorize, regulate, and control commercial airline flights according to government or company regulations to expedite and ensure flight safety. Monitor aircraft within a specific airspace, using radar, computer equipment, and visual references. Monitor and direct the movement of aircraft within an assigned airspace and on the ground at airports to minimize delays and maximize safety. Organize flight plans and traffic management plans to prepare for planes about to enter assigned airspace. Provide flight path changes or directions to emergency landing fields for pilots traveling in bad weather or in emergency situations. Compile information about flights from flight plans, pilot reports, radar, and observations. Relay to control centers such air traffic information as courses, altitudes, and expected arrival times. Transfer control of departing flights to traffic control centers and accept control of arriving flights. Complete daily activity reports and keep records of messages from aircraft. Initiate and coordinate searches for missing aircraft. Inspect, adjust, and control radio equipment and airport lights. Review records and reports for clarity and completeness and maintain records and reports as required under federal law. Alert airport emergency services in cases of emergency and when aircraft are experiencing difficulties. Analyze factors such as weather reports, fuel requirements, and maps in order to determine air routes. Check conditions and traffic at different altitudes in response to pilots' requests for altitude changes. Conduct pre-flight briefings on weather conditions, suggested routes, altitudes, indications of turbulence, and other flight safety information. Contact pilots by radio to provide meteorological, navigational, and other information. Determine the timing and procedures for flight vector changes. Direct ground traffic, including taxiing aircraft, maintenance and baggage vehicles, and airport workers. Direct pilots to runways when space is available or direct them to maintain a traffic pattern until there is space for them to land. Inform pilots about nearby planes as well as potentially hazardous conditions such as weather, speed and direction of wind, and visibility problems. Issue landing and take-off authorizations and instructions. **SKILLS—Operation and Control:** Controlling operations of equipment or systems. **Operation Monitoring:** Watching gauges, dials, or other indicators to make sure a machine is working properly. **Active Listening:** Giving full attention to what other people are saying, taking time to understand the points being made, asking questions as appropriate, and not interrupting at inappropriate times. **Coordination:** Adjusting actions in relation to others' actions. **Critical Thinking:** Using logic and reasoning to identify the strengths and weaknesses of alternative solutions, conclusions, or approaches to problems. **Systems Analysis:** Determining how a system should work and how changes in conditions, operations, and the environment will affect outcomes. **Active Learning:** Understanding the implications of new information for both current and future problem-solving and decision-making. **Troubleshooting:** Determining causes of operating errors and deciding what to do about them. **Judgment and Decision Making:** Considering the relative costs and benefits of potential actions to choose the most appropriate one. **GOE—Interest Area:** 03. Arts and Communication. **Work Group:** 03.10. Communications Technology. **Other Jobs in This Work Group:** Airfield Operations Specialists; Central Office Operators; Directory Assistance Operators; Dispatchers, Except Police, Fire, and Ambulance; Police, Fire, and Ambulance Dispatchers. **PERSONALITY TYPE:** Conventional.

EDUCATION/TRAINING PROGRAM(S)—Air Traffic Controller. **RELATED KNOWLEDGE/ COURSES—Transportation:** Knowledge of principles and methods for moving people or goods by air, rail, sea, or road, including the relative costs and benefits. **Physics:** Knowledge and prediction of physical principles and laws and their interrelationships and applications to understanding fluid, material, and atmospheric dynamics and mechanical, electrical, atomic, and subatomic structures and processes. **Telecommunications:** Knowledge of transmission, broadcasting, switching, control, and operation of telecommunications systems. **Geography:** Knowledge of principles and methods for describing the features of land, sea, and air masses, including their physical characteristics; locations; interrelationships; and distribution of plant, animal, and human life. **Computers and Electronics:** Knowledge of circuit boards, processors, chips, electronic equipment, and computer hardware and software, including applications and programming. **Engineering and Technology:** Knowledge of the practical application of engineering science and technology. This includes applying principles, techniques, procedures, and equipment to the design and production of various goods and services.

Aircraft Body and Bonded Structure Repairers

◎ Education/Training Required: Postsecondary vocational training
◎ Annual Earnings: $45,290
◎ Growth: 11.0%
◎ Annual Job Openings: 12,000
◎ Self-Employed: 1.0%
◎ Part-Time: 1.2%

Repair body or structure of aircraft according to specifications. Locates and marks dimension and reference lines on defective or replacement part, using templates, scribes, compass, and steel rule. Trims and shapes replacement section to specified size and fits and secures section in place, using adhesives, hand tools, and power tools. Cleans, strips, primes, and sands structural surfaces and materials prior to bonding. Spreads plastic film over area to be repaired to prevent damage to surrounding area. Cures bonded structure, using portable or stationary curing equipment. Reinstalls repaired or replacement parts for subsequent riveting or welding, using clamps and wrenches. Repairs or fabricates defective section or part, using metal fabricating machines, saws, brakes, shears, and grinders. Reads work orders, blueprints, and specifications or examines sample or damaged part or structure to determine repair or fabrication procedures and sequence of operations. Communicates with other workers to fit and align heavy parts or expedite processing of repair parts. Removes or cuts out defective part or drills holes to gain access to internal defect or damage, using drill and punch. **SKILLS—Installation:** Installing equipment, machines, wiring, or programs to meet specifications. **Repairing:** Repairing machines or systems by using the needed tools. **Equipment Maintenance:** Performing routine maintenance on equipment and determining when and what kind of maintenance is needed. **Equipment Selection:** Determining the kind of tools and equipment needed to do a job. **Mathematics:** Using mathematics to solve problems. **Operation Monitoring:** Watching gauges, dials, or other indicators to make sure a machine is working properly. **Operation and Control:** Controlling operations of equipment or systems. **Troubleshooting:** Determining causes of operating errors and deciding what to do about them. **GOE—Interest**

Area: 13. Manufacturing. **Work Group:** 13.14. Vehicle and Facility Mechanical Work. **Other Jobs in This Work Group:** Aircraft Engine Specialists; Aircraft Rigging Assemblers; Aircraft Structure Assemblers, Precision; Aircraft Systems Assemblers, Precision; Airframe-and-Power-Plant Mechanics; Automotive Body and Related Repairers; Automotive Glass Installers and Repairers; Automotive Master Mechanics; Automotive Specialty Technicians; Bus and Truck Mechanics and Diesel Engine Specialists; Farm Equipment Mechanics; Fiberglass Laminators and Fabricators; Mobile Heavy Equipment Mechanics, Except Engines; Motorboat Mechanics; Motorcycle Mechanics; Outdoor Power Equipment and Other Small Engine Mechanics; Rail Car Repairers; Recreational Vehicle Service Technicians; Tire Repairers and Changers. **PERSONALITY TYPE:** Realistic.

EDUCATION/TRAINING PROGRAM(S)—Agricultural Mechanics and Equipment/Machine Technology; Airframe Mechanics and Aircraft Maintenance Technology/Technician. **RELATED KNOWLEDGE/COURSES—Mechanical Devices:** Knowledge of machines and tools, including their designs, uses, repair, and maintenance. **Building and Construction:** Knowledge of the materials, methods, and tools involved in the construction or repair of houses, buildings, or other structures such as highways and roads. **Design:** Knowledge of design techniques, tools, and principles involved in production of precision technical plans, blueprints, drawings, and models. **Engineering and Technology:** Knowledge of the practical application of engineering science and technology. This includes applying principles, techniques, procedures, and equipment to the design and production of various goods and services. **Production and Processing:** Knowledge of raw materials, production processes, quality control, costs, and other techniques for maximizing the effective manufacture and distribution of goods. **Physics:** Knowledge and prediction of physical principles and laws and their interrelationships and applications to understanding fluid, material, and atmospheric dynamics and mechanical, electrical, atomic, and subatomic structures and processes.

Aircraft Engine Specialists

- Education/Training Required: Postsecondary vocational training
- Annual Earnings: $45,290
- Growth: 11.0%
- Annual Job Openings: 12,000
- Self-Employed: 1.0%
- Part-Time: 1.2%

Repair and maintain the operating condition of aircraft engines. Includes helicopter engine mechanics. Replaces or repairs worn, defective, or damaged components, using hand tools, gauges, and testing equipment. Tests engine operation, using test equipment such as ignition analyzer, compression checker, distributor timer, and ammeter, to identify malfunction. Listens to operating engine to detect and diagnose malfunctions, such as sticking or burned valves. Reassembles engine and installs engine in aircraft. Disassembles and inspects engine parts, such as turbine blades and cylinders, for wear, warping, cracks, and leaks. Removes engine from aircraft, using hoist or forklift truck. Services, repairs, and rebuilds aircraft structures, such as wings, fuselage, rigging, and surface and hydraulic controls, using hand or power tools and equipment. Adjusts, repairs, or replaces electrical wiring system and aircraft accessories. Reads and interprets manufacturers' maintenance manuals, service bulletins, and other specifications to determine feasibility and methods of repair. Services and maintains aircraft and related apparatus by performing activities such as flushing crankcase, cleaning screens, and lubricating moving parts. **SKILLS—Equipment Maintenance:** Performing routine maintenance on equipment and determining when and what kind of maintenance is needed. **Repairing:** Repairing machines or systems by using the needed tools. **Installation:** Installing equipment, machines, wiring, or programs to meet specifications. **Troubleshooting:** Determining causes of operating errors and deciding what to do about them. **Operation Monitoring:** Watching gauges, dials, or other indicators to make sure a machine is working properly. **Quality Control Analysis:** Conducting tests and inspections of products, services, or processes to evaluate quality or performance. **Judgment and Decision Making:** Considering the relative costs and benefits of potential actions to choose the most appropriate one. **Systems Analysis:** Determining how a system should work and how changes in conditions, operations, and the environment will affect outcomes. **GOE—Interest Area:** 13. Manufacturing. **Work Group:** 13.14. Vehicle and Facility Mechanical Work. **Other Jobs in This Work Group:** Aircraft Body and Bonded Structure Repairers; Aircraft Rigging Assemblers; Aircraft Structure Assemblers, Precision; Aircraft Systems Assemblers, Precision; Airframe-and-Power-Plant Mechanics; Automotive Body and Related Repairers; Automotive Glass Installers and Repairers; Automotive Master Mechanics; Automotive Specialty Technicians; Bus and Truck Mechanics and Diesel Engine Specialists; Farm Equipment Mechanics; Fiberglass Laminators and Fabricators; Mobile Heavy Equipment Mechanics, Except Engines; Motorboat Mechanics; Motorcycle Mechanics; Outdoor Power Equipment and Other Small Engine Mechanics; Rail Car Repairers; Recreational Vehicle Service Technicians; Tire Repairers and Changers. **PERSONALITY TYPE:** Realistic.

EDUCATION/TRAINING PROGRAM(S)—Agricultural Mechanics and Equipment/Machine Technology; Aircraft Powerplant Technology/Technician. **RELATED KNOWLEDGE/COURSES—Mechanical Devices:** Knowledge of machines and tools, including their designs, uses, repair, and maintenance. **Engineering and Technology:** Knowledge of the practical application of engineering science and technology. This includes applying principles, techniques, procedures, and equipment to the design and production of various goods and services. **Physics:** Knowledge and prediction of physical principles and laws and their interrelationships and applications to understanding fluid, material, and atmospheric dynamics and mechanical, electrical, atomic, and subatomic structures and processes. **Building and Construction:** Knowledge of the materials, methods, and tools involved in the construction or repair of houses, buildings, or other structures such as highways and roads. **Design:** Knowledge of design techniques, tools, and principles involved in production of precision technical plans, blueprints, drawings, and models. **Mathematics:** Knowledge of arithmetic, algebra, geometry, calculus, and statistics and their applications.

Airframe-and-Power-Plant Mechanics

- ◎ Education/Training Required: Postsecondary vocational training
- ◎ Annual Earnings: $45,290
- ◎ Growth: 11.0%
- ◎ Annual Job Openings: 12,000
- ◎ Self-Employed: 1.0%
- ◎ Part-Time: 1.2%

Inspect, test, repair, maintain, and service aircraft. Adjusts, aligns, and calibrates aircraft systems, using hand tools, gauges, and test equipment. Examines and inspects engines or other components for cracks, breaks, or leaks. Disassembles and inspects parts for wear, warping, or other defects. Assembles and installs electrical, plumbing, mechanical, hydraulic, and structural components and accessories, using hand tools and power tools. Services and maintains aircraft systems by performing tasks such as flushing crankcase, cleaning screens, greasing moving parts, and checking brakes. Repairs, replaces, and rebuilds aircraft structures, functional components, and parts, such as wings and fuselage, rigging, and hydraulic units. Tests engine and system operations, using testing equipment, and listens to engine sounds to detect and diagnose malfunctions. Removes engine from aircraft or installs engine, using hoist or forklift truck. Modifies aircraft structures, space vehicles, systems, or components, following drawings, engineering orders, and technical publications. Reads and interprets aircraft maintenance manuals and specifications to determine feasibility and method of repairing or replacing malfunctioning or damaged components. **SKILLS— Equipment Maintenance:** Performing routine maintenance on equipment and determining when and what kind of maintenance is needed. **Installation:** Installing equipment, machines, wiring, or programs to meet specifications. **Repairing:** Repairing machines or systems by using the needed tools. **Troubleshooting:** Determining causes of operating errors and deciding what to do about them. **Operation Monitoring:** Watching gauges, dials, or other indicators to make sure a machine is working properly. **Quality Control Analysis:** Conducting tests and inspections of products, services, or processes to evaluate quality or performance. **Science:** Using scientific rules and methods to solve problems. **Equipment Selection:** Determining the kind of tools and equipment needed to do a job. **GOE—Interest Area:** 13. Manufacturing. **Work Group:** 13.14. Vehicle and Facility Mechanical Work. **Other Jobs in This Work Group:** Aircraft Body and Bonded Structure Repairers; Aircraft Engine Specialists; Aircraft Rigging Assemblers; Aircraft Structure Assemblers, Precision; Aircraft Systems Assemblers, Precision; Automotive Body and Related Repairers; Automotive Glass Installers and Repairers; Automotive Master Mechanics; Automotive Specialty Technicians; Bus and Truck Mechanics and Diesel Engine Specialists; Farm Equipment Mechanics; Fiberglass Laminators and Fabricators; Mobile Heavy Equipment Mechanics, Except Engines; Motorboat Mechanics; Motorcycle Mechanics; Outdoor Power Equipment and Other Small Engine Mechanics; Rail Car Repairers; Recreational Vehicle Service Technicians; Tire Repairers and Changers. **PERSONALITY TYPE:** Realistic.

EDUCATION/TRAINING PROGRAM(S)—Agricultural Mechanics and Equipment/Machine Technology; Aircraft Powerplant Technology/Technician; Airframe Mechanics and Aircraft Maintenance Technology/Technician. **RELATED KNOWLEDGE/ COURSES—Mechanical Devices:** Knowledge of machines and tools, including their designs, uses, repair, and maintenance. **Engineering and Technology:** Knowledge of the practical application of engineering science and technology. This includes applying principles, techniques, procedures, and equipment to the design and production of various goods and services. **Building and Construction:** Knowledge of the materials, methods, and tools involved in the construction or repair of houses, buildings, or other structures such as highways and roads. **Design:** Knowledge of design techniques, tools, and principles involved in production of precision technical plans, blueprints, drawings, and models. **Physics:** Knowledge and prediction of physical principles and laws and their interrelationships and applications to understanding fluid, material, and atmospheric dynamics and mechanical, electrical, atomic, and subatomic structures and processes. **Public Safety and Security:** Knowledge of relevant equipment, policies, procedures, and strategies to promote effective local, state, or national security operations for the protection of people, data, property, and institutions.

Airline Pilots, Copilots, and Flight Engineers

- ◎ Education/Training Required: Bachelor's degree
- ◎ Annual Earnings: $129,250
- ◎ Growth: 18.5%
- ◎ Annual Job Openings: 6,000
- ◎ Self-Employed: 0%
- ◎ Part-Time: 12.9%

Pilot and navigate the flight of multi-engine aircraft in regularly scheduled service for the transport of passengers and cargo. Requires Federal Air Transport rating and certification in specific aircraft type used. Brief crews about flight details such as destinations, duties, and responsibilities. Check passenger and cargo distributions and fuel amounts to ensure that weight and balance specifications are met. Choose routes, altitudes, and speeds that will provide the fastest, safest, and smoothest flights. Confer with flight dispatchers and weather forecasters to keep abreast of flight conditions. Contact control towers for takeoff clearances, arrival instructions, and other information, using radio equipment. Coordinate flight activities with ground crews and air-traffic control and inform crew members of flight and test procedures. Direct activities of aircraft crews during flights. File instrument flight plans with air traffic control to ensure that flights are coordinated with other air traffic. Inspect aircraft for defects and malfunctions according to pre-flight checklists. Make announcements regarding flights, using public address systems. Monitor engine operation, fuel consumption, and functioning of aircraft systems during flights. Monitor gauges, warning devices, and control panels to verify aircraft performance and to regulate engine speed. Order changes in fuel supplies, loads, routes, or schedules to ensure safety of flights. Plan and formulate flight activities and test schedules and prepare flight evaluation reports. Respond to and report in-flight emergencies and malfunctions. Start engines, operate controls, and pilot airplanes to transport passengers, mail, or freight while adhering to flight plans, regulations, and procedures. Steer aircraft along planned routes with the assistance of autopilot and flight management computers. Work as part of a flight team with other crew members, especially during takeoffs and landings. Conduct in-flight tests and evaluations at specified altitudes and in all types of weather in order to determine the receptivity and other characteristics of equipment and systems. Evaluate other pilots or pilot-license applicants for proficiency. Instruct other pilots and student pilots in aircraft operations and the principles of flight. Load smaller aircraft, handling passenger luggage and supervising refueling. **SKILLS—Operation and Control:** Controlling operations of equipment or systems. **Operation Monitoring:** Watching gauges, dials, or other indicators to make sure a machine is working properly. **Instructing:** Teaching others how to do something. **Science:** Using scientific rules and methods to solve problems. **Coordination:** Adjusting actions in relation to others' actions. **Systems Analysis:** Determining how a system should work and how changes in conditions, operations, and the environment will affect outcomes. **Systems Evaluation:** Identifying measures or indicators of system performance and the actions needed to improve or correct performance relative to the goals of the system. **Judgment and Decision Making:** Considering the relative costs and benefits of potential actions to choose the most appropriate one. **GOE—Interest Area:** 16. Transportation, Distribution, and Logistics. **Work Group:** 16.02. Air Vehicle Operation. **Other Jobs in This Work Group:** Commercial Pilots. **PERSONALITY TYPE:** Realistic.

EDUCATION/TRAINING PROGRAM(S)—Airline/Commercial/Professional Pilot and Flight Crew; Flight Instructor. **RELATED KNOWLEDGE/ COURSES—Transportation:** Knowledge of principles and methods for moving people or goods by air, rail, sea, or road, including the relative costs and benefits. **Geography:** Knowledge of principles and methods for describing the features of land, sea, and air masses, including their physical characteristics; locations; interrelationships; and distribution of plant, animal, and human life. **Public Safety and Security:** Knowledge of relevant equipment, policies, procedures, and strategies to promote effective local, state, or national security operations for the protection of people, data, property, and institutions. **Mechanical Devices:** Knowledge of machines and tools, including their designs, uses, repair, and maintenance. **Education and Training:** Knowledge of principles and methods for curriculum and training design, teaching and instruction for individuals and groups, and the measurement of training effects. **Physics:** Knowledge and prediction of physical principles and laws and their interrelationships and applications to understanding fluid, material, and atmospheric dynamics and mechanical, electrical, atomic, and subatomic structures and processes.

Amusement and Recreation Attendants

- ◎ Education/Training Required: Short-term on-the-job training
- ◎ Annual Earnings: $15,550
- ◎ Growth: 27.8%
- ◎ Annual Job Openings: 66,000
- ◎ Self-Employed: 0.4%
- ◎ Part-Time: 51.9%

Perform variety of attending duties at amusement or recreation facility. May schedule use of recreation facilities, maintain and provide equipment to participants of sporting events or recreational pursuits, or operate amusement concessions and rides. Provide information about facilities, entertainment options, and rules and regulations. Record details of attendance, sales, receipts, reservations, and repair activities. Monitor activities to ensure adherence to rules and safety procedures and arrange for the removal of unruly patrons. Sell tickets and collect fees from customers. Keep informed of shut-down and emergency evacuation procedures. Clean sporting equipment, vehicles, rides, booths, facilities, and grounds. Operate machines to clean, smooth, and prepare the ice surfaces of rinks for activities such as skating, hockey, and curling. Announce and describe amusement park attractions to patrons in order to entice customers to games and other entertainment. Fasten safety devices for patrons or provide them with directions for fastening devices. Inspect equipment to detect wear and damage and perform minor repairs, adjustments, and maintenance tasks such as oiling parts. Operate, drive, or explain the use of mechanical riding devices or other automatic equipment in amusement parks, carnivals, or recreation areas. Rent, sell, or issue sporting equipment and supplies such as bowling shoes, golf balls, swimming suits, and beach chairs. Verify, collect, or punch tickets before admitting patrons to venues such as amusement parks and rides. Tend amusement booths in parks, carnivals, or stadiums, performing duties such as conducting games, photographing patrons, and awarding prizes. Direct patrons to rides, seats, or attractions. Provide assistance to patrons entering or exiting amusement rides, boats, or ski lifts or mounting or dismounting animals. Sell and serve refreshments to customers. Schedule the use of recreation facilities such as golf courses, tennis courts, bowling alleys, and softball diamonds. **SKILLS—Learning Strategies:** Selecting and using training/instructional methods and procedures appropriate for the situation when learning or teaching new things. **Social Perceptiveness:** Being aware of others' reactions and understanding why they react as they do. **Service Orientation:** Actively looking for ways to help people. **Active Listening:** Giving full attention to what other people are saying, taking time to understand the points being made, asking questions as appropriate, and not interrupting at inappropriate times. **Instructing:** Teaching others how to do something. **Reading Comprehension:** Understanding written sentences and paragraphs in work-related documents. **Speaking:** Talking to others to convey information effectively. **Critical Thinking:** Using logic and reasoning to identify the strengths and weaknesses of alternative solutions, conclusions, or approaches to problems. **GOE—Interest Area:** 09. Hospitality, Tourism, and Recreation. **Work Group:** 09.02. Recreational Services. **Other Jobs in This Work Group:** Gaming and Sports Book Writers and Runners; Gaming Dealers; Locker Room, Coatroom, and Dressing Room Attendants; Motion Picture Projectionists; Recreation Workers; Slot Key Persons; Ushers, Lobby Attendants, and Ticket Takers. **PERSONALITY TYPE:** Realistic.

EDUCATION/TRAINING PROGRAM(S)—No data available. **RELATED KNOWLEDGE/COURSES—Customer and Personal Service:** Knowledge of principles and processes for providing customer and personal services. This includes customer needs assessment, meeting quality standards for services, and evaluation of customer satisfaction. **Public Safety and Security:** Knowledge of relevant equipment, policies, procedures, and strategies to promote effective local, state, or national security operations for the protection of people, data, property, and institutions. **Medicine and Dentistry:** Knowledge of the information and techniques needed to diagnose and treat human injuries, diseases, and deformities. This includes symptoms, treatment alternatives, drug properties and interactions, and preventive health-care measures. **Sales and Marketing:** Knowledge of principles and methods for showing, promoting, and selling products or services. This includes marketing strategy and tactics, product demonstrations, sales techniques, and sales control systems. **Sociology and Anthropology:** Knowledge of group behavior and dynamics, societal trends and influences, human migrations, ethnicity, and cultures and their history and origins. **History and Archeology:** Knowledge of historical events and their causes, indicators, and effects on civilizations and cultures.

Anesthesiologists

- ◎ Education/Training Required: First professional degree
- ◎ Annual Earnings: more than $145,600
- ◎ Growth: 19.5%
- ◎ Annual Job Openings: 38,000
- ◎ Self-Employed: 16.9%
- ◎ Part-Time: 8.1%

Administer anesthetics during surgery or other medical procedures. Administer anesthetic or sedation during medical procedures, using local, intravenous, spinal, or caudal methods. Confer with other medical professionals to determine type and method of anesthetic or sedation to render patient insensible to pain. Coordinate administration of anesthetics with surgeons during operation. Decide when patients have recovered or stabilized enough to be sent to another room or ward or to be sent home following outpatient surgery. Examine patient; obtain medical history; and use diagnostic tests to determine risk during surgical, obstetrical, and other medical procedures. Monitor patient before, during, and after anesthesia and counteract adverse reactions or complications. Record type and amount of anesthesia and patient condition throughout procedure. Conduct medical research to aid in controlling and curing disease, to investigate new medications, and to develop and test new medical techniques. Coordinate and direct work of nurses, medical technicians, and other health-care providers. Diagnose illnesses, using examinations, tests, and reports. Inform students and staff of types and methods of anesthesia administration, signs of complications, and emergency methods to counteract reactions. Manage anesthesiological services, coordinating them with other medical activities and formulating plans and procedures. Order laboratory tests, X rays, and other diagnostic procedures. Position patient on operating table to maximize patient comfort and surgical accessibility. Provide and maintain life support and airway management and help prepare patients for emer-gency surgery. Provide medical care and consultation in many settings, prescribing medication and treatment and referring patients for surgery. Instruct individuals and groups on ways to preserve health and prevent disease. Schedule and maintain use of surgical suite, including operating, wash-up, and waiting rooms and anesthetic and sterilizing equipment. **SKILLS—Operation Monitoring:** Watching gauges, dials, or other indicators to make sure a machine is working properly. **Judgment and Decision Making:** Considering the relative costs and benefits of potential actions to choose the most appropriate one. **Reading Comprehension:** Understanding written sentences and paragraphs in work-related documents. **Systems Evaluation:** Identifying measures or indicators of system performance and the actions needed to improve or correct performance relative to the goals of the system. **Systems Analysis:** Determining how a system should work and how changes in conditions, operations, and the environment will affect outcomes. **Instructing:** Teaching others how to do something. **Operation and Control:** Controlling operations of equipment or systems. **Critical Thinking:** Using logic and reasoning to identify the strengths and weaknesses of alternative solutions, conclusions, or approaches to problems. **Coordination:** Adjusting actions in relation to others' actions. **GOE—Interest Area:** 08. Health Science. **Work Group:** 08.02. Medicine and Surgery. **Other Jobs in This Work Group:** Family and General Practitioners; Internists, General; Medical Assistants; Medical Transcriptionists; Obstetricians and Gynecologists; Pediatricians, General; Pharmacists; Pharmacy Aides; Pharmacy Technicians; Physician Assistants; Psychiatrists; Registered Nurses; Surgeons; Surgical Technologists. **PERSONALITY TYPE:** Investigative.

EDUCATION/TRAINING PROGRAM(S)—Anesthesiology; Critical Care Anesthesiology. **RELATED KNOWLEDGE/COURSES—Medicine and Dentistry:** Knowledge of the information and techniques needed to diagnose and treat human injuries, diseases, and deformities. This includes symptoms, treatment alternatives, drug properties and interactions, and preventive health-care measures. **Biology:** Knowledge of plant and animal organisms and their tissues, cells, functions, interdependencies, and interactions with each other and the environment. **Chemistry:** Knowledge of the chemical composition, structure, and properties of substances and of the chemical processes and transformations that they undergo. This includes uses of chemicals and their danger signs, production techniques, and disposal methods. **English Language:** Knowledge of the structure and content of the English language, including the meaning and spelling of words, rules of composition, and grammar. **Physics:** Knowledge and prediction of physical principles and laws and their interrelationships and applications to understanding fluid, material, and atmospheric dynamics and mechanical, electrical, atomic, and subatomic structures and processes. **Mathematics:** Knowledge of arithmetic, algebra, geometry, calculus, and statistics and their applications.

Anthropology and Archeology Teachers, Postsecondary

- Education/Training Required: Master's degree
- Annual Earnings: $60,860
- Growth: 38.1%
- Annual Job Openings: 216,000
- Self-Employed: 0.3%
- Part-Time: 27.7%

Teach courses in anthropology or archeology. Conduct research in a particular field of knowledge and publish findings in professional journals, books, and/or electronic media. Keep abreast of developments in their field by reading current literature, talking with colleagues, and participating in professional conferences. Prepare and deliver lectures to undergraduate and/or graduate students on topics such as research methods, urban anthropology, and language and culture. Evaluate and grade students' class work, assignments, and papers. Initiate, facilitate, and moderate classroom discussions. Write grant proposals to procure external research funding. Supervise undergraduate and/or graduate teaching, internship, and research work. Prepare course materials such as syllabi, homework assignments, and handouts. Compile, administer, and grade examinations or assign this work to others. Supervise students' laboratory or field work. Plan, evaluate, and revise curricula, course content, and course materials and methods of instruction. Advise students on academic and vocational curricula, career issues, and laboratory and field research. Maintain student attendance records, grades, and other required records. Maintain regularly scheduled office

hours in order to advise and assist students. Collaborate with colleagues to address teaching and research issues. Compile bibliographies of specialized materials for outside reading assignments. Perform administrative duties such as serving as department head. Select and obtain materials and supplies such as textbooks and laboratory equipment. Serve on academic or administrative committees that deal with institutional policies, departmental matters, and academic issues. Participate in student recruitment, registration, and placement activities. **SKILLS—Instructing:** Teaching others how to do something. **Writing:** Communicating effectively in writing as appropriate for the needs of the audience. **Critical Thinking:** Using logic and reasoning to identify the strengths and weaknesses of alternative solutions, conclusions, or approaches to problems. **Active Learning:** Understanding the implications of new information for both current and future problem-solving and decision-making. **Reading Comprehension:** Understanding written sentences and paragraphs in work-related documents. **Science:** Using scientific rules and methods to solve problems. **Learning Strategies:** Selecting and using training/instructional methods and procedures appropriate for the situation when learning or teaching new things. **Active Listening:** Giving full attention to what other people are saying, taking time to understand the points being made, asking questions as appropriate, and not interrupting at inappropriate times. **Social Perceptiveness:** Being aware of others' reactions and understanding why they react as they do. **GOE—Interest Area:** 05. Education and Training. **Work Group:** 05.03. Postsecondary and Adult Teaching and Instructing. **Other Jobs in This Work Group:** Adult Literacy, Remedial Education, and GED Teachers and Instructors; Agricultural Sciences Teachers, Postsecondary; Architecture Teachers, Postsecondary; Area, Ethnic, and Cultural Studies Teachers, Postsecondary; Art, Drama, and Music Teachers, Postsecondary; Atmospheric, Earth, Marine, and Space Sciences Teachers, Postsecondary; Biological Science Teachers, Postsecondary; Business Teachers, Postsecondary; Chemistry Teachers, Postsecondary; Communications Teachers, Postsecondary; Computer Science Teachers, Postsecondary; Criminal Justice and Law Enforcement Teachers, Postsecondary; Economics Teachers, Postsecondary; Education Teachers, Postsecondary; Engineering Teachers, Postsecondary; English Language and Literature Teachers, Postsecondary; Environmental Science Teachers, Postsecondary; Farm and Home Management Advisors;

Foreign Language and Literature Teachers, Postsecondary; Forestry and Conservation Science Teachers, Postsecondary; Geography Teachers, Postsecondary; Graduate Teaching Assistants; Health Specialties Teachers, Postsecondary; History Teachers, Postsecondary; Home Economics Teachers, Postsecondary; Law Teachers, Postsecondary; Library Science Teachers, Postsecondary; Mathematical Science Teachers, Postsecondary; Nursing Instructors and Teachers, Postsecondary; Philosophy and Religion Teachers, Postsecondary; Physics Teachers, Postsecondary; Political Science Teachers, Postsecondary; Psychology Teachers, Postsecondary; Recreation and Fitness Studies Teachers, Postsecondary; Self-Enrichment Education Teachers; Social Work Teachers, Postsecondary; Sociology Teachers, Postsecondary; Vocational Education Teachers, Postsecondary. **PERSONALITY TYPE:** Social.

EDUCATION/TRAINING PROGRAM(S)— Anthropology; Archeology; Physical Anthropology; Social Science Teacher Education. **RELATED KNOWLEDGE/COURSES—Sociology and Anthropology:** Knowledge of group behavior and dynamics, societal trends and influences, human migrations, ethnicity, and cultures and their history and origins. **History and Archeology:** Knowledge of historical events and their causes, indicators, and effects on civilizations and cultures. **Geography:** Knowledge of principles and methods for describing the features of land, sea, and air masses, including their physical characteristics; locations; interrelationships; and distribution of plant, animal, and human life. **Foreign Language:** Knowledge of the structure and content of a foreign (non-English) language, including the meaning and spelling of words, rules of composition and grammar, and pronunciation. **Philosophy and Theology:** Knowledge of different philosophical systems and religions. This includes their basic principles, values, ethics, ways of thinking, customs, and practices and their impact on human culture. **Education and Training:** Knowledge of principles and methods for curriculum and training design, teaching and instruction for individuals and groups, and the measurement of training effects.

Appraisers, Real Estate

- ◎ Education/Training Required: Postsecondary vocational training
- ◎ Annual Earnings: $43,390
- ◎ Growth: 17.6%
- ◎ Annual Job Openings: 11,000
- ◎ Self-Employed: 34.8%
- ◎ Part-Time: 8.9%

Appraise real property to determine its value for purchase, sales, investment, mortgage, or loan purposes. Compute final estimation of property values, taking into account such factors as depreciation, replacement costs, value comparisons of similar properties, and income potential. Draw land diagrams that will be used in appraisal reports to support findings. Estimate building replacement costs, using building valuation manuals and professional cost estimators. Evaluate land and neighborhoods where properties are situated, considering locations and trends or impending changes that could influence future values. Examine the type and location of nearby services such as shopping centers, schools, parks, and other neighborhood features in order to evaluate their impact on property values. Inspect properties to evaluate construction, condition, special features, and functional design and to take property measurements. Obtain county land values and sales information about nearby properties in order to aid in establishment of property values. Photograph interiors and exteriors of properties in order to assist in estimating property value, substantiate findings, and complete appraisal reports. Prepare written reports that estimate property values, outline methods by which the estimations were made, and meet appraisal standards. Search public records for transactions such as sales, leases, and assessments. Verify legal descriptions of properties by comparing them to county records. Check building codes and zoning bylaws in order to determine any effects on the properties being appraised. Examine income records and operating costs of income properties. Interview persons familiar with properties and immediate surroundings, such as contractors, homeowners, and real estate agents, in order to obtain pertinent information. Testify in court as to the value of a piece of real estate property. **SKILLS—Writing:** Communicating effectively in writing as appropriate for the needs of the audience. **Mathematics:** Using mathematics to solve problems. **Management of Personnel Resources:** Motivating, developing, and directing people as they work, identifying the best people for the job. **Systems Analysis:** Determining how a system should work and how changes in conditions, operations, and the environment will affect outcomes. **Speaking:** Talking to others to convey information effectively. **Reading Comprehension:** Understanding written sentences and paragraphs in work-related documents. **Time Management:** Managing one's own time and the time of others. **Active Listening:** Giving full attention to what other people are saying, taking time to understand the points being made, asking questions as appropriate, and not interrupting at inappropriate times. **Management of Financial Resources:** Determining how money will be spent to get the work done and accounting for these expenditures. **GOE—Interest Area:** 06. Finance and Insurance. **Work Group:** 06.02. Finance/Insurance Investigation and Analysis. **Other Jobs in This Work Group:** Assessors; Claims Examiners, Property and Casualty Insurance; Cost Estimators; Credit Analysts; Financial Analysts; Insurance Adjusters, Examiners, and Investigators; Insurance Appraisers, Auto Damage; Insurance Underwriters; Loan Counselors; Loan Officers; Market Research Analysts; Survey Researchers. **PERSONALITY TYPE:** Enterprising.

EDUCATION/TRAINING PROGRAM(S)—Real Estate. **RELATED KNOWLEDGE/COURSES**— **Building and Construction:** Knowledge of the materials, methods, and tools involved in the construction or repair of houses, buildings, or other structures such as highways and roads. **Personnel and Human Resources:** Knowledge of principles and procedures for personnel recruitment, selection, training, compensation and benefits, labor relations and negotiation, and personnel information systems. **Economics and Accounting:** Knowledge of economic and accounting principles and practices, the financial markets, banking, and the analysis and reporting of financial data. **Law and Government:** Knowledge of laws, legal codes, court procedures, precedents, government regulations, executive orders, agency rules, and the democratic political process. **Geography:** Knowledge of principles and methods for describing the features of land, sea, and air masses, including their physical characteristics; locations; interrelationships; and distribution of plant, animal, and human life. **Administration and Management:** Knowledge of business and management principles involved in strategic planning, resource allocation, human resources modeling, leadership technique, production methods, and coordination of people and resources. **Communications and Media:** Knowledge of media production, communication, and dissemination techniques and methods. This includes alternative ways to inform and entertain via written, oral, and visual media.

Arbitrators, Mediators, and Conciliators

- ◉ Education/Training Required: Work experience plus degree
- ◉ Annual Earnings: $54,760
- ◉ Growth: 13.7%
- ◉ Annual Job Openings: Fewer than 500
- ◉ Self-Employed: 11.2%
- ◉ Part-Time: 6.2%

Facilitate negotiation and conflict resolution through dialogue. Resolve conflicts outside of the court system by mutual consent of parties involved. Review and evaluate information from documents such as claim applications, birth or death certificates, and physician or employer records. Set up appointments for parties to meet for mediation. Use mediation techniques to facilitate communication between disputants, to further parties' understanding of different perspectives, and to guide parties toward mutual agreement. Authorize payment of valid claims. Determine existence and amount of liability according to evidence, laws, and administrative and judicial precedents. Issue subpoenas and administer oaths to prepare for formal hearings. Notify claimants of denied claims and appeal rights. Analyze evidence and apply relevant laws, regulations, policies, and precedents in order to reach conclusions. Arrange and conduct hearings to obtain information and evidence relative to disposition of claims. Conduct initial meetings with disputants to outline the arbitration process, settle procedural matters such as fees, and determine details such as witness numbers and time requirements. Confer with disputants to clarify issues, identify underlying concerns, and develop an understanding of their respective needs and interests. Interview claimants, agents, or witnesses to obtain information about disputed issues. Participate in court proceedings. Prepare settlement agreements for disputants to sign. Recommend acceptance or rejection of compromise settlement offers. Research laws, regulations, policies, and precedent decisions to prepare for hearings. Prepare written opinions and decisions regarding cases. Rule on exceptions, motions, and admissibility of evidence. Conduct studies of appeals procedures in order to ensure adherence to legal requirements and to facilitate disposition of cases. Organize and deliver public presentations about mediation to organizations such as community agencies and schools. **SKILLS—Judgment and Decision Making:** Considering the relative costs and benefits of potential actions to choose the most appropriate one. **Active Listening:** Giving full attention to what other people are saying, taking time to understand the points being made, asking questions as appropriate, and not interrupting at inappropriate times. **Critical Thinking:** Using logic and reasoning to identify the strengths and weaknesses of alternative solutions, conclusions, or approaches to problems. **Writing:** Communicating effectively in writing as appropriate for the needs of the audience. **Reading Comprehension:** Understanding written sentences and paragraphs in work-related documents. **Speaking:** Talking to others to convey information effectively. **Active Learning:** Understanding the implications of new information for both current and future problem-solving and decision-making. **Negotiation:** Bringing others together and trying to reconcile differences. **GOE—Interest Area:** 12. Law and Public Safety. **Work Group:** 12.02. Legal Practice and Justice Administration. **Other Jobs in This Work Group:** Administrative Law Judges, Adjudicators, and Hearing Officers; Judges, Magistrate Judges, and Magistrates; Lawyers. **PERSONALITY TYPE:** Enterprising.

EDUCATION/TRAINING PROGRAM(S)—Law (LL.B., J.D.); Legal Professions and Studies, Other. **RELATED KNOWLEDGE/COURSES—Law and Government:** Knowledge of laws, legal codes, court procedures, precedents, government regulations, executive orders, agency rules, and the democratic political process. **Therapy and Counseling:** Knowledge of principles, methods, and procedures for diagnosis, treatment, and rehabilitation of physical and mental dysfunctions and for career counseling and guidance. **Psychology:** Knowledge of human behavior and performance; individual differences in ability, personality, and interests; learning and motivation; psychological research methods; and the assessment and treatment of behavioral and affective disorders. **Administration and Management:** Knowledge of business and management principles involved in strategic planning, resource allocation, human resources modeling, leadership technique, production methods, and coordination of people and resources. **English Language:** Knowledge of the structure and content of the English language, including the meaning and spelling of words, rules of composition, and grammar. **Sociology and Anthropology:** Knowledge of group behavior and dynamics, societal trends and influences, human migrations, ethnicity, and cultures and their history and origins.

Architects, Except Landscape and Naval

- Education/Training Required: Bachelor's degree
- Annual Earnings: $60,300
- Growth: 17.3%
- Annual Job Openings: 8,000
- Self-Employed: 21.4%
- Part-Time: 5.5%

Plan and design structures such as private residences, office buildings, theaters, factories, and other structural property. Prepare information regarding design, structure specifications, materials, color, equipment, estimated costs, and construction time. Consult with client to determine functional and spatial requirements of structure. Direct activities of workers engaged in preparing drawings and specification documents. Plan layout of project. Prepare contract documents for building contractors. Prepare scale drawings. Integrate engineering element into unified design. Conduct periodic on-site observation of work during construction to monitor compliance with plans. Administer construction contracts. Represent client in obtaining bids and awarding construction contracts. **SKILLS— Operations Analysis:** Analyzing needs and product requirements to create a design. **Management of Financial Resources:** Determining how money will be spent to get the work done and accounting for these expenditures. **Coordination:** Adjusting actions in relation to others' actions. **Management of Personnel Resources:** Motivating, developing, and directing people as they work, identifying the best people for the job. **Complex Problem Solving:** Identifying complex problems and reviewing related information to develop and evaluate options and implement solutions. **Negotiation:** Bringing others together and trying to reconcile differences. **Persuasion:** Persuading others to change their minds or behavior. **Active Listening:** Giving full attention to what other people are saying, taking time to understand the points being made, asking questions as appropriate, and not interrupting at inappropriate times. **GOE—Interest Area:** 02. Architecture and Construction. **Work Group:** 02.02. Architectural Design. **Other Jobs in This Work Group:** Landscape Architects. **PERSONALITY TYPE:** Artistic.

EDUCATION/TRAINING   PROGRAM(S)— Architectural History and Criticism, General; Architecture (BArch, BA/BS, MArch, MA/MS, PhD); Architecture and Related Services, Other; Environmental Design/Architecture. **RELATED KNOWLEDGE/COURSES—Building and Construction:** Knowledge of the materials, methods, and tools involved in the construction or repair of houses, buildings, or other structures such as highways and roads. **Design:** Knowledge of design techniques, tools, and principles involved in production of precision technical plans, blueprints, drawings, and models. **Engineering and Technology:** Knowledge of the practical application of engineering science and technology. This includes applying principles, techniques, procedures, and equipment to the design and production of various goods and services. **Law and Government:** Knowledge of laws, legal codes, court procedures, precedents, government regulations, executive orders, agency rules, and the democratic political process. **Public Safety and Security:** Knowledge of relevant equipment, policies, procedures, and strategies to promote effective local, state, or national security operations for the protection of people, data, property, and institutions. **Physics:** Knowledge and prediction of physical principles and laws and their interrelationships and applications to understanding fluid, material, and atmospheric dynamics and mechanical, electrical, atomic, and subatomic structures and processes.

Architectural Drafters

- Education/Training Required: Associate degree
- Annual Earnings: $39,190
- Growth: 4.2%
- Annual Job Openings: 14,000
- Self-Employed: 3.7%
- Part-Time: 5.1%

Prepare detailed drawings of architectural designs and plans for buildings and structures according to specifications provided by architect. Analyze building codes, bylaws, space and site requirements, and other technical documents and reports to determine their effect on architectural designs. Operate computer-aided drafting equipment or conventional drafting station to produce designs, working drawings, charts, forms, and records. Coordinate structural, electrical, and mechanical designs and determine a method of presentation in order to graphically represent building plans. Obtain and assemble data to complete architectural designs, visiting job sites to compile measurements as necessary. Draw rough and detailed scale plans for foundations, buildings, and structures based on preliminary concepts, sketches, engineering calculations, specification sheets, and other data. Lay out and plan interior room arrangements for commercial buildings, using computer-assisted drafting (CAD) equipment and software. Supervise, coordinate, and inspect the work of draftspersons, technicians, and technologists on construction projects. Represent architect on construction site, ensuring builder compliance with design specifications and advising on design corrections under architect's supervision. Check dimensions of materials to be used and assign numbers to lists of materials. Determine procedures and instructions to be followed according to design specifications and quantity of required materials. Analyze technical implications of architect's design concept, calculating weights, volumes, and stress factors. Create freehand drawings and lettering to accompany drawings. Prepare colored drawings of landscape and interior designs for presentation to client. Reproduce drawings on copy machines or trace copies of plans and drawings, using transparent paper or cloth, ink, pencil, and standard drafting instruments. Prepare cost estimates, contracts, bidding documents, and technical reports for specific projects under an architect's supervision. Calculate heat loss and gain of buildings and structures to determine required equipment specifications, following standard procedures. **SKILLS—Coordination:** Adjusting actions in relation to others' actions. **Operations Analysis:** Analyzing needs and product requirements to create a design. **Active Learning:** Understanding the implications of new information for both current and future problem-solving and decision-making. **Technology Design:** Generating or adapting equipment and technology to serve user needs. **Persuasion:** Persuading others to change their minds or behavior. **Complex Problem Solving:** Identifying complex problems and reviewing related information to develop and evaluate options and implement solutions. **Mathematics:** Using mathematics to solve problems. **Critical Thinking:** Using logic and reasoning to identify the strengths and weaknesses of alternative solutions, conclusions, or approaches to problems. **Service Orientation:** Actively looking for ways to help people. **GOE—Interest Area:** 02. Architecture and Construction. **Work Group:** 02.03. Architecture/Construction Engineering Technologies. **Other Jobs in This Work Group:** Civil Drafters; Construction and Building Inspectors; Electrical Drafters; Surveyors. **PERSONALITY TYPE:** Realistic.

EDUCATION/TRAINING PROGRAM(S)— Architectural Drafting and Architectural CAD/CADD; Architectural Technology/Technician; CAD/CADD Drafting and/or Design Technology/Technician; Civil Drafting and Civil Engineering CAD/CADD; Drafting and Design Technology/Technician, General. **RELATED KNOWLEDGE/ COURSES—Design:** Knowledge of design techniques, tools, and principles involved in production of precision technical plans, blueprints, drawings, and models. **Building and Construction:** Knowledge of the materials, methods, and tools involved in the construction or repair of houses, buildings, or other structures such as highways and roads. **Computers and Electronics:** Knowledge of circuit boards, processors, chips, electronic equipment, and computer hardware and software, including applications and programming. **Engineering and Technology:** Knowledge of the practical application of engineering science and technology. This includes applying principles, techniques, procedures, and equipment to the design and production of various goods and services. **Mathematics:** Knowledge of arithmetic, algebra, geometry, calculus, and statistics and their applications. **Public Safety and Security:** Knowledge of relevant equipment, policies, procedures, and strategies to promote effective

local, state, or national security operations for the protection of people, data, property, and institutions.

Architecture Teachers, Postsecondary

- ◎ Education/Training Required: Master's degree
- ◎ Annual Earnings: $59,990
- ◎ Growth: 38.1%
- ◎ Annual Job Openings: 216,000
- ◎ Self-Employed: 0.3%
- ◎ Part-Time: 27.7%

Teach courses in architecture and architectural design, such as architectural environmental design, interior architecture/design, and landscape architecture. Evaluate and grade students' work, including work performed in design studios. Prepare and deliver lectures to undergraduate and/or graduate students on topics such as architectural design methods, aesthetics and design, and structures and materials. Prepare course materials such as syllabi, homework assignments, and handouts. Initiate, facilitate, and moderate classroom discussions. Plan, evaluate, and revise curricula, course content, and course materials and methods of instruction. Keep abreast of developments in their field by reading current literature, talking with colleagues, and participating in professional conferences. Maintain student attendance records, grades, and other required records. Maintain regularly scheduled office hours in order to advise and assist students. Compile, administer, and grade examinations or assign this work to others. Conduct research in a particular field of knowledge and publish findings in professional journals, books, and/or electronic media. Supervise undergraduate and/or graduate teaching, internship, and research work. Advise students on academic and vocational curricula and on career issues. Collaborate with colleagues to address teaching and research issues. Compile bibliographies of specialized materials for outside reading assignments. Serve on academic or administrative committees that deal with institutional policies, departmental matters, and academic issues. Participate in student recruitment, registration, and placement activities. Select and obtain materials and supplies such as textbooks and laboratory equipment. Write grant proposals to procure external research funding. Provide professional consulting services to government and/or industry. Perform administrative duties such as serving as department head. **SKILLS—Instructing:** Teaching others how to do something. **Technology Design:** Generating or adapting equipment and technology to serve user needs. **Learning Strategies:** Selecting and using training/instructional methods and procedures appropriate for the situation when learning or teaching new things. **Writing:** Communicating effectively in writing as appropriate for the needs of the audience. **Active Learning:** Understanding the implications of new information for both current and future problem-solving and decision-making. **Critical Thinking:** Using logic and reasoning to identify the strengths and weaknesses of alternative solutions, conclusions, or approaches to problems. **Operations Analysis:** Analyzing needs and product requirements to create a design. **Coordination:** Adjusting actions in relation to others' actions. **Persuasion:** Persuading others to change their minds or behavior. **GOE—Interest Area:** 05. Education and Training. **Work Group:** 05.03. Postsecondary and Adult Teaching and Instructing. **Other Jobs in This Work Group:** Adult Literacy, Remedial Education, and GED Teachers and Instructors; Agricultural Sciences Teachers, Postsecondary; Anthropology and Archeology Teachers, Postsecondary; Area, Ethnic, and Cultural Studies Teachers, Postsecondary; Art, Drama, and Music Teachers, Postsecondary; Atmospheric, Earth, Marine, and Space Sciences Teachers, Postsecondary; Biological Science Teachers, Postsecondary; Business Teachers, Postsecondary; Chemistry Teachers, Postsecondary; Communications Teachers, Postsecondary; Computer Science Teachers, Postsecondary; Criminal Justice and Law Enforcement Teachers, Postsecondary; Economics Teachers, Postsecondary; Education Teachers, Postsecondary; Engineering Teachers, Postsecondary; English Language and Literature Teachers, Postsecondary; Environmental Science Teachers, Postsecondary; Farm and Home Management Advisors; Foreign Language and Literature Teachers, Postsecondary; Forestry and Conservation Science Teachers, Postsecondary; Geography Teachers, Postsecondary; Graduate Teaching Assistants; Health Specialties Teachers, Postsecondary; History Teachers, Postsecondary; Home Economics Teachers, Postsecondary; Law Teachers, Postsecondary; Library Science Teachers, Postsecondary; Mathematical Science Teachers, Postsecondary; Nursing Instructors and Teachers, Postsecondary; Philosophy and Religion Teachers, Postsecondary; Physics Teachers, Postsecondary; Political Science Teachers, Postsec-

ondary; Psychology Teachers, Postsecondary; Recreation and Fitness Studies Teachers, Postsecondary; Self-Enrichment Education Teachers; Social Work Teachers, Postsecondary; Sociology Teachers, Postsecondary; Vocational Education Teachers, Postsecondary. **PERSONALITY TYPE:** No data available.

EDUCATION/TRAINING PROGRAM(S)— Architectural Engineering; Architecture (BArch, BA/BS, MArch, MA/MS, PhD); City/Urban, Community, and Regional Planning; Environmental Design/Architecture; Interior Architecture; Landscape Architecture (BS, BSLA, BLA, MSLA, MLA, PhD); Teacher Education and Professional Development, Specific Subject Areas, Other. **RELATED KNOWLEDGE/COURSES—Design:** Knowledge of design techniques, tools, and principles involved in production of precision technical plans, blueprints, drawings, and models. **Fine Arts:** Knowledge of the theory and techniques required to compose, produce, and perform works of music, dance, the visual arts, drama, and sculpture. **Building and Construction:** Knowledge of the materials, methods, and tools involved in the construction or repair of houses, buildings, or other structures such as highways and roads. **History and Archeology:** Knowledge of historical events and their causes, indicators, and effects on civilizations and cultures. **Education and Training:** Knowledge of principles and methods for curriculum and training design, teaching and instruction for individuals and groups, and the measurement of training effects. **Philosophy and Theology:** Knowledge of different philosophical systems and religions. This includes their basic principles, values, ethics, ways of thinking, customs, and practices and their impact on human culture.

Archivists

- Education/Training Required: Master's degree
- Annual Earnings: $36,470
- Growth: 17.0%
- Annual Job Openings: 2,000
- Self-Employed: 3.4%
- Part-Time: 11.8%

Appraise, edit, and direct safekeeping of permanent records and historically valuable documents. Participate in research activities based on archival materials. Authenticate and appraise historical documents and

archival materials. Create and maintain accessible, retrievable computer archives and databases, incorporating current advances in electric information storage technology. Direct activities of workers who assist in arranging, cataloguing, exhibiting, and maintaining collections of valuable materials. Locate new materials and direct their acquisition and display. Organize archival records and develop classification systems to facilitate access to archival materials. Prepare archival records, such as document descriptions, to allow easy access to information. Preserve records, documents, and objects, copying records to film, videotape, audiotape, disk, or computer formats as necessary. Research and record the origins and historical significance of archival materials. Select and edit documents for publication and display, applying knowledge of subject, literary expression, and presentation techniques. Coordinate educational and public outreach programs, such as tours, workshops, lectures, and classes. Establish and administer policy guidelines concerning public access and use of materials. Provide reference services and assistance for users needing archival materials. Specialize in an area of history or technology, researching topics or items relevant to collections to determine what should be retained or acquired. **SKILLS—Management of Personnel Resources:** Motivating, developing, and directing people as they work, identifying the best people for the job. **Writing:** Communicating effectively in writing as appropriate for the needs of the audience. **Management of Material Resources:** Obtaining and seeing to the appropriate use of equipment, facilities, and materials needed to do certain work. **Systems Evaluation:** Identifying measures or indicators of system performance and the actions needed to improve or correct performance relative to the goals of the system. **Judgment and Decision Making:** Considering the relative costs and benefits of potential actions to choose the most appropriate one. **Reading Comprehension:** Understanding written sentences and paragraphs in work-related documents. **Operations Analysis:** Analyzing needs and product requirements to create a design. **Speaking:** Talking to others to convey information effectively. **Systems Analysis:** Determining how a system should work and how changes in conditions, operations, and the environment will affect outcomes. **GOE—Interest Area:** 05. Education and Training. **Work Group:** 05.05. Archival and Museum Services. **Other Jobs in This Work Group:** Audio-Visual Collections Specialists; Curators; Museum Technicians and Conservators. **PERSONALITY TYPE:** Investigative.

EDUCATION/TRAINING PROGRAM(S)—Art History, Criticism, and Conservation; Cultural Resource Management and Policy Analysis; Historic Preservation and Conservation; Historic Preservation and Conservation, Other; Museology/Museum Studies; Public/Applied History and Archival Administration. **RELATED KNOWLEDGE/COURSES—History and Archeology:** Knowledge of historical events and their causes, indicators, and effects on civilizations and cultures. **Communications and Media:** Knowledge of media production, communication, and dissemination techniques and methods. This includes alternative ways to inform and entertain via written, oral, and visual media. **Sociology and Anthropology:** Knowledge of group behavior and dynamics, societal trends and influences, human migrations, ethnicity, and cultures and their history and origins. **Administration and Management:** Knowledge of business and management principles involved in strategic planning, resource allocation, human resources modeling, leadership technique, production methods, and coordination of people and resources. **Clerical Practices:** Knowledge of administrative and clerical procedures and systems such as word processing, managing files and records, stenography and transcription, designing forms, and other office procedures and terminology. **English Language:** Knowledge of the structure and content of the English language, including the meaning and spelling of words, rules of composition, and grammar.

Area, Ethnic, and Cultural Studies Teachers, Postsecondary

- ◉ Education/Training Required: Master's degree
- ◉ Annual Earnings: $56,200
- ◉ Growth: 38.1%
- ◉ Annual Job Openings: 216,000
- ◉ Self-Employed: 0.3%
- ◉ Part-Time: 27.7%

Teach courses pertaining to the culture and development of an area (e.g., Latin America), an ethnic group, or any other group (e.g., women's studies, urban affairs). Keep abreast of developments in their field by reading current literature, talking with colleagues, and participating in professional conferences. Conduct research in a particular field of knowledge and publish findings in professional journals, books, and/or electronic media. Evaluate and grade students' class work, assignments, and papers. Prepare course materials such as syllabi, homework assignments, and handouts. Prepare and deliver lectures to undergraduate and/or graduate students on topics such as race and ethnic relations, gender studies, and cross-cultural perspectives. Initiate, facilitate, and moderate classroom discussions. Compile, administer, and grade examinations or assign this work to others. Maintain regularly scheduled office hours in order to advise and assist students. Plan, evaluate, and revise curricula, course content, and course materials and methods of instruction. Maintain student attendance records, grades, and other required records. Advise students on academic and vocational curricula and on career issues. Supervise undergraduate and/or graduate teaching, internship, and research work. Collaborate with colleagues to address teaching and research issues. Select and obtain materials and supplies such as textbooks. Serve on academic or administrative committees that deal with institutional policies, departmental matters, and academic issues. Compile bibliographies of specialized materials for outside reading assignments. Write grant proposals to procure external research funding. Participate in campus and community events. Participate in student recruitment, registration, and placement activities. Act as advisers to student organizations. Incorporate experiential/site visit components into courses. Perform administrative duties such as serving as department head. **SKILLS—Writing:** Communicating effectively in writing as appropriate for the needs of the audience. **Instructing:** Teaching others how to do something. **Critical Thinking:** Using logic and reasoning to identify the strengths and weaknesses of alternative solutions, conclusions, or approaches to problems. **Persuasion:** Persuading others to change their minds or behavior. **Learning Strategies:** Selecting and using training/instructional methods and procedures appropriate for the situation when learning or teaching new things. **Active Learning:** Understanding the implications of new information for both current and future problem-solving and decision-making. **Social Perceptiveness:** Being aware of others' reactions and understanding why they react as they do. **Speaking:** Talking to others to convey information effectively. **GOE— Interest Area:** 05. Education and Training. **Work Group:** 05.03. Postsecondary and Adult Teaching and Instructing. **Other Jobs in This Work Group:** Adult Literacy, Remedial Education, and GED Teachers and Instructors; Agricultural Sciences Teachers, Postsecondary; Anthropology and Archeology Teachers, Postsecondary; Architecture Teachers, Postsecondary; Art, Drama, and Music Teachers, Postsecondary; Atmospheric, Earth, Marine, and Space Sciences Teachers, Postsecondary; Biological Science Teachers, Postsecondary; Business Teachers, Postsecondary; Chemistry Teachers, Postsecondary; Communications Teachers, Postsecondary; Computer Science Teachers, Postsecondary; Criminal Justice and Law Enforcement Teachers, Postsecondary; Economics Teachers, Postsecondary; Education Teachers, Postsecondary; Engineering Teachers, Postsecondary; English Language and Literature Teachers, Postsecondary; Environmental Science Teachers, Postsecondary; Farm and Home Management Advisors; Foreign Language and Literature Teachers, Postsecondary; Forestry and Conservation Science Teachers, Postsecondary; Geography Teachers, Postsecondary; Graduate Teaching Assistants; Health Specialties Teachers, Postsecondary; History Teachers, Postsecondary; Home Economics Teachers, Postsecondary; Law Teachers, Postsecondary; Library Science Teachers, Postsecondary; Mathematical Science Teachers, Postsecondary; Nursing Instructors and Teachers, Postsecondary; Philosophy and Religion Teachers, Postsecondary; Physics Teachers, Postsecondary; Political Science Teachers, Postsecondary; Psychology Teachers, Postsecondary; Recreation and Fitness Studies Teachers, Postsecondary; Self-Enrichment Education Teachers; Social Work Teachers, Postsecondary; Sociology Teachers, Postsecondary; Vocational Education Teachers, Postsecondary. **PERSONALITY TYPE:** Social.

EDUCATION/TRAINING PROGRAM(S)— African Studies; African-American/Black Studies; American Indian/Native American Studies; American/United States Studies/Civilization; Area Studies, Other; Area, Ethnic, Cultural, and Gender Studies, Other; Asian Studies/Civilization; Asian-American Studies; Balkans Studies; Baltic Studies; Canadian Studies; Caribbean Studies; Central/Middle and Eastern European Studies; Chinese Studies; Commonwealth Studies; East Asian Studies; Ethnic, Cultural Minority, and Gender Studies, Other; European Studies/Civilization; French Studies; Gay/Lesbian Studies; German Studies; Hispanic-American, Puerto Rican, and Mexican-American/Chicano Studies; Intercultural/Multicultural and Diversity Studies; Islamic Studies;

Italian Studies; Japanese Studies; Jewish/Judaic Studies; Korean Studies; Latin American Studies; Near and Middle Eastern Studies; Pacific Area/Pacific Rim Studies; Polish Studies; Regional Studies (U.S., Canadian, Foreign); Religion/Religious Studies, Other; Russian Studies; Scandinavian Studies; Slavic Studies; Social Studies Teacher Education; South Asian Studies; Southeast Asian Studies; Spanish and Iberian Studies; Tibetan Studies; Ukraine Studies; Ural-Altaic and Central Asian Studies; Western European Studies; Women's Studies. **RELATED KNOWLEDGE/ COURSES—Sociology and Anthropology:** Knowledge of group behavior and dynamics, societal trends and influences, human migrations, ethnicity, and cultures and their history and origins. **History and Archeology:** Knowledge of historical events and their causes, indicators, and effects on civilizations and cultures. **Foreign Language:** Knowledge of the structure and content of a foreign (non-English) language, including the meaning and spelling of words, rules of composition and grammar, and pronunciation. **Philosophy and Theology:** Knowledge of different philosophical systems and religions. This includes their basic principles, values, ethics, ways of thinking, customs, and practices and their impact on human culture. **Education and Training:** Knowledge of principles and methods for curriculum and training design, teaching and instruction for individuals and groups, and the measurement of training effects. **Geography:** Knowledge of principles and methods for describing the features of land, sea, and air masses, including their physical characteristics; locations; interrelationships; and distribution of plant, animal, and human life.

Art Directors

- ◎ Education/Training Required: Work experience plus degree
- ◎ Annual Earnings: $63,840
- ◎ Growth: 11.4%
- ◎ Annual Job Openings: 8,000
- ◎ Self-Employed: 53.6%
- ◎ Part-Time: 23.1%

Formulate design concepts and presentation approaches and direct workers engaged in art work, layout design, and copy writing for visual communications media, such as magazines, books, newspapers, **and packaging.** Formulate basic layout design or presentation approach and specify material details, such as style and size of type, photographs, graphics, animation, video, and sound. Review and approve proofs of printed copy and art and copy materials developed by staff members. Manage own accounts and projects, working within budget and scheduling requirements. Confer with creative, art, copy-writing, or production department heads to discuss client requirements and presentation concepts and to coordinate creative activities. Present final layouts to clients for approval. Confer with clients to determine objectives; budget; background information; and presentation approaches, styles, and techniques. Hire, train, and direct staff members who develop design concepts into art layouts or who prepare layouts for printing. Work with creative directors to develop design solutions. Review illustrative material to determine if it conforms to standards and specifications. Attend photo shoots and printing sessions to ensure that the products needed are obtained. Create custom illustrations or other graphic elements. Mark up, paste, and complete layouts and write typography instructions to prepare materials for typesetting or printing. Negotiate with printers and estimators to determine what services will be performed. Conceptualize and help design interfaces for multimedia games, products, and devices. **SKILLS—Coordination:** Adjusting actions in relation to others' actions. **Negotiation:** Bringing others together and trying to reconcile differences. **Persuasion:** Persuading others to change their minds or behavior. **Service Orientation:** Actively looking for ways to help people. **Management of Financial Resources:** Determining how money will be spent to get the work done and accounting for these expenditures. **Instructing:** Teaching others how to do something. **Operations Analysis:** Analyzing needs and product requirements to create a design. **Time Management:** Managing one's own time and the time of others. **GOE—Interest Area:** 03. Arts and Communication. **Work Group:** 03.01. Managerial Work in Arts and Communication. **Other Jobs in This Work Group:** Agents and Business Managers of Artists, Performers, and Athletes; Producers; Program Directors; Public Relations Managers; Technical Directors/Managers. **PERSONALITY TYPE:** Artistic.

EDUCATION/TRAINING PROGRAM(S)— Graphic Design; Intermedia/Multimedia. **RELATED KNOWLEDGE/COURSES—Design:** Knowledge of design techniques, tools, and principles involved in production of precision technical plans, blueprints, drawings, and models. **Fine Arts:** Knowledge of the theory and techniques required to compose, produce, and perform works of music, dance, the visual arts, drama, and sculpture. **Computers and Electronics:** Knowledge of circuit boards, processors, chips, electronic equipment, and computer hardware and software, including applications and programming. **Communications and Media:** Knowledge of media production, communication, and dissemination techniques and methods. This includes alternative ways to inform and entertain via written, oral, and visual media. **Production and Processing:** Knowledge of raw materials, production processes, quality control, costs, and other techniques for maximizing the effective manufacture and distribution of goods. **Customer and Personal Service:** Knowledge of principles and processes for providing customer and personal services. This includes customer needs assessment, meeting quality standards for services, and evaluation of customer satisfaction. **Education and Training:** Knowledge of principles and methods for curriculum and training design, teaching and instruction for individuals and groups, and the measurement of training effects.

Art, Drama, and Music Teachers, Postsecondary

◉ Education/Training Required: Master's degree
◉ Annual Earnings: $48,780
◉ Growth: 38.1%
◉ Annual Job Openings: 216,000
◉ Self-Employed: 0.3%
◉ Part-Time: 27.7%

Teach courses in drama, music, and the arts, including fine and applied art, such as painting and sculpture or design and crafts. Evaluate and grade students' class work, performances, projects, assignments, and papers. Explain and demonstrate artistic techniques. Prepare students for performances, exams, or assessments. Prepare and deliver lectures to undergraduate and/or graduate students on topics such as acting techniques, fundamentals of music, and art history. Organize performance groups and direct their rehearsals. Prepare course materials such as syllabi, homework assignments, and handouts. Initiate, facilitate, and

moderate classroom discussions. Keep abreast of developments in their field by reading current literature, talking with colleagues, and participating in professional conferences. Advise students on academic and vocational curricula and on career issues. Maintain student attendance records, grades, and other required records. Conduct research in a particular field of knowledge and publish findings in professional journals, books, and/or electronic media. Supervise undergraduate and/or graduate teaching, internship, and research work. Plan, evaluate, and revise curricula, course content, and course materials and methods of instruction. Maintain regularly scheduled office hours in order to advise and assist students. Compile, administer, and grade examinations or assign this work to others. Participate in student recruitment, registration, and placement activities. Select and obtain materials and supplies such as textbooks and performance pieces. Collaborate with colleagues to address teaching and research issues. Serve on academic or administrative committees that deal with institutional policies, departmental matters, and academic issues. Participate in campus and community events. Keep students informed of community events such as plays and concerts. Compile bibliographies of specialized materials for outside reading assignments. Display students' work in schools, galleries, and exhibitions. Perform administrative duties such as serving as department head. **SKILLS—Instructing:** Teaching others how to do something. **Social Perceptiveness:** Being aware of others' reactions and understanding why they react as they do. **Learning Strategies:** Selecting and using training/instructional methods and procedures appropriate for the situation when learning or teaching new things. **Persuasion:** Persuading others to change their minds or behavior. **Speaking:** Talking to others to convey information effectively. **Active Listening:** Giving full attention to what other people are saying, taking time to understand the points being made, asking questions as appropriate, and not interrupting at inappropriate times. **Critical Thinking:** Using logic and reasoning to identify the strengths and weaknesses of alternative solutions, conclusions, or approaches to problems. **Active Learning:** Understanding the implications of new information for both current and future problem-solving and decision-making. **GOE—Interest Area:** 05. Education and Training. **Work Group:** 05.03. Postsecondary and Adult Teaching and Instructing. **Other Jobs in This Work Group:** Adult Literacy, Remedial Education, and GED Teachers and

Instructors; Agricultural Sciences Teachers, Postsecondary; Anthropology and Archeology Teachers, Postsecondary; Architecture Teachers, Postsecondary; Area, Ethnic, and Cultural Studies Teachers, Postsecondary; Atmospheric, Earth, Marine, and Space Sciences Teachers, Postsecondary; Biological Science Teachers, Postsecondary; Business Teachers, Postsecondary; Chemistry Teachers, Postsecondary; Communications Teachers, Postsecondary; Computer Science Teachers, Postsecondary; Criminal Justice and Law Enforcement Teachers, Postsecondary; Economics Teachers, Postsecondary; Education Teachers, Postsecondary; Engineering Teachers, Postsecondary; English Language and Literature Teachers, Postsecondary; Environmental Science Teachers, Postsecondary; Farm and Home Management Advisors; Foreign Language and Literature Teachers, Postsecondary; Forestry and Conservation Science Teachers, Postsecondary; Geography Teachers, Postsecondary; Graduate Teaching Assistants; Health Specialties Teachers, Postsecondary; History Teachers, Postsecondary; Home Economics Teachers, Postsecondary; Law Teachers, Postsecondary; Library Science Teachers, Postsecondary; Mathematical Science Teachers, Postsecondary; Nursing Instructors and Teachers, Postsecondary; Philosophy and Religion Teachers, Postsecondary; Physics Teachers, Postsecondary; Political Science Teachers, Postsecondary; Psychology Teachers, Postsecondary; Recreation and Fitness Studies Teachers, Postsecondary; Self-Enrichment Education Teachers; Social Work Teachers, Postsecondary; Sociology Teachers, Postsecondary; Vocational Education Teachers, Postsecondary. **PERSONALITY TYPE:** Artistic.

EDUCATION/TRAINING PROGRAM(S)—Art History, Criticism, and Conservation; Art/Art Studies, General; Arts Management; Ceramic Arts and Ceramics; Cinematography and Film/Video Production; Commercial Photography; Conducting; Crafts/Craft Design, Folk Art, and Artisanry; Dance, General; Design and Applied Arts, Other; Design and Visual Communications, General; Directing and Theatrical Production; Drama and Dramatics/Theatre Arts, General; Dramatic/Theatre Arts and Stagecraft, Other; Fashion/Apparel Design; Fiber, Textile, and Weaving Arts; Film/Cinema Studies; Film/Video and Photographic Arts, Other; Fine Arts and Art Studies, Other; Fine/Studio Arts, General; Graphic Design; Industrial Design; Interior Design; Intermedia/Multimedia; Jazz/Jazz Studies; Metal and Jewelry Arts; Music History, Literature, and Theory; Music Management and Merchandising; Music Pedagogy; Music Performance, General; Music Theory and Composition; Music, Other; Musicology and Ethnomusicology; Painting; Photography; Piano and Organ; Playwriting and Screenwriting; Printmaking; Sculpture; Technical Theatre/Theatre Design and Technology; Theatre Literature, History, and Criticism; Theatre/Theatre Arts Management; Violin, Viola, Guitar, and Other Stringed Instruments; Visual and Performing Arts, General; Visual and Performing Arts, Other; Voice and Opera. **RELATED KNOWLEDGE/COURSES—Fine Arts:** Knowledge of the theory and techniques required to compose, produce, and perform works of music, dance, the visual arts, drama, and sculpture. **Education and Training:** Knowledge of principles and methods for curriculum and training design, teaching and instruction for individuals and groups, and the measurement of training effects. **History and Archeology:** Knowledge of historical events and their causes, indicators, and effects on civilizations and cultures. **Philosophy and Theology:** Knowledge of different philosophical systems and religions. This includes their basic principles, values, ethics, ways of thinking, customs, and practices and their impact on human culture. **English Language:** Knowledge of the structure and content of the English language, including the meaning and spelling of words, rules of composition, and grammar. **Communications and Media:** Knowledge of media production, communication, and dissemination techniques and methods. This includes alternative ways to inform and entertain via written, oral, and visual media.

Assessors

◎ Education/Training Required: Postsecondary vocational training
◎ Annual Earnings: $43,390
◎ Growth: 17.6%
◎ Annual Job Openings: 11,000
◎ Self-Employed: 34.8%
◎ Part-Time: 8.9%

Appraise real and personal property to determine its fair value. May assess taxes in accordance with prescribed schedules. Determine taxability and value of properties, using methods such as field inspection, structural measurement, calculation, sales analysis, market trend studies, and income and expense analysis. Inspect new construction and major improvements to existing structures in order to determine values. Explain assessed values to property owners and defend appealed assessments at public hearings. Inspect properties, considering factors such as market value, location, and building or replacement costs to determine appraisal value. Prepare and maintain current data on each parcel assessed, including maps of boundaries, inventories of land and structures, property characteristics, and any applicable exemptions. Identify the ownership of each piece of taxable property. Conduct regular reviews of property within jurisdictions in order to determine changes in property due to construction or demolition. Complete and maintain assessment rolls that show the assessed values and status of all property in a municipality. Issue notices of assessments and taxes. Review information about transfers of property to ensure its accuracy, checking basic information on buyers, sellers, and sales prices and making corrections as necessary. Maintain familiarity with aspects of local real estate markets. Analyze trends in sales prices, construction costs, and rents in order to assess property values and/or determine the accuracy of assessments. Approve applications for property tax exemptions or deductions. Establish uniform and equitable systems for assessing all classes and kinds of property. Write and submit appraisal and tax reports for public record. Serve on assessment review boards. Hire staff members. Provide sales analyses to be used for equalization of school aid. Calculate tax bills for properties by multiplying assessed values by jurisdiction tax rates. **SKILLS—Social Perceptiveness:** Being aware of others' reactions and understanding why they react as they do. **Mathematics:** Using mathematics to solve problems. **Negotiation:** Bringing others together and trying to reconcile differences. **Persuasion:** Persuading others to change their minds or behavior. **Active Listening:** Giving full attention to what other people are saying, taking time to understand the points being made, asking questions as appropriate, and not interrupting at inappropriate times. **Speaking:** Talking to others to convey information effectively. **Service Orientation:** Actively looking for ways to help people. **Instructing:** Teaching others how to do something. **Systems Analysis:** Determining how a system should work and how changes in conditions, operations, and the environment will affect outcomes. **GOE—Interest Area:** 06. Finance and Insurance. **Work Group:** 06.02. Finance/Insurance Investigation and Analysis. **Other Jobs in This Work**

Group: Appraisers, Real Estate; Claims Examiners, Property and Casualty Insurance; Cost Estimators; Credit Analysts; Financial Analysts; Insurance Adjusters, Examiners, and Investigators; Insurance Appraisers, Auto Damage; Insurance Underwriters; Loan Counselors; Loan Officers; Market Research Analysts; Survey Researchers. **PERSONALITY TYPE:** Conventional.

EDUCATION/TRAINING PROGRAM(S)—Real Estate. **RELATED KNOWLEDGE/COURSES—Customer and Personal Service:** Knowledge of principles and processes for providing customer and personal services. This includes customer needs assessment, meeting quality standards for services, and evaluation of customer satisfaction. **Building and Construction:** Knowledge of the materials, methods, and tools involved in the construction or repair of houses, buildings, or other structures such as highways and roads. **Clerical Practices:** Knowledge of administrative and clerical procedures and systems such as word processing, managing files and records, stenography and transcription, designing forms, and other office procedures and terminology. **Law and Government:** Knowledge of laws, legal codes, court procedures, precedents, government regulations, executive orders, agency rules, and the democratic political process. **Mathematics:** Knowledge of arithmetic, algebra, geometry, calculus, and statistics and their applications. **Computers and Electronics:** Knowledge of circuit boards, processors, chips, electronic equipment, and computer hardware and software, including applications and programming.

Athletes and Sports Competitors

- Education/Training Required: Long-term on-the-job training
- Annual Earnings: $48,310
- Growth: 19.2%
- Annual Job Openings: 3,000
- Self-Employed: 31.5%
- Part-Time: 36.3%

Compete in athletic events. Assess performance following athletic competition, identifying strengths and weaknesses and making adjustments to improve future performance. Attend scheduled practice and training sessions. Exercise and practice under the direction of athletic trainers or professional coaches in order to develop skills, improve physical condition, and prepare for competitions. Maintain optimum physical fitness levels by training regularly, following nutrition plans, and consulting with health professionals. Participate in athletic events and competitive sports according to established rules and regulations. Receive instructions from coaches and other sports staff prior to events and discuss their performance afterwards. Lead teams by serving as captains. Maintain equipment used in a particular sport. Represent teams or professional sports clubs, performing such activities as meeting with members of the media, making speeches, or participating in charity events. **SKILLS—Monitoring:** Monitoring or assessing your performance or that of other individuals or organizations to make improvements or take corrective action. **Coordination:** Adjusting actions in relation to others' actions. **Social Perceptiveness:** Being aware of others' reactions and understanding why they react as they do. **GOE—Interest Area:** 09. Hospitality, Tourism, and Recreation. **Work Group:** 09.06. Sports. **Other Jobs in This Work Group:** Coaches and Scouts; Umpires, Referees, and Other Sports Officials. **PERSONALITY TYPE:** Enterprising.

EDUCATION/TRAINING PROGRAM(S)— Health and Physical Education, General. **RELATED KNOWLEDGE/COURSES—Biology:** Knowledge of plant and animal organisms and their tissues, cells, functions, interdependencies, and interactions with each other and the environment. **Medicine and Dentistry:** Knowledge of the information and techniques needed to diagnose and treat human injuries, diseases, and deformities. This includes symptoms, treatment alternatives, drug properties and interactions, and preventive health-care measures. **Communications and Media:** Knowledge of media production, communication, and dissemination techniques and methods. This includes alternative ways to inform and entertain via written, oral, and visual media.

Athletic Trainers

- ◎ Education/Training Required: Bachelor's degree
- ◎ Annual Earnings: $33,940
- ◎ Growth: 29.9%
- ◎ Annual Job Openings: 2,000
- ◎ Self-Employed: 0.1%
- ◎ Part-Time: 6.5%

Evaluate, advise, and treat athletes to assist recovery from injury, avoid injury, or maintain peak physical fitness. Conduct an initial assessment of an athlete's injury or illness in order to provide emergency or continued care and to determine whether they should be referred to physicians for definitive diagnosis and treatment. Care for athletic injuries, using physical therapy equipment, techniques, and medication. Evaluate athletes' readiness to play and provide participation clearances when necessary and warranted. Apply protective or injury-preventive devices such as tape, bandages, or braces to body parts such as ankles, fingers, or wrists. Assess and report the progress of recovering athletes to coaches and physicians. Collaborate with physicians in order to develop and implement comprehensive rehabilitation programs for athletic injuries. Advise athletes on the proper use of equipment. Plan and implement comprehensive athletic injury and illness prevention programs. Develop training programs and routines designed to improve athletic performance. Travel with athletic teams in order to be available at sporting events. Instruct coaches, athletes, parents, medical personnel, and community members in the care and prevention of athletic injuries. Inspect playing fields in order to locate any items that could injure players. Conduct research and provide instruction on subject matter related to athletic training or sports medicine. Recommend special diets in order to improve athletes' health, increase their stamina, and/or alter their weight. Massage body parts in order to relieve soreness, strains, and bruises. Confer with coaches in order to select protective equipment. Accompany injured athletes to hospitals. Perform team-support duties such as running errands, maintaining equipment, and stocking supplies. Lead stretching exercises for team members prior to games and practices. **SKILLS—Social Perceptiveness:** Being aware of others' reactions and understanding why they react as they do. **Time Management:** Managing one's own time and the time of others. **Service Orientation:** Actively looking for ways to help people. **Management of Material Resources:** Obtaining and seeing to the appropriate use of equipment, facilities, and materials needed to do certain work. **Management of Personnel Resources:** Motivating, developing, and directing people as they work, identifying the best people for the job. **Instructing:** Teaching others how to do something. **Coordination:** Adjusting actions in relation to others' actions. **Management of Financial Resources:** Determining how money will be spent to get the work done and accounting for these expenditures. **GOE—Interest Area:** 08. Health Science. **Work Group:** 08.09. Health Protection and Promotion. **Other Jobs in This Work Group:** Dietetic Technicians; Dietitians and Nutritionists; Embalmers. **PERSONALITY TYPE:** Social.

EDUCATION/TRAINING PROGRAM(S)—Athletic Training/Trainer. **RELATED KNOWLEDGE/ COURSES—Therapy and Counseling:** Knowledge of principles, methods, and procedures for diagnosis, treatment, and rehabilitation of physical and mental dysfunctions and for career counseling and guidance. **Medicine and Dentistry:** Knowledge of the information and techniques needed to diagnose and treat human injuries, diseases, and deformities. This includes symptoms, treatment alternatives, drug properties and interactions, and preventive health-care measures. **Psychology:** Knowledge of human behavior and performance; individual differences in ability, personality, and interests; learning and motivation; psychological research methods; and the assessment and treatment of behavioral and affective disorders. **Customer and Personal Service:** Knowledge of principles and processes for providing customer and personal services. This includes customer needs assessment, meeting quality standards for services, and evaluation of customer satisfaction. **Biology:** Knowledge of plant and animal organisms and their tissues, cells, functions, interdependencies, and interactions with each other and the environment. **Education and Training:** Knowledge of principles and methods for curriculum and training design, teaching and instruction for individuals and groups, and the measurement of training effects.

Atmospheric and Space Scientists

- Education/Training Required: Bachelor's degree
- Annual Earnings: $70,100
- Growth: 16.2%
- Annual Job Openings: 1,000
- Self-Employed: 2.1%
- Part-Time: 4.3%

Investigate atmospheric phenomena and interpret meteorological data gathered by surface and air stations, satellites, and radar to prepare reports and forecasts for public and other uses. Collect and analyze historical climate information such as precipitation and temperature records in order to help predict future weather and climate trends. Conduct basic or applied meteorological research into the processes and determinants of atmospheric phenomena, weather, and climate. Conduct numerical simulations of climate conditions in order to understand and predict global and regional weather patterns. Gather data from sources such as surface and upper air stations, satellites, weather bureaus, and radar for use in meteorological reports and forecasts. Operate computer graphic equipment to produce weather reports and maps for analysis, distribution, or use in weather broadcasts. Prepare forecasts and briefings to meet the needs of industry, business, government, and other groups. Study and interpret data, reports, maps, photographs, and charts to predict long- and short-range weather conditions, using computer models and knowledge of climate theory, physics, and mathematics. Apply meteorological knowledge to problems in areas including agriculture, pollution control, and water management and to issues such as global warming or ozone depletion. Broadcast weather conditions, forecasts, and severe weather warnings to the public via television, radio, and the Internet and/or provide this information to the news media. Collect air samples from planes and ships over land and sea to study atmospheric composition. Consult with agencies, professionals, or researchers regarding the use and interpretation of climatological information. Design and develop new equipment and methods for meteorological data collection, remote sensing, or related applications. Develop and use weather forecasting tools such as mathematical and computer models. Measure wind, temperature, and humidity in the upper atmosphere, using weather balloons. Research and analyze the impact of industrial projects and pollution on climate, air quality, and weather phenomena. Direct forecasting services at weather stations or at radio or television broadcasting facilities. Make scientific presentations and publish reports, articles, or texts. **SKILLS—Science:** Using scientific rules and methods to solve problems. **Management of Personnel Resources:** Motivating, developing, and directing people as they work, identifying the best people for the job. **Active Learning:** Understanding the implications of new information for both current and future problem-solving and decision-making. **Speaking:** Talking to others to convey information effectively. **Systems Analysis:** Determining how a system should work and how changes in conditions, operations, and the environment will affect outcomes. **Critical Thinking:** Using logic and reasoning to identify the strengths and weaknesses of alternative solutions, conclusions, or approaches to problems. **Judgment and Decision Making:** Considering the relative costs and benefits of potential actions to choose the most appropriate one. **Complex Problem Solving:** Identifying complex problems and reviewing related information to develop and evaluate options and implement solutions. **GOE— Interest Area:** 15. Scientific Research, Engineering, and Mathematics. **Work Group:** 15.02. Physical Sciences. **Other Jobs in This Work Group:** Astronomers; Chemists; Geographers; Geologists; Hydrologists; Materials Scientists; Physicists. **PERSONALITY TYPE:** Investigative.

EDUCATION/TRAINING PROGRAM(S)— Atmospheric Chemistry and Climatology; Atmospheric Physics and Dynamics; Atmospheric Sciences and Meteorology, General; Atmospheric Sciences and Meteorology, Other; Meteorology. **RELATED KNOWLEDGE/COURSES—Physics:** Knowledge and prediction of physical principles and laws and their interrelationships and applications to understanding fluid, material, and atmospheric dynamics and mechanical, electrical, atomic, and subatomic structures and processes. **Geography:** Knowledge of principles and methods for describing the features of land, sea, and air masses, including their physical characteristics; locations; interrelationships; and distribution of plant, animal, and human life. **Communications and Media:** Knowledge of media production, communication, and dissemination techniques and methods. This includes alternative ways to inform and entertain via written, oral, and visual media. **Telecommunications:** Knowledge of transmission, broadcasting, switching, control, and operation of telecommunications systems. **Administration and Management:** Knowledge of business and management principles involved in strategic planning, resource allocation, human resources modeling, leadership technique, production methods, and coordination of people and resources. **Mathematics:** Knowledge of arithmetic, algebra, geometry, calculus, and statistics and their applications.

Atmospheric, Earth, Marine, and Space Sciences Teachers, Postsecondary

- Education/Training Required: Master's degree
- Annual Earnings: $65,350
- Growth: 38.1%
- Annual Job Openings: 216,000
- Self-Employed: 0.3%
- Part-Time: 27.7%

Teach courses in the physical sciences, except chemistry and physics. Conduct research in a particular field of knowledge and publish findings in professional journals, books, and/or electronic media. Write grant proposals to procure external research funding. Keep abreast of developments in their field by reading current literature, talking with colleagues, and participating in professional conferences. Supervise undergraduate and/or graduate teaching, internship, and research work. Prepare and deliver lectures to undergraduate and/or graduate students on topics such as structural geology, micrometeorology, and atmospheric thermodynamics. Supervise laboratory work and field work. Evaluate and grade students' class work, assignments, and papers. Prepare course materials such as syllabi, homework assignments, and handouts. Collaborate with colleagues to address teaching and research issues. Compile, administer, and grade examinations or assign this work to others. Plan, evaluate, and revise curricula, course content, and course materials and methods of instruction. Initiate, facilitate, and moderate classroom discussions. Maintain regularly scheduled office hours in order to advise and assist students. Advise students on academic and vocational curricula and on career issues. Maintain student attendance records, grades, and other required records. Participate in student recruitment, registration, and placement activities. Perform administrative duties such as serving as department head. Select and obtain materials and supplies such as textbooks and laboratory equipment. Serve on academic or administrative committees that deal with institutional policies, departmental matters, and academic issues. Compile bibliographies of specialized materials for outside reading assignments. **SKILLS—Science:** Using scientific rules and methods to solve problems. **Instructing:** Teaching others how to do something. **Programming:** Writing computer programs for various purposes. **Active Learning:** Understanding the implications of new information for both current and future problem-solving and decision-making. **Management of Financial Resources:** Determining how money will be spent to get the work done and accounting for these expenditures. **Complex Problem Solving:** Identifying complex problems and reviewing related information to develop and evaluate options and implement solutions. **Mathematics:** Using mathematics to solve problems. **Writing:** Communicating effectively in writing as appropriate for the needs of the audience. **GOE—Interest Area:** 05. Education and Training. **Work Group:** 05.03. Postsecondary and Adult Teaching and Instructing. **Other Jobs in This Work Group:** Adult Literacy, Remedial Education, and GED Teachers and Instructors; Agricultural Sciences Teachers, Postsecondary; Anthropology and Archeology Teachers, Postsecondary; Architecture Teachers, Postsecondary; Area, Ethnic, and Cultural Studies Teachers, Postsecondary; Art, Drama, and Music Teachers, Postsecondary; Biological Science Teachers, Postsecondary; Business Teachers, Postsecondary; Chemistry Teachers, Postsecondary; Communications Teachers, Postsecondary; Computer Science Teachers, Postsecondary; Criminal Justice and Law Enforcement Teachers, Postsecondary; Economics Teachers, Postsecondary; Education Teachers, Postsecondary; Engineering Teachers, Postsecondary; English Language and Literature Teachers, Postsecondary; Environmental Science Teachers, Postsecondary; Farm and Home Management Advisors; Foreign Language and Literature Teachers, Postsecondary; Forestry and Conservation Science Teachers, Postsecondary; Geography Teachers, Postsecondary; Graduate Teaching Assistants; Health Specialties Teachers, Postsecondary; History Teachers, Postsecondary; Home Economics Teachers, Postsecondary; Law Teachers, Postsecondary; Library Science Teachers, Postsecondary; Mathematical Science Teachers, Postsecondary; Nursing Instructors and Teachers, Postsecondary; Philosophy and Religion Teachers, Postsecondary; Physics Teachers, Postsecondary; Political Science Teachers, Postsecondary; Psychology Teachers, Postsecondary; Recreation and Fitness Studies Teachers, Postsecondary; Self-Enrichment Education Teachers; Social Work Teachers, Postsecondary; Sociology Teachers, Postsecondary; Vocational Education Teachers, Postsecondary. **PERSONALITY TYPE:** No data available.

EDUCATION/TRAINING PROGRAM(S)— Acoustics; Astronomy; Astrophysics; Atmospheric Chemistry and Climatology; Atmospheric Physics and Dynamics; Atmospheric Sciences and Meteorology, General; Atmospheric Sciences and Meteorology, Other; Atomic/Molecular Physics; Elementary Particle Physics; Geochemistry; Geochemistry and Petrology; Geological and Earth Sciences/Geosciences, Other; Geology/Earth Science, General; Geophysics and Seismology; Hydrology and Water Resources Science; Meteorology; Nuclear Physics; Oceanography, Chemical and Physical; Optics/Optical Sciences; Paleontology; Physics Teacher Education; Physics, Other; Planetary Astronomy and Science; Plasma and High-Temperature Physics; Science Teacher Education/General Science Teacher Education; Solid State and Low-Temperature Physics; Theoretical and Mathematical Physics. **RELATED KNOWLEDGE/COURSES—Physics:** Knowledge and prediction of physical principles and laws and their interrelationships and applications to understanding fluid, material, and atmospheric dynamics and mechanical, electrical, atomic, and subatomic structures and processes. **Geography:** Knowledge of principles and methods for describing the features of land, sea, and air masses, including their physical characteristics; locations; interrelationships; and distribution of plant, animal, and human life. **Education and Training:** Knowledge of principles and methods for curriculum and training design, teaching and instruction for individuals and groups, and the measurement of training effects. **Mathematics:** Knowledge of arithmetic, algebra, geometry, calculus, and statistics and their applications. **Chemistry:** Knowledge of the chemical composition, structure, and properties of substances and of the chemical processes and transformations that they undergo. This includes uses of chemicals and their danger signs, production techniques, and disposal methods. **English Language:** Knowledge of the structure and content of the English language, including the meaning and spelling of words, rules of composition, and grammar.

Audio and Video Equipment Technicians

- Education/Training Required: Long-term on-the-job training
- Annual Earnings: $32,570
- Growth: 26.7%
- Annual Job Openings: 5,000
- Self-Employed: 9.1%
- Part-Time: 12.5%

Set up or set up and operate audio and video equipment, including microphones, sound speakers, video screens, projectors, video monitors, recording equipment, connecting wires and cables, sound and mixing boards, and related electronic equipment, for concerts, sports events, meetings and conventions, presentations, and news conferences. May also set up and operate associated spotlights and other custom lighting systems. Notify supervisors when major equipment repairs are needed. Monitor incoming and outgoing pictures and sound feeds to ensure quality and notify directors of any possible problems. Mix and regulate sound inputs and feeds or coordinate audio feeds with television pictures. Install, adjust, and operate electronic equipment used to record, edit, and transmit radio and television programs, cable programs, and motion pictures. Design layouts of audio and video equipment and perform upgrades and maintenance. Perform minor repairs and routine cleaning of audio and video equipment. Diagnose and resolve media system problems in classrooms. Switch sources of video input from one camera or studio to another, from film to live programming, or from network to local programming. Meet with directors and senior members of camera crews to discuss assignments and determine filming sequences, camera movements, and picture composition. Construct and position properties, sets, lighting equipment, and other equipment. Compress, digitize, duplicate, and store audio and video data. Obtain, set up, and load videotapes for

scheduled productions or broadcasts. Edit videotapes by erasing and removing portions of programs and adding video and/or sound as required. Direct and coordinate activities of assistants and other personnel during production. Plan and develop pre-production ideas into outlines, scripts, storyboards, and graphics, using own ideas or specifications of assignments. Maintain inventories of audiotapes, videotapes, and related supplies. Determine formats, approaches, content, levels, and mediums to effectively meet objectives within budgetary constraints, utilizing research, knowledge, and training. Record and edit audio material such as movie soundtracks, using audio recording and editing equipment. Inform users of audiotaping and videotaping service policies and procedures. Obtain and preview musical performance programs prior to events in order to become familiar with the order and approximate times of pieces. Produce rough and finished graphics and graphic designs. Locate and secure settings, properties, effects, and other production necessities. **SKILLS—Troubleshooting:** Determining causes of operating errors and deciding what to do about them. **Installation:** Installing equipment, machines, wiring, or programs to meet specifications. **Equipment Maintenance:** Performing routine maintenance on equipment and determining when and what kind of maintenance is needed. **Operation and Control:** Controlling operations of equipment or systems. **Operation Monitoring:** Watching gauges, dials, or other indicators to make sure a machine is working properly. **Service Orientation:** Actively looking for ways to help people. **Repairing:** Repairing machines or systems by using the needed tools. **Technology Design:** Generating or adapting equipment and technology to serve user needs. **GOE—Interest Area:** 03. Arts and Communication. **Work Group:** 03.09. Media Technology. **Other Jobs in This Work Group:** Broadcast Technicians; Camera Operators, Television, Video, and Motion Picture; Film and Video Editors; Multi-Media Artists and Animators; Photographic Hand Developers; Photographic Reproduction Technicians; Photographic Retouchers and Restorers; Professional Photographers; Radio Operators; Sound Engineering Technicians. **PERSONALITY TYPE:** Conventional.

EDUCATION/TRAINING PROGRAM(S)—Agricultural Communication/Journalism; Photographic and Film/Video Technology/Technician and Assistant; Recording Arts Technology/Technician. **RELATED KNOWLEDGE/COURSES—Computers and Elec-**

tronics: Knowledge of circuit boards, processors, chips, electronic equipment, and computer hardware and software, including applications and programming. **Telecommunications:** Knowledge of transmission, broadcasting, switching, control, and operation of telecommunications systems. **Engineering and Technology:** Knowledge of the practical application of engineering science and technology. This includes applying principles, techniques, procedures, and equipment to the design and production of various goods and services. **Communications and Media:** Knowledge of media production, communication, and dissemination techniques and methods. This includes alternative ways to inform and entertain via written, oral, and visual media. **Mechanical Devices:** Knowledge of machines and tools, including their designs, uses, repair, and maintenance. **Design:** Knowledge of design techniques, tools, and principles involved in production of precision technical plans, blueprints, drawings, and models.

Audiologists

- Education/Training Required: Master's degree
- Annual Earnings: $51,470
- Growth: 29.0%
- Annual Job Openings: 1,000
- Self-Employed: 7.1%
- Part-Time: 22.7%

Assess and treat persons with hearing and related disorders. May fit hearing aids and provide auditory training. May perform research related to hearing problems. Educate and supervise audiology students and health-care personnel. Fit and tune cochlear implants, providing rehabilitation for adjustment to listening with implant amplification systems. Instruct clients, parents, teachers, or employers in how to avoid behavior patterns that lead to miscommunication. Participate in conferences or training to update or share knowledge of new hearing or speech disorder treatment methods or technologies. Measure noise levels in workplaces and conduct hearing protection programs in industry, schools, and communities. Work with multi-disciplinary teams to assess and rehabilitate recipients of implanted hearing devices. Administer hearing or speech/language evaluations, tests, or examinations to patients to collect information on type and degree of impairment, using specialized instruments and electronic equipment. Counsel and instruct clients in techniques to improve hearing or speech impairment, including sign language or lipreading. Evaluate hearing and speech/language disorders to determine diagnoses and courses of treatment. Examine and clean patients' ear canals. Fit and dispense assistive devices, such as hearing aids. Maintain client records at all stages, including initial evaluation and discharge. Monitor clients' progress and discharge them from treatment when goals have been attained. Plan and conduct treatment programs for clients' hearing or speech problems, consulting with physicians, nurses, psychologists, and other health-care personnel as necessary. Recommend assistive devices according to clients' needs or nature of impairments. Refer clients to additional medical or educational services if needed. Advise educators or other medical staff on speech or hearing topics. Conduct or direct research on hearing or speech topics and report findings to help in the development of procedures, technology, or treatments. Develop and supervise hearing screening programs. **SKILLS—Instructing:** Teaching others how to do something. **Management of Personnel Resources:** Motivating, developing, and directing people as they work, identifying the best people for the job. **Writing:** Communicating effectively in writing as appropriate for the needs of the audience. **Management of Financial Resources:** Determining how money will be spent to get the work done and accounting for these expenditures. **Learning Strategies:** Selecting and using training/instructional methods and procedures appropriate for the situation when learning or teaching new things. **Service Orientation:** Actively looking for ways to help people. **Speaking:** Talking to others to convey information effectively. **Technology Design:** Generating or adapting equipment and technology to serve user needs. **GOE—Interest Area:** 08. Health Science. **Work Group:** 08.07. Medical Therapy. **Other Jobs in This Work Group:** Massage Therapists; Occupational Therapist Aides; Occupational Therapist Assistants; Occupational Therapists; Physical Therapist Aides; Physical Therapist Assistants; Physical Therapists; Radiation Therapists; Recreational Therapists; Respiratory Therapists; Respiratory Therapy Technicians; Speech-Language Pathologists. **PERSONALITY TYPE:** Social.

EDUCATION/TRAINING PROGRAM(S)—Audiology/Audiologist and Hearing Sciences; Audiology/Audiologist and Speech-Language Pathology/Pathologist; Communication Disorders Sciences and Services, Other; Communication Disorders, General. **RELATED KNOWLEDGE/COURSES—Therapy and Counseling:** Knowledge of principles, methods, and procedures for diagnosis, treatment, and rehabilitation of physical and mental dysfunctions and for career counseling and guidance. **Medicine and Dentistry:** Knowledge of the information and techniques needed to diagnose and treat human injuries, diseases, and deformities. This includes symptoms, treatment alternatives, drug properties and interactions, and preventive health-care measures. **Education and Training:** Knowledge of principles and methods for curriculum and training design, teaching and instruction for individuals and groups, and the measurement of training effects. **Personnel and Human Resources:** Knowledge of principles and procedures for personnel recruitment, selection, training, compensation and benefits, labor relations and negotiation, and personnel information systems. **Economics and Accounting:** Knowledge of economic and accounting principles and practices, the financial markets, banking, and the analysis and reporting of financial data. **Biology:** Knowledge of plant and animal organisms and their tissues, cells, functions, interdependencies, and interactions with each other and the environment.

Auditors

- ◎ Education/Training Required: Bachelor's degree
- ◎ Annual Earnings: $50,770
- ◎ Growth: 19.5%
- ◎ Annual Job Openings: 119,000
- ◎ Self-Employed: 10.6%
- ◎ Part-Time: 8.8%

Examine and analyze accounting records to determine financial status of establishment and prepare financial reports concerning operating procedures. Collect and analyze data to detect deficient controls; duplicated effort; extravagance; fraud; or non-compliance with laws, regulations, and management policies. Report to management about asset utilization and audit results and recommend changes in operations and financial activities. Prepare detailed reports on audit findings. Review data about material assets, net worth, liabilities, capital stock, surplus, income, and expenditures. Inspect account books and accounting

systems for efficiency, effectiveness, and use of accepted accounting procedures to record transactions. Examine and evaluate financial and information systems, recommending controls to ensure system reliability and data integrity. Supervise auditing of establishments and determine scope of investigation required. Prepare, analyze, and verify annual reports, financial statements, and other records, using accepted accounting and statistical procedures to assess financial condition and facilitate financial planning. Confer with company officials about financial and regulatory matters. Inspect cash on hand, notes receivable and payable, negotiable securities, and canceled checks to confirm records are accurate. Examine inventory to verify journal and ledger entries. Examine whether the organization's objectives are reflected in its management activities and whether employees understand the objectives. Examine records and interview workers to ensure recording of transactions and compliance with laws and regulations. Direct activities of personnel engaged in filing, recording, compiling, and transmitting financial records. Produce up-to-the-minute information, using internal computer systems, to allow management to base decisions on actual, not historical, data. Conduct pre-implementation audits to determine if systems and programs under development will work as planned. **SKILLS—Management of Financial Resources:** Determining how money will be spent to get the work done and accounting for these expenditures. **Time Management:** Managing one's own time and the time of others. **Instructing:** Teaching others how to do something. **Negotiation:** Bringing others together and trying to reconcile differences. **Service Orientation:** Actively looking for ways to help people. **Writing:** Communicating effectively in writing as appropriate for the needs of the audience. **Critical Thinking:** Using logic and reasoning to identify the strengths and weaknesses of alternative solutions, conclusions, or approaches to problems. **Persuasion:** Persuading others to change their minds or behavior. **GOE—Interest Area:** 04. Business and Administration. **Work Group:** 04.05. Accounting, Auditing, and Analytical Support. **Other Jobs in This Work Group:** Accountants; Budget Analysts; Industrial Engineering Technicians; Logisticians; Management Analysts; Operations Research Analysts. **PERSONALITY TYPE:** Conventional.

EDUCATION/TRAINING PROGRAM(S)— Accounting; Accounting and Business/Management; Accounting and Computer Science; Accounting and

Finance; Auditing; Taxation. **RELATED KNOWL-EDGE/COURSES—Economics and Accounting:** Knowledge of economic and accounting principles and practices, the financial markets, banking, and the analysis and reporting of financial data. **Customer and Personal Service:** Knowledge of principles and processes for providing customer and personal services. This includes customer needs assessment, meeting quality standards for services, and evaluation of customer satisfaction. **Mathematics:** Knowledge of arithmetic, algebra, geometry, calculus, and statistics and their applications. **Sales and Marketing:** Knowledge of principles and methods for showing, promoting, and selling products or services. This includes marketing strategy and tactics, product demonstrations, sales techniques, and sales control systems. **Law and Government:** Knowledge of laws, legal codes, court procedures, precedents, government regulations, executive orders, agency rules, and the democratic political process. **Computers and Electronics:** Knowledge of circuit boards, processors, chips, electronic equipment, and computer hardware and software, including applications and programming.

Automatic Teller Machine Servicers

- Education/Training Required: Long-term on-the-job training
- Annual Earnings: $35,150
- Growth: 15.1%
- Annual Job Openings: 19,000
- Self-Employed: 12.2%
- Part-Time: 8.2%

Collect deposits and replenish automatic teller machines with cash and supplies. Tests machine functions and balances machine cash account, using electronic keypad. Corrects malfunctions, such as jammed cash or paper, or calls repair personnel when ATM needs repair. Removes money canisters from ATM and replenishes machine supplies, such as deposit envelopes, receipt paper, and cash. Counts cash and items deposited by customers and compares to transactions indicated on transaction tape from ATM. Records transaction information on form or log and notifies designated personnel of discrepancies. **SKILLS—Repairing:** Repairing machines or systems

by using the needed tools. **Programming:** Writing computer programs for various purposes. **Management of Financial Resources:** Determining how money will be spent to get the work done and accounting for these expenditures. **GOE—Interest Area:** 11. Information Technology. **Work Group:** 11.03. Digital Equipment Repair. **Other Jobs in This Work Group:** Coin, Vending, and Amusement Machine Servicers and Repairers; Data Processing Equipment Repairers; Office Machine and Cash Register Servicers. **PERSONALITY TYPE:** Realistic.

EDUCATION/TRAINING PROGRAM(S)—Business Machine Repair; Computer Installation and Repair Technology/Technician. **RELATED KNOWL-EDGE/COURSES—Telecommunications:** Knowledge of transmission, broadcasting, switching, control, and operation of telecommunications systems. **Computers and Electronics:** Knowledge of circuit boards, processors, chips, electronic equipment, and computer hardware and software, including applications and programming.

Automotive Body and Related Repairers

- Education/Training Required: Long-term on-the-job training
- Annual Earnings: $34,690
- Growth: 13.2%
- Annual Job Openings: 23,000
- Self-Employed: 11.3%
- Part-Time: 3.3%

Repair and refinish automotive vehicle bodies and straighten vehicle frames. File, grind, sand, and smooth filled or repaired surfaces, using power tools and hand tools. Sand body areas to be painted and cover bumpers, windows, and trim with masking tape or paper to protect them from the paint. Follow supervisors' instructions as to which parts to restore or replace and how much time the job should take. Remove damaged sections of vehicles, using metal-cutting guns, air grinders, and wrenches, and install replacement parts, using wrenches or welding equipment. Cut and tape plastic separating film to outside repair areas in order to avoid damaging surrounding surfaces during repair procedure and remove tape and wash surfaces after repairs are complete. Prime and paint repaired surfaces, using paint spray guns and motorized sanders. Inspect repaired vehicles for dimensional accuracy and test drive them to ensure proper alignment and handling. Mix polyester resins and hardeners to be used in restoring damaged areas. Chain or clamp frames and sections to alignment machines that use hydraulic pressure to align damaged components. Fill small dents that cannot be worked out with plastic or solder. Fit and weld replacement parts into place, using wrenches and welding equipment, and grind down welds to smooth them, using power grinders and other tools. Position dolly blocks against surfaces of dented areas and beat opposite surfaces to remove dents, using hammers. Remove damaged panels and identify the family and properties of the plastic used on a vehicle. Review damage reports, prepare or review repair cost estimates, and plan work to be performed. Remove small pits and dimples in body metal, using pick hammers and punches. Remove upholstery, accessories, electrical window-and-seat-operating equipment, and trim in order to gain access to vehicle bodies and fenders. Clean work areas, using air hoses, in order to remove damaged material and discarded fiberglass strips used in repair procedures. Adjust or align headlights, wheels, and brake systems. Apply heat to plastic panels, using hot-air welding guns or immersion in hot water, and press the softened panels back into shape by hand. **SKILLS—Repairing:** Repairing machines or systems by using the needed tools. **Installation:** Installing equipment, machines, wiring, or programs to meet specifications. **Equipment Maintenance:** Performing routine maintenance on equipment and determining when and what kind of maintenance is needed. **Troubleshooting:** Determining causes of operating errors and deciding what to do about them. **Equipment Selection:** Determining the kind of tools and equipment needed to do a job. **Learning Strategies:** Selecting and using training/instructional methods and procedures appropriate for the situation when learning or teaching new things. **Negotiation:** Bringing others together and trying to reconcile differences. **Complex Problem Solving:** Identifying complex problems and reviewing related information to develop and evaluate options and implement solutions. **GOE—Interest Area:** 13. Manufacturing. **Work Group:** 13.14. Vehicle and Facility Mechanical Work. **Other Jobs in This Work Group:** Aircraft Body and Bonded Structure Repairers; Aircraft Engine Specialists; Aircraft Rigging Assemblers; Aircraft Structure Assemblers, Precision; Aircraft Systems Assemblers, Precision; Airframe-and-Power-Plant Mechanics; Automotive Glass Installers and Repairers; Automotive Master Mechanics; Automotive Specialty Technicians; Bus and Truck Mechanics and Diesel Engine Specialists; Farm Equipment Mechanics; Fiberglass Laminators and Fabricators; Mobile Heavy Equipment Mechanics, Except Engines; Motorboat Mechanics; Motorcycle Mechanics; Outdoor Power Equipment and Other Small Engine Mechanics; Rail Car Repairers; Recreational Vehicle Service Technicians; Tire Repairers and Changers. **PERSONALITY TYPE:** Realistic.

EDUCATION/TRAINING PROGRAM(S)— Autobody/Collision and Repair Technology/Technician. **RELATED KNOWLEDGE/COURSES—Mechanical Devices:** Knowledge of machines and tools, including their designs, uses, repair, and maintenance. **Building and Construction:** Knowledge of the materials, methods, and tools involved in the construction or repair of houses, buildings, or other structures such as highways and roads. **Customer and Personal Service:** Knowledge of principles and processes for providing customer and personal services. This includes customer needs assessment, meeting quality standards for services, and evaluation of customer satisfaction. **Administration and Management:** Knowledge of business and management principles involved in strategic planning, resource allocation, human resources modeling, leadership technique, production methods, and coordination of people and resources. **Chemistry:** Knowledge of the chemical composition, structure, and properties of substances and of the chemical processes and transformations that they undergo. This includes uses of chemicals and their danger signs, production techniques, and disposal methods. **Transportation:** Knowledge of principles and methods for moving people or goods by air, rail, sea, or road, including the relative costs and benefits. **Production and Processing:** Knowledge of raw materials, production processes, quality control, costs, and other techniques for maximizing the effective manufacture and distribution of goods.

Automotive Master Mechanics

- ◎ Education/Training Required: Postsecondary vocational training
- ◎ Annual Earnings: $32,450
- ◎ Growth: 12.4%
- ◎ Annual Job Openings: 100,000
- ◎ Self-Employed: 15.5%
- ◎ Part-Time: 4.3%

Repair automobiles, trucks, buses, and other vehicles. Master mechanics repair virtually any part on the vehicle or specialize in the transmission system. Examine vehicles to determine extent of damage or malfunctions. Test drive vehicles and test components and systems, using equipment such as infrared engine analyzers, compression gauges, and computerized diagnostic devices. Repair, reline, replace, and adjust brakes. Review work orders and discuss work with supervisors. Follow checklists to ensure all important parts are examined, including belts, hoses, steering systems, spark plugs, brake and fuel systems, wheel bearings, and other potentially troublesome areas. Plan work procedures, using charts, technical manuals, and experience. Test and adjust repaired systems to meet manufacturers' performance specifications. Confer with customers to obtain descriptions of vehicle problems and to discuss work to be performed and future repair requirements. Perform routine and scheduled maintenance services such as oil changes, lubrications, and tune-ups. Disassemble units and inspect parts for wear, using micrometers, calipers, and gauges. Overhaul or replace carburetors, blowers, generators, distributors, starters, and pumps. Repair and service air conditioning, heating, engine-cooling, and electrical systems. Repair or replace parts such as pistons, rods, gears, valves, and bearings. Tear down, repair, and rebuild faulty assemblies such as power systems, steering systems, and linkages. Rewire ignition systems, lights, and instrument panels. Repair radiator leaks. Install and repair accessories such as radios, heaters, mirrors, and windshield wipers. Repair manual and automatic transmissions. Repair or replace shock absorbers. Align vehicles' front ends. Rebuild parts such as crankshafts and cylinder blocks. **SKILLS—Troubleshooting:** Determining causes of operating errors and deciding what to do about them. **Repairing:** Repairing machines or systems by using the needed tools. **Installation:** Installing equipment, machines, wiring, or programs to meet specifications. **Equipment Maintenance:** Performing routine maintenance on equipment and determining when and what kind of maintenance is needed. **Active Learning:** Understanding the implications of new information for both current and future problem-solving and decision-making. **Complex Problem Solving:** Identifying complex problems and reviewing related information to develop and evaluate options and implement solutions. **Equipment Selection:** Determining the kind of tools and equipment needed to do a job. **Instructing:** Teaching others how to do something. **GOE—Interest Area:** 13. Manufacturing. **Work Group:** 13.14. Vehicle and Facility Mechanical Work. **Other Jobs in This Work Group:** Aircraft Body and Bonded Structure Repairers; Aircraft Engine Specialists; Aircraft Rigging Assemblers; Aircraft Structure Assemblers, Precision; Aircraft Systems Assemblers, Precision; Airframe-and-Power-Plant Mechanics; Automotive Body and Related Repairers; Automotive Glass Installers and Repairers; Automotive Specialty Technicians; Bus and Truck Mechanics and Diesel Engine Specialists; Farm Equipment Mechanics; Fiberglass Laminators and Fabricators; Mobile Heavy Equipment Mechanics, Except Engines; Motorboat Mechanics; Motorcycle Mechanics; Outdoor Power Equipment and Other Small Engine Mechanics; Rail Car Repairers; Recreational Vehicle Service Technicians; Tire Repairers and Changers. **PERSONALITY TYPE:** Realistic.

EDUCATION/TRAINING PROGRAM(S)— Alternative Fuel Vehicle Technology/Technician; Automobile/Automotive Mechanics Technology/Technician; Automotive Engineering Technology/Technician; Medium/Heavy Vehicle and Truck Technology/Technician; Vehicle Emissions Inspection and Maintenance Technology/Technician. **RELATED KNOWLEDGE/COURSES—Mechanical Devices:** Knowledge of machines and tools, including their designs, uses, repair, and maintenance. **Computers and Electronics:** Knowledge of circuit boards, processors, chips, electronic equipment, and computer hardware and software, including applications and programming. **Physics:** Knowledge and prediction of physical principles and laws and their interrelationships and applications to understanding fluid, material, and atmospheric dynamics and mechanical, electrical, atomic, and subatomic structures and processes. **Engineering and Technology:** Knowledge of the practical application of engineering science and technology. This includes applying principles, techniques, procedures, and equipment to the design and production of various goods and services. **Education and Training:** Knowledge of principles and methods for curriculum and training design, teaching and instruction for individuals and groups, and the measurement of training effects. **Customer and Personal Service:** Knowledge of principles and processes for providing customer and personal services. This includes customer needs assessment, meeting quality standards for services, and evaluation of customer satisfaction.

Automotive Specialty Technicians

- Education/Training Required: Postsecondary vocational training
- Annual Earnings: $32,450
- Growth: 12.4%
- Annual Job Openings: 100,000
- Self-Employed: 15.5%
- Part-Time: 4.3%

Repair only one system or component on a vehicle, such as brakes, suspension, or radiator. Align and repair wheels, axles, frames, torsion bars, and steering mechanisms of automobiles, using special alignment equipment and wheel-balancing machines. Examine vehicles, compile estimates of repair costs, and secure customers' approval to perform repairs. Install and repair air conditioners and service components such as compressors, condensers, and controls. Rebuild, repair, and test automotive fuel injection units. Remove and replace defective mufflers and tailpipes. Repair and rebuild clutch systems. Repair and replace automobile leaf springs. Repair and replace defective ball joint suspensions, brake shoes, and wheel bearings. Repair, overhaul, and adjust automobile brake systems. Repair, replace, and adjust defective carburetor parts and gasoline filters. Test electronic computer components in automobiles to ensure that they are working properly. Tune automobile engines to ensure proper and efficient functioning. Use electronic test equipment to locate and correct malfunctions in fuel, ignition, and emissions control systems. Convert vehicle fuel systems from gasoline to butane gas operations and repair

and service operating butane fuel units. Inspect and test new vehicles for damage and then record findings so that necessary repairs can be made. Repair, install, and adjust hydraulic and electromagnetic automatic lift mechanisms used to raise and lower automobile windows, seats, and tops. **SKILLS—Installation:** Installing equipment, machines, wiring, or programs to meet specifications. **Repairing:** Repairing machines or systems by using the needed tools. **Troubleshooting:** Determining causes of operating errors and deciding what to do about them. **Equipment Maintenance:** Performing routine maintenance on equipment and determining when and what kind of maintenance is needed. **Quality Control Analysis:** Conducting tests and inspections of products, services, or processes to evaluate quality or performance. **Operation Monitoring:** Watching gauges, dials, or other indicators to make sure a machine is working properly. **Technology Design:** Generating or adapting equipment and technology to serve user needs. **Management of Material Resources:** Obtaining and seeing to the appropriate use of equipment, facilities, and materials needed to do certain work. **GOE—Interest Area:** 13. Manufacturing. **Work Group:** 13.14. Vehicle and Facility Mechanical Work. **Other Jobs in This Work Group:** Aircraft Body and Bonded Structure Repairers; Aircraft Engine Specialists; Aircraft Rigging Assemblers; Aircraft Structure Assemblers, Precision; Aircraft Systems Assemblers, Precision; Airframe-and-Power-Plant Mechanics; Automotive Body and Related Repairers; Automotive Glass Installers and Repairers; Automotive Master Mechanics; Bus and Truck Mechanics and Diesel Engine Specialists; Farm Equipment Mechanics; Fiberglass Laminators and Fabricators; Mobile Heavy Equipment Mechanics, Except Engines; Motorboat Mechanics; Motorcycle Mechanics; Outdoor Power Equipment and Other Small Engine Mechanics; Rail Car Repairers; Recreational Vehicle Service Technicians; Tire Repairers and Changers. **PERSONALITY TYPE:** Realistic.

EDUCATION/TRAINING   PROGRAM(S)— Alternative Fuel Vehicle Technology/Technician; Automobile/Automotive Mechanics Technology/Technician; Automotive Engineering Technology/Technician; Medium/Heavy Vehicle and Truck Technology/Technician; Vehicle Emissions Inspection and Maintenance Technology/Technician. **RELATED KNOWLEDGE/COURSES—Mechanical Devices:** Knowledge of machines and tools, including their designs, uses, repair, and maintenance. **Design:**

Knowledge of design techniques, tools, and principles involved in production of precision technical plans, blueprints, drawings, and models. **Computers and Electronics:** Knowledge of circuit boards, processors, chips, electronic equipment, and computer hardware and software, including applications and programming. **Physics:** Knowledge and prediction of physical principles and laws and their interrelationships and applications to understanding fluid, material, and atmospheric dynamics and mechanical, electrical, atomic, and subatomic structures and processes. **Engineering and Technology:** Knowledge of the practical application of engineering science and technology. This includes applying principles, techniques, procedures, and equipment to the design and production of various goods and services. **Chemistry:** Knowledge of the chemical composition, structure, and properties of substances and of the chemical processes and transformations that they undergo. This includes uses of chemicals and their danger signs, production techniques, and disposal methods.

Aviation Inspectors

- Education/Training Required: Work experience in a related occupation
- Annual Earnings: $50,380
- Growth: 7.7%
- Annual Job Openings: 5,000
- Self-Employed: 0.4%
- Part-Time: 3.2%

Inspect aircraft, maintenance procedures, air navigational aids, air traffic controls, and communications equipment to ensure conformance with federal safety regulations. Analyze training programs and conduct oral and written examinations to ensure the competency of persons operating, installing, and repairing aircraft equipment. Approve or deny issuance of certificates of airworthiness. Conduct flight test programs to test equipment, instruments, and systems under a variety of conditions, using both manual and automatic controls. Examine landing gear; tires; and exteriors of fuselage, wings, and engines for evidence of damage or corrosion and to determine whether repairs are needed. Examine maintenance records and flight logs to determine if service and maintenance checks and overhauls were performed at prescribed intervals. Inspect new, repaired, or modified aircraft to identify damage or defects and to assess airworthiness and conformance to standards, using checklists, hand tools, and test instruments. Inspect work of aircraft mechanics performing maintenance, modification, or repair and overhaul of aircraft and aircraft mechanical systems in order to ensure adherence to standards and procedures. Prepare and maintain detailed repair, inspection, investigation, and certification records and reports. Recommend replacement, repair, or modification of aircraft equipment. Start aircraft and observe gauges, meters, and other instruments to detect evidence of malfunctions. Examine aircraft access plates and doors for security. Investigate air accidents and complaints to determine causes. Issue pilots' licenses to individuals meeting standards. Observe flight activities of pilots to assess flying skills and to ensure conformance to flight and safety regulations. Recommend changes in rules, policies, standards, and regulations based on knowledge of operating conditions, aircraft improvements, and other factors. Schedule and coordinate in-flight testing programs with ground crews and air traffic control to ensure availability of ground tracking, equipment monitoring, and related services. **SKILLS—Operation Monitoring:** Watching gauges, dials, or other indicators to make sure a machine is working properly. **Quality Control Analysis:** Conducting tests and inspections of products, services, or processes to evaluate quality or performance. **Science:** Using scientific rules and methods to solve problems. **Systems Analysis:** Determining how a system should work and how changes in conditions, operations, and the environment will affect outcomes. **Systems Evaluation:** Identifying measures or indicators of system performance and the actions needed to improve or correct performance relative to the goals of the system. **Writing:** Communicating effectively in writing as appropriate for the needs of the audience. **Critical Thinking:** Using logic and reasoning to identify the strengths and weaknesses of alternative solutions, conclusions, or approaches to problems. **Reading Comprehension:** Understanding written sentences and paragraphs in work-related documents. **GOE—Interest Area:** 07. Government and Public Administration. **Work Group:** 07.03. Regulations Enforcement. **Other Jobs in This Work Group:** Agricultural Inspectors; Child Support, Missing Persons, and Unemployment Insurance Fraud Investigators; Environmental Compliance Inspectors; Equal Opportunity Representatives and Officers; Financial Examiners; Fire Inspectors; Fish and Game Wardens; Forest Fire Inspectors and Prevention Specialists; Government Property Inspectors and Investigators; Immigration and Customs Inspectors; Licensing Examiners and Inspectors; Marine Cargo Inspectors; Mechanical Inspectors; Motor Vehicle Inspectors; Nuclear Monitoring Technicians; Occupational Health and Safety Specialists; Pressure Vessel Inspectors; Railroad Inspectors; Tax Examiners, Collectors, and Revenue Agents. **PERSONALITY TYPE:** Realistic.

EDUCATION/TRAINING PROGRAM(S)—No data available. **RELATED KNOWLEDGE/COURSES—Engineering and Technology:** Knowledge of the practical application of engineering science and technology. This includes applying principles, techniques, procedures, and equipment to the design and production of various goods and services. **Public Safety and Security:** Knowledge of relevant equipment, policies, procedures, and strategies to promote effective local, state, or national security operations for the protection of people, data, property, and institutions. **Mechanical Devices:** Knowledge of machines and tools, including their designs, uses, repair, and maintenance. **Physics:** Knowledge and prediction of physical principles and laws and their interrelationships and applications to understanding fluid, material, and atmospheric dynamics and mechanical, electrical, atomic, and subatomic structures and processes. **Law and Government:** Knowledge of laws, legal codes, court procedures, precedents, government regulations, executive orders, agency rules, and the democratic political process. **Transportation:** Knowledge of principles and methods for moving people or goods by air, rail, sea, or road, including the relative costs and benefits.

Bill and Account Collectors

- ◎ Education/Training Required: Short-term on-the-job training
- ◎ Annual Earnings: $27,450
- ◎ Growth: 24.5%
- ◎ Annual Job Openings: 76,000
- ◎ Self-Employed: 0.9%
- ◎ Part-Time: 11.3%

Locate and notify customers of delinquent accounts by mail, telephone, or personal visit to solicit payment. Duties include receiving payment and posting

amount to customer's account, preparing statements to credit department if customer fails to respond, initiating repossession proceedings or service disconnection, and keeping records of collection and status of accounts. Receive payments and post amounts paid to customer accounts. Locate and monitor overdue accounts, using computers and a variety of automated systems. Record information about financial status of customers and status of collection efforts. Locate and notify customers of delinquent accounts by mail, telephone, or personal visits in order to solicit payment. Confer with customers by telephone or in person to determine reasons for overdue payments and to review the terms of sales, service, or credit contracts. Advise customers of necessary actions and strategies for debt repayment. Persuade customers to pay amounts due on credit accounts, damage claims, or nonpayable checks or to return merchandise. Sort and file correspondence and perform miscellaneous clerical duties such as answering correspondence and writing reports. Perform various administrative functions for assigned accounts, such as recording address changes and purging the records of deceased customers. Arrange for debt repayment or establish repayment schedules based on customers' financial situations. Negotiate credit extensions when necessary. Trace delinquent customers to new addresses by inquiring at post offices, telephone companies, or credit bureaus or through the questioning of neighbors. Notify credit departments, order merchandise repossession or service disconnection, and turn over account records to attorneys when customers fail to respond to collection attempts. **SKILLS—Social Perceptiveness:** Being aware of others' reactions and understanding why they react as they do. **Service Orientation:** Actively looking for ways to help people. **Time Management:** Managing one's own time and the time of others. **Management of Financial Resources:** Determining how money will be spent to get the work done and accounting for these expenditures. **Management of Personnel Resources:** Motivating, developing, and directing people as they work, identifying the best people for the job. **Persuasion:** Persuading others to change their minds or behavior. **Speaking:** Talking to others to convey information effectively. **Judgment and Decision Making:** Considering the relative costs and benefits of potential actions to choose the most appropriate one. **GOE—Interest Area:** 06. Finance and Insurance. **Work Group:** 06.04. Finance/Insurance Customer Service. **Other Jobs in This Work Group:** Loan Interviewers and Clerks; New Accounts Clerks; Tellers. **PERSONALITY TYPE:** Conventional.

EDUCATION/TRAINING PROGRAM(S)— Banking and Financial Support Services. **RELATED KNOWLEDGE/COURSES—Clerical Practices:** Knowledge of administrative and clerical procedures and systems such as word processing, managing files and records, stenography and transcription, designing forms, and other office procedures and terminology. **Customer and Personal Service:** Knowledge of principles and processes for providing customer and personal services. This includes customer needs assessment, meeting quality standards for services, and evaluation of customer satisfaction. **Computers and Electronics:** Knowledge of circuit boards, processors, chips, electronic equipment, and computer hardware and software, including applications and programming. **Law and Government:** Knowledge of laws, legal codes, court procedures, precedents, government regulations, executive orders, agency rules, and the democratic political process. **Economics and Accounting:** Knowledge of economic and accounting principles and practices, the financial markets, banking, and the analysis and reporting of financial data. **Personnel and Human Resources:** Knowledge of principles and procedures for personnel recruitment, selection, training, compensation and benefits, labor relations and negotiation, and personnel information systems.

Billing, Cost, and Rate Clerks

- Education/Training Required: Short-term on-the-job training
- Annual Earnings: $27,040
- Growth: 7.9%
- Annual Job Openings: 78,000
- Self-Employed: 2.2%
- Part-Time: 16.1%

Compile data, compute fees and charges, and prepare invoices for billing purposes. Duties include computing costs and calculating rates for goods, services, and shipment of goods; posting data; and keeping other relevant records. May involve use of computer or typewriter, calculator, and adding and bookkeeping machines. Verify accuracy of billing data and revise any errors. Operate typing, adding, calculating, and billing machines. Prepare itemized statements, bills, or invoices and record amounts due for items purchased or services rendered. Review documents such as purchase orders, sales tickets, charge slips, or hospital records in order to compute fees and charges due. Perform bookkeeping work, including posting data and keeping other records concerning costs of goods and services and the shipment of goods. Keep records of invoices and support documents. Resolve discrepancies in accounting records. Type billing documents, shipping labels, credit memorandums, and credit forms, using typewriters or computers. Contact customers in order to obtain or relay account information. Compute credit terms, discounts, shipment charges, and rates for goods and services in order to complete billing documents. Answer mail and telephone inquiries regarding rates, routing, and procedures. Track accumulated hours and dollar amounts charged to each client job in order to calculate client fees for professional services such as legal and accounting services. Review compiled data on operating costs and revenues in order to set rates. Compile reports of cost factors, such as labor, production, storage, and equipment. Consult sources such as rate books, manuals, and insurance company representatives in order to determine specific charges and information such as rules, regulations, and government tax and tariff information. Update manuals when rates, rules, or regulations are amended. Estimate market value of products or services. **SKILLS—Instructing:** Teaching others how to do something. **Service Orientation:** Actively looking for ways to help people. **Active Listening:** Giving full attention to what other people are saying, taking time to understand the points being made, asking questions as appropriate, and not interrupting at inappropriate times. **Social Perceptiveness:** Being aware of others' reactions and understanding why they react as they do. **Writing:** Communicating effectively in writing as appropriate for the needs of the audience. **Reading Comprehension:** Understanding written sentences and paragraphs in work-related documents. **Learning Strategies:** Selecting and using training/instructional methods and procedures appropriate for the situation when learning or teaching new things. **Speaking:** Talking to others to convey information effectively. **Negotiation:** Bringing others together and trying to reconcile differences. **GOE—Interest Area:** 04. Business and Administration. **Work Group:** 04.06. Mathematical Clerical Support. **Other Jobs in This Work

Group: Bookkeeping, Accounting, and Auditing Clerks; Brokerage Clerks; Payroll and Timekeeping Clerks; Statement Clerks; Tax Preparers. **PERSONALITY TYPE:** Conventional.

EDUCATION/TRAINING PROGRAM(S)—Accounting Technology/Technician and Bookkeeping. **RELATED KNOWLEDGE/COURSES**—**Clerical Practices:** Knowledge of administrative and clerical procedures and systems such as word processing, managing files and records, stenography and transcription, designing forms, and other office procedures and terminology. **Computers and Electronics:** Knowledge of circuit boards, processors, chips, electronic equipment, and computer hardware and software, including applications and programming. **Customer and Personal Service:** Knowledge of principles and processes for providing customer and personal services. This includes customer needs assessment, meeting quality standards for services, and evaluation of customer satisfaction. **Economics and Accounting:** Knowledge of economic and accounting principles and practices, the financial markets, banking, and the analysis and reporting of financial data. **English Language:** Knowledge of the structure and content of the English language, including the meaning and spelling of words, rules of composition, and grammar. **Mathematics:** Knowledge of arithmetic, algebra, geometry, calculus, and statistics and their applications.

Billing, Posting, and Calculating Machine Operators

- Education/Training Required: Short-term on-the-job training
- Annual Earnings: $27,040
- Growth: 7.9%
- Annual Job Openings: 78,000
- Self-Employed: 2.2%
- Part-Time: 16.1%

Operate machines that automatically perform mathematical processes, such as addition, subtraction, multiplication, and division, to calculate and record billing, accounting, statistical, and other numerical data. Duties include operating special billing machines to prepare statements, bills, and invoices and operating bookkeeping machines to copy and post data, make computations, and compile records of transactions. Enter into machines all information needed for bill generation. Train other calculating machine operators and review their work. Operate special billing machines to prepare statements, bills, and invoices. Operate bookkeeping machines to copy and post data, make computations, and compile records of transactions. Reconcile and post receipts for cash received by various departments. Prepare transmittal reports for changes to assessment and tax rolls and redemption file changes and for warrants, deposits, and invoices. Encode and add amounts of transaction documents, such as checks or money orders, using encoding machines. Balance and reconcile batch control totals with source documents or computer listings in order to locate errors, encode correct amounts, or prepare correction records. Compute payroll and retirement amounts, applying knowledge of payroll deductions, actuarial tables, disability factors, and survivor allowances. Maintain ledgers and registers, posting charges and refunds to individual funds and computing and verifying balances. Compute monies due on personal and real property, inventories, redemption payments, and other amounts, applying specialized knowledge of tax rates, formulas, interest rates, and other relevant information. Verify and post to ledgers purchase orders, reports of goods received, invoices, paid vouchers, and other information. Assign purchase order numbers to invoices, requisitions, and formal and informal bids. Verify completeness and accuracy of original documents such as business property statements, tax rolls, invoices, bonds and coupons, and redemption certificates. Bundle sorted documents to prepare those drawn on other banks for collection. Transcribe data from office records, using specified forms, billing machines, and transcribing machines. Sort and list items for proof or collection. Send completed bills to billing clerks for information verification. Transfer data from machines, such as encoding machines, to computers. Sort and microfilm transaction documents, such as checks, using sorting machines. Observe operation of sorters to locate documents that machines cannot read and manually record amounts of these documents. **SKILLS**—**Active Listening:** Giving full attention to what other people are saying, taking time to understand the points being made, asking questions as appropriate, and not interrupting at inappropriate times. **Speaking:** Talking to others to convey information effectively. **Writing:** Communicating effectively in writing as appropriate for the needs of the audience. **Instructing:** Teaching others how to do something. **Management of Financial Resources:** Determining how money will be spent to get the work done and accounting for these expenditures. **Reading Comprehension:** Understanding written sentences and paragraphs in work-related documents. **Persuasion:** Persuading others to change their minds or behavior. **Critical Thinking:** Using logic and reasoning to identify the strengths and weaknesses of alternative solutions, conclusions, or approaches to problems. **Monitoring**: Monitoring or assessing your performance or that of other individuals or organizations to make improvements or take corrective action. **Negotiation:** Bringing others together and trying to reconcile differences. **GOE—Interest Area:** 04. Business and Administration. **Work Group:** 04.08. Clerical Machine Operation. **Other Jobs in This Work Group:** Data Entry Keyers; Duplicating Machine Operators; Mail Machine Operators, Preparation and Handling; Switchboard Operators, Including Answering Service; Word Processors and Typists. **PERSONALITY TYPE:** Conventional.

EDUCATION/TRAINING PROGRAM(S)— Accounting Technology/Technician and Bookkeeping. **RELATED KNOWLEDGE/COURSES—Economics and Accounting:** Knowledge of economic and accounting principles and practices, the financial markets, banking, and the analysis and reporting of financial data. **Clerical Practices:** Knowledge of administrative and clerical procedures and systems such as word processing, managing files and records, stenography and transcription, designing forms, and other office procedures and terminology. **Personnel and Human Resources:** Knowledge of principles and procedures for personnel recruitment, selection, training, compensation and benefits, labor relations and negotiation, and personnel information systems. **English Language:** Knowledge of the structure and content of the English language, including the meaning and spelling of words, rules of composition, and grammar. **Computers and Electronics:** Knowledge of circuit boards, processors, chips, electronic equipment, and computer hardware and software, including applications and programming. **Telecommunications:** Knowledge of transmission, broadcasting, switching, control, and operation of telecommunications systems.

Biochemists

- ◎ Education/Training Required: Doctoral degree
- ◎ Annual Earnings: $68,950
- ◎ Growth: 22.9%
- ◎ Annual Job Openings: 2,000
- ◎ Self-Employed: 2.6%
- ◎ Part-Time: 7.1%

Research or study chemical composition and processes of living organisms that affect vital processes such as growth and aging to determine chemical actions and effects on organisms such as the action of foods, drugs, or other substances on body functions and tissues. Studies chemistry of living processes, such as cell development, breathing, and digestion, and living energy changes, such as growth, aging, and death. Researches methods of transferring characteristics, such as resistance to disease, from one organism to another. Examines chemical aspects of formation of antibodies and researches chemistry of cells and blood corpuscles. Develops and executes tests to detect disease, genetic disorders, or other abnormalities. Develops and tests new drugs and medications used for commercial distribution. Designs and builds laboratory equipment needed for special research projects. Analyzes foods to determine nutritional value and effects of cooking, canning, and processing on this value. Cleans, purifies, refines, and otherwise prepares pharmaceutical compounds for commercial distribution. Prepares reports and recommendations based upon research outcomes. Develops methods to process, store, and use food, drugs, and chemical compounds. Isolates, analyzes, and identifies hormones, vitamins, allergens, minerals, and enzymes and determines their effects on body functions. Researches and determines chemical action of substances such as drugs, serums, hormones, and food on tissues and vital processes. **SKILLS—Science:** Using scientific rules and methods to solve problems. **Writing:** Communicating effectively in writing as appropriate for the needs of the audience. **Programming:** Writing computer programs for various purposes. **Reading Comprehension:** Understanding written sentences and paragraphs in work-related documents. **Active Learning:** Understanding the implications of new information for both current and future problem-solving and decision-making. **Mathematics:** Using mathematics to solve problems. **Critical Thinking:** Using logic and reasoning to identify the strengths and weaknesses of alternative solutions, conclusions, or approaches to problems. **Equipment Selection:** Determining the kind of tools and equipment needed to do a job. **GOE—Interest Area:** 15. Scientific Research, Engineering, and Mathematics. **Work Group:** 15.03. Life Sciences. **Other Jobs in This Work Group:** Biologists; Biophysicists; Environmental Scientists and Specialists, Including Health; Epidemiologists; Medical Scientists, Except Epidemiologists; Microbiologists. **PERSONALITY TYPE:** Investigative.

EDUCATION/TRAINING PROGRAM(S)—Biochemistry; Biochemistry/Biophysics and Molecular Biology; Biophysics; Cell/Cellular Biology and Anatomical Sciences, Other; Molecular Biochemistry; Molecular Biophysics; Soil Chemistry and Physics; Soil Microbiology. **RELATED KNOWLEDGE/ COURSES—Biology:** Knowledge of plant and animal organisms and their tissues, cells, functions, interdependencies, and interactions with each other and the environment. **Chemistry:** Knowledge of the chemical composition, structure, and properties of substances and of the chemical processes and transformations that they undergo. This includes uses of chemicals and their danger signs, production techniques, and disposal methods. **Mathematics:** Knowledge of arithmetic, algebra, geometry, calculus, and statistics and their applications. **Building and Construction:** Knowledge of the materials, methods, and tools involved in the construction or repair of houses, buildings, or other structures such as highways and roads. **Engineering and Technology:** Knowledge of the practical application of engineering science and technology. This includes applying principles, techniques, procedures, and equipment to the design and production of various goods and services.

Biological Science Teachers, Postsecondary

- Education/Training Required: Master's degree
- Annual Earnings: $61,940
- Growth: 38.1%
- Annual Job Openings: 216,000
- Self-Employed: 0.3%
- Part-Time: 27.7%

Teach courses in biological sciences. Prepare and deliver lectures to undergraduate and/or graduate students on topics such as molecular biology, marine biology, and botany. Evaluate and grade students' class work, laboratory work, assignments, and papers. Prepare course materials such as syllabi, homework assignments, and handouts. Compile, administer, and grade examinations or assign this work to others. Supervise students' laboratory work. Keep abreast of developments in their field by reading current literature, talking with colleagues, and participating in professional conferences. Maintain student attendance records, grades, and other required records. Initiate, facilitate, and moderate classroom discussions. Plan, evaluate, and revise curricula, course content, and course materials and methods of instruction. Advise students on academic and vocational curricula and on career issues. Maintain regularly scheduled office hours in order to advise and assist students. Supervise undergraduate and/or graduate teaching, internship, and research work. Select and obtain materials and supplies such as textbooks and laboratory equipment. Collaborate with colleagues to address teaching and research issues. Conduct research in a particular field of knowledge and publish findings in professional journals, books, and/or electronic media. Serve on academic or administrative committees that deal with institutional policies, departmental matters, and academic issues. Participate in student recruitment, registration, and placement activities. Write grant proposals to procure external research funding. Perform administrative duties such as serving as department head. **SKILLS— Science:** Using scientific rules and methods to solve problems. **Instructing:** Teaching others how to do something. **Learning Strategies:** Selecting and using training/instructional methods and procedures appropriate for the situation when learning or teaching new things. **Reading Comprehension:** Understanding written sentences and paragraphs in work-related documents. **Writing:** Communicating effectively in writing as appropriate for the needs of the audience. **Active Learning:** Understanding the implications of new information for both current and future problem-solving and decision-making. **Speaking:** Talking to others to convey information effectively. **Critical Thinking:** Using logic and reasoning to identify the strengths and weaknesses of alternative solutions, conclusions, or approaches to problems. **GOE—Interest Area:** 05. Education and Training. **Work Group:** 05.03. Postsecondary and Adult Teaching and Instructing. **Other**

Jobs in This Work Group: Adult Literacy, Remedial Education, and GED Teachers and Instructors; Agricultural Sciences Teachers, Postsecondary; Anthropology and Archeology Teachers, Postsecondary; Architecture Teachers, Postsecondary; Area, Ethnic, and Cultural Studies Teachers, Postsecondary; Art, Drama, and Music Teachers, Postsecondary; Atmospheric, Earth, Marine, and Space Sciences Teachers, Postsecondary; Business Teachers, Postsecondary; Chemistry Teachers, Postsecondary; Communications Teachers, Postsecondary; Computer Science Teachers, Postsecondary; Criminal Justice and Law Enforcement Teachers, Postsecondary; Economics Teachers, Postsecondary; Education Teachers, Postsecondary; Engineering Teachers, Postsecondary; English Language and Literature Teachers, Postsecondary; Environmental Science Teachers, Postsecondary; Farm and Home Management Advisors; Foreign Language and Literature Teachers, Postsecondary; Forestry and Conservation Science Teachers, Postsecondary; Geography Teachers, Postsecondary; Graduate Teaching Assistants; Health Specialties Teachers, Postsecondary; History Teachers, Postsecondary; Home Economics Teachers, Postsecondary; Law Teachers, Postsecondary; Library Science Teachers, Postsecondary; Mathematical Science Teachers, Postsecondary; Nursing Instructors and Teachers, Postsecondary; Philosophy and Religion Teachers, Postsecondary; Physics Teachers, Postsecondary; Political Science Teachers, Postsecondary; Psychology Teachers, Postsecondary; Recreation and Fitness Studies Teachers, Postsecondary; Self-Enrichment Education Teachers; Social Work Teachers, Postsecondary; Sociology Teachers, Postsecondary; Vocational Education Teachers, Postsecondary. **PERSONALITY TYPE:** Investigative.

EDUCATION/TRAINING PROGRAM(S)— Anatomy; Animal Physiology; Biochemistry; Biological and Biomedical Sciences, Other; Biology/Biological Sciences, General; Biometry/Biometrics; Biophysics; Biotechnology; Botany/Plant Biology; Cell/Cellular Biology and Histology; Ecology; Ecology, Evolution, Systematics, and Population Biology, Other; Entomology; Evolutionary Biology; Immunology; Marine Biology and Biological Oceanography; Microbiology, General; Molecular Biology; Neuroscience; Nutrition Sciences; Parasitology; Pathology/Experimental Pathology; Pharmacology; Plant Genetics; Plant Pathology/Phytopathology; Plant Physiology; Radiation Biology/Radiobiology; Toxicology; Virology; Zoology/Animal Biology.

RELATED KNOWLEDGE/COURSES—Biology: Knowledge of plant and animal organisms and their tissues, cells, functions, interdependencies, and interactions with each other and the environment. **Education and Training:** Knowledge of principles and methods for curriculum and training design, teaching and instruction for individuals and groups, and the measurement of training effects. **Chemistry:** Knowledge of the chemical composition, structure, and properties of substances and of the chemical processes and transformations that they undergo. This includes uses of chemicals and their danger signs, production techniques, and disposal methods. **English Language:** Knowledge of the structure and content of the English language, including the meaning and spelling of words, rules of composition, and grammar. **Medicine and Dentistry:** Knowledge of the information and techniques needed to diagnose and treat human injuries, diseases, and deformities. This includes symptoms, treatment alternatives, drug properties and interactions, and preventive health-care measures. **Mathematics:** Knowledge of arithmetic, algebra, geometry, calculus, and statistics and their applications. **Physics:** Knowledge and prediction of physical principles and laws and their interrelationships and applications to understanding fluid, material, and atmospheric dynamics and mechanical, electrical, atomic, and subatomic structures and processes.

Biological Technicians

- Education/Training Required: Associate degree
- Annual Earnings: $33,210
- Growth: 19.4%
- Annual Job Openings: 7,000
- Self-Employed: 0.1%
- Part-Time: 9.7%

Assist biological and medical scientists in laboratories. Set up, operate, and maintain laboratory instruments and equipment; monitor experiments; make observations; and calculate and record results. May analyze organic substances, such as blood, food, and drugs. Keep detailed logs of all work-related activities. Monitor laboratory work to ensure compliance with set standards. Isolate, identify, and prepare specimens for examination. Use computers, computer-interfaced equipment, robotics, and high-technology industrial applications to perform work duties. Conduct or assist in conducting research, including the collection of information and samples such as blood, water, soil, plants and animals. Set up, adjust, calibrate, clean, maintain, and troubleshoot laboratory and field equipment. Provide technical support and services for scientists and engineers working in fields such as agriculture, environmental science, resource management, biology, and health sciences. Clean, maintain, and prepare supplies and work areas. Participate in the research, development, and manufacturing of medicinal and pharmaceutical preparations. Conduct standardized biological, microbiological, and biochemical tests and laboratory analyses to evaluate the quantity or quality of physical or chemical substances in food and other products. Analyze experimental data and interpret results to write reports and summaries of findings. Measure or weigh compounds and solutions for use in testing or animal feed. Monitor and observe experiments, recording production and test data for evaluation by research personnel. Examine animals and specimens to detect the presence of disease or other problems. Conduct or supervise operational programs such as fish hatcheries, greenhouses, and livestock production programs. **SKILLS—Science:** Using scientific rules and methods to solve problems. **Learning Strategies:** Selecting and using training/instructional methods and procedures appropriate for the situation when learning or teaching new things. **Active Learning:** Understanding the implications of new information for both current and future problem-solving and decision-making. **Instructing:** Teaching others how to do something. **Equipment Maintenance:** Performing routine maintenance on equipment and determining when and what kind of maintenance is needed. **Troubleshooting:** Determining causes of operating errors and deciding what to do about them. **Technology Design:** Generating or adapting equipment and technology to serve user needs. **Quality Control Analysis:** Conducting tests and inspections of products, services, or processes to evaluate quality or performance. **GOE—Interest Area:** 08. Health Science. **Work Group:** 08.06. Medical Technology. **Other Jobs in This Work Group:** Cardiovascular Technologists and Technicians; Diagnostic Medical Sonographers; Medical and Clinical Laboratory Technicians; Medical and Clinical Laboratory Technologists; Medical Equipment Preparers; Medical Records and Health Information Technicians; Nuclear Medicine Technologists; Opticians, Dispensing; Orthotists and Prosthetists; Radiologic Technicians; Radiologic Technologists.

PERSONALITY TYPE: Realistic.

EDUCATION/TRAINING PROGRAM(S)—Biology Technician/Biotechnology Laboratory Technician. **RELATED KNOWLEDGE/COURSES—Chemistry:** Knowledge of the chemical composition, structure, and properties of substances and of the chemical processes and transformations that they undergo. This includes uses of chemicals and their danger signs, production techniques, and disposal methods. **Biology:** Knowledge of plant and animal organisms and their tissues, cells, functions, interdependencies, and interactions with each other and the environment. **Mathematics:** Knowledge of arithmetic, algebra, geometry, calculus, and statistics and their applications. **English Language:** Knowledge of the structure and content of the English language, including the meaning and spelling of words, rules of composition, and grammar. **Production and Processing:** Knowledge of raw materials, production processes, quality control, costs, and other techniques for maximizing the effective manufacture and distribution of goods.

Biomedical Engineers

- Education/Training Required: Bachelor's degree
- Annual Earnings: $67,690
- Growth: 26.1%
- Annual Job Openings: Fewer than 500
- Self-Employed: 4.9%
- Part-Time: 2.8%

Apply knowledge of engineering, biology, and biomechanical principles to the design, development, and evaluation of biological and health systems and products, such as artificial organs, prostheses, instrumentation, medical information systems, and health management and care-delivery systems. Advise and assist in the application of instrumentation in clinical environments. Conduct research, along with life scientists, chemists, and medical scientists, on the engineering aspects of the biological systems of humans and animals. Design and develop medical diagnostic and clinical instrumentation, equipment, and procedures, utilizing the principles of engineering and bio-behavioral sciences. Develop models or computer simulations of human bio-behavioral systems in order to obtain data for measuring or controlling life processes.

Evaluate the safety, efficiency, and effectiveness of biomedical equipment. Install, adjust, maintain, and/or repair biomedical equipment. Research new materials to be used for products such as implanted artificial organs. Adapt or design computer hardware or software for medical science uses. Advise hospital administrators on the planning, acquisition, and use of medical equipment. Analyze new medical procedures in order to forecast likely outcomes. Design and deliver technology to assist people with disabilities. Develop new applications for energy sources, such as using nuclear power for biomedical implants. Diagnose and interpret bioelectric data, using signal processing techniques. Teach biomedical engineering or disseminate knowledge about field through writing or consulting. **SKILLS**—No data available. **GOE—Interest Area:** 15. Scientific Research, Engineering, and Mathematics. **Work Group:** 15.07. Research and Design Engineering. **Other Jobs in This Work Group:** Aerospace Engineers; Chemical Engineers; Civil Engineers; Computer Hardware Engineers; Electrical Engineers; Electronics Engineers, Except Computer; Marine Architects; Marine Engineers; Materials Engineers; Mechanical Engineers; Nuclear Engineers. **PERSONALITY TYPE:** No data available.

EDUCATION/TRAINING PROGRAM(S)—Biomedical/Medical Engineering. **RELATED KNOWLEDGE/COURSES**—No data available.

Biophysicists

- Education/Training Required: Doctoral degree
- Annual Earnings: $68,950
- Growth: 22.9%
- Annual Job Openings: 2,000
- Self-Employed: 2.6%
- Part-Time: 7.1%

Research or study physical principles of living cells and organisms, their electrical and mechanical energy, and related phenomena. Studies physical principles of living cells and organisms and their electrical and mechanical energy. Investigates transmission of electrical impulses along nerves and muscles. Studies absorption of light by chlorophyll in photosynthesis or by pigments of eye involved in vision. Researches cancer treatment, using radiation and nuclear particles. Analyzes functions of electronic and human brains,

such as learning, thinking, and memory. Investigates dynamics of seeing and hearing. Studies spatial configuration of submicroscopic molecules, such as proteins, using X-ray and electron microscope. Researches manner in which characteristics of plants and animals are carried through successive generations. Investigates damage to cells and tissues caused by X rays and nuclear particles. Researches transformation of substances in cells, using atomic isotopes. **SKILLS—Science:** Using scientific rules and methods to solve problems. **Reading Comprehension:** Understanding written sentences and paragraphs in work-related documents. **Writing:** Communicating effectively in writing as appropriate for the needs of the audience. **Mathematics:** Using mathematics to solve problems. **Active Learning:** Understanding the implications of new information for both current and future problem-solving and decision-making. **Critical Thinking:** Using logic and reasoning to identify the strengths and weaknesses of alternative solutions, conclusions, or approaches to problems. **Complex Problem Solving:** Identifying complex problems and reviewing related information to develop and evaluate options and implement solutions. **Programming:** Writing computer programs for various purposes. **GOE—Interest Area:** 15. Scientific Research, Engineering, and Mathematics. **Work Group:** 15.03. Life Sciences. **Other Jobs in This Work Group:** Biochemists; Biologists; Environmental Scientists and Specialists, Including Health; Epidemiologists; Medical Scientists, Except Epidemiologists; Microbiologists. **PERSONALITY TYPE:** Investigative.

EDUCATION/TRAINING PROGRAM(S)—Biochemistry; Biochemistry/Biophysics and Molecular Biology; Biophysics; Cell/Cellular Biology and Anatomical Sciences, Other; Molecular Biochemistry; Molecular Biophysics; Soil Chemistry and Physics; Soil Microbiology. **RELATED KNOWLEDGE/COURSES—Biology:** Knowledge of plant and animal organisms and their tissues, cells, functions, interdependencies, and interactions with each other and the environment. **Physics:** Knowledge and prediction of physical principles and laws and their interrelationships and applications to understanding fluid, material, and atmospheric dynamics and mechanical, electrical, atomic, and subatomic structures and processes. **Mathematics:** Knowledge of arithmetic, algebra, geometry, calculus, and statistics and their applications. **Chemistry:** Knowledge of the chemical composition, structure, and properties of

B

substances and of the chemical processes and transformations that they undergo. This includes uses of chemicals and their danger signs, production techniques, and disposal methods.

Boat Builders and Shipwrights

◎ Education/Training Required: Long-term on-the-job training

◎ Annual Earnings: $34,900

◎ Growth: 10.1%

◎ Annual Job Openings: 193,000

◎ Self-Employed: 29.7%

◎ Part-Time: 5.3%

Construct and repair ships or boats according to blueprints. Cuts and forms parts, such as keel, ribs, sidings, and support structures and blocks, using woodworking hand tools and power tools. Constructs and shapes wooden frames, structures, and other parts according to blueprint specifications, using hand tools, power tools, and measuring instruments. Attaches metal parts, such as fittings, plates, and bulkheads, to ship, using brace and bits, augers, and wrenches. Establishes dimensional reference points on layout and hull to make template of parts and locate machinery and equipment. Smoothes and finishes ship surfaces, using power sander, broadax, adz, and paint, and waxes and buffs surface to specified finish. Cuts out defect, using power tools and hand tools, and fits and secures replacement part, using caulking gun, adhesive, or hand tools. Assembles and installs hull timbers and other structures in ship, using adhesive, measuring instruments, and hand tools or power tools. Measures and marks dimensional lines on lumber, following template and using scriber. Consults with customer or supervisor and reads blueprint to determine necessary repairs. Attaches hoist to sections of hull and directs hoist operator to align parts over blocks according to layout of boat. Marks outline of boat on building dock, shipway, or mold loft according to blueprint specifications, using measuring instruments and crayon. Inspects boat to determine location and extent of defect. Positions and secures support structures on construction area. **SKILLS—Installation:** Installing equipment, machines, wiring, or programs to meet specifications. **Repairing:** Repairing machines or systems by using the needed tools. **Operations Analysis:** Analyzing needs and product requirements to create a design. **Technology Design:** Generating or adapting equipment and technology to serve user needs. **Equipment Selection:** Determining the kind of tools and equipment needed to do a job. **Equipment Maintenance:** Performing routine maintenance on equipment and determining when and what kind of maintenance is needed. **Mathematics:** Using mathematics to solve problems. **Quality Control Analysis:** Conducting tests and inspections of products, services, or processes to evaluate quality or performance. **GOE—Interest Area:** 02. Architecture and Construction. **Work Group:** 02.04. Construction Crafts. **Other Jobs in This Work Group:** Boilermakers; Brattice Builders; Brickmasons and Blockmasons; Carpet Installers; Ceiling Tile Installers; Cement Masons and Concrete Finishers; Commercial Divers; Construction Carpenters; Crane and Tower Operators; Dragline Operators; Drywall Installers; Electricians; Fence Erectors; Floor Layers, Except Carpet, Wood, and Hard Tiles; Floor Sanders and Finishers; Glaziers; Grader, Bulldozer, and Scraper Operators; Hazardous Materials Removal Workers; Insulation Workers, Floor, Ceiling, and Wall; Insulation Workers, Mechanical; Manufactured Building and Mobile Home Installers; Operating Engineers; Painters, Construction and Maintenance; Paperhangers; Paving, Surfacing, and Tamping Equipment Operators; Pile-Driver Operators; Pipe Fitters; Pipelayers; Pipelaying Fitters; Plasterers and Stucco Masons; Plumbers; Rail-Track Laying and Maintenance Equipment Operators; Refractory Materials Repairers, Except Brickmasons; Reinforcing Iron and Rebar Workers; Riggers; Roofers; Rough Carpenters; Security and Fire Alarm Systems Installers; Segmental Pavers; Sheet Metal Workers; Ship Carpenters and Joiners; Stone Cutters and Carvers; Stonemasons; Structural Iron and Steel Workers; Tapers; Terrazzo Workers and Finishers; Tile and Marble Setters. **PERSONALITY TYPE:** Realistic.

EDUCATION/TRAINING PROGRAM(S)—Carpentry/Carpenter. **RELATED KNOWLEDGE/ COURSES—Building and Construction:** Knowledge of the materials, methods, and tools involved in the construction or repair of houses, buildings, or other structures such as highways and roads. **Design:** Knowledge of design techniques, tools, and principles involved in production of precision technical plans, blueprints, drawings, and models. **Mechanical Devices:** Knowledge of machines and tools, including their designs, uses, repair, and maintenance. **Engineering and Technology:** Knowledge of the practical application of engineering science and technology. This includes applying principles, techniques, procedures, and equipment to the design and production of various goods and services. **Production and Processing:** Knowledge of raw materials, production processes, quality control, costs, and other techniques for maximizing the effective manufacture and distribution of goods. **Physics:** Knowledge and prediction of physical principles and laws and their interrelationships and applications to understanding fluid, material, and atmospheric dynamics and mechanical, electrical, atomic, and subatomic structures and processes.

Bookkeeping, Accounting, and Auditing Clerks

- Education/Training Required: Moderate-term on-the-job training
- Annual Earnings: $28,570
- Growth: 3.0%
- Annual Job Openings: 274,000
- Self-Employed: 7.9%
- Part-Time: 25.0%

Compute, classify, and record numerical data to keep financial records complete. Perform any combination of routine calculating, posting, and verifying duties to obtain primary financial data for use in maintaining accounting records. May also check the accuracy of figures, calculations, and postings pertaining to business transactions recorded by other workers. Check figures, postings, and documents for correct entry, mathematical accuracy, and proper codes. Operate computers programmed with accounting software to record, store, and analyze information. Comply with federal, state, and company policies, procedures, and regulations. Debit, credit, and total accounts on computer spreadsheets and databases, using specialized accounting software. Classify, record, and summarize numerical and financial data in order to compile and keep financial records, using journals and ledgers or computers. Calculate, prepare, and issue bills, invoices, account statements, and other financial statements according to established procedures. Compile statistical, financial, accounting, or auditing reports and tables pertaining to such matters as cash receipts, expenditures, accounts payable and receivable, and profits and losses. Code documents according to company procedures. Access computerized financial information to answer general questions as well as those related to specific accounts. Operate 10-key calculators, typewriters, and copy machines to perform calculations and produce documents. Reconcile or note and report discrepancies found in records. Perform financial calculations such as amounts due, interest charges, balances, discounts, equity, and principal. Perform general office duties such as filing, answering telephones, and handling routine correspondence. Prepare bank deposits by compiling data from cashiers; verifying and balancing receipts; and sending cash, checks, or other forms of payment to banks. Receive, record, and bank cash, checks, and vouchers. Calculate and prepare checks for utilities, taxes, and other payments. Compare computer printouts to manually maintained journals in order to determine if they match. Reconcile records of bank transactions. Prepare trial balances of books. Monitor status of loans and accounts to ensure that payments are up to date. Transfer details from separate journals to general ledgers and/or data processing sheets. Compile budget data and documents based on estimated revenues and expenses and previous budgets. **SKILLS—Management of Financial Resources:** Determining how money will be spent to get the work done and accounting for these expenditures. **Time Management:** Managing one's own time and the time of others. **Instructing:** Teaching others how to do something. **Critical Thinking:** Using logic and reasoning to identify the strengths and weaknesses of alternative solutions, conclusions, or approaches to problems. **Negotiation:** Bringing others together and trying to reconcile differences. **Active Learning:** Understanding the implications of new information for both current and future problem-solving and decision-making. **Learning Strategies:** Selecting and using training/instructional methods and procedures appropriate for the situation when learning or teaching new things. **Mathematics:** Using mathematics to solve problems. **Persuasion:** Persuading others to change their minds or behavior. **GOE—Interest Area:** 04. Business and Administration. **Work Group:** 04.06. Mathematical Clerical Support. **Other Jobs in This Work Group:** Billing, Cost, and Rate Clerks; Brokerage Clerks; Payroll and Timekeeping Clerks; Statement Clerks; Tax Preparers. **PERSONALITY TYPE:** Conventional.

EDUCATION/TRAINING PROGRAM(S)— Accounting and Related Services, Other; Accounting Technology/Technician and Bookkeeping. **RELATED KNOWLEDGE/COURSES—Clerical Practices:** Knowledge of administrative and clerical procedures and systems such as word processing, managing files and records, stenography and transcription, designing forms, and other office procedures and terminology. **Economics and Accounting:** Knowledge of economic and accounting principles and practices, the financial markets, banking, and the analysis and reporting of financial data. **Mathematics:** Knowledge of arithmetic, algebra, geometry, calculus, and statistics and their applications. **Computers and Electronics:** Knowledge of circuit boards, processors, chips, electronic equipment, and computer hardware and software, including applications and programming. **Customer and Personal Service:** Knowledge of principles and processes for providing customer and personal services. This includes customer needs assessment, meeting quality standards for services, and evaluation of customer satisfaction. **English Language:** Knowledge of the structure and content of the English language, including the meaning and spelling of words, rules of composition, and grammar.

Brattice Builders

- Education/Training Required: Moderate-term on-the-job training
- Annual Earnings: $34,900
- Growth: 10.1%
- Annual Job Openings: 193,000
- Self-Employed: 29.7%
- Part-Time: 5.3%

Build doors or brattices (ventilation walls or partitions) in underground passageways to control the proper circulation of air through the passageways and to the working places. Installs rigid and flexible air ducts to transport air to work areas. Drills and blasts obstructing boulders to reopen ventilation shafts. Erects partitions to support roof in areas unsuited to timbering or bolting. **SKILLS—Installation:** Installing equipment, machines, wiring, or programs to meet specifications. **Technology Design:** Generating or adapting equipment and technology to serve user needs. **Operations Analysis:** Analyzing needs and product requirements to create a design. **Equipment**

Selection: Determining the kind of tools and equipment needed to do a job. **Quality Control Analysis:** Conducting tests and inspections of products, services, or processes to evaluate quality or performance. **GOE—Interest Area:** 02. Architecture and Construction. **Work Group:** 02.04. Construction Crafts. **Other Jobs in This Work Group:** Boat Builders and Shipwrights; Boilermakers; Brickmasons and Blockmasons; Carpet Installers; Ceiling Tile Installers; Cement Masons and Concrete Finishers; Commercial Divers; Construction Carpenters; Crane and Tower Operators; Dragline Operators; Drywall Installers; Electricians; Fence Erectors; Floor Layers, Except Carpet, Wood, and Hard Tiles; Floor Sanders and Finishers; Glaziers; Grader, Bulldozer, and Scraper Operators; Hazardous Materials Removal Workers; Insulation Workers, Floor, Ceiling, and Wall; Insulation Workers, Mechanical; Manufactured Building and Mobile Home Installers; Operating Engineers; Painters, Construction and Maintenance; Paperhangers; Paving, Surfacing, and Tamping Equipment Operators; Pile-Driver Operators; Pipe Fitters; Pipelayers; Pipelaying Fitters; Plasterers and Stucco Masons; Plumbers; Rail-Track Laying and Maintenance Equipment Operators; Refractory Materials Repairers, Except Brickmasons; Reinforcing Iron and Rebar Workers; Riggers; Roofers; Rough Carpenters; Security and Fire Alarm Systems Installers; Segmental Pavers; Sheet Metal Workers; Ship Carpenters and Joiners; Stone Cutters and Carvers; Stonemasons; Structural Iron and Steel Workers; Tapers; Terrazzo Workers and Finishers; Tile and Marble Setters. **PERSONALITY TYPE:** Realistic.

EDUCATION/TRAINING PROGRAM(S)—Carpentry/Carpenter. **RELATED KNOWLEDGE/ COURSES—Building and Construction:** Knowledge of the materials, methods, and tools involved in the construction or repair of houses, buildings, or other structures such as highways and roads. **Physics:** Knowledge and prediction of physical principles and laws and their interrelationships and applications to understanding fluid, material, and atmospheric dynamics and mechanical, electrical, atomic, and subatomic structures and processes. **Engineering and Technology:** Knowledge of the practical application of engineering science and technology. This includes applying principles, techniques, procedures, and equipment to the design and production of various goods and services. **Mechanical Devices:** Knowledge of machines and tools, including their designs, uses, repair, and maintenance.

Brazers

- Education/Training Required: Short-term on-the-job training
- Annual Earnings: $30,620
- Growth: 17.0%
- Annual Job Openings: 71,000
- Self-Employed: 5.6%
- Part-Time: 2.1%

Braze together components to assemble fabricated metal parts, using torch or welding machine and flux. Guides torch and rod along joint of workpieces to heat to brazing temperature, melt braze alloy, and bond workpieces together. Cuts carbon electrodes to specified size and shape, using cutoff saw. Removes workpiece from fixture, using tongs, and cools workpiece, using air or water. Cleans joints of workpieces by dipping them into cleaning solution or using wire brush. Examines seam and rebrazes defective joints or broken parts. Connects hoses from torch to regulator valves and cylinders of oxygen and specified fuel gas (acetylene or natural). Turns valves to start flow of gases, lights flame, and adjusts valves to obtain desired color and size of flame. Brushes flux onto joint of workpiece or dips braze rod into flux to prevent oxidation of metal. Aligns and secures workpieces in fixtures, jigs, or vise, using rule, square, or template. Melts and separates brazed joints to remove and straighten damaged or misaligned components, using hand torch or furnace. Selects torch tip, flux, and brazing alloy from data charts or work order. Adjusts electric current and timing cycle of resistance welding machine to heat metal to bonding temperature. **SKILLS—Operation and Control:** Controlling operations of equipment or systems. **Operation Monitoring:** Watching gauges, dials, or other indicators to make sure a machine is working properly. **Installation:** Installing equipment, machines, wiring, or programs to meet specifications. **Equipment Selection:** Determining the kind of tools and equipment needed to do a job. **Science:** Using scientific rules and methods to solve problems. **GOE—Interest Area:** 13. Manufacturing. **Work Group:** 13.04. Welding, Brazing, and Soldering. **Other Jobs in This Work Group:** Fitters, Structural Metal—Precision; Metal Fabricators, Structural Metal Products; Solderers; Soldering and Brazing Machine Operators and Tenders; Welder-Fitters; Welders and Cutters; Welders, Production; Welding Machine Operators and Tenders; Welding Machine Setters and Set-Up Operators. **PERSONALITY TYPE:** Realistic.

EDUCATION/TRAINING PROGRAM(S)— Welding Technology/Welder. **RELATED KNOWLEDGE/COURSES—Engineering and Technology:** Knowledge of the practical application of engineering science and technology. This includes applying principles, techniques, procedures, and equipment to the design and production of various goods and services. **Building and Construction:** Knowledge of the materials, methods, and tools involved in the construction or repair of houses, buildings, or other structures such as highways and roads. **Mechanical Devices:** Knowledge of machines and tools, including their designs, uses, repair, and maintenance. **Chemistry:** Knowledge of the chemical composition, structure, and properties of substances and of the chemical processes and transformations that they undergo. This includes uses of chemicals and their danger signs, production techniques, and disposal methods.

Brickmasons and Blockmasons

- Education/Training Required: Long-term on-the-job training
- Annual Earnings: $41,740
- Growth: 14.2%
- Annual Job Openings: 21,000
- Self-Employed: 27.9%
- Part-Time: 5.3%

Lay and bind building materials, such as brick, structural tile, concrete block, cinder block, glass block, and terra-cotta block, with mortar and other substances to construct or repair walls, partitions, arches, sewers, and other structures. Construct corners by fastening in plumb position a corner pole or building a corner pyramid of bricks and then filling in between the corners, using a line from corner to corner to guide each course, or layer, of brick. Measure distance from reference points and mark guidelines to lay out work, using plumb bobs and levels. Calculate angles and courses and determine vertical and horizontal alignment of courses. Fasten or fuse brick or other building material to structure with wire clamps, anchor holes, torch, or cement. Break or cut bricks, tiles, or blocks to size, using trowel edge, hammer, or power saw. Remove excess mortar with trowels and hand tools and finish mortar joints with jointing tools for a sealed, uniform appearance. Interpret blueprints and drawings to determine specifications and to calculate the materials required. Apply and smooth mortar or other mixture over work surface. Mix specified amounts of sand, clay, dirt, or mortar powder with water to form refractory mixtures. Examine brickwork or structure to determine need for repair. Clean working surface to remove scale, dust, soot, or chips of brick and mortar, using broom, wire brush, or scraper. Lay and align bricks, blocks, or tiles to build or repair structures or high-temperature equipment, such as cupola, kilns, ovens, or furnaces. Remove burned or damaged brick or mortar, using sledgehammer, crowbar, chipping gun, or chisel. **SKILLS—Equipment Maintenance:** Performing routine maintenance on equipment and determining when and what kind of maintenance is needed. **Mathematics:** Using mathematics to solve problems. **Installation:** Installing equipment, machines, wiring, or programs to meet specifications. **Instructing:** Teaching others how to do something. **Coordination:** Adjusting actions in relation to others' actions. **Social Perceptiveness:** Being aware of others' reactions and understanding why they react as they do. **Technology Design:** Generating or adapting equipment and technology to serve user needs. **Management of Financial Resources:** Determining how money will be spent to get the work done and accounting for these expenditures. **GOE—Interest Area:** 02. Architecture and Construction. **Work Group:** 02.04. Construction Crafts. **Other Jobs in This Work Group:** Boat Builders and Shipwrights; Boilermakers; Brattice Builders; Carpet Installers; Ceiling Tile Installers; Cement Masons and Concrete Finishers; Commercial Divers; Construction Carpenters; Crane and Tower Operators; Dragline Operators; Drywall Installers; Electricians; Fence Erectors; Floor Layers, Except Carpet, Wood, and Hard Tiles; Floor Sanders and Finishers; Glaziers; Grader, Bulldozer, and Scraper Operators; Hazardous Materials Removal Workers; Insulation Workers, Floor, Ceiling, and Wall; Insulation Workers, Mechanical; Manufactured Building and Mobile Home Installers; Operating Engineers; Painters, Construction and Maintenance; Paperhangers; Paving, Surfacing, and Tamping Equipment Operators; Pile-Driver Operators; Pipe Fitters; Pipelayers; Pipelaying Fitters; Plasterers and Stucco Masons; Plumbers; Rail-Track Laying and Maintenance Equip-

ment Operators; Refractory Materials Repairers, Except Brickmasons; Reinforcing Iron and Rebar Workers; Riggers; Roofers; Rough Carpenters; Security and Fire Alarm Systems Installers; Segmental Pavers; Sheet Metal Workers; Ship Carpenters and Joiners; Stone Cutters and Carvers; Stonemasons; Structural Iron and Steel Workers; Tapers; Terrazzo Workers and Finishers; Tile and Marble Setters. **PERSONALITY TYPE:** Realistic.

EDUCATION/TRAINING PROGRAM(S)— Mason/Masonry. **RELATED KNOWLEDGE/ COURSES—Building and Construction:** Knowledge of the materials, methods, and tools involved in the construction or repair of houses, buildings, or other structures such as highways and roads. **Design:** Knowledge of design techniques, tools, and principles involved in production of precision technical plans, blueprints, drawings, and models. **Public Safety and Security:** Knowledge of relevant equipment, policies, procedures, and strategies to promote effective local, state, or national security operations for the protection of people, data, property, and institutions. **Production and Processing:** Knowledge of raw materials, production processes, quality control, costs, and other techniques for maximizing the effective manufacture and distribution of goods. **Mathematics:** Knowledge of arithmetic, algebra, geometry, calculus, and statistics and their applications. **Mechanical Devices:** Knowledge of machines and tools, including their designs, uses, repair, and maintenance.

Budget Analysts

◎ Education/Training Required: Bachelor's degree
◎ Annual Earnings: $56,040
◎ Growth: 14.0%
◎ Annual Job Openings: 8,000
◎ Self-Employed: 0%
◎ Part-Time: 4.7%

Examine budget estimates for completeness, accuracy, and conformance with procedures and regulations. Analyze budgeting and accounting reports for the purpose of maintaining expenditure controls. Analyze monthly department budgeting and accounting reports to maintain expenditure controls. Direct the preparation of regular and special budget reports.

Consult with managers to ensure that budget adjustments are made in accordance with program changes. Match appropriations for specific programs with appropriations for broader programs, including items for emergency funds. Provide advice and technical assistance with cost analysis, fiscal allocation, and budget preparation. Summarize budgets and submit recommendations for the approval or disapproval of funds requests. Seek new ways to improve efficiency and increase profits. Review operating budgets to analyze trends affecting budget needs. Examine budget estimates for completeness, accuracy, and conformance with procedures and regulations. Perform cost-benefits analyses to compare operating programs, review financial requests, and explore alternative financing methods. Interpret budget directives and establish policies for carrying out directives. Compile and analyze accounting records and other data to determine the financial resources required to implement a program. Testify before examining and fund-granting authorities, clarifying and promoting the proposed budgets. SKILLS—Management of Financial Resources: Determining how money will be spent to get the work done and accounting for these expenditures. Operations Analysis: Analyzing needs and product requirements to create a design. Mathematics: Using mathematics to solve problems. Service Orientation: Actively looking for ways to help people. Negotiation: Bringing others together and trying to reconcile differences. Time Management: Managing one's own time and the time of others. Active Learning: Understanding the implications of new information for both current and future problem-solving and decision-making. Complex Problem Solving: Identifying complex problems and reviewing related information to develop and evaluate options and implement solutions. Quality Control Analysis: Conducting tests and inspections of products, services, or processes to evaluate quality or performance. GOE—Interest Area: 04. Business and Administration. Work Group: 04.05. Accounting, Auditing, and Analytical Support. Other Jobs in This Work Group: Accountants; Auditors; Industrial Engineering Technicians; Logisticians; Management Analysts; Operations Research Analysts. PERSONALITY TYPE: Conventional.

EDUCATION/TRAINING PROGRAM(S)—Accounting; Finance, General. RELATED KNOWLEDGE/COURSES—Economics and Accounting: Knowledge of economic and accounting principles and practices, the financial markets, banking, and the analysis and reporting of financial data. Administration and Management: Knowledge of business and management principles involved in strategic planning, resource allocation, human resources modeling, leadership technique, production methods, and coordination of people and resources. Clerical Practices: Knowledge of administrative and clerical procedures and systems such as word processing, managing files and records, stenography and transcription, designing forms, and other office procedures and terminology. Computers and Electronics: Knowledge of circuit boards, processors, chips, electronic equipment, and computer hardware and software, including applications and programming. Mathematics: Knowledge of arithmetic, algebra, geometry, calculus, and statistics and their applications. English Language: Knowledge of the structure and content of the English language, including the meaning and spelling of words, rules of composition, and grammar.

Bus and Truck Mechanics and Diesel Engine Specialists

- Education/Training Required: Postsecondary vocational training
- Annual Earnings: $35,780
- Growth: 14.2%
- Annual Job Openings: 28,000
- Self-Employed: 3.9%
- Part-Time: 2.5%

Diagnose, adjust, repair, or overhaul trucks, buses, and all types of diesel engines. Includes mechanics working primarily with automobile diesel engines. Use hand tools, such as screwdrivers, pliers, wrenches, pressure gauges, and precision instruments, as well as power tools, such as pneumatic wrenches, lathes, welding equipment, and jacks and hoists. Inspect brake systems, steering mechanisms, wheel bearings, and other important parts to ensure that they are in proper operating condition. Perform routine maintenance such as changing oil, checking batteries, and lubricating equipment and machinery. Adjust and reline brakes, align wheels, tighten bolts and screws, and reassemble equipment. Raise trucks, buses, and heavy parts or equipment, using hydraulic jacks or hoists. Test-drive trucks and buses to diagnose malfunctions or to ensure that they are working properly. Inspect, test, and listen to defective equipment to diagnose malfunctions, using test instruments such as handheld computers, motor analyzers, chassis charts, and pressure gauges. Examine and adjust protective guards, loose bolts, and specified safety devices. Inspect and verify dimensions and clearances of parts to ensure conformance to factory specifications. Specialize in repairing and maintaining parts of the engine, such as fuel injection systems. Attach test instruments to equipment and read dials and gauges in order to diagnose malfunctions. Rewire ignition systems, lights, and instrument panels. Recondition and replace parts, pistons, bearings, gears, and valves. Repair and adjust seats, doors, and windows and install and repair accessories. Inspect, repair, and maintain automotive and mechanical equipment and machinery such as pumps and compressors. Disassemble and overhaul internal combustion engines, pumps, generators, transmissions, clutches, and differential units. Rebuild gas and/or diesel engines. Align front ends and suspension systems. **SKILLS—Equipment Maintenance:** Performing routine maintenance on equipment and determining when and what kind of maintenance is needed. **Repairing:** Repairing machines or systems by using the needed tools. **Troubleshooting:** Determining causes of operating errors and deciding what to do about them. **Installation:** Installing equipment, machines, wiring, or programs to meet specifications. **Learning Strategies:** Selecting and using training/instructional methods and procedures appropriate for the situation when learning or teaching new things. **Technology Design:** Generating or adapting equipment and technology to serve user needs. **Science:** Using scientific rules and methods to solve problems. **Social Perceptiveness:** Being aware of others' reactions and understanding why they react as they do. **Coordination:** Adjusting actions in relation to others' actions. **Instructing:** Teaching others how to do something. **GOE—Interest Area:** 13. Manufacturing. **Work Group:** 13.14. Vehicle and Facility Mechanical Work. **Other Jobs in This Work Group:** Aircraft Body and Bonded Structure Repairers; Aircraft Engine Specialists; Aircraft Rigging Assemblers; Aircraft Structure Assemblers, Precision; Aircraft Systems Assemblers, Precision; Airframe-and-Power-Plant Mechanics; Automotive Body and Related Repairers; Automotive Glass Installers and Repairers; Automotive Master Mechanics; Automotive Specialty Technicians; Farm Equipment Mechanics; Fiberglass Laminators and Fabricators; Mobile Heavy Equipment Mechanics, Except Engines; Motorboat Mechanics; Motorcycle Mechanics; Outdoor Power Equipment and Other Small Engine Mechanics; Rail Car Repairers; Recreational Vehicle Service Technicians; Tire Repairers and Changers. **PERSONALITY TYPE:** Realistic.

EDUCATION/TRAINING PROGRAM(S)— Diesel Mechanics Technology/Technician; Medium/Heavy Vehicle and Truck Technology/Technician. **RELATED KNOWLEDGE/COURSES—Mechanical Devices:** Knowledge of machines and tools, including their designs, uses, repair, and maintenance. **Transportation:** Knowledge of principles and methods for moving people or goods by air, rail, sea, or road, including the relative costs and benefits. **Public Safety and Security:** Knowledge of relevant equipment, policies, procedures, and strategies to promote effective local, state, or national security operations for the protection of people, data, property, and institutions. **Engineering and Technology:** Knowledge of the practical application of engineering science and technology. This includes applying principles, techniques, procedures, and equipment to the design and production of various goods and services. **Physics:** Knowledge and prediction of physical principles and laws and their interrelationships and applications to understanding fluid, material, and atmospheric dynamics and mechanical, electrical, atomic, and subatomic structures and processes. **Chemistry:** Knowledge of the chemical composition, structure, and properties of substances and of the chemical processes and transformations that they undergo. This includes uses of chemicals and their danger signs, production techniques, and disposal methods. **Law and Government:** Knowledge of laws, legal codes, court procedures, precedents, government regulations, executive orders, agency rules, and the democratic political process.

Bus Drivers, School

- Education/Training Required: Short-term on-the-job training
- Annual Earnings: $23,250
- Growth: 16.7%
- Annual Job Openings: 76,000
- Self-Employed: 0.7%
- Part-Time: 35.6%

Transport students or special clients such as the elderly or persons with disabilities. Ensure adherence to safety rules. May assist passengers in boarding or exiting. Drive gasoline, diesel, or electrically powered multi-passenger vehicles to transport students between neighborhoods, schools, and school activities. Check the condition of a vehicle's tires, brakes, windshield wipers, lights, oil, fuel, water, and safety equipment to ensure that everything is in working order. Comply with traffic regulations in order to operate vehicles in a safe and courteous manner. Follow safety rules as students are boarding and exiting buses and as they cross streets near bus stops. Pick up and drop off students at regularly scheduled neighborhood locations, following strict time schedules. Read maps and follow written and verbal geographic directions. Regulate heating, lighting, and ventilation systems for passenger comfort. Escort small children across roads and highways. Keep bus interiors clean for passengers. Maintain knowledge of first-aid procedures. Maintain order among pupils during trips in order to ensure safety. Make minor repairs to vehicles. Prepare and submit reports that may include the number of passengers or trips, hours worked, mileage, fuel consumption, and/or fares received. Report any bus malfunctions or needed repairs. Report delays, accidents, or other traffic and transportation situations, using telephones or mobile two-way radios. **SKILLS—Repairing:** Repairing machines or systems by using the needed tools. **Operation and Control:** Controlling operations of equipment or systems. **Operation Monitoring:** Watching gauges, dials, or other indicators to make sure a machine is working properly. **Equipment Maintenance:** Performing routine maintenance on equipment and determining when and what kind of maintenance is needed. **GOE—Interest Area:** 16. Transportation, Distribution, and Logistics. **Work Group:** 16.06. Other Services Requiring Driving. **Other Jobs in This Work Group:** Ambulance Drivers and Attendants, Except Emergency Medical Technicians; Bus Drivers, Transit and Intercity; Couriers and Messengers; Driver/Sales Workers; Parking Lot Attendants; Postal Service Mail Carriers; Taxi Drivers and Chauffeurs. **PERSONALITY TYPE:** Realistic.

EDUCATION/TRAINING PROGRAM(S)— Truck and Bus Driver/Commercial Vehicle Operation. **RELATED KNOWLEDGE/COURSES—Transportation:** Knowledge of principles and methods for moving people or goods by air, rail, sea, or road, including the relative costs and benefits. **Public Safety**

and Security: Knowledge of relevant equipment, policies, procedures, and strategies to promote effective local, state, or national security operations for the protection of people, data, property, and institutions. **Customer and Personal Service:** Knowledge of principles and processes for providing customer and personal services. This includes customer needs assessment, meeting quality standards for services, and evaluation of customer satisfaction. **Mechanical Devices:** Knowledge of machines and tools, including their designs, uses, repair, and maintenance. **Geography:** Knowledge of principles and methods for describing the features of land, sea, and air masses, including their physical characteristics; locations; interrelationships; and distribution of plant, animal, and human life. **Law and Government:** Knowledge of laws, legal codes, court procedures, precedents, government regulations, executive orders, agency rules, and the democratic political process.

Bus Drivers, Transit and Intercity

- Education/Training Required: Moderate-term on-the-job training
- Annual Earnings: $29,730
- Growth: 15.2%
- Annual Job Openings: 33,000
- Self-Employed: 0.7%
- Part-Time: 35.6%

Drive bus or motor coach, including regular route operations, charters, and private carriage. May assist passengers with baggage. May collect fares or tickets. Inspect vehicles and check gas, oil, and water levels prior to departure. Drive vehicles over specified routes or to specified destinations according to time schedules in order to transport passengers, complying with traffic regulations. Park vehicles at loading areas so that passengers can board. Assist passengers with baggage and collect tickets or cash fares. Report delays or accidents. Advise passengers to be seated and orderly while on vehicles. Regulate heating, lighting, and ventilating systems for passenger comfort. Load and unload baggage in baggage compartments. Record cash receipts and ticket fares. Make minor repairs to vehicle and change tires. **SKILLS—Social Perceptiveness:** Being aware of others' reactions and understanding why they react as they do. **Equipment Maintenance:** Performing routine maintenance on equipment and determining when and what kind of maintenance is needed. **Operation and Control:** Controlling operations of equipment or systems. **Troubleshooting:** Determining causes of operating errors and deciding what to do about them. **Negotiation:** Bringing others together and trying to reconcile differences. **Operation Monitoring:** Watching gauges, dials, or other indicators to make sure a machine is working properly. **Service Orientation:** Actively looking for ways to help people. **Instructing:** Teaching others how to do something. **GOE—Interest Area:** 16. Transportation, Distribution, and Logistics. **Work Group:** 16.06. Other Services Requiring Driving. **Other Jobs in This Work Group:** Ambulance Drivers and Attendants, Except Emergency Medical Technicians; Bus Drivers, School; Couriers and Messengers; Driver/Sales Workers; Parking Lot Attendants; Postal Service Mail Carriers; Taxi Drivers and Chauffeurs. **PERSONALITY TYPE:** Realistic.

EDUCATION/TRAINING PROGRAM(S)— Truck and Bus Driver/Commercial Vehicle Operation. **RELATED KNOWLEDGE/COURSES—Transportation:** Knowledge of principles and methods for moving people or goods by air, rail, sea, or road, including the relative costs and benefits. **Customer and Personal Service:** Knowledge of principles and processes for providing customer and personal services. This includes customer needs assessment, meeting quality standards for services, and evaluation of customer satisfaction. **Geography:** Knowledge of principles and methods for describing the features of land, sea, and air masses, including their physical characteristics; locations; interrelationships; and distribution of plant, animal, and human life. **Public Safety and Security:** Knowledge of relevant equipment, policies, procedures, and strategies to promote effective local, state, or national security operations for the protection of people, data, property, and institutions. **Psychology:** Knowledge of human behavior and performance; individual differences in ability, personality, and interests; learning and motivation; psychological research methods; and the assessment and treatment of behavioral and affective disorders. **Law and Government:** Knowledge of laws, legal codes, court procedures, precedents, government regulations, executive orders, agency rules, and the democratic political process.

Business Teachers, Postsecondary

◎ Education/Training Required: Master's degree
◎ Annual Earnings: $57,210
◎ Growth: 38.1%
◎ Annual Job Openings: 216,000
◎ Self-Employed: 0.3%
◎ Part-Time: 27.7%

Teach courses in business administration and management, such as accounting, finance, human resources, labor relations, marketing, and operations research. Prepare and deliver lectures to undergraduate and/or graduate students on topics such as financial accounting, principles of marketing, and operations management. Evaluate and grade students' class work, assignments, and papers. Compile, administer, and grade examinations or assign this work to others. Prepare course materials such as syllabi, homework assignments, and handouts. Maintain student attendance records, grades, and other required records. Initiate, facilitate, and moderate classroom discussions. Plan, evaluate, and revise curricula, course content, and course materials and methods of instruction. Maintain regularly scheduled office hours in order to advise and assist students. Keep abreast of developments in their field by reading current literature, talking with colleagues, and participating in professional organizations and conferences. Advise students on academic and vocational curricula and on career issues. Select and obtain materials and supplies such as textbooks. Collaborate with colleagues to address teaching and research issues. Collaborate with members of the business community to improve programs, to develop new programs, and to provide student access to learning opportunities such as internships. Participate in student recruitment, registration, and placement activities. Serve on academic or administrative committees that deal with institutional policies, departmental matters, and academic issues. Participate in campus and community events. Compile bibliographies of specialized materials for outside reading assignments. Perform administrative duties such as serving as department head. Supervise undergraduate and/or graduate teaching, internship, and research work. Conduct research in a particular field of knowledge and publish findings in professional journals, books, and/or electronic media. Act as advisers to student organizations. **SKILLS—Instructing:** Teaching others how to do something. **Learning Strategies:** Selecting and using training/instructional methods and procedures appropriate for the situation when learning or teaching new things. **Writing:** Communicating effectively in writing as appropriate for the needs of the audience. **Active Learning:** Understanding the implications of new information for both current and future problem-solving and decision-making. **Monitoring:** Monitoring or assessing your performance or that of other individuals or organizations to make improvements or take corrective action. **Social Perceptiveness:** Being aware of others' reactions and understanding why they react as they do. **Persuasion:** Persuading others to change their minds or behavior. **Time Management:** Managing one's own time and the time of others. **GOE—Interest Area:** 05. Education and Training. **Work Group:** 05.03. Postsecondary and Adult Teaching and Instructing. **Other Jobs in This Work Group:** Adult Literacy, Remedial Education, and GED Teachers and Instructors; Agricultural Sciences Teachers, Postsecondary; Anthropology and Archeology Teachers, Postsecondary; Architecture Teachers, Postsecondary; Area, Ethnic, and Cultural Studies Teachers, Postsecondary; Art, Drama, and Music Teachers, Postsecondary; Atmospheric, Earth, Marine, and Space Sciences Teachers, Postsecondary; Biological Science Teachers, Postsecondary; Chemistry Teachers, Postsecondary; Communications Teachers, Postsecondary; Computer Science Teachers, Postsecondary; Criminal Justice and Law Enforcement Teachers, Postsecondary; Economics Teachers, Postsecondary; Education Teachers, Postsecondary; Engineering Teachers, Postsecondary; English Language and Literature Teachers, Postsecondary; Environmental Science Teachers, Postsecondary; Farm and Home Management Advisors; Foreign Language and Literature Teachers, Postsecondary; Forestry and Conservation Science Teachers, Postsecondary; Geography Teachers, Postsecondary; Graduate Teaching Assistants; Health Specialties Teachers, Postsecondary; History Teachers, Postsecondary; Home Economics Teachers, Postsecondary; Law Teachers, Postsecondary; Library Science Teachers, Postsecondary; Mathematical Science Teachers, Postsecondary; Nursing Instructors and Teachers, Postsecondary; Philosophy and Religion Teachers, Postsecondary; Physics Teachers, Postsecondary; Political Science Teachers, Postsecondary; Psychology Teachers, Postsecondary; Recre-

ation and Fitness Studies Teachers, Postsecondary; Self-Enrichment Education Teachers; Social Work Teachers, Postsecondary; Sociology Teachers, Postsecondary; Vocational Education Teachers, Postsecondary. **PERSONALITY TYPE:** No data available.

EDUCATION/TRAINING PROGRAM(S)— Accounting; Actuarial Science; Business Administration and Management, General; Business Statistics; Business Teacher Education; Business/Commerce, General; Business/Corporate Communications; Entrepreneurship/Entrepreneurial Studies; Finance, General; Financial Planning and Services; Franchising and Franchise Operations; Human Resources Management/Personnel Administration, General; Insurance; International Business/Trade/Commerce; International Finance; International Marketing; Investments and Securities; Labor and Industrial Relations; Logistics and Materials Management; Management Science, General; Marketing Research; Marketing/Marketing Management, General; Operations Management and Supervision; Organizational Behavior Studies; Public Finance; Purchasing, Procurement/Acquisitions, and Contracts Management. **RELATED KNOWLEDGE/COURSES—Education and Training:** Knowledge of principles and methods for curriculum and training design, teaching and instruction for individuals and groups, and the measurement of training effects. **Economics and Accounting:** Knowledge of economic and accounting principles and practices, the financial markets, banking, and the analysis and reporting of financial data. **English Language:** Knowledge of the structure and content of the English language, including the meaning and spelling of words, rules of composition, and grammar. **Sales and Marketing:** Knowledge of principles and methods for showing, promoting, and selling products or services. This includes marketing strategy and tactics, product demonstrations, sales techniques, and sales control systems. **Personnel and Human Resources:** Knowledge of principles and procedures for personnel recruitment, selection, training, compensation and benefits, labor relations and negotiation, and personnel information systems. **Customer and Personal Service:** Knowledge of principles and processes for providing customer and personal services. This includes customer needs assessment, meeting quality standards for services, and evaluation of customer satisfaction.

B

Calibration and Instrumentation Technicians

- ◎ Education/Training Required: Associate degree
- ◎ Annual Earnings: $46,310
- ◎ Growth: 10.0%
- ◎ Annual Job Openings: 24,000
- ◎ Self-Employed: 0.4%
- ◎ Part-Time: 5.0%

Develop, test, calibrate, operate, and repair electrical, mechanical, electromechanical, electrohydraulic, or electronic measuring and recording instruments, apparatus, and equipment. Plans sequence of testing and calibration program for instruments and equipment according to blueprints, schematics, technical manuals, and other specifications. Performs preventative and corrective maintenance of test apparatus and peripheral equipment. Confers with engineers, supervisor, and other technical workers to assist with equipment installation, maintenance, and repair techniques. Analyzes and converts test data, using mathematical formulas, and reports results and proposed modifications. Sets up test equipment and conducts tests on performance and reliability of mechanical, structural, or electromechanical equipment. Selects sensing, telemetering, and recording instrumentation and circuitry. Disassembles and reassembles instruments and equipment, using hand tools, and inspects instruments and equipment for defects. Sketches plans for developing jigs, fixtures, instruments, and related nonstandard apparatus. Modifies performance and operation of component parts and circuitry to specifications, using test equipment and precision instruments. **SKILLS— Technology Design:** Generating or adapting equipment and technology to serve user needs. **Equipment Maintenance:** Performing routine maintenance on equipment and determining when and what kind of maintenance is needed. **Quality Control Analysis:** Conducting tests and inspections of products, services, or processes to evaluate quality or performance. **Science:** Using scientific rules and methods to solve problems. **Equipment Selection:** Determining the kind of tools and equipment needed to do a job. **Troubleshooting:** Determining causes of operating errors

and deciding what to do about them. **Installation:** Installing equipment, machines, wiring, or programs to meet specifications. **Operation Monitoring:** Watching gauges, dials, or other indicators to make sure a machine is working properly. **GOE—Interest Area:** 15. Scientific Research, Engineering, and Mathematics. **Work Group:** 15.09. Engineering Technology. **Other Jobs in This Work Group:** Aerospace Engineering and Operations Technicians; Cartographers and Photogrammetrists; Civil Engineering Technicians; Electrical Engineering Technicians; Electro-Mechanical Technicians; Electronic Drafters; Electronics Engineering Technicians; Environmental Engineering Technicians; Mapping Technicians; Mechanical Drafters; Mechanical Engineering Technicians; Surveying Technicians. **PERSONALITY TYPE:** Realistic.

EDUCATION/TRAINING PROGRAM(S)— Computer Engineering Technology/Technician; Computer Technology/Computer Systems Technology; Electrical and Electronic Engineering Technologies/Technicians, Other; Electrical, Electronic, and Communications Engineering Technology/Technician; Telecommunications Technology/Technician. **RELATED KNOWLEDGE/COURSES—Design:** Knowledge of design techniques, tools, and principles involved in production of precision technical plans, blueprints, drawings, and models. **Mathematics:** Knowledge of arithmetic, algebra, geometry, calculus, and statistics and their applications. **Engineering and Technology:** Knowledge of the practical application of engineering science and technology. This includes applying principles, techniques, procedures, and equipment to the design and production of various goods and services. **Computers and Electronics:** Knowledge of circuit boards, processors, chips, electronic equipment, and computer hardware and software, including applications and programming. **Mechanical Devices:** Knowledge of machines and tools, including their designs, uses, repair, and maintenance. **Physics:** Knowledge and prediction of physical principles and laws and their interrelationships and applications to understanding fluid, material, and atmospheric dynamics and mechanical, electrical, atomic, and subatomic structures and processes.

Camera Operators, Television, Video, and Motion Picture

- Education/Training Required: Moderate-term on-the-job training
- Annual Earnings: $37,610
- Growth: 13.4%
- Annual Job Openings: 4,000
- Self-Employed: 23.8%
- Part-Time: 20.4%

Operate television, video, or motion picture camera to photograph images or scenes for various purposes, such as TV broadcasts, advertising, video production, or motion pictures. Operate television or motion picture cameras to record scenes for television broadcasts, advertising, or motion pictures. Compose and frame each shot, applying the technical aspects of light, lenses, film, filters, and camera settings in order to achieve the effects sought by directors. Operate zoom lenses, changing images according to specifications and rehearsal instructions. Use cameras in any of several different camera mounts, such as stationary, track-mounted, or crane-mounted. Test, clean, and maintain equipment to ensure proper working condition. Adjust positions and controls of cameras, printers, and related equipment in order to change focus, exposure, and lighting. Gather and edit raw footage on location to send to television affiliates for broadcast, using electronic news-gathering or film-production equipment. Confer with directors, sound and lighting technicians, electricians, and other crew members to discuss assignments and determine filming sequences, desired effects, camera movements, and lighting requirements. Observe sets or locations for potential problems and to determine filming and lighting requirements. Instruct camera operators regarding camera setups, angles, distances, movement, and variables and cues for starting and stopping filming. Select and assemble cameras, accessories, equipment, and film stock to be used during filming, using knowledge of filming techniques, requirements, and computations. Label and record contents of exposed film and note details on report forms. Read charts and compute ratios to determine variables such as lighting, shutter angles, filter factors, and camera distances. Set up cameras, optical printers, and related equipment to produce photographs and special effects. View films to resolve problems of exposure control, subject and camera movement, changes in subject distance, and related variables. Reload camera magazines with fresh raw film stock. Read and analyze work orders and specifications to determine locations of subject material, work procedures, sequences of operations, and machine setups. Receive raw film stock and maintain film inventories. **SKILLS—Operation Monitoring:** Watching gauges, dials, or other indicators to make sure a machine is working properly. **Equipment Maintenance:** Performing routine maintenance on equipment and determining when and what kind of maintenance is needed. **Troubleshooting:** Determining causes of operating errors and deciding what to do about them. **Operation and Control:** Controlling operations of equipment or systems. **Active Listening:** Giving full attention to what other people are saying, taking time to understand the points being made, asking questions as appropriate, and not interrupting at inappropriate times. **Coordination:** Adjusting actions in relation to others' actions. **Time Management:** Managing one's own time and the time of others. **Social Perceptiveness:** Being aware of others' reactions and understanding why they react as they do. **Persuasion:** Persuading others to change their minds or behavior. **GOE— Interest Area:** 03. Arts and Communication. **Work Group:** 03.09. Media Technology. **Other Jobs in This Work Group:** Audio and Video Equipment Technicians; Broadcast Technicians; Film and Video Editors; Multi-Media Artists and Animators; Photographic Hand Developers; Photographic Reproduction Technicians; Photographic Retouchers and Restorers; Professional Photographers; Radio Operators; Sound Engineering Technicians. **PERSONALITY TYPE:** Artistic.

EDUCATION/TRAINING PROGRAM(S)— Audiovisual Communications Technologies/Technicians, Other; Cinematography and Film/Video Production; Radio and Television Broadcasting Technology/Technician. **RELATED KNOWLEDGE/ COURSES—Communications and Media:** Knowledge of media production, communication, and dissemination techniques and methods. This includes alternative ways to inform and entertain via written, oral, and visual media. **Computers and Electronics:** Knowledge of circuit boards, processors, chips, electronic equipment, and computer hardware and software, including applications and programming. **Telecommunications:** Knowledge of transmission, broadcasting, switching, control, and operation of telecommunications systems. **Customer and Personal Service:** Knowledge of principles and processes for providing customer and personal services. This includes customer needs assessment, meeting quality standards for services, and evaluation of customer satisfaction. **Engineering and Technology:** Knowledge of the practical application of engineering science and technology. This includes applying principles, techniques, procedures, and equipment to the design and production of various goods and services. **Sales and Marketing:** Knowledge of principles and methods for showing, promoting, and selling products or services. This includes marketing strategy and tactics, product demonstrations, sales techniques, and sales control systems. **Fine Arts:** Knowledge of the theory and techniques required to compose, produce, and perform works of music, dance, the visual arts, drama, and sculpture.

Caption Writers

- ◎ Education/Training Required: Moderate-term on-the-job training
- ◎ Annual Earnings: $44,350
- ◎ Growth: 16.1%
- ◎ Annual Job Openings: 23,000
- ◎ Self-Employed: 67.9%
- ◎ Part-Time: 24.2%

Write caption phrases of dialogue for hearing-impaired and foreign language–speaking viewers of movie or television productions. Writes captions to describe music and background noises. Watches production and reviews captions simultaneously to determine which caption phrases require editing. Enters commands to synchronize captions with dialogue and place on the screen. Translates foreign-language dialogue into English-language captions or English dialogue into foreign-language captions. Operates computerized captioning system for movies or television productions for hearing-impaired and foreign language–speaking viewers. Oversees encoding of captions to master tape of television production. Discusses captions with directors or producers of movie and television productions. Edits translations for cor-

rectness of grammar, punctuation, and clarity of expression. **SKILLS—Writing:** Communicating effectively in writing as appropriate for the needs of the audience. **Reading Comprehension:** Understanding written sentences and paragraphs in work-related documents. **Operation and Control:** Controlling operations of equipment or systems. **GOE—Interest Area:** 03. Arts and Communication. **Work Group:** 03.03. News, Broadcasting, and Public Relations. **Other Jobs in This Work Group:** Broadcast News Analysts; Interpreters and Translators; Public Relations Specialists; Reporters and Correspondents. **PERSONALITY TYPE:** Artistic.

EDUCATION/TRAINING PROGRAM(S)— Broadcast Journalism; Business/Corporate Communications; Communication Studies/Speech Communication and Rhetoric; Communication, Journalism, and Related Programs, Other; Creative Writing; English Composition; Family and Consumer Sciences/Human Sciences Communication; Journalism; Mass Communication/Media Studies; Playwriting and Screenwriting; Technical and Business Writing. **RELATED KNOWLEDGE/COURSES—Foreign Language:** Knowledge of the structure and content of a foreign (non-English) language, including the meaning and spelling of words, rules of composition and grammar, and pronunciation. **Communications and Media:** Knowledge of media production, communication, and dissemination techniques and methods. This includes alternative ways to inform and entertain via written, oral, and visual media. **English Language:** Knowledge of the structure and content of the English language, including the meaning and spelling of words, rules of composition, and grammar. **Computers and Electronics:** Knowledge of circuit boards, processors, chips, electronic equipment, and computer hardware and software, including applications and programming. **Telecommunications:** Knowledge of transmission, broadcasting, switching, control, and operation of telecommunications systems.

Cardiovascular Technologists and Technicians

- ◎ Education/Training Required: Associate degree
- ◎ Annual Earnings: $38,690
- ◎ Growth: 33.5%
- ◎ Annual Job Openings: 6,000
- ◎ Self-Employed: 0.2%
- ◎ Part-Time: 17.5%

Conduct tests on pulmonary or cardiovascular systems of patients for diagnostic purposes. May conduct or assist in electrocardiograms, cardiac catheterizations, pulmonary function tests, lung capacity tests, and similar tests. Monitor patients' blood pressure and heart rate, using electrocardiogram (EKG) equipment, during diagnostic and therapeutic procedures in order to notify the physician if something appears wrong. Monitor patients' comfort and safety during tests, alerting physicians to abnormalities or changes in patient responses. Explain testing procedures to patient to obtain cooperation and reduce anxiety. Prepare reports of diagnostic procedures for interpretation by physician. Observe gauges, recorder, and video screens of data analysis system during imaging of cardiovascular system. Conduct electrocardiogram, phonocardiogram, echocardiogram, stress testing, and other cardiovascular tests to record patients' cardiac activity, using specialized electronic test equipment, recording devices, and laboratory instruments. Prepare and position patients for testing. Obtain and record patient identification, medical history, and test results. Attach electrodes to the patients' chests, arms, and legs, connect electrodes to leads from the electrocardiogram (EKG) machine, and operate the EKG machine to obtain a reading. Adjust equipment and controls according to physicians' orders or established protocol. Check, test, and maintain cardiology equipment, making minor repairs when necessary, to ensure proper operation. Supervise and train other cardiology technologists and students. Assist physicians in diagnosis and treatment of cardiac and peripheral vascular treatments, for example, assisting with balloon angioplasties to treat blood vessel blockages. Operate diagnostic imaging equipment to produce contrast-enhanced radiographs of heart and cardiovascular system. Inject contrast medium into patients' blood vessels. Observe ultrasound display screen and listen to signals to record vascular information such as blood pressure, limb volume changes, oxygen saturation, and cerebral circulation. Assess cardiac physiology and calculate valve areas from blood flow velocity measurements. Compare measurements of heart wall thickness and chamber sizes to standard norms to identify abnormalities. Activate fluoroscope and camera to produce images used to guide catheter through cardiovascular system. **SKILLS—Instructing:** Teaching others how to do something. **Service Orientation:** Actively looking for ways to help people. **Operation Monitoring:** Watching gauges, dials, or other indicators to make sure a machine is working properly. **Active Learning:** Understanding the implications of new information for both current and future problem-solving and decision-making. **Equipment Maintenance:** Performing routine maintenance on equipment and determining when and what kind of maintenance is needed. **Learning Strategies:** Selecting and using training/instructional methods and procedures appropriate for the situation when learning or teaching new things. **Social Perceptiveness:** Being aware of others' reactions and understanding why they react as they do. **Time Management:** Managing one's own time and the time of others. **GOE—Interest Area:** 08. Health Science. **Work Group:** 08.06. Medical Technology. **Other Jobs in This Work Group:** Biological Technicians; Diagnostic Medical Sonographers; Medical and Clinical Laboratory Technicians; Medical and Clinical Laboratory Technologists; Medical Equipment Preparers; Medical Records and Health Information Technicians; Nuclear Medicine Technologists; Opticians, Dispensing; Orthotists and Prosthetists; Radiologic Technicians; Radiologic Technologists. **PERSONALITY TYPE:** Investigative.

EDUCATION/TRAINING PROGRAM(S)—Cardiopulmonary Technology/Technologist; Cardiovascular Technology/Technologist; Electrocardiograph Technology/Technician; Perfusion Technology/Perfusionist. **RELATED KNOWLEDGE/COURSES— Medicine and Dentistry:** Knowledge of the information and techniques needed to diagnose and treat human injuries, diseases, and deformities. This includes symptoms, treatment alternatives, drug properties and interactions, and preventive health-care measures. **Customer and Personal Service:** Knowledge of principles and processes for providing customer and personal services. This includes customer needs assessment, meeting quality standards for services, and evaluation of customer satisfaction. **Psychology:** Knowledge of human behavior and performance; individual differences in ability, personality, and interests; learning and motivation; psychological research methods; and the assessment and treatment of behavioral and affective disorders. **Physics:** Knowledge and prediction of physical principles and laws and their interrelationships and applications to understanding fluid, material, and atmospheric dynamics and mechanical, electrical, atomic, and subatomic structures and processes. **Education and Training:** Knowledge of principles and methods for curriculum and training design, teaching and instruction for individuals and groups, and the measurement of training effects. **Computers and Electronics:** Knowledge of circuit boards, processors, chips, electronic equipment, and computer hardware and software, including applications and programming. **Biology:** Knowledge of plant and animal organisms and their tissues, cells, functions, interdependencies, and interactions with each other and the environment.

Cargo and Freight Agents

- ◎ Education/Training Required: Moderate-term on-the-job training
- ◎ Annual Earnings: $34,250
- ◎ Growth: 15.5%
- ◎ Annual Job Openings: 8,000
- ◎ Self-Employed: 0.1%
- ◎ Part-Time: 5.5%

Expedite and route movement of incoming and outgoing cargo and freight shipments in airline, train, and trucking terminals and shipping docks. Take orders from customers and arrange pickup of freight and cargo for delivery to loading platform. Prepare and examine bills of lading to determine shipping charges and tariffs. Advise clients on transportation and payment methods. Arrange insurance coverage for goods. Check import/export documentation to determine cargo contents and classify goods into different fee or tariff groups, using a tariff coding system. Contact vendors and/or claims adjustment departments in order to resolve problems with shipments or contact service depots to arrange for repairs. Determine method of shipment and prepare bills of lading, invoices, and other shipping documents. Direct deliv-

ery trucks to shipping doors or designated marshalling areas and help load and unload goods safely. Direct or participate in cargo loading in order to ensure completeness of load and even distribution of weight. Enter shipping information into a computer by hand or by using a hand-held scanner that reads bar codes on goods. Estimate freight or postal rates and record shipment costs and weights. Inspect and count items received and check them against invoices or other documents, recording shortages and rejecting damaged goods. Keep records of all goods shipped, received, and stored. Negotiate and arrange transport of goods with shipping or freight companies. Notify consignees, passengers, or customers of the arrival of freight or baggage and arrange for delivery. Retrieve stored items and trace lost shipments as necessary. Route received goods to first available flight or to appropriate storage areas or departments, using forklifts, handtrucks, or other equipment. Assemble containers and crates used to transport items such as machines or vehicles. Attach address labels, identification codes, and shipping instructions to containers. Coordinate and supervise activities of workers engaged in packing and shipping merchandise. Inspect trucks and vans to ensure cleanliness when shipping such items as grain, flour, and milk. Install straps, braces, and padding to loads in order to prevent shifting or damage during shipment. Maintain a supply of packing materials. Obtain flight numbers, airplane numbers, and names of crew members from dispatchers and record data on airplane flight papers. Open cargo containers and unwrap contents, using steel cutters, crowbars, or other hand tools. **SKILLS—Service Orientation:** Actively looking for ways to help people. **Operation and Control:** Controlling operations of equipment or systems. **Coordination:** Adjusting actions in relation to others' actions. **GOE—Interest Area:** 16. Transportation, Distribution, and Logistics. **Work Group:** 16.07. Transportation Support Work. **Other Jobs in This Work Group:** Bridge and Lock Tenders; Cleaners of Vehicles and Equipment; Freight Inspectors; Public Transportation Inspectors; Railroad Yard Workers; Stevedores, Except Equipment Operators; Traffic Technicians; Train Crew Members. **PERSONALITY TYPE:** Conventional.

EDUCATION/TRAINING PROGRAM(S)—General Office Occupations and Clerical Services. **RELATED KNOWLEDGE/COURSES—Transportation:** Knowledge of principles and methods for moving people or goods by air, rail, sea, or road, including the relative costs and benefits. **Telecommu-**

nications: Knowledge of transmission, broadcasting, switching, control, and operation of telecommunications systems. **Clerical Practices:** Knowledge of administrative and clerical procedures and systems such as word processing, managing files and records, stenography and transcription, designing forms, and other office procedures and terminology. **Geography:** Knowledge of principles and methods for describing the features of land, sea, and air masses, including their physical characteristics; locations; interrelationships; and distribution of plant, animal, and human life. **Customer and Personal Service:** Knowledge of principles and processes for providing customer and personal services. This includes customer needs assessment, meeting quality standards for services, and evaluation of customer satisfaction.

Carpenter Assemblers and Repairers

- ◎ Education/Training Required: Moderate-term on-the-job training
- ◎ Annual Earnings: $34,900
- ◎ Growth: 10.1%
- ◎ Annual Job Openings: 193,000
- ◎ Self-Employed: 29.7%
- ◎ Part-Time: 5.3%

Perform a variety of tasks requiring a limited knowledge of carpentry, such as applying siding and weatherboard to building exteriors or assembling and erecting prefabricated buildings. Measures and marks location of studs, leaders, and receptacle openings, using tape measure, template, and marker. Cuts sidings and moldings, sections of weatherboard, openings in sheetrock, and lumber, using hand tools and power tools. Lays out and aligns materials on worktable or in assembly jig according to specified instructions. Removes surface defects, using knife, scraper, wet sponge, electric iron, and sanding tools. Trims overlapping edges of wood or weatherboard, using portable router or power saw and hand tools. Installs prefabricated windows and doors; insulation; wall, ceiling, and floor panels; or siding, using adhesives, hoists, hand tools, and power tools. Aligns and fastens materials together, using hand tools and power tools, to form building or bracing. Repairs or replaces defective locks, hinges, cranks, and pieces of wood, using glue, hand tools, and power tools. Applies stain, paint, or crayons to defects and filters to touch up the repaired area. Directs crane operator in positioning floor, wall, ceiling, and roof panel on house foundation. Moves panel or roof section to other workstations or to storage or shipping area, using electric hoist. Studies blueprints, specification sheets, and drawings to determine style and type of window or wall panel required. Fills cracks, seams, depressions, and nail holes with filler. Examines wood surfaces for defects, such as nicks, cracks, or blisters. Measures cut materials to determine conformance to specifications, using tape measure. Realigns windows and screens to fit casements and oils moving parts. **SKILLS—Repairing:** Repairing machines or systems by using the needed tools. **Installation:** Installing equipment, machines, wiring, or programs to meet specifications. **Management of Material Resources:** Obtaining and seeing to the appropriate use of equipment, facilities, and materials needed to do certain work. **Operation and Control:** Controlling operations of equipment or systems. **Equipment Maintenance:** Performing routine maintenance on equipment and determining when and what kind of maintenance is needed. **GOE—Interest Area:** 02. Architecture and Construction. **Work Group:** 02.06. Construction Support/Labor. **Other Jobs in This Work Group:** Construction Laborers; Grips and Set-Up Workers, Motion Picture Sets, Studios, and Stages; Helpers—Brickmasons, Blockmasons, Stonemasons, and Tile and Marble Setters; Helpers—Carpenters; Helpers—Electricians; Helpers—Installation, Maintenance, and Repair Workers; Helpers—Painters, Paperhangers, Plasterers, and Stucco Masons; Helpers—Pipelayers, Plumbers, Pipefitters, and Steamfitters; Highway Maintenance Workers; Septic Tank Servicers and Sewer Pipe Cleaners. **PERSONALITY TYPE:** Realistic.

EDUCATION/TRAINING PROGRAM(S)—Carpentry/Carpenter. **RELATED KNOWLEDGE/COURSES—Building and Construction:** Knowledge of the materials, methods, and tools involved in the construction or repair of houses, buildings, or other structures such as highways and roads. **Design:** Knowledge of design techniques, tools, and principles involved in production of precision technical plans, blueprints, drawings, and models. **Engineering and Technology:** Knowledge of the practical application of engineering science and technology. This includes applying principles, techniques, procedures, and equipment to the design and production of various goods and services.

Carpet Installers

- Education/Training Required: Moderate-term on-the-job training
- Annual Earnings: $34,090
- Growth: 16.8%
- Annual Job Openings: 10,000
- Self-Employed: 53.5%
- Part-Time: 6.9%

Lay and install carpet from rolls or blocks on floors. Install padding and trim flooring materials. Join edges of carpet and seam edges where necessary by sewing or by using tape with glue and heated carpet iron. Cut and trim carpet to fit along wall edges, openings, and projections, finishing the edges with a wall trimmer. Inspect the surface to be covered to determine its condition and correct any imperfections that might show through carpet or cause carpet to wear unevenly. Roll out, measure, mark, and cut carpeting to size with a carpet knife, following floor sketches and allowing extra carpet for final fitting. Plan the layout of the carpet, allowing for expected traffic patterns and placing seams for best appearance and longest wear. Stretch carpet to align with walls and ensure a smooth surface and press carpet in place over tack strips or use staples, tape, tacks, or glue to hold carpet in place. Take measurements and study floor sketches to calculate the area to be carpeted and the amount of material needed. Cut carpet padding to size and install padding, following prescribed method. Install carpet on some floors by using adhesive, following prescribed method. Nail tack strips around area to be carpeted or use old strips to attach edges of new carpet. Fasten metal treads across door openings or where carpet meets flooring to hold carpet in place. Measure, cut, and install tackless strips along the baseboard or wall. Draw building diagrams and record dimensions. Move furniture from area to be carpeted and remove old carpet and padding. Cut and bind material. **SKILLS—Installation:** Installing equipment, machines, wiring, or programs to meet specifications. **Equipment Selection:** Determining the kind of tools and equipment needed to do a job. **Repairing:** Repairing machines or systems by using the needed tools. **Management of Personnel Resources:** Motivating, developing, and directing people as they work, identifying the best people for the job. **Coordination:** Adjusting actions in relation to others' actions. **Mathematics:** Using mathematics to solve problems. **Complex Problem Solving:** Identifying complex problems and reviewing related information to develop and evaluate options and implement solutions. **Learning Strategies:** Selecting and using training/instructional methods and procedures appropriate for the situation when learning or teaching new things. **GOE—Interest Area:** 02. Architecture and Construction. **Work Group:** 02.04. Construction Crafts. **Other Jobs in This Work Group:** Boat Builders and Shipwrights; Boilermakers; Brattice Builders; Brickmasons and Blockmasons; Ceiling Tile Installers; Cement Masons and Concrete Finishers; Commercial Divers; Construction Carpenters; Crane and Tower Operators; Dragline Operators; Drywall Installers; Electricians; Fence Erectors; Floor Layers, Except Carpet, Wood, and Hard Tiles; Floor Sanders and Finishers; Glaziers; Grader, Bulldozer, and Scraper Operators; Hazardous Materials Removal Workers; Insulation Workers, Floor, Ceiling, and Wall; Insulation Workers, Mechanical; Manufactured Building and Mobile Home Installers; Operating Engineers; Painters, Construction and Maintenance; Paperhangers; Paving, Surfacing, and Tamping Equipment Operators; Pile-Driver Operators; Pipe Fitters; Pipelayers; Pipelaying Fitters; Plasterers and Stucco Masons; Plumbers; Rail-Track Laying and Maintenance Equipment Operators; Refractory Materials Repairers, Except Brickmasons; Reinforcing Iron and Rebar Workers; Riggers; Roofers; Rough Carpenters; Security and Fire Alarm Systems Installers; Segmental Pavers; Sheet Metal Workers; Ship Carpenters and Joiners; Stone Cutters and Carvers; Stonemasons; Structural Iron and Steel Workers; Tapers; Terrazzo Workers and Finishers; Tile and Marble Setters. **PERSONALITY TYPE:** Realistic.

EDUCATION/TRAINING PROGRAM(S)—Construction Trades, Other. **RELATED KNOWLEDGE/COURSES—Public Safety and Security:** Knowledge of relevant equipment, policies, procedures, and strategies to promote effective local, state, or national security operations for the protection of people, data, property, and institutions. **Transportation:** Knowledge of principles and methods for moving people or goods by air, rail, sea, or road, including the relative costs and benefits. **Building and Construction:** Knowledge of the materials, methods, and tools involved in the construction or repair of houses, buildings, or other structures such as highways and roads. **Sales and Marketing:** Knowledge of principles and methods for showing, promoting, and selling products or services. This includes marketing strategy and tactics, product demonstrations, sales techniques, and sales control systems. **Customer and Personal Service:** Knowledge of principles and processes for providing customer and personal services. This includes customer needs assessment, meeting quality standards for services, and evaluation of customer satisfaction. **Personnel and Human Resources:** Knowledge of principles and procedures for personnel recruitment, selection, training, compensation and benefits, labor relations and negotiation, and personnel information systems. **Design:** Knowledge of design techniques, tools, and principles involved in production of precision technical plans, blueprints, drawings, and models.

Cartographers and Photogrammetrists

- Education/Training Required: Bachelor's degree
- Annual Earnings: $46,080
- Growth: 15.1%
- Annual Job Openings: 1,000
- Self-Employed: 3.3%
- Part-Time: 7.7%

Collect, analyze, and interpret geographic information provided by geodetic surveys, aerial photographs, and satellite data. Research, study, and prepare maps and other spatial data in digital or graphic form for legal, social, political, educational, and design purposes. May work with Geographic Information Systems (GIS). May design and evaluate algorithms, data structures, and user interfaces for GIS and mapping systems. Identify, scale, and orient geodetic points, elevations, and other planimetric or topographic features, applying standard mathematical formulas. Collect information about specific features of the Earth, using aerial photography and other digital remote sensing techniques. Revise existing maps and charts, making all necessary corrections and adjustments. Compile data required for map preparation, including aerial photographs, survey notes, records, reports, and original maps. Inspect final compositions in order to ensure completeness and accuracy. Determine map content and layout, as well as production specifications such as scale, size, projection, and colors, and direct production in order to ensure

that specifications are followed. Examine and analyze data from ground surveys, reports, aerial photographs, and satellite images in order to prepare topographic maps, aerial-photograph mosaics, and related charts. Select aerial photographic and remote-sensing techniques and plotting equipment needed to meet required standards of accuracy. Delineate aerial photographic detail, such as control points, hydrography, topography, and cultural features, using precision stereoplotting apparatus or drafting instruments. Build and update digital databases. Prepare and alter trace maps, charts, tables, detailed drawings, and three-dimensional optical models of terrain, using stereoscopic plotting and computer graphics equipment. Determine guidelines that specify which source material is acceptable for use. Study legal records in order to establish boundaries of local, national, and international properties. Travel over photographed areas in order to observe, identify, record, and verify all relevant features. **SKILLS—Active Learning:** Understanding the implications of new information for both current and future problem-solving and decision-making. **Technology Design:** Generating or adapting equipment and technology to serve user needs. **Science:** Using scientific rules and methods to solve problems. **Mathematics:** Using mathematics to solve problems. **Troubleshooting:** Determining causes of operating errors and deciding what to do about them. **Reading Comprehension:** Understanding written sentences and paragraphs in work-related documents. **Critical Thinking:** Using logic and reasoning to identify the strengths and weaknesses of alternative solutions, conclusions, or approaches to problems. **Complex Problem Solving:** Identifying complex problems and reviewing related information to develop and evaluate options and implement solutions. **GOE—Interest Area:** 15. Scientific Research, Engineering, and Mathematics. **Work Group:** 15.09. Engineering Technology. **Other Jobs in This Work Group:** Aerospace Engineering and Operations Technicians; Calibration and Instrumentation Technicians; Civil Engineering Technicians; Electrical Engineering Technicians; Electro-Mechanical Technicians; Electronic Drafters; Electronics Engineering Technicians; Environmental Engineering Technicians; Mapping Technicians; Mechanical Drafters; Mechanical Engineering Technicians; Surveying Technicians. **PERSONALITY TYPE:** Conventional.

EDUCATION/TRAINING PROGRAM(S)—Cartography; Surveying Technology/Surveying. **RELAT-**

C

ED KNOWLEDGE/COURSES—**Geography:** Knowledge of principles and methods for describing the features of land, sea, and air masses, including their physical characteristics; locations; interrelationships; and distribution of plant, animal, and human life. **Design:** Knowledge of design techniques, tools, and principles involved in production of precision technical plans, blueprints, drawings, and models. **Computers and Electronics:** Knowledge of circuit boards, processors, chips, electronic equipment, and computer hardware and software, including applications and programming. **Engineering and Technology:** Knowledge of the practical application of engineering science and technology. This includes applying principles, techniques, procedures, and equipment to the design and production of various goods and services. **Production and Processing:** Knowledge of raw materials, production processes, quality control, costs, and other techniques for maximizing the effective manufacture and distribution of goods. **Mathematics:** Knowledge of arithmetic, algebra, geometry, calculus, and statistics and their applications.

Cartoonists

- ◎ Education/Training Required: Long-term on-the-job training
- ◎ Annual Earnings: $38,060
- ◎ Growth: 16.5%
- ◎ Annual Job Openings: 4,000
- ◎ Self-Employed: 55.5%
- ◎ Part-Time: 23.1%

Create original artwork by using any of a wide variety of mediums and techniques, such as painting and sculpture. Sketches and submits cartoon or animation for approval. Develops personal ideas for cartoons, comic strips, or animations or reads written material to develop ideas. Makes changes and corrections to cartoon, comic strip, or animation as necessary. Creates and prepares sketches and model drawings of characters, providing details from memory, live models, manufactured products, or reference material. Renders sequential drawings of characters or other subject material which, when photographed and projected at specific speed, become animated. Develops color patterns and moods and paints background layouts to dramatize action for animated cartoon scenes. Discusses ideas for cartoons, comic strips, or animations with

editor or publisher's representative. Labels each section with designated colors when colors are used. **SKILLS—Operations Analysis:** Analyzing needs and product requirements to create a design. **GOE—Interest Area:** 03. Arts and Communication. **Work Group:** 03.04. Studio Art. **Other Jobs in This Work Group:** Craft Artists; Painters and Illustrators; Potters; Sculptors; Sketch Artists. **PERSONALITY TYPE:** Artistic.

EDUCATION/TRAINING PROGRAM(S)— Art/Art Studies, General; Drawing; Fine Arts and Art Studies, Other; Fine/Studio Arts, General; Intermedia/Multimedia; Medical Illustration/Medical Illustrator; Painting; Visual and Performing Arts, General. **RELATED KNOWLEDGE/COURSES—Fine Arts:** Knowledge of the theory and techniques required to compose, produce, and perform works of music, dance, the visual arts, drama, and sculpture. **Communications and Media:** Knowledge of media production, communication, and dissemination techniques and methods. This includes alternative ways to inform and entertain via written, oral, and visual media. **Design:** Knowledge of design techniques, tools, and principles involved in production of precision technical plans, blueprints, drawings, and models. **Sales and Marketing:** Knowledge of principles and methods for showing, promoting, and selling products or services. This includes marketing strategy and tactics, product demonstrations, sales techniques, and sales control systems. **Telecommunications:** Knowledge of transmission, broadcasting, switching, control, and operation of telecommunications systems.

Cashiers

- ◎ Education/Training Required: Short-term on-the-job training
- ◎ Annual Earnings: $16,240
- ◎ Growth: 13.2%
- ◎ Annual Job Openings: 1,221,000
- ◎ Self-Employed: 1.0%
- ◎ Part-Time: 44.8%

Receive and disburse money in establishments other than financial institutions. Usually involves use of electronic scanners, cash registers, or related equipment. Often involved in processing credit or debit card transactions and validating checks. Receive payment by cash, check, credit cards, vouchers, or automatic debits. Issue receipts, refunds, credits, or change due to customers. Count money in cash drawers at the beginning of shifts to ensure that amounts are correct and that there is adequate change. Greet customers entering establishments. Maintain clean and orderly checkout areas. Establish or identify prices of goods, services, or admission and tabulate bills, using calculators, cash registers, or optical price scanners. Issue trading stamps and redeem food stamps and coupons. Resolve customer complaints. Answer customers' questions and provide information on procedures or policies. Cash checks for customers. Weigh items sold by weight in order to determine prices. Calculate total payments received during a time period and reconcile this with total sales. Compute and record totals of transactions. Sell tickets and other items to customers. Keep periodic balance sheets of amounts and numbers of transactions. Bag, box, wrap, or gift-wrap merchandise and prepare packages for shipment. Sort, count, and wrap currency and coins. Process merchandise returns and exchanges. Pay company bills by cash, vouchers, or checks. Request information or assistance by using paging systems. Stock shelves and mark prices on shelves and items. Compile and maintain non-monetary reports and records. Monitor checkout stations to ensure that they have adequate cash available and that they are staffed appropriately. Post charges against guests' or patients' accounts. Offer customers carry-out service at the completion of transactions. **SKILLS—Social Perceptiveness:** Being aware of others' reactions and understanding why they react as they do. **Learning Strategies:** Selecting and using training/instructional methods and procedures appropriate for the situation when learning or teaching new things. **Service Orientation:** Actively looking for ways to help people. **Management of Personnel Resources:** Motivating, developing, and directing people as they work, identifying the best people for the job. **Systems Analysis:** Determining how a system should work and how changes in conditions, operations, and the environment will affect outcomes. **Instructing:** Teaching others how to do something. **Negotiation:** Bringing others together and trying to reconcile differences. **Persuasion:** Persuading others to change their minds or behavior. **GOE—Interest Area:** 14. Retail and Wholesale Sales and Service. **Work Group:** 14.06. Customer Service. **Other Jobs in This Work Group:** Adjustment Clerks; Counter and Rental Clerks; Customer Service Representatives, Utilities; Gaming Change Persons and Booth Cashiers; Order Clerks; Receptionists and

Information Clerks. **PERSONALITY TYPE:** Conventional.

EDUCATION/TRAINING PROGRAM(S)— Retailing and Retail Operations. **RELATED KNOWLEDGE/COURSES—Customer and Personal Service:** Knowledge of principles and processes for providing customer and personal services. This includes customer needs assessment, meeting quality standards for services, and evaluation of customer satisfaction. **Education and Training:** Knowledge of principles and methods for curriculum and training design, teaching and instruction for individuals and groups, and the measurement of training effects. **Foreign Language:** Knowledge of the structure and content of a foreign (non-English) language, including the meaning and spelling of words, rules of composition and grammar, and pronunciation. **English Language:** Knowledge of the structure and content of the English language, including the meaning and spelling of words, rules of composition, and grammar. **Administration and Management:** Knowledge of business and management principles involved in strategic planning, resource allocation, human resources modeling, leadership technique, production methods, and coordination of people and resources. **Mathematics:** Knowledge of arithmetic, algebra, geometry, calculus, and statistics and their applications.

Ceiling Tile Installers

- Education/Training Required: Moderate-term on-the-job training
- Annual Earnings: $34,030
- Growth: 21.4%
- Annual Job Openings: 17,000
- Self-Employed: 18.4%
- Part-Time: 5.9%

Apply or mount acoustical tiles or blocks, strips, or sheets of shock-absorbing materials to ceilings and walls of buildings to reduce or reflect sound. Materials may be of decorative quality. Includes lathers who fasten wooden, metal, or rockboard lath to walls, ceilings, or partitions of buildings to provide support base for plaster, fire-proofing, or acoustical material. Applies acoustical tiles or shock-absorbing materials to ceilings and walls of buildings to reduce or reflect sound and to decorate rooms. Washes concrete sur-

faces with washing soda and zinc sulfate solution before mounting tile to increase adhesive qualities of surfaces. Inspects furrings, mechanical mountings, and masonry surface for plumbness and level, using spirit or water level. Hangs dry lines (stretched string) to wall molding to guide positioning of main runners. Nails or screws molding to wall to support and seals joint between ceiling tile and wall. Scribes and cuts edges of tile to fit wall where wall molding is not specified. Nails channels or wood furring strips to surfaces to provide mounting for tile. Measures and marks surface to lay out work according to blueprints and drawings. Cuts tiles for fixture and borders, using keyhole saw, and inserts tiles into supporting framework. Applies cement to back of tile and presses tile into place, aligning with layout marks and joints of previously laid tile. **SKILLS**—None met the criteria. **GOE—Interest Area:** 02. Architecture and Construction. **Work Group:** 02.04. Construction Crafts. **Other Jobs in This Work Group:** Boat Builders and Shipwrights; Boilermakers; Brattice Builders; Brickmasons and Blockmasons; Carpet Installers; Cement Masons and Concrete Finishers; Commercial Divers; Construction Carpenters; Crane and Tower Operators; Dragline Operators; Drywall Installers; Electricians; Fence Erectors; Floor Layers, Except Carpet, Wood, and Hard Tiles; Floor Sanders and Finishers; Glaziers; Grader, Bulldozer, and Scraper Operators; Hazardous Materials Removal Workers; Insulation Workers, Floor, Ceiling, and Wall; Insulation Workers, Mechanical; Manufactured Building and Mobile Home Installers; Operating Engineers; Painters, Construction and Maintenance; Paperhangers; Paving, Surfacing, and Tamping Equipment Operators; Pile-Driver Operators; Pipe Fitters; Pipelayers; Pipelaying Fitters; Plasterers and Stucco Masons; Plumbers; Rail-Track Laying and Maintenance Equipment Operators; Refractory Materials Repairers, Except Brickmasons; Reinforcing Iron and Rebar Workers; Riggers; Roofers; Rough Carpenters; Security and Fire Alarm Systems Installers; Segmental Pavers; Sheet Metal Workers; Ship Carpenters and Joiners; Stone Cutters and Carvers; Stonemasons; Structural Iron and Steel Workers; Tapers; Terrazzo Workers and Finishers; Tile and Marble Setters. **PERSONALITY TYPE:** Realistic.

EDUCATION/TRAINING PROGRAM(S)—Drywall Installation/Drywaller. **RELATED KNOWLEDGE/COURSES—Building and Construction:** Knowledge of the materials, methods, and tools involved in the construction or repair of houses, buildings, or other structures such as highways and roads. **Design:** Knowledge of design techniques, tools, and principles involved in production of precision technical plans, blueprints, drawings, and models. **Physics:** Knowledge and prediction of physical principles and laws and their interrelationships and applications to understanding fluid, material, and atmospheric dynamics and mechanical, electrical, atomic, and subatomic structures and processes.

Cement Masons and Concrete Finishers

- Education/Training Required: Long-term on-the-job training
- Annual Earnings: $31,400
- Growth: 26.1%
- Annual Job Openings: 24,000
- Self-Employed: 5.2%
- Part-Time: 5.0%

Smooth and finish surfaces of poured concrete, such as floors, walks, sidewalks, roads, or curbs, using a variety of hand and power tools. Align forms for sidewalks, curbs, or gutters; patch voids; use saws to cut expansion joints. Check the forms that hold the concrete to see that they are properly constructed. Set the forms that hold concrete to the desired pitch and depth and align them. Spread, level, and smooth concrete, using rake, shovel, hand or power trowel, hand or power screed, and float. Mold expansion joints and edges, using edging tools, jointers, and straightedge. Monitor how the wind, heat, or cold affect the curing of the concrete throughout the entire process. Signal truck driver to position truck to facilitate pouring concrete and move chute to direct concrete on forms. Produce rough concrete surface, using broom. Operate power vibrator to compact concrete. Direct the casting of the concrete and supervise laborers who use shovels or special tools to spread it. Mix cement, sand, and water to produce concrete, grout, or slurry, using hoe, trowel, tamper, scraper, or concrete-mixing machine. Cut out damaged areas, drill holes for reinforcing rods, and position reinforcing rods to repair concrete, using power saw and drill. Wet concrete surface and rub with stone to smooth surface and obtain specified finish. Wet surface to prepare for bonding, fill holes and cracks with grout or slurry, and smooth, using trowel.

Clean chipped area, using wire brush, and feel and observe surface to determine if it is rough or uneven. Apply hardening and sealing compounds to cure surface of concrete and waterproof or restore surface. Chip, scrape, and grind high spots, ridges, and rough projections to finish concrete, using pneumatic chisels, power grinders, or hand tools. Spread roofing paper on surface of foundation and spread concrete onto roofing paper with trowel to form terrazzo base. Build wooden molds and clamp molds around area to be repaired, using hand tools. Sprinkle colored marble or stone chips, powdered steel, or coloring powder over surface to produce prescribed finish. Cut metal division strips and press them into terrazzo base so that top edges form desired design or pattern. Fabricate concrete beams, columns, and panels. Waterproof or restore concrete surfaces, using appropriate compounds. **SKILLS—Coordination:** Adjusting actions in relation to others' actions. **Mathematics:** Using mathematics to solve problems. **Installation:** Installing equipment, machines, wiring, or programs to meet specifications. **Repairing:** Repairing machines or systems by using the needed tools. **Equipment Maintenance:** Performing routine maintenance on equipment and determining when and what kind of maintenance is needed. **Persuasion:** Persuading others to change their minds or behavior. **Equipment Selection:** Determining the kind of tools and equipment needed to do a job. **Active Learning:** Understanding the implications of new information for both current and future problem-solving and decision-making. **GOE—Interest Area:** 02. Architecture and Construction. **Work Group:** 02.04. Construction Crafts. **Other Jobs in This Work Group:** Boat Builders and Shipwrights; Boilermakers; Brattice Builders; Brickmasons and Blockmasons; Carpet Installers; Ceiling Tile Installers; Commercial Divers; Construction Carpenters; Crane and Tower Operators; Dragline Operators; Drywall Installers; Electricians; Fence Erectors; Floor Layers, Except Carpet, Wood, and Hard Tiles; Floor Sanders and Finishers; Glaziers; Grader, Bulldozer, and Scraper Operators; Hazardous Materials Removal Workers; Insulation Workers, Floor, Ceiling, and Wall; Insulation Workers, Mechanical; Manufactured Building and Mobile Home Installers; Operating Engineers; Painters, Construction and Maintenance; Paperhangers; Paving, Surfacing, and Tamping Equipment Operators; Pile-Driver Operators; Pipe Fitters; Pipelayers; Pipelaying Fitters; Plasterers and Stucco Masons; Plumbers; Rail-Track Laying and Maintenance Equipment Operators; Refractory Materials Repairers,

Except Brickmasons; Reinforcing Iron and Rebar Workers; Riggers; Roofers; Rough Carpenters; Security and Fire Alarm Systems Installers; Segmental Pavers; Sheet Metal Workers; Ship Carpenters and Joiners; Stone Cutters and Carvers; Stonemasons; Structural Iron and Steel Workers; Tapers; Terrazzo Workers and Finishers; Tile and Marble Setters. **PERSONALITY TYPE:** Realistic.

EDUCATION/TRAINING PROGRAM(S)—Concrete Finishing/Concrete Finisher. **RELATED KNOWLEDGE/COURSES—Building and Construction:** Knowledge of the materials, methods, and tools involved in the construction or repair of houses, buildings, or other structures such as highways and roads. **Public Safety and Security:** Knowledge of relevant equipment, policies, procedures, and strategies to promote effective local, state, or national security operations for the protection of people, data, property, and institutions. **Foreign Language:** Knowledge of the structure and content of a foreign (non-English) language, including the meaning and spelling of words, rules of composition and grammar, and pronunciation. **Economics and Accounting:** Knowledge of economic and accounting principles and practices, the financial markets, banking, and the analysis and reporting of financial data. **Administration and Management:** Knowledge of business and management principles involved in strategic planning, resource allocation, human resources modeling, leadership technique, production methods, and coordination of people and resources. **Mathematics:** Knowledge of arithmetic, algebra, geometry, calculus, and statistics and their applications.

Central Office and PBX Installers and Repairers

- ◎ Education/Training Required: Postsecondary vocational training
- ◎ Annual Earnings: $49,840
- ◎ Growth: –0.6%
- ◎ Annual Job Openings: 23,000
- ◎ Self-Employed: 4.6%
- ◎ Part-Time: 1.7%

Test, analyze, and repair telephone or telegraph circuits and equipment at a central office location, using

test meters and hand tools. Analyze and repair defects in communications equipment on customers' premises, using circuit diagrams, polarity probes, meters, and a telephone test set. May install equipment. Tests circuits and components of malfunctioning telecommunication equipment to isolate source of malfunction, using test instruments and circuit diagrams. Analyzes test readings, computer printouts, and trouble reports to determine method of repair. Tests and adjusts installed equipment to ensure circuit continuity and operational performance, using test instruments. Connects wires to equipment, using hand tools, soldering iron, or wire wrap gun. Installs preassembled or partially assembled switching equipment, switchboards, wiring frames, and power apparatus according to floor plans. Retests repaired equipment to ensure that malfunction has been corrected. Repairs or replaces defective components, such as switches, relays, amplifiers, and circuit boards, using hand tools and soldering iron. Removes and remakes connections on wire distributing frame to change circuit layout, following diagrams. Routes cables and trunklines from entry points to specified equipment, following diagrams. Enters codes to correct programming of electronic switching systems. **SKILLS—Repairing:** Repairing machines or systems by using the needed tools. **Installation:** Installing equipment, machines, wiring, or programs to meet specifications. **Troubleshooting:** Determining causes of operating errors and deciding what to do about them. **Technology Design:** Generating or adapting equipment and technology to serve user needs. **Operation Monitoring:** Watching gauges, dials, or other indicators to make sure a machine is working properly. **Science:** Using scientific rules and methods to solve problems. **Equipment Maintenance:** Performing routine maintenance on equipment and determining when and what kind of maintenance is needed. **Quality Control Analysis:** Conducting tests and inspections of products, services, or processes to evaluate quality or performance. **GOE—Interest Area:** 02. Architecture and Construction. **Work Group:** 02.05. Systems and Equipment Installation, Maintenance, and Repair. **Other Jobs in This Work Group:** Communication Equipment Mechanics, Installers, and Repairers; Electric Meter Installers and Repairers; Electrical and Electronics Repairers, Powerhouse, Substation, and Relay; Electrical Power-Line Installers and Repairers; Elevator Installers and Repairers; Frame Wirers, Central Office; Heating and Air Conditioning Mechanics; Home Appliance Installers; Maintenance and Repair Work-

ers, General; Meter Mechanics; Refrigeration Mechanics; Station Installers and Repairers, Telephone; Telecommunications Facility Examiners; Telecommunications Line Installers and Repairers. **PERSONALITY TYPE:** Realistic.

EDUCATION/TRAINING PROGRAM(S)— Communications Systems Installation and Repair Technology. **RELATED KNOWLEDGE/COURSES—Telecommunications:** Knowledge of transmission, broadcasting, switching, control, and operation of telecommunications systems. **Computers and Electronics:** Knowledge of circuit boards, processors, chips, electronic equipment, and computer hardware and software, including applications and programming. **Design:** Knowledge of design techniques, tools, and principles involved in production of precision technical plans, blueprints, drawings, and models. **Engineering and Technology:** Knowledge of the practical application of engineering science and technology. This includes applying principles, techniques, procedures, and equipment to the design and production of various goods and services. **Physics:** Knowledge and prediction of physical principles and laws and their interrelationships and applications to understanding fluid, material, and atmospheric dynamics and mechanical, electrical, atomic, and subatomic structures and processes.

Chefs and Head Cooks

- Education/Training Required: Postsecondary vocational training
- Annual Earnings: $30,680
- Growth: 15.8%
- Annual Job Openings: 33,000
- Self-Employed: 7.4%
- Part-Time: 8.6%

Direct the preparation, seasoning, and cooking of salads, soups, fish, meats, vegetables, desserts, or other foods. May plan and price menu items, order supplies, and keep records and accounts. May participate in cooking. Prepare and cook foods of all types, either on a regular basis or for special guests or functions. Supervise and coordinate activities of cooks and workers engaged in food preparation. Collaborate with other personnel to plan and develop recipes and menus, taking into account such factors as seasonal availability of ingredients and the likely number of customers. Check the quality of raw and cooked food products to ensure that standards are met. Check the quantity and quality of received products. Demonstrate new cooking techniques and equipment to staff. Determine how food should be presented and create decorative food displays. Determine production schedules and staff requirements necessary to ensure timely delivery of services. Estimate amounts and costs of required supplies, such as food and ingredients. Inspect supplies, equipment, and work areas to ensure conformance to established standards. Instruct cooks and other workers in the preparation, cooking, garnishing, and presentation of food. Monitor sanitation practices to ensure that employees follow standards and regulations. Order or requisition food and other supplies needed to ensure efficient operation. Recruit and hire staff, including cooks and other kitchen workers. Analyze recipes to assign prices to menu items based on food, labor, and overhead costs. Arrange for equipment purchases and repairs. Meet with customers to discuss menus for special occasions such as weddings, parties, and banquets. Meet with sales representatives in order to negotiate prices and order supplies. Record production and operational data on specified forms. Coordinate planning, budgeting, and purchasing for all the food operations within establishments such as clubs, hotels, or restaurant chains. Plan, direct, and supervise the food preparation and cooking activities of multiple kitchens or restaurants in an establishment such as a restaurant chain, hospital, or hotel. **SKILLS—Management of Financial Resources:** Determining how money will be spent to get the work done and accounting for these expenditures. **Management of Material Resources:** Obtaining and seeing to the appropriate use of equipment, facilities, and materials needed to do certain work. **Management of Personnel Resources:** Motivating, developing, and directing people as they work, identifying the best people for the job. **Coordination:** Adjusting actions in relation to others' actions. **Instructing:** Teaching others how to do something. **Systems Evaluation:** Identifying measures or indicators of system performance and the actions needed to improve or correct performance relative to the goals of the system. **Time Management:** Managing one's own time and the time of others. **Systems Analysis:** Determining how a system should work and how changes in conditions, operations, and the environment will affect outcomes. **GOE—Interest Area:** 09. Hospitality,

Tourism, and Recreation. **Work Group:** 09.04. Food and Beverage Preparation. **Other Jobs in This Work Group:** Bakers, Bread and Pastry; Butchers and Meat Cutters; Cooks, Fast Food; Cooks, Institution and Cafeteria; Cooks, Restaurant; Cooks, Short Order; Dishwashers; Food Preparation Workers. **PERSONALITY TYPE:** Enterprising.

EDUCATION/TRAINING PROGRAM(S)— Cooking and Related Culinary Arts, General; Culinary Arts/Chef Training. **RELATED KNOWLEDGE/ COURSES—Administration and Management:** Knowledge of business and management principles involved in strategic planning, resource allocation, human resources modeling, leadership technique, production methods, and coordination of people and resources. **Personnel and Human Resources:** Knowledge of principles and procedures for personnel recruitment, selection, training, compensation and benefits, labor relations and negotiation, and personnel information systems. **Economics and Accounting:** Knowledge of economic and accounting principles and practices, the financial markets, banking, and the analysis and reporting of financial data. **Education and Training:** Knowledge of principles and methods for curriculum and training design, teaching and instruction for individuals and groups, and the measurement of training effects. **Food Production:** Knowledge of techniques and equipment for planting, growing, and harvesting food products (both plant and animal) for consumption, including storage/handling techniques. **Biology:** Knowledge of plant and animal organisms and their tissues, cells, functions, interdependencies, and interactions with each other and the environment.

Chemistry Teachers, Postsecondary

- Education/Training Required: Master's degree
- Annual Earnings: $56,660
- Growth: 38.1%
- Annual Job Openings: 216,000
- Self-Employed: 0.3%
- Part-Time: 27.7%

Teach courses pertaining to the chemical and physical properties and compositional changes of substances. Work may include instruction in the methods of qualitative and quantitative chemical analysis. Includes both teachers primarily engaged in teaching and those who do a combination of both teaching and research. Prepare and deliver lectures to undergraduate and/or graduate students on topics such as organic chemistry, analytical chemistry, and chemical separation. Supervise students' laboratory work. Evaluate and grade students' class work, laboratory performance, assignments, and papers. Compile, administer, and grade examinations or assign this work to others. Maintain student attendance records, grades, and other required records. Prepare course materials such as syllabi, homework assignments, and handouts. Maintain regularly scheduled office hours in order to advise and assist students. Plan, evaluate, and revise curricula, course content, and course materials and methods of instruction. Supervise undergraduate and/or graduate teaching, internship, and research work. Keep abreast of developments in their field by reading current literature, talking with colleagues, and participating in professional conferences. Initiate, facilitate, and moderate classroom discussions. Select and obtain materials and supplies such as textbooks and laboratory equipment. Conduct research in a particular field of knowledge and publish findings in professional journals, books, and/or electronic media. Advise students on academic and vocational curricula and on career issues. Collaborate with colleagues to address teaching and research issues. Serve on academic or administrative committees that deal with institutional policies, departmental matters, and academic issues. Write grant proposals to procure external research funding. Participate in student recruitment, registration, and placement activities. Prepare and submit required reports related to instruction. Perform administrative duties such as serving as a department head. **SKILLS—Science:** Using scientific rules and methods to solve problems. **Instructing:** Teaching others how to do something. **Active Learning:** Understanding the implications of new information for both current and future problem-solving and decision-making. **Mathematics:** Using mathematics to solve problems. **Learning Strategies:** Selecting and using training/instructional methods and procedures appropriate for the situation when learning or teaching new things. **Reading Comprehension:** Understanding written sentences and paragraphs in work-related documents. **Critical Thinking:** Using logic and reasoning to identify the strengths and weaknesses of alternative solutions, conclusions, or approaches to problems.

Writing: Communicating effectively in writing as appropriate for the needs of the audience. **GOE— Interest Area:** 05. Education and Training. **Work Group:** 05.03. Postsecondary and Adult Teaching and Instructing. **Other Jobs in This Work Group:** Adult Literacy, Remedial Education, and GED Teachers and Instructors; Agricultural Sciences Teachers, Postsecondary; Anthropology and Archeology Teachers, Postsecondary; Architecture Teachers, Postsecondary; Area, Ethnic, and Cultural Studies Teachers, Postsecondary; Art, Drama, and Music Teachers, Postsecondary; Atmospheric, Earth, Marine, and Space Sciences Teachers, Postsecondary; Biological Science Teachers, Postsecondary; Business Teachers, Postsecondary; Communications Teachers, Postsecondary; Computer Science Teachers, Postsecondary; Criminal Justice and Law Enforcement Teachers, Postsecondary; Economics Teachers, Postsecondary; Education Teachers, Postsecondary; Engineering Teachers, Postsecondary; English Language and Literature Teachers, Postsecondary; Environmental Science Teachers, Postsecondary; Farm and Home Management Advisors; Foreign Language and Literature Teachers, Postsecondary; Forestry and Conservation Science Teachers, Postsecondary; Geography Teachers, Postsecondary; Graduate Teaching Assistants; Health Specialties Teachers, Postsecondary; History Teachers, Postsecondary; Home Economics Teachers, Postsecondary; Law Teachers, Postsecondary; Library Science Teachers, Postsecondary; Mathematical Science Teachers, Postsecondary; Nursing Instructors and Teachers, Postsecondary; Philosophy and Religion Teachers, Postsecondary; Physics Teachers, Postsecondary; Political Science Teachers, Postsecondary; Psychology Teachers, Postsecondary; Recreation and Fitness Studies Teachers, Postsecondary; Self-Enrichment Education Teachers; Social Work Teachers, Postsecondary; Sociology Teachers, Postsecondary; Vocational Education Teachers, Postsecondary. **PERSONALITY TYPE:** Investigative.

EDUCATION/TRAINING PROGRAM(S)—Analytical Chemistry; Chemical Physics; Chemistry, General; Chemistry, Other; Geochemistry; Inorganic Chemistry; Organic Chemistry; Physical and Theoretical Chemistry; Polymer Chemistry. **RELATED KNOWLEDGE/COURSES—Chemistry:** Knowledge of the chemical composition, structure, and properties of substances and of the chemical processes and transformations that they undergo. This includes uses of chemicals and their danger signs, production techniques, and disposal methods. **Education and Training:** Knowledge of principles and methods for curriculum and training design, teaching and instruction for individuals and groups, and the measurement of training effects. **Physics:** Knowledge and prediction of physical principles and laws and their interrelationships and applications to understanding fluid, material, and atmospheric dynamics and mechanical, electrical, atomic, and subatomic structures and processes. **Biology:** Knowledge of plant and animal organisms and their tissues, cells, functions, interdependencies, and interactions with each other and the environment. **Mathematics:** Knowledge of arithmetic, algebra, geometry, calculus, and statistics and their applications. **English Language:** Knowledge of the structure and content of the English language, including the meaning and spelling of words, rules of composition, and grammar.

Chemists

- ◎ Education/Training Required: Bachelor's degree
- ◎ Annual Earnings: $56,060
- ◎ Growth: 12.7%
- ◎ Annual Job Openings: 7,000
- ◎ Self-Employed: 0.2%
- ◎ Part-Time: 4.2%

Conduct qualitative and quantitative chemical analyses or chemical experiments in laboratories for quality or process control or to develop new products or knowledge. Analyze organic and inorganic compounds to determine chemical and physical properties, composition, structure, relationships, and reactions, utilizing chromatography, spectroscopy, and spectrophotometry techniques. Develop, improve, and customize products, equipment, formulas, processes, and analytical methods. Compile and analyze test information to determine process or equipment operating efficiency and to diagnose malfunctions. Confer with scientists and engineers to conduct analyses of research projects, interpret test results, or develop nonstandard tests. Direct, coordinate, and advise personnel in test procedures for analyzing components and physical properties of materials. Induce changes in composition of substances by introducing heat, light, energy, and chemical catalysts for quantitative and qualitative analysis. Write technical papers and reports; prepare standards and specifications for processes, facilities, products, and tests. Study effects of various methods of processing, preserving, and packaging on composition and properties of foods. Prepare test solutions, compounds, and reagents for laboratory personnel to conduct test. **SKILLS—Science:** Using scientific rules and methods to solve problems. **Quality Control Analysis:** Conducting tests and inspections of products, services, or processes to evaluate quality or performance. **Technology Design:** Generating or adapting equipment and technology to serve user needs. **Operation Monitoring:** Watching gauges, dials, or other indicators to make sure a machine is working properly. **Time Management:** Managing one's own time and the time of others. **Equipment Selection:** Determining the kind of tools and equipment needed to do a job. **Management of Material Resources:** Obtaining and seeing to the appropriate use of equipment, facilities, and materials needed to do certain work. **Instructing:** Teaching others how to do something. **Troubleshooting:** Determining causes of operating errors and deciding what to do about them. **Management of Financial Resources:** Determining how money will be spent to get the work done and accounting for these expenditures. **GOE—Interest Area:** 15. Scientific Research, Engineering, and Mathematics. **Work Group:** 15.02. Physical Sciences. **Other Jobs in This Work Group:** Astronomers; Atmospheric and Space Scientists; Geographers; Geologists; Hydrologists; Materials Scientists; Physicists. **PERSONALITY TYPE:** Investigative.

EDUCATION/TRAINING PROGRAM(S)—Analytical Chemistry; Chemical Physics; Chemistry, General; Chemistry, Other; Inorganic Chemistry; Organic Chemistry; Physical and Theoretical Chemistry; Polymer Chemistry. **RELATED KNOWLEDGE/COURSES—Chemistry:** Knowledge of the chemical composition, structure, and properties of substances and of the chemical processes and transformations that they undergo. This includes uses of chemicals and their danger signs, production techniques, and disposal methods. **Mathematics:** Knowledge of arithmetic, algebra, geometry, calculus, and statistics and their applications. **Engineering and Technology:** Knowledge of the practical application of engineering science and technology. This includes applying principles, techniques, procedures, and equipment to the design and production of various goods and services. **Com-**

puters and Electronics: Knowledge of circuit boards, processors, chips, electronic equipment, and computer hardware and software, including applications and programming. **Production and Processing:** Knowledge of raw materials, production processes, quality control, costs, and other techniques for maximizing the effective manufacture and distribution of goods. **Physics:** Knowledge and prediction of physical principles and laws and their interrelationships and applications to understanding fluid, material, and atmospheric dynamics and mechanical, electrical, atomic, and subatomic structures and processes. **Education and Training:** Knowledge of principles and methods for curriculum and training design, teaching and instruction for individuals and groups, and the measurement of training effects.

Chief Executives

- ◎ Education/Training Required: Work experience plus degree
- ◎ Annual Earnings: $140,350
- ◎ Growth: 16.7%
- ◎ Annual Job Openings: 63,000
- ◎ Self-Employed: 14.6%
- ◎ Part-Time: 5.3%

Determine and formulate policies and provide the overall direction of companies or private- and public-sector organizations within the guidelines set up by a board of directors or similar governing body. Plan, direct, or coordinate operational activities at the highest level of management with the help of subordinate executives and staff managers. Analyze operations to evaluate performance of a company and its staff in meeting objectives and to determine areas of potential cost reduction, program improvement, or policy change. Appoint department heads or managers and assign or delegate responsibilities to them. Confer with board members, organization officials, and staff members to discuss issues, coordinate activities, and resolve problems. Coordinate the development and implementation of budgetary control systems, record-keeping systems, and other administrative control processes. Direct and coordinate an organization's financial and budget activities in order to fund operations, maximize investments, and increase efficiency. Direct human resources activities, including the approval of human resource plans and activities, the selection of directors and other high-level staff, and establishment and organization of major departments. Direct, plan, and implement policies, objectives, and activities of organizations or businesses in order to ensure continuing operations, to maximize returns on investments, and to increase productivity. Establish departmental responsibilities and coordinate functions among departments and sites. Implement corrective action plans to solve organizational or departmental problems. Prepare and present reports concerning activities, expenses, budgets, government statutes and rulings, and other items affecting businesses or program services. Preside over or serve on boards of directors, management committees, or other governing boards. Represent organizations and promote their objectives at official functions or delegate representatives to do so. Serve as liaisons between organizations, shareholders, and outside organizations. Administer programs for selection of sites, construction of buildings, and provision of equipment and supplies. Attend and participate in meetings of municipal councils and council committees. Deliver speeches, write articles, and present information at meetings or conventions in order to promote services, exchange ideas, and accomplish objectives. Direct and conduct studies and research on issues affecting areas of responsibility. **SKILLS**—No data available. **GOE—Interest Area:** 04. Business and Administration. **Work Group:** 04.01. Managerial Work in General Business. **Other Jobs in This Work Group:** Compensation and Benefits Managers; General and Operations Managers; Human Resources Managers; Private Sector Executives; Training and Development Managers. **PERSONALITY TYPE:** No data available.

EDUCATION/TRAINING PROGRAM(S)—Business Administration and Management, General; Business/Commerce, General; Entrepreneurship/Entrepreneurial Studies; International Business/Trade/Commerce; Public Administration; Public Administration and Social Service Professions, Other; Public Policy Analysis. **RELATED KNOWLEDGE/COURSES**—No data available.

Child Care Workers

- Education/Training Required: Short-term on-the-job training
- Annual Earnings: $16,760
- Growth: 11.7%
- Annual Job Openings: 406,000
- Self-Employed: 43.4%
- Part-Time: 35.2%

Attend to children at schools, businesses, private households, and child care institutions. Perform a variety of tasks, such as dressing, feeding, bathing, and overseeing play. Support children's emotional and social development, encouraging understanding of others and positive self-concepts. Care for children in institutional setting, such as group homes, nursery schools, private businesses, or schools for the handicapped. Sanitize toys and play equipment. Discipline children and recommend or initiate other measures to control behavior, such as caring for own clothing and picking up toys and books. Identify signs of emotional or developmental problems in children and bring them to parents' or guardians' attention. Observe and monitor children's play activities. Keep records on individual children, including daily observations and information about activities, meals served, and medications administered. Instruct children in health and personal habits such as eating, resting, and toilet habits. Read to children and teach them simple painting, drawing, handicrafts, and songs. Organize and participate in recreational activities, such as games. Assist in preparing food for children, serve meals and refreshments to children, and regulate rest periods. Organize and store toys and materials to ensure order in activity areas. Operate in-house day care centers within businesses. Sterilize bottles and prepare formulas. Provide counseling or therapy to mentally disturbed, delinquent, or handicapped children. Dress children and change diapers. Help children with homework and school work. Perform housekeeping duties such as laundry, cleaning, dishwashing, and changing of linens. Accompany children to and from school, on outings, and to medical appointments. **SKILLS—Learning Strategies:** Selecting and using training/instructional methods and procedures appropriate for the situation when learning or teaching new things. **Social Perceptiveness:** Being aware of others' reactions and understanding why they react as they do.

Negotiation: Bringing others together and trying to reconcile differences. **Service Orientation:** Actively looking for ways to help people. **Persuasion:** Persuading others to change their minds or behavior. **Time Management:** Managing one's own time and the time of others. **Critical Thinking:** Using logic and reasoning to identify the strengths and weaknesses of alternative solutions, conclusions, or approaches to problems. **Monitoring:** Monitoring or assessing your performance or that of other individuals or organizations to make improvements or take corrective action. **GOE—Interest Area:** 10. Human Service. **Work Group:** 10.03. Child/Personal Care and Services. **Other Jobs in This Work Group:** Funeral Attendants; Nannies; Personal and Home Care Aides. **PERSONALITY TYPE:** Social.

EDUCATION/TRAINING PROGRAM(S)— Child Care Provider/Assistant. **RELATED KNOWLEDGE/COURSES—Psychology:** Knowledge of human behavior and performance; individual differences in ability, personality, and interests; learning and motivation; psychological research methods; and the assessment and treatment of behavioral and affective disorders. **Customer and Personal Service:** Knowledge of principles and processes for providing customer and personal services. This includes customer needs assessment, meeting quality standards for services, and evaluation of customer satisfaction. **Sociology and Anthropology:** Knowledge of group behavior and dynamics, societal trends and influences, human migrations, ethnicity, and cultures and their history and origins. **Public Safety and Security:** Knowledge of relevant equipment, policies, procedures, and strategies to promote effective local, state, or national security operations for the protection of people, data, property, and institutions. **Philosophy and Theology:** Knowledge of different philosophical systems and religions. This includes their basic principles, values, ethics, ways of thinking, customs, and practices and their impact on human culture. **Medicine and Dentistry:** Knowledge of the information and techniques needed to diagnose and treat human injuries, diseases, and deformities. This includes symptoms, treatment alternatives, drug properties and interactions, and preventive health-care measures.

C

Child Support, Missing Persons, and Unemployment Insurance Fraud Investigators

- ◉ Education/Training Required: Work experience in a related occupation
- ◉ Annual Earnings: $53,990
- ◉ Growth: 22.4%
- ◉ Annual Job Openings: 11,000
- ◉ Self-Employed: 0%
- ◉ Part-Time: 0.5%

Conduct investigations to locate, arrest, and return fugitives and persons wanted for non-payment of support payments and unemployment insurance fraud and to locate missing persons. Serves warrants and makes arrests to return persons sought in connection with crimes or for non-payment of child support. Computes amount of child support payments. Testifies in court to present evidence regarding cases. Examines medical and dental X rays, fingerprints, and other information to identify bodies held in morgue. Examines case file to determine that divorce decree and court-ordered judgment for payment are in order. Completes reports to document information acquired during criminal and child support cases and actions taken. Monitors child support payments awarded by court to ensure compliance and enforcement of child support laws. Determines types of court jurisdiction, according to facts and circumstances surrounding case, and files court action. Confers with prosecuting attorney to prepare court case and with court clerk to obtain arrest warrant and schedule court date. Interviews client to obtain information such as relocation of absent parent, amount of child support awarded, and names of witnesses. Interviews and discusses case with parent charged with nonpayment of support to resolve issues in lieu of filing court proceedings. Reviews files and criminal records to develop possible leads, such as previous addresses and aliases. Prepares file indicating data such as wage records of accused, witnesses, and blood test results. Obtains extradition papers to bring about return of fugitive. Contacts employers, neighbors, relatives, and law enforcement agencies to locate person sought and verify information gathered about case. **SKILLS—Active Listening:** Giving full attention to what other people are saying, taking time to understand the points being made, asking questions as appropriate, and not interrupting at inappropriate times. **Speaking:** Talking to others to convey information effectively. **Negotiation:** Bringing others together and trying to reconcile differences. **Critical Thinking:** Using logic and reasoning to identify the strengths and weaknesses of alternative solutions, conclusions, or approaches to problems. **Reading Comprehension:** Understanding written sentences and paragraphs in work-related documents. **Judgment and Decision Making:** Considering the relative costs and benefits of potential actions to choose the most appropriate one. **Writing:** Communicating effectively in writing as appropriate for the needs of the audience. **Persuasion:** Persuading others to change their minds or behavior. **GOE—Interest Area:** 07. Government and Public Administration. **Work Group:** 07.03. Regulations Enforcement. **Other Jobs in This Work Group:** Agricultural Inspectors; Aviation Inspectors; Environmental Compliance Inspectors; Equal Opportunity Representatives and Officers; Financial Examiners; Fire Inspectors; Fish and Game Wardens; Forest Fire Inspectors and Prevention Specialists; Government Property Inspectors and Investigators; Immigration and Customs Inspectors; Licensing Examiners and Inspectors; Marine Cargo Inspectors; Mechanical Inspectors; Motor Vehicle Inspectors; Nuclear Monitoring Technicians; Occupational Health and Safety Specialists; Pressure Vessel Inspectors; Railroad Inspectors; Tax Examiners, Collectors, and Revenue Agents. **PERSONALITY TYPE:** Enterprising.

EDUCATION/TRAINING PROGRAM(S)— Criminal Justice/Police Science; Criminalistics and Criminal Science. **RELATED KNOWLEDGE/ COURSES—Law and Government:** Knowledge of laws, legal codes, court procedures, precedents, government regulations, executive orders, agency rules, and the democratic political process. **Public Safety and Security:** Knowledge of relevant equipment, policies, procedures, and strategies to promote effective local, state, or national security operations for the protection of people, data, property, and institutions. **Economics and Accounting:** Knowledge of economic and accounting principles and practices, the financial markets, banking, and the analysis and reporting of financial data. **Geography:** Knowledge of principles and methods for describing the features of land, sea, and air masses, including their physical characteristics; locations; interrelationships; and distribution of plant, animal, and human life. **English Language:** Knowledge of the structure and content of the English language, including the meaning and spelling of words, rules of composition, and grammar. **Sociology and Anthropology:** Knowledge of group behavior and dynamics, societal trends and influences, human migrations, ethnicity, and cultures and their history and origins.

Child, Family, and School Social Workers

- ◎ Education/Training Required: Bachelor's degree
- ◎ Annual Earnings: $34,820
- ◎ Growth: 23.2%
- ◎ Annual Job Openings: 45,000
- ◎ Self-Employed: 1.7%
- ◎ Part-Time: 8.7%

Provide social services and assistance to improve the social and psychological functioning of children and their families and to maximize the family well-being and the academic functioning of children. May assist single parents, arrange adoptions, and find foster homes for abandoned or abused children. In schools, they address such problems as teenage pregnancy, misbehavior, and truancy. May also advise teachers on how to deal with problem children. Interview clients individually, in families, or in groups, assessing their situations, capabilities, and problems, to determine what services are required to meet their needs. Counsel individuals, groups, families, or communities regarding issues including mental health, poverty, unemployment, substance abuse, physical abuse, rehabilitation, social adjustment, child care, and/or medical care. Maintain case history records and prepare reports. Counsel students whose behavior, school progress, or mental or physical impairment indicate a need for assistance, diagnosing students' problems and arranging for needed services. Consult with parents, teachers, and other school personnel to determine causes of problems such as truancy and misbehavior and to implement solutions. Counsel parents with child-rearing problems, interviewing the child and family to determine whether further action is required. Develop and review service plans in consultation with clients and perform follow-ups assessing the quantity and quality of services provided. Collect supplemen-

tary information needed to assist client, such as employment records, medical records, or school reports. Address legal issues, such as child abuse and discipline, assisting with hearings and providing testimony to inform custody arrangements. Provide, find, or arrange for support services, such as child care, homemaker service, prenatal care, substance abuse treatment, job training, counseling, or parenting classes, to prevent more serious problems from developing. Refer clients to community resources for services such as job placement, debt counseling, legal aid, housing, medical treatment, or financial assistance and provide concrete information, such as where to go and how to apply. Arrange for medical, psychiatric, and other tests that may disclose causes of difficulties and indicate remedial measures. Work in child and adolescent residential institutions. Administer welfare programs. Evaluate personal characteristics and home conditions of foster home or adoption applicants. Serve as liaisons between students, homes, schools, family services, child guidance clinics, courts, protective services, doctors, and other contacts to help children who face problems such as disabilities, abuse, or poverty. **SKILLS—Social Perceptiveness:** Being aware of others' reactions and understanding why they react as they do. **Service Orientation:** Actively looking for ways to help people. **Learning Strategies:** Selecting and using training/instructional methods and procedures appropriate for the situation when learning or teaching new things. **Negotiation:** Bringing others together and trying to reconcile differences. **Speaking:** Talking to others to convey information effectively. **Monitoring:** Monitoring or assessing your performance or that of other individuals or organizations to make improvements or take corrective action. **Active Listening:** Giving full attention to what other people are saying, taking time to understand the points being made, asking questions as appropriate, and not interrupting at inappropriate times. **Persuasion:** Persuading others to change their minds or behavior. **GOE—Interest Area:** 10. Human Service. **Work Group:** 10.01. Counseling and Social Work. **Other Jobs in This Work Group:** Clinical Psychologists; Counseling Psychologists; Marriage and Family Therapists; Medical and Public Health Social Workers; Mental Health and Substance Abuse Social Workers; Mental Health Counselors; Probation Officers and Correctional Treatment Specialists; Rehabilitation Counselors; Residential Advisors; Social and Human Service Assistants; Substance Abuse and Behavioral Disorder Counselors. **PERSONALITY TYPE:** Social.

C

EDUCATION/TRAINING PROGRAM(S)—Juvenile Corrections; Social Work; Youth Services/Administration. **RELATED KNOWLEDGE/COURSES— Therapy and Counseling:** Knowledge of principles, methods, and procedures for diagnosis, treatment, and rehabilitation of physical and mental dysfunctions and for career counseling and guidance. **Psychology:** Knowledge of human behavior and performance; individual differences in ability, personality, and interests; learning and motivation; psychological research methods; and the assessment and treatment of behavioral and affective disorders. **Sociology and Anthropology:** Knowledge of group behavior and dynamics, societal trends and influences, human migrations, ethnicity, and cultures and their history and origins. **Customer and Personal Service:** Knowledge of principles and processes for providing customer and personal services. This includes customer needs assessment, meeting quality standards for services, and evaluation of customer satisfaction. **Law and Government:** Knowledge of laws, legal codes, court procedures, precedents, government regulations, executive orders, agency rules, and the democratic political process. **Philosophy and Theology:** Knowledge of different philosophical systems and religions. This includes their basic principles, values, ethics, ways of thinking, customs, and practices and their impact on human culture.

Chiropractors

- ◎ Education/Training Required: First professional degree
- ◎ Annual Earnings: $69,910
- ◎ Growth: 23.3%
- ◎ Annual Job Openings: 3,000
- ◎ Self-Employed: 58.5%
- ◎ Part-Time: 22.2%

Adjust spinal column and other articulations of the body to correct abnormalities of the human body believed to be caused by interference with the nervous system. Examine patient to determine nature and extent of disorder. Manipulate spine or other involved area. May utilize supplementary measures, such as exercise, rest, water, light, heat, and nutritional therapy. Perform a series of manual adjustments to the spine or other articulations of the body in order to correct the musculoskeletal system. Evaluate the functioning of the neuromuscularskeletal system and

the spine, using systems of chiropractic diagnosis. Diagnose health problems by reviewing patients' health and medical histories; questioning, observing, and examining patients; and interpreting X rays. Maintain accurate case histories of patients. Advise patients about recommended courses of treatment. Obtain and record patients' medical histories. Analyze X rays in order to locate the sources of patients' difficulties and to rule out fractures or diseases as sources of problems. Counsel patients about nutrition, exercise, sleeping habits, stress management, and other matters. Arrange for diagnostic X rays to be taken. Consult with and refer patients to appropriate health practitioners when necessary. Suggest and apply the use of supports such as straps, tapes, bandages, and braces if necessary. **SKILLS—Social Perceptiveness:** Being aware of others' reactions and understanding why they react as they do. **Persuasion:** Persuading others to change their minds or behavior. **Service Orientation:** Actively looking for ways to help people. **Management of Financial Resources:** Determining how money will be spent to get the work done and accounting for these expenditures. **Science:** Using scientific rules and methods to solve problems. **Reading Comprehension:** Understanding written sentences and paragraphs in work-related documents. **Instructing:** Teaching others how to do something. **Critical Thinking:** Using logic and reasoning to identify the strengths and weaknesses of alternative solutions, conclusions, or approaches to problems. **GOE—Interest Area:** 08. Health Science. **Work Group:** 08.04. Health Specialties. **Other Jobs in This Work Group:** Optometrists; Podiatrists. **PERSONALITY TYPE:** Investigative.

EDUCATION/TRAINING PROGRAM(S)— Chiropractic (DC). **RELATED KNOWLEDGE/ COURSES—Medicine and Dentistry:** Knowledge of the information and techniques needed to diagnose and treat human injuries, diseases, and deformities. This includes symptoms, treatment alternatives, drug properties and interactions, and preventive health-care measures. **Therapy and Counseling:** Knowledge of principles, methods, and procedures for diagnosis, treatment, and rehabilitation of physical and mental dysfunctions and for career counseling and guidance. **Psychology:** Knowledge of human behavior and performance; individual differences in ability, personality, and interests; learning and motivation; psychological research methods; and the assessment and treatment of behavioral and affective disorders. **Customer and Personal Service:** Knowledge of principles and processes for providing customer and personal services. This includes customer needs assessment, meeting quality standards for services, and evaluation of customer satisfaction. **Biology:** Knowledge of plant and animal organisms and their tissues, cells, functions, interdependencies, and interactions with each other and the environment. **Sales and Marketing:** Knowledge of principles and methods for showing, promoting, and selling products or services. This includes marketing strategy and tactics, product demonstrations, sales techniques, and sales control systems.

City and Regional Planning Aides

- ◎ Education/Training Required: Associate degree
- ◎ Annual Earnings: $34,360
- ◎ Growth: 17.5%
- ◎ Annual Job Openings: 18,000
- ◎ Self-Employed: 1.1%
- ◎ Part-Time: 20.2%

Compile data from various sources, such as maps, reports, and field and file investigations, for use by city planner in making planning studies. Prepare, maintain, and update files and records, including land use data and statistics. Respond to public inquiries and complaints. Research, compile, analyze, and organize information from maps, reports, investigations, and books for use in reports and special projects. Prepare, develop, and maintain maps and databases. Serve as a liaison between planning department and other departments and agencies. Prepare reports, using statistics, charts, and graphs, to illustrate planning studies in areas such as population, land use, or zoning. Participate in and support team planning efforts. Provide and process zoning and project permits and applications. Perform clerical duties such as composing, typing, and proofreading documents; scheduling appointments and meetings; handling mail; and posting public notices. Conduct interviews, surveys, and site inspections concerning factors that affect land usage, such as zoning, traffic flow, and housing. Perform code enforcement tasks. Inspect sites and review plans for minor development permit applications. **SKILLS—Service Orientation:** Actively looking for ways to help people. **Coordination:** Adjusting actions

in relation to others' actions. **Social Perceptiveness:** Being aware of others' reactions and understanding why they react as they do. **Persuasion:** Persuading others to change their minds or behavior. **Writing:** Communicating effectively in writing as appropriate for the needs of the audience. **Active Learning:** Understanding the implications of new information for both current and future problem-solving and decision-making. **Negotiation:** Bringing others together and trying to reconcile differences. **Learning Strategies:** Selecting and using training/instructional methods and procedures appropriate for the situation when learning or teaching new things. **Complex Problem Solving:** Identifying complex problems and reviewing related information to develop and evaluate options and implement solutions. **GOE—Interest Area:** 07. Government and Public Administration. **Work Group:** 07.02. Public Planning. **Other Jobs in This Work Group:** Urban and Regional Planners. **PERSONALITY TYPE:** Conventional.

EDUCATION/TRAINING PROGRAM(S)— Social Sciences, General. **RELATED KNOWLEDGE/COURSES—Geography:** Knowledge of principles and methods for describing the features of land, sea, and air masses, including their physical characteristics; locations; interrelationships; and distribution of plant, animal, and human life. **Design:** Knowledge of design techniques, tools, and principles involved in production of precision technical plans, blueprints, drawings, and models. **Clerical Practices:** Knowledge of administrative and clerical procedures and systems such as word processing, managing files and records, stenography and transcription, designing forms, and other office procedures and terminology. **Law and Government:** Knowledge of laws, legal codes, court procedures, precedents, government regulations, executive orders, agency rules, and the democratic political process. **English Language:** Knowledge of the structure and content of the English language, including the meaning and spelling of words, rules of composition, and grammar. **Customer and Personal Service:** Knowledge of principles and processes for providing customer and personal services. This includes customer needs assessment, meeting quality standards for services, and evaluation of customer satisfaction.

C

Civil Drafters

- ◎ Education/Training Required: Postsecondary vocational training
- ◎ Annual Earnings: $39,190
- ◎ Growth: 4.2%
- ◎ Annual Job Openings: 14,000
- ◎ Self-Employed: 3.7%
- ◎ Part-Time: 5.1%

Prepare drawings and topographical and relief maps used in civil engineering projects, such as highways, bridges, pipelines, flood control projects, and water and sewerage control systems. Produce drawings by using computer assisted drafting systems (CAD) or drafting machines or by hand, using compasses, dividers, protractors, triangles, and other drafting devices. Draft plans and detailed drawings for structures, installations, and construction projects such as highways, sewage disposal systems, and dikes, working from sketches or notes. Draw maps, diagrams, and profiles, using cross-sections and surveys, to represent elevations, topographical contours, subsurface formations, and structures. Correlate, interpret, and modify data obtained from topographical surveys, well logs, and geophysical prospecting reports. Finish and duplicate drawings and documentation packages according to required mediums and specifications for reproduction, using blueprinting, photography, or other duplicating methods. Review rough sketches, drawings, specifications, and other engineering data received from civil engineers to ensure that they conform to design concepts. Supervise and train other technologists, technicians, and drafters. Supervise or conduct field surveys, inspections, or technical investigations to obtain data required to revise construction drawings. Determine the order of work and method of presentation, such as orthographic or isometric drawing. Calculate excavation tonnage and prepare graphs and fill-hauling diagrams for use in earth-moving operations. Explain drawings to production or construction teams and provide adjustments as necessary. Locate and identify symbols located on topographical surveys to denote geological and geophysical formations or oil field installations. **SKILLS—Mathematics:** Using mathematics to solve problems. **Coordination:** Adjusting actions in relation to others' actions. **Instructing:** Teaching others how to do something. **Operations Analysis:** Analyzing needs and product requirements to create a design. **Active Learning:** Understanding the implications of new information for both current and future problem-solving and decision-making. **Technology Design:** Generating or adapting equipment and technology to serve user needs. **Time Management:** Managing one's own time and the time of others. **Active Listening:** Giving full attention to what other people are saying, taking time to understand the points being made, asking questions as appropriate, and not interrupting at inappropriate times. **GOE—Interest Area:** 02. Architecture and Construction. **Work Group:** 02.03. Architecture/Construction Engineering Technologies. **Other Jobs in This Work Group:** Architectural Drafters; Construction and Building Inspectors; Electrical Drafters; Surveyors. **PERSONALITY TYPE:** Realistic.

EDUCATION/TRAINING PROGRAM(S)— Architectural Drafting and Architectural CAD/CADD; Architectural Technology/Technician; CAD/CADD Drafting and/or Design Technology/Technician; Civil Drafting and Civil Engineering CAD/CADD; Drafting and Design Technology/Technician, General. **RELATED KNOWLEDGE/COURSES—Design:** Knowledge of design techniques, tools, and principles involved in production of precision technical plans, blueprints, drawings, and models. **Engineering and Technology:** Knowledge of the practical application of engineering science and technology. This includes applying principles, techniques, procedures, and equipment to the design and production of various goods and services. **Computers and Electronics:** Knowledge of circuit boards, processors, chips, electronic equipment, and computer hardware and software, including applications and programming. **Geography:** Knowledge of principles and methods for describing the features of land, sea, and air masses, including their physical characteristics; locations; interrelationships; and distribution of plant, animal, and human life. **Mathematics:** Knowledge of arithmetic, algebra, geometry, calculus, and statistics and their applications. **Law and Government:** Knowledge of laws, legal codes, court procedures, precedents, government regulations, executive orders, agency rules, and the democratic political process.

Civil Engineering Technicians

- Education/Training Required: Associate degree
- Annual Earnings: $38,480
- Growth: 7.6%
- Annual Job Openings: 10,000
- Self-Employed: 0.4%
- Part-Time: 5.0%

Apply theory and principles of civil engineering in planning, designing, and overseeing construction and maintenance of structures and facilities under the direction of engineering staff or physical scientists. Calculate dimensions, square footage, profile and component specifications, and material quantities, using calculator or computer. Draft detailed dimensional drawings and design layouts for projects and to ensure conformance to specifications. Analyze proposed site factors and design maps, graphs, tracings, and diagrams to illustrate findings. Read and review project blueprints and structural specifications to determine dimensions of structure or system and material requirements. Prepare reports and document project activities and data. Confer with supervisor to determine project details, such as plan preparation, acceptance testing, and evaluation of field conditions. Inspect project site and evaluate contractor work to detect design malfunctions and ensure conformance to design specifications and applicable codes. Plan and conduct field surveys to locate new sites and analyze details of project sites. Develop plans and estimate costs for installation of systems, utilization of facilities, or construction of structures. Report maintenance problems occurring at project site to supervisor and negotiate changes to resolve system conflicts. Conduct materials test and analysis, using tools and equipment and applying engineering knowledge. Respond to public suggestions and complaints. Evaluate facility to determine suitability for occupancy and square footage availability. **SKILLS—Mathematics:** Using mathematics to solve problems. **Instructing:** Teaching others how to do something. **Active Learning:** Understanding the implications of new information for both current and future problem-solving and decision-making. **Operations Analysis:** Analyzing needs and product requirements to create a design. **Critical Thinking:** Using logic and reasoning to identify the strengths and weaknesses of alternative solutions, conclusions, or approaches to problems. **Complex Problem Solving:** Identifying complex problems and reviewing related information to develop and evaluate options and implement solutions. **Writing:** Communicating effectively in writing as appropriate for the needs of the audience. **Science:** Using scientific rules and methods to solve problems. **Learning Strategies:** Selecting and using training/instructional methods and procedures appropriate for the situation when learning or teaching new things. **GOE—Interest Area:** 15. Scientific Research, Engineering, and Mathematics. **Work Group:** 15.09. Engineering Technology. **Other Jobs in This Work Group:** Aerospace Engineering and Operations Technicians; Calibration and Instrumentation Technicians; Cartographers and Photogrammetrists; Electrical Engineering Technicians; Electro-Mechanical Technicians; Electronic Drafters; Electronics Engineering Technicians; Environmental Engineering Technicians; Mapping Technicians; Mechanical Drafters; Mechanical Engineering Technicians; Surveying Technicians. **PERSONALITY TYPE:** Realistic.

EDUCATION/TRAINING PROGRAM(S)—Civil Engineering Technology/Technician; Construction Engineering Technology/Technician. **RELATED KNOWLEDGE/COURSES—Design:** Knowledge of design techniques, tools, and principles involved in production of precision technical plans, blueprints, drawings, and models. **Building and Construction:** Knowledge of the materials, methods, and tools involved in the construction or repair of houses, buildings, or other structures such as highways and roads. **Engineering and Technology:** Knowledge of the practical application of engineering science and technology. This includes applying principles, techniques, procedures, and equipment to the design and production of various goods and services. **Mathematics:** Knowledge of arithmetic, algebra, geometry, calculus, and statistics and their applications. **Computers and Electronics:** Knowledge of circuit boards, processors, chips, electronic equipment, and computer hardware and software, including applications and programming. **Transportation:** Knowledge of principles and methods for moving people or goods by air, rail, sea, or road, including the relative costs and benefits.

C

Civil Engineers

- Education/Training Required: Bachelor's degree
- Annual Earnings: $64,230
- Growth: 8.0%
- Annual Job Openings: 17,000
- Self-Employed: 6.7%
- Part-Time: 3.3%

Perform engineering duties in planning, designing, and overseeing construction and maintenance of building structures and facilities, such as roads, railroads, airports, bridges, harbors, channels, dams, irrigation projects, pipelines, power plants, water and sewage systems, and waste disposal units. Includes architectural, structural, traffic, ocean, and geo-technical engineers. Analyze survey reports, maps, drawings, blueprints, aerial photography, and other topographical or geologic data to plan projects. Plan and design transportation or hydraulic systems and structures, following construction and government standards and using design software and drawing tools. Compute load and grade requirements, water flow rates, and material stress factors to determine design specifications. Inspect project sites to monitor progress and ensure conformance to design specifications and safety or sanitation standards. Direct construction, operations, and maintenance activities at project site. Direct or participate in surveying to lay out installations and establish reference points, grades, and elevations to guide construction. Estimate quantities and cost of materials, equipment, or labor to determine project feasibility. Prepare or present public reports, such as bid proposals, deeds, environmental impact statements, and property and right-of-way descriptions. Test soils and materials to determine the adequacy and strength of foundations, concrete, asphalt, or steel. Provide technical advice regarding design, construction, or program modifications and structural repairs to industrial and managerial personnel. **SKILLS—Science:** Using scientific rules and methods to solve problems. **Coordination:** Adjusting actions in relation to others' actions. **Negotiation:** Bringing others together and trying to reconcile differences. **Persuasion:** Persuading others to change their minds or behavior. **Mathematics:** Using mathematics to solve problems. **Operations Analysis:** Analyzing needs and product requirements to create a design. **Instructing:** Teaching others how to do something. **Complex Problem Solving:** Identifying complex problems and reviewing related information to develop and evaluate options and implement solutions. **Technology Design:** Generating or adapting equipment and technology to serve user needs. GOE—**Interest Area:** 15. Scientific Research, Engineering, and Mathematics. **Work Group:** 15.07. Research and Design Engineering. **Other Jobs in This Work Group:** Aerospace Engineers; Biomedical Engineers; Chemical Engineers; Computer Hardware Engineers; Electrical Engineers; Electronics Engineers, Except Computer; Marine Architects; Marine Engineers; Materials Engineers; Mechanical Engineers; Nuclear Engineers. **PERSONALITY TYPE:** Realistic.

EDUCATION/TRAINING PROGRAM(S)—Civil Engineering, General; Civil Engineering, Other; Transportation and Highway Engineering; Water Resources Engineering. **RELATED KNOWLEDGE/COURSES—Engineering and Technology:** Knowledge of the practical application of engineering science and technology. This includes applying principles, techniques, procedures, and equipment to the design and production of various goods and services. **Design:** Knowledge of design techniques, tools, and principles involved in production of precision technical plans, blueprints, drawings, and models. **Building and Construction:** Knowledge of the materials, methods, and tools involved in the construction or repair of houses, buildings, or other structures such as highways and roads. **Mathematics:** Knowledge of arithmetic, algebra, geometry, calculus, and statistics and their applications. **Customer and Personal Service:** Knowledge of principles and processes for providing customer and personal services. This includes customer needs assessment, meeting quality standards for services, and evaluation of customer satisfaction. **Physics:** Knowledge and prediction of physical principles and laws and their interrelationships and applications to understanding fluid, material, and atmospheric dynamics and mechanical, electrical, atomic, and subatomic structures and processes.

Claims Examiners, Property and Casualty Insurance

- Education/Training Required: Long-term on-the-job training
- Annual Earnings: $44,220
- Growth: 14.2%
- Annual Job Openings: 31,000
- Self-Employed: 1.9%
- Part-Time: 4.9%

Review settled insurance claims to determine that payments and settlements have been made in accordance with company practices and procedures. Report overpayments, underpayments, and other irregularities. Confer with legal counsel on claims requiring litigation. Investigate, evaluate, and settle claims, applying technical knowledge and human relations skills to effect fair and prompt disposal of cases and to contribute to a reduced loss ratio. Pay and process claims within designated authority level. Adjust reserves and provide reserve recommendations to ensure reserving activities consistent with corporate policies. Enter claim payments, reserves, and new claims on computer system, inputting concise yet sufficient file documentation. Resolve complex, severe exposure claims, using high-service-oriented file handling. Maintain claim files, such as records of settled claims and an inventory of claims requiring detailed analysis. Verify and analyze data used in settling claims to ensure that claims are valid and that settlements are made according to company practices and procedures. Examine claims investigated by insurance adjusters, further investigating questionable claims to determine whether to authorize payments. Present cases and participate in their discussion at claim committee meetings. Contact and/or interview claimants, doctors, medical specialists, or employers to get additional information. Confer with legal counsel on claims requiring litigation. Report overpayments, underpayments, and other irregularities. Communicate with reinsurance brokers to obtain information necessary for processing claims. Supervise claims adjusters to ensure that adjusters have followed proper methods. Conduct detailed bill reviews to implement sound litigation management and expense control. Prepare reports to be submitted to company's data processing department. SKILLS—Judgment and Decision Making: Considering the relative costs and benefits of potential actions to choose the most appropriate one. Persuasion: Persuading others to change their minds or behavior. Instructing: Teaching others how to do something. Negotiation: Bringing others together and trying to reconcile differences. Writing: Communicating effectively in writing as appropriate for the needs of the audience. Critical Thinking: Using logic and reasoning to identify the strengths and weaknesses of alternative solutions, conclusions, or approaches to problems. Time Management: Managing one's own time and the time of others. Reading Comprehension: Understanding written sentences and paragraphs in work-related documents. Active Listening: Giving full attention to what other people are saying, taking time to understand the points being made, asking questions as appropriate, and not interrupting at inappropriate times. Social Perceptiveness: Being aware of others' reactions and understanding why they react as they do. GOE—Interest Area: 06. Finance and Insurance. Work Group: 06.02. Finance/Insurance Investigation and Analysis. Other Jobs in This Work Group: Appraisers, Real Estate; Assessors; Cost Estimators; Credit Analysts; Financial Analysts; Insurance Adjusters, Examiners, and Investigators; Insurance Appraisers, Auto Damage; Insurance Underwriters; Loan Counselors; Loan Officers; Market Research Analysts; Survey Researchers. PERSONALITY TYPE: Conventional.

EDUCATION/TRAINING PROGRAM(S)— Health/Medical Claims Examiner; Insurance. RELATED KNOWLEDGE/COURSES—Customer and Personal Service: Knowledge of principles and processes for providing customer and personal services. This includes customer needs assessment, meeting quality standards for services, and evaluation of customer satisfaction. Clerical Practices: Knowledge of administrative and clerical procedures and systems such as word processing, managing files and records, stenography and transcription, designing forms, and other office procedures and terminology. Medicine and Dentistry: Knowledge of the information and techniques needed to diagnose and treat human injuries, diseases, and deformities. This includes symptoms, treatment alternatives, drug properties and interactions, and preventive health-care measures. Law and Government: Knowledge of laws, legal codes, court procedures, precedents, government regulations, executive orders, agency rules, and the democratic political process. **Computers and Electronics:** Knowledge of circuit boards, processors, chips, electronic equipment, and computer hardware and software, including applications and programming. **English Language:** Knowledge of the structure and content of the English language, including the meaning and spelling of words, rules of composition, and grammar.

Clergy

- Education/Training Required: First professional degree
- Annual Earnings: $36,690
- Growth: 15.5%
- Annual Job Openings: 34,000
- Self-Employed: 0.3%
- Part-Time: 9.4%

Conduct religious worship and perform other spiritual functions associated with beliefs and practices of religious faith or denomination. Provide spiritual and moral guidance and assistance to members. Administer religious rites or ordinances. Study and interpret religious laws, doctrines, and/or traditions. Counsel individuals and groups concerning their spiritual, emotional, and personal needs. Organize and lead regular religious services. Conduct special ceremonies such as weddings, funerals, and confirmations. Instruct people who seek conversion to a particular faith. Pray and promote spirituality. Prepare and deliver sermons and other talks. Prepare people for participation in religious ceremonies. Read from sacred texts such as the Bible, Torah, or Koran. Collaborate with committees and individuals to address financial and administrative issues pertaining to congregations. Devise ways in which congregation membership can be expanded. Organize and engage in interfaith, community, civic, educational, and recreational activities sponsored by or related to their religion. Participate in fundraising activities to support congregation activities and facilities. Perform administrative duties such as overseeing building management, ordering supplies, contracting for services and repairs, and supervising the work of staff members and volunteers. Plan and lead religious education programs for their congregations. Refer people to community support services, psychologists, and/or doctors as necessary. Respond to requests for assistance during emergencies or crises.

Share information about religious issues by writing articles, giving speeches, or teaching. Train leaders of church, community, and youth groups. Visit people in homes, hospitals, and prisons to provide them with comfort and support. **SKILLS—Service Orientation:** Actively looking for ways to help people. **Social Perceptiveness:** Being aware of others' reactions and understanding why they react as they do. **Speaking:** Talking to others to convey information effectively. **Writing:** Communicating effectively in writing as appropriate for the needs of the audience. **Active Listening:** Giving full attention to what other people are saying, taking time to understand the points being made, asking questions as appropriate, and not interrupting at inappropriate times. **Reading Comprehension:** Understanding written sentences and paragraphs in work-related documents. **Learning Strategies:** Selecting and using training/instructional methods and procedures appropriate for the situation when learning or teaching new things. **Persuasion:** Persuading others to change their minds or behavior. **GOE—Interest Area:** 10. Human Service. **Work Group:** 10.02. Religious Work. **Other Jobs in This Work Group:** Directors, Religious Activities and Education. **PERSONALITY TYPE:** Social.

EDUCATION/TRAINING PROGRAM(S)—Clinical Pastoral Counseling/Patient Counseling; Divinity/Ministry (BD, MDiv.); Pastoral Counseling and Specialized Ministries, Other; Pastoral Studies/Counseling; Pre-Theology/Pre-Ministerial Studies; Rabbinical Studies; Theological and Ministerial Studies, Other; Theology and Religious Vocations, Other; Theology/Theological Studies; Youth Ministry. **RELATED KNOWLEDGE/COURSES—Philosophy and Theology:** Knowledge of different philosophical systems and religions. This includes their basic principles, values, ethics, ways of thinking, customs, and practices and their impact on human culture. **Education and Training:** Knowledge of principles and methods for curriculum and training design, teaching and instruction for individuals and groups, and the measurement of training effects. **Therapy and Counseling:** Knowledge of principles, methods, and procedures for diagnosis, treatment, and rehabilitation of physical and mental dysfunctions and for career counseling and guidance. **Psychology:** Knowledge of human behavior and performance; individual differences in ability, personality, and interests; learning and motivation; psychological research methods; and the assessment and treatment of behavioral and affective disorders. **English Language:** Knowledge of the structure and content of the English language, including the meaning and spelling of words, rules of composition, and grammar. **Communications and Media:** Knowledge of media production, communication, and dissemination techniques and methods. This includes alternative ways to inform and entertain via written, oral, and visual media.

Clinical Psychologists

- Education/Training Required: Master's degree
- Annual Earnings: $54,950
- Growth: 24.4%
- Annual Job Openings: 17,000
- Self-Employed: 25.4%
- Part-Time: 27.2%

Diagnose or evaluate mental and emotional disorders of individuals through observation, interview, and psychological tests and formulate and administer programs of treatment. Consult reference material such as textbooks, manuals, and journals in order to identify symptoms, to make diagnoses, and to develop approaches to treatment. Counsel individuals and groups regarding problems such as stress, substance abuse, and family situations in order to modify behavior and/or to improve personal, social, and vocational adjustment. Develop and implement individual treatment plans, specifying type, frequency, intensity, and duration of therapy. Discuss the treatment of problems with clients. Evaluate the effectiveness of counseling or treatments and the accuracy and completeness of diagnoses and then modify plans and diagnoses as necessary. Identify psychological, emotional, or behavioral issues and diagnose disorders, using information obtained from interviews, tests, records, and reference materials. Interact with clients to assist them in gaining insight, defining goals, and planning action to achieve effective personal, social, educational, and vocational development and adjustment. Observe individuals at play, in group interactions, or in other contexts to detect indications of mental deficiency, abnormal behavior, or maladjustment. Obtain and study medical, psychological, social, and family histories by interviewing individuals, couples, or families and by reviewing records. Provide occupational, edu-cational, and other information to individuals so that they can make educational and vocational plans. Select, administer, score, and interpret psychological tests in order to obtain information on individuals' intelligence, achievements, interests, and personalities. Utilize a variety of treatment methods such as psychotherapy, hypnosis, behavior modification, stress reduction therapy, psychodrama, and play therapy. Maintain current knowledge of relevant research. Plan, supervise, and conduct psychological research and write papers describing research results. Refer clients to other specialists, institutions, or support services as necessary. Write reports on clients and maintain required paperwork. Develop, direct, and participate in training programs for staff and students. **SKILLS— Social Perceptiveness:** Being aware of others' reactions and understanding why they react as they do. **Active Listening:** Giving full attention to what other people are saying, taking time to understand the points being made, asking questions as appropriate, and not interrupting at inappropriate times. **Systems Evaluation:** Identifying measures or indicators of system performance and the actions needed to improve or correct performance relative to the goals of the system. **Persuasion:** Persuading others to change their minds or behavior. **Systems Analysis:** Determining how a system should work and how changes in conditions, operations, and the environment will affect outcomes. **Speaking:** Talking to others to convey information effectively. **Reading Comprehension:** Understanding written sentences and paragraphs in work-related documents. **Science:** Using scientific rules and methods to solve problems. **Complex Problem Solving:** Identifying complex problems and reviewing related information to develop and evaluate options and implement solutions. **GOE—Interest Area:** 10. Human Service. **Work Group:** 10.01. Counseling and Social Work. **Other Jobs in This Work Group:** Child, Family, and School Social Workers; Counseling Psychologists; Marriage and Family Therapists; Medical and Public Health Social Workers; Mental Health and Substance Abuse Social Workers; Mental Health Counselors; Probation Officers and Correctional Treatment Specialists; Rehabilitation Counselors; Residential Advisors; Social and Human Service Assistants; Substance Abuse and Behavioral Disorder Counselors. **PERSONALITY TYPE:** Investigative.

EDUCATION/TRAINING PROGRAM(S)—Clinical Child Psychology; Clinical Psychology; Counseling Psychology; Developmental and Child Psychology; Psychoanalysis and Psychotherapy; Psychology, General; School Psychology. **RELATED KNOWLEDGE/COURSES—Therapy and Counseling:** Knowledge of principles, methods, and procedures for diagnosis, treatment, and rehabilitation of physical and mental dysfunctions and for career counseling and guidance. **Psychology:** Knowledge of human behavior and performance; individual differences in ability, personality, and interests; learning and motivation; psychological research methods; and the assessment and treatment of behavioral and affective disorders. **Administration and Management:** Knowledge of business and management principles involved in strategic planning, resource allocation, human resources modeling, leadership technique, production methods, and coordination of people and resources. **Sociology and Anthropology:** Knowledge of group behavior and dynamics, societal trends and influences, human migrations, ethnicity, and cultures and their history and origins. **Customer and Personal Service:** Knowledge of principles and processes for providing customer and personal services. This includes customer needs assessment, meeting quality standards for services, and evaluation of customer satisfaction. **English Language:** Knowledge of the structure and content of the English language, including the meaning and spelling of words, rules of composition, and grammar.

Coaches and Scouts

- ◉ Education/Training Required: Long-term on-the-job training
- ◉ Annual Earnings: $26,350
- ◉ Growth: 18.3%
- ◉ Annual Job Openings: 26,000
- ◉ Self-Employed: 26.6%
- ◉ Part-Time: 36.3%

Instruct or coach groups or individuals in the fundamentals of sports. Demonstrate techniques and methods of participation. May evaluate athletes' strengths and weaknesses as possible recruits or to improve the athletes' technique to prepare them for competition. Those required to hold teaching degrees should be reported in the appropriate teaching category. Plan, organize, and conduct practice sessions.

Provide training direction, encouragement, and motivation in order to prepare athletes for games, competitive events, and/or tours. Identify and recruit potential athletes, arranging and offering incentives such as athletic scholarships. Plan strategies and choose team members for individual games and/or sports seasons. Plan and direct physical conditioning programs that will enable athletes to achieve maximum performance. Adjust coaching techniques based on the strengths and weaknesses of athletes. File scouting reports that detail player assessments, provide recommendations on athlete recruitment, and identify locations and individuals to be targeted for future recruitment efforts. Keep records of athlete, team, and opposing team performance. Instruct individuals or groups in sports rules, game strategies, and performance principles such as specific ways of moving the body, hands, and/or feet in order to achieve desired results. Analyze the strengths and weaknesses of opposing teams in order to develop game strategies. Evaluate athletes' skills and review performance records in order to determine their fitness and potential in a particular area of athletics. Keep abreast of changing rules, techniques, technologies, and philosophies relevant to their sport. Monitor athletes' use of equipment in order to ensure safe and proper use. Develop and arrange competition schedules and programs. Explain and enforce safety rules and regulations. Serve as organizer, leader, instructor, or referee for outdoor and indoor games, such as volleyball, football, and soccer. Explain and demonstrate the use of sports and training equipment, such as trampolines or weights. Perform activities that support a team or a specific sport, such as meeting with media representatives and appearing at fundraising events. Arrange and conduct sports-related activities such as training camps, skill-improvement courses, clinics, and/or pre-season tryouts. Select, acquire, store, and issue equipment and other materials as necessary. **SKILLS—Social Perceptiveness:** Being aware of others' reactions and understanding why they react as they do. **Instructing:** Teaching others how to do something. **Management of Personnel Resources:** Motivating, developing, and directing people as they work, identifying the best people for the job. **Persuasion:** Persuading others to change their minds or behavior. **Negotiation:** Bringing others together and trying to reconcile differences. **Learning Strategies:** Selecting and using training/instructional methods and procedures appropriate for the situation when learning or teaching new things. **Time Management:** Managing one's own time and the time of others. **Management of Financial Resources:** Determining how money will be spent to get the work done and accounting for these expenditures. **GOE—Interest Area:** 09. Hospitality, Tourism, and Recreation. **Work Group:** 09.06. Sports. **Other Jobs in This Work Group:** Athletes and Sports Competitors; Umpires, Referees, and Other Sports Officials. **PERSONALITY TYPE:** Enterprising.

EDUCATION/TRAINING PROGRAM(S)— Health and Physical Education, General; Physical Education Teaching and Coaching; Sport and Fitness Administration/Management. **RELATED KNOWLEDGE/COURSES—Psychology:** Knowledge of human behavior and performance; individual differences in ability, personality, and interests; learning and motivation; psychological research methods; and the assessment and treatment of behavioral and affective disorders. **Education and Training:** Knowledge of principles and methods for curriculum and training design, teaching and instruction for individuals and groups, and the measurement of training effects. **Sales and Marketing:** Knowledge of principles and methods for showing, promoting, and selling products or services. This includes marketing strategy and tactics, product demonstrations, sales techniques, and sales control systems. **Therapy and Counseling:** Knowledge of principles, methods, and procedures for diagnosis, treatment, and rehabilitation of physical and mental dysfunctions and for career counseling and guidance. **Personnel and Human Resources:** Knowledge of principles and procedures for personnel recruitment, selection, training, compensation and benefits, labor relations and negotiation, and personnel information systems. **Customer and Personal Service:** Knowledge of principles and processes for providing customer and personal services. This includes customer needs assessment, meeting quality standards for services, and evaluation of customer satisfaction.

Combined Food Preparation and Serving Workers, Including Fast Food

- ◎ Education/Training Required: Short-term on-the-job training
- ◎ Annual Earnings: $14,690
- ◎ Growth: 22.8%
- ◎ Annual Job Openings: 734,000
- ◎ Self-Employed: 0.1%
- ◎ Part-Time: 40.4%

Perform duties which combine both food preparation and food service. Accept payment from customers and make change as necessary. Request and record customer orders and compute bills, using cash registers, multicounting machines, or pencil and paper. Clean and organize eating and service areas. Serve customers in eating places that specialize in fast service and inexpensive carry-out food. Prepare and serve cold drinks or frozen milk drinks or desserts, using drink-dispensing, milkshake, or frozen custard machines. Select food items from serving or storage areas and place them in dishes, on serving trays, or in takeout bags. Prepare simple foods and beverages such as sandwiches, salads, and coffee. Notify kitchen personnel of shortages or special orders. Cook or re-heat food items such as french fries. Wash dishes, glassware, and silverware after meals. Collect and return dirty dishes to the kitchen for washing. Relay food orders to cooks. Distribute food to servers. Serve food and beverages to guests at banquets or other social functions. Provide caterers with assistance in food preparation or service. Pack food, dishes, utensils, tablecloths, and accessories for transportation from catering or food preparation establishments to locations designated by customers. Arrange tables and decorations according to instructions. **SKILLS—Instructing:** Teaching others how to do something. **Service Orientation:** Actively looking for ways to help people. **Social Perceptiveness:** Being aware of others' reactions and understanding why they react as they do. **GOE—Interest Area:** 09. Hospitality, Tourism, and Recreation. **Work Group:** 09.05. Food and Beverage Service. **Other Jobs in This Work Group:** Bartenders; Counter Attendants, Cafeteria, Food Concession, and Coffee Shop; Dining Room and Cafeteria Attendants and Bartender Helpers; Food Servers, Nonrestaurant; Hosts and Hostesses, Restaurant, Lounge, and Coffee Shop; Waiters and Waitresses. **PERSONALITY TYPE:** Realistic.

EDUCATION/TRAINING PROGRAM(S)—Food Preparation/Professional Cooking/Kitchen Assistant; Institutional Food Workers. **RELATED KNOWLEDGE/COURSES—Food Production:** Knowledge of techniques and equipment for planting, growing, and harvesting food products (both plant and animal) for consumption, including storage/handling techniques. **Sales and Marketing:** Knowledge of principles and methods for showing, promoting, and selling products or services. This includes marketing strategy and tactics, product demonstrations, sales techniques, and sales control systems. **Customer and Personal Service:** Knowledge of principles and processes for providing customer and personal services. This includes customer needs assessment, meeting quality standards for services, and evaluation of customer satisfaction. **Production and Processing:** Knowledge of raw materials, production processes, quality control, costs, and other techniques for maximizing the effective manufacture and distribution of goods. **Economics and Accounting:** Knowledge of economic and accounting principles and practices, the financial markets, banking, and the analysis and reporting of financial data. **Personnel and Human Resources:** Knowledge of principles and procedures for personnel recruitment, selection, training, compensation and benefits, labor relations and negotiation, and personnel information systems.

Commercial and Industrial Designers

- ◎ Education/Training Required: Bachelor's degree
- ◎ Annual Earnings: $52,310
- ◎ Growth: 14.7%
- ◎ Annual Job Openings: 7,000
- ◎ Self-Employed: 31.0%
- ◎ Part-Time: 16.5%

Develop and design manufactured products, such as cars, home appliances, and children's toys. Combine artistic talent with research on product use, market-ing, and materials to create the most functional and appealing product design. Prepare sketches of ideas, detailed drawings, illustrations, artwork, and/or blueprints, using drafting instruments, paints and brushes, or computer-aided design equipment. Direct and coordinate the fabrication of models or samples and the drafting of working drawings and specification sheets from sketches. Modify and refine designs, using working models, to conform with customer specifications, production limitations, or changes in design trends. Coordinate the look and function of product lines. Confer with engineering, marketing, production, and/or sales departments or with customers to establish and evaluate design concepts for manufactured products. Present designs and reports to customers or design committees for approval and discuss need for modification. Evaluate feasibility of design ideas, based on factors such as appearance, safety, function, serviceability, budget, production costs/methods, and market characteristics. Read publications, attend showings, and study competing products and design styles and motifs to obtain perspective and generate design concepts. Research production specifications, costs, production materials, and manufacturing methods and provide cost estimates and itemized production requirements. Design graphic material for use as ornamentation, illustration, or advertising on manufactured materials and packaging or containers. Develop manufacturing procedures and monitor the manufacture of their designs in a factory to improve operations and product quality. Supervise assistants' work throughout the design process. Fabricate models or samples in paper, wood, glass, fabric, plastic, metal, or other materials, using hand and/or power tools. Investigate product characteristics such as the product's safety and handling qualities; its market appeal; how efficiently it can be produced; and ways of distributing, using and maintaining it. Develop industrial standards and regulatory guidelines. Participate in new product planning or market research, including studying the potential need for new products. **SKILLS—Technology Design:** Generating or adapting equipment and technology to serve user needs. **Operations Analysis:** Analyzing needs and product requirements to create a design. **Troubleshooting:** Determining causes of operating errors and deciding what to do about them. **Time Management:** Managing one's own time and the time of others. **Quality Control Analysis:** Conducting tests and inspections of products, services, or processes to evaluate quality or performance. **Equipment Selec-**

tion: Determining the kind of tools and equipment needed to do a job. **Coordination:** Adjusting actions in relation to others' actions. **Judgment and Decision Making:** Considering the relative costs and benefits of potential actions to choose the most appropriate one. **GOE—Interest Area:** 03. Arts and Communication. **Work Group:** 03.05. Design. **Other Jobs in This Work Group:** Exhibit Designers; Fashion Designers; Floral Designers; Graphic Designers; Interior Designers; Merchandise Displayers and Window Trimmers; Set Designers. **PERSONALITY TYPE:** Artistic.

EDUCATION/TRAINING PROGRAM(S)— Commercial and Advertising Art; Design and Applied Arts, Other; Design and Visual Communications, General; Industrial Design. **RELATED KNOWLEDGE/COURSES—Design:** Knowledge of design techniques, tools, and principles involved in production of precision technical plans, blueprints, drawings, and models. **Engineering and Technology:** Knowledge of the practical application of engineering science and technology. This includes applying principles, techniques, procedures, and equipment to the design and production of various goods and services. **Mathematics:** Knowledge of arithmetic, algebra, geometry, calculus, and statistics and their applications. **Clerical Practices:** Knowledge of administrative and clerical procedures and systems such as word processing, managing files and records, stenography and transcription, designing forms, and other office procedures and terminology. **Computers and Electronics:** Knowledge of circuit boards, processors, chips, electronic equipment, and computer hardware and software, including applications and programming. **Production and Processing:** Knowledge of raw materials, production processes, quality control, costs, and other techniques for maximizing the effective manufacture and distribution of goods.

Commercial Pilots

◉ Education/Training Required: Postsecondary vocational training

◉ Annual Earnings: $53,870

◉ Growth: 14.9%

◉ Annual Job Openings: 2,000

◉ Self-Employed: 11.2%

◉ Part-Time: 12.9%

Pilot and navigate the flight of small fixed or rotary winged aircraft, primarily for the transport of cargo and passengers. Requires commercial rating. Check aircraft prior to flights to ensure that the engines, controls, instruments, and other systems are functioning properly. Check baggage or cargo to ensure that it has been loaded correctly. Choose routes, altitudes, and speeds that will provide the fastest, safest, and smoothest flights. Consider airport altitudes, outside temperatures, plane weights, and wind speeds and directions in order to calculate the speed needed to become airborne. Contact control towers for takeoff clearances, arrival instructions, and other information, using radio equipment. Coordinate flight activities with ground crews and air traffic control and inform crew members of flight and test procedures. File instrument flight plans with air traffic control so that flights can be coordinated with other air traffic. Monitor engine operation, fuel consumption, and functioning of aircraft systems during flights. Obtain and review data such as load weights, fuel supplies, weather conditions, and flight schedules in order to determine flight plans and to see if changes might be necessary. Order changes in fuel supplies, loads, routes, or schedules to ensure safety of flights. Plan and formulate flight activities and test schedules and prepare flight evaluation reports. Plan flights, following government and company regulations, using aeronautical charts and navigation instruments. Request changes in altitudes or routes as circumstances dictate. Start engines, operate controls, and pilot airplanes to transport passengers, mail, or freight while adhering to flight plans, regulations, and procedures. Use instrumentation to pilot aircraft when visibility is poor. Check the flight performance of new and experimental planes. Conduct in-flight tests and evaluations at specified altitudes and in all types of weather in order to determine the receptivity and other characteristics of equipment and systems. Co-pilot aircraft or perform captain's duties if required. Fly with other pilots or pilot-license applicants to evaluate their proficiency. Instruct other pilots and student pilots in aircraft operations. Perform minor aircraft maintenance and repair work or arrange for major maintenance. **SKILLS— Operation and Control:** Controlling operations of equipment or systems. **Operation Monitoring:** Watching gauges, dials, or other indicators to make sure a machine is working properly. **Instructing:** Teaching others how to do something. **Science:** Using scientific rules and methods to solve problems. **Coor-**

C

dination: Adjusting actions in relation to others' actions. **Systems Analysis:** Determining how a system should work and how changes in conditions, operations, and the environment will affect outcomes. **Systems Evaluation:** Identifying measures or indicators of system performance and the actions needed to improve or correct performance relative to the goals of the system. **Judgment and Decision Making:** Considering the relative costs and benefits of potential actions to choose the most appropriate one. **GOE—Interest Area:** 16. Transportation, Distribution, and Logistics. **Work Group:** 16.02. Air Vehicle Operation. **Other Jobs in This Work Group:** Airline Pilots, Copilots, and Flight Engineers. **PERSONALITY TYPE:** Realistic.

EDUCATION/TRAINING PROGRAM(S)—Airline/Commercial/Professional Pilot and Flight Crew; Flight Instructor. **RELATED KNOWLEDGE/ COURSES—Transportation:** Knowledge of principles and methods for moving people or goods by air, rail, sea, or road, including the relative costs and benefits. **Geography:** Knowledge of principles and methods for describing the features of land, sea, and air masses, including their physical characteristics; locations; interrelationships; and distribution of plant, animal, and human life. **Public Safety and Security:** Knowledge of relevant equipment, policies, procedures, and strategies to promote effective local, state, or national security operations for the protection of people, data, property, and institutions. **Mechanical Devices:** Knowledge of machines and tools, including their designs, uses, repair, and maintenance. **Education and Training:** Knowledge of principles and methods for curriculum and training design, teaching and instruction for individuals and groups, and the measurement of training effects. **Physics:** Knowledge and prediction of physical principles and laws and their interrelationships and applications to understanding fluid, material, and atmospheric dynamics and mechanical, electrical, atomic, and subatomic structures and processes.

Communication Equipment Mechanics, Installers, and Repairers

- ◉ Education/Training Required: Postsecondary vocational training
- ◉ Annual Earnings: $49,840
- ◉ Growth: –0.6%
- ◉ Annual Job Openings: 23,000
- ◉ Self-Employed: 4.6%
- ◉ Part-Time: 1.7%

Install, maintain, test, and repair communication cables and equipment. Examines and tests malfunctioning equipment to determine defects, using blueprints and electrical measuring instruments. Tests installed equipment for conformance to specifications, using test equipment. Assembles and installs communication equipment, such as data communication lines and equipment, computer systems, and antennas and towers, using hand tools. Repairs, replaces, or adjusts defective components. Disassembles equipment to adjust, repair, or replace parts, using hand tools. Evaluates quality of performance of installed equipment by observance and using test equipment. Digs holes or trenches. Answers customers' inquiries or complaints. Cleans and maintains tools, test equipment, and motor vehicle. Communicates with base, using telephone or two-way radio to receive instructions or technical advice or to report unauthorized use of equipment. Demonstrates equipment and instructs customer in use of equipment. Determines viability of site through observation and discusses site location and construction requirements with customer. Measures distance from landmarks to identify exact installation site. Climbs poles and ladders; constructs pole, roof mounts, or reinforcements; and mixes concrete to enable equipment installation. Plans layout and installation of data communications equipment. Reviews work orders, building permits, manufacturer's instructions, and ordinances to move, change, install, repair, or remove communication equipment. Adjusts or modifies equipment in accordance with customer request or to enhance performance of equipment. Performs routine maintenance on equipment, which includes adjustment, repair, and painting. Measures, cuts, splices, connects, solders, and installs wires and cables. **SKILLS—Repairing:** Repairing machines or systems by using the needed tools. **Installation:** Installing equipment, machines, wiring, or programs to meet specifications. **Troubleshooting:** Determining causes of operating errors and deciding what to do about them. **Equipment Maintenance:** Performing routine maintenance on equipment and determining when and what kind of maintenance is needed. **Quality Control Analysis:** Conducting tests and inspections of products, services, or processes to evaluate quality or performance. **Technology Design:** Generating or adapting equipment and technology to serve user needs. **Operation Monitoring:** Watching gauges, dials, or other indicators to make sure a machine is working properly. **Operation and Control:** Controlling operations of equipment or systems. **GOE—Interest Area:** 02. Architecture and Construction. **Work Group:** 02.05. Systems and Equipment Installation, Maintenance, and Repair. **Other Jobs in This Work Group:** Central Office and PBX Installers and Repairers; Electric Meter Installers and Repairers; Electrical and Electronics Repairers, Powerhouse, Substation, and Relay; Electrical Power-Line Installers and Repairers; Elevator Installers and Repairers; Frame Wirers, Central Office; Heating and Air Conditioning Mechanics; Home Appliance Installers; Maintenance and Repair Workers, General; Meter Mechanics; Refrigeration Mechanics; Station Installers and Repairers, Telephone; Telecommunications Facility Examiners; Telecommunications Line Installers and Repairers. **PERSONALITY TYPE:** Realistic.

EDUCATION/TRAINING PROGRAM(S)— Communications Systems Installation and Repair Technology. **RELATED KNOWLEDGE/COURSES—Telecommunications:** Knowledge of transmission, broadcasting, switching, control, and operation of telecommunications systems. **Computers and Electronics:** Knowledge of circuit boards, processors, chips, electronic equipment, and computer hardware and software, including applications and programming. **Design:** Knowledge of design techniques, tools, and principles involved in production of precision technical plans, blueprints, drawings, and models. **Mechanical Devices:** Knowledge of machines and tools, including their designs, uses, repair, and maintenance. **Engineering and Technology:** Knowledge of the practical application of engineering science and technology. This includes applying principles, techniques, procedures, and equipment to the design and production of various goods and services.

Communications Teachers, Postsecondary

- Education/Training Required: Master's degree
- Annual Earnings: $49,800
- Growth: 38.1%
- Annual Job Openings: 216,000
- Self-Employed: 0.3%
- Part-Time: 27.7%

Teach courses in communications, such as organizational communications, public relations, radio/television broadcasting, and journalism. Evaluate and grade students' class work, assignments, and papers. Prepare course materials such as syllabi, homework assignments, and handouts. Initiate, facilitate, and moderate classroom discussions. Prepare and deliver lectures to undergraduate and/or graduate students on topics such as public speaking, media criticism, and oral traditions. Compile, administer, and grade examinations or assign this work to others. Maintain student attendance records, grades, and other required records. Plan, evaluate, and revise curricula, course content, and course materials and methods of instruction. Maintain regularly scheduled office hours in order to advise and assist students. Keep abreast of developments in their field by reading current literature, talking with colleagues, and participating in professional conferences. Advise students on academic and vocational curricula and on career issues. Supervise undergraduate and/or graduate teaching, internship, and research work. Select and obtain materials and supplies such as textbooks. Collaborate with colleagues to address teaching and research issues. Conduct research in a particular field of knowledge and publish findings in professional journals, books, and/or electronic media. Participate in student recruitment, registration, and placement activities. Serve on academic or administrative committees that deal with institutional policies, departmental matters, and academic issues. Compile bibliographies of specialized materials for outside reading assignments. Act as advisers to student organizations. Participate in campus and community events. Perform administrative duties such as serving as department head. **SKILLS—Instructing:** Teaching others how to do something. **Learning Strategies:** Selecting and using training/instructional methods and procedures appropriate for the situation when learning or teaching new things. **Persuasion:** Persuading others to change their minds or behavior. **Writing:** Communicating effectively in writing as appropriate for the needs of the audience. **Social Perceptiveness:** Being aware of others' reactions and understanding why they react as they do. **Monitoring:** Monitoring or assessing your performance or that of other individuals or organizations to make improvements or take corrective action. **Active Learning:** Understanding the implications of new information for both current and future problem-solving and decision-making. **Critical Thinking:** Using logic and reasoning to identify the strengths and weaknesses of alternative solutions, conclusions, or approaches to problems. **GOE—Interest Area:** 05. Education and Training. **Work Group:** 05.03. Postsecondary and Adult Teaching and Instructing. **Other Jobs in This Work Group:** Adult Literacy, Remedial Education, and GED Teachers and Instructors; Agricultural Sciences Teachers, Postsecondary; Anthropology and Archeology Teachers, Postsecondary; Architecture Teachers, Postsecondary; Area, Ethnic, and Cultural Studies Teachers, Postsecondary; Art, Drama, and Music Teachers, Postsecondary; Atmospheric, Earth, Marine, and Space Sciences Teachers, Postsecondary; Biological Science Teachers, Postsecondary; Business Teachers, Postsecondary; Chemistry Teachers, Postsecondary; Computer Science Teachers, Postsecondary; Criminal Justice and Law Enforcement Teachers, Postsecondary; Economics Teachers, Postsecondary; Education Teachers, Postsecondary; Engineering Teachers, Postsecondary; English Language and Literature Teachers, Postsecondary; Environmental Science Teachers, Postsecondary; Farm and Home Management Advisors; Foreign Language and Literature Teachers, Postsecondary; Forestry and Conservation Science Teachers, Postsecondary; Geography Teachers, Postsecondary; Graduate Teaching Assistants; Health Specialties Teachers, Postsecondary; History Teachers, Postsecondary; Home Economics Teachers, Postsecondary; Law Teachers, Postsecondary; Library Science Teachers, Postsecondary; Mathematical Science Teachers, Postsecondary; Nursing Instructors and Teachers, Postsecondary; Philosophy and Religion Teachers, Postsecondary; Physics Teachers, Postsecondary; Political Science Teachers, Postsecondary; Psychology Teachers, Postsecondary; Recreation and Fitness Studies Teachers, Postsecondary; Self-Enrichment Education Teachers; Social Work Teachers, Postsecondary; Sociology Teachers, Post-

secondary; Vocational Education Teachers, Postsecondary. **PERSONALITY TYPE:** No data available.

EDUCATION/TRAINING PROGRAM(S)— Advertising; Broadcast Journalism; Communication Studies/Speech Communication and Rhetoric; Communication, Journalism, and Related Programs, Other; Digital Communication and Media/Multimedia; Health Communication; Journalism; Journalism, Other; Mass Communication/Media Studies; Political Communication; Public Relations/Image Management; Radio and Television. **RELATED KNOWLEDGE/COURSES—Communications and Media:** Knowledge of media production, communication, and dissemination techniques and methods. This includes alternative ways to inform and entertain via written, oral, and visual media. **Education and Training:** Knowledge of principles and methods for curriculum and training design, teaching and instruction for individuals and groups, and the measurement of training effects. **English Language:** Knowledge of the structure and content of the English language, including the meaning and spelling of words, rules of composition, and grammar. **Sociology and Anthropology:** Knowledge of group behavior and dynamics, societal trends and influences, human migrations, ethnicity, and cultures and their history and origins. **Philosophy and Theology:** Knowledge of different philosophical systems and religions. This includes their basic principles, values, ethics, ways of thinking, customs, and practices and their impact on human culture. **History and Archeology:** Knowledge of historical events and their causes, indicators, and effects on civilizations and cultures.

Compensation and Benefits Managers

- Education/Training Required: Work experience plus degree
- Annual Earnings: $66,530
- Growth: 19.4%
- Annual Job Openings: 21,000
- Self-Employed: 0%
- Part-Time: 3.7%

Plan, direct, or coordinate compensation and benefits activities and staff of an organization. Advise management on such matters as equal employment opportunity, sexual harassment, and discrimination. Direct preparation and distribution of written and verbal information to inform employees of benefits, compensation, and personnel policies. Administer, direct, and review employee benefit programs, including the integration of benefit programs following mergers and acquisition. Plan and conduct new employee orientations to foster positive attitude toward organizational objectives. Plan, direct, supervise, and coordinate work activities of subordinates and staff relating to employment, compensation, labor relations, and employee relations. Identify and implement benefits to increase the quality of life for employees by working with brokers and researching benefits issues. Design, evaluate, and modify benefits policies to ensure that programs are current, competitive, and in compliance with legal requirements. Analyze compensation policies, government regulations, and prevailing wage rates to develop competitive compensation plan. Formulate policies, procedures, and programs for recruitment, testing, placement, classification, orientation, benefits and compensation, and labor and industrial relations. Mediate between benefit providers and employees, such as by assisting in handling employees' benefit-related questions or taking suggestions. Fulfill all reporting requirements of all relevant government rules and regulations, including the Employee Retirement Income Security Act (ERISA). Maintain records and compile statistical reports concerning personnel-related data such as hires, transfers, performance appraisals, and absenteeism rates. Analyze statistical data and reports to identify and determine causes of personnel problems and develop recommendations for improvement of organization's personnel policies and practices. Develop methods to improve employment policies, processes, and practices and recommend changes to management. Negotiate bargaining agreements. Investigate and report on industrial accidents for insurance carriers. Represent organization at personnel-related hearings and investigations. **SKILLS— Management of Personnel Resources:** Motivating, developing, and directing people as they work, identifying the best people for the job. **Management of Financial Resources:** Determining how money will be spent to get the work done and accounting for these expenditures. **Social Perceptiveness:** Being aware of others' reactions and understanding why they react as they do. **Time Management:** Managing one's own time and the time of others. **Management of Material**

Resources: Obtaining and seeing to the appropriate use of equipment, facilities, and materials needed to do certain work. **Monitoring:** Monitoring or assessing your performance or that of other individuals or organizations to make improvements or take corrective action. **Instructing:** Teaching others how to do something. **Negotiation:** Bringing others together and trying to reconcile differences. **GOE—Interest Area:** 04. Business and Administration. **Work Group:** 04.01. Managerial Work in General Business. **Other Jobs in This Work Group:** Chief Executives; General and Operations Managers; Human Resources Managers; Private Sector Executives; Training and Development Managers. **PERSONALITY TYPE:** Enterprising.

EDUCATION/TRAINING PROGRAM(S)— Human Resources Management/Personnel Administration, General; Labor and Industrial Relations. **RELATED KNOWLEDGE/COURSES—Personnel and Human Resources:** Knowledge of principles and procedures for personnel recruitment, selection, training, compensation and benefits, labor relations and negotiation, and personnel information systems. **Clerical Practices:** Knowledge of administrative and clerical procedures and systems such as word processing, managing files and records, stenography and transcription, designing forms, and other office procedures and terminology. **Administration and Management:** Knowledge of business and management principles involved in strategic planning, resource allocation, human resources modeling, leadership technique, production methods, and coordination of people and resources. **Economics and Accounting:** Knowledge of economic and accounting principles and practices, the financial markets, banking, and the analysis and reporting of financial data. **Law and Government:** Knowledge of laws, legal codes, court procedures, precedents, government regulations, executive orders, agency rules, and the democratic political process. **Education and Training:** Knowledge of principles and methods for curriculum and training design, teaching and instruction for individuals and groups, and the measurement of training effects.

Compensation, Benefits, and Job Analysis Specialists

- ◎ Education/Training Required: Bachelor's degree
- ◎ Annual Earnings: $47,490
- ◎ Growth: 28.0%
- ◎ Annual Job Openings: 15,000
- ◎ Self-Employed: 0.8%
- ◎ Part-Time: 7.7%

Conduct programs of compensation and benefits and job analysis for employer. May specialize in specific areas, such as position classification and pension programs. Evaluate job positions, determining classification, exempt or non-exempt status, and salary. Ensure company compliance with federal and state laws, including reporting requirements. Advise managers and employees on state and federal employment regulations, collective agreements, benefit and compensation policies, personnel procedures, and classification programs. Plan, develop, evaluate, improve, and communicate methods and techniques for selecting, promoting, compensating, evaluating, and training workers. Provide advice on the resolution of classification and salary complaints. Prepare occupational classifications, job descriptions, and salary scales. Assist in preparing and maintaining personnel records and handbooks. Prepare reports such as organization and flow charts and career path reports to summarize job analysis and evaluation and compensation analysis information. Administer employee insurance, pension, and savings plans, working with insurance brokers and plan carriers. Negotiate collective agreements on behalf of employers or workers and mediate labor disputes and grievances. Develop, implement, administer, and evaluate personnel and labor relations programs, including performance appraisal, affirmative action, and employment equity programs. Perform multifactor data and cost analyses that may be used in areas such as support of collective bargaining agreements. Research employee benefit and health and safety practices and recommend changes or modifications to existing policies. Analyze organizational, occupational, and industrial data to facilitate organizational functions and provide technical information to business, industry, and government. Advise staff of individuals' qualifications. Assess need for and develop job analysis instruments and materials. Review occupational data on Alien Employment Certification Applications to determine the appropriate occupational title and code and provide local offices with information about immigration and occupations. Research job and worker requirements, structural and functional relationships among jobs and occupations, and occupational trends. **SKILLS—Service Orientation:** Actively looking for ways to help people. **Persuasion:** Persuading others to change their minds or behavior. **Coordination:** Adjusting actions in relation to others' actions. **Negotiation:** Bringing others together and trying to reconcile differences. **Active Listening:** Giving full attention to what other people are saying, taking time to understand the points being made, asking questions as appropriate, and not interrupting at inappropriate times. **Social Perceptiveness:** Being aware of others' reactions and understanding why they react as they do. **Judgment and Decision Making:** Considering the relative costs and benefits of potential actions to choose the most appropriate one. **Critical Thinking:** Using logic and reasoning to identify the strengths and weaknesses of alternative solutions, conclusions, or approaches to problems. **Time Management:** Managing one's own time and the time of others. **GOE— Interest Area:** 04. Business and Administration. **Work Group:** 04.03. Human Resources Support. **Other Jobs in This Work Group:** Employment Interviewers, Private or Public Employment Service; Personnel Recruiters; Training and Development Specialists. **PERSONALITY TYPE:** Investigative.

EDUCATION/TRAINING PROGRAM(S)— Human Resources Management/Personnel Administration, General; Labor and Industrial Relations. **RELATED KNOWLEDGE/COURSES—Personnel and Human Resources:** Knowledge of principles and procedures for personnel recruitment, selection, training, compensation and benefits, labor relations and negotiation, and personnel information systems. **Clerical Practices:** Knowledge of administrative and clerical procedures and systems such as word processing, managing files and records, stenography and transcription, designing forms, and other office procedures and terminology. **Customer and Personal Service:** Knowledge of principles and processes for providing customer and personal services. This includes customer needs assessment, meeting quality standards for services, and evaluation of customer satisfaction. **Administration and Management:** Knowledge of business and management principles involved in strategic planning, resource allocation, human resources modeling, leadership technique, production methods, and coordination of people and resources. **English Language:** Knowledge of the structure and content of the English language, including the meaning and spelling of words, rules of composition, and grammar. **Education and Training:** Knowledge of principles and methods for curriculum and training design, teaching and instruction for individuals and groups, and the measurement of training effects.

Composers

- ◎ Education/Training Required: Master's degree
- ◎ Annual Earnings: $34,570
- ◎ Growth: 13.5%
- ◎ Annual Job Openings: 8,000
- ◎ Self-Employed: 39.3%
- ◎ Part-Time: 39.5%

Compose music for orchestra, choral group, or band. Creates original musical form or writes within circumscribed musical form, such as sonata, symphony, or opera. Transcribes or records musical ideas into notes on scored music paper. Develops pattern of harmony, applying knowledge of music theory. Synthesizes ideas for melody of musical scores for choral group or band. Creates musical and tonal structure, applying elements of music theory such as instrumental and vocal capabilities. Determines basic pattern of melody, applying knowledge of music theory. **SKILLS**—None met the criteria. **GOE—Interest Area:** 03. Arts and Communication. **Work Group:** 03.07. Music. **Other Jobs in This Work Group:** Music Arrangers and Orchestrators; Music Directors; Musicians, Instrumental; Singers; Talent Directors. **PERSONALITY TYPE:** Artistic.

EDUCATION/TRAINING PROGRAM(S)—Conducting; Music Management and Merchandising; Music Performance, General; Music Theory and Composition; Music, Other; Musicology and Ethnomusicology; Religious/Sacred Music; Voice and Opera. **RELATED KNOWLEDGE/COURSES—Fine Arts:** Knowledge of the theory and techniques required to compose, produce, and perform works of music, dance, the visual arts, drama, and sculpture. **History and Archeology:** Knowledge of historical events and their causes, indicators, and effects on civilizations and cultures.

Computer and Information Systems Managers

- ◎ Education/Training Required: Work experience plus degree
- ◎ Annual Earnings: $92,570
- ◎ Growth: 36.1%
- ◎ Annual Job Openings: 39,000
- ◎ Self-Employed: 1.1%
- ◎ Part-Time: 1.8%

Plan, direct, or coordinate activities in such fields as electronic data processing, information systems, systems analysis, and computer programming. Manage backup, security, and user help systems. Consult with users, management, vendors, and technicians to assess computing needs and system requirements. Direct daily operations of department, analyzing workflow, establishing priorities, developing standards, and setting deadlines. Assign and review the work of systems analysts, programmers, and other computer-related workers. Stay abreast of advances in technology. Develop computer information resources, providing for data security and control, strategic computing, and disaster recovery. Review and approve all systems charts and programs prior to their implementation. Evaluate the organization's technology use and needs and recommend improvements, such as hardware and software upgrades. Control operational budget and expenditures. Meet with department heads, managers, supervisors, vendors, and others to solicit cooperation and resolve problems. Develop and interpret organizational goals, policies, and procedures. Recruit, hire, train, and supervise staff and/or participate in staffing decisions. Review project plans in order to plan and coordinate project activity. Evaluate data processing proposals to assess project feasibility and requirements. Prepare and review operational reports or project progress reports. Purchase necessary equipment. **SKILLS—Management of Financial Resources:** Determining how money will be spent to get the work done and accounting for these expenditures. **Operations Analysis:** Analyzing needs and product requirements to create a design. **Programming:** Writing computer programs for various purposes. **Negotiation:**

Bringing others together and trying to reconcile differences. **Systems Analysis:** Determining how a system should work and how changes in conditions, operations, and the environment will affect outcomes. **Management of Material Resources:** Obtaining and seeing to the appropriate use of equipment, facilities, and materials needed to do certain work. **Persuasion:** Persuading others to change their minds or behavior. **Systems Evaluation:** Identifying measures or indicators of system performance and the actions needed to improve or correct performance relative to the goals of the system. **GOE—Interest Area:** 11. Information Technology. **Work Group:** 11.01. Managerial Work in Information Technology. **Other Jobs in This Work Group:** Network and Computer Systems Administrators. **PERSONALITY TYPE:** Enterprising.

EDUCATION/TRAINING   PROGRAM(S)— Computer and Information Sciences, General; Computer Science; Information Resources Management/CIO Training; Information Science/Studies; Knowledge Management; Management Information Systems, General; Operations Management and Supervision; System Administration/Administrator. **RELATED KNOWLEDGE/COURSES—Clerical Practices:** Knowledge of administrative and clerical procedures and systems such as word processing, managing files and records, stenography and transcription, designing forms, and other office procedures and terminology. **Computers and Electronics:** Knowledge of circuit boards, processors, chips, electronic equipment, and computer hardware and software, including applications and programming. **Economics and Accounting:** Knowledge of economic and accounting principles and practices, the financial markets, banking, and the analysis and reporting of financial data. **Engineering and Technology:** Knowledge of the practical application of engineering science and technology. This includes applying principles, techniques, procedures, and equipment to the design and production of various goods and services. **Design:** Knowledge of design techniques, tools, and principles involved in production of precision technical plans, blueprints, drawings, and models. **Administration and Management:** Knowledge of business and management principles involved in strategic planning, resource allocation, human resources modeling, leadership technique, production methods, and coordination of people and resources.

Computer Hardware Engineers

◎ Education/Training Required: Bachelor's degree
◎ Annual Earnings: $81,150
◎ Growth: 6.1%
◎ Annual Job Openings: 6,000
◎ Self-Employed: 4.7%
◎ Part-Time: 3.4%

Research, design, develop, and test computer or computer-related equipment for commercial, industrial, military, or scientific use. May supervise the manufacturing and installation of computer or computer-related equipment and components. Analyze information to determine, recommend, and plan layout, including type of computers and peripheral equipment modifications. Analyze user needs and recommend appropriate hardware. Build, test, and modify product prototypes, using working models or theoretical models constructed using computer simulation. Confer with engineering staff and consult specifications to evaluate interface between hardware and software and operational and performance requirements of overall system. Design and develop computer hardware and support peripherals, including central processing units (CPUs), support logic, microprocessors, custom integrated circuits, and printers and disk drives. Evaluate factors such as reporting formats required, cost constraints, and need for security restrictions to determine hardware configuration. Monitor functioning of equipment and make necessary modifications to ensure system operates in conformance with specifications. Specify power supply requirements and configuration, drawing on system performance expectations and design specifications. Store, retrieve, and manipulate data for analysis of system capabilities and requirements. Test and verify hardware and support peripherals to ensure that they meet specifications and requirements, analyzing and recording test data. Write detailed functional specifications that document the hardware development process and support hardware introduction. Assemble and modify existing pieces of equipment to meet special needs. Direct technicians, engineering designers, or other technical support personnel as needed. Provide technical support to designers, marketing and sales departments, suppliers, engineers, and other team members throughout the product development and implementation process. Provide training and support to system designers and users. Recommend purchase of equipment to control dust, temperature, and humidity in area of system installation. Select hardware and material, assuring compliance with specifications and product requirements. Update knowledge and skills to keep up with rapid advancements in computer technology. **SKILLS—Programming:** Writing computer programs for various purposes. **Troubleshooting:** Determining causes of operating errors and deciding what to do about them. **Installation:** Installing equipment, machines, wiring, or programs to meet specifications. **Science:** Using scientific rules and methods to solve problems. **Operations Analysis:** Analyzing needs and product requirements to create a design. **Technology Design:** Generating or adapting equipment and technology to serve user needs. **Management of Material Resources:** Obtaining and seeing to the appropriate use of equipment, facilities, and materials needed to do certain work. **Active Learning:** Understanding the implications of new information for both current and future problem-solving and decision-making. **GOE— Interest Area:** 15. Scientific Research, Engineering, and Mathematics. **Work Group:** 15.07. Research and Design Engineering. **Other Jobs in This Work Group:** Aerospace Engineers; Biomedical Engineers; Chemical Engineers; Civil Engineers; Electrical Engineers; Electronics Engineers, Except Computer; Marine Architects; Marine Engineers; Materials Engineers; Mechanical Engineers; Nuclear Engineers. **PERSONALITY TYPE:** Investigative.

EDUCATION/TRAINING PROGRAM(S)— Computer Engineering, General; Computer Hardware Engineering. **RELATED KNOWLEDGE/ COURSES—Computers and Electronics:** Knowledge of circuit boards, processors, chips, electronic equipment, and computer hardware and software, including applications and programming. **Mathematics:** Knowledge of arithmetic, algebra, geometry, calculus, and statistics and their applications. **Engineering and Technology:** Knowledge of the practical application of engineering science and technology. This includes applying principles, techniques, procedures, and equipment to the design and production of various goods and services. **Design:** Knowledge of design techniques, tools, and principles involved in production of precision technical plans, blueprints, drawings, and models. **Telecommunications:** Knowledge of

transmission, broadcasting, switching, control, and operation of telecommunications systems. **Economics and Accounting:** Knowledge of economic and accounting principles and practices, the financial markets, banking, and the analysis and reporting of financial data.

Computer Programmers

- Education/Training Required: Bachelor's degree
- Annual Earnings: $62,890
- Growth: 14.6%
- Annual Job Openings: 45,000
- Self-Employed: 3.7%
- Part-Time: 4.6%

Convert project specifications and statements of problems and procedures to detailed logical flow charts for coding into computer language. Develop and write computer programs to store, locate, and retrieve specific documents, data, and information. May program Web sites. Correct errors by making appropriate changes and then rechecking the program to ensure that the desired results are produced. Conduct trial runs of programs and software applications to be sure that they will produce the desired information and that the instructions are correct. Compile and write documentation of program development and subsequent revisions, inserting comments in the coded instructions so others can understand the program. Write, update, and maintain computer programs or software packages to handle specific jobs, such as tracking inventory, storing or retrieving data, or controlling other equipment. Consult with managerial, engineering, and technical personnel to clarify program intent, identify problems, and suggest changes. Perform or direct revision, repair, or expansion of existing programs to increase operating efficiency or adapt to new requirements. Write, analyze, review, and rewrite programs, using workflow chart and diagram and applying knowledge of computer capabilities, subject matter, and symbolic logic. Write or contribute to instructions or manuals to guide end users. Investigate whether networks, workstations, the central processing unit of the system, and/or peripheral equipment are responding to a program's instructions. Prepare detailed workflow charts and diagrams that describe

C

input, output, and logical operation and convert them into a series of instructions coded in a computer language. Perform systems analysis and programming tasks to maintain and control the use of computer systems software as a systems programmer. Consult with and assist computer operators or system analysts to define and resolve problems in running computer programs. Assign, coordinate, and review work and activities of programming personnel. **SKILLS—Programming:** Writing computer programs for various purposes. **Operations Analysis:** Analyzing needs and product requirements to create a design. **Technology Design:** Generating or adapting equipment and technology to serve user needs. **Troubleshooting:** Determining causes of operating errors and deciding what to do about them. **Systems Analysis:** Determining how a system should work and how changes in conditions, operations, and the environment will affect outcomes. **Critical Thinking:** Using logic and reasoning to identify the strengths and weaknesses of alternative solutions, conclusions, or approaches to problems. **Complex Problem Solving:** Identifying complex problems and reviewing related information to develop and evaluate options and implement solutions. **Active Learning:** Understanding the implications of new information for both current and future problem-solving and decision-making. **GOE—Interest Area:** 11. Information Technology. **Work Group:** 11.02. Information Technology Specialties. **Other Jobs in This Work Group:** Computer Operators; Computer Security Specialists; Computer Software Engineers, Applications; Computer Software Engineers, Systems Software; Computer Support Specialists; Computer Systems Analysts; Database Administrators; Network Systems and Data Communications Analysts. **PERSONALITY TYPE:** Investigative.

EDUCATION/TRAINING PROGRAM(S)—Artificial Intelligence and Robotics; Bioinformatics; Computer Graphics; Computer Programming, Specific Applications; Computer Programming, Vendor/Product Certification; Computer Programming/Programmer, General; E-Commerce/Electronic Commerce; Management Information Systems, General; Medical Informatics; Medical Office Computer Specialist/Assistant; Web Page, Digital/Multimedia, and Information Resources Design; Web/Multimedia Management and Webmaster. **RELATED KNOWLEDGE/COURSES—Computers and Electronics:** Knowledge of circuit boards, processors, chips, electronic equipment, and computer hardware and soft-

ware, including applications and programming. **Design:** Knowledge of design techniques, tools, and principles involved in production of precision technical plans, blueprints, drawings, and models. **Mathematics:** Knowledge of arithmetic, algebra, geometry, calculus, and statistics and their applications. **Telecommunications:** Knowledge of transmission, broadcasting, switching, control, and operation of telecommunications systems. **Economics and Accounting:** Knowledge of economic and accounting principles and practices, the financial markets, banking, and the analysis and reporting of financial data. **English Language:** Knowledge of the structure and content of the English language, including the meaning and spelling of words, rules of composition, and grammar.

Computer Science Teachers, Postsecondary

- Education/Training Required: Master's degree
- Annual Earnings: $52,630
- Growth: 38.1%
- Annual Job Openings: 216,000
- Self-Employed: 0.3%
- Part-Time: 27.7%

Teach courses in computer science. May specialize in a field of computer science, such as the design and function of computers or operations and research analysis. Evaluate and grade students' class work, laboratory work, assignments, and papers. Maintain student attendance records, grades, and other required records. Prepare and deliver lectures to undergraduate and/or graduate students on topics such as programming, data structures, and software design. Prepare course materials such as syllabi, homework assignments, and handouts. Compile, administer, and grade examinations or assign this work to others. Keep abreast of developments in their field by reading current literature, talking with colleagues, and participating in professional conferences. Initiate, facilitate, and moderate classroom discussions. Plan, evaluate, and revise curricula, course content, and course materials and methods of instruction. Supervise students' laboratory work. Maintain regularly scheduled office hours in order to advise and assist students. Select and obtain materials and supplies such as textbooks and laboratory equipment. Advise students on academic and vocational curricula and on career issues. Participate in student recruitment, registration, and placement activities. Collaborate with colleagues to address teaching and research issues. Serve on academic or administrative committees that deal with institutional policies, departmental matters, and academic issues. Act as advisers to student organizations. Supervise undergraduate and/or graduate teaching, internship, and research work. Perform administrative duties such as serving as department head. Conduct research in a particular field of knowledge and publish findings in professional journals, books, and/or electronic media. Direct research of other teachers or of graduate students working for advanced academic degrees. **SKILLS—Instructing:** Teaching others how to do something. **Programming:** Writing computer programs for various purposes. **Learning Strategies:** Selecting and using training/instructional methods and procedures appropriate for the situation when learning or teaching new things. **Technology Design:** Generating or adapting equipment and technology to serve user needs. **Active Learning:** Understanding the implications of new information for both current and future problem-solving and decision-making. **Operations Analysis:** Analyzing needs and product requirements to create a design. **Critical Thinking:** Using logic and reasoning to identify the strengths and weaknesses of alternative solutions, conclusions, or approaches to problems. **Complex Problem Solving:** Identifying complex problems and reviewing related information to develop and evaluate options and implement solutions. **GOE—Interest Area:** 05. Education and Training. **Work Group:** 05.03. Postsecondary and Adult Teaching and Instructing. **Other Jobs in This Work Group:** Adult Literacy, Remedial Education, and GED Teachers and Instructors; Agricultural Sciences Teachers, Postsecondary; Anthropology and Archeology Teachers, Postsecondary; Architecture Teachers, Postsecondary; Area, Ethnic, and Cultural Studies Teachers, Postsecondary; Art, Drama, and Music Teachers, Postsecondary; Atmospheric, Earth, Marine, and Space Sciences Teachers, Postsecondary; Biological Science Teachers, Postsecondary; Business Teachers, Postsecondary; Chemistry Teachers, Postsecondary; Communications Teachers, Postsecondary; Criminal Justice and Law Enforcement Teachers, Postsecondary; Economics Teachers, Postsecondary; Education Teachers, Postsecondary; Engineering Teachers, Postsecondary; English Language and Literature Teachers, Postsecondary; Environmental Science Teachers, Postsecondary; Farm and Home Management Advisors; Foreign Language and Literature Teachers, Postsecondary; Forestry and Conservation Science Teachers, Postsecondary; Geography Teachers, Postsecondary; Graduate Teaching Assistants; Health Specialties Teachers, Postsecondary; History Teachers, Postsecondary; Home Economics Teachers, Postsecondary; Law Teachers, Postsecondary; Library Science Teachers, Postsecondary; Mathematical Science Teachers, Postsecondary; Nursing Instructors and Teachers, Postsecondary; Philosophy and Religion Teachers, Postsecondary; Physics Teachers, Postsecondary; Political Science Teachers, Postsecondary; Psychology Teachers, Postsecondary; Recreation and Fitness Studies Teachers, Postsecondary; Self-Enrichment Education Teachers; Social Work Teachers, Postsecondary; Sociology Teachers, Postsecondary; Vocational Education Teachers, Postsecondary. **PERSONALITY TYPE:** Investigative.

EDUCATION/TRAINING PROGRAM(S)— Computer and Information Sciences, General; Computer Programming/Programmer, General; Computer Science; Computer Systems Analysis/Analyst; Information Science/Studies. **RELATED KNOWLEDGE/COURSES—Education and Training:** Knowledge of principles and methods for curriculum and training design, teaching and instruction for individuals and groups, and the measurement of training effects. **Computers and Electronics:** Knowledge of circuit boards, processors, chips, electronic equipment, and computer hardware and software, including applications and programming. **Telecommunications:** Knowledge of transmission, broadcasting, switching, control, and operation of telecommunications systems. **Mathematics:** Knowledge of arithmetic, algebra, geometry, calculus, and statistics and their applications. **English Language:** Knowledge of the structure and content of the English language, including the meaning and spelling of words, rules of composition, and grammar. **Engineering and Technology:** Knowledge of the practical application of engineering science and technology. This includes applying principles, techniques, procedures, and equipment to the design and production of various goods and services.

Computer Security Specialists

- Education/Training Required: Bachelor's degree
- Annual Earnings: $58,190
- Growth: 37.4%
- Annual Job Openings: 35,000
- Self-Employed: 0.5%
- Part-Time: 3.9%

Plan, coordinate, and implement security measures for information systems to regulate access to computer data files and prevent unauthorized modification, destruction, or disclosure of information. Train users and promote security awareness to ensure system security and to improve server and network efficiency. Develop plans to safeguard computer files against accidental or unauthorized modification, destruction, or disclosure and to meet emergency data processing needs. Confer with users to discuss issues such as computer data access needs, security violations, and programming changes. Monitor current reports of computer viruses to determine when to update virus protection systems. Modify computer security files to incorporate new software, correct errors, or change individual access status. Coordinate implementation of computer system plan with establishment personnel and outside vendors. Monitor use of data files and regulate access to safeguard information in computer files. Perform risk assessments and execute tests of data processing system to ensure functioning of data processing activities and security measures. Encrypt data transmissions and erect firewalls to conceal confidential information as it is being transmitted and to keep out tainted digital transfers. Document computer security and emergency measures policies, procedures, and tests. Review violations of computer security procedures and discuss procedures with violators to ensure violations are not repeated. **SKILLS—Systems Analysis:** Determining how a system should work and how changes in conditions, operations, and the environment will affect outcomes. **Systems Evaluation:** Identifying measures or indicators of system performance and the actions needed to improve or correct performance relative to the goals of the system. **Troubleshooting:** Determining causes of operating errors and deciding what to do about them. **Management of Material Resources:** Obtaining and seeing to the appropriate use of equipment, facilities, and materials needed to do certain work. **Active Learning:** Understanding the implications of new information for both current and future problem-solving and decision-making. **Operations Analysis:** Analyzing needs and product requirements to create a design. **Management of Financial Resources:** Determining how money will be spent to get the work done and accounting for these expenditures. **Installation:** Installing equipment, machines, wiring, or programs to meet specifications. **GOE—Interest Area:** 11. Information Technology. **Work Group:** 11.02. Information Technology Specialties. **Other Jobs in This Work Group:** Computer Operators; Computer Programmers; Computer Software Engineers, Applications; Computer Software Engineers, Systems Software; Computer Support Specialists; Computer Systems Analysts; Database Administrators; Network Systems and Data Communications Analysts. **PERSONALITY TYPE:** Investigative.

EDUCATION/TRAINING PROGRAM(S)—Computer and Information Sciences and Support Services, Other; Computer and Information Sciences, General; Computer and Information Systems Security; Computer Systems Analysis/Analyst; Computer Systems Networking and Telecommunications; Information Science/Studies; System Administration/Administrator; System, Networking, and LAN/WAN Management/Manager. **RELATED KNOWLEDGE/COURSES—Computers and Electronics:** Knowledge of circuit boards, processors, chips, electronic equipment, and computer hardware and software, including applications and programming. **Telecommunications:** Knowledge of transmission, broadcasting, switching, control, and operation of telecommunications systems. **Education and Training:** Knowledge of principles and methods for curriculum and training design, teaching and instruction for individuals and groups, and the measurement of training effects. **Engineering and Technology:** Knowledge of the practical application of engineering science and technology. This includes applying principles, techniques, procedures, and equipment to the design and production of various goods and services. **Design:** Knowledge of design techniques, tools, and principles involved in production of precision technical plans, blueprints, drawings, and models. **Customer and Personal Service:** Knowledge of principles and processes for providing customer and personal services. This includes customer needs assessment, meeting quality standards for services, and evaluation of customer satisfaction.

Computer Software Engineers, Applications

◎ Education/Training Required: Bachelor's degree
◎ Annual Earnings: $74,980
◎ Growth: 45.5%
◎ Annual Job Openings: 55,000
◎ Self-Employed: 3.1%
◎ Part-Time: 2.4%

Develop, create, and modify general computer applications software or specialized utility programs. Analyze user needs and develop software solutions. Design software or customize software for client use with the aim of optimizing operational efficiency. May analyze and design databases within an application area, working individually or coordinating database development as part of a team. Confer with systems analysts, engineers, programmers, and others to design system and to obtain information on project limitations and capabilities, performance requirements, and interfaces. Modify existing software to correct errors, allow it to adapt to new hardware, or improve its performance. Analyze user needs and software requirements to determine feasibility of design within time and cost constraints. Consult with customers about software system design and maintenance. Coordinate software system installation and monitor equipment functioning to ensure specifications are met. Design, develop, and modify software systems, using scientific analysis and mathematical models to predict and measure outcome and consequences of design. Develop and direct software system testing and validation procedures, programming, and documentation. Analyze information to determine, recommend, and plan computer specifications and layouts and peripheral equipment modifications. Supervise the work of programmers, technologists and technicians, and other engineering and scientific personnel. Obtain and evaluate information on factors such as reporting formats required, costs, and security needs to determine hardware configuration. Determine system performance standards. Train users to use new or modified equipment. Store, retrieve, and manipulate data for analysis of system capabilities and requirements. **SKILLS—Programming:** Writing computer programs for various purposes. **Troubleshooting:** Determining causes of operating errors and deciding what to do about them. **Technology Design:** Generating or adapting equipment and technology to serve user needs. **Systems Analysis:** Determining how a system should work and how changes in conditions, operations, and the environment will affect outcomes. **Quality Control Analysis:** Conducting tests and inspections of products, services, or processes to evaluate quality or performance. **Complex Problem Solving:** Identifying complex problems and reviewing related information to develop and evaluate options and implement solutions. **Operations Analysis:** Analyzing needs and product requirements to create a design. **Critical Thinking:** Using logic and reasoning to identify the strengths and weaknesses of alternative solutions, conclusions, or approaches to problems. **GOE—Interest Area:** 11. Information Technology. **Work Group:** 11.02. Information Technology Specialties. **Other Jobs in This Work Group:** Computer Operators; Computer Programmers; Computer Security Specialists; Computer Software Engineers, Systems Software; Computer Support Specialists; Computer Systems Analysts; Database Administrators; Network Systems and Data Communications Analysts. **PERSONALITY TYPE:** Investigative.

EDUCATION/TRAINING PROGRAM(S)—Artificial Intelligence and Robotics; Bioinformatics; Computer Engineering Technologies/Technicians, Other; Computer Engineering, General; Computer Science; Computer Software Engineering; Information Technology; Medical Illustration and Informatics, Other; Medical Informatics. **RELATED KNOWLEDGE/COURSES—Computers and Electronics:** Knowledge of circuit boards, processors, chips, electronic equipment, and computer hardware and software, including applications and programming. **Telecommunications:** Knowledge of transmission, broadcasting, switching, control, and operation of telecommunications systems. **Engineering and Technology:** Knowledge of the practical application of engineering science and technology. This includes applying principles, techniques, procedures, and equipment to the design and production of various goods and services. **Design:** Knowledge of design techniques, tools, and principles involved in production of precision technical plans, blueprints, drawings, and models. **Mathematics:** Knowledge of arithmetic, algebra, geometry, calculus, and statistics and their applications. **English Language:** Knowledge of the structure and content of the English language, including the meaning and spelling of words, rules of composition, and grammar.

C

Computer Software Engineers, Systems Software

- Education/Training Required: Bachelor's degree
- Annual Earnings: $79,740
- Growth: 45.5%
- Annual Job Openings: 39,000
- Self-Employed: 3.0%
- Part-Time: 2.4%

Research, design, develop, and test operating system–level software, compilers, and network distribution software for medical, industrial, military, communications, aerospace, business, scientific, and general computing applications. Set operational specifications and formulate and analyze software requirements. Apply principles and techniques of computer science, engineering, and mathematical analysis. Modify existing software to correct errors, to adapt it to new hardware, or to upgrade interfaces and improve performance. Design and develop software systems, using scientific analysis and mathematical models to predict and measure outcome and consequences of design. Consult with engineering staff to evaluate interface between hardware and software, develop specifications and performance requirements, and resolve customer problems. Analyze information to determine, recommend, and plan installation of a new system or modification of an existing system. Develop and direct software system testing and validation procedures. Direct software programming and development of documentation. Consult with customers and/or other departments on project status, proposals, and technical issues such as software system design and maintenance. Advise customer about, or perform, maintenance of software system. Coordinate installation of software system. Monitor functioning of equipment to ensure system operates in conformance with specifications. Store, retrieve, and manipulate data for analysis of system capabilities and requirements. Confer with data processing and project managers to obtain information on limitations and capabilities for data processing projects. Prepare reports and correspondence concerning project specifications, activities, and status. Evaluate factors such as reporting formats required, cost constraints, and need for security restrictions to determine hardware configuration. Supervise and assign work to programmers, designers, technologists and technicians, and other engineering and scientific personnel. Train users to use new or modified equipment. Utilize microcontrollers to develop control signals, implement control algorithms, and measure process variables such as temperatures, pressures, and positions. **SKILLS—Programming:** Writing computer programs for various purposes. **Technology Design:** Generating or adapting equipment and technology to serve user needs. **Troubleshooting:** Determining causes of operating errors and deciding what to do about them. **Systems Analysis:** Determining how a system should work and how changes in conditions, operations, and the environment will affect outcomes. **Complex Problem Solving:** Identifying complex problems and reviewing related information to develop and evaluate options and implement solutions. **Operations Analysis:** Analyzing needs and product requirements to create a design. **Active Learning:** Understanding the implications of new information for both current and future problem-solving and decision-making. **Critical Thinking:** Using logic and reasoning to identify the strengths and weaknesses of alternative solutions, conclusions, or approaches to problems. **GOE—Interest Area:** 11. Information Technology. **Work Group:** 11.02. Information Technology Specialties. **Other Jobs in This Work Group:** Computer Operators; Computer Programmers; Computer Security Specialists; Computer Software Engineers, Applications; Computer Support Specialists; Computer Systems Analysts; Database Administrators; Network Systems and Data Communications Analysts. **PERSONALITY TYPE:** Investigative.

EDUCATION/TRAINING PROGRAM(S)—Artificial Intelligence and Robotics; Computer Engineering Technologies/Technicians, Other; Computer Engineering, General; Computer Science; Information Science/Studies; Information Technology. **RELATED KNOWLEDGE/COURSES—Computers and Electronics:** Knowledge of circuit boards, processors, chips, electronic equipment, and computer hardware and software, including applications and programming. **Design:** Knowledge of design techniques, tools, and principles involved in production of precision technical plans, blueprints, drawings, and models. **Engineering and Technology:** Knowledge of the practical application of engineering science and technology.

This includes applying principles, techniques, procedures, and equipment to the design and production of various goods and services. **Telecommunications:** Knowledge of transmission, broadcasting, switching, control, and operation of telecommunications systems. **Mathematics:** Knowledge of arithmetic, algebra, geometry, calculus, and statistics and their applications. **Education and Training:** Knowledge of principles and methods for curriculum and training design, teaching and instruction for individuals and groups, and the measurement of training effects.

Computer Support Specialists

- Education/Training Required: Associate degree
- Annual Earnings: $40,430
- Growth: 30.3%
- Annual Job Openings: 71,000
- Self-Employed: 0.6%
- Part-Time: 6.8%

Provide technical assistance to computer system users. Answer questions or resolve computer problems for clients in person, via telephone, or from remote location. May provide assistance concerning the use of computer hardware and software, including printing, installation, word processing, electronic mail, and operating systems. Answer users' inquiries regarding computer software and hardware operation to resolve problems. Enter commands and observe system functioning to verify correct operations and detect errors. Install and perform minor repairs to hardware, software, and peripheral equipment, following design or installation specifications. Oversee the daily performance of computer systems. Set up equipment for employee use, performing or ensuring proper installation of cable, operating systems, and appropriate software. Maintain record of daily data communication transactions, problems and remedial action taken, and installation activities. Read technical manuals, confer with users, and conduct computer diagnostics to investigate and resolve problems and to provide technical assistance and support. Confer with staff, users, and management to establish requirements for new systems or modifications. Develop training materials and procedures and/or train users in the proper use of hard-

ware and software. Refer major hardware or software problems or defective products to vendors or technicians for service. Prepare evaluations of software or hardware and recommend improvements or upgrades. Read trade magazines and technical manuals and attend conferences and seminars to maintain knowledge of hardware and software. Supervise and coordinate workers engaged in problem-solving, monitoring, and installing data communication equipment and software. Inspect equipment and read order sheets to prepare for delivery to users. Modify and customize commercial programs for internal needs. **SKILLS— Troubleshooting:** Determining causes of operating errors and deciding what to do about them. **Repairing:** Repairing machines or systems by using the needed tools. **Social Perceptiveness:** Being aware of others' reactions and understanding why they react as they do. **Installation:** Installing equipment, machines, wiring, or programs to meet specifications. **Persuasion:** Persuading others to change their minds or behavior. **Equipment Maintenance:** Performing routine maintenance on equipment and determining when and what kind of maintenance is needed. **Writing:** Communicating effectively in writing as appropriate for the needs of the audience. **Instructing:** Teaching others how to do something. **GOE—Interest Area:** 11. Information Technology. **Work Group:** 11.02. Information Technology Specialties. **Other Jobs in This Work Group:** Computer Operators; Computer Programmers; Computer Security Specialists; Computer Software Engineers, Applications; Computer Software Engineers, Systems Software; Computer Systems Analysts; Database Administrators; Network Systems and Data Communications Analysts. **PERSONALITY TYPE:** Investigative.

EDUCATION/TRAINING PROGRAM(S)— Accounting and Computer Science; Agricultural Business Technology; Computer Hardware Technology/ Technician; Computer Software Technology/Technician; Data Processing and Data Processing Technology/Technician; Medical Office Computer Specialist/Assistant. **RELATED KNOWLEDGE/ COURSES—Computers and Electronics:** Knowledge of circuit boards, processors, chips, electronic equipment, and computer hardware and software, including applications and programming. **Customer and Personal Service:** Knowledge of principles and processes for providing customer and personal services. This includes customer needs assessment, meeting quality standards for services, and evaluation of customer satisfaction. **Telecommunications:** Knowledge of transmission, broadcasting, switching, control, and operation of telecommunications systems. **Production and Processing:** Knowledge of raw materials, production processes, quality control, costs, and other techniques for maximizing the effective manufacture and distribution of goods. **Engineering and Technology:** Knowledge of the practical application of engineering science and technology. This includes applying principles, techniques, procedures, and equipment to the design and production of various goods and services. **Design:** Knowledge of design techniques, tools, and principles involved in production of precision technical plans, blueprints, drawings, and models.

Computer Systems Analysts

◎ Education/Training Required: Bachelor's degree
◎ Annual Earnings: $66,460
◎ Growth: 39.4%
◎ Annual Job Openings: 68,000
◎ Self-Employed: 6.4%
◎ Part-Time: 5.7%

Analyze science, engineering, business, and all other data processing problems for application to electronic data processing systems. Analyze user requirements, procedures, and problems to automate or improve existing systems and review computer system capabilities, workflow, and scheduling limitations. May analyze or recommend commercially available software. May supervise computer programmers. Provide staff and users with assistance solving computer-related problems, such as malfunctions and program problems. Test, maintain, and monitor computer programs and systems, including coordinating the installation of computer programs and systems. Use object-oriented programming languages, as well as client/server applications development processes and multimedia and Internet technology. Confer with clients regarding the nature of the information processing or computation needs a computer program is to address. Coordinate and link the computer systems within an organization to increase compatibility and so information can be shared. Consult with management to ensure agreement on system principles. Expand or

modify system to serve new purposes or improve work flow. Interview or survey workers, observe job performance, and/or perform the job in order to determine what information is processed and how it is processed. Determine computer software or hardware needed to set up or alter system. Train staff and users to work with computer systems and programs. Analyze information processing or computation needs and plan and design computer systems, using techniques such as structured analysis, data modeling, and information engineering. Assess the usefulness of pre-developed application packages and adapt them to a user environment. Define the goals of the system and devise flow charts and diagrams describing logical operational steps of programs. Develop, document, and revise system design procedures, test procedures, and quality standards. Review and analyze computer printouts and performance indicators to locate code problems and correct errors by correcting codes. Recommend new equipment or software packages. Read manuals, periodicals, and technical reports to learn how to develop programs that meet staff and user requirements. Supervise computer programmers or other systems analysts or serve as project leaders for particular systems projects. Utilize the computer in the analysis and solution of business problems such as development of integrated production and inventory control and cost analysis systems. **SKILLS—Quality Control Analysis:** Conducting tests and inspections of products, services, or processes to evaluate quality or performance. **Installation:** Installing equipment, machines, wiring, or programs to meet specifications. **Troubleshooting:** Determining causes of operating errors and deciding what to do about them. **Technology Design:** Generating or adapting equipment and technology to serve user needs. **Systems Analysis:** Determining how a system should work and how changes in conditions, operations, and the environment will affect outcomes. **Time Management:** Managing one's own time and the time of others. **Service Orientation:** Actively looking for ways to help people. **Programming:** Writing computer programs for various purposes. **GOE—Interest Area:** 11. Information Technology. **Work Group:** 11.02. Information Technology Specialties. **Other Jobs in This Work Group:** Computer Operators; Computer Programmers; Computer Security Specialists; Computer Software Engineers, Applications; Computer Software Engineers, Systems Software; Computer Support Specialists; Database Administrators; Network Systems and Data

Communications Analysts. **PERSONALITY TYPE:** Investigative.

EDUCATION/TRAINING PROGRAM(S)— Computer and Information Sciences, General; Computer Systems Analysis/Analyst; Information Technology; Web/Multimedia Management and Webmaster. **RELATED KNOWLEDGE/COURSES— Computers and Electronics:** Knowledge of circuit boards, processors, chips, electronic equipment, and computer hardware and software, including applications and programming. **Telecommunications:** Knowledge of transmission, broadcasting, switching, control, and operation of telecommunications systems. **Customer and Personal Service:** Knowledge of principles and processes for providing customer and personal services. This includes customer needs assessment, meeting quality standards for services, and evaluation of customer satisfaction. **Design:** Knowledge of design techniques, tools, and principles involved in production of precision technical plans, blueprints, drawings, and models. **Education and Training:** Knowledge of principles and methods for curriculum and training design, teaching and instruction for individuals and groups, and the measurement of training effects. **Law and Government:** Knowledge of laws, legal codes, court procedures, precedents, government regulations, executive orders, agency rules, and the democratic political process.

Construction and Building Inspectors

- Education/Training Required: Work experience in a related occupation
- Annual Earnings: $43,670
- Growth: 13.8%
- Annual Job Openings: 10,000
- Self-Employed: 8.1%
- Part-Time: 5.9%

Inspect structures, using engineering skills to determine structural soundness and compliance with specifications, building codes, and other regulations. Inspections may be general in nature or may be limited to a specific area, such as electrical systems or plumbing. Use survey instruments; metering devices; tape measures; and test equipment, such as concrete strength measurers, to perform inspections. Inspect bridges, dams, highways, buildings, wiring, plumbing, electrical circuits, sewers, heating systems, and foundations during and after construction for structural quality, general safety, and conformance to specifications and codes. Maintain daily logs and supplement inspection records with photographs. Review and interpret plans, blueprints, site layouts, specifications, and construction methods to ensure compliance to legal requirements and safety regulations. Inspect and monitor construction sites to ensure adherence to safety standards, building codes, and specifications. Measure dimensions and verify level, alignment, and elevation of structures and fixtures to ensure compliance to building plans and codes. Issue violation notices and stop-work orders, conferring with owners, violators, and authorities to explain regulations and recommend rectifications. Issue permits for construction, relocation, demolition, and occupancy. Approve and sign plans that meet required specifications. Compute estimates of work completed or of needed renovations or upgrades and approve payment for contractors. Monitor installation of plumbing, wiring, equipment, and appliances to ensure that installation is performed properly and is in compliance with applicable regulations. Examine lifting and conveying devices, such as elevators, escalators, moving sidewalks, lifts and hoists, inclined railways, ski lifts, and amusement rides, to ensure safety and proper functioning. Train, direct, and supervise other construction inspectors. Evaluate premises for cleanliness, including proper garbage disposal and lack of vermin infestation. **SKILLS—Persuasion:** Persuading others to change their minds or behavior. **Mathematics:** Using mathematics to solve problems. **Time Management:** Managing one's own time and the time of others. **Reading Comprehension:** Understanding written sentences and paragraphs in work-related documents. **Active Listening:** Giving full attention to what other people are saying, taking time to understand the points being made, asking questions as appropriate, and not interrupting at inappropriate times. **Coordination:** Adjusting actions in relation to others' actions. **Active Learning:** Understanding the implications of new information for both current and future problem-solving and decision-making. **Social Perceptiveness:** Being aware of others' reactions and understanding why they react as they do. **Negotiation:** Bringing others together and trying to reconcile differences. **Instructing:** Teaching others how to do something. **GOE—Interest Area:** 02. Architecture and

Construction. **Work Group:** 02.03. Architecture/Construction Engineering Technologies. **Other Jobs in This Work Group:** Architectural Drafters; Civil Drafters; Electrical Drafters; Surveyors. **PERSONALITY TYPE:** Conventional.

EDUCATION/TRAINING PROGRAM(S)—Building/Home/Construction Inspection/Inspector. **RELATED KNOWLEDGE/COURSES—Building and Construction:** Knowledge of the materials, methods, and tools involved in the construction or repair of houses, buildings, or other structures such as highways and roads. **Design:** Knowledge of design techniques, tools, and principles involved in production of precision technical plans, blueprints, drawings, and models. **Engineering and Technology:** Knowledge of the practical application of engineering science and technology. This includes applying principles, techniques, procedures, and equipment to the design and production of various goods and services. **Public Safety and Security:** Knowledge of relevant equipment, policies, procedures, and strategies to promote effective local, state, or national security operations for the protection of people, data, property, and institutions. **Customer and Personal Service:** Knowledge of principles and processes for providing customer and personal services. This includes customer needs assessment, meeting quality standards for services, and evaluation of customer satisfaction. **Administration and Management:** Knowledge of business and management principles involved in strategic planning, resource allocation, human resources modeling, leadership technique, production methods, and coordination of people and resources. **Mechanical Devices:** Knowledge of machines and tools, including their designs, uses, repair, and maintenance.

Construction Carpenters

- Education/Training Required: Long-term on-the-job training
- Annual Earnings: $34,900
- Growth: 10.1%
- Annual Job Openings: 193,000
- Self-Employed: 29.7%
- Part-Time: 5.3%

Construct, erect, install, and repair structures and fixtures of wood, plywood, and wallboard, using carpenter's hand tools and power tools. Measure and mark cutting lines on materials, using ruler, pencil, chalk, and marking gauge. Follow established safety rules and regulations and maintain a safe and clean environment. Verify trueness of structure, using plumb bob and level. Shape or cut materials to specified measurements, using hand tools, machines, or power saw. Study specifications in blueprints, sketches, or building plans to prepare project layout and determine dimensions and materials required. Assemble and fasten materials to make framework or props, using hand tools and wood screws, nails, dowel pins, or glue. Build or repair cabinets, doors, frameworks, floors, and other wooden fixtures used in buildings, using woodworking machines, carpenter's hand tools, and power tools. Erect scaffolding and ladders for assembling structures above ground level. Remove damaged or defective parts or sections of structures and repair or replace, using hand tools. Install structures and fixtures, such as windows, frames, floorings, and trim, or hardware, using carpenter's hand and power tools. Select and order lumber and other required materials. Maintain records, document actions, and present written progress reports. Finish surfaces of woodwork or wallboard in houses and buildings, using paint, hand tools, and paneling. Prepare cost estimates for clients or employers. Arrange for subcontractors to deal with special areas such as heating and electrical wiring work. **SKILLS—Management of Personnel Resources:** Motivating, developing, and directing people as they work, identifying the best people for the job. **Management of Material Resources:** Obtaining and seeing to the appropriate use of equipment, facilities, and materials needed to do certain work. **Management of Financial Resources:** Determining how money will be spent to get the work done and accounting for these expenditures. **Equipment Maintenance:** Performing routine maintenance on equipment and determining when and what kind of maintenance is needed. **Repairing:** Repairing machines or systems by using the needed tools. **Quality Control Analysis:** Conducting tests and inspections of products, services, or processes to evaluate quality or performance. **Service Orientation:** Actively looking for ways to help people. **Speaking:** Talking to others to convey information effectively. **GOE—Interest Area:** 02. Architecture and Construction. **Work Group:** 02.04. Construction Crafts. **Other Jobs in This Work Group:** Boat Builders and Shipwrights; Boilermakers; Brattice Builders; Brickmasons and Blockmasons; Carpet

Installers; Ceiling Tile Installers; Cement Masons and Concrete Finishers; Commercial Divers; Crane and Tower Operators; Dragline Operators; Drywall Installers; Electricians; Fence Erectors; Floor Layers, Except Carpet, Wood, and Hard Tiles; Floor Sanders and Finishers; Glaziers; Grader, Bulldozer, and Scraper Operators; Hazardous Materials Removal Workers; Insulation Workers, Floor, Ceiling, and Wall; Insulation Workers, Mechanical; Manufactured Building and Mobile Home Installers; Operating Engineers; Painters, Construction and Maintenance; Paperhangers; Paving, Surfacing, and Tamping Equipment Operators; Pile-Driver Operators; Pipe Fitters; Pipelayers; Pipelaying Fitters; Plasterers and Stucco Masons; Plumbers; Rail-Track Laying and Maintenance Equipment Operators; Refractory Materials Repairers, Except Brickmasons; Reinforcing Iron and Rebar Workers; Riggers; Roofers; Rough Carpenters; Security and Fire Alarm Systems Installers; Segmental Pavers; Sheet Metal Workers; Ship Carpenters and Joiners; Stone Cutters and Carvers; Stonemasons; Structural Iron and Steel Workers; Tapers; Terrazzo Workers and Finishers; Tile and Marble Setters. **PERSONALITY TYPE:** Realistic.

EDUCATION/TRAINING   PROGRAM(S)— Carpentry/Carpenter. **RELATED KNOWLEDGE/ COURSES—Building and Construction:** Knowledge of the materials, methods, and tools involved in the construction or repair of houses, buildings, or other structures such as highways and roads. **Production and Processing:** Knowledge of raw materials, production processes, quality control, costs, and other techniques for maximizing the effective manufacture and distribution of goods. **Engineering and Technology:** Knowledge of the practical application of engineering science and technology. This includes applying principles, techniques, procedures, and equipment to the design and production of various goods and services. **Design:** Knowledge of design techniques, tools, and principles involved in production of precision technical plans, blueprints, drawings, and models. **Public Safety and Security:** Knowledge of relevant equipment, policies, procedures, and strategies to promote effective local, state, or national security operations for the protection of people, data, property, and institutions. **Mechanical Devices:** Knowledge of machines and tools, including their designs, uses, repair, and maintenance.

Construction Laborers

- Education/Training Required: Moderate-term on-the-job training
- Annual Earnings: $25,160
- Growth: 14.2%
- Annual Job Openings: 166,000
- Self-Employed: 13.3%
- Part-Time: 7.9%

Perform tasks involving physical labor at building, highway, and heavy construction projects; tunnel and shaft excavations; and demolition sites. May operate hand and power tools of all types: air hammers, earth tampers, cement mixers, small mechanical hoists, surveying and measuring equipment, and a variety of other equipment and instruments. May clean and prepare sites; dig trenches; set braces to support the sides of excavations; erect scaffolding; clean up rubble and debris; and remove asbestos, lead, and other hazardous waste materials. May assist other craft workers. Apply caulking compounds by hand or using caulking guns. Build and position forms for pouring concrete and dismantle forms after use, using saws, hammers, nails, or bolts. Clean and prepare construction sites to eliminate possible hazards. Control traffic passing near, in, and around work zones. Dig ditches or trenches, backfill excavations, and compact and level earth to grade specifications, using picks, shovels, pneumatic tampers, and rakes. Erect and disassemble scaffolding, shoring, braces, traffic barricades, ramps, and other temporary structures. Grind, scrape, sand, or polish surfaces such as concrete, marble, terrazzo, or wood flooring, using abrasive tools or machines. Install sewer, water, and storm drain pipes, using pipe-laying machinery and laser guidance equipment. Load, unload, and identify building materials, machinery, and tools and distribute them to the appropriate locations according to project plans and specifications. Measure, mark, and record openings and distances to lay out areas where construction work will be performed. Mix ingredients to create compounds for covering or cleaning surfaces. Mop, brush, or spread paints, cleaning solutions, or other compounds over surfaces to clean them or to provide protection. Operate jackhammers and drills to break up concrete or pavement. Place, consolidate, and protect case-in-place concrete or masonry structures. Position, join, align, and seal structural components, such as concrete wall sections and pipes. Shovel cement and other materials into portable cement mixers and mix, pour, and spread concrete. Signal equipment operators to facilitate alignment, movement, and adjustment of machinery, equipment, and materials. Smooth and finish freshly poured cement or concrete, using floats, trowels, screeds, or powered cement-finishing tools. Spray materials such as water, sand, steam, vinyl, paint, or stucco through hoses to clean, coat, or seal surfaces. Tend machines that pump concrete, grout, cement, sand, plaster, or stucco through spray guns for application to ceilings and walls. Tend pumps, compressors, and generators to provide power for tools, machinery, and equipment or to heat and move materials such as asphalt. **SKILLS—Equipment Maintenance:** Performing routine maintenance on equipment and determining when and what kind of maintenance is needed. **GOE—Interest Area:** 02. Architecture and Construction. **Work Group:** 02.06. Construction Support/Labor. **Other Jobs in This Work Group:** Carpenter Assemblers and Repairers; Grips and Set-Up Workers, Motion Picture Sets, Studios, and Stages; Helpers—Brickmasons, Blockmasons, Stonemasons, and Tile and Marble Setters; Helpers—Carpenters; Helpers—Electricians; Helpers—Installation, Maintenance, and Repair Workers; Helpers—Painters, Paperhangers, Plasterers, and Stucco Masons; Helpers—Pipelayers, Plumbers, Pipefitters, and Steamfitters; Highway Maintenance Workers; Septic Tank Servicers and Sewer Pipe Cleaners. **PERSONALITY TYPE:** Realistic.

EDUCATION/TRAINING PROGRAM(S)—Construction Trades, Other. **RELATED KNOWLEDGE/COURSES—Building and Construction:** Knowledge of the materials, methods, and tools involved in the construction or repair of houses, buildings, or other structures such as highways and roads. **Mechanical Devices:** Knowledge of machines and tools, including their designs, uses, repair, and maintenance. **Production and Processing:** Knowledge of raw materials, production processes, quality control, costs, and other techniques for maximizing the effective manufacture and distribution of goods. **Engineering and Technology:** Knowledge of the practical application of engineering science and technology. This includes applying principles, techniques, procedures, and equipment to the design and production of various goods and services. **Physics:** Knowledge and prediction of physical principles and laws and their interrelationships and applications to understanding fluid, material, and atmospheric dynamics and mechanical, electrical, atomic, and subatomic structures and processes. **Design:** Knowledge of design techniques, tools, and principles involved in production of precision technical plans, blueprints, drawings, and models.

Construction Managers

- Education/Training Required: Bachelor's degree
- Annual Earnings: $69,870
- Growth: 12.0%
- Annual Job Openings: 47,000
- Self-Employed: 46.9%
- Part-Time: 3.6%

Plan, direct, coordinate, or budget, usually through subordinate supervisory personnel, activities concerned with the construction and maintenance of structures, facilities, and systems. Participate in the conceptual development of a construction project and oversee its organization, scheduling, and implementation. Confer with supervisory personnel, owners, contractors, and design professionals to discuss and resolve matters such as work procedures, complaints, and construction problems. Plan, organize, and direct activities concerned with the construction and maintenance of structures, facilities, and systems. Schedule the project in logical steps and budget time required to meet deadlines. Determine labor requirements and dispatch workers to construction sites. Inspect and review projects to monitor compliance with building and safety codes and other regulations. Interpret and explain plans and contract terms to administrative staff, workers, and clients, representing the owner or developer. Prepare contracts and negotiate revisions, changes, and additions to contractual agreements with architects, consultants, clients, suppliers, and subcontractors. Obtain all necessary permits and licenses. Direct and supervise workers. Study job specifications to determine appropriate construction methods. Select, contract, and oversee workers who complete specific pieces of the project, such as painting or plumbing. Requisition supplies and materials to complete construction projects. Prepare and submit budget estimates and progress and cost tracking reports. Develop and implement quality control programs. Take actions to deal with the results of delays, bad weather, or emergencies at construction site. Investigate damage, accidents, or delays at construction sites to ensure that proper procedures are being carried out. Evaluate construction methods and determine cost-effectiveness of plans, using computers. **SKILLS—Coordination:** Adjusting actions in relation to others' actions. **Troubleshooting:** Determining causes of operating errors and deciding what to do about them. **Installation:** Installing equipment, machines, wiring, or programs to meet specifications. **Repairing:** Repairing machines or systems by using the needed tools. **Negotiation:** Bringing others together and trying to reconcile differences. **Management of Material Resources:** Obtaining and seeing to the appropriate use of equipment, facilities, and materials needed to do certain work. **Instructing:** Teaching others how to do something. **Persuasion:** Persuading others to change their minds or behavior. **Management of Financial Resources:** Determining how money will be spent to get the work done and accounting for these expenditures. **GOE—Interest Area:** 02. Architecture and Construction. **Work Group:** 02.01. Managerial Work in Architecture and Construction. **Other Jobs in This Work Group:** First-Line Supervisors and Manager/Supervisors—Construction Trades Workers. **PERSONALITY TYPE:** Enterprising.

EDUCATION/TRAINING PROGRAM(S)—Business Administration and Management, General; Business/Commerce, General; Construction Engineering Technology/Technician; Operations Management and Supervision. **RELATED KNOWLEDGE/COURSES—Building and Construction:** Knowledge of the materials, methods, and tools involved in the construction or repair of houses, buildings, or other structures such as highways and roads. **Design:** Knowledge of design techniques, tools, and principles involved in production of precision technical plans, blueprints, drawings, and models. **Administration and Management:** Knowledge of business and management principles involved in strategic planning, resource allocation, human resources modeling, leadership technique, production methods, and coordination of people and resources. **Mechanical Devices:** Knowledge of machines and tools, including their designs, uses, repair, and maintenance. **Public Safety and Security:** Knowledge of relevant equipment, policies, procedures, and strategies to promote effective local, state, or national security operations for the protection of people, data, property, and institutions. **Customer and Personal Service:** Knowledge of principles and processes for providing customer and personal services. This includes customer needs assessment, meeting quality standards for services, and evaluation of customer satisfaction. **Mathematics:** Knowledge of arithmetic, algebra, geometry, calculus, and statistics and their applications.

Cooks, Restaurant

- Education/Training Required: Long-term on-the-job training
- Annual Earnings: $19,520
- Growth: 15.9%
- Annual Job Openings: 211,000
- Self-Employed: 1.3%
- Part-Time: 31.6%

Prepare, season, and cook soups, meats, vegetables, desserts, or other foodstuffs in restaurants. May order supplies, keep records and accounts, price items on menu, or plan menu. Inspect food preparation and serving areas to ensure observance of safe, sanitary food-handling practices. Turn or stir foods to ensure even cooking. Season and cook food according to recipes or personal judgment and experience. Observe and test foods to determine if they have been cooked sufficiently, using methods such as tasting, smelling, or piercing them with utensils. Weigh, measure, and mix ingredients according to recipes or personal judgment, using various kitchen utensils and equipment. Portion, arrange, and garnish food and serve food to waiters or patrons. Regulate temperature of ovens, broilers, grills, and roasters. Substitute for or assist other cooks during emergencies or rush periods. Bake, roast, broil, and steam meats, fish, vegetables, and other foods. Wash, peel, cut, and seed fruits and vegetables to prepare them for consumption. Estimate expected food consumption; then requisition or purchase supplies or procure food from storage. Carve and trim meats such as beef, veal, ham, pork, and lamb for hot or cold service or for sandwiches. Coordinate and supervise work of kitchen staff. Consult with supervisory staff to plan menus, taking into consideration factors such as costs and special event needs. Butcher and dress animals, fowl, or shellfish or cut and bone meat prior to cooking. Bake breads, rolls, cakes, and pastries. Prepare relishes and hors d'oeuvres. Keep records and accounts. Plan and price menu items. **SKILLS—Equipment Maintenance:** Performing routine maintenance on equipment and determining when and what kind of maintenance is needed. **Instructing:** Teaching others how to do something. **Active Learning:** Understanding the implications of new information for both current and future problem-solving and decision-making. **Learning Strategies:** Selecting and using training/instructional methods and procedures appropriate for the situation when learning or teaching new things. **Time Management:** Managing one's own time and the time of others. **Management of Personnel Resources:** Motivating, developing, and directing people as they work, identifying the best people for the job. **Social Perceptiveness:** Being aware of others' reactions and understanding why they react as they do. **Repairing:** Repairing machines or systems by using the needed tools. **GOE—Interest Area:** 09. Hospitality, Tourism, and Recreation. **Work Group:** 09.04. Food and Beverage Preparation. **Other Jobs in This Work Group:** Bakers, Bread and Pastry; Butchers and Meat Cutters; Chefs and Head Cooks; Cooks, Fast Food; Cooks, Institution and Cafeteria; Cooks, Short Order; Dishwashers; Food Preparation Workers. **PERSONALITY TYPE:** Realistic.

EDUCATION/TRAINING PROGRAM(S)— Cooking and Related Culinary Arts, General; Culinary Arts/Chef Training. **RELATED KNOWLEDGE/COURSES—Food Production:** Knowledge of techniques and equipment for planting, growing, and harvesting food products (both plant and animal) for consumption, including storage/handling techniques. **Production and Processing:** Knowledge of raw materials, production processes, quality control, costs, and other techniques for maximizing the effective manufacture and distribution of goods. **Customer and Personal Service:** Knowledge of principles and processes for providing customer and personal services. This includes customer needs assessment, meeting quality standards for services, and evaluation of customer satisfaction. **Foreign Language:** Knowledge of the structure and content of a foreign (non-English) language, including the meaning and spelling of words, rules of composition and grammar, and pronunciation. **Chemistry:** Knowledge of the chemical composition, structure, and properties of substances and of the chemical processes and transformations that they undergo. This includes uses of chemicals and their danger signs, production techniques, and disposal methods. **Administration and Management:** Knowledge of business and management principles involved in strategic planning, resource allocation, human

resources modeling, leadership technique, production methods, and coordination of people and resources. **Education and Training:** Knowledge of principles and methods for curriculum and training design, teaching and instruction for individuals and groups, and the measurement of training effects.

Copy Writers

◎ Education/Training Required: Bachelor's degree
◎ Annual Earnings: $44,350
◎ Growth: 16.1%
◎ Annual Job Openings: 23,000
◎ Self-Employed: 67.9%
◎ Part-Time: 24.2%

Write advertising copy for use by publication or broadcast media to promote sale of goods and services. Write advertising copy for use by publication, broadcast, or Internet media to promote the sale of goods and services. Present drafts and ideas to clients. Discuss with the client the product, advertising themes and methods, and any changes that should be made in advertising copy. Vary language and tone of messages based on product and medium. Consult with sales, media, and marketing representatives to obtain information on product or service and discuss style and length of advertising copy. Edit or rewrite existing copy as necessary and submit copy for approval by supervisor. Write to customers in their terms and on their level so that the advertiser's sales message is more readily received. Write articles, bulletins, sales letters, speeches, and other related informative, marketing, and promotional material. Invent names for products and write the slogans that appear on packaging, brochures, and other promotional material. Review advertising trends, consumer surveys, and other data regarding marketing of goods and services to determine the best way to promote products. Develop advertising campaigns for a wide range of clients, working with an advertising agency's creative director and art director to determine the best way to present advertising information. Conduct research and interviews to determine which of a product's selling features should be promoted. **SKILLS—Persuasion:** Persuading others to change their minds or behavior. **Time Management:** Managing one's own time and the time of others. **Instructing:** Teaching others how to do something. **Technology Design:** Generating or adapting equipment and technology to serve user needs. **Coordination:** Adjusting actions in relation to others' actions. **Negotiation:** Bringing others together and trying to reconcile differences. **Active Listening:** Giving full attention to what other people are saying, taking time to understand the points being made, asking questions as appropriate, and not interrupting at inappropriate times. **Critical Thinking:** Using logic and reasoning to identify the strengths and weaknesses of alternative solutions, conclusions, or approaches to problems. **GOE—Interest Area:** 03. Arts and Communication. **Work Group:** 03.02. Writing and Editing. **Other Jobs in This Work Group:** Creative Writers; Editors; Poets and Lyricists; Technical Writers. **PERSONALITY TYPE:** Artistic.

EDUCATION/TRAINING PROGRAM(S)— Broadcast Journalism; Business/Corporate Communications; Communication Studies/Speech Communication and Rhetoric; Communication, Journalism, and Related Programs, Other; Creative Writing; English Composition; Family and Consumer Sciences/Human Sciences Communication; Journalism; Mass Communication/Media Studies; Playwriting and Screenwriting; Technical and Business Writing. **RELATED KNOWLEDGE/COURSES— Communications and Media:** Knowledge of media production, communication, and dissemination techniques and methods. This includes alternative ways to inform and entertain via written, oral, and visual media. **Sales and Marketing:** Knowledge of principles and methods for showing, promoting, and selling products or services. This includes marketing strategy and tactics, product demonstrations, sales techniques, and sales control systems. **Sociology and Anthropology:** Knowledge of group behavior and dynamics, societal trends and influences, human migrations, ethnicity, and cultures and their history and origins. **English Language:** Knowledge of the structure and content of the English language, including the meaning and spelling of words, rules of composition, and grammar. **Computers and Electronics:** Knowledge of circuit boards, processors, chips, electronic equipment, and computer hardware and software, including applications and programming. **Administration and Management:** Knowledge of business and management principles involved in strategic planning, resource allocation, human resources modeling, leadership technique, production methods, and coordination of people and resources. **History and Archeology:** Knowledge of historical events and their causes, indicators, and effects on civilizations and cultures.

Coroners

- ◎ Education/Training Required: Work experience in a related occupation
- ◎ Annual Earnings: $47,390
- ◎ Growth: 9.8%
- ◎ Annual Job Openings: 20,000
- ◎ Self-Employed: 0.9%
- ◎ Part-Time: 5.3%

Direct activities such as autopsies, pathological and toxicological analyses, and inquests relating to the investigation of deaths occurring within a legal jurisdiction to determine cause of death or to fix responsibility for accidental, violent, or unexplained deaths. Collect and document any pertinent medical history information. Complete death certificates, including the assignment of a cause and manner of death. Complete reports and forms required to finalize cases. Direct activities of workers who conduct autopsies, perform pathological and toxicological analyses, and prepare documents for permanent records. Inquire into the cause, manner, and circumstances of human deaths and establish the identities of deceased persons. Interview persons present at death scenes to obtain information useful in determining the manner of death. Observe and record the positions and conditions of bodies and of related evidence. Observe, record, and preserve any objects or personal property related to deaths, including objects such as medication containers and suicide notes. Perform medico-legal examinations and autopsies, conducting preliminary examinations of the body in order to identify victims, to locate signs of trauma, and to identify factors that would indicate time of death. Testify at inquests, hearings, and court trials. Arrange for the next of kin to be notified of deaths. Collect wills, burial instructions, and other documentation needed for investigations and for handling of the remains. Confer with officials of public health and law enforcement agencies in order to coordinate interdepartmental activities. Coordinate the release of personal effects to authorized persons and facilitate the disposition of unclaimed corpses and personal effects. Inventory personal effects, such as jewelry or wallets, that are recovered from bodies. Locate and document information regarding the next of kin, including their relationship to the deceased and the status of notification attempts. Provide information concerning the circumstances of death to relatives of the deceased. Remove or supervise removal of bodies from death scenes, using the proper equipment and supplies, and arrange for transportation to morgues. Witness and certify deaths that are the result of a judicial order. Record the disposition of minor children, as well as details of arrangements made for their care. **SKILLS—Science:** Using scientific rules and methods to solve problems. **Reading Comprehension:** Understanding written sentences and paragraphs in work-related documents. **Speaking:** Talking to others to convey information effectively. **Writing:** Communicating effectively in writing as appropriate for the needs of the audience. **Critical Thinking:** Using logic and reasoning to identify the strengths and weaknesses of alternative solutions, conclusions, or approaches to problems. **Mathematics:** Using mathematics to solve problems. **Management of Personnel Resources:** Motivating, developing, and directing people as they work, identifying the best people for the job. **Active Listening:** Giving full attention to what other people are saying, taking time to understand the points being made, asking questions as appropriate, and not interrupting at inappropriate times. **Complex Problem Solving:** Identifying complex problems and reviewing related information to develop and evaluate options and implement solutions. **GOE—Interest Area:** 08. Health Science. **Work Group:** 08.01. Managerial Work in Medical and Health Services. **Other Jobs in This Work Group:** First-Line Supervisors and Manager/Supervisors—Animal Care Workers, Except Livestock; Medical and Health Services Managers. **PERSONALITY TYPE:** Investigative.

EDUCATION/TRAINING PROGRAM(S)—No data available. **RELATED KNOWLEDGE/COURSES—Medicine and Dentistry:** Knowledge of the information and techniques needed to diagnose and treat human injuries, diseases, and deformities. This includes symptoms, treatment alternatives, drug properties and interactions, and preventive health-care measures. **Biology:** Knowledge of plant and animal organisms and their tissues, cells, functions, interdependencies, and interactions with each other and the environment. **Chemistry:** Knowledge of the chemical composition, structure, and properties of substances and of the chemical processes and transformations that they undergo. This includes uses of chemicals and their danger signs, production techniques, and disposal

methods. **Administration and Management:** Knowledge of business and management principles involved in strategic planning, resource allocation, human resources modeling, leadership technique, production methods, and coordination of people and resources. **Law and Government:** Knowledge of laws, legal codes, court procedures, precedents, government regulations, executive orders, agency rules, and the democratic political process. **Public Safety and Security:** Knowledge of relevant equipment, policies, procedures, and strategies to promote effective local, state, or national security operations for the protection of people, data, property, and institutions.

Correctional Officers and Jailers

- Education/Training Required: Moderate-term on-the-job training
- Annual Earnings: $33,600
- Growth: 24.2%
- Annual Job Openings: 49,000
- Self-Employed: 0%
- Part-Time: 1.3%

Guard inmates in penal or rehabilitative institution in accordance with established regulations and procedures. May guard prisoners in transit between jail, courtroom, prison, or other point. Includes deputy sheriffs and police who spend the majority of their time guarding prisoners in correctional institutions. Monitor conduct of prisoners according to established policies, regulations, and procedures in order to prevent escape or violence. Inspect conditions of locks, window bars, grills, doors, and gates at correctional facilities in order to ensure that they will prevent escapes. Search prisoners, cells, and vehicles for weapons, valuables, or drugs. Guard facility entrances in order to screen visitors. Search for and recapture escapees. Inspect mail for the presence of contraband. Take prisoners into custody and escort to locations within and outside of facility, such as visiting room, courtroom, or airport. Record information such as prisoner identification, charges, and incidences of inmate disturbance. Use weapons, handcuffs, and physical force to maintain discipline and order among prisoners. Conduct fire, safety, and sanitation inspections. Provide to supervisors oral and written reports of the quality and quantity of work performed by inmates, inmate disturbances and rule violations, and unusual occurrences. Settle disputes between inmates. Drive passenger vehicles and trucks used to transport inmates to other institutions, courtrooms, hospitals, and work sites. Arrange daily schedules for prisoners, including library visits, work assignments, family visits, and counseling appointments. Assign duties to inmates, providing instructions as needed. Issue clothing, tools, and other authorized items to inmates. Serve meals and distribute commissary items to prisoners. Investigate crimes that have occurred within an institution or assist police in their investigations of crimes and inmates. Maintain records of prisoners' identification and charges. Supervise and coordinate work of other correctional service officers. Sponsor inmate recreational activities such as newspapers and self-help groups. **SKILLS—Social Perceptiveness:** Being aware of others' reactions and understanding why they react as they do. **Persuasion:** Persuading others to change their minds or behavior. **Negotiation:** Bringing others together and trying to reconcile differences. **Speaking:** Talking to others to convey information effectively. **Instructing:** Teaching others how to do something. **Writing:** Communicating effectively in writing as appropriate for the needs of the audience. **Monitoring:** Monitoring or assessing your performance or that of other individuals or organizations to make improvements or take corrective action. **Active Listening:** Giving full attention to what other people are saying, taking time to understand the points being made, asking questions as appropriate, and not interrupting at inappropriate times. **GOE—Interest Area:** 12. Law and Public Safety. **Work Group:** 12.04. Law Enforcement and Public Safety. **Other Jobs in This Work Group:** Bailiffs; Criminal Investigators and Special Agents; Fire Investigators; Forensic Science Technicians; Highway Patrol Pilots; Parking Enforcement Workers; Police Detectives; Police Identification and Records Officers; Police Patrol Officers; Sheriffs and Deputy Sheriffs; Transit and Railroad Police. **PERSONALITY TYPE:** Realistic.

EDUCATION/TRAINING PROGRAM(S)—Corrections; Corrections and Criminal Justice, Other; Juvenile Corrections. **RELATED KNOWLEDGE/ COURSES—Psychology:** Knowledge of human behavior and performance; individual differences in ability, personality, and interests; learning and motivation; psychological research methods; and the assessment and treatment of behavioral and affective disorders. **Public Safety and Security:** Knowledge of relevant equipment, policies, procedures, and strategies to promote effective local, state, or national security operations for the protection of people, data, property, and institutions. **Law and Government:** Knowledge of laws, legal codes, court procedures, precedents, government regulations, executive orders, agency rules, and the democratic political process. **Philosophy and Theology:** Knowledge of different philosophical systems and religions. This includes their basic principles, values, ethics, ways of thinking, customs, and practices and their impact on human culture. **Sociology and Anthropology:** Knowledge of group behavior and dynamics, societal trends and influences, human migrations, ethnicity, and cultures and their history and origins. **Transportation:** Knowledge of principles and methods for moving people or goods by air, rail, sea, or road, including the relative costs and benefits.

Cost Estimators

- Education/Training Required: Bachelor's degree
- Annual Earnings: $49,940
- Growth: 18.6%
- Annual Job Openings: 25,000
- Self-Employed: 1.7%
- Part-Time: 5.9%

Prepare cost estimates for product manufacturing, construction projects, or services to aid management in bidding on or determining price of product or service. May specialize according to particular service performed or type of product manufactured. Analyze blueprints and other documentation to prepare time, cost, materials, and labor estimates. Assess cost-effectiveness of products, projects, or services, tracking actual costs relative to bids as the project develops. Consult with clients, vendors, personnel in other departments, or construction foremen to discuss and formulate estimates and resolve issues. Confer with engineers, architects, owners, contractors, and subcontractors on changes and adjustments to cost estimates. Prepare estimates used by management for purposes such as planning, organizing, and scheduling work. Prepare estimates for use in selecting vendors or subcontractors. Review material and labor requirements to decide whether it is more cost-effective to produce or purchase components. Prepare cost and expenditure statements and other necessary documentation at regular intervals for the duration of the project. Prepare and maintain a directory of suppliers, contractors, and subcontractors. Set up cost monitoring and reporting systems and procedures. Establish and maintain tendering process and conduct negotiations. Conduct special studies to develop and establish standard hour and related cost data or to effect cost reduction. Visit site and record information about access, drainage and topography, and availability of services such as water and electricity. **SKILLS—Negotiation:** Bringing others together and trying to reconcile differences. **Management of Financial Resources:** Determining how money will be spent to get the work done and accounting for these expenditures. **Management of Personnel Resources:** Motivating, developing, and directing people as they work, identifying the best people for the job. **Coordination:** Adjusting actions in relation to others' actions. **Active Listening:** Giving full attention to what other people are saying, taking time to understand the points being made, asking questions as appropriate, and not interrupting at inappropriate times. **Mathematics:** Using mathematics to solve problems. **Persuasion:** Persuading others to change their minds or behavior. **Time Management:** Managing one's own time and the time of others. **GOE—Interest Area:** 06. Finance and Insurance. **Work Group:** 06.02. Finance/Insurance Investigation and Analysis. **Other Jobs in This Work Group:** Appraisers, Real Estate; Assessors; Claims Examiners, Property and Casualty Insurance; Credit Analysts; Financial Analysts; Insurance Adjusters, Examiners, and Investigators; Insurance Appraisers, Auto Damage; Insurance Underwriters; Loan Counselors; Loan Officers; Market Research Analysts; Survey Researchers. **PERSONALITY TYPE:** Conventional.

EDUCATION/TRAINING PROGRAM(S)—Business Administration and Management, General; Business/Commerce, General; Construction Engineering; Construction Engineering Technology/Technician; Manufacturing Engineering; Materials Engineering; Mechanical Engineering. **RELATED KNOWLEDGE/COURSES—Administration and Management:** Knowledge of business and management principles involved in strategic planning, resource allocation, human resources modeling, leadership technique, production methods, and coordination of people and resources. **Production and Processing:** Knowledge of raw materials, production processes, quality control, costs, and other techniques for maximizing the effective manufacture and distribution of goods. **Economics and Accounting:** Knowledge of economic and accounting principles and practices, the financial markets, banking, and the analysis and reporting of financial data. **Clerical Practices:** Knowledge of administrative and clerical procedures and systems such as word processing, managing files and records, stenography and transcription, designing forms, and other office procedures and terminology. **Sales and Marketing:** Knowledge of principles and methods for showing, promoting, and selling products or services. This includes marketing strategy and tactics, product demonstrations, sales techniques, and sales control systems. **Mathematics:** Knowledge of arithmetic, algebra, geometry, calculus, and statistics and their applications.

Costume Attendants

- ◉ Education/Training Required: Moderate-term on-the-job training
- ◉ Annual Earnings: $25,050
- ◉ Growth: 27.8%
- ◉ Annual Job Openings: 66,000
- ◉ Self-Employed: 0.4%
- ◉ Part-Time: 51.9%

Select, fit, and take care of costumes for cast members and aid entertainers. Arrange costumes in order of use to facilitate quick-change procedures for performances. Assign lockers to employees and maintain locker rooms, dressing rooms, wig rooms, and costume storage and laundry areas. Care for non-clothing items such as flags, table skirts, and draperies. Check the appearance of costumes on stage and under lights in order to determine whether desired effects are being achieved. Clean and press costumes before and after performances and perform any minor repairs. Collaborate with production designers, costume designers, and other production staff in order to discuss and execute costume design details. Create worksheets for dressing lists, show notes, and costume checks. Distribute costumes and related equipment and keep records of item status. Examine costume fit on cast members and sketch or write notes for alterations. Inventory stock in order to determine types and conditions of available costuming. Monitor, maintain, and secure inventories of costumes, wigs, and makeup, providing keys or access to assigned directors, costume designers, and wardrobe mistresses/masters. Provide assistance to cast members in wearing costumes or assign cast dressers to assist specific cast members with costume changes. Return borrowed or rented items when productions are complete and return other items to storage. Design and construct costumes or send them to tailors for construction, major repairs, or alterations. Direct the work of wardrobe crews during dress rehearsals and performances. Participate in the hiring, training, scheduling, and supervision of alteration workers. Provide managers with budget recommendations and take responsibility for budgetary line items related to costumes, storage, and makeup needs. Purchase, rent, or requisition costumes and other wardrobe necessities. Recommend vendors and monitor their work. Review scripts or other production information in order to determine a story's locale and period as well as the number of characters and required costumes. Study books, pictures, and examples of period clothing in order to determine styles worn during specific periods in history. **SKILLS—Management of Material Resources:** Obtaining and seeing to the appropriate use of equipment, facilities, and materials needed to do certain work. **Management of Financial Resources:** Determining how money will be spent to get the work done and accounting for these expenditures. **Repairing:** Repairing machines or systems by using the needed tools. **GOE—Interest Area:** 03. Arts and Communication. **Work Group:** 03.06. Drama. **Other Jobs in This Work Group:** Actors; Directors—Stage, Motion Pictures, Television, and Radio; Makeup Artists, Theatrical and Performance; Public Address System and Other Announcers; Radio and Television Announcers. **PERSONALITY TYPE:** Artistic.

EDUCATION/TRAINING PROGRAM(S)—No data available. **RELATED KNOWLEDGE/COURSES—Fine Arts:** Knowledge of the theory and techniques required to compose, produce, and perform works of music, dance, the visual arts, drama, and sculpture. **Design:** Knowledge of design techniques, tools, and principles involved in production of precision technical plans, blueprints, drawings, and models. **Sociology and Anthropology:** Knowledge of group behavior and dynamics, societal trends and influences, human migrations, ethnicity, and cultures and their history and origins. **Geography:** Knowledge of principles and methods for describing the features of land, sea, and air masses, including their physical characteristics; locations; interrelationships; and distribution of plant, animal, and human life. **History and Archeology:** Knowledge of historical events and their causes, indicators, and effects on civilizations and cultures.

Counseling Psychologists

- Education/Training Required: Master's degree
- Annual Earnings: $54,950
- Growth: 24.4%
- Annual Job Openings: 17,000
- Self-Employed: 25.4%
- Part-Time: 27.2%

Assess and evaluate individuals' problems through the use of case history, interview, and observation and provide individual or group counseling services to assist individuals in achieving more effective personal, social, educational, and vocational development and adjustment. Advise clients on how they could be helped by counseling. Analyze data such as interview notes, test results, and reference manuals in order to identify symptoms and to diagnose the nature of clients' problems. Collect information about individuals or clients, using interviews, case histories, observational techniques, and other assessment methods. Counsel individuals, groups, or families to help them understand problems, define goals, and develop realistic action plans. Develop therapeutic and treatment plans based on clients' interests, abilities, and needs. Evaluate the results of counseling methods to determine the reliability and validity of treatments. Select, administer, and interpret psychological tests to assess intelligence, aptitudes, abilities, or interests. Consult with other professionals to discuss therapies, treatments, counseling resources, or techniques and to share occupational information. Refer clients to specialists or to other institutions for non-counseling treatment of problems. Conduct research to develop or improve diagnostic or therapeutic counseling techniques. Provide consulting services to schools, social service agencies, and businesses. **SKILLS—Social Perceptiveness:** Being aware of others' reactions and understanding why they react as they do. **Active Listening:** Giving full attention to what other people are saying, taking time to understand the points being made, asking questions as appropriate, and not interrupting at inappropriate times. **Learning Strategies:** Selecting and using training/instructional methods and procedures appropriate for the situation when

C

learning or teaching new things. **Reading Comprehension:** Understanding written sentences and paragraphs in work-related documents. **Critical Thinking:** Using logic and reasoning to identify the strengths and weaknesses of alternative solutions, conclusions, or approaches to problems. **Persuasion:** Persuading others to change their minds or behavior. **Active Learning:** Understanding the implications of new information for both current and future problem-solving and decision-making. **Science:** Using scientific rules and methods to solve problems. **GOE—Interest Area:** 10. Human Service. **Work Group:** 10.01. Counseling and Social Work. **Other Jobs in This Work Group:** Child, Family, and School Social Workers; Clinical Psychologists; Marriage and Family Therapists; Medical and Public Health Social Workers; Mental Health and Substance Abuse Social Workers; Mental Health Counselors; Probation Officers and Correctional Treatment Specialists; Rehabilitation Counselors; Residential Advisors; Social and Human Service Assistants; Substance Abuse and Behavioral Disorder Counselors. **PERSONALITY TYPE:** Social.

EDUCATION/TRAINING PROGRAM(S)—Clinical Child Psychology; Clinical Psychology; Counseling Psychology; Developmental and Child Psychology; Psychoanalysis and Psychotherapy; Psychology, General; School Psychology. **RELATED KNOWLEDGE/COURSES—Therapy and Counseling:** Knowledge of principles, methods, and procedures for diagnosis, treatment, and rehabilitation of physical and mental dysfunctions and for career counseling and guidance. **Psychology:** Knowledge of human behavior and performance; individual differences in ability, personality, and interests; learning and motivation; psychological research methods; and the assessment and treatment of behavioral and affective disorders. **Sociology and Anthropology:** Knowledge of group behavior and dynamics, societal trends and influences, human migrations, ethnicity, and cultures and their history and origins. **Philosophy and Theology:** Knowledge of different philosophical systems and religions. This includes their basic principles, values, ethics, ways of thinking, customs, and practices and their impact on human culture. **Mathematics:** Knowledge of arithmetic, algebra, geometry, calculus, and statistics and their applications. **Education and Training:** Knowledge of principles and methods for curriculum and training design, teaching and instruction for individuals and groups, and the measurement of training effects.

Counter and Rental Clerks

- Education/Training Required: Short-term on-the-job training
- Annual Earnings: $18,280
- Growth: 26.3%
- Annual Job Openings: 144,000
- Self-Employed: 1.3%
- Part-Time: 35.9%

Receive orders for repairs, rentals, and services. May describe available options, compute cost, and accept payment. Compute charges for merchandise or services and receive payments. Prepare merchandise for display or for purchase or rental. Recommend and provide advice on a wide variety of products and services. Answer telephones to provide information and receive orders. Greet customers and discuss the type, quality, and quantity of merchandise sought for rental. Keep records of transactions and of the number of customers entering an establishment. Prepare rental forms, obtaining customer signature and other information, such as required licenses. Receive, examine, and tag articles to be altered, cleaned, stored, or repaired. Inspect and adjust rental items to meet needs of customer. Explain rental fees, policies, and procedures. Reserve items for requested times and keep records of items rented. Receive orders for services such as rentals, repairs, dry cleaning, and storage. Rent items, arrange for provision of services to customers, and accept returns. Provide information about rental items, such as availability, operation, or description. Advise customers on use and care of merchandise. **SKILLS—Instructing:** Teaching others how to do something. **Service Orientation:** Actively looking for ways to help people. **GOE—Interest Area:** 14. Retail and Wholesale Sales and Service. **Work Group:** 14.06. Customer Service. **Other Jobs in This Work Group:** Adjustment Clerks; Cashiers; Customer Service Representatives, Utilities; Gaming Change Persons and Booth Cashiers; Order Clerks; Receptionists and Information Clerks. **PERSONALITY TYPE:** Conventional.

EDUCATION/TRAINING PROGRAM(S)—Selling Skills and Sales Operations. **RELATED KNOWLEDGE/COURSES—Food Production:** Knowledge of techniques and equipment for planting, growing, and harvesting food products (both plant and animal) for consumption, including storage/handling techniques. **Administration and Management:** Knowledge of business and management principles involved in strategic planning, resource allocation, human resources modeling, leadership technique, production methods, and coordination of people and resources. **Sales and Marketing:** Knowledge of principles and methods for showing, promoting, and selling products or services. This includes marketing strategy and tactics, product demonstrations, sales techniques, and sales control systems. **Personnel and Human Resources:** Knowledge of principles and procedures for personnel recruitment, selection, training, compensation and benefits, labor relations and negotiation, and personnel information systems. **Clerical Practices:** Knowledge of administrative and clerical procedures and systems such as word processing, managing files and records, stenography and transcription, designing forms, and other office procedures and terminology. **Mathematics:** Knowledge of arithmetic, algebra, geometry, calculus, and statistics and their applications. **English Language:** Knowledge of the structure and content of the English language, including the meaning and spelling of words, rules of composition, and grammar.

Counter Attendants, Cafeteria, Food Concession, and Coffee Shop

- ◎ Education/Training Required: Short-term on-the-job training
- ◎ Annual Earnings: $15,660
- ◎ Growth: 16.7%
- ◎ Annual Job Openings: 190,000
- ◎ Self-Employed: 0.9%
- ◎ Part-Time: 65.8%

Serve food to diners at counter or from a steam table. Scrub and polish counters, steam tables, and other equipment and clean glasses, dishes, and fountain equipment. Serve food, beverages, or desserts to customers in such settings as take-out counters of restaurants or lunchrooms, business or industrial establishments, hotel rooms, and cars. Replenish foods at serving stations. Take customers' orders and write ordered items on tickets, giving ticket stubs to customers when needed to identify filled orders. Prepare food such as sandwiches, salads, and ice cream dishes, using standard formulas or following directions. Wrap menu items such as sandwiches, hot entrees, and desserts for serving or for takeout. Prepare bills for food, using cash registers, calculators, or adding machines, and accept payment and make change. Deliver orders to kitchens and pick up and serve food when it is ready. Serve salads, vegetables, meat, breads, and cocktails; ladle soups and sauces; portion desserts; and fill beverage cups and glasses. Add relishes and garnishes to food orders according to instructions. Carve meat. Order items needed to replenish supplies. Set up dining areas for meals and clear them following meals. Brew coffee and tea and fill containers with requested beverages. Balance receipts and payments in cash registers. Arrange reservations for patrons of dining establishments. **SKILLS—Social Perceptiveness:** Being aware of others' reactions and understanding why they react as they do. **Management of Personnel Resources:** Motivating, developing, and directing people as they work, identifying the best people for the job. **Negotiation:** Bringing others together and trying to reconcile differences. **Equipment Maintenance:** Performing routine maintenance on equipment and determining when and what kind of maintenance is needed. **Service Orientation:** Actively looking for ways to help people. **Troubleshooting:** Determining causes of operating errors and deciding what to do about them. **Repairing:** Repairing machines or systems by using the needed tools. **Learning Strategies:** Selecting and using training/instructional methods and procedures appropriate for the situation when learning or teaching new things. **GOE—Interest Area:** 09. Hospitality, Tourism, and Recreation. **Work Group:** 09.05. Food and Beverage Service. **Other Jobs in This Work Group:** Bartenders; Combined Food Preparation and Serving Workers, Including Fast Food; Dining Room and Cafeteria Attendants and Bartender Helpers; Food Servers, Nonrestaurant; Hosts and Hostesses, Restaurant, Lounge, and Coffee Shop; Waiters and Waitresses. **PERSONALITY TYPE:** Social.

EDUCATION/TRAINING PROGRAM(S)—Food Service, Waiter/Waitress, and Dining Room Management/Manager. **RELATED KNOWLEDGE/COURSES—Food Production:** Knowledge of techniques and equipment for planting, growing, and harvesting food products (both plant and animal) for consumption, including storage/handling techniques.

Sales and Marketing: Knowledge of principles and methods for showing, promoting, and selling products or services. This includes marketing strategy and tactics, product demonstrations, sales techniques, and sales control systems. **Customer and Personal Service:** Knowledge of principles and processes for providing customer and personal services. This includes customer needs assessment, meeting quality standards for services, and evaluation of customer satisfaction. **Psychology:** Knowledge of human behavior and performance; individual differences in ability, personality, and interests; learning and motivation; psychological research methods; and the assessment and treatment of behavioral and affective disorders. **Public Safety and Security:** Knowledge of relevant equipment, policies, procedures, and strategies to promote effective local, state, or national security operations for the protection of people, data, property, and institutions. **Administration and Management:** Knowledge of business and management principles involved in strategic planning, resource allocation, human resources modeling, leadership technique, production methods, and coordination of people and resources. **Chemistry:** Knowledge of the chemical composition, structure, and properties of substances and of the chemical processes and transformations that they undergo. This includes uses of chemicals and their danger signs, production techniques, and disposal methods.

Court Clerks

- ◎ Education/Training Required: Short-term on-the-job training
- ◎ Annual Earnings: $28,430
- ◎ Growth: 12.3%
- ◎ Annual Job Openings: 14,000
- ◎ Self-Employed: 2.6%
- ◎ Part-Time: 8.3%

Perform clerical duties in court of law; prepare docket of cases to be called; secure information for judges; and contact witnesses, attorneys, and litigants to obtain information for court. Prepare dockets or calendars of cases to be called, using typewriters or computers. Record case dispositions, court orders, and arrangements made for payment of court fees. Answer inquiries from the general public regarding judicial procedures, court appearances, trial dates, adjournments, outstanding warrants, summonses, subpoenas, witness fees, and payment of fines. Prepare and issue orders of the court, including probation orders, release documentation, sentencing information, and summonses. Prepare documents recording the outcomes of court proceedings. Instruct parties about timing of court appearances. Explain procedures or forms to parties in cases or to the general public. Search files and contact witnesses, attorneys, and litigants in order to obtain information for the court. Follow procedures to secure courtrooms and exhibits such as money, drugs, and weapons. Amend indictments when necessary and endorse indictments with pertinent information. Read charges and related information to the court and, if necessary, record defendants' pleas. Swear in jury members, interpreters, witnesses, and defendants. Collect court fees or fines and record amounts collected. Direct support staff in handling of paperwork processed by clerks' offices. Prepare and mark all applicable court exhibits and evidence. Examine legal documents submitted to courts for adherence to laws or court procedures. Record court proceedings, using recording equipment, or record minutes of court proceedings, using stenotype machines or shorthand. Prepare courtrooms with paper, pens, water, easels, and electronic equipment and ensure that recording equipment is working. Conduct roll calls and poll jurors. Open courts, calling them to order and announcing judges. Meet with judges, lawyers, parole officers, police, and social agency officials in order to coordinate the functions of the court. SKILLS—**Instructing:** Teaching others how to do something. **Active Listening:** Giving full attention to what other people are saying, taking time to understand the points being made, asking questions as appropriate, and not interrupting at inappropriate times. **Service Orientation:** Actively looking for ways to help people. **Coordination:** Adjusting actions in relation to others' actions. **Learning Strategies:** Selecting and using training/instructional methods and procedures appropriate for the situation when learning or teaching new things. **Critical Thinking:** Using logic and reasoning to identify the strengths and weaknesses of alternative solutions, conclusions, or approaches to problems. **Writing:** Communicating effectively in writing as appropriate for the needs of the audience. **Time Management:** Managing one's own time and the time of others. GOE—**Interest Area:** 07. Government and Public Administration. **Work Group:** 07.04. Public Administration Clerical Support. **Other Jobs in This Work Group:** Court Reporters; License Clerks; Municipal Clerks. **PERSONALITY TYPE:** Conventional.

EDUCATION/TRAINING PROGRAM(S)—General Office Occupations and Clerical Services. **RELATED KNOWLEDGE/COURSES—Clerical Practices:** Knowledge of administrative and clerical procedures and systems such as word processing, managing files and records, stenography and transcription, designing forms, and other office procedures and terminology. **Customer and Personal Service:** Knowledge of principles and processes for providing customer and personal services. This includes customer needs assessment, meeting quality standards for services, and evaluation of customer satisfaction. **Law and Government:** Knowledge of laws, legal codes, court procedures, precedents, government regulations, executive orders, agency rules, and the democratic political process. **Computers and Electronics:** Knowledge of circuit boards, processors, chips, electronic equipment, and computer hardware and software, including applications and programming. **English Language:** Knowledge of the structure and content of the English language, including the meaning and spelling of words, rules of composition, and grammar.

Court Reporters

◎ Education/Training Required: Postsecondary vocational training
◎ Annual Earnings: $42,920
◎ Growth: 12.7%
◎ Annual Job Openings: 2,000
◎ Self-Employed: 11.0%
◎ Part-Time: 12.6%

Use verbatim methods and equipment to capture, store, retrieve, and transcribe pretrial and trial proceedings or other information. Includes stenocaptioners who operate computerized stenographic captioning equipment to provide captions of live or prerecorded broadcasts for hearing-impaired viewers. Ask speakers to clarify inaudible statements. File a legible transcript of records of a court case with the court clerk's office. Provide transcripts of proceedings upon request of judges, lawyers, or the public. Record verbatim proceedings of courts, legislative assemblies, committee meetings, and other proceedings, using computerized recording equipment, electronic stenograph machines, or stenomasks. Respond to requests during court sessions to read portions of the proceedings already recorded. Transcribe recorded proceedings

in accordance with established formats. Verify accuracy of transcripts by checking copies against original records of proceedings and accuracy of rulings by checking with judges. Caption news, emergency broadcasts, sporting events, and other programming for television networks or cable stations. File and store shorthand notes of court session. Record depositions and other proceedings for attorneys. Record symbols on computer disks or CD-ROM and then translate and display them as text in computer-aided transcription process. Take notes in shorthand or use a stenotype or shorthand machine that prints letters on a paper tape. **SKILLS**—No data available. **GOE**—**Interest Area:** 07. Government and Public Administration. **Work Group:** 07.04. Public Administration Clerical Support. **Other Jobs in This Work Group:** Court Clerks; License Clerks; Municipal Clerks. **PERSONALITY TYPE:** No data available.

EDUCATION/TRAINING PROGRAM(S)—Court Reporting/Court Reporter. **RELATED KNOWLEDGE/COURSES**—No data available.

Crane and Tower Operators

◎ Education/Training Required: Moderate-term on-the-job training
◎ Annual Earnings: $37,410
◎ Growth: 10.8%
◎ Annual Job Openings: 5,000
◎ Self-Employed: 1.9%
◎ Part-Time: 1.2%

Operate mechanical boom and cable or tower and cable equipment to lift and move materials, machines, or products in many directions. Determine load weights and check them against lifting capacities in order to prevent overload. Direct helpers engaged in placing blocking and outrigging under cranes. Load and unload bundles from trucks and move containers to storage bins, using moving equipment. Move levers, depress foot pedals, and turn dials to operate cranes, cherry pickers, electromagnets, or other moving equipment for lifting, moving, and placing loads. Review daily work and delivery schedules to determine orders, sequences of deliveries, and special loading instructions. Weigh bundles, using floor scales, and record weights for company records. Clean, lubricate, and maintain mechanisms such as cables, pulleys, and grappling devices, making repairs as necessary. Direct truck drivers backing vehicles into loading bays and cover, uncover, and secure loads for delivery. Inspect and adjust crane mechanisms and lifting accessories in order to prevent malfunctions and damage. Inspect bundle packaging for conformance to regulations and customer requirements and remove and batch packaging tickets. Inspect cables and grappling devices for wear and install or replace cables as needed. **SKILLS— Operation and Control:** Controlling operations of equipment or systems. **Repairing:** Repairing machines or systems by using the needed tools. **Installation:** Installing equipment, machines, wiring, or programs to meet specifications. **Operation Monitoring:** Watching gauges, dials, or other indicators to make sure a machine is working properly. **Equipment Maintenance:** Performing routine maintenance on equipment and determining when and what kind of maintenance is needed. **GOE—Interest Area:** 02. Architecture and Construction. **Work Group:** 02.04. Construction Crafts. **Other Jobs in This Work Group:** Boat Builders and Shipwrights; Boilermakers; Brattice Builders; Brickmasons and Blockmasons; Carpet Installers; Ceiling Tile Installers; Cement Masons and Concrete Finishers; Commercial Divers; Construction Carpenters; Dragline Operators; Drywall Installers; Electricians; Fence Erectors; Floor Layers, Except Carpet, Wood, and Hard Tiles; Floor Sanders and Finishers; Glaziers; Grader, Bulldozer, and Scraper Operators; Hazardous Materials Removal Workers; Insulation Workers, Floor, Ceiling, and Wall; Insulation Workers, Mechanical; Manufactured Building and Mobile Home Installers; Operating Engineers; Painters, Construction and Maintenance; Paperhangers; Paving, Surfacing, and Tamping Equipment Operators; Pile-Driver Operators; Pipe Fitters; Pipelayers; Pipelaying Fitters; Plasterers and Stucco Masons; Plumbers; Rail-Track Laying and Maintenance Equipment Operators; Refractory Materials Repairers, Except Brickmasons; Reinforcing Iron and Rebar Workers; Riggers; Roofers; Rough Carpenters; Security and Fire Alarm Systems Installers; Segmental Pavers; Sheet Metal Workers; Ship Carpenters and Joiners; Stone Cutters and Carvers; Stonemasons; Structural Iron and Steel Workers; Tapers; Terrazzo Workers and Finishers; Tile and Marble Setters. **PERSONALITY TYPE:** Realistic.

EDUCATION/TRAINING PROGRAM(S)—Construction/Heavy Equipment/Earthmoving Equipment Operation; Mobil Crane Operation/Operator. **RELATED KNOWLEDGE/COURSES—Mechanical Devices:** Knowledge of machines and tools, including their designs, uses, repair, and maintenance. **Transportation:** Knowledge of principles and methods for moving people or goods by air, rail, sea, or road, including the relative costs and benefits. **Building and Construction:** Knowledge of the materials, methods, and tools involved in the construction or repair of houses, buildings, or other structures such as highways and roads.

Creative Writers

- ◎ Education/Training Required: Bachelor's degree
- ◎ Annual Earnings: $44,350
- ◎ Growth: 16.1%
- ◎ Annual Job Openings: 23,000
- ◎ Self-Employed: 67.9%
- ◎ Part-Time: 24.2%

Create original written works, such as plays or prose, for publication or performance. Writes fiction or nonfiction prose work, such as short story, novel, biography, article, descriptive or critical analysis, or essay. Writes play or script for moving pictures or television, based on original ideas or adapted from fictional, historical, or narrative sources. Organizes material for project, plans arrangement or outline, and writes synopsis. Collaborates with other writers on specific projects. Confers with client, publisher, or producer to discuss development changes or revisions. Conducts research to obtain factual information and authentic detail, utilizing sources such as newspaper accounts, diaries, and interviews. Reviews, submits for approval, and revises written material to meet personal standards and satisfy needs of client, publisher, director, or producer. Selects subject or theme for writing project based on personal interest and writing specialty or assignment from publisher, client, producer, or director. Develops factors, such as theme, plot, characterization, psychological analysis, historical environment, action, and dialogue, to create material. Writes humorous material for publication or performance, such as comedy routines, gags, comedy shows, or scripts for entertainers. **SKILLS—Writing:** Communicating effectively in writing as appropriate for the needs of the audience. **Reading Comprehension:** Understanding written sentences and paragraphs in work-related documents. **Coordination:** Adjusting actions in relation to others' actions. **Critical Thinking:** Using logic and reasoning to identify the strengths and weaknesses of alternative solutions, conclusions, or approaches to problems. **Complex Problem Solving:** Identifying complex problems and reviewing related information to develop and evaluate options and implement solutions. **Social Perceptiveness:** Being aware of others' reactions and understanding why they react as they do. **Systems Analysis:** Determining how a system should work and how changes in conditions, operations, and the environment will affect outcomes. **Monitoring:** Monitoring or assessing your performance or that of other individuals or organizations to make improvements or take corrective action. **Negotiation:** Bringing others together and trying to reconcile differences. **GOE—Interest Area:** 03. Arts and Communication. **Work Group:** 03.02. Writing and Editing. **Other Jobs in This Work Group:** Copy Writers; Editors; Poets and Lyricists; Technical Writers. **PERSONALITY TYPE:** Artistic.

EDUCATION/TRAINING PROGRAM(S)— Broadcast Journalism; Business/Corporate Communications; Communication Studies/Speech Communication and Rhetoric; Communication, Journalism, and Related Programs, Other; Creative Writing; English Composition; Family and Consumer Sciences/Human Sciences Communication; Journalism; Mass Communication/Media Studies; Playwriting and Screenwriting; Technical and Business Writing. **RELATED KNOWLEDGE/COURSES— Communications and Media:** Knowledge of media production, communication, and dissemination techniques and methods. This includes alternative ways to inform and entertain via written, oral, and visual media. **English Language:** Knowledge of the structure and content of the English language, including the meaning and spelling of words, rules of composition, and grammar. **Fine Arts:** Knowledge of the theory and techniques required to compose, produce, and perform works of music, dance, the visual arts, drama, and sculpture. **Sociology and Anthropology:** Knowledge of group behavior and dynamics, societal trends and influences, human migrations, ethnicity, and cultures and their history and origins. **Computers and Electronics:** Knowledge of circuit boards, processors,

chips, electronic equipment, and computer hardware and software, including applications and programming.

Credit Analysts

- Education/Training Required: Bachelor's degree
- Annual Earnings: $47,260
- Growth: 18.7%
- Annual Job Openings: 9,000
- Self-Employed: 0%
- Part-Time: 4.1%

Analyze current credit data and financial statements of individuals or firms to determine the degree of risk involved in extending credit or lending money. Prepare reports with this credit information for use in decision-making. Analyze credit data and financial statements to determine the degree of risk involved in extending credit or lending money. Prepare reports that include the degree of risk involved in extending credit or lending money. Evaluate customer records and recommend payment plans based on earnings, savings data, payment history, and purchase activity. Confer with credit association and other business representatives to exchange credit information. Complete loan applications, including credit analyses and summaries of loan requests, and submit to loan committees for approval. Generate financial ratios, using computer programs, to evaluate customers' financial status. Review individual or commercial customer files to identify and select delinquent accounts for collection. Compare liquidity, profitability, and credit histories of establishments being evaluated with those of similar establishments in the same industries and geographic locations. Consult with customers to resolve complaints and verify financial and credit transactions. Analyze financial data such as income growth, quality of management, and market share to determine expected profitability of loans. **SKILLS—Speaking:** Talking to others to convey information effectively. **Writing:** Communicating effectively in writing as appropriate for the needs of the audience. **Negotiation:** Bringing others together and trying to reconcile differences. **Instructing:** Teaching others how to do something. **Active Listening:** Giving full attention to what other people are saying, taking time to understand the points being made, asking questions as appropriate, and not interrupting at inappropriate times. **Social Perceptiveness:** Being aware of others' reactions and understanding why they react as they do. **Operations Analysis:** Analyzing needs and product requirements to create a design. **Judgment and Decision Making:** Considering the relative costs and benefits of potential actions to choose the most appropriate one. **GOE—Interest Area:** 06. Finance and Insurance. **Work Group:** 06.02. Finance/Insurance Investigation and Analysis. **Other Jobs in This Work Group:** Appraisers, Real Estate; Assessors; Claims Examiners, Property and Casualty Insurance; Cost Estimators; Financial Analysts; Insurance Adjusters, Examiners, and Investigators; Insurance Appraisers, Auto Damage; Insurance Underwriters; Loan Counselors; Loan Officers; Market Research Analysts; Survey Researchers. **PERSONALITY TYPE:** Conventional.

EDUCATION/TRAINING PROGRAM(S)— Accounting; Credit Management; Finance, General. **RELATED KNOWLEDGE/COURSES—Economics and Accounting:** Knowledge of economic and accounting principles and practices, the financial markets, banking, and the analysis and reporting of financial data. **Clerical Practices:** Knowledge of administrative and clerical procedures and systems such as word processing, managing files and records, stenography and transcription, designing forms, and other office procedures and terminology. **Mathematics:** Knowledge of arithmetic, algebra, geometry, calculus, and statistics and their applications. **Customer and Personal Service:** Knowledge of principles and processes for providing customer and personal services. This includes customer needs assessment, meeting quality standards for services, and evaluation of customer satisfaction. **Administration and Management:** Knowledge of business and management principles involved in strategic planning, resource allocation, human resources modeling, leadership technique, production methods, and coordination of people and resources. **Law and Government:** Knowledge of laws, legal codes, court procedures, precedents, government regulations, executive orders, agency rules, and the democratic political process.

Criminal Investigators and Special Agents

- Education/Training Required: Work experience in a related occupation
- Annual Earnings: $53,990
- Growth: 22.4%
- Annual Job Openings: 11,000
- Self-Employed: 0%
- Part-Time: 0.5%

Investigate alleged or suspected criminal violations of federal, state, or local laws to determine if evidence is sufficient to recommend prosecution. Determine scope, timing, and direction of investigations. Develop relationships with informants in order to obtain information related to cases. Examine records in order to locate links in chains of evidence or information. Identify case issues and evidence needed based on analysis of charges, complaints, or allegations of law violations. Obtain and use search and arrest warrants. Obtain and verify evidence by interviewing and observing suspects and witnesses or by analyzing records. Perform undercover assignments and maintain surveillance, including monitoring authorized wiretaps. Prepare reports that detail investigation findings. Analyze evidence in laboratories or in the field. Collaborate with other authorities on activities such as surveillance, transcription, and research. Collaborate with other offices and agencies in order to exchange information and coordinate activities. Collect and record physical information about arrested suspects, including fingerprints, height and weight measurements, and photographs. Compare crime scene fingerprints with those from suspects or fingerprint files to identify perpetrators, using computers. Investigate organized crime, public corruption, financial crime, copyright infringement, civil rights violations, bank robbery, extortion, kidnapping, and other violations of federal or state statutes. Manage security programs designed to protect personnel, facilities, and information. Record evidence and documents, using equipment such as cameras and photocopy machines. Search for and collect evidence such as fingerprints, using investigative equipment. Serve subpoenas or other official papers. Testify before grand juries concerning criminal activity investigations. Administer counter-terrorism and counter-narcotics reward programs. Issue security clearances. Provide protection for individuals such as government leaders, political candidates and visiting foreign dignitaries. Train foreign civilian police. **SKILLS—Social Perceptiveness:** Being aware of others' reactions and understanding why they react as they do. **Speaking:** Talking to others to convey information effectively. **Active Listening:** Giving full attention to what other people are saying, taking time to understand the points being made, asking questions as appropriate, and not interrupting at inappropriate times. **Persuasion:** Persuading others to change their minds or behavior. **Writing:** Communicating effectively in writing as appropriate for the needs of the audience. **Complex Problem Solving:** Identifying complex problems and reviewing related information to develop and evaluate options and implement solutions. **Judgment and Decision Making:** Considering the relative costs and benefits of potential actions to choose the most appropriate one. **Critical Thinking:** Using logic and reasoning to identify the strengths and weaknesses of alternative solutions, conclusions, or approaches to problems. **Coordination:** Adjusting actions in relation to others' actions. **GOE—Interest Area:** 12. Law and Public Safety. **Work Group:** 12.04. Law Enforcement and Public Safety. **Other Jobs in This Work Group:** Bailiffs; Correctional Officers and Jailers; Fire Investigators; Forensic Science Technicians; Highway Patrol Pilots; Parking Enforcement Workers; Police Detectives; Police Identification and Records Officers; Police Patrol Officers; Sheriffs and Deputy Sheriffs; Transit and Railroad Police. **PERSONALITY TYPE:** Enterprising.

EDUCATION/TRAINING PROGRAM(S)— Criminal Justice/Police Science; Criminalistics and Criminal Science. **RELATED KNOWLEDGE/ COURSES—Public Safety and Security:** Knowledge of relevant equipment, policies, procedures, and strategies to promote effective local, state, or national security operations for the protection of people, data, property, and institutions. **Law and Government:** Knowledge of laws, legal codes, court procedures, precedents, government regulations, executive orders, agency rules, and the democratic political process. **Psychology:** Knowledge of human behavior and performance; individual differences in ability, personality, and interests; learning and motivation; psychological research methods; and the assessment and treatment of behavioral and affective disorders. **Telecommunications:** Knowledge of transmission, broadcasting, switching, control, and operation of telecommunica-

tions systems. **Sociology and Anthropology:** Knowledge of group behavior and dynamics, societal trends and influences, human migrations, ethnicity, and cultures and their history and origins. **Geography:** Knowledge of principles and methods for describing the features of land, sea, and air masses, including their physical characteristics; locations; interrelationships; and distribution of plant, animal, and human life.

Criminal Justice and Law Enforcement Teachers, Postsecondary

- Education/Training Required: Master's degree
- Annual Earnings: $47,800
- Growth: 38.1%
- Annual Job Openings: 216,000
- Self-Employed: 0.3%
- Part-Time: 27.7%

Teach courses in criminal justice, corrections, and law enforcement administration. Initiate, facilitate, and moderate classroom discussions. Keep abreast of developments in their field by reading current literature, talking with colleagues, and participating in professional conferences. Evaluate and grade students' class work, assignments, and papers. Compile, administer, and grade examinations or assign this work to others. Prepare and deliver lectures to undergraduate and/or graduate students on topics such as criminal law, defensive policing, and investigation techniques. Prepare course materials such as syllabi, homework assignments, and handouts. Conduct research in a particular field of knowledge and publish findings in professional journals, books, and/or electronic media. Plan, evaluate, and revise curricula, course content, and course materials and methods of instruction. Supervise undergraduate and/or graduate teaching, internship, and research work. Maintain student attendance records, grades, and other required records. Select and obtain materials and supplies such as textbooks. Advise students on academic and vocational curricula and on career issues. Maintain regularly scheduled office hours in order to advise and assist students. Collaborate with colleagues to address teaching and research issues. Write grant proposals to procure external research funding. Serve on academic or administrative committees that deal with institutional policies, departmental matters, and academic issues. Compile bibliographies of specialized materials for outside reading assignments. Participate in student recruitment, registration, and placement activities. Provide professional consulting services to government and/or industry. Perform administrative duties such as serving as department head. **SKILLS—Instructing:** Teaching others how to do something. **Critical Thinking:** Using logic and reasoning to identify the strengths and weaknesses of alternative solutions, conclusions, or approaches to problems. **Writing:** Communicating effectively in writing as appropriate for the needs of the audience. **Active Learning:** Understanding the implications of new information for both current and future problem-solving and decision-making. **Persuasion:** Persuading others to change their minds or behavior. **Learning Strategies:** Selecting and using training/instructional methods and procedures appropriate for the situation when learning or teaching new things. **Reading Comprehension:** Understanding written sentences and paragraphs in work-related documents. **Time Management:** Managing one's own time and the time of others. **GOE—Interest Area:** 05. Education and Training. **Work Group:** 05.03. Postsecondary and Adult Teaching and Instructing. **Other Jobs in This Work Group:** Adult Literacy, Remedial Education, and GED Teachers and Instructors; Agricultural Sciences Teachers, Postsecondary; Anthropology and Archeology Teachers, Postsecondary; Architecture Teachers, Postsecondary; Area, Ethnic, and Cultural Studies Teachers, Postsecondary; Art, Drama, and Music Teachers, Postsecondary; Atmospheric, Earth, Marine, and Space Sciences Teachers, Postsecondary; Biological Science Teachers, Postsecondary; Business Teachers, Postsecondary; Chemistry Teachers, Postsecondary; Communications Teachers, Postsecondary; Computer Science Teachers, Postsecondary; Economics Teachers, Postsecondary; Education Teachers, Postsecondary; Engineering Teachers, Postsecondary; English Language and Literature Teachers, Postsecondary; Environmental Science Teachers, Postsecondary; Farm and Home Management Advisors; Foreign Language and Literature Teachers, Postsecondary; Forestry and Conservation Science Teachers, Postsecondary; Geography Teachers, Postsecondary; Graduate Teaching Assistants; Health Specialties Teachers, Postsecondary; History Teachers, Postsecondary; Home Economics Teachers, Postsecondary; Law Teachers, Postsecondary; Library Science Teachers, Postsecondary; Mathematical Science Teachers, Postsecondary; Nursing Instructors and Teachers, Postsecondary; Philosophy and Religion Teachers, Postsecondary; Physics Teachers, Postsecondary; Political Science Teachers, Postsecondary; Psychology Teachers, Postsecondary; Recreation and Fitness Studies Teachers, Postsecondary; Self-Enrichment Education Teachers; Social Work Teachers, Postsecondary; Sociology Teachers, Postsecondary; Vocational Education Teachers, Postsecondary. **PERSONALITY TYPE:** No data available.

EDUCATION/TRAINING PROGRAM(S)—Corrections; Corrections Administration; Corrections and Criminal Justice, Other; Criminal Justice/Law Enforcement Administration; Criminal Justice/Police Science; Criminal Justice/Safety Studies; Criminalistics and Criminal Science; Forensic Science and Technology; Juvenile Corrections; Security and Loss Prevention Services; Teacher Education and Professional Development, Specific Subject Areas, Other. **RELATED KNOWLEDGE/COURSES—Sociology and Anthropology:** Knowledge of group behavior and dynamics, societal trends and influences, human migrations, ethnicity, and cultures and their history and origins. **Philosophy and Theology:** Knowledge of different philosophical systems and religions. This includes their basic principles, values, ethics, ways of thinking, customs, and practices and their impact on human culture. **Law and Government:** Knowledge of laws, legal codes, court procedures, precedents, government regulations, executive orders, agency rules, and the democratic political process. **Education and Training:** Knowledge of principles and methods for curriculum and training design, teaching and instruction for individuals and groups, and the measurement of training effects. **English Language:** Knowledge of the structure and content of the English language, including the meaning and spelling of words, rules of composition, and grammar. **History and Archeology:** Knowledge of historical events and their causes, indicators, and effects on civilizations and cultures.

Curators

- Education/Training Required: Master's degree
- Annual Earnings: $43,620
- Growth: 17.0%
- Annual Job Openings: 2,000
- Self-Employed: 3.4%
- Part-Time: 11.8%

Administer affairs of museum and conduct research programs. Direct instructional, research, and public service activities of institution. Plan and organize the acquisition, storage, and exhibition of collections and related materials, including the selection of exhibition themes and designs. Develop and maintain an institution's registration, cataloging, and basic record-keeping systems, using computer databases. Provide information from the institution's holdings to other curators and to the public. Inspect premises to assess the need for repairs and to ensure that climate and pest-control issues are addressed. Train and supervise curatorial, fiscal, technical, research, and clerical staff, as well as volunteers or interns. Negotiate and authorize purchase, sale, exchange, or loan of collections. Plan and conduct special research projects in area of interest or expertise. Conduct or organize tours, workshops, and instructional sessions to acquaint individuals with an institution's facilities and materials. Confer with the board of directors to formulate and interpret policies, to determine budget requirements, and to plan overall operations. Attend meetings, conventions, and civic events to promote use of institution's services, to seek financing, and to maintain community alliances. Schedule events and organize details including refreshment, entertainment, decorations, and the collection of any fees. Write and review grant proposals, journal articles, institutional reports, and publicity materials. Study, examine, and test acquisitions to authenticate their origin, composition, and history and to assess their current value. Arrange insurance coverage for objects on loan or for special exhibits and recommend changes in coverage for the entire collection. **SKILLS—Management of Financial Resources:** Determining how money will be spent to get the work done and accounting for these expenditures. **Management of Personnel Resources:** Motivating, developing, and directing people as they work, identifying the best people for the job. **Time Management:** Managing one's own time and the time of others. **Persuasion:** Persuading others to change their minds or behavior. **Writing:** Communicating effectively in writing as appropriate for the needs of the audience. **Negotiation:** Bringing others together and trying to reconcile differences. **Service Orientation:** Actively looking for ways to help people. **Speaking:** Talking to others to convey information effectively. **GOE—Interest Area:** 05. Education and Training. **Work Group:** 05.05. Archival and Museum Services. **Other Jobs in This Work Group:** Archivists; Audio-Visual Collections Specialists; Museum Technicians and Conservators. **PERSONALITY TYPE:** Artistic.

EDUCATION/TRAINING PROGRAM(S)—Art History, Criticism, and Conservation; Museology/Museum Studies; Public/Applied History and Archival Administration. RELATED KNOWLEDGE/COURSES—Clerical Practices: Knowledge of administrative and clerical procedures and systems such as word processing, managing files and records, stenography and transcription, designing forms, and other office procedures and terminology. **History and Archeology:** Knowledge of historical events and their causes, indicators, and effects on civilizations and cultures. **Fine Arts:** Knowledge of the theory and techniques required to compose, produce, and perform works of music, dance, the visual arts, drama, and sculpture. **Sociology and Anthropology:** Knowledge of group behavior and dynamics, societal trends and influences, human migrations, ethnicity, and cultures and their history and origins. **Philosophy and Theology:** Knowledge of different philosophical systems and religions. This includes their basic principles, values, ethics, ways of thinking, customs, and practices and their impact on human culture. **Education and Training:** Knowledge of principles and methods for curriculum and training design, teaching and instruction for individuals and groups, and the measurement of training effects.

Customer Service Representatives, Utilities

- Education/Training Required: Moderate-term on-the-job training
- Annual Earnings: $27,020
- Growth: 24.3%
- Annual Job Openings: 419,000
- Self-Employed: 0.5%
- Part-Time: 14.8%

Interview applicants for water, gas, electric, or telephone service. Talk with customer by phone or in person and receive orders for installation, turn-on, discontinuance, or change in services. Confers with customer by phone or in person to receive orders for installation, turn-on, discontinuance, or change in service. Completes contract forms, prepares change of address records, and issues discontinuance orders, using computer. Determines charges for service requested and collects deposits. Solicits sale of new or additional utility services. Resolves billing or service complaints and refers grievances to designated departments for investigation. **SKILLS—Service Orientation:** Actively looking for ways to help people. **Active Listening:** Giving full attention to what other people are saying, taking time to understand the points being made, asking questions as appropriate, and not interrupting at inappropriate times. **Speaking:** Talking to others to convey information effectively. **GOE—Interest Area:** 14. Retail and Wholesale Sales and Service. **Work Group:** 14.06. Customer Service. **Other Jobs in This Work Group:** Adjustment Clerks; Cashiers; Counter and Rental Clerks; Gaming Change Persons and Booth Cashiers; Order Clerks; Receptionists and Information Clerks. **PERSONALITY TYPE:** Conventional.

EDUCATION/TRAINING PROGRAM(S)— Customer Service Support/Call Center/Teleservice Operation; Receptionist. **RELATED KNOWLEDGE/COURSES—Sales and Marketing:** Knowledge of principles and methods for showing, promoting, and selling products or services. This includes marketing strategy and tactics, product demonstrations, sales techniques, and sales control systems. **Customer and Personal Service:** Knowledge of principles and processes for providing customer and personal services. This includes customer needs assessment, meeting quality standards for services, and evaluation of customer satisfaction. **Economics and Accounting:** Knowledge of economic and accounting principles and practices, the financial markets, banking, and the analysis and reporting of financial data. **Telecommunications:** Knowledge of transmission, broadcasting, switching, control, and operation of telecommunications systems. **Clerical Practices:** Knowledge of administrative and clerical procedures and systems such as word processing, managing files and records, stenography and transcription, designing forms, and other office procedures and terminology.

Data Processing Equipment Repairers

- Education/Training Required: Postsecondary vocational training
- Annual Earnings: $35,150
- Growth: 15.1%
- Annual Job Openings: 19,000
- Self-Employed: 12.2%
- Part-Time: 8.2%

Repair, maintain, and install computer hardware such as peripheral equipment and word-processing systems. Replaces defective components and wiring. Tests faulty equipment and applies knowledge of functional operation of electronic units and systems to diagnose cause of malfunction. Aligns, adjusts, and calibrates equipment according to specifications. Calibrates testing instruments. Adjusts mechanical parts, using hand tools and soldering iron. Converses with equipment operators to ascertain problems with equipment before breakdown or cause of breakdown. Tests electronic components and circuits to locate defects, using oscilloscopes, signal generators, ammeters, and voltmeters. Maintains records of repairs, calibrations, and tests. Enters information into computer to copy program from one electronic component to another or to draw, modify, or store schematics. **SKILLS—Installation:** Installing equipment, machines, wiring, or programs to meet specifications. **Repairing:** Repairing machines or systems by using the needed tools. **Troubleshooting:** Determining causes of operating errors and deciding what to do about them. **Science:** Using scientific rules and methods to solve problems. **Equipment Maintenance:** Performing routine maintenance on equipment and determining when and what kind of maintenance is needed. **Operation Monitoring:** Watching gauges, dials, or other indicators to make sure a machine is working properly. **Quality Control Analysis:** Conducting tests and inspections of products, services, or processes to evaluate quality or performance. **Operation and Control:** Controlling operations of equipment or systems. **GOE—Interest Area:** 11. Information Technology. **Work Group:** 11.03. Digital Equipment Repair. **Other Jobs in This Work Group:** Automatic Teller Machine Servicers; Coin, Vending, and Amusement Machine Servicers and Repairers; Office Machine and

Cash Register Servicers. **PERSONALITY TYPE:** Realistic.

EDUCATION/TRAINING PROGRAM(S)—Business Machine Repair; Computer Installation and Repair Technology/Technician. **RELATED KNOWLEDGE/COURSES**—**Computers and Electronics:** Knowledge of circuit boards, processors, chips, electronic equipment, and computer hardware and software, including applications and programming. **Telecommunications:** Knowledge of transmission, broadcasting, switching, control, and operation of telecommunications systems. **Design:** Knowledge of design techniques, tools, and principles involved in production of precision technical plans, blueprints, drawings, and models. **Mechanical Devices:** Knowledge of machines and tools, including their designs, uses, repair, and maintenance. **Physics:** Knowledge and prediction of physical principles and laws and their interrelationships and applications to understanding fluid, material, and atmospheric dynamics and mechanical, electrical, atomic, and subatomic structures and processes. **Engineering and Technology:** Knowledge of the practical application of engineering science and technology. This includes applying principles, techniques, procedures, and equipment to the design and production of various goods and services.

Database Administrators

- ◎ Education/Training Required: Bachelor's degree
- ◎ Annual Earnings: $60,650
- ◎ Growth: 44.2%
- ◎ Annual Job Openings: 16,000
- ◎ Self-Employed: 0.6%
- ◎ Part-Time: 4.6%

Coordinate changes to computer databases. Test and implement the database, applying knowledge of database management systems. May plan, coordinate, and implement security measures to safeguard computer databases. Develop standards and guidelines to guide the use and acquisition of software and to protect vulnerable information. Modify existing databases and database management systems or direct programmers and analysts to make changes. Test programs or databases, correct errors, and make necessary modifi-

cations. Plan, coordinate, and implement security measures to safeguard information in computer files against accidental or unauthorized damage, modification, or disclosure. Approve, schedule, plan, and supervise the installation and testing of new products and improvements to computer systems, such as the installation of new databases. Train users and answer questions. Establish and calculate optimum values for database parameters, using manuals and calculator. Specify users and user access levels for each segment of database. Develop data model describing data elements and how they are used, following procedures and using pen, template, or computer software. Develop methods for integrating different products so they work properly together, such as customizing commercial databases to fit specific needs. Review project requests describing database user needs to estimate time and cost required to accomplish project. Review procedures in database management system manuals for making changes to database. Work as part of a project team to coordinate database development and determine project scope and limitations. Select and enter codes to monitor database performance and to create production database. Identify and evaluate industry trends in database systems to serve as a source of information and advice for upper management. Write and code logical and physical database descriptions and specify identifiers of database to management system or direct others in coding descriptions. Review workflow charts developed by programmer analyst to understand tasks computer will perform, such as updating records. Revise company definition of data as defined in data dictionary. **SKILLS—Troubleshooting:** Determining causes of operating errors and deciding what to do about them. **Persuasion:** Persuading others to change their minds or behavior. **Systems Evaluation:** Identifying measures or indicators of system performance and the actions needed to improve or correct performance relative to the goals of the system. **Operations Analysis:** Analyzing needs and product requirements to create a design. **Management of Personnel Resources:** Motivating, developing, and directing people as they work, identifying the best people for the job. **Instructing:** Teaching others how to do something. **Systems Analysis:** Determining how a system should work and how changes in conditions, operations, and the environment will affect outcomes. **Technology Design:** Generating or adapting equipment and technology to serve user needs. **Time Management:** Managing one's own time and the time of others. **GOE—Interest Area:** 11. Information Technology. **Work Group:** 11.02. Information Technology Specialties. **Other Jobs in This Work Group:** Computer Operators; Computer Programmers; Computer Security Specialists; Computer Software Engineers, Applications; Computer Software Engineers, Systems Software; Computer Support Specialists; Computer Systems Analysts; Network Systems and Data Communications Analysts. **PERSONALITY TYPE:** Investigative.

EDUCATION/TRAINING PROGRAM(S)— Computer and Information Sciences, General; Computer and Information Systems Security; Computer Systems Analysis/Analyst; Data Modeling/Warehousing and Database Administration; Management Information Systems, General. **RELATED KNOWLEDGE/COURSES—Computers and Electronics:** Knowledge of circuit boards, processors, chips, electronic equipment, and computer hardware and software, including applications and programming. **Economics and Accounting:** Knowledge of economic and accounting principles and practices, the financial markets, banking, and the analysis and reporting of financial data. **Clerical Practices:** Knowledge of administrative and clerical procedures and systems such as word processing, managing files and records, stenography and transcription, designing forms, and other office procedures and terminology. **Customer and Personal Service:** Knowledge of principles and processes for providing customer and personal services. This includes customer needs assessment, meeting quality standards for services, and evaluation of customer satisfaction. **Administration and Management:** Knowledge of business and management principles involved in strategic planning, resource allocation, human resources modeling, leadership technique, production methods, and coordination of people and resources. **Mathematics:** Knowledge of arithmetic, algebra, geometry, calculus, and statistics and their applications.

Demonstrators and Product Promoters

- Education/Training Required: Moderate-term on-the-job training
- Annual Earnings: $20,700
- Growth: 17.0%
- Annual Job Openings: 38,000
- Self-Employed: 42.1%
- Part-Time: 52.5%

Demonstrate merchandise and answer questions for the purpose of creating public interest in buying the product. May sell demonstrated merchandise. Demonstrate and explain products, methods, or services in order to persuade customers to purchase products or utilize services. Identify interested and qualified customers in order to provide them with additional information. Keep areas neat while working and return items to correct locations following demonstrations. Practice demonstrations to ensure that they will run smoothly. Prepare and alter presentation contents to target specific audiences. Provide product information, using lectures, films, charts, and/or slide shows. Provide product samples, coupons, informational brochures, and other incentives to persuade people to buy products. Record and report demonstration-related information such as the number of questions asked by the audience and the number of coupons distributed. Research and investigate products to be presented to prepare for demonstrations. Sell products being promoted and keep records of sales. Set up and arrange displays and demonstration areas to attract the attention of prospective customers. Stock shelves with products. Suggest specific product purchases to meet customers' needs. Transport, assemble, and disassemble materials used in presentations. Visit trade shows, stores, community organizations, and other venues to demonstrate products or services and to answer questions from potential customers. Collect fees or accept donations. Contact businesses and civic establishments to arrange to exhibit and sell merchandise. Develop lists of prospective clients from sources such as newspaper items, company records, local merchants, and customers. Give tours of plants where specific products are made. Instruct customers in alteration of products. Learn about competitors' products and consumers' interests and concerns in order to answer questions and provide more-complete information. Recommend product or service improvements to employers. Train demonstrators to present a company's products or services. Wear costumes or signboards and walk in public to promote merchandise, services, or events. Work as part of a team of demonstrators to accommodate large crowds. **SKILLS—Persuasion:** Persuading others to change their minds or behavior. **Speaking:** Talking to others to convey information effectively. **Social Perceptiveness:** Being aware of others' reactions and understanding why they react as they do. **Learning Strategies:** Selecting and using training/instructional methods and procedures appropriate for the situation when learning or teaching new things. **Instructing:** Teaching others how to do something. **Writing:** Communicating effectively in writing as appropriate for the needs of the audience. **Active Learning:** Understanding the implications of new information for both current and future problem-solving and decision-making. **Systems Evaluation:** Identifying measures or indicators of system performance and the actions needed to improve or correct performance relative to the goals of the system. **GOE—Interest Area:** 14. Retail and Wholesale Sales and Service. **Work Group:** 14.04. Personal Soliciting. **Other Jobs in This Work Group:** Door-To-Door Sales Workers, News and Street Vendors, and Related Workers; Models; Telemarketers. **PERSONALITY TYPE:** Enterprising.

EDUCATION/TRAINING PROGRAM(S)— Retailing and Retail Operations. **RELATED KNOWLEDGE/COURSES—Sales and Marketing:** Knowledge of principles and methods for showing, promoting, and selling products or services. This includes marketing strategy and tactics, product demonstrations, sales techniques, and sales control systems. **Communications and Media:** Knowledge of media production, communication, and dissemination techniques and methods. This includes alternative ways to inform and entertain via written, oral, and visual media. **Education and Training:** Knowledge of principles and methods for curriculum and training design, teaching and instruction for individuals and groups, and the measurement of training effects. **English Language:** Knowledge of the structure and content of the English language, including the meaning and spelling of words, rules of composition, and grammar. **Economics and Accounting:** Knowledge of economic and accounting principles and practices, the financial markets, banking, and the analysis and reporting of financial data. **Clerical Practices:** Knowledge of administrative and clerical procedures and systems such as word processing, managing files and records, stenography and transcription, designing forms, and other office procedures and terminology.

Dental Assistants

- Education/Training Required: Moderate-term on-the-job training
- Annual Earnings: $28,330
- Growth: 42.5%
- Annual Job Openings: 35,000
- Self-Employed: 0%
- Part-Time: 35.6%

Assist dentist, set up patient and equipment, and keep records. Prepare patient, sterilize and disinfect instruments, set up instrument trays, prepare materials, and assist dentist during dental procedures. Expose dental diagnostic X rays. Record treatment information in patient records. Take and record medical and dental histories and vital signs of patients. Provide postoperative instructions prescribed by dentist. Assist dentist in management of medical and dental emergencies. Pour, trim, and polish study casts. Instruct patients in oral hygiene and plaque control programs. Make preliminary impressions for study casts and occlusal registrations for mounting study casts. Clean and polish removable appliances. Clean teeth, using dental instruments. Apply protective coating of fluoride to teeth. Fabricate temporary restorations and custom impressions from preliminary impressions. Schedule appointments, prepare bills and receive payment for dental services, complete insurance forms, and maintain records, manually or using computer. **SKILLS—Social Perceptiveness:** Being aware of others' reactions and understanding why they react as they do. **Equipment Maintenance:** Performing routine maintenance on equipment and determining when and what kind of maintenance is needed. **Management of Material Resources:** Obtaining and seeing to the appropriate use of equipment, facilities, and materials needed to do certain work. **Instructing:** Teaching others how to do something. **Service Orientation:** Actively looking for ways to help people. **Operation and Control:** Controlling operations of equipment or systems. **Persuasion:** Persuading others to change their minds or behavior. **Time Management:** Managing one's own time and the time of others. **GOE—Interest Area:** 08. Health Science. **Work Group:** 08.03.

Dentistry. **Other Jobs in This Work Group:** Dental Hygienists; Dentists, General; Oral and Maxillofacial Surgeons; Orthodontists; Prosthodontists. **PERSONALITY TYPE:** Social.

EDUCATION/TRAINING PROGRAM(S)—Dental Assisting/Assistant. **RELATED KNOWLEDGE/COURSES—Medicine and Dentistry:** Knowledge of the information and techniques needed to diagnose and treat human injuries, diseases, and deformities. This includes symptoms, treatment alternatives, drug properties and interactions, and preventive health-care measures. **Customer and Personal Service:** Knowledge of principles and processes for providing customer and personal services. This includes customer needs assessment, meeting quality standards for services, and evaluation of customer satisfaction. **Chemistry:** Knowledge of the chemical composition, structure, and properties of substances and of the chemical processes and transformations that they undergo. This includes uses of chemicals and their danger signs, production techniques, and disposal methods. **Clerical Practices:** Knowledge of administrative and clerical procedures and systems such as word processing, managing files and records, stenography and transcription, designing forms, and other office procedures and terminology. **Psychology:** Knowledge of human behavior and performance; individual differences in ability, personality, and interests; learning and motivation; psychological research methods; and the assessment and treatment of behavioral and affective disorders. **Computers and Electronics:** Knowledge of circuit boards, processors, chips, electronic equipment, and computer hardware and software, including applications and programming.

Dental Hygienists

◎ Education/Training Required: Associate degree

◎ Annual Earnings: $58,350

◎ Growth: 43.1%

◎ Annual Job Openings: 9,000

◎ Self-Employed: 0.7%

◎ Part-Time: 57.8%

Clean teeth and examine oral areas, head, and neck for signs of oral disease. May educate patients on oral hygiene, take and develop X rays, or apply fluoride or

sealants. Clean calcareous deposits, accretions, and stains from teeth and beneath margins of gums, using dental instruments. Feel and visually examine gums for sores and signs of disease. Chart conditions of decay and disease for diagnosis and treatment by dentist. Feel lymph nodes under patient's chin to detect swelling or tenderness that could indicate presence of oral cancer. Apply fluorides and other cavity-preventing agents to arrest dental decay. Examine gums, using probes, to locate periodontal recessed gums and signs of gum disease. Expose and develop X-ray film. Provide clinical services and health education to improve and maintain oral health of schoolchildren. Remove excess cement from coronal surfaces of teeth. Make impressions for study casts. Place, carve, and finish amalgam restorations. Administer local anesthetic agents. Conduct dental health clinics for community groups to augment services of dentist. **SKILLS—Time Management:** Managing one's own time and the time of others. **Active Learning:** Understanding the implications of new information for both current and future problem-solving and decision-making. **Social Perceptiveness:** Being aware of others' reactions and understanding why they react as they do. **Instructing:** Teaching others how to do something. **Persuasion:** Persuading others to change their minds or behavior. **Learning Strategies:** Selecting and using training/instructional methods and procedures appropriate for the situation when learning or teaching new things. **Reading Comprehension:** Understanding written sentences and paragraphs in work-related documents. **Active Listening:** Giving full attention to what other people are saying, taking time to understand the points being made, asking questions as appropriate, and not interrupting at inappropriate times. **Service Orientation:** Actively looking for ways to help people. **GOE—Interest Area:** 08. Health Science. **Work Group:** 08.03. Dentistry. **Other Jobs in This Work Group:** Dental Assistants; Dentists, General; Oral and Maxillofacial Surgeons; Orthodontists; Prosthodontists. **PERSONALITY TYPE:** Social.

EDUCATION/TRAINING PROGRAM(S)—Dental Hygiene/Hygienist. **RELATED KNOWLEDGE/COURSES—Medicine and Dentistry:** Knowledge of the information and techniques needed to diagnose and treat human injuries, diseases, and deformities. This includes symptoms, treatment alternatives, drug properties and interactions, and preventive health-care measures. **Biology:** Knowledge of plant and animal organisms and their tissues, cells, functions, interdependencies, and interactions with each other and the environment. **Customer and Personal Service:** Knowledge of principles and processes for providing customer and personal services. This includes customer needs assessment, meeting quality standards for services, and evaluation of customer satisfaction. **Chemistry:** Knowledge of the chemical composition, structure, and properties of substances and of the chemical processes and transformations that they undergo. This includes uses of chemicals and their danger signs, production techniques, and disposal methods. **Psychology:** Knowledge of human behavior and performance; individual differences in ability, personality, and interests; learning and motivation; psychological research methods; and the assessment and treatment of behavioral and affective disorders. **Sales and Marketing:** Knowledge of principles and methods for showing, promoting, and selling products or services. This includes marketing strategy and tactics, product demonstrations, sales techniques, and sales control systems.

Dentists, General

- ◎ Education/Training Required: First professional degree
- ◎ Annual Earnings: $123,060
- ◎ Growth: 4.1%
- ◎ Annual Job Openings: 7,000
- ◎ Self-Employed: 39.9%
- ◎ Part-Time: 22.3%

Diagnose and treat diseases, injuries, and malformations of teeth and gums and related oral structures. May treat diseases of nerve, pulp, and other dental tissues affecting vitality of teeth. Use masks, gloves, and safety glasses to protect themselves and their patients from infectious diseases. Administer anesthetics to limit the amount of pain experienced by patients during procedures. Examine teeth, gums, and related tissues, using dental instruments, X rays, and other diagnostic equipment, to evaluate dental health, diagnose diseases or abnormalities, and plan appropriate treatments. Formulate plan of treatment for patient's teeth and mouth tissue. Use air turbine and hand instruments, dental appliances, and surgical implements. Advise and instruct patients regarding preventive dental care, the causes and treatment of dental problems, and oral health care services. Design, make, and fit prosthodontic appliances such as space maintainers, bridges, and dentures or write fabrication instructions or prescriptions for denturists and dental technicians. Diagnose and treat diseases, injuries, and malformations of teeth, gums, and related oral structures and provide preventive and corrective services. Fill pulp chamber and canal with endodontic materials. Write prescriptions for antibiotics and other medications. Analyze and evaluate dental needs to determine changes and trends in patterns of dental disease. Treat exposure of pulp by pulp capping, removal of pulp from pulp chamber, or root canal, using dental instruments. Eliminate irritating margins of fillings and correct occlusions, using dental instruments. Perform oral and periodontal surgery on the jaw or mouth. Remove diseased tissue, using surgical instruments. Apply fluoride and sealants to teeth. Manage business, employing and supervising staff and handling paperwork and insurance claims. Bleach, clean, or polish teeth to restore natural color. Plan, organize, and maintain dental health programs. Produce and evaluate dental health educational materials. **SKILLS—Science:** Using scientific rules and methods to solve problems. **Management of Material Resources:** Obtaining and seeing to the appropriate use of equipment, facilities, and materials needed to do certain work. **Management of Financial Resources:** Determining how money will be spent to get the work done and accounting for these expenditures. **Service Orientation:** Actively looking for ways to help people. **Complex Problem Solving:** Identifying complex problems and reviewing related information to develop and evaluate options and implement solutions. **Persuasion:** Persuading others to change their minds or behavior. **Equipment Selection:** Determining the kind of tools and equipment needed to do a job. **Management of Personnel Resources:** Motivating, developing, and directing people as they work, identifying the best people for the job. **GOE—Interest Area:** 08. Health Science. **Work Group:** 08.03. Dentistry. **Other Jobs in This Work Group:** Dental Assistants; Dental Hygienists; Oral and Maxillofacial Surgeons; Orthodontists; Prosthodontists. **PERSONALITY TYPE:** Investigative.

EDUCATION/TRAINING PROGRAM(S)— Advanced General Dentistry (Cert, MS, PhD); Dental Public Health and Education (Cert, MS/MPH, PhD/DPH); Dental Public Health Specialty; Dentistry (DDS, DMD); Pediatric Dentistry/Pedodontics (Cert, MS, PhD); Pedodontics Specialty. **RELATED**

KNOWLEDGE/COURSES—**Medicine and Dentistry:** Knowledge of the information and techniques needed to diagnose and treat human injuries, diseases, and deformities. This includes symptoms, treatment alternatives, drug properties and interactions, and preventive health-care measures. **Biology:** Knowledge of plant and animal organisms and their tissues, cells, functions, interdependencies, and interactions with each other and the environment. **Psychology:** Knowledge of human behavior and performance; individual differences in ability, personality, and interests; learning and motivation; psychological research methods; and the assessment and treatment of behavioral and affective disorders. **Personnel and Human Resources:** Knowledge of principles and procedures for personnel recruitment, selection, training, compensation and benefits, labor relations and negotiation, and personnel information systems. **Chemistry:** Knowledge of the chemical composition, structure, and properties of substances and of the chemical processes and transformations that they undergo. This includes uses of chemicals and their danger signs, production techniques, and disposal methods. **Customer and Personal Service:** Knowledge of principles and processes for providing customer and personal services. This includes customer needs assessment, meeting quality standards for services, and evaluation of customer satisfaction.

Design Printing Machine Setters and Set-Up Operators

◎ Education/Training Required: Postsecondary vocational training

◎ Annual Earnings: $29,900

◎ Growth: 4.6%

◎ Annual Job Openings: 30,000

◎ Self-Employed: 2.7%

◎ Part-Time: 6.2%

Set up or set up and operate machines to print designs on materials. Installs printing plates, cylinders, or rollers on machine, using hand tools and gauges. Measures and records amount of product produced. Repairs or replaces worn or broken parts, using hand tools. Cleans and lubricates equipment. Inspects prod-

uct to detect defects. Mixes colors of paint according to formulas. Adjusts and changes gears, using hand tools. Fills reservoirs with paint or ink. Adjusts feed guides, gauges, and rollers, using hand tools. Monitors machines and gauges to ensure and maintain standards. SKILLS—**Repairing:** Repairing machines or systems by using the needed tools. **Operation Monitoring:** Watching gauges, dials, or other indicators to make sure a machine is working properly. **Equipment Maintenance:** Performing routine maintenance on equipment and determining when and what kind of maintenance is needed. **Operation and Control:** Controlling operations of equipment or systems. **Technology Design:** Generating or adapting equipment and technology to serve user needs. **Installation:** Installing equipment, machines, wiring, or programs to meet specifications. **Troubleshooting:** Determining causes of operating errors and deciding what to do about them. GOE—**Interest Area:** 13. Manufacturing. **Work Group:** 13.08. Graphic Arts Production. **Other Jobs in This Work Group:** Bindery Machine Operators and Tenders; Camera Operators; Desktop Publishers; Dot Etchers; Electronic Masking System Operators; Electrotypers and Stereotypers; Embossing Machine Set-Up Operators; Engraver Set-Up Operators; Engravers, Hand; Engravers/Carvers; Etchers; Etchers, Hand; Film Laboratory Technicians; Hand Compositors and Typesetters; Job Printers; Letterpress Setters and Set-Up Operators; Marking and Identification Printing Machine Setters and Set-Up Operators; Offset Lithographic Press Setters and Set-Up Operators; Pantograph Engravers; Paste-Up Workers; Photoengravers; Photoengraving and Lithographing Machine Operators and Tenders; Photographic Processing Machine Operators; Plate Finishers; Platemakers; Precision Etchers and Engravers, Hand or Machine; Precision Printing Workers; Printing Press Machine Operators and Tenders; Scanner Operators; Strippers; Typesetting and Composing Machine Operators and Tenders. **PERSONALITY TYPE:** Realistic.

EDUCATION/TRAINING PROGRAM(S)— Graphic and Printing Equipment Operator, General Production; Graphic Communications, Other; Printing Management; Printing Press Operator. **RELATED KNOWLEDGE/COURSES—Mechanical Devices:** Knowledge of machines and tools, including their designs, uses, repair, and maintenance. **Engineering and Technology:** Knowledge of the practical application of engineering science and technology. This includes applying principles, techniques, procedures, and equipment to the design and production of various goods and services. **Production and Processing:** Knowledge of raw materials, production processes, quality control, costs, and other techniques for maximizing the effective manufacture and distribution of goods.

Desktop Publishers

- Education/Training Required: Postsecondary vocational training
- Annual Earnings: $32,340
- Growth: 29.2%
- Annual Job Openings: 4,000
- Self-Employed: 0%
- Part-Time: 17.5%

Format typescript and graphic elements, using computer software to produce publication-ready material. Check preliminary and final proofs for errors and make necessary corrections. Operate desktop publishing software and equipment to design, lay out, and produce camera-ready copy. View monitors for visual representation of work in progress and for instructions and feedback throughout process, making modifications as necessary. Enter text into computer keyboard and select the size and style of type, column width, and appropriate spacing for printed materials. Store copies of publications on paper, magnetic tape, film, or diskette. Position text and art elements from a variety of databases in a visually appealing way in order to design print or Web pages, using knowledge of type styles and size and layout patterns. Enter digitized data into electronic prepress system computer memory, using scanner, camera, keyboard, or mouse. Edit graphics and photos, using pixel or bitmap editing, airbrushing, masking, or image retouching. Import text and art elements such as electronic clip art or electronic files from photographs that have been scanned or produced with a digital camera, using computer software. Prepare sample layouts for approval, using computer software. Study layout or other design instructions to determine work to be done and sequence of operations. Load floppy disks or tapes containing information into system. Convert various types of files for printing or for the Internet, using computer software. Enter data, such as coordinates of images and color specifications, into system to retouch and make color corrections. Select number of colors and determine color separations. Transmit, deliver, or mail publication master to printer for production into film and plates. Collaborate with graphic artists, editors, and writers to produce master copies according to design specifications. Create special effects such as vignettes, mosaics, and image combining and add elements such as sound and animation to electronic publications. **SKILLS—Time Management:** Managing one's own time and the time of others. **Service Orientation:** Actively looking for ways to help people. **Operation and Control:** Controlling operations of equipment or systems. **Instructing:** Teaching others how to do something. **Active Listening:** Giving full attention to what other people are saying, taking time to understand the points being made, asking questions as appropriate, and not interrupting at inappropriate times. **Operations Analysis:** Analyzing needs and product requirements to create a design. **Technology Design:** Generating or adapting equipment and technology to serve user needs. **Reading Comprehension:** Understanding written sentences and paragraphs in work-related documents. **GOE—Interest Area:** 13. Manufacturing. **Work Group:** 13.08. Graphic Arts Production. **Other Jobs in This Work Group:** Bindery Machine Operators and Tenders; Camera Operators; Design Printing Machine Setters and Set-Up Operators; Dot Etchers; Electronic Masking System Operators; Electrotypers and Stereotypers; Embossing Machine Set-Up Operators; Engraver Set-Up Operators; Engravers, Hand; Engravers/Carvers; Etchers; Etchers, Hand; Film Laboratory Technicians; Hand Compositors and Typesetters; Job Printers; Letterpress Setters and Set-Up Operators; Marking and Identification Printing Machine Setters and Set-Up Operators; Offset Lithographic Press Setters and Set-Up Operators; Pantograph Engravers; Paste-Up Workers; Photoengravers; Photoengraving and Lithographing Machine Operators and Tenders; Photographic Processing Machine Operators; Plate Finishers; Platemakers; Precision Etchers and Engravers, Hand or Machine; Precision Printing Workers; Printing Press Machine Operators and Tenders; Scanner Operators; Strippers; Typesetting and Composing Machine Operators and Tenders. **PERSONALITY TYPE:** Realistic.

EDUCATION/TRAINING PROGRAM(S)—Prepress/Desktop Publishing and Digital Imaging Design. **RELATED KNOWLEDGE/COURSES—Computers and Electronics:** Knowledge of circuit boards, processors, chips, electronic equipment, and computer hardware and software, including applications and programming. **Production and Processing:** Knowledge of raw materials, production processes, quality control, costs, and other techniques for maximizing the effective manufacture and distribution of goods. **English Language:** Knowledge of the structure and content of the English language, including the meaning and spelling of words, rules of composition, and grammar. **Clerical Practices:** Knowledge of administrative and clerical procedures and systems such as word processing, managing files and records, stenography and transcription, designing forms, and other office procedures and terminology. **Customer and Personal Service:** Knowledge of principles and processes for providing customer and personal services. This includes customer needs assessment, meeting quality standards for services, and evaluation of customer satisfaction. **Telecommunications:** Knowledge of transmission, broadcasting, switching, control, and operation of telecommunications systems.

Diagnostic Medical Sonographers

- Education/Training Required: Associate degree
- Annual Earnings: $52,490
- Growth: 24.0%
- Annual Job Openings: 4,000
- Self-Employed: 0.2%
- Part-Time: 17.5%

Produce ultrasonic recordings of internal organs for use by physicians. Decide which images to include, looking for differences between healthy and pathological areas. Observe screen during scan to ensure that image produced is satisfactory for diagnostic purposes, making adjustments to equipment as required. Observe and care for patients throughout examinations to ensure their safety and comfort. Provide sonogram and oral or written summary of technical findings to physician for use in medical diagnosis. Operate ultrasound equipment to produce and record images of the motion, shape, and composition of blood, organs, tissues, and bodily masses such as fluid accumulations. Select appropriate equipment settings and adjust patient positions to obtain the best sites and angles. Determine whether scope of exam should be

extended, based on findings. Process and code film from procedures and complete appropriate documentation. Obtain and record accurate patient history, including prior test results and information from physical examinations. Prepare patient for exam by explaining procedure, transferring them to ultrasound table, scrubbing skin and applying gel, and positioning them properly. Record and store suitable images, using camera unit connected to the ultrasound equipment. Coordinate work with physicians and other healthcare team members, including providing assistance during invasive procedures. Maintain records that include patient information, sonographs and interpretations, files of correspondence, publications and regulations, and quality assurance records (e.g., pathology, biopsy, post-operative reports). Perform legal and ethical duties, including preparing safety and accident reports, obtaining written consent from patient to perform invasive procedures, and reporting symptoms of abuse and neglect. Supervise and train students and other medical sonographers. Maintain stock and supplies, preparing supplies for special examinations and ordering supplies when necessary. Clean, check, and maintain sonographic equipment, submitting maintenance requests or performing minor repairs as necessary. Perform clerical duties such as scheduling exams and special procedures, keeping records, and archiving computerized images. **SKILLS—Social Perceptiveness:** Being aware of others' reactions and understanding why they react as they do. **Reading Comprehension:** Understanding written sentences and paragraphs in work-related documents. **Learning Strategies:** Selecting and using training/instructional methods and procedures appropriate for the situation when learning or teaching new things. **Instructing:** Teaching others how to do something. **Operation and Control:** Controlling operations of equipment or systems. **Active Listening:** Giving full attention to what other people are saying, taking time to understand the points being made, asking questions as appropriate, and not interrupting at inappropriate times. **Service Orientation:** Actively looking for ways to help people. **Active Learning:** Understanding the implications of new information for both current and future problem-solving and decision-making. **GOE—Interest Area:** 08. Health Science. **Work Group:** 08.06. Medical Technology. **Other Jobs in This Work Group:** Biological Technicians; Cardiovascular Technologists and Technicians; Medical and Clinical Laboratory Technicians; Medical and Clinical Laboratory Technologists; Medical Equipment Preparers; Medical Records and

Health Information Technicians; Nuclear Medicine Technologists; Opticians, Dispensing; Orthotists and Prosthetists; Radiologic Technicians; Radiologic Technologists. **PERSONALITY TYPE:** No data available.

EDUCATION/TRAINING PROGRAM(S)— Allied Health Diagnostic, Intervention, and Treatment Professions, Other; Diagnostic Medical Sonography/Sonographer and Ultrasound Technician. **RELATED KNOWLEDGE/COURSES—Medicine and Dentistry:** Knowledge of the information and techniques needed to diagnose and treat human injuries, diseases, and deformities. This includes symptoms, treatment alternatives, drug properties and interactions, and preventive health-care measures. **Physics:** Knowledge and prediction of physical principles and laws and their interrelationships and applications to understanding fluid, material, and atmospheric dynamics and mechanical, electrical, atomic, and subatomic structures and processes. **Biology:** Knowledge of plant and animal organisms and their tissues, cells, functions, interdependencies, and interactions with each other and the environment. **Customer and Personal Service:** Knowledge of principles and processes for providing customer and personal services. This includes customer needs assessment, meeting quality standards for services, and evaluation of customer satisfaction. **Education and Training:** Knowledge of principles and methods for curriculum and training design, teaching and instruction for individuals and groups, and the measurement of training effects. **Psychology:** Knowledge of human behavior and performance; individual differences in ability, personality, and interests; learning and motivation; psychological research methods; and the assessment and treatment of behavioral and affective disorders.

Dietitians and Nutritionists

- Education/Training Required: Bachelor's degree
- Annual Earnings: $43,630
- Growth: 17.8%
- Annual Job Openings: 8,000
- Self-Employed: 6.3%
- Part-Time: 24.3%

Plan and conduct food service or nutritional programs to assist in the promotion of health and control of disease. **May supervise activities of a department providing quantity food services, counsel individuals, or conduct nutritional research.** Assess nutritional needs, diet restrictions, and current health plans to develop and implement dietary-care plans and provide nutritional counseling. Consult with physicians and health-care personnel to determine nutritional needs and diet restrictions of patient or client. Advise patients and their families on nutritional principles, dietary plans and diet modifications, and food selection and preparation. Counsel individuals and groups on basic rules of good nutrition, healthy eating habits, and nutrition monitoring to improve their quality of life. Monitor food service operations to ensure conformance to nutritional, safety, sanitation, and quality standards. Coordinate recipe development and standardization and develop new menus for independent food service operations. Develop policies for food service or nutritional programs to assist in health promotion and disease control. Inspect meals served for conformance to prescribed diets and standards of palatability and appearance. Develop curriculum and prepare manuals, visual aids, course outlines, and other materials used in teaching. Prepare and administer budgets for food, equipment, and supplies. Purchase food in accordance with health and safety codes. Select, train, and supervise workers who plan, prepare, and serve meals. Manage quantity food service departments or clinical and community nutrition services. Coordinate diet counseling services. Advise food service managers and organizations on sanitation, safety procedures, menu development, budgeting, and planning to assist with the establishment, operation, and evaluation of food service facilities and nutrition programs. Organize, develop, analyze, test, and prepare special meals such as low-fat, low-cholesterol, and chemical-free meals. Plan, conduct, and evaluate dietary, nutritional, and epidemiological research. Plan and conduct training programs in dietetics, nutrition, and institutional management and administration for medical students, health-care personnel, and the general public. Make recommendations regarding public policy, such as nutrition labeling, food fortification, and nutrition standards for school programs. **SKILLS—Instructing:** Teaching others how to do something. **Social Perceptiveness:** Being aware of others' reactions and understanding why they react as they do. **Learning Strategies:** Selecting and using training/instructional methods and procedures appropriate for the situation when learning or teaching new things.

Science: Using scientific rules and methods to solve problems. Writing: Communicating effectively in writing as appropriate for the needs of the audience. Persuasion: Persuading others to change their minds or behavior. Speaking: Talking to others to convey information effectively. Service Orientation: Actively looking for ways to help people. GOE—Interest Area: 08. Health Science. Work Group: 08.09. Health Protection and Promotion. Other Jobs in This Work Group: Athletic Trainers; Dietetic Technicians; Embalmers. PERSONALITY TYPE: Investigative.

EDUCATION/TRAINING PROGRAM(S)—Clinical Nutrition/Nutritionist; Dietetics and Clinical Nutrition Services, Other; Dietetics/Dietitian (RD); Foods, Nutrition, and Related Services, Other; Foods, Nutrition, and Wellness Studies, General; Foodservice Systems Administration/Management; Human Nutrition; Nutrition Sciences. RELATED KNOWLEDGE/COURSES—Food Production: Knowledge of techniques and equipment for planting, growing, and harvesting food products (both plant and animal) for consumption, including storage/handling techniques. Sociology and Anthropology: Knowledge of group behavior and dynamics, societal trends and influences, human migrations, ethnicity, and cultures and their history and origins. Therapy and Counseling: Knowledge of principles, methods, and procedures for diagnosis, treatment, and rehabilitation of physical and mental dysfunctions and for career counseling and guidance. Psychology: Knowledge of human behavior and performance; individual differences in ability, personality, and interests; learning and motivation; psychological research methods; and the assessment and treatment of behavioral and affective disorders. Education and Training: Knowledge of principles and methods for curriculum and training design, teaching and instruction for individuals and groups, and the measurement of training effects. Medicine and Dentistry: Knowledge of the information and techniques needed to diagnose and treat human injuries, diseases, and deformities. This includes symptoms, treatment alternatives, drug properties and interactions, and preventive health-care measures.

Dining Room and Cafeteria Attendants and Bartender Helpers

- Education/Training Required: Short-term on-the-job training
- Annual Earnings: $14,770
- Growth: 14.9%
- Annual Job Openings: 143,000
- Self-Employed: 0.1%
- Part-Time: 54.0%

Facilitate food service. Clean tables, carry dirty dishes, replace soiled table linens; set tables; replenish supply of clean linens, silverware, glassware, and dishes; supply service bar with food; and serve water, butter, and coffee to patrons. Perform serving, cleaning, and stocking duties in establishments such as cafeterias or dining rooms in order to facilitate customer service. Clean up spilled food, drink, and broken dishes and remove empty bottles and trash. Carry food, dishes, trays, and silverware from kitchens and supply departments to serving counters. Carry trays from food counters to tables for cafeteria patrons. Fill beverage and ice dispensers. Garnish foods and position them on tables to make them visible and accessible. Maintain adequate supplies of items such as clean linens, silverware, glassware, dishes, and trays. Mix and prepare flavors for mixed drinks. Replenish supplies of food and equipment at steam tables and service bars. Scrape and stack dirty dishes and carry dishes and other tableware to kitchens for cleaning. Serve food to customers when waiters and waitresses need assistance. Serve ice water, coffee, rolls, and butter to patrons. Set tables with clean linens, condiments, and other supplies. Slice and pit fruit used to garnish drinks. Stock cabinets and serving areas with condiments and refill condiment containers as necessary. Stock refrigerating units with wines and bottled beer and replace empty beer kegs. Wash glasses and other serving equipment at bars. Wipe tables and seats with dampened cloths and replace dirty tablecloths. Carry linens to and from laundry areas. Clean and polish counters, shelves, walls, furniture, and equipment in food service areas and other areas of restaurants and mop and vacuum floors. Locate items requested by customers. Run cash registers. Stock vending machines with food. SKILLS—None met the criteria. GOE—Interest

Area: 09. Hospitality, Tourism, and Recreation. **Work Group:** 09.05. Food and Beverage Service. **Other Jobs in This Work Group:** Bartenders; Combined Food Preparation and Serving Workers, Including Fast Food; Counter Attendants, Cafeteria, Food Concession, and Coffee Shop; Food Servers, Nonrestaurant; Hosts and Hostesses, Restaurant, Lounge, and Coffee Shop; Waiters and Waitresses. **PERSONALITY TYPE:** Realistic.

EDUCATION/TRAINING PROGRAM(S)—Food Service, Waiter/Waitress, and Dining Room Management/Manager. **RELATED KNOWLEDGE/ COURSES—Administration and Management:** Knowledge of business and management principles involved in strategic planning, resource allocation, human resources modeling, leadership technique, production methods, and coordination of people and resources. **Clerical Practices:** Knowledge of administrative and clerical procedures and systems such as word processing, managing files and records, stenography and transcription, designing forms, and other office procedures and terminology.

Directors—Stage, Motion Pictures, Television, and Radio

- Education/Training Required: Work experience plus degree
- Annual Earnings: $52,840
- Growth: 18.3%
- Annual Job Openings: 10,000
- Self-Employed: 32.8%
- Part-Time: 9.1%

Interpret script, conduct rehearsals, and direct activities of cast and technical crew for stage, motion pictures, television, or radio programs. Direct live broadcasts, films and recordings, or non-broadcast programming for public entertainment or education. Supervise and coordinate the work of camera, lighting, design, and sound crew members. Study and research scripts in order to determine how they should be directed. Cut and edit film or tape in order to integrate component parts into desired sequences. Collaborate with film and sound editors during the post-produc-tion process as films are edited and soundtracks are added. Confer with technical directors, managers, crew members, and writers to discuss details of production, such as photography, script, music, sets, and costumes. Plan details such as framing, composition, camera movement, sound, and actor movement for each shot or scene. Communicate to actors the approach, characterization, and movement needed for each scene in such a way that rehearsals and takes are minimized. Establish pace of programs and sequences of scenes according to time requirements and cast and set accessibility. Choose settings and locations for films and determine how scenes will be shot in these settings. Identify and approve equipment and elements required for productions, such as scenery, lights, props, costumes, choreography, and music. Compile scripts, program notes, and other material related to productions. Perform producers' duties such as securing financial backing, establishing and administering budgets, and recruiting cast and crew. Select plays or scripts for production and determine how material should be interpreted and performed. Compile cue words and phrases and cue announcers, cast members, and technicians during performances. Consult with writers, producers, and/or actors about script changes or "workshop" scripts through rehearsal with writers and actors to create final drafts. Review film daily in order to check on work in progress and to plan for future filming. Collaborate with producers in order to hire crew members such as art directors, cinematographers, and costumer designers. Interpret stage-set diagrams to determine stage layouts and supervise placement of equipment and scenery. **SKILLS—Management of Personnel Resources:** Motivating, developing, and directing people as they work, identifying the best people for the job. **Time Management:** Managing one's own time and the time of others. **Judgment and Decision Making:** Considering the relative costs and benefits of potential actions to choose the most appropriate one. **Active Listening:** Giving full attention to what other people are saying, taking time to understand the points being made, asking questions as appropriate, and not interrupting at inappropriate times. **Critical Thinking:** Using logic and reasoning to identify the strengths and weaknesses of alternative solutions, conclusions, or approaches to problems. **Operations Analysis:** Analyzing needs and product requirements to create a design. **Speaking:** Talking to others to convey information effectively. **Equipment Selection:** Determining the kind of tools and equipment needed to do a job. **GOE—Interest Area:** 03. Arts and Communication. **Work Group:** 03.06. Drama. **Other Jobs in This Work Group:** Actors; Costume Attendants; Makeup Artists, Theatrical and Performance; Public Address System and Other Announcers; Radio and Television Announcers. **PERSONALITY TYPE:** Artistic.

EDUCATION/TRAINING PROGRAM(S)—Cinematography and Film/Video Production; Directing and Theatrical Production; Drama and Dramatics/Theatre Arts, General; Dramatic/Theatre Arts and Stagecraft, Other; Film/Cinema Studies; Radio and Television; Theatre/Theatre Arts Management. **RELATED KNOWLEDGE/COURSES— Communications and Media:** Knowledge of media production, communication, and dissemination techniques and methods. This includes alternative ways to inform and entertain via written, oral, and visual media. **Telecommunications:** Knowledge of transmission, broadcasting, switching, control, and operation of telecommunications systems. **Computers and Electronics:** Knowledge of circuit boards, processors, chips, electronic equipment, and computer hardware and software, including applications and programming. **Geography:** Knowledge of principles and methods for describing the features of land, sea, and air masses, including their physical characteristics; locations; interrelationships; and distribution of plant, animal, and human life. **Education and Training:** Knowledge of principles and methods for curriculum and training design, teaching and instruction for individuals and groups, and the measurement of training effects. **Fine Arts:** Knowledge of the theory and techniques required to compose, produce, and perform works of music, dance, the visual arts, drama, and sculpture.

Directors, Religious Activities and Education

- ⊚ Education/Training Required: Bachelor's degree
- ⊚ Annual Earnings: $30,700
- ⊚ Growth: 24.1%
- ⊚ Annual Job Openings: 16,000
- ⊚ Self-Employed: 0%
- ⊚ Part-Time: 28.2%

Direct and coordinate activities of a denominational group to meet religious needs of students. Plan, direct, or coordinate church school programs designed to promote religious education among church membership. May provide counseling and guidance relative to marital, health, financial, and religious problems. Analyze member participation and changes in congregation emphasis to determine needs for religious education. Collaborate with other ministry members to establish goals and objectives for religious education programs and to develop ways to encourage program participation. Confer with clergy members, congregation officials, and congregation organizations to encourage support of and participation in religious education activities. Develop and direct study courses and religious education programs within congregations. Identify and recruit potential volunteer workers. Implement program plans by ordering needed materials, scheduling speakers, reserving space, and handling other administrative details. Locate and distribute resources such as periodicals and curricula in order to enhance the effectiveness of educational programs. Publicize programs through sources such as newsletters, bulletins, and mailings. Schedule special events such as camps, conferences, meetings, seminars, and retreats. Select appropriate curricula and class structures for educational programs. Train and supervise religious education instructional staff. Analyze revenue and program cost data to determine budget priorities. Attend workshops, seminars, and conferences to obtain program ideas, information, and resources. Counsel individuals regarding interpersonal, health, financial, and religious problems. Interpret religious education activities to the public through speaking, leading discussions, and writing articles for local and national publications. Participate in denominational activities aimed at goals such as promoting interfaith understanding or providing aid to new or small congregations. Plan and conduct conferences dealing with the interpretation of religious ideas and convictions. Visit congregation members' homes, or arrange for pastoral visits, in order to provide information and resources regarding religious education programs. **SKILLS—Management of Financial Resources:** Determining how money will be spent to get the work done and accounting for these expenditures. **Social Perceptiveness:** Being aware of others' reactions and understanding why they react as they do. **Management of Personnel Resources:** Motivating, developing, and directing people as they work, identifying the best people for the job. **Service Orientation:** Actively looking for ways to help people. **Management of Material Resources:** Obtaining and seeing to the appropriate use of equipment, facilities, and materials needed to do certain work. **Systems Analysis:** Determining how a system should work and how changes in conditions, operations, and the environment will affect outcomes. **Instructing:** Teaching others how to do something. **Systems Evaluation:** Identifying measures or indicators of system performance and the actions needed to improve or correct performance relative to the goals of the system. **GOE—Interest Area:** 10. Human Service. **Work Group:** 10.02. Religious Work. **Other Jobs in This Work Group:** Clergy. **PERSONALITY TYPE:** Social.

EDUCATION/TRAINING PROGRAM(S)— Bible/Biblical Studies; Missions/Missionary Studies and Missiology; Religious Education; Youth Ministry. **RELATED KNOWLEDGE/COURSES—Therapy and Counseling:** Knowledge of principles, methods, and procedures for diagnosis, treatment, and rehabilitation of physical and mental dysfunctions and for career counseling and guidance. **Philosophy and Theology:** Knowledge of different philosophical systems and religions. This includes their basic principles, values, ethics, ways of thinking, customs, and practices and their impact on human culture. **Administration and Management:** Knowledge of business and management principles involved in strategic planning, resource allocation, human resources modeling, leadership technique, production methods, and coordination of people and resources. **Sociology and Anthropology:** Knowledge of group behavior and dynamics, societal trends and influences, human migrations, ethnicity, and cultures and their history and origins. **Psychology:** Knowledge of human behavior and performance; individual differences in ability, personality, and interests; learning and motivation; psychological research methods; and the assessment and treatment of behavioral and affective disorders. **Economics and Accounting:** Knowledge of economic and accounting principles and practices, the financial markets, banking, and the analysis and reporting of financial data.

Dispatchers, Except Police, Fire, and Ambulance

- Education/Training Required: Moderate-term on-the-job training
- Annual Earnings: $30,920
- Growth: 14.4%
- Annual Job Openings: 28,000
- Self-Employed: 0.6%
- Part-Time: 8.5%

Schedule and dispatch workers, work crews, equipment, or service vehicles for conveyance of materials, freight, or passengers or for normal installation, service, or emergency repairs rendered outside the place of business. Duties may include using radio, telephone, or computer to transmit assignments and compiling statistics and reports on work progress. Schedule and dispatch workers, work crews, equipment, or service vehicles to appropriate locations according to customer requests, specifications, or needs, using radios or telephones. Arrange for necessary repairs in order to restore service and schedules. Relay work orders, messages, and information to or from work crews, supervisors, and field inspectors, using telephones or two-way radios. Confer with customers or supervising personnel in order to address questions, problems, and requests for service or equipment. Prepare daily work and run schedules. Receive or prepare work orders. Oversee all communications within specifically assigned territories. Monitor personnel and/or equipment locations and utilization in order to coordinate service and schedules. Record and maintain files and records of customer requests, work or services performed, charges, expenses, inventory, and other dispatch information. Determine types or amounts of equipment, vehicles, materials, or personnel required according to work orders or specifications. Advise personnel about traffic problems such as construction areas, accidents, congestion, weather conditions, and other hazards. Ensure timely and efficient movement of trains according to train orders and schedules. Order supplies and equipment and issue them to personnel. **SKILLS—Service Orientation:** Actively looking for ways to help people. **Operations Analysis:** Analyzing needs and product requirements to create a design. **Management of Personnel**

Resources: Motivating, developing, and directing people as they work, identifying the best people for the job. **Learning Strategies:** Selecting and using training/instructional methods and procedures appropriate for the situation when learning or teaching new things. **Critical Thinking:** Using logic and reasoning to identify the strengths and weaknesses of alternative solutions, conclusions, or approaches to problems. **Social Perceptiveness:** Being aware of others' reactions and understanding why they react as they do. **Instructing:** Teaching others how to do something. **Troubleshooting:** Determining causes of operating errors and deciding what to do about them. **GOE—Interest Area:** 03. Arts and Communication. **Work Group:** 03.10. Communications Technology. **Other Jobs in This Work Group:** Air Traffic Controllers; Airfield Operations Specialists; Central Office Operators; Directory Assistance Operators; Police, Fire, and Ambulance Dispatchers. **PERSONALITY TYPE:** Conventional.

EDUCATION/TRAINING PROGRAM(S)—No data available. **RELATED KNOWLEDGE/COURSES—Transportation:** Knowledge of principles and methods for moving people or goods by air, rail, sea, or road, including the relative costs and benefits. **Clerical Practices:** Knowledge of administrative and clerical procedures and systems such as word processing, managing files and records, stenography and transcription, designing forms, and other office procedures and terminology. **Public Safety and Security:** Knowledge of relevant equipment, policies, procedures, and strategies to promote effective local, state, or national security operations for the protection of people, data, property, and institutions. **Customer and Personal Service:** Knowledge of principles and processes for providing customer and personal services. This includes customer needs assessment, meeting quality standards for services, and evaluation of customer satisfaction. **Computers and Electronics:** Knowledge of circuit boards, processors, chips, electronic equipment, and computer hardware and software, including applications and programming. **Telecommunications:** Knowledge of transmission, broadcasting, switching, control, and operation of telecommunications systems.

Dragline Operators

- Education/Training Required: Moderate-term on-the-job training
- Annual Earnings: $31,970
- Growth: 8.9%
- Annual Job Openings: 14,000
- Self-Employed: 16.9%
- Part-Time: 2.7%

Operate power-driven crane equipment with dragline bucket to excavate or move sand, gravel, mud, or other materials. Moves controls to position boom, lower and drag bucket through material, and release material at unloading point. Directs workers engaged in placing blocks and outriggers to prevent capsizing of machine when lifting heavy loads. Drives machine to work site. **SKILLS—Operation and Control:** Controlling operations of equipment or systems. **Operation Monitoring:** Watching gauges, dials, or other indicators to make sure a machine is working properly. **GOE—Interest Area:** 02. Architecture and Construction. **Work Group:** 02.04. Construction Crafts. **Other Jobs in This Work Group:** Boat Builders and Shipwrights; Boilermakers; Brattice Builders; Brickmasons and Blockmasons; Carpet Installers; Ceiling Tile Installers; Cement Masons and Concrete Finishers; Commercial Divers; Construction Carpenters; Crane and Tower Operators; Drywall Installers; Electricians; Fence Erectors; Floor Layers, Except Carpet, Wood, and Hard Tiles; Floor Sanders and Finishers; Glaziers; Grader, Bulldozer, and Scraper Operators; Hazardous Materials Removal Workers; Insulation Workers, Floor, Ceiling, and Wall; Insulation Workers, Mechanical; Manufactured Building and Mobile Home Installers; Operating Engineers; Painters, Construction and Maintenance; Paperhangers; Paving, Surfacing, and Tamping Equipment Operators; Pile-Driver Operators; Pipe Fitters; Pipelayers; Pipelaying Fitters; Plasterers and Stucco Masons; Plumbers; Rail-Track Laying and Maintenance Equipment Operators; Refractory Materials Repairers, Except Brickmasons; Reinforcing Iron and Rebar Workers; Riggers; Roofers; Rough Carpenters; Security and Fire Alarm Systems Installers; Segmental Pavers; Sheet Metal Workers; Ship Carpenters and Joiners; Stone Cutters and Carvers; Stonemasons; Structural Iron and Steel Workers; Tapers; Terrazzo Workers and Finishers; Tile and Marble Setters. **PERSONALITY TYPE:** Realistic.

EDUCATION/TRAINING PROGRAM(S)—Construction/Heavy Equipment/Earthmoving Equipment Operation. **RELATED KNOWLEDGE/COURSES—Building and Construction:** Knowledge of the materials, methods, and tools involved in the construction or repair of houses, buildings, or other structures such as highways and roads. **Transportation:** Knowledge of principles and methods for moving people or goods by air, rail, sea, or road, including the relative costs and benefits. **Physics:** Knowledge and prediction of physical principles and laws and their interrelationships and applications to understanding fluid, material, and atmospheric dynamics and mechanical, electrical, atomic, and subatomic structures and processes. **Engineering and Technology:** Knowledge of the practical application of engineering science and technology. This includes applying principles, techniques, procedures, and equipment to the design and production of various goods and services. **Mechanical Devices:** Knowledge of machines and tools, including their designs, uses, repair, and maintenance. **Public Safety and Security:** Knowledge of relevant equipment, policies, procedures, and strategies to promote effective local, state, or national security operations for the protection of people, data, property, and institutions.

Drywall Installers

- Education/Training Required: Moderate-term on-the-job training
- Annual Earnings: $34,030
- Growth: 21.4%
- Annual Job Openings: 17,000
- Self-Employed: 18.4%
- Part-Time: 5.9%

Apply plasterboard or other wallboard to ceilings and interior walls of buildings. Trims rough edges from wallboard to maintain even joints, using knife. Fits and fastens wallboard or sheetrock into specified position, using hand tools, portable power tools, or adhesive. Measures and marks cutting lines on framing, drywall, and trim, using tape measure, straightedge or square, and marking devices. Installs blanket insulation between studs and tacks plastic moisture barrier over insulation. Removes plaster, drywall, or paneling, using crowbar and hammer. Assembles and installs metal framing and decorative trim for windows, doorways, and bents. Reads blueprints and other specifications to determine method of installation, work procedures, and material and tool requirements. Lays out reference lines and points, computes position of framing and furring channels, and marks position, using chalkline. Suspends angle iron grid and channel iron from ceiling, using wire. Installs horizontal and vertical metal or wooden studs for attachment of wallboard on interior walls, using hand tools. Cuts metal or wood framing, angle and channel iron, and trim to size, using cutting tools. Cuts openings into board for electrical outlets, windows, vents, or fixtures, using keyhole saw or other cutting tools. **SKILLS—Installation:** Installing equipment, machines, wiring, or programs to meet specifications. **GOE—Interest Area:** 02. Architecture and Construction. **Work Group:** 02.04. Construction Crafts. **Other Jobs in This Work Group:** Boat Builders and Shipwrights; Boilermakers; Brattice Builders; Brickmasons and Blockmasons; Carpet Installers; Ceiling Tile Installers; Cement Masons and Concrete Finishers; Commercial Divers; Construction Carpenters; Crane and Tower Operators; Dragline Operators; Electricians; Fence Erectors; Floor Layers, Except Carpet, Wood, and Hard Tiles; Floor Sanders and Finishers; Glaziers; Grader, Bulldozer, and Scraper Operators; Hazardous Materials Removal Workers; Insulation Workers, Floor, Ceiling, and Wall; Insulation Workers, Mechanical; Manufactured Building and Mobile Home Installers; Operating Engineers; Painters, Construction and Maintenance; Paperhangers; Paving, Surfacing, and Tamping Equipment Operators; Pile-Driver Operators; Pipe Fitters; Pipelayers; Pipelaying Fitters; Plasterers and Stucco Masons; Plumbers; Rail-Track Laying and Maintenance Equipment Operators; Refractory Materials Repairers, Except Brickmasons; Reinforcing Iron and Rebar Workers; Riggers; Roofers; Rough Carpenters; Security and Fire Alarm Systems Installers; Segmental Pavers; Sheet Metal Workers; Ship Carpenters and Joiners; Stone Cutters and Carvers; Stonemasons; Structural Iron and Steel Workers; Tapers; Terrazzo Workers and Finishers; Tile and Marble Setters. **PERSONALITY TYPE:** Realistic.

EDUCATION/TRAINING PROGRAM(S)—Drywall Installation/Drywaller. **RELATED KNOWLEDGE/COURSES—Building and Construction:** Knowledge of the materials, methods, and tools involved in the construction or repair of houses, buildings, or other structures such as highways and roads.

Design: Knowledge of design techniques, tools, and principles involved in production of precision technical plans, blueprints, drawings, and models. **Engineering and Technology:** Knowledge of the practical application of engineering science and technology. This includes applying principles, techniques, procedures, and equipment to the design and production of various goods and services. **Mechanical Devices:** Knowledge of machines and tools, including their designs, uses, repair, and maintenance.

Economics Teachers, Postsecondary

- Education/Training Required: Master's degree
- Annual Earnings: $67,520
- Growth: 38.1%
- Annual Job Openings: 216,000
- Self-Employed: 0.3%
- Part-Time: 27.7%

Teach courses in economics. Prepare and deliver lectures to undergraduate and/or graduate students on topics such as econometrics, price theory, and macroeconomics. Prepare course materials such as syllabi, homework assignments, and handouts. Evaluate and grade students' class work, assignments, and papers. Compile, administer, and grade examinations or assign this work to others. Keep abreast of developments in their field by reading current literature, talking with colleagues, and participating in professional conferences. Maintain student attendance records, grades, and other required records. Initiate, facilitate, and moderate classroom discussions. Maintain regularly scheduled office hours in order to advise and assist students. Select and obtain materials and supplies such as textbooks. Plan, evaluate, and revise curricula, course content, and course materials and methods of instruction. Conduct research in a particular field of knowledge and publish findings in professional journals, books, and/or electronic media. Supervise undergraduate and/or graduate teaching, internship, and research work. Advise students on academic and vocational curricula and on career issues. Serve on academic or administrative committees that deal with institutional policies, departmental matters, and academic issues. Collaborate with colleagues to address teaching and research issues. Compile bibliographies of specialized materials for outside reading assignments. Participate in student recruitment, registration, and placement activities. Perform administrative duties such as serving as department head. **SKILLS—Instructing:** Teaching others how to do something. **Writing:** Communicating effectively in writing as appropriate for the needs of the audience. **Speaking:** Talking to others to convey information effectively. **Mathematics:** Using mathematics to solve problems. **Critical Thinking:** Using logic and reasoning to identify the strengths and weaknesses of alternative solutions, conclusions, or approaches to problems. **Reading Comprehension:** Understanding written sentences and paragraphs in work-related documents. **Learning Strategies:** Selecting and using training/instructional methods and procedures appropriate for the situation when learning or teaching new things. **Active Learning:** Understanding the implications of new information for both current and future problem-solving and decision-making. **GOE—Interest Area:** 05. Education and Training. **Work Group:** 05.03. Postsecondary and Adult Teaching and Instructing. **Other Jobs in This Work Group:** Adult Literacy, Remedial Education, and GED Teachers and Instructors; Agricultural Sciences Teachers, Postsecondary; Anthropology and Archeology Teachers, Postsecondary; Architecture Teachers, Postsecondary; Area, Ethnic, and Cultural Studies Teachers, Postsecondary; Art, Drama, and Music Teachers, Postsecondary; Atmospheric, Earth, Marine, and Space Sciences Teachers, Postsecondary; Biological Science Teachers, Postsecondary; Business Teachers, Postsecondary; Chemistry Teachers, Postsecondary; Communications Teachers, Postsecondary; Computer Science Teachers, Postsecondary; Criminal Justice and Law Enforcement Teachers, Postsecondary; Education Teachers, Postsecondary; Engineering Teachers, Postsecondary; English Language and Literature Teachers, Postsecondary; Environmental Science Teachers, Postsecondary; Farm and Home Management Advisors; Foreign Language and Literature Teachers, Postsecondary; Forestry and Conservation Science Teachers, Postsecondary; Geography Teachers, Postsecondary; Graduate Teaching Assistants; Health Specialties Teachers, Postsecondary; History Teachers, Postsecondary; Home Economics Teachers, Postsecondary; Law Teachers, Postsecondary; Library Science Teachers, Postsecondary; Mathematical Science Teachers, Postsecondary; Nursing Instructors and Teachers, Postsecondary; Philosophy and Religion Teachers, Postsecondary; Physics Teachers, Postsecondary; Political

Science Teachers, Postsecondary; Psychology Teachers, Postsecondary; Recreation and Fitness Studies Teachers, Postsecondary; Self-Enrichment Education Teachers; Social Work Teachers, Postsecondary; Sociology Teachers, Postsecondary; Vocational Education Teachers, Postsecondary. **PERSONALITY TYPE:** Social.

EDUCATION/TRAINING PROGRAM(S)— Applied Economics; Business/Managerial Economics; Development Economics and International Development; Econometrics and Quantitative Economics; Economics, General; Economics, Other; International Economics; Social Science Teacher Education. **RELATED KNOWLEDGE/COURSES—Economics and Accounting:** Knowledge of economic and accounting principles and practices, the financial markets, banking, and the analysis and reporting of financial data. **Mathematics:** Knowledge of arithmetic, algebra, geometry, calculus, and statistics and their applications. **Education and Training:** Knowledge of principles and methods for curriculum and training design, teaching and instruction for individuals and groups, and the measurement of training effects. **History and Archeology:** Knowledge of historical events and their causes, indicators, and effects on civilizations and cultures. **English Language:** Knowledge of the structure and content of the English language, including the meaning and spelling of words, rules of composition, and grammar. **Philosophy and Theology:** Knowledge of different philosophical systems and religions. This includes their basic principles, values, ethics, ways of thinking, customs, and practices and their impact on human culture.

Economists

- ◉ Education/Training Required: Bachelor's degree
- ◉ Annual Earnings: $72,780
- ◉ Growth: 13.4%
- ◉ Annual Job Openings: 2,000
- ◉ Self-Employed: 11.5%
- ◉ Part-Time: 8.3%

Conduct research, prepare reports, or formulate plans to aid in solution of economic problems arising from production and distribution of goods and services. May collect and process economic and statistical data using econometric and sampling techniques. Study economic and statistical data in area of specialization, such as finance, labor, or agriculture. Formulate recommendations, policies, or plans to solve economic problems or to interpret markets. Provide advice and consultation on economic relationships to businesses, public and private agencies, and other employers. Supervise research projects and students' study projects. Teach theories, principles, and methods of economics. Testify at regulatory or legislative hearings concerning the estimated effects of changes in legislation or public policy and present recommendations based on cost-benefit analyses. Compile, analyze, and report data to explain economic phenomena and forecast market trends, applying mathematical models and statistical techniques. Develop economic guidelines and standards and prepare points of view used in forecasting trends and formulating economic policy. Forecast production and consumption of renewable resources and supply, consumption, and depletion of non-renewable resources. **SKILLS—Systems Evaluation:** Identifying measures or indicators of system performance and the actions needed to improve or correct performance relative to the goals of the system. **Systems Analysis:** Determining how a system should work and how changes in conditions, operations, and the environment will affect outcomes. **Judgment and Decision Making:** Considering the relative costs and benefits of potential actions to choose the most appropriate one. **Persuasion:** Persuading others to change their minds or behavior. **Complex Problem Solving:** Identifying complex problems and reviewing related information to develop and evaluate options and implement solutions. **Learning Strategies:** Selecting and using training/instructional methods and procedures appropriate for the situation when learning or teaching new things. **Writing:** Communicating effectively in writing as appropriate for the needs of the audience. **Instructing:** Teaching others how to do something. **GOE—Interest Area:** 15. Scientific Research, Engineering, and Mathematics. **Work Group:** 15.04. Social Sciences. **Other Jobs in This Work Group:** Anthropologists; Archeologists; Educational Psychologists; Historians; Industrial-Organizational Psychologists; Political Scientists; Sociologists. **PERSONALITY TYPE:** Investigative.

EDUCATION/TRAINING PROGRAM(S)—Agricultural Economics; Applied Economics; Business/Managerial Economics; Development Economics and International Development; Econometrics and Quantitative Economics; Economics, General;

E

Economics, Other; International Economics. **RELAT-ED KNOWLEDGE/COURSES—Economics and Accounting:** Knowledge of economic and accounting principles and practices, the financial markets, banking, and the analysis and reporting of financial data. **Mathematics:** Knowledge of arithmetic, algebra, geometry, calculus, and statistics and their applications. **Education and Training:** Knowledge of principles and methods for curriculum and training design, teaching and instruction for individuals and groups, and the measurement of training effects. **Production and Processing:** Knowledge of raw materials, production processes, quality control, costs, and other techniques for maximizing the effective manufacture and distribution of goods. **Personnel and Human Resources:** Knowledge of principles and procedures for personnel recruitment, selection, training, compensation and benefits, labor relations and negotiation, and personnel information systems. **Computers and Electronics:** Knowledge of circuit boards, processors, chips, electronic equipment, and computer hardware and software, including applications and programming.

Editors

- Education/Training Required: Bachelor's degree
- Annual Earnings: $43,890
- Growth: 11.8%
- Annual Job Openings: 14,000
- Self-Employed: 12.9%
- Part-Time: 13.0%

Perform variety of editorial duties, such as laying out, indexing, and revising content of written materials, in preparation for final publication. Prepare, rewrite, and edit copy to improve readability or supervise others who do this work. Read copy or proof to detect and correct errors in spelling, punctuation, and syntax. Allocate print space for story text, photos, and illustrations according to space parameters and copy significance, using knowledge of layout principles. Plan the contents of publications according to the publication's style, editorial policy, and publishing requirements. Verify facts, dates, and statistics, using standard reference sources. Review and approve proofs submitted by composing room prior to publication production.

Develop story or content ideas, considering reader or audience appeal. Oversee publication production, including artwork, layout, computer typesetting, and printing, ensuring adherence to deadlines and budget requirements. Confer with management and editorial staff members regarding placement and emphasis of developing news stories. Assign topics, events, and stories to individual writers or reporters for coverage. Read, evaluate, and edit manuscripts or other materials submitted for publication and confer with authors regarding changes in content, style or organization, or publication. Monitor news-gathering operations to ensure utilization of all news sources, such as press releases, telephone contacts, radio, television, wire services, and other reporters. Meet frequently with artists, typesetters, layout personnel, marketing directors, and production managers to discuss projects and resolve problems. Supervise and coordinate work of reporters and other editors. Make manuscript acceptance or revision recommendations to the publisher. Select local, state, national, and international news items received from wire services based on assessment of items' significance and interest value. Interview and hire writers and reporters or negotiate contracts, royalties, and payments for authors or freelancers. **SKILLS—Writing:** Communicating effectively in writing as appropriate for the needs of the audience. **Reading Comprehension:** Understanding written sentences and paragraphs in work-related documents. **Active Listening:** Giving full attention to what other people are saying, taking time to understand the points being made, asking questions as appropriate, and not interrupting at inappropriate times. **Time Management:** Managing one's own time and the time of others. **Persuasion:** Persuading others to change their minds or behavior. **Critical Thinking:** Using logic and reasoning to identify the strengths and weaknesses of alternative solutions, conclusions, or approaches to problems. **Social Perceptiveness:** Being aware of others' reactions and understanding why they react as they do. **Active Learning:** Understanding the implications of new information for both current and future problem-solving and decision-making. **Negotiation:** Bringing others together and trying to reconcile differences. **GOE—Interest Area:** 03. Arts and Communication. **Work Group:** 03.02. Writing and Editing. **Other Jobs in This Work Group:** Copy Writers; Creative Writers; Poets and Lyricists; Technical Writers. **PERSONALITY TYPE:** Artistic.

EDUCATION/TRAINING PROGRAM(S)— Broadcast Journalism; Business/Corporate Communications; Communication, Journalism, and Related Programs, Other; Creative Writing; Journalism; Mass Communication/Media Studies; Publishing; Technical and Business Writing. **RELATED KNOWLEDGE/COURSES—Communications and Media:** Knowledge of media production, communication, and dissemination techniques and methods. This includes alternative ways to inform and entertain via written, oral, and visual media. **English Language:** Knowledge of the structure and content of the English language, including the meaning and spelling of words, rules of composition, and grammar. **Geography:** Knowledge of principles and methods for describing the features of land, sea, and air masses, including their physical characteristics; locations; interrelationships; and distribution of plant, animal, and human life. **History and Archeology:** Knowledge of historical events and their causes, indicators, and effects on civilizations and cultures. **Clerical Practices:** Knowledge of administrative and clerical procedures and systems such as word processing, managing files and records, stenography and transcription, designing forms, and other office procedures and terminology. **Computers and Electronics:** Knowledge of circuit boards, processors, chips, electronic equipment, and computer hardware and software, including applications and programming.

Education Administrators, Elementary and Secondary School

◎ Education/Training Required: Work experience plus degree

◎ Annual Earnings: $74,190

◎ Growth: 20.7%

◎ Annual Job Openings: 31,000

◎ Self-Employed: 3.2%

◎ Part-Time: 7.2%

Plan, direct, or coordinate the academic, clerical, or auxiliary activities of public or private elementary or secondary-level schools. Review and approve new programs or recommend modifications to existing programs, submitting program proposals for school board approval as necessary. Prepare, maintain, or oversee the preparation/maintenance of attendance, activity, planning, or personnel reports and records. Confer with parents and staff to discuss educational activities, policies, and student behavioral or learning problems. Prepare and submit budget requests and recommendations or grant proposals to solicit program funding. Direct and coordinate school maintenance services and the use of school facilities. Counsel and provide guidance to students regarding personal, academic, vocational, or behavioral issues. Organize and direct committees of specialists, volunteers, and staff to provide technical and advisory assistance for programs. Teach classes or courses to students. Advocate for new schools to be built or for existing facilities to be repaired or remodeled. Plan and develop instructional methods and content for educational, vocational, or student activity programs. Develop partnerships with businesses, communities, and other organizations to help meet identified educational needs and to provide school-to-work programs. Direct and coordinate activities of teachers, administrators, and support staff at schools, public agencies, and institutions. Evaluate curricula, teaching methods, and programs to determine their effectiveness, efficiency, and utilization and to ensure that school activities comply with federal, state, and local regulations. Set educational standards and goals and help establish policies and procedures to carry them out. Recruit, hire, train, and evaluate primary and supplemental staff. Enforce discipline and attendance rules. Observe teaching methods and examine learning materials in order to evaluate and standardize curricula and teaching techniques and to determine areas where improvement is needed. Establish, coordinate, and oversee particular programs across school districts, such as programs to evaluate student academic achievement. Review and interpret government codes and develop programs to ensure adherence to codes and facility safety, security, and maintenance. **SKILLS—Management of Personnel Resources:** Motivating, developing, and directing people as they work, identifying the best people for the job. **Management of Financial Resources:** Determining how money will be spent to get the work done and accounting for these expenditures. **Learning Strategies:** Selecting and using training/instructional methods and procedures appropriate for the situation when learning or teaching new things. **Negotiation:** Bringing others together and trying to reconcile differences. **Social Perceptiveness:** Being aware of others' reactions and understanding why they react as they do. **Persuasion:**

E

Persuading others to change their minds or behavior. **Monitoring:** Monitoring or assessing your performance or that of other individuals or organizations to make improvements or take corrective action. **Coordination:** Adjusting actions in relation to others' actions. **Service Orientation:** Actively looking for ways to help people. **GOE—Interest Area:** 05. Education and Training. **Work Group:** 05.01. Managerial Work in Education. **Other Jobs in This Work Group:** Education Administrators, Postsecondary; Education Administrators, Preschool and Child Care Center/Program; Instructional Coordinators. **PERSONALITY TYPE:** Social.

EDUCATION/TRAINING PROGRAM(S)—Educational Administration and Supervision, Other; Educational Leadership and Administration, General; Educational, Instructional, and Curriculum Supervision; Elementary and Middle School Administration/Principalship; Secondary School Administration/Principalship. **RELATED KNOWLEDGE/COURSES—Education and Training:** Knowledge of principles and methods for curriculum and training design, teaching and instruction for individuals and groups, and the measurement of training effects. **Personnel and Human Resources:** Knowledge of principles and procedures for personnel recruitment, selection, training, compensation and benefits, labor relations and negotiation, and personnel information systems. **Therapy and Counseling:** Knowledge of principles, methods, and procedures for diagnosis, treatment, and rehabilitation of physical and mental dysfunctions and for career counseling and guidance. **Customer and Personal Service:** Knowledge of principles and processes for providing customer and personal services. This includes customer needs assessment, meeting quality standards for services, and evaluation of customer satisfaction. **Psychology:** Knowledge of human behavior and performance; individual differences in ability, personality, and interests; learning and motivation; psychological research methods; and the assessment and treatment of behavioral and affective disorders. **English Language:** Knowledge of the structure and content of the English language, including the meaning and spelling of words, rules of composition, and grammar.

Education Administrators, Postsecondary

- Education/Training Required: Work experience plus degree
- Annual Earnings: $68,340
- Growth: 25.9%
- Annual Job Openings: 19,000
- Self-Employed: 2.6%
- Part-Time: 7.2%

Plan, direct, or coordinate research, instructional, student administration and services, and other educational activities at postsecondary institutions, including universities, colleges, and junior and community colleges. Recruit, hire, train, and terminate departmental personnel. Plan, administer, and control budgets; maintain financial records; and produce financial reports. Represent institutions at community and campus events, in meetings with other institution personnel, and during accreditation processes. Participate in faculty and college committee activities. Provide assistance to faculty and staff in duties such as teaching classes, conducting orientation programs, issuing transcripts, and scheduling events. Establish operational policies and procedures and make any necessary modifications based on analysis of operations, demographics, and other research information. Confer with other academic staff to explain and formulate admission requirements and course credit policies. Appoint individuals to faculty positions and evaluate their performance. Direct activities of administrative departments, such as admissions, registration, and career services. Develop curricula and recommend curriculum revisions and additions. Determine course schedules and coordinate teaching assignments and room assignments in order to ensure optimum use of buildings and equipment. Consult with government regulatory and licensing agencies in order to ensure the institution's conformance with applicable standards. Direct, coordinate, and evaluate the activities of personnel engaged in administering academic institutions, departments, and/or alumni organizations. Teach courses within their department. Participate in student recruitment, selection, and admission, making admissions recommendations when required to do so. Review student misconduct reports requiring disciplinary action and counsel students regarding such reports. Supervise coaches. Assess and collect tuition and fees. Direct scholarship, fellowship, and loan programs, performing activities such as selecting recipients and distributing aid. Coordinate the production and dissemination of university publications such as course catalogs and class schedules. Review registration statistics and consult with faculty officials to develop registration policies. **SKILLS—Management of Personnel Resources:** Motivating, developing, and directing people as they work, identifying the best people for the job. **Management of Financial Resources:** Determining how money will be spent to get the work done and accounting for these expenditures. **Social Perceptiveness:** Being aware of others' reactions and understanding why they react as they do. **Persuasion:** Persuading others to change their minds or behavior. **Coordination:** Adjusting actions in relation to others' actions. **Service Orientation:** Actively looking for ways to help people. **Negotiation:** Bringing others together and trying to reconcile differences. **Monitoring:** Monitoring or assessing your performance or that of other individuals or organizations to make improvements or take corrective action. **GOE—Interest Area:** 05. Education and Training. **Work Group:** 05.01. Managerial Work in Education. **Other Jobs in This Work Group:** Education Administrators, Elementary and Secondary School; Education Administrators, Preschool and Child Care Center/Program; Instructional Coordinators. **PERSONALITY TYPE:** Enterprising.

EDUCATION/TRAINING PROGRAM(S)— Community College Education; Educational Administration and Supervision, Other; Educational Leadership and Administration, General; Educational, Instructional, and Curriculum Supervision; Higher Education/Higher Education Administration. **RELATED KNOWLEDGE/COURSES—Education and Training:** Knowledge of principles and methods for curriculum and training design, teaching and instruction for individuals and groups, and the measurement of training effects. **Customer and Personal Service:** Knowledge of principles and processes for providing customer and personal services. This includes customer needs assessment, meeting quality standards for services, and evaluation of customer satisfaction. **Personnel and Human Resources:** Knowledge of principles and procedures for personnel recruitment, selection, training, compensation and benefits, labor relations and negotiation, and personnel information systems. **Administration and Management:** Knowledge of business and management principles involved in strategic planning, resource allocation, human resources modeling, leadership technique, production methods, and coordination of people and resources. **Sociology and Anthropology:** Knowledge of group behavior and dynamics, societal trends and influences, human migrations, ethnicity, and cultures and their history and origins. **English Language:** Knowledge of the structure and content of the English language, including the meaning and spelling of words, rules of composition, and grammar.

Education Administrators, Preschool and Child Care Center/Program

- Education/Training Required: Work experience plus degree
- Annual Earnings: $35,730
- Growth: 32.0%
- Annual Job Openings: 9,000
- Self-Employed: 3.0%
- Part-Time: 7.2%

Plan, direct, or coordinate the academic and nonacademic activities of preschool and child care centers or programs. Confer with parents and staff to discuss educational activities and policies and students' behavioral or learning problems. Prepare and maintain attendance, activity, planning, accounting, or personnel reports and records for officials and agencies or direct preparation and maintenance activities. Set educational standards and goals and help establish policies, procedures, and programs to carry them out. Monitor students' progress and provide students and teachers with assistance in resolving any problems. Determine allocations of funds for staff, supplies, materials, and equipment and authorize purchases. Recruit, hire, train, and evaluate primary and supplemental staff and recommend personnel actions for programs and services. Direct and coordinate activities of teachers or administrators at day care centers, schools, public agencies, and/or institutions. Plan, direct, and monitor instructional methods and content of educational, vocational, or student activity programs. Review and interpret government codes and develop procedures to meet codes and to ensure facility safety, security, and maintenance. Determine the scope of educational program offerings and prepare drafts of program schedules and descriptions in order to estimate staffing and facility requirements. Review and evaluate new and current programs to determine their efficiency, effectiveness, and compliance with state, local, and federal regulations; recommend any necessary modifications. Teach classes or courses and/or provide direct care to children. Prepare and submit budget requests or grant proposals to solicit program funding. Write articles, manuals, and other publications and assist in the distribution of promotional literature about programs and facilities. Collect and analyze survey data, regulatory information, and demographic and employment trends in order to forecast enrollment patterns and the need for curriculum changes. Inform businesses, community groups, and governmental agencies about educational needs, available programs, and program policies. Organize and direct committees of specialists, volunteers, and staff to provide technical and advisory assistance for programs. **SKILLS—Management of Personnel Resources:** Motivating, developing, and directing people as they work, identifying the best people for the job. **Management of Financial Resources:** Determining how money will be spent to get the work done and accounting for these expenditures. **Learning Strategies:** Selecting and using training/instructional methods and procedures appropriate for the situation when learning or teaching new things. **Social Perceptiveness:** Being aware of others' reactions and understanding why they react as they do. **Persuasion:** Persuading others to change their minds or behavior. **Monitoring:** Monitoring or assessing your performance or that of other individuals or organizations to make improvements or take corrective action. **Negotiation:** Bringing others together and trying to reconcile differences. **Service Orientation:** Actively looking for ways to help people. **GOE—Interest Area:** 05. Education and Training. **Work Group:** 05.01. Managerial Work in Education. **Other Jobs in This Work Group:** Education Administrators, Elementary and Secondary School; Education Administrators, Postsecondary; Instructional Coordinators. **PERSONALITY TYPE:** Social.

EDUCATION/TRAINING PROGRAM(S)—Educational Administration and Supervision, Other; Educational Leadership and Administration, General; Educational, Instructional, and Curriculum Supervision. **RELATED KNOWLEDGE/COURSES— Education and Training:** Knowledge of principles and methods for curriculum and training design, teaching and instruction for individuals and groups, and the measurement of training effects. **Personnel and Human Resources:** Knowledge of principles and procedures for personnel recruitment, selection, training, compensation and benefits, labor relations and negotiation, and personnel information systems. **Clerical Practices:** Knowledge of administrative and clerical procedures and systems such as word processing, managing files and records, stenography and transcription, designing forms, and other office procedures and terminology. **Customer and Personal Service:** Knowledge of principles and processes for providing customer and personal services. This includes customer needs assessment, meeting quality standards for services, and evaluation of customer satisfaction. **Philosophy and Theology:** Knowledge of different philosophical systems and religions. This includes their basic principles, values, ethics, ways of thinking, customs, and practices and their impact on human culture. **Psychology:** Knowledge of human behavior and performance; individual differences in ability, personality, and interests; learning and motivation; psychological research methods; and the assessment and treatment of behavioral and affective disorders.

Education Teachers, Postsecondary

- Education/Training Required: Master's degree
- Annual Earnings: $49,530
- Growth: 38.1%
- Annual Job Openings: 216,000
- Self-Employed: 0.3%
- Part-Time: 27.7%

Teach courses pertaining to education, such as counseling, curriculum, guidance, instruction, teacher education, and teaching English as a second language. Prepare course materials such as syllabi, homework assignments, and handouts. Prepare and deliver lectures to undergraduate and/or graduate students on topics such as children's literature, learning and development, and reading instruction. Initiate, facilitate, and moderate classroom discussions. Evaluate and grade students' class work, assignments, and papers. Plan, evaluate, and revise curricula, course content, and course materials and methods of instruction. Supervise students' fieldwork, internship, and research work. Keep abreast of developments in their field by reading current literature, talking with colleagues, and participating in professional conferences. Advise students on academic and vocational curricula and on career issues. Maintain regularly scheduled office hours in order to advise and assist students. Maintain student attendance records, grades, and other required records. Collaborate with colleagues to address teaching and research issues. Compile, administer, and grade examinations or assign this work to others. Conduct research in a particular field of knowledge and publish findings in professional journals, books, and/or electronic media. Select and obtain materials and supplies such as textbooks. Participate in student recruitment, registration, and placement activities. Advise and instruct teachers employed in school systems by providing activities such as in-service seminars. Serve on academic or administrative committees that deal with institutional policies, departmental matters, and academic issues. Compile bibliographies of specialized materials for outside reading assignments. Write grant proposals to procure external research funding. Participate in campus and community events. Perform administrative duties such as serving as department head. Act as advisers to student organizations. **SKILLS—Instructing:** Teaching others how to do something. **Learning Strategies:** Selecting and using training/instructional methods and procedures appropriate for the situation when learning or teaching new things. **Social Perceptiveness:** Being aware of others' reactions and understanding why they react as they do. **Writing:** Communicating effectively in writing as appropriate for the needs of the audience. **Persuasion:** Persuading others to change their minds or behavior. **Service Orientation:** Actively looking for ways to help people. **Speaking:** Talking to others to convey information effectively. **Active Learning:** Understanding the implications of new information for both current and future problem-solving and decision-making. **GOE—Interest Area:** 05. Education and Training. **Work Group:** 05.03. Postsecondary and Adult Teaching and Instructing. **Other Jobs in This Work Group:** Adult Literacy, Remedial Education, and GED Teachers and Instructors; Agricultural Sciences Teachers, Postsecondary; Anthropology and Archeology Teachers, Postsecondary; Architecture Teachers, Postsecondary; Area, Ethnic, and Cultural Studies Teachers, Postsecondary; Art, Drama, and Music Teachers, Postsecondary; Atmospheric, Earth, Marine, and Space Sciences Teachers, Postsecondary; Biological Science Teachers, Postsecondary; Business Teachers, Postsecondary; Chemistry Teachers, Postsecondary; Communications Teachers, Postsecondary; Computer Science Teachers, Postsecondary; Criminal Justice and Law Enforcement Teachers, Postsecondary; Economics Teachers, Postsecondary; Engineering Teachers, Postsecondary; English Language and Literature Teachers, Postsecondary; Environmental Science Teachers, Postsecondary; Farm and Home Management Advisors; Foreign Language and Literature Teachers, Postsecondary; Forestry and Conservation Science Teachers, Postsecondary; Geography Teachers, Postsecondary; Graduate Teaching Assistants; Health Specialties Teachers, Postsecondary; History Teachers, Postsecondary; Home Economics Teachers, Postsecondary; Law Teachers, Postsecondary; Library Science Teachers, Postsecondary; Mathematical Science Teachers, Postsecondary; Nursing Instructors and Teachers, Postsecondary; Philosophy and Religion Teachers, Postsecondary; Physics Teachers, Postsecondary; Political Science Teachers, Postsecondary; Psychology Teachers, Postsecondary; Recreation and Fitness Studies Teachers, Postsecondary; Self-Enrichment Education Teachers; Social Work Teachers, Postsecondary; Sociology Teachers, Postsecondary; Vocational Education Teachers, Postsecondary. **PERSONALITY TYPE:** No data available.

EDUCATION/TRAINING PROGRAM(S)—Agricultural Teacher Education; Art Teacher Education; Biology Teacher Education; Business Teacher Education; Chemistry Teacher Education; Computer Teacher Education; Drama and Dance Teacher Education; Driver and Safety Teacher Education; Education, General; English/Language Arts Teacher Education; Family and Consumer Sciences/Home Economics Teacher Education; Foreign Language Teacher Education; French Language Teacher Education; Geography Teacher Education; German Language Teacher Education; Health Occupations Teacher Education; Health Teacher Education; History Teacher Education; Mathematics Teacher Education; Music Teacher Education; Physical Education Teaching and Coaching; Physics Teacher Education; Reading Teacher Education; Sales and Marketing Operations/Marketing and Distribution Teacher Education; Science Teacher Education/General Science Teacher Education; Social Science Teacher Education; Social Studies Teacher Education; Spanish Language Teacher Education; Speech Teacher Education; Teacher Education and Professional Development, Specific Subject Areas,

E

Other; Technical Teacher Education; Technology Teacher Education/Industrial Arts Teacher Education; Trade and Industrial Teacher Education. **RELATED KNOWLEDGE/COURSES—Education and Training:** Knowledge of principles and methods for curriculum and training design, teaching and instruction for individuals and groups, and the measurement of training effects. **Sociology and Anthropology:** Knowledge of group behavior and dynamics, societal trends and influences, human migrations, ethnicity, and cultures and their history and origins. **Psychology:** Knowledge of human behavior and performance; individual differences in ability, personality, and interests; learning and motivation; psychological research methods; and the assessment and treatment of behavioral and affective disorders. **Therapy and Counseling:** Knowledge of principles, methods, and procedures for diagnosis, treatment, and rehabilitation of physical and mental dysfunctions and for career counseling and guidance. **Philosophy and Theology:** Knowledge of different philosophical systems and religions. This includes their basic principles, values, ethics, ways of thinking, customs, and practices and their impact on human culture. **English Language:** Knowledge of the structure and content of the English language, including the meaning and spelling of words, rules of composition, and grammar.

Educational, Vocational, and School Counselors

- Education/Training Required: Master's degree
- Annual Earnings: $45,570
- Growth: 15.0%
- Annual Job Openings: 32,000
- Self-Employed: 4.4%
- Part-Time: 14.6%

Counsel individuals and provide group educational and vocational guidance services. Counsel students regarding educational issues such as course and program selection, class scheduling, school adjustment, truancy, study habits, and career planning. Counsel individuals to help them understand and overcome personal, social, or behavioral problems affecting their educational or vocational situations. Maintain accurate and complete student records as required by laws, district policies, and administrative regulations. Confer with parents or guardians, teachers, other counselors, and administrators to resolve students' behavioral, academic, and other problems. Provide crisis intervention to students when difficult situations occur at schools. Identify cases involving domestic abuse or other family problems affecting students' development. Meet with parents and guardians to discuss their children's progress and to determine their priorities for their children and their resource needs. Prepare students for later educational experiences by encouraging them to explore learning opportunities and to persevere with challenging tasks. Encourage students and/or parents to seek additional assistance from mental health professionals when necessary. Observe and evaluate students' performance, behavior, social development, and physical health. Enforce all administration policies and rules governing students. Meet with other professionals to discuss individual students' needs and progress. Provide students with information on such topics as college degree programs and admission requirements, financial aid opportunities, trade and technical schools, and apprenticeship programs. Evaluate individuals' abilities, interests, and personality characteristics, using tests, records, interviews, and professional sources. Collaborate with teachers and administrators in the development, evaluation, and revision of school programs. Teach classes and present self-help or information sessions on subjects related to education and career planning. Establish and enforce behavioral rules and procedures to maintain order among students. Conduct follow-up interviews with counselees to determine if their needs have been met. **SKILLS— Social Perceptiveness:** Being aware of others' reactions and understanding why they react as they do. **Service Orientation:** Actively looking for ways to help people. **Negotiation:** Bringing others together and trying to reconcile differences. **Persuasion:** Persuading others to change their minds or behavior. **Active Listening:** Giving full attention to what other people are saying, taking time to understand the points being made, asking questions as appropriate, and not interrupting at inappropriate times. **Learning Strategies:** Selecting and using training/instructional methods and procedures appropriate for the situation when learning or teaching new things. **Coordination:** Adjusting actions in relation to others' actions. **Instructing:** Teaching others how to do something. **GOE—Interest Area:** 05. Education and Training. **Work Group:** 05.06. Counseling, Health, and Fitness Education. **Other Jobs in This**

Work Group: Fitness Trainers and Aerobics Instructors; Health Educators. **PERSONALITY TYPE:** Social.

EDUCATION/TRAINING PROGRAM(S)—College Student Counseling and Personnel Services; Counselor Education/School Counseling and Guidance Services. **RELATED KNOWLEDGE/COURSES**—**Therapy and Counseling:** Knowledge of principles, methods, and procedures for diagnosis, treatment, and rehabilitation of physical and mental dysfunctions and for career counseling and guidance. **Psychology:** Knowledge of human behavior and performance; individual differences in ability, personality, and interests; learning and motivation; psychological research methods; and the assessment and treatment of behavioral and affective disorders. **Education and Training:** Knowledge of principles and methods for curriculum and training design, teaching and instruction for individuals and groups, and the measurement of training effects. **Sociology and Anthropology:** Knowledge of group behavior and dynamics, societal trends and influences, human migrations, ethnicity, and cultures and their history and origins. **Customer and Personal Service:** Knowledge of principles and processes for providing customer and personal services. This includes customer needs assessment, meeting quality standards for services, and evaluation of customer satisfaction. **Clerical Practices:** Knowledge of administrative and clerical procedures and systems such as word processing, managing files and records, stenography and transcription, designing forms, and other office procedures and terminology.

Electric Meter Installers and Repairers

- ◎ Education/Training Required: Moderate-term on-the-job training
- ◎ Annual Earnings: $43,710
- ◎ Growth: 12.0%
- ◎ Annual Job Openings: 5,000
- ◎ Self-Employed: 0.7%
- ◎ Part-Time: 2.0%

Install electric meters on customers' premises or on pole. Test meters and perform necessary repairs. Turn current on/off by connecting/disconnecting service drop. Mounts and installs meter and other electric equipment, such as time clocks, transformers, and circuit breakers, using electrician's hand tools. Inspects and tests electric meters, relays, and power to detect cause of malfunction and inaccuracy, using hand tools and testing equipment. Splices and connects cable from meter or current transformer to pull box or switchboard, using hand tools, to provide power. Disconnects and removes electric power meters when defective or when customer accounts are in default, using hand tools. Records meter reading and installation data on meter cards, work orders, or field service orders. Cleans meter parts, using chemical solutions, brushes, sandpaper, and soap and water. Makes adjustments to meter components, such as setscrews or timing mechanism, to conform to specifications. Repairs electric meters and components, such as transformers and relays, and changes faulty or incorrect wiring, using hand tools. **SKILLS**—**Installation:** Installing equipment, machines, wiring, or programs to meet specifications. **Troubleshooting:** Determining causes of operating errors and deciding what to do about them. **Repairing:** Repairing machines or systems by using the needed tools. **Technology Design:** Generating or adapting equipment and technology to serve user needs. **Equipment Maintenance:** Performing routine maintenance on equipment and determining when and what kind of maintenance is needed. **Quality Control Analysis:** Conducting tests and inspections of products, services, or processes to evaluate quality or performance. **Science:** Using scientific rules and methods to solve problems. **Operation Monitoring:** Watching gauges, dials, or other indicators to make sure a machine is working properly. **GOE**—**Interest Area:** 02. Architecture and Construction. **Work Group:** 02.05. Systems and Equipment Installation, Maintenance, and Repair. **Other Jobs in This Work Group:** Central Office and PBX Installers and Repairers; Communication Equipment Mechanics, Installers, and Repairers; Electrical and Electronics Repairers, Powerhouse, Substation, and Relay; Electrical Power-Line Installers and Repairers; Elevator Installers and Repairers; Frame Wirers, Central Office; Heating and Air Conditioning Mechanics; Home Appliance Installers; Maintenance and Repair Workers, General; Meter Mechanics; Refrigeration Mechanics; Station Installers and Repairers, Telephone; Telecommunications Facility Examiners; Telecommunications Line Installers and Repairers. **PERSONALITY TYPE:** Realistic.

E

EDUCATION/TRAINING PROGRAM(S)—Electromechanical and Instrumentation and Maintenance Technologies/Technicians, Other. **RELATED KNOWLEDGE/COURSES—Mechanical Devices:** Knowledge of machines and tools, including their designs, uses, repair, and maintenance. **Computers and Electronics:** Knowledge of circuit boards, processors, chips, electronic equipment, and computer hardware and software, including applications and programming. **Engineering and Technology:** Knowledge of the practical application of engineering science and technology. This includes applying principles, techniques, procedures, and equipment to the design and production of various goods and services. **Design:** Knowledge of design techniques, tools, and principles involved in production of precision technical plans, blueprints, drawings, and models. **Telecommunications:** Knowledge of transmission, broadcasting, switching, control, and operation of telecommunications systems. **Building and Construction:** Knowledge of the materials, methods, and tools involved in the construction or repair of houses, buildings, or other structures such as highways and roads. **Geography:** Knowledge of principles and methods for describing the features of land, sea, and air masses, including their physical characteristics; locations; interrelationships; and distribution of plant, animal, and human life.

Electrical and Electronic Inspectors and Testers

- ◎ Education/Training Required: Moderate-term on-the-job training
- ◎ Annual Earnings: $28,410
- ◎ Growth: 4.7%
- ◎ Annual Job Openings: 87,000
- ◎ Self-Employed: 1.2%
- ◎ Part-Time: 5.0%

Inspect and test electrical and electronic systems, such as radar navigational equipment, computer memory units, and television and radio transmitters, using precision measuring instruments. Tests and measures finished products, components, or assemblies for functioning, operation, accuracy, or assembly to verify adherence to functional specifications. Reads dials and meters to verify functioning of equipment according to specifications. Analyzes and interprets blueprints, sample data, and other materials to determine, change, or measure specifications or inspection and testing procedures. Marks items for acceptance or rejection, records test results and inspection data, and compares findings with specifications to ensure conformance to standards. Inspects materials, products, and work in progress for conformance to specifications and adjusts process or assembly equipment to meet standards. Computes and/or calculates sample data and test results. Confers with vendors and others regarding inspection results; recommends corrective procedures; and compiles reports of results, recommendations, and needed repairs. Writes and installs computer programs to control test equipment. Installs, positions, or connects new or replacement parts, components, and instruments. Reviews maintenance records to ensure that plant equipment functions properly. Disassembles defective parts and components. Cleans and maintains test equipment and instruments to ensure proper functioning. Positions or directs other workers to position products, components, or parts for testing. Operates or tends machinery and equipment and uses hand tools. Examines and adjusts or repairs finished products and components or parts. **SKILLS—Programming:** Writing computer programs for various purposes. **Quality Control Analysis:** Conducting tests and inspections of products, services, or processes to evaluate quality or performance. **Installation:** Installing equipment, machines, wiring, or programs to meet specifications. **Troubleshooting:** Determining causes of operating errors and deciding what to do about them. **Repairing:** Repairing machines or systems by using the needed tools. **Operation Monitoring:** Watching gauges, dials, or other indicators to make sure a machine is working properly. **Science:** Using scientific rules and methods to solve problems. **Equipment Maintenance:** Performing routine maintenance on equipment and determining when and what kind of maintenance is needed. **GOE—Interest Area:** 13. Manufacturing. **Work Group:** 13.07. Production Quality Control. **Other Jobs in This Work Group:** Graders and Sorters, Agricultural Products; Materials Inspectors; Precision Devices Inspectors and Testers; Production Inspectors, Testers, Graders, Sorters, Samplers, Weighers. **PERSONALITY TYPE:** Realistic.

EDUCATION/TRAINING PROGRAM(S)—Quality Control Technology/Technician. **RELATED KNOWLEDGE/COURSES—Computers and Electronics:** Knowledge of circuit boards, processors, chips, electronic equipment, and computer hardware and software, including applications and programming. **Telecommunications:** Knowledge of transmission, broadcasting, switching, control, and operation of telecommunications systems. **Design:** Knowledge of design techniques, tools, and principles involved in production of precision technical plans, blueprints, drawings, and models. **Mechanical Devices:** Knowledge of machines and tools, including their designs, uses, repair, and maintenance. **Engineering and Technology:** Knowledge of the practical application of engineering science and technology. This includes applying principles, techniques, procedures, and equipment to the design and production of various goods and services. **Production and Processing:** Knowledge of raw materials, production processes, quality control, costs, and other techniques for maximizing the effective manufacture and distribution of goods.

Electrical and Electronics Repairers, Commercial and Industrial Equipment

- ◎ Education/Training Required: Postsecondary vocational training
- ◎ Annual Earnings: $42,600
- ◎ Growth: 10.3%
- ◎ Annual Job Openings: 10,000
- ◎ Self-Employed: 0.7%
- ◎ Part-Time: 1.2%

Repair, test, adjust, or install electronic equipment, such as industrial controls, transmitters, and antennas. Perform scheduled preventive maintenance tasks, such as checking, cleaning, and repairing equipment, to detect and prevent problems. Examine work orders and converse with equipment operators to detect equipment problems and to ascertain whether mechanical or human errors contributed to the problems. Set up and test industrial equipment to ensure that it functions properly. Operate equipment to demonstrate proper use and to analyze malfunctions. Test faulty equipment to diagnose malfunctions, using test equipment and software and applying knowledge of the functional operation of electronic units and systems. Repair and adjust equipment, machines, and

defective components, replacing worn parts such as gaskets and seals in watertight electrical equipment. Calibrate testing instruments and installed or repaired equipment to prescribed specifications. Advise management regarding customer satisfaction, product performance, and suggestions for product improvements. Inspect components of industrial equipment for accurate assembly and installation and for defects such as loose connections and frayed wires. Study blueprints, schematics, manuals, and other specifications to determine installation procedures. Maintain equipment logs that record performance problems, repairs, calibrations, and tests. Coordinate efforts with other workers involved in installing and maintaining equipment or components. Maintain inventory of spare parts. Consult with customers, supervisors, and engineers to plan layout of equipment and to resolve problems in system operation and maintenance. Send defective units to the manufacturer or to a specialized repair shop for repair. Install repaired equipment in various settings, such as industrial or military establishments. Determine feasibility of using standardized equipment and develop specifications for equipment required to perform additional functions. Enter information into computer to copy program or to draw, modify, or store schematics, applying knowledge of software package used. Sign overhaul documents for equipment replaced or repaired. Develop or modify industrial electronic devices, circuits, and equipment according to available specifications. **SKILLS—Installation:** Installing equipment, machines, wiring, or programs to meet specifications. **Troubleshooting:** Determining causes of operating errors and deciding what to do about them. **Repairing:** Repairing machines or systems by using the needed tools. **Operation Monitoring:** Watching gauges, dials, or other indicators to make sure a machine is working properly. **Equipment Maintenance:** Performing routine maintenance on equipment and determining when and what kind of maintenance is needed. **Systems Analysis:** Determining how a system should work and how changes in conditions, operations, and the environment will affect outcomes. **Operation and Control:** Controlling operations of equipment or systems. **Coordination:** Adjusting actions in relation to others' actions. **GOE—Interest Area:** 13. Manufacturing. **Work Group:** 13.12. Electrical and Electronic Repair. **Other Jobs in This Work Group:** Avionics Technicians; Battery Repairers; Electric Home Appliance and Power Tool Repairers; Electric Motor and Switch

Assemblers and Repairers; Electrical and Electronics Installers and Repairers, Transportation Equipment; Electrical Parts Reconditioners; Electronic Equipment Installers and Repairers, Motor Vehicles; Electronic Home Entertainment Equipment Installers and Repairers; Radio Mechanics; Transformer Repairers. **PERSONALITY TYPE:** Realistic.

EDUCATION/TRAINING PROGRAM(S)— Computer Installation and Repair Technology/Technician; Industrial Electronics Technology/Technician. **RELATED KNOWLEDGE/COURSES—Mechanical Devices:** Knowledge of machines and tools, including their designs, uses, repair, and maintenance. **Computers and Electronics:** Knowledge of circuit boards, processors, chips, electronic equipment, and computer hardware and software, including applications and programming. **Telecommunications:** Knowledge of transmission, broadcasting, switching, control, and operation of telecommunications systems. **Design:** Knowledge of design techniques, tools, and principles involved in production of precision technical plans, blueprints, drawings, and models. **Engineering and Technology:** Knowledge of the practical application of engineering science and technology. This includes applying principles, techniques, procedures, and equipment to the design and production of various goods and services. **Transportation:** Knowledge of principles and methods for moving people or goods by air, rail, sea, or road, including the relative costs and benefits.

Electrical Engineering Technicians

- ◉ Education/Training Required: Associate degree
- ◉ Annual Earnings: $46,310
- ◉ Growth: 10.0%
- ◉ Annual Job Openings: 24,000
- ◉ Self-Employed: 0.4%
- ◉ Part-Time: 5.0%

Apply electrical theory and related knowledge to test and modify developmental or operational electrical machinery and electrical control equipment and circuitry in industrial or commercial plants and laboratories. Usually work under direction of engineering

staff. Provide technical assistance and resolution when electrical or engineering problems are encountered before, during, and after construction. Assemble electrical and electronic systems and prototypes according to engineering data and knowledge of electrical principles, using hand tools and measuring instruments. Install and maintain electrical control systems and solid state equipment. Modify electrical prototypes, parts, assemblies, and systems to correct functional deviations. Set up and operate test equipment to evaluate performance of developmental parts, assemblies, or systems under simulated operating conditions and record results. Collaborate with electrical engineers and other personnel to identify, define, and solve developmental problems. Build, calibrate, maintain, troubleshoot, and repair electrical instruments or testing equipment. Analyze and interpret test information to resolve design-related problems. Write commissioning procedures for electrical installations. Prepare project cost and work-time estimates. Evaluate engineering proposals, shop drawings, and design comments for sound electrical engineering practice and conformance with established safety and design criteria and recommend approval or disapproval. Draw or modify diagrams and write engineering specifications to clarify design details and functional criteria of experimental electronics units. Conduct inspections for quality control and assurance programs, reporting findings and recommendations. Prepare contracts and initiate, review, and coordinate modifications to contract specifications and plans throughout the construction process. Plan, schedule, and monitor work of support personnel to assist supervisor. Review existing electrical engineering criteria to identify necessary revisions, deletions, or amendments to outdated material. Perform supervisory duties such as recommending work assignments, approving leaves, and completing performance evaluations. Plan method and sequence of operations for developing and testing experimental electronic and electrical equipment. **SKILLS—Troubleshooting:** Determining causes of operating errors and deciding what to do about them. **Repairing:** Repairing machines or systems by using the needed tools. **Installation:** Installing equipment, machines, wiring, or programs to meet specifications. **Technology Design:** Generating or adapting equipment and technology to serve user needs. **Operations Analysis:** Analyzing needs and product requirements to create a design. **Equipment Maintenance:** Performing routine maintenance on equipment and determining when and what kind of maintenance is needed. **Mathematics:** Using mathematics to solve problems. **Science:** Using scientific rules and methods to solve problems. **GOE—Interest Area:** 15. Scientific Research, Engineering, and Mathematics. **Work Group:** 15.09. Engineering Technology. **Other Jobs in This Work Group:** Aerospace Engineering and Operations Technicians; Calibration and Instrumentation Technicians; Cartographers and Photogrammetrists; Civil Engineering Technicians; Electro-Mechanical Technicians; Electronic Drafters; Electronics Engineering Technicians; Environmental Engineering Technicians; Mapping Technicians; Mechanical Drafters; Mechanical Engineering Technicians; Surveying Technicians. **PERSONALITY TYPE:** Realistic.

EDUCATION/TRAINING PROGRAM(S)— Computer Engineering Technology/Technician; Computer Technology/Computer Systems Technology; Electrical and Electronic Engineering Technologies/ Technicians, Other; Electrical, Electronic, and Communications Engineering Technology/Technician; Telecommunications Technology/Technician. **RELATED KNOWLEDGE/COURSES—Engineering and Technology:** Knowledge of the practical application of engineering science and technology. This includes applying principles, techniques, procedures, and equipment to the design and production of various goods and services. **Design:** Knowledge of design techniques, tools, and principles involved in production of precision technical plans, blueprints, drawings, and models. **Computers and Electronics:** Knowledge of circuit boards, processors, chips, electronic equipment, and computer hardware and software, including applications and programming. **Physics:** Knowledge and prediction of physical principles and laws and their interrelationships and applications to understanding fluid, material, and atmospheric dynamics and mechanical, electrical, atomic, and subatomic structures and processes. **Mechanical Devices:** Knowledge of machines and tools, including their designs, uses, repair, and maintenance. **Telecommunications:** Knowledge of transmission, broadcasting, switching, control, and operation of telecommunications systems.

Electrical Engineers

◎ Education/Training Required: Bachelor's degree
◎ Annual Earnings: $71,610
◎ Growth: 2.5%
◎ Annual Job Openings: 11,000
◎ Self-Employed: 3.3%
◎ Part-Time: 2.4%

Design, develop, test, or supervise the manufacturing and installation of electrical equipment, components, or systems for commercial, industrial, military, or scientific use. Confer with engineers, customers, and others to discuss existing or potential engineering projects and products. Design, implement, maintain, and improve electrical instruments, equipment, facilities, components, products, and systems for commercial, industrial, and domestic purposes. Operate computer-assisted engineering and design software and equipment to perform engineering tasks. Direct and coordinate manufacturing, construction, installation, maintenance, support, documentation, and testing activities to ensure compliance with specifications, codes, and customer requirements. Perform detailed calculations to compute and establish manufacturing, construction, and installation standards and specifications. Inspect completed installations and observe operations to ensure conformance to design and equipment specifications and compliance with operational and safety standards. Plan and implement research methodology and procedures to apply principles of electrical theory to engineering projects. Prepare specifications for purchase of materials and equipment. Supervise and train project team members as necessary. Investigate and test vendors' and competitors' products. Oversee project production efforts to assure projects are completed satisfactorily, on time, and within budget. Prepare and study technical drawings, specifications of electrical systems, and topographical maps to ensure that installation and operations conform to standards and customer requirements. Investigate customer or public complaints, determine nature and extent of problem, and recommend remedial measures. Plan layout of electric power–generating plants and distribution lines and stations. Assist in developing capital project programs for new equipment and major repairs. Develop budgets, estimating labor, material, and construction costs.

E

SKILLS—Troubleshooting: Determining causes of operating errors and deciding what to do about them. **Technology Design:** Generating or adapting equipment and technology to serve user needs. **Systems Analysis:** Determining how a system should work and how changes in conditions, operations, and the environment will affect outcomes. **Science:** Using scientific rules and methods to solve problems. **Systems Evaluation:** Identifying measures or indicators of system performance and the actions needed to improve or correct performance relative to the goals of the system. **Complex Problem Solving:** Identifying complex problems and reviewing related information to develop and evaluate options and implement solutions. **Equipment Selection:** Determining the kind of tools and equipment needed to do a job. **Management of Material Resources:** Obtaining and seeing to the appropriate use of equipment, facilities, and materials needed to do certain work. **GOE—Interest Area:** 15. Scientific Research, Engineering, and Mathematics. **Work Group:** 15.07. Research and Design Engineering. **Other Jobs in This Work Group:** Aerospace Engineers; Biomedical Engineers; Chemical Engineers; Civil Engineers; Computer Hardware Engineers; Electronics Engineers, Except Computer; Marine Architects; Marine Engineers; Materials Engineers; Mechanical Engineers; Nuclear Engineers. **PERSONALITY TYPE:** Investigative.

EDUCATION/TRAINING PROGRAM(S)—Electrical, Electronics, and Communications Engineering. **RELATED KNOWLEDGE/COURSES—Engineering and Technology:** Knowledge of the practical application of engineering science and technology. This includes applying principles, techniques, procedures, and equipment to the design and production of various goods and services. **Design:** Knowledge of design techniques, tools, and principles involved in production of precision technical plans, blueprints, drawings, and models. **Physics:** Knowledge and prediction of physical principles and laws and their interrelationships and applications to understanding fluid, material, and atmospheric dynamics and mechanical, electrical, atomic, and subatomic structures and processes. **Computers and Electronics:** Knowledge of circuit boards, processors, chips, electronic equipment, and computer hardware and software, including applications and programming. **Mathematics:** Knowledge of arithmetic, algebra, geometry, calculus, and statistics and their applications. **Telecommunications:** Knowl-edge of transmission, broadcasting, switching, control, and operation of telecommunications systems.

Electrical Power-Line Installers and Repairers

- Education/Training Required: Long-term on-the-job training
- Annual Earnings: $49,100
- Growth: 1.6%
- Annual Job Openings: 9,000
- Self-Employed: 3.1%
- Part-Time: 1.3%

Install or repair cables or wires used in electrical power or distribution systems. May erect poles and light- or heavy-duty transmission towers. Adhere to safety practices and procedures, such as checking equipment regularly and erecting barriers around work areas. Attach crossarms, insulators, and auxiliary equipment to poles prior to installing them. Clean, tin, and splice corresponding conductors by twisting ends together or by joining ends with metal clamps and soldering connections. Climb poles or use truck-mounted buckets to access equipment. Cut and peel lead sheathing and insulation from defective or newly installed cables and conduits prior to splicing. Identify defective sectionalizing devices, circuit breakers, fuses, voltage regulators, transformers, switches, relays, or wiring, using wiring diagrams and electrical-testing instruments. Inspect and test power lines and auxiliary equipment to locate and identify problems, using reading and testing instruments. Install, maintain, and repair electrical distribution and transmission systems, including conduits, cables, wires, and related equipment such as transformers, circuit breakers, and switches. Lay underground cable directly in trenches or string it through conduit running through the trenches. Open switches or attach grounding devices in order to remove electrical hazards from disturbed or fallen lines or to facilitate repairs. Place insulating or fireproofing materials over conductors and joints. Pull up cable by hand from large reels mounted on trucks. Replace damaged poles with new poles and straighten the poles. Splice or solder cables together or to overhead transmission lines, customer service lines, or street light lines, using hand tools, epoxies, or specialized equipment. String wire conductors and cables between poles, towers, trenches, pylons, and buildings, setting lines in place and using winches to adjust tension. Test conductors according to electrical diagrams and specifications to identify corresponding conductors and to prevent incorrect connections. Coordinate work assignment preparation and completion with other workers. Cut trenches for laying underground cables, using trenchers and cable plows. Dig holes, using augers, and set poles, using cranes and power equipment. **SKILLS—Installation:** Installing equipment, machines, wiring, or programs to meet specifications. **Repairing:** Repairing machines or systems by using the needed tools. **Troubleshooting:** Determining causes of operating errors and deciding what to do about them. **Equipment Maintenance:** Performing routine maintenance on equipment and determining when and what kind of maintenance is needed. **Science:** Using scientific rules and methods to solve problems. **Quality Control Analysis:** Conducting tests and inspections of products, services, or processes to evaluate quality or performance. **Technology Design:** Generating or adapting equipment and technology to serve user needs. **Operation and Control:** Controlling operations of equipment or systems. **GOE—Interest Area:** 02. Architecture and Construction. **Work Group:** 02.05. Systems and Equipment Installation, Maintenance, and Repair. **Other Jobs in This Work Group:** Central Office and PBX Installers and Repairers; Communication Equipment Mechanics, Installers, and Repairers; Electric Meter Installers and Repairers; Electrical and Electronics Repairers, Powerhouse, Substation, and Relay; Elevator Installers and Repairers; Frame Wirers, Central Office; Heating and Air Conditioning Mechanics; Home Appliance Installers; Maintenance and Repair Workers, General; Meter Mechanics; Refrigeration Mechanics; Station Installers and Repairers, Telephone; Telecommunications Facility Examiners; Telecommunications Line Installers and Repairers. **PERSONALITY TYPE:** Realistic.

EDUCATION/TRAINING PROGRAM(S)—Electrical and Power Transmission Installation/Installer, General; Electrical and Power Transmission Installers, Other; Lineworker. **RELATED KNOWLEDGE/ COURSES—Mechanical Devices:** Knowledge of machines and tools, including their designs, uses, repair, and maintenance. **Public Safety and Security:** Knowledge of relevant equipment, policies, procedures, and strategies to promote effective local, state, or

national security operations for the protection of people, data, property, and institutions. **Design:** Knowledge of design techniques, tools, and principles involved in production of precision technical plans, blueprints, drawings, and models. **Engineering and Technology:** Knowledge of the practical application of engineering science and technology. This includes applying principles, techniques, procedures, and equipment to the design and production of various goods and services. **Building and Construction:** Knowledge of the materials, methods, and tools involved in the construction or repair of houses, buildings, or other structures such as highways and roads. **Computers and Electronics:** Knowledge of circuit boards, processors, chips, electronic equipment, and computer hardware and software, including applications and programming.

Electricians

- ◎ Education/Training Required: Long-term on-the-job training
- ◎ Annual Earnings: $42,300
- ◎ Growth: 23.4%
- ◎ Annual Job Openings: 65,000
- ◎ Self-Employed: 9.1%
- ◎ Part-Time: 2.2%

Install, maintain, and repair electrical wiring, equipment, and fixtures. Ensure that work is in accordance with relevant codes. May install or service street lights, intercom systems, or electrical control systems. Assemble, install, test, and maintain electrical or electronic wiring, equipment, appliances, apparatus, and fixtures, using hand tools and power tools. Diagnose malfunctioning systems, apparatus, and components, using test equipment and hand tools, to locate the cause of a breakdown and correct the problem. Connect wires to circuit breakers, transformers, or other components. Inspect electrical systems, equipment, and components to identify hazards, defects, and the need for adjustment or repair and to ensure compliance with codes. Advise management on whether continued operation of equipment could be hazardous. Test electrical systems and continuity of circuits in electrical wiring, equipment, and fixtures, using testing devices such as ohmmeters, voltmeters, and oscilloscopes, to ensure compatibility and safety of system.

Maintain current electrician's license or identification card to meet governmental regulations. Plan layout and installation of electrical wiring, equipment, and fixtures based on job specifications and local codes. Direct and train workers to install, maintain, or repair electrical wiring, equipment, and fixtures. Prepare sketches or follow blueprints to determine the location of wiring and equipment and to ensure conformance to building and safety codes. Use a variety of tools and equipment, such as power construction equipment; measuring devices; power tools; and testing equipment, including oscilloscopes, ammeters, and test lamps. Install ground leads and connect power cables to equipment such as motors. Perform business management duties such as maintaining records and files, preparing reports, and ordering supplies and equipment. Repair or replace wiring, equipment, and fixtures, using hand tools and power tools. Work from ladders, scaffolds, and roofs to install, maintain, or repair electrical wiring, equipment, and fixtures. Place conduit (pipes or tubing) inside designated partitions, walls, or other concealed areas and pull insulated wires or cables through the conduit to complete circuits between boxes. Construct and fabricate parts, using hand tools and specifications. **SKILLS—Installation:** Installing equipment, machines, wiring, or programs to meet specifications. **Repairing:** Repairing machines or systems by using the needed tools. **Troubleshooting:** Determining causes of operating errors and deciding what to do about them. **Equipment Maintenance:** Performing routine maintenance on equipment and determining when and what kind of maintenance is needed. **Technology Design:** Generating or adapting equipment and technology to serve user needs. **Equipment Selection:** Determining the kind of tools and equipment needed to do a job. **Operations Analysis:** Analyzing needs and product requirements to create a design. **Operation Monitoring:** Watching gauges, dials, or other indicators to make sure a machine is working properly. **Management of Financial Resources:** Determining how money will be spent to get the work done and accounting for these expenditures. **GOE—Interest Area:** 02. Architecture and Construction. **Work Group:** 02.04. Construction Crafts. **Other Jobs in This Work Group:** Boat Builders and Shipwrights; Boilermakers; Brattice Builders; Brickmasons and Blockmasons; Carpet Installers; Ceiling Tile Installers; Cement Masons and Concrete Finishers; Commercial Divers; Construction Carpenters; Crane and Tower Operators; Dragline Operators; Drywall Installers; Fence Erectors; Floor Layers, Except Carpet, Wood, and Hard Tiles; Floor Sanders and Finishers; Glaziers; Grader, Bulldozer, and Scraper Operators; Hazardous Materials Removal Workers; Insulation Workers, Floor, Ceiling, and Wall; Insulation Workers, Mechanical; Manufactured Building and Mobile Home Installers; Operating Engineers; Painters, Construction and Maintenance; Paperhangers; Paving, Surfacing, and Tamping Equipment Operators; Pile-Driver Operators; Pipe Fitters; Pipelayers; Pipelaying Fitters; Plasterers and Stucco Masons; Plumbers; Rail-Track Laying and Maintenance Equipment Operators; Refractory Materials Repairers, Except Brickmasons; Reinforcing Iron and Rebar Workers; Riggers; Roofers; Rough Carpenters; Security and Fire Alarm Systems Installers; Segmental Pavers; Sheet Metal Workers; Ship Carpenters and Joiners; Stone Cutters and Carvers; Stonemasons; Structural Iron and Steel Workers; Tapers; Terrazzo Workers and Finishers; Tile and Marble Setters. **PERSONALITY TYPE:** Realistic.

EDUCATION/TRAINING PROGRAM(S)—Electrician. **RELATED KNOWLEDGE/COURSES—Building and Construction:** Knowledge of the materials, methods, and tools involved in the construction or repair of houses, buildings, or other structures such as highways and roads. **Mechanical Devices:** Knowledge of machines and tools, including their designs, uses, repair, and maintenance. **Design:** Knowledge of design techniques, tools, and principles involved in production of precision technical plans, blueprints, drawings, and models. **Production and Processing:** Knowledge of raw materials, production processes, quality control, costs, and other techniques for maximizing the effective manufacture and distribution of goods. **Physics:** Knowledge and prediction of physical principles and laws and their interrelationships and applications to understanding fluid, material, and atmospheric dynamics and mechanical, electrical, atomic, and subatomic structures and processes. **Customer and Personal Service:** Knowledge of principles and processes for providing customer and personal services. This includes customer needs assessment, meeting quality standards for services, and evaluation of customer satisfaction.

Electro-Mechanical Technicians

- ◉ Education/Training Required: Associate degree
- ◉ Annual Earnings: $41,440
- ◉ Growth: 11.5%
- ◉ Annual Job Openings: 4,000
- ◉ Self-Employed: 0.6%
- ◉ Part-Time: 5.0%

Operate, test, and maintain unmanned, automated, servo-mechanical, or electromechanical equipment. May operate unmanned submarines, aircraft, or other equipment at work sites, such as oil rigs, deep ocean exploration, or hazardous waste removal. May assist engineers in testing and designing robotics equipment. Analyze and record test results and prepare written testing documentation. Inspect parts for surface defects. Install electrical and electronic parts and hardware in housings or assemblies, using soldering equipment and hand tools. Read blueprints, schematics, diagrams, and technical orders to determine methods and sequences of assembly. Repair, rework, and calibrate hydraulic and pneumatic assemblies and systems to meet operational specifications and tolerances. Test performance of electromechanical assemblies, using test instruments such as oscilloscopes, electronic voltmeters, and bridges. Verify dimensions and clearances of parts to ensure conformance to specifications, using precision measuring instruments. Develop, test, and program new robots. Operate metalworking machines to fabricate housings, jigs, fittings, and fixtures. Train others to install, use, and maintain robots. Align, fit, and assemble component parts, using hand tools, power tools, fixtures, templates, and microscopes. **SKILLS—Repairing:** Repairing machines or systems by using the needed tools. **Troubleshooting:** Determining causes of operating errors and deciding what to do about them. **Equipment Maintenance:** Performing routine maintenance on equipment and determining when and what kind of maintenance is needed. **Quality Control Analysis:** Conducting tests and inspections of products, services, or processes to evaluate quality or performance. **Installation:** Installing equipment, machines, wiring, or programs to meet specifications. **Operation Monitoring:** Watching gauges, dials, or other indicators to make sure a machine is working properly. **Science:** Using scientific rules and methods to solve problems. **Operation and Control:** Controlling operations of equipment or systems. **GOE—Interest Area:** 15. Scientific Research, Engineering, and Mathematics. **Work Group:** 15.09. Engineering Technology. **Other Jobs in This Work Group:** Aerospace Engineering and Operations Technicians; Calibration and Instrumentation Technicians; Cartographers and Photogrammetrists; Civil Engineering Technicians; Electrical Engineering Technicians; Electronic Drafters; Electronics Engineering Technicians; Environmental Engineering Technicians; Mapping Technicians; Mechanical Drafters; Mechanical Engineering Technicians; Surveying Technicians. **PERSONALITY TYPE:** Realistic.

EDUCATION/TRAINING PROGRAM(S)—Engineering Technologies/Technicians, Other. **RELATED KNOWLEDGE/COURSES—Mechanical Devices:** Knowledge of machines and tools, including their designs, uses, repair, and maintenance. **Production and Processing:** Knowledge of raw materials, production processes, quality control, costs, and other techniques for maximizing the effective manufacture and distribution of goods. **Engineering and Technology:** Knowledge of the practical application of engineering science and technology. This includes applying principles, techniques, procedures, and equipment to the design and production of various goods and services. **Computers and Electronics:** Knowledge of circuit boards, processors, chips, electronic equipment, and computer hardware and software, including applications and programming. **Design:** Knowledge of design techniques, tools, and principles involved in production of precision technical plans, blueprints, drawings, and models. **Physics:** Knowledge and prediction of physical principles and laws and their interrelationships and applications to understanding fluid, material, and atmospheric dynamics and mechanical, electrical, atomic, and subatomic structures and processes.

E

Electronics Engineering Technicians

◎ Education/Training Required: Associate degree
◎ Annual Earnings: $46,310
◎ Growth: 10.0%
◎ Annual Job Openings: 24,000
◎ Self-Employed: 0.4%
◎ Part-Time: 5.0%

Lay out, build, test, troubleshoot, repair, and modify developmental and production electronic components, parts, equipment, and systems, such as computer equipment, missile control instrumentation, electron tubes, test equipment, and machine tool numerical controls, applying principles and theories of electronics, electrical circuitry, engineering mathematics, electronic and electrical testing, and physics. Usually work under direction of engineering staff. Test electronics units, using standard test equipment, and analyze results to evaluate performance and determine need for adjustment. Perform preventative maintenance and calibration of equipment and systems. Read blueprints, wiring diagrams, schematic drawings, and engineering instructions for assembling electronics units, applying knowledge of electronic theory and components. Identify and resolve equipment malfunctions, working with manufacturers and field representatives as necessary to procure replacement parts. Maintain system logs and manuals to document testing and operation of equipment. Assemble, test, and maintain circuitry or electronic components according to engineering instructions, technical manuals, and knowledge of electronics, using hand and power tools. Adjust and replace defective or improperly functioning circuitry and electronics components, using hand tools and soldering iron. Procure parts and maintain inventory and related documentation. Maintain working knowledge of state-of-the-art tools, software, etc., through reading and/or attending conferences, workshops, or other training. Provide user applications and engineering support and recommendations for new and existing equipment with regard to installation, upgrades, and enhancement. Write reports and record data on testing techniques, laboratory equipment, and specifications to assist engineers. Provide customer support and education, working with users to identify needs, determine sources of problems, and provide information on product use. Design basic circuitry and draft sketches for clarification of details and design documentation under engineers' direction, using drafting instruments and computer-aided design equipment. Build prototypes from rough sketches or plans. Develop and upgrade preventative maintenance procedures for components, equipment, parts, and systems. Fabricate parts, such as coils, terminal boards, and chassis, using bench lathes, drills, or other machine tools. Research equipment and component needs, sources, competitive prices, delivery times, and ongoing operational costs. **SKILLS—Repairing:** Repairing machines or systems by using the needed tools. **Troubleshooting:** Determining causes of operating errors and deciding what to do about them. **Equipment Maintenance:** Performing routine maintenance on equipment and determining when and what kind of maintenance is needed. **Installation:** Installing equipment, machines, wiring, or programs to meet specifications. **Technology Design:** Generating or adapting equipment and technology to serve user needs. **Operation Monitoring:** Watching gauges, dials, or other indicators to make sure a machine is working properly. **Systems Evaluation:** Identifying measures or indicators of system performance and the actions needed to improve or correct performance relative to the goals of the system. **Systems Analysis:** Determining how a system should work and how changes in conditions, operations, and the environment will affect outcomes. **GOE—Interest Area:** 15. Scientific Research, Engineering, and Mathematics. **Work Group:** 15.09. Engineering Technology. **Other Jobs in This Work Group:** Aerospace Engineering and Operations Technicians; Calibration and Instrumentation Technicians; Cartographers and Photogrammetrists; Civil Engineering Technicians; Electrical Engineering Technicians; Electro-Mechanical Technicians; Electronic Drafters; Environmental Engineering Technicians; Mapping Technicians; Mechanical Drafters; Mechanical Engineering Technicians; Surveying Technicians. **PERSONALITY TYPE:** Realistic.

EDUCATION/TRAINING PROGRAM(S)— Computer Engineering Technology/Technician; Computer Technology/Computer Systems Technology; Electrical and Electronic Engineering Technologies/Technicians, Other; Electrical, Electronic, and Communications Engineering Technology/Technician; Telecommunications Technology/Technician. **RELATED KNOWLEDGE/COURSES—Engineer-**

ing and **Technology:** Knowledge of the practical application of engineering science and technology. This includes applying principles, techniques, procedures, and equipment to the design and production of various goods and services. **Computers and Electronics:** Knowledge of circuit boards, processors, chips, electronic equipment, and computer hardware and software, including applications and programming. **Mechanical Devices:** Knowledge of machines and tools, including their designs, uses, repair, and maintenance. **Design:** Knowledge of design techniques, tools, and principles involved in production of precision technical plans, blueprints, drawings, and models. **Mathematics:** Knowledge of arithmetic, algebra, geometry, calculus, and statistics and their applications. **Telecommunications:** Knowledge of transmission, broadcasting, switching, control, and operation of telecommunications systems.

Electronics Engineers, Except Computer

- Education/Training Required: Bachelor's degree
- Annual Earnings: $75,770
- Growth: 9.4%
- Annual Job Openings: 11,000
- Self-Employed: 3.1%
- Part-Time: 2.4%

Research, design, develop, and test electronic components and systems for commercial, industrial, military, or scientific use, utilizing knowledge of electronic theory and materials properties. Design electronic circuits and components for use in fields such as telecommunications, aerospace guidance and propulsion control, acoustics, or instruments and controls. Design electronic components and software, products, and systems for commercial, industrial, medical, military, and scientific applications. Provide technical support and instruction to staff and customers regarding equipment standards and help solve specific difficult in-service engineering problems. Operate computer-assisted engineering and design software and equipment to perform engineering tasks. Analyze system requirements, capacity, cost, and customer needs to determine feasibility of project and develop system plan. Confer with engineers, cus-

tomers, vendors, and others to discuss existing and potential engineering projects or products. Review and evaluate work of others, inside and outside the organization, to ensure effectiveness, technical adequacy, and compatibility in the resolution of complex engineering problems. Determine material and equipment needs and order supplies. Inspect electronic equipment, instruments, products, and systems to ensure conformance to specifications, safety standards, and applicable codes and regulations. Evaluate operational systems, prototypes, and proposals and recommend repair or design modifications based on factors such as environment, service, cost, and system capabilities. Prepare documentation containing information such as confidential descriptions and specifications of proprietary hardware and software, product development and introduction schedules, product costs, and information about product performance weaknesses. Direct and coordinate activities concerned with manufacture, construction, installation, maintenance, operation, and modification of electronic equipment, products, and systems. Develop and perform operational, maintenance, and testing procedures for electronic products, components, equipment, and systems. Plan and develop applications and modifications for electronic properties used in components, products, and systems to improve technical performance. Prepare engineering sketches and specifications for construction, relocation, and installation of equipment, facilities, products, and systems. Plan and implement research, methodology, and procedures to apply principles of electronic theory to engineering projects. **SKILLS— Troubleshooting:** Determining causes of operating errors and deciding what to do about them. **Technology Design:** Generating or adapting equipment and technology to serve user needs. **Operations Analysis:** Analyzing needs and product requirements to create a design. **Installation:** Installing equipment, machines, wiring, or programs to meet specifications. **Science:** Using scientific rules and methods to solve problems. **Complex Problem Solving:** Identifying complex problems and reviewing related information to develop and evaluate options and implement solutions. **Equipment Selection:** Determining the kind of tools and equipment needed to do a job. **Active Learning:** Understanding the implications of new information for both current and future problem-solving and decision-making. **Systems Evaluation:** Identifying measures or indicators of system performance and the actions needed to improve or correct performance relative to the goals of the system. **GOE—Interest Area:** 15. Scientific Research, Engineering, and Mathematics. **Work Group:** 15.07. Research and Design Engineering. **Other Jobs in This Work Group:** Aerospace Engineers; Biomedical Engineers; Chemical Engineers; Civil Engineers; Computer Hardware Engineers; Electrical Engineers; Marine Architects; Marine Engineers; Materials Engineers; Mechanical Engineers; Nuclear Engineers. **PERSONALITY TYPE:** Investigative.

EDUCATION/TRAINING PROGRAM(S)—Electrical, Electronics, and Communications Engineering. **RELATED KNOWLEDGE/COURSES—Engineering and Technology:** Knowledge of the practical application of engineering science and technology. This includes applying principles, techniques, procedures, and equipment to the design and production of various goods and services. **Design:** Knowledge of design techniques, tools, and principles involved in production of precision technical plans, blueprints, drawings, and models. **Computers and Electronics:** Knowledge of circuit boards, processors, chips, electronic equipment, and computer hardware and software, including applications and programming. **Physics:** Knowledge and prediction of physical principles and laws and their interrelationships and applications to understanding fluid, material, and atmospheric dynamics and mechanical, electrical, atomic, and subatomic structures and processes. **Telecommunications:** Knowledge of transmission, broadcasting, switching, control, and operation of telecommunications systems. **Mathematics:** Knowledge of arithmetic, algebra, geometry, calculus, and statistics and their applications.

Elementary School Teachers, Except Special Education

- Education/Training Required: Bachelor's degree
- Annual Earnings: $43,160
- Growth: 15.2%
- Annual Job Openings: 183,000
- Self-Employed: 0.1%
- Part-Time: 9.2%

Teach pupils in public or private schools at the elementary level basic academic, social, and other formative skills. Establish and enforce rules for behavior and procedures for maintaining order among the students for whom they are responsible. Observe and evaluate students' performance, behavior, social development, and physical health. Prepare materials and classrooms for class activities. Adapt teaching methods and instructional materials to meet students' varying needs and interests. Plan and conduct activities for a balanced program of instruction, demonstration, and work time that provides students with opportunities to observe, question, and investigate. Instruct students individually and in groups, using various teaching methods such as lectures, discussions, and demonstrations. Establish clear objectives for all lessons, units, and projects and communicate those objectives to students. Assign and grade class work and homework. Read books to entire classes or small groups. Prepare, administer, and grade tests and assignments in order to evaluate students' progress. Confer with parents or guardians, teachers, counselors, and administrators in order to resolve students' behavioral and academic problems. Meet with parents and guardians to discuss their children's progress and to determine their priorities for their children and their resource needs. Maintain accurate and complete student records as required by laws, district policies, and administrative regulations. Prepare students for later grades by encouraging them to explore learning opportunities and to persevere with challenging tasks. Guide and counsel students with adjustment and/or academic problems or special academic interests. Prepare and implement remedial programs for students requiring extra help. Prepare objectives and outlines for courses of study, following curriculum guidelines or requirements of states and schools. Provide a variety of materials and resources for children to explore, manipulate, and use, both in learning activities and in imaginative play. Enforce administration policies and rules governing students. Confer with other staff members to plan and schedule lessons promoting learning, following approved curricula. **SKILLS—Instructing:** Teaching others how to do something. **Learning Strategies:** Selecting and using training/instructional methods and procedures appropriate for the situation when learning or teaching new things. **Social Perceptiveness:** Being aware of others' reactions and understanding why they react as they do. **Monitoring:** Monitoring or assessing your performance or that of other individuals or organizations to make improvements or take corrective action. **Service Orientation:** Actively looking for ways to help people. **Persuasion:** Persuading others to change their minds or behavior. **Time Management:** Managing one's own time and the time of others. **Negotiation:** Bringing others together and trying to reconcile differences. **GOE—Interest Area:** 05. Education and Training. **Work Group:** 05.02. Preschool, Elementary, and Secondary Teaching and Instructing. **Other Jobs in This Work Group:** Kindergarten Teachers, Except Special Education; Middle School Teachers, Except Special and Vocational Education; Preschool Teachers, Except Special Education; Secondary School Teachers, Except Special and Vocational Education; Special Education Teachers, Middle School; Special Education Teachers, Preschool, Kindergarten, and Elementary School; Special Education Teachers, Secondary School; Teacher Assistants; Vocational Education Teachers, Middle School; Vocational Education Teachers, Secondary School. **PERSONALITY TYPE:** Social.

EDUCATION/TRAINING PROGRAM(S)— Elementary Education and Teaching; Teacher Education, Multiple Levels. **RELATED KNOWLEDGE/COURSES—Geography:** Knowledge of principles and methods for describing the features of land, sea, and air masses, including their physical characteristics; locations; interrelationships; and distribution of plant, animal, and human life. **History and Archeology:** Knowledge of historical events and their causes, indicators, and effects on civilizations and cultures. **Education and Training:** Knowledge of principles and methods for curriculum and training design, teaching and instruction for individuals and groups, and the measurement of training effects. **Psychology:** Knowledge of human behavior and performance; individual differences in ability, personality, and interests; learning and motivation; psychological research methods; and the assessment and treatment of behavioral and affective disorders. **English Language:** Knowledge of the structure and content of the English language, including the meaning and spelling of words, rules of composition, and grammar. **Sociology and Anthropology:** Knowledge of group behavior and dynamics, societal trends and influences, human migrations, ethnicity, and cultures and their history and origins.

Elevator Installers and Repairers

- Education/Training Required: Long-term on-the-job training
- Annual Earnings: $58,710
- Growth: 17.1%
- Annual Job Openings: 3,000
- Self-Employed: 0%
- Part-Time: 0.2%

Assemble, install, repair, or maintain electric or hydraulic freight or passenger elevators, escalators, or dumbwaiters. Adjust safety controls; counterweights; door mechanisms; and components such as valves, ratchets, seals, and brake linings. Assemble electrically powered stairs, steel frameworks, and tracks and install associated motors and electrical wiring. Assemble elevator cars, installing each car's platform, walls, and doors. Assemble, install, repair, and maintain elevators, escalators, moving sidewalks, and dumbwaiters, using hand and power tools and testing devices such as test lamps, ammeters, and voltmeters. Attach guide shoes and rollers to minimize the lateral motion of cars as they travel through shafts. Bolt or weld steel rails to the walls of shafts to guide elevators, working from scaffolding or platforms. Check that safety regulations and building codes are met and complete service reports verifying conformance to standards. Connect car frames to counterweights, using steel cables. Connect electrical wiring to control panels and electric motors. Cut prefabricated sections of framework, rails, and other components to specified dimensions. Disassemble defective units and repair or replace parts such as locks, gears, cables, and electric wiring. Inspect wiring connections, control panel hookups, door installations, and alignments and clearances of cars and hoistways to ensure that equipment will operate properly. Install electrical wires and controls by attaching conduit along shaft walls from floor to floor and then pulling plastic-covered wires through the conduit. Install outer doors and door frames at elevator entrances on each floor of a structure. Locate malfunctions in brakes, motors, switches, and signal and control systems, using test equipment. Maintain logbooks that detail all repairs and checks performed. Operate elevators to determine power demands and test power consumption to detect overload factors. Read and interpret blueprints to determine the layout of system components, frameworks, and foundations and to select installation equipment. Test newly installed equipment to ensure that it meets specifications, such as stopping at floors for set amounts of time. **SKILLS—Installation:** Installing equipment, machines, wiring, or programs to meet specifications. **Repairing:** Repairing machines or systems by using the needed tools. **Equipment Maintenance:** Performing routine maintenance on equipment and determining when and what kind of maintenance is needed. **Troubleshooting:** Determining causes of operating errors and deciding what to do about them. **Quality Control Analysis:** Conducting tests and inspections of products, services, or processes to evaluate quality or performance. **Operation Monitoring:** Watching gauges, dials, or other indicators to make sure a machine is working properly. **Systems Analysis:** Determining how a system should work and how changes in conditions, operations, and the environment will affect outcomes. **Operation and Control:** Controlling operations of equipment or systems. **GOE—Interest Area:** 02. Architecture and Construction. **Work Group:** 02.05. Systems and Equipment Installation, Maintenance, and Repair. **Other Jobs in This Work Group:** Central Office and PBX Installers and Repairers; Communication Equipment Mechanics, Installers, and Repairers; Electric Meter Installers and Repairers; Electrical and Electronics Repairers, Powerhouse, Substation, and Relay; Electrical Power-Line Installers and Repairers; Frame Wirers, Central Office; Heating and Air Conditioning Mechanics; Home Appliance Installers; Maintenance and Repair Workers, General; Meter Mechanics; Refrigeration Mechanics; Station Installers and Repairers, Telephone; Telecommunications Facility Examiners; Telecommunications Line Installers and Repairers. **PERSONALITY TYPE:** Realistic.

EDUCATION/TRAINING PROGRAM(S)— Industrial Mechanics and Maintenance Technology. **RELATED KNOWLEDGE/COURSES—Building and Construction:** Knowledge of the materials, methods, and tools involved in the construction or repair of houses, buildings, or other structures such as highways and roads. **Mechanical Devices:** Knowledge of machines and tools, including their designs, uses, repair, and maintenance. **Engineering and Technology:** Knowledge of the practical application of engineering science and technology. This includes applying principles, techniques, procedures, and equipment to the design and production of various goods and services. **Physics:** Knowledge and prediction of physical principles and laws and their interrelationships and applications to understanding fluid, material, and atmospheric dynamics and mechanical, electrical, atomic, and subatomic structures and processes. **Telecommunications:** Knowledge of transmission, broadcasting, switching, control, and operation of telecommunications systems. **Public Safety and Security:** Knowledge of relevant equipment, policies, procedures, and strategies to promote effective local, state, or national security operations for the protection of people, data, property, and institutions.

Embossing Machine Set-Up Operators

- ◎ Education/Training Required: Postsecondary vocational training
- ◎ Annual Earnings: $29,900
- ◎ Growth: 4.6%
- ◎ Annual Job Openings: 30,000
- ◎ Self-Employed: 2.7%
- ◎ Part-Time: 6.2%

Set up and operate embossing machines. Sets guides to hold cover in position and adjusts table height to obtain correct depth of impression. Positions, installs, and locks embossed plate in chase and locks chase in bed of press. Makes impression of embossing to desired depth in composition on platen, trims off excess, and allows composition to harden. Stamps embossing design on workpiece, using heated work tools. Starts machine to lower ram and impress cardboard. Sets sheets singly in gauge pins and starts press. Scrapes high spots on counter die to prevent from puncturing paper. Removes and stacks embossed covers. Cuts surface of cardboard, leaving design or letters, using hand tools. Mixes embossing composition to putty-like consistency, spreads glue on paten, and applies thin pad of composition over glue. **SKILLS—Installation:** Installing equipment, machines, wiring, or programs to meet specifications. **Operation and Control:** Controlling operations of equipment or systems. **Operation Monitoring:** Watching gauges, dials, or other indicators to make sure a machine is working properly. **Equipment Maintenance:** Performing routine maintenance on equipment and determining when and what kind of maintenance is needed. **Repairing:** Repairing machines or systems by using the needed tools. **GOE—Interest Area:** 13. Manufacturing. **Work Group:** 13.08. Graphic Arts Production. **Other Jobs in This Work Group:** Bindery Machine Operators and Tenders; Camera Operators; Design Printing Machine Setters and Set-Up Operators; Desktop Publishers; Dot Etchers; Electronic Masking System Operators; Electrotypers and Stereotypers; Engraver Set-Up Operators; Engravers, Hand; Engravers/Carvers; Etchers; Etchers, Hand; Film Laboratory Technicians; Hand Compositors and Typesetters; Job Printers; Letterpress Setters and Set-Up Operators; Marking and Identification Printing Machine Setters and Set-Up Operators; Offset Lithographic Press Setters and Set-Up Operators; Pantograph Engravers; Paste-Up Workers; Photoengravers; Photoengraving and Lithographing Machine Operators and Tenders; Photographic Processing Machine Operators; Plate Finishers; Platemakers; Precision Etchers and Engravers, Hand or Machine; Precision Printing Workers; Printing Press Machine Operators and Tenders; Scanner Operators; Strippers; Typesetting and Composing Machine Operators and Tenders. **PERSONALITY TYPE:** Realistic.

EDUCATION/TRAINING PROGRAM(S)— Graphic and Printing Equipment Operator, General Production; Graphic Communications, Other; Printing Management; Printing Press Operator. **RELATED KNOWLEDGE/COURSES—Production and Processing:** Knowledge of raw materials, production processes, quality control, costs, and other techniques for maximizing the effective manufacture and distribution of goods. **Administration and Management:** Knowledge of business and management principles involved in strategic planning, resource allocation, human resources modeling, leadership technique, production methods, and coordination of people and resources.

Emergency Management Specialists

- Education/Training Required: Work experience in a related occupation
- Annual Earnings: $45,390
- Growth: 28.2%
- Annual Job Openings: 2,000
- Self-Employed: 0%
- Part-Time: 7.4%

Coordinate disaster response or crisis management activities; provide disaster-preparedness training; and prepare emergency plans and procedures for natural (e.g., hurricanes, floods, earthquakes), wartime, or technological (e.g., nuclear power plant emergencies, hazardous materials spills) disasters or hostage situations. Collaborate with other officials in order to prepare and analyze damage assessments following disasters or emergencies. Conduct surveys to determine the types of emergency-related needs that will need to be addressed in disaster planning or provide technical support to others conducting such surveys. Consult with officials of local and area governments, schools, hospitals, and other institutions in order to determine their needs and capabilities in the event of a natural disaster or other emergency. Coordinate disaster response or crisis management activities such as ordering evacuations, opening public shelters, and implementing special needs plans and programs. Design and administer emergency/disaster-preparedness training courses that teach people how to effectively respond to major emergencies and disasters. Develop and maintain liaisons with municipalities, county departments, and similar entities in order to facilitate plan development, response effort coordination, and exchanges of personnel and equipment. Develop and perform tests and evaluations of emergency management plans in accordance with state and federal regulations. Inspect facilities and equipment such as emergency management centers and communications equipment in order to determine their operational and functional capabilities in emergency situations. Keep informed of activities or changes that could affect the likelihood of an emergency, as well as those that could affect response efforts and details of plan implementation. Keep informed of federal, state, and local regulations affecting emergency plans and

E

ensure that plans adhere to these regulations. Maintain and update all resource materials associated with emergency-preparedness plans. Prepare emergency situation status reports that describe response and recovery efforts, needs, and preliminary damage assessments. Prepare plans that outline operating procedures to be used in response to disasters/emergencies such as hurricanes, nuclear accidents, and terrorist attacks and in recovery from these events. Propose alteration of emergency response procedures based on regulatory changes, technological changes, or knowledge gained from outcomes of previous emergency situations. **SKILLS**—No data available. **GOE—Interest Area:** 12. Law and Public Safety. **Work Group:** 12.01. Managerial Work in Law and Public Safety. **Other Jobs in This Work Group:** First-Line Supervisors/Managers of Correctional Officers; First-Line Supervisors/Managers of Police and Detectives; Forest Fire Fighting and Prevention Supervisors; Municipal Fire Fighting and Prevention Supervisors. **PERSONALITY TYPE:** No data available.

EDUCATION/TRAINING PROGRAM(S)— Community Organization and Advocacy; Public Administration. **RELATED KNOWLEDGE/ COURSES**—No data available.

Emergency Medical Technicians and Paramedics

- ◎ Education/Training Required: Postsecondary vocational training
- ◎ Annual Earnings: $25,310
- ◎ Growth: 33.1%
- ◎ Annual Job Openings: 32,000
- ◎ Self-Employed: 0.8%
- ◎ Part-Time: 8.4%

Assess injuries, administer emergency medical care, and extricate trapped individuals. Transport injured or sick persons to medical facilities. Administer first-aid treatment and life-support care to sick or injured persons in prehospital setting. Operate equipment such as EKGs, external defibrillators, and bag-valve mask resuscitators in advanced life-support environments. Assess nature and extent of illness or injury to establish and prioritize medical procedures. Maintain vehicles and medical and communication equipment and replenish first-aid equipment and supplies. Observe, record, and report to physician the patient's condition or injury, the treatment provided, and reactions to drugs and treatment. Perform emergency diagnostic and treatment procedures, such as stomach suction, airway management, and heart monitoring, during ambulance ride. Administer drugs, orally or by injection, and perform intravenous procedures under a physician's direction. Comfort and reassure patients. Coordinate work with other emergency medical team members and police and fire department personnel. Communicate with dispatchers and treatment center personnel to provide information about situation, to arrange reception of victims, and to receive instructions for further treatment. Immobilize patient for placement on stretcher and ambulance transport, using backboard or other spinal immobilization device. Decontaminate ambulance interior following treatment of patient with infectious disease and report case to proper authorities. Drive mobile intensive care unit to specified location, following instructions from emergency medical dispatcher. Coordinate with treatment center personnel to obtain patients' vital statistics and medical history, to determine the circumstances of the emergency, and to administer emergency treatment. **SKILLS—Equipment Maintenance:** Performing routine maintenance on equipment and determining when and what kind of maintenance is needed. **Social Perceptiveness:** Being aware of others' reactions and understanding why they react as they do. **Service Orientation:** Actively looking for ways to help people. **Coordination:** Adjusting actions in relation to others' actions. **Instructing:** Teaching others how to do something. **Negotiation:** Bringing others together and trying to reconcile differences. **Speaking:** Talking to others to convey information effectively. **Operation Monitoring:** Watching gauges, dials, or other indicators to make sure a machine is working properly. **GOE—Interest Area:** 12. Law and Public Safety. **Work Group:** 12.06. Emergency Responding. **Other Jobs in This Work Group:** Forest Fire Fighters; Municipal Fire Fighters. **PERSONALITY TYPE:** Social.

EDUCATION/TRAINING PROGRAM(S)— Emergency Care Attendant (EMT Ambulance); Emergency Medical Technology/Technician (EMT Paramedic). **RELATED KNOWLEDGE/COURSES—Customer and Personal Service:** Knowledge of principles and processes for providing customer and personal services. This includes customer needs assessment, meeting quality standards for services, and evaluation of customer satisfaction. **Medicine and Dentistry:** Knowledge of the information and techniques needed to diagnose and treat human injuries, diseases, and deformities. This includes symptoms, treatment alternatives, drug properties and interactions, and preventive health-care measures. **Psychology:** Knowledge of human behavior and performance; individual differences in ability, personality, and interests; learning and motivation; psychological research methods; and the assessment and treatment of behavioral and affective disorders. **Chemistry:** Knowledge of the chemical composition, structure, and properties of substances and of the chemical processes and transformations that they undergo. This includes uses of chemicals and their danger signs, production techniques, and disposal methods. **Public Safety and Security:** Knowledge of relevant equipment, policies, procedures, and strategies to promote effective local, state, or national security operations for the protection of people, data, property, and institutions. **Therapy and Counseling:** Knowledge of principles, methods, and procedures for diagnosis, treatment, and rehabilitation of physical and mental dysfunctions and for career counseling and guidance.

Employment Interviewers, Private or Public Employment Service

- Education/Training Required: Bachelor's degree
- Annual Earnings: $41,190
- Growth: 27.3%
- Annual Job Openings: 29,000
- Self-Employed: 0.8%
- Part-Time: 7.7%

Interview job applicants in employment office and refer them to prospective employers for consideration. Search application files, notify selected applicants of job openings, and refer qualified applicants to prospective employers. Contact employers to verify referral results. Record and evaluate various pertinent data. Inform applicants of job openings and details such as duties and responsibilities, compensation, benefits, schedules, working conditions, and promotion opportunities. Interview job applicants to match their qualifications with employers' needs, recording and evaluating applicant experience, education, training, and skills. Review employment applications and job orders to match applicants with job requirements, using manual or computerized file searches. Select qualified applicants or refer them to employers, according to organization policy. Perform reference and background checks on applicants. Maintain records of applicants not selected for employment. Instruct job applicants in presenting a positive image by providing help with resume writing, personal appearance, and interview techniques. Refer applicants to services such as vocational counseling, literacy or language instruction, transportation assistance, vocational training, and child care. Contact employers to solicit orders for job vacancies, determining their requirements and recording relevant data such as job descriptions. Conduct workshops and demonstrate the use of job listings to assist applicants with skill building. Search for and recruit applicants for open positions through campus job fairs and advertisements. Provide background information on organizations with which interviews are scheduled. Administer assessment tests to identify skill-building needs. Conduct or arrange for skill, intelligence, or psychological testing of applicants and current employees. Hire workers and place them with employers needing temporary help. Evaluate selection and testing techniques by conducting research or follow-up activities and conferring with management and supervisory personnel. **SKILLS—Social Perceptiveness:** Being aware of others' reactions and understanding why they react as they do. **Service Orientation:** Actively looking for ways to help people. **Management of Personnel Resources:** Motivating, developing, and directing people as they work, identifying the best people for the job. **Persuasion:** Persuading others to change their minds or behavior. **Negotiation:** Bringing others together and trying to reconcile differences. **Instructing:** Teaching others how to do something. **Speaking:** Talking to others to convey information effectively. **Active Listening:** Giving full attention to what other people are saying, taking time to understand the points being made, asking questions as appropriate, and not interrupting at inappropriate times. **Time Management:** Managing one's own time and the time of others. **GOE—Interest Area:** 04. Business and Administration. **Work**

Group: 04.03. Human Resources Support. **Other Jobs in This Work Group:** Compensation, Benefits, and Job Analysis Specialists; Personnel Recruiters; Training and Development Specialists. **PERSONALITY TYPE:** Social.

EDUCATION/TRAINING PROGRAM(S)—Human Resources Management/Personnel Administration, General; Labor and Industrial Relations. **RELATED KNOWLEDGE/COURSES—Customer and Personal Service:** Knowledge of principles and processes for providing customer and personal services. This includes customer needs assessment, meeting quality standards for services, and evaluation of customer satisfaction. **Clerical Practices:** Knowledge of administrative and clerical procedures and systems such as word processing, managing files and records, stenography and transcription, designing forms, and other office procedures and terminology. **Foreign Language:** Knowledge of the structure and content of a foreign (non-English) language, including the meaning and spelling of words, rules of composition and grammar, and pronunciation. **Personnel and Human Resources:** Knowledge of principles and procedures for personnel recruitment, selection, training, compensation and benefits, labor relations and negotiation, and personnel information systems. **English Language:** Knowledge of the structure and content of the English language, including the meaning and spelling of words, rules of composition, and grammar. **Sales and Marketing:** Knowledge of principles and methods for showing, promoting, and selling products or services. This includes marketing strategy and tactics, product demonstrations, sales techniques, and sales control systems.

Engineering Managers

- ☉ Education/Training Required: Work experience plus degree
- ☉ Annual Earnings: $97,630
- ☉ Growth: 9.2%
- ☉ Annual Job Openings: 16,000
- ☉ Self-Employed: 0.1%
- ☉ Part-Time: 1.0%

Plan, direct, or coordinate activities in such fields as architecture and engineering or research and development in these fields. Confer with management, production, and marketing staff to discuss project specifications and procedures. Coordinate and direct projects, making detailed plans to accomplish goals and directing the integration of technical activities. Analyze technology, resource needs, and market demand to plan and assess the feasibility of projects. Plan and direct the installation, testing, operation, maintenance, and repair of facilities and equipment. Direct, review, and approve product design and changes. Recruit employees; assign, direct, and evaluate their work; and oversee the development and maintenance of staff competence. Prepare budgets, bids, and contracts and direct the negotiation of research contracts. Develop and implement policies, standards, and procedures for the engineering and technical work performed in the department, service, laboratory, or firm. Perform administrative functions such as reviewing and writing reports, approving expenditures, enforcing rules, and making decisions about the purchase of materials or services. Review and recommend or approve contracts and cost estimates. Present and explain proposals, reports, and findings to clients. Consult or negotiate with clients to prepare project specifications. Set scientific and technical goals within broad outlines provided by top management. Administer highway planning, construction, and maintenance. Direct the engineering of water control, treatment, and distribution projects. Plan, direct, and coordinate survey work with other staff activities, certifying survey work and writing land legal descriptions. Confer with and report to officials and the public to provide information and solicit support for projects. **SKILLS—Technology Design:** Generating or adapting equipment and technology to serve user needs. **Operations Analysis:** Analyzing needs and product requirements to create a design. **Science:** Using scientific rules and methods to solve problems. **Installation:** Installing equipment, machines, wiring, or programs to meet specifications. **Management of Financial Resources:** Determining how money will be spent to get the work done and accounting for these expenditures. **Negotiation:** Bringing others together and trying to reconcile differences. **Persuasion:** Persuading others to change their minds or behavior. **Judgment and Decision Making:** Considering the relative costs and benefits of potential actions to choose the most appropriate one. **GOE—Interest Area:** 15. Scientific Research, Engineering, and Mathematics. **Work Group:** 15.01. Managerial Work in Scientific

Research, Engineering, and Mathematics. **Other Jobs in This Work Group:** Natural Sciences Managers. **PERSONALITY TYPE:** Enterprising.

EDUCATION/TRAINING PROGRAM(S)—Aerospace, Aeronautical, and Astronautical Engineering; Agricultural/Biological Engineering and Bioengineering; Architectural Engineering; Architecture (BArch, BA/BS, MArch, MA/MS, PhD); Biomedical/Medical Engineering; Ceramic Sciences and Engineering; Chemical Engineering; City/Urban, Community, and Regional Planning; Civil Engineering, General; Civil Engineering, Other; Computer Engineering, General; Computer Engineering, Other; Computer Hardware Engineering; Computer Software Engineering; Construction Engineering; Electrical, Electronics, and Communications Engineering; Engineering Mechanics; Engineering Physics; Engineering Science; Engineering, General; Engineering, Other; Environmental Design/Architecture; Environmental/Environmental Health Engineering; Forest Engineering; Geological/Geophysical Engineering; Geotechnical Engineering; Industrial Engineering; Interior Architecture; Landscape Architecture (BS, BSLA, BLA, MSLA, MLA, PhD); Manufacturing Engineering; Materials Engineering; Materials Science; Mechanical Engineering; Metallurgical Engineering; Mining and Mineral Engineering; Naval Architecture and Marine Engineering; Nuclear Engineering; Ocean Engineering; Petroleum Engineering; Polymer/Plastics Engineering; Structural Engineering; Surveying Engineering; Systems Engineering; Textile Sciences and Engineering; Transportation and Highway Engineering; Water Resources Engineering. **RELATED KNOWLEDGE/COURSES**—**Engineering and Technology:** Knowledge of the practical application of engineering science and technology. This includes applying principles, techniques, procedures, and equipment to the design and production of various goods and services. **Design:** Knowledge of design techniques, tools, and principles involved in production of precision technical plans, blueprints, drawings, and models. **Physics:** Knowledge and prediction of physical principles and laws and their interrelationships and applications to understanding fluid, material, and atmospheric dynamics and mechanical, electrical, atomic, and subatomic structures and processes. **Mathematics:** Knowledge of arithmetic, algebra, geometry, calculus, and statistics and their applications. **Personnel and Human Resources:** Knowledge of principles and procedures for personnel recruitment, selection, training,

compensation and benefits, labor relations and negotiation, and personnel information systems. **Building and Construction:** Knowledge of the materials, methods, and tools involved in the construction or repair of houses, buildings, or other structures such as highways and roads.

Engineering Teachers, Postsecondary

◎ Education/Training Required: Master's degree
◎ Annual Earnings: $72,140
◎ Growth: 38.1%
◎ Annual Job Openings: 216,000
◎ Self-Employed: 0.3%
◎ Part-Time: 27.7%

Teach courses pertaining to the application of physical laws and principles of engineering for the development of machines, materials, instruments, processes, and services. Includes teachers of subjects such as chemical, civil, electrical, industrial, mechanical, mineral, and petroleum engineering. Includes both teachers primarily engaged in teaching and those who do a combination of both teaching and research. Prepare and deliver lectures to undergraduate and/or graduate students on topics such as mechanics, hydraulics, and robotics. Keep abreast of developments in their field by reading current literature, talking with colleagues, and participating in professional conferences. Supervise undergraduate and/or graduate teaching, internship, and research work. Evaluate and grade students' class work, laboratory work, assignments, and papers. Conduct research in a particular field of knowledge and publish findings in professional journals, books, and/or electronic media. Prepare course materials such as syllabi, homework assignments, and handouts. Compile, administer, and grade examinations or assign this work to others. Write grant proposals to procure external research funding. Supervise students' laboratory work. Initiate, facilitate, and moderate class discussions. Maintain regularly scheduled office hours in order to advise and assist students. Plan, evaluate, and revise curricula, course content, and course materials and methods of instruction. Advise students on academic and vocational curricula and on career issues. Maintain student attendance records, grades, and other required records. Collaborate with colleagues to address teaching and research issues. Select and obtain materials and supplies such as textbooks and laboratory equipment. Participate in student recruitment, registration, and placement activities. Serve on academic or administrative committees that deal with institutional policies, departmental matters, and academic issues. Perform administrative duties such as serving as department head. **SKILLS—Science:** Using scientific rules and methods to solve problems. **Programming:** Writing computer programs for various purposes. **Instructing:** Teaching others how to do something. **Mathematics:** Using mathematics to solve problems. **Critical Thinking:** Using logic and reasoning to identify the strengths and weaknesses of alternative solutions, conclusions, or approaches to problems. **Technology Design:** Generating or adapting equipment and technology to serve user needs. **Active Learning:** Understanding the implications of new information for both current and future problem-solving and decision-making. **Complex Problem Solving:** Identifying complex problems and reviewing related information to develop and evaluate options and implement solutions. **GOE—Interest Area:** 05. Education and Training. **Work Group:** 05.03. Postsecondary and Adult Teaching and Instructing. **Other Jobs in This Work Group:** Adult Literacy, Remedial Education, and GED Teachers and Instructors; Agricultural Sciences Teachers, Postsecondary; Anthropology and Archeology Teachers, Postsecondary; Architecture Teachers, Postsecondary; Area, Ethnic, and Cultural Studies Teachers, Postsecondary; Art, Drama, and Music Teachers, Postsecondary; Atmospheric, Earth, Marine, and Space Sciences Teachers, Postsecondary; Biological Science Teachers, Postsecondary; Business Teachers, Postsecondary; Chemistry Teachers, Postsecondary; Communications Teachers, Postsecondary; Computer Science Teachers, Postsecondary; Criminal Justice and Law Enforcement Teachers, Postsecondary; Economics Teachers, Postsecondary; Education Teachers, Postsecondary; English Language and Literature Teachers, Postsecondary; Environmental Science Teachers, Postsecondary; Farm and Home Management Advisors; Foreign Language and Literature Teachers, Postsecondary; Forestry and Conservation Science Teachers, Postsecondary; Geography Teachers, Postsecondary; Graduate Teaching Assistants; Health Specialties Teachers, Postsecondary; History Teachers, Postsecondary; Home Economics Teachers, Postsecondary; Law Teachers, Postsecondary; Library Science Teachers, Postsecondary; Mathemati-

cal Science Teachers, Postsecondary; Nursing Instructors and Teachers, Postsecondary; Philosophy and Religion Teachers, Postsecondary; Physics Teachers, Postsecondary; Political Science Teachers, Postsecondary; Psychology Teachers, Postsecondary; Recreation and Fitness Studies Teachers, Postsecondary; Self-Enrichment Education Teachers; Social Work Teachers, Postsecondary; Sociology Teachers, Postsecondary; Vocational Education Teachers, Postsecondary. **PERSONALITY TYPE:** Investigative.

EDUCATION/TRAINING PROGRAM(S)—Aerospace, Aeronautical, and Astronautical Engineering; Agricultural/Biological Engineering and Bioengineering; Architectural Engineering; Biomedical/Medical Engineering; Ceramic Sciences and Engineering; Chemical Engineering; Civil Engineering, General; Civil Engineering, Other; Computer Engineering, General; Computer Engineering, Other; Computer Hardware Engineering; Computer Software Engineering; Construction Engineering; Electrical, Electronics and Communications Engineering; Engineering Mechanics; Engineering Physics; Engineering Science; Engineering, General; Engineering, Other; Environmental/Environmental Health Engineering; Forest Engineering; Geological/Geophysical Engineering; Geotechnical Engineering; Industrial Engineering; Manufacturing Engineering; Materials Engineering; Materials Science; Mechanical Engineering; Metallurgical Engineering; Mining and Mineral Engineering; Naval Architecture and Marine Engineering; Nuclear Engineering; Ocean Engineering; Petroleum Engineering; Polymer/Plastics Engineering; Structural Engineering; Surveying Engineering; Systems Engineering; Teacher Education and Professional Development, Specific Subject Areas, Other; Textile Sciences and Engineering; Transportation and Highway Engineering; Water Resources Engineering. **RELATED KNOWLEDGE/COURSES—Engineering and Technology:** Knowledge of the practical application of engineering science and technology. This includes applying principles, techniques, procedures, and equipment to the design and production of various goods and services. **Design:** Knowledge of design techniques, tools, and principles involved in production of precision technical plans, blueprints, drawings, and models. **Physics:** Knowledge and prediction of physical principles and laws and their interrelationships and applications to understanding fluid, material, and atmospheric dynamics and mechanical, electrical, atomic, and subatomic structures and processes.

Mathematics: Knowledge of arithmetic, algebra, geometry, calculus, and statistics and their applications. **Education and Training:** Knowledge of principles and methods for curriculum and training design, teaching and instruction for individuals and groups, and the measurement of training effects. **Computers and Electronics:** Knowledge of circuit boards, processors, chips, electronic equipment, and computer hardware and software, including applications and programming.

English Language and Literature Teachers, Postsecondary

◉ Education/Training Required: Master's degree
◉ Annual Earnings: $47,900
◉ Growth: 38.1%
◉ Annual Job Openings: 216,000
◉ Self-Employed: 0.3%
◉ Part-Time: 27.7%

Teach courses in English language and literature, including linguistics and comparative literature. Initiate, facilitate, and moderate classroom discussions. Evaluate and grade students' class work, assignments, and papers. Prepare course materials such as syllabi, homework assignments, and handouts. Prepare and deliver lectures to undergraduate and/or graduate students on topics such as poetry, novel structure, and translation and adaptation. Maintain student attendance records, grades, and other required records. Plan, evaluate, and revise curricula, course content, and course materials and methods of instruction. Compile, administer, and grade examinations or assign this work to others. Maintain regularly scheduled office hours in order to advise and assist students. Keep abreast of developments in their field by reading current literature, talking with colleagues, and participating in professional conferences. Select and obtain materials and supplies such as textbooks. Advise students on academic and vocational curricula and on career issues. Conduct research in a particular field of knowledge and publish findings in professional journals, books, and/or electronic media. Collaborate with colleagues to address teaching and research issues. Serve on academic or administrative committees that deal with institutional policies, departmental matters, and academic issues. Participate in campus and community events. Participate in student recruitment, registration, and placement activities. Compile bibliographies of specialized materials for outside reading assignments. Supervise undergraduate and/or graduate teaching, internship, and research work. Provide assistance to students in college writing centers. Perform administrative duties such as serving as department head. Recruit, train, and supervise student writing instructors. Act as advisers to student organizations. **SKILLS—Instructing:** Teaching others how to do something. **Learning Strategies:** Selecting and using training/instructional methods and procedures appropriate for the situation when learning or teaching new things. **Social Perceptiveness:** Being aware of others' reactions and understanding why they react as they do. **Persuasion:** Persuading others to change their minds or behavior. **Writing:** Communicating effectively in writing as appropriate for the needs of the audience. **Reading Comprehension:** Understanding written sentences and paragraphs in work-related documents. **Critical Thinking:** Using logic and reasoning to identify the strengths and weaknesses of alternative solutions, conclusions, or approaches to problems. **Active Learning:** Understanding the implications of new information for both current and future problem-solving and decision-making. **GOE—Interest Area:** 05. Education and Training. **Work Group:** 05.03. Postsecondary and Adult Teaching and Instructing. **Other Jobs in This Work Group:** Adult Literacy, Remedial Education, and GED Teachers and Instructors; Agricultural Sciences Teachers, Postsecondary; Anthropology and Archeology Teachers, Postsecondary; Architecture Teachers, Postsecondary; Area, Ethnic, and Cultural Studies Teachers, Postsecondary; Art, Drama, and Music Teachers, Postsecondary; Atmospheric, Earth, Marine, and Space Sciences Teachers, Postsecondary; Biological Science Teachers, Postsecondary; Business Teachers, Postsecondary; Chemistry Teachers, Postsecondary; Communications Teachers, Postsecondary; Computer Science Teachers, Postsecondary; Criminal Justice and Law Enforcement Teachers, Postsecondary; Economics Teachers, Postsecondary; Education Teachers, Postsecondary; Engineering Teachers, Postsecondary; Environmental Science Teachers, Postsecondary; Farm and Home Management Advisors; Foreign Language and Literature Teachers, Postsecondary; Forestry and Conservation Science Teachers, Postsecondary; Geography Teachers,

E

Postsecondary; Graduate Teaching Assistants; Health Specialties Teachers, Postsecondary; History Teachers, Postsecondary; Home Economics Teachers, Postsecondary; Law Teachers, Postsecondary; Library Science Teachers, Postsecondary; Mathematical Science Teachers, Postsecondary; Nursing Instructors and Teachers, Postsecondary; Philosophy and Religion Teachers, Postsecondary; Physics Teachers, Postsecondary; Political Science Teachers, Postsecondary; Psychology Teachers, Postsecondary; Recreation and Fitness Studies Teachers, Postsecondary; Self-Enrichment Education Teachers; Social Work Teachers, Postsecondary; Sociology Teachers, Postsecondary; Vocational Education Teachers, Postsecondary. **PERSONALITY TYPE:** Artistic.

EDUCATION/TRAINING PROGRAM(S)— American Literature (Canadian); American Literature (United States); Comparative Literature; Creative Writing; English Composition; English Language and Literature, General; English Language and Literature/Letters, Other; English Literature (British and Commonwealth); Technical and Business Writing. **RELATED KNOWLEDGE/COURSES—English Language:** Knowledge of the structure and content of the English language, including the meaning and spelling of words, rules of composition, and grammar. **Education and Training:** Knowledge of principles and methods for curriculum and training design, teaching and instruction for individuals and groups, and the measurement of training effects. **Philosophy and Theology:** Knowledge of different philosophical systems and religions. This includes their basic principles, values, ethics, ways of thinking, customs, and practices and their impact on human culture. **History and Archeology:** Knowledge of historical events and their causes, indicators, and effects on civilizations and cultures. **Communications and Media:** Knowledge of media production, communication, and dissemination techniques and methods. This includes alternative ways to inform and entertain via written, oral, and visual media. **Sociology and Anthropology:** Knowledge of group behavior and dynamics, societal trends and influences, human migrations, ethnicity, and cultures and their history and origins.

Engraver Set-Up Operators

◎ Education/Training Required: Long-term on-the-job training
◎ Annual Earnings: $29,900
◎ Growth: 4.6%
◎ Annual Job Openings: 30,000
◎ Self-Employed: 2.7%
◎ Part-Time: 6.2%

Set up and operate machines to transfer printing designs. Positions machine mechanisms and depresses levers to apply marks on roller. Aligns plate with markings on machine table and tacks to table. Turns screws to align machine components. Determines ground setting according to weight of fabric, type of design, and colors in design. Examines marks on roller to verify alignment and detect defects. Records ground setting, length of roller, width of engraving, and circumference of roller on production sheet. Measures depth of engraving and weighs diamond points, using gauges and scales. Inserts mandrel through roller and lifts into position on machine. Adjusts and tightens levers in position, using hand tools. **SKILLS—Operation and Control:** Controlling operations of equipment or systems. **Operation Monitoring:** Watching gauges, dials, or other indicators to make sure a machine is working properly. **Installation:** Installing equipment, machines, wiring, or programs to meet specifications. **GOE— Interest Area:** 13. Manufacturing. **Work Group:** 13.08. Graphic Arts Production. **Other Jobs in This Work Group:** Bindery Machine Operators and Tenders; Camera Operators; Design Printing Machine Setters and Set-Up Operators; Desktop Publishers; Dot Etchers; Electronic Masking System Operators; Electrotypers and Stereotypers; Embossing Machine Set-Up Operators; Engravers, Hand; Engravers/Carvers; Etchers; Etchers, Hand; Film Laboratory Technicians; Hand Compositors and Typesetters; Job Printers; Letterpress Setters and Set-Up Operators; Marking and Identification Printing Machine Setters and Set-Up Operators; Offset Lithographic Press Setters and Set-Up Operators; Pantograph Engravers; Paste-Up Workers; Photoengravers; Photoengraving and Lithographing Machine Operators and Tenders; Photographic Processing Machine Operators; Plate Finishers; Platemakers; Precision Etchers and Engravers, Hand or Machine; Precision Printing Workers; Printing Press Machine Operators and Tenders; Scanner Operators; Strippers; Typesetting and Composing Machine Operators and Tenders. **PERSONALITY TYPE:** Realistic.

EDUCATION/TRAINING PROGRAM(S)— Graphic and Printing Equipment Operator, General Production; Graphic Communications, Other; Printing Management; Printing Press Operator. **RELATED KNOWLEDGE/COURSES—Production and Processing:** Knowledge of raw materials, production processes, quality control, costs, and other techniques for maximizing the effective manufacture and distribution of goods. **Mechanical Devices:** Knowledge of machines and tools, including their designs, uses, repair, and maintenance.

Environmental Compliance Inspectors

- Education/Training Required: Long-term on-the-job training
- Annual Earnings: $47,390
- Growth: 9.8%
- Annual Job Openings: 20,000
- Self-Employed: 0.9%
- Part-Time: 5.3%

Inspect and investigate sources of pollution to protect the public and environment and ensure conformance with federal, state, and local regulations and ordinances. Inform health professionals, property owners, and the public about harmful properties and related problems of water pollution and contaminated wastewater. Participate in the development of spill prevention programs and hazardous waste rules and regulations and recommend corrective actions for hazardous waste problems. Prepare data to calculate sewer service charges and capacity fees. Prepare written, oral, tabular, and graphic reports summarizing requirements and regulations, including enforcement and chain of custody documentation. Research and keep informed of pertinent information and developments in areas such as EPA laws and regulations. Respond to questions and inquiries, such as those concerning service charges and capacity fees, or refer them to supervisors. Maintain and repair materials, work sites, and equipment. Analyze and implement state, federal, or local requirements as necessary to maintain approved pretreatment, pollution prevention, and storm water

runoff programs. Conduct research on hazardous waste management projects in order to determine the magnitude of problems and treatment or disposal alternatives and costs. Determine the nature of code violations and actions to be taken and issue written notices of violation; participate in enforcement hearings as necessary. Determine sampling locations and methods and collect water or wastewater samples for analysis, preserving samples with appropriate containers and preservation methods. Determine which sites and violation reports to investigate and coordinate compliance and enforcement activities with other government agencies. Examine permits, licenses, applications, and records to ensure compliance with licensing requirements. Inform individuals and groups of pollution control regulations and inspection findings and explain how problems can be corrected. Inspect waste pretreatment, treatment, and disposal facilities and systems for conformance to federal, state, or local regulations. Interview individuals to determine the nature of suspected violations and to obtain evidence of violations. Investigate complaints and suspected violations regarding illegal dumping, pollution, pesticides, product quality, or labeling laws. **SKILLS—Science:** Using scientific rules and methods to solve problems. **Systems Evaluation:** Identifying measures or indicators of system performance and the actions needed to improve or correct performance relative to the goals of the system. **Reading Comprehension:** Understanding written sentences and paragraphs in work-related documents. **Systems Analysis:** Determining how a system should work and how changes in conditions, operations, and the environment will affect outcomes. **Speaking:** Talking to others to convey information effectively. **Negotiation:** Bringing others together and trying to reconcile differences. **Critical Thinking:** Using logic and reasoning to identify the strengths and weaknesses of alternative solutions, conclusions, or approaches to problems. **Writing:** Communicating effectively in writing as appropriate for the needs of the audience. **Judgment and Decision Making:** Considering the relative costs and benefits of potential actions to choose the most appropriate one. **GOE—Interest Area:** 07. Government and Public Administration. **Work Group:** 07.03. Regulations Enforcement. **Other Jobs in This Work Group:** Agricultural Inspectors; Aviation Inspectors; Child Support, Missing Persons, and Unemployment Insurance Fraud Investigators; Equal Opportunity Representatives and Officers; Financial Examiners; Fire Inspectors; Fish and Game Wardens; Forest Fire Inspectors and Prevention Specialists; Government Property Inspectors and Investigators; Immigration and Customs Inspectors; Licensing Examiners and Inspectors; Marine Cargo Inspectors; Mechanical Inspectors; Motor Vehicle Inspectors; Nuclear Monitoring Technicians; Occupational Health and Safety Specialists; Pressure Vessel Inspectors; Railroad Inspectors; Tax Examiners, Collectors, and Revenue Agents. **PERSONALITY TYPE:** Investigative.

EDUCATION/TRAINING PROGRAM(S)—No data available. **RELATED KNOWLEDGE/COURSES**—**Chemistry:** Knowledge of the chemical composition, structure, and properties of substances and of the chemical processes and transformations that they undergo. This includes uses of chemicals and their danger signs, production techniques, and disposal methods. **Public Safety and Security:** Knowledge of relevant equipment, policies, procedures, and strategies to promote effective local, state, or national security operations for the protection of people, data, property, and institutions. **Law and Government:** Knowledge of laws, legal codes, court procedures, precedents, government regulations, executive orders, agency rules, and the democratic political process. **Physics:** Knowledge and prediction of physical principles and laws and their interrelationships and applications to understanding fluid, material, and atmospheric dynamics and mechanical, electrical, atomic, and subatomic structures and processes. **Production and Processing:** Knowledge of raw materials, production processes, quality control, costs, and other techniques for maximizing the effective manufacture and distribution of goods. **Biology:** Knowledge of plant and animal organisms and their tissues, cells, functions, interdependencies, and interactions with each other and the environment.

Environmental Engineering Technicians

- ◉ Education/Training Required: Associate degree
- ◉ Annual Earnings: $38,550
- ◉ Growth: 28.4%
- ◉ Annual Job Openings: 3,000
- ◉ Self-Employed: 0.4%
- ◉ Part-Time: 5.0%

Apply theory and principles of environmental engineering to modify, test, and operate equipment and devices used in the prevention, control, and remediation of environmental pollution, including waste treatment and site remediation. May assist in the development of environmental pollution remediation devices under direction of engineer. Receive, set up, test, and decontaminate equipment. Maintain project logbook records and computer program files. Conduct pollution surveys, collecting and analyzing samples such as air and groundwater. Perform environmental quality work in field and office settings. Review technical documents to ensure completeness and conformance to requirements. Perform laboratory work such as logging numerical and visual observations, preparing and packaging samples, recording test results, and performing photo documentation. Review work plans to schedule activities. Obtain product information, identify vendors and suppliers, and order materials and equipment to maintain inventory. Arrange for the disposal of lead, asbestos, and other hazardous materials. Inspect facilities to monitor compliance with regulations governing substances such as asbestos, lead, and wastewater. Provide technical engineering support in the planning of projects, such as wastewater treatment plants, to ensure compliance with environmental regulations and policies. Improve chemical processes to reduce toxic emissions. Oversee support staff. Assist in the cleanup of hazardous material spills. Produce environmental assessment reports, tabulating data and preparing charts, graphs, and sketches. Maintain process parameters and evaluate process anomalies. Work with customers to assess the environmental impact of proposed construction and to develop pollution prevention programs. Perform statistical analysis and correction of air and/or water pollution data submitted by industry and other agencies. Develop work plans, including writing specifications and establishing material, manpower, and facilities needs. **SKILLS**—**Troubleshooting:** Determining causes of operating errors and deciding what to do about them. **Science:** Using scientific rules and methods to solve problems. **Repairing:** Repairing machines or systems by using the needed tools. **Coordination:** Adjusting actions in relation to others' actions. **Equipment Maintenance:** Performing routine maintenance on equipment and determining when and what kind of maintenance is needed. **Operation Monitoring:** Watching gauges, dials, or other indicators to make sure a machine is working properly. **Time Manage-**

ment: Managing one's own time and the time of others. **Service Orientation:** Actively looking for ways to help people. **Management of Financial Resources:** Determining how money will be spent to get the work done and accounting for these expenditures. **GOE—Interest Area:** 15. Scientific Research, Engineering, and Mathematics. **Work Group:** 15.09. Engineering Technology. **Other Jobs in This Work Group:** Aerospace Engineering and Operations Technicians; Calibration and Instrumentation Technicians; Cartographers and Photogrammetrists; Civil Engineering Technicians; Electrical Engineering Technicians; Electro-Mechanical Technicians; Electronic Drafters; Electronics Engineering Technicians; Mapping Technicians; Mechanical Drafters; Mechanical Engineering Technicians; Surveying Technicians. **PERSONALITY TYPE:** No data available.

EDUCATION/TRAINING PROGRAM(S)—Environmental Engineering Technology/Environmental Technology; Hazardous Materials Information Systems Technology/Technician. **RELATED KNOWLEDGE/COURSES—Engineering and Technology:** Knowledge of the practical application of engineering science and technology. This includes applying principles, techniques, procedures, and equipment to the design and production of various goods and services. **Design:** Knowledge of design techniques, tools, and principles involved in production of precision technical plans, blueprints, drawings, and models. **Building and Construction:** Knowledge of the materials, methods, and tools involved in the construction or repair of houses, buildings, or other structures such as highways and roads. **Physics:** Knowledge and prediction of physical principles and laws and their interrelationships and applications to understanding fluid, material, and atmospheric dynamics and mechanical, electrical, atomic, and subatomic structures and processes. **Law and Government:** Knowledge of laws, legal codes, court procedures, precedents, government regulations, executive orders, agency rules, and the democratic political process. **Administration and Management:** Knowledge of business and management principles involved in strategic planning, resource allocation, human resources modeling, leadership technique, production methods, and coordination of people and resources. **Customer and Personal Service:** Knowledge of principles and processes for providing customer and personal services. This includes customer needs assessment, meeting quality standards for services, and evaluation of customer sat-

isfaction. **Chemistry:** Knowledge of the chemical composition, structure, and properties of substances and of the chemical processes and transformations that they undergo. This includes uses of chemicals and their danger signs, production techniques, and disposal methods.

Environmental Engineers

- Education/Training Required: Bachelor's degree
- Annual Earnings: $66,480
- Growth: 38.2%
- Annual Job Openings: 6,000
- Self-Employed: 0.4%
- Part-Time: 4.6%

Design, plan, or perform engineering duties in the prevention, control, and remediation of environmental health hazards, utilizing various engineering disciplines. Work may include waste treatment, site remediation, or pollution control technology. Prepare, review, and update environmental investigation and recommendation reports. Collaborate with environmental scientists, planners, hazardous waste technicians, engineers, and other specialists and experts in law and business to address environmental problems. Obtain, update, and maintain plans, permits, and standard operating procedures. Provide technical-level support for environmental remediation and litigation projects, including remediation system design and determination of regulatory applicability. Monitor progress of environmental improvement programs. Inspect industrial and municipal facilities and programs in order to evaluate operational effectiveness and ensure compliance with environmental regulations. Provide administrative support for projects by collecting data, providing project documentation, training staff, and performing other general administrative duties. Develop proposed project objectives and targets and report to management on progress in attaining them. Advise corporations and government agencies of procedures to follow in cleaning up contaminated sites in order to protect people and the environment. Advise industries and government agencies about environmental policies and standards. Inform company employees and other interested parties of environmental issues. Assess the existing or potential environmental impact of land use projects on air, water, and land.

E

Assist in budget implementation, forecasts, and administration. Develop site-specific health and safety protocols, such as spill contingency plans and methods for loading and transporting waste. Coordinate and manage environmental protection programs and projects, assigning and evaluating work. Serve as liaison with federal, state, and local agencies and officials on issues pertaining to solid and hazardous waste program requirements. Design systems, processes, and equipment for control, management, and remediation of water, air, and soil quality. Prepare hazardous waste manifests and land disposal restriction notifications. Serve on teams conducting multimedia inspections at complex facilities, providing assistance with planning, quality assurance, safety inspection protocols, and sampling. **SKILLS—Science:** Using scientific rules and methods to solve problems. **Management of Financial Resources:** Determining how money will be spent to get the work done and accounting for these expenditures. **Coordination:** Adjusting actions in relation to others' actions. **Writing:** Communicating effectively in writing as appropriate for the needs of the audience. **Mathematics:** Using mathematics to solve problems. **Negotiation:** Bringing others together and trying to reconcile differences. **Persuasion:** Persuading others to change their minds or behavior. **Technology Design:** Generating or adapting equipment and technology to serve user needs. **GOE—Interest Area:** 01. Agriculture and Natural Resources. **Work Group:** 01.02. Resource Science/Engineering for Plants, Animals, and the Environment. **Other Jobs in This Work Group:** Agricultural Engineers; Animal Scientists; Foresters; Mining and Geological Engineers, Including Mining Safety Engineers; Petroleum Engineers; Plant Scientists; Range Managers; Soil Conservationists; Soil Scientists; Zoologists and Wildlife Biologists. **PERSONALITY TYPE:** No data available.

EDUCATION/TRAINING PROGRAM(S)—Environmental/Environmental Health Engineering. **RELATED KNOWLEDGE/COURSES—Education and Training:** Knowledge of principles and methods for curriculum and training design, teaching and instruction for individuals and groups, and the measurement of training effects. **Chemistry:** Knowledge of the chemical composition, structure, and properties of substances and of the chemical processes and transformations that they undergo. This includes uses of chemicals and their danger signs, production techniques, and disposal methods. **Law and Government:** Knowledge of laws, legal codes, court procedures, precedents, government regulations, executive orders, agency rules, and the democratic political process. **Public Safety and Security:** Knowledge of relevant equipment, policies, procedures, and strategies to promote effective local, state, or national security operations for the protection of people, data, property, and institutions. **Engineering and Technology:** Knowledge of the practical application of engineering science and technology. This includes applying principles, techniques, procedures, and equipment to the design and production of various goods and services. **Design:** Knowledge of design techniques, tools, and principles involved in production of precision technical plans, blueprints, drawings, and models.

Environmental Science and Protection Technicians, Including Health

- Education/Training Required: Associate degree
- Annual Earnings: $35,340
- Growth: 36.8%
- Annual Job Openings: 4,000
- Self-Employed: 1.1%
- Part-Time: 20.2%

Performs laboratory and field tests to monitor the environment and investigate sources of pollution, including those that affect health. Under direction of an environmental scientist or specialist, may collect samples of gases, soil, water, and other materials for testing and take corrective actions as assigned. Record test data and prepare reports, summaries, and charts that interpret test results. Collect samples of gases, soils, water, industrial wastewater, and asbestos products to conduct tests on pollutant levels and identify sources of pollution. Respond to and investigate hazardous conditions or spills or outbreaks of disease or food poisoning, collecting samples for analysis. Provide information and technical and program assistance to government representatives, employers, and the general public on the issues of public health, environmental protection, or workplace safety. Calibrate microscopes and test instruments. Make recommendations to control or eliminate unsafe conditions at workplaces or public facilities. Inspect sanitary conditions at public facilities. Prepare samples or photomicrographs for testing and analysis. Calculate amount of pollutant in samples or compute air pollution or gas flow in industrial processes, using chemical and mathematical formulas. Initiate procedures to close down or fine establishments violating environmental and/or health regulations. Determine amounts and kinds of chemicals to use in destroying harmful organisms and removing impurities from purification systems. Discuss test results and analyses with customers. Maintain files such as hazardous waste databases, chemical usage data, personnel exposure information, and diagrams showing equipment locations. Perform statistical analysis of environmental data. Set up equipment or stations to monitor and collect pollutants from sites such as smoke stacks, manufacturing plants, or mechanical equipment. Distribute permits, closure plans, and cleanup plans. Inspect workplaces to ensure the absence of health and safety hazards such as high noise levels, radiation, or potential lighting hazards. Weigh, analyze, and measure collected sample particles, such as lead, coal dust, or rock, to determine concentration of pollutants. Examine and analyze material for presence and concentration of contaminants such as asbestos, using variety of microscopes. Develop testing procedures and direct activities of workers in laboratory. **SKILLS—Science:** Using scientific rules and methods to solve problems. **Persuasion:** Persuading others to change their minds or behavior. **Active Learning:** Understanding the implications of new information for both current and future problem-solving and decision-making. **Instructing:** Teaching others how to do something. **Reading Comprehension:** Understanding written sentences and paragraphs in work-related documents. **Critical Thinking:** Using logic and reasoning to identify the strengths and weaknesses of alternative solutions, conclusions, or approaches to problems. **Social Perceptiveness:** Being aware of others' reactions and understanding why they react as they do. **Troubleshooting:** Determining causes of operating errors and deciding what to do about them. **GOE—Interest Area:** 01. Agriculture and Natural Resources. **Work Group:** 01.03. Resource Technologies for Plants, Animals, and the Environment. **Other Jobs in This Work Group:** Agricultural Technicians; Food Science Technicians; Food Scientists and Technologists; Geological Data Technicians; Geological Sample Test Technicians. **PERSONALITY TYPE:** Investigative.

EDUCATION/TRAINING PROGRAM(S)—Environmental Science; Environmental Studies; Physical Science Technologies/Technicians, Other; Science Technologies/Technicians, Other. **RELATED KNOWLEDGE/COURSES—Biology:** Knowledge of plant and animal organisms and their tissues, cells, functions, interdependencies, and interactions with each other and the environment. **Engineering and Technology:** Knowledge of the practical application of engineering science and technology. This includes applying principles, techniques, procedures, and equipment to the design and production of various goods and services. **Chemistry:** Knowledge of the chemical composition, structure, and properties of substances and of the chemical processes and transformations that they undergo. This includes uses of chemicals and their danger signs, production techniques, and disposal methods. **Physics:** Knowledge and prediction of physical principles and laws and their interrelationships and applications to understanding fluid, material, and atmospheric dynamics and mechanical, electrical, atomic, and subatomic structures and processes. **Customer and Personal Service:** Knowledge of principles and processes for providing customer and personal services. This includes customer needs assessment, meeting quality standards for services, and evaluation of customer satisfaction. **Education and Training:** Knowledge of principles and methods for curriculum and training design, teaching and instruction for individuals and groups, and the measurement of training effects.

Environmental Science Teachers, Postsecondary

- Education/Training Required: Master's degree
- Annual Earnings: $62,330
- Growth: 38.1%
- Annual Job Openings: 216,000
- Self-Employed: 0.3%
- Part-Time: 27.7%

Teach courses in environmental science. Supervise undergraduate and/or graduate teaching, internship, and research work. Conduct research in a particular field of knowledge and publish findings in professional journals, books, and/or electronic media. Keep abreast of developments in their field by reading current literature, talking with colleagues, and participating in professional conferences. Evaluate and grade students' class work, laboratory work, assignments, and papers. Write grant proposals to procure external research funding. Supervise students' laboratory and field work. Prepare course materials such as syllabi, homework assignments, and handouts. Plan, evaluate, and revise curricula, course content, and course materials and methods of instruction. Initiate, facilitate, and moderate classroom discussions. Compile, administer, and grade examinations or assign this work to others. Advise students on academic and vocational curricula and on career issues. Prepare and deliver lectures to undergraduate and/or graduate students on topics such as hazardous waste management, industrial safety, and environmental toxicology. Maintain student attendance records, grades, and other required records. Select and obtain materials and supplies such as textbooks and laboratory equipment. Maintain regularly scheduled office hours in order to advise and assist students. Collaborate with colleagues to address teaching and research issues. Perform administrative duties such as serving as department head. Participate in student recruitment, registration, and placement activities. Provide professional consulting services to government and/or industry. Serve on academic or administrative committees that deal with institutional policies, departmental matters, and academic issues. Compile bibliographies of specialized materials for outside reading assignments. **SKILLS—Science:** Using scientific rules and methods to solve problems. **Instructing:** Teaching others how to do something. **Writing:** Communicating effectively in writing as appropriate for the needs of the audience. **Critical Thinking:** Using logic and reasoning to identify the strengths and weaknesses of alternative solutions, conclusions, or approaches to problems. **Reading Comprehension:** Understanding written sentences and paragraphs in work-related documents. **Active Learning:** Understanding the implications of new information for both current and future problem-solving and decision-making. **Learning Strategies:** Selecting and using training/instructional methods and procedures appropriate for the situation when learning or teaching new things. **Management of Financial Resources:** Determining how money will be spent to get the work done and accounting for these expenditures. **GOE— Interest Area:** 05. Education and Training. **Work Group:** 05.03. Postsecondary and Adult Teaching and Instructing. **Other Jobs in This Work Group:** Adult Literacy, Remedial Education, and GED Teachers and Instructors; Agricultural Sciences Teachers, Postsecondary; Anthropology and Archeology Teachers, Postsecondary; Architecture Teachers, Postsecondary; Area, Ethnic, and Cultural Studies Teachers, Postsecondary; Art, Drama, and Music Teachers, Postsecondary; Atmospheric, Earth, Marine, and Space Sciences Teachers, Postsecondary; Biological Science Teachers, Postsecondary; Business Teachers, Postsecondary; Chemistry Teachers, Postsecondary; Communications Teachers, Postsecondary; Computer Science Teachers, Postsecondary; Criminal Justice and Law Enforcement Teachers, Postsecondary; Economics Teachers, Postsecondary; Education Teachers, Postsecondary; Engineering Teachers, Postsecondary; English Language and Literature Teachers, Postsecondary; Farm and Home Management Advisors; Foreign Language and Literature Teachers, Postsecondary; Forestry and Conservation Science Teachers, Postsecondary; Geography Teachers, Postsecondary; Graduate Teaching Assistants; Health Specialties Teachers, Postsecondary; History Teachers, Postsecondary; Home Economics Teachers, Postsecondary; Law Teachers, Postsecondary; Library Science Teachers, Postsecondary; Mathematical Science Teachers, Postsecondary; Nursing Instructors and Teachers, Postsecondary; Philosophy and Religion Teachers, Postsecondary; Physics Teachers, Postsecondary; Political Science Teachers, Postsecondary; Psychology Teachers, Postsecondary; Recreation and Fitness Studies Teachers, Postsecondary; Self-Enrichment Education Teachers; Social Work Teachers, Postsecondary; Sociology Teachers, Postsecondary; Vocational Education Teachers, Postsecondary. **PERSONALITY TYPE:** No data available.

EDUCATION/TRAINING PROGRAM(S)—Environmental Science; Environmental Studies; Science Teacher Education/General Science Teacher Education. **RELATED KNOWLEDGE/COURSES— Biology:** Knowledge of plant and animal organisms and their tissues, cells, functions, interdependencies, and interactions with each other and the environment. **Geography:** Knowledge of principles and methods for describing the features of land, sea, and air masses, including their physical characteristics; locations; interrelationships; and distribution of plant, animal, and human life. **Education and Training:** Knowledge of principles and methods for curriculum and training design, teaching and instruction for individuals and groups, and the measurement of training effects. **Chemistry:** Knowledge of the chemical composition, structure, and properties of substances and of the chemical processes and transformations that they undergo. This includes uses of chemicals and their danger signs, production techniques, and disposal methods. **English Language:** Knowledge of the structure and content of the English language, including the meaning and spelling of words, rules of composition, and grammar. **Mathematics:** Knowledge of arithmetic, algebra, geometry, calculus, and statistics and their applications. **Physics:** Knowledge and prediction of physical principles and laws and their interrelationships and applications to understanding fluid, material, and atmospheric dynamics and mechanical, electrical, atomic, and subatomic structures and processes.

Environmental Scientists and Specialists, Including Health

- Education/Training Required: Bachelor's degree
- Annual Earnings: $51,080
- Growth: 23.7%
- Annual Job Openings: 6,000
- Self-Employed: 2.9%
- Part-Time: 7.7%

Conduct research or perform investigation for the purpose of identifying, abating, or eliminating sources of pollutants or hazards that affect either the environment or the health of the population. Utilizing knowledge of various scientific disciplines, may collect, synthesize, study, report, and take action based on data derived from measurements or observations of air, food, soil, water, and other sources. Conduct environmental audits and inspections and investigations of violations. Evaluate violations or problems discovered during inspections in order to determine appropriate regulatory actions or to provide advice on the development and prosecution of regulatory cases. Communicate scientific and technical information through oral briefings, written documents, workshops, conferences, and public hearings. Review and implement environmental technical standards, guidelines, policies, and formal regulations that meet all appropriate requirements. Provide technical

guidance, support, and oversight to environmental programs, industry, and the public. Provide advice on proper standards and regulations and the development of policies, strategies, and codes of practice for environmental management. Analyze data to determine validity, quality, and scientific significance and to interpret correlations between human activities and environmental effects. Collect, synthesize, and analyze data derived from pollution emission measurements, atmospheric monitoring, meteorological and mineralogical information, and soil or water samples. Determine data collection methods to be employed in research projects and surveys. Prepare charts or graphs from data samples and provide summary information on the environmental relevance of the data. Develop the technical portions of legal documents, administrative orders, or consent decrees. Investigate and report on accidents affecting the environment. Monitor environmental impacts of development activities. Supervise environmental technologists and technicians. Develop programs designed to obtain the most productive, non-damaging use of land. Research sources of pollution to determine their effects on the environment and to develop theories or methods of pollution abatement or control. Monitor effects of pollution and land degradation and recommend means of prevention or control. Design and direct studies to obtain technical environmental information about planned projects. Conduct applied research on topics such as waste control and treatment and pollution control methods. **SKILLS—Science:** Using scientific rules and methods to solve problems. **Service Orientation:** Actively looking for ways to help people. **Negotiation:** Bringing others together and trying to reconcile differences. **Coordination:** Adjusting actions in relation to others' actions. **Reading Comprehension:** Understanding written sentences and paragraphs in work-related documents. **Persuasion:** Persuading others to change their minds or behavior. **Learning Strategies:** Selecting and using training/instructional methods and procedures appropriate for the situation when learning or teaching new things. **Social Perceptiveness:** Being aware of others' reactions and understanding why they react as they do. **Complex Problem Solving:** Identifying complex problems and reviewing related information to develop and evaluate options and implement solutions. **GOE—Interest Area:** 15. Scientific Research, Engineering, and Mathematics. **Work Group:** 15.03. Life Sciences. **Other Jobs in This Work Group:** Biochemists; Biologists; Biophysicists; Epidemiologists;

E

Medical Scientists, Except Epidemiologists; Microbiologists. **PERSONALITY TYPE:** Investigative.

EDUCATION/TRAINING PROGRAM(S)— Environmental Science; Environmental Studies. **RELATED KNOWLEDGE/COURSES—Biology:** Knowledge of plant and animal organisms and their tissues, cells, functions, interdependencies, and interactions with each other and the environment. **Geography:** Knowledge of principles and methods for describing the features of land, sea, and air masses, including their physical characteristics; locations; interrelationships; and distribution of plant, animal, and human life. **Chemistry:** Knowledge of the chemical composition, structure, and properties of substances and of the chemical processes and transformations that they undergo. This includes uses of chemicals and their danger signs, production techniques, and disposal methods. **Law and Government:** Knowledge of laws, legal codes, court procedures, precedents, government regulations, executive orders, agency rules, and the democratic political process. **Customer and Personal Service:** Knowledge of principles and processes for providing customer and personal services. This includes customer needs assessment, meeting quality standards for services, and evaluation of customer satisfaction. **Engineering and Technology:** Knowledge of the practical application of engineering science and technology. This includes applying principles, techniques, procedures, and equipment to the design and production of various goods and services. **Public Safety and Security:** Knowledge of relevant equipment, policies, procedures, and strategies to promote effective local, state, or national security operations for the protection of people, data, property, and institutions.

Epidemiologists

- Education/Training Required: Doctoral degree
- Annual Earnings: $54,800
- Growth: 32.5%
- Annual Job Openings: Fewer than 500
- Self-Employed: 2.1%
- Part-Time: 8.8%

Investigate and describe the determinants and distribution of disease, disability, and other health outcomes and develop the means for prevention and control. Oversee public health programs, including statistical analysis, health care planning, surveillance systems, and public health improvement. Investigate diseases or parasites to determine cause and risk factors, progress, life cycle, or mode of transmission. Plan and direct studies to investigate human or animal disease, preventive methods, and treatments for disease. Plan, administer, and evaluate health safety standards and programs to improve public health, conferring with health department, industry personnel, physicians, and others. Provide expertise in the design, management, and evaluation of study protocols and health status questionnaires, sample selection, and analysis. Conduct research to develop methodologies, instrumentation, and procedures for medical application, analyzing data and presenting findings. Consult with and advise physicians, educators, researchers, government health officials, and others regarding medical applications of sciences such as physics, biology, and chemistry. Supervise professional, technical, and clerical personnel. Identify and analyze public health issues related to foodborne parasitic diseases and their impact on public policies or scientific studies or surveys. Teach principles of medicine and medical and laboratory procedures to physicians, residents, students, and technicians. Standardize drug dosages, methods of immunization, and procedures for manufacture of drugs and medicinal compounds. Prepare and analyze samples to study effects of drugs, gases, pesticides, or microorganisms on cell structure and tissue. **SKILLS—Science:** Using scientific rules and methods to solve problems. **Reading Comprehension:** Understanding written sentences and paragraphs in work-related documents. **Active Learning:** Understanding the implications of new information for both current and future problem-solving and decision-making. **Programming:** Writing computer programs for various purposes. **Social Perceptiveness:** Being aware of others' reactions and understanding why they react as they do. **Persuasion:** Persuading others to change their minds or behavior. **Writing:** Communicating effectively in writing as appropriate for the needs of the audience. **Complex Problem Solving:** Identifying complex problems and reviewing related information to develop and evaluate options and implement solutions. **GOE—Interest Area:** 15. Scientific Research, Engineering, and Mathematics. **Work Group:** 15.03. Life Sciences. **Other Jobs in This Work Group:** Biochemists; Biologists; Biophysicists; Environmental Scientists and Specialists, Including Health; Medical Scientists, Except Epidemiologists; Microbiologists. **PERSONALITY TYPE:** Investigative.

EDUCATION/TRAINING PROGRAM(S)— Cell/Cellular Biology and Histology; Epidemiology; Medical Scientist (MS, PhD). **RELATED KNOWL-EDGE/COURSES—Biology:** Knowledge of plant and animal organisms and their tissues, cells, functions, interdependencies, and interactions with each other and the environment. **Sociology and Anthropology:** Knowledge of group behavior and dynamics, societal trends and influences, human migrations, ethnicity, and cultures and their history and origins. **Medicine and Dentistry:** Knowledge of the information and techniques needed to diagnose and treat human injuries, diseases, and deformities. This includes symptoms, treatment alternatives, drug properties and interactions, and preventive health-care measures. **English Language:** Knowledge of the structure and content of the English language, including the meaning and spelling of words, rules of composition, and grammar. **Education and Training:** Knowledge of principles and methods for curriculum and training design, teaching and instruction for individuals and groups, and the measurement of training effects. **Computers and Electronics:** Knowledge of circuit boards, processors, chips, electronic equipment, and computer hardware and software, including applications and programming.

Equal Opportunity Representatives and Officers

- Education/Training Required: Long-term on-the-job training
- Annual Earnings: $47,390
- Growth: 9.8%
- Annual Job Openings: 20,000
- Self-Employed: 0.9%
- Part-Time: 5.3%

Monitor and evaluate compliance with equal opportunity laws, guidelines, and policies to ensure that employment practices and contracting arrangements give equal opportunity without regard to race, religion, color, national origin, sex, age, or disability. Conduct surveys and evaluate findings in order to determine if systematic discrimination exists. Counsel newly hired members of minority and disadvantaged groups, informing them about details of civil rights laws. Interpret civil rights laws and equal opportunity regulations for individuals and employers. Investigate employment practices and alleged violations of laws in order to document and correct discriminatory factors. Meet with persons involved in equal opportunity complaints in order to verify case information and to arbitrate and settle disputes. Prepare reports of selection, survey, and other statistics and recommendations for corrective action. Provide information, technical assistance, and training to supervisors, managers, and employees on topics such as employee supervision, hiring, grievance procedures, and staff development. Review company contracts to determine actions required to meet governmental equal opportunity provisions. Study equal opportunity complaints in order to clarify issues. Act as liaisons between minority placement agencies and employers or between job search committees and other equal opportunity administrators. Consult with community representatives to develop technical assistance agreements in accordance with governmental regulations. Coordinate, monitor, and revise complaint procedures to ensure timely processing and review of complaints. Develop guidelines for non-discriminatory employment practices and monitor their implementation and impact. Meet with job search committees or coordinators to explain the role of the equal opportunity coordinator, to provide resources for advertising, and to explain expectations for future contacts. Participate in the recruitment of employees through job fairs, career days, and advertising plans. Verify that all job descriptions are submitted for review and approval and that descriptions meet regulatory standards. **SKILLS—Negotiation:** Bringing others together and trying to reconcile differences. **Writing:** Communicating effectively in writing as appropriate for the needs of the audience. **Speaking:** Talking to others to convey information effectively. **Persuasion:** Persuading others to change their minds or behavior. **Systems Analysis:** Determining how a system should work and how changes in conditions, operations, and the environment will affect outcomes. **Reading Comprehension:** Understanding written sentences and paragraphs in work-related documents. **Active Listening:** Giving full attention to what other people are saying, taking time to understand the points being made, asking questions as appropriate, and not interrupting at inappropriate times. **Systems Evalua-**

E

tion: Identifying measures or indicators of system performance and the actions needed to improve or correct performance relative to the goals of the system. **GOE—Interest Area:** 07. Government and Public Administration. **Work Group:** 07.03. Regulations Enforcement. **Other Jobs in This Work Group:** Agricultural Inspectors; Aviation Inspectors; Child Support, Missing Persons, and Unemployment Insurance Fraud Investigators; Environmental Compliance Inspectors; Financial Examiners; Fire Inspectors; Fish and Game Wardens; Forest Fire Inspectors and Prevention Specialists; Government Property Inspectors and Investigators; Immigration and Customs Inspectors; Licensing Examiners and Inspectors; Marine Cargo Inspectors; Mechanical Inspectors; Motor Vehicle Inspectors; Nuclear Monitoring Technicians; Occupational Health and Safety Specialists; Pressure Vessel Inspectors; Railroad Inspectors; Tax Examiners, Collectors, and Revenue Agents. **PERSONALITY TYPE:** Social.

EDUCATION/TRAINING PROGRAM(S)—No data available. **RELATED KNOWLEDGE/COURSES—Personnel and Human Resources:** Knowledge of principles and procedures for personnel recruitment, selection, training, compensation and benefits, labor relations and negotiation, and personnel information systems. **Law and Government:** Knowledge of laws, legal codes, court procedures, precedents, government regulations, executive orders, agency rules, and the democratic political process. **Sociology and Anthropology:** Knowledge of group behavior and dynamics, societal trends and influences, human migrations, ethnicity, and cultures and their history and origins. **English Language:** Knowledge of the structure and content of the English language, including the meaning and spelling of words, rules of composition, and grammar. **Mathematics:** Knowledge of arithmetic, algebra, geometry, calculus, and statistics and their applications. **Communications and Media:** Knowledge of media production, communication, and dissemination techniques and methods. This includes alternative ways to inform and entertain via written, oral, and visual media.

Excavating and Loading Machine Operators

- Education/Training Required: Moderate-term on-the-job training
- Annual Earnings: $31,970
- Growth: 8.9%
- Annual Job Openings: 14,000
- Self-Employed: 16.9%
- Part-Time: 2.7%

Operate machinery equipped with scoops, shovels, or buckets to excavate and load loose materials. Operates power machinery, such as powered shovel, stripping shovel, scraper loader (mucking machine), or backhoe (trench-excavating machine) to excavate and load material. Observes hand signals, grade stakes, and other markings when operating machines. Receives written or oral instructions to move or excavate material. Measures and verifies levels of rock or gravel, base, and other excavated material. Lubricates and repairs machinery and replaces parts such as gears, bearings, and bucket teeth. Directs ground workers engaged in activities such as moving stakes or markers. **SKILLS—Operation and Control:** Controlling operations of equipment or systems. **Operation Monitoring:** Watching gauges, dials, or other indicators to make sure a machine is working properly. **Repairing:** Repairing machines or systems by using the needed tools. **Equipment Maintenance:** Performing routine maintenance on equipment and determining when and what kind of maintenance is needed. **Management of Personnel Resources:** Motivating, developing, and directing people as they work, identifying the best people for the job. **Troubleshooting:** Determining causes of operating errors and deciding what to do about them. **Equipment Selection:** Determining the kind of tools and equipment needed to do a job. **Installation:** Installing equipment, machines, wiring, or programs to meet specifications. **GOE—Interest Area:** 01. Agriculture and Natural Resources. **Work Group:** 01.08. Mining and Drilling. **Other Jobs in This Work Group:** Construction Drillers; Continuous Mining Machine Operators; Derrick Operators, Oil and Gas; Explosives Workers, Ordnance Handling Experts, and Blasters; Helpers—Extraction Workers; Loading Machine Operators, Underground Mining; Mine Cutting and Channeling Machine Operators; Rock Splitters, Quarry; Roof Bolters, Mining; Rotary Drill

Operators, Oil and Gas; Roustabouts, Oil and Gas; Service Unit Operators, Oil, Gas, and Mining; Shuttle Car Operators; Well and Core Drill Operators; Wellhead Pumpers. **PERSONALITY TYPE:** Realistic.

EDUCATION/TRAINING PROGRAM(S)—Construction/Heavy Equipment/Earthmoving Equipment Operation. **RELATED KNOWLEDGE/COURSES**—**Mechanical Devices:** Knowledge of machines and tools, including their designs, uses, repair, and maintenance. **Engineering and Technology:** Knowledge of the practical application of engineering science and technology. This includes applying principles, techniques, procedures, and equipment to the design and production of various goods and services. **Physics:** Knowledge and prediction of physical principles and laws and their interrelationships and applications to understanding fluid, material, and atmospheric dynamics and mechanical, electrical, atomic, and subatomic structures and processes.

Executive Secretaries and Administrative Assistants

- Education/Training Required: Moderate-term on-the-job training
- Annual Earnings: $34,970
- Growth: 8.7%
- Annual Job Openings: 210,000
- Self-Employed: 1.6%
- Part-Time: 17.5%

Provide high-level administrative support by conducting research; preparing statistical reports; handling information requests; and performing clerical functions such as preparing correspondence, receiving visitors, arranging conference calls, and scheduling meetings. May also train and supervise lower-level clerical staff. Manage and maintain executives' schedules. Prepare invoices, reports, memos, letters, financial statements, and other documents, using word-processing, spreadsheet, database, and/or presentation software. Read and analyze incoming memos, submissions, and reports in order to determine their significance and plan their distribution. Open, sort, and distribute incoming correspondence, including faxes and e-mail. File and retrieve corporate documents, records, and reports. Greet visitors and deter-

mine whether they should be given access to specific individuals. Prepare responses to correspondence containing routine inquiries. Perform general office duties such as ordering supplies, maintaining records management systems, and performing basic bookkeeping work. Prepare agendas and make arrangements for committee, board, and other meetings. Make travel arrangements for executives. Conduct research, compile data, and prepare papers for consideration and presentation by executives, committees, and boards of directors. Compile, transcribe, and distribute minutes of meetings. Attend meetings in order to record minutes. Coordinate and direct office services, such as records and budget preparation, personnel, and housekeeping, in order to aid executives. Meet with individuals, special interest groups, and others on behalf of executives, committees, and boards of directors. Set up and oversee administrative policies and procedures for offices and/or organizations. Supervise and train other clerical staff. Review operating practices and procedures in order to determine whether improvements can be made in areas such as workflow, reporting procedures, or expenditures. Interpret administrative and operating policies and procedures for employees. **SKILLS**—**Active Listening:** Giving full attention to what other people are saying, taking time to understand the points being made, asking questions as appropriate, and not interrupting at inappropriate times. **Time Management:** Managing one's own time and the time of others. **Writing:** Communicating effectively in writing as appropriate for the needs of the audience. **Speaking:** Talking to others to convey information effectively. **Service Orientation:** Actively looking for ways to help people. **Management of Material Resources:** Obtaining and seeing to the appropriate use of equipment, facilities, and materials needed to do certain work. **Instructing:** Teaching others how to do something. **Management of Financial Resources:** Determining how money will be spent to get the work done and accounting for these expenditures. **GOE**—**Interest Area:** 04. Business and Administration. **Work Group:** 04.04. Secretarial Support. **Other Jobs in This Work Group:** Legal Secretaries; Medical Secretaries; Secretaries, Except Legal, Medical, and Executive. **PERSONALITY TYPE:** Conventional.

EDUCATION/TRAINING PROGRAM(S)—Administrative Assistant and Secretarial Science, General; Executive Assistant/Executive Secretary; Medical Administrative/Executive Assistant and Medical Secretary. **RELATED KNOWLEDGE/COURSES**—Clerical Practices: Knowledge of administrative and clerical procedures and systems such as word processing, managing files and records, stenography and transcription, designing forms, and other office procedures and terminology. **Customer and Personal Service:** Knowledge of principles and processes for providing customer and personal services. This includes customer needs assessment, meeting quality standards for services, and evaluation of customer satisfaction. **English Language:** Knowledge of the structure and content of the English language, including the meaning and spelling of words, rules of composition, and grammar. **Computers and Electronics:** Knowledge of circuit boards, processors, chips, electronic equipment, and computer hardware and software, including applications and programming. **Communications and Media:** Knowledge of media production, communication, and dissemination techniques and methods. This includes alternative ways to inform and entertain via written, oral, and visual media. **Administration and Management:** Knowledge of business and management principles involved in strategic planning, resource allocation, human resources modeling, leadership technique, production methods, and coordination of people and resources.

Exhibit Designers

◎ Education/Training Required: Bachelor's degree

◎ Annual Earnings: $35,800

◎ Growth: 20.9%

◎ Annual Job Openings: 2,000

◎ Self-Employed: 32.2%

◎ Part-Time: 16.5%

Plan, design, and oversee construction and installation of permanent and temporary exhibits and displays. Prepares preliminary drawings of proposed exhibit, including detailed construction, layout, material specifications, or special effects diagrams. Arranges for acquisition of specimens or graphics or building of exhibit structures by outside contractors to complete exhibit. Inspects installed exhibit for conformance to specifications and satisfactory operation of special effects components. Submits plans for approval and adapts plan to serve intended purpose or to conform to budget or fabrication restrictions. Designs, draws, paints, or sketches backgrounds and fixtures for use in

windows or interior displays. Oversees preparation of artwork, construction of exhibit components, and placement of collection to ensure intended interpretation of concepts and conformance to specifications. Confers with client or staff regarding theme, interpretative or informational purpose, planned location, budget, materials, or promotion. Designs display to decorate streets, fairgrounds, building, or other places for celebrations, using paper, cloth, plastic, or other materials. **SKILLS—Management of Financial Resources:** Determining how money will be spent to get the work done and accounting for these expenditures. **Management of Material Resources:** Obtaining and seeing to the appropriate use of equipment, facilities, and materials needed to do certain work. **Systems Evaluation:** Identifying measures or indicators of system performance and the actions needed to improve or correct performance relative to the goals of the system. **Negotiation:** Bringing others together and trying to reconcile differences. **Systems Analysis:** Determining how a system should work and how changes in conditions, operations, and the environment will affect outcomes. **Operations Analysis:** Analyzing needs and product requirements to create a design. **Social Perceptiveness:** Being aware of others' reactions and understanding why they react as they do. **Management of Personnel Resources:** Motivating, developing, and directing people as they work, identifying the best people for the job. **GOE—Interest Area:** 03. Arts and Communication. **Work Group:** 03.05. Design. **Other Jobs in This Work Group:** Commercial and Industrial Designers; Fashion Designers; Floral Designers; Graphic Designers; Interior Designers; Merchandise Displayers and Window Trimmers; Set Designers. **PERSONALITY TYPE:** Artistic.

EDUCATION/TRAINING PROGRAM(S)— Design and Applied Arts, Other; Design and Visual Communications, General; Illustration; Technical Theatre/Theatre Design and Technology. **RELATED KNOWLEDGE/COURSES—Design:** Knowledge of design techniques, tools, and principles involved in production of precision technical plans, blueprints, drawings, and models. **Fine Arts:** Knowledge of the theory and techniques required to compose, produce, and perform works of music, dance, the visual arts, drama, and sculpture. **Building and Construction:** Knowledge of the materials, methods, and tools involved in the construction or repair of houses, buildings, or other structures such as highways and roads. **Sales and Marketing:** Knowledge of principles and methods for showing, promoting, and selling products or services. This includes marketing strategy and tactics, product demonstrations, sales techniques, and sales control systems. **Computers and Electronics:** Knowledge of circuit boards, processors, chips, electronic equipment, and computer hardware and software, including applications and programming. **Economics and Accounting:** Knowledge of economic and accounting principles and practices, the financial markets, banking, and the analysis and reporting of financial data.

Family and General Practitioners

- ◎ Education/Training Required: First professional degree
- ◎ Annual Earnings: $137,090
- ◎ Growth: 19.5%
- ◎ Annual Job Openings: 38,000
- ◎ Self-Employed: 16.9%
- ◎ Part-Time: 8.1%

Diagnose, treat, and help prevent diseases and injuries that commonly occur in the general population. Advise patients and community members concerning diet, activity, hygiene, and disease prevention. Collect, record, and maintain patient information, such as medical history, reports, and examination results. Explain procedures and discuss test results or prescribed treatments with patients. Monitor the patients' conditions and progress and re-evaluate treatments as necessary. Order, perform, and interpret tests and analyze records, reports, and examination information to diagnose patients' condition. Prescribe or administer treatment, therapy, medication, vaccination, and other specialized medical care to treat or prevent illness, disease, or injury. Refer patients to medical specialists or other practitioners when necessary. Conduct research to study anatomy and develop or test medications, treatments, or procedures to prevent or control disease or injury. Coordinate work with nurses, social workers, rehabilitation therapists, pharmacists, psychologists, and other health care providers. Deliver babies. Direct and coordinate activities of nurses, students, assistants, specialists, therapists, and other medical staff. Operate on patients to remove, repair, or improve functioning of diseased or injured body parts and systems. Plan, implement, or administer health programs or standards in hospital, business, or community for information, prevention, or treatment of injury or illness. Prepare reports for government or management of birth, death, and disease statistics; workforce evaluations; or medical status of individuals. **SKILLS—Science:** Using scientific rules and methods to solve problems. **Systems Evaluation:** Identifying measures or indicators of system performance and the actions needed to improve or correct performance relative to the goals of the system. **Reading Comprehension:** Understanding written sentences and paragraphs in work-related documents. **Active Learning:** Understanding the implications of new information for both current and future problem-solving and decision-making. **Judgment and Decision Making:** Considering the relative costs and benefits of potential actions to choose the most appropriate one. **Management of Personnel Resources:** Motivating, developing, and directing people as they work, identifying the best people for the job. **Systems Analysis:** Determining how a system should work and how changes in conditions, operations, and the environment will affect outcomes. **Social Perceptiveness:** Being aware of others' reactions and understanding why they react as they do. **GOE—Interest Area:** 08. Health Science. **Work Group:** 08.02. Medicine and Surgery. **Other Jobs in This Work Group:** Anesthesiologists; Internists, General; Medical Assistants; Medical Transcriptionists; Obstetricians and Gynecologists; Pediatricians, General; Pharmacists; Pharmacy Aides; Pharmacy Technicians; Physician Assistants; Psychiatrists; Registered Nurses; Surgeons; Surgical Technologists. **PERSONALITY TYPE:** Investigative.

EDUCATION/TRAINING PROGRAM(S)—Family Medicine; Medicine (MD); Osteopathic Medicine/Osteopathy (DO). **RELATED KNOWLEDGE/ COURSES—Medicine and Dentistry:** Knowledge of the information and techniques needed to diagnose and treat human injuries, diseases, and deformities. This includes symptoms, treatment alternatives, drug properties and interactions, and preventive health-care measures. **Biology:** Knowledge of plant and animal organisms and their tissues, cells, functions, interdependencies, and interactions with each other and the environment. **Therapy and Counseling:** Knowledge of principles, methods, and procedures for diagnosis, treatment, and rehabilitation of physical and mental dysfunctions and for career counseling and guidance. **Chemistry:** Knowledge of the chemical composition, structure, and properties of substances and of the chemical processes and transformations that they undergo. This includes uses of chemicals and their danger signs, production techniques, and disposal methods. **Administration and Management:** Knowledge of business and management principles involved in strategic planning, resource allocation, human resources modeling, leadership technique, production methods, and coordination of people and resources. **Physics:** Knowledge and prediction of physical principles and laws and their interrelationships and applications to understanding fluid, material, and atmospheric dynamics and mechanical, electrical, atomic, and subatomic structures and processes.

Farmers and Ranchers

- ◉ Education/Training Required: Long-term on-the-job training
- ◉ Annual Earnings: $40,440
- ◉ Growth: –20.6%
- ◉ Annual Job Openings: 118,000
- ◉ Self-Employed: 99.3%
- ◉ Part-Time: 17.7%

On an ownership or rental basis, operate farms, ranches, greenhouses, nurseries, timber tracts, or other agricultural production establishments that produce crops, horticultural specialties, livestock, poultry, finfish, shellfish, or animal specialties. May plant, cultivate, harvest, perform post-harvest activities for, and market crops and livestock; may hire, train, and supervise farm workers or supervise a farm labor contractor; may prepare cost, production, and other records. May maintain and operate machinery and perform physical work. Assist in animal births and care for newborn livestock. Breed and raise stock such as cattle, poultry, and honeybees, using recognized breeding practices to ensure continued improvement in stock. Clean and disinfect buildings and yards and remove manure. Clean and sanitize milking equipment, storage tanks, collection cups, and cows' udders or ensure that procedures are followed to maintain sanitary conditions for handling of milk. Clean, grade, and package crops for marketing. Control the spread of disease and parasites in herds by using vaccination and medication and by separating sick animals. Destroy diseased or superfluous crops. Determine types and quantities of crops or livestock to be raised according to factors such as market conditions, federal program availability, and soil conditions. Evaluate product marketing alternatives and then promote and market farm products, acting as the sales agent for livestock and crops. Harvest crops and collect specialty products such as royal jelly, wax, pollen, and honey from bee colonies. Install and shift irrigation systems to irrigate fields evenly or according to crop need. Maintain pastures or grazing lands to ensure that animals have enough feed, employing pasture-conservation measures such as arranging rotational grazing. Milk cows, using milking machinery. Monitor crops as they grow in order to ensure that they are growing properly and are free from diseases and contaminants. Negotiate and arrange with buyers for the sale, storage, and shipment of crops. Perform crop production duties such as planning, tilling, planting, fertilizing, cultivating, spraying, and harvesting. Plan crop activities based on factors such as crop maturity and weather conditions. Purchase and store livestock feed. Remove lower-quality or older animals from herds and purchase other livestock to replace culled animals. Select and purchase supplies and equipment such as seed, fertilizers, and farm machinery. Select animals for market and provide transportation of livestock to market. Set up and operate farm machinery to cultivate, harvest, and haul crops. **SKILLS—Management of Financial Resources:** Determining how money will be spent to get the work done and accounting for these expenditures. **Management of Personnel Resources:** Motivating, developing, and directing people as they work, identifying the best people for the job. **Installation:** Installing equipment, machines, wiring, or programs to meet specifications. **Management of Material Resources:** Obtaining and seeing to the appropriate use of equipment, facilities, and materials needed to do certain work. **Equipment Selection:** Determining the kind of tools and equipment needed to do a job. **Operation and Control:** Controlling operations of equipment or systems. **Equipment Maintenance:** Performing routine maintenance on equipment and determining when and what kind of maintenance is needed. **Repairing:** Repairing machines or systems by using the needed tools. **GOE—Interest Area:** 01. Agriculture and Natural Resources. **Work Group:** 01.01. Managerial Work in Agriculture and Natural Resources. **Other Jobs in This Work Group:** Agricultural Crop Farm Managers; First-Line Supervisors and Manager/Supervisors—Agricultural Crop Workers;

First-Line Supervisors and Manager/Supervisors—Animal Husbandry Workers; First-Line Supervisors and Manager/Supervisors—Extractive Workers; First-Line Supervisors and Manager/Supervisors—Fishery Workers; First-Line Supervisors and Manager/Supervisors—Horticultural Workers; First-Line Supervisors and Manager/Supervisors—Landscaping Workers; First-Line Supervisors and Manager/Supervisors—Logging Workers; Fish Hatchery Managers; Lawn Service Managers; Nursery and Greenhouse Managers; Park Naturalists; Purchasing Agents and Buyers, Farm Products. **PERSONALITY TYPE:** Realistic.

EDUCATION/TRAINING PROGRAM(S)—Agribusiness/Agricultural Business Operations; Agricultural Animal Breeding; Agricultural Business and Management, General; Agricultural Production Operations, General; Agricultural Production Operations, Other; Agronomy and Crop Science; Animal Nutrition; Animal Sciences, General; Animal/Livestock Husbandry and Production; Aquaculture; Crop Production; Dairy Husbandry and Production; Dairy Science; Farm/Farm and Ranch Management; Greenhouse Operations and Management; Horticultural Science; Livestock Management; Ornamental Horticulture; Plant Nursery Operations and Management; Plant Protection and Integrated Pest Management; Plant Sciences, General; Poultry Science; Range Science and Management. **RELATED KNOWLEDGE/COURSES—Food Production:** Knowledge of techniques and equipment for planting, growing, and harvesting food products (both plant and animal) for consumption, including storage/handling techniques. **Economics and Accounting:** Knowledge of economic and accounting principles and practices, the financial markets, banking, and the analysis and reporting of financial data. **Personnel and Human Resources:** Knowledge of principles and procedures for personnel recruitment, selection, training, compensation and benefits, labor relations and negotiation, and personnel information systems. **Production and Processing:** Knowledge of raw materials, production processes, quality control, costs, and other techniques for maximizing the effective manufacture and distribution of goods. **Sales and Marketing:** Knowledge of principles and methods for showing, promoting, and selling products or services. This includes marketing strategy and tactics, product demonstrations, sales techniques, and sales control systems. **Transportation:** Knowledge of principles and methods for moving people or goods by air, rail, sea, or road, including the relative costs and benefits.

Fashion Designers

- Education/Training Required: Bachelor's degree
- Annual Earnings: $55,840
- Growth: 10.6%
- Annual Job Openings: 2,000
- Self-Employed: 29.3%
- Part-Time: 16.5%

Design clothing and accessories. Create original garments or design garments that follow well-established fashion trends. May develop the line of color and kinds of materials. Attend fashion shows and review garment magazines and manuals in order to gather information about fashion trends and consumer preferences. Design custom clothing and accessories for individuals; retailers; or theatrical, television, or film productions. Draw patterns for articles designed; then cut patterns and cut material according to patterns, using measuring instruments and scissors. Examine sample garments on and off models; then modify designs to achieve desired effects. Select materials and production techniques to be used for products. Sketch rough and detailed drawings of apparel or accessories and write specifications such as color schemes, construction, material types, and accessory requirements. Adapt other designers' ideas for the mass market. Collaborate with other designers to coordinate special products and designs. Confer with sales and management executives or with clients in order to discuss design ideas. Determine prices for styles. Develop a group of products and/or accessories and market them through venues such as boutiques or mail-order catalogs. Direct and coordinate workers involved in drawing and cutting patterns and constructing samples or finished garments. Identify target markets for designs, looking at factors such as age, gender, and socioeconomic status. Provide sample garments to agents and sales representatives and arrange for showings of sample garments at sales meetings or fashion shows. Purchase new or used clothing and accessory items as needed to complete designs. Read scripts and consult directors and other production staff in order to develop design concepts and plan productions.

Research the styles and periods of clothing needed for film or theatrical productions. Sew together sections of material to form mockups or samples of garments or articles, using sewing equipment. Visit textile showrooms to keep up to date on the latest fabrics. Test fabrics or oversee testing so that garment care labels can be created. **SKILLS—Systems Analysis:** Determining how a system should work and how changes in conditions, operations, and the environment will affect outcomes. **Persuasion:** Persuading others to change their minds or behavior. **Operations Analysis:** Analyzing needs and product requirements to create a design. **Management of Financial Resources:** Determining how money will be spent to get the work done and accounting for these expenditures. **Negotiation:** Bringing others together and trying to reconcile differences. **Management of Material Resources:** Obtaining and seeing to the appropriate use of equipment, facilities, and materials needed to do certain work. **Systems Evaluation:** Identifying measures or indicators of system performance and the actions needed to improve or correct performance relative to the goals of the system. **Social Perceptiveness:** Being aware of others' reactions and understanding why they react as they do. **Coordination:** Adjusting actions in relation to others' actions. **Service Orientation:** Actively looking for ways to help people. **GOE—Interest Area:** 03. Arts and Communication. **Work Group:** 03.05. Design. **Other Jobs in This Work Group:** Commercial and Industrial Designers; Exhibit Designers; Floral Designers; Graphic Designers; Interior Designers; Merchandise Displayers and Window Trimmers; Set Designers. **PERSONALITY TYPE:** Artistic.

EDUCATION/TRAINING PROGRAM(S)— Apparel and Textile Manufacture; Fashion and Fabric Consultant; Fashion/Apparel Design; Textile Science. **RELATED KNOWLEDGE/COURSES—Design:** Knowledge of design techniques, tools, and principles involved in production of precision technical plans, blueprints, drawings, and models. **Fine Arts:** Knowledge of the theory and techniques required to compose, produce, and perform works of music, dance, the visual arts, drama, and sculpture. **Production and Processing:** Knowledge of raw materials, production processes, quality control, costs, and other techniques for maximizing the effective manufacture and distribution of goods. **Sales and Marketing:** Knowledge of principles and methods for showing, promoting, and selling products or services. This includes marketing strategy and tactics, product demonstrations, sales

techniques, and sales control systems. **Education and Training:** Knowledge of principles and methods for curriculum and training design, teaching and instruction for individuals and groups, and the measurement of training effects. **Customer and Personal Service:** Knowledge of principles and processes for providing customer and personal services. This includes customer needs assessment, meeting quality standards for services, and evaluation of customer satisfaction.

Film and Video Editors

- Education/Training Required: Bachelor's degree
- Annual Earnings: $43,590
- Growth: 26.4%
- Annual Job Openings: 3,000
- Self-Employed: 21.9%
- Part-Time: 20.4%

Edit motion picture soundtracks, film, and video. Cut shot sequences to different angles at specific points in scenes, making each individual cut as fluid and seamless as possible. Study scripts to become familiar with production concepts and requirements. Edit films and videotapes to insert music, dialogue, and sound effects; to arrange films into sequences; and to correct errors, using editing equipment. Select and combine the most effective shots of each scene in order to form a logical and smoothly running story. Mark frames where a particular shot or piece of sound is to begin or end. Determine the specific audio and visual effects and music necessary to complete films. Verify key numbers and time codes on materials. Organize and string together raw footage into a continuous whole according to scripts and/or the instructions of directors and producers. Review assembled films or edited videotapes on screens or monitors in order to determine if corrections are necessary. Program computerized graphic effects. Review footage sequence by sequence in order to become familiar with it before assembling it into a final product. Set up and operate computer editing systems, electronic titling systems, video switching equipment, and digital video effects units in order to produce a final product. Record needed sounds or obtain them from sound effects libraries. Confer with producers and directors concerning layout or editing approaches needed to increase dramatic or entertainment value of productions. Manipulate plot, score, sound, and graphics to make the parts into a continuous whole, working closely with people in audio, visual, music, optical, and/or special effects departments. Supervise and coordinate activities of workers engaged in film editing, assembling, and recording activities. Trim film segments to specified lengths and reassemble segments in sequences that present stories with maximum effect. Develop post-production models for films. Piece sounds together to develop film soundtracks. Conduct film screenings for directors and members of production staffs. Collaborate with music editors to select appropriate passages of music and develop production scores. **SKILLS— Equipment Selection:** Determining the kind of tools and equipment needed to do a job. **Coordination:** Adjusting actions in relation to others' actions. **Operations Analysis:** Analyzing needs and product requirements to create a design. **Equipment Maintenance:** Performing routine maintenance on equipment and determining when and what kind of maintenance is needed. **Troubleshooting:** Determining causes of operating errors and deciding what to do about them. **Time Management:** Managing one's own time and the time of others. **Active Learning:** Understanding the implications of new information for both current and future problem-solving and decision-making. **Operation and Control:** Controlling operations of equipment or systems. **GOE—Interest Area:** 03. Arts and Communication. **Work Group:** 03.09. Media Technology. **Other Jobs in This Work Group:** Audio and Video Equipment Technicians; Broadcast Technicians; Camera Operators, Television, Video, and Motion Picture; Multi-Media Artists and Animators; Photographic Hand Developers; Photographic Reproduction Technicians; Photographic Retouchers and Restorers; Professional Photographers; Radio Operators; Sound Engineering Technicians. **PERSONALITY TYPE:** Artistic.

EDUCATION/TRAINING PROGRAM(S)— Audiovisual Communications Technologies/Technicians, Other; Cinematography and Film/Video Production; Communications Technology/Technician; Photojournalism; Radio and Television; Radio and Television Broadcasting Technology/Technician. **RELATED KNOWLEDGE/COURSES—Communications and Media:** Knowledge of media production, communication, and dissemination techniques and methods. This includes alternative ways to inform and entertain via written, oral, and visual media. **Fine Arts:** Knowledge of the theory and techniques required to compose, produce, and perform works of music, dance, the visual arts, drama, and sculpture. **Computers and Electronics:** Knowledge of circuit boards, processors, chips, electronic equipment, and computer hardware and software, including applications and programming. **Design:** Knowledge of design techniques, tools, and principles involved in production of precision technical plans, blueprints, drawings, and models. **Education and Training:** Knowledge of principles and methods for curriculum and training design, teaching and instruction for individuals and groups, and the measurement of training effects. **English Language:** Knowledge of the structure and content of the English language, including the meaning and spelling of words, rules of composition, and grammar.

Financial Analysts

- ◎ Education/Training Required: Bachelor's degree
- ◎ Annual Earnings: $61,910
- ◎ Growth: 18.7%
- ◎ Annual Job Openings: 22,000
- ◎ Self-Employed: 4.8%
- ◎ Part-Time: 10.2%

Conduct quantitative analyses of information affecting investment programs of public or private institutions. Analyze financial information to produce forecasts of business, industry, and economic conditions for use in making investment decisions. Assemble spreadsheets and draw charts and graphs used to illustrate technical reports, using computer. Evaluate and compare the relative quality of various securities in a given industry. Interpret data affecting investment programs, such as price, yield, stability, future trends in investment risks, and economic influences. Maintain knowledge and stay abreast of developments in the fields of industrial technology, business, finance, and economic theory. Monitor fundamental economic, industrial, and corporate developments through the analysis of information obtained from financial publications and services, investment banking firms, government agencies, trade publications, company sources, and personal interviews. Prepare plans of action for investment based on financial analyses. Present oral and written reports on general economic trends, individual corporations, and entire industries. Recommend investments and investment timing to companies, investment firm staff, or the investing public. Collaborate with investment bankers to attract new corporate clients to securities firms. Contact brokers and purchase investments for companies according to company policy. Determine the prices at which securities should be syndicated and offered to the public. **SKILLS—Judgment and Decision Making:** Considering the relative costs and benefits of potential actions to choose the most appropriate one. **Systems Analysis:** Determining how a system should work and how changes in conditions, operations, and the environment will affect outcomes. **Systems Evaluation:** Identifying measures or indicators of system performance and the actions needed to improve or correct performance relative to the goals of the system. **Critical Thinking:** Using logic and reasoning to identify the strengths and weaknesses of alternative solutions, conclusions, or approaches to problems. **Active Learning:** Understanding the implications of new information for both current and future problem-solving and decision-making. **Reading Comprehension:** Understanding written sentences and paragraphs in work-related documents. **Mathematics:** Using mathematics to solve problems. **Management of Financial Resources:** Determining how money will be spent to get the work done and accounting for these expenditures. **GOE—Interest Area:** 06. Finance and Insurance. **Work Group:** 06.02. Finance/Insurance Investigation and Analysis. **Other Jobs in This Work Group:** Appraisers, Real Estate; Assessors; Claims Examiners, Property and Casualty Insurance; Cost Estimators; Credit Analysts; Insurance Adjusters, Examiners, and Investigators; Insurance Appraisers, Auto Damage; Insurance Underwriters; Loan Counselors; Loan Officers; Market Research Analysts; Survey Researchers. **PERSONALITY TYPE:** Investigative.

EDUCATION/TRAINING PROGRAM(S)— Accounting and Business/Management; Accounting and Finance; Finance, General. **RELATED KNOWLEDGE/COURSES—Economics and Accounting:** Knowledge of economic and accounting principles and practices, the financial markets, banking, and the analysis and reporting of financial data. **Mathematics:** Knowledge of arithmetic, algebra, geometry, calculus, and statistics and their applications. **Law and Government:** Knowledge of laws, legal codes, court procedures, precedents, government regulations, executive

orders, agency rules, and the democratic political process. **Computers and Electronics:** Knowledge of circuit boards, processors, chips, electronic equipment, and computer hardware and software, including applications and programming. **Sales and Marketing:** Knowledge of principles and methods for showing, promoting, and selling products or services. This includes marketing strategy and tactics, product demonstrations, sales techniques, and sales control systems. **Telecommunications:** Knowledge of transmission, broadcasting, switching, control, and operation of telecommunications systems.

Financial Examiners

- Education/Training Required: Bachelor's degree
- Annual Earnings: $60,310
- Growth: 8.9%
- Annual Job Openings: 3,000
- Self-Employed: 0%
- Part-Time: 10.2%

Enforce or ensure compliance with laws and regulations governing financial and securities institutions and financial and real estate transactions. May examine, verify correctness of, or establish authenticity of records. Direct and participate in formal and informal meetings with bank directors, trustees, senior management, counsels, outside accountants, and consultants in order to gather information and discuss findings. Investigate activities of institutions in order to enforce laws and regulations and to ensure legality of transactions and operations or financial solvency. Prepare reports, exhibits, and other supporting schedules that detail an institution's safety and soundness, compliance with laws and regulations, and recommended solutions to questionable financial conditions. Recommend actions to ensure compliance with laws and regulations or to protect solvency of institutions. Resolve problems concerning the overall financial integrity of banking institutions, including loan investment portfolios, capital, earnings, and specific or large troubled accounts. Review audit reports of internal and external auditors in order to monitor adequacy of scope of reports or to discover specific weaknesses in internal routines. Review balance sheets, operating income and expense accounts, and loan documentation in order to confirm institution assets and liabilities. Verify and inspect cash reserves, assigned collateral, and bank-owned securities in order to check internal control procedures. Confer with officials of real estate, securities, or financial institution industries in order to exchange views and discuss issues or pending cases. Establish guidelines for procedures and policies that comply with new and revised regulations and direct their implementation. Evaluate data-processing applications for institutions under examination in order to develop recommendations for coordinating existing systems with examination procedures. Examine the minutes of meetings of directors, stockholders, and committees in order to investigate the specific authority extended at various levels of management. Plan, supervise, and review work of assigned subordinates. Review and analyze new, proposed, or revised laws, regulations, policies, and procedures in order to interpret their meaning and determine their impact. **SKILLS—Reading Comprehension:** Understanding written sentences and paragraphs in work-related documents. **Judgment and Decision Making:** Considering the relative costs and benefits of potential actions to choose the most appropriate one. **Negotiation:** Bringing others together and trying to reconcile differences. **Writing:** Communicating effectively in writing as appropriate for the needs of the audience. **Mathematics:** Using mathematics to solve problems. **Management of Financial Resources:** Determining how money will be spent to get the work done and accounting for these expenditures. **Speaking:** Talking to others to convey information effectively. **Systems Analysis:** Determining how a system should work and how changes in conditions, operations, and the environment will affect outcomes. **GOE—Interest Area:** 07. Government and Public Administration. **Work Group:** 07.03. Regulations Enforcement. **Other Jobs in This Work Group:** Agricultural Inspectors; Aviation Inspectors; Child Support, Missing Persons, and Unemployment Insurance Fraud Investigators; Environmental Compliance Inspectors; Equal Opportunity Representatives and Officers; Fire Inspectors; Fish and Game Wardens; Forest Fire Inspectors and Prevention Specialists; Government Property Inspectors and Investigators; Immigration and Customs Inspectors; Licensing Examiners and Inspectors; Marine Cargo Inspectors; Mechanical Inspectors; Motor Vehicle Inspectors; Nuclear Monitoring Technicians; Occupational Health and Safety Specialists; Pressure Vessel Inspectors; Railroad Inspectors; Tax Examiners,

Collectors, and Revenue Agents. **PERSONALITY TYPE:** Enterprising.

EDUCATION/TRAINING PROGRAM(S)— Accounting; Taxation. **RELATED KNOWLEDGE/COURSES—Economics and Accounting:** Knowledge of economic and accounting principles and practices, the financial markets, banking, and the analysis and reporting of financial data. **Education and Training:** Knowledge of principles and methods for curriculum and training design, teaching and instruction for individuals and groups, and the measurement of training effects. **Mathematics:** Knowledge of arithmetic, algebra, geometry, calculus, and statistics and their applications. **Law and Government:** Knowledge of laws, legal codes, court procedures, precedents, government regulations, executive orders, agency rules, and the democratic political process. **Administration and Management:** Knowledge of business and management principles involved in strategic planning, resource allocation, human resources modeling, leadership technique, production methods, and coordination of people and resources. **English Language:** Knowledge of the structure and content of the English language, including the meaning and spelling of words, rules of composition, and grammar.

Financial Managers, Branch or Department

- Education/Training Required: Work experience plus degree
- Annual Earnings: $81,880
- Growth: 18.3%
- Annual Job Openings: 71,000
- Self-Employed: 3.1%
- Part-Time: 4.8%

Direct and coordinate financial activities of workers in a branch, office, or department of an establishment, such as branch bank, brokerage firm, risk and insurance department, or credit department. Prepare operational and risk reports for management analysis. Communicate with stockholders and other investors to provide information and to raise capital. Direct floor operations of brokerage firm engaged in buying and selling securities at exchange. Direct insurance negotiations, select insurance brokers and carriers, and place insurance. Establish and maintain relationships with individual and business customers and provide assistance with problems these customers may encounter. Examine, evaluate, and process loan applications. Monitor order flow and transactions that brokerage firm executes on the floor of exchange. Recruit staff members and oversee training programs. Review collection reports to determine the status of collections and the amounts of outstanding balances. Review reports of securities transactions and price lists in order to analyze market conditions. Submit delinquent accounts to attorneys or outside agencies for collection. Analyze and classify risks and investments to determine their potential impacts on companies. Approve or reject, or coordinate the approval and rejection of, lines of credit and commercial, real estate, and personal loans. Develop and analyze information to assess the current and future financial status of firms. Establish procedures for custody and control of assets, records, loan collateral, and securities in order to ensure safekeeping. Evaluate data pertaining to costs in order to plan budgets. Evaluate financial reporting systems, accounting and collection procedures, and investment activities and make recommendations for changes to procedures, operating systems, budgets, and other financial control functions. Network within communities to find and attract new business. Oversee the flow of cash and financial instruments. Plan, direct, and coordinate risk and insurance programs of establishments to control risks and losses. Plan, direct, and coordinate the activities of workers in branches, offices, or departments of such establishments as branch banks, brokerage firms, risk and insurance departments, or credit departments. Prepare financial and regulatory reports required by laws, regulations, and boards of directors. **SKILLS—Management of Financial Resources:** Determining how money will be spent to get the work done and accounting for these expenditures. **Management of Personnel Resources:** Motivating, developing, and directing people as they work, identifying the best people for the job. **Systems Analysis:** Determining how a system should work and how changes in conditions, operations, and the environment will affect outcomes. **Systems Evaluation:** Identifying measures or indicators of system performance and the actions needed to improve or correct performance relative to the goals of the system. **Judgment and Decision Making:** Considering the relative costs and benefits of potential actions to choose the most appropriate one. **Writing:** Communicating effectively in writing as appropriate for the needs of the audience. **Monitoring:** Monitoring or assessing your performance or that of other individuals or organizations to make improvements or take corrective action. **Complex Problem Solving:** Identifying complex problems and reviewing related information to develop and evaluate options and implement solutions. **GOE—Interest Area:** 06. Finance and Insurance. **Work Group:** 06.01. Managerial Work in Finance and Insurance. **Other Jobs in This Work Group:** Treasurers, Controllers, and Chief Financial Officers. **PERSONALITY TYPE:** Enterprising.

EDUCATION/TRAINING PROGRAM(S)— Accounting and Business/Management; Accounting and Finance; Credit Management; Finance and Financial Management Services, Other; Finance, General; International Finance; Public Finance. **RELATED KNOWLEDGE/COURSES—Economics and Accounting:** Knowledge of economic and accounting principles and practices, the financial markets, banking, and the analysis and reporting of financial data. **Administration and Management:** Knowledge of business and management principles involved in strategic planning, resource allocation, human resources modeling, leadership technique, production methods, and coordination of people and resources. **Law and Government:** Knowledge of laws, legal codes, court procedures, precedents, government regulations, executive orders, agency rules, and the democratic political process. **Mathematics:** Knowledge of arithmetic, algebra, geometry, calculus, and statistics and their applications. **Personnel and Human Resources:** Knowledge of principles and procedures for personnel recruitment, selection, training, compensation and benefits, labor relations and negotiation, and personnel information systems. **Psychology:** Knowledge of human behavior and performance; individual differences in ability, personality, and interests; learning and motivation; psychological research methods; and the assessment and treatment of behavioral and affective disorders.

Fire-Prevention and Protection Engineers

- ◎ Education/Training Required: Bachelor's degree
- ◎ Annual Earnings: $63,730
- ◎ Growth: 7.9%
- ◎ Annual Job Openings: 4,000
- ◎ Self-Employed: 1.6%
- ◎ Part-Time: 1.5%

Research causes of fires; determine fire protection methods; and design or recommend materials or equipment such as structural components or fire-detection equipment to assist organizations in safeguarding life and property against fire, explosion, and related hazards. Advise architects, builders, and other construction personnel on fire prevention equipment and techniques and on fire code and standard interpretation and compliance. Conduct research on fire retardants and the fire safety of materials and devices. Consult with authorities to discuss safety regulations and to recommend changes as necessary. Design fire detection equipment, alarm systems, and fire extinguishing devices and systems. Determine causes of fires and ways in which they could have been prevented. Direct the purchase, modification, installation, maintenance, and operation of fire protection systems. Inspect buildings or building designs to determine fire protection system requirements and potential problems in areas such as water supplies, exit locations, and construction materials. Study the relationships between ignition sources and materials to determine how fires start. Attend workshops, seminars, or conferences to present or obtain information regarding fire prevention and protection. Develop plans for the prevention of destruction by fire, wind, and water. Develop training materials and conduct training sessions on fire protection. Evaluate fire department performance and the laws and regulations affecting fire prevention or fire safety. Prepare and write reports detailing specific fire prevention and protection issues such as work performed and proposed review schedules. **SKILLS—Technology Design:** Generating or adapting equipment and technology to serve user needs. **Instructing:** Teaching others how to do something. **Operations Analysis:** Analyzing needs and product requirements to create a design. **Systems Evaluation:** Identifying measures or indicators of system performance and the actions needed to improve or correct performance relative to the goals of the system. **Science:** Using scientific rules and methods to solve problems. **Quality Control Analysis:** Conducting tests and inspections of products, services, or processes to evaluate quality or performance. **Systems Analysis:** Determining how a system should work and how changes in conditions, operations, and the environment will affect outcomes. **Speaking:** Talking to others to convey information effectively. **Active Learning:** Understanding the implications of new information for both current and future problem-solving and decision-making. **GOE—Interest Area:** 15. Scientific Research, Engineering, and Mathematics. **Work Group:** 15.08. Industrial and Safety Engineering. **Other Jobs in This Work Group:** Industrial Engineers; Industrial Safety and Health Engineers; Product Safety Engineers. **PERSONALITY TYPE:** Investigative.

EDUCATION/TRAINING PROGRAM(S)—Environmental/Environmental Health Engineering. **RELATED KNOWLEDGE/COURSES—Public Safety and Security:** Knowledge of relevant equipment, policies, procedures, and strategies to promote effective local, state, or national security operations for the protection of people, data, property, and institutions. **Engineering and Technology:** Knowledge of the practical application of engineering science and technology. This includes applying principles, techniques, procedures, and equipment to the design and production of various goods and services. **Education and Training:** Knowledge of principles and methods for curriculum and training design, teaching and instruction for individuals and groups, and the measurement of training effects. **Design:** Knowledge of design techniques, tools, and principles involved in production of precision technical plans, blueprints, drawings, and models. **Chemistry:** Knowledge of the chemical composition, structure, and properties of substances and of the chemical processes and transformations that they undergo. This includes uses of chemicals and their danger signs, production techniques, and disposal methods. **Law and Government:** Knowledge of laws, legal codes, court procedures, precedents, government regulations, executive orders, agency rules, and the democratic political process.

First-Line Supervisors and Manager/Supervisors— Agricultural Crop Workers

- Education/Training Required: Associate degree
- Annual Earnings: $35,490
- Growth: 11.4%
- Annual Job Openings: 6,000
- Self-Employed: 0.9%
- Part-Time: 6.1%

Directly supervise and coordinate activities of agricultural crop workers. Manager/supervisors are generally found in smaller establishments, where they perform both supervisory and management functions, such as accounting, marketing, and personnel work, and may also engage in the same agricultural work as the workers they supervise. Assigns duties, such as tilling soil, planting, irrigating, storing crops, and maintaining machines, and assigns fields or rows to workers. Determines number and kind of workers needed to perform required work and schedules activities. Observes workers to detect inefficient and unsafe work procedures or identify problems and initiates actions to correct improper procedure or solve problem. Issues farm implements and machinery, ladders, or containers to workers and collects them at end of workday. Investigates grievances and settles disputes to maintain harmony among workers. Opens gate to permit entry of water into ditches or pipes and signals worker to start flow of water to irrigate fields. Drives and operates farm machinery, such as trucks, tractors, or self-propelled harvesters, to transport workers or cultivate and harvest fields. Requisitions and purchases farm supplies, such as insecticides, machine parts or lubricants, and tools. Confers with manager to evaluate weather and soil conditions and to develop and revise plans and procedures. Prepares time, payroll, and production reports, such as farm conditions, amount of yield, machinery breakdowns, and labor problems. Directs or assists in adjustment, repair, and maintenance of farm machinery and equipment. Trains workers in methods of field work and safety regulations and briefs them on identifying characteristic of insects and diseases. Contracts with seasonal workers and farmers to provide employment and arranges for transportation, equipment, and living quarters. Recruits, hires, and discharges workers. Inspects crops and fields to determine maturity, yield, infestation, or work requirements, such as cultivating, spraying, weeding, or harvesting. **SKILLS—Management of Personnel Resources:** Motivating, developing, and directing people as they work, identifying the best people for the job. **Management of Material Resources:** Obtaining and seeing to the appropriate use of equipment, facilities, and materials needed to do certain work. **Coordination:** Adjusting actions in relation to others' actions. **Equipment Maintenance:** Performing routine maintenance on equipment and determining when and what kind of maintenance is needed. **Repairing:** Repairing machines or systems by using the needed tools. **Time Management:** Managing one's own time and the time of others. **Instructing:** Teaching others how to do something. **Management of Financial Resources:** Determining how money will be spent to get the work done and accounting for these expenditures. **GOE—Interest Area:** 01. Agriculture and Natural Resources. **Work Group:** 01.01. Managerial Work in Agriculture and Natural Resources. **Other Jobs in This Work Group:** Agricultural Crop Farm Managers; Farmers and Ranchers; First-Line Supervisors and Manager/Supervisors—Animal Husbandry Workers; First-Line Supervisors and Manager/Supervisors—Extractive Workers; First-Line Supervisors and Manager/Supervisors—Fishery Workers; First-Line Supervisors and Manager/Supervisors—Horticultural Workers; First-Line Supervisors and Manager/Supervisors—Landscaping Workers; First-Line Supervisors and Manager/Supervisors—Logging Workers; Fish Hatchery Managers; Lawn Service Managers; Nursery and Greenhouse Managers; Park Naturalists; Purchasing Agents and Buyers, Farm Products. **PERSONALITY TYPE:** Enterprising.

EDUCATION/TRAINING PROGRAM(S)—Agricultural Business and Management, Other; Agricultural Production Operations, General; Agricultural Production Operations, Other; Agriculture, Agriculture Operations, and Related Sciences, Other; Agronomy and Crop Science; Aquaculture; Crop Production; Farm/Farm and Ranch Management; Fishing and Fisheries Sciences and Management; Plant Sciences, General; Range Science and Management. **RELATED KNOWLEDGE/COURSES—Food Production:** Knowledge of techniques and equipment for planting, growing, and harvesting food products (both plant and animal) for consumption, including storage/handling techniques. **Personnel and Human**

Resources: Knowledge of principles and procedures for personnel recruitment, selection, training, compensation and benefits, labor relations and negotiation, and personnel information systems. **Administration and Management:** Knowledge of business and management principles involved in strategic planning, resource allocation, human resources modeling, leadership technique, production methods, and coordination of people and resources. **Biology:** Knowledge of plant and animal organisms and their tissues, cells, functions, interdependencies, and interactions with each other and the environment. **Mechanical Devices:** Knowledge of machines and tools, including their designs, uses, repair, and maintenance. **Chemistry:** Knowledge of the chemical composition, structure, and properties of substances and of the chemical processes and transformations that they undergo. This includes uses of chemicals and their danger signs, production techniques, and disposal methods.

First-Line Supervisors and Manager/Supervisors— Animal Care Workers, Except Livestock

- ◎ Education/Training Required: Associate degree
- ◎ Annual Earnings: $35,490
- ◎ Growth: 11.4%
- ◎ Annual Job Openings: 6,000
- ◎ Self-Employed: 0.9%
- ◎ Part-Time: 6.1%

Directly supervise and coordinate activities of animal care workers. Manager/supervisors are generally found in smaller establishments, where they perform both supervisory and management functions, such as accounting, marketing, and personnel work, and may also engage in the same animal care work as the workers they supervise. Assigns workers to tasks such as feeding and treatment of animals and cleaning and maintenance of animal quarters. Establishes work schedule and procedures of animal care. Monitors animal care, inspects facilities to identify problems, and discusses solutions with workers. Trains workers in ani-

mal care procedures, maintenance duties, and safety precautions. Plans budget and arranges for purchase of animals, feed, or supplies. Prepares reports concerning activity of facility, employees' time records, and animal treatment. Delivers lectures to public to stimulate interest in animals and communicate humane philosophy to public. Operates euthanasia equipment to destroy animals. Investigates complaints of animal neglect or cruelty and follows up on complaints appearing to justify prosecution. Observes and examines animals to detect signs of illness and determine need of services from veterinarian. Directs and assists workers in maintenance and repair of facilities. **SKILLS—Management of Financial Resources:** Determining how money will be spent to get the work done and accounting for these expenditures. **Management of Personnel Resources:** Motivating, developing, and directing people as they work, identifying the best people for the job. **Instructing:** Teaching others how to do something. **Management of Material Resources:** Obtaining and seeing to the appropriate use of equipment, facilities, and materials needed to do certain work. **Systems Evaluation:** Identifying measures or indicators of system performance and the actions needed to improve or correct performance relative to the goals of the system. **Writing:** Communicating effectively in writing as appropriate for the needs of the audience. **Speaking:** Talking to others to convey information effectively. **Systems Analysis:** Determining how a system should work and how changes in conditions, operations, and the environment will affect outcomes. **GOE—Interest Area:** 08. Health Science. **Work Group:** 08.01. Managerial Work in Medical and Health Services. **Other Jobs in This Work Group:** Coroners; Medical and Health Services Managers. **PERSONALITY TYPE:** Realistic.

EDUCATION/TRAINING PROGRAM(S)—Agricultural Business and Management, Other; Agricultural Production Operations, General; Agricultural Production Operations, Other; Agriculture, Agriculture Operations, and Related Sciences, Other; Animal Nutrition; Animal Sciences, General; Aquaculture; Farm/Farm and Ranch Management; Fishing and Fisheries Sciences and Management; Range Science and Management. **RELATED KNOWLEDGE/ COURSES—Administration and Management:** Knowledge of business and management principles involved in strategic planning, resource allocation, human resources modeling, leadership technique, production methods, and coordination of people and resources. **Biology:** Knowledge of plant and animal organisms and their tissues, cells, functions, interdependencies, and interactions with each other and the environment. **Medicine and Dentistry:** Knowledge of the information and techniques needed to diagnose and treat human injuries, diseases, and deformities. This includes symptoms, treatment alternatives, drug properties and interactions, and preventive health-care measures. **Economics and Accounting:** Knowledge of economic and accounting principles and practices, the financial markets, banking, and the analysis and reporting of financial data. **Personnel and Human Resources:** Knowledge of principles and procedures for personnel recruitment, selection, training, compensation and benefits, labor relations and negotiation, and personnel information systems. **Education and Training:** Knowledge of principles and methods for curriculum and training design, teaching and instruction for individuals and groups, and the measurement of training effects.

First-Line Supervisors and Manager/Supervisors— Animal Husbandry Workers

◎ Education/Training Required: Associate degree

◎ Annual Earnings: $35,490

◎ Growth: 11.4%

◎ Annual Job Openings: 6,000

◎ Self-Employed: 16.9%

◎ Part-Time: 6.1%

Directly supervise and coordinate activities of animal husbandry workers. Manager/supervisors are generally found in smaller establishments, where they perform both supervisory and management functions, such as accounting, marketing, and personnel work, and may also engage in the same animal husbandry work as the workers they supervise. Assigns workers to tasks such as feeding and treating animals, cleaning quarters, transferring animals, and maintaining facilities. Notifies veterinarian and manager of serious illnesses or injuries to animals. Monitors eggs and adjusts incubator thermometer and gauges to ascertain hatching progress and maintain specified conditions. Treats animal illness or injury, following experience or instructions of veterinarian. Inseminates livestock artificially to produce desired offspring and to demonstrate techniques to farmers. Transports or arranges for transport of animals, equipment, food, animal feed, and other supplies to and from work site. Requisitions equipment, materials, and supplies. Prepares animal condition, production, feed consumption, and worker attendance reports. Trains workers in animal care, artificial insemination techniques, egg candling and sorting, and transfer of animals. Observes animals, such as cattle, sheep, poultry, or game animals, for signs of illness, injury, nervousness, or unnatural behavior. Plans and prepares work schedules. Recruits, hires, and pays workers. Confers with manager to discuss and ascertain production requirements, condition of equipment and supplies, and work schedules. Inspects buildings, fences, fields or range, supplies, and equipment to determine work to be done. Studies feed, weight, health, genetic, or milk production records to determine feed formula and rations or breeding schedule. Oversees animal care, maintenance, breeding, or packing and transfer activities to ensure work is done correctly and to identify and solve problems. **SKILLS—Management of Personnel Resources:** Motivating, developing, and directing people as they work, identifying the best people for the job. **Management of Material Resources:** Obtaining and seeing to the appropriate use of equipment, facilities, and materials needed to do certain work. **Systems Evaluation:** Identifying measures or indicators of system performance and the actions needed to improve or correct performance relative to the goals of the system. **Instructing:** Teaching others how to do something. **Systems Analysis:** Determining how a system should work and how changes in conditions, operations, and the environment will affect outcomes. **Time Management:** Managing one's own time and the time of others. **Coordination:** Adjusting actions in relation to others' actions. **Equipment Selection:** Determining the kind of tools and equipment needed to do a job. **Management of Financial Resources:** Determining how money will be spent to get the work done and accounting for these expenditures. **GOE—Interest Area:** 01. Agriculture and Natural Resources. **Work Group:** 01.01. Managerial Work in Agriculture and Natural Resources. **Other Jobs in This Work Group:** Agricultural Crop Farm Managers; Farmers and Ranchers; First-Line Supervisors and Manager/Supervisors—Agricultural Crop Workers; First-Line Supervisors and Manager/Supervisors—Extractive Workers;

First-Line Supervisors and Manager/Supervisors—Fishery Workers; First-Line Supervisors and Manager/Supervisors—Horticultural Workers; First-Line Supervisors and Manager/Supervisors—Landscaping Workers; First-Line Supervisors and Manager/Supervisors—Logging Workers; Fish Hatchery Managers; Lawn Service Managers; Nursery and Greenhouse Managers; Park Naturalists; Purchasing Agents and Buyers, Farm Products. **PERSONALITY TYPE:** Enterprising.

EDUCATION/TRAINING PROGRAM(S)—Agricultural Animal Breeding; Agricultural Business and Management, Other; Agricultural Production Operations, General; Agricultural Production Operations, Other; Agriculture, Agriculture Operations, and Related Sciences, Other; Animal Nutrition; Animal Sciences, General; Animal/Livestock Husbandry and Production; Aquaculture; Dairy Husbandry and Production; Dairy Science; Farm/Farm and Ranch Management; Fishing and Fisheries Sciences and Management; Horse Husbandry/Equine Science and Management; Livestock Management; Poultry Science; Range Science and Management. **RELATED KNOWLEDGE/COURSES**—**Food Production:** Knowledge of techniques and equipment for planting, growing, and harvesting food products (both plant and animal) for consumption, including storage/handling techniques. **Biology:** Knowledge of plant and animal organisms and their tissues, cells, functions, interdependencies, and interactions with each other and the environment. **Personnel and Human Resources:** Knowledge of principles and procedures for personnel recruitment, selection, training, compensation and benefits, labor relations and negotiation, and personnel information systems. **Administration and Management:** Knowledge of business and management principles involved in strategic planning, resource allocation, human resources modeling, leadership technique, production methods, and coordination of people and resources. **Medicine and Dentistry:** Knowledge of the information and techniques needed to diagnose and treat human injuries, diseases, and deformities. This includes symptoms, treatment alternatives, drug properties and interactions, and preventive health-care measures. **Transportation:** Knowledge of principles and methods for moving people or goods by air, rail, sea, or road, including the relative costs and benefits.

First-Line Supervisors and Manager/Supervisors—Construction Trades Workers

- Education/Training Required: Work experience in a related occupation
- Annual Earnings: $50,450
- Growth: 14.1%
- Annual Job Openings: 67,000
- Self-Employed: 20.1%
- Part-Time: 2.1%

Directly supervise and coordinate activities of construction trades workers and their helpers. Manager/supervisors are generally found in smaller establishments, where they perform both supervisory and management functions, such as accounting, marketing, and personnel work, and may also engage in the same construction trades work as the workers they supervise. Suggests and initiates personnel actions, such as promotions, transfers, and hires. Analyzes and resolves worker problems and recommends motivational plans. Examines and inspects work progress, equipment, and construction sites to verify safety and ensure that specifications are met. Estimates material and worker requirements to complete job. Reads specifications, such as blueprints and data, to determine construction requirements. Analyzes and plans installation and construction of equipment and structures. Locates, measures, and marks location and placement of structures and equipment. Records information, such as personnel, production, and operational data, on specified forms and reports. Trains workers in construction methods and operation of equipment. Recommends measures to improve production methods and equipment performance to increase efficiency and safety. Assists workers engaged in construction activities, using hand tools and equipment. Supervises and coordinates activities of construction trades workers. Directs and leads workers engaged in construction activities. Assigns work to employees, using material and worker requirements data. Confers with staff and worker to ensure production and personnel problems are resolved. **SKILLS**—**Management of Personnel Resources:** Motivating, developing, and directing people as they work, identifying the best people for the job. **Management of Material Resources:** Obtaining and seeing to the appropriate use of equipment, facilities, and materials needed to do certain work. **Installation:** Installing equipment, machines, wiring, or programs to meet specifications. **Systems Analysis:** Determining how a system should work and how changes in conditions, operations, and the environment will affect outcomes. **Systems Evaluation:** Identifying measures or indicators of system performance and the actions needed to improve or correct performance relative to the goals of the system. **Time Management:** Managing one's own time and the time of others. **Coordination:** Adjusting actions in relation to others' actions. **Quality Control Analysis:** Conducting tests and inspections of products, services, or processes to evaluate quality or performance. **GOE—Interest Area:** 02. Architecture and Construction. **Work Group:** 02.01. Managerial Work in Architecture and Construction. **Other Jobs in This Work Group:** Construction Managers. **PERSONALITY TYPE:** Enterprising.

EDUCATION/TRAINING   PROGRAM(S)— Building/Construction Finishing, Management, and Inspection, Other; Building/Construction Site Management/Manager;   Building/Home/Construction Inspection/Inspector; Building/Property Maintenance and Management; Carpentry/Carpenter; Concrete Finishing/Concrete Finisher; Construction Trades, Other; Drywall Installation/Drywaller; Electrical and Power Transmission Installation/Installer, General; Electrical and Power Transmission Installers, Other; Electrician; Glazier; Lineworker; Mason/Masonry; Painting/Painter and Wall Coverer; Plumbing Technology/Plumber; Roofer; Well Drilling/Driller. **RELATED KNOWLEDGE/COURSES—Building and Construction:** Knowledge of the materials, methods, and tools involved in the construction or repair of houses, buildings, or other structures such as highways and roads. **Personnel and Human Resources:** Knowledge of principles and procedures for personnel recruitment, selection, training, compensation and benefits, labor relations and negotiation, and personnel information systems. **Administration and Management:** Knowledge of business and management principles involved in strategic planning, resource allocation, human resources modeling, leadership technique, production methods, and coordination of people and resources. **Design:** Knowledge of design techniques, tools, and principles involved in production of precision technical plans, blueprints, drawings,

and models. **Engineering and Technology:** Knowledge of the practical application of engineering science and technology. This includes applying principles, techniques, procedures, and equipment to the design and production of various goods and services. **Mechanical Devices:** Knowledge of machines and tools, including their designs, uses, repair, and maintenance.

First-Line Supervisors and Manager/Supervisors— Extractive Workers

- ◎ Education/Training Required: Work experience in a related occupation
- ◎ Annual Earnings: $50,450
- ◎ Growth: 14.1%
- ◎ Annual Job Openings: 67,000
- ◎ Self-Employed: 20.1%
- ◎ Part-Time: 2.1%

Directly supervise and coordinate activities of extractive workers and their helpers. Manager/supervisors are generally found in smaller establishments, where they perform both supervisory and management functions, such as accounting, marketing, and personnel work, and may also engage in the same extractive work as the workers they supervise. Supervises and coordinates activities of workers engaged in the extraction of geological materials. Directs and leads workers engaged in extraction of geological materials. Assigns work to employees, using material and worker requirements data. Confers with staff and workers to ensure production personnel problems are resolved. Analyzes and resolves worker problems and recommends motivational plans. Analyzes and plans extraction process of geological materials. Trains workers in construction methods and operation of equipment. Examines and inspects equipment, site, and materials to verify specifications are met. Recommends measures to improve production methods and equipment performance to increase efficiency and safety. Suggests and initiates personnel actions, such as promotions, transfers, and hires. Records information such as personnel, production, and operational data on specified forms. Assists workers engaged in extraction activities, using hand tools and equipment. Locates, measures, and marks materials and site location, using measuring and marking equipment. Orders materials, supplies, and repair of equipment and machinery. **SKILLS—Management of Personnel Resources:** Motivating, developing, and directing people as they work, identifying the best people for the job. **Management of Material Resources:** Obtaining and seeing to the appropriate use of equipment, facilities, and materials needed to do certain work. **Instructing:** Teaching others how to do something. **Systems Evaluation:** Identifying measures or indicators of system performance and the actions needed to improve or correct performance relative to the goals of the system. **Systems Analysis:** Determining how a system should work and how changes in conditions, operations, and the environment will affect outcomes. **Coordination:** Adjusting actions in relation to others' actions. **Operation Monitoring:** Watching gauges, dials, or other indicators to make sure a machine is working properly. **Social Perceptiveness:** Being aware of others' reactions and understanding why they react as they do. **Negotiation:** Bringing others together and trying to reconcile differences. **Time Management:** Managing one's own time and the time of others. **GOE—Interest Area:** 01. Agriculture and Natural Resources. **Work Group:** 01.01. Managerial Work in Agriculture and Natural Resources. **Other Jobs in This Work Group:** Agricultural Crop Farm Managers; Farmers and Ranchers; First-Line Supervisors and Manager/Supervisors—Agricultural Crop Workers; First-Line Supervisors and Manager/Supervisors—Animal Husbandry Workers; First-Line Supervisors and Manager/Supervisors—Fishery Workers; First-Line Supervisors and Manager/Supervisors—Horticultural Workers; First-Line Supervisors and Manager/Supervisors—Landscaping Workers; First-Line Supervisors and Manager/Supervisors—Logging Workers; Fish Hatchery Managers; Lawn Service Managers; Nursery and Greenhouse Managers; Park Naturalists; Purchasing Agents and Buyers, Farm Products. **PERSONALITY TYPE:** Enterprising.

EDUCATION/TRAINING PROGRAM(S)—Blasting/Blaster; Well Drilling/Driller. **RELATED KNOWLEDGE/COURSES—Personnel and Human Resources:** Knowledge of principles and procedures for personnel recruitment, selection, training, compensation and benefits, labor relations and negotiation, and personnel information systems. **Administration and Management:** Knowledge of business and management principles involved in strategic planning, resource allocation, human resources modeling, leader-ship technique, production methods, and coordination of people and resources. **Engineering and Technology:** Knowledge of the practical application of engineering science and technology. This includes applying principles, techniques, procedures, and equipment to the design and production of various goods and services. **Physics:** Knowledge and prediction of physical principles and laws and their interrelationships and applications to understanding fluid, material, and atmospheric dynamics and mechanical, electrical, atomic, and subatomic structures and processes. **Production and Processing:** Knowledge of raw materials, production processes, quality control, costs, and other techniques for maximizing the effective manufacture and distribution of goods. **Mechanical Devices:** Knowledge of machines and tools, including their designs, uses, repair, and maintenance.

First-Line Supervisors and Manager/Supervisors—Fishery Workers

- Education/Training Required: Associate degree
- Annual Earnings: $35,490
- Growth: 11.4%
- Annual Job Openings: 6,000
- Self-Employed: 16.9%
- Part-Time: 6.1%

Directly supervise and coordinate activities of fishery workers. Manager/supervisors are generally found in smaller establishments, where they perform both supervisory and management functions, such as accounting, marketing, and personnel work, and may also engage in the same fishery work as the workers they supervise. Assigns workers to duties such as fertilizing and incubating spawn; feeding and transferring fish; and planting, cultivating, and harvesting shellfish beds. Oversees worker activities, such as treatment and rearing of fingerlings, maintenance of equipment, and harvesting of fish or shellfish. Directs workers to correct deviations or problems, such as disease, quality of seed distribution, or adequacy of cultivation. Plans work schedules according to availability of personnel and equipment, tidal levels, feeding schedules, or need for transfer or harvest. Observes fish and beds or ponds to detect diseases, determine quality of fish, or determine completeness of harvesting. Records number and type of fish or shellfish reared and harvested and keeps workers' time records. Confers with manager to determine time and place of seed planting and cultivating, feeding, or harvesting of fish or shellfish. Trains workers in spawning, rearing, cultivating, and harvesting methods and use of equipment. **SKILLS—Management of Personnel Resources:** Motivating, developing, and directing people as they work, identifying the best people for the job. **Instructing:** Teaching others how to do something. **Management of Material Resources:** Obtaining and seeing to the appropriate use of equipment, facilities, and materials needed to do certain work. **Systems Analysis:** Determining how a system should work and how changes in conditions, operations, and the environment will affect outcomes. **Time Management:** Managing one's own time and the time of others. **Coordination:** Adjusting actions in relation to others' actions. **Systems Evaluation:** Identifying measures or indicators of system performance and the actions needed to improve or correct performance relative to the goals of the system. **Learning Strategies:** Selecting and using training/instructional methods and procedures appropriate for the situation when learning or teaching new things. **GOE—Interest Area:** 01. Agriculture and Natural Resources. **Work Group:** 01.01. Managerial Work in Agriculture and Natural Resources. **Other Jobs in This Work Group:** Agricultural Crop Farm Managers; Farmers and Ranchers; First-Line Supervisors and Manager/Supervisors—Agricultural Crop Workers; First-Line Supervisors and Manager/Supervisors—Animal Husbandry Workers; First-Line Supervisors and Manager/Supervisors—Extractive Workers; First-Line Supervisors and Manager/Supervisors—Horticultural Workers; First-Line Supervisors and Manager/Supervisors—Landscaping Workers; First-Line Supervisors and Manager/Supervisors—Logging Workers; Fish Hatchery Managers; Lawn Service Managers; Nursery and Greenhouse Managers; Park Naturalists; Purchasing Agents and Buyers, Farm Products. **PERSONALITY TYPE:** Realistic.

EDUCATION/TRAINING PROGRAM(S)—Agricultural Animal Breeding; Agricultural Business and Management, Other; Agricultural Production Operations, General; Agricultural Production Operations, Other; Agriculture, Agriculture Operations, and Related Sciences, Other; Animal Nutrition; Animal Sciences, General; Animal/Livestock Husbandry and Production; Farm/Farm and Ranch Management; Fishing and Fisheries Sciences and Management. **RELATED KNOWLEDGE/COURSES—Food Production:** Knowledge of techniques and equipment for planting, growing, and harvesting food products (both plant and animal) for consumption, including storage/handling techniques. **Biology:** Knowledge of plant and animal organisms and their tissues, cells, functions, interdependencies, and interactions with each other and the environment. **Personnel and Human Resources:** Knowledge of principles and procedures for personnel recruitment, selection, training, compensation and benefits, labor relations and negotiation, and personnel information systems. **Production and Processing:** Knowledge of raw materials, production processes, quality control, costs, and other techniques for maximizing the effective manufacture and distribution of goods. **Administration and Management:** Knowledge of business and management principles involved in strategic planning, resource allocation, human resources modeling, leadership technique, production methods, and coordination of people and resources. **Chemistry:** Knowledge of the chemical composition, structure, and properties of substances and of the chemical processes and transformations that they undergo. This includes uses of chemicals and their danger signs, production techniques, and disposal methods.

First-Line Supervisors and Manager/Supervisors— Horticultural Workers

- Education/Training Required: Associate degree
- Annual Earnings: $35,490
- Growth: 11.4%
- Annual Job Openings: 6,000
- Self-Employed: 16.9%
- Part-Time: 6.1%

Directly supervise and coordinate activities of horticultural workers. Manager/supervisors are generally found in smaller establishments, where they perform both supervisory and management functions, such as

accounting, marketing, and personnel work, and may also engage in the same horticultural work as the workers they supervise. Assigns workers to duties such as cultivation, harvesting, maintenance, grading and packing products, or altering greenhouse environmental conditions. Estimates work-hour requirements to plant, cultivate, or harvest and prepares work schedule. Confers with management to report conditions; plan planting and harvesting schedules; and discuss changes in fertilizer, herbicides, or cultivating techniques. Drives and operates heavy machinery, such as dump truck, tractor, or growth-media tiller, to transport materials and supplies. Maintains records of employees' hours worked and work completed. Prepares and submits written or oral reports of personnel actions, such as performance evaluations, hires, promotions, and discipline. Trains employees in horticultural techniques, such as transplanting and weeding, shearing and harvesting trees, and grading and packing flowers. Inspects facilities to determine maintenance needs, such as malfunctioning environmental-control system, clogged sprinklers, or missing glass panes in greenhouse. Observes plants, flowers, shrubs, and trees in greenhouses, cold frames, or fields to ascertain condition. Reads inventory records, customer orders, and shipping schedules to ascertain day's activities. Reviews employees' work to ascertain quality and quantity of work performed. **SKILLS—Management of Personnel Resources:** Motivating, developing, and directing people as they work, identifying the best people for the job. **Management of Material Resources:** Obtaining and seeing to the appropriate use of equipment, facilities, and materials needed to do certain work. **Instructing:** Teaching others how to do something. **Coordination:** Adjusting actions in relation to others' actions. **Operation Monitoring:** Watching gauges, dials, or other indicators to make sure a machine is working properly. **Systems Analysis:** Determining how a system should work and how changes in conditions, operations, and the environment will affect outcomes. **Repairing:** Repairing machines or systems by using the needed tools. **Troubleshooting:** Determining causes of operating errors and deciding what to do about them. **Time Management:** Managing one's own time and the time of others. **GOE—Interest Area:** 01. Agriculture and Natural Resources. **Work Group:** 01.01. Managerial Work in Agriculture and Natural Resources. **Other Jobs in This Work Group:** Agricultural Crop Farm Managers; Farmers and Ranchers; First-Line Supervisors and Manager/Supervisors— Agricultural Crop Workers; First-Line Supervisors and Manager/Supervisors—Animal Husbandry Workers; First-Line Supervisors and Manager/Supervisors— Extractive Workers; First-Line Supervisors and Manager/Supervisors—Fishery Workers; First-Line Supervisors and Manager/Supervisors—Landscaping Workers; First-Line Supervisors and Manager/Supervisors—Logging Workers; Fish Hatchery Managers; Lawn Service Managers; Nursery and Greenhouse Managers; Park Naturalists; Purchasing Agents and Buyers, Farm Products. **PERSONALITY TYPE:** Realistic.

EDUCATION/TRAINING PROGRAM(S)—Agricultural Business and Management, Other; Agricultural Production Operations, General; Agricultural Production Operations, Other; Agriculture, Agriculture Operations, and Related Sciences, Other; Agronomy and Crop Science; Crop Production; Farm/Farm and Ranch Management; Plant Sciences, General. **RELATED KNOWLEDGE/COURSES—Biology:** Knowledge of plant and animal organisms and their tissues, cells, functions, interdependencies, and interactions with each other and the environment. **Personnel and Human Resources:** Knowledge of principles and procedures for personnel recruitment, selection, training, compensation and benefits, labor relations and negotiation, and personnel information systems. **Food Production:** Knowledge of techniques and equipment for planting, growing, and harvesting food products (both plant and animal) for consumption, including storage/handling techniques. **Administration and Management:** Knowledge of business and management principles involved in strategic planning, resource allocation, human resources modeling, leadership technique, production methods, and coordination of people and resources. **Chemistry:** Knowledge of the chemical composition, structure, and properties of substances and of the chemical processes and transformations that they undergo. This includes uses of chemicals and their danger signs, production techniques, and disposal methods. **Production and Processing:** Knowledge of raw materials, production processes, quality control, costs, and other techniques for maximizing the effective manufacture and distribution of goods.

First-Line Supervisors and Manager/Supervisors— Landscaping Workers

◎ Education/Training Required: Work experience in a related occupation

◎ Annual Earnings: $35,340

◎ Growth: 21.6%

◎ Annual Job Openings: 18,000

◎ Self-Employed: 34.7%

◎ Part-Time: 5.9%

Directly supervise and coordinate activities of landscaping workers. Manager/supervisors are generally found in smaller establishment, where they perform both supervisory and management functions, such as accounting, marketing, and personnel work, and may also engage in the same landscaping work as the workers they supervise. Directs workers in maintenance and repair of driveways, walkways, benches, graves, and mausoleums. Observes ongoing work to ascertain if work is being performed according to instructions and will be completed on time. Determines work priority and crew and equipment requirements and assigns workers tasks, such as planting, fertilizing, irrigating, and mowing. Directs and assists workers engaged in maintenance and repair of equipment such as power mower and backhoe, using hand tools and power tools. Confers with manager to develop plans and schedules for maintenance and improvement of grounds. Keeps employee time records and records daily work performed. Interviews, hires, and discharges workers. Assists workers in performing work when completion is critical. Tours grounds, such as park, botanical garden, cemetery, or golf course, to inspect conditions. Trains workers in tasks such as transplanting and pruning trees and shrubs, finishing cement, using equipment, and caring for turf. Mixes and prepares spray and dust solutions and directs application of fertilizer, insecticide, and fungicide. **SKILLS—Management of Personnel Resources:** Motivating, developing, and directing people as they work, identifying the best people for the job. **Management of Material Resources:** Obtaining and seeing to the appropriate use of equipment, facilities, and materials needed to do certain work. **Coordination:** Adjusting actions in relation to others' actions. **Systems Analysis:** Determining how a system should work and how changes in conditions, operations, and the environment will affect outcomes. **Systems Evaluation:** Identifying measures or indicators of system performance and the actions needed to improve or correct performance relative to the goals of the system. **Instructing:** Teaching others how to do something. **Time Management:** Managing one's own time and the time of others. **Speaking:** Talking to others to convey information effectively. **GOE—Interest Area:** 01. Agriculture and Natural Resources. **Work Group:** 01.01. Managerial Work in Agriculture and Natural Resources. **Other Jobs in This Work Group:** Agricultural Crop Farm Managers; Farmers and Ranchers; First-Line Supervisors and Manager/Supervisors—Agricultural Crop Workers; First-Line Supervisors and Manager/Supervisors—Animal Husbandry Workers; First-Line Supervisors and Manager/Supervisors—Extractive Workers; First-Line Supervisors and Manager/Supervisors—Fishery Workers; First-Line Supervisors and Manager/Supervisors—Horticultural Workers; First-Line Supervisors and Manager/Supervisors—Logging Workers; Fish Hatchery Managers; Lawn Service Managers; Nursery and Greenhouse Managers; Park Naturalists; Purchasing Agents and Buyers, Farm Products. **PERSONALITY TYPE:** Realistic.

EDUCATION/TRAINING PROGRAM(S)— Landscaping and Groundskeeping; Ornamental Horticulture; Turf and Turfgrass Management. **RELATED KNOWLEDGE/COURSES—Personnel and Human Resources:** Knowledge of principles and procedures for personnel recruitment, selection, training, compensation and benefits, labor relations and negotiation, and personnel information systems. **Administration and Management:** Knowledge of business and management principles involved in strategic planning, resource allocation, human resources modeling, leadership technique, production methods, and coordination of people and resources. **Chemistry:** Knowledge of the chemical composition, structure, and properties of substances and of the chemical processes and transformations that they undergo. This includes uses of chemicals and their danger signs, production techniques, and disposal methods. **Mechanical Devices:** Knowledge of machines and tools, including their designs, uses, repair, and maintenance. **Biology:** Knowledge of plant and animal organisms and their tissues, cells, functions, interdependencies, and interactions with each other and the environment. **Building and Construction:** Knowledge of the materials, methods, and tools involved in the construction or repair of houses, buildings, or other structures such as highways and roads.

First-Line Supervisors and Manager/Supervisors— Logging Workers

◎ Education/Training Required: Bachelor's degree
◎ Annual Earnings: $35,490
◎ Growth: 11.4%
◎ Annual Job Openings: 6,000
◎ Self-Employed: 16.9%
◎ Part-Time: 6.1%

Directly supervise and coordinate activities of logging workers. Manager/supervisors are generally found in smaller establishments, where they perform both supervisory and management functions, such as accounting, marketing, and personnel work, and may also engage in the same logging work as the workers they supervise. Assign to workers duties such as trees to be cut; cutting sequences and specifications; and loading of trucks, railcars, or rafts. Change logging operations or methods to eliminate unsafe conditions. Communicate with forestry personnel regarding forest harvesting and forest management plans, procedures, and schedules. Determine logging operation methods, crew sizes, and equipment requirements, conferring with mill, company, and forestry officials as necessary. Monitor logging operations to identify and solve problems; improve work methods; and ensure compliance with safety, company, and government regulations. Monitor workers to ensure that safety regulations are followed, warning or disciplining those who violate safety regulations. Plan and schedule logging operations such as felling and bucking trees and grading, sorting, yarding, or loading logs. Schedule work crews, equipment, and transportation for several different work locations. Supervise and coordinate the activities of workers engaged in logging operations and silvicultural operations. Train workers in tree felling and bucking, operation of tractors and loading machines, yarding and loading techniques, and safety regulations. Coordinate dismantling, moving, and setting up equipment at new work sites. Coordinate the selection

and movement of logs from storage areas according to transportation schedules or production requirements. Prepare production and personnel time records for management. **SKILLS—Management of Personnel Resources:** Motivating, developing, and directing people as they work, identifying the best people for the job. **Management of Material Resources:** Obtaining and seeing to the appropriate use of equipment, facilities, and materials needed to do certain work. **Instructing:** Teaching others how to do something. **Time Management:** Managing one's own time and the time of others. **Coordination:** Adjusting actions in relation to others' actions. **Systems Analysis:** Determining how a system should work and how changes in conditions, operations, and the environment will affect outcomes. **Systems Evaluation:** Identifying measures or indicators of system performance and the actions needed to improve or correct performance relative to the goals of the system. **Operation and Control:** Controlling operations of equipment or systems. **GOE—Interest Area:** 01. Agriculture and Natural Resources. **Work Group:** 01.01. Managerial Work in Agriculture and Natural Resources. **Other Jobs in This Work Group:** Agricultural Crop Farm Managers; Farmers and Ranchers; First-Line Supervisors and Manager/Supervisors— Agricultural Crop Workers; First-Line Supervisors and Manager/Supervisors—Animal Husbandry Workers; First-Line Supervisors and Manager/Supervisors— Extractive Workers; First-Line Supervisors and Manager/Supervisors—Fishery Workers; First-Line Supervisors and Manager/Supervisors—Horticultural Workers; First-Line Supervisors and Manager/Supervisors—Landscaping Workers; Fish Hatchery Managers; Lawn Service Managers; Nursery and Greenhouse Managers; Park Naturalists; Purchasing Agents and Buyers, Farm Products. **PERSONALITY TYPE:** Realistic.

EDUCATION/TRAINING PROGRAM(S)—Agricultural Business and Management, Other; Agricultural Production Operations, General; Agricultural Production Operations, Other; Agriculture, Agriculture Operations, and Related Sciences, Other; Agronomy and Crop Science; Crop Production; Farm/Farm and Ranch Management; Plant Sciences, General. **RELATED KNOWLEDGE/COURSES—Administration and Management:** Knowledge of business and management principles involved in strategic planning, resource allocation, human resources modeling, leadership technique, production methods, and coordination of people and resources. **Production and**

Processing: Knowledge of raw materials, production processes, quality control, costs, and other techniques for maximizing the effective manufacture and distribution of goods. **Personnel and Human Resources:** Knowledge of principles and procedures for personnel recruitment, selection, training, compensation and benefits, labor relations and negotiation, and personnel information systems. **Public Safety and Security:** Knowledge of relevant equipment, policies, procedures, and strategies to promote effective local, state, or national security operations for the protection of people, data, property, and institutions. **Transportation:** Knowledge of principles and methods for moving people or goods by air, rail, sea, or road, including the relative costs and benefits. **Education and Training:** Knowledge of principles and methods for curriculum and training design, teaching and instruction for individuals and groups, and the measurement of training effects.

First-Line Supervisors, Administrative Support

- Education/Training Required: Work experience in a related occupation
- Annual Earnings: $41,030
- Growth: 6.6%
- Annual Job Openings: 140,000
- Self-Employed: 0.9%
- Part-Time: 6.7%

Supervise and coordinate activities of workers involved in providing administrative support. Supervises and coordinates activities of workers engaged in clerical or administrative support activities. Plans, prepares, and revises work schedules and duty assignments according to budget allotments, customer needs, problems, workloads, and statistical forecasts. Verifies completeness and accuracy of subordinates' work, computations, and records. Interviews, selects, and discharges employees. Oversees, coordinates, or performs activities associated with shipping, receiving, distribution, and transportation. Evaluates subordinate job performance and conformance to regulations and recommends appropriate personnel action. Consults with supervisor and other personnel to resolve problems such as equipment performance, output quality, and work schedules. Trains employees in work and safety

procedures and company policies. Computes figures such as balances, totals, and commissions. Analyzes financial activities of establishment or department and assists in planning budget. Inspects equipment for defects and notifies maintenance personnel or outside service contractors for repairs. Plans layout of stockroom, warehouse, or other storage areas, considering turnover, size, weight, and related factors pertaining to items stored. Compiles reports and information required by management or governmental agencies. Identifies and resolves discrepancies or errors. Maintains records of such matters as inventory, personnel, orders, supplies, and machine maintenance. Examines procedures and recommends changes to save time, labor, and other costs and to improve quality control and operating efficiency. Participates in work of subordinates to facilitate productivity or overcome difficult aspects of work. Requisitions supplies. Reviews records and reports pertaining to such activities as production, operation, payroll, customer accounts, and shipping. **SKILLS—Management of Personnel Resources:** Motivating, developing, and directing people as they work, identifying the best people for the job. **Management of Financial Resources:** Determining how money will be spent to get the work done and accounting for these expenditures. **Management of Material Resources:** Obtaining and seeing to the appropriate use of equipment, facilities, and materials needed to do certain work. **Social Perceptiveness:** Being aware of others' reactions and understanding why they react as they do. **Systems Evaluation:** Identifying measures or indicators of system performance and the actions needed to improve or correct performance relative to the goals of the system. **Time Management:** Managing one's own time and the time of others. **Systems Analysis:** Determining how a system should work and how changes in conditions, operations, and the environment will affect outcomes. **Learning Strategies:** Selecting and using training/instructional methods and procedures appropriate for the situation when learning or teaching new things. **GOE—Interest Area:** 04. Business and Administration. **Work Group:** 04.02. Managerial Work in Business Detail. **Other Jobs in This Work Group:** Administrative Services Managers; First-Line Supervisors, Customer Service; Housekeeping Supervisors; Janitorial Supervisors; Meeting and Convention Planners. **PERSONALITY TYPE:** Enterprising.

EDUCATION/TRAINING PROGRAM(S)—Agricultural Business Technology; Customer Service Management; Medical/Health Management and Clinical Assistant/Specialist; Office Management and Supervision. **RELATED KNOWLEDGE/COURSES— Clerical Practices:** Knowledge of administrative and clerical procedures and systems such as word processing, managing files and records, stenography and transcription, designing forms, and other office procedures and terminology. **Personnel and Human Resources:** Knowledge of principles and procedures for personnel recruitment, selection, training, compensation and benefits, labor relations and negotiation, and personnel information systems. **Transportation:** Knowledge of principles and methods for moving people or goods by air, rail, sea, or road, including the relative costs and benefits. **Economics and Accounting:** Knowledge of economic and accounting principles and practices, the financial markets, banking, and the analysis and reporting of financial data. **Administration and Management:** Knowledge of business and management principles involved in strategic planning, resource allocation, human resources modeling, leadership technique, production methods, and coordination of people and resources. **Law and Government:** Knowledge of laws, legal codes, court procedures, precedents, government regulations, executive orders, agency rules, and the democratic political process.

First-Line Supervisors, Customer Service

- ◎ Education/Training Required: Work experience in a related occupation
- ◎ Annual Earnings: $41,030
- ◎ Growth: 6.6%
- ◎ Annual Job Openings: 140,000
- ◎ Self-Employed: 0.9%
- ◎ Part-Time: 6.7%

Supervise and coordinate activities of workers involved in providing customer service. Supervises and coordinates activities of workers engaged in customer service activities. Plans, prepares, and devises work schedules according to budgets and workloads. Observes and evaluates workers' performance. Issues instructions and assigns duties to workers. Trains and instructs employees. Hires and discharges workers. Communicates with other departments and management to resolve problems and expedite work. Inter-

prets and communicates work procedures and company policies to staff. Helps workers in resolving problems and completing work. Resolves complaints and answers questions of customers regarding services and procedures. Reviews and checks work of subordinates, such as reports, records, and applications, for accuracy and content and corrects errors. Prepares, maintains, and submits reports and records, such as budgets and operational and personnel reports. Makes recommendations to management concerning staff and improvement of procedures. Plans and develops improved procedures. Requisitions or purchases supplies. **SKILLS—Management of Personnel Resources:** Motivating, developing, and directing people as they work, identifying the best people for the job. **Management of Financial Resources:** Determining how money will be spent to get the work done and accounting for these expenditures. **Service Orientation:** Actively looking for ways to help people. **Social Perceptiveness:** Being aware of others' reactions and understanding why they react as they do. **Systems Evaluation:** Identifying measures or indicators of system performance and the actions needed to improve or correct performance relative to the goals of the system. **Coordination:** Adjusting actions in relation to others' actions. **Time Management:** Managing one's own time and the time of others. **Learning Strategies:** Selecting and using training/instructional methods and procedures appropriate for the situation when learning or teaching new things. **Systems Analysis:** Determining how a system should work and how changes in conditions, operations, and the environment will affect outcomes. **GOE—Interest Area:** 04. Business and Administration. **Work Group:** 04.02. Managerial Work in Business Detail. **Other Jobs in This Work Group:** Administrative Services Managers; First-Line Supervisors, Administrative Support; Housekeeping Supervisors; Janitorial Supervisors; Meeting and Convention Planners. **PERSONALITY TYPE:** Enterprising.

EDUCATION/TRAINING PROGRAM(S)—Agricultural Business Technology; Customer Service Management; Medical/Health Management and Clinical Assistant/Specialist; Office Management and Supervision. **RELATED KNOWLEDGE/COURSES—Customer and Personal Service:** Knowledge of principles and processes for providing customer and personal services. This includes customer needs assessment, meeting quality standards for services, and evaluation of customer satisfaction. **Personnel and Human**

Resources: Knowledge of principles and procedures for personnel recruitment, selection, training, compensation and benefits, labor relations and negotiation, and personnel information systems. **Economics and Accounting:** Knowledge of economic and accounting principles and practices, the financial markets, banking, and the analysis and reporting of financial data. **Administration and Management:** Knowledge of business and management principles involved in strategic planning, resource allocation, human resources modeling, leadership technique, production methods, and coordination of people and resources. **Clerical Practices:** Knowledge of administrative and clerical procedures and systems such as word processing, managing files and records, stenography and transcription, designing forms, and other office procedures and terminology. **Education and Training:** Knowledge of principles and methods for curriculum and training design, teaching and instruction for individuals and groups, and the measurement of training effects.

First-Line Supervisors/ Managers of Correctional Officers

- ◎ Education/Training Required: Work experience in a related occupation
- ◎ Annual Earnings: $44,720
- ◎ Growth: 19.0%
- ◎ Annual Job Openings: 4,000
- ◎ Self-Employed: 0%
- ◎ Part-Time: 1.4%

Supervise and coordinate activities of correctional officers and jailers. Complete administrative paperwork and supervise the preparation and maintenance of records, forms, and reports. Conduct roll calls of correctional officers. Develop work and security procedures. Instruct employees and provide on-the-job training. Maintain knowledge of, comply with, and enforce all institutional policies, rules, procedures, and regulations. Maintain order, discipline, and security within assigned areas in accordance with relevant rules, regulations, policies, and laws. Monitor behavior of subordinates to ensure alert, courteous, and professional behavior toward inmates, parolees, fellow employees, visitors, and the public. Read and review offender information to identify issues that require special attention. Respond to emergencies such as escapes. Restrain, secure, and control offenders, using chemical agents, firearms, and other weapons of force as necessary. Set up employee work schedules. Supervise and direct the work of correctional officers to ensure the safe custody, discipline, and welfare of inmates. Supervise and perform searches of inmates and their quarters to locate contraband items. Supervise activities such as searches, shakedowns, riot control, and institutional tours. Take, receive, and check periodic inmate counts. Carry injured offenders or employees to safety and provide emergency first aid when necessary. Convey correctional officers' and inmates' complaints to superiors. Examine incoming and outgoing mail to ensure conformance with regulations. Rate behavior of inmates, promoting acceptable attitudes and behaviors to those with low ratings. Resolve problems between inmates. Supervise and provide security for offenders performing tasks such as construction, maintenance, laundry, food service, and other industrial or agricultural operations. Transfer and transport offenders on foot or by driving vehicles such as trailers, vans, and buses. **SKILLS**—No data available. **GOE—Interest Area:** 12. Law and Public Safety. **Work Group:** 12.01. Managerial Work in Law and Public Safety. **Other Jobs in This Work Group:** Emergency Management Specialists; First-Line Supervisors/Managers of Police and Detectives; Forest Fire Fighting and Prevention Supervisors; Municipal Fire Fighting and Prevention Supervisors. **PERSONALITY TYPE:** No data available.

EDUCATION/TRAINING PROGRAM(S)—Corrections; Corrections Administration. **RELATED KNOWLEDGE/COURSES**—No data available.

First-Line Supervisors/ Managers of Food Preparation and Serving Workers

- ◉ Education/Training Required: Work experience in a related occupation
- ◉ Annual Earnings: $25,410
- ◉ Growth: 15.5%
- ◉ Annual Job Openings: 154,000
- ◉ Self-Employed: 4.5%
- ◉ Part-Time: 14.7%

Supervise workers engaged in preparing and serving food. Compile and balance cash receipts at the end of the day or shift. Resolve customer complaints regarding food service. Train workers in food preparation and in service, sanitation, and safety procedures. Inspect supplies, equipment, and work areas in order to ensure efficient service and conformance to standards. Control inventories of food, equipment, smallware, and liquor and report shortages to designated personnel. Observe and evaluate workers and work procedures in order to ensure quality standards and service. Assign duties, responsibilities, and work stations to employees in accordance with work requirements. Estimate ingredients and supplies required to prepare a recipe. Perform personnel actions such as hiring and firing staff, consulting with other managers as necessary. Analyze operational problems, such as theft and wastage, and establish procedures to alleviate these problems. Specify food portions and courses, production and time sequences, and workstation and equipment arrangements. Recommend measures for improving work procedures and worker performance in order to increase service quality and enhance job safety. Greet and seat guests and present menus and wine lists. Present bills and accept payments. Forecast staff, equipment, and supply requirements based on a master menu. Perform serving duties such as carving meat, preparing flambe dishes, or serving wine and liquor. Record production and operational data on specified forms. Purchase or requisition supplies and equipment needed to ensure quality and timely delivery of services. Collaborate with other personnel in order to plan menus, serving arrangements, and related details. Supervise and check the assembly of regular and spe-cial diet trays and the delivery of food trolleys to hospital patients. Schedule parties and take reservations. Develop departmental objectives, budgets, policies, procedures, and strategies. Develop equipment maintenance schedules and arrange for repairs. Evaluate new products for usefulness and suitability. **SKILLS— Management of Personnel Resources:** Motivating, developing, and directing people as they work, identifying the best people for the job. **Management of Financial Resources:** Determining how money will be spent to get the work done and accounting for these expenditures. **Equipment Maintenance:** Performing routine maintenance on equipment and determining when and what kind of maintenance is needed. **Instructing:** Teaching others how to do something. **Learning Strategies:** Selecting and using training/instructional methods and procedures appropriate for the situation when learning or teaching new things. **Service Orientation:** Actively looking for ways to help people. **Monitoring:** Monitoring or assessing your performance or that of other individuals or organizations to make improvements or take corrective action. **Speaking:** Talking to others to convey information effectively. **GOE—Interest Area:** 09. Hospitality, Tourism, and Recreation. **Work Group:** 09.01. Managerial Work in Hospitality and Tourism. **Other Jobs in This Work Group:** First-Line Supervisors/Managers of Personal Service Workers; Food Service Managers; Gaming Managers; Gaming Supervisors; Lodging Managers. **PERSONALITY TYPE:** Enterprising.

EDUCATION/TRAINING PROGRAM(S)— Cooking and Related Culinary Arts, General; Foodservice Systems Administration/Management; Restaurant, Culinary, and Catering Management/ Manager. **RELATED KNOWLEDGE/COURSES— Customer and Personal Service:** Knowledge of principles and processes for providing customer and personal services. This includes customer needs assessment, meeting quality standards for services, and evaluation of customer satisfaction. **Food Production:** Knowledge of techniques and equipment for planting, growing, and harvesting food products (both plant and animal) for consumption, including storage/handling techniques. **Administration and Management:** Knowledge of business and management principles involved in strategic planning, resource allocation, human resources modeling, leadership technique, production methods, and coordination of people and resources. **Sales and Marketing:** Knowledge of principles and methods for showing, promoting, and selling products or services. This includes marketing strategy and tactics, product demonstrations, sales techniques, and sales control systems. **Production and Processing:** Knowledge of raw materials, production processes, quality control, costs, and other techniques for maximizing the effective manufacture and distribution of goods. **Personnel and Human Resources:** Knowledge of principles and procedures for personnel recruitment, selection, training, compensation and benefits, labor relations and negotiation, and personnel information systems. **Education and Training:** Knowledge of principles and methods for curriculum and training design, teaching and instruction for individuals and groups, and the measurement of training effects.

First-Line Supervisors/ Managers of Helpers, Laborers, and Material Movers, Hand

- ◎ Education/Training Required: Work experience in a related occupation
- ◎ Annual Earnings: $38,280
- ◎ Growth: 14.0%
- ◎ Annual Job Openings: 16,000
- ◎ Self-Employed: 0.2%
- ◎ Part-Time: 6.6%

Supervise and coordinate the activities of helpers, laborers, or material movers. Assess training needs of staff; then arrange for or provide appropriate instruction. Collaborate with workers and managers to solve work-related problems. Conduct staff meetings to relay general information or to address specific topics such as safety. Estimate material, time, and staffing requirements for a given project, based on work orders, job specifications, and experience. Evaluate employee performance and prepare performance appraisals. Examine freight to determine loading sequences. Perform the same work duties as those whom they supervise and/or perform more difficult or skilled tasks or assist in their performance. Plan work schedules and assign duties to maintain adequate staffing levels, to ensure that activities are performed effectively, and to respond to fluctuating workloads. Prepare and maintain work records and reports that include information such as employee time and wages, daily receipts, and inspection results. Provide assistance in balancing books, tracking, monitoring, and projecting a unit's budget needs and in developing unit policies and procedures. Recommend or initiate personnel actions such as promotions, transfers, and disciplinary measures. Resolve personnel problems, complaints, and formal grievances when possible, or refer them to higher-level supervisors for resolution. Review work throughout the work process and at completion in order to ensure that it has been performed properly. Transmit and explain work orders to laborers. Check specifications of materials loaded or unloaded against information contained in work orders. Counsel employees in work-related activities, personal growth, and career development. Inform designated employees or departments of items loaded and problems encountered. Inspect equipment for wear and for conformance to specifications. Inspect job sites to determine the extent of maintenance or repairs needed. Inventory supplies and requisition or purchase additional items as necessary. Participate in the hiring process by reviewing credentials, conducting interviews, and/or making hiring decisions or recommendations. **SKILLS—Management of Personnel Resources:** Motivating, developing, and directing people as they work, identifying the best people for the job. **Social Perceptiveness:** Being aware of others' reactions and understanding why they react as they do. **Systems Analysis:** Determining how a system should work and how changes in conditions, operations, and the environment will affect outcomes. **Instructing:** Teaching others how to do something. **Systems Evaluation:** Identifying measures or indicators of system performance and the actions needed to improve or correct performance relative to the goals of the system. **Learning Strategies:** Selecting and using training/instructional methods and procedures appropriate for the situation when learning or teaching new things. **Management of Material Resources:** Obtaining and seeing to the appropriate use of equipment, facilities, and materials needed to do certain work. **Time Management:** Managing one's own time and the time of others. **GOE— Interest Area:** 13. Manufacturing. **Work Group:** 13.01. Managerial Work in Manufacturing. **Other Jobs in This Work Group:** First-Line Supervisors/Managers of Mechanics, Installers, and Repairers; First-Line Supervisors/Managers of Production and Operating Workers; Industrial Production Managers. **PERSONALITY TYPE:** Enterprising.

EDUCATION/TRAINING PROGRAM(S)—No data available. **RELATED KNOWLEDGE/COURS-ES—Production and Processing:** Knowledge of raw materials, production processes, quality control, costs, and other techniques for maximizing the effective manufacture and distribution of goods. **Economics and Accounting:** Knowledge of economic and accounting principles and practices, the financial markets, banking, and the analysis and reporting of financial data. **Administration and Management:** Knowledge of business and management principles involved in strategic planning, resource allocation, human resources modeling, leadership technique, production methods, and coordination of people and resources. **Personnel and Human Resources:** Knowledge of principles and procedures for personnel recruitment, selection, training, compensation and benefits, labor relations and negotiation, and personnel information systems. **Education and Training:** Knowledge of principles and methods for curriculum and training design, teaching and instruction for individuals and groups, and the measurement of training effects. **Mathematics:** Knowledge of arithmetic, algebra, geometry, calculus, and statistics and their applications.

First-Line Supervisors/ Managers of Mechanics, Installers, and Repairers

- Education/Training Required: Work experience in a related occupation
- Annual Earnings: $50,340
- Growth: 15.4%
- Annual Job Openings: 42,000
- Self-Employed: 0.1%
- Part-Time: 1.3%

Supervise and coordinate the activities of mechanics, installers, and repairers. Determine schedules, sequences, and assignments for work activities based on work priority, quantity of equipment and skill of personnel. Patrol and monitor work areas and examine tools and equipment in order to detect unsafe conditions or violations of procedures or safety rules. Monitor employees' work levels and review work performance. Examine objects, systems, or facilities and analyze information to determine needed installations, services, or repairs. Participate in budget preparation and administration, coordinating purchasing and documentation and monitoring departmental expenditures. Counsel employees about work-related issues and assist employees in correcting job-skill deficiencies. Requisition materials and supplies, such as tools, equipment, and replacement parts. Compute estimates and actual costs of factors such as materials, labor, and outside contractors. Interpret specifications, blueprints, and job orders in order to construct templates and lay out reference points for workers. Conduct or arrange for worker training in safety, repair, and maintenance techniques; operational procedures; and equipment use. Investigate accidents and injuries and prepare reports of findings. Confer with personnel, such as management, engineering, quality control, customer, and union workers' representatives, in order to coordinate work activities, resolve employee grievances, and identify and review resource needs. Recommend or initiate personnel actions, such as hires, promotions, transfers, discharges, and disciplinary measures. Perform skilled repair and maintenance operations, using equipment such as hand and power tools, hydraulic presses and shears, and welding equipment. Compile operational and personnel records, such as time and production records, inventory data, repair and maintenance statistics, and test results. Develop, implement, and evaluate maintenance policies and procedures. Monitor tool inventories and the condition and maintenance of shops in order to ensure adequate working conditions. Inspect, test, and measure completed work, using devices such as hand tools and gauges to verify conformance to standards and repair requirements. **SKILLS—Management of Personnel Resources:** Motivating, developing, and directing people as they work, identifying the best people for the job. **Installation:** Installing equipment, machines, wiring, or programs to meet specifications. **Repairing:** Repairing machines or systems by using the needed tools. **Management of Material Resources:** Obtaining and seeing to the appropriate use of equipment, facilities, and materials needed to do certain work. **Management of Financial Resources:** Determining how money will be spent to get the work done and accounting for these expenditures. **Equipment Maintenance:** Performing routine maintenance on equipment and determining when and what kind of maintenance is needed. **Negotiation:** Bringing others together and trying to reconcile differences. **Troubleshooting:**

F

Determining causes of operating errors and deciding what to do about them. **GOE—Interest Area:** 13. Manufacturing. **Work Group:** 13.01. Managerial Work in Manufacturing. **Other Jobs in This Work Group:** First-Line Supervisors/Managers of Helpers, Laborers, and Material Movers, Hand; First-Line Supervisors/Managers of Production and Operating Workers; Industrial Production Managers. **PERSONALITY TYPE:** Enterprising.

EDUCATION/TRAINING PROGRAM(S)— Operations Management and Supervision. **RELATED KNOWLEDGE/COURSES—Mechanical Devices:** Knowledge of machines and tools, including their designs, uses, repair, and maintenance. **Building and Construction:** Knowledge of the materials, methods, and tools involved in the construction or repair of houses, buildings, or other structures such as highways and roads. **Design:** Knowledge of design techniques, tools, and principles involved in production of precision technical plans, blueprints, drawings, and models. **Personnel and Human Resources:** Knowledge of principles and procedures for personnel recruitment, selection, training, compensation and benefits, labor relations and negotiation, and personnel information systems. **Administration and Management:** Knowledge of business and management principles involved in strategic planning, resource allocation, human resources modeling, leadership technique, production methods, and coordination of people and resources. **Customer and Personal Service:** Knowledge of principles and processes for providing customer and personal services. This includes customer needs assessment, meeting quality standards for services, and evaluation of customer satisfaction.

First-Line Supervisors/Managers of Non-Retail Sales Workers

◉ Education/Training Required: Work experience in a related occupation

◉ Annual Earnings: $59,300

◉ Growth: 6.8%

◉ Annual Job Openings: 72,000

◉ Self-Employed: 44.7%

◉ Part-Time: 5.7%

Directly supervise and coordinate activities of sales workers other than retail sales workers. May perform duties such as budgeting, accounting, and personnel work in addition to supervisory duties. Analyze details of sales territories to assess their growth potential and to set quotas. Direct and supervise employees engaged in sales, inventory-taking, reconciling cash receipts, or performing specific services such as pumping gasoline for customers. Hire, train, and evaluate personnel. Inventory stock and reorder when inventories drop to specified levels. Keep records pertaining to purchases, sales, and requisitions. Listen to and resolve customer complaints regarding services, products, or personnel. Monitor sales staff performance to ensure that goals are met. Plan and prepare work schedules and assign employees to specific duties. Prepare sales and inventory reports for management and budget departments. Provide staff with assistance in performing difficult or complicated duties. Attend company meetings to exchange product information and coordinate work activities with other departments. Confer with company officials to develop methods and procedures to increase sales, expand markets, and promote business. Coordinate sales promotion activities and prepare merchandise displays and advertising copy. Examine merchandise to ensure correct pricing and display and that it functions as advertised. Examine products purchased for resale or received for storage to determine product condition. Formulate pricing policies on merchandise according to profitability requirements. Prepare rental or lease agreements, specifying charges and payment procedures for use of machinery, tools, or other items. Visit retailers and sales representatives to promote products and gather information. **SKILLS—Management of Personnel Resources:** Motivating, developing, and directing people as they work, identifying the best people for the job. **Management of Material Resources:** Obtaining and seeing to the appropriate use of equipment, facilities, and materials needed to do certain work. **Management of Financial Resources:** Determining how money will be spent to get the work done and accounting for these expenditures. **Systems Evaluation:** Identifying measures or indicators of system performance and the actions needed to improve or correct performance relative to the goals of the system. **Systems Analysis:** Determining how a system should work and how changes in conditions, operations, and the environment will affect outcomes. **Negotiation:** Bringing others together and trying to reconcile differences.

Social Perceptiveness: Being aware of others' reactions and understanding why they react as they do. Coordination: Adjusting actions in relation to others' actions. GOE—Interest Area: 14. Retail and Wholesale Sales and Service. Work Group: 14.01. Managerial Work in Retail/Wholesale Sales and Service. Other Jobs in This Work Group: Advertising and Promotions Managers; First-Line Supervisors/Managers of Retail Sales Workers; Funeral Directors; Marketing Managers; Property, Real Estate, and Community Association Managers; Purchasing Managers; Sales Managers. PERSONALITY TYPE: Enterprising.

EDUCATION/TRAINING PROGRAM(S)—Business, Management, Marketing, and Related Support Services, Other; General Merchandising, Sales, and Related Marketing Operations, Other; Special Products Marketing Operations; Specialized Merchandising, Sales, and Related Marketing Operations, Other. RELATED KNOWLEDGE/COURSES—Sales and Marketing: Knowledge of principles and methods for showing, promoting, and selling products or services. This includes marketing strategy and tactics, product demonstrations, sales techniques, and sales control systems. Economics and Accounting: Knowledge of economic and accounting principles and practices, the financial markets, banking, and the analysis and reporting of financial data. Personnel and Human Resources: Knowledge of principles and procedures for personnel recruitment, selection, training, compensation and benefits, labor relations and negotiation, and personnel information systems. Administration and Management: Knowledge of business and management principles involved in strategic planning, resource allocation, human resources modeling, leadership technique, production methods, and coordination of people and resources. Mathematics: Knowledge of arithmetic, algebra, geometry, calculus, and statistics and their applications. Customer and Personal Service: Knowledge of principles and processes for providing customer and personal services. This includes customer needs assessment, meeting quality standards for services, and evaluation of customer satisfaction.

First-Line Supervisors/ Managers of Personal Service Workers

- Education/Training Required: Work experience in a related occupation
- Annual Earnings: $30,350
- Growth: 9.4%
- Annual Job Openings: 26,000
- Self-Employed: 49.4%
- Part-Time: 16.1%

Supervise and coordinate activities of personal service workers, such as flight attendants, hairdressers, or caddies. Analyze and record personnel and operational data and write related activity reports. Apply customer/guest feedback to service improvement efforts. Assign work schedules, following work requirements, to ensure quality and timely delivery of service. Direct and coordinate the activities of workers such as flight attendants, hotel staff, or hairstylists. Inspect work areas and operating equipment to ensure conformance to established standards in areas such as cleanliness and maintenance. Meet with managers and other supervisors to stay informed of changes affecting operations. Observe and evaluate workers' appearance and performance to ensure quality service and compliance with specifications. Recruit and hire staff members. Requisition necessary supplies, equipment, and services. Resolve customer complaints regarding worker performance and services rendered. Take disciplinary action to address performance problems. Train workers in proper operational procedures and functions and explain company policies. Collaborate with staff members to plan and develop programs of events, schedules of activities, or menus. Direct marketing, advertising, and other customer recruitment efforts. Furnish customers with information on events and activities. Inform workers about interests and special needs of specific groups. Participate in continuing education to stay abreast of industry trends and developments. SKILLS—Service Orientation: Actively looking for ways to help people. Management of Personnel Resources: Motivating, developing, and directing people as they work, identifying the best people for the job. Coordination: Adjusting actions in relation to others' actions. Time Management: Managing one's own time and the time of others. Management of

Financial Resources: Determining how money will be spent to get the work done and accounting for these expenditures. **Management of Material Resources:** Obtaining and seeing to the appropriate use of equipment, facilities, and materials needed to do certain work. **Learning Strategies:** Selecting and using training/instructional methods and procedures appropriate for the situation when learning or teaching new things. **Systems Evaluation:** Identifying measures or indicators of system performance and the actions needed to improve or correct performance relative to the goals of the system. **GOE—Interest Area:** 09. Hospitality, Tourism, and Recreation. **Work Group:** 09.01. Managerial Work in Hospitality and Tourism. **Other Jobs in This Work Group:** First-Line Supervisors/Managers of Food Preparation and Serving Workers; Food Service Managers; Gaming Managers; Gaming Supervisors; Lodging Managers. **PERSONALITY TYPE:** Enterprising.

EDUCATION/TRAINING PROGRAM(S)—No data available. **RELATED KNOWLEDGE/COURSES—Administration and Management:** Knowledge of business and management principles involved in strategic planning, resource allocation, human resources modeling, leadership technique, production methods, and coordination of people and resources. **Customer and Personal Service:** Knowledge of principles and processes for providing customer and personal services. This includes customer needs assessment, meeting quality standards for services, and evaluation of customer satisfaction. **Personnel and Human Resources:** Knowledge of principles and procedures for personnel recruitment, selection, training, compensation and benefits, labor relations and negotiation, and personnel information systems. **Psychology:** Knowledge of human behavior and performance; individual differences in ability, personality, and interests; learning and motivation; psychological research methods; and the assessment and treatment of behavioral and affective disorders. **Economics and Accounting:** Knowledge of economic and accounting principles and practices, the financial markets, banking, and the analysis and reporting of financial data. **Education and Training:** Knowledge of principles and methods for curriculum and training design, teaching and instruction for individuals and groups, and the measurement of training effects.

First-Line Supervisors/ Managers of Police and Detectives

◉ Education/Training Required: Work experience in a related occupation

◉ Annual Earnings: $64,430

◉ Growth: 15.3%

◉ Annual Job Openings: 14,000

◉ Self-Employed: 0%

◉ Part-Time: 1.4%

Supervise and coordinate activities of members of police force. Explain police operations to subordinates to assist them in performing their job duties. Inform personnel of changes in regulations and policies, implications of new or amended laws, and new techniques of police work. Supervise and coordinate the investigation of criminal cases, offering guidance and expertise to investigators and ensuring that procedures are conducted in accordance with laws and regulations. Investigate and resolve personnel problems within organization and charges of misconduct against staff. Train staff in proper police work procedures. Maintain logs; prepare reports; and direct the preparation, handling, and maintenance of departmental records. Monitor and evaluate the job performance of subordinates and authorize promotions and transfers. Direct collection, preparation, and handling of evidence and personal property of prisoners. Develop, implement, and revise departmental policies and procedures. Conduct raids and order detention of witnesses and suspects for questioning. Prepare work schedules and assign duties to subordinates. Discipline staff for violation of department rules and regulations. Cooperate with court personnel and officials from other law enforcement agencies and testify in court as necessary. Review contents of written orders to ensure adherence to legal requirements. Inspect facilities, supplies, vehicles, and equipment to ensure conformance to standards. Prepare news releases and respond to police correspondence. Requisition and issue equipment and supplies. Meet with civic, educational, and community groups to develop community programs and events and to discuss law enforcement subjects. Direct release or transfer of prisoners. Prepare budgets and manage expenditures of department funds. **SKILLS—Management of Personnel Resources:** Motivating, developing, and directing people as they work, identifying the best people for the job. **Persuasion:** Persuading others to change their minds or behavior. **Negotiation:** Bringing others together and trying to reconcile differences. **Social Perceptiveness:** Being aware of others' reactions and understanding why they react as they do. **Service Orientation:** Actively looking for ways to help people. **Monitoring:** Monitoring or assessing your performance or that of other individuals or organizations to make improvements or take corrective action. **Instructing:** Teaching others how to do something. **Learning Strategies:** Selecting and using training/instructional methods and procedures appropriate for the situation when learning or teaching new things. **Coordination:** Adjusting actions in relation to others' actions. **GOE—Interest Area:** 12. Law and Public Safety. **Work Group:** 12.01. Managerial Work in Law and Public Safety. **Other Jobs in This Work Group:** Emergency Management Specialists; First-Line Supervisors/Managers of Correctional Officers; Forest Fire Fighting and Prevention Supervisors; Municipal Fire Fighting and Prevention Supervisors. **PERSONALITY TYPE:** Enterprising.

EDUCATION/TRAINING PROGRAM(S)—Corrections; Criminal Justice/Law Enforcement Administration; Criminal Justice/Safety Studies. **RELATED KNOWLEDGE/COURSES—Public Safety and Security:** Knowledge of relevant equipment, policies, procedures, and strategies to promote effective local, state, or national security operations for the protection of people, data, property, and institutions. **Psychology:** Knowledge of human behavior and performance; individual differences in ability, personality, and interests; learning and motivation; psychological research methods; and the assessment and treatment of behavioral and affective disorders. **Law and Government:** Knowledge of laws, legal codes, court procedures, precedents, government regulations, executive orders, agency rules, and the democratic political process. **Customer and Personal Service:** Knowledge of principles and processes for providing customer and personal services. This includes customer needs assessment, meeting quality standards for services, and evaluation of customer satisfaction. **Personnel and Human Resources:** Knowledge of principles and procedures for personnel recruitment, selection, training, compensation and benefits, labor relations and negotiation, and personnel information systems. **Education and Training:**

Knowledge of principles and methods for curriculum and training design, teaching and instruction for individuals and groups, and the measurement of training effects.

First-Line Supervisors/ Managers of Production and Operating Workers

- Education/Training Required: Work experience in a related occupation
- Annual Earnings: $44,740
- Growth: 9.5%
- Annual Job Openings: 66,000
- Self-Employed: 2.2%
- Part-Time: 1.9%

Supervise and coordinate the activities of production and operating workers, such as inspectors, precision workers, machine setters and operators, assemblers, fabricators, and plant and system operators. Calculate labor and equipment requirements and production specifications, using standard formulas. Confer with management or subordinates to resolve worker problems, complaints, or grievances. Confer with other supervisors to coordinate operations and activities within or between departments. Demonstrate equipment operations and work and safety procedures to new employees or assign employees to experienced workers for training. Direct and coordinate the activities of employees engaged in the production or processing of goods, such as inspectors, machine setters, and fabricators. Inspect materials, products, or equipment to detect defects or malfunctions. Interpret specifications, blueprints, job orders, and company policies and procedures for workers. Maintain operations data such as time, production, and cost records and prepare management reports of production results. Observe work and monitor gauges, dials, and other indicators to ensure that operators conform to production or processing standards. Plan and establish work schedules, assignments, and production sequences to meet production goals. Recommend or implement measures to motivate employees and to improve production methods, equipment performance, product quality, or efficiency. Requisition materials, supplies, equipment parts, or repair services. Determine standards, budgets, production goals, and rates based on company policies, equipment and labor availability, and workloads. Enforce safety and sanitation regulations. Plan and develop new products and production processes. Read and analyze charts, work orders, production schedules, and other records and reports in order to determine production requirements and to evaluate current production estimates and outputs. Recommend personnel actions such as hirings and promotions. Set up and adjust machines and equipment. **SKILLS—Management of Personnel Resources:** Motivating, developing, and directing people as they work, identifying the best people for the job. **Management of Material Resources:** Obtaining and seeing to the appropriate use of equipment, facilities, and materials needed to do certain work. **Systems Analysis:** Determining how a system should work and how changes in conditions, operations, and the environment will affect outcomes. **Negotiation:** Bringing others together and trying to reconcile differences. **Operation Monitoring:** Watching gauges, dials, or other indicators to make sure a machine is working properly. **Coordination:** Adjusting actions in relation to others' actions. **Social Perceptiveness:** Being aware of others' reactions and understanding why they react as they do. **Systems Evaluation:** Identifying measures or indicators of system performance and the actions needed to improve or correct performance relative to the goals of the system. **Management of Financial Resources:** Determining how money will be spent to get the work done and accounting for these expenditures. **GOE—Interest Area:** 13. Manufacturing. **Work Group:** 13.01. Managerial Work in Manufacturing. **Other Jobs in This Work Group:** First-Line Supervisors/Managers of Helpers, Laborers, and Material Movers, Hand; First-Line Supervisors/Managers of Mechanics, Installers, and Repairers; Industrial Production Managers. **PERSONALITY TYPE:** Enterprising.

EDUCATION/TRAINING PROGRAM(S)— Operations Management and Supervision. **RELATED KNOWLEDGE/COURSES—Production and Processing:** Knowledge of raw materials, production processes, quality control, costs, and other techniques for maximizing the effective manufacture and distribution of goods. **Personnel and Human Resources:** Knowledge of principles and procedures for personnel recruitment, selection, training, compensation and benefits, labor relations and negotiation, and personnel information systems. **Administration and Man-**

agement: Knowledge of business and management principles involved in strategic planning, resource allocation, human resources modeling, leadership technique, production methods, and coordination of people and resources. **Economics and Accounting:** Knowledge of economic and accounting principles and practices, the financial markets, banking, and the analysis and reporting of financial data. **Psychology:** Knowledge of human behavior and performance; individual differences in ability, personality, and interests; learning and motivation; psychological research methods; and the assessment and treatment of behavioral and affective disorders. **Mathematics:** Knowledge of arithmetic, algebra, geometry, calculus, and statistics and their applications.

First-Line Supervisors/ Managers of Retail Sales Workers

- ◉ Education/Training Required: Work experience in a related occupation
- ◉ Annual Earnings: $32,720
- ◉ Growth: 9.1%
- ◉ Annual Job Openings: 251,000
- ◉ Self-Employed: 33.0%
- ◉ Part-Time: 7.3%

Directly supervise sales workers in a retail establishment or department. Duties may include management functions, such as purchasing, budgeting, accounting, and personnel work, in addition to supervisory duties. Provide customer service by greeting and assisting customers and responding to customer inquiries and complaints. Monitor sales activities to ensure that customers receive satisfactory service and quality goods. Assign employees to specific duties. Direct and supervise employees engaged in sales, inventory-taking, reconciling cash receipts, or performing services for customers. Inventory stock and reorder when inventory drops to a specified level. Keep records of purchases, sales, and requisitions. Enforce safety, health, and security rules. Examine products purchased for resale or received for storage to assess the condition of each product or item. Hire, train, and evaluate personnel in sales or marketing establishments, promoting or firing workers when appropriate. Perform work activities of subordinates, such as cleaning and organizing shelves and displays and selling merchandise. Establish and implement policies, goals, objectives, and procedures for their department. Instruct staff on how to handle difficult and complicated sales. Formulate pricing policies for merchandise according to profitability requirements. Estimate consumer demand and determine the types and amounts of goods to be sold. Examine merchandise to ensure that it is correctly priced and displayed and that it functions as advertised. Plan and prepare work schedules and keep records of employees' work schedules and time cards. Review inventory and sales records to prepare reports for management and budget departments. Plan and coordinate advertising campaigns and sales promotions and prepare merchandise displays and advertising copy. Confer with company officials to develop methods and procedures to increase sales, expand markets, and promote business. Establish credit policies and operating procedures. Plan budgets and authorize payments and merchandise returns. **SKILLS—Management of Personnel Resources:** Motivating, developing, and directing people as they work, identifying the best people for the job. **Persuasion:** Persuading others to change their minds or behavior. **Instructing:** Teaching others how to do something. **Management of Financial Resources:** Determining how money will be spent to get the work done and accounting for these expenditures. **Social Perceptiveness:** Being aware of others' reactions and understanding why they react as they do. **Service Orientation:** Actively looking for ways to help people. **Time Management:** Managing one's own time and the time of others. **Monitoring:** Monitoring or assessing your performance or that of other individuals or organizations to make improvements or take corrective action. **Negotiation:** Bringing others together and trying to reconcile differences. **GOE—Interest Area:** 14. Retail and Wholesale Sales and Service. **Work Group:** 14.01. Managerial Work in Retail/Wholesale Sales and Service. **Other Jobs in This Work Group:** Advertising and Promotions Managers; First-Line Supervisors/Managers of Non-Retail Sales Workers; Funeral Directors; Marketing Managers; Property, Real Estate, and Community Association Managers; Purchasing Managers; Sales Managers. **PERSONALITY TYPE:** Enterprising.

EDUCATION/TRAINING PROGRAM(S)—Business, Management, Marketing, and Related Support Services, Other; Consumer Merchandising/Retailing Management; E-Commerce/Electronic Commerce; Floriculture/Floristry Operations and Management; Retailing and Retail Operations; Selling Skills and Sales Operations; Special Products Marketing Operations; Specialized Merchandising, Sales, and Related Marketing Operations, Other. **RELATED KNOWLEDGE/COURSES—Sales and Marketing:** Knowledge of principles and methods for showing, promoting, and selling products or services. This includes marketing strategy and tactics, product demonstrations, sales techniques, and sales control systems. **Customer and Personal Service:** Knowledge of principles and processes for providing customer and personal services. This includes customer needs assessment, meeting quality standards for services, and evaluation of customer satisfaction. **Administration and Management:** Knowledge of business and management principles involved in strategic planning, resource allocation, human resources modeling, leadership technique, production methods, and coordination of people and resources. **Personnel and Human Resources:** Knowledge of principles and procedures for personnel recruitment, selection, training, compensation and benefits, labor relations and negotiation, and personnel information systems. **Food Production:** Knowledge of techniques and equipment for planting, growing, and harvesting food products (both plant and animal) for consumption, including storage/handling techniques. **Economics and Accounting:** Knowledge of economic and accounting principles and practices, the financial markets, banking, and the analysis and reporting of financial data. **Public Safety and Security:** Knowledge of relevant equipment, policies, procedures, and strategies to promote effective local, state, or national security operations for the protection of people, data, property, and institutions.

First-Line Supervisors/ Managers of Transportation and Material-Moving Machine and Vehicle Operators

◉ Education/Training Required: Work experience in a related occupation

◉ Annual Earnings: $44,810

◉ Growth: 12.1%

◉ Annual Job Openings: 23,000

◉ Self-Employed: 0.2%

◉ Part-Time: 6.6%

Directly supervise and coordinate activities of transportation and material-moving machine and vehicle operators and helpers. Confer with customers, supervisors, contractors, and other personnel to exchange information and to resolve problems. Direct workers in transportation or related services, such as pumping, moving, storing, and loading/unloading of materials or people. Enforce safety rules and regulations. Explain and demonstrate work tasks to new workers or assign workers to more experienced workers for further training. Interpret transportation and tariff regulations, shipping orders, safety regulations, and company policies and procedures for workers. Maintain or verify records of time, materials, expenditures, and crew activities. Monitor fieldwork to ensure that it is being performed properly and that materials are being used as they should be. Plan work assignments and equipment allocations in order to meet transportation, operations, or production goals. Prepare, compile, and submit reports on work activities, operations, production, and work-related accidents. Recommend or implement personnel actions such as employee selection, evaluation, and rewards or disciplinary actions. Requisition needed personnel, supplies, equipment, parts, or repair services. Resolve worker problems or collaborate with employees to assist in problem resolution. Review orders, production schedules, blueprints, and shipping/receiving notices to determine work sequences and material shipping dates, types, volumes, and destinations. Compute and estimate cash, payroll, transportation, personnel, and storage requirements. Dispatch personnel and vehicles in response to telephone or radio reports of emergencies. Drive vehicles or operate machines or equipment to complete work assignments or to assist workers. Examine, measure, and weigh cargo or materials to determine specific handling requirements. Inspect or test materials, stock, vehicles, equipment, and facilities to ensure that they are safe, are free of defects, and meet specifications. Perform or schedule repairs and preventive maintenance of vehicles and other equipment. Plan and establish transportation routes. Provide workers with assistance in performing tasks such as coupling railroad cars or loading vehicles. **SKILLS—Management of Financial Resources:** Determining how money will be spent to get the work done and accounting for these expenditures. **Management of Personnel Resources:** Motivating, developing, and directing people as they work, identifying the best people for the job. **Management of Material Resources:** Obtaining and seeing to the appropriate use of equipment, facilities, and materials needed to do certain work. **Systems Analysis:** Determining how a system should work and how changes in conditions, operations, and the environment will affect outcomes. **Operations Analysis:** Analyzing needs and product requirements to create a design. **Equipment Maintenance:** Performing routine maintenance on equipment and determining when and what kind of maintenance is needed. **Negotiation:** Bringing others together and trying to reconcile differences. **Coordination:** Adjusting actions in relation to others' actions. **Systems Evaluation:** Identifying measures or indicators of system performance and the actions needed to improve or correct performance relative to the goals of the system. **GOE—Interest Area:** 16. Transportation, Distribution, and Logistics. **Work Group:** 16.01. Managerial Work in Transportation. **Other Jobs in This Work Group:** Aircraft Cargo Handling Supervisors; Postmasters and Mail Superintendents; Railroad Conductors and Yardmasters; Storage and Distribution Managers; Transportation Managers. **PERSONALITY TYPE:** Enterprising.

EDUCATION/TRAINING PROGRAM(S)—No data available. **RELATED KNOWLEDGE/COURSES—Economics and Accounting:** Knowledge of economic and accounting principles and practices, the financial markets, banking, and the analysis and reporting of financial data. **Transportation:** Knowledge of principles and methods for moving people or goods by air, rail, sea, or road, including the relative costs and benefits. **Personnel and Human Resources:** Knowledge of principles and procedures for personnel recruitment, selection, training, compensation and benefits, labor relations and negotiation, and personnel information systems. **Administration and Management:** Knowledge of business and management principles involved in strategic planning, resource allocation, human resources modeling, leadership technique, production methods, and coordination of people and resources. **Production and Processing:** Knowledge of raw materials, production processes, quality control, costs, and other techniques for maximizing the effective manufacture and distribution of goods. **Sales and Marketing:** Knowledge of principles and methods for showing, promoting, and selling products or services. This includes marketing strategy and tactics, product demonstrations, sales techniques, and sales control systems.

Fish Hatchery Managers

◎ Education/Training Required: Work experience in a related occupation
◎ Annual Earnings: $50,700
◎ Growth: 5.1%
◎ Annual Job Openings: 25,000
◎ Self-Employed: 0.9%
◎ Part-Time: 9.2%

Direct and coordinate, through subordinate supervisory personnel, activities of workers engaged in fish hatchery production for corporations, cooperatives, or other owners. Determines, administers, and executes policies relating to administration, standards of hatchery operations, and facility maintenance. Oversees trapping and spawning of fish, egg incubation, and fry rearing, applying knowledge of management and fish culturing techniques. Oversees movement of mature fish to lakes, ponds, streams, or commercial tanks. Collects information regarding techniques for collecting, fertilizing, incubating spawn, and treatment of spawn and fry. Accounts for and dispenses funds. Prepares reports required by state and federal laws. Prepares budget reports. Confers with biologists and other fishery personnel to obtain data concerning fish habits, food, and environmental requirements. Approves employment and discharge of employees, signs payrolls, and performs personnel duties. **SKILLS—Management of Financial Resources:** Determining how money will be spent to get the work done and accounting for these expenditures. **Management of Personnel**

Resources: Motivating, developing, and directing people as they work, identifying the best people for the job. **Management of Material Resources:** Obtaining and seeing to the appropriate use of equipment, facilities, and materials needed to do certain work. **Science:** Using scientific rules and methods to solve problems. **Reading Comprehension:** Understanding written sentences and paragraphs in work-related documents. **Systems Analysis:** Determining how a system should work and how changes in conditions, operations, and the environment will affect outcomes. **Writing:** Communicating effectively in writing as appropriate for the needs of the audience. **Time Management:** Managing one's own time and the time of others. **GOE—Interest Area:** 01. Agriculture and Natural Resources. **Work Group:** 01.01. Managerial Work in Agriculture and Natural Resources. **Other Jobs in This Work Group:** Agricultural Crop Farm Managers; Farmers and Ranchers; First-Line Supervisors and Manager/Supervisors—Agricultural Crop Workers; First-Line Supervisors and Manager/Supervisors—Animal Husbandry Workers; First-Line Supervisors and Manager/Supervisors—Extractive Workers; First-Line Supervisors and Manager/Supervisors—Fishery Workers; First-Line Supervisors and Manager/Supervisors—Horticultural Workers; First-Line Supervisors and Manager/Supervisors—Landscaping Workers; First-Line Supervisors and Manager/Supervisors—Logging Workers; Lawn Service Managers; Nursery and Greenhouse Managers; Park Naturalists; Purchasing Agents and Buyers, Farm Products. **PERSONALITY TYPE:** Enterprising.

EDUCATION/TRAINING PROGRAM(S)— Agribusiness/Agricultural Business Operations; Agricultural Animal Breeding; Agricultural Business and Management, General; Agricultural Business and Management, Other; Agricultural Production Operations, General; Agricultural Production Operations, Other; Animal Nutrition; Animal Sciences, General; Animal/Livestock Husbandry and Production; Farm/Farm and Ranch Management; Livestock Management. **RELATED KNOWLEDGE/COURSES—Food Production:** Knowledge of techniques and equipment for planting, growing, and harvesting food products (both plant and animal) for consumption, including storage/handling techniques. **Administration and Management:** Knowledge of business and management principles involved in strategic planning, resource allocation, human resources modeling, leadership technique, production methods, and coordination of people and resources. **Personnel and Human**

Resources: Knowledge of principles and procedures for personnel recruitment, selection, training, compensation and benefits, labor relations and negotiation, and personnel information systems. **Economics and Accounting:** Knowledge of economic and accounting principles and practices, the financial markets, banking, and the analysis and reporting of financial data. **Biology:** Knowledge of plant and animal organisms and their tissues, cells, functions, interdependencies, and interactions with each other and the environment. **Law and Government:** Knowledge of laws, legal codes, court procedures, precedents, government regulations, executive orders, agency rules, and the democratic political process.

Fitness Trainers and Aerobics Instructors

- Education/Training Required: Postsecondary vocational training
- Annual Earnings: $25,470
- Growth: 44.5%
- Annual Job Openings: 38,000
- Self-Employed: 5.4%
- Part-Time: 35.6%

Instruct or coach groups or individuals in exercise activities and the fundamentals of sports. Demonstrate techniques and methods of participation. Observe participants and inform them of corrective measures necessary to improve their skills. Those required to hold teaching degrees should be reported in the appropriate teaching category. Explain and enforce safety rules and regulations governing sports, recreational activities, and the use of exercise equipment. Offer alternatives during classes to accommodate different levels of fitness. Plan routines, choose appropriate music, and choose different movements for each set of muscles, depending on participants' capabilities and limitations. Observe participants and inform them of corrective measures necessary for skill improvement. Teach proper breathing techniques used during physical exertion. Instruct participants in maintaining exertion levels in order to maximize benefits from exercise routines. Teach and demonstrate use of gymnastic and training equipment such as trampolines and weights. Maintain fitness equipment. Conduct therapeutic, recreational, or athletic activities. Monitor participants' progress and adapt programs as needed. Evaluate individuals' abilities, needs, and physical conditions and develop suitable training programs to meet any special requirements. Plan physical education programs to promote development of participants' physical attributes and social skills. Provide students with information and resources regarding nutrition, weight control, and lifestyle issues. Administer emergency first aid, wrap injuries, treat minor chronic disabilities, or refer injured persons to physicians. Advise clients about proper clothing and shoes. Wrap ankles, fingers, wrists, or other body parts with synthetic skin, gauze, or adhesive tape in order to support muscles and ligaments. Teach individual and team sports to participants through instruction and demonstration, utilizing knowledge of sports techniques and of participants' physical capabilities. Promote health clubs through membership sales and record member information. Organize, lead, and referee indoor and outdoor games such as volleyball, baseball, and basketball. Maintain equipment inventories and select, store, and issue equipment as needed. Organize and conduct competitions and tournaments. Advise participants in use of heat or ultraviolet treatments and hot baths. Massage body parts to relieve soreness, strains, and bruises. **SKILLS—Instructing:** Teaching others how to do something. **Service Orientation:** Actively looking for ways to help people. **Coordination:** Adjusting actions in relation to others' actions. **Monitoring:** Monitoring or assessing your performance or that of other individuals or organizations to make improvements or take corrective action. **Equipment Selection:** Determining the kind of tools and equipment needed to do a job. **Social Perceptiveness:** Being aware of others' reactions and understanding why they react as they do. **Learning Strategies:** Selecting and using training/instructional methods and procedures appropriate for the situation when learning or teaching new things. **Time Management:** Managing one's own time and the time of others. **GOE—Interest Area:** 05. Education and Training. **Work Group:** 05.06. Counseling, Health, and Fitness Education. **Other Jobs in This Work Group:** Educational, Vocational, and School Counselors; Health Educators. **PERSONALITY TYPE:** Social.

EDUCATION/TRAINING PROGRAM(S)— Health and Physical Education, General; Physical Education Teaching and Coaching; Sport and Fitness Administration/Management. **RELATED KNOWLEDGE/COURSES—Customer and Personal Ser-**

vice: Knowledge of principles and processes for providing customer and personal services. This includes customer needs assessment, meeting quality standards for services, and evaluation of customer satisfaction. **Psychology:** Knowledge of human behavior and performance; individual differences in ability, personality, and interests; learning and motivation; psychological research methods; and the assessment and treatment of behavioral and affective disorders. **Medicine and Dentistry:** Knowledge of the information and techniques needed to diagnose and treat human injuries, diseases, and deformities. This includes symptoms, treatment alternatives, drug properties and interactions, and preventive health-care measures. **Education and Training:** Knowledge of principles and methods for curriculum and training design, teaching and instruction for individuals and groups, and the measurement of training effects. **Sociology and Anthropology:** Knowledge of group behavior and dynamics, societal trends and influences, human migrations, ethnicity, and cultures and their history and origins. **Fine Arts:** Knowledge of the theory and techniques required to compose, produce, and perform works of music, dance, the visual arts, drama, and sculpture.

Flight Attendants

- ◎ Education/Training Required: Long-term on-the-job training
- ◎ Annual Earnings: $43,440
- ◎ Growth: 15.9%
- ◎ Annual Job Openings: 23,000
- ◎ Self-Employed: 0%
- ◎ Part-Time: 29.9%

Provide personal services to ensure the safety and comfort of airline passengers during flight. Greet passengers, verify tickets, explain use of safety equipment, and serve food or beverages. Administer first aid to passengers in distress. Inspect and clean cabins, checking for any problems and making sure that cabins are in order. Inspect passenger tickets to verify information and to obtain destination information. Operate audio and video systems. Prepare reports showing places of departure and destination, passenger ticket numbers, meal and beverage inventories, the conditions of cabin equipment, and any problems encountered by passengers. Reassure passengers when situations such as turbulence are encountered. Verify that first aid kits and other emergency equipment, including fire extinguishers and oxygen bottles, are in working order. Announce and demonstrate safety and emergency procedures such as the use of oxygen masks, seat belts, and life jackets. Answer passengers' questions about flights, aircraft, weather, travel routes and services, arrival times, and/or schedules. Assist passengers in placing carry-on luggage in overhead, garment, or under-seat storage. Assist passengers while entering or disembarking the aircraft. Attend preflight briefings concerning weather, altitudes, routes, emergency procedures, crew coordination, lengths of flights, food and beverage services offered, and numbers of passengers. Check to ensure that food, beverages, blankets, reading material, emergency equipment, and other supplies are aboard and are in adequate supply. Collect money for meals and beverages. Conduct periodic trips through the cabin to ensure passenger comfort and to distribute reading material, headphones, pillows, playing cards, and blankets. Determine special assistance needs of passengers such as small children, the elderly, or disabled persons. Direct and assist passengers in the event of an emergency, such as directing passengers to evacuate a plane following an emergency landing. Prepare passengers and aircraft for landing, following procedures. Greet passengers boarding aircraft and direct them to assigned seats. Heat and serve prepared foods. Announce flight delays and descent preparations. Sell alcoholic beverages to passengers. Take inventory of headsets, alcoholic beverages, and money collected. **SKILLS—Service Orientation:** Actively looking for ways to help people. **Social Perceptiveness:** Being aware of others' reactions and understanding why they react as they do. **GOE—Interest Area:** 09. Hospitality, Tourism, and Recreation. **Work Group:** 09.03. Hospitality and Travel Services. **Other Jobs in This Work Group:** Baggage Porters and Bellhops; Concierges; Hotel, Motel, and Resort Desk Clerks; Janitors and Cleaners, Except Maids and Housekeeping Cleaners; Maids and Housekeeping Cleaners; Reservation and Transportation Ticket Agents; Tour Guides and Escorts; Transportation Attendants, Except Flight Attendants and Baggage Porters; Travel Agents; Travel Clerks; Travel Guides. **PERSONALITY TYPE:** Enterprising.

EDUCATION/TRAINING PROGRAM(S)—Airline Flight Attendant. **RELATED KNOWLEDGE/ COURSES—Customer and Personal Service:** Knowledge of principles and processes for providing customer and personal services. This includes customer needs assessment, meeting quality standards for services, and evaluation of customer satisfaction. **Medicine and Dentistry:** Knowledge of the information and techniques needed to diagnose and treat human injuries, diseases, and deformities. This includes symptoms, treatment alternatives, drug properties and interactions, and preventive health-care measures. **Transportation:** Knowledge of principles and methods for moving people or goods by air, rail, sea, or road, including the relative costs and benefits. **Geography:** Knowledge of principles and methods for describing the features of land, sea, and air masses, including their physical characteristics; locations; interrelationships; and distribution of plant, animal, and human life. **Public Safety and Security:** Knowledge of relevant equipment, policies, procedures, and strategies to promote effective local, state, or national security operations for the protection of people, data, property, and institutions. **Psychology:** Knowledge of human behavior and performance; individual differences in ability, personality, and interests; learning and motivation; psychological research methods; and the assessment and treatment of behavioral and affective disorders.

Food Preparation Workers

- ◎ Education/Training Required: Short-term on-the-job training
- ◎ Annual Earnings: $16,710
- ◎ Growth: 20.2%
- ◎ Annual Job Openings: 267,000
- ◎ Self-Employed: 0.6%
- ◎ Part-Time: 41.9%

Perform a variety of food preparation duties other than cooking, such as preparing cold foods and shellfish, slicing meat, and brewing coffee or tea. Clean work areas, equipment, utensils, dishes, and silverware. Store food in designated containers and storage areas to prevent spoilage. Prepare a variety of foods according to customers' orders or supervisors' instructions, following approved procedures. Package take-out foods and/or serve food to customers. Portion and wrap the food or place it directly on plates for service to patrons. Place food trays over food warmers for immediate service or store them in refrigerated storage cabinets. Inform supervisors when supplies are getting low or equipment is not working properly. Weigh or measure ingredients. Assist cooks and kitchen staff with various tasks as needed and provide cooks with needed items. Wash, peel, and/or cut various foods to prepare for cooking or serving. Receive and store food supplies, equipment, and utensils in refrigerators, cupboards, and other storage areas. Stock cupboards and refrigerators and tend salad bars and buffet meals. Remove trash and clean kitchen garbage containers. Prepare and serve a variety of beverages such as coffee, tea, and soft drinks. Carry food supplies, equipment, and utensils to and from storage and work areas. Make special dressings and sauces as condiments for sandwiches. Scrape leftovers from dishes into garbage containers. Use manual and/or electric appliances to clean, peel, slice, and trim foods. Stir and strain soups and sauces. Distribute food to waiters and waitresses to serve to customers. Keep records of the quantities of food used. Load dishes, glasses, and tableware into dishwashing machines. Butcher and clean fowl, fish, poultry, and shellfish to prepare for cooking or serving. Cut, slice, and/or grind meat, poultry, and seafood to prepare for cooking. Work on assembly lines, adding cutlery, napkins, food, and other items to trays in hospitals, cafeterias, airline kitchens, and similar establishments. Mix ingredients for green salads, molded fruit salads, vegetable salads, and pasta salads. Distribute menus to hospital patients, collect diet sheets, and deliver food trays and snacks to nursing units or directly to patients. **SKILLS—Management of Personnel Resources:** Motivating, developing, and directing people as they work, identifying the best people for the job. **Service Orientation:** Actively looking for ways to help people. **Instructing:** Teaching others how to do something. **Social Perceptiveness:** Being aware of others' reactions and understanding why they react as they do. **Learning Strategies:** Selecting and using training/instructional methods and procedures appropriate for the situation when learning or teaching new things. **Negotiation:** Bringing others together and trying to reconcile differences. **Persuasion:** Persuading others to change their minds or behavior. **Operation Monitoring:** Watching gauges, dials, or other indicators to make sure a machine is working properly. **Equipment Maintenance:** Performing routine maintenance on equipment and determining when and what kind of maintenance is needed. **GOE—Interest Area:** 09. Hospitality, Tourism, and Recreation. **Work Group:** 09.04. Food and Beverage Preparation. **Other Jobs in This Work Group:** Bakers, Bread and Pastry; Butchers and Meat Cutters; Chefs and Head Cooks; Cooks, Fast Food; Cooks, Institution and Cafeteria; Cooks,

Restaurant; Cooks, Short Order; Dishwashers. **PERSONALITY TYPE:** Realistic.

EDUCATION/TRAINING PROGRAM(S)— Cooking and Related Culinary Arts, General; Food Preparation/Professional Cooking/Kitchen Assistant; Institutional Food Workers. **RELATED KNOWLEDGE/COURSES—Food Production:** Knowledge of techniques and equipment for planting, growing, and harvesting food products (both plant and animal) for consumption, including storage/handling techniques. **Customer and Personal Service:** Knowledge of principles and processes for providing customer and personal services. This includes customer needs assessment, meeting quality standards for services, and evaluation of customer satisfaction. **Production and Processing:** Knowledge of raw materials, production processes, quality control, costs, and other techniques for maximizing the effective manufacture and distribution of goods. **Administration and Management:** Knowledge of business and management principles involved in strategic planning, resource allocation, human resources modeling, leadership technique, production methods, and coordination of people and resources. **Sales and Marketing:** Knowledge of principles and methods for showing, promoting, and selling products or services. This includes marketing strategy and tactics, product demonstrations, sales techniques, and sales control systems. **Economics and Accounting:** Knowledge of economic and accounting principles and practices, the financial markets, banking, and the analysis and reporting of financial data. **Public Safety and Security:** Knowledge of relevant equipment, policies, procedures, and strategies to promote effective local, state, or national security operations for the protection of people, data, property, and institutions.

Food Scientists and Technologists

- Education/Training Required: Bachelor's degree
- Annual Earnings: $50,840
- Growth: 9.1%
- Annual Job Openings: 2,000
- Self-Employed: 8.9%
- Part-Time: 7.0%

Use chemistry, microbiology, engineering, and other sciences to study the principles underlying the processing and deterioration of foods; analyze food content to determine levels of vitamins, fat, sugar, and protein; discover new food sources; research ways to make processed foods safe, palatable, and healthful; and apply food science knowledge to determine best ways to process, package, preserve, store, and distribute food. Study methods to improve aspects of foods such as chemical composition, flavor, color, texture, nutritional value, and convenience. Study the structure and composition of food or the changes foods undergo in storage and processing. Test new products for flavor, texture, color, nutritional content, and adherence to government and industry standards. Confer with process engineers, plant operators, flavor experts, and packaging and marketing specialists in order to resolve problems in product development. Evaluate food processing and storage operations and assist in the development of quality assurance programs for such operations. Inspect food processing areas in order to ensure compliance with government regulations and standards for sanitation, safety, quality, and waste management standards. Demonstrate products to clients. Check raw ingredients for maturity or stability for processing and finished products for safety, quality, and nutritional value. Develop food standards and production specifications, safety and sanitary regulations, and waste management and water supply specifications. Develop new or improved ways of preserving, processing, packaging, storing, and delivering foods, using knowledge of chemistry, microbiology, and other sciences. Search for substitutes for harmful or undesirable additives, such as nitrites. **SKILLS—Science:** Using scientific rules and methods to solve problems. **Active Learning:** Understanding the implications of new information for both current and future problem-solving and decision-making. **Quality Control Analysis:** Conducting tests and inspections of products, services, or processes to evaluate quality or performance. **Systems Analysis:** Determining how a system should work and how changes in conditions, operations, and the environment will affect outcomes. **Operations Analysis:** Analyzing needs and product requirements to create a design. **Systems Evaluation:** Identifying measures or indicators of system performance and the actions needed to improve or correct performance relative to the goals of the system. **Judgment and Decision Making:** Considering the relative costs and benefits of potential actions to choose the most appropriate one. **Complex Problem Solving:** Identifying complex problems and reviewing related information to develop and evaluate options and implement solutions. **GOE— Interest Area:** 01. Agriculture and Natural Resources. **Work Group:** 01.03. Resource Technologies for Plants, Animals, and the Environment. **Other Jobs in This Work Group:** Agricultural Technicians; Environmental Science and Protection Technicians, Including Health; Food Science Technicians; Geological Data Technicians; Geological Sample Test Technicians. **PERSONALITY TYPE:** Investigative.

EDUCATION/TRAINING PROGRAM(S)—Agriculture, General; Food Science; Food Technology and Processing; International Agriculture. **RELATED KNOWLEDGE/COURSES—Food Production:** Knowledge of techniques and equipment for planting, growing, and harvesting food products (both plant and animal) for consumption, including storage/handling techniques. **Production and Processing:** Knowledge of raw materials, production processes, quality control, costs, and other techniques for maximizing the effective manufacture and distribution of goods. **Chemistry:** Knowledge of the chemical composition, structure, and properties of substances and of the chemical processes and transformations that they undergo. This includes uses of chemicals and their danger signs, production techniques, and disposal methods. **Biology:** Knowledge of plant and animal organisms and their tissues, cells, functions, interdependencies, and interactions with each other and the environment. **Law and Government:** Knowledge of laws, legal codes, court procedures, precedents, government regulations, executive orders, agency rules, and the democratic political process. **Administration and Management:** Knowledge of business and management principles involved in strategic planning, resource allocation, human resources modeling, leadership technique, production methods, and coordination of people and resources.

Food Service Managers

- ◎ Education/Training Required: Work experience in a related occupation
- ◎ Annual Earnings: $39,610
- ◎ Growth: 11.5%
- ◎ Annual Job Openings: 58,000
- ◎ Self-Employed: 34.7%
- ◎ Part-Time: 8.6%

Plan, direct, or coordinate activities of an organization or department that serves food and beverages. Test cooked food by tasting and smelling it in order to ensure palatability and flavor conformity. Investigate and resolve complaints regarding food quality, service, or accommodations. Schedule and receive food and beverage deliveries, checking delivery contents in order to verify product quality and quantity. Monitor food preparation methods, portion sizes, and garnishing and presentation of food in order to ensure that food is prepared and presented in an acceptable manner. Monitor budgets and payroll records and review financial transactions in order to ensure that expenditures are authorized and budgeted. Schedule staff hours and assign duties. Monitor compliance with health and fire regulations regarding food preparation and serving and building maintenance in lodging and dining facilities. Coordinate assignments of cooking personnel in order to ensure economical use of food and timely preparation. Keep records required by government agencies regarding sanitation and food subsidies when appropriate. Establish standards for personnel performance and customer service. Estimate food, liquor, wine, and other beverage consumption in order to anticipate amounts to be purchased or requisitioned. Review work procedures and operational problems in order to determine ways to improve service, performance, and/or safety. Perform some food preparation or service tasks such as cooking, clearing tables, and serving food and drinks when necessary. Maintain food and equipment inventories and keep inventory records. Organize and direct worker training programs, resolve personnel problems, hire new staff, and evaluate employee performance in dining and lodging facilities. Order and purchase equipment and supplies. Review menus and analyze recipes in order to determine labor and overhead costs and assign prices to menu items. Record the number, type, and cost of items sold in order to determine which items may be unpopular or less profitable. Assess staffing needs and recruit staff, using methods such as newspaper advertisements or attendance at job fairs. Arrange for equipment maintenance and repairs and coordinate a variety of services such as waste removal and pest control. **SKILLS— Management of Personnel Resources:** Motivating, developing, and directing people as they work, identifying the best people for the job. **Management of Financial Resources:** Determining how money will be spent to get the work done and accounting for these expenditures. **Time Management:** Managing one's own time and the time of others. **Learning Strategies:**

Selecting and using training/instructional methods and procedures appropriate for the situation when learning or teaching new things. **Monitoring:** Monitoring or assessing your performance or that of other individuals or organizations to make improvements or take corrective action. **Instructing:** Teaching others how to do something. **Service Orientation:** Actively looking for ways to help people. **Management of Material Resources:** Obtaining and seeing to the appropriate use of equipment, facilities, and materials needed to do certain work. **GOE—Interest Area:** 09. Hospitality, Tourism, and Recreation. **Work Group:** 09.01. Managerial Work in Hospitality and Tourism. **Other Jobs in This Work Group:** First-Line Supervisors/Managers of Food Preparation and Serving Workers; First-Line Supervisors/Managers of Personal Service Workers; Gaming Managers; Gaming Supervisors; Lodging Managers. **PERSONALITY TYPE:** Enterprising.

EDUCATION/TRAINING PROGRAM(S)—Hospitality Administration/Management, General; Hotel/Motel Administration/Management; Restaurant, Culinary, and Catering Management/Manager; Restaurant/Food Services Management. **RELATED KNOWLEDGE/COURSES—Customer and Personal Service:** Knowledge of principles and processes for providing customer and personal services. This includes customer needs assessment, meeting quality standards for services, and evaluation of customer satisfaction. **Food Production:** Knowledge of techniques and equipment for planting, growing, and harvesting food products (both plant and animal) for consumption, including storage/handling techniques. **Sales and Marketing:** Knowledge of principles and methods for showing, promoting, and selling products or services. This includes marketing strategy and tactics, product demonstrations, sales techniques, and sales control systems. **Production and Processing:** Knowledge of raw materials, production processes, quality control, costs, and other techniques for maximizing the effective manufacture and distribution of goods. **Administration and Management:** Knowledge of business and management principles involved in strategic planning, resource allocation, human resources modeling, leadership technique, production methods, and coordination of people and resources. **Personnel and Human Resources:** Knowledge of principles and procedures for personnel recruitment, selection, training, compensation and benefits, labor relations and negotiation, and personnel information systems.

Foreign Language and Literature Teachers, Postsecondary

- Education/Training Required: Master's degree
- Annual Earnings: $47,600
- Growth: 38.1%
- Annual Job Openings: 216,000
- Self-Employed: 0.3%
- Part-Time: 27.7%

Teach courses in foreign (i.e., other than English) languages and literature. Evaluate and grade students' class work, assignments, and papers. Prepare course materials such as syllabi, homework assignments, and handouts. Initiate, facilitate, and moderate classroom discussions. Maintain student attendance records, grades, and other required records. Compile, administer, and grade examinations or assign this work to others. Plan, evaluate, and revise curricula, course content, and course materials and methods of instruction. Prepare and deliver lectures to undergraduate and/or graduate students on topics such as how to speak and write a foreign language and the cultural aspects of areas where a particular language is used. Maintain regularly scheduled office hours in order to advise and assist students. Select and obtain materials and supplies such as textbooks. Keep abreast of developments in their field by reading current literature, talking with colleagues, and participating in professional organizations and activities. Advise students on academic and vocational curricula and on career issues. Conduct research in a particular field of knowledge and publish findings in scholarly journals, books, and/or electronic media. Collaborate with colleagues to address teaching and research issues. Serve on academic or administrative committees that deal with institutional policies, departmental matters, and academic issues. Participate in student recruitment, registration, and placement activities. Compile bibliographies of specialized materials for outside reading assignments. Participate in campus and community events. Act as advisers to student organizations. Perform administrative duties such as serving as department head. Supervise undergraduate and/or graduate teaching, internship, and research work. **SKILLS—Instructing:** Teaching others how to do something. **Learning Strategies:** Selecting and using training/instructional methods and procedures appropriate for the situation when learning or teaching new things. **Social Perceptiveness:** Being aware of others' reactions and understanding why they react as they do. **Persuasion:** Persuading others to change their minds or behavior. **Writing:** Communicating effectively in writing as appropriate for the needs of the audience. **Speaking:** Talking to others to convey information effectively. **Reading Comprehension:** Understanding written sentences and paragraphs in work-related documents. **Critical Thinking:** Using logic and reasoning to identify the strengths and weaknesses of alternative solutions, conclusions, or approaches to problems. **GOE—Interest Area:** 05. Education and Training. **Work Group:** 05.03. Postsecondary and Adult Teaching and Instructing. **Other Jobs in This Work Group:** Adult Literacy, Remedial Education, and GED Teachers and Instructors; Agricultural Sciences Teachers, Postsecondary; Anthropology and Archeology Teachers, Postsecondary; Architecture Teachers, Postsecondary; Area, Ethnic, and Cultural Studies Teachers, Postsecondary; Art, Drama, and Music Teachers, Postsecondary; Atmospheric, Earth, Marine, and Space Sciences Teachers, Postsecondary; Biological Science Teachers, Postsecondary; Business Teachers, Postsecondary; Chemistry Teachers, Postsecondary; Communications Teachers, Postsecondary; Computer Science Teachers, Postsecondary; Criminal Justice and Law Enforcement Teachers, Postsecondary; Economics Teachers, Postsecondary; Education Teachers, Postsecondary; Engineering Teachers, Postsecondary; English Language and Literature Teachers, Postsecondary; Environmental Science Teachers, Postsecondary; Farm and Home Management Advisors; Forestry and Conservation Science Teachers, Postsecondary; Geography Teachers, Postsecondary; Graduate Teaching Assistants; Health Specialties Teachers, Postsecondary; History Teachers, Postsecondary; Home Economics Teachers, Postsecondary; Law Teachers, Postsecondary; Library Science Teachers, Postsecondary; Mathematical Science Teachers, Postsecondary; Nursing Instructors and Teachers, Postsecondary; Philosophy and Religion Teachers, Postsecondary; Physics Teachers, Postsecondary; Political Science Teachers, Postsecondary; Psychology Teachers, Postsecondary; Recreation and Fitness Studies Teachers, Postsecondary; Self-Enrichment Education Teachers; Social Work Teachers, Postsecondary; Sociology Teachers, Postsecondary; Vocational Education Teachers, Postsecondary. **PERSONALITY TYPE:** Artistic.

EDUCATION/TRAINING PROGRAM(S)— African Languages, Literatures, and Linguistics; Albanian Language and Literature; American Indian/Native American Languages, Literatures, and Linguistics; Ancient Near Eastern and Biblical Languages, Literatures, and Linguistics; Ancient/Classical Greek Language and Literature; Arabic Language and Literature; Australian/Oceanic/Pacific Languages, Literatures, and Linguistics; Bahasa Indonesian/Bahasa Malay Languages and Literatures; Baltic Languages, Literatures, and Linguistics; Bengali Language and Literature; Bulgarian Language and Literature; Burmese Language and Literature; Catalan Language and Literature; Celtic Languages, Literatures, and Linguistics; Chinese Language and Literature; Classics and Classical Languages, Literatures, and Linguistics, General; Classics and Classical Languages, Literatures, and Linguistics, Other; Czech Language and Literature; Danish Language and Literature; Dutch/Flemish Language and Literature; East Asian Languages, Literatures, and Linguistics, General; East Asian Languages, Literatures, and Linguistics, Other; Filipino/Tagalog Language and Literature; Finnish and Related Languages, Literatures, and Linguistics; Foreign Languages and Literatures, General; Foreign Languages, Literatures, and Linguistics, Other; French Language and Literature; German Language and Literature; Germanic Languages, Literatures, and Linguistics, General; Germanic Languages, Literatures, and Linguistics, Other; Hebrew Language and Literature; Hindi Language and Literature; Hungarian/Magyar Language and Literature; Iranian/Persian Languages, Literatures, and Linguistics; Italian Language and Literature; Japanese Language and Literature; Khmer/Cambodian Language and Literature; Korean Language and Literature; Language Interpretation and Translation; Lao/Laotian Language and Literature; Latin Language and Literature; Latin Teacher Education; Linguistics; Middle/Near Eastern and Semitic Languages, Literatures, and Linguistics, Other; others. **RELATED KNOWLEDGE/COURSES—Foreign Language:** Knowledge of the structure and content of a foreign (non-English) language, including the meaning and spelling of words, rules of composition and grammar, and pronunciation. **Philosophy and Theology:** Knowledge of different philosophical systems and religions. This includes their basic principles, values, ethics, ways of thinking, customs, and practices and their impact on human culture. **History and Archeology:** Knowledge of historical events and their causes, indicators, and effects on civilizations and cultures. **English Language:** Knowledge of the structure and content of the English language, including the meaning and spelling of words, rules of composition, and grammar. **Sociology and Anthropology:** Knowledge of group behavior and dynamics, societal trends and influences, human migrations, ethnicity, and cultures and their history and origins. **Education and Training:** Knowledge of principles and methods for curriculum and training design, teaching and instruction for individuals and groups, and the measurement of training effects.

Forensic Science Technicians

- Education/Training Required: Associate degree
- Annual Earnings: $44,010
- Growth: 18.9%
- Annual Job Openings: 1,000
- Self-Employed: 1.0%
- Part-Time: 20.2%

Collect, identify, classify, and analyze physical evidence related to criminal investigations. Perform tests on weapons or substances such as fiber, hair, and tissue to determine significance to investigation. May testify as expert witnesses on evidence or crime laboratory techniques. May serve as specialists in area of expertise, such as ballistics, fingerprinting, handwriting, or biochemistry. Testify in court about investigative and analytical methods and findings. Keep records and prepare reports detailing findings, investigative methods, and laboratory techniques. Interpret laboratory findings and test results in order to identify and classify substances, materials, and other evidence collected at crime scenes. Operate and maintain laboratory equipment and apparatus. Prepare solutions, reagents, and sample formulations needed for laboratory work. Analyze and classify biological fluids, using DNA typing or serological techniques. Collect evidence from crime scenes, storing it in conditions that preserve its integrity. Identify and quantify drugs and poisons found in biological fluids and tissues, in foods, and at crime scenes. Analyze handwritten and machine-produced textual evidence to decipher altered or obliterated text or to determine authorship, age, and/or source. Reconstruct crime scenes in order to determine relationships among pieces of evidence. Examine DNA samples to determine if they match other samples. Collect impressions of dust from surfaces in order to obtain and identify fingerprints. Analyze gunshot residue and bullet paths in order to determine how shootings occurred. Visit morgues, examine scenes of crimes, or contact other sources in order to obtain evidence or information to be used in investigations. Examine physical evidence such as hair, fiber, wood, or soil residues in order to obtain information about its source and composition. Determine types of bullets used in shooting and if they were fired from a specific weapon. Examine firearms in order to determine mechanical condition and legal status, performing restoration work on damaged firearms in order to obtain information such as serial numbers. Interpret the pharmacological effects of a drug or a combination of drugs on an individual. Confer with ballistics, fingerprinting, handwriting, documents, electronics, medical, chemical, or metallurgical experts concerning evidence and its interpretation. Compare objects such as tools with impression marks in order to determine whether a specific object is responsible for a specific mark. **SKILLS—Science:** Using scientific rules and methods to solve problems. **Quality Control Analysis:** Conducting tests and inspections of products, services, or processes to evaluate quality or performance. **Troubleshooting:** Determining causes of operating errors and deciding what to do about them. **Active Learning:** Understanding the implications of new information for both current and future problem-solving and decision-making. **Instructing:** Teaching others how to do something. **Speaking:** Talking to others to convey information effectively. **Reading Comprehension:** Understanding written sentences and paragraphs in work-related documents. **Critical Thinking:** Using logic and reasoning to identify the strengths and weaknesses of alternative solutions, conclusions, or approaches to problems. **GOE—Interest Area:** 12. Law and Public Safety. **Work Group:** 12.04. Law Enforcement and Public Safety. **Other Jobs in This Work Group:** Bailiffs; Correctional Officers and Jailers; Criminal Investigators and Special Agents; Fire Investigators; Highway Patrol Pilots; Parking Enforcement Workers; Police Detectives; Police Identification and Records Officers; Police Patrol Officers; Sheriffs and Deputy Sheriffs; Transit and Railroad Police. **PERSONALITY TYPE:** Investigative.

EDUCATION/TRAINING PROGRAM(S)—Forensic Science and Technology. **RELATED KNOWLEDGE/COURSES—Chemistry:** Knowledge of the chemical composition, structure, and properties of substances and of the chemical processes and transformations that they undergo. This includes uses of chemicals and their danger signs, production techniques, and disposal methods. **Law and Government:** Knowledge of laws, legal codes, court procedures, precedents, government regulations, executive orders, agency rules, and the democratic political process. **Customer and Personal Service:** Knowledge of principles and processes for providing customer and personal services. This includes customer needs assessment, meeting quality standards for services, and evaluation of customer satisfaction. **Public Safety and Security:** Knowledge of relevant equipment, policies, procedures, and strategies to promote effective local, state, or national security operations for the protection of people, data, property, and institutions. **English Language:** Knowledge of the structure and content of the English language, including the meaning and spelling of words, rules of composition, and grammar. **Biology:** Knowledge of plant and animal organisms and their tissues, cells, functions, interdependencies, and interactions with each other and the environment.

Forest Fire Fighters

- ◉ Education/Training Required: Long-term on-the-job training
- ◉ Annual Earnings: $38,330
- ◉ Growth: 20.7%
- ◉ Annual Job Openings: 29,000
- ◉ Self-Employed: 0%
- ◉ Part-Time: 1.1%

Control and suppress fires in forests or vacant public land. Maintain contact with fire dispatchers at all times in order to notify them of the need for additional fire fighters and supplies or to detail any difficulties encountered. Rescue fire victims and administer emergency medical aid. Collaborate with other fire fighters as a member of a firefighting crew. Patrol burned areas after fires to locate and eliminate hot spots that may restart fires. Extinguish flames and embers to suppress fires, using shovels or engine- or hand-driven water or chemical pumps. Fell trees, cut and clear brush, and dig trenches in order to create firelines, using axes,

chain saws, or shovels. Maintain knowledge of current firefighting practices by participating in drills and by attending seminars, conventions, and conferences. Operate pumps connected to high-pressure hoses. Participate in physical training in order to maintain high levels of physical fitness. Establish water supplies, connect hoses, and direct water onto fires. Maintain fire equipment and firehouse living quarters. Inform and educate the public about fire prevention. Take action to contain any hazardous chemicals that could catch fire, leak, or spill. Organize fire caches, positioning equipment for the most effective response. Transport personnel and cargo to and from fire areas. Participate in fire prevention and inspection programs. Perform forest maintenance and improvement tasks such as cutting brush, planting trees, building trails, and marking timber. Test and maintain tools, equipment, jump gear, and parachutes in order to ensure readiness for fire-suppression activities. Observe forest areas from fire lookout towers in order to spot potential problems. Orient self in relation to fire, using compass and map, and collect supplies and equipment dropped by parachute. Serve as fully trained lead helicopter crew member and as helispot manager. Drop weighted paper streamers from aircraft to determine the speed and direction of the wind at fire sites. **SKILLS—Management of Personnel Resources:** Motivating, developing, and directing people as they work, identifying the best people for the job. **Service Orientation:** Actively looking for ways to help people. **Equipment Maintenance:** Performing routine maintenance on equipment and determining when and what kind of maintenance is needed. **Repairing:** Repairing machines or systems by using the needed tools. **Coordination:** Adjusting actions in relation to others' actions. **Operation Monitoring:** Watching gauges, dials, or other indicators to make sure a machine is working properly. **Equipment Selection:** Determining the kind of tools and equipment needed to do a job. **Systems Analysis:** Determining how a system should work and how changes in conditions, operations, and the environment will affect outcomes. **GOE—Interest Area:** 12. Law and Public Safety. **Work Group:** 12.06. Emergency Responding. **Other Jobs in This Work Group:** Emergency Medical Technicians and Paramedics; Municipal Fire Fighters. **PERSONALITY TYPE:** Realistic.

EDUCATION/TRAINING PROGRAM(S)—Fire Protection, Other; Fire Science/Firefighting. **RELATED KNOWLEDGE/COURSES—Customer and**

Personal Service: Knowledge of principles and processes for providing customer and personal services. This includes customer needs assessment, meeting quality standards for services, and evaluation of customer satisfaction. **Geography:** Knowledge of principles and methods for describing the features of land, sea, and air masses, including their physical characteristics; locations; interrelationships; and distribution of plant, animal, and human life. **Education and Training:** Knowledge of principles and methods for curriculum and training design, teaching and instruction for individuals and groups, and the measurement of training effects. **Mechanical Devices:** Knowledge of machines and tools, including their designs, uses, repair, and maintenance. **Public Safety and Security:** Knowledge of relevant equipment, policies, procedures, and strategies to promote effective local, state, or national security operations for the protection of people, data, property, and institutions. **Psychology:** Knowledge of human behavior and performance; individual differences in ability, personality, and interests; learning and motivation; psychological research methods; and the assessment and treatment of behavioral and affective disorders.

Forest Fire Fighting and Prevention Supervisors

- Education/Training Required: Work experience in a related occupation
- Annual Earnings: $58,920
- Growth: 18.7%
- Annual Job Openings: 8,000
- Self-Employed: 0%
- Part-Time: 0.1%

Supervise fire fighters who control and suppress fires in forests or vacant public land. Communicate fire details to superiors, subordinates, and interagency dispatch centers, using two-way radios. Direct investigations of suspected arsons in wildfires, working closely with other investigating agencies. Direct the loading of fire suppression equipment into aircraft and the parachuting of equipment to crews on the ground. Evaluate size, location, and condition of forest fires in order to request and dispatch crews and position equipment so fires can be contained safely and effectively. Identify staff training and development needs in order to ensure that appropriate training can be arranged. Maintain fire suppression equipment in good condition, checking equipment periodically in order to ensure that it is ready for use. Maintain knowledge of forest fire laws and fire prevention techniques and tactics. Monitor prescribed burns to ensure that they are conducted safely and effectively. Observe fires and crews from air to determine firefighting force requirements and to note changing conditions that will affect firefighting efforts. Operate wildland fire engines and hoselays. Perform administrative duties such as compiling and maintaining records, completing forms, preparing reports, and composing correspondence. Recruit and hire forest fire—fighting personnel. Review and evaluate employee performance. Schedule employee work assignments and set work priorities. Serve as working leader of an engine, hand, helicopter, or prescribed fire crew of three or more fire fighters. Train workers in such skills as parachute jumping, fire suppression, aerial observation, and radio communication both in the classroom and on the job. Appraise damage caused by fires in order to prepare damage reports. Direct and supervise prescribed burn projects and prepare post-burn reports analyzing burn conditions and results. Drive crew carriers in order to transport fire fighters to fire sites. Educate the public about forest fire prevention by participating in activities such as exhibits and presentations and by distributing promotional materials. Inspect all stations, uniforms, equipment, and recreation areas in order to ensure compliance with safety standards, taking corrective action as necessary. **SKILLS—Management of Personnel Resources:** Motivating, developing, and directing people as they work, identifying the best people for the job. **Management of Material Resources:** Obtaining and seeing to the appropriate use of equipment, facilities, and materials needed to do certain work. **Systems Analysis:** Determining how a system should work and how changes in conditions, operations, and the environment will affect outcomes. **Systems Evaluation:** Identifying measures or indicators of system performance and the actions needed to improve or correct performance relative to the goals of the system. **Service Orientation:** Actively looking for ways to help people. **Coordination:** Adjusting actions in relation to others' actions. **Instructing:** Teaching others how to do something. **Judgment and Decision Making:** Considering the relative costs and benefits of potential actions to choose the most appropriate one. **GOE—Interest Area:** 12. Law and Public Safety. **Work Group:** 12.01. Managerial Work in Law and Public Safety. **Other Jobs**

in This Work Group: Emergency Management Specialists; First-Line Supervisors/Managers of Correctional Officers; First-Line Supervisors/Managers of Police and Detectives; Municipal Fire Fighting and Prevention Supervisors. **PERSONALITY TYPE:** Realistic.

EDUCATION/TRAINING PROGRAM(S)—Fire Protection and Safety Technology/Technician; Fire Services Administration. **RELATED KNOWLEDGE/COURSES**—**Public Safety and Security:** Knowledge of relevant equipment, policies, procedures, and strategies to promote effective local, state, or national security operations for the protection of people, data, property, and institutions. **Transportation:** Knowledge of principles and methods for moving people or goods by air, rail, sea, or road, including the relative costs and benefits. **Education and Training:** Knowledge of principles and methods for curriculum and training design, teaching and instruction for individuals and groups, and the measurement of training effects. **Administration and Management:** Knowledge of business and management principles involved in strategic planning, resource allocation, human resources modeling, leadership technique, production methods, and coordination of people and resources. **Geography:** Knowledge of principles and methods for describing the features of land, sea, and air masses, including their physical characteristics; locations; interrelationships; and distribution of plant, animal, and human life. **Chemistry:** Knowledge of the chemical composition, structure, and properties of substances and of the chemical processes and transformations that they undergo. This includes uses of chemicals and their danger signs, production techniques, and disposal methods.

Forestry and Conservation Science Teachers, Postsecondary

- Education/Training Required: Master's degree
- Annual Earnings: $65,530
- Growth: 38.1%
- Annual Job Openings: 216,000
- Self-Employed: 0.3%
- Part-Time: 27.7%

Teach courses in environmental and conservation science. Conduct research in a particular field of knowledge and publish findings in books, professional journals, and/or electronic media. Keep abreast of developments in their field by reading current literature, talking with colleagues, and participating in professional conferences. Prepare and deliver lectures to undergraduate and/or graduate students on topics such as forest resource policy, forest pathology, and mapping. Evaluate and grade students' class work, assignments, and papers. Write grant proposals to procure external research funding. Supervise undergraduate and/or graduate teaching, internship, and research work. Plan, evaluate, and revise curricula, course content, and course materials and methods of instruction. Prepare course materials such as syllabi, homework assignments, and handouts. Compile, administer, and grade examinations or assign this work to others. Advise students on academic and vocational curricula and on career issues. Initiate, facilitate, and moderate classroom discussions. Supervise students' laboratory and/or field work. Maintain student attendance records, grades, and other required records. Collaborate with colleagues to address teaching and research issues. Maintain regularly scheduled office hours in order to advise and assist students. Select and obtain materials and supplies such as textbooks and laboratory equipment. Participate in student recruitment, registration, and placement activities. Serve on academic or administrative committees that deal with institutional policies, departmental matters, and academic issues. Provide professional consulting services to government and/or industry. Perform administrative duties such as serving as department head. **SKILLS**—**Science:** Using scientific rules and methods to solve problems. **Instructing:** Teaching others how to do something. **Management of Financial Resources:** Determining how money will be spent to get the work done and accounting for these expenditures. **Management of Personnel Resources:** Motivating, developing, and directing people as they work, identifying the best people for the job. **Writing:** Communicating effectively in writing as appropriate for the needs of the audience. **Active Learning:** Understanding the implications of new information for both current and future problem-solving and decision-making. **Learning Strategies:** Selecting and using training/instructional methods and procedures appropriate for the situation when learning or teaching new things. **Critical Thinking:** Using logic and reasoning to identify the strengths and weaknesses of alternative solutions, conclusions, or approaches to problems. **Time Management:** Managing one's own time and the time of others. **GOE—Interest Area:** 05. Education and Training. **Work Group:** 05.03. Postsecondary and Adult Teaching and Instructing. **Other Jobs in This Work Group:** Adult Literacy, Remedial Education, and GED Teachers and Instructors; Agricultural Sciences Teachers, Postsecondary; Anthropology and Archeology Teachers, Postsecondary; Architecture Teachers, Postsecondary; Area, Ethnic, and Cultural Studies Teachers, Postsecondary; Art, Drama, and Music Teachers, Postsecondary; Atmospheric, Earth, Marine, and Space Sciences Teachers, Postsecondary; Biological Science Teachers, Postsecondary; Business Teachers, Postsecondary; Chemistry Teachers, Postsecondary; Communications Teachers, Postsecondary; Computer Science Teachers, Postsecondary; Criminal Justice and Law Enforcement Teachers, Postsecondary; Economics Teachers, Postsecondary; Education Teachers, Postsecondary; Engineering Teachers, Postsecondary; English Language and Literature Teachers, Postsecondary; Environmental Science Teachers, Postsecondary; Farm and Home Management Advisors; Foreign Language and Literature Teachers, Postsecondary; Geography Teachers, Postsecondary; Graduate Teaching Assistants; Health Specialties Teachers, Postsecondary; History Teachers, Postsecondary; Home Economics Teachers, Postsecondary; Law Teachers, Postsecondary; Library Science Teachers, Postsecondary; Mathematical Science Teachers, Postsecondary; Nursing Instructors and Teachers, Postsecondary; Philosophy and Religion Teachers, Postsecondary; Physics Teachers, Postsecondary; Political Science Teachers, Postsecondary; Psychology Teachers, Postsecondary; Recreation and Fitness Studies Teachers, Postsecondary; Self-Enrichment Education Teachers; Social Work Teachers, Postsecondary; Sociology Teachers, Postsecondary; Vocational Education Teachers, Postsecondary. **PERSONALITY TYPE:** Investigative.

EDUCATION/TRAINING PROGRAM(S)—Science Teacher Education/General Science Teacher Education. **RELATED KNOWLEDGE/COURSES** —**Biology:** Knowledge of plant and animal organisms and their tissues, cells, functions, interdependencies, and interactions with each other and the environment. **Education and Training:** Knowledge of principles and methods for curriculum and training design, teaching and instruction for individuals and groups, and the measurement of training effects. **Geography:** Knowledge of principles and methods for describing the features of land, sea, and air masses, including their physical characteristics; locations; interrelationships; and distribution of plant, animal, and human life. **English Language:** Knowledge of the structure and content of the English language, including the meaning and spelling of words, rules of composition, and grammar. **Mathematics:** Knowledge of arithmetic, algebra, geometry, calculus, and statistics and their applications. **Computers and Electronics:** Knowledge of circuit boards, processors, chips, electronic equipment, and computer hardware and software, including applications and programming.

Frame Wirers, Central Office

- Education/Training Required: Postsecondary vocational training
- Annual Earnings: $49,840
- Growth: –0.6%
- Annual Job Openings: 23,000
- Self-Employed: 4.6%
- Part-Time: 1.7%

Connect wires from telephone lines and cables to distributing frames in telephone company central office, using soldering iron and other hand tools. Solders connections, following diagram or oral instructions. Strings distributing frames with connecting wires. Tests circuit connections, using voltmeter or ammeter. Assists in locating and correcting malfunction in wiring on distributing frame. Lubricates moving switch parts. Cleans switches and replaces contact points, using vacuum hose, solvents, and hand tools. Removes and remakes connections to change circuit layouts. **SKILLS—Installation:** Installing equipment, machines, wiring, or programs to meet specifications. **Repairing:** Repairing machines or systems by using the needed tools. **Quality Control Analysis:** Conducting tests and inspections of products, services, or processes to evaluate quality or performance. **Troubleshooting:** Determining causes of operating errors and deciding what to do about them. **Operation Monitoring:** Watching gauges, dials, or other indicators to make sure a machine is working properly. **Equipment Maintenance:** Performing routine maintenance on equipment and determining when and what kind of maintenance is needed. **GOE—Interest Area:** 02. Architecture and Construction. **Work Group:** 02.05. Systems and Equipment Installation, Maintenance, and Repair. **Other Jobs in This Work Group:** Central Office and PBX Installers and Repairers; Communication Equipment Mechanics, Installers, and Repairers; Electric Meter Installers and Repairers; Electrical and Electronics Repairers, Powerhouse, Substation, and Relay; Electrical Power-Line Installers and Repairers; Elevator Installers and Repairers; Heating and Air Conditioning Mechanics; Home Appliance Installers; Maintenance and Repair Workers, General; Meter Mechanics; Refrigeration Mechanics; Station Installers and Repairers, Telephone; Telecommunications Facility Examiners; Telecommunications Line Installers and Repairers. **PERSONALITY TYPE:** Realistic.

EDUCATION/TRAINING PROGRAM(S)— Communications Systems Installation and Repair Technology. **RELATED KNOWLEDGE/COURSES—Telecommunications:** Knowledge of transmission, broadcasting, switching, control, and operation of telecommunications systems. **Engineering and Technology:** Knowledge of the practical application of engineering science and technology. This includes applying principles, techniques, procedures, and equipment to the design and production of various goods and services. **Mechanical Devices:** Knowledge of machines and tools, including their designs, uses, repair, and maintenance. **Physics:** Knowledge and prediction of physical principles and laws and their interrelationships and applications to understanding fluid, material, and atmospheric dynamics and mechanical, electrical, atomic, and subatomic structures and processes. **Design:** Knowledge of design techniques, tools, and principles involved in production of precision technical plans, blueprints, drawings, and models.

Freight Inspectors

- Education/Training Required: Work experience in a related occupation
- Annual Earnings: $50,380
- Growth: 7.7%
- Annual Job Openings: 5,000
- Self-Employed: 0.4%
- Part-Time: 3.2%

Inspect freight for proper storage according to specifications. Inspects shipment to ascertain that freight is securely braced and blocked. Observes loading of freight to ensure that crews comply with procedures. Monitors temperature and humidity of freight storage area. Records freight condition and handling and notifies crews to reload freight or insert additional bracing or packing. Measures height and width of loads that will pass over bridges or through tunnels. Notifies workers of special treatment required for shipments. Prepares and submits report after trip. Posts warning signs on vehicles containing explosives or inflammatory or radioactive materials. **SKILLS—Systems Analysis:** Determining how a system should work and how changes in conditions, operations, and the environment will affect outcomes. **GOE—Interest Area:** 16. Transportation, Distribution, and Logistics. **Work Group:** 16.07. Transportation Support Work. **Other Jobs in This Work Group:** Bridge and Lock Tenders; Cargo and Freight Agents; Cleaners of Vehicles and Equipment; Public Transportation Inspectors; Railroad Yard Workers; Stevedores, Except Equipment Operators; Traffic Technicians; Train Crew Members. **PERSONALITY TYPE:** Conventional.

EDUCATION/TRAINING PROGRAM(S)—No data available. **RELATED KNOWLEDGE/COURSES—Transportation:** Knowledge of principles and methods for moving people or goods by air, rail, sea, or road, including the relative costs and benefits. **Public Safety and Security:** Knowledge of relevant equipment, policies, procedures, and strategies to promote effective local, state, or national security operations for the protection of people, data, property, and institutions. **Production and Processing:** Knowledge of raw materials, production processes, quality control, costs, and other techniques for maximizing the effective manufacture and distribution of goods. **Geography:** Knowledge of principles and methods for describing the features of land, sea, and air masses, including their physical characteristics; locations; interrelationships; and distribution of plant, animal, and human life.

Freight, Stock, and Material Movers, Hand

- ◎ Education/Training Required: Short-term on-the-job training
- ◎ Annual Earnings: $20,120
- ◎ Growth: 6.6%
- ◎ Annual Job Openings: 525,000
- ◎ Self-Employed: 0.8%
- ◎ Part-Time: 21.0%

Load, unload, and move materials at plant, yard, or other work site. Loads and unloads materials to and from designated storage areas, such as racks and shelves, or vehicles, such as trucks. Stacks or piles materials such as lumber, boards, or pallets. Bundles and bands material such as fodder and tobacco leaves, using banding machines. Sorts and stores items according to specifications. Assembles product containers and crates, using hand tools and precut lumber. Adjusts or replaces equipment parts, such as rollers, belts, plugs and caps, using hand tools. Records number of units handled and moved, using daily production sheet or work tickets. Attaches identifying tags or marks information on containers. Cleans work area, using brooms, rags, and cleaning compounds. Installs protective devices, such as bracing, padding, or strapping, to prevent shifting or damage to items being transported. Reads work orders or receives and listens to oral instructions to determine work assignment. Shovels materials, such as gravel, ice, or spilled concrete, into containers or bins or onto conveyors. Directs spouts and positions receptacles, such as bins, carts, and containers, to receive loads. Transports receptacles to and from designated areas by hand or using dollies, handtrucks, and wheelbarrows. Secures lifting attachments to materials and conveys load to destination, using crane or hoist. **SKILLS—Installation:** Installing equipment, machines, wiring, or programs to meet specifications. **GOE—Interest Area:** 13. Manufacturing. **Work Group:** 13.17. Loading, Moving, Hoisting, and Conveying. **Other Jobs in This Work Group:** Conveyor Operators and Tenders; Hoist and Winch Operators; Industrial Truck and Tractor Operators; Irradiated-Fuel Handlers; Machine Feeders and Offbearers; Packers and Packagers, Hand; Pump Operators, Except Wellhead Pumpers; Refuse and Recyclable Material Collectors; Tank Car, Truck, and Ship Loaders. **PERSONALITY TYPE:** Realistic.

EDUCATION/TRAINING PROGRAM(S)—No data available. **RELATED KNOWLEDGE/COURSES—Production and Processing:** Knowledge of raw materials, production processes, quality control, costs, and other techniques for maximizing the effective manufacture and distribution of goods. **Transportation:** Knowledge of principles and methods for moving people or goods by air, rail, sea, or road, including the relative costs and benefits. **Mechanical Devices:** Knowledge of machines and tools, including their designs, uses, repair, and maintenance. **Physics:** Knowledge and prediction of physical principles and laws and their interrelationships and applications to understanding fluid, material, and atmospheric dynamics and mechanical, electrical, atomic, and subatomic structures and processes.

Gaming Change Persons and Booth Cashiers

- ◎ Education/Training Required: Short-term on-the-job training
- ◎ Annual Earnings: $20,530
- ◎ Growth: 24.1%
- ◎ Annual Job Openings: 12,000
- ◎ Self-Employed: 1.0%
- ◎ Part-Time: 44.8%

Exchange coins and tokens for patrons' money. May issue payoffs and obtain customer's signature on receipt when winnings exceed the amount held in the slot machine. May operate a booth in the slot machine area and furnish change persons with money bank at the start of the shift or count and audit money in drawers. Count money and audit money drawers. Keep accurate records of monetary exchanges, authorization forms, and transaction reconciliations. Exchange money, credit, and casino chips and make change for customers. Work in and monitor an assigned area on the casino floor where slot machines are located. Listen for jackpot alarm bells and issue payoffs to winners. Maintain cage security according to rules. Obtain customers' signatures on receipts when winnings exceed the amount held in a slot machine. Reconcile daily summaries of transactions to balance books. Sell gambling chips, tokens, or tickets to patrons or to other workers for resale to patrons. Calculate the value of chips won or lost by players. Furnish change persons with a money bank at the start of each shift. Accept credit applications and verify credit references in order to provide check-cashing authorization or to establish house credit accounts. **SKILLS—Service Orientation:** Actively looking for ways to help people. **Time Management:** Managing one's own time and the time of others. **GOE—Interest Area:** 14. Retail and Wholesale Sales and Service. **Work Group:** 14.06. Customer Service. **Other Jobs in This Work Group:** Adjustment Clerks; Cashiers; Counter and Rental Clerks; Customer Service Representatives, Utilities; Order Clerks; Receptionists and Information Clerks. **PERSONALITY TYPE:** No data available.

EDUCATION/TRAINING PROGRAM(S)— Retailing and Retail Operations. **RELATED KNOWLEDGE/COURSES—Customer and Personal Service:** Knowledge of principles and processes for providing customer and personal services. This includes customer needs assessment, meeting quality standards for services, and evaluation of customer satisfaction. **Public Safety and Security:** Knowledge of relevant equipment, policies, procedures, and strategies to promote effective local, state, or national security operations for the protection of people, data, property, and institutions. **Sales and Marketing:** Knowledge of principles and methods for showing, promoting, and selling products or services. This includes marketing strategy and tactics, product demonstrations, sales techniques, and sales control systems. **Engineering and Technology:** Knowledge of the practical application of engineering science and technology. This includes applying principles, techniques, procedures, and equipment to the design and production of various goods and services. **Administration and Management:** Knowledge of business and management principles involved in strategic planning, resource allocation, human resources modeling, leadership technique, production methods, and coordination of people and resources. **Economics and Accounting:** Knowledge of economic and accounting principles and practices, the financial markets, banking, and the analysis and reporting of financial data.

Gaming Dealers

- Education/Training Required: Postsecondary vocational training
- Annual Earnings: $14,340
- Growth: 24.7%
- Annual Job Openings: 26,000
- Self-Employed: 2.5%
- Part-Time: 16.3%

Operate table games. Stand or sit behind table and operate games of chance by dispensing the appropriate number of cards or blocks to players or operating other gaming equipment. Compare the house's hand against players' hands and pay off or collect players' money or chips. Exchange paper currency for playing chips or coin money. Pay winnings or collect losing bets as established by the rules and procedures of a specific game. Deal cards to house hands and compare these with players' hands to determine winners, as in blackjack. Conduct gambling games such as dice, roulette, cards, or keno, following all applicable rules and regulations. Check to ensure that all players have placed bets before play begins. Stand behind a gaming table and deal the appropriate number of cards to each player. Inspect cards and equipment to be used in games to ensure that they are in good condition. Start and control games and gaming equipment and announce winning numbers or colors. Open and close cash floats and game tables. Compute amounts of players' wins or losses or scan winning tickets presented by patrons to calculate the amount of money won. Apply rule variations to card games such as poker, in which players bet on the value of their hands. Receive, verify, and record patrons' cash wagers. Answer questions about game rules and casino policies. Refer patrons to gaming cashiers to collect winnings. Work as part of a team of dealers in games such as baccarat or craps. Participate in games for gambling establishments in order to provide the minimum complement of players at a table. Seat patrons at gaming tables. Prepare collection reports for submission to supervisors. Monitor gambling tables and supervise staff. Train new dealers. **SKILLS—Service Orientation:** Actively looking for ways to help people. **Speaking:** Talking to others to convey information effectively. **Social Perceptiveness:** Being aware of others' reactions and understanding why they react as they do. **Mathematics:** Using mathematics to solve problems. **Coordina-**

tion: Adjusting actions in relation to others' actions. **Critical Thinking:** Using logic and reasoning to identify the strengths and weaknesses of alternative solutions, conclusions, or approaches to problems. **Active Listening:** Giving full attention to what other people are saying, taking time to understand the points being made, asking questions as appropriate, and not interrupting at inappropriate times. **Learning Strategies:** Selecting and using training/instructional methods and procedures appropriate for the situation when learning or teaching new things. **Instructing:** Teaching others how to do something. **GOE—Interest Area:** 09. Hospitality, Tourism, and Recreation. **Work Group:** 09.02. Recreational Services. **Other Jobs in This Work Group:** Amusement and Recreation Attendants; Gaming and Sports Book Writers and Runners; Locker Room, Coatroom, and Dressing Room Attendants; Motion Picture Projectionists; Recreation Workers; Slot Key Persons; Ushers, Lobby Attendants, and Ticket Takers. **PERSONALITY TYPE:** Enterprising.

EDUCATION/TRAINING PROGRAM(S)—No data available. **RELATED KNOWLEDGE/COURSES—Customer and Personal Service:** Knowledge of principles and processes for providing customer and personal services. This includes customer needs assessment, meeting quality standards for services, and evaluation of customer satisfaction. **Psychology:** Knowledge of human behavior and performance; individual differences in ability, personality, and interests; learning and motivation; psychological research methods; and the assessment and treatment of behavioral and affective disorders. **Mathematics:** Knowledge of arithmetic, algebra, geometry, calculus, and statistics and their applications. **Sales and Marketing:** Knowledge of principles and methods for showing, promoting, and selling products or services. This includes marketing strategy and tactics, product demonstrations, sales techniques, and sales control systems. **Economics and Accounting:** Knowledge of economic and accounting principles and practices, the financial markets, banking, and the analysis and reporting of financial data. **Law and Government:** Knowledge of laws, legal codes, court procedures, precedents, government regulations, executive orders, agency rules, and the democratic political process.

Gaming Managers

- ◎ Education/Training Required: Work experience plus degree
- ◎ Annual Earnings: $58,580
- ◎ Growth: 12.4%
- ◎ Annual Job Openings: 1,000
- ◎ Self-Employed: 38.6%
- ◎ Part-Time: 6.9%

Plan, organize, direct, control, or coordinate gaming operations in a casino. Formulate gaming policies for their area of responsibility. Circulate among gaming tables to ensure that operations are conducted properly, that dealers follow house rules, and that players are not cheating. Direct the distribution of complimentary hotel rooms, meals, and other discounts or free items given to players based on their length of play and betting totals. Direct workers compiling summary sheets that show wager amounts and payoffs for races and events. Establish policies on issues such as the type of gambling offered and the odds, the extension of credit, and the serving of food and beverages. Maintain familiarity with all games used at a facility, as well as strategies and tricks employed in those games. Monitor credit extended to players. Monitor staffing levels to ensure that games and tables are adequately staffed for each shift, arranging for staff rotations and breaks and locating substitute employees as necessary. Prepare work schedules and station assignments and keep attendance records. Resolve customer complaints regarding problems such as payout errors. Review operational expenses, budget estimates, betting accounts, and collection reports for accuracy. Set and maintain a bank and table limit for each game. Track supplies of money to tables and perform any required paperwork. Explain and interpret house rules, such as game rules and betting limits. Interview and hire workers. Notify board attendants of table vacancies so that waiting patrons can play. Record, collect, and pay off bets, issuing receipts as necessary. Remove suspected cheaters, such as card counters and other players who may have systems that shift the odds of winning to their favor. Train new workers and evaluate their performance. **SKILLS—Management of Financial Resources:** Determining how money will be spent to get the work done and accounting for these expenditures. **Management of Personnel Resources:** Motivating, developing, and directing people as they work, identifying the best people for the job. **Negotiation:** Bringing others together and trying to reconcile differences. **Management of Material Resources:** Obtaining and seeing to the appropriate use of equipment, facilities, and materials needed to do certain work. **Speaking:** Talking to others to convey information effectively. **Social Perceptiveness:** Being aware of others' reactions and understanding why they react as they do. **Systems Evaluation:** Identifying measures or indicators of system performance and the actions needed to improve or correct performance relative to the goals of the system. **Time Management:** Managing one's own time and the time of others. **GOE—Interest Area:** 09. Hospitality, Tourism, and Recreation. **Work Group:** 09.01. Managerial Work in Hospitality and Tourism. **Other Jobs in This Work Group:** First-Line Supervisors/Managers of Food Preparation and Serving Workers; First-Line Supervisors/Managers of Personal Service Workers; Food Service Managers; Gaming Supervisors; Lodging Managers. **PERSONALITY TYPE:** Enterprising.

EDUCATION/TRAINING PROGRAM(S)—Personal and Culinary Services, Other. **RELATED KNOWLEDGE/COURSES—Economics and Accounting:** Knowledge of economic and accounting principles and practices, the financial markets, banking, and the analysis and reporting of financial data. **Administration and Management:** Knowledge of business and management principles involved in strategic planning, resource allocation, human resources modeling, leadership technique, production methods, and coordination of people and resources. **Personnel and Human Resources:** Knowledge of principles and procedures for personnel recruitment, selection, training, compensation and benefits, labor relations and negotiation, and personnel information systems. **Customer and Personal Service:** Knowledge of principles and processes for providing customer and personal services. This includes customer needs assessment, meeting quality standards for services, and evaluation of customer satisfaction. **Mathematics:** Knowledge of arithmetic, algebra, geometry, calculus, and statistics and their applications. **Education and Training:** Knowledge of principles and methods for curriculum and training design, teaching and instruction for individuals and groups, and the measurement of training effects.

Gaming Supervisors

- Education/Training Required: Postsecondary vocational training
- Annual Earnings: $40,840
- Growth: 15.7%
- Annual Job Openings: 6,000
- Self-Employed: 33.8%
- Part-Time: 15.2%

Supervise gaming operations and personnel in an assigned area. Circulate among tables and observe operations. Ensure that stations and games are covered for each shift. May explain and interpret operating rules of house to patrons. May plan and organize activities and create friendly atmosphere for guests in hotels/casinos. May adjust service complaints. Monitor game operations to ensure that house rules are followed; that tribal, state, and federal regulations are adhered to; and that employees provide prompt and courteous service. Observe gamblers' behavior for signs of cheating such as marking, switching, or counting cards; notify security staff of suspected cheating. Maintain familiarity with the games at a facility and with strategies and tricks used by cheaters at such games. Perform paperwork required for monetary transactions. Resolve customer and employee complaints. Greet customers and ask about the quality of service they are receiving. Establish and maintain banks and table limits for each game. Monitor stations and games and move dealers from game to game to ensure adequate staffing. Report customer-related incidents occurring in gaming areas to supervisors. Explain and interpret house rules, such as game rules and betting limits, for patrons. Supervise the distribution of complimentary meals, hotel rooms, discounts, and other items given to players based on length of play and amount bet. Evaluate workers' performance and prepare written performance evaluations. Monitor patrons for signs of compulsive gambling, offering assistance if necessary. Record, issue receipts for, and pay off bets. Monitor and verify the counting, wrapping, weighing, and distribution of currency and coins. Direct workers compiling summary sheets for each race or event to record amounts wagered and amounts to be paid to winners. Determine how many gaming tables to open each day and schedule staff accordingly. Establish policies on types of gambling offered, odds, and extension of credit. Interview, hire, and train workers. Provide fire protection and first-aid assistance when necessary. Review operational expenses, budget estimates, betting accounts, and collection reports for accuracy. **SKILLS—Instructing:** Teaching others how to do something. **Management of Personnel Resources:** Motivating, developing, and directing people as they work, identifying the best people for the job. **Social Perceptiveness:** Being aware of others' reactions and understanding why they react as they do. **Service Orientation:** Actively looking for ways to help people. **Monitoring:** Monitoring or assessing your performance or that of other individuals or organizations to make improvements or take corrective action. **Critical Thinking:** Using logic and reasoning to identify the strengths and weaknesses of alternative solutions, conclusions, or approaches to problems. **Learning Strategies:** Selecting and using training/instructional methods and procedures appropriate for the situation when learning or teaching new things. **Persuasion:** Persuading others to change their minds or behavior. **GOE—Interest Area:** 09. Hospitality, Tourism, and Recreation. **Work Group:** 09.01. Managerial Work in Hospitality and Tourism. **Other Jobs in This Work Group:** First-Line Supervisors/Managers of Food Preparation and Serving Workers; First-Line Supervisors/Managers of Personal Service Workers; Food Service Managers; Gaming Managers; Lodging Managers. **PERSONALITY TYPE:** Enterprising.

EDUCATION/TRAINING PROGRAM(S)—No data available. **RELATED KNOWLEDGE/COURSES—Customer and Personal Service:** Knowledge of principles and processes for providing customer and personal services. This includes customer needs assessment, meeting quality standards for services, and evaluation of customer satisfaction. **Psychology:** Knowledge of human behavior and performance; individual differences in ability, personality, and interests; learning and motivation; psychological research methods; and the assessment and treatment of behavioral and affective disorders. **Education and Training:** Knowledge of principles and methods for curriculum and training design, teaching and instruction for individuals and groups, and the measurement of training effects. **Mathematics:** Knowledge of arithmetic, algebra, geometry, calculus, and statistics and their applications. **Law and Government:** Knowledge of laws, legal codes, court procedures, precedents, government regulations, executive orders, agency rules, and the democratic political process. **Administration and Management:** Knowledge of business and manage-

ment principles involved in strategic planning, resource allocation, human resources modeling, leadership technique, production methods, and coordination of people and resources. **Personnel and Human Resources:** Knowledge of principles and procedures for personnel recruitment, selection, training, compensation and benefits, labor relations and negotiation, and personnel information systems.

General and Operations Managers

◉ Education/Training Required: Work experience plus degree
◉ Annual Earnings: $77,420
◉ Growth: 18.4%
◉ Annual Job Openings: 260,000
◉ Self-Employed: 0.7%
◉ Part-Time: 2.6%

Plan, direct, or coordinate the operations of companies or public and private sector organizations. Duties and responsibilities include formulating policies, managing daily operations, and planning the use of materials and human resources, but are too diverse and general in nature to be classified in any one functional area of management or administration, such as personnel, purchasing, or administrative services. Includes owners and managers who head small business establishments whose duties are primarily managerial. Direct and coordinate activities of businesses or departments concerned with the production, pricing, sales, and/or distribution of products. Manage staff, preparing work schedules and assigning specific duties. Review financial statements, sales and activity reports, and other performance data to measure productivity and goal achievement and to determine areas needing cost reduction and program improvement. Establish and implement departmental policies, goals, objectives, and procedures, conferring with board members, organization officials, and staff members as necessary. Determine staffing requirements and interview, hire, and train new employees or oversee those personnel processes. Monitor businesses and agencies to ensure that they efficiently and effectively provide needed services while staying within budgetary limits. Oversee activities directly related to making products or providing services. Direct and coordinate organization's financial and budget activities to fund operations, maximize investments, and increase efficiency. Determine goods and services to be sold and set prices and credit terms based on forecasts of customer demand. Manage the movement of goods into and out of production facilities. Locate, select, and procure merchandise for resale, representing management in purchase negotiations. Perform sales floor work such as greeting and assisting customers, stocking shelves, and taking inventory. Develop and implement product marketing strategies, including advertising campaigns and sales promotions. Plan and direct activities such as sales promotions, coordinating with other department heads as required. Direct non-merchandising departments of businesses, such as advertising and purchasing. **SKILLS—Management of Financial Resources:** Determining how money will be spent to get the work done and accounting for these expenditures. **Management of Personnel Resources:** Motivating, developing, and directing people as they work, identifying the best people for the job. **Management of Material Resources:** Obtaining and seeing to the appropriate use of equipment, facilities, and materials needed to do certain work. **Negotiation:** Bringing others together and trying to reconcile differences. **Monitoring:** Monitoring or assessing your performance or that of other individuals or organizations to make improvements or take corrective action. **Persuasion:** Persuading others to change their minds or behavior. **Coordination:** Adjusting actions in relation to others' actions. **Social Perceptiveness:** Being aware of others' reactions and understanding why they react as they do. **GOE—Interest Area:** 04. Business and Administration. **Work Group:** 04.01. Managerial Work in General Business. **Other Jobs in This Work Group:** Chief Executives; Compensation and Benefits Managers; Human Resources Managers; Private Sector Executives; Training and Development Managers. **PERSONALITY TYPE:** No data available.

EDUCATION/TRAINING PROGRAM(S)—Business Administration and Management, General; Business/Commerce, General; Entrepreneurship/ Entrepreneurial Studies; International Business/ Trade/Commerce; Public Administration. **RELATED KNOWLEDGE/COURSES—Sales and Marketing:** Knowledge of principles and methods for showing, promoting, and selling products or services. This includes marketing strategy and tactics, product demonstrations, sales techniques, and sales control systems. **Administration and Management:** Knowledge of business and management principles involved in strategic planning, resource allocation, human resources modeling, leadership technique, production methods, and coordination of people and resources. **Customer and Personal Service:** Knowledge of principles and processes for providing customer and personal services. This includes customer needs assessment, meeting quality standards for services, and evaluation of customer satisfaction. **Personnel and Human Resources:** Knowledge of principles and procedures for personnel recruitment, selection, training, compensation and benefits, labor relations and negotiation, and personnel information systems. **Economics and Accounting:** Knowledge of economic and accounting principles and practices, the financial markets, banking, and the analysis and reporting of financial data. **Law and Government:** Knowledge of laws, legal codes, court procedures, precedents, government regulations, executive orders, agency rules, and the democratic political process.

Geographers

- Education/Training Required: Bachelor's degree
- Annual Earnings: $58,970
- Growth: 19.5%
- Annual Job Openings: Fewer than 500
- Self-Employed: 3.7%
- Part-Time: 16.8%

Study nature and use of areas of earth's surface, relating and interpreting interactions of physical and cultural phenomena. Conduct research on physical aspects of a region, including land forms, climates, soils, plants, and animals, and conduct research on the spatial implications of human activities within a given area, including social characteristics, economic activities, and political organization, as well as researching interdependence between regions at scales ranging from local to global. Create and modify maps, graphs, and/or diagrams, using geographical information software and related equipment and principles of cartography such as coordinate systems, longitude, latitude, elevation, topography, and map scales. Write and present reports of research findings. Develop, operate, and maintain geographical information (GIS) computer systems, including hardware, software, plotters, digitizers, printers, and video cameras. Locate and obtain existing geographic information databases. Analyze geographic distributions of physical and cultural phenomena on local, regional, continental, and/or global scales. Teach geography. Gather and compile geographic data from sources including censuses, field observations, satellite imagery, aerial photographs, and existing maps. Conduct fieldwork at outdoor sites. Study the economic, political, and cultural characteristics of a specific region's population. Provide consulting services in fields including resource development and management, business location and market area analysis, environmental hazards, regional cultural history, and urban social planning. Collect data on physical characteristics of specified areas, such as geological formations, climates, and vegetation, using surveying or meteorological equipment. Provide geographical information systems support to the private and public sectors. **SKILLS—Programming:** Writing computer programs for various purposes. **Science:** Using scientific rules and methods to solve problems. **Complex Problem Solving:** Identifying complex problems and reviewing related information to develop and evaluate options and implement solutions. **Reading Comprehension:** Understanding written sentences and paragraphs in work-related documents. **Critical Thinking:** Using logic and reasoning to identify the strengths and weaknesses of alternative solutions, conclusions, or approaches to problems. **Writing:** Communicating effectively in writing as appropriate for the needs of the audience. **Instructing:** Teaching others how to do something. **Management of Financial Resources:** Determining how money will be spent to get the work done and accounting for these expenditures. **GOE—Interest Area:** 15. Scientific Research, Engineering, and Mathematics. **Work Group:** 15.02. Physical Sciences. **Other Jobs in This Work Group:** Astronomers; Atmospheric and Space Scientists; Chemists; Geologists; Hydrologists; Materials Scientists; Physicists. **PERSONALITY TYPE:** Investigative.

EDUCATION/TRAINING PROGRAM(S)— Geography. **RELATED KNOWLEDGE/COURSES—Geography:** Knowledge of principles and methods for describing the features of land, sea, and air masses, including their physical characteristics; locations; interrelationships; and distribution of plant, animal, and human life. **Sociology and Anthropology:** Knowledge of group behavior and dynamics, societal trends and influences, human migrations, ethnicity,

and cultures and their history and origins. **Education and Training:** Knowledge of principles and methods for curriculum and training design, teaching and instruction for individuals and groups, and the measurement of training effects. **History and Archeology:** Knowledge of historical events and their causes, indicators, and effects on civilizations and cultures. **Biology:** Knowledge of plant and animal organisms and their tissues, cells, functions, interdependencies, and interactions with each other and the environment. **Computers and Electronics:** Knowledge of circuit boards, processors, chips, electronic equipment, and computer hardware and software, including applications and programming.

Geography Teachers, Postsecondary

◎ Education/Training Required: Master's degree
◎ Annual Earnings: $57,510
◎ Growth: 38.1%
◎ Annual Job Openings: 216,000
◎ Self-Employed: 0.3%
◎ Part-Time: 27.7%

Teach courses in geography. Prepare and deliver lectures to undergraduate and/or graduate students on topics such as urbanization, environmental systems, and cultural geography. Evaluate and grade students' class work, assignments, and papers. Compile, administer, and grade examinations or assign this work to others. Initiate, facilitate, and moderate classroom discussions. Maintain student attendance records, grades, and other required records. Prepare course materials such as syllabi, homework assignments, and handouts. Keep abreast of developments in their field by reading current literature, talking with colleagues, and participating in professional conferences. Supervise undergraduate and/or graduate teaching, internship, and research work. Plan, evaluate, and revise curricula, course content, and course materials and methods of instruction. Maintain regularly scheduled office hours in order to advise and assist students. Supervise students' laboratory and field work. Conduct research in a particular field of knowledge and publish findings in professional journals, books, and/or electronic media. Collaborate with colleagues to address teaching and research issues. Select and obtain materials and supplies such as textbooks. Advise students on academic and vocational curricula and on career issues. Serve on academic or administrative committees that deal with institutional policies, departmental matters, and academic issues. Participate in student recruitment, registration, and placement activities. Participate in campus and community events. Compile bibliographies of specialized materials for outside reading assignments. Perform administrative duties such as serving as department head. Write grant proposals to procure external research funding. Maintain geographic information systems laboratories, performing duties such as updating software. Perform spatial analysis and modeling, using geographic information system techniques. **SKILLS—Instructing:** Teaching others how to do something. **Learning Strategies:** Selecting and using training/instructional methods and procedures appropriate for the situation when learning or teaching new things. **Writing:** Communicating effectively in writing as appropriate for the needs of the audience. **Science:** Using scientific rules and methods to solve problems. **Active Learning:** Understanding the implications of new information for both current and future problem-solving and decision-making. **Critical Thinking:** Using logic and reasoning to identify the strengths and weaknesses of alternative solutions, conclusions, or approaches to problems. **Speaking:** Talking to others to convey information effectively. **Reading Comprehension:** Understanding written sentences and paragraphs in work-related documents. **GOE—Interest Area:** 05. Education and Training. **Work Group:** 05.03. Postsecondary and Adult Teaching and Instructing. **Other Jobs in This Work Group:** Adult Literacy, Remedial Education, and GED Teachers and Instructors; Agricultural Sciences Teachers, Postsecondary; Anthropology and Archeology Teachers, Postsecondary; Architecture Teachers, Postsecondary; Area, Ethnic, and Cultural Studies Teachers, Postsecondary; Art, Drama, and Music Teachers, Postsecondary; Atmospheric, Earth, Marine, and Space Sciences Teachers, Postsecondary; Biological Science Teachers, Postsecondary; Business Teachers, Postsecondary; Chemistry Teachers, Postsecondary; Communications Teachers, Postsecondary; Computer Science Teachers, Postsecondary; Criminal Justice and Law Enforcement Teachers, Postsecondary; Economics Teachers, Postsecondary; Education Teachers, Postsecondary; Engineering Teachers, Postsecondary; English Language and Literature Teachers, Postsecondary; Environmental Science Teachers, Postsecondary; Farm and Home

Management Advisors; Foreign Language and Literature Teachers, Postsecondary; Forestry and Conservation Science Teachers, Postsecondary; Graduate Teaching Assistants; Health Specialties Teachers, Postsecondary; History Teachers, Postsecondary; Home Economics Teachers, Postsecondary; Law Teachers, Postsecondary; Library Science Teachers, Postsecondary; Mathematical Science Teachers, Postsecondary; Nursing Instructors and Teachers, Postsecondary; Philosophy and Religion Teachers, Postsecondary; Physics Teachers, Postsecondary; Political Science Teachers, Postsecondary; Psychology Teachers, Postsecondary; Recreation and Fitness Studies Teachers, Postsecondary; Self-Enrichment Education Teachers; Social Work Teachers, Postsecondary; Sociology Teachers, Postsecondary; Vocational Education Teachers, Postsecondary. **PERSONALITY TYPE:** No data available.

EDUCATION/TRAINING PROGRAM(S)— Geography; Geography Teacher Education. **RELATED KNOWLEDGE/COURSES—Geography:** Knowledge of principles and methods for describing the features of land, sea, and air masses, including their physical characteristics; locations; interrelationships; and distribution of plant, animal, and human life. **Sociology and Anthropology:** Knowledge of group behavior and dynamics, societal trends and influences, human migrations, ethnicity, and cultures and their history and origins. **History and Archeology:** Knowledge of historical events and their causes, indicators, and effects on civilizations and cultures. **Education and Training:** Knowledge of principles and methods for curriculum and training design, teaching and instruction for individuals and groups, and the measurement of training effects. **Philosophy and Theology:** Knowledge of different philosophical systems and religions. This includes their basic principles, values, ethics, ways of thinking, customs, and practices and their impact on human culture. **English Language:** Knowledge of the structure and content of the English language, including the meaning and spelling of words, rules of composition, and grammar.

Geologists

◎ Education/Training Required: Bachelor's degree
◎ Annual Earnings: $68,730
◎ Growth: 11.5%
◎ Annual Job Openings: 2,000
◎ Self-Employed: 2.7%
◎ Part-Time: 7.7%

Study composition, structure, and history of the earth's crust; examine rocks, minerals, and fossil remains to identify and determine the sequence of processes affecting the development of the earth; apply knowledge of chemistry, physics, biology, and mathematics to explain these phenomena and to help locate mineral and petroleum deposits and underground water resources; prepare geologic reports and maps; and interpret research data to recommend further action for study. Analyze and interpret geological, geochemical, and geophysical information from sources such as survey data, well logs, boreholes, and aerial photos. Plan and conduct geological, geochemical, and geophysical field studies and surveys; sample collection; and drilling and testing programs used to collect data for research and/or application. Investigate the composition, structure, and history of the Earth's crust through the collection, examination, measurement, and classification of soils, minerals, rocks, and fossil remains. Prepare geological maps; cross-sectional diagrams; charts; and reports concerning mineral extraction, land use, and resource management, using results of field work and laboratory research. Locate and estimate probable natural gas, oil, and mineral ore deposits and underground water resources, using aerial photographs, charts, and research and survey results. Assess ground and surface water movement in order to provide advice regarding issues such as waste management, route and site selection, and the restoration of contaminated sites. Identify risks for natural disasters such as mudslides, earthquakes, and volcanic eruptions and provide advice on ways in which potential damage can be mitigated. Conduct geological and geophysical studies to provide information for use in regional development, site selection, and the development of public works projects. Inspect construction projects in order to analyze engineering problems, applying geological knowledge and using test equipment and drilling machinery. Advise construction firms and government agencies on dam and road construction, foundation design, and land use and resource management. **SKILLS—Science:** Using scientific rules and methods to solve problems. **Management of Financial Resources:** Determining how money will be spent to get the work done and accounting for these expenditures. **Time Management:** Managing one's own time and the time of others. **Active Learning:** Understanding the implications of new information for both current and future problem-solving and decision-making. **Coordination:** Adjusting actions in relation to others' actions. **Negotiation:** Bringing others together and trying to reconcile differences. **Critical Thinking:** Using logic and reasoning to identify the strengths and weaknesses of alternative solutions, conclusions, or approaches to problems. **Persuasion:** Persuading others to change their minds or behavior. **GOE—Interest Area:** 15. Scientific Research, Engineering, and Mathematics. **Work Group:** 15.02. Physical Sciences. **Other Jobs in This Work Group:** Astronomers; Atmospheric and Space Scientists; Chemists; Geographers; Hydrologists; Materials Scientists; Physicists. **PERSONALITY TYPE:** Investigative.

EDUCATION/TRAINING PROGRAM(S)—Geochemistry; Geochemistry and Petrology; Geological and Earth Sciences/Geosciences, Other; Geology/Earth Science, General; Geophysics and Seismology; Oceanography, Chemical and Physical; Paleontology. **RELATED KNOWLEDGE/COURSES—Geography:** Knowledge of principles and methods for describing the features of land, sea, and air masses, including their physical characteristics; locations; interrelationships; and distribution of plant, animal, and human life. **Physics:** Knowledge and prediction of physical principles and laws and their interrelationships and applications to understanding fluid, material, and atmospheric dynamics and mechanical, electrical, atomic, and subatomic structures and processes. **Chemistry:** Knowledge of the chemical composition, structure, and properties of substances and of the chemical processes and transformations that they undergo. This includes uses of chemicals and their danger signs, production techniques, and disposal methods. **Engineering and Technology:** Knowledge of the practical application of engineering science and technology. This includes applying principles, techniques, procedures, and equipment to the design and production of various goods and services. **Mathematics:** Knowledge of arithmetic, algebra, geometry, calculus, and statistics and their applications. **Biology:** Knowledge of plant and animal organisms and their tissues, cells, functions, interdependencies, and interactions with each other and the environment.

Glaziers

◎ Education/Training Required: Long-term on-the-job training

◎ Annual Earnings: $32,650

◎ Growth: 17.2%

◎ Annual Job Openings: 7,000

◎ Self-Employed: 5.6%

◎ Part-Time: 3.1%

Install glass in windows, skylights, store fronts, and display cases or on surfaces such as building fronts, interior walls, ceilings, and tabletops. Cut and attach mounting strips, metal or wood moldings, rubber gaskets, or metal clips to surfaces in preparation for mirror installation. Secure mirrors in position, using mastic cement, putty, bolts, or screws. Cut and remove broken glass prior to installing replacement glass. Cut, fit, install, repair, and replace glass and glass substitutes, such as plastic and aluminum, in building interiors or exteriors and in furniture or other products. Determine plumb of walls or ceilings, using plumb lines and levels. Fasten glass panes into wood sashes or frames with clips, points, or moldings, adding weather seals or putty around pane edges to seal joints. Grind and polish glass and smooth edges when necessary. Measure and mark outlines or patterns on glass to indicate cutting lines. Score glass with cutters' wheels, breaking off excess glass by hand or with notched tools. Measure mirrors and dimensions of areas to be covered in order to determine work procedures. Measure, cut, fit, and press anti-glare adhesive film to glass or spray glass with tinting solution to prevent light glare. Pack spaces between moldings and glass with glazing compounds and trim excess material with glazing knives. Prepare glass for cutting by resting it on rack edges or against cutting tables and brushing thin layer of oil along cutting lines or dipping cutting tools in oil. Read and interpret blueprints and specifications to determine size, shape, color, type, and thickness of glass; location of framing; installation procedures; and staging and scaffolding materials required. Select the type and color of glass or mirror according to specifications. Assemble and cement sections of stained glass together. Assemble, erect, and dismantle scaffolds, rigging, and hoisting equipment. Confer with customers to determine project requirements and to provide cost estimates. Create patterns on glass by etching, sandblasting, or painting designs. Cut, assemble, fit, and attach metal-framed glass enclosures for showers, bathtubs, display cases, skylights, solariums, and other structures. Drive trucks to installation sites and unload mirrors, glass equipment, and tools. **SKILLS—Installation:** Installing equipment, machines, wiring, or programs to meet specifications. **Technology Design:** Generating or adapting equipment and technology to serve user needs. **Repairing:** Repairing machines or systems by using the needed tools. **Mathematics:** Using mathematics to solve problems. **GOE—Interest Area:** 02. Architecture and Construction. **Work Group:** 02.04. Construction Crafts. **Other Jobs in This Work Group:** Boat Builders and Shipwrights; Boilermakers; Brattice Builders; Brickmasons and Blockmasons; Carpet Installers; Ceiling Tile Installers; Cement Masons and Concrete Finishers; Commercial Divers; Construction Carpenters; Crane and Tower Operators; Dragline Operators; Drywall Installers; Electricians; Fence Erectors; Floor Layers, Except Carpet, Wood, and Hard Tiles; Floor Sanders and Finishers; Grader, Bulldozer, and Scraper Operators; Hazardous Materials Removal Workers; Insulation Workers, Floor, Ceiling, and Wall; Insulation Workers, Mechanical; Manufactured Building and Mobile Home Installers; Operating Engineers; Painters, Construction and Maintenance; Paperhangers; Paving, Surfacing, and Tamping Equipment Operators; Pile-Driver Operators; Pipe Fitters; Pipelayers; Pipelaying Fitters; Plasterers and Stucco Masons; Plumbers; Rail-Track Laying and Maintenance Equipment Operators; Refractory Materials Repairers, Except Brickmasons; Reinforcing Iron and Rebar Workers; Riggers; Roofers; Rough Carpenters; Security and Fire Alarm Systems Installers; Segmental Pavers; Sheet Metal Workers; Ship Carpenters and Joiners; Stone Cutters and Carvers; Stonemasons; Structural Iron and Steel Workers; Tapers; Terrazzo Workers and Finishers; Tile and Marble Setters. **PERSONALITY TYPE:** Realistic.

EDUCATION/TRAINING PROGRAM(S)— Glazier. **RELATED KNOWLEDGE/COURSES— Building and Construction:** Knowledge of the materials, methods, and tools involved in the construction or repair of houses, buildings, or other structures such as highways and roads. **Production and Processing:** Knowledge of raw materials, production processes, quality control, costs, and other techniques for maximizing the effective manufacture and distribution of goods. **Design:** Knowledge of design techniques, tools, and principles involved in production of precision technical plans, blueprints, drawings, and models. **Engineering and Technology:** Knowledge of the practical application of engineering science and technology. This includes applying principles, techniques, procedures, and equipment to the design and production of various goods and services. **Geography:** Knowledge of principles and methods for describing the features of land, sea, and air masses, including their physical characteristics; locations; interrelationships; and distribution of plant, animal, and human life.

Government Property Inspectors and Investigators

- Education/Training Required: Long-term on-the-job training
- Annual Earnings: $47,390
- Growth: 9.8%
- Annual Job Openings: 20,000
- Self-Employed: 0.9%
- Part-Time: 5.3%

Investigate or inspect government property to ensure compliance with contract agreements and government regulations. Collect, identify, evaluate, and preserve case evidence. Examine records, reports, and documents in order to establish facts and detect discrepancies. Inspect government-owned equipment and materials in the possession of private contractors in order to ensure compliance with contracts and regulations and to prevent misuse. Inspect manufactured or processed products to ensure compliance with contract specifications and legal requirements. Locate and interview plaintiffs, witnesses, or representatives of business or government in order to gather facts relevant to inspections or alleged violations. Prepare correspondence, reports of inspections or investigations, and recommendations for action. Recommend legal or administrative action to protect government property. Submit samples of products to government laboratories for testing as required. Coordinate with and assist law enforcement agencies in matters of mutual con-

cern. Investigate applications for special licenses or permits, as well as alleged license or permit violations. Testify in court or at administrative proceedings concerning investigation findings. Monitor investigations of suspected offenders to ensure that they are conducted in accordance with constitutional requirements. **SKILLS—Systems Analysis:** Determining how a system should work and how changes in conditions, operations, and the environment will affect outcomes. **Negotiation:** Bringing others together and trying to reconcile differences. **Speaking:** Talking to others to convey information effectively. **Judgment and Decision Making:** Considering the relative costs and benefits of potential actions to choose the most appropriate one. **Writing:** Communicating effectively in writing as appropriate for the needs of the audience. **Reading Comprehension:** Understanding written sentences and paragraphs in work-related documents. **Critical Thinking:** Using logic and reasoning to identify the strengths and weaknesses of alternative solutions, conclusions, or approaches to problems. **Systems Evaluation:** Identifying measures or indicators of system performance and the actions needed to improve or correct performance relative to the goals of the system. **GOE—Interest Area:** 07. Government and Public Administration. **Work Group:** 07.03. Regulations Enforcement. **Other Jobs in This Work Group:** Agricultural Inspectors; Aviation Inspectors; Child Support, Missing Persons, and Unemployment Insurance Fraud Investigators; Environmental Compliance Inspectors; Equal Opportunity Representatives and Officers; Financial Examiners; Fire Inspectors; Fish and Game Wardens; Forest Fire Inspectors and Prevention Specialists; Immigration and Customs Inspectors; Licensing Examiners and Inspectors; Marine Cargo Inspectors; Mechanical Inspectors; Motor Vehicle Inspectors; Nuclear Monitoring Technicians; Occupational Health and Safety Specialists; Pressure Vessel Inspectors; Railroad Inspectors; Tax Examiners, Collectors, and Revenue Agents. **PERSONALITY TYPE:** Enterprising.

EDUCATION/TRAINING PROGRAM(S)—No data available. **RELATED KNOWLEDGE/COURSES—Law and Government:** Knowledge of laws, legal codes, court procedures, precedents, government regulations, executive orders, agency rules, and the democratic political process. **Personnel and Human Resources:** Knowledge of principles and procedures for personnel recruitment, selection, training, compensation and benefits, labor relations and negotiation, and personnel information systems. **Public Safety and Security:** Knowledge of relevant equipment, policies, procedures, and strategies to promote effective local, state, or national security operations for the protection of people, data, property, and institutions. **English Language:** Knowledge of the structure and content of the English language, including the meaning and spelling of words, rules of composition, and grammar. **Communications and Media:** Knowledge of media production, communication, and dissemination techniques and methods. This includes alternative ways to inform and entertain via written, oral, and visual media. **Production and Processing:** Knowledge of raw materials, production processes, quality control, costs, and other techniques for maximizing the effective manufacture and distribution of goods.

Government Service Executives

- ◎ Education/Training Required: Work experience plus degree
- ◎ Annual Earnings: $140,350
- ◎ Growth: 16.7%
- ◎ Annual Job Openings: 63,000
- ◎ Self-Employed: 14.6%
- ◎ Part-Time: 5.3%

Determine and formulate policies and provide overall direction of federal, state, local, or international government activities. Plan, direct, and coordinate operational activities at the highest level of management with the help of subordinate managers. Directs organization charged with administering and monitoring regulated activities to interpret and clarify laws and ensure compliance with laws. Administers, interprets, and explains policies, rules, regulations, and laws to organizations and individuals under authority of commission or applicable legislation. Develops, plans, organizes, and administers policies and procedures for organization to ensure administrative and operational objectives are met. Directs and coordinates activities of workers in public organization to ensure continuing operations, maximize returns on investments, and increase productivity. Negotiates contracts and agreements with federal and state agencies and other organizations and prepares budget for funding and implementation of programs. Implements corrective action plan to solve problems. Reviews and analyzes legislation, laws, and public policy and recommends changes to promote and support interests of general population as well as special groups. Develops, directs, and coordinates testing, hiring, training, and evaluation of staff personnel. Establishes and maintains comprehensive and current record-keeping system of activities and operational procedures in business office. Testifies in court, before control or review board, or at legislature. Participates in activities to promote business and expand services and provides technical assistance in conducting of conferences, seminars, and workshops. Delivers speeches, writes articles, and presents information for organization at meetings or conventions to promote services, exchange ideas, and accomplish objectives. Plans, promotes, organizes, and coordinates public community service program and maintains cooperative working relationships among public and agency participants. Conducts or directs investigations or hearings to resolve complaints and violations of laws. Prepares, reviews, and submits reports concerning activities, expenses, budget, government statutes and rulings, and other items affecting business or program services. Directs, coordinates, and conducts activities between United States government and foreign entities to provide information to promote international interest and harmony. **SKILLS—Management of Financial Resources:** Determining how money will be spent to get the work done and accounting for these expenditures. **Systems Analysis:** Determining how a system should work and how changes in conditions, operations, and the environment will affect outcomes. **Systems Evaluation:** Identifying measures or indicators of system performance and the actions needed to improve or correct performance relative to the goals of the system. **Coordination:** Adjusting actions in relation to others' actions. **Management of Personnel Resources:** Motivating, developing, and directing people as they work, identifying the best people for the job. **Judgment and Decision Making:** Considering the relative costs and benefits of potential actions to choose the most appropriate one. **Negotiation:** Bringing others together and trying to reconcile differences. **Persuasion:** Persuading others to change their minds or behavior. **GOE—Interest Area:** 07. Government and Public Administration. **Work Group:** 07.01. Managerial Work in Government and Public Administration. **Other Jobs in This Work Group:** Social and Community Service Managers. **PERSONALITY TYPE:** Enterprising.

EDUCATION/TRAINING PROGRAM(S)—Business Administration and Management, General; Business/Commerce, General; Entrepreneurship/Entrepreneurial Studies; International Business/Trade/Commerce; Public Administration; Public Administration and Social Service Professions, Other; Public Policy Analysis. **RELATED KNOWLEDGE/COURSES**—**Administration and Management:** Knowledge of business and management principles involved in strategic planning, resource allocation, human resources modeling, leadership technique, production methods, and coordination of people and resources. **Law and Government:** Knowledge of laws, legal codes, court procedures, precedents, government regulations, executive orders, agency rules, and the democratic political process. **Economics and Accounting:** Knowledge of economic and accounting principles and practices, the financial markets, banking, and the analysis and reporting of financial data. **Personnel and Human Resources:** Knowledge of principles and procedures for personnel recruitment, selection, training, compensation and benefits, labor relations and negotiation, and personnel information systems. **Education and Training:** Knowledge of principles and methods for curriculum and training design, teaching and instruction for individuals and groups, and the measurement of training effects. **Psychology:** Knowledge of human behavior and performance; individual differences in ability, personality, and interests; learning and motivation; psychological research methods; and the assessment and treatment of behavioral and affective disorders.

Grader, Bulldozer, and Scraper Operators

- Education/Training Required: Moderate-term on-the-job training
- Annual Earnings: $35,360
- Growth: 10.4%
- Annual Job Openings: 45,000
- Self-Employed: 3.7%
- Part-Time: 2.6%

Operate machines or vehicles equipped with blades to remove, distribute, level, or grade earth. Connects hydraulic hoses, belts, mechanical linkage, or power takeoff shaft to tractor. Starts engine; moves throttle, switches, and levers; and depresses pedals to operate machines, equipment, and attachments. Drives equipment in successive passes over working area to achieve specified result, such as grading terrain or removing, dumping, or spreading earth and rock. Aligns machine, cutterhead, or depth gauge marker with reference stakes and guidelines on ground or positions equipment, following hand signals of assistant. Fastens bulldozer blade or other attachment to tractor, using hitches. Greases, oils, and performs minor repairs on tractor, using grease gun, oilcans, and hand tools. Signals operator to guide movement of tractor-drawn machine. **SKILLS—Operation and Control:** Controlling operations of equipment or systems. **Repairing:** Repairing machines or systems by using the needed tools. **Operation Monitoring:** Watching gauges, dials, or other indicators to make sure a machine is working properly. **Equipment Selection:** Determining the kind of tools and equipment needed to do a job. **Equipment Maintenance:** Performing routine maintenance on equipment and determining when and what kind of maintenance is needed. **GOE—Interest Area:** 02. Architecture and Construction. **Work Group:** 02.04. Construction Crafts. **Other Jobs in This Work Group:** Boat Builders and Shipwrights; Boilermakers; Brattice Builders; Brickmasons and Blockmasons; Carpet Installers; Ceiling Tile Installers; Cement Masons and Concrete Finishers; Commercial Divers; Construction Carpenters; Crane and Tower Operators; Dragline Operators; Drywall Installers; Electricians; Fence Erectors; Floor Layers, Except Carpet, Wood, and Hard Tiles; Floor Sanders and Finishers; Glaziers; Hazardous Materials Removal Workers; Insulation Workers, Floor, Ceiling, and Wall; Insulation Workers, Mechanical; Manufactured Building and Mobile Home Installers; Operating Engineers; Painters, Construction and Maintenance; Paperhangers; Paving, Surfacing, and Tamping Equipment Operators; Pile-Driver Operators; Pipe Fitters; Pipelayers; Pipelaying Fitters; Plasterers and Stucco Masons; Plumbers; Rail-Track Laying and Maintenance Equipment Operators; Refractory Materials Repairers, Except Brickmasons; Reinforcing Iron and Rebar Workers; Riggers; Roofers; Rough Carpenters; Security and Fire Alarm Systems Installers; Segmental Pavers; Sheet Metal Workers; Ship Carpenters and Joiners; Stone Cutters and Carvers; Stonemasons; Structural Iron and Steel Workers; Tapers; Terrazzo Workers and Finishers; Tile and Marble Setters. **PERSONALITY TYPE:** Realistic.

EDUCATION/TRAINING PROGRAM(S)—Construction/Heavy Equipment/Earthmoving Equipment Operation; Mobil Crane Operation/Operator. **RELATED KNOWLEDGE/COURSES—Mechanical Devices:** Knowledge of machines and tools, including their designs, uses, repair, and maintenance. **Transportation:** Knowledge of principles and methods for moving people or goods by air, rail, sea, or road, including the relative costs and benefits. **Physics:** Knowledge and prediction of physical principles and laws and their interrelationships and applications to understanding fluid, material, and atmospheric dynamics and mechanical, electrical, atomic, and subatomic structures and processes.

Graduate Teaching Assistants

- ◎ Education/Training Required: Master's degree
- ◎ Annual Earnings: $26,120
- ◎ Growth: 38.1%
- ◎ Annual Job Openings: 216,000
- ◎ Self-Employed: 0.3%
- ◎ Part-Time: 27.7%

Assist department chairperson, faculty members, or other professional staff members in college or university by performing teaching or teaching-related duties, such as teaching lower-level courses, developing teaching materials, preparing and giving examinations, and grading examinations or papers. Graduate assistants must be enrolled in a graduate school program. Graduate assistants who primarily perform non-teaching duties, such as laboratory research, should be reported in the occupational category related to the work performed. Evaluate and grade examinations, assignments, and papers and record grades. Lead discussion sections, tutorials, and laboratory sections. Teach undergraduate-level courses. Develop teaching materials such as syllabi, visual aids, answer keys, supplementary notes, and course Web sites. Attend lectures given by the instructor whom they are assisting. Complete laboratory projects prior to assigning them to students so that any needed modifications can be made. Copy and distribute classroom materials. Demonstrate use of laboratory equipment and enforce laboratory rules. Inform students of the procedures for completing and submitting class work such as lab reports. Meet with supervisors to discuss students' grades and to complete required grade-related paperwork. Notify instructors of errors or problems with assignments. Order or obtain materials needed for classes. Prepare and proctor examinations. Return assignments to students in accordance with established deadlines. Schedule and maintain regular office hours to meet with students. Arrange for supervisors to conduct teaching observations; meet with supervisors to receive feedback about teaching performance. Assist faculty members or staff with student conferences. Provide assistance to faculty members or staff with laboratory or field research. Provide instructors with assistance in the use of audiovisual equipment. Provide assistance to library staff in maintaining library collections. **SKILLS—Instructing:** Teaching others how to do something. **Learning Strategies:** Selecting and using training/instructional methods and procedures appropriate for the situation when learning or teaching new things. **Speaking:** Talking to others to convey information effectively. **Reading Comprehension:** Understanding written sentences and paragraphs in work-related documents. **Science:** Using scientific rules and methods to solve problems. **Writing:** Communicating effectively in writing as appropriate for the needs of the audience. **Mathematics:** Using mathematics to solve problems. **Critical Thinking:** Using logic and reasoning to identify the strengths and weaknesses of alternative solutions, conclusions, or approaches to problems. **GOE—Interest Area:** 05. Education and Training. **Work Group:** 05.03. Postsecondary and Adult Teaching and Instructing. **Other Jobs in This Work Group:** Adult Literacy, Remedial Education, and GED Teachers and Instructors; Agricultural Sciences Teachers, Postsecondary; Anthropology and Archeology Teachers, Postsecondary; Architecture Teachers, Postsecondary; Area, Ethnic, and Cultural Studies Teachers, Postsecondary; Art, Drama, and Music Teachers, Postsecondary; Atmospheric, Earth, Marine, and Space Sciences Teachers, Postsecondary; Biological Science Teachers, Postsecondary; Business Teachers, Postsecondary; Chemistry Teachers, Postsecondary; Communications Teachers, Postsecondary; Computer Science Teachers, Postsecondary; Criminal Justice and Law Enforcement Teachers, Postsecondary; Economics Teachers, Postsecondary; Education Teachers, Postsecondary; Engineering Teachers, Postsecondary; English Language and Literature Teachers, Postsecondary; Environmental Science Teachers, Postsecondary; Farm and Home Management Advisors; Foreign Language and Literature Teachers, Postsecondary; Forestry and Conservation Science Teachers, Postsecondary; Geography Teachers, Postsecondary; Health Specialties Teachers, Postsecondary; History Teachers, Postsecondary; Home Economics Teachers, Postsecondary; Law Teachers, Postsecondary; Library Science Teachers, Postsecondary; Mathematical Science Teachers, Postsecondary; Nursing Instructors and Teachers, Postsecondary; Philosophy and Religion Teachers, Postsecondary; Physics Teachers, Postsecondary; Political Science Teachers, Postsecondary; Psychology Teachers, Postsecondary; Recreation and Fitness Studies Teachers, Postsecondary; Self-Enrichment Education Teachers; Social Work Teachers, Postsecondary; Sociology Teachers, Postsecondary; Vocational Education Teachers, Postsecondary. **PERSONALITY TYPE:** Social.

EDUCATION/TRAINING PROGRAM(S)—No data available. **RELATED KNOWLEDGE/COURSES—Education and Training:** Knowledge of principles and methods for curriculum and training design, teaching and instruction for individuals and groups, and the measurement of training effects. **English Language:** Knowledge of the structure and content of the English language, including the meaning and spelling of words, rules of composition, and grammar. **Clerical Practices:** Knowledge of administrative and clerical procedures and systems such as word processing, managing files and records, stenography and transcription, designing forms, and other office procedures and terminology. **Mathematics:** Knowledge of arithmetic, algebra, geometry, calculus, and statistics and their applications. **Administration and Management:** Knowledge of business and management principles involved in strategic planning, resource allocation, human resources modeling, leadership technique, production methods, and coordination of people and resources. **Computers and Electronics:** Knowledge of circuit boards, processors, chips, electronic equipment, and computer hardware and software, including applications and programming.

Graphic Designers

- Education/Training Required: Bachelor's degree
- Annual Earnings: $38,030
- Growth: 21.9%
- Annual Job Openings: 29,000
- Self-Employed: 31.8%
- Part-Time: 16.5%

Design or create graphics to meet specific commercial or promotional needs, such as packaging, displays, or logos. May use a variety of mediums to achieve artistic or decorative effects. Create designs, concepts, and sample layouts based on knowledge of layout principles and esthetic design concepts. Determine size and arrangement of illustrative material and copy and select style and size of type. Use computer software to generate new images. Mark up, paste, and assemble final layouts to prepare layouts for printer. Draw and print charts, graphs, illustrations, and other artwork, using computer. Review final layouts and suggest improvements as needed. Confer with clients to discuss and determine layout design. Develop graphics and layouts for product illustrations, company logos, and Internet Web sites. Key information into computer equipment to create layouts for client or supervisor. Prepare illustrations or rough sketches of material, discussing them with clients and/or supervisors and making necessary changes. Study illustrations and photographs to plan presentation of materials, products, or services. Prepare notes and instructions for workers who assemble and prepare final layouts for printing. Develop negatives and prints to produce layout photographs, using negative- and print-developing equipment and tools. Photograph layouts, using camera, to make layout prints for supervisors or clients. Produce still and animated graphics for on-air and taped portions of television news broadcasts, using electronic video equipment. **SKILLS—Persuasion:** Persuading others to change their minds or behavior. **Time Management:** Managing one's own time and the time of others. **Troubleshooting:** Determining causes of operating errors and deciding what to do about them. **Instructing:** Teaching others how to do something. **Coordination:** Adjusting actions in relation to others' actions. **Social Perceptiveness:** Being aware of others' reactions and understanding why they react as they do. **Operations Analysis:** Analyzing needs and

G

product requirements to create a design. **Complex Problem Solving:** Identifying complex problems and reviewing related information to develop and evaluate options and implement solutions. **GOE—Interest Area:** 03. Arts and Communication. **Work Group:** 03.05. Design. **Other Jobs in This Work Group:** Commercial and Industrial Designers; Exhibit Designers; Fashion Designers; Floral Designers; Interior Designers; Merchandise Displayers and Window Trimmers; Set Designers. **PERSONALITY TYPE:** Artistic.

EDUCATION/TRAINING PROGRAM(S)—Agricultural Communication/Journalism; Commercial and Advertising Art; Computer Graphics; Design and Visual Communications, General; Graphic Design; Industrial Design; Web Page, Digital/Multimedia, and Information Resources Design. **RELATED KNOWLEDGE/COURSES—Fine Arts:** Knowledge of the theory and techniques required to compose, produce, and perform works of music, dance, the visual arts, drama, and sculpture. **Design:** Knowledge of design techniques, tools, and principles involved in production of precision technical plans, blueprints, drawings, and models. **Computers and Electronics:** Knowledge of circuit boards, processors, chips, electronic equipment, and computer hardware and software, including applications and programming. **Communications and Media:** Knowledge of media production, communication, and dissemination techniques and methods. This includes alternative ways to inform and entertain via written, oral, and visual media. **Sales and Marketing:** Knowledge of principles and methods for showing, promoting, and selling products or services. This includes marketing strategy and tactics, product demonstrations, sales techniques, and sales control systems. **Clerical Practices:** Knowledge of administrative and clerical procedures and systems such as word processing, managing files and records, stenography and transcription, designing forms, and other office procedures and terminology.

Grips and Set-Up Workers, Motion Picture Sets, Studios, and Stages

- Education/Training Required: Short-term on-the-job training
- Annual Earnings: $20,120
- Growth: 6.6%
- Annual Job Openings: 525,000
- Self-Employed: 0.8%
- Part-Time: 21.0%

Arrange equipment; raise and lower scenery; move dollies, cranes, and booms; and perform other duties for motion-picture, recording, or television industry. Arranges equipment preparatory to sessions and performances, following work order specifications, and handles props during performances. Rigs and dismantles stage or set equipment such as frames, scaffolding, platforms, or backdrops, using carpenter's hand tools. Adjusts controls to raise and lower scenery and stage curtain during performance, following cues. Adjusts controls to guide, position, and move equipment, such as cranes, booms, and cameras. Erects canvas covers to protect equipment from weather. Reads work orders and follows oral instructions to determine specified material and equipment to be moved and its relocation. Connects electrical equipment to power source and tests equipment before performance. Orders equipment and maintains equipment storage areas. Sews and repairs items using materials and hand tools such as canvas and sewing machines. Produces special lighting and sound effects during performances, using various machines and devices. **SKILLS—Installation:** Installing equipment, machines, wiring, or programs to meet specifications. **Repairing:** Repairing machines or systems by using the needed tools. **Operation and Control:** Controlling operations of equipment or systems. **Technology Design:** Generating or adapting equipment and technology to serve user needs. **Management of Material Resources:** Obtaining and seeing to the appropriate use of equipment, facilities, and materials needed to do certain work. **Operation Monitoring:** Watching gauges, dials, or other indicators to make sure a machine is working properly. **GOE—Interest Area:** 02. Architecture and Construction. **Work Group:** 02.06. Construction Support/Labor. **Other Jobs in This Work Group:** Carpenter Assemblers and Repairers; Construction Laborers; Helpers—Brickmasons, Blockmasons, Stonemasons, and Tile and Marble Setters; Helpers—Carpenters; Helpers—Electricians; Helpers—Installation, Maintenance, and Repair Workers; Helpers—Painters, Paperhangers, Plasterers, and Stucco Masons; Helpers—Pipelayers, Plumbers, Pipefitters, and Steamfitters; Highway Maintenance Workers; Septic Tank Servicers and Sewer Pipe Cleaners. **PERSONALITY TYPE:** Realistic.

EDUCATION/TRAINING PROGRAM(S)—No data available. **RELATED KNOWLEDGE/COURSES—Building and Construction:** Knowledge of the materials, methods, and tools involved in the construction or repair of houses, buildings, or other structures such as highways and roads. **Fine Arts:** Knowledge of the theory and techniques required to compose, produce, and perform works of music, dance, the visual arts, drama, and sculpture. **Mechanical Devices:** Knowledge of machines and tools, including their designs, uses, repair, and maintenance.

Hairdressers, Hairstylists, and Cosmetologists

- ◎ Education/Training Required: Postsecondary vocational training
- ◎ Annual Earnings: $19,800
- ◎ Growth: 14.7%
- ◎ Annual Job Openings: 68,000
- ◎ Self-Employed: 44.3%
- ◎ Part-Time: 31.1%

Provide beauty services, such as shampooing, cutting, coloring, and styling hair and massaging and treating scalp. May also apply makeup, dress wigs, perform hair removal, and provide nail and skin care services. Keep work stations clean and sanitize tools such as scissors and combs. Cut, trim, and shape hair or hairpieces, based on customers' instructions, hair type, and facial features, using clippers, scissors, trimmers, and razors. Analyze patrons' hair and other physical features to determine and recommend beauty treatment or suggest hairstyles. Schedule client appointments. Bleach, dye, or tint hair, using applicator or brush. Update and maintain customer information records, such as beauty services provided. Shampoo, rinse, con-

dition, and dry hair and scalp or hairpieces with water, liquid soap, or other solutions. Operate cash registers to receive payments from patrons. Demonstrate and sell hair care products and cosmetics. Develop new styles and techniques. Apply water or setting, straightening, or waving solutions to hair and use curlers, rollers, hot combs, and curling irons to press and curl hair. Comb, brush, and spray hair or wigs to set style. Shape eyebrows and remove facial hair, using depilatory cream, tweezers, electrolysis, or wax. Administer therapeutic medication and advise patron to seek medical treatment for chronic or contagious scalp conditions. Massage and treat scalp for hygienic and remedial purposes, using hands, fingers, or vibrating equipment. Shave, trim, and shape beards and moustaches. Train or supervise other hairstylists, hairdressers, and assistants. Recommend and explain the use of cosmetics, lotions, and creams to soften and lubricate skin and enhance and restore natural appearance. Give facials to patrons, using special compounds such as lotions and creams. Clean, shape, and polish fingernails and toenails, using files and nail polish. Apply artificial fingernails. **SKILLS—Learning Strategies:** Selecting and using training/instructional methods and procedures appropriate for the situation when learning or teaching new things. **Social Perceptiveness:** Being aware of others' reactions and understanding why they react as they do. **Time Management:** Managing one's own time and the time of others. **Management of Financial Resources:** Determining how money will be spent to get the work done and accounting for these expenditures. **Science:** Using scientific rules and methods to solve problems. **Service Orientation:** Actively looking for ways to help people. **Operations Analysis:** Analyzing needs and product requirements to create a design. **Persuasion:** Persuading others to change their minds or behavior. **Equipment Selection:** Determining the kind of tools and equipment needed to do a job. **GOE—Interest Area:** 09. Hospitality, Tourism, and Recreation. **Work Group:** 09.07. Barber and Beauty Services. **Other Jobs in This Work Group:** Barbers; Manicurists and Pedicurists; Shampooers; Skin Care Specialists. **PERSONALITY TYPE:** Enterprising.

EDUCATION/TRAINING PROGRAM(S)—Cosmetology and Related Personal Grooming Arts, Other; Cosmetology, Barber/Styling, and Nail Instructor; Cosmetology/Cosmetologist, General; Electrolysis/Electrology and Electrolysis Technician; Hair Styling/Stylist and Hair Design; Make-Up Artist/

Specialist; Permanent Cosmetics/Makeup and Tattooing; Salon/Beauty Salon Management/Manager. **RELATED KNOWLEDGE/COURSES—Chemistry:** Knowledge of the chemical composition, structure, and properties of substances and of the chemical processes and transformations that they undergo. This includes uses of chemicals and their danger signs, production techniques, and disposal methods. **Customer and Personal Service:** Knowledge of principles and processes for providing customer and personal services. This includes customer needs assessment, meeting quality standards for services, and evaluation of customer satisfaction. **Sales and Marketing:** Knowledge of principles and methods for showing, promoting, and selling products or services. This includes marketing strategy and tactics, product demonstrations, sales techniques, and sales control systems. **Education and Training:** Knowledge of principles and methods for curriculum and training design, teaching and instruction for individuals and groups, and the measurement of training effects. **Administration and Management:** Knowledge of business and management principles involved in strategic planning, resource allocation, human resources modeling, leadership technique, production methods, and coordination of people and resources. **Psychology:** Knowledge of human behavior and performance; individual differences in ability, personality, and interests; learning and motivation; psychological research methods; and the assessment and treatment of behavioral and affective disorders.

Hazardous Materials Removal Workers

- Education/Training Required: Moderate-term on-the-job training
- Annual Earnings: $33,320
- Growth: 43.1%
- Annual Job Openings: 8,000
- Self-Employed: 0%
- Part-Time: 5.7%

Identify, remove, pack, transport, or dispose of hazardous materials, including asbestos, lead-based paint, waste oil, fuel, transmission fluid, radioactive materials, contaminated soil, etc. Specialized training and certification in hazardous materials handling or a confined entry permit are generally required. May

operate earth-moving equipment or trucks. Clean contaminated equipment or areas for re-use, using detergents and solvents, sandblasters, filter pumps, and steam cleaners. Drive trucks or other heavy equipment to convey contaminated waste to designated sea or ground locations. Follow prescribed safety procedures and comply with federal laws regulating waste disposal methods. Identify asbestos, lead, or other hazardous materials that need to be removed, using monitoring devices. Load and unload materials into containers and onto trucks, using hoists or forklifts. Mix and pour concrete into forms to encase waste material for disposal. Operate cranes to move and load baskets, casks, and canisters. Operate machines and equipment to remove, package, store, or transport loads of waste materials. Record numbers of containers stored at disposal sites and specify amounts and types of equipment and waste disposed. Apply chemical compounds to lead-based paint, allow compounds to dry, and then scrape the hazardous material into containers for removal and/or storage. Construct scaffolding or build containment areas prior to beginning abatement or decontamination work. Manipulate handgrips of mechanical arms to place irradiated fuel elements into baskets. Organize and track the locations of hazardous items in landfills. Package, store, and move irradiated fuel elements in the underwater storage basin of a nuclear reactor plant, using machines and equipment. Pull tram cars along underwater tracks and position cars to receive irradiated fuel elements; then pull loaded cars to mechanisms that automatically unload elements onto underwater tables. Remove asbestos and/or lead from surfaces, using hand and power tools such as scrapers, vacuums, and high-pressure sprayers. Unload baskets of irradiated elements onto packaging machines that automatically insert fuel elements into canisters and secure lids. **SKILLS—**No data available. **GOE—Interest Area:** 02. Architecture and Construction. **Work Group:** 02.04. Construction Crafts. **Other Jobs in This Work Group:** Boat Builders and Shipwrights; Boilermakers; Brattice Builders; Brickmasons and Blockmasons; Carpet Installers; Ceiling Tile Installers; Cement Masons and Concrete Finishers; Commercial Divers; Construction Carpenters; Crane and Tower Operators; Dragline Operators; Drywall Installers; Electricians; Fence Erectors; Floor Layers, Except Carpet, Wood, and Hard Tiles; Floor Sanders and Finishers; Glaziers; Grader, Bulldozer, and Scraper Operators; Insulation Workers, Floor, Ceiling, and Wall; Insulation Workers, Mechanical; Manufactured

Building and Mobile Home Installers; Operating Engineers; Painters, Construction and Maintenance; Paperhangers; Paving, Surfacing, and Tamping Equipment Operators; Pile-Driver Operators; Pipe Fitters; Pipelayers; Pipelaying Fitters; Plasterers and Stucco Masons; Plumbers; Rail-Track Laying and Maintenance Equipment Operators; Refractory Materials Repairers, Except Brickmasons; Reinforcing Iron and Rebar Workers; Riggers; Roofers; Rough Carpenters; Security and Fire Alarm Systems Installers; Segmental Pavers; Sheet Metal Workers; Ship Carpenters and Joiners; Stone Cutters and Carvers; Stonemasons; Structural Iron and Steel Workers; Tapers; Terrazzo Workers and Finishers; Tile and Marble Setters. **PERSONALITY TYPE:** No data available.

EDUCATION/TRAINING PROGRAM(S)—Construction Trades, Other; Hazardous Materials Management and Waste Technology/Technician; Mechanic and Repair Technologies/Technicians, Other. **RELATED KNOWLEDGE/COURSES**—No data available.

Health Educators

- Education/Training Required: Master's degree
- Annual Earnings: $38,480
- Growth: 21.9%
- Annual Job Openings: 8,000
- Self-Employed: 0.2%
- Part-Time: 10.6%

Promote, maintain, and improve individual and community health by assisting individuals and communities in adopting healthy behaviors. Collect and analyze data to identify community needs prior to planning, implementing, monitoring, and evaluating programs designed to encourage healthy lifestyles, policies, and environments. May also serve as a resource to assist individuals, other professionals, or the community, and may administer fiscal resources for health education programs. Collaborate with health specialists and civic groups to determine community health needs and the availability of services and to develop goals for meeting needs. Design and conduct evaluations and diagnostic studies to assess the quality and performance of health education programs. Develop and present health education and promotion programs such as training workshops, conferences, and school or community presentations. Develop operational plans and policies necessary to achieve health education objectives and services. Develop, conduct, or coordinate health needs assessments and other public health surveys. Prepare and distribute health education materials, including reports; bulletins; and visual aids such as films, videotapes, photographs, and posters. Provide guidance to agencies and organizations in the assessment of health education needs and in the development and delivery of health education programs. Provide program information to the public by preparing and presenting press releases, conducting media campaigns, and/or maintaining program-related Web sites. Develop and maintain cooperative working relationships with agencies and organizations interested in public health care. Develop and maintain health education libraries to provide resources for staff and community agencies. Develop, prepare, and coordinate grant applications and grant-related activities to obtain funding for health education programs and related work. Document activities, recording information such as the numbers of applications completed, presentations conducted, and persons assisted. Maintain databases, mailing lists, telephone networks, and other information to facilitate the functioning of health education programs. Supervise professional and technical staff in implementing health programs, objectives, and goals. **SKILLS—Speaking:** Talking to others to convey information effectively. **Systems Analysis:** Determining how a system should work and how changes in conditions, operations, and the environment will affect outcomes. **Coordination:** Adjusting actions in relation to others' actions. **Writing:** Communicating effectively in writing as appropriate for the needs of the audience. **Systems Evaluation:** Identifying measures or indicators of system performance and the actions needed to improve or correct performance relative to the goals of the system. **Persuasion:** Persuading others to change their minds or behavior. **Complex Problem Solving:** Identifying complex problems and reviewing related information to develop and evaluate options and implement solutions. **Active Learning:** Understanding the implications of new information for both current and future problem-solving and decision-making. **GOE—Interest Area:** 05. Education and Training. **Work Group:** 05.06. Counseling, Health, and Fitness Education. **Other Jobs in This Work Group:** Educational, Vocational, and School Counselors; Fitness Trainers and Aerobics Instructors. **PERSONALITY TYPE:** Social.

EDUCATION/TRAINING PROGRAM(S)—Community Health Services/Liaison/Counseling; Health Communication; International Public Health/International Health; Maternal and Child Health; Public Health Education and Promotion. **RELATED KNOWLEDGE/COURSES—Education and Training:** Knowledge of principles and methods for curriculum and training design, teaching and instruction for individuals and groups, and the measurement of training effects. **Communications and Media:** Knowledge of media production, communication, and dissemination techniques and methods. This includes alternative ways to inform and entertain via written, oral, and visual media. **Therapy and Counseling:** Knowledge of principles, methods, and procedures for diagnosis, treatment, and rehabilitation of physical and mental dysfunctions and for career counseling and guidance. **Sales and Marketing:** Knowledge of principles and methods for showing, promoting, and selling products or services. This includes marketing strategy and tactics, product demonstrations, sales techniques, and sales control systems. **Medicine and Dentistry:** Knowledge of the information and techniques needed to diagnose and treat human injuries, diseases, and deformities. This includes symptoms, treatment alternatives, drug properties and interactions, and preventive health-care measures. **English Language:** Knowledge of the structure and content of the English language, including the meaning and spelling of words, rules of composition, and grammar.

Health Specialties Teachers, Postsecondary

- Education/Training Required: Master's degree
- Annual Earnings: $64,630
- Growth: 38.1%
- Annual Job Openings: 216,000
- Self-Employed: 0.3%
- Part-Time: 27.7%

Teach courses in health specialties, such as veterinary medicine, dentistry, pharmacy, therapy, laboratory technology, and public health. Initiate, facilitate, and moderate classroom discussions. Keep abreast of developments in their field by reading current literature, talking with colleagues, and participating in professional conferences. Compile, administer, and grade examinations or assign this work to others. Evaluate and grade students' class work, assignments, and papers. Prepare course materials such as syllabi, homework assignments, and handouts. Prepare and deliver lectures to undergraduate and/or graduate students on topics such as public health, stress management, and work-site health promotion. Plan, evaluate, and revise curricula, course content, and course materials and methods of instruction. Supervise undergraduate and/or graduate teaching, internship, and research work. Conduct research in a particular field of knowledge and publish findings in professional journals, books, and/or electronic media. Collaborate with colleagues to address teaching and research issues. Supervise laboratory sessions. Maintain student attendance records, grades, and other required records. Maintain regularly scheduled office hours in order to advise and assist students. Advise students on academic and vocational curricula and on career issues. Participate in student recruitment, registration, and placement activities. Write grant proposals to procure external research funding. Serve on academic or administrative committees that deal with institutional policies, departmental matters, and academic issues. Select and obtain materials and supplies such as textbooks and laboratory equipment. Act as advisers to student organizations. Perform administrative duties such as serving as department head. **SKILLS—Science:** Using scientific rules and methods to solve problems. **Instructing:** Teaching others how to do something. **Learning Strategies:** Selecting and using training/instructional methods and procedures appropriate for the situation when learning or teaching new things. **Writing:** Communicating effectively in writing as appropriate for the needs of the audience. **Critical Thinking:** Using logic and reasoning to identify the strengths and weaknesses of alternative solutions, conclusions, or approaches to problems. **Reading Comprehension:** Understanding written sentences and paragraphs in work-related documents. **Time Management:** Managing one's own time and the time of others. **Active Learning:** Understanding the implications of new information for both current and future problem-solving and decision-making. **GOE—Interest Area:** 05. Education and Training. **Work Group:** 05.03. Postsecondary and Adult Teaching and Instructing. **Other Jobs in This Work Group:** Adult Literacy, Remedial Education, and GED Teachers and Instructors; Agricultural Sciences Teachers, Postsecondary; Anthropology and Archeology Teachers, Postsecondary; Architecture Teachers, Postsecondary; Area, Ethnic, and Cultural Studies Teachers, Postsecondary; Art, Drama, and Music Teachers, Postsecondary; Atmospheric, Earth, Marine, and Space Sciences Teachers, Postsecondary; Biological Science Teachers, Postsecondary; Business Teachers, Postsecondary; Chemistry Teachers, Postsecondary; Communications Teachers, Postsecondary; Computer Science Teachers, Postsecondary; Criminal Justice and Law Enforcement Teachers, Postsecondary; Economics Teachers, Postsecondary; Education Teachers, Postsecondary; Engineering Teachers, Postsecondary; English Language and Literature Teachers, Postsecondary; Environmental Science Teachers, Postsecondary; Farm and Home Management Advisors; Foreign Language and Literature Teachers, Postsecondary; Forestry and Conservation Science Teachers, Postsecondary; Geography Teachers, Postsecondary; Graduate Teaching Assistants; History Teachers, Postsecondary; Home Economics Teachers, Postsecondary; Law Teachers, Postsecondary; Library Science Teachers, Postsecondary; Mathematical Science Teachers, Postsecondary; Nursing Instructors and Teachers, Postsecondary; Philosophy and Religion Teachers, Postsecondary; Physics Teachers, Postsecondary; Political Science Teachers, Postsecondary; Psychology Teachers, Postsecondary; Recreation and Fitness Studies Teachers, Postsecondary; Self-Enrichment Education Teachers; Social Work Teachers, Postsecondary; Sociology Teachers, Postsecondary; Vocational Education Teachers, Postsecondary. **PERSONALITY TYPE:** Investigative.

EDUCATION/TRAINING PROGRAM(S)— Allied Health and Medical Assisting Services, Other; Allied Health Diagnostic, Intervention, and Treatment Professions, Other; Art Therapy/Therapist; Asian Bodywork Therapy; Audiology/Audiologist and Hearing Sciences; Audiology/Audiologist and Speech-Language Pathology/Pathologist; Biostatistics; Blood Bank Technology Specialist; Cardiovascular Technology/Technologist; Chiropractic (DC); Clinical Laboratory Science/Medical Technology/Technologist; Clinical/Medical Laboratory Assistant; Clinical/Medical Laboratory Technician; Communication Disorders, General; Cytotechnology/Cytotechnologist; Dance Therapy/Therapist; Dental Assisting/Assistant; Dental Clinical Sciences, General (MS, PhD); Dental Hygiene/Hygienist; Dental Laboratory Technology/Technician; Dental Services and Allied Professions,

Other; Dentistry (DDS, DMD); Diagnostic Medical Sonography/Sonographer and Ultrasound Technician; Electrocardiograph Technology/Technician; Electroneurodiagnostic/Electroencephalographic Technology/Technologist; Emergency Medical Technology/Technician (EMT Paramedic); Environmental Health; Epidemiology; Health Occupations Teacher Education; Health/Medical Physics; Health/Medical Preparatory Programs, Other; Hematology Technology/Technician; Hypnotherapy/Hypnotherapist; Massage Therapy/Therapeutic Massage; Medical Radiologic Technology/Science—Radiation Therapist; Music Therapy/Therapist; Nuclear Medical Technology/Technologist; Occupational Health and Industrial Hygiene; Occupational Therapist Assistant; Occupational Therapy/Therapist; Orthotist/Prosthetist; Perfusion Technology/Perfusionist; Pharmacy (PharmD [USA]; PharmD, BS/BPharm [Canada]); Pharmacy Administration and Pharmacy Policy and Regulatory Affairs (MS, PhD); Pharmacy Technician/Assistant; Pharmacy, Pharmaceutical Sciences, and Administration, Other; Physical Therapist Assistant; Physical Therapy/Therapist; Physician Assistant; Pre-Dentistry Studies; Pre-Medicine/Pre-Medical Studies; Pre-Nursing Studies; others. **RELATED KNOWLEDGE/ COURSES—Education and Training:** Knowledge of principles and methods for curriculum and training design, teaching and instruction for individuals and groups, and the measurement of training effects. **Medicine and Dentistry:** Knowledge of the information and techniques needed to diagnose and treat human injuries, diseases, and deformities. This includes symptoms, treatment alternatives, drug properties and interactions, and preventive health-care measures. **Biology:** Knowledge of plant and animal organisms and their tissues, cells, functions, interdependencies, and interactions with each other and the environment. **Psychology:** Knowledge of human behavior and performance; individual differences in ability, personality, and interests; learning and motivation; psychological research methods; and the assessment and treatment of behavioral and affective disorders. **Sociology and Anthropology:** Knowledge of group behavior and dynamics, societal trends and influences, human migrations, ethnicity, and cultures and their history and origins. **Therapy and Counseling:** Knowledge of principles, methods, and procedures for diagnosis, treatment, and rehabilitation of physical and mental dysfunctions and for career counseling and guidance.

Heating and Air Conditioning Mechanics

- Education/Training Required: Long-term on-the-job training
- Annual Earnings: $36,260
- Growth: 31.8%
- Annual Job Openings: 35,000
- Self-Employed: 15.4%
- Part-Time: 3.1%

Install, service, and repair heating and air conditioning systems in residences and commercial establishments. Obtain and maintain required certification(s). Comply with all applicable standards, policies, and procedures, including safety procedures and the maintenance of a clean work area. Repair or replace defective equipment, components, or wiring. Test electrical circuits and components for continuity, using electrical test equipment. Reassemble and test equipment following repairs. Inspect and test system to verify system compliance with plans and specifications and to detect and locate malfunctions. Discuss heating-cooling system malfunctions with users to isolate problems or to verify that malfunctions have been corrected. Record and report all faults, deficiencies, and other unusual occurrences, as well as the time and materials expended on work orders. Test pipe or tubing joints and connections for leaks, using pressure gauge or soap-and-water solution. Adjust system controls to setting recommended by manufacturer to balance system, using hand tools. Recommend, develop, and perform preventive and general maintenance procedures such as cleaning, power-washing, and vacuuming equipment; oiling parts; and changing filters. Lay out and connect electrical wiring between controls and equipment according to wiring diagram, using electrician's hand tools. Install auxiliary components to heating-cooling equipment, such as expansion and discharge valves, air ducts, pipes, blowers, dampers, flues, and stokers, following blueprints. Assist with other work in coordination with repair and maintenance teams. Install, connect, and adjust thermostats, humidistats and timers, using hand tools. Generate work orders that address deficiencies in need of correction. Join pipes or tubing to equipment and to fuel, water, or refrigerant source to form complete circuit. Assemble, position, and mount heating or cooling equipment, following blueprints. Study blueprints, design specifications, and manufacturers' recommendations to ascertain the configuration of heating or cooling equipment components and to ensure the proper installation of components. Cut and drill holes in floors, walls, and roof to install equipment, using power saws and drills. **SKILLS—Repairing:** Repairing machines or systems by using the needed tools. **Installation:** Installing equipment, machines, wiring, or programs to meet specifications. **Equipment Maintenance:** Performing routine maintenance on equipment and determining when and what kind of maintenance is needed. **Troubleshooting:** Determining causes of operating errors and deciding what to do about them. **Systems Evaluation:** Identifying measures or indicators of system performance and the actions needed to improve or correct performance relative to the goals of the system. **Coordination:** Adjusting actions in relation to others' actions. **Negotiation:** Bringing others together and trying to reconcile differences. **Persuasion:** Persuading others to change their minds or behavior. **GOE—Interest Area:** 02. Architecture and Construction. **Work Group:** 02.05. Systems and Equipment Installation, Maintenance, and Repair. **Other Jobs in This Work Group:** Central Office and PBX Installers and Repairers; Communication Equipment Mechanics, Installers, and Repairers; Electric Meter Installers and Repairers; Electrical and Electronics Repairers, Powerhouse, Substation, and Relay; Electrical Power-Line Installers and Repairers; Elevator Installers and Repairers; Frame Wirers, Central Office; Home Appliance Installers; Maintenance and Repair Workers, General; Meter Mechanics; Refrigeration Mechanics; Station Installers and Repairers, Telephone; Telecommunications Facility Examiners; Telecommunications Line Installers and Repairers. **PERSONALITY TYPE:** Realistic.

EDUCATION/TRAINING PROGRAM(S)— Heating, Air Conditioning, and Refrigeration Technology/Technician (ACH/ACR/ACHR/HRAC/ HVAC/AC Technology); Heating, Air Conditioning, Ventilation, and Refrigeration Maintenance Technology/Technician (HAC, HACR, HVAC, HVACR); Solar Energy Technology/Technician. **RELATED KNOWLEDGE/COURSES—Mechanical Devices:** Knowledge of machines and tools, including their designs, uses, repair, and maintenance. **Building and Construction:** Knowledge of the materials, methods, and tools involved in the construction or repair of houses, buildings, or other structures such as highways and roads. **Design:** Knowledge of design techniques, tools, and principles involved in production of precision technical plans, blueprints, drawings, and models. **Engineering and Technology:** Knowledge of the practical application of engineering science and technology. This includes applying principles, techniques, procedures, and equipment to the design and production of various goods and services. **Physics:** Knowledge and prediction of physical principles and laws and their interrelationships and applications to understanding fluid, material, and atmospheric dynamics and mechanical, electrical, atomic, and subatomic structures and processes. **Customer and Personal Service:** Knowledge of principles and processes for providing customer and personal services. This includes customer needs assessment, meeting quality standards for services, and evaluation of customer satisfaction.

Helpers—Electricians

- ◎ Education/Training Required: Short-term on-the-job training
- ◎ Annual Earnings: $23,420
- ◎ Growth: 17.9%
- ◎ Annual Job Openings: 17,000
- ◎ Self Employed: 0.4%
- ◎ Part-Time: 13.2%

Help electricians by performing duties of lesser skill. Duties include using, supplying or holding materials or tools and cleaning work area and equipment. Trace out short circuits in wiring, using test meter. Measure, cut, and bend wire and conduit, using measuring instruments and hand tools. Maintain tools, vehicles, and equipment and keep parts and supplies in order. Drill holes and pull or push wiring through openings, using hand and power tools. Perform semi-skilled and unskilled laboring duties related to the installation, maintenance, and repair of a wide variety of electrical systems and equipment. Disassemble defective electrical equipment, replace defective or worn parts, and reassemble equipment, using hand tools. Transport tools, materials, equipment, and supplies to work site by hand; handtruck; or heavy, motorized truck. Examine electrical units for loose connections and broken insulation and tighten connections, using hand tools. Strip insulation from wire ends, using wire-stripping pliers, and attach wires to terminals for subsequent sol-

dering. Thread conduit ends, connect couplings, and fabricate and secure conduit support brackets, using hand tools. Construct controllers and panels, using power drills, drill presses, taps, saws, and punches. String transmission lines or cables through ducts or conduits, under the ground, through equipment, or to towers. Clean work area and wash parts. Erect electrical system components and barricades and rig scaffolds, hoists, and shoring. Install copper-clad ground rods, using a manual post driver. Raise, lower, or position equipment, tools, and materials, using hoist, hand line, or block and tackle. Dig trenches or holes for installation of conduit or supports. Requisition materials, using warehouse requisition or release forms. Bolt component parts together to form tower assemblies, using hand tools. Paint a variety of objects related to electrical functions. Operate cutting torches and welding equipment while working with conduit and metal components to construct devices associated with electrical functions. **SKILLS—Installation:** Installing equipment, machines, wiring, or programs to meet specifications. **Troubleshooting:** Determining causes of operating errors and deciding what to do about them. **Repairing:** Repairing machines or systems by using the needed tools. **Complex Problem Solving:** Identifying complex problems and reviewing related information to develop and evaluate options and implement solutions. **Mathematics:** Using mathematics to solve problems. **Equipment Selection:** Determining the kind of tools and equipment needed to do a job. **Instructing:** Teaching others how to do something. **Critical Thinking:** Using logic and reasoning to identify the strengths and weaknesses of alternative solutions, conclusions, or approaches to problems. **Learning Strategies:** Selecting and using training/instructional methods and procedures appropriate for the situation when learning or teaching new things. **Time Management:** Managing one's own time and the time of others. **GOE—Interest Area:** 02. Architecture and Construction. **Work Group:** 02.06. Construction Support/Labor. **Other Jobs in This Work Group:** Carpenter Assemblers and Repairers; Construction Laborers; Grips and Set-Up Workers, Motion Picture Sets, Studios, and Stages; Helpers—Brickmasons, Blockmasons, Stonemasons, and Tile and Marble Setters; Helpers—Carpenters; Helpers—Installation, Maintenance, and Repair Workers; Helpers—Painters, Paperhangers, Plasterers, and Stucco Masons; Helpers—Pipelayers, Plumbers, Pipefitters, and Steamfitters; Highway Maintenance Workers;

Septic Tank Servicers and Sewer Pipe Cleaners. **PER-SONALITY TYPE:** Realistic.

EDUCATION/TRAINING PROGRAM(S)—Electrician. **RELATED KNOWLEDGE/COURSES—Building and Construction:** Knowledge of the materials, methods, and tools involved in the construction or repair of houses, buildings, or other structures such as highways and roads. **Mechanical Devices:** Knowledge of machines and tools, including their designs, uses, repair, and maintenance. **Design:** Knowledge of design techniques, tools, and principles involved in production of precision technical plans, blueprints, drawings, and models. **Public Safety and Security:** Knowledge of relevant equipment, policies, procedures, and strategies to promote effective local, state, or national security operations for the protection of people, data, property, and institutions. **Mathematics:** Knowledge of arithmetic, algebra, geometry, calculus, and statistics and their applications. **Engineering and Technology:** Knowledge of the practical application of engineering science and technology. This includes applying principles, techniques, procedures, and equipment to the design and production of various goods and services.

Helpers—Installation, Maintenance, and Repair Workers

- ◎ Education/Training Required: Short-term on-the-job training
- ◎ Annual Earnings: $21,310
- ◎ Growth: 20.3%
- ◎ Annual Job Openings: 33,000
- ◎ Self-Employed: 0%
- ◎ Part-Time: 19.2%

Help installation, maintenance, and repair workers in maintenance, parts replacement, and repair of vehicles, industrial machinery, and electrical and electronic equipment. Perform duties such as furnishing tools, materials, and supplies to other workers; cleaning work area, machines, and tools; and holding materials or tools for other workers. Tend and observe equipment and machinery in order to verify efficient and safe operation. Examine and test machinery,

equipment, components, and parts for defects and to ensure proper functioning. Adjust, connect, or disconnect wiring, piping, tubing, and other parts, using hand tools or power tools. Install or replace machinery, equipment, and new or replacement parts and instruments, using hand tools or power tools. Clean or lubricate vehicles, machinery, equipment, instruments, tools, work areas, and other objects, using hand tools, power tools, and cleaning equipment. Apply protective materials to equipment, components, and parts in order to prevent defects and corrosion. Transfer tools, parts, equipment, and supplies to and from work stations and other areas. Disassemble broken or defective equipment in order to facilitate repair; reassemble equipment when repairs are complete. Assemble and maintain physical structures, using hand tools or power tools. Provide assistance to more-skilled workers involved in the adjustment, maintenance, part replacement, and repair of tools, equipment, and machines. Position vehicles, machinery, equipment, physical structures, and other objects for assembly or installation, using hand tools, power tools, and moving equipment. Hold or supply tools, parts, equipment, and supplies for other workers. Prepare work stations so mechanics and repairers can conduct work. **SKILLS—Installation:** Installing equipment, machines, wiring, or programs to meet specifications. **Operation Monitoring:** Watching gauges, dials, or other indicators to make sure a machine is working properly. **Repairing:** Repairing machines or systems by using the needed tools. **Equipment Maintenance:** Performing routine maintenance on equipment and determining when and what kind of maintenance is needed. **Troubleshooting:** Determining causes of operating errors and deciding what to do about them. **Operations Analysis:** Analyzing needs and product requirements to create a design. **Persuasion:** Persuading others to change their minds or behavior. **Operation and Control:** Controlling operations of equipment or systems. **GOE—Interest Area:** 02. Architecture and Construction. **Work Group:** 02.06. Construction Support/Labor. **Other Jobs in This Work Group:** Carpenter Assemblers and Repairers; Construction Laborers; Grips and Set-Up Workers, Motion Picture Sets, Studios, and Stages; Helpers—Brickmasons, Blockmasons, Stonemasons, and Tile and Marble Setters; Helpers—Carpenters; Helpers—Electricians; Helpers—Painters, Paperhangers, Plasterers, and Stucco Masons; Helpers—Pipelayers, Plumbers, Pipefitters, and Steamfitters; Highway Maintenance Workers;

Septic Tank Servicers and Sewer Pipe Cleaners. **PERSONALITY TYPE:** Realistic.

EDUCATION/TRAINING PROGRAM(S)—Industrial Mechanics and Maintenance Technology. **RELATED KNOWLEDGE/COURSES—Mechanical Devices:** Knowledge of machines and tools, including their designs, uses, repair, and maintenance. **Engineering and Technology:** Knowledge of the practical application of engineering science and technology. This includes applying principles, techniques, procedures, and equipment to the design and production of various goods and services. **Design:** Knowledge of design techniques, tools, and principles involved in production of precision technical plans, blueprints, drawings, and models. **Chemistry:** Knowledge of the chemical composition, structure, and properties of substances and of the chemical processes and transformations that they undergo. This includes uses of chemicals and their danger signs, production techniques, and disposal methods. **Building and Construction:** Knowledge of the materials, methods, and tools involved in the construction or repair of houses, buildings, or other structures such as highways and roads. **Public Safety and Security:** Knowledge of relevant equipment, policies, procedures, and strategies to promote effective local, state, or national security operations for the protection of people, data, property, and institutions.

Highway Maintenance Workers

- Education/Training Required: Moderate-term on-the-job training
- Annual Earnings: $29,550
- Growth: 10.4%
- Annual Job Openings: 25,000
- Self-Employed: 1.6%
- Part-Time: 1.8%

Maintain highways, municipal and rural roads, airport runways, and rights-of-way. Duties include patching broken or eroded pavement, repairing guard rails, highway markers, and snow fences. May also mow or clear brush from along road or plow snow from roadway. Flag motorists to warn them of obstacles or repair work ahead. Set out signs and cones around work areas to divert traffic. Drive trucks or tractors with adjustable attachments to sweep debris from paved surfaces, mow grass and weeds, and remove snow and ice. Dump, spread, and tamp asphalt, using pneumatic tampers, to repair joints and patch broken pavement. Drive trucks to transport crews and equipment to work sites. Inspect, clean, and repair drainage systems, bridges, tunnels, and other structures. Haul and spread sand, gravel, and clay to fill washouts and repair road shoulders. Erect, install, or repair guardrails, road shoulders, berms, highway markers, warning signals, and highway lighting, using hand tools and power tools. Remove litter and debris from roadways, including debris from rock and mud slides. Clean and clear debris from culverts, catch basins, drop inlets, ditches, and other drain structures. Perform roadside landscaping work, such as clearing weeds and brush and planting and trimming trees. Paint traffic control lines and place pavement traffic messages by hand or using machines. Inspect markers to verify accurate installation. Apply poisons along roadsides and in animal burrows to eliminate unwanted roadside vegetation and rodents. Measure and mark locations for installation of markers, using tape, string, or chalk. Apply oil to road surfaces, using sprayers. Blend compounds to form adhesive mixtures used for marker installation. Place and remove snow fences used to prevent the accumulation of drifting snow on highways. **SKILLS—Equipment Maintenance:** Performing routine maintenance on equipment and determining when and what kind of maintenance is needed. **Repairing:** Repairing machines or systems by using the needed tools. **Installation:** Installing equipment, machines, wiring, or programs to meet specifications. **Management of Material Resources:** Obtaining and seeing to the appropriate use of equipment, facilities, and materials needed to do certain work. **Troubleshooting:** Determining causes of operating errors and deciding what to do about them. **Management of Personnel Resources:** Motivating, developing, and directing people as they work, identifying the best people for the job. **Coordination:** Adjusting actions in relation to others' actions. **Instructing:** Teaching others how to do something. **GOE—Interest Area:** 02. Architecture and Construction. **Work Group:** 02.06. Construction Support/Labor. **Other Jobs in This Work Group:** Carpenter Assemblers and Repairers; Construction Laborers; Grips and Set-Up Workers, Motion Picture Sets, Studios, and Stages; Helpers—Brickmasons, Blockmasons, Stonemasons, and Tile and Marble Setters; Helpers—Carpenters; Helpers—Electricians; Helpers—Installation, Maintenance, and Repair Workers; Helpers—Painters, Paperhangers, Plasterers, and Stucco Masons; Helpers—Pipelayers, Plumbers, Pipefitters, and Steamfitters; Septic Tank Servicers and Sewer Pipe Cleaners. **PERSONALITY TYPE:** Realistic.

EDUCATION/TRAINING PROGRAM(S)—Construction/Heavy Equipment/Earthmoving Equipment Operation. **RELATED KNOWLEDGE/COURSES**—**Transportation:** Knowledge of principles and methods for moving people or goods by air, rail, sea, or road, including the relative costs and benefits. **Building and Construction:** Knowledge of the materials, methods, and tools involved in the construction or repair of houses, buildings, or other structures such as highways and roads. **Customer and Personal Service:** Knowledge of principles and processes for providing customer and personal services. This includes customer needs assessment, meeting quality standards for services, and evaluation of customer satisfaction. **Public Safety and Security:** Knowledge of relevant equipment, policies, procedures, and strategies to promote effective local, state, or national security operations for the protection of people, data, property, and institutions. **Mechanical Devices:** Knowledge of machines and tools, including their designs, uses, repair, and maintenance. **Geography:** Knowledge of principles and methods for describing the features of land, sea, and air masses, including their physical characteristics; locations; interrelationships; and distribution of plant, animal, and human life.

Highway Patrol Pilots

- ◎ Education/Training Required: Long-term on-the-job training
- ◎ Annual Earnings: $45,210
- ◎ Growth: 24.7%
- ◎ Annual Job Openings: 67,000
- ◎ Self-Employed: 0%
- ◎ Part-Time: 1.4%

Pilot aircraft to patrol highway and enforce traffic laws. Pilots airplane to maintain order, respond to emergencies, enforce traffic and criminal laws, and apprehend criminals. Investigates traffic accidents and other accidents to determine causes and to determine if crime was committed. Arrests perpetrator of criminal act or submits citation or warning to violator of motor vehicle ordinance. Informs ground personnel where to re-route traffic in case of emergencies. Informs ground personnel of traffic congestion or unsafe driving conditions to ensure traffic flow and reduce incidence of accidents. Reviews facts to determine if criminal act or statute violation was involved. Expedites processing of prisoners, prepares and maintains records of prisoner bookings, and maintains record of prisoner status during booking and pre-trial process. Prepares reports to document activities. Relays complaint and emergency request information to appropriate agency dispatcher. Evaluates complaint and emergency request information to determine response requirements. Renders aid to accident victims and other persons requiring first aid for physical injuries. Testifies in court to present evidence or act as witness in traffic and criminal cases. Records facts, photographs and diagrams crime or accident scene, and interviews witnesses to gather information for possible use in legal action or safety programs. **SKILLS**—**Operation and Control:** Controlling operations of equipment or systems. **Social Perceptiveness:** Being aware of others' reactions and understanding why they react as they do. **Service Orientation:** Actively looking for ways to help people. **Operation Monitoring:** Watching gauges, dials, or other indicators to make sure a machine is working properly. **Judgment and Decision Making:** Considering the relative costs and benefits of potential actions to choose the most appropriate one. **Active Listening:** Giving full attention to what other people are saying, taking time to understand the points being made, asking questions as appropriate, and not interrupting at inappropriate times. **Critical Thinking:** Using logic and reasoning to identify the strengths and weaknesses of alternative solutions, conclusions, or approaches to problems. **Reading Comprehension:** Understanding written sentences and paragraphs in work-related documents. **GOE—Interest Area:** 12. Law and Public Safety. **Work Group:** 12.04. Law Enforcement and Public Safety. **Other Jobs in This Work Group:** Bailiffs; Correctional Officers and Jailers; Criminal Investigators and Special Agents; Fire Investigators; Forensic Science Technicians; Parking Enforcement Workers; Police Detectives; Police Identification and Records Officers; Police Patrol Officers; Sheriffs and Deputy Sheriffs; Transit and Railroad Police. **PERSONALITY TYPE:** Realistic.

EDUCATION/TRAINING PROGRAM(S)—Criminal Justice/Police Science; Criminalistics and Criminal Science. **RELATED KNOWLEDGE/COURSES—Public Safety and Security:** Knowledge of relevant equipment, policies, procedures, and strategies to promote effective local, state, or national security operations for the protection of people, data, property, and institutions. **Transportation:** Knowledge of principles and methods for moving people or goods by air, rail, sea, or road, including the relative costs and benefits. **Law and Government:** Knowledge of laws, legal codes, court procedures, precedents, government regulations, executive orders, agency rules, and the democratic political process. **Customer and Personal Service:** Knowledge of principles and processes for providing customer and personal services. This includes customer needs assessment, meeting quality standards for services, and evaluation of customer satisfaction. **Medicine and Dentistry:** Knowledge of the information and techniques needed to diagnose and treat human injuries, diseases, and deformities. This includes symptoms, treatment alternatives, drug properties and interactions, and preventive health-care measures. **Psychology:** Knowledge of human behavior and performance; individual differences in ability, personality, and interests; learning and motivation; psychological research methods; and the assessment and treatment of behavioral and affective disorders.

History Teachers, Postsecondary

- Education/Training Required: Master's degree
- Annual Earnings: $54,040
- Growth: 38.1%
- Annual Job Openings: 216,000
- Self-Employed: 0.3%
- Part-Time: 27.7%

Teach courses in human history and historiography. Prepare and deliver lectures to undergraduate and/or graduate students on topics such as ancient history, postwar civilizations, and the history of third-world countries. Evaluate and grade students' class work, assignments, and papers. Prepare course materials such as syllabi, homework assignments, and handouts. Compile, administer, and grade examinations or assign this work to others. Initiate, facilitate, and moderate classroom discussions. Keep abreast of developments in their field by reading current literature, talking with colleagues, and participating in professional conferences. Maintain student attendance records, grades, and other required records. Plan, evaluate, and revise curricula, course content, and course materials and methods of instruction. Maintain regularly scheduled office hours in order to advise and assist students. Conduct research in a particular field of knowledge and publish findings in professional journals, books, and/or electronic media. Select and obtain materials and supplies such as textbooks. Advise students on academic and vocational curricula and on career issues. Collaborate with colleagues to address teaching and research issues. Serve on academic or administrative committees that deal with institutional policies, departmental matters, and academic issues. Participate in campus and community events. Act as advisers to student organizations. Participate in student recruitment, registration, and placement activities. Compile bibliographies of specialized materials for outside reading assignments. Supervise undergraduate and/or graduate teaching, internship, and research work. Perform administrative duties such as serving as department head. **SKILLS—Instructing:** Teaching others how to do something. **Writing:** Communicating effectively in writing as appropriate for the needs of the audience. **Learning Strategies:** Selecting and using training/instructional methods and procedures appropriate for the situation when learning or teaching new things. **Persuasion:** Persuading others to change their minds or behavior. **Critical Thinking:** Using logic and reasoning to identify the strengths and weaknesses of alternative solutions, conclusions, or approaches to problems. **Social Perceptiveness:** Being aware of others' reactions and understanding why they react as they do. **Reading Comprehension:** Understanding written sentences and paragraphs in work-related documents. **Speaking:** Talking to others to convey information effectively. **Active Learning:** Understanding the implications of new information for both current and future problem-solving and decision-making. **GOE—Interest Area:** 05. Education and Training. **Work Group:** 05.03. Postsecondary and Adult Teaching and Instructing. **Other Jobs in This Work Group:** Adult Literacy, Remedial Education, and GED Teachers and Instructors; Agricultural Sciences Teachers, Postsecondary; Anthropology and Archeology Teachers, Postsecondary; Architecture Teachers, Postsecondary; Area, Ethnic, and Cultural Studies Teachers, Postsecondary;

Art, Drama, and Music Teachers, Postsecondary; Atmospheric, Earth, Marine, and Space Sciences Teachers, Postsecondary; Biological Science Teachers, Postsecondary; Business Teachers, Postsecondary; Chemistry Teachers, Postsecondary; Communications Teachers, Postsecondary; Computer Science Teachers, Postsecondary; Criminal Justice and Law Enforcement Teachers, Postsecondary; Economics Teachers, Postsecondary; Education Teachers, Postsecondary; Engineering Teachers, Postsecondary; English Language and Literature Teachers, Postsecondary; Environmental Science Teachers, Postsecondary; Farm and Home Management Advisors; Foreign Language and Literature Teachers, Postsecondary; Forestry and Conservation Science Teachers, Postsecondary; Geography Teachers, Postsecondary; Graduate Teaching Assistants; Health Specialties Teachers, Postsecondary; Home Economics Teachers, Postsecondary; Law Teachers, Postsecondary; Library Science Teachers, Postsecondary; Mathematical Science Teachers, Postsecondary; Nursing Instructors and Teachers, Postsecondary; Philosophy and Religion Teachers, Postsecondary; Physics Teachers, Postsecondary; Political Science Teachers, Postsecondary; Psychology Teachers, Postsecondary; Recreation and Fitness Studies Teachers, Postsecondary; Self-Enrichment Education Teachers; Social Work Teachers, Postsecondary; Sociology Teachers, Postsecondary; Vocational Education Teachers, Postsecondary. **PERSONALITY TYPE:** Social.

EDUCATION/TRAINING PROGRAM(S)— American History (United States); Asian History; Canadian History; European History; History and Philosophy of Science and Technology; History, General; History, Other; Public/Applied History and Archival Administration. **RELATED KNOWLEDGE/COURSES—History and Archeology:** Knowledge of historical events and their causes, indicators, and effects on civilizations and cultures. **Philosophy and Theology:** Knowledge of different philosophical systems and religions. This includes their basic principles, values, ethics, ways of thinking, customs, and practices and their impact on human culture. **Geography:** Knowledge of principles and methods for describing the features of land, sea, and air masses, including their physical characteristics; locations; interrelationships; and distribution of plant, animal, and human life. **Education and Training:** Knowledge of principles and methods for curriculum

and training design, teaching and instruction for individuals and groups, and the measurement of training effects. **Sociology and Anthropology:** Knowledge of group behavior and dynamics, societal trends and influences, human migrations, ethnicity, and cultures and their history and origins. **English Language:** Knowledge of the structure and content of the English language, including the meaning and spelling of words, rules of composition, and grammar.

Home Economics Teachers, Postsecondary

- Education/Training Required: Master's degree
- Annual Earnings: $47,280
- Growth: 38.1%
- Annual Job Openings: 216,000
- Self-Employed: 0.3%
- Part-Time: 27.7%

Teach courses in child care, family relations, finance, nutrition, and related subjects as pertaining to home management. Evaluate and grade students' class work, laboratory work, projects, assignments, and papers. Initiate, facilitate, and moderate classroom discussions. Prepare and deliver lectures to undergraduate and/or graduate students on topics such as food science, nutrition, and child care. Prepare course materials such as syllabi, homework assignments, and handouts. Keep abreast of developments in their field by reading current literature, talking with colleagues, and participating in professional conferences. Maintain student attendance records, grades, and other required records. Plan, evaluate, and revise curricula, course content, and course materials and methods of instruction. Compile, administer, and grade examinations or assign this work to others. Advise students on academic and vocational curricula and on career issues. Maintain regularly scheduled office hours in order to advise and assist students. Supervise undergraduate and/or graduate teaching, internship, and research work. Select and obtain materials and supplies such as textbooks. Conduct research in a particular field of knowledge and publish findings in professional journals, books, and/or electronic media. Collaborate with colleagues to address teaching and research issues. Act as advisers to student organizations. Participate in student recruitment, registration, and placement activities. Serve on academic or administrative committees that deal with institutional policies, departmental matters, and academic issues. Participate in campus and community events. Compile bibliographies of specialized materials for outside reading assignments. Perform administrative duties such as serving as department head. Write grant proposals to procure external research funding. Provide professional consulting services to government and/or industry. **SKILLS—Instructing:** Teaching others how to do something. **Learning Strategies:** Selecting and using training/instructional methods and procedures appropriate for the situation when learning or teaching new things. **Writing:** Communicating effectively in writing as appropriate for the needs of the audience. **Social Perceptiveness:** Being aware of others' reactions and understanding why they react as they do. **Service Orientation:** Actively looking for ways to help people. **Active Learning:** Understanding the implications of new information for both current and future problem-solving and decision-making. **Persuasion:** Persuading others to change their minds or behavior. **Negotiation:** Bringing others together and trying to reconcile differences. **GOE—Interest Area:** 05. Education and Training. **Work Group:** 05.03. Postsecondary and Adult Teaching and Instructing. **Other Jobs in This Work Group:** Adult Literacy, Remedial Education, and GED Teachers and Instructors; Agricultural Sciences Teachers, Postsecondary; Anthropology and Archeology Teachers, Postsecondary; Architecture Teachers, Postsecondary; Area, Ethnic, and Cultural Studies Teachers, Postsecondary; Art, Drama, and Music Teachers, Postsecondary; Atmospheric, Earth, Marine, and Space Sciences Teachers, Postsecondary; Biological Science Teachers, Postsecondary; Business Teachers, Postsecondary; Chemistry Teachers, Postsecondary; Communications Teachers, Postsecondary; Computer Science Teachers, Postsecondary; Criminal Justice and Law Enforcement Teachers, Postsecondary; Economics Teachers, Postsecondary; Education Teachers, Postsecondary; Engineering Teachers, Postsecondary; English Language and Literature Teachers, Postsecondary; Environmental Science Teachers, Postsecondary; Farm and Home Management Advisors; Foreign Language and Literature Teachers, Postsecondary; Forestry and Conservation Science Teachers, Postsecondary; Geography Teachers, Postsecondary; Graduate Teaching Assistants; Health Specialties Teachers, Postsecondary; History Teachers, Postsecondary; Law Teachers, Postsecondary; Library Science Teachers, Postsecondary; Mathematical Science Teachers, Postsecondary; Nursing Instructors and Teachers, Postsecondary; Philosophy and Religion Teachers, Postsecondary; Physics Teachers, Postsecondary; Political Science Teachers, Postsecondary; Psychology Teachers, Postsecondary; Recreation and Fitness Studies Teachers, Postsecondary; Self-Enrichment Education Teachers; Social Work Teachers, Postsecondary; Sociology Teachers, Postsecondary; Vocational Education Teachers, Postsecondary. **PERSONALITY TYPE:** No data available.

EDUCATION/TRAINING PROGRAM(S)—Business Family and Consumer Sciences/Human Sciences; Child Care and Support Services Management; Family and Consumer Sciences/Human Sciences, General; Foodservice Systems Administration/Management; Human Development and Family Studies, General. **RELATED KNOWLEDGE/COURSES—Education and Training:** Knowledge of principles and methods for curriculum and training design, teaching and instruction for individuals and groups, and the measurement of training effects. **Sociology and Anthropology:** Knowledge of group behavior and dynamics, societal trends and influences, human migrations, ethnicity, and cultures and their history and origins. **Philosophy and Theology:** Knowledge of different philosophical systems and religions. This includes their basic principles, values, ethics, ways of thinking, customs, and practices and their impact on human culture. **Psychology:** Knowledge of human behavior and performance; individual differences in ability, personality, and interests; learning and motivation; psychological research methods; and the assessment and treatment of behavioral and affective disorders. **English Language:** Knowledge of the structure and content of the English language, including the meaning and spelling of words, rules of composition, and grammar. **Customer and Personal Service:** Knowledge of principles and processes for providing customer and personal services. This includes customer needs assessment, meeting quality standards for services, and evaluation of customer satisfaction.

Home Health Aides

- Education/Training Required: Short-term on-the-job training
- Annual Earnings: $18,330
- Growth: 48.1%
- Annual Job Openings: 141,000
- Self-Employed: 1.6%
- Part-Time: 21.9%

Provide routine, personal health care, such as bathing, dressing, or grooming, to elderly, convalescent, or disabled persons in the home of patients or in a residential care facility. Maintain records of patient care, condition, progress, and problems in order to report and discuss observations with a supervisor or case manager. Provide patients with help moving in and out of beds, baths, wheelchairs, or automobiles and with dressing and grooming. Provide patients and families with emotional support and instruction in areas such as infant care, preparing healthy meals, independent living, and adaptation to disability or illness. Change bed linens, wash and iron patients' laundry, and clean patients' quarters. Entertain, converse with, or read aloud to patients to keep them mentally healthy and alert. Plan, purchase, prepare, and serve meals to patients and other family members according to prescribed diets. Direct patients in simple prescribed exercises and in the use of braces or artificial limbs. Check patients' pulse, temperature, and respiration. Change dressings. Perform a variety of duties as requested by client, such as obtaining household supplies and running errands. Accompany clients to doctors' offices and on other trips outside the home, providing transportation, assistance, and companionship. Administer prescribed oral medications under written direction of physician or as directed by home care nurse and aide. Care for children who are disabled or who have sick or disabled parents. Massage patients and apply preparations and treatments such as liniment, alcohol rubs, and heat-lamp stimulation. **SKILLS—Social Perceptiveness:** Being aware of others' reactions and understanding why they react as they do. **Service Orientation:** Actively looking for ways to help people. **Reading Comprehension:** Understanding written sentences and paragraphs in work-related documents. **Writing:** Communicating effectively in writing as appropriate for the needs of the audience. **Instructing:** Teaching others how to do something.

Active Listening: Giving full attention to what other people are saying, taking time to understand the points being made, asking questions as appropriate, and not interrupting at inappropriate times. **Learning Strategies:** Selecting and using training/instructional methods and procedures appropriate for the situation when learning or teaching new things. **Persuasion:** Persuading others to change their minds or behavior. **GOE— Interest Area:** 08. Health Science. **Work Group:** 08.08. Patient Care and Assistance. **Other Jobs in This Work Group:** Licensed Practical and Licensed Vocational Nurses; Nursing Aides, Orderlies, and Attendants; Psychiatric Aides; Psychiatric Technicians. **PERSONALITY TYPE:** Social.

EDUCATION/TRAINING PROGRAM(S)— Home Health Aide/Home Attendant. **RELATED KNOWLEDGE/COURSES—Medicine and Dentistry:** Knowledge of the information and techniques needed to diagnose and treat human injuries, diseases, and deformities. This includes symptoms, treatment alternatives, drug properties and interactions, and preventive health-care measures. **Psychology:** Knowledge of human behavior and performance; individual differences in ability, personality, and interests; learning and motivation; psychological research methods; and the assessment and treatment of behavioral and affective disorders. **Therapy and Counseling:** Knowledge of principles, methods, and procedures for diagnosis, treatment, and rehabilitation of physical and mental dysfunctions and for career counseling and guidance. **Philosophy and Theology:** Knowledge of different philosophical systems and religions. This includes their basic principles, values, ethics, ways of thinking, customs, and practices and their impact on human culture. **Food Production:** Knowledge of techniques and equipment for planting, growing, and harvesting food products (both plant and animal) for consumption, including storage/handling techniques. **Public Safety and Security:** Knowledge of relevant equipment, policies, procedures, and strategies to promote effective local, state, or national security operations for the protection of people, data, property, and institutions.

Hosts and Hostesses, Restaurant, Lounge, and Coffee Shop

- Education/Training Required: Short-term on-the-job training
- Annual Earnings: $15,630
- Growth: 16.4%
- Annual Job Openings: 95,000
- Self-Employed: 0.6%
- Part-Time: 66.9%

Welcome patrons, seat them at tables or in lounge, and help ensure quality of facilities and service. Provide guests with menus. Greet guests and seat them at tables or in waiting areas. Assign patrons to tables suitable for their needs. Inspect dining and serving areas to ensure cleanliness and proper setup. Speak with patrons to ensure satisfaction with food and service and to respond to complaints. Receive and record patrons' dining reservations. Maintain contact with kitchen staff, management, serving staff, and customers to ensure that dining details are handled properly and customers' concerns are addressed. Inform patrons of establishment specialties and features. Direct patrons to coatrooms and waiting areas such as lounges. Operate cash registers to accept payments for food and beverages. Prepare cash receipts after establishments close and make bank deposits. Supervise and coordinate activities of dining room staff to ensure that patrons receive prompt and courteous service. Prepare staff work schedules. Order or requisition supplies and equipment for tables and serving stations. Hire, train, and supervise food and beverage service staff. Plan parties or other special events and services. Confer with other staff to help plan establishments' menus. Perform marketing and advertising services. **SKILLS— Service Orientation:** Actively looking for ways to help people. **Persuasion:** Persuading others to change their minds or behavior. **Instructing:** Teaching others how to do something. **Social Perceptiveness:** Being aware of others' reactions and understanding why they react as they do. **Learning Strategies:** Selecting and using training/instructional methods and procedures appropriate for the situation when learning or teaching new things. **Negotiation:** Bringing others together and trying to reconcile differences. **GOE—Interest Area:** 09. Hospitality, Tourism, and Recreation. **Work Group:**

09.05. Food and Beverage Service. **Other Jobs in This Work Group:** Bartenders; Combined Food Preparation and Serving Workers, Including Fast Food; Counter Attendants, Cafeteria, Food Concession, and Coffee Shop; Dining Room and Cafeteria Attendants and Bartender Helpers; Food Servers, Nonrestaurant; Waiters and Waitresses. **PERSONALITY TYPE:** Enterprising.

EDUCATION/TRAINING PROGRAM(S)—Food Service, Waiter/Waitress, and Dining Room Management/Manager. **RELATED KNOWLEDGE/ COURSES—Customer and Personal Service:** Knowledge of principles and processes for providing customer and personal services. This includes customer needs assessment, meeting quality standards for services, and evaluation of customer satisfaction. **Food Production:** Knowledge of techniques and equipment for planting, growing, and harvesting food products (both plant and animal) for consumption, including storage/handling techniques. **Sales and Marketing:** Knowledge of principles and methods for showing, promoting, and selling products or services. This includes marketing strategy and tactics, product demonstrations, sales techniques, and sales control systems. **Public Safety and Security:** Knowledge of relevant equipment, policies, procedures, and strategies to promote effective local, state, or national security operations for the protection of people, data, property, and institutions. **Administration and Management:** Knowledge of business and management principles involved in strategic planning, resource allocation, human resources modeling, leadership technique, production methods, and coordination of people and resources.

Hotel, Motel, and Resort Desk Clerks

- Education/Training Required: Short-term on-the-job training
- Annual Earnings: $17,700
- Growth: 23.9%
- Annual Job Openings: 46,000
- Self-Employed: 0%
- Part-Time: 27.2%

Accommodate hotel, motel, and resort patrons by registering and assigning rooms to guests, issuing

room keys, transmitting and receiving messages, keeping records of occupied rooms and guests' accounts, making and confirming reservations, and presenting statements to and collecting payments from departing guests. Greet, register, and assign rooms to guests of hotels or motels. Verify customers' credit and establish how the customer will pay for the accommodation. Keep records of room availability and guests' accounts manually or by using computers. Compute bills, collect payments, and make change for guests. Perform simple bookkeeping activities such as balancing cash accounts. Issue room keys and escort instructions to bellhops. Review accounts and charges with guests during the checkout process. Post charges, such as those for rooms, food, liquor, or telephone calls, to ledgers manually or by using computers. Transmit and receive messages, using telephones or telephone switchboards. Contact housekeeping or maintenance staff when guests report problems. Make and confirm reservations. Answer inquiries pertaining to hotel services; registration of guests; and shopping, dining, entertainment, and travel directions. Record guest comments or complaints, referring customers to managers as necessary. Advise housekeeping staff when rooms have been vacated and are ready for cleaning. Arrange tours, taxis, and restaurants for customers. Deposit guests' valuables in hotel safes or safe-deposit boxes. Date-stamp, sort, and rack incoming mail and messages. **SKILLS—Service Orientation:** Actively looking for ways to help people. **Instructing:** Teaching others how to do something. **Learning Strategies:** Selecting and using training/instructional methods and procedures appropriate for the situation when learning or teaching new things. **Critical Thinking:** Using logic and reasoning to identify the strengths and weaknesses of alternative solutions, conclusions, or approaches to problems. **Social Perceptiveness:** Being aware of others' reactions and understanding why they react as they do. **Active Listening:** Giving full attention to what other people are saying, taking time to understand the points being made, asking questions as appropriate, and not interrupting at inappropriate times. **Persuasion:** Persuading others to change their minds or behavior. **Negotiation:** Bringing others together and trying to reconcile differences. **GOE— Interest Area:** 09. Hospitality, Tourism, and Recreation. **Work Group:** 09.03. Hospitality and Travel Services. **Other Jobs in This Work Group:** Baggage Porters and Bellhops; Concierges; Flight Attendants; Janitors and Cleaners, Except Maids and Housekeep-

ing Cleaners; Maids and Housekeeping Cleaners; Reservation and Transportation Ticket Agents; Tour Guides and Escorts; Transportation Attendants, Except Flight Attendants and Baggage Porters; Travel Agents; Travel Clerks; Travel Guides. **PERSONALITY TYPE:** Conventional.

EDUCATION/TRAINING PROGRAM(S)—Selling Skills and Sales Operations. **RELATED KNOWL-EDGE/COURSES—Customer and Personal Service:** Knowledge of principles and processes for providing customer and personal services. This includes customer needs assessment, meeting quality standards for services, and evaluation of customer satisfaction. **Clerical Practices:** Knowledge of administrative and clerical procedures and systems such as word processing, managing files and records, stenography and transcription, designing forms, and other office procedures and terminology. **Sales and Marketing:** Knowledge of principles and methods for showing, promoting, and selling products or services. This includes marketing strategy and tactics, product demonstrations, sales techniques, and sales control systems. **Computers and Electronics:** Knowledge of circuit boards, processors, chips, electronic equipment, and computer hardware and software, including applications and programming. **Administration and Management:** Knowledge of business and management principles involved in strategic planning, resource allocation, human resources modeling, leadership technique, production methods, and coordination of people and resources. **Economics and Accounting:** Knowledge of economic and accounting principles and practices, the financial markets, banking, and the analysis and reporting of financial data.

Housekeeping Supervisors

- ◎ Education/Training Required: Work experience in a related occupation
- ◎ Annual Earnings: $29,510
- ◎ Growth: 16.2%
- ◎ Annual Job Openings: 28,000
- ◎ Self-Employed: 5.6%
- ◎ Part-Time: 6.6%

Supervise work activities of cleaning personnel to ensure clean, orderly, and attractive rooms in hotels,

hospitals, educational institutions, and similar establishments. Assign duties, inspect work, and investigate complaints regarding housekeeping service and equipment and take corrective action. May purchase housekeeping supplies and equipment, take periodic inventories, screen applicants, train new employees, and recommend dismissals. Assigns workers their duties and inspects work for conformance to prescribed standards of cleanliness. Investigates complaints regarding housekeeping service and equipment and takes corrective action. Obtains list of rooms to be cleaned immediately and list of prospective check-outs or discharges to prepare work assignments. Coordinates work activities among departments. Conducts orientation training and in-service training to explain policies and work procedures and to demonstrate use and maintenance of equipment. Inventories stock to ensure adequate supplies. Evaluates records to forecast department personnel requirements. Makes recommendations to improve service and ensure more efficient operation. Prepares reports concerning room occupancy, payroll, and department expenses. Selects and purchases new furnishings. Performs cleaning duties in cases of emergency or staff shortage. Examines building to determine need for repairs or replacement of furniture or equipment and makes recommendations to management. Attends staff meetings to discuss company policies and patrons' complaints. Issues supplies and equipment to workers. Establishes standards and procedures for work of housekeeping staff. Advises manager, desk clerk, or admitting personnel of rooms ready for occupancy. Records data regarding work assignments, personnel actions, and time cards and prepares periodic reports. Screens job applicants; hires new employees; and recommends promotions, transfers, and dismissals. **SKILLS—Management of Personnel Resources:** Motivating, developing, and directing people as they work, identifying the best people for the job. **Time Management:** Managing one's own time and the time of others. **Management of Material Resources:** Obtaining and seeing to the appropriate use of equipment, facilities, and materials needed to do certain work. **Management of Financial Resources:** Determining how money will be spent to get the work done and accounting for these expenditures. **Systems Analysis:** Determining how a system should work and how changes in conditions, operations, and the environment will affect outcomes. **Coordination:** Adjusting actions in relation to others' actions. **Systems Evalua-**

tion: Identifying measures or indicators of system performance and the actions needed to improve or correct performance relative to the goals of the system. **Speaking:** Talking to others to convey information effectively. **GOE—Interest Area:** 04. Business and Administration. **Work Group:** 04.02. Managerial Work in Business Detail. **Other Jobs in This Work Group:** Administrative Services Managers; First-Line Supervisors, Administrative Support; First-Line Supervisors, Customer Service; Janitorial Supervisors; Meeting and Convention Planners. **PERSONALITY TYPE:** Enterprising.

EDUCATION/TRAINING PROGRAM(S)—No data available. RELATED KNOWLEDGE/COURSES—**Personnel and Human Resources:** Knowledge of principles and procedures for personnel recruitment, selection, training, compensation and benefits, labor relations and negotiation, and personnel information systems. **Administration and Management:** Knowledge of business and management principles involved in strategic planning, resource allocation, human resources modeling, leadership technique, production methods, and coordination of people and resources. **Customer and Personal Service:** Knowledge of principles and processes for providing customer and personal services. This includes customer needs assessment, meeting quality standards for services, and evaluation of customer satisfaction. **Clerical Practices:** Knowledge of administrative and clerical procedures and systems such as word processing, managing files and records, stenography and transcription, designing forms, and other office procedures and terminology. **Education and Training:** Knowledge of principles and methods for curriculum and training design, teaching and instruction for individuals and groups, and the measurement of training effects. **Foreign Language:** Knowledge of the structure and content of a foreign (non-English) language, including the meaning and spelling of words, rules of composition and grammar, and pronunciation.

Human Resources Assistants, Except Payroll and Timekeeping

- Education/Training Required: Short-term on-the-job training
- Annual Earnings: $31,750
- Growth: 19.3%
- Annual Job Openings: 36,000
- Self-Employed: 0%
- Part-Time: 15.1%

Compile and keep personnel records. Record data for each employee, such as address, weekly earnings, absences, amount of sales or production, supervisory reports on ability, and date of and reason for termination. Compile and type reports from employment records. File employment records. Search employee files and furnish information to authorized persons. Explain company personnel policies, benefits, and procedures to employees or job applicants. Process, verify, and maintain documentation relating to personnel activities such as staffing, recruitment, training, grievances, performance evaluations, and classifications. Record data for each employee, including such information as addresses, weekly earnings, absences, amount of sales or production, supervisory reports on performance, and dates of and reasons for terminations. Process and review employment applications in order to evaluate qualifications or eligibility of applicants. Answer questions regarding examinations, eligibility, salaries, benefits, and other pertinent information. Examine employee files to answer inquiries and provide information for personnel actions. Gather personnel records from other departments and/or employees. Search employee files in order to obtain information for authorized persons and organizations, such as credit bureaus and finance companies. Interview job applicants to obtain and verify information used to screen and evaluate them. Request information from law enforcement officials, previous employers, and other references in order to determine applicants' employment acceptability. Compile and prepare reports and documents pertaining to personnel activities. Inform job applicants of their acceptance or rejection of employment. Select applicants meeting specified job requirements and refer them to hiring personnel. Arrange for in-house and external training activities. Arrange for advertising or posting of job vacancies and notify eligible workers of position availability. Provide assistance in administering employee benefit programs and worker's compensation plans. Prepare badges, passes, and identification cards and perform other security-related duties. Administer and score applicant and employee aptitude, personality, and interest assessment instruments. **SKILLS—Active Listening:** Giving full attention to what other people are saying, taking time to understand the points being made, asking questions as appropriate, and not interrupting at inappropriate times. **Social Perceptiveness:** Being aware of others' reactions and understanding why they react as they do. **Management of Personnel Resources:** Motivating, developing, and directing people as they work, identifying the best people for the job. **Service Orientation:** Actively looking for ways to help people. **Time Management:** Managing one's own time and the time of others. **Writing:** Communicating effectively in writing as appropriate for the needs of the audience. **Speaking:** Talking to others to convey information effectively. **Instructing:** Teaching others how to do something. **GOE—Interest Area:** 04. Business and Administration. **Work Group:** 04.07. Records and Materials Processing. **Other Jobs in This Work Group:** Correspondence Clerks; File Clerks; Mail Clerks, Except Mail Machine Operators and Postal Service; Marking Clerks; Meter Readers, Utilities; Office Clerks, General; Order Fillers, Wholesale and Retail Sales; Postal Service Clerks; Postal Service Mail Sorters, Processors, and Processing Machine Operators; Procurement Clerks; Production, Planning, and Expediting Clerks; Shipping, Receiving, and Traffic Clerks; Stock Clerks, Sales Floor; Stock Clerks—Stockroom, Warehouse, or Storage Yard; Weighers, Measurers, Checkers, and Samplers, Recordkeeping. **PERSONALITY TYPE:** Conventional.

EDUCATION/TRAINING PROGRAM(S)—General Office Occupations and Clerical Services. **RELATED KNOWLEDGE/COURSES—Clerical Practices:** Knowledge of administrative and clerical procedures and systems such as word processing, managing files and records, stenography and transcription, designing forms, and other office procedures and terminology. **Personnel and Human Resources:** Knowledge of principles and procedures for personnel recruitment, selection, training, compensation and benefits, labor relations and negotiation, and personnel information systems. **Customer and Personal Ser-**

vice: Knowledge of principles and processes for providing customer and personal services. This includes customer needs assessment, meeting quality standards for services, and evaluation of customer satisfaction. **Computers and Electronics:** Knowledge of circuit boards, processors, chips, electronic equipment, and computer hardware and software, including applications and programming. **Education and Training:** Knowledge of principles and methods for curriculum and training design, teaching and instruction for individuals and groups, and the measurement of training effects. **English Language:** Knowledge of the structure and content of the English language, including the meaning and spelling of words, rules of composition, and grammar.

Hydrologists

- Education/Training Required: Bachelor's degree
- Annual Earnings: $61,510
- Growth: 21.0%
- Annual Job Openings: 1,000
- Self-Employed: 3.0%
- Part-Time: 7.7%

Research the distribution, circulation, and physical properties of underground and surface waters; study the form and intensity of precipitation, its rate of infiltration into the soil, its movement through the earth, and its return to the ocean and atmosphere. Apply research findings to help minimize the environmental impacts of pollution, water-borne diseases, erosion, and sedimentation. Compile and evaluate hydrologic information in order to prepare navigational charts and maps and to predict atmospheric conditions. Conduct research and communicate information to promote the conservation and preservation of water resources. Conduct short-term and long-term climate assessments and study storm occurrences. Design and conduct scientific hydrogeological investigations to ensure that accurate and appropriate information is available for use in water resource management decisions. Evaluate research data in terms of its impact on issues such as soil and water conservation, flood control planning, and water supply forecasting. Investigate properties, origins, and activities of glaciers, ice, snow, and permafrost. Measure and graph phenomena such as lake levels, stream flows, and changes in water volumes. Study and analyze the physical aspects of the Earth in terms of the hydrological components, including atmosphere, hydrosphere, and interior structure. Study and document quantities, distribution, disposition, and development of underground and surface waters. Study public water supply issues, including flood and drought risks, water quality, wastewater, and impacts on wetland habitats. Answer questions and provide technical assistance and information to contractors and/or the public regarding issues such as well drilling, code requirements, hydrology, and geology. Collect and analyze water samples as part of field investigations and/or to validate data from automatic monitors. Coordinate and supervise the work of professional and technical staff, including research assistants, technologists, and technicians. Design civil works associated with hydrographic activities and supervise their construction, installation, and maintenance. Develop or modify methods of conducting hydrologic studies. Draft final reports describing research results, including illustrations, appendices, maps, and other attachments. Evaluate data and provide recommendations regarding the feasibility of municipal projects such as hydroelectric power plants, irrigation systems, flood warning systems, and waste treatment facilities. **SKILLS—Science:** Using scientific rules and methods to solve problems. **Mathematics:** Using mathematics to solve problems. **Systems Analysis:** Determining how a system should work and how changes in conditions, operations, and the environment will affect outcomes. **Writing:** Communicating effectively in writing as appropriate for the needs of the audience. **Active Learning:** Understanding the implications of new information for both current and future problem-solving and decision-making. **Critical Thinking:** Using logic and reasoning to identify the strengths and weaknesses of alternative solutions, conclusions, or approaches to problems. **Complex Problem Solving:** Identifying complex problems and reviewing related information to develop and evaluate options and implement solutions. **Judgment and Decision Making:** Considering the relative costs and benefits of potential actions to choose the most appropriate one. **GOE—Interest Area:** 15. Scientific Research, Engineering, and Mathematics. **Work Group:** 15.02. Physical Sciences. **Other Jobs in This Work Group:** Astronomers; Atmospheric and Space Scientists; Chemists; Geographers; Geologists; Materials Scientists; Physicists. **PERSONALITY TYPE:** Investigative.

EDUCATION/TRAINING PROGRAM(S)—Geology/Earth Science, General; Hydrology and Water Resources Science; Oceanography, Chemical and Physical. **RELATED KNOWLEDGE/COURSES—Physics:** Knowledge and prediction of physical principles and laws and their interrelationships and applications to understanding fluid, material, and atmospheric dynamics and mechanical, electrical, atomic, and subatomic structures and processes. **Geography:** Knowledge of principles and methods for describing the features of land, sea, and air masses, including their physical characteristics; locations; interrelationships; and distribution of plant, animal, and human life. **Mathematics:** Knowledge of arithmetic, algebra, geometry, calculus, and statistics and their applications. **Chemistry:** Knowledge of the chemical composition, structure, and properties of substances and of the chemical processes and transformations that they undergo. This includes uses of chemicals and their danger signs, production techniques, and disposal methods. **History and Archeology:** Knowledge of historical events and their causes, indicators, and effects on civilizations and cultures. **Communications and Media:** Knowledge of media production, communication, and dissemination techniques and methods. This includes alternative ways to inform and entertain via written, oral, and visual media.

Immigration and Customs Inspectors

◎ Education/Training Required: Work experience in a related occupation
◎ Annual Earnings: $53,990
◎ Growth: 22.4%
◎ Annual Job Openings: 11,000
◎ Self-Employed: 0%
◎ Part-Time: 0.5%

Investigate and inspect persons, common carriers, goods, and merchandise arriving in or departing from the United States or moving between states to detect violations of immigration and customs laws and regulations. Detain persons found to be in violation of customs or immigration laws and arrange for legal action such as deportation. Determine duty and taxes to be paid on goods. Examine immigration applications, visas, and passports and interview persons in order to determine eligibility for admission, residence, and travel in the United States. Inspect cargo, baggage, and personal articles entering or leaving the United States for compliance with revenue laws and U.S. Customs Service regulations. Interpret and explain laws and regulations to travelers, prospective immigrants, shippers, and manufacturers. Investigate applications for duty refunds and petition for remission or mitigation of penalties when warranted. Locate and seize contraband; undeclared merchandise; and vehicles, aircraft, or boats that contain such merchandise. Record and report job-related activities, findings, transactions, violations, discrepancies, and decisions. Collect samples of merchandise for examination, appraisal, or testing. Institute civil and criminal prosecutions and cooperate with other law enforcement agencies in the investigation and prosecution of those in violation of immigration or customs laws. Testify regarding decisions at immigration appeals or in federal court. **SKILLS—Writing:** Communicating effectively in writing as appropriate for the needs of the audience. **Speaking:** Talking to others to convey information effectively. **Negotiation:** Bringing others together and trying to reconcile differences. **Judgment and Decision Making:** Considering the relative costs and benefits of potential actions to choose the most appropriate one. **Systems Analysis:** Determining how a system should work and how changes in conditions, operations, and the environment will affect outcomes. **GOE—Interest Area:** 07. Government and Public Administration. **Work Group:** 07.03. Regulations Enforcement. **Other Jobs in This Work Group:** Agricultural Inspectors; Aviation Inspectors; Child Support, Missing Persons, and Unemployment Insurance Fraud Investigators; Environmental Compliance Inspectors; Equal Opportunity Representatives and Officers; Financial Examiners; Fire Inspectors; Fish and Game Wardens; Forest Fire Inspectors and Prevention Specialists; Government Property Inspectors and Investigators; Licensing Examiners and Inspectors; Marine Cargo Inspectors; Mechanical Inspectors; Motor Vehicle Inspectors; Nuclear Monitoring Technicians; Occupational Health and Safety Specialists; Pressure Vessel Inspectors; Railroad Inspectors; Tax Examiners, Collectors, and Revenue Agents. **PERSONALITY TYPE:** Conventional.

EDUCATION/TRAINING PROGRAM(S)— Criminal Justice/Police Science; Criminalistics and Criminal Science. **RELATED KNOWLEDGE/**

COURSES—**Law and Government:** Knowledge of laws, legal codes, court procedures, precedents, government regulations, executive orders, agency rules, and the democratic political process. **Geography:** Knowledge of principles and methods for describing the features of land, sea, and air masses, including their physical characteristics; locations; interrelationships; and distribution of plant, animal, and human life. **Public Safety and Security:** Knowledge of relevant equipment, policies, procedures, and strategies to promote effective local, state, or national security operations for the protection of people, data, property, and institutions. **Transportation:** Knowledge of principles and methods for moving people or goods by air, rail, sea, or road, including the relative costs and benefits. **Foreign Language:** Knowledge of the structure and content of a foreign (non-English) language, including the meaning and spelling of words, rules of composition and grammar, and pronunciation. **Communications and Media:** Knowledge of media production, communication, and dissemination techniques and methods. This includes alternative ways to inform and entertain via written, oral, and visual media.

Industrial Engineering Technicians

- Education/Training Required: Associate degree
- Annual Earnings: $43,590
- Growth: 8.7%
- Annual Job Openings: 7,000
- Self-Employed: 0.4%
- Part-Time: 5.0%

Apply engineering theory and principles to problems of industrial layout or manufacturing production, usually under the direction of engineering staff. May study and record time, motion, method, and speed involved in performance of production, maintenance, clerical, and other worker operations for such purposes as establishing standard production rates or improving efficiency. Recommend revision to methods of operation, material handling, equipment layout, or other changes to increase production or improve standards. Study time, motion, methods, and speed involved in maintenance, production, and other operations to establish standard production rate and improve efficiency. Interpret engineering drawings, schematic diagrams, or formulas and confer with management or engineering staff to determine quality and reliability standards. Recommend modifications to existing quality or production standards to achieve optimum quality within limits of equipment capability. Aid in planning work assignments in accordance with worker performance, machine capacity, production schedules, and anticipated delays. Observe worker using equipment to verify that equipment is being operated and maintained according to quality assurance standards. Observe workers operating equipment or performing tasks to determine time involved and fatigue rate, using timing devices. Prepare charts, graphs, and diagrams to illustrate workflow, routing, floor layouts, material handling, and machine utilization. Evaluate data and write reports to validate or indicate deviations from existing standards. Read worker logs, product processing sheets, and specification sheets to verify that records adhere to quality assurance specifications. Prepare graphs or charts of data or enter data into computer for analysis. Record test data, applying statistical quality control procedures. Select products for tests at specified stages in production process and test products for performance characteristics and adherence to specifications. Compile and evaluate statistical data to determine and maintain quality and reliability of products. SKILLS—**Troubleshooting:** Determining causes of operating errors and deciding what to do about them. **Coordination:** Adjusting actions in relation to others' actions. **Persuasion:** Persuading others to change their minds or behavior. **Technology Design:** Generating or adapting equipment and technology to serve user needs. **Instructing:** Teaching others how to do something. **Operations Analysis:** Analyzing needs and product requirements to create a design. **Active Learning:** Understanding the implications of new information for both current and future problem-solving and decision-making. **Negotiation:** Bringing others together and trying to reconcile differences. GOE—**Interest Area:** 04. Business and Administration. **Work Group:** 04.05. Accounting, Auditing, and Analytical Support. **Other Jobs in This Work Group:** Accountants; Auditors; Budget Analysts; Logisticians; Management Analysts; Operations Research Analysts. **PERSONALITY TYPE:** Investigative.

EDUCATION/TRAINING PROGRAM(S)—Engineering/Industrial Management; Industrial Production Technologies/Technicians, Other; Industrial

Technology/Technician; Manufacturing Technology/Technician. **RELATED KNOWLEDGE/ COURSES—Production and Processing:** Knowledge of raw materials, production processes, quality control, costs, and other techniques for maximizing the effective manufacture and distribution of goods. **Engineering and Technology:** Knowledge of the practical application of engineering science and technology. This includes applying principles, techniques, procedures, and equipment to the design and production of various goods and services. **Clerical Practices:** Knowledge of administrative and clerical procedures and systems such as word processing, managing files and records, stenography and transcription, designing forms, and other office procedures and terminology. **Design:** Knowledge of design techniques, tools, and principles involved in production of precision technical plans, blueprints, drawings, and models. **Mathematics:** Knowledge of arithmetic, algebra, geometry, calculus, and statistics and their applications. **Education and Training:** Knowledge of principles and methods for curriculum and training design, teaching and instruction for individuals and groups, and the measurement of training effects.

Industrial Engineers

◎ Education/Training Required: Bachelor's degree

◎ Annual Earnings: $65,020

◎ Growth: 10.6%

◎ Annual Job Openings: 16,000

◎ Self-Employed: 1.5%

◎ Part-Time: 1.5%

Design, develop, test, and evaluate integrated systems for managing industrial production processes, including human work factors, quality control, inventory control, logistics and material flow, cost analysis, and production coordination. Analyze statistical data and product specifications to determine standards and establish quality and reliability objectives of finished product. Develop manufacturing methods, labor utilization standards, and cost analysis systems to promote efficient staff and facility utilization. Recommend methods for improving utilization of personnel, material, and utilities. Plan and establish sequence of operations to fabricate and assemble parts or products and to promote efficient utilization. Apply statistical

methods and perform mathematical calculations to determine manufacturing processes, staff requirements, and production standards. Coordinate quality control objectives and activities to resolve production problems, maximize product reliability, and minimize cost. Confer with vendors, staff, and management personnel regarding purchases, procedures, product specifications, manufacturing capabilities, and project status. Draft and design layout of equipment, materials, and workspace to illustrate maximum efficiency, using drafting tools and computer. Review production schedules, engineering specifications, orders, and related information to obtain knowledge of manufacturing methods, procedures, and activities. Communicate with management and user personnel to develop production and design standards. Estimate production cost and effect of product design changes for management review, action, and control. Formulate sampling procedures and designs and develop forms and instructions for recording, evaluating, and reporting quality and reliability data. Record or oversee recording of information to ensure currency of engineering drawings and documentation of production problems. Study operations sequence, material flow, functional statements, organization charts, and project information to determine worker functions and responsibilities. Direct workers engaged in product measurement, inspection, and testing activities to ensure quality control and reliability. Implement methods and procedures for disposition of discrepant material and defective or damaged parts and assess cost and responsibility. **SKILLS—Equipment Selection:** Determining the kind of tools and equipment needed to do a job. **Technology Design:** Generating or adapting equipment and technology to serve user needs. **Negotiation:** Bringing others together and trying to reconcile differences. **Troubleshooting:** Determining causes of operating errors and deciding what to do about them. **Judgment and Decision Making:** Considering the relative costs and benefits of potential actions to choose the most appropriate one. **Active Learning:** Understanding the implications of new information for both current and future problem-solving and decision-making. **Persuasion:** Persuading others to change their minds or behavior. **Complex Problem Solving:** Identifying complex problems and reviewing related information to develop and evaluate options and implement solutions. **Systems Analysis:** Determining how a system should work and how changes in conditions, operations, and the environment will affect outcomes. **GOE—Interest Area:** 15. Scientific Research,

Engineering, and Mathematics. **Work Group:** 15.08. Industrial and Safety Engineering. **Other Jobs in This Work Group:** Fire-Prevention and Protection Engineers; Industrial Safety and Health Engineers; Product Safety Engineers. **PERSONALITY TYPE:** Enterprising.

EDUCATION/TRAINING PROGRAM(S)—Industrial Engineering. **RELATED KNOWLEDGE/COURSES—Engineering and Technology:** Knowledge of the practical application of engineering science and technology. This includes applying principles, techniques, procedures, and equipment to the design and production of various goods and services. **Design:** Knowledge of design techniques, tools, and principles involved in production of precision technical plans, blueprints, drawings, and models. **Production and Processing:** Knowledge of raw materials, production processes, quality control, costs, and other techniques for maximizing the effective manufacture and distribution of goods. **Mathematics:** Knowledge of arithmetic, algebra, geometry, calculus, and statistics and their applications. **Mechanical Devices:** Knowledge of machines and tools, including their designs, uses, repair, and maintenance. **Education and Training:** Knowledge of principles and methods for curriculum and training design, teaching and instruction for individuals and groups, and the measurement of training effects.

Industrial Machinery Mechanics

- ◎ Education/Training Required: Long-term on-the-job training
- ◎ Annual Earnings: $39,060
- ◎ Growth: 5.5%
- ◎ Annual Job Openings: 19,000
- ◎ Self-Employed: 6.3%
- ◎ Part-Time: 2.1%

Repair, install, adjust, or maintain industrial production and processing machinery or refinery and pipeline distribution systems. Analyze test results, machine error messages, and information obtained from operators in order to diagnose equipment problems. Clean, lubricate, and adjust parts, equipment, and machinery. Disassemble machinery and equip-

ment to remove parts and make repairs. Examine parts for defects such as breakage and excessive wear. Observe and test the operation of machinery and equipment in order to diagnose malfunctions, using voltmeters and other testing devices. Operate newly repaired machinery and equipment to verify the adequacy of repairs. Reassemble equipment after completion of inspections, testing, or repairs. Repair and maintain the operating condition of industrial production and processing machinery and equipment. Repair and replace broken or malfunctioning components of machinery and equipment. Study blueprints and manufacturers' manuals to determine correct installation and operation of machinery. Cut and weld metal to repair broken metal parts, fabricate new parts, and assemble new equipment. Demonstrate equipment functions and features to machine operators. Enter codes and instructions to program computer-controlled machinery. Record parts and materials used and order or requisition new parts and materials as necessary. Record repairs and maintenance performed. **SKILLS—Repairing:** Repairing machines or systems by using the needed tools. **Equipment Maintenance:** Performing routine maintenance on equipment and determining when and what kind of maintenance is needed. **Troubleshooting:** Determining causes of operating errors and deciding what to do about them. **Operation Monitoring:** Watching gauges, dials, or other indicators to make sure a machine is working properly. **Quality Control Analysis:** Conducting tests and inspections of products, services, or processes to evaluate quality or performance. **Installation:** Installing equipment, machines, wiring, or programs to meet specifications. **Operation and Control:** Controlling operations of equipment or systems. **Technology Design:** Generating or adapting equipment and technology to serve user needs. **GOE—Interest Area:** 13. Manufacturing. **Work Group:** 13.13. Machinery Repair. **Other Jobs in This Work Group:** Bicycle Repairers; Gas Appliance Repairers; Hand and Portable Power Tool Repairers; Locksmiths and Safe Repairers; Maintenance Workers, Machinery; Mechanical Door Repairers; Millwrights; Signal and Track Switch Repairers; Valve and Regulator Repairers. **PERSONALITY TYPE:** Realistic.

EDUCATION/TRAINING PROGRAM(S)—Heavy/Industrial Equipment Maintenance Technologies, Other; Industrial Mechanics and Maintenance Technology. **RELATED KNOWLEDGE/COURSES—Mechanical Devices:** Knowledge of machines and tools, including their designs, uses, repair, and maintenance. **Engineering and Technology:** Knowledge of the practical application of engineering science and technology. This includes applying principles, techniques, procedures, and equipment to the design and production of various goods and services. **Computers and Electronics:** Knowledge of circuit boards, processors, chips, electronic equipment, and computer hardware and software, including applications and programming. **Physics:** Knowledge and prediction of physical principles and laws and their interrelationships and applications to understanding fluid, material, and atmospheric dynamics and mechanical, electrical, atomic, and subatomic structures and processes. **Public Safety and Security:** Knowledge of relevant equipment, policies, procedures, and strategies to promote effective local, state, or national security operations for the protection of people, data, property, and institutions. **Design:** Knowledge of design techniques, tools, and principles involved in production of precision technical plans, blueprints, drawings, and models.

Industrial Production Managers

◎ Education/Training Required: Bachelor's degree

◎ Annual Earnings: $73,000

◎ Growth: 7.9%

◎ Annual Job Openings: 18,000

◎ Self-Employed: 1.5%

◎ Part-Time: 1.8%

Plan, direct, or coordinate the work activities and resources necessary for manufacturing products in accordance with cost, quality, and quantity specifications. Direct and coordinate production, processing, distribution, and marketing activities of industrial organization. Develop budgets and approve expenditures for supplies, materials, and human resources, ensuring that materials, labor, and equipment are used efficiently to meet production targets. Review processing schedules and production orders to make decisions concerning inventory requirements, staffing requirements, work procedures, and duty assignments, considering budgetary limitations and time constraints.

Review operations and confer with technical or administrative staff to resolve production or processing problems. Hire, train, evaluate, and discharge staff and resolve personnel grievances. Initiate and coordinate inventory and cost control programs. Prepare and maintain production reports and personnel records. Set and monitor product standards, examining samples of raw products or directing testing during processing to ensure finished products are of prescribed quality. Develop and implement production tracking and quality control systems, analyzing production, quality control, maintenance, and other operational reports to detect production problems. Review plans and confer with research and support staff to develop new products and processes. Institute employee suggestion or involvement programs. Coordinate and recommend procedures for facility and equipment maintenance or modification, including the replacement of machines. Maintain current knowledge of the quality control field, relying on current literature pertaining to materials use, technological advances, and statistical studies. Negotiate materials prices with suppliers. **SKILLS—Management of Material Resources:** Obtaining and seeing to the appropriate use of equipment, facilities, and materials needed to do certain work. **Management of Personnel Resources:** Motivating, developing, and directing people as they work, identifying the best people for the job. **Persuasion:** Persuading others to change their minds or behavior. **Systems Evaluation:** Identifying measures or indicators of system performance and the actions needed to improve or correct performance relative to the goals of the system. **Coordination:** Adjusting actions in relation to others' actions. **Monitoring:** Monitoring or assessing your performance or that of other individuals or organizations to make improvements or take corrective action. **Operations Analysis:** Analyzing needs and product requirements to create a design. **Time Management:** Managing one's own time and the time of others. **GOE—Interest Area:** 13. Manufacturing. **Work Group:** 13.01. Managerial Work in Manufacturing. **Other Jobs in This Work Group:** First-Line Supervisors/Managers of Helpers, Laborers, and Material Movers, Hand; First-Line Supervisors/Managers of Mechanics, Installers, and Repairers; First-Line Supervisors/Managers of Production and Operating Workers. **PERSONALITY TYPE:** Enterprising.

EDUCATION/TRAINING PROGRAM(S)—Business Administration and Management, General; Business/Commerce, General; Operations Management and Supervision. **RELATED KNOWLEDGE/ COURSES—Production and Processing:** Knowledge of raw materials, production processes, quality control, costs, and other techniques for maximizing the effective manufacture and distribution of goods. **Personnel and Human Resources:** Knowledge of principles and procedures for personnel recruitment, selection, training, compensation and benefits, labor relations and negotiation, and personnel information systems. **Education and Training:** Knowledge of principles and methods for curriculum and training design, teaching and instruction for individuals and groups, and the measurement of training effects. **Administration and Management:** Knowledge of business and management principles involved in strategic planning, resource allocation, human resources modeling, leadership technique, production methods, and coordination of people and resources. **Mechanical Devices:** Knowledge of machines and tools, including their designs, uses, repair, and maintenance. **Engineering and Technology:** Knowledge of the practical application of engineering science and technology. This includes applying principles, techniques, procedures, and equipment to the design and production of various goods and services.

Industrial Safety and Health Engineers

◎ Education/Training Required: Bachelor's degree
◎ Annual Earnings: $63,730
◎ Growth: 7.9%
◎ Annual Job Openings: 4,000
◎ Self-Employed: 1.6%
◎ Part-Time: 1.5%

Plan, implement, and coordinate safety programs requiring application of engineering principles and technology to prevent or correct unsafe environmental working conditions. Investigate industrial accidents, injuries, or occupational diseases to determine causes and preventive measures. Report or review findings from accident investigations, facilities inspections, or environmental testing. Maintain and apply knowledge of current policies, regulations, and industrial processes. Inspect facilities, machinery, and safety equipment in order to identify and correct potential hazards and to ensure safety regulation compliance. Conduct or coordinate worker training in areas such as safety laws and regulations, hazardous condition monitoring, and use of safety equipment. Review employee safety programs to determine their adequacy. Interview employers and employees to obtain information about work environments and workplace incidents. Review plans and specifications for construction of new machinery or equipment in order to determine if all safety requirements have been met. Compile, analyze, and interpret statistical data related to occupational illnesses and accidents. Interpret safety regulations for others interested in industrial safety, such as safety engineers, labor representatives, and safety inspectors. Recommend process and product safety features that will reduce employees' exposure to chemical, physical, and biological work hazards. Conduct or direct testing of air quality, noise, temperature, and/or radiation levels to verify compliance with health and safety regulations. Provide technical advice and guidance to organizations on how to handle health-related problems and make needed changes. Confer with medical professionals to assess health risks and to develop ways to manage health issues and concerns. Install safety devices on machinery or direct device installation. Maintain liaisons with outside organizations, such as fire departments, mutual aid societies, and rescue teams, so that emergency responses can be facilitated. Evaluate adequacy of actions taken to correct health inspection violations. Write and revise safety regulations and codes. Check floors of plants to ensure that they are strong enough to support heavy machinery. Plan and conduct industrial hygiene research. **SKILLS—Management of Financial Resources:** Determining how money will be spent to get the work done and accounting for these expenditures. **Persuasion:** Persuading others to change their minds or behavior. **Service Orientation:** Actively looking for ways to help people. **Negotiation:** Bringing others together and trying to reconcile differences. **Systems Analysis:** Determining how a system should work and how changes in conditions, operations, and the environment will affect outcomes. **Science:** Using scientific rules and methods to solve problems. **Management of Personnel Resources:** Motivating, developing, and directing people as they work, identifying the best people for the job. **Management of Material Resources:** Obtaining and seeing to the appropriate use of equipment, facilities, and materials needed to do certain work. **GOE—Interest Area:** 15. Scientific Research, Engineering, and Mathematics. **Work Group:** 15.08. Industrial and Safety Engineering. **Other Jobs in This Work Group:** Fire-Prevention and Protection Engineers; Industrial Engineers; Product Safety Engineers. **PERSONALITY TYPE:** Investigative.

EDUCATION/TRAINING PROGRAM(S)—Environmental/Environmental Health Engineering. **RELATED KNOWLEDGE/COURSES—Education and Training:** Knowledge of principles and methods for curriculum and training design, teaching and instruction for individuals and groups, and the measurement of training effects. **Public Safety and Security:** Knowledge of relevant equipment, policies, procedures, and strategies to promote effective local, state, or national security operations for the protection of people, data, property, and institutions. **Chemistry:** Knowledge of the chemical composition, structure, and properties of substances and of the chemical processes and transformations that they undergo. This includes uses of chemicals and their danger signs, production techniques, and disposal methods. **Engineering and Technology:** Knowledge of the practical application of engineering science and technology. This includes applying principles, techniques, procedures, and equipment to the design and production of various goods and services. **Physics:** Knowledge and prediction of physical principles and laws and their interrelationships and applications to understanding fluid, material, and atmospheric dynamics and mechanical, electrical, atomic, and subatomic structures and processes. **Building and Construction:** Knowledge of the materials, methods, and tools involved in the construction or repair of houses, buildings, or other structures such as highways and roads. **Psychology:** Knowledge of human behavior and performance; individual differences in ability, personality, and interests; learning and motivation; psychological research methods; and the assessment and treatment of behavioral and affective disorders.

Industrial Truck and Tractor Operators

- Education/Training Required: Short-term on-the-job training
- Annual Earnings: $26,580
- Growth: 11.1%
- Annual Job Openings: 94,000
- Self-Employed: 0.1%
- Part-Time: 2.1%

Operate industrial trucks or tractors equipped to move materials around a warehouse, storage yard, factory, construction site, or similar location. Move controls to drive gasoline- or electric-powered trucks, cars, or tractors and transport materials between loading, processing, and storage areas. Move levers and controls that operate lifting devices, such as forklifts, lift beams and swivel-hooks, hoists, and elevating platforms, in order to load, unload, transport, and stack material. Position lifting devices under, over, or around loaded pallets, skids, and boxes and secure material or products for transport to designated areas. Manually load or unload materials onto or off pallets, skids, platforms, cars, or lifting devices. Perform routine maintenance on vehicles and auxiliary equipment, such as cleaning, lubricating, recharging batteries, fueling, or replacing liquefied-gas tank. Weigh materials or products and record weight and other production data on tags or labels. Operate or tend automatic stacking, loading, packaging, or cutting machines. Signal workers to discharge, dump, or level materials. Hook tow trucks to trailer hitches and fasten attachments such as graders, plows, rollers, and winch cables to tractors, using hitchpins. **SKILLS—Operation Monitoring:** Watching gauges, dials, or other indicators to make sure a machine is working properly. **Equipment Maintenance:** Performing routine maintenance on equipment and determining when and what kind of maintenance is needed. **Instructing:** Teaching others how to do something. **Repairing:** Repairing machines or systems by using the needed tools. **Operation and Control:** Controlling operations of equipment or systems. **Troubleshooting:** Determining causes of operating errors and deciding what to do about them. **Systems Analysis:** Determining how a system should work and how changes in conditions, operations, and the environment will affect outcomes. **Learning**

Strategies: Selecting and using training/instructional methods and procedures appropriate for the situation when learning or teaching new things. **Equipment Selection**: Determining the kind of tools and equipment needed to do a job. **GOE—Interest Area**: 13. Manufacturing. **Work Group**: 13.17. Loading, Moving, Hoisting, and Conveying. **Other Jobs in This Work Group**: Conveyor Operators and Tenders; Freight, Stock, and Material Movers, Hand; Hoist and Winch Operators; Irradiated-Fuel Handlers; Machine Feeders and Offbearers; Packers and Packagers, Hand; Pump Operators, Except Wellhead Pumpers; Refuse and Recyclable Material Collectors; Tank Car, Truck, and Ship Loaders. **PERSONALITY TYPE**: Realistic.

EDUCATION/TRAINING PROGRAM(S)— Ground Transportation, Other. **RELATED KNOWLEDGE/COURSES—Transportation**: Knowledge of principles and methods for moving people or goods by air, rail, sea, or road, including the relative costs and benefits. **Mechanical Devices**: Knowledge of machines and tools, including their designs, uses, repair, and maintenance. **Chemistry**: Knowledge of the chemical composition, structure, and properties of substances and of the chemical processes and transformations that they undergo. This includes uses of chemicals and their danger signs, production techniques, and disposal methods. **Geography**: Knowledge of principles and methods for describing the features of land, sea, and air masses, including their physical characteristics; locations; interrelationships; and distribution of plant, animal, and human life. **Production and Processing**: Knowledge of raw materials, production processes, quality control, costs, and other techniques for maximizing the effective manufacture and distribution of goods. **Mathematics**: Knowledge of arithmetic, algebra, geometry, calculus, and statistics and their applications. **Telecommunications**: Knowledge of transmission, broadcasting, switching, control, and operation of telecommunications systems.

Industrial-Organizational Psychologists

- Education/Training Required: Master's degree
- Annual Earnings: $71,400
- Growth: 16.0%
- Annual Job Openings: Fewer than 500
- Self-Employed: 26.8%
- Part-Time: 27.2%

Apply principles of psychology to personnel, administration, management, sales, and marketing problems. Activities may include policy planning; employee screening, training, and development; and organizational development and analysis. May work with management to reorganize the work setting to improve worker productivity. Analyze data, using statistical methods and applications, in order to evaluate the outcomes and effectiveness of workplace programs. Analyze job requirements and content in order to establish criteria for classification, selection, training, and other related personnel functions. Conduct research studies of physical work environments, organizational structures, communication systems, group interactions, morale, and motivation in order to assess organizational functioning. Develop and implement employee selection and placement programs. Develop interview techniques, rating scales, and psychological tests used to assess skills, abilities, and interests for the purpose of employee selection, placement, and promotion. Facilitate organizational development and change. Formulate and implement training programs, applying principles of learning and individual differences. Identify training and development needs. Observe and interview workers in order to obtain information about the physical, mental, and educational requirements of jobs as well as information about aspects such as job satisfaction. Study organizational effectiveness, productivity, and efficiency, including the nature of workplace supervision and leadership. Advise management concerning personnel, managerial, and marketing policies and practices and their potential effects on organizational effectiveness and efficiency. Assess employee performance. Counsel workers about job and career-related issues. Participate in mediation and dispute resolution. Study consumers' reactions to new products and package designs and to advertising efforts, using surveys and tests. Write reports on research findings and implications in order to contribute to general knowledge and to suggest potential changes in organizational functioning. **SKILLS—Systems Evaluation:** Identifying measures or indicators of system performance and the actions needed to improve or correct performance relative to the goals of the system. **Management of Personnel Resources:** Motivating, developing, and directing people as they work, identifying the best people for the job. **Systems Analysis:** Determining how a system should work and how changes in conditions, operations, and the environment will affect outcomes. **Science:** Using scientific rules and methods to solve problems. **Complex Problem Solving:** Identifying complex problems and reviewing related information to develop and evaluate options and implement solutions. **Mathematics:** Using mathematics to solve problems. **Social Perceptiveness:** Being aware of others' reactions and understanding why they react as they do. **Writing:** Communicating effectively in writing as appropriate for the needs of the audience. **Active Learning:** Understanding the implications of new information for both current and future problem-solving and decision-making. **Judgment and Decision Making:** Considering the relative costs and benefits of potential actions to choose the most appropriate one. **GOE—Interest Area:** 15. Scientific Research, Engineering, and Mathematics. **Work Group:** 15.04. Social Sciences. **Other Jobs in This Work Group:** Anthropologists; Archeologists; Economists; Educational Psychologists; Historians; Political Scientists; Sociologists. **PERSONALITY TYPE:** Investigative.

EDUCATION/TRAINING PROGRAM(S)— Industrial and Organizational Psychology; Psychology, General. **RELATED KNOWLEDGE/COURSES— Personnel and Human Resources:** Knowledge of principles and procedures for personnel recruitment, selection, training, compensation and benefits, labor relations and negotiation, and personnel information systems. **Psychology:** Knowledge of human behavior and performance; individual differences in ability, personality, and interests; learning and motivation; psychological research methods; and the assessment and treatment of behavioral and affective disorders. **Education and Training:** Knowledge of principles and methods for curriculum and training design, teaching and instruction for individuals and groups, and the measurement of training effects. **Administration and Management:** Knowledge of business and management principles involved in strategic planning, resource allo-

cation, human resources modeling, leadership technique, production methods, and coordination of people and resources. **Mathematics:** Knowledge of arithmetic, algebra, geometry, calculus, and statistics and their applications. **Therapy and Counseling:** Knowledge of principles, methods, and procedures for diagnosis, treatment, and rehabilitation of physical and mental dysfunctions and for career counseling and guidance.

Instructional Coordinators

- Education/Training Required: Master's degree
- Annual Earnings: $48,790
- Growth: 25.4%
- Annual Job Openings: 18,000
- Self-Employed: 2.7%
- Part-Time: 16.5%

Develop instructional material, coordinate educational content, and incorporate current technology in specialized fields that provide guidelines to educators and instructors for developing curricula and conducting courses. Conduct or participate in workshops, committees, and conferences designed to promote the intellectual, social, and physical welfare of students. Plan and conduct teacher training programs and conferences dealing with new classroom procedures, instructional materials and equipment, and teaching aids. Advise teaching and administrative staff in curriculum development, use of materials and equipment, and implementation of state and federal programs and procedures. Recommend, order, or authorize purchase of instructional materials, supplies, equipment, and visual aids designed to meet student educational needs and district standards. Interpret and enforce provisions of state education codes and rules and regulations of state education boards. Confer with members of educational committees and advisory groups to obtain knowledge of subject areas and to relate curriculum materials to specific subjects, individual student needs, and occupational areas. Organize production and design of curriculum materials. Research, evaluate, and prepare recommendations on curricula, instructional methods, and materials for school systems. Observe work of teaching staff in order to evaluate performance and to recommend changes that could strengthen teaching skills. Develop instructional materials to be used by educators and instructors. Prepare grant proposals, budgets, and program policies and goals or assist in their preparation. Develop tests, questionnaires, and procedures that measure the effectiveness of curricula and use these tools to determine whether program objectives are being met. Update the content of educational programs to ensure that students are being trained with equipment and processes that are technologically current. Address public audiences to explain program objectives and to elicit support. Advise and teach students. Prepare or approve manuals, guidelines, and reports on state educational policies and practices for distribution to school districts. Develop classroom-based and distance-learning training courses, using needs assessments and skill-level analyses. Inspect instructional equipment to determine if repairs are needed; authorize necessary repairs. **SKILLS—Learning Strategies:** Selecting and using training/instructional methods and procedures appropriate for the situation when learning or teaching new things. **Management of Financial Resources:** Determining how money will be spent to get the work done and accounting for these expenditures. **Social Perceptiveness:** Being aware of others' reactions and understanding why they react as they do. **Coordination:** Adjusting actions in relation to others' actions. **Time Management:** Managing one's own time and the time of others. **Monitoring:** Monitoring or assessing your performance or that of other individuals or organizations to make improvements or take corrective action. **Management of Personnel Resources:** Motivating, developing, and directing people as they work, identifying the best people for the job. **Instructing:** Teaching others how to do something. **GOE—Interest Area:** 05. Education and Training. **Work Group:** 05.01. Managerial Work in Education. **Other Jobs in This Work Group:** Education Administrators, Elementary and Secondary School; Education Administrators, Postsecondary; Education Administrators, Preschool and Child Care Center/Program. **PERSONALITY TYPE:** Social.

EDUCATION/TRAINING PROGRAM(S)—Curriculum and Instruction; Educational/Instructional Media Design. **RELATED KNOWLEDGE/ COURSES—Education and Training:** Knowledge of principles and methods for curriculum and training design, teaching and instruction for individuals and groups, and the measurement of training effects. **Customer and Personal Service:** Knowledge of principles and processes for providing customer and personal

services. This includes customer needs assessment, meeting quality standards for services, and evaluation of customer satisfaction. **English Language:** Knowledge of the structure and content of the English language, including the meaning and spelling of words, rules of composition, and grammar. **Personnel and Human Resources:** Knowledge of principles and procedures for personnel recruitment, selection, training, compensation and benefits, labor relations and negotiation, and personnel information systems. **Psychology:** Knowledge of human behavior and performance; individual differences in ability, personality, and interests; learning and motivation; psychological research methods; and the assessment and treatment of behavioral and affective disorders. **Sociology and Anthropology:** Knowledge of group behavior and dynamics, societal trends and influences, human migrations, ethnicity, and cultures and their history and origins.

Insulation Workers, Floor, Ceiling, and Wall

- Education/Training Required: Moderate-term on-the-job training
- Annual Earnings: $30,310
- Growth: 15.8%
- Annual Job Openings: 9,000
- Self-Employed: 3.9%
- Part-Time: 2.0%

Line and cover structures with insulating materials. May work with batt, roll, or blown insulation materials. Cover and line structures with blown or rolled forms of materials to insulate against cold, heat, or moisture, using saws, knives, rasps, trowels, blowers, and other tools and implements. Cover, seal, or finish insulated surfaces or access holes with plastic covers, canvas ships, sealants, tape, cement, or asphalt mastic. Distribute insulating materials evenly into small spaces within floors, ceilings, or walls, using blowers and hose attachments or cement mortars. Fill blower hoppers with insulating materials. Fit, wrap, staple, or glue insulating materials to structures or surfaces, using hand tools or wires. Measure and cut insulation for covering surfaces, using tape measures, handsaws, power saws, knives, or scissors. Move controls, buttons, or levers to start blowers and regulate flow of materials through nozzles. Prepare surfaces for insulation application by brushing or spreading on adhesives, cement, or asphalt or by attaching metal pins to surfaces. Read blueprints and select appropriate insulation, based on space characteristics and the heat-retaining or -excluding characteristics of the material. Remove old insulation such as asbestos, following safety procedures. **SKILLS—Installation:** Installing equipment, machines, wiring, or programs to meet specifications. **GOE—Interest Area:** 02. Architecture and Construction. **Work Group:** 02.04. Construction Crafts. **Other Jobs in This Work Group:** Boat Builders and Shipwrights; Boilermakers; Brattice Builders; Brickmasons and Blockmasons; Carpet Installers; Ceiling Tile Installers; Cement Masons and Concrete Finishers; Commercial Divers; Construction Carpenters; Crane and Tower Operators; Dragline Operators; Drywall Installers; Electricians; Fence Erectors; Floor Layers, Except Carpet, Wood, and Hard Tiles; Floor Sanders and Finishers; Glaziers; Grader, Bulldozer, and Scraper Operators; Hazardous Materials Removal Workers; Insulation Workers, Mechanical; Manufactured Building and Mobile Home Installers; Operating Engineers; Painters, Construction and Maintenance; Paperhangers; Paving, Surfacing, and Tamping Equipment Operators; Pile-Driver Operators; Pipe Fitters; Pipelayers; Pipelaying Fitters; Plasterers and Stucco Masons; Plumbers; Rail-Track Laying and Maintenance Equipment Operators; Refractory Materials Repairers, Except Brickmasons; Reinforcing Iron and Rebar Workers; Riggers; Roofers; Rough Carpenters; Security and Fire Alarm Systems Installers; Segmental Pavers; Sheet Metal Workers; Ship Carpenters and Joiners; Stone Cutters and Carvers; Stonemasons; Structural Iron and Steel Workers; Tapers; Terrazzo Workers and Finishers; Tile and Marble Setters. **PERSONALITY TYPE:** Realistic.

EDUCATION/TRAINING PROGRAM(S)—Construction Trades, Other. **RELATED KNOWLEDGE/COURSES—Building and Construction:** Knowledge of the materials, methods, and tools involved in the construction or repair of houses, buildings, or other structures such as highways and roads. **Mechanical Devices:** Knowledge of machines and tools, including their designs, uses, repair, and maintenance.

Insulation Workers, Mechanical

- Education/Training Required: Moderate-term on-the-job training
- Annual Earnings: $33,330
- Growth: 15.8%
- Annual Job Openings: 9,000
- Self-Employed: 3.9%
- Part-Time: 2.0%

Apply insulating materials to pipes or ductwork or other mechanical systems in order to help control and maintain temperature. Apply, remove, and repair insulation on industrial equipment, pipes, ductwork, or other mechanical systems such as heat exchangers, tanks, and vessels to help control noise and maintain temperatures. Cover, seal, and finish insulated surfaces or access holes with plastic covers, canvas ships, sealant, tape, cement, or asphalt mastic. Determine the amounts and types of insulation needed and methods of installation, based on factors such as location, surface shape, and equipment use. Fit insulation around obstructions and shape insulating materials and protective coverings as required. Install sheet metal around insulated pipes with screws in order to protect the insulation from weather conditions or physical damage. Measure and cut insulation for covering surfaces, using tape measures, handsaws, knives, and scissors. Prepare surfaces for insulation application by brushing or spreading on adhesives, cement, or asphalt or by attaching metal pins to surfaces. Read blueprints and specifications to determine job requirements. Select appropriate insulation such as fiberglass, Styrofoam, or cork, based on the heat-retaining or -excluding characteristics of the material. Distribute insulating materials evenly into small spaces within floors, ceilings, or walls, using blowers and hose attachments or cement mortar. Fill blower hoppers with insulating materials. Move controls, buttons, or levers to start blowers and to regulate flow of materials through nozzles. Remove or seal off old asbestos insulation, following safety procedures. **SKILLS—Installation:** Installing equipment, machines, wiring, or programs to meet specifications. **GOE—Interest Area:** 02. Architecture and Construction. **Work Group:** 02.04. Construction Crafts. **Other Jobs in This Work Group:** Boat Builders and Shipwrights; Boilermakers; Brattice Builders; Brickmasons and Blockmasons; Carpet Installers; Ceiling Tile Installers; Cement Masons and Concrete Finishers; Commercial Divers; Construction Carpenters; Crane and Tower Operators; Dragline Operators; Drywall Installers; Electricians; Fence Erectors; Floor Layers, Except Carpet, Wood, and Hard Tiles; Floor Sanders and Finishers; Glaziers; Grader, Bulldozer, and Scraper Operators; Hazardous Materials Removal Workers; Insulation Workers, Floor, Ceiling, and Wall; Manufactured Building and Mobile Home Installers; Operating Engineers; Painters, Construction and Maintenance; Paperhangers; Paving, Surfacing, and Tamping Equipment Operators; Pile-Driver Operators; Pipe Fitters; Pipelayers; Pipelaying Fitters; Plasterers and Stucco Masons; Plumbers; Rail-Track Laying and Maintenance Equipment Operators; Refractory Materials Repairers, Except Brickmasons; Reinforcing Iron and Rebar Workers; Riggers; Roofers; Rough Carpenters; Security and Fire Alarm Systems Installers; Segmental Pavers; Sheet Metal Workers; Ship Carpenters and Joiners; Stone Cutters and Carvers; Stonemasons; Structural Iron and Steel Workers; Tapers; Terrazzo Workers and Finishers; Tile and Marble Setters. **PERSONALITY TYPE:** Realistic.

EDUCATION/TRAINING PROGRAM(S)—Construction Trades, Other. **RELATED KNOWLEDGE/COURSES—Building and Construction:** Knowledge of the materials, methods, and tools involved in the construction or repair of houses, buildings, or other structures such as highways and roads. **Mechanical Devices:** Knowledge of machines and tools, including their designs, uses, repair, and maintenance.

Insurance Adjusters, Examiners, and Investigators

- Education/Training Required: Long-term on-the-job training
- Annual Earnings: $44,220
- Growth: 14.2%
- Annual Job Openings: 31,000
- Self-Employed: 1.9%
- Part-Time: 4.9%

Investigate, analyze, and determine the extent of insurance company's liability concerning personal, casualty, or property loss or damages and attempt to effect settlement with claimants. Correspond with or interview medical specialists, agents, witnesses, or claimants to compile information. Calculate benefit payments and approve payment of claims within a certain monetary limit. Interview or correspond with claimant and witnesses, consult police and hospital records, and inspect property damage to determine extent of liability. Investigate and assess damage to property. Examine claims form and other records to determine insurance coverage. Analyze information gathered by investigation and report findings and recommendations. Negotiate claim settlements and recommend litigation when settlement cannot be negotiated. Prepare report of findings of investigation. Collect evidence to support contested claims in court. Interview or correspond with agents and claimants to correct errors or omissions and to investigate questionable claims. Refer questionable claims to investigator or claims adjuster for investigation or settlement. Examine titles to property to determine validity and act as company agent in transactions with property owners. Obtain credit information from banks and other credit services. Communicate with former associates to verify employment record and to obtain background information regarding persons or businesses applying for credit. **SKILLS—Negotiation:** Bringing others together and trying to reconcile differences. **Persuasion:** Persuading others to change their minds or behavior. **Time Management:** Managing one's own time and the time of others. **Judgment and Decision Making:** Considering the relative costs and benefits of potential actions to choose the most appropriate one. **Social Perceptiveness:** Being aware of others' reactions and understanding why they react as they do. **Reading Comprehension:** Understanding written sentences and paragraphs in work-related documents. **Learning Strategies:** Selecting and using training/instructional methods and procedures appropriate for the situation when learning or teaching new things. **Service Orientation:** Actively looking for ways to help people. **GOE—Interest Area:** 06. Finance and Insurance. **Work Group:** 06.02. Finance/Insurance Investigation and Analysis. **Other Jobs in This Work Group:** Appraisers, Real Estate; Assessors; Claims Examiners, Property and Casualty Insurance; Cost Estimators; Credit Analysts; Financial Analysts; Insurance Appraisers, Auto Damage; Insurance Underwriters; Loan

Counselors; Loan Officers; Market Research Analysts; Survey Researchers. **PERSONALITY TYPE:** Enterprising.

EDUCATION/TRAINING PROGRAM(S)—Health/Medical Claims Examiner; Insurance. **RELATED KNOWLEDGE/COURSES—Customer and Personal Service:** Knowledge of principles and processes for providing customer and personal services. This includes customer needs assessment, meeting quality standards for services, and evaluation of customer satisfaction. **Clerical Practices:** Knowledge of administrative and clerical procedures and systems such as word processing, managing files and records, stenography and transcription, designing forms, and other office procedures and terminology. **Computers and Electronics:** Knowledge of circuit boards, processors, chips, electronic equipment, and computer hardware and software, including applications and programming. **Law and Government:** Knowledge of laws, legal codes, court procedures, precedents, government regulations, executive orders, agency rules, and the democratic political process. **English Language:** Knowledge of the structure and content of the English language, including the meaning and spelling of words, rules of composition, and grammar. **Mathematics:** Knowledge of arithmetic, algebra, geometry, calculus, and statistics and their applications. **Medicine and Dentistry:** Knowledge of the information and techniques needed to diagnose and treat human injuries, diseases, and deformities. This includes symptoms, treatment alternatives, drug properties and interactions, and preventive health-care measures.

Insurance Appraisers, Auto Damage

- Education/Training Required: Long-term on-the-job training
- Annual Earnings: $45,330
- Growth: 11.7%
- Annual Job Openings: 2,000
- Self-Employed: 1.8%
- Part-Time: 4.9%

Appraise automobile or other vehicle damage to determine cost of repair for insurance claim settlement and seek agreement with automotive repair shop on cost of repair. **Prepare insurance forms to indicate repair cost or cost estimates and recommendations.** Estimate parts and labor to repair damage, using standard automotive labor and parts-cost manuals and knowledge of automotive repair. Review repair-cost estimates with automobile-repair shop to secure agreement on cost of repairs. Prepare insurance forms to indicate repair-cost estimates and recommendations. Examine damaged vehicle to determine extent of structural, body, mechanical, electrical, or interior damage. Arrange to have damage appraised by another appraiser to resolve disagreement with shop on repair cost. Determine salvage value on total-loss vehicle. Evaluate practicality of repair as opposed to payment of market value of vehicle before accident. **SKILLS—Negotiation:** Bringing others together and trying to reconcile differences. **Mathematics:** Using mathematics to solve problems. **Judgment and Decision Making:** Considering the relative costs and benefits of potential actions to choose the most appropriate one. **Management of Financial Resources:** Determining how money will be spent to get the work done and accounting for these expenditures. **Systems Evaluation:** Identifying measures or indicators of system performance and the actions needed to improve or correct performance relative to the goals of the system. **Writing:** Communicating effectively in writing as appropriate for the needs of the audience. **Speaking:** Talking to others to convey information effectively. **GOE—Interest Area:** 06. Finance and Insurance. **Work Group:** 06.02. Finance/Insurance Investigation and Analysis. **Other Jobs in This Work Group:** Appraisers, Real Estate; Assessors; Claims Examiners, Property and Casualty Insurance; Cost Estimators; Credit Analysts; Financial Analysts; Insurance Adjusters, Examiners, and Investigators; Insurance Underwriters; Loan Counselors; Loan Officers; Market Research Analysts; Survey Researchers. **PERSONALITY TYPE:** Conventional.

EDUCATION/TRAINING PROGRAM(S)—Insurance. **RELATED KNOWLEDGE/COURSES—Economics and Accounting:** Knowledge of economic and accounting principles and practices, the financial markets, banking, and the analysis and reporting of financial data. **Mechanical Devices:** Knowledge of machines and tools, including their designs, uses, repair, and maintenance. **Clerical Practices:** Knowledge of administrative and clerical procedures and systems such as word processing, managing files and records, stenography and transcription, designing forms, and other office procedures and terminology. **Mathematics:** Knowledge of arithmetic, algebra, geometry, calculus, and statistics and their applications. **Telecommunications:** Knowledge of transmission, broadcasting, switching, control, and operation of telecommunications systems.

Insurance Sales Agents

- Education/Training Required: Bachelor's degree
- Annual Earnings: $41,720
- Growth: 8.4%
- Annual Job Openings: 52,000
- Self-Employed: 26.2%
- Part-Time: 9.2%

Sell life, property, casualty, health, automotive, or other types of insurance. May refer clients to independent brokers, work as independent broker, or be employed by an insurance company. Call on policyholders to deliver and explain policy, to analyze insurance program and suggest additions or changes, or to change beneficiaries. Calculate premiums and establish payment method. Customize insurance programs to suit individual customers, often covering a variety of risks. Sell various types of insurance policies to businesses and individuals on behalf of insurance companies, including automobile, fire, life, property, medical, and dental insurance or specialized policies such as marine, farm/crop, and medical malpractice. Interview prospective clients to obtain data about their financial resources and needs and the physical condition of the person or property to be insured and to discuss any existing coverage. Seek out new clients and develop clientele by networking to find new customers and generate lists of prospective clients. Explain features, advantages, and disadvantages of various policies to promote sale of insurance plans. Contact underwriter and submit forms to obtain binder coverage. Ensure that policy requirements are fulfilled, including any necessary medical examinations and the completion of appropriate forms. Confer with clients to obtain and provide information when claims are made on a policy. Perform administrative tasks, such as maintaining records and handling policy renewals. Select company that offers type of coverage requested by client to underwrite policy. Monitor insurance claims to ensure they are settled equitably for both the client and the insurer. Develop marketing strategies to compete with other individuals or companies who sell insurance. Attend meetings, seminars, and programs to learn about new products and services, learn new skills, and receive technical assistance in developing new accounts. Inspect property, examining its general condition, type of construction, age, and other characteristics to decide if it is a good insurance risk. Install bookkeeping systems and resolve system problems. Plan and oversee incorporation of insurance program into bookkeeping system of company. Explain necessary bookkeeping requirements for customer to implement and provide group insurance program. **SKILLS—Persuasion:** Persuading others to change their minds or behavior. **Time Management:** Managing one's own time and the time of others. **Negotiation:** Bringing others together and trying to reconcile differences. **Service Orientation:** Actively looking for ways to help people. **Social Perceptiveness:** Being aware of others' reactions and understanding why they react as they do. **Judgment and Decision Making:** Considering the relative costs and benefits of potential actions to choose the most appropriate one. **Active Listening:** Giving full attention to what other people are saying, taking time to understand the points being made, asking questions as appropriate, and not interrupting at inappropriate times. **Speaking:** Talking to others to convey information effectively. GOE—**Interest Area:** 06. Finance and Insurance. **Work Group:** 06.05. Finance/Insurance Sales and Support. **Other Jobs in This Work Group:** Advertising Sales Agents; Personal Financial Advisors; Sales Agents, Financial Services; Sales Agents, Securities and Commodities. **PERSONALITY TYPE:** Enterprising.

EDUCATION/TRAINING PROGRAM(S)— Insurance. RELATED KNOWLEDGE/COURSES—**Sales and Marketing:** Knowledge of principles and methods for showing, promoting, and selling products or services. This includes marketing strategy and tactics, product demonstrations, sales techniques, and sales control systems. **Customer and Personal Service:** Knowledge of principles and processes for providing customer and personal services. This includes customer needs assessment, meeting quality standards for services, and evaluation of customer satisfaction. **Economics and Accounting:** Knowledge of economic and accounting principles and practices, the financial markets, banking, and the analysis and reporting of financial data. **Clerical Practices:** Knowledge of administrative and clerical procedures and systems such as word processing, managing files and records, stenography and transcription, designing forms, and other office procedures and terminology. **Computers and Electronics:** Knowledge of circuit boards, processors, chips, electronic equipment, and computer hardware and software, including applications and programming. **Mathematics:** Knowledge of arithmetic, algebra, geometry, calculus, and statistics and their applications. **Law and Government:** Knowledge of laws, legal codes, court procedures, precedents, government regulations, executive orders, agency rules, and the democratic political process.

Insurance Underwriters

- ◎ Education/Training Required: Bachelor's degree
- ◎ Annual Earnings: $48,550
- ◎ Growth: 10.0%
- ◎ Annual Job Openings: 12,000
- ◎ Self-Employed: 1.0%
- ◎ Part-Time: 4.5%

Review individual applications for insurance to evaluate degree of risk involved and determine acceptance of applications. Examine documents to determine degree of risk from such factors as applicant financial standing and value and condition of property. Decline excessive risks. Write to field representatives, medical personnel, and others to obtain further information, quote rates, or explain company underwriting policies. Evaluate possibility of losses due to catastrophe or excessive insurance. Decrease value of policy when risk is substandard and specify applicable endorsements or apply rating to ensure safe profitable distribution of risks, using reference materials. Review company records to determine amount of insurance in force on single risk or group of closely related risks. Authorize reinsurance of policy when risk is high. **SKILLS—Service Orientation:** Actively looking for ways to help people. **Writing:** Communicating effectively in writing as appropriate for the needs of the audience. **Learning Strategies:** Selecting and using training/instructional methods and procedures appropriate for the situation when learning or teaching new things. **Active Learning:** Understanding the implications of new information for both current and future

problem-solving and decision-making. **Active Listening:** Giving full attention to what other people are saying, taking time to understand the points being made, asking questions as appropriate, and not interrupting at inappropriate times. **Persuasion:** Persuading others to change their minds or behavior. **Speaking:** Talking to others to convey information effectively. **Monitoring:** Monitoring or assessing your performance or that of other individuals or organizations to make improvements or take corrective action. **Negotiation:** Bringing others together and trying to reconcile differences. **GOE—Interest Area:** 06. Finance and Insurance. **Work Group:** 06.02. Finance/Insurance Investigation and Analysis. **Other Jobs in This Work Group:** Appraisers, Real Estate; Assessors; Claims Examiners, Property and Casualty Insurance; Cost Estimators; Credit Analysts; Financial Analysts; Insurance Adjusters, Examiners, and Investigators; Insurance Appraisers, Auto Damage; Loan Counselors; Loan Officers; Market Research Analysts; Survey Researchers. **PERSONALITY TYPE:** Conventional.

EDUCATION/TRAINING PROGRAM(S)— Insurance. **RELATED KNOWLEDGE/COURSES—Customer and Personal Service:** Knowledge of principles and processes for providing customer and personal services. This includes customer needs assessment, meeting quality standards for services, and evaluation of customer satisfaction. **Clerical Practices:** Knowledge of administrative and clerical procedures and systems such as word processing, managing files and records, stenography and transcription, designing forms, and other office procedures and terminology. **Sales and Marketing:** Knowledge of principles and methods for showing, promoting, and selling products or services. This includes marketing strategy and tactics, product demonstrations, sales techniques, and sales control systems. **Economics and Accounting:** Knowledge of economic and accounting principles and practices, the financial markets, banking, and the analysis and reporting of financial data. **Computers and Electronics:** Knowledge of circuit boards, processors, chips, electronic equipment, and computer hardware and software, including applications and programming. **Law and Government:** Knowledge of laws, legal codes, court procedures, precedents, government regulations, executive orders, agency rules, and the democratic political process.

Interior Designers

- ◎ Education/Training Required: Bachelor's degree
- ◎ Annual Earnings: $40,670
- ◎ Growth: 21.7%
- ◎ Annual Job Openings: 8,000
- ◎ Self-Employed: 32.2%
- ◎ Part-Time: 16.5%

Plan, design, and furnish interiors of residential, commercial, or industrial buildings. Formulate design which is practical, aesthetic, and conducive to intended purposes, such as raising productivity, selling merchandise, or improving lifestyle. May specialize in a particular field, style, or phase of interior design. Estimate material requirements and costs and present design to client for approval. Confer with client to determine factors affecting planning interior environments, such as budget, architectural preferences, and purpose and function. Advise client on interior design factors, such as space planning, layout and utilization of furnishings and equipment, and color coordination. Select or design and purchase furnishings, artwork, and accessories. Formulate environmental plan to be practical, esthetic, and conducive to intended purposes, such as raising productivity or selling merchandise. Subcontract fabrication, installation, and arrangement of carpeting, fixtures, accessories, draperies, paint and wall coverings, artwork, furniture, and related items. Render design ideas in form of paste-ups or drawings. **SKILLS—Installation:** Installing equipment, machines, wiring, or programs to meet specifications. **Persuasion:** Persuading others to change their minds or behavior. **Management of Financial Resources:** Determining how money will be spent to get the work done and accounting for these expenditures. **Active Learning:** Understanding the implications of new information for both current and future problem-solving and decision-making. **Negotiation:** Bringing others together and trying to reconcile differences. **Speaking:** Talking to others to convey information effectively. **Troubleshooting:** Determining causes of operating errors and deciding what to do about them. **Mathematics:** Using mathematics to solve problems. **Critical Thinking:** Using logic and reasoning to identify the strengths and weaknesses of alternative solutions, conclusions, or approaches to problems. **Operations Analysis:** Analyzing needs and product

requirements to create a design. **GOE—Interest Area:** 03. Arts and Communication. **Work Group:** 03.05. Design. **Other Jobs in This Work Group:** Commercial and Industrial Designers; Exhibit Designers; Fashion Designers; Floral Designers; Graphic Designers; Merchandise Displayers and Window Trimmers; Set Designers. **PERSONALITY TYPE:** Artistic.

EDUCATION/TRAINING PROGRAM(S)—Facilities Planning and Management; Interior Architecture; Interior Design; Textile Science. **RELATED KNOWLEDGE/COURSES—Design:** Knowledge of design techniques, tools, and principles involved in production of precision technical plans, blueprints, drawings, and models. **Sales and Marketing:** Knowledge of principles and methods for showing, promoting, and selling products or services. This includes marketing strategy and tactics, product demonstrations, sales techniques, and sales control systems. **Administration and Management:** Knowledge of business and management principles involved in strategic planning, resource allocation, human resources modeling, leadership technique, production methods, and coordination of people and resources. **Customer and Personal Service:** Knowledge of principles and processes for providing customer and personal services. This includes customer needs assessment, meeting quality standards for services, and evaluation of customer satisfaction. **Clerical Practices:** Knowledge of administrative and clerical procedures and systems such as word processing, managing files and records, stenography and transcription, designing forms, and other office procedures and terminology. **Building and Construction:** Knowledge of the materials, methods, and tools involved in the construction or repair of houses, buildings, or other structures such as highways and roads.

Internists, General

- ◎ Education/Training Required: First professional degree
- ◎ Annual Earnings: More than $145,600
- ◎ Growth: 19.5%
- ◎ Annual Job Openings: 38,000
- ◎ Self-Employed: 16.9%
- ◎ Part-Time: 8.1%

Diagnose and provide non-surgical treatment of diseases and injuries of internal organ systems. Provide care mainly for adults who have a wide range of problems associated with the internal organs. Advise patients and community members concerning diet, activity, hygiene, and disease prevention. Analyze records, reports, test results, or examination information to diagnose medical condition of patient. Collect, record, and maintain patient information, such as medical history, reports, and examination results. Make diagnoses when different illnesses occur together or in situations where the diagnosis may be obscure. Explain procedures and discuss test results or prescribed treatments with patients. Immunize patients to protect them from preventable diseases. Manage and treat common health problems, such as infections, influenza, and pneumonia, as well as serious, chronic, and complex illnesses, in adolescents, adults, and the elderly. Monitor patients' conditions and progress and re-evaluate treatments as necessary. Prescribe or administer medication, therapy, and other specialized medical care to treat or prevent illness, disease, or injury. Provide and manage long-term comprehensive medical care, including diagnosis and non-surgical treatment of diseases, for adult patients in an office or hospital. Refer patient to medical specialist or other practitioner when necessary. Treat internal disorders, such as hypertension; heart disease; diabetes; and problems of the lung, brain, kidney, and gastrointestinal tract. Advise surgeon of a patient's risk status and recommend appropriate intervention to minimize risk. Conduct research to develop or test medications, treatments, or procedures to prevent or control disease or injury. Direct and coordinate activities of nurses, students, assistants, specialists, therapists, and other medical staff. Operate on patients to remove, repair, or improve functioning of diseased or injured body parts and systems. Provide consulting services to other doctors caring for patients with special or difficult problems. Plan, implement, or administer health programs in hospitals, businesses, or communities for prevention and treatment of injuries or illnesses. Prepare government or organizational reports on birth, death, and disease statistics; workforce evaluations; or the medical status of individuals. **SKILLS—Science:** Using scientific rules and methods to solve problems. **Systems Evaluation:** Identifying measures or indicators of system performance and the actions needed to improve or correct performance relative to the goals of the system. **Reading Comprehension:** Understanding written sentences and paragraphs in work-related documents. **Active Learning:** Understanding the implications of new information for both current and future problem-solving and decision-making. **Judgment and Decision Making:** Considering the relative costs and benefits of potential actions to choose the most appropriate one. **Management of Personnel Resources:** Motivating, developing, and directing people as they work, identifying the best people for the job. **Systems Analysis:** Determining how a system should work and how changes in conditions, operations, and the environment will affect outcomes. **Social Perceptiveness:** Being aware of others' reactions and understanding why they react as they do. **GOE—Interest Area:** 08. Health Science. **Work Group:** 08.02. Medicine and Surgery. **Other Jobs in This Work Group:** Anesthesiologists; Family and General Practitioners; Medical Assistants; Medical Transcriptionists; Obstetricians and Gynecologists; Pediatricians, General; Pharmacists; Pharmacy Aides; Pharmacy Technicians; Physician Assistants; Psychiatrists; Registered Nurses; Surgeons; Surgical Technologists. **PERSONALITY TYPE:** Investigative.

EDUCATION/TRAINING PROGRAM(S)—Cardiology; Critical Care Medicine; Endocrinology and Metabolism; Gastroenterology; Geriatric Medicine; Hematology; Infectious Disease; Internal Medicine; Nephrology; Neurology; Nuclear Medicine; Oncology; Pulmonary Disease; Rheumatology. **RELATED KNOWLEDGE/COURSES—Medicine and Dentistry:** Knowledge of the information and techniques needed to diagnose and treat human injuries, diseases, and deformities. This includes symptoms, treatment alternatives, drug properties and interactions, and preventive health-care measures. **Biology:** Knowledge of plant and animal organisms and their tissues, cells, functions, interdependencies, and interactions with each other and the environment. **Therapy and Counseling:** Knowledge of principles, methods, and procedures for diagnosis, treatment, and rehabilitation of physical and mental dysfunctions and for career counseling and guidance. **Chemistry:** Knowledge of the chemical composition, structure, and properties of substances and of the chemical processes and transformations that they undergo. This includes uses of chemicals and their danger signs, production techniques, and disposal methods. **Administration and Management:** Knowledge of business and management principles involved in strategic planning, resource allocation, human resources modeling, leadership technique, production methods, and coordination of people and resources. **Physics:** Knowledge and prediction of physical principles and laws and their interrelationships and applications to understanding fluid, material, and atmospheric dynamics and mechanical, electrical, atomic, and subatomic structures and processes.

Interpreters and Translators

- ◉ Education/Training Required: Long-term on-the-job training
- ◉ Annual Earnings: $33,860
- ◉ Growth: 22.1%
- ◉ Annual Job Openings: 4,000
- ◉ Self-Employed: 19.6%
- ◉ Part-Time: 26.3%

Translate or interpret written, oral, or sign language text into another language for others. Check original texts or confer with authors to ensure that translations retain the content, meaning, and feeling of the original material. Check translations of technical terms and terminology to ensure that they are accurate and remain consistent throughout translation revisions. Compile terminology and information to be used in translations, including technical terms such as those for legal or medical material. Discuss translation requirements with clients and determine any fees to be charged for services provided. Listen to speakers' statements in order to determine meanings and to prepare translations, using electronic listening systems as necessary. Proofread, edit, and revise translated materials. Read written materials such as legal documents, scientific works, or news reports and rewrite material into specified languages. Refer to reference materials such as dictionaries, lexicons, encyclopedias, and computerized terminology banks as needed to ensure translation accuracy. Translate messages simultaneously or consecutively into specified languages orally or by using hand signs, maintaining message content, context, and style as much as possible. Adapt translations to students' cognitive and grade levels, collaborating with educational team members as necessary. Follow ethical codes that protect the confidentiality of information. Identify and resolve conflicts related to the meanings of words, concepts, practices, or behaviors. Compile information about the content and context of information to be translated, as well as details of the groups for whom translation or interpretation is being performed. Adapt software and accompanying technical documents to another language and culture. Educate students, parents, staff, and teachers about the roles and functions of educational interpreters. Train and supervise other translators/interpreters. Travel with or guide tourists who speak another language. **SKILLS—Active Listening:** Giving full attention to what other people are saying, taking time to understand the points being made, asking questions as appropriate, and not interrupting at inappropriate times. **Writing:** Communicating effectively in writing as appropriate for the needs of the audience. **Reading Comprehension:** Understanding written sentences and paragraphs in work-related documents. **Speaking:** Talking to others to convey information effectively. **Service Orientation:** Actively looking for ways to help people. **GOE— Interest Area:** 03. Arts and Communication. **Work Group:** 03.03. News, Broadcasting, and Public Relations. **Other Jobs in This Work Group:** Broadcast News Analysts; Caption Writers; Public Relations Specialists; Reporters and Correspondents. **PERSONALITY TYPE:** Artistic.

EDUCATION/TRAINING PROGRAM(S)— African Languages, Literatures, and Linguistics; Albanian Language and Literature; American Indian/Native American Languages, Literatures, and Linguistics; Ancient Near Eastern and Biblical Languages, Literatures, and Linguistics; Ancient/Classical Greek Language and Literature; Arabic Language and Literature; Australian/Oceanic/Pacific Languages, Literatures, and Linguistics; Bahasa Indonesian/Bahasa Malay Languages and Literatures; Baltic Languages, Literatures, and Linguistics; Bengali Language and Literature; Bulgarian Language and Literature; Burmese Language and Literature; Catalan Language and Literature; Celtic Languages, Literatures, and Linguistics; Chinese Language and Literature; Classics and Classical Languages, Literatures, and Linguistics, General; Classics and Classical Languages, Literatures, and Linguistics, Other; Czech Language and Literature; Danish Language and Literature; Dutch/Flemish Language and Literature; East Asian Languages, Literatures, and Linguistics, General; East Asian Languages, Literatures, and Linguistics, Other; Filipino/Tagalog Language and Literature; Finnish and Related Languages, Literatures, and Linguistics; Foreign Languages and Literatures, General; Foreign Languages, Literatures, and

Linguistics, Other; French Language and Literature; German Language and Literature; Germanic Languages, Literatures, and Linguistics, General; Germanic Languages, Literatures, and Linguistics, Other; Hebrew Language and Literature; Hindi Language and Literature; Hungarian/Magyar Language and Literature; Iranian/Persian Languages, Literatures, and Linguistics; Italian Language and Literature; Japanese Language and Literature; Khmer/Cambodian Language and Literature; Korean Language and Literature; Language Interpretation and Translation; Lao/Laotian Language and Literature; Latin Language and Literature; Latin Teacher Education; Linguistics; Middle/Near Eastern and Semitic Languages, Literatures, and Linguistics, Other; others. **RELATED KNOWLEDGE/COURSES—Foreign Language:** Knowledge of the structure and content of a foreign (non-English) language, including the meaning and spelling of words, rules of composition and grammar, and pronunciation. **Communications and Media:** Knowledge of media production, communication, and dissemination techniques and methods. This includes alternative ways to inform and entertain via written, oral, and visual media. **English Language:** Knowledge of the structure and content of the English language, including the meaning and spelling of words, rules of composition, and grammar. **Sociology and Anthropology:** Knowledge of group behavior and dynamics, societal trends and influences, human migrations, ethnicity, and cultures and their history and origins. **History and Archeology:** Knowledge of historical events and their causes, indicators, and effects on civilizations and cultures.

Interviewers, Except Eligibility and Loan

- Education/Training Required: Short-term on-the-job training
- Annual Earnings: $23,670
- Growth: 28.0%
- Annual Job Openings: 46,000
- Self-Employed: 0.7%
- Part-Time: 30.4%

Interview persons by telephone, by mail, in person, or by other means for the purpose of completing forms, applications, or questionnaires. Ask specific questions, record answers, and assist persons with completing form. May sort, classify, and file forms. Ask questions in accordance with instructions to obtain various specified information, such as person's name, address, age, religious preference, and state of residency. Identify and resolve inconsistencies in interviewees' responses by means of appropriate questioning and/or explanation. Compile, record, and code results and data from interview or survey, using computer or specified form. Review data obtained from interview for completeness and accuracy. Contact individuals to be interviewed at home, place of business, or field location by telephone, by mail, or in person. Assist individuals in filling out applications or questionnaires. Ensure payment for services by verifying benefits with the person's insurance provider or working out financing options. Identify and report problems in obtaining valid data. Explain survey objectives and procedures to interviewees and interpret survey questions to help interviewees' comprehension. Perform patient services, such as answering the telephone and assisting patients with financial and medical questions. Prepare reports to provide answers in response to specific problems. Locate and list addresses and households. Perform other office duties as needed, such as telemarketing and customer service inquiries, billing patients, and receiving payments. Meet with supervisor daily to submit completed assignments and discuss progress. Collect and analyze data, such as studying old records; tallying the number of outpatients entering each day or week; or participating in federal, state, or local population surveys as a Census Enumerator. **SKILLS—Service Orientation:** Actively looking for ways to help people. **Social Perceptiveness:** Being aware of others' reactions and understanding why they react as they do. **Speaking:** Talking to others to convey information effectively. **Active Listening:** Giving full attention to what other people are saying, taking time to understand the points being made, asking questions as appropriate, and not interrupting at inappropriate times. **Persuasion:** Persuading others to change their minds or behavior. **Learning Strategies:** Selecting and using training/instructional methods and procedures appropriate for the situation when learning or teaching new things. **Negotiation:** Bringing others together and trying to reconcile differences. **Writing:** Communicating effectively in writing as appropriate for the needs of the audience. **GOE—Interest Area:** 10. Human Service. **Work Group:** 10.04. Client Interviewing. **Other Jobs in This Work Group:** Claims Takers, Unemployment Benefits; Welfare Eligibility Workers and Interviewers. **PERSONALITY TYPE:** Conventional.

EDUCATION/TRAINING PROGRAM(S)— Receptionist. **RELATED KNOWLEDGE/COURSES—Customer and Personal Service:** Knowledge of principles and processes for providing customer and personal services. This includes customer needs assessment, meeting quality standards for services, and evaluation of customer satisfaction. **Therapy and Counseling:** Knowledge of principles, methods, and procedures for diagnosis, treatment, and rehabilitation of physical and mental dysfunctions and for career counseling and guidance. **Sales and Marketing:** Knowledge of principles and methods for showing, promoting, and selling products or services. This includes marketing strategy and tactics, product demonstrations, sales techniques, and sales control systems. **Education and Training:** Knowledge of principles and methods for curriculum and training design, teaching and instruction for individuals and groups, and the measurement of training effects. **Psychology:** Knowledge of human behavior and performance; individual differences in ability, personality, and interests; learning and motivation; psychological research methods; and the assessment and treatment of behavioral and affective disorders. **Philosophy and Theology:** Knowledge of different philosophical systems and religions. This includes their basic principles, values, ethics, ways of thinking, customs, and practices and their impact on human culture.

Irradiated-Fuel Handlers

- ◎ Education/Training Required: Moderate-term on-the-job training
- ◎ Annual Earnings: $33,320
- ◎ Growth: 43.1%
- ◎ Annual Job Openings: 8,000
- ◎ Self-Employed: 0%
- ◎ Part-Time: 5.7%

Package, store, and convey irradiated fuels and wastes, using hoists, mechanical arms, shovels, and industrial truck. Operates machines and equipment to package, store, or transport loads of waste materials. Follows prescribed safety procedures and complies with federal laws regulating waste disposal methods.

Cleans contaminated equipment for reuse, using detergents and solvents, sandblasters, filter pumps, and steam cleaners. Records number of containers stored at disposal site and specifies amount and type of equipment and waste disposed. Mixes and pours concrete into forms to encase waste material for disposal. Drives truck to convey contaminated waste to designated sea or ground location. Loads and unloads materials into containers and onto trucks, using hoists or forklift. **SKILLS—Operation and Control:** Controlling operations of equipment or systems. **GOE—Interest Area:** 13. Manufacturing. **Work Group:** 13.17. Loading, Moving, Hoisting, and Conveying. **Other Jobs in This Work Group:** Conveyor Operators and Tenders; Freight, Stock, and Material Movers, Hand; Hoist and Winch Operators; Industrial Truck and Tractor Operators; Machine Feeders and Offbearers; Packers and Packagers, Hand; Pump Operators, Except Wellhead Pumpers; Refuse and Recyclable Material Collectors; Tank Car, Truck, and Ship Loaders. **PERSONALITY TYPE:** Realistic.

EDUCATION/TRAINING PROGRAM(S)—Hazardous Materials Management and Waste Technology/Technician. **RELATED KNOWLEDGE/ COURSES—Transportation:** Knowledge of principles and methods for moving people or goods by air, rail, sea, or road, including the relative costs and benefits. **Production and Processing:** Knowledge of raw materials, production processes, quality control, costs, and other techniques for maximizing the effective manufacture and distribution of goods. **Chemistry:** Knowledge of the chemical composition, structure, and properties of substances and of the chemical processes and transformations that they undergo. This includes uses of chemicals and their danger signs, production techniques, and disposal methods. **Public Safety and Security:** Knowledge of relevant equipment, policies, procedures, and strategies to promote effective local, state, or national security operations for the protection of people, data, property, and institutions. **Law and Government:** Knowledge of laws, legal codes, court procedures, precedents, government regulations, executive orders, agency rules, and the democratic political process. **Building and Construction:** Knowledge of the materials, methods, and tools involved in the construction or repair of houses, buildings, or other structures such as highways and roads.

Janitorial Supervisors

- Education/Training Required: Work experience in a related occupation
- Annual Earnings: $29,510
- Growth: 16.2%
- Annual Job Openings: 28,000
- Self-Employed: 5.6%
- Part-Time: 6.6%

Supervise work activities of janitorial personnel in commercial and industrial establishments. Assign duties, inspect work, and investigate complaints regarding janitorial services and take corrective action. May purchase janitorial supplies and equipment, take periodic inventories, screen applicants, train new employees, and recommend dismissals. Supervises and coordinates activities of workers engaged in janitorial services. Assigns janitorial work to employees, following material and work requirements. Inspects work performed to ensure conformance to specifications and established standards. Records personnel data on specified forms. Recommends personnel actions, such as hires and discharges, to ensure proper staffing. Confers with staff to resolve production and personnel problems. Trains workers in janitorial methods and procedures and proper operation of equipment. Issues janitorial supplies and equipment to workers to ensure quality and timely delivery of services. **SKILLS—Management of Personnel Resources:** Motivating, developing, and directing people as they work, identifying the best people for the job. **Coordination:** Adjusting actions in relation to others' actions. **Time Management:** Managing one's own time and the time of others. **Social Perceptiveness:** Being aware of others' reactions and understanding why they react as they do. **Persuasion:** Persuading others to change their minds or behavior. **Negotiation:** Bringing others together and trying to reconcile differences. **Management of Material Resources:** Obtaining and seeing to the appropriate use of equipment, facilities, and materials needed to do certain work. **Speaking:** Talking to others to convey information effectively. **GOE—Interest Area:** 04. Business and Administration. **Work Group:** 04.02. Managerial Work in Business Detail. **Other Jobs in This Work Group:** Administrative Services Managers; First-Line Supervisors, Administrative Support; First-Line Supervisors, Customer Service; Housekeeping Supervisors;

Meeting and Convention Planners. **PERSONALITY TYPE:** Enterprising.

EDUCATION/TRAINING PROGRAM(S)—No data available. **RELATED KNOWLEDGE/COURSES—Personnel and Human Resources:** Knowledge of principles and procedures for personnel recruitment, selection, training, compensation and benefits, labor relations and negotiation, and personnel information systems. **Administration and Management:** Knowledge of business and management principles involved in strategic planning, resource allocation, human resources modeling, leadership technique, production methods, and coordination of people and resources. **Customer and Personal Service:** Knowledge of principles and processes for providing customer and personal services. This includes customer needs assessment, meeting quality standards for services, and evaluation of customer satisfaction.

Janitors and Cleaners, Except Maids and Housekeeping Cleaners

- Education/Training Required: Short-term on-the-job training
- Annual Earnings: $18,790
- Growth: 18.3%
- Annual Job Openings: 454,000
- Self-Employed: 4.7%
- Part-Time: 21.7%

Keep buildings in clean and orderly condition. Perform heavy cleaning duties, such as cleaning floors, shampooing rugs, washing walls and glass, and removing rubbish. Duties may include tending furnace and boiler, performing routine maintenance activities, notifying management of need for repairs, and cleaning snow or debris from sidewalk. Clean building floors by sweeping, mopping, scrubbing, or vacuuming them. Gather and empty trash. Service, clean, and supply restrooms. Clean and polish furniture and fixtures. Clean windows, glass partitions, and mirrors, using soapy water or other cleaners, sponges, and squeegees. Dust furniture, walls, machines, and equipment. Make adjustments and minor repairs to heating, cooling, ventilating, plumbing, and electrical systems. Mix water and detergents or acids in containers to prepare cleaning solutions according to specifications. Steam-clean or shampoo carpets. Strip, seal, finish, and polish floors. Clean and restore building interiors damaged by fire, smoke, or water, using commercial cleaning equipment. Clean chimneys, flues, and connecting pipes, using power and hand tools. Clean laboratory equipment, such as glassware and metal instruments, using solvents, brushes, rags, and power-cleaning equipment. Drive vehicles required to perform or travel to cleaning work, including vans, industrial trucks, or industrial vacuum cleaners. Follow procedures for the use of chemical cleaners and power equipment in order to prevent damage to floors and fixtures. Monitor building security and safety by performing such tasks as locking doors after operating hours and checking electrical appliance use to ensure that hazards are not created. Move heavy furniture, equipment, and supplies either manually or by using hand trucks. Mow and trim lawns and shrubbery, using mowers and hand and power trimmers, and clear debris from grounds. Notify managers concerning the need for major repairs or additions to building operating systems. Remove snow from sidewalks, driveways, and parking areas, using snowplows, snow blowers, and snow shovels, and spread snow-melting chemicals. Requisition supplies and equipment needed for cleaning and maintenance duties. Set up, arrange, and remove decorations, tables, chairs, ladders, and scaffolding to prepare facilities for events such as banquets and meetings. Spray insecticides and fumigants to prevent insect and rodent infestation. **SKILLS—Repairing:** Repairing machines or systems by using the needed tools. **Equipment Maintenance:** Performing routine maintenance on equipment and determining when and what kind of maintenance is needed. **Installation:** Installing equipment, machines, wiring, or programs to meet specifications. **Troubleshooting:** Determining causes of operating errors and deciding what to do about them. **GOE—Interest Area:** 09. Hospitality, Tourism, and Recreation. **Work Group:** 09.03. Hospitality and Travel Services. **Other Jobs in This Work Group:** Baggage Porters and Bellhops; Concierges; Flight Attendants; Hotel, Motel, and Resort Desk Clerks; Maids and Housekeeping Cleaners; Reservation and Transportation Ticket Agents; Tour Guides and Escorts; Transportation Attendants, Except Flight Attendants and Baggage Porters; Travel Agents; Travel Clerks; Travel Guides. **PERSONALITY TYPE:** Realistic.

EDUCATION/TRAINING PROGRAM(S)—No data available. **RELATED KNOWLEDGE/COURSES—Mechanical Devices:** Knowledge of machines and tools, including their designs, uses, repair, and maintenance. **Chemistry:** Knowledge of the chemical composition, structure, and properties of substances and of the chemical processes and transformations that they undergo. This includes uses of chemicals and their danger signs, production techniques, and disposal methods. **Building and Construction:** Knowledge of the materials, methods, and tools involved in the construction or repair of houses, buildings, or other structures such as highways and roads. **Transportation:** Knowledge of principles and methods for moving people or goods by air, rail, sea, or road, including the relative costs and benefits. **Physics:** Knowledge and prediction of physical principles and laws and their interrelationships and applications to understanding fluid, material, and atmospheric dynamics and mechanical, electrical, atomic, and subatomic structures and processes. **Public Safety and Security:** Knowledge of relevant equipment, policies, procedures, and strategies to promote effective local, state, or national security operations for the protection of people, data, property, and institutions.

Judges, Magistrate Judges, and Magistrates

- Education/Training Required: Work experience plus degree
- Annual Earnings: $93,070
- Growth: 8.7%
- Annual Job Openings: 2,000
- Self-Employed: 0%
- Part-Time: 6.2%

Arbitrate, advise, adjudicate, or administer justice in a court of law. May sentence defendant in criminal cases according to government statutes. May determine liability of defendant in civil cases. May issue marriage licenses and perform wedding ceremonies. Instruct juries on applicable laws, direct juries to deduce the facts from the evidence presented, and hear their verdicts. Sentence defendants in criminal cases on conviction by jury according to applicable government statutes. Rule on admissibility of evidence and methods of conducting testimony. Preside over hearings and listen to allegations made by plaintiffs to determine whether the evidence supports the charges. Read documents on pleadings and motions to ascertain facts and issues. Interpret and enforce rules of procedure or establish new rules in situations where there are no procedures already established by law. Monitor proceedings to ensure that all applicable rules and procedures are followed. Advise attorneys, juries, litigants, and court personnel regarding conduct, issues, and proceedings. Research legal issues and write opinions on the issues. Conduct preliminary hearings to decide issues such as whether there is reasonable and probable cause to hold defendants in felony cases. Write decisions on cases. Award compensation for damages to litigants in civil cases in relation to findings by juries or by the court. Settle disputes between opposing attorneys. Supervise other judges, court officers, and the court's administrative staff. Impose restrictions upon parties in civil cases until trials can be held. Rule on custody and access disputes and enforce court orders regarding custody and support of children. Grant divorces and divide assets between spouses. Participate in judicial tribunals to help resolve disputes. **SKILLS—Judgment and Decision Making:** Considering the relative costs and benefits of potential actions to choose the most appropriate one. **Persuasion:** Persuading others to change their minds or behavior. **Negotiation:** Bringing others together and trying to reconcile differences. **Social Perceptiveness:** Being aware of others' reactions and understanding why they react as they do. **Critical Thinking:** Using logic and reasoning to identify the strengths and weaknesses of alternative solutions, conclusions, or approaches to problems. **Active Listening:** Giving full attention to what other people are saying, taking time to understand the points being made, asking questions as appropriate, and not interrupting at inappropriate times. **Service Orientation:** Actively looking for ways to help people. **Management of Personnel Resources:** Motivating, developing, and directing people as they work, identifying the best people for the job. **GOE— Interest Area:** 12. Law and Public Safety. **Work Group:** 12.02. Legal Practice and Justice Administration. **Other Jobs in This Work Group:** Administrative Law Judges, Adjudicators, and Hearing Officers; Arbitrators, Mediators, and Conciliators; Lawyers. **PERSONALITY TYPE:** Enterprising.

EDUCATION/TRAINING PROGRAM(S)—Law (LL.B., J.D.); Legal Professions and Studies, Other.

RELATED KNOWLEDGE/COURSES—Law and Government: Knowledge of laws, legal codes, court procedures, precedents, government regulations, executive orders, agency rules, and the democratic political process. **English Language:** Knowledge of the structure and content of the English language, including the meaning and spelling of words, rules of composition, and grammar. **Psychology:** Knowledge of human behavior and performance; individual differences in ability, personality, and interests; learning and motivation; psychological research methods; and the assessment and treatment of behavioral and affective disorders. **Philosophy and Theology:** Knowledge of different philosophical systems and religions. This includes their basic principles, values, ethics, ways of thinking, customs, and practices and their impact on human culture. **Public Safety and Security:** Knowledge of relevant equipment, policies, procedures, and strategies to promote effective local, state, or national security operations for the protection of people, data, property, and institutions. **Therapy and Counseling:** Knowledge of principles, methods, and procedures for diagnosis, treatment, and rehabilitation of physical and mental dysfunctions and for career counseling and guidance.

Kindergarten Teachers, Except Special Education

- ◎ Education/Training Required: Bachelor's degree
- ◎ Annual Earnings: $41,400
- ◎ Growth: 27.2%
- ◎ Annual Job Openings: 34,000
- ◎ Self-Employed: 2.2%
- ◎ Part-Time: 24.9%

Teach elemental natural and social science, personal hygiene, music, art, and literature to children from 4 to 6 years old. Promote physical, mental, and social development. May be required to hold state certification. Teach basic skills such as color, shape, number, and letter recognition; personal hygiene; and social skills. Establish and enforce rules for behavior and policies and procedures to maintain order among students. Observe and evaluate children's performance, behavior, social development, and physical health.

Instruct students individually and in groups, adapting teaching methods to meet students' varying needs and interests. Read books to entire classes or to small groups. Demonstrate activities to children. Provide a variety of materials and resources for children to explore, manipulate, and use, both in learning activities and in imaginative play. Plan and conduct activities for a balanced program of instruction, demonstration, and work time that provides students with opportunities to observe, question, and investigate. Confer with parents or guardians, other teachers, counselors, and administrators to resolve students' behavioral and academic problems. Prepare children for later grades by encouraging them to explore learning opportunities and to persevere with challenging tasks. Establish clear objectives for all lessons, units, and projects and communicate those objectives to children. Prepare and implement remedial programs for students requiring extra help. Meet with parents and guardians to discuss their children's progress and to determine their priorities for their children and their resource needs. Organize and lead activities designed to promote physical, mental, and social development, such as games, arts and crafts, music, and storytelling. Prepare objectives and outlines for courses of study, following curriculum guidelines or requirements of states and schools. Guide and counsel students with adjustment and/or academic problems or special academic interests. Instruct and monitor students in the use and care of equipment and materials in order to prevent injuries and damage. Identify children showing signs of emotional, developmental, or health-related problems and discuss them with supervisors, parents or guardians, and child development specialists. Assimilate arriving children to the school environment by greeting them, helping them remove outerwear, and selecting activities of interest to them. **SKILLS—Instructing:** Teaching others how to do something. **Learning Strategies:** Selecting and using training/instructional methods and procedures appropriate for the situation when learning or teaching new things. **Social Perceptiveness:** Being aware of others' reactions and understanding why they react as they do. **Monitoring:** Monitoring or assessing your performance or that of other individuals or organizations to make improvements or take corrective action. **Time Management:** Managing one's own time and the time of others. **Coordination:** Adjusting actions in relation to others' actions. **Persuasion:** Persuading others to change their minds or behavior. **Negotiation:** Bringing others together and trying to reconcile differences. **Service Orientation:** Actively looking for ways to help people. **GOE—Interest Area:** 05. Education and Training. **Work Group:** 05.02. Preschool, Elementary, and Secondary Teaching and Instructing. **Other Jobs in This Work Group:** Elementary School Teachers, Except Special Education; Middle School Teachers, Except Special and Vocational Education; Preschool Teachers, Except Special Education; Secondary School Teachers, Except Special and Vocational Education; Special Education Teachers, Middle School; Special Education Teachers, Preschool, Kindergarten, and Elementary School; Special Education Teachers, Secondary School; Teacher Assistants; Vocational Education Teachers, Middle School; Vocational Education Teachers, Secondary School. **PERSONALITY TYPE:** Social.

EDUCATION/TRAINING PROGRAM(S)— Early Childhood Education and Teaching; Kindergarten/Preschool Education and Teaching. **RELATED KNOWLEDGE/COURSES—Education and Training:** Knowledge of principles and methods for curriculum and training design, teaching and instruction for individuals and groups, and the measurement of training effects. **History and Archeology:** Knowledge of historical events and their causes, indicators, and effects on civilizations and cultures. **Psychology:** Knowledge of human behavior and performance; individual differences in ability, personality, and interests; learning and motivation; psychological research methods; and the assessment and treatment of behavioral and affective disorders. **Sociology and Anthropology:** Knowledge of group behavior and dynamics, societal trends and influences, human migrations, ethnicity, and cultures and their history and origins. **Geography:** Knowledge of principles and methods for describing the features of land, sea, and air masses, including their physical characteristics; locations; interrelationships; and distribution of plant, animal, and human life. **Philosophy and Theology:** Knowledge of different philosophical systems and religions. This includes their basic principles, values, ethics, ways of thinking, customs, and practices and their impact on human culture.

Landscape Architects

- Education/Training Required: Bachelor's degree
- Annual Earnings: $53,120
- Growth: 22.2%
- Annual Job Openings: 2,000
- Self-Employed: 23.4%
- Part-Time: 5.5%

Plan and design land areas for such projects as parks and other recreational facilities; airports; highways; hospitals; schools; land subdivisions; and commercial, industrial, and residential sites. Prepare site plans, specifications, and cost estimates for land development, coordinating arrangement of existing and proposed land features and structures. Confer with clients, engineering personnel, and architects on overall program. Compile and analyze data on conditions such as location, drainage, and location of structures for environmental reports and landscaping plans. Inspect landscape work to ensure compliance with specifications, approve quality of materials and work, and advise client and construction personnel. **SKILLS— Coordination:** Adjusting actions in relation to others' actions. **Operations Analysis:** Analyzing needs and product requirements to create a design. **Management of Financial Resources:** Determining how money will be spent to get the work done and accounting for these expenditures. **Social Perceptiveness:** Being aware of others' reactions and understanding why they react as they do. **Persuasion:** Persuading others to change their minds or behavior. **Complex Problem Solving:** Identifying complex problems and reviewing related information to develop and evaluate options and implement solutions. **Time Management:** Managing one's own time and the time of others. **Instructing:** Teaching others how to do something. **GOE—Interest Area:** 02. Architecture and Construction. **Work Group:** 02.02. Architectural Design. **Other Jobs in This Work Group:** Architects, Except Landscape and Naval. **PERSONALITY TYPE:** Artistic.

EDUCATION/TRAINING PROGRAM(S)—Environmental Design/Architecture; Landscape Architecture (BS, BSLA, BLA, MSLA, MLA, PhD). **RELATED KNOWLEDGE/COURSES—Design:** Knowledge of design techniques, tools, and principles involved in production of precision technical plans, blueprints, drawings, and models. **Building and Con-** struction: Knowledge of the materials, methods, and tools involved in the construction or repair of houses, buildings, or other structures such as highways and roads. **Geography:** Knowledge of principles and methods for describing the features of land, sea, and air masses, including their physical characteristics; locations; interrelationships; and distribution of plant, animal, and human life. **Engineering and Technology:** Knowledge of the practical application of engineering science and technology. This includes applying principles, techniques, procedures, and equipment to the design and production of various goods and services. **Biology:** Knowledge of plant and animal organisms and their tissues, cells, functions, interdependencies, and interactions with each other and the environment. **Administration and Management:** Knowledge of business and management principles involved in strategic planning, resource allocation, human resources modeling, leadership technique, production methods, and coordination of people and resources. **Sales and Marketing:** Knowledge of principles and methods for showing, promoting, and selling products or services. This includes marketing strategy and tactics, product demonstrations, sales techniques, and sales control systems.

Landscaping and Groundskeeping Workers

- Education/Training Required: Short-term on-the-job training
- Annual Earnings: $20,420
- Growth: 22.0%
- Annual Job Openings: 203,000
- Self-Employed: 23.3%
- Part-Time: 15.3%

Landscape or maintain grounds of property, using hand or power tools or equipment. Workers typically perform a variety of tasks, which may include any combination of the following: sod laying, mowing, trimming, planting, watering, fertilizing, digging, raking, sprinkler installation, and installation of mortarless segmental concrete masonry wall units. Care for established lawns by mulching; aerating; weeding; grubbing and removing thatch; and trimming and edging around flowerbeds, walks, and walls. Mix and spray or spread fertilizers, herbicides, or insecticides onto grass, shrubs, and trees, using hand or automatic sprayers or spreaders. Mow and edge lawns, using power mowers and edgers. Plant seeds, bulbs, foliage, flowering plants, grass, ground cover, trees, and shrubs and apply mulch for protection, using gardening tools. Attach wires from planted trees to support stakes. Decorate gardens with stones and plants. Follow planned landscaping designs to determine where to lay sod, sow grass, or plant flowers and foliage. Gather and remove litter. Haul or spread topsoil and spread straw over seeded soil to hold soil in place. Maintain irrigation systems, including winterizing the systems and starting them up in spring. Plan and cultivate lawns and gardens. Prune and trim trees, shrubs, and hedges, using shears, pruners, or chain saws. Rake, mulch, and compost leaves. Trim and pick flowers and clean flowerbeds. Water lawns, trees, and plants, using portable sprinkler systems, hoses, or watering cans. Advise customers on plant selection and care. Build forms and mix and pour cement to form garden borders. Install rock gardens, ponds, decks, drainage systems, irrigation systems, retaining walls, fences, planters, and/or playground equipment. Maintain and repair tools; equipment; and structures such as buildings, greenhouses, fences, and benches, using hand and power tools. Provide proper upkeep of sidewalks, driveways, parking lots, fountains, planters, burial sites, and other grounds features. Shovel snow from walks, driveways, and parking lots and spread salt in those areas. Use irrigation methods to adjust the amount of water consumption and to prevent waste. Care for artificial turf fields, periodically removing the turf and replacing cushioning pads and vacuuming and disinfecting the turf after use to prevent the growth of harmful bacteria. Care for natural turf fields, making sure the underlying soil has the required composition to allow proper drainage and to support the grasses used on the fields. **SKILLS—Repairing:** Repairing machines or systems by using the needed tools. **Operation and Control:** Controlling operations of equipment or systems. **Equipment Maintenance:** Performing routine maintenance on equipment and determining when and what kind of maintenance is needed. **Installation:** Installing equipment, machines, wiring, or programs to meet specifications. **GOE— Interest Area:** 01. Agriculture and Natural Resources. **Work Group:** 01.05. Nursery, Groundskeeping, and Pest Control. **Other Jobs in This Work Group:** Nursery Workers; Pest Control Workers; Pesticide Handlers, Sprayers, and Applicators, Vegetation; Tree Trimmers and Pruners. **PERSONALITY TYPE:** Realistic.

EDUCATION/TRAINING PROGRAM(S)— Landscaping and Groundskeeping; Turf and Turfgrass Management. **RELATED KNOWLEDGE/COURSES—Chemistry:** Knowledge of the chemical composition, structure, and properties of substances and of the chemical processes and transformations that they undergo. This includes uses of chemicals and their danger signs, production techniques, and disposal methods. **Building and Construction:** Knowledge of the materials, methods, and tools involved in the construction or repair of houses, buildings, or other structures such as highways and roads. **Mechanical Devices:** Knowledge of machines and tools, including their designs, uses, repair, and maintenance.

Laundry and Drycleaning Machine Operators and Tenders, Except Pressing

- Education/Training Required: Moderate-term on-the-job training
- Annual Earnings: $17,220
- Growth: 12.3%
- Annual Job Openings: 47,000
- Self-Employed: 6.8%
- Part-Time: 16.9%

Operate or tend washing or dry-cleaning machines to wash or dry-clean commercial, industrial, or household articles, such as cloth garments, suede, leather, furs, blankets, draperies, fine linens, rugs, and carpets. Starts washer, dry cleaner, drier, or extractor, and turns valves or levers to regulate and monitor cleaning or drying operations. Loads or directs other workers to load articles into washer or dry-cleaning machine. Starts pumps to operate distilling system that drains and reclaims dry-cleaning solvents. Adjusts switches to tend and regulate equipment that fumigates and removes foreign matter from furs. Cleans machine filters and lubricates equipment. Mends and sews articles, using hand stitching, adhesive patch, or power sewing machine. Hangs curtains, drapes, blankets, pants, and other garments on stretch frames to dry and transports items between specified locations. Irons or presses articles, fabrics, and furs, using hand iron or pressing machine. Receives and marks articles for laundry or dry cleaning with identifying code number or name, using hand or machine marker. Sorts and counts articles removed from dryer and folds, wraps, or hangs items for airing out, pickup, or delivery. Examines and sorts articles to be cleaned into lots according to color, fabric, dirt content, and cleaning technique required. Pre-soaks, sterilizes, scrubs, spot-cleans, and dries contaminated or stained articles, using neutralizer solutions and portable machines. Washes, dry cleans, or glazes delicate articles or fur garment linings by hand, using mild detergent or dry-cleaning solutions. Removes or directs other workers to remove items from washer or dry-cleaning machine and into extractor or tumbler. Tends variety of automatic machines that comb and polish furs; clean, sterilize, and fluff feathers and blankets; and roll and package towels. Mixes and adds detergents, dyes, bleach, starch, and other solutions and chemicals to clean, color, dry, or stiffen articles. **SKILLS—Operation Monitoring:** Watching gauges, dials, or other indicators to make sure a machine is working properly. **Operation and Control:** Controlling operations of equipment or systems. **Equipment Maintenance:** Performing routine maintenance on equipment and determining when and what kind of maintenance is needed. **Installation:** Installing equipment, machines, wiring, or programs to meet specifications. **GOE—Interest Area:** 13. Manufacturing. **Work Group:** 13.11. Apparel, Shoes, Leather, and Fabric Care. **Other Jobs in This Work Group:** Custom Tailors; Fabric Menders, Except Garment; Precision Dyers; Pressers, Delicate Fabrics; Pressers, Hand; Shoe and Leather Workers and Repairers; Shop and Alteration Tailors; Spotters, Dry Cleaning; Upholsterers. **PERSONALITY TYPE:** Realistic.

EDUCATION/TRAINING PROGRAM(S)—No data available. **RELATED KNOWLEDGE/COURSES—Chemistry:** Knowledge of the chemical composition, structure, and properties of substances and of the chemical processes and transformations that they undergo. This includes uses of chemicals and their danger signs, production techniques, and disposal methods. **Production and Processing:** Knowledge of raw materials, production processes, quality control, costs, and other techniques for maximizing the effective manufacture and distribution of goods.

Law Teachers, Postsecondary

- Education/Training Required: First professional degree
- Annual Earnings: $87,290
- Growth: 38.1%
- Annual Job Openings: 216,000
- Self-Employed: 0.3%
- Part-Time: 27.7%

Teach courses in law. Evaluate and grade students' class work, assignments, papers, and oral presentations. Compile, administer, and grade examinations or assign this work to others. Prepare and deliver lectures to undergraduate and/or graduate students on topics such as civil procedure, contracts, and torts. Initiate, facilitate, and moderate classroom discussions. Prepare course materials such as syllabi, homework assignments, and handouts. Keep abreast of developments in their field by reading current literature, talking with colleagues, and participating in professional conferences. Plan, evaluate, and revise curricula, course content, and course materials and methods of instruction. Maintain regularly scheduled office hours in order to advise and assist students. Conduct research in a particular field of knowledge and publish findings in professional journals, books, and/or electronic media. Advise students on academic and vocational curricula and on career issues. Supervise undergraduate and/or graduate teaching, internship, and research work. Select and obtain materials and supplies such as textbooks. Maintain student attendance records, grades, and other required records. Serve on academic or administrative committees that deal with institutional policies, departmental matters, and academic issues. Perform administrative duties such as serving as department head. Collaborate with colleagues to address teaching and research issues. Participate in student recruitment, registration, and placement activities. Compile bibliographies of specialized materials for outside reading assignments. Participate in campus and community events. Act as advisers to student organizations. Assign cases for students to hear and try. **SKILLS—Instructing:** Teaching others how to do something. **Critical Thinking:** Using logic and reasoning to identify the strengths and weaknesses of alternative solutions, conclusions, or approaches to problems.

Persuasion: Persuading others to change their minds or behavior. **Reading Comprehension:** Understanding written sentences and paragraphs in work-related documents. **Writing:** Communicating effectively in writing as appropriate for the needs of the audience. **Speaking:** Talking to others to convey information effectively. **Learning Strategies:** Selecting and using training/instructional methods and procedures appropriate for the situation when learning or teaching new things. **Active Listening:** Giving full attention to what other people are saying, taking time to understand the points being made, asking questions as appropriate, and not interrupting at inappropriate times. **GOE— Interest Area:** 05. Education and Training. **Work Group:** 05.03. Postsecondary and Adult Teaching and Instructing. **Other Jobs in This Work Group:** Adult Literacy, Remedial Education, and GED Teachers and Instructors; Agricultural Sciences Teachers, Postsecondary; Anthropology and Archeology Teachers, Postsecondary; Architecture Teachers, Postsecondary; Area, Ethnic, and Cultural Studies Teachers, Postsecondary; Art, Drama, and Music Teachers, Postsecondary; Atmospheric, Earth, Marine, and Space Sciences Teachers, Postsecondary; Biological Science Teachers, Postsecondary; Business Teachers, Postsecondary; Chemistry Teachers, Postsecondary; Communications Teachers, Postsecondary; Computer Science Teachers, Postsecondary; Criminal Justice and Law Enforcement Teachers, Postsecondary; Economics Teachers, Postsecondary; Education Teachers, Postsecondary; Engineering Teachers, Postsecondary; English Language and Literature Teachers, Postsecondary; Environmental Science Teachers, Postsecondary; Farm and Home Management Advisors; Foreign Language and Literature Teachers, Postsecondary; Forestry and Conservation Science Teachers, Postsecondary; Geography Teachers, Postsecondary; Graduate Teaching Assistants; Health Specialties Teachers, Postsecondary; History Teachers, Postsecondary; Home Economics Teachers, Postsecondary; Library Science Teachers, Postsecondary; Mathematical Science Teachers, Postsecondary; Nursing Instructors and Teachers, Postsecondary; Philosophy and Religion Teachers, Postsecondary; Physics Teachers, Postsecondary; Political Science Teachers, Postsecondary; Psychology Teachers, Postsecondary; Recreation and Fitness Studies Teachers, Postsecondary; Self-Enrichment Education Teachers; Social Work Teachers, Postsecondary; Sociology Teachers, Postsecondary; Vocational Education Teachers, Postsecondary. **PERSONALITY TYPE:** No data available.

EDUCATION/TRAINING PROGRAM(S)—Law (LL.B., J.D.); Legal Studies, General. **RELATED KNOWLEDGE/COURSES—Law and Government:** Knowledge of laws, legal codes, court procedures, precedents, government regulations, executive orders, agency rules, and the democratic political process. **English Language:** Knowledge of the structure and content of the English language, including the meaning and spelling of words, rules of composition, and grammar. **Education and Training:** Knowledge of principles and methods for curriculum and training design, teaching and instruction for individuals and groups, and the measurement of training effects. **History and Archeology:** Knowledge of historical events and their causes, indicators, and effects on civilizations and cultures. **Philosophy and Theology:** Knowledge of different philosophical systems and religions. This includes their basic principles, values, ethics, ways of thinking, customs, and practices and their impact on human culture. **Communications and Media:** Knowledge of media production, communication, and dissemination techniques and methods. This includes alternative ways to inform and entertain via written, oral, and visual media.

Lawn Service Managers

- Education/Training Required: Work experience in a related occupation
- Annual Earnings: $35,340
- Growth: 21.6%
- Annual Job Openings: 18,000
- Self-Employed: 34.7%
- Part-Time: 5.9%

Plan, direct, and coordinate activities of workers engaged in pruning trees and shrubs, cultivating lawns, and applying pesticides and other chemicals according to service contract specifications. Supervises workers who provide groundskeeping services on a contract basis. Investigates customer complaints. Prepares work activity and personnel reports. Suggests changes in work procedures and orders corrective work done. Spot-checks completed work to improve quality of service and to ensure contract compliance. Schedules work for crew according to weather conditions, availability of equipment, and seasonal limitations. Reviews contracts to ascertain service, machine, and workforce requirements for job. Prepares service cost estimates for customers. Answers customers' questions about groundskeeping care requirements. **SKILLS— Management of Personnel Resources:** Motivating, developing, and directing people as they work, identifying the best people for the job. **Time Management:** Managing one's own time and the time of others. **Management of Financial Resources:** Determining how money will be spent to get the work done and accounting for these expenditures. **Systems Analysis:** Determining how a system should work and how changes in conditions, operations, and the environment will affect outcomes. **Systems Evaluation:** Identifying measures or indicators of system performance and the actions needed to improve or correct performance relative to the goals of the system. **Management of Material Resources:** Obtaining and seeing to the appropriate use of equipment, facilities, and materials needed to do certain work. **Coordination:** Adjusting actions in relation to others' actions. **Mathematics:** Using mathematics to solve problems. **Negotiation:** Bringing others together and trying to reconcile differences. **GOE—Interest Area:** 01. Agriculture and Natural Resources. **Work Group:** 01.01. Managerial Work in Agriculture and Natural Resources. **Other Jobs in This Work Group:** Agricultural Crop Farm Managers; Farmers and Ranchers; First-Line Supervisors and Manager/Supervisors—Agricultural Crop Workers; First-Line Supervisors and Manager/Supervisors—Animal Husbandry Workers; First-Line Supervisors and Manager/Supervisors—Extractive Workers; First-Line Supervisors and Manager/Supervisors—Fishery Workers; First-Line Supervisors and Manager/Supervisors—Horticultural Workers; First-Line Supervisors and Manager/Supervisors—Landscaping Workers; First-Line Supervisors and Manager/Supervisors—Logging Workers; Fish Hatchery Managers; Nursery and Greenhouse Managers; Park Naturalists; Purchasing Agents and Buyers, Farm Products. **PERSONALITY TYPE:** Enterprising.

EDUCATION/TRAINING PROGRAM(S)— Landscaping and Groundskeeping; Ornamental Horticulture; Turf and Turfgrass Management. **RELATED KNOWLEDGE/COURSES—Administration and Management:** Knowledge of business and management principles involved in strategic planning, resource allocation, human resources modeling, leadership technique, production methods, and coordination of people and resources. **Economics and Accounting:** Knowledge of economic and accounting principles and practices, the financial markets, bank-

ing, and the analysis and reporting of financial data. **Customer and Personal Service:** Knowledge of principles and processes for providing customer and personal services. This includes customer needs assessment, meeting quality standards for services, and evaluation of customer satisfaction. **Personnel and Human Resources:** Knowledge of principles and procedures for personnel recruitment, selection, training, compensation and benefits, labor relations and negotiation, and personnel information systems. **Sales and Marketing:** Knowledge of principles and methods for showing, promoting, and selling products or services. This includes marketing strategy and tactics, product demonstrations, sales techniques, and sales control systems. **Chemistry:** Knowledge of the chemical composition, structure, and properties of substances and of the chemical processes and transformations that they undergo. This includes uses of chemicals and their danger signs, production techniques, and disposal methods.

Lawyers

- Education/Training Required: First professional degree
- Annual Earnings: $94,930
- Growth: 17.0%
- Annual Job Openings: 53,000
- Self-Employed: 26.8%
- Part-Time: 6.2%

Represent clients in criminal and civil litigation and other legal proceedings, draw up legal documents, and manage or advise clients on legal transactions. May specialize in a single area or may practice broadly in many areas of law. Advise clients concerning business transactions, claim liability, advisability of prosecuting or defending lawsuits, or legal rights and obligations. Interpret laws, rulings, and regulations for individuals and businesses. Analyze the probable outcomes of cases, using knowledge of legal precedents. Present and summarize cases to judges and juries. Evaluate findings and develop strategies and arguments in preparation for presentation of cases. Gather evidence to formulate defense or to initiate legal actions by such means as interviewing clients and witnesses to ascertain the facts of a case. Represent clients in court or before government agencies. Examine legal data to determine advisability of defending or prosecuting lawsuit. Select jurors, argue motions, meet with judges, and question witnesses during the course of a trial. Present evidence to defend clients or prosecute defendants in criminal or civil litigation. Study Constitution, statutes, decisions, regulations, and ordinances of quasi-judicial bodies to determine ramifications for cases. Prepare and draft legal documents, such as wills, deeds, patent applications, mortgages, leases, and contracts. Prepare legal briefs and opinions and file appeals in state and federal courts of appeal. Negotiate settlements of civil disputes. Confer with colleagues with specialties in appropriate areas of legal issue to establish and verify bases for legal proceedings. Search for and examine public and other legal records to write opinions or establish ownership. Supervise legal assistants. Perform administrative and management functions related to the practice of law. Act as agent, trustee, guardian, or executor for businesses or individuals. Probate wills and represent and advise executors and administrators of estates. Help develop federal and state programs, draft and interpret laws and legislation, and establish enforcement procedures. Work in environmental law, representing public interest groups, waste disposal companies, or construction firms in their dealings with state and federal agencies. **SKILLS—Persuasion:** Persuading others to change their minds or behavior. **Negotiation:** Bringing others together and trying to reconcile differences. **Critical Thinking:** Using logic and reasoning to identify the strengths and weaknesses of alternative solutions, conclusions, or approaches to problems. **Social Perceptiveness:** Being aware of others' reactions and understanding why they react as they do. **Writing:** Communicating effectively in writing as appropriate for the needs of the audience. **Judgment and Decision Making:** Considering the relative costs and benefits of potential actions to choose the most appropriate one. **Speaking:** Talking to others to convey information effectively. **Active Learning:** Understanding the implications of new information for both current and future problem-solving and decision-making. **GOE—Interest Area:** 12. Law and Public Safety. **Work Group:** 12.02. Legal Practice and Justice Administration. **Other Jobs in This Work Group:** Administrative Law Judges, Adjudicators, and Hearing Officers; Arbitrators, Mediators, and Conciliators; Judges, Magistrate Judges, and Magistrates. **PERSONALITY TYPE:** Enterprising.

EDUCATION/TRAINING PROGRAM(S)— Advanced Legal Research/Studies, General (LL.M., M.C.L., M.L.I., M.S.L., J.S.D./S.J.D.); American/U.S. Law/Legal Studies/Jurisprudence (LL.M., M.C.J., J.S.D./S.J.D.); Banking, Corporate, Finance, and Securities Law (LL.M., J.S.D./S.J.D.); Canadian Law/Legal Studies/Jurisprudence (LL.M., M.C.J., J.S.D./S.J.D.); Comparative Law (LL.M., M.C.L., J.S.D./S.J.D.); Energy, Environment, and Natural Resources Law (LL.M., M.S., J.S.D./S.J.D.); Health Law (LL.M., M.J., J.S.D./S.J.D.); International Business, Trade, and Tax Law (LL.M., J.S.D./S.J.D.); International Law and Legal Studies (LL.M., J.S.D./S.J.D.); Law (LL.B., J.D.); Legal Professions and Studies, Other; Legal Research and Advanced Professional Studies, Other; Programs for Foreign Lawyers (LL.M., M.C.L.); Tax Law/Taxation (LL.M, J.S.D./S.J.D.). **RELATED KNOWLEDGE/COURSES—Law and Government:** Knowledge of laws, legal codes, court procedures, precedents, government regulations, executive orders, agency rules, and the democratic political process. **English Language:** Knowledge of the structure and content of the English language, including the meaning and spelling of words, rules of composition, and grammar. **Customer and Personal Service:** Knowledge of principles and processes for providing customer and personal services. This includes customer needs assessment, meeting quality standards for services, and evaluation of customer satisfaction. **Personnel and Human Resources:** Knowledge of principles and procedures for personnel recruitment, selection, training, compensation and benefits, labor relations and negotiation, and personnel information systems. **Psychology:** Knowledge of human behavior and performance; individual differences in ability, personality, and interests; learning and motivation; psychological research methods; and the assessment and treatment of behavioral and affective disorders. **Administration and Management:** Knowledge of business and management principles involved in strategic planning, resource allocation, human resources modeling, leadership technique, production methods, and coordination of people and resources.

Legal Secretaries

- Education/Training Required: Postsecondary vocational training
- Annual Earnings: $36,720
- Growth: 18.8%
- Annual Job Openings: 39,000
- Self-Employed: 1.7%
- Part-Time: 17.5%

Perform secretarial duties, utilizing legal terminology, procedures, and documents. Prepare legal papers and correspondence, such as summonses, complaints, motions, and subpoenas. May also assist with legal research. Prepare and process legal documents and papers, such as summonses, subpoenas, complaints, appeals, motions, and pretrial agreements. Mail, fax, or arrange for delivery of legal correspondence to clients, witnesses, and court officials. Receive and place telephone calls. Schedule and make appointments. Make photocopies of correspondence, document, and other printed matter. Organize and maintain law libraries and document and case files. Assist attorneys in collecting information such as employment, medical, and other records. Attend legal meetings, such as client interviews, hearings, or depositions, and take notes. Draft and type office memos. Review legal publications and perform database searches to identify laws and court decisions relevant to pending cases. Submit articles and information from searches to attorneys for review and approval for use. Complete various forms, such as accident reports, trial and courtroom requests, and applications for clients. **SKILLS—Writing:** Communicating effectively in writing as appropriate for the needs of the audience. **Time Management:** Managing one's own time and the time of others. **Social Perceptiveness:** Being aware of others' reactions and understanding why they react as they do. **Reading Comprehension:** Understanding written sentences and paragraphs in work-related documents. **Learning Strategies:** Selecting and using training/instructional methods and procedures appropriate for the situation when learning or teaching new things. **Negotiation:** Bringing others together and trying to reconcile differences. **Active Listening:** Giving full attention to what other people are saying, taking time to understand the points being made, asking questions as appropriate, and not interrupting at inappropriate times. **Persuasion:** Persuading others to change their minds or

behavior. **GOE—Interest Area:** 04. Business and Administration. **Work Group:** 04.04. Secretarial Support. **Other Jobs in This Work Group:** Executive Secretaries and Administrative Assistants; Medical Secretaries; Secretaries, Except Legal, Medical, and Executive. **PERSONALITY TYPE:** Conventional.

EDUCATION/TRAINING PROGRAM(S)—Legal Administrative Assistant/Secretary. **RELATED KNOWLEDGE/COURSES—Clerical Practices:** Knowledge of administrative and clerical procedures and systems such as word processing, managing files and records, stenography and transcription, designing forms, and other office procedures and terminology. **Law and Government:** Knowledge of laws, legal codes, court procedures, precedents, government regulations, executive orders, agency rules, and the democratic political process. **Customer and Personal Service:** Knowledge of principles and processes for providing customer and personal services. This includes customer needs assessment, meeting quality standards for services, and evaluation of customer satisfaction. **Economics and Accounting:** Knowledge of economic and accounting principles and practices, the financial markets, banking, and the analysis and reporting of financial data. **Computers and Electronics:** Knowledge of circuit boards, processors, chips, electronic equipment, and computer hardware and software, including applications and programming. **English Language:** Knowledge of the structure and content of the English language, including the meaning and spelling of words, rules of composition, and grammar.

Letterpress Setters and Set-Up Operators

- Education/Training Required: Moderate-term on-the-job training
- Annual Earnings: $29,900
- Growth: 4.6%
- Annual Job Openings: 30,000
- Self-Employed: 2.7%
- Part-Time: 6.2%

Set up or set up and operate direct relief letterpresses, either sheet or roll (web) fed, to produce single-color or multicolor printed material, such as newspapers,

books, and periodicals. Dismantles and reassembles printing unit or parts, using hand tools, to repair, clean, maintain, or adjust press. Operates specially-equipped presses and auxiliary equipment, such as cutting, folding, numbering, and pasting devices. Reads work orders and job specifications to select ink and paper stock. Records and maintains production logsheet. Directs and monitors activities of apprentices and feeding or stacking workers. Inspects printed materials for irregularities such as off-level areas, variations in ink volume, register slippage, and poor color register. Moves controls to set or adjust ink flow, tension rollers, paper guides, and feed controls. Positions and installs printing plates, cylinder packing, die, and type forms in press according to specifications, using hand tools. Loads, positions, and adjusts unprinted materials on holding fixtures or in feeding mechanism of press. Pushes buttons or moves controls to start printing press and control operation. Mixes colors or inks and fills reservoirs. Monitors feeding and printing operations to maintain specified operating levels and detect malfunctions. **SKILLS—Installation:** Installing equipment, machines, wiring, or programs to meet specifications. **Operation Monitoring:** Watching gauges, dials, or other indicators to make sure a machine is working properly. **Operation and Control:** Controlling operations of equipment or systems. **Equipment Maintenance:** Performing routine maintenance on equipment and determining when and what kind of maintenance is needed. **Troubleshooting:** Determining causes of operating errors and deciding what to do about them. **Quality Control Analysis:** Conducting tests and inspections of products, services, or processes to evaluate quality or performance. **Equipment Selection:** Determining the kind of tools and equipment needed to do a job. **Management of Personnel Resources:** Motivating, developing, and directing people as they work, identifying the best people for the job. **GOE—Interest Area:** 13. Manufacturing. **Work Group:** 13.08. Graphic Arts Production. **Other Jobs in This Work Group:** Bindery Machine Operators and Tenders; Camera Operators; Design Printing Machine Setters and Set-Up Operators; Desktop Publishers; Dot Etchers; Electronic Masking System Operators; Electrotypers and Stereotypers; Embossing Machine Set-Up Operators; Engraver Set-Up Operators; Engravers, Hand; Engravers/Carvers; Etchers; Etchers, Hand; Film Laboratory Technicians; Hand Compositors and Typesetters; Job Printers; Marking and Identification Printing Machine Setters and Set-

Up Operators; Offset Lithographic Press Setters and Set-Up Operators; Pantograph Engravers; Paste-Up Workers; Photoengravers; Photoengraving and Lithographing Machine Operators and Tenders; Photographic Processing Machine Operators; Plate Finishers; Platemakers; Precision Etchers and Engravers, Hand or Machine; Precision Printing Workers; Printing Press Machine Operators and Tenders; Scanner Operators; Strippers; Typesetting and Composing Machine Operators and Tenders. **PERSONALITY TYPE:** Realistic.

EDUCATION/TRAINING PROGRAM(S)— Graphic and Printing Equipment Operator, General Production; Graphic Communications, Other; Printing Management; Printing Press Operator. **RELATED KNOWLEDGE/COURSES—Production and Processing:** Knowledge of raw materials, production processes, quality control, costs, and other techniques for maximizing the effective manufacture and distribution of goods. **Economics and Accounting:** Knowledge of economic and accounting principles and practices, the financial markets, banking, and the analysis and reporting of financial data.

Librarians

- ◉ Education/Training Required: Master's degree
- ◉ Annual Earnings: $45,900
- ◉ Growth: 10.1%
- ◉ Annual Job Openings: 15,000
- ◉ Self-Employed: 0.1%
- ◉ Part-Time: 23.1%

Administer libraries and perform related library services. Work in a variety of settings, including public libraries, schools, colleges and universities, museums, corporations, government agencies, law firms, nonprofit organizations, and health-care providers. Tasks may include selecting, acquiring, cataloguing, classifying, circulating, and maintaining library materials and furnishing reference, bibliographical, and readers' advisory services. May perform in-depth, strategic research and synthesize, analyze, edit, and filter information. May set up or work with databases and information systems to catalogue and access information. Search standard reference materials, including online sources and the Internet, in order to answer patrons' reference questions. Analyze patrons' requests to determine needed information and assist in furnishing or locating that information. Teach library patrons to search for information by using databases. Keep records of circulation and materials. Supervise budgeting, planning, and personnel activities. Check books in and out of the library. Explain use of library facilities, resources, equipment, and services and provide information about library policies. Review and evaluate resource material, such as book reviews and catalogs, in order to select and order print, audiovisual, and electronic resources. Code, classify, and catalog books, publications, films, audiovisual aids, and other library materials based on subject matter or standard library classification systems. Locate unusual or unique information in response to specific requests. Direct and train library staff in duties such as receiving, shelving, researching, cataloging, and equipment use. Respond to customer complaints, taking action as necessary. Organize collections of books, publications, documents, audiovisual aids, and other reference materials for convenient access. Develop library policies and procedures. Evaluate materials to determine outdated or unused items to be discarded. Develop information access aids such as indexes and annotated bibliographies, Web pages, electronic pathfinders, and online tutorials. Plan and deliver client-centered programs and services such as special services for corporate clients, storytelling for children, newsletters, or programs for special groups. Compile lists of books, periodicals, articles, and audiovisual materials on particular subjects. Arrange for interlibrary loans of materials not available in a particular library. Assemble and arrange display materials. Confer with teachers, parents, and community organizations to develop, plan, and conduct programs in reading, viewing, and communication skills. Compile lists of overdue materials and notify borrowers that their materials are overdue. **SKILLS—Learning Strategies:** Selecting and using training/instructional methods and procedures appropriate for the situation when learning or teaching new things. **Management of Financial Resources:** Determining how money will be spent to get the work done and accounting for these expenditures. **Service Orientation:** Actively looking for ways to help people. **Instructing:** Teaching others how to do something. **Persuasion:** Persuading others to change their minds or behavior. **Management of Material Resources:** Obtaining and seeing to the appropriate use of equipment, facilities, and materials needed to do certain work. **Social Perceptiveness:** Being aware of others' reactions and understanding why they react as they do. **Monitoring:** Monitoring or assessing your performance or that of other individuals or organizations to make improvements or take corrective action. **GOE— Interest Area:** 05. Education and Training. **Work Group:** 05.04. Library Services. **Other Jobs in This Work Group:** Library Assistants, Clerical; Library Technicians. **PERSONALITY TYPE:** Artistic.

EDUCATION/TRAINING PROGRAM(S)— Library Science, Other; Library Science/Librarianship; School Librarian/School Library Media Specialist. **RELATED KNOWLEDGE/COURSES—Customer and Personal Service:** Knowledge of principles and processes for providing customer and personal services. This includes customer needs assessment, meeting quality standards for services, and evaluation of customer satisfaction. **Clerical Practices:** Knowledge of administrative and clerical procedures and systems such as word processing, managing files and records, stenography and transcription, designing forms, and other office procedures and terminology. **English Language:** Knowledge of the structure and content of the English language, including the meaning and spelling of words, rules of composition, and grammar. **Communications and Media:** Knowledge of media production, communication, and dissemination techniques and methods. This includes alternative ways to inform and entertain via written, oral, and visual media. **Personnel and Human Resources:** Knowledge of principles and procedures for personnel recruitment, selection, training, compensation and benefits, labor relations and negotiation, and personnel information systems. **Geography:** Knowledge of principles and methods for describing the features of land, sea, and air masses, including their physical characteristics; locations; interrelationships; and distribution of plant, animal, and human life.

Library Assistants, Clerical

- Education/Training Required: Short-term on-the-job training
- Annual Earnings: $20,720
- Growth: 21.5%
- Annual Job Openings: 27,000
- Self-Employed: 0.1%
- Part-Time: 50.4%

Compile records, sort and shelve books, and issue and receive library materials such as pictures, cards, slides and microfilm. Locate library materials for loan and replace material in shelving area, stacks, or files according to identification number and title. Register patrons to permit them to borrow books, periodicals, and other library materials. Lend and collect books, periodicals, videotapes, and other materials at circulation desks. Enter and update patrons' records on computers. Process new materials, including books, audiovisual materials, and computer software. Sort books, publications, and other items according to established procedure and return them to shelves, files, or other designated storage areas. Locate library materials for patrons, including books, periodicals, tape cassettes, Braille volumes, and pictures. Instruct patrons on how to use reference sources, card catalogs, and automated information systems. Inspect returned books for condition and due-date status and compute any applicable fines. Answer routine inquiries and refer patrons in need of professional assistance to librarians. Maintain records of items received, stored, issued, and returned and file catalog cards according to system used. Perform clerical activities such as filing, typing, word processing, photocopying and mailing out material, and mail sorting. Provide assistance to librarians in the maintenance of collections of books, periodicals, magazines, newspapers, and audiovisual and other materials. Take action to deal with disruptive or problem patrons. Classify and catalog items according to content and purpose. Register new patrons and issue borrower identification cards that permit patrons to borrow books and other materials. Send out notices and accept fine payments for lost or overdue books. Operate small branch libraries under the direction of off-site librarian supervisors. Prepare, store, and retrieve classification and catalog information, lecture notes, or other information related to stored documents, using computers. Schedule and supervise clerical workers, volunteers, and student assistants. Operate and maintain audiovisual equipment. Review records, such as microfilm and issue cards, in order to identify titles of overdue materials and delinquent borrowers. Select substitute titles when requested materials are unavailable, following criteria such as age, education, and interests. Repair books, using mending tape, paste, and brushes. **SKILLS—Service Orientation:** Actively looking for ways to help people. **Reading Comprehension:** Understanding written sentences and paragraphs in work-related documents. **Instructing:** Teaching others how to do something. **Learning Strategies:** Selecting and using training/instructional methods and procedures appropriate for the situation when learning or teaching new things. **Active Listening:** Giving full attention to what other people are saying, taking time to understand the points being made, asking questions as appropriate, and not interrupting at inappropriate times. **Social Perceptiveness:** Being aware of others' reactions and understanding why they react as they do. **Time Management:** Managing one's own time and the time of others. **Writing:** Communicating effectively in writing as appropriate for the needs of the audience. **GOE—Interest Area:** 05. Education and Training. **Work Group:** 05.04. Library Services. **Other Jobs in This Work Group:** Librarians; Library Technicians. **PERSONALITY TYPE:** Conventional.

EDUCATION/TRAINING PROGRAM(S)— Library Assistant/Technician. **RELATED KNOWLEDGE/COURSES—Clerical Practices:** Knowledge of administrative and clerical procedures and systems such as word processing, managing files and records, stenography and transcription, designing forms, and other office procedures and terminology. **Computers and Electronics:** Knowledge of circuit boards, processors, chips, electronic equipment, and computer hardware and software, including applications and programming. **Customer and Personal Service:** Knowledge of principles and processes for providing customer and personal services. This includes customer needs assessment, meeting quality standards for services, and evaluation of customer satisfaction. **English Language:** Knowledge of the structure and content of the English language, including the meaning and spelling of words, rules of composition, and grammar. **History and Archeology:** Knowledge of historical events and their causes, indicators, and effects on civilizations and cultures. **Communications and Media:** Knowledge of media production, communication, and dissemination techniques and methods. This includes alternative ways to inform and entertain via written, oral, and visual media.

Library Science Teachers, Postsecondary

- Education/Training Required: Master's degree
- Annual Earnings: $51,600
- Growth: 38.1%
- Annual Job Openings: 216,000
- Self-Employed: 0.3%
- Part-Time: 27.7%

Teach courses in library science. Prepare course materials such as syllabi, homework assignments, and handouts. Prepare and deliver lectures to undergraduate and/or graduate students on topics such as collection development, archival methods, and indexing and abstracting. Evaluate and grade students' class work, assignments, and papers. Keep abreast of developments in their field by reading current literature, talking with colleagues, and participating in professional conferences. Initiate, facilitate, and moderate classroom discussions. Plan, evaluate, and revise curricula, course content, and course materials and methods of instruction. Conduct research in a particular field of knowledge and publish findings in professional journals, books, and/or electronic media. Maintain student attendance records, grades, and other required records. Collaborate with colleagues to address teaching and research issues. Advise students on academic and vocational curricula and on career issues. Compile, administer, and grade examinations or assign this work to others. Supervise undergraduate and/or graduate teaching, internship, and research work. Maintain regularly scheduled office hours in order to advise and assist students. Write grant proposals to procure external research funding. Select and obtain materials and supplies such as textbooks. Serve on academic or administrative committees that deal with institutional policies, departmental matters, and academic issues. Participate in student recruitment, registration, and placement activities. Compile bibliographies of specialized materials for outside reading assignments. Perform administrative duties such as serving as department head. **SKILLS—Instructing:** Teaching others how to do something. **Learning Strategies:** Selecting and using training/instructional methods and procedures appropriate for the situation when learning or teaching new things. **Writing:** Communicating effectively in writing as appropriate for the needs of the audience. **Active Learning:** Understanding the implications of new information for both current and future problem-solving and decision-making. **Persuasion:** Persuading others to change their minds or behavior. **Service Orientation:** Actively looking for ways to help people. **Reading Comprehension:** Understanding written sentences and paragraphs in work-related documents. **Social Perceptiveness:** Being aware of others' reactions and understanding why they react as they do. **GOE—Interest Area:** 05. Education and Training. **Work Group:** 05.03. Postsecondary and Adult Teaching and Instructing. **Other Jobs in This Work Group:** Adult Literacy, Remedial Education, and GED Teachers and Instructors; Agricultural Sciences Teachers, Postsecondary; Anthropology and Archeology Teachers, Postsecondary; Architecture Teachers, Postsecondary; Area, Ethnic, and Cultural Studies Teachers, Postsecondary; Art, Drama, and Music Teachers, Postsecondary; Atmospheric, Earth, Marine, and Space Sciences Teachers, Postsecondary; Biological Science Teachers, Postsecondary; Business Teachers, Postsecondary; Chemistry Teachers, Postsecondary; Communications Teachers, Postsecondary; Computer Science Teachers, Postsecondary; Criminal Justice and Law Enforcement Teachers, Postsecondary; Economics Teachers, Postsecondary; Education Teachers, Postsecondary; Engineering Teachers, Postsecondary; English Language and Literature Teachers, Postsecondary; Environmental Science Teachers, Postsecondary; Farm and Home Management Advisors; Foreign Language and Literature Teachers, Postsecondary; Forestry and Conservation Science Teachers, Postsecondary; Geography Teachers, Postsecondary; Graduate Teaching Assistants; Health Specialties Teachers, Postsecondary; History Teachers, Postsecondary; Home Economics Teachers, Postsecondary; Law Teachers, Postsecondary; Mathematical Science Teachers, Postsecondary; Nursing Instructors and Teachers, Postsecondary; Philosophy and Religion Teachers, Postsecondary; Physics Teachers, Postsecondary; Political Science Teachers, Postsecondary; Psychology Teachers, Postsecondary; Recreation and Fitness Studies Teachers, Postsecondary; Self-Enrichment Education Teachers; Social Work Teachers, Postsecondary; Sociology Teachers, Postsecondary; Vocational Education Teachers, Postsecondary. **PERSONALITY TYPE:** No data available.

EDUCATION/TRAINING PROGRAM(S)— Library Science/Librarianship; Teacher Education and Professional Development, Specific Subject Areas, Other. **RELATED KNOWLEDGE/COURSES—**

Education and Training: Knowledge of principles and methods for curriculum and training design, teaching and instruction for individuals and groups, and the measurement of training effects. **English Language:** Knowledge of the structure and content of the English language, including the meaning and spelling of words, rules of composition, and grammar. **Sociology and Anthropology:** Knowledge of group behavior and dynamics, societal trends and influences, human migrations, ethnicity, and cultures and their history and origins. **Communications and Media:** Knowledge of media production, communication, and dissemination techniques and methods. This includes alternative ways to inform and entertain via written, oral, and visual media. **Computers and Electronics:** Knowledge of circuit boards, processors, chips, electronic equipment, and computer hardware and software, including applications and programming. **History and Archeology:** Knowledge of historical events and their causes, indicators, and effects on civilizations and cultures.

Library Technicians

- ⊚ Education/Training Required: Short-term on-the-job training
- ⊚ Annual Earnings: $24,940
- ⊚ Growth: 16.8%
- ⊚ Annual Job Openings: 22,000
- ⊚ Self-Employed: 0%
- ⊚ Part-Time: 53.4%

Assist librarians by helping readers in the use of library catalogs, databases, and indexes to locate books and other materials and by answering questions that require only brief consultation of standard reference. Compile records; sort and shelve books; remove or repair damaged books; register patrons; check materials in and out of the circulation process. Replace materials in shelving area (stacks) or files. Includes bookmobile drivers who operate bookmobiles or light trucks that pull trailers to specific locations on a predetermined schedule and assist with providing services in mobile libraries. Reserve, circulate, renew, and discharge books and other materials. Enter and update patrons' records on computers. Provide assistance to teachers and students by locating materials and helping to complete special projects. Answer routine reference inquiries and refer patrons needing further assistance to librarians. Guide patrons in finding and using library resources, including reference materials, audiovisual equipment, computers, and electronic resources. Train other staff, volunteers, and/or student assistants and schedule and supervise their work. Sort books, publications, and other items according to procedure and return them to shelves, files, or other designated storage areas. Conduct reference searches, using printed materials and in-house and online databases. Deliver and retrieve items throughout the library by hand or using pushcart. Take actions to halt disruption of library activities by problem patrons. Process interlibrary loans for patrons. Process print and non-print library materials to prepare them for inclusion in library collections. Retrieve information from central databases for storage in a library's computer. Organize and maintain periodicals and reference materials. Compile and maintain records relating to circulation, materials, and equipment. Collect fines and respond to complaints about fines. Issue identification cards to borrowers. Verify bibliographical data for materials, including author, title, publisher, publication date, and edition. Review subject matter of materials to be classified and select classification numbers and headings according to classification systems. Send out notices about lost or overdue books. Prepare order slips for materials to be acquired, checking prices and figuring costs. Design, customize, and maintain databases, Web pages, and local area networks. Operate and maintain audiovisual equipment such as projectors, tape recorders, and videocassette recorders. File catalog cards according to system used. Prepare volumes for binding. Conduct children's programs and other specialized programs such as library tours. Compose explanatory summaries of contents of books and other reference materials. **SKILLS—Service Orientation:** Actively looking for ways to help people. **Instructing:** Teaching others how to do something. **Learning Strategies:** Selecting and using training/instructional methods and procedures appropriate for the situation when learning or teaching new things. **Social Perceptiveness:** Being aware of others' reactions and understanding why they react as they do. **Reading Comprehension:** Understanding written sentences and paragraphs in work-related documents. **Active Listening:** Giving full attention to what other people are saying, taking time to understand the points being made, asking questions as appropriate, and not interrupting at inappropriate times. **Management of Personnel Resources:** Motivating, developing, and directing people as they work, identifying the best people for the job. **Writing:** Communicating effectively in writing as appropriate for the needs of the audience. **Critical Thinking**: Using logic and reasoning to identify the strengths and weaknesses of alternative solutions, conclusions, or approaches to problems. **Time Management**: Managing one's own time and the time of others. **GOE—Interest Area**: 05. Education and Training. **Work Group**: 05.04. Library Services. **Other Jobs in This Work Group**: Librarians; Library Assistants, Clerical. **PERSONALITY TYPE**: Conventional.

EDUCATION/TRAINING PROGRAM(S)— Library Assistant/Technician. **RELATED KNOWLEDGE/COURSES—Clerical Practices**: Knowledge of administrative and clerical procedures and systems such as word processing, managing files and records, stenography and transcription, designing forms, and other office procedures and terminology. **Customer and Personal Service**: Knowledge of principles and processes for providing customer and personal services. This includes customer needs assessment, meeting quality standards for services, and evaluation of customer satisfaction. **Computers and Electronics**: Knowledge of circuit boards, processors, chips, electronic equipment, and computer hardware and software, including applications and programming. **Geography**: Knowledge of principles and methods for describing the features of land, sea, and air masses, including their physical characteristics; locations; interrelationships; and distribution of plant, animal, and human life. **Education and Training**: Knowledge of principles and methods for curriculum and training design, teaching and instruction for individuals and groups, and the measurement of training effects. **English Language**: Knowledge of the structure and content of the English language, including the meaning and spelling of words, rules of composition, and grammar.

License Clerks

- Education/Training Required: Short-term on-the-job training
- Annual Earnings: $28,430
- Growth: 12.3%
- Annual Job Openings: 14,000
- Self-Employed: 2.6%
- Part-Time: 8.3%

Issue licenses or permits to qualified applicants. Obtain necessary information, record data, advise applicants on requirements, collect fees, and issue licenses. May conduct oral, written, visual, or performance testing. Answer questions and provide advice to the public regarding licensing policies, procedures, and regulations. Assemble photographs with printed license information in order to produce completed documents. Collect prescribed fees for licenses. Conduct and score oral, visual, written, or performance tests to determine applicant qualifications and notify applicants of their scores. Evaluate information on applications to verify completeness and accuracy and to determine whether applicants are qualified to obtain desired licenses. Instruct customers in the completion of drivers' license application forms and other forms such as voter registration cards and organ donor forms. Maintain records of applications made and licensing fees collected. Operate specialized photographic equipment in order to obtain photographs for drivers' licenses and photo identification cards. Perform routine data entry and other office support activities, including creating, sorting, photocopying, distributing, and filing documents. Question applicants to obtain required information, such as name, address, and age, and record data on prescribed forms. Stock counters with adequate supplies of forms, film, licenses, and other required materials. Update operational records and licensing information, using computer terminals. Code information on license applications for entry into computers. Inform customers by mail or telephone of additional steps they need to take to obtain licenses. Perform record checks on past and current licensees as required by investigations. Prepare bank deposits and take them to banks. Prepare lists of overdue accounts and license suspensions and issuances. Train other workers and coordinate their work as necessary. Send drivers' licenses by mail to out-of-county or out-of-state applicants. Enforce canine licensing regulations, contacting noncompliant owners in person or by mail to inform them of the required regulations and potential enforcement actions. Perform driver education program enrollments for participating schools. Provide assistance in the preparation of insurance examinations covering a variety of types of insurance. **SKILLS—Speaking**: Talking to others to convey information effectively. **GOE—Interest Area**: 07. Government and Public Administration. **Work Group**: 07.04. Public Administration Clerical Support. **Other Jobs in This Work**

Group: Court Clerks; Court Reporters; Municipal Clerks. **PERSONALITY TYPE:** Conventional.

EDUCATION/TRAINING PROGRAM(S)—General Office Occupations and Clerical Services. **RELATED KNOWLEDGE/COURSES—Clerical Practices:** Knowledge of administrative and clerical procedures and systems such as word processing, managing files and records, stenography and transcription, designing forms, and other office procedures and terminology. **Law and Government:** Knowledge of laws, legal codes, court procedures, precedents, government regulations, executive orders, agency rules, and the democratic political process. **Economics and Accounting:** Knowledge of economic and accounting principles and practices, the financial markets, banking, and the analysis and reporting of financial data. **Transportation:** Knowledge of principles and methods for moving people or goods by air, rail, sea, or road, including the relative costs and benefits. **Telecommunications:** Knowledge of transmission, broadcasting, switching, control, and operation of telecommunications systems.

Licensed Practical and Licensed Vocational Nurses

◎ Education/Training Required: Postsecondary vocational training
◎ Annual Earnings: $33,970
◎ Growth: 20.2%
◎ Annual Job Openings: 105,000
◎ Self-Employed: 0.6%
◎ Part-Time: 19.1%

Care for ill, injured, convalescent, or disabled persons in hospitals, nursing homes, clinics, private homes, group homes, and similar institutions. May work under the supervision of a registered nurse. Licensing required. Observe patients, charting and reporting changes in patients' conditions such as adverse reactions to medication or treatment and taking any necessary action. Administer prescribed medications or start intravenous fluids and note times and amounts on patients' charts. Answer patients' calls and determine how to assist them. Measure and record patients' vital signs, such as height, weight, temperature, blood pressure, pulse, and respiration. Provide basic patient care and treatments, such as taking temperatures and blood pressure; dressing wounds; treating bedsores; giving enemas, douches, alcohol rubs, and massages; or performing catheterizations. Help patients with bathing, dressing, personal hygiene, moving in bed, and standing and walking. Supervise nurses' aides and assistants. Work as part of a health-care team to assess patient needs, plan and modify care, and implement interventions. Record food and fluid intake and output. Evaluate nursing intervention outcomes, conferring with other health-care team members as necessary. Assemble and use equipment such as catheters, tracheotomy tubes, and oxygen suppliers. Collect samples such as blood, urine, and sputum from patients and perform routine laboratory tests on samples. Prepare patients for examinations, tests, and treatments and explain procedures. Prepare food trays and examine them for conformance to prescribed diet. Apply compresses, ice bags, and hot water bottles. Clean rooms and make beds. Inventory and requisition supplies and instruments. Provide medical treatment and personal care to patients in private home settings, such as cooking, keeping rooms orderly, seeing that patients are comfortable and in good spirits, and instructing family members in simple nursing tasks. Sterilize equipment and supplies, using germicides, sterilizer, or autoclave. Assist in delivery, care, and feeding of infants. Wash and dress bodies of deceased persons. Make appointments, keep records, and perform other clerical duties in doctors' offices and clinics. Set up equipment and prepare medical treatment rooms. **SKILLS—Service Orientation:** Actively looking for ways to help people. **Science:** Using scientific rules and methods to solve problems. **Active Listening:** Giving full attention to what other people are saying, taking time to understand the points being made, asking questions as appropriate, and not interrupting at inappropriate times. **Judgment and Decision Making:** Considering the relative costs and benefits of potential actions to choose the most appropriate one. **Time Management:** Managing one's own time and the time of others. **Operation Monitoring:** Watching gauges, dials, or other indicators to make sure a machine is working properly. **Management of Personnel Resources:** Motivating, developing, and directing people as they work, identifying the best people for the job. **Instructing:** Teaching others how to do something. **GOE—Interest Area:** 08. Health Science.

Work Group: 08.08. Patient Care and Assistance. **Other Jobs in This Work Group:** Home Health Aides; Nursing Aides, Orderlies, and Attendants; Psychiatric Aides; Psychiatric Technicians. **PERSONALITY TYPE:** Social.

EDUCATION/TRAINING PROGRAM(S)—Licensed Practical/Vocational Nurse Training (LPN, LVN, Cert, Dipl, AAS). **RELATED KNOWLEDGE/COURSES—Psychology:** Knowledge of human behavior and performance; individual differences in ability, personality, and interests; learning and motivation; psychological research methods; and the assessment and treatment of behavioral and affective disorders. **Customer and Personal Service:** Knowledge of principles and processes for providing customer and personal services. This includes customer needs assessment, meeting quality standards for services, and evaluation of customer satisfaction. **Therapy and Counseling:** Knowledge of principles, methods, and procedures for diagnosis, treatment, and rehabilitation of physical and mental dysfunctions and for career counseling and guidance. **Medicine and Dentistry:** Knowledge of the information and techniques needed to diagnose and treat human injuries, diseases, and deformities. This includes symptoms, treatment alternatives, drug properties and interactions, and preventive health-care measures. **Philosophy and Theology:** Knowledge of different philosophical systems and religions. This includes their basic principles, values, ethics, ways of thinking, customs, and practices and their impact on human culture. **Education and Training:** Knowledge of principles and methods for curriculum and training design, teaching and instruction for individuals and groups, and the measurement of training effects.

Licensing Examiners and Inspectors

- ◎ Education/Training Required: Long-term on-the-job training
- ◎ Annual Earnings: $47,390
- ◎ Growth: 9.8%
- ◎ Annual Job Openings: 20,000
- ◎ Self-Employed: 0.9%
- ◎ Part-Time: 5.3%

Examine, evaluate, and investigate eligibility for, conformity with, or liability under licenses or permits. Administer oral, written, road, or flight tests to license applicants. Advise licensees and other individuals or groups concerning licensing, permit, or passport regulations. Evaluate applications, records, and documents in order to gather information about eligibility or liability issues. Issue licenses to individuals meeting standards. Prepare correspondence to inform concerned parties of licensing decisions and of appeals processes. Prepare reports of activities, evaluations, recommendations, and decisions. Report law or regulation violations to appropriate boards and agencies. Score tests and observe equipment operation and control in order to rate ability of applicants. Confer with and interview officials, technical or professional specialists, and applicants in order to obtain information or to clarify facts relevant to licensing decisions. Visit establishments to verify that valid licenses and permits are displayed and that licensing standards are being upheld. Warn violators of infractions or penalties. **SKILLS—Speaking:** Talking to others to convey information effectively. **Reading Comprehension:** Understanding written sentences and paragraphs in work-related documents. **Active Listening:** Giving full attention to what other people are saying, taking time to understand the points being made, asking questions as appropriate, and not interrupting at inappropriate times. **Writing:** Communicating effectively in writing as appropriate for the needs of the audience. **Monitoring:** Monitoring or assessing your performance or that of other individuals or organizations to make improvements or take corrective action. **Judgment and Decision Making:** Considering the relative costs and benefits of potential actions to choose the most appropriate one. **Mathematics:** Using mathematics to solve problems. **Quality Control Analysis:** Conducting tests and inspections of products, services, or processes to evaluate quality or performance. **Systems Analysis:** Determining how a system should work and how changes in conditions, operations, and the environment will affect outcomes. **GOE—Interest Area:** 07. Government and Public Administration. **Work Group:** 07.03. Regulations Enforcement. **Other Jobs in This Work Group:** Agricultural Inspectors; Aviation Inspectors; Child Support, Missing Persons, and Unemployment Insurance Fraud Investigators; Environmental Compliance Inspectors; Equal Opportunity Representatives and Officers; Financial Examiners; Fire Inspectors; Fish and Game Wardens; Forest Fire Inspectors and Prevention Specialists; Government Property Inspectors and Investigators; Immigration and Customs Inspectors; Marine Cargo Inspectors; Mechanical Inspectors; Motor Vehicle Inspectors; Nuclear Monitoring Technicians; Occupational Health and Safety Specialists; Pressure Vessel Inspectors; Railroad Inspectors; Tax Examiners, Collectors, and Revenue Agents. **PERSONALITY TYPE:** Conventional.

EDUCATION/TRAINING PROGRAM(S)—No data available. **RELATED KNOWLEDGE/COURSES—Law and Government:** Knowledge of laws, legal codes, court procedures, precedents, government regulations, executive orders, agency rules, and the democratic political process. **Transportation:** Knowledge of principles and methods for moving people or goods by air, rail, sea, or road, including the relative costs and benefits. **Clerical Practices:** Knowledge of administrative and clerical procedures and systems such as word processing, managing files and records, stenography and transcription, designing forms, and other office procedures and terminology. **Communications and Media:** Knowledge of media production, communication, and dissemination techniques and methods. This includes alternative ways to inform and entertain via written, oral, and visual media. **English Language:** Knowledge of the structure and content of the English language, including the meaning and spelling of words, rules of composition, and grammar.

Lifeguards, Ski Patrol, and Other Recreational Protective Service Workers

- Education/Training Required: Short-term on-the-job training
- Annual Earnings: $16,540
- Growth: 14.3%
- Annual Job Openings: 60,000
- Self-Employed: 0%
- Part-Time: 57.1%

Monitor recreational areas such as pools, beaches, or ski slopes to provide assistance and protection to participants. Rescue distressed persons, using rescue techniques and equipment. Contact emergency medical personnel in case of serious injury. Patrol or monitor recreational areas such as trails, slopes, and swimming areas on foot, in vehicles, or from towers. Examine injured persons and administer first aid or cardiopulmonary resuscitation if necessary, utilizing training and medical supplies and equipment. Instruct participants in skiing, swimming, or other recreational activities and provide safety precaution information. Warn recreational participants of inclement weather, unsafe areas, or illegal conduct. Complete and maintain records of weather and beach conditions, emergency medical treatments performed, and other relevant incident information. Inspect recreational equipment, such as rope tows, T-bars, J-bars, and chair lifts, for safety hazards and damage or wear. Provide assistance with staff selection, training, and supervision. Inspect recreational facilities for cleanliness. Observe activities in assigned areas, using binoculars, in order to detect hazards, disturbances, or safety infractions. Provide assistance in the safe use of equipment such as ski lifts. **SKILLS—Social Perceptiveness:** Being aware of others' reactions and understanding why they react as they do. **Monitoring:** Monitoring or assessing your performance or that of other individuals or organizations to make improvements or take corrective action. **Instructing:** Teaching others how to do something. **Learning Strategies:** Selecting and using training/instructional methods and procedures appropriate for the situation when learning or teaching new things. **Service Orientation:** Actively looking for ways to help people. **Critical Thinking:** Using logic and reasoning to identify the strengths and weaknesses of alternative solutions, conclusions, or approaches to problems. **Equipment Maintenance:** Performing routine maintenance on equipment and determining when and what kind of maintenance is needed. **Operation Monitoring:** Watching gauges, dials, or other indicators to make sure a machine is working properly. **GOE—Interest Area:** 12. Law and Public Safety. **Work Group:** 12.05. Safety and Security. **Other Jobs in This Work Group:** Animal Control Workers; Crossing Guards; Gaming Surveillance Officers and Gaming Investigators; Private Detectives and Investigators; Security Guards. **PERSONALITY TYPE:** Realistic.

EDUCATION/TRAINING PROGRAM(S)—Security and Protective Services, Other. **RELATED KNOWLEDGE/COURSES—Customer and Personal Service:** Knowledge of principles and processes for providing customer and personal services. This includes customer needs assessment, meeting quality standards for services, and evaluation of customer satisfaction. **Medicine and Dentistry:** Knowledge of the information and techniques needed to diagnose and treat human injuries, diseases, and deformities. This includes symptoms, treatment alternatives, drug properties and interactions, and preventive health-care measures. **Chemistry:** Knowledge of the chemical composition, structure, and properties of substances and of the chemical processes and transformations that they undergo. This includes uses of chemicals and their danger signs, production techniques, and disposal methods. **Psychology:** Knowledge of human behavior and performance; individual differences in ability, personality, and interests; learning and motivation; psychological research methods; and the assessment and treatment of behavioral and affective disorders. **Public Safety and Security:** Knowledge of relevant equipment, policies, procedures, and strategies to promote effective local, state, or national security operations for the protection of people, data, property, and institutions. **Education and Training:** Knowledge of principles and methods for curriculum and training design, teaching and instruction for individuals and groups, and the measurement of training effects.

Loading Machine Operators, Underground Mining

◎ Education/Training Required: Moderate-term on-the-job training

◎ Annual Earnings: $33,250

◎ Growth: 8.9%

◎ Annual Job Openings: 14,000

◎ Self-Employed: 16.5%

◎ Part-Time: 2.7%

Operate underground loading machine to load coal, ore, or rock into shuttle or mine car or onto conveyors. Loading equipment may include power shovels, hoisting engines equipped with cable-drawn scraper or scoop, or machines equipped with gathering arms and conveyor. Advance machines in order to gather material and convey it into cars. Drive machines into piles of material blasted from working faces. Operate levers to move conveyor booms or shovels so that mine contents such as coal, rock, and ore can be placed into cars or onto conveyors. Signal workers to move loaded cars. Start conveyor booms and gathering-arm motors and operate winches to position cars under boom-conveyors for loading. Stop gathering arms when cars are full. Clean hoppers and clean spillage from tracks, walks, driveways, and conveyor decking. Estimate and record amounts of material in bins. Inspect boarding and locking of open-top box cars and wedging of side-drop and hopper cars in order to prevent loss of material in transit. Move trailing electrical cables clear of obstructions, using rubber safety gloves. Notify switching departments to deliver specific types of cars. Observe and record car numbers, carriers, customers, tonnages, and grades and conditions of material. Oil, lubricate, and adjust conveyors, crushers, and other equipment, using hand tools and lubricating equipment. Pry off loose material from roofs and move it into the paths of machines, using crowbars. Replace hydraulic hoses, headlight bulbs, and gathering-arm teeth. **SKILLS—Repairing:** Repairing machines or systems by using the needed tools. **Equipment Maintenance:** Performing routine maintenance on equipment and determining when and what kind of maintenance is needed. **Operation and Control:** Controlling operations of equipment or systems. **Operation Monitoring:** Watching gauges, dials, or other indicators to make sure a machine is working properly. **GOE—Interest Area:** 01. Agriculture and Natural Resources. **Work Group:** 01.08. Mining and Drilling. **Other Jobs in This Work Group:** Construction Drillers; Continuous Mining Machine Operators; Derrick Operators, Oil and Gas; Excavating and Loading Machine Operators; Explosives Workers, Ordnance Handling Experts, and Blasters; Helpers—Extraction Workers; Mine Cutting and Channeling Machine Operators; Rock Splitters, Quarry; Roof Bolters, Mining; Rotary Drill Operators, Oil and Gas; Roustabouts, Oil and Gas; Service Unit Operators, Oil, Gas, and Mining; Shuttle Car Operators; Well and Core Drill Operators; Wellhead Pumpers. **PERSONALITY TYPE:** Realistic.

EDUCATION/TRAINING PROGRAM(S)—Ground Transportation, Other. **RELATED KNOWLEDGE/COURSES—Mechanical Devices:** Knowledge of machines and tools, including their designs, uses, repair, and maintenance. **Engineering and Technology:** Knowledge of the practical application of engineering science and technology. This includes applying principles, techniques, procedures, and equipment to the design and production of various goods and services. **Physics:** Knowledge and prediction of physical principles and laws and their interrelationships and applications to understanding fluid, material, and atmospheric dynamics and mechanical, electrical, atomic, and subatomic structures and processes. **Public Safety and Security:** Knowledge of relevant equipment, policies, procedures, and strategies to promote effective local, state, or national security operations for the protection of people, data, property, and institutions. **Transportation:** Knowledge of principles and methods for moving people or goods by air, rail, sea, or road, including the relative costs and benefits. **Production and Processing:** Knowledge of raw materials, production processes, quality control, costs, and other techniques for maximizing the effective manufacture and distribution of goods.

Loan Counselors

- ◎ Education/Training Required: Bachelor's degree
- ◎ Annual Earnings: $33,970
- ◎ Growth: 17.8%
- ◎ Annual Job Openings: 4,000
- ◎ Self-Employed: 2.3%
- ◎ Part-Time: 5.0%

Provide guidance to prospective loan applicants who have problems qualifying for traditional loans. Guidance may include determining the best type of loan and explaining loan requirements or restrictions. Analyze applicants' financial status, credit, and property evaluations to determine feasibility of granting loans. Approve loans within specified limits. Calculate amount of debt and funds available in order to plan methods of payoff and to estimate time for debt liquidation. Check loan agreements to ensure that they are complete and accurate according to policies. Contact applicants or creditors to resolve questions about applications or to assist with completion of paperwork. Interview applicants and request specified information for loan applications. Maintain and review account records, updating and recategorizing them according to status changes. Maintain current knowledge of credit regulations. Refer loans to loan committees for approval. Review accounts to determine write-offs for collection agencies. Submit applications to credit analysts for verification and recommendation. Analyze

potential loan markets to find opportunities to promote loans and financial services. Arrange for maintenance and liquidation of delinquent properties. Assist in selection of financial award candidates, using electronic databases to certify loan eligibility. Authorize and sign mail collection letters. Compare data on student aid applications with eligibility requirements of assistance programs. Confer with underwriters to resolve mortgage application problems. Contact borrowers with delinquent accounts to obtain payment in full or to negotiate repayment plans. Contact creditors to explain clients' financial situations and to arrange for payment adjustments so that payments are feasible for clients and agreeable to creditors. Counsel clients on personal and family financial problems, such as excessive spending and borrowing of funds. Establish payment priorities according to credit terms and interest rates in order to reduce clients' overall costs. Inform individuals and groups about the financial assistance available to college or university students. Locate debtors, using post office directories, utility services account listings, and mailing lists. Match students' needs and eligibility with available financial aid programs in order to provide informed recommendations. **SKILLS—Management of Personnel Resources:** Motivating, developing, and directing people as they work, identifying the best people for the job. **Speaking:** Talking to others to convey information effectively. **Judgment and Decision Making:** Considering the relative costs and benefits of potential actions to choose the most appropriate one. **Reading Comprehension:** Understanding written sentences and paragraphs in work-related documents. **Mathematics:** Using mathematics to solve problems. **Active Listening:** Giving full attention to what other people are saying, taking time to understand the points being made, asking questions as appropriate, and not interrupting at inappropriate times. **Writing:** Communicating effectively in writing as appropriate for the needs of the audience. **Systems Evaluation:** Identifying measures or indicators of system performance and the actions needed to improve or correct performance relative to the goals of the system. **GOE—Interest Area:** 06. Finance and Insurance. **Work Group:** 06.02. Finance/Insurance Investigation and Analysis. **Other Jobs in This Work Group:** Appraisers, Real Estate; Assessors; Claims Examiners, Property and Casualty Insurance; Cost Estimators; Credit Analysts; Financial Analysts; Insurance Adjusters, Examiners, and Investigators; Insurance Appraisers, Auto Damage; Insurance

Underwriters; Loan Officers; Market Research Analysts; Survey Researchers. **PERSONALITY TYPE:** Enterprising.

EDUCATION/TRAINING PROGRAM(S)— Banking and Financial Support Services; Finance and Financial Management Services, Other. **RELATED KNOWLEDGE/COURSES—Economics and Accounting:** Knowledge of economic and accounting principles and practices, the financial markets, banking, and the analysis and reporting of financial data. **Mathematics:** Knowledge of arithmetic, algebra, geometry, calculus, and statistics and their applications. **Law and Government:** Knowledge of laws, legal codes, court procedures, precedents, government regulations, executive orders, agency rules, and the democratic political process. **Sales and Marketing:** Knowledge of principles and methods for showing, promoting, and selling products or services. This includes marketing strategy and tactics, product demonstrations, sales techniques, and sales control systems. **Clerical Practices:** Knowledge of administrative and clerical procedures and systems such as word processing, managing files and records, stenography and transcription, designing forms, and other office procedures and terminology. **Personnel and Human Resources:** Knowledge of principles and procedures for personnel recruitment, selection, training, compensation and benefits, labor relations and negotiation, and personnel information systems.

Loan Officers

- ◎ Education/Training Required: Bachelor's degree
- ◎ Annual Earnings: $48,830
- ◎ Growth: 18.8%
- ◎ Annual Job Openings: 30,000
- ◎ Self-Employed: 2.3%
- ◎ Part-Time: 5.0%

Evaluate, authorize, or recommend approval of commercial, real estate, or credit loans. Advise borrowers on financial status and methods of payments. Includes mortgage loan officers and agents, collection analysts, loan servicing officers, and loan underwriters. Approve loans within specified limits and refer loan applications outside those limits to management for approval. Meet with applicants to obtain information for loan applications and to answer questions about the process. Analyze applicants' financial status, credit, and property evaluations to determine feasibility of granting loans. Explain to customers the different types of loans and credit options that are available, as well as the terms of those services. Obtain and compile copies of loan applicants' credit histories, corporate financial statements, and other financial information. Review and update credit and loan files. Review loan agreements to ensure that they are complete and accurate according to policy. Compute payment schedules. Stay abreast of new types of loans and other financial services and products in order to better meet customers' needs. Submit applications to credit analysts for verification and recommendation. Handle customer complaints and take appropriate action to resolve them. Work with clients to identify their financial goals and to find ways of reaching those goals. Confer with underwriters to aid in resolving mortgage application problems. Negotiate payment arrangements with customers who have delinquent loans. Market bank products to individuals and firms, promoting bank services that may meet customers' needs. Supervise loan personnel. Set credit policies, credit lines, procedures, and standards in conjunction with senior managers. Provide special services such as investment banking for clients with more specialized needs. Analyze potential loan markets and develop referral networks in order to locate prospects for loans. Prepare reports to send to customers whose accounts are delinquent and forward irreconcilable accounts for collector action. Arrange for maintenance and liquidation of delinquent properties. Interview, hire, and train new employees. Petition courts to transfer titles and deeds of collateral to banks. **SKILLS—Persuasion:** Persuading others to change their minds or behavior. **Social Perceptiveness:** Being aware of others' reactions and understanding why they react as they do. **Service Orientation:** Actively looking for ways to help people. **Instructing:** Teaching others how to do something. **Negotiation:** Bringing others together and trying to reconcile differences. **Learning Strategies:** Selecting and using training/instructional methods and procedures appropriate for the situation when learning or teaching new things. **Complex Problem Solving:** Identifying complex problems and reviewing related information to develop and evaluate options and implement solutions. **Speaking:** Talking to others to convey information effectively. **GOE—Interest Area:** 06. Finance and Insurance. **Work Group:** 06.02.

Finance/Insurance Investigation and Analysis. **Other Jobs in This Work Group:** Appraisers, Real Estate; Assessors; Claims Examiners, Property and Casualty Insurance; Cost Estimators; Credit Analysts; Financial Analysts; Insurance Adjusters, Examiners, and Investigators; Insurance Appraisers, Auto Damage; Insurance Underwriters; Loan Counselors; Market Research Analysts; Survey Researchers. **PERSONALITY TYPE:** Enterprising.

EDUCATION/TRAINING PROGRAM(S)— Credit Management; Finance, General. **RELATED KNOWLEDGE/COURSES—Economics and Accounting:** Knowledge of economic and accounting principles and practices, the financial markets, banking, and the analysis and reporting of financial data. **Sales and Marketing:** Knowledge of principles and methods for showing, promoting, and selling products or services. This includes marketing strategy and tactics, product demonstrations, sales techniques, and sales control systems. **Law and Government:** Knowledge of laws, legal codes, court procedures, precedents, government regulations, executive orders, agency rules, and the democratic political process. **Customer and Personal Service:** Knowledge of principles and processes for providing customer and personal services. This includes customer needs assessment, meeting quality standards for services, and evaluation of customer satisfaction. **English Language:** Knowledge of the structure and content of the English language, including the meaning and spelling of words, rules of composition, and grammar. **Mathematics:** Knowledge of arithmetic, algebra, geometry, calculus, and statistics and their applications.

Locker Room, Coatroom, and Dressing Room Attendants

- Education/Training Required: Short-term on-the-job training
- Annual Earnings: $17,550
- Growth: 27.8%
- Annual Job Openings: 66,000
- Self-Employed: 0.3%
- Part-Time: 51.9%

Provide personal items to patrons or customers in locker rooms, dressing rooms, or coatrooms. Assign dressing room facilities, locker space, or clothing containers to patrons of athletic or bathing establishments. Answer customer inquiries and explain cost, availability, policies, and procedures of facilities. Check supplies to ensure adequate availability and order new supplies when necessary. Refer guest problems or complaints to supervisors. Clean and polish footwear, using brushes, sponges, cleaning fluid, polishes, waxes, liquid or sole dressing, and daubers. Report and document safety hazards, potentially hazardous conditions, and unsafe practices and procedures. Operate washing machines and dryers in order to clean soiled apparel and towels. Monitor patrons' facility use in order to ensure that rules and regulations are followed and safety and order are maintained. Procure beverages, food, and other items as requested. Activate emergency action plans and administer first aid as necessary. Store personal possessions for patrons, issue claim checks for articles stored, and return articles on receipt of checks. Provide towels and sheets to clients in public baths, steam rooms, and restrooms. Collect soiled linen or clothing for laundering. Operate controls that regulate temperatures or room environments. Attend to needs of athletic teams in clubhouses. Provide assistance to patrons by performing duties such as opening doors and carrying bags. Stencil identifying information on equipment. Maintain inventories of clothing or uniforms, accessories, equipment, and/or linens. **SKILLS—Service Orientation:** Actively looking for ways to help people. **Negotiation:** Bringing others together and trying to reconcile differences. **Social Perceptiveness:** Being aware of others' reactions and understanding why they react as they do. **Instructing:** Teaching others how to do something. **Critical Thinking:** Using logic and reasoning to identify the strengths and weaknesses of alternative solutions, conclusions, or approaches to problems. **Persuasion:** Persuading others to change their minds or behavior. **Reading Comprehension:** Understanding written sentences and paragraphs in work-related documents. **Speaking:** Talking to others to convey information effectively. **GOE—Interest Area:** 09. Hospitality, Tourism, and Recreation. **Work Group:** 09.02. Recreational Services. **Other Jobs in This Work Group:** Amusement and Recreation Attendants; Gaming and Sports Book Writers and Runners; Gaming Dealers; Motion Picture Projectionists; Recreation Workers; Slot Key Persons; Ushers, Lobby Attendants, and Ticket Takers. **PERSONALITY TYPE:** Social.

EDUCATION/TRAINING PROGRAM(S)—No data available. **RELATED KNOWLEDGE/COURS-ES—Customer and Personal Service:** Knowledge of principles and processes for providing customer and personal services. This includes customer needs assessment, meeting quality standards for services, and evaluation of customer satisfaction. **Sales and Marketing:** Knowledge of principles and methods for showing, promoting, and selling products or services. This includes marketing strategy and tactics, product demonstrations, sales techniques, and sales control systems.

Locksmiths and Safe Repairers

- ◎ Education/Training Required: Moderate-term on-the-job training
- ◎ Annual Earnings: $30,360
- ◎ Growth: 21.0%
- ◎ Annual Job Openings: 3,000
- ◎ Self-Employed: 16.8%
- ◎ Part-Time: 6.9%

Repair and open locks, make keys, change locks and safe combinations, and install and repair safes. Cut new or duplicate keys, using key-cutting machines. Keep records of company locks and keys. Insert new or repaired tumblers into locks in order to change combinations. Move picklocks in cylinders in order to open door locks without keys. Disassemble mechanical or electrical locking devices and repair or replace worn tumblers, springs, and other parts, using hand tools. Repair and adjust safes, vault doors, and vault components, using hand tools, lathes, drill presses, and welding and acetylene cutting apparatus. Install safes, vault doors, and deposit boxes according to blueprints, using equipment such as powered drills, taps, dies, truck cranes, and dollies. Open safe locks by drilling. **SKILLS—Installation:** Installing equipment, machines, wiring, or programs to meet specifications. **Repairing:** Repairing machines or systems by using the needed tools. **Equipment Maintenance:** Performing routine maintenance on equipment and determining when and what kind of maintenance is needed. **Troubleshooting:** Determining causes of operating errors and deciding what to do about them. **Service Orienta-** tion: Actively looking for ways to help people. **Equipment Selection:** Determining the kind of tools and equipment needed to do a job. **Technology Design:** Generating or adapting equipment and technology to serve user needs. **Management of Material Resources:** Obtaining and seeing to the appropriate use of equipment, facilities, and materials needed to do certain work. **GOE—Interest Area:** 13. Manufacturing. **Work Group:** 13.13. Machinery Repair. **Other Jobs in This Work Group:** Bicycle Repairers; Gas Appliance Repairers; Hand and Portable Power Tool Repairers; Industrial Machinery Mechanics; Maintenance Workers, Machinery; Mechanical Door Repairers; Millwrights; Signal and Track Switch Repairers; Valve and Regulator Repairers. **PERSONALITY TYPE:** Realistic.

EDUCATION/TRAINING PROGRAM(S)—Locksmithing and Safe Repair. **RELATED KNOWL-EDGE/COURSES—Customer and Personal Service:** Knowledge of principles and processes for providing customer and personal services. This includes customer needs assessment, meeting quality standards for services, and evaluation of customer satisfaction. **Administration and Management:** Knowledge of business and management principles involved in strategic planning, resource allocation, human resources modeling, leadership technique, production methods, and coordination of people and resources. **Clerical Practices:** Knowledge of administrative and clerical procedures and systems such as word processing, managing files and records, stenography and transcription, designing forms, and other office procedures and terminology. **Sales and Marketing:** Knowledge of principles and methods for showing, promoting, and selling products or services. This includes marketing strategy and tactics, product demonstrations, sales techniques, and sales control systems. **Public Safety and Security:** Knowledge of relevant equipment, policies, procedures, and strategies to promote effective local, state, or national security operations for the protection of people, data, property, and institutions. **Mechanical Devices:** Knowledge of machines and tools, including their designs, uses, repair, and maintenance. **Law and Government:** Knowledge of laws, legal codes, court procedures, precedents, government regulations, executive orders, agency rules, and the democratic political process.

Lodging Managers

- Education/Training Required: Work experience in a related occupation
- Annual Earnings: $37,660
- Growth: 6.6%
- Annual Job Openings: 10,000
- Self-Employed: 50.3%
- Part-Time: 7.2%

Plan, direct, or coordinate activities of an organization or department that provides lodging and other accommodations. Greet and register guests. Answer inquiries pertaining to hotel policies and services and resolve occupants' complaints. Assign duties to workers and schedule shifts. Coordinate front-office activities of hotels or motels and resolve problems. Participate in financial activities such as the setting of room rates, the establishment of budgets, and the allocation of funds to departments. Confer and cooperate with other managers in order to ensure coordination of hotel activities. Collect payments and record data pertaining to funds and expenditures. Manage and maintain temporary or permanent lodging facilities. Observe and monitor staff performance in order to ensure efficient operations and adherence to facility's policies and procedures. Train staff members in their duties. Show, rent, or assign accommodations. Develop and implement policies and procedures for the operation of a department or establishment. Inspect guest rooms, public areas, and grounds for cleanliness and appearance. Prepare required paperwork pertaining to departmental functions. Interview and hire applicants. Purchase supplies and arrange for outside services, such as deliveries, laundry, maintenance and repair, and trash collection. Arrange telephone answering services, deliver mail and packages, and answer questions regarding locations for eating and entertainment. Perform marketing and public relations activities. Organize and coordinate the work of staff and convention personnel for meetings to be held at a particular facility. Receive and process advance registration payments, send out letters of confirmation, and return checks when registrations cannot be accepted. Meet with clients in order to schedule and plan details of conventions, banquets, receptions, and other functions. Provide assistance to staff members by performing activities such as inspecting rooms, setting tables, and doing laundry. **SKILLS—Management of Finan-**cial Resources: Determining how money will be spent to get the work done and accounting for these expenditures. **Social Perceptiveness:** Being aware of others' reactions and understanding why they react as they do. **Negotiation:** Bringing others together and trying to reconcile differences. **Management of Material Resources:** Obtaining and seeing to the appropriate use of equipment, facilities, and materials needed to do certain work. **Monitoring:** Monitoring or assessing your performance or that of other individuals or organizations to make improvements or take corrective action. **Management of Personnel Resources:** Motivating, developing, and directing people as they work, identifying the best people for the job. **Persuasion:** Persuading others to change their minds or behavior. **Time Management:** Managing one's own time and the time of others. **GOE—Interest Area:** 09. Hospitality, Tourism, and Recreation. **Work Group:** 09.01. Managerial Work in Hospitality and Tourism. **Other Jobs in This Work Group:** First-Line Supervisors/Managers of Food Preparation and Serving Workers; First-Line Supervisors/Managers of Personal Service Workers; Food Service Managers; Gaming Managers; Gaming Supervisors. **PERSONALITY TYPE:** Enterprising.

EDUCATION/TRAINING PROGRAM(S)—Hospitality Administration/Management, General; Hospitality and Recreation Marketing Operations; Hotel/Motel Administration/Management; Resort Management; Selling Skills and Sales Operations. **RELATED KNOWLEDGE/COURSES—Clerical Practices:** Knowledge of administrative and clerical procedures and systems such as word processing, managing files and records, stenography and transcription, designing forms, and other office procedures and terminology. **Sales and Marketing:** Knowledge of principles and methods for showing, promoting, and selling products or services. This includes marketing strategy and tactics, product demonstrations, sales techniques, and sales control systems. **Customer and Personal Service:** Knowledge of principles and processes for providing customer and personal services. This includes customer needs assessment, meeting quality standards for services, and evaluation of customer satisfaction. **Personnel and Human Resources:** Knowledge of principles and procedures for personnel recruitment, selection, training, compensation and benefits, labor relations and negotiation, and personnel information systems. **Psychology:** Knowledge of human behavior and performance; individual differences in ability, personality, and interests; learning and motivation; psychological research methods; and the assessment and treatment of behavioral and affective disorders. **Economics and Accounting:** Knowledge of economic and accounting principles and practices, the financial markets, banking, and the analysis and reporting of financial data.

Logisticians

- Education/Training Required: Bachelor's degree
- Annual Earnings: $57,110
- Growth: 27.5%
- Annual Job Openings: 162,000
- Self-Employed: No data available
- Part-Time: 7.4%

Analyze and coordinate the logistical functions of a firm or organization. Responsible for the entire life cycle of a product, including acquisition, distribution, internal allocation, delivery, and final disposal of resources. Develop and implement technical project management tools such as plans, schedules, and responsibility and compliance matrices. Develop proposals that include documentation for estimates. Direct and support the compilation and analysis of technical source data necessary for product development. Direct availability and allocation of materials, supplies, and finished products. Direct team activities, establishing task priorities, scheduling and tracking work assignments, providing guidance, and ensuring the availability of resources. Manage the logistical aspects of product life cycles, including coordination or provisioning of samples and the minimization of obsolescence. Participate in the assessment and review of design alternatives and design change proposal impacts. Perform system life-cycle cost analysis and develop component studies. Plan, organize, and execute logistics support activities such as maintenance planning, repair analysis, and test equipment recommendations. Provide project management services, including the provision and analysis of technical data. Redesign the movement of goods in order to maximize value and minimize costs. Report project plans, progress, and results. Stay informed of logistics technology advances and apply appropriate technology in order to improve logistics processes. Collaborate with other departments as necessary to meet customer requirements, to take advantage of sales opportunities,

or, in the case of shortages, to minimize negative impacts on a business. Develop an understanding of customers' needs and take actions to ensure that such needs are met. Explain proposed solutions to customers, management, or other interested parties through written proposals and oral presentations. Maintain and develop positive business relationships with a customer's key personnel involved in or directly relevant to a logistics activity. Manage subcontractor activities, reviewing proposals, developing performance specifications, and serving as liaisons between subcontractors and organizations. Protect and control proprietary materials. Review logistics performance with customers against targets, benchmarks, and service agreements. **SKILLS**—No data available. **GOE— Interest Area:** 04. Business and Administration. **Work Group:** 04.05. Accounting, Auditing, and Analytical Support. **Other Jobs in This Work Group:** Accountants; Auditors; Budget Analysts; Industrial Engineering Technicians; Management Analysts; Operations Research Analysts. **PERSONALITY TYPE:** No data available.

EDUCATION/TRAINING PROGRAM(S)— Logistics and Materials Management; Operations Management and Supervision. **RELATED KNOWLEDGE/COURSES**—No data available.

Machinists

- Education/Training Required: Long-term on-the-job training
- Annual Earnings: $33,960
- Growth: 8.2%
- Annual Job Openings: 30,000
- Self-Employed: 2.7%
- Part-Time: 2.1%

Set up and operate a variety of machine tools to produce precision parts and instruments. Includes precision instrument makers who fabricate, modify, or repair mechanical instruments. May also fabricate and modify parts to make or repair machine tools or maintain industrial machines, applying knowledge of mechanics, shop mathematics, metal properties, layout, and machining procedures. Calculate dimensions and tolerances, using knowledge of mathematics and instruments such as micrometers and vernier calipers. Machine parts to specifications, using machine tools such as lathes, milling machines, shapers, or grinders. Measure, examine, and test completed units in order to detect defects and ensure conformance to specifications, using precision instruments such as micrometers. Set up, adjust, and operate all of the basic machine tools and many specialized or advanced variation tools in order to perform precision machining operations. Align and secure holding fixtures, cutting tools, attachments, accessories, and materials onto machines. Monitor the feed and speed of machines during the machining process. Study sample parts, blueprints, drawings, and engineering information in order to determine methods and sequences of operations needed to fabricate products and determine product dimensions and tolerances. Select the appropriate tools, machines, and materials to be used in preparation of machinery work. Lay out, measure, and mark metal stock in order to display placement of cuts. Observe and listen to operating machines or equipment in order to diagnose machine malfunctions and to determine need for adjustments or repairs. Check workpieces to ensure that they are properly lubricated and cooled. Maintain industrial machines, applying knowledge of mechanics, shop mathematics, metal properties, layout, and machining procedures. Position and fasten workpieces. Operate equipment to verify operational efficiency. Install repaired parts into equipment or install new equipment. Clean and lubricate machines, tools, and equipment in order to remove grease, rust, stains, and foreign matter. Advise clients about the materials being used for finished products. Program computers and electronic instruments such as numerically controlled machine tools. Set controls to regulate machining or enter commands to retrieve, input, or edit computerized machine control media. Confer with engineering, supervisory, and manufacturing personnel in order to exchange technical information. **SKILLS—Operation Monitoring:** Watching gauges, dials, or other indicators to make sure a machine is working properly. **Operation and Control:** Controlling operations of equipment or systems. **Equipment Maintenance:** Performing routine maintenance on equipment and determining when and what kind of maintenance is needed. **Quality Control Analysis:** Conducting tests and inspections of products, services, or processes to evaluate quality or performance. **Installation:** Installing equipment, machines, wiring, or programs to meet specifications. **Troubleshooting:** Determining causes of operating errors and deciding what to do about them. **Equip-**

ment Selection: Determining the kind of tools and equipment needed to do a job. **Repairing:** Repairing machines or systems by using the needed tools. **GOE—Interest Area:** 13. Manufacturing. **Work Group:** 13.05. Production Machining Technology. **Other Jobs in This Work Group:** Foundry Mold and Coremakers; Lay-Out Workers, Metal and Plastic; Model Makers, Metal and Plastic; Numerical Control Machine Tool Operators and Tenders, Metal and Plastic; Numerical Tool and Process Control Programmers; Patternmakers, Metal and Plastic; Tool and Die Makers; Tool Grinders, Filers, and Sharpeners. **PERSONALITY TYPE:** Realistic.

EDUCATION/TRAINING PROGRAM(S)— Machine Shop Technology/Assistant; Machine Tool Technology/Machinist. **RELATED KNOWLEDGE/COURSES—Mechanical Devices:** Knowledge of machines and tools, including their designs, uses, repair, and maintenance. **Mathematics:** Knowledge of arithmetic, algebra, geometry, calculus, and statistics and their applications. **Engineering and Technology:** Knowledge of the practical application of engineering science and technology. This includes applying principles, techniques, procedures, and equipment to the design and production of various goods and services. **Design:** Knowledge of design techniques, tools, and principles involved in production of precision technical plans, blueprints, drawings, and models. **Production and Processing:** Knowledge of raw materials, production processes, quality control, costs, and other techniques for maximizing the effective manufacture and distribution of goods. **Computers and Electronics:** Knowledge of circuit boards, processors, chips, electronic equipment, and computer hardware and software, including applications and programming.

Maids and Housekeeping Cleaners

- Education/Training Required: Short-term on-the-job training
- Annual Earnings: $16,900
- Growth: 9.2%
- Annual Job Openings: 352,000
- Self-Employed: 9.0%
- Part-Time: 31.9%

Perform any combination of light cleaning duties to maintain private households or commercial establishments, such as hotels, restaurants, and hospitals, in a clean and orderly manner. Duties include making beds, replenishing linens, cleaning rooms and halls, and vacuuming. Move and arrange furniture and turn mattresses. Observe precautions required to protect hotel and guest property and report damage, theft, and found articles to supervisors. Plan menus and cook and serve meals and refreshments, following employer's instructions or own methods. Prepare rooms for meetings and arrange decorations, media equipment, and furniture for social or business functions. Take care of pets by grooming, exercising, and/or feeding them. Wash dishes and clean kitchens, cooking utensils, and silverware. Answer telephones and doorbells. Care for children and/or elderly persons by overseeing their activities; providing companionship; and assisting them with dressing, bathing, eating, and other needs. Carry linens, towels, toilet items, and cleaning supplies, using wheeled carts. Purchase or order groceries and household supplies to keep kitchens stocked and record expenditures. Run errands such as taking laundry to the cleaners and buying groceries. Clean rooms, hallways, lobbies, lounges, restrooms, corridors, elevators, stairways, locker rooms, and other work areas so that health standards are met. Clean rugs, carpets, upholstered furniture, and/or draperies, using vacuum cleaners and/or shampooers. Empty wastebaskets, empty and clean ashtrays, and transport other trash and waste to disposal areas. Sweep, scrub, wax, and/or polish floors, using brooms, mops, and/or powered scrubbing and waxing machines. Dust and polish furniture and equipment. Keep storage areas and carts well stocked, clean, and tidy. Polish silver accessories and metalwork such as fixtures and fittings. Remove debris from driveways, garages, and swimming pool areas. Replace light bulbs. Replenish supplies such as drinking glasses, linens, writing supplies, and bathroom items. Sort clothing and other articles, load washing machines, and iron and fold dried items. Sort, count, and mark clean linens and store them in linen closets. Wash windows, walls, ceilings, and woodwork, waxing and polishing as necessary. Assign duties to other staff and give instructions regarding work methods and routines. **SKILLS**—None met the criteria. **GOE**—**Interest Area:** 09. Hospitality, Tourism, and Recreation. **Work Group:** 09.03. Hospitality and Travel Services. **Other Jobs in This Work Group:** Baggage Porters and Bellhops; Concierges; Flight Attendants; Hotel, Motel, and Resort Desk Clerks; Janitors and Cleaners, Except Maids and Housekeeping Cleaners; Reservation and Transportation Ticket Agents; Tour Guides and Escorts; Transportation Attendants, Except Flight Attendants and Baggage Porters; Travel Agents; Travel Clerks; Travel Guides. **PERSONALITY TYPE:** Realistic.

EDUCATION/TRAINING PROGRAM(S)—No data available. **RELATED KNOWLEDGE/COURSES—Customer and Personal Service:** Knowledge of principles and processes for providing customer and personal services. This includes customer needs assessment, meeting quality standards for services, and evaluation of customer satisfaction. **Chemistry:** Knowledge of the chemical composition, structure, and properties of substances and of the chemical processes and transformations that they undergo. This includes uses of chemicals and their danger signs, production techniques, and disposal methods.

Maintenance and Repair Workers, General

- ◉ Education/Training Required: Long-term on-the-job training
- ◉ Annual Earnings: $30,710
- ◉ Growth: 16.3%
- ◉ Annual Job Openings: 155,000
- ◉ Self-Employed: 0.9%
- ◉ Part-Time: 4.5%

Perform work involving the skills of two or more maintenance or craft occupations to keep machines, mechanical equipment, or the structure of an establishment in repair. Duties may involve pipe fitting; boilermaking; insulating; welding; machining; carpentry; repairing electrical or mechanical equipment; installing, aligning, and balancing new equipment; and repairing buildings, floors, or stairs. Repair or replace defective equipment parts, using hand tools and power tools, and reassemble equipment. Perform routine preventive maintenance to ensure that machines continue to run smoothly, building systems operate efficiently, and the physical condition of buildings does not deteriorate. Inspect drives, motors, and belts; check fluid levels; replace filters; and perform other maintenance actions, following checklists. Use tools ranging from common hand and power tools, such as hammers, hoists, saws, drills, and wrenches, to precision measuring instruments and electrical and electronic testing devices. Assemble, install, and/or repair wiring, electrical and electronic components, pipe systems and plumbing, machinery, and equipment. Diagnose mechanical problems and determine how to correct them, checking blueprints, repair manuals, and parts catalogs as necessary. Inspect, operate, and test machinery and equipment in order to diagnose machine malfunctions. Record maintenance and repair work performed and the costs of the work. Clean and lubricate shafts, bearings, gears, and other parts of machinery. Dismantle devices to gain access to and remove defective parts, using hoists, cranes, hand tools, and power tools. Plan and lay out repair work, using diagrams, drawings, blueprints, maintenance manuals, and schematic diagrams. Order parts, supplies, and equipment from catalogs and suppliers or obtain them from storerooms. Adjust functional parts of devices and control instruments, using hand tools, levels, plumb bobs, and straightedges. Paint and repair roofs, windows, doors, floors, woodwork, plaster, drywall, and other parts of building structures. Operate cutting torches or welding equipment to cut or join metal parts. Align and balance new equipment after installation. Inspect used parts to determine changes in dimensional requirements, using rules, calipers, micrometers, and other measuring instruments. Set up and operate machine tools to repair or fabricate machine parts, jigs and fixtures, and tools. Maintain and repair specialized equipment and machinery found in cafeterias, laundries, hospitals, stores, offices, and factories. **SKILLS—Equipment Maintenance:** Performing routine maintenance on equipment and determining when and what kind of maintenance is needed. **Installation:** Installing equipment, machines, wiring, or programs to meet specifications. **Repairing:** Repairing machines or systems by using the needed tools. **Troubleshooting:** Determining causes of operating errors and deciding what to do about them. **Operation Monitoring:** Watching gauges, dials, or other indicators to make sure a machine is working properly. **Equipment Selection:** Determining the kind of tools and equipment needed to do a job. **Operation and Control:** Controlling operations of equipment or systems. **Technology Design:** Generating or adapting equipment and technology to serve user needs. **GOE—Interest Area:** 02. Architecture and Construction. **Work Group:** 02.05. Systems and Equipment Installation, Maintenance, and Repair. **Other Jobs in This Work Group:** Central Office and PBX Installers and Repairers; Communication Equipment Mechan-

ics, Installers, and Repairers; Electric Meter Installers and Repairers; Electrical and Electronics Repairers, Powerhouse, Substation, and Relay; Electrical Power-Line Installers and Repairers; Elevator Installers and Repairers; Frame Wirers, Central Office; Heating and Air Conditioning Mechanics; Home Appliance Installers; Meter Mechanics; Refrigeration Mechanics; Station Installers and Repairers, Telephone; Telecommunications Facility Examiners; Telecommunications Line Installers and Repairers. **PERSONALITY TYPE:** Realistic.

EDUCATION/TRAINING PROGRAM(S)— Building/Construction Site Management/Manager. **RELATED KNOWLEDGE/COURSES—Mechanical Devices:** Knowledge of machines and tools, including their designs, uses, repair, and maintenance. **Building and Construction:** Knowledge of the materials, methods, and tools involved in the construction or repair of houses, buildings, or other structures such as highways and roads. **Design:** Knowledge of design techniques, tools, and principles involved in production of precision technical plans, blueprints, drawings, and models. **Public Safety and Security:** Knowledge of relevant equipment, policies, procedures, and strategies to promote effective local, state, or national security operations for the protection of people, data, property, and institutions. **Engineering and Technology:** Knowledge of the practical application of engineering science and technology. This includes applying principles, techniques, procedures, and equipment to the design and production of various goods and services. **Physics:** Knowledge and prediction of physical principles and laws and their interrelationships and applications to understanding fluid, material, and atmospheric dynamics and mechanical, electrical, atomic, and subatomic structures and processes.

Management Analysts

- Education/Training Required: Work experience plus degree
- Annual Earnings: $63,450
- Growth: 30.4%
- Annual Job Openings: 78,000
- Self-Employed: 29.8%
- Part-Time: 14.0%

Conduct organizational studies and evaluations, design systems and procedures, conduct work simplifications and measurement studies, and prepare operations and procedures manuals to assist management in operating more efficiently and effectively. Includes program analysts and management consultants. Review forms and reports and confer with management and users about format, distribution, and purpose and to identify problems and improvements. Develop and implement records-management program for filing, protection, and retrieval of records and assure compliance with program. Interview personnel and conduct on-site observation to ascertain unit functions; work performed; and methods, equipment, and personnel used. Prepare manuals and train workers in use of new forms, reports, procedures, or equipment according to organizational policy. Design, evaluate, recommend, and approve changes of forms and reports. Recommend purchase of storage equipment and design area layout to locate equipment in space available. Plan study of work problems and procedures, such as organizational change, communications, information flow, integrated production methods, inventory control, or cost analysis. Gather and organize information on problems or procedures. Analyze data gathered and develop solutions or alternative methods of proceeding. Document findings of study and prepare recommendations for implementation of new systems, procedures, or organizational changes. Confer with personnel concerned to ensure successful functioning of newly implemented systems or procedures. SKILLS—Systems Evaluation: Identifying measures or indicators of system performance and the actions needed to improve or correct performance relative to the goals of the system. Systems Analysis: Determining how a system should work and how changes in conditions, operations, and the environment will affect outcomes. Management of Personnel Resources: Motivating, developing, and directing people as they work, identifying the best people for the job. Management of Material Resources: Obtaining and seeing to the appropriate use of equipment, facilities, and materials needed to do certain work. Operations Analysis: Analyzing needs and product requirements to create a design. Judgment and Decision Making: Considering the relative costs and benefits of potential actions to choose the most appropriate one. Complex Problem Solving: Identifying complex problems and reviewing related information to develop and evaluate options and implement solutions. Writing: Communicating effectively in writing as appropriate for the needs of the audience. Monitoring: Monitoring or assessing your performance or that of

other individuals or organizations to make improvements or take corrective action. GOE—Interest Area: 04. Business and Administration. Work Group: 04.05. Accounting, Auditing, and Analytical Support. Other Jobs in This Work Group: Accountants; Auditors; Budget Analysts; Industrial Engineering Technicians; Logisticians; Operations Research Analysts. PERSONALITY TYPE: Enterprising.

EDUCATION/TRAINING PROGRAM(S)—Business Administration and Management, General; Business/Commerce, General. RELATED KNOWLEDGE/COURSES—Administration and Management: Knowledge of business and management principles involved in strategic planning, resource allocation, human resources modeling, leadership technique, production methods, and coordination of people and resources. Economics and Accounting: Knowledge of economic and accounting principles and practices, the financial markets, banking, and the analysis and reporting of financial data. Personnel and Human Resources: Knowledge of principles and procedures for personnel recruitment, selection, training, compensation and benefits, labor relations and negotiation, and personnel information systems. Education and Training: Knowledge of principles and methods for curriculum and training design, teaching and instruction for individuals and groups, and the measurement of training effects. Clerical Practices: Knowledge of administrative and clerical procedures and systems such as word processing, managing files and records, stenography and transcription, designing forms, and other office procedures and terminology. Mathematics: Knowledge of arithmetic, algebra, geometry, calculus, and statistics and their applications. English Language: Knowledge of the structure and content of the English language, including the meaning and spelling of words, rules of composition, and grammar.

Mapping Technicians

- Education/Training Required: Moderate-term on-the-job training
- Annual Earnings: $30,380
- Growth: 23.1%
- Annual Job Openings: 10,000
- Self-Employed: 5.5%
- Part-Time: 7.0%

Calculate mapmaking information from field notes and draw and verify accuracy of topographical maps. Analyze aerial photographs in order to detect and interpret significant military, industrial, resource, or topographical data. Calculate latitudes, longitudes, angles, areas, and other information for mapmaking, using survey field notes and reference tables. Check all layers of maps in order to ensure accuracy, identifying and marking errors and making corrections. Compare topographical features and contour lines with images from aerial photographs, old maps, and other reference materials in order to verify the accuracy of their identification. Compute and measure scaled distances between reference points in order to establish relative positions of adjoining prints and enable the creation of photographic mosaics. Form three-dimensional images of aerial photographs taken from different locations, using mathematical techniques and plotting instruments. Lay out and match aerial photographs in sequences in which they were taken and identify any areas missing from photographs. Monitor mapping work and the updating of maps in order to ensure accuracy, the inclusion of new and/or changed information, and compliance with rules and regulations. Produce and update overlay maps in order to show information boundaries, water locations, and topographic features on various base maps and at different scales. Redraw and correct maps, such as revising parcel maps to reflect tax code area changes, using information from official records and surveys. Trace contours and topographic details in order to generate maps that denote specific land and property locations and geographic attributes. Trim, align, and join prints in order to form photographic mosaics, maintaining scaled distances between reference points. Complete detailed source and method notes detailing the location of routine and complex land parcels. Create survey description pages and historical records related to the mapping activities and specifications of section plats. Determine scales, line sizes, and colors to be used for hard copies of computerized maps, using plotters. Enter GPS data, legal deeds, field notes, and land survey reports into GIS workstations so that information can be transformed into graphic land descriptions, such as maps and drawings. **SKILLS—Mathematics:** Using mathematics to solve problems. **Technology Design:** Generating or adapting equipment and technology to serve user needs. **Management of Personnel Resources:** Motivating, developing, and directing people as they work, identifying the best people for the job. **Operations Analysis:** Analyzing needs and prod-

uct requirements to create a design. **GOE—Interest Area:** 15. Scientific Research, Engineering, and Mathematics. **Work Group:** 15.09. Engineering Technology. **Other Jobs in This Work Group:** Aerospace Engineering and Operations Technicians; Calibration and Instrumentation Technicians; Cartographers and Photogrammetrists; Civil Engineering Technicians; Electrical Engineering Technicians; Electro-Mechanical Technicians; Electronic Drafters; Electronics Engineering Technicians; Environmental Engineering Technicians; Mechanical Drafters; Mechanical Engineering Technicians; Surveying Technicians. **PERSONALITY TYPE:** Conventional.

EDUCATION/TRAINING PROGRAM(S)—Cartography; Surveying Technology/Surveying. **RELATED KNOWLEDGE/COURSES—Geography:** Knowledge of principles and methods for describing the features of land, sea, and air masses, including their physical characteristics; locations; interrelationships; and distribution of plant, animal, and human life. **Design:** Knowledge of design techniques, tools, and principles involved in production of precision technical plans, blueprints, drawings, and models. **Mathematics:** Knowledge of arithmetic, algebra, geometry, calculus, and statistics and their applications. **Computers and Electronics:** Knowledge of circuit boards, processors, chips, electronic equipment, and computer hardware and software, including applications and programming. **Administration and Management:** Knowledge of business and management principles involved in strategic planning, resource allocation, human resources modeling, leadership technique, production methods, and coordination of people and resources. **Engineering and Technology:** Knowledge of the practical application of engineering science and technology. This includes applying principles, techniques, procedures, and equipment to the design and production of various goods and services.

Marine Cargo Inspectors

- ◎ Education/Training Required: Work experience in a related occupation
- ◎ Annual Earnings: $50,380
- ◎ Growth: 7.7%
- ◎ Annual Job Openings: 5,000
- ◎ Self-Employed: 0.4%
- ◎ Part-Time: 3.2%

M

Inspect cargoes of seagoing vessels to certify compliance with health and safety regulations in cargo handling and stowage. Inspects loaded cargo in holds and cargo-handling devices to determine compliance with regulations and need for maintenance. Reads vessel documents to ascertain cargo capabilities according to design and cargo regulations. Calculates gross and net tonnage, hold capacities, volume of stored fuel and water, cargo weight, and ship stability factors, using mathematical formulas. Determines type of license and safety equipment required and computes applicable tolls and wharfage fees. Examines blueprints of ship and takes physical measurements to determine capacity and depth of vessel in water, using measuring instruments. Writes certificates of admeasurement, listing details such as design, length, depth, and breadth of vessel and method of propulsion. Issues certificate of compliance when violations are not detected or recommends remedial procedures to correct deficiencies. Times roll of ship, using stopwatch. Analyzes data, formulates recommendations, and writes reports of findings. Advises crew in techniques of stowing dangerous and heavy cargo according to knowledge of hazardous cargo. **SKILLS—Mathematics:** Using mathematics to solve problems. **Writing:** Communicating effectively in writing as appropriate for the needs of the audience. **Systems Evaluation:** Identifying measures or indicators of system performance and the actions needed to improve or correct performance relative to the goals of the system. **Systems Analysis:** Determining how a system should work and how changes in conditions, operations, and the environment will affect outcomes. **Reading Comprehension:** Understanding written sentences and paragraphs in work-related documents. **Active Listening:** Giving full attention to what other people are saying, taking time to understand the points being made, asking questions as appropriate, and not interrupting at inappropriate times. **Speaking:** Talking to others to convey information effectively. **Judgment and Decision Making:** Considering the relative costs and benefits of potential actions to choose the most appropriate one. **GOE—Interest Area:** 07. Government and Public Administration. **Work Group:** 07.03. Regulations Enforcement. **Other Jobs in This Work Group:** Agricultural Inspectors; Aviation Inspectors; Child Support, Missing Persons, and Unemployment Insurance Fraud Investigators; Environmental Compliance Inspectors; Equal Opportunity Representatives and Officers; Financial Examiners; Fire Inspectors; Fish and Game Wardens; Forest Fire Inspectors and Prevention Specialists; Government Property Inspectors and Investigators; Immigration and Customs Inspectors; Licensing Examiners and Inspectors; Mechanical Inspectors; Motor Vehicle Inspectors; Nuclear Monitoring Technicians; Occupational Health and Safety Specialists; Pressure Vessel Inspectors; Railroad Inspectors; Tax Examiners, Collectors, and Revenue Agents. **PERSONALITY TYPE:** Conventional.

EDUCATION/TRAINING PROGRAM(S)—No data available. **RELATED KNOWLEDGE/COURSES—Public Safety and Security:** Knowledge of relevant equipment, policies, procedures, and strategies to promote effective local, state, or national security operations for the protection of people, data, property, and institutions. **Mathematics:** Knowledge of arithmetic, algebra, geometry, calculus, and statistics and their applications. **Transportation:** Knowledge of principles and methods for moving people or goods by air, rail, sea, or road, including the relative costs and benefits. **Design:** Knowledge of design techniques, tools, and principles involved in production of precision technical plans, blueprints, drawings, and models. **Physics:** Knowledge and prediction of physical principles and laws and their interrelationships and applications to understanding fluid, material, and atmospheric dynamics and mechanical, electrical, atomic, and subatomic structures and processes. **Law and Government:** Knowledge of laws, legal codes, court procedures, precedents, government regulations, executive orders, agency rules, and the democratic political process.

Market Research Analysts

- Education/Training Required: Bachelor's degree
- Annual Earnings: $56,140
- Growth: 23.4%
- Annual Job Openings: 18,000
- Self-Employed: 7.3%
- Part-Time: 11.7%

Research market conditions in local, regional, or national areas to determine potential sales of a product or service. May gather information on competitors, prices, sales, and methods of marketing and distribution. May use survey results to create a mar-

keting campaign based on regional preferences and buying habits. Collect and analyze data on customer demographics, preferences, needs, and buying habits to identify potential markets and factors affecting product demand. Prepare reports of findings, illustrating data graphically and translating complex findings into written text. Measure and assess customer and employee satisfaction. Forecast and track marketing and sales trends, analyzing collected data. Seek and provide information to help companies determine their position in the marketplace. Measure the effectiveness of marketing, advertising, and communications programs and strategies. Conduct research on consumer opinions and marketing strategies, collaborating with marketing professionals, statisticians, pollsters, and other professionals. Attend staff conferences to provide management with information and proposals concerning the promotion, distribution, design, and pricing of company products or services. Gather data on competitors and analyze their prices, sales, and method of marketing and distribution. Monitor industry statistics and follow trends in trade literature. Devise and evaluate methods and procedures for collecting data (such as surveys, opinion polls, or questionnaires) or arrange to obtain existing data. Develop and implement procedures for identifying advertising needs. Direct trained survey interviewers. **SKILLS— Negotiation:** Bringing others together and trying to reconcile differences. **Persuasion:** Persuading others to change their minds or behavior. **Coordination:** Adjusting actions in relation to others' actions. **Writing:** Communicating effectively in writing as appropriate for the needs of the audience. **Social Perceptiveness:** Being aware of others' reactions and understanding why they react as they do. **Time Management:** Managing one's own time and the time of others. **Judgment and Decision Making:** Considering the relative costs and benefits of potential actions to choose the most appropriate one. **Reading Comprehension:** Understanding written sentences and paragraphs in work-related documents. **GOE—Interest Area:** 06. Finance and Insurance. **Work Group:** 06.02. Finance/Insurance Investigation and Analysis. **Other Jobs in This Work Group:** Appraisers, Real Estate; Assessors; Claims Examiners, Property and Casualty Insurance; Cost Estimators; Credit Analysts; Financial Analysts; Insurance Adjusters, Examiners, and Investigators; Insurance Appraisers, Auto Damage; Insurance Underwriters; Loan Counselors; Loan Officers; Survey Researchers. **PERSONALITY TYPE:** Investigative.

EDUCATION/TRAINING PROGRAM(S)— Applied Economics; Business/Managerial Economics; Econometrics and Quantitative Economics; Economics, General; International Economics; Marketing Research. **RELATED KNOWLEDGE/COURSES— Sales and Marketing:** Knowledge of principles and methods for showing, promoting, and selling products or services. This includes marketing strategy and tactics, product demonstrations, sales techniques, and sales control systems. **Administration and Management:** Knowledge of business and management principles involved in strategic planning, resource allocation, human resources modeling, leadership technique, production methods, and coordination of people and resources. **Communications and Media:** Knowledge of media production, communication, and dissemination techniques and methods. This includes alternative ways to inform and entertain via written, oral, and visual media. **Customer and Personal Service:** Knowledge of principles and processes for providing customer and personal services. This includes customer needs assessment, meeting quality standards for services, and evaluation of customer satisfaction. **Economics and Accounting:** Knowledge of economic and accounting principles and practices, the financial markets, banking, and the analysis and reporting of financial data. **Clerical Practices:** Knowledge of administrative and clerical procedures and systems such as word processing, managing files and records, stenography and transcription, designing forms, and other office procedures and terminology.

M

Marketing Managers

- ◎ Education/Training Required: Work experience plus degree
- ◎ Annual Earnings: $87,640
- ◎ Growth: 21.3%
- ◎ Annual Job Openings: 30,000
- ◎ Self-Employed: 3.1%
- ◎ Part-Time: 4.7%

Determine the demand for products and services offered by a firm and its competitors and identify potential customers. Develop pricing strategies with the goal of maximizing the firm's profits or share of the market while ensuring the firm's customers are satisfied. Oversee product development or monitor

trends that indicate the need for new products and services. Develop pricing strategies, balancing firm objectives and customer satisfaction. Identify, develop, and evaluate marketing strategy, based on knowledge of establishment objectives, market characteristics, and cost and markup factors. Evaluate the financial aspects of product development, such as budgets, expenditures, research and development appropriations, and return-on-investment and profit-loss projections. Formulate, direct, and coordinate marketing activities and policies to promote products and services, working with advertising and promotion managers. Direct the hiring, training, and performance evaluations of marketing and sales staff and oversee their daily activities. Negotiate contracts with vendors and distributors to manage product distribution, establishing distribution networks and developing distribution strategies. Consult with product development personnel on product specifications such as design, color, and packaging. Compile lists describing product or service offerings. Use sales forecasting and strategic planning to ensure the sale and profitability of products, lines, or services, analyzing business developments and monitoring market trends. Select products and accessories to be displayed at trade or special production shows. Confer with legal staff to resolve problems such as copyright infringement and royalty sharing with outside producers and distributors. Coordinate and participate in promotional activities and trade shows, working with developers, advertisers, and production managers to market products and services. Advise business and other groups on local, national, and international factors affecting the buying and selling of products and services. Initiate market research studies and analyze their findings. Consult with buying personnel to gain advice regarding the types of products or services expected to be in demand. Conduct economic and commercial surveys to identify potential markets for products and services. **SKILLS—Management of Financial Resources:** Determining how money will be spent to get the work done and accounting for these expenditures. **Management of Personnel Resources:** Motivating, developing, and directing people as they work, identifying the best people for the job. **Negotiation:** Bringing others together and trying to reconcile differences. **Operations Analysis:** Analyzing needs and product requirements to create a design. **Persuasion:** Persuading others to change their minds or behavior. **Coordination:** Adjusting actions in relation to others' actions. **Instructing:** Teaching others how to do some-

thing. **Learning Strategies:** Selecting and using training/instructional methods and procedures appropriate for the situation when learning or teaching new things. **GOE—Interest Area:** 14. Retail and Wholesale Sales and Service. **Work Group:** 14.01. Managerial Work in Retail/Wholesale Sales and Service. **Other Jobs in This Work Group:** Advertising and Promotions Managers; First-Line Supervisors/Managers of Non-Retail Sales Workers; First-Line Supervisors/Managers of Retail Sales Workers; Funeral Directors; Property, Real Estate, and Community Association Managers; Purchasing Managers; Sales Managers. **PERSONALITY TYPE:** Enterprising.

EDUCATION/TRAINING PROGRAM(S)— Apparel and Textile Marketing Management; Consumer Merchandising/Retailing Management; International Marketing; Marketing Research; Marketing, Other; Marketing/Marketing Management, General. **RELATED KNOWLEDGE/COURSES—Sales and Marketing:** Knowledge of principles and methods for showing, promoting, and selling products or services. This includes marketing strategy and tactics, product demonstrations, sales techniques, and sales control systems. **Customer and Personal Service:** Knowledge of principles and processes for providing customer and personal services. This includes customer needs assessment, meeting quality standards for services, and evaluation of customer satisfaction. **Administration and Management:** Knowledge of business and management principles involved in strategic planning, resource allocation, human resources modeling, leadership technique, production methods, and coordination of people and resources. **Personnel and Human Resources:** Knowledge of principles and procedures for personnel recruitment, selection, training, compensation and benefits, labor relations and negotiation, and personnel information systems. **Education and Training:** Knowledge of principles and methods for curriculum and training design, teaching and instruction for individuals and groups, and the measurement of training effects. **English Language:** Knowledge of the structure and content of the English language, including the meaning and spelling of words, rules of composition, and grammar. **Communications and Media:** Knowledge of media production, communication, and dissemination techniques and methods. This includes alternative ways to inform and entertain via written, oral, and visual media.

Marriage and Family Therapists

- Education/Training Required: Master's degree
- Annual Earnings: $38,980
- Growth: 22.4%
- Annual Job Openings: 3,000
- Self-Employed: 4.2%
- Part-Time: 14.6%

Diagnose and treat mental and emotional disorders, whether cognitive, affective, or behavioral, within the context of marriage and family systems. Apply psychotherapeutic and family systems theories and techniques in the delivery of professional services to individuals, couples, and families for the purpose of treating such diagnosed nervous and mental disorders. Ask questions that will help clients identify their feelings and behaviors. Collect information about clients, using techniques such as testing, interviewing, discussion, and observation. Confer with clients in order to develop plans for post-treatment activities. Counsel clients on concerns such as unsatisfactory relationships, divorce and separation, child rearing, home management, and financial difficulties. Determine whether clients should be counseled or referred to other specialists in such fields as medicine, psychiatry, and legal aid. Develop and implement individualized treatment plans addressing family relationship problems. Encourage individuals and family members to develop and use skills and strategies for confronting their problems in a constructive manner. Maintain case files that include activities, progress notes, evaluations, and recommendations. Confer with other counselors in order to analyze individual cases and to coordinate counseling services. Contact doctors, schools, social workers, juvenile counselors, law enforcement personnel, and others to gather information in order to make recommendations to courts for the resolution of child custody or visitation disputes. Follow up on results of counseling programs and clients' adjustments in order to determine effectiveness of programs. Provide family counseling and treatment services to inmates participating in substance abuse programs. Provide instructions to clients on how to obtain help with legal, financial, and other personal issues. Supervise other counselors, social service staff, and assistants. Write evaluations of parents and children for use by courts deciding divorce and custody cases, testifying in court if necessary. Provide public education and consultation to other professionals or groups regarding counseling services, issues, and methods. **SKILLS**—No data available. **GOE—Interest Area:** 10. Human Service. **Work Group:** 10.01. Counseling and Social Work. **Other Jobs in This Work Group:** Child, Family, and School Social Workers; Clinical Psychologists; Counseling Psychologists; Medical and Public Health Social Workers; Mental Health and Substance Abuse Social Workers; Mental Health Counselors; Probation Officers and Correctional Treatment Specialists; Rehabilitation Counselors; Residential Advisors; Social and Human Service Assistants; Substance Abuse and Behavioral Disorder Counselors. **PERSONALITY TYPE:** No data available.

EDUCATION/TRAINING PROGRAM(S)—Clinical Pastoral Counseling/Patient Counseling; Marriage and Family Therapy/Counseling; Social Work. **RELATED KNOWLEDGE/COURSES**—No data available.

Massage Therapists

- Education/Training Required: Postsecondary vocational training
- Annual Earnings: $31,960
- Growth: 27.1%
- Annual Job Openings: 24,000
- Self-Employed: 70.1%
- Part-Time: 41.2%

Massage customers for hygienic or remedial purposes. Apply finger and hand pressure to specific points of the body. Assess clients' soft tissue condition, joint quality and function, muscle strength, and range of motion. Confer with clients about their medical histories and any problems with stress and/or pain in order to determine whether massage would be helpful. Develop and propose client treatment plans that specify which types of massage are to be used. Massage and knead the muscles and soft tissues of the human body in order to provide courses of treatment for medical conditions and injuries or wellness maintenance. Prepare and blend oils and apply the blends to clients' skin. Consult with other health care professionals such as physiotherapists, chiropractors, physicians, and psychologists in order to develop treatment plans for clients. Maintain treatment records. Provide clients with guidance and information about techniques for postural improvement and stretching, strengthening, relaxation, and rehabilitative exercises. Refer clients to other types of therapists when necessary. Use complementary aids such as infrared lamps, wet compresses, ice, and whirlpool baths in order to promote clients' recovery, relaxation, and well-being. Treat clients in own offices or travel to clients' offices and homes. **SKILLS**—No data available. **GOE—Interest Area:** 08. Health Science. **Work Group:** 08.07. Medical Therapy. **Other Jobs in This Work Group:** Audiologists; Occupational Therapist Aides; Occupational Therapist Assistants; Occupational Therapists; Physical Therapist Aides; Physical Therapist Assistants; Physical Therapists; Radiation Therapists; Recreational Therapists; Respiratory Therapists; Respiratory Therapy Technicians; Speech-Language Pathologists. **PERSONALITY TYPE:** No data available.

EDUCATION/TRAINING PROGRAM(S)—Asian Bodywork Therapy; Massage Therapy/Therapeutic Massage; Somatic Bodywork; Somatic Bodywork and Related Therapeutic Services, Other. **RELATED KNOWLEDGE/COURSES**—No data available.

Materials Inspectors

- Education/Training Required: Moderate-term on-the-job training
- Annual Earnings: $28,410
- Growth: 4.7%
- Annual Job Openings: 87,000
- Self-Employed: 1.2%
- Part-Time: 5.0%

Examine and inspect materials and finished parts and products for defects and wear and to ensure conformance with work orders, diagrams, blueprints, and template specifications. Usually specialize in a single phase of inspection. Inspects materials, products, and work in progress for conformance to specifications and adjusts process or assembly equipment to meet standards. Collects samples for testing and computes findings. Reads dials and meters to verify functioning of equipment according to specifications. Analyzes and interprets blueprints, sample data, and other materials to determine, change, or measure specifications or

inspection and testing procedures. Tests and measures finished products, components, or assemblies for functioning, operation, accuracy, or assembly to verify adherence to functional specifications. Observes and monitors production operations and equipment to ensure proper assembly of parts or assists in testing and monitoring activities. Marks items for acceptance or rejection, records test results and inspection data, and compares findings with specifications to ensure conformance to standards. Confers with vendors and others regarding inspection results; recommends corrective procedures; and compiles reports of results, recommendations, and needed repairs. Supervises testing or drilling activities and adjusts equipment to obtain sample fluids or to direct drilling. Operates or tends machinery and equipment and uses hand tools. Fabricates, installs, positions, or connects components, parts, finished products, or instruments for testing or operational purposes. **SKILLS—Quality Control Analysis:** Conducting tests and inspections of products, services, or processes to evaluate quality or performance. **Operation Monitoring:** Watching gauges, dials, or other indicators to make sure a machine is working properly. **Troubleshooting:** Determining causes of operating errors and deciding what to do about them. **Operation and Control:** Controlling operations of equipment or systems. **Technology Design:** Generating or adapting equipment and technology to serve user needs. **Installation:** Installing equipment, machines, wiring, or programs to meet specifications. **Science:** Using scientific rules and methods to solve problems. **Mathematics:** Using mathematics to solve problems. **GOE—Interest Area:** 13. Manufacturing. **Work Group:** 13.07. Production Quality Control. **Other Jobs in This Work Group:** Electrical and Electronic Inspectors and Testers; Graders and Sorters, Agricultural Products; Precision Devices Inspectors and Testers; Production Inspectors, Testers, Graders, Sorters, Samplers, Weighers. **PERSONALITY TYPE:** Realistic.

EDUCATION/TRAINING PROGRAM(S)— Quality Control Technology/Technician. **RELATED KNOWLEDGE/COURSES—Design:** Knowledge of design techniques, tools, and principles involved in production of precision technical plans, blueprints, drawings, and models. **Mechanical Devices:** Knowledge of machines and tools, including their designs, uses, repair, and maintenance. **Production and Processing:** Knowledge of raw materials, production processes, quality control, costs, and other techniques for maximizing the effective manufacture and distribution of goods. **Engineering and Technology:** Knowledge of the practical application of engineering science and technology. This includes applying principles, techniques, procedures, and equipment to the design and production of various goods and services. **Physics:** Knowledge and prediction of physical principles and laws and their interrelationships and applications to understanding fluid, material, and atmospheric dynamics and mechanical, electrical, atomic, and subatomic structures and processes. **Public Safety and Security:** Knowledge of relevant equipment, policies, procedures, and strategies to promote effective local, state, or national security operations for the protection of people, data, property, and institutions.

Materials Scientists

- ◎ Education/Training Required: Bachelor's degree
- ◎ Annual Earnings: $72,390
- ◎ Growth: 8.5%
- ◎ Annual Job Openings: 1,000
- ◎ Self-Employed: 0.2%
- ◎ Part-Time: 4.2%

Research and study the structures and chemical properties of various natural and manmade materials, including metals, alloys, rubber, ceramics, semiconductors, polymers, and glass. Determine ways to strengthen or combine materials or develop new materials with new or specific properties for use in a variety of products and applications. Conduct research into the structures and properties of materials such as metals, alloys, polymers, and ceramics in order to obtain information that could be used to develop new products or enhance existing ones. Determine ways to strengthen or combine materials or develop new materials with new or specific properties for use in a variety of products and applications. Devise testing methods to evaluate the effects of various conditions on particular materials. Plan laboratory experiments to confirm feasibility of processes and techniques used in the production of materials having special characteristics. Prepare reports of materials-study findings for the use of other scientists and requestors. Recommend materials for reliable performance in various environments. Research methods of processing, forming, and firing materials in order to develop such products as ceramic fillings for teeth, unbreakable dinner plates, and telescope lenses. Study the nature, structure, and physical properties of metals and their alloys and their responses to applied forces. Test material samples for tolerance under tension, compression, and shear to determine the cause of metal failures. Confer with customers in order to determine how materials can be tailored to suit their needs. Monitor production processes in order to ensure that equipment is used efficiently and that projects are completed within appropriate time frames and budgets. Receive molten metal from smelters and further alloy and refine it in oxygen, open-hearth, or other kinds of furnaces. Teach in colleges and universities. Test individual parts and products in order to ensure that manufacturer and governmental quality and safety standards are met. Test metals in order to determine whether they meet specifications of mechanical strength; strength-weight ratio; ductility; magnetic and electrical properties; and resistance to abrasion, corrosion, heat, and cold. Visit suppliers of materials or users of products in order to gather specific information. **SKILLS—Science:** Using scientific rules and methods to solve problems. **Writing:** Communicating effectively in writing as appropriate for the needs of the audience. **Active Learning:** Understanding the implications of new information for both current and future problem-solving and decision-making. **Mathematics:** Using mathematics to solve problems. **Reading Comprehension:** Understanding written sentences and paragraphs in work-related documents. **Operations Analysis:** Analyzing needs and product requirements to create a design. **Quality Control Analysis:** Conducting tests and inspections of products, services, or processes to evaluate quality or performance. **Systems Analysis:** Determining how a system should work and how changes in conditions, operations, and the environment will affect outcomes. **Systems Evaluation:** Identifying measures or indicators of system performance and the actions needed to improve or correct performance relative to the goals of the system. **GOE—Interest Area:** 15. Scientific Research, Engineering, and Mathematics. **Work Group:** 15.02. Physical Sciences. **Other Jobs in This Work Group:** Astronomers; Atmospheric and Space Scientists; Chemists; Geographers; Geologists; Hydrologists; Physicists. **PERSONALITY TYPE:** Investigative.

EDUCATION/TRAINING PROGRAM(S)— Materials Science. **RELATED KNOWLEDGE/**

M

COURSES—**Chemistry:** Knowledge of the chemical composition, structure, and properties of substances and of the chemical processes and transformations that they undergo. This includes uses of chemicals and their danger signs, production techniques, and disposal methods. **Physics:** Knowledge and prediction of physical principles and laws and their interrelationships and applications to understanding fluid, material, and atmospheric dynamics and mechanical, electrical, atomic, and subatomic structures and processes. **Engineering and Technology:** Knowledge of the practical application of engineering science and technology. This includes applying principles, techniques, procedures, and equipment to the design and production of various goods and services. **Mathematics:** Knowledge of arithmetic, algebra, geometry, calculus, and statistics and their applications. **Administration and Management:** Knowledge of business and management principles involved in strategic planning, resource allocation, human resources modeling, leadership technique, production methods, and coordination of people and resources. **English Language:** Knowledge of the structure and content of the English language, including the meaning and spelling of words, rules of composition, and grammar.

Mathematical Science Teachers, Postsecondary

- ◎ Education/Training Required: Master's degree
- ◎ Annual Earnings: $52,450
- ◎ Growth: 38.1%
- ◎ Annual Job Openings: 216,000
- ◎ Self-Employed: 0.3%
- ◎ Part-Time: 27.7%

Teach courses pertaining to mathematical concepts, statistics, and actuarial science and to the application of original and standardized mathematical techniques in solving specific problems and situations. Evaluate and grade students' class work, assignments, and papers. Compile, administer, and grade examinations or assign this work to others. Prepare and deliver lectures to undergraduate and/or graduate students on topics such as linear algebra, differential equations, and discrete mathematics. Prepare course materials such as syllabi, homework assignments, and handouts. Maintain student attendance records, grades, and other required records. Maintain regularly scheduled office hours in order to advise and assist students. Plan, evaluate, and revise curricula, course content, and course materials and methods of instruction. Initiate, facilitate, and moderate classroom discussions. Select and obtain materials and supplies such as textbooks. Keep abreast of developments in their field by reading current literature, talking with colleagues, and participating in professional conferences. Advise students on academic and vocational curricula and on career issues. Collaborate with colleagues to address teaching and research issues. Serve on academic or administrative committees that deal with institutional policies, departmental matters, and academic issues. Participate in student recruitment, registration, and placement activities. Perform administrative duties such as serving as department head. Conduct research in a particular field of knowledge and publish findings in books, professional journals, and/or electronic media. Supervise undergraduate and/or graduate teaching, internship, and research work. Act as advisers to student organizations. SKILLS—**Instructing:** Teaching others how to do something. **Mathematics:** Using mathematics to solve problems. **Learning Strategies:** Selecting and using training/instructional methods and procedures appropriate for the situation when learning or teaching new things. **Critical Thinking:** Using logic and reasoning to identify the strengths and weaknesses of alternative solutions, conclusions, or approaches to problems. **Active Learning:** Understanding the implications of new information for both current and future problem-solving and decision-making. **Speaking:** Talking to others to convey information effectively. **Social Perceptiveness:** Being aware of others' reactions and understanding why they react as they do. **Persuasion:** Persuading others to change their minds or behavior. **Complex Problem Solving:** Identifying complex problems and reviewing related information to develop and evaluate options and implement solutions. GOE—**Interest Area:** 05. Education and Training. **Work Group:** 05.03. Postsecondary and Adult Teaching and Instructing. **Other Jobs in This Work Group:** Adult Literacy, Remedial Education, and GED Teachers and Instructors; Agricultural Sciences Teachers, Postsecondary; Anthropology and Archeology Teachers, Postsecondary; Architecture Teachers, Postsecondary; Area, Ethnic, and Cultural Studies Teachers, Postsecondary; Art, Drama, and Music Teachers, Postsecondary; Atmospheric, Earth, Marine, and Space Sciences Teachers, Postsecondary; Biological

Science Teachers, Postsecondary; Business Teachers, Postsecondary; Chemistry Teachers, Postsecondary; Communications Teachers, Postsecondary; Computer Science Teachers, Postsecondary; Criminal Justice and Law Enforcement Teachers, Postsecondary; Economics Teachers, Postsecondary; Education Teachers, Postsecondary; Engineering Teachers, Postsecondary; English Language and Literature Teachers, Postsecondary; Environmental Science Teachers, Postsecondary; Farm and Home Management Advisors; Foreign Language and Literature Teachers, Postsecondary; Forestry and Conservation Science Teachers, Postsecondary; Geography Teachers, Postsecondary; Graduate Teaching Assistants; Health Specialties Teachers, Postsecondary; History Teachers, Postsecondary; Home Economics Teachers, Postsecondary; Law Teachers, Postsecondary; Library Science Teachers, Postsecondary; Nursing Instructors and Teachers, Postsecondary; Philosophy and Religion Teachers, Postsecondary; Physics Teachers, Postsecondary; Political Science Teachers, Postsecondary; Psychology Teachers, Postsecondary; Recreation and Fitness Studies Teachers, Postsecondary; Self-Enrichment Education Teachers; Social Work Teachers, Postsecondary; Sociology Teachers, Postsecondary; Vocational Education Teachers, Postsecondary. **PERSONALITY TYPE:** Investigative.

EDUCATION/TRAINING PROGRAM(S)—Algebra and Number Theory; Analysis and Functional Analysis; Applied Mathematics; Business Statistics; Geometry/Geometric Analysis; Logic; Mathematical Statistics and Probability; Mathematics and Statistics, Other; Mathematics, General; Mathematics, Other; Statistics, General; Topology and Foundations. **RELATED KNOWLEDGE/COURSES—Mathematics:** Knowledge of arithmetic, algebra, geometry, calculus, and statistics and their applications. **Education and Training:** Knowledge of principles and methods for curriculum and training design, teaching and instruction for individuals and groups, and the measurement of training effects. **Computers and Electronics:** Knowledge of circuit boards, processors, chips, electronic equipment, and computer hardware and software, including applications and programming. **Physics:** Knowledge and prediction of physical principles and laws and their interrelationships and applications to understanding fluid, material, and atmospheric dynamics and mechanical, electrical, atomic, and subatomic structures and processes. **English Language:** Knowledge of the structure and content of the English language, including the meaning

and spelling of words, rules of composition, and grammar. **Psychology:** Knowledge of human behavior and performance; individual differences in ability, personality, and interests; learning and motivation; psychological research methods; and the assessment and treatment of behavioral and affective disorders.

Meat, Poultry, and Fish Cutters and Trimmers

- Education/Training Required: Short-term on-the-job training
- Annual Earnings: $18,900
- Growth: 16.4%
- Annual Job Openings: 27,000
- Self-Employed: 1.1%
- Part-Time: 7.0%

Use hand tools to perform routine cutting and trimming of meat, poultry, and fish. Separate meats and byproducts into specified containers and seal containers. Weigh meats and tag containers for weight and contents. Clean and salt hides. Prepare ready-to-heat foods by filleting meat or fish or cutting it into bite-sized pieces, preparing and adding vegetables, or applying sauces or breading. Prepare sausages, luncheon meats, hot dogs, and other fabricated meat products, using meat trimmings and hamburger meat. Slaughter live animals, using stunning devices and knives. Use knives, cleavers, meat saws, band saws, or other equipment to perform meat cutting and trimming. Clean, trim, slice, and section carcasses for future processing. Cut and trim meat to prepare for packing. Inspect meat products for defects, bruises, or blemishes and remove them along with any excess fat. Obtain and distribute specified meat or carcass. Process primal parts into cuts that are ready for retail use. Produce hamburger meat and meat trimmings. Remove parts such as skin, feathers, scales or bones from carcass. **SKILLS**—None met the criteria. **GOE—Interest Area:** 13. Manufacturing. **Work Group:** 13.03. Production Work, Assorted Materials Processing. **Other Jobs in This Work Group:** Bakers, Manufacturing; Cementing and Gluing Machine Operators and Tenders; Chemical Equipment Controllers and Operators; Chemical Equipment Tenders; Cleaning, Washing, and Metal Pickling Equipment Operators and Tenders; Coating, Painting, and Spraying Machine Oper-

M

ators and Tenders; Combination Machine Tool Operators and Tenders, Metal and Plastic; Cooling and Freezing Equipment Operators and Tenders; Cutting and Slicing Machine Operators and Tenders; Electrolytic Plating and Coating Machine Operators and Tenders, Metal and Plastic; Extruding and Forming Machine Operators and Tenders, Synthetic or Glass Fibers; Extruding, Forming, Pressing, and Compacting Machine Operators and Tenders; Food and Tobacco Roasting, Baking, and Drying Machine Operators and Tenders; Food Batchmakers; Food Cooking Machine Operators and Tenders; Furnace, Kiln, Oven, Drier, and Kettle Operators and Tenders; Heat Treating, Annealing, and Tempering Machine Operators and Tenders, Metal and Plastic; Heaters, Metal and Plastic; Metal-Refining Furnace Operators and Tenders; Mixing and Blending Machine Setters, Operators, and Tenders; Nonelectrolytic Plating and Coating Machine Operators and Tenders, Metal and Plastic; Packaging and Filling Machine Operators and Tenders; Plastic Molding and Casting Machine Operators and Tenders; Pourers and Casters, Metal; Pressing Machine Operators and Tenders—Textile, Garment, and Related Materials; Production Helpers; Production Laborers; Sawing Machine Operators and Tenders; Separating, Filtering, Clarifying, Precipitating, and Still Machine Setters, Operators, and Tenders; Sewing Machine Operators, Garment; Sewing Machine Operators, Non-Garment; Shoe Machine Operators and Tenders; Slaughterers and Meat Packers; Stone Sawyers; Team Assemblers; Textile Bleaching and Dyeing Machine Operators and Tenders; Tire Builders; Woodworking Machine Operators and Tenders, Except Sawing. **PERSONALITY TYPE:** Realistic.

EDUCATION/TRAINING PROGRAM(S)—Meat Cutting/Meat Cutter. **RELATED KNOWLEDGE/ COURSES**—**Food Production:** Knowledge of techniques and equipment for planting, growing, and harvesting food products (both plant and animal) for consumption, including storage/handling techniques. **Biology:** Knowledge of plant and animal organisms and their tissues, cells, functions, interdependencies, and interactions with each other and the environment. **Production and Processing:** Knowledge of raw materials, production processes, quality control, costs, and other techniques for maximizing the effective manufacture and distribution of goods. **Law and Government:** Knowledge of laws, legal codes, court procedures, precedents, government regulations, exec-

utive orders, agency rules, and the democratic political process. **Public Safety and Security:** Knowledge of relevant equipment, policies, procedures, and strategies to promote effective local, state, or national security operations for the protection of people, data, property, and institutions.

Mechanical Engineering Technicians

- Education/Training Required: Associate degree
- Annual Earnings: $43,400
- Growth: 11.0%
- Annual Job Openings: 6,000
- Self-Employed: 0.4%
- Part-Time: 5.0%

Apply theory and principles of mechanical engineering to modify, develop, and test machinery and equipment under direction of engineering staff or physical scientists. Prepare parts sketches and write work orders and purchase requests to be furnished by outside contractors. Draft detail drawing or sketch for drafting room completion or to request parts fabrication by machine, sheet, or wood shops. Review project instructions and blueprints to ascertain test specifications, procedures, and objectives and test nature of technical problems, such as redesign. Review project instructions and specifications to identify, modify, and plan requirements fabrication, assembly, and testing. Devise, fabricate, and assemble new or modified mechanical components for products such as industrial machinery or equipment and measuring instruments. Discuss changes in design, method of manufacture and assembly, and drafting techniques and procedures with staff and coordinate corrections. Set up and conduct tests of complete units and components under operational conditions to investigate proposals for improving equipment performance. Inspect lines and figures for clarity and return erroneous drawings to designer for correction. Analyze test results in relation to design or rated specifications and test objectives and modify or adjust equipment to meet specifications. Evaluate tool drawing designs by measuring drawing dimensions and comparing with original specifications for form and function, using engineering skills. Confer with technicians, submit reports of test results to engineering department, and recommend design or material changes. Calculate required capacities for equipment of proposed system to obtain specified performance and submit data to engineering personnel for approval. Record test procedures and results, numerical and graphical data, and recommendations for changes in product or test methods. Read dials and meters to determine amperage, voltage, and electrical output and input at specific operating temperature to analyze parts performance. Estimate cost factors, including labor and material for purchased and fabricated parts and costs for assembly, testing, and installing. Set up prototype and test apparatus and operate test, controlling equipment to observe and record prototype test results. **SKILLS—Troubleshooting:** Determining causes of operating errors and deciding what to do about them. **Installation:** Installing equipment, machines, wiring, or programs to meet specifications. **Coordination:** Adjusting actions in relation to others' actions. **Technology Design:** Generating or adapting equipment and technology to serve user needs. **Equipment Selection:** Determining the kind of tools and equipment needed to do a job. **Service Orientation:** Actively looking for ways to help people. **Operations Analysis:** Analyzing needs and product requirements to create a design. **Time Management:** Managing one's own time and the time of others. **GOE—Interest Area:** 15. Scientific Research, Engineering, and Mathematics. **Work Group:** 15.09. Engineering Technology. **Other Jobs in This Work Group:** Aerospace Engineering and Operations Technicians; Calibration and Instrumentation Technicians; Cartographers and Photogrammetrists; Civil Engineering Technicians; Electrical Engineering Technicians; Electro-Mechanical Technicians; Electronic Drafters; Electronics Engineering Technicians; Environmental Engineering Technicians; Mapping Technicians; Mechanical Drafters; Surveying Technicians. **PERSONALITY TYPE:** Realistic.

EDUCATION/TRAINING PROGRAM(S)—Mechanical Engineering–Related Technologies/Technicians, Other; Mechanical Engineering/Mechanical Technology/Technician. **RELATED KNOWLEDGE/COURSES—Engineering and Technology:** Knowledge of the practical application of engineering science and technology. This includes applying principles, techniques, procedures, and equipment to the design and production of various goods and services. **Design:** Knowledge of design techniques, tools, and principles involved in production of precision technical plans, blueprints, drawings, and models. **Mechanical Devices:** Knowledge of machines and tools, including their designs, uses, repair, and maintenance. **Physics:** Knowledge and prediction of physical principles and laws and their interrelationships and applications to understanding fluid, material, and atmospheric dynamics and mechanical, electrical, atomic, and subatomic structures and processes. **Computers and Electronics:** Knowledge of circuit boards, processors, chips, electronic equipment, and computer hardware and software, including applications and programming. **Production and Processing:** Knowledge of raw materials, production processes, quality control, costs, and other techniques for maximizing the effective manufacture and distribution of goods.

Mechanical Engineers

- Education/Training Required: Bachelor's degree
- Annual Earnings: $66,320
- Growth: 4.8%
- Annual Job Openings: 14,000
- Self-Employed: 3.0%
- Part-Time: 2.4%

Perform engineering duties in planning and designing tools, engines, machines, and other mechanically functioning equipment. Oversee installation, operation, maintenance, and repair of such equipment as centralized heat, gas, water, and steam systems. Read and interpret blueprints, technical drawings, schematics, and computer-generated reports. Confer with engineers and other personnel to implement operating procedures, resolve system malfunctions, and provide technical information. Research and analyze customer design proposals, specifications, manuals, and other data to evaluate the feasibility, cost, and maintenance requirements of designs or applications. Specify system components or direct modification of products to ensure conformance with engineering design and performance specifications. Research, design, evaluate, install, operate, and maintain mechanical products, equipment, systems, and processes to meet requirements, applying knowledge of engineering principles. Investigate equipment failures and difficulties to diagnose faulty operation and to make recommendations to maintenance crew. Assist drafters in developing the structural design of products, using drafting tools or

M

computer-assisted design/drafting equipment and software. Provide feedback to design engineers on customer problems and needs. Oversee installation, operation, maintenance, and repair to ensure that machines and equipment are installed and functioning according to specifications. Conduct research that tests and analyzes the feasibility, design, operation, and performance of equipment, components, and systems. Recommend design modifications to eliminate machine or system malfunctions. Develop and test models of alternate designs and processing methods to assess feasibility, operating condition effects, possible new applications, and necessity of modification. Develop, coordinate, and monitor all aspects of production, including selection of manufacturing methods, fabrication, and operation of product designs. Estimate costs and submit bids for engineering, construction, or extraction projects and prepare contract documents. Perform personnel functions, such as supervision of production workers, technicians, technologists, and other engineers and design of evaluation programs. Solicit new business and provide technical customer service. Establish and coordinate the maintenance and safety procedures, service schedule, and supply of materials required to maintain machines and equipment in the prescribed condition. **SKILLS—Science:** Using scientific rules and methods to solve problems. **Operations Analysis:** Analyzing needs and product requirements to create a design. **Complex Problem Solving:** Identifying complex problems and reviewing related information to develop and evaluate options and implement solutions. **Installation:** Installing equipment, machines, wiring, or programs to meet specifications. **Coordination:** Adjusting actions in relation to others' actions. **Mathematics:** Using mathematics to solve problems. **Judgment and Decision Making:** Considering the relative costs and benefits of potential actions to choose the most appropriate one. **Negotiation:** Bringing others together and trying to reconcile differences. **GOE—Interest Area:** 15. Scientific Research, Engineering, and Mathematics. **Work Group:** 15.07. Research and Design Engineering. **Other Jobs in This Work Group:** Aerospace Engineers; Biomedical Engineers; Chemical Engineers; Civil Engineers; Computer Hardware Engineers; Electrical Engineers; Electronics Engineers, Except Computer; Marine Architects; Marine Engineers; Materials Engineers; Nuclear Engineers. **PERSONALITY TYPE:** Realistic.

EDUCATION/TRAINING PROGRAM(S)— Mechanical Engineering. **RELATED KNOWLEDGE/COURSES—Design:** Knowledge of design techniques, tools, and principles involved in production of precision technical plans, blueprints, drawings, and models. **Engineering and Technology:** Knowledge of the practical application of engineering science and technology. This includes applying principles, techniques, procedures, and equipment to the design and production of various goods and services. **Mechanical Devices:** Knowledge of machines and tools, including their designs, uses, repair, and maintenance. **Production and Processing:** Knowledge of raw materials, production processes, quality control, costs, and other techniques for maximizing the effective manufacture and distribution of goods. **Administration and Management:** Knowledge of business and management principles involved in strategic planning, resource allocation, human resources modeling, leadership technique, production methods, and coordination of people and resources. **Physics:** Knowledge and prediction of physical principles and laws and their interrelationships and applications to understanding fluid, material, and atmospheric dynamics and mechanical, electrical, atomic, and subatomic structures and processes.

Mechanical Inspectors

- Education/Training Required: Long-term on-the-job training
- Annual Earnings: $28,410
- Growth: 4.7%
- Annual Job Openings: 87,000
- Self-Employed: 1.2%
- Part-Time: 5.0%

Inspect and test mechanical assemblies and systems, such as motors, vehicles, and transportation equipment, for defects and wear to ensure compliance with specifications. Tests and measures finished products, components, or assemblies for functioning, operation, accuracy, or assembly to verify adherence to functional specifications. Inspects materials, products, and work in progress for conformance to specifications and adjusts process or assembly equipment to meet standards. Starts and operates finished products for testing or inspection. Reads dials and meters to ensure that equipment is operating according to specifications.

Collects samples for testing and computes findings. Marks items for acceptance or rejection, records test results and inspection data, and compares findings with specifications to ensure conformance to standards. Discards or rejects products, materials, and equipment not meeting specifications. Reads and interprets materials such as work orders, inspection manuals, and blueprints to determine inspection and test procedures. Analyzes and interprets sample data. Installs and positions new or replacement parts, components, and instruments. Estimates and records operational data. Completes necessary procedures to satisfy licensing requirements and indicates concurrence with acceptance or rejection decisions. Confers with vendors and others regarding inspection results; recommends corrective procedures; and compiles reports of results, recommendations, and needed repairs. Cleans and maintains test equipment and instruments to ensure proper functioning. **SKILLS—Quality Control Analysis:** Conducting tests and inspections of products, services, or processes to evaluate quality or performance. **Science:** Using scientific rules and methods to solve problems. **Installation:** Installing equipment, machines, wiring, or programs to meet specifications. **Operation Monitoring:** Watching gauges, dials, or other indicators to make sure a machine is working properly. **Troubleshooting:** Determining causes of operating errors and deciding what to do about them. **Operation and Control:** Controlling operations of equipment or systems. **Equipment Maintenance:** Performing routine maintenance on equipment and determining when and what kind of maintenance is needed. **Repairing:** Repairing machines or systems by using the needed tools. **GOE—Interest Area:** 07. Government and Public Administration. **Work Group:** 07.03. Regulations Enforcement. **Other Jobs in This Work Group:** Agricultural Inspectors; Aviation Inspectors; Child Support, Missing Persons, and Unemployment Insurance Fraud Investigators; Environmental Compliance Inspectors; Equal Opportunity Representatives and Officers; Financial Examiners; Fire Inspectors; Fish and Game Wardens; Forest Fire Inspectors and Prevention Specialists; Government Property Inspectors and Investigators; Immigration and Customs Inspectors; Licensing Examiners and Inspectors; Marine Cargo Inspectors; Motor Vehicle Inspectors; Nuclear Monitoring Technicians; Occupational Health and Safety Specialists; Pressure Vessel Inspectors; Railroad Inspectors; Tax Examiners, Collectors, and Revenue Agents. **PERSONALITY TYPE:** Realistic.

EDUCATION/TRAINING PROGRAM(S)— Quality Control Technology/Technician. **RELATED KNOWLEDGE/COURSES—Mechanical Devices:** Knowledge of machines and tools, including their designs, uses, repair, and maintenance. **Design:** Knowledge of design techniques, tools, and principles involved in production of precision technical plans, blueprints, drawings, and models. **Engineering and Technology:** Knowledge of the practical application of engineering science and technology. This includes applying principles, techniques, procedures, and equipment to the design and production of various goods and services. **Production and Processing:** Knowledge of raw materials, production processes, quality control, costs, and other techniques for maximizing the effective manufacture and distribution of goods. **Public Safety and Security:** Knowledge of relevant equipment, policies, procedures, and strategies to promote effective local, state, or national security operations for the protection of people, data, property, and institutions. **Physics:** Knowledge and prediction of physical principles and laws and their interrelationships and applications to understanding fluid, material, and atmospheric dynamics and mechanical, electrical, atomic, and subatomic structures and processes.

Medical and Clinical Laboratory Technicians

- Education/Training Required: Associate degree
- Annual Earnings: $30,840
- Growth: 19.4%
- Annual Job Openings: 21,000
- Self-Employed: 1.6%
- Part-Time: 16.0%

Perform routine medical laboratory tests for the diagnosis, treatment, and prevention of disease. May work under the supervision of a medical technologist. Conduct chemical analyses of body fluids, such as blood and urine, using microscope or automatic analyzer to detect abnormalities or diseases, and enter findings into computer. Set up, adjust, maintain, and clean medical laboratory equipment. Analyze the results of tests and experiments to ensure conformity to specifications, using special mechanical and electrical devices. Analyze and record test data to issue reports that use charts, graphs, and narratives. Perform medical research to further control and cure disease. Conduct blood tests for transfusion purposes and perform blood counts. Obtain specimens, cultivating, isolating, and identifying microorganisms for analysis. Examine cells stained with dye to locate abnormalities. Collect blood or tissue samples from patients, observing principles of asepsis to obtain blood sample. Consult with a pathologist to determine a final diagnosis when abnormal cells are found. Inoculate fertilized eggs, broths, or other bacteriological media with organisms. Cut, stain, and mount tissue samples for examination by pathologists. Supervise and instruct other technicians and laboratory assistants. Prepare standard volumetric solutions and reagents to be combined with samples, following standardized formulas or experimental procedures. Prepare vaccines and serums by standard laboratory methods, testing for virus inactivity and sterility. Test raw materials, processes, and finished products to determine quality and quantity of materials or characteristics of a substance. **SKILLS—Equipment Maintenance:** Performing routine maintenance on equipment and determining when and what kind of maintenance is needed. **Science:** Using scientific rules and methods to solve problems. **Troubleshooting:** Determining causes of operating errors and deciding what to do about them. **Instructing:** Teaching others how to do something. **Monitoring:** Monitoring or assessing your performance or that of other individuals or organizations to make improvements or take corrective action. **Service Orientation:** Actively looking for ways to help people. **Operation Monitoring:** Watching gauges, dials, or other indicators to make sure a machine is working properly. **Quality Control Analysis:** Conducting tests and inspections of products, services, or processes to evaluate quality or performance. **Time Management:** Managing one's own time and the time of others. **GOE—Interest Area:** 08. Health Science. **Work Group:** 08.06. Medical Technology. **Other Jobs in This Work Group:** Biological Technicians; Cardiovascular Technologists and Technicians; Diagnostic Medical Sonographers; Medical and Clinical Laboratory Technologists; Medical Equipment Preparers; Medical Records and Health Information Technicians; Nuclear Medicine Technologists; Opticians, Dispensing; Orthotists and Prosthetists; Radiologic Technicians; Radiologic Technologists. **PERSONALITY TYPE:** Realistic.

EDUCATION/TRAINING PROGRAM(S)— Blood Bank Technology Specialist; Clinical/Medical Laboratory Assistant; Clinical/Medical Laboratory Technician; Hematology Technology/Technician; Histologic Technician. **RELATED KNOWLEDGE/ COURSES—Medicine and Dentistry:** Knowledge of the information and techniques needed to diagnose and treat human injuries, diseases, and deformities. This includes symptoms, treatment alternatives, drug properties and interactions, and preventive health-care measures. **Therapy and Counseling:** Knowledge of principles, methods, and procedures for diagnosis, treatment, and rehabilitation of physical and mental dysfunctions and for career counseling and guidance. **Clerical Practices:** Knowledge of administrative and clerical procedures and systems such as word processing, managing files and records, stenography and transcription, designing forms, and other office procedures and terminology. **Biology:** Knowledge of plant and animal organisms and their tissues, cells, functions, interdependencies, and interactions with each other and the environment. **Chemistry:** Knowledge of the chemical composition, structure, and properties of substances and of the chemical processes and transformations that they undergo. This includes uses of chemicals and their danger signs, production techniques, and disposal methods. **Customer and Personal Service:** Knowledge of principles and processes for providing customer and personal services. This includes customer needs assessment, meeting quality standards for services, and evaluation of customer satisfaction.

Medical and Clinical Laboratory Technologists

◉ Education/Training Required: Bachelor's degree
◉ Annual Earnings: $45,730
◉ Growth: 19.3%
◉ Annual Job Openings: 21,000
◉ Self-Employed: 1.6%
◉ Part-Time: 16.0%

Perform complex medical laboratory tests for diagnosis, treatment, and prevention of disease. May train or supervise staff. Analyze laboratory findings to check the accuracy of the results. Conduct chemical analysis of body fluids, including blood, urine, and spinal fluid, to determine presence of normal and abnormal components. Operate, calibrate, and maintain equipment used in quantitative and qualitative analysis, such as spectrophotometers, calorimeters, flame photometers, and computer-controlled analyzers. Enter data from analysis of medical tests and clinical results into computer for storage. Analyze samples of biological material for chemical content or reaction. Establish and monitor programs to ensure the accuracy of laboratory results. Set up, clean, and maintain laboratory equipment. Provide technical information about test results to physicians, family members, and researchers. Supervise, train, and direct lab assistants, medical and clinical laboratory technicians and technologists, and other medical laboratory workers engaged in laboratory testing. Develop, standardize, evaluate, and modify procedures, techniques, and tests used in the analysis of specimens and in medical laboratory experiments. Cultivate, isolate, and assist in identifying microbial organisms and perform various tests on these microorganisms. Study blood samples to determine the number of cells and their morphology, as well as the blood group, type, and compatibility for transfusion purposes, using microscopic technique. Obtain, cut, stain, and mount biological material on slides for microscopic study and diagnosis, following standard laboratory procedures. Select and prepare specimen and media for cell culture, using aseptic technique and knowledge of medium components and cell requirements. Conduct medical research under direction of microbiologist or biochemist. Harvest cell cultures at optimum time based on knowledge of cell cycle differences and culture conditions. **SKILLS—Equipment Maintenance:** Performing routine maintenance on equipment and determining when and what kind of maintenance is needed. **Operation Monitoring:** Watching gauges, dials, or other indicators to make sure a machine is working properly. **Quality Control Analysis:** Conducting tests and inspections of products, services, or processes to evaluate quality or performance. **Science:** Using scientific rules and methods to solve problems. **Troubleshooting:** Determining causes of operating errors and deciding what to do about them. **Repairing:** Repairing machines or systems by using the needed tools. **Operation and Control:** Controlling operations of equipment or systems. **Instructing:** Teaching others how to do something. **GOE—Interest Area:** 08. Health Science. **Work Group:** 08.06. Medical Technology. **Other Jobs in This Work Group:** Biological Technicians; Cardiovascular Technologists and Technicians; Diagnostic Medical Sonographers; Medical and Clinical Laboratory Technicians; Medical Equipment Preparers; Medical Records and Health Information Technicians; Nuclear Medicine Technologists; Opticians, Dispensing; Orthotists and Prosthetists; Radiologic Technicians; Radiologic Technologists. **PERSONALITY TYPE:** Investigative.

EDUCATION/TRAINING PROGRAM(S)—Clinical Laboratory Science/Medical Technology/Technologist; Clinical/Medical Laboratory Science and Allied Professions, Other; Cytogenetics/Genetics/Clinical Genetics Technology/Technologist; Cytotechnology/Cytotechnologist; Histologic Technology/Histotechnologist; Renal/Dialysis Technologist/Technician. **RELATED KNOWLEDGE/COURSES—Biology:** Knowledge of plant and animal organisms and their tissues, cells, functions, interdependencies, and interactions with each other and the environment. **Chemistry:** Knowledge of the chemical composition, structure, and properties of substances and of the chemical processes and transformations that they undergo. This includes uses of chemicals and their danger signs, production techniques, and disposal methods. **Public Safety and Security:** Knowledge of relevant equipment, policies, procedures, and strategies to promote effective local, state, or national security operations for the protection of people, data, property, and institutions. **Computers and Electronics:** Knowledge of circuit boards, processors, chips, electronic equipment, and computer hardware and software, including applications and programming. **Customer and Personal Service:** Knowledge of principles and processes for providing customer and personal services. This includes customer needs assessment, meeting quality standards for services, and evaluation of customer satisfaction. **Mathematics:** Knowledge of arithmetic, algebra, geometry, calculus, and statistics and their applications.

M

Medical and Health Services Managers

- Education/Training Required: Work experience plus degree
- Annual Earnings: $67,430
- Growth: 29.3%
- Annual Job Openings: 33,000
- Self-Employed: 5.3%
- Part-Time: 5.4%

Plan, direct, or coordinate medicine and health services in hospitals, clinics, managed care organizations, public health agencies, or similar organizations. Direct, supervise, and evaluate work activities of medical, nursing, technical, clerical, service, maintenance, and other personnel. Establish objectives and evaluative or operational criteria for units they manage. Direct or conduct recruitment, hiring, and training of personnel. Develop and maintain computerized record management systems to store and process data, such as personnel activities and information, and to produce reports. Develop and implement organizational policies and procedures for the facility or medical unit. Conduct and administer fiscal operations, including accounting, planning budgets, authorizing expenditures, establishing rates for services, and coordinating financial reporting. Establish work schedules and assignments for staff according to workload, space, and equipment availability. Maintain communication between governing boards, medical staff, and department heads by attending board meetings and coordinating interdepartmental functioning. Monitor the use of diagnostic services, inpatient beds, facilities, and staff to ensure effective use of resources and assess the need for additional staff, equipment, and services. Maintain awareness of advances in medicine, computerized diagnostic and treatment equipment, data processing technology, government regulations, health insurance changes, and financing options. Manage change in integrated health-care delivery systems, such as work restructuring, technological innovations, and shifts in the focus of care. Prepare activity reports to inform management of the status and implementation plans of programs, services, and quality initiatives. Plan, implement, and administer programs and services in a health-care or medical facility, including personnel administration, training, and coordination of medical, nursing, and physical plant staff. Consult with medical, business, and community groups to discuss service problems, respond to community needs, enhance public relations, coordinate activities and plans, and promote health programs. Inspect facilities and recommend building or equipment modifications to ensure emergency readiness and compliance to access, safety, and sanitation regulations. **SKILLS—Management of Personnel Resources:** Motivating, developing, and directing people as they work, identifying the best people for the job. **Persuasion:** Persuading others to change their minds or behavior. **Service Orientation:** Actively looking for ways to help people. **Management of Material Resources:** Obtaining and seeing to the appropriate use of equipment, facilities, and materials needed to do certain work. **Learning Strategies:** Selecting and using training/instructional methods and procedures appropriate for the situation when learning or teaching new things. **Social Perceptiveness:** Being aware of others' reactions and understanding why they react as they do. **Monitoring:** Monitoring or assessing your performance or that of other individuals or organizations to make improvements or take corrective action. **Management of Financial Resources:** Determining how money will be spent to get the work done and accounting for these expenditures. **GOE—Interest Area:** 08. Health Science. **Work Group:** 08.01. Managerial Work in Medical and Health Services. **Other Jobs in This Work Group:** Coroners; First-Line Supervisors and Manager/Supervisors—Animal Care Workers, Except Livestock. **PERSONALITY TYPE:** Enterprising.

EDUCATION/TRAINING PROGRAM(S)— Community Health and Preventive Medicine; Health and Medical Administrative Services, Other; Health Information/Medical Records Administration/Administrator; Health Services Administration; Health Unit Manager/Ward Supervisor; Health/Health Care Administration/Management; Hospital and Health Care Facilities Administration/Management; Medical Staff Services Technology/Technician; Nursing Administration (MSN, MS, PhD); Public Health, General (MPH, DPH). **RELATED KNOWLEDGE/COURSES—Therapy and Counseling:** Knowledge of principles, methods, and procedures for diagnosis, treatment, and rehabilitation of physical and mental dysfunctions and for career counseling and guidance. **Customer and Personal Service:** Knowledge of principles and processes for providing customer and personal services. This includes customer needs assessment, meeting quality standards for services, and evaluation of customer satisfaction. **Medicine and Dentistry:** Knowledge of the information and techniques needed to diagnose and treat human injuries, diseases, and deformities. This includes symptoms, treatment alternatives, drug properties and interactions, and preventive health-care measures. **Psychology:** Knowledge of human behavior and performance; individual differences in ability, personality, and interests; learning and motivation; psychological research methods; and the assessment and treatment of behavioral and affective disorders. **Personnel and Human Resources:** Knowledge of principles and procedures for personnel recruitment, selection, training, compensation and benefits, labor relations and negotiation, and personnel information systems. **Education and Training:** Knowledge of principles and methods for curriculum and training design, teaching and instruction for individuals and groups, and the measurement of training effects.

Medical and Public Health Social Workers

- ◎ Education/Training Required: Bachelor's degree
- ◎ Annual Earnings: $40,080
- ◎ Growth: 28.6%
- ◎ Annual Job Openings: 18,000
- ◎ Self-Employed: 1.7%
- ◎ Part-Time: 8.7%

Provide persons, families, or vulnerable populations with the psychosocial support needed to cope with chronic, acute, or terminal illnesses, such as Alzheimer's, cancer, or AIDS. Services include advising family caregivers, providing patient education and counseling, and making necessary referrals for other social services. Collaborate with other professionals to evaluate patients' medical or physical condition and to assess client needs. Investigate child abuse or neglect cases and take authorized protective action when necessary. Refer patient, client, or family to community resources to assist in recovery from mental or physical illness and to provide access to services such as financial assistance, legal aid, housing, job placement, or education. Counsel clients and patients in individual and group sessions to help them overcome dependencies, recover from illness, and adjust to life. Organize support groups or counsel family members to assist them in understanding, dealing with, and supporting the client or patient. Advocate for clients or patients to resolve crises. Identify environmental impediments to client or patient progress through interviews and review of patient records. Utilize consultation data and social work experience to plan and coordinate client or patient care and rehabilitation, following through to ensure service efficacy. Modify treatment plans to comply with changes in clients' status. Monitor, evaluate, and record client progress according to measurable goals described in treatment and care plan. Supervise and direct other workers providing services to clients or patients. Develop or advise on social policy and assist in community development. Oversee Medicaid- and Medicare-related paperwork and record keeping in hospitals. Conduct social research to advance knowledge in the social work field. Plan and conduct programs to combat social problems, prevent substance abuse, or improve community health and counseling services. **SKILLS—Social Perceptiveness:** Being aware of others' reactions and understanding why they react as they do. **Service Orientation:** Actively looking for ways to help people. **Negotiation:** Bringing others together and trying to reconcile differences. **Coordination:** Adjusting actions in relation to others' actions. **Active Listening:** Giving full attention to what other people are saying, taking time to understand the points being made, asking questions as appropriate, and not interrupting at inappropriate times. **Learning Strategies:** Selecting and using training/instructional methods and procedures appropriate for the situation when learning or teaching new things. **Critical Thinking:** Using logic and reasoning to identify the strengths and weaknesses of alternative solutions, conclusions, or approaches to problems. **Speaking:** Talking to others to convey information effectively. **Instructing:** Teaching others how to do something. **GOE—Interest Area:** 10. Human Service. **Work Group:** 10.01. Counseling and Social Work. **Other Jobs in This Work Group:** Child, Family, and School Social Workers; Clinical Psychologists; Counseling Psychologists; Marriage and Family Therapists; Mental Health and Substance Abuse Social Workers; Mental Health Counselors; Probation Officers and Correctional Treatment Specialists; Rehabilitation Counselors; Residential Advisors; Social and Human Service Assistants; Substance Abuse and Behavioral Disorder Counselors. **PERSONALITY TYPE:** Social.

M

EDUCATION/TRAINING PROGRAM(S)—Clinical/Medical Social Work. **RELATED KNOWLEDGE/COURSES—Psychology:** Knowledge of human behavior and performance; individual differences in ability, personality, and interests; learning and motivation; psychological research methods; and the assessment and treatment of behavioral and affective disorders. **Therapy and Counseling:** Knowledge of principles, methods, and procedures for diagnosis, treatment, and rehabilitation of physical and mental dysfunctions and for career counseling and guidance. **Customer and Personal Service:** Knowledge of principles and processes for providing customer and personal services. This includes customer needs assessment, meeting quality standards for services, and evaluation of customer satisfaction. **Sociology and Anthropology:** Knowledge of group behavior and dynamics, societal trends and influences, human migrations, ethnicity, and cultures and their history and origins. **Philosophy and Theology:** Knowledge of different philosophical systems and religions. This includes their basic principles, values, ethics, ways of thinking, customs, and practices and their impact on human culture. **Medicine and Dentistry:** Knowledge of the information and techniques needed to diagnose and treat human injuries, diseases, and deformities. This includes symptoms, treatment alternatives, drug properties and interactions, and preventive health-care measures.

Medical Assistants

◎ Education/Training Required: Moderate-term on-the-job training

◎ Annual Earnings: $24,610

◎ Growth: 58.9%

◎ Annual Job Openings: 78,000

◎ Self-Employed: 2.3%

◎ Part-Time: 25.3%

Perform administrative and certain clinical duties under the direction of physician. Administrative duties may include scheduling appointments, maintaining medical records, billing, and coding for insurance purposes. Clinical duties may include taking and recording vital signs and medical histories, preparing patients for examination, drawing blood, and administering medications as directed by physi-

cian. Interview patients to obtain medical information and measure their vital signs, weight, and height. Show patients to examination rooms and prepare them for the physician. Record patients' medical history, vital statistics, and information such as test results in medical records. Prepare and administer medications as directed by a physician. Collect blood, tissue, or other laboratory specimens; log the specimens; and prepare them for testing. Explain treatment procedures, medications, diets, and physicians' instructions to patients. Help physicians examine and treat patients, handing them instruments and materials or performing such tasks as giving injections and removing sutures. Authorize drug refills and provide prescription information to pharmacies. Prepare treatment rooms for patient examinations, keeping the rooms neat and clean. Clean and sterilize instruments and dispose of contaminated supplies. Schedule appointments for patients. Change dressings on wounds. Greet and log in patients arriving at office or clinic. Contact medical facilities or departments to schedule patients for tests and/or admission. Perform general office duties such as answering telephones, taking dictation, and completing insurance forms. Inventory and order medical, lab, and office supplies and equipment. Perform routine laboratory tests and sample analyses. Set up medical laboratory equipment. Keep financial records and perform other bookkeeping duties, such as handling credit and collections and mailing monthly statements to patients. Operate X-ray, electrocardiogram (EKG), and other equipment to administer routine diagnostic tests. **SKILLS—Social Perceptiveness:** Being aware of others' reactions and understanding why they react as they do. **Service Orientation:** Actively looking for ways to help people. **Instructing:** Teaching others how to do something. **Active Listening:** Giving full attention to what other people are saying, taking time to understand the points being made, asking questions as appropriate, and not interrupting at inappropriate times. **Learning Strategies:** Selecting and using training/instructional methods and procedures appropriate for the situation when learning or teaching new things. **Negotiation:** Bringing others together and trying to reconcile differences. **Troubleshooting:** Determining causes of operating errors and deciding what to do about them. **Reading Comprehension:** Understanding written sentences and paragraphs in work-related documents. **Operation Monitoring:** Watching gauges, dials, or other indicators to make sure a machine is working properly. **GOE—Interest Area:** 08. Health

Science. **Work Group:** 08.02. Medicine and Surgery. **Other Jobs in This Work Group:** Anesthesiologists; Family and General Practitioners; Internists, General; Medical Transcriptionists; Obstetricians and Gynecologists; Pediatricians, General; Pharmacists; Pharmacy Aides; Pharmacy Technicians; Physician Assistants; Psychiatrists; Registered Nurses; Surgeons; Surgical Technologists. **PERSONALITY TYPE:** Social.

EDUCATION/TRAINING PROGRAM(S)— Allied Health and Medical Assisting Services, Other; Anesthesiologist Assistant; Chiropractic Assistant/ Technician; Medical Administrative/Executive Assistant and Medical Secretary; Medical Insurance Coding Specialist/Coder; Medical Office Assistant/Specialist; Medical Office Management/Administration; Medical Reception/Receptionist; Medical/Clinical Assistant; Opthalmic Technician/Technologist; Optomeric Technician/Assistant; Orthoptics/Orthoptist. **RELATED KNOWLEDGE/COURSES—Medicine and Dentistry:** Knowledge of the information and techniques needed to diagnose and treat human injuries, diseases, and deformities. This includes symptoms, treatment alternatives, drug properties and interactions, and preventive health-care measures. **Customer and Personal Service:** Knowledge of principles and processes for providing customer and personal services. This includes customer needs assessment, meeting quality standards for services, and evaluation of customer satisfaction. **Clerical Practices:** Knowledge of administrative and clerical procedures and systems such as word processing, managing files and records, stenography and transcription, designing forms, and other office procedures and terminology. **Psychology:** Knowledge of human behavior and performance; individual differences in ability, personality, and interests; learning and motivation; psychological research methods; and the assessment and treatment of behavioral and affective disorders. **Therapy and Counseling:** Knowledge of principles, methods, and procedures for diagnosis, treatment, and rehabilitation of physical and mental dysfunctions and for career counseling and guidance. **English Language:** Knowledge of the structure and content of the English language, including the meaning and spelling of words, rules of composition, and grammar.

Medical Equipment Repairers

- Education/Training Required: Moderate-term on-the-job training
- Annual Earnings: $37,220
- Growth: 14.8%
- Annual Job Openings: 4,000
- Self-Employed: 23.2%
- Part-Time: 10.1%

Test, adjust, or repair biomedical or electromedical equipment. Inspect and test malfunctioning medical and related equipment, following manufacturers' specifications and using test and analysis instruments. Examine medical equipment and facility's structural environment and check for proper use of equipment to protect patients and staff from electrical or mechanical hazards and to ensure compliance with safety regulations. Disassemble malfunctioning equipment and remove, repair, and replace defective parts such as motors, clutches, or transformers. Keep records of maintenance, repair, and required updates of equipment. Perform preventive maintenance or service such as cleaning, lubricating, and adjusting equipment. Test and calibrate components and equipment, following manufacturers' manuals and troubleshooting techniques and using hand tools, power tools, and measuring devices. Explain and demonstrate correct operation and preventive maintenance of medical equipment to personnel. Study technical manuals and attend training sessions provided by equipment manufacturers to maintain current knowledge. Plan and carry out work assignments, using blueprints, schematic drawings, technical manuals, wiring diagrams, and liquid and air flow sheets, while following prescribed regulations, directives, and other instructions as required. Solder loose connections, using soldering iron. Test, evaluate, and classify excess or in-use medial equipment and determine serviceability, condition, and disposition in accordance with regulations. Research catalogs and repair part lists to locate sources for repair parts, requisitioning parts and recording their receipt. Evaluate technical specifications to identify equipment and systems best suited for intended use and possible purchase based on specifications, user needs, and technical requirements. Contribute expertise to develop medical maintenance standard operating procedures. Compute

M

power and space requirements for installing medical, dental, or related equipment and install units to manufacturers' specifications. Supervise and advise subordinate personnel. **SKILLS—Repairing:** Repairing machines or systems by using the needed tools. **Installation:** Installing equipment, machines, wiring, or programs to meet specifications. **Equipment Maintenance:** Performing routine maintenance on equipment and determining when and what kind of maintenance is needed. **Troubleshooting:** Determining causes of operating errors and deciding what to do about them. **Systems Analysis:** Determining how a system should work and how changes in conditions, operations, and the environment will affect outcomes. **Service Orientation:** Actively looking for ways to help people. **Operation Monitoring:** Watching gauges, dials, or other indicators to make sure a machine is working properly. **Instructing:** Teaching others how to do something. **GOE—Interest Area:** 13. Manufacturing. **Work Group:** 13.15. Medical and Technical Equipment Repair. **Other Jobs in This Work Group:** Camera and Photographic Equipment Repairers; Watch Repairers. **PERSONALITY TYPE:** Realistic.

EDUCATION/TRAINING PROGRAM(S)—Biomedical Technology/Technician. **RELATED KNOWLEDGE/COURSES—Computers and Electronics:** Knowledge of circuit boards, processors, chips, electronic equipment, and computer hardware and software, including applications and programming. **Mechanical Devices:** Knowledge of machines and tools, including their designs, uses, repair, and maintenance. **Engineering and Technology:** Knowledge of the practical application of engineering science and technology. This includes applying principles, techniques, procedures, and equipment to the design and production of various goods and services. **Customer and Personal Service:** Knowledge of principles and processes for providing customer and personal services. This includes customer needs assessment, meeting quality standards for services, and evaluation of customer satisfaction. **Physics:** Knowledge and prediction of physical principles and laws and their interrelationships and applications to understanding fluid, material, and atmospheric dynamics and mechanical, electrical, atomic, and subatomic structures and processes. **Chemistry:** Knowledge of the chemical composition, structure, and properties of substances and of the chemical processes and transformations that they undergo. This includes uses of chemicals and their danger signs, production techniques, and disposal

methods. **Telecommunications:** Knowledge of transmission, broadcasting, switching, control, and operation of telecommunications systems.

Medical Records and Health Information Technicians

- Education/Training Required: Associate degree
- Annual Earnings: $25,590
- Growth: 46.8%
- Annual Job Openings: 24,000
- Self-Employed: 1.1%
- Part-Time: 17.6%

Compile, process, and maintain medical records of hospital and clinic patients in a manner consistent with medical, administrative, ethical, legal, and regulatory requirements of the health-care system. Process, maintain, compile, and report patient information for health requirements and standards. Protect the security of medical records to ensure that confidentiality is maintained. Process patient admission and discharge documents. Review records for completeness, accuracy, and compliance with regulations. Compile and maintain patients' medical records to document condition and treatment and to provide data for research or cost control and care improvement efforts. Enter data such as demographic characteristics, history and extent of disease, diagnostic procedures, and treatment into computer. Release information to persons and agencies according to regulations. Plan, develop, maintain, and operate a variety of health record indexes and storage and retrieval systems to collect, classify, store, and analyze information. Manage the department and supervise clerical workers, directing and controlling activities of personnel in the medical records department. Transcribe medical reports. Identify, compile, abstract, and code patient data, using standard classification systems. Resolve/clarify codes and diagnoses with conflicting, missing, or unclear information by consulting with doctors or others to get additional information and by participating in the coding team's regular meetings. Train medical records staff. Assign the patient to one of several hundred "diagnosis-related groups," or DRGs, using appropriate computer software. Post medical insurance billings. Process and prepare business and government forms. Contact discharged patients, their families, and physicians to maintain registry with follow-up information, such as quality of life and length of survival of cancer patients. Prepare statistical reports, narrative reports, and graphic presentations of information such as tumor registry data for use by hospital staff, researchers, and other users. Consult classification manuals to locate information about disease processes. Compile medical care and census data for statistical reports on diseases treated, surgery performed, and use of hospital beds. Develop in-service educational materials. **SKILLS—Instructing:** Teaching others how to do something. **Systems Evaluation:** Identifying measures or indicators of system performance and the actions needed to improve or correct performance relative to the goals of the system. **Active Listening:** Giving full attention to what other people are saying, taking time to understand the points being made, asking questions as appropriate, and not interrupting at inappropriate times. **Learning Strategies:** Selecting and using training/instructional methods and procedures appropriate for the situation when learning or teaching new things. **Time Management:** Managing one's own time and the time of others. **Service Orientation:** Actively looking for ways to help people. **Critical Thinking:** Using logic and reasoning to identify the strengths and weaknesses of alternative solutions, conclusions, or approaches to problems. **Reading Comprehension:** Understanding written sentences and paragraphs in work-related documents. **Social Perceptiveness:** Being aware of others' reactions and understanding why they react as they do. **GOE— Interest Area:** 08. Health Science. **Work Group:** 08.06. Medical Technology. **Other Jobs in This Work Group:** Biological Technicians; Cardiovascular Technologists and Technicians; Diagnostic Medical Sonographers; Medical and Clinical Laboratory Technicians; Medical and Clinical Laboratory Technologists; Medical Equipment Preparers; Nuclear Medicine Technologists; Opticians, Dispensing; Orthotists and Prosthetists; Radiologic Technicians; Radiologic Technologists. **PERSONALITY TYPE:** Conventional.

EDUCATION/TRAINING PROGRAM(S)— Health Information/Medical Records Technology/ Technician; Medical Insurance Coding Specialist/Coder. **RELATED KNOWLEDGE/ COURSES—Clerical Practices:** Knowledge of administrative and clerical procedures and systems

such as word processing, managing files and records, stenography and transcription, designing forms, and other office procedures and terminology. **Customer and Personal Service:** Knowledge of principles and processes for providing customer and personal services. This includes customer needs assessment, meeting quality standards for services, and evaluation of customer satisfaction. **Medicine and Dentistry:** Knowledge of the information and techniques needed to diagnose and treat human injuries, diseases, and deformities. This includes symptoms, treatment alternatives, drug properties and interactions, and preventive health-care measures. **Administration and Management:** Knowledge of business and management principles involved in strategic planning, resource allocation, human resources modeling, leadership technique, production methods, and coordination of people and resources. **Personnel and Human Resources:** Knowledge of principles and procedures for personnel recruitment, selection, training, compensation and benefits, labor relations and negotiation, and personnel information systems. **Computers and Electronics:** Knowledge of circuit boards, processors, chips, electronic equipment, and computer hardware and software, including applications and programming.

Medical Scientists, Except Epidemiologists

◎ Education/Training Required: Doctoral degree
◎ Annual Earnings: $61,320
◎ Growth: 26.9%
◎ Annual Job Openings: 6,000
◎ Self-Employed: 1.7%
◎ Part-Time: 8.8%

Conduct research dealing with the understanding of human diseases and the improvement of human health. Engage in clinical investigation or other research, production, technical writing, or related activities. Conduct research to develop methodologies, instrumentation, and procedures for medical application, analyzing data and presenting findings. Evaluate effects of drugs, gases, pesticides, parasites, and microorganisms at various levels. Follow strict safety procedures when handling toxic materials to avoid contamination. Investigate cause, progress, life cycle, or mode of transmission of diseases or parasites. Plan and direct studies to investigate human or animal disease, preventive methods, and treatments for disease. Prepare and analyze organ, tissue, and cell samples to identify toxicity, bacteria, or microorganisms or to study cell structure. Standardize drug dosages, methods of immunization, and procedures for manufacture of drugs and medicinal compounds. Confer with health department, industry personnel, physicians, and others to develop health safety standards and public health improvement programs. Study animal and human health and physiological processes. Consult with and advise physicians, educators, researchers, and others regarding medical applications of physics, biology, and chemistry. Teach principles of medicine and medical and laboratory procedures to physicians, residents, students, and technicians. Use equipment such as atomic absorption spectrometers, electron microscopes, flow cytometers, and chromatography systems. **SKILLS—Instructing:** Teaching others how to do something. **Science:** Using scientific rules and methods to solve problems. **Active Learning:** Understanding the implications of new information for both current and future problem-solving and decision-making. **Systems Analysis:** Determining how a system should work and how changes in conditions, operations, and the environment will affect outcomes. **Systems Evaluation:** Identifying measures or indicators of system performance and the actions needed to improve or correct performance relative to the goals of the system. **Writing:** Communicating effectively in writing as appropriate for the needs of the audience. **Reading Comprehension:** Understanding written sentences and paragraphs in work-related documents. **Learning Strategies:** Selecting and using training/instructional methods and procedures appropriate for the situation when learning or teaching new things. **Service Orientation:** Actively looking for ways to help people. **GOE—Interest Area:** 15. Scientific Research, Engineering, and Mathematics. **Work Group:** 15.03. Life Sciences. **Other Jobs in This Work Group:** Biochemists; Biologists; Biophysicists; Environmental Scientists and Specialists, Including Health; Epidemiologists; Microbiologists. **PERSONALITY TYPE:** Investigative.

EDUCATION/TRAINING PROGRAM(S)— Anatomy; Biochemistry; Biomedical Sciences, General; Biophysics; Biostatistics; Cardiovascular Science; Cell Physiology; Cell/Cellular Biology and Histology; Endocrinology; Environmental Toxicology; Epidemiology; Exercise Physiology; Human/Medical Genetics;

Immunology; Medical Microbiology and Bacteriology; Medical Scientist (MS, PhD); Molecular Biology; Molecular Pharmacology; Molecular Physiology; Molecular Toxicology; Neurobiology and Neurophysiology; Neuropharmacology; Oncology and Cancer Biology; Pathology/Experimental Pathology; Pharmacology; Pharmacology and Toxicology; Pharmacology and Toxicology, Other; Physiology, General; Physiology, Pathology, and Related Sciences, Other; Reproductive Biology; Toxicology; Vision Science/Physiological Optics. **RELATED KNOWLEDGE/COURSES— Biology:** Knowledge of plant and animal organisms and their tissues, cells, functions, interdependencies, and interactions with each other and the environment. **Medicine and Dentistry:** Knowledge of the information and techniques needed to diagnose and treat human injuries, diseases, and deformities. This includes symptoms, treatment alternatives, drug properties and interactions, and preventive health-care measures. **Chemistry:** Knowledge of the chemical composition, structure, and properties of substances and of the chemical processes and transformations that they undergo. This includes uses of chemicals and their danger signs, production techniques, and disposal methods. **Mathematics:** Knowledge of arithmetic, algebra, geometry, calculus, and statistics and their applications. **Education and Training:** Knowledge of principles and methods for curriculum and training design, teaching and instruction for individuals and groups, and the measurement of training effects. **Communications and Media:** Knowledge of media production, communication, and dissemination techniques and methods. This includes alternative ways to inform and entertain via written, oral, and visual media.

Medical Secretaries

- Education/Training Required: Postsecondary vocational training
- Annual Earnings: $26,540
- Growth: 17.2%
- Annual Job Openings: 50,000
- Self-Employed: 1.6%
- Part-Time: 17.5%

Perform secretarial duties, utilizing specific knowledge of medical terminology and hospital, clinic, or laboratory procedures. Duties include scheduling

appointments; billing patients; and compiling and recording medical charts, reports, and correspondence. Schedule and confirm patient diagnostic appointments, surgeries, and medical consultations. Compile and record medical charts, reports, and correspondence, using typewriter or personal computer. Answer telephones and direct calls to appropriate staff. Receive and route messages and documents such as laboratory results to appropriate staff. Greet visitors, ascertain purpose of visit, and direct them to appropriate staff. Interview patients in order to complete documents, case histories, and forms such as intake and insurance forms. Maintain medical records, technical library, and correspondence files. Operate office equipment such as voice mail messaging systems and use word-processing, spreadsheet, and other software applications to prepare reports, invoices, financial statements, letters, case histories, and medical records. Transmit correspondence and medical records by mail, e-mail, or fax. Perform various clerical and administrative functions, such as ordering and maintaining an inventory of supplies. Arrange hospital admissions for patients. Transcribe recorded messages and practitioners' diagnoses and recommendations into patients' medical records. Perform bookkeeping duties, such as credits and collections, preparing and sending financial statements and bills, and keeping financial records. Complete insurance and other claim forms. Prepare correspondence and assist physicians or medical scientists with preparation of reports, speeches, articles, and conference proceedings. **SKILLS—Social Perceptiveness:** Being aware of others' reactions and understanding why they react as they do. **Active Listening:** Giving full attention to what other people are saying, taking time to understand the points being made, asking questions as appropriate, and not interrupting at inappropriate times. **Instructing:** Teaching others how to do something. **Writing:** Communicating effectively in writing as appropriate for the needs of the audience. **Management of Personnel Resources:** Motivating, developing, and directing people as they work, identifying the best people for the job. **Time Management:** Managing one's own time and the time of others. **Reading Comprehension:** Understanding written sentences and paragraphs in work-related documents. **Management of Material Resources:** Obtaining and seeing to the appropriate use of equipment, facilities, and materials needed to do certain work. **GOE— Interest Area:** 04. Business and Administration. **Work Group:** 04.04. Secretarial Support. **Other Jobs in This**

Work Group: Executive Secretaries and Administrative Assistants; Legal Secretaries; Secretaries, Except Legal, Medical, and Executive. **PERSONALITY TYPE:** Conventional.

EDUCATION/TRAINING PROGRAM(S)—Medical Administrative/Executive Assistant and Medical Secretary; Medical Insurance Specialist/Medical Biller; Medical Office Assistant/Specialist. **RELATED KNOWLEDGE/COURSES—Customer and Personal Service:** Knowledge of principles and processes for providing customer and personal services. This includes customer needs assessment, meeting quality standards for services, and evaluation of customer satisfaction. **Clerical Practices:** Knowledge of administrative and clerical procedures and systems such as word processing, managing files and records, stenography and transcription, designing forms, and other office procedures and terminology. **Telecommunications:** Knowledge of transmission, broadcasting, switching, control, and operation of telecommunications systems. **Computers and Electronics:** Knowledge of circuit boards, processors, chips, electronic equipment, and computer hardware and software, including applications and programming. **English Language:** Knowledge of the structure and content of the English language, including the meaning and spelling of words, rules of composition, and grammar. **Communications and Media:** Knowledge of media production, communication, and dissemination techniques and methods. This includes alternative ways to inform and entertain via written, oral, and visual media.

Medical Transcriptionists

- Education/Training Required: Associate degree
- Annual Earnings: $28,380
- Growth: 22.6%
- Annual Job Openings: 18,000
- Self-Employed: 2.3%
- Part-Time: 25.3%

Use transcribing machines with headset and foot pedal to listen to recordings of physicians and other health-care professionals dictating a variety of medical reports, such as emergency room visits, diagnostic imaging studies, operations, chart reviews, and final summaries. Transcribe dictated reports and translate medical jargon and abbreviations into their expanded forms. Edit as necessary and return reports in either printed or electronic form to the dictator for review and signature or correction. Decide which information should be included or excluded in reports. Distinguish between homonyms and recognize inconsistencies and mistakes in medical terms, referring to dictionaries; drug references; and other sources on anatomy, physiology, and medicine. Identify mistakes in reports and check with doctors to obtain the correct information. Perform data entry and data retrieval services, providing data for inclusion in medical records and for transmission to physicians. Produce medical reports, correspondence, records, patient-care information, statistics, medical research, and administrative material. Return dictated reports in printed or electronic form for physicians' review, signature, and corrections and for inclusion in patients' medical records. Review and edit transcribed reports or dictated material for spelling, grammar, clarity, consistency, and proper medical terminology. Take dictation, using either shorthand or a stenotype machine or using headsets and transcribing machines; then convert dictated materials or rough notes to written form. Transcribe dictation for a variety of medical reports, such as patient histories, physical examinations, emergency room visits, operations, chart reviews, consultation, and/or discharge summaries. Translate medical jargon and abbreviations into their expanded forms to ensure the accuracy of patient and health-care facility records. Answer inquiries concerning the progress of medical cases within the limits of confidentiality laws. Perform a variety of clerical and office tasks, such as handling incoming and outgoing mail, completing and submitting insurance claims, typing, filing, and operating office machines. Receive patients, schedule appointments, and maintain patient records. Set up and maintain medical files and databases, including records such as X-ray, lab, and procedure reports; medical histories; diagnostic workups; admission and discharge summaries; and clinical resumes. Receive and screen telephone calls and visitors. **SKILLS**—No data available. **GOE—Interest Area:** 08. Health Science. **Work Group:** 08.02. Medicine and Surgery. **Other Jobs in This Work Group:** Anesthesiologists; Family and General Practitioners; Internists, General; Medical Assistants; Obstetricians and Gynecologists; Pediatricians, General; Pharmacists; Pharmacy Aides; Pharmacy Technicians; Physician Assistants; Psychiatrists; Registered Nurses; Surgeons; Surgical Technologists. **PERSONALITY TYPE:** No data available.

EDUCATION/TRAINING PROGRAM(S)—Medical Transcription/Transcriptionist. **RELATED KNOWLEDGE/COURSES**—No data available.

Meeting and Convention Planners

- Education/Training Required: Bachelor's degree
- Annual Earnings: $39,620
- Growth: 21.3%
- Annual Job Openings: 7,000
- Self-Employed: 1.8%
- Part-Time: 14.4%

Coordinate activities of staff and convention personnel to make arrangements for group meetings and conventions. Consult with customers in order to determine objectives and requirements for events such as meetings, conferences, and conventions. Monitor event activities in order to ensure compliance with applicable regulations and laws, satisfaction of participants, and resolution of any problems that arise. Confer with staff at a chosen event site in order to coordinate details. Review event bills for accuracy and approve payment. Plan and develop programs, agendas, budgets, and services according to customer requirements. Coordinate services for events, such as accommodation and transportation for participants, facilities, catering, signage, displays, special needs requirements, printing, and event security. Arrange the availability of audiovisual equipment, transportation, displays, and other event needs. Inspect event facilities in order to ensure that they conform to customer requirements. Maintain records of event aspects, including financial details. Conduct post-event evaluations in order to determine how future events could be improved. Negotiate contracts with such service providers and suppliers as hotels, convention centers, and speakers. Meet with sponsors and organizing committees in order to plan scope and format of events, to establish and monitor budgets, and to review administrative procedures and event progress. Direct administrative details such as financial operations, dissemination of promotional materials, and responses to inquiries. Evaluate and select providers of services according to customer requirements. Read trade publications, attend seminars, and consult with other meeting professionals in order to keep abreast of meeting management standards and trends. Organize registration of event participants. Design and implement efforts to publicize events and promote sponsorships. Hire, train, and supervise volunteers and support staff required for events. Obtain permits from fire and health departments to erect displays and exhibits and serve food at events. Promote conference, convention, and trades show services by performing tasks such as meeting with professional and trade associations and producing brochures and other publications. **SKILLS—Service Orientation:** Actively looking for ways to help people. **Coordination:** Adjusting actions in relation to others' actions. **Negotiation:** Bringing others together and trying to reconcile differences. **Social Perceptiveness:** Being aware of others' reactions and understanding why they react as they do. **Time Management:** Managing one's own time and the time of others. **Persuasion:** Persuading others to change their minds or behavior. **Operations Analysis:** Analyzing needs and product requirements to create a design. **Management of Personnel Resources:** Motivating, developing, and directing people as they work, identifying the best people for the job. **GOE—Interest Area:** 04. Business and Administration. **Work Group:** 04.02. Managerial Work in Business Detail. **Other Jobs in This Work Group:** Administrative Services Managers; First-Line Supervisors, Administrative Support; First-Line Supervisors, Customer Service; Housekeeping Supervisors; Janitorial Supervisors. **PERSONALITY TYPE:** Enterprising.

EDUCATION/TRAINING PROGRAM(S)—Selling Skills and Sales Operations. **RELATED KNOWLEDGE/COURSES—Sales and Marketing:** Knowledge of principles and methods for showing, promoting, and selling products or services. This includes marketing strategy and tactics, product demonstrations, sales techniques, and sales control systems. **Customer and Personal Service:** Knowledge of principles and processes for providing customer and personal services. This includes customer needs assessment, meeting quality standards for services, and evaluation of customer satisfaction. **Personnel and Human Resources:** Knowledge of principles and procedures for personnel recruitment, selection, training, compensation and benefits, labor relations and negotiation, and personnel information systems. **Administration and Management:** Knowledge of business and management principles involved in strategic planning, resource allocation, human resources modeling, leader-

ship technique, production methods, and coordination of people and resources. **Economics and Accounting:** Knowledge of economic and accounting principles and practices, the financial markets, banking, and the analysis and reporting of financial data. **Clerical Practices:** Knowledge of administrative and clerical procedures and systems such as word processing, managing files and records, stenography and transcription, designing forms, and other office procedures and terminology. **Education and Training:** Knowledge of principles and methods for curriculum and training design, teaching and instruction for individuals and groups, and the measurement of training effects.

Mental Health and Substance Abuse Social Workers

- Education/Training Required: Master's degree
- Annual Earnings: $33,920
- Growth: 34.5%
- Annual Job Openings: 17,000
- Self-Employed: 1.6%
- Part-Time: 8.7%

Assess and treat individuals with mental, emotional, or substance abuse problems, including abuse of alcohol, tobacco, and/or other drugs. Activities may include individual and group therapy, crisis intervention, case management, client advocacy, prevention, and education. Counsel clients in individual and group sessions to assist them in dealing with substance abuse, mental and physical illness, poverty, unemployment, or physical abuse. Interview clients, review records, and confer with other professionals to evaluate mental or physical condition of client or patient. Collaborate with counselors, physicians, and nurses to plan and coordinate treatment, drawing on social work experience and patient needs. Monitor, evaluate, and record client progress with respect to treatment goals. Refer patient, client, or family to community resources for housing or treatment to assist in recovery from mental or physical illness, following through to ensure service efficacy. Counsel and aid family members to assist them in understanding, dealing with, and supporting the client or patient. Modify treatment plans according to changes in client status. Plan and conduct programs to prevent substance abuse, to combat social problems, or to improve health and counseling services in community. Supervise and direct other workers who provide services to clients or patients. Develop or advise on social policy and assist in community development. **SKILLS—Social Perceptiveness:** Being aware of others' reactions and understanding why they react as they do. **Service Orientation:** Actively looking for ways to help people. **Negotiation:** Bringing others together and trying to reconcile differences. **Persuasion:** Persuading others to change their minds or behavior. **Active Listening:** Giving full attention to what other people are saying, taking time to understand the points being made, asking questions as appropriate, and not interrupting at inappropriate times. **Judgment and Decision Making:** Considering the relative costs and benefits of potential actions to choose the most appropriate one. **Critical Thinking:** Using logic and reasoning to identify the strengths and weaknesses of alternative solutions, conclusions, or approaches to problems. **Learning Strategies:** Selecting and using training/instructional methods and procedures appropriate for the situation when learning or teaching new things. **Coordination:** Adjusting actions in relation to others' actions. **GOE—Interest Area:** 10. Human Service. **Work Group:** 10.01. Counseling and Social Work. **Other Jobs in This Work Group:** Child, Family, and School Social Workers; Clinical Psychologists; Counseling Psychologists; Marriage and Family Therapists; Medical and Public Health Social Workers; Mental Health Counselors; Probation Officers and Correctional Treatment Specialists; Rehabilitation Counselors; Residential Advisors; Social and Human Service Assistants; Substance Abuse and Behavioral Disorder Counselors. **PERSONALITY TYPE:** Social.

EDUCATION/TRAINING PROGRAM(S)—Clinical/Medical Social Work. **RELATED KNOWLEDGE/COURSES—Psychology:** Knowledge of human behavior and performance; individual differences in ability, personality, and interests; learning and motivation; psychological research methods; and the assessment and treatment of behavioral and affective disorders. **Therapy and Counseling:** Knowledge of principles, methods, and procedures for diagnosis, treatment, and rehabilitation of physical and mental dysfunctions and for career counseling and guidance. **Customer and Personal Service:** Knowledge of principles and processes for providing customer and personal services. This includes customer needs assessment, meeting quality standards for services, and evaluation

of customer satisfaction. **Sociology and Anthropology:** Knowledge of group behavior and dynamics, societal trends and influences, human migrations, ethnicity, and cultures and their history and origins. **Medicine and Dentistry:** Knowledge of the information and techniques needed to diagnose and treat human injuries, diseases, and deformities. This includes symptoms, treatment alternatives, drug properties and interactions, and preventive health-care measures. **Philosophy and Theology:** Knowledge of different philosophical systems and religions. This includes their basic principles, values, ethics, ways of thinking, customs, and practices and their impact on human culture.

Mental Health Counselors

- Education/Training Required: Master's degree
- Annual Earnings: $32,960
- Growth: 26.7%
- Annual Job Openings: 13,000
- Self-Employed: 4.1%
- Part-Time: 14.6%

Counsel with emphasis on prevention. Work with individuals and groups to promote optimum mental health. May help individuals deal with addictions and substance abuse; family, parenting, and marital problems; suicide; stress management; problems with self-esteem; and issues associated with aging and mental and emotional health. Maintain confidentiality of records relating to clients' treatment. Encourage clients to express their feelings and discuss what is happening in their lives and help them to develop insight into themselves and their relationships. Guide clients in the development of skills and strategies for dealing with their problems. Prepare and maintain all required treatment records and reports. Counsel clients and patients, individually and in group sessions, to assist in overcoming dependencies, adjusting to life, and making changes. Collect information about clients through interviews, observation, and tests. Act as client advocates in order to coordinate required services or to resolve emergency problems in crisis situations. Develop and implement treatment plans based on clinical experience and knowledge. Collaborate with other staff members to perform clinical assessments and develop treatment plans. Evaluate clients' physical or mental condition based on review of client information. Meet with families, probation officers, police, and other interested parties in order to exchange necessary information during the treatment process. Refer patients, clients, or family members to community resources or to specialists as necessary. Counsel family members to assist them in understanding, dealing with, and supporting clients or patients. Evaluate the effectiveness of counseling programs and clients' progress in resolving identified problems and moving towards defined objectives. Plan, organize, and lead structured programs of counseling, work, study, recreation, and social activities for clients. Modify treatment activities and approaches as needed in order to comply with changes in clients' status. Learn about new developments in their field by reading professional literature, attending courses and seminars, and establishing and maintaining contact with other social service agencies. Discuss with individual patients their plans for life after leaving therapy. Gather information about community mental health needs and resources that could be used in conjunction with therapy. Monitor clients' use of medications. **SKILLS—Social Perceptiveness:** Being aware of others' reactions and understanding why they react as they do. **Service Orientation:** Actively looking for ways to help people. **Learning Strategies:** Selecting and using training/instructional methods and procedures appropriate for the situation when learning or teaching new things. **Negotiation:** Bringing others together and trying to reconcile differences. **Persuasion:** Persuading others to change their minds or behavior. **Active Listening:** Giving full attention to what other people are saying, taking time to understand the points being made, asking questions as appropriate, and not interrupting at inappropriate times. **Critical Thinking:** Using logic and reasoning to identify the strengths and weaknesses of alternative solutions, conclusions, or approaches to problems. **Speaking:** Talking to others to convey information effectively. **Active Learning:** Understanding the implications of new information for both current and future problem-solving and decision-making. **Instructing:** Teaching others how to do something. **GOE—Interest Area:** 10. Human Service. **Work Group:** 10.01. Counseling and Social Work. **Other Jobs in This Work Group:** Child, Family, and School Social Workers; Clinical Psychologists; Counseling Psychologists; Marriage and Family Therapists; Medical and Public Health Social Workers; Mental Health and Substance Abuse Social Workers; Probation Officers and Correctional Treatment Specialists; Rehabilitation Counselors; Residential Advisors; Social

and Human Service Assistants; Substance Abuse and Behavioral Disorder Counselors. **PERSONALITY TYPE:** Social.

EDUCATION/TRAINING PROGRAM(S)—Clinical/Medical Social Work; Mental and Social Health Services and Allied Professions, Other; Mental Health Counseling/Counselor; Substance Abuse/Addiction Counseling. **RELATED KNOWLEDGE/COURSES—Therapy and Counseling:** Knowledge of principles, methods, and procedures for diagnosis, treatment, and rehabilitation of physical and mental dysfunctions and for career counseling and guidance. **Psychology:** Knowledge of human behavior and performance; individual differences in ability, personality, and interests; learning and motivation; psychological research methods; and the assessment and treatment of behavioral and affective disorders. **Sociology and Anthropology:** Knowledge of group behavior and dynamics, societal trends and influences, human migrations, ethnicity, and cultures and their history and origins. **Customer and Personal Service:** Knowledge of principles and processes for providing customer and personal services. This includes customer needs assessment, meeting quality standards for services, and evaluation of customer satisfaction. **Education and Training:** Knowledge of principles and methods for curriculum and training design, teaching and instruction for individuals and groups, and the measurement of training effects. **Philosophy and Theology:** Knowledge of different philosophical systems and religions. This includes their basic principles, values, ethics, ways of thinking, customs, and practices and their impact on human culture.

Meter Mechanics

- ◎ Education/Training Required: Moderate-term on-the-job training
- ◎ Annual Earnings: $43,710
- ◎ Growth: 12.0%
- ◎ Annual Job Openings: 5,000
- ◎ Self-Employed: 0.7%
- ◎ Part-Time: 2.0%

Test, adjust, and repair gas, water, and oil meters. Adjusts meter and repeats test until meter registration is within specified limits. Inspects, repairs, and maintains gas meters at wells or processing plants. Dismantles meter and replaces defective parts, such as case, shafts, gears, disks, and recording mechanisms, using soldering iron and hand tools. Connects gas, oil, water, or air meter to test apparatus to detect leaks. Reassembles meter and meter parts, using soldering gun, power tools, and hand tools. Lubricates moving meter parts, using oil gun. Records test results, materials used, and meters needing repair on log or card and segregates meters requiring repair. Caps meter housing and activates controls on paint booth to spray-paint meter case. Cleans plant growth, scale, and rust from meter housing, using wire brush, buffer, sandblaster, or cleaning compounds. Analyzes test results to determine cause of persistent meter registration errors. **SKILLS—Repairing:** Repairing machines or systems by using the needed tools. **Installation:** Installing equipment, machines, wiring, or programs to meet specifications. **Equipment Maintenance:** Performing routine maintenance on equipment and determining when and what kind of maintenance is needed. **Quality Control Analysis:** Conducting tests and inspections of products, services, or processes to evaluate quality or performance. **Troubleshooting:** Determining causes of operating errors and deciding what to do about them. **Operation Monitoring:** Watching gauges, dials, or other indicators to make sure a machine is working properly. **Operation and Control:** Controlling operations of equipment or systems. **GOE—Interest Area:** 02. Architecture and Construction. **Work Group:** 02.05. Systems and Equipment Installation, Maintenance, and Repair. **Other Jobs in This Work Group:** Central Office and PBX Installers and Repairers; Communication Equipment Mechanics, Installers, and Repairers; Electric Meter Installers and Repairers; Electrical and Electronics Repairers, Powerhouse, Substation, and Relay; Electrical Power-Line Installers and Repairers; Elevator Installers and Repairers; Frame Wirers, Central Office; Heating and Air Conditioning Mechanics; Home Appliance Installers; Maintenance and Repair Workers, General; Refrigeration Mechanics; Station Installers and Repairers, Telephone; Telecommunications Facility Examiners; Telecommunications Line Installers and Repairers. **PERSONALITY TYPE:** Realistic.

EDUCATION/TRAINING PROGRAM(S)— Electromechanical and Instrumentation and Maintenance Technologies/Technicians, Other. **RELATED KNOWLEDGE/COURSES—Mechanical Devices:** Knowledge of machines and tools, including their designs, uses, repair, and maintenance. **Engineering**

and Technology: Knowledge of the practical application of engineering science and technology. This includes applying principles, techniques, procedures, and equipment to the design and production of various goods and services.

Microbiologists

◎ Education/Training Required: Doctoral degree
◎ Annual Earnings: $54,840
◎ Growth: 20.0%
◎ Annual Job Openings: 1,000
◎ Self-Employed: 2.6%
◎ Part-Time: 7.1%

Investigate the growth, structure, development, and other characteristics of microscopic organisms, such as bacteria, algae, or fungi. Includes medical microbiologists who study the relationship between organisms and disease or the effects of antibiotics on microorganisms. Isolate and make cultures of bacteria or other microorganisms in prescribed media, controlling moisture, aeration, temperature, and nutrition. Perform tests on water, food, and the environment to detect harmful microorganisms and to obtain information about sources of pollution and contamination. Examine physiological, morphological, and cultural characteristics, using microscope, to identify and classify microorganisms in human, water, and food specimens. Provide laboratory services for health departments, for community environmental health programs, and for physicians needing information for diagnosis and treatment. Observe action of microorganisms upon living tissues of plants, higher animals, and other microorganisms and on dead organic matter. Investigate the relationship between organisms and disease, including the control of epidemics and the effects of antibiotics on microorganisms. Supervise biological technologists and technicians and other scientists. Study growth, structure, development, and general characteristics of bacteria and other microorganisms to understand their relationship to human, plant, and animal health. Prepare technical reports and recommendations based upon research outcomes. Study the structure and function of human, animal, and plant tissues, cells, pathogens, and toxins. Use a variety of specialized equipment, such as electron microscopes, gas chromatographs and high-pressure liquid chromatographs, electrophoresis units, thermocyclers, fluorescence-activated cell sorters, and phosphoimagers. Conduct chemical analyses of substances such as acids, alcohols, and enzymes. **SKILLS—Science:** Using scientific rules and methods to solve problems. **Operation Monitoring:** Watching gauges, dials, or other indicators to make sure a machine is working properly. **Equipment Maintenance:** Performing routine maintenance on equipment and determining when and what kind of maintenance is needed. **Active Listening:** Giving full attention to what other people are saying, taking time to understand the points being made, asking questions as appropriate, and not interrupting at inappropriate times. **Instructing:** Teaching others how to do something. **Repairing:** Repairing machines or systems by using the needed tools. **Troubleshooting:** Determining causes of operating errors and deciding what to do about them. **Technology Design:** Generating or adapting equipment and technology to serve user needs. **Quality Control Analysis:** Conducting tests and inspections of products, services, or processes to evaluate quality or performance. **GOE—Interest Area:** 15. Scientific Research, Engineering, and Mathematics. **Work Group:** 15.03. Life Sciences. **Other Jobs in This Work Group:** Biochemists; Biologists; Biophysicists; Environmental Scientists and Specialists, Including Health; Epidemiologists; Medical Scientists, Except Epidemiologists. **PERSONALITY TYPE:** Investigative.

EDUCATION/TRAINING PROGRAM(S)—Biochemistry/Biophysics and Molecular Biology; Cell/Cellular Biology and Anatomical Sciences, Other; Microbiology, General; Neuroanatomy; Soil Microbiology; Structural Biology. **RELATED KNOWLEDGE/COURSES—Biology:** Knowledge of plant and animal organisms and their tissues, cells, functions, interdependencies, and interactions with each other and the environment. **Chemistry:** Knowledge of the chemical composition, structure, and properties of substances and of the chemical processes and transformations that they undergo. This includes uses of chemicals and their danger signs, production techniques, and disposal methods. **Clerical Practices:** Knowledge of administrative and clerical procedures and systems such as word processing, managing files and records, stenography and transcription, designing forms, and other office procedures and terminology. **English Language:** Knowledge of the structure and content of the English language, including the meaning and spelling of words, rules of composition, and grammar. **Computers and Electronics:** Knowledge of

circuit boards, processors, chips, electronic equipment, and computer hardware and software, including applications and programming. **Administration and Management:** Knowledge of business and management principles involved in strategic planning, resource allocation, human resources modeling, leadership technique, production methods, and coordination of people and resources.

Middle School Teachers, Except Special and Vocational Education

- ◉ Education/Training Required: Bachelor's degree
- ◉ Annual Earnings: $43,670
- ◉ Growth: 9.0%
- ◉ Annual Job Openings: 69,000
- ◉ Self-Employed: 0.1%
- ◉ Part-Time: 9.2%

Teach students in public or private schools in one or more subjects at the middle, intermediate, or junior high level, which falls between elementary and senior high school as defined by applicable state laws and regulations. Establish and enforce rules for behavior and procedures for maintaining order among the students for whom they are responsible. Adapt teaching methods and instructional materials to meet students' varying needs and interests. Instruct through lectures, discussions, and demonstrations in one or more subjects, such as English, mathematics, or social studies. Prepare, administer, and grade tests and assignments in order to evaluate students' progress. Establish clear objectives for all lessons, units, and projects and communicate these objectives to students. Plan and conduct activities for a balanced program of instruction, demonstration, and work time that provides students with opportunities to observe, question, and investigate. Maintain accurate, complete, and correct student records as required by laws, district policies, and administrative regulations. Observe and evaluate students' performance, behavior, social development, and physical health. Prepare materials and classrooms for class activities. Assign lessons and correct homework. Enforce all administration policies and rules governing students. Confer with parents or guardians, other teachers, counselors, and administrators in order to resolve students' behavioral and academic problems. Prepare students for later grades by encouraging them to explore learning opportunities and to persevere with challenging tasks. Prepare objectives and outlines for courses of study, following curriculum guidelines or requirements of states and schools. Meet with parents and guardians to discuss their children's progress and to determine their priorities for their children and their resource needs. Guide and counsel students with adjustment and/or academic problems or special academic interests. Meet with other professionals to discuss individual students' needs and progress. Prepare and implement remedial programs for students requiring extra help. Prepare for assigned classes and show written evidence of preparation upon request of immediate supervisors. Use computers, audiovisual aids, and other equipment and materials to supplement presentations. **SKILLS—Instructing:** Teaching others how to do something. **Learning Strategies:** Selecting and using training/instructional methods and procedures appropriate for the situation when learning or teaching new things. **Social Perceptiveness:** Being aware of others' reactions and understanding why they react as they do. **Time Management:** Managing one's own time and the time of others. **Monitoring:** Monitoring or assessing your performance or that of other individuals or organizations to make improvements or take corrective action. **Negotiation:** Bringing others together and trying to reconcile differences. **Persuasion:** Persuading others to change their minds or behavior. **Service Orientation:** Actively looking for ways to help people. **GOE—Interest Area:** 05. Education and Training. **Work Group:** 05.02. Preschool, Elementary, and Secondary Teaching and Instructing. **Other Jobs in This Work Group:** Elementary School Teachers, Except Special Education; Kindergarten Teachers, Except Special Education; Preschool Teachers, Except Special Education; Secondary School Teachers, Except Special and Vocational Education; Special Education Teachers, Middle School; Special Education Teachers, Preschool, Kindergarten, and Elementary School; Special Education Teachers, Secondary School; Teacher Assistants; Vocational Education Teachers, Middle School; Vocational Education Teachers, Secondary School. **PERSONALITY TYPE:** Social.

EDUCATION/TRAINING PROGRAM(S)—Art Teacher Education; Computer Teacher Education; English/Language Arts Teacher Education; Family and Consumer Sciences/Home Economics Teacher Education; Foreign Language Teacher Education; Health Occupations Teacher Education; Health Teacher Education; History Teacher Education; Junior High/Intermediate/Middle School Education and Teaching; Mathematics Teacher Education; Music Teacher Education; Physical Education Teaching and Coaching; Reading Teacher Education; Science Teacher Education/General Science Teacher Education; Social Science Teacher Education; Social Studies Teacher Education; Teacher Education and Professional Development, Specific Subject Areas, Other; Technology Teacher Education/Industrial Arts Teacher Education. **RELATED KNOWLEDGE/COURSES—Education and Training:** Knowledge of principles and methods for curriculum and training design, teaching and instruction for individuals and groups, and the measurement of training effects. **Sociology and Anthropology:** Knowledge of group behavior and dynamics, societal trends and influences, human migrations, ethnicity, and cultures and their history and origins. **Psychology:** Knowledge of human behavior and performance; individual differences in ability, personality, and interests; learning and motivation; psychological research methods; and the assessment and treatment of behavioral and affective disorders. **English Language:** Knowledge of the structure and content of the English language, including the meaning and spelling of words, rules of composition, and grammar. **History and Archeology:** Knowledge of historical events and their causes, indicators, and effects on civilizations and cultures. **Geography:** Knowledge of principles and methods for describing the features of land, sea, and air masses, including their physical characteristics; locations; interrelationships; and distribution of plant, animal, and human life. **Philosophy and Theology:** Knowledge of different philosophical systems and religions. This includes their basic principles, values, ethics, ways of thinking, customs, and practices and their impact on human culture.

Millwrights

- Education/Training Required: Long-term on-the-job training
- Annual Earnings: $43,720
- Growth: 5.3%
- Annual Job Openings: 7,000
- Self-Employed: 1.5%
- Part-Time: 1.6%

Install, dismantle, or move machinery and heavy equipment according to layout plans, blueprints, or other drawings. Replace defective parts of machine or adjust clearances and alignment of moving parts. Align machines and equipment, using hoists, jacks, hand tools, squares, rules, micrometers, and plumb bobs. Connect power unit to machines or steam piping to equipment and test unit to evaluate its mechanical operation. Repair and lubricate machines and equipment. Assemble and install equipment, using hand tools and power tools. Position steel beams to support bedplates of machines and equipment, using blueprints and schematic drawings to determine work procedures. Signal crane operator to lower basic assembly units to bedplate and align unit to centerline. Insert shims, adjust tension on nuts and bolts, or position parts, using hand tools and measuring instruments, to set specified clearances between moving and stationary parts. Move machinery and equipment, using hoists, dollies, rollers, and trucks. Attach moving parts and subassemblies to basic assembly unit, using hand tools and power tools. Assemble machines and bolt, weld, rivet, or otherwise fasten them to foundation or other structures, using hand tools and power tools. Lay out mounting holes, using measuring instruments, and drill holes with power drill. Bolt parts, such as side and deck plates, jaw plates, and journals, to basic assembly unit. Level bedplate and establish centerline, using straightedge, levels, and transit. Dismantle machines, using hammers, wrenches, crowbars, and other hand tools. Shrink-fit bushings, sleeves, rings, liners, gears, and wheels to specified items, using portable gas heating equipment. Dismantle machinery and equipment for shipment to installation site, usually performing installation and maintenance work as part of team. Construct foundation for machines, using hand tools and building materials such as wood, cement, and steel. **SKILLS—Installation:** Installing equipment, machines, wiring, or programs to meet specifications. **Repairing:** Repairing machines or systems by using the needed tools. **Troubleshooting:** Determining causes of operating errors and deciding what to do about them. **Equipment Maintenance:** Performing routine maintenance on equipment and determining when and what kind of maintenance is needed. **Mathematics:** Using mathematics to solve problems. **Equipment Selection:** Determining the kind of tools and equipment needed to do a job. **Technology Design:** Generating or adapting equipment and technology to serve user needs. **Coordination:** Adjusting actions in relation to others' actions. **GOE—Interest Area:** 13. Manufacturing.

Work Group: 13.13. Machinery Repair. **Other Jobs in This Work Group:** Bicycle Repairers; Gas Appliance Repairers; Hand and Portable Power Tool Repairers; Industrial Machinery Mechanics; Locksmiths and Safe Repairers; Maintenance Workers, Machinery; Mechanical Door Repairers; Signal and Track Switch Repairers; Valve and Regulator Repairers. **PERSONALITY TYPE:** Realistic.

EDUCATION/TRAINING PROGRAM(S)—Heavy/Industrial Equipment Maintenance Technologies, Other; Industrial Mechanics and Maintenance Technology. **RELATED KNOWLEDGE/COURSES—Mechanical Devices:** Knowledge of machines and tools, including their designs, uses, repair, and maintenance. **Building and Construction:** Knowledge of the materials, methods, and tools involved in the construction or repair of houses, buildings, or other structures such as highways and roads. **Engineering and Technology:** Knowledge of the practical application of engineering science and technology. This includes applying principles, techniques, procedures, and equipment to the design and production of various goods and services. **Design:** Knowledge of design techniques, tools, and principles involved in production of precision technical plans, blueprints, drawings, and models. **Physics:** Knowledge and prediction of physical principles and laws and their interrelationships and applications to understanding fluid, material, and atmospheric dynamics and mechanical, electrical, atomic, and subatomic structures and processes. **Public Safety and Security:** Knowledge of relevant equipment, policies, procedures, and strategies to promote effective local, state, or national security operations for the protection of people, data, property, and institutions.

Mobile Heavy Equipment Mechanics, Except Engines

- Education/Training Required: Postsecondary vocational training
- Annual Earnings: $38,150
- Growth: 9.6%
- Annual Job Openings: 12,000
- Self-Employed: 4.4%
- Part-Time: 2.8%

Diagnose, adjust, repair, or overhaul mobile mechanical, hydraulic, and pneumatic equipment, such as cranes, bulldozers, graders, and conveyors, used in construction, logging, and surface mining. Test mechanical products and equipment after repair or assembly to ensure proper performance and compliance with manufacturers' specifications. Repair and replace damaged or worn parts. Operate and inspect machines or heavy equipment in order to diagnose defects. Diagnose faults or malfunctions to determine required repairs, using engine diagnostic equipment such as computerized test equipment and calibration devices. Dismantle and reassemble heavy equipment, using hoists and hand tools. Clean, lubricate, and perform other routine maintenance work on equipment and vehicles. Examine parts for damage or excessive wear, using micrometers and gauges. Schedule maintenance for industrial machines and equipment and keep equipment service records. Read and understand operating manuals, blueprints, and technical drawings. Overhaul and test machines or equipment to ensure operating efficiency. Assemble gear systems and align frames and gears. Fit bearings to adjust, repair, or overhaul mobile mechanical, hydraulic, and pneumatic equipment. Weld or solder broken parts and structural members, using electric or gas welders and soldering tools. Clean parts by spraying them with grease solvent or immersing them in tanks of solvent. Adjust, maintain, and repair or replace subassemblies, such as transmissions and crawler heads, using hand tools, jacks, and cranes. Adjust and maintain industrial machinery, using control and regulating devices. Fabricate needed parts or items from sheet metal. Direct workers who are assembling or disassembling equipment or cleaning parts. **SKILLS—Installation:** Installing equipment, machines, wiring, or programs to meet specifications. **Equipment Maintenance:** Performing routine maintenance on equipment and determining when and what kind of maintenance is needed. **Repairing:** Repairing machines or systems by using the needed tools. **Troubleshooting:** Determining causes of operating errors and deciding what to do about them. **Operation Monitoring:** Watching gauges, dials, or other indicators to make sure a machine is working properly. **Equipment Selection:** Determining the kind of tools and equipment needed to do a job. **Operation and Control:** Controlling operations of equipment or systems. **Technology Design:** Generating or adapting equipment and technology to serve user needs. **GOE— Interest Area:** 13. Manufacturing. **Work Group:**

13.14. Vehicle and Facility Mechanical Work. **Other Jobs in This Work Group:** Aircraft Body and Bonded Structure Repairers; Aircraft Engine Specialists; Aircraft Rigging Assemblers; Aircraft Structure Assemblers, Precision; Aircraft Systems Assemblers, Precision; Airframe-and-Power-Plant Mechanics; Automotive Body and Related Repairers; Automotive Glass Installers and Repairers; Automotive Master Mechanics; Automotive Specialty Technicians; Bus and Truck Mechanics and Diesel Engine Specialists; Farm Equipment Mechanics; Fiberglass Laminators and Fabricators; Motorboat Mechanics; Motorcycle Mechanics; Outdoor Power Equipment and Other Small Engine Mechanics; Rail Car Repairers; Recreational Vehicle Service Technicians; Tire Repairers and Changers. **PERSONALITY TYPE:** Realistic.

EDUCATION/TRAINING PROGRAM(S)—Agricultural Mechanics and Equipment/Machine Technology; Heavy Equipment Maintenance Technology/ Technician. **RELATED KNOWLEDGE/COURSES—Mechanical Devices:** Knowledge of machines and tools, including their designs, uses, repair, and maintenance. **Engineering and Technology:** Knowledge of the practical application of engineering science and technology. This includes applying principles, techniques, procedures, and equipment to the design and production of various goods and services. **Physics:** Knowledge and prediction of physical principles and laws and their interrelationships and applications to understanding fluid, material, and atmospheric dynamics and mechanical, electrical, atomic, and subatomic structures and processes. **Customer and Personal Service:** Knowledge of principles and processes for providing customer and personal services. This includes customer needs assessment, meeting quality standards for services, and evaluation of customer satisfaction. **Chemistry:** Knowledge of the chemical composition, structure, and properties of substances and of the chemical processes and transformations that they undergo. This includes uses of chemicals and their danger signs, production techniques, and disposal methods. **Transportation:** Knowledge of principles and methods for moving people or goods by air, rail, sea, or road, including the relative costs and benefits.

Model Makers, Metal and Plastic

◎ Education/Training Required: Moderate-term on-the-job training
◎ Annual Earnings: $44,250
◎ Growth: 14.6%
◎ Annual Job Openings: 1,000
◎ Self-Employed: 0%
◎ Part-Time: 6.0%

Set up and operate machines such as lathes, milling and engraving machines, and jig borers to make working models of metal or plastic objects. Align, fit, and join parts by using bolts and screws or by welding or gluing. Cut, shape, and form metal parts, using lathes, power saws, snips, power brakes and shears, files, and mallets. Drill, countersink, and ream holes in parts and assemblies for bolts, screws, and other fasteners, using power tools. Grind, file, and sand parts to finished dimensions. Inspect and test products to verify conformance to specifications, using precision measuring instruments or circuit testers. Lay out and mark reference points and dimensions on materials, using measuring instruments and drawing or scribing tools. Set up and operate machines such as lathes, drill presses, punch presses, or bandsaws to fabricate prototypes or models. Study blueprints, drawings, and sketches to determine material dimensions, required equipment, and operations sequences. Assemble mechanical, electrical, and electronic components into models or prototypes, using hand tools, power tools, and fabricating machines. Consult and confer with engineering personnel to discuss developmental problems and to recommend product modifications. Devise and construct tools, dies, molds, jigs, and fixtures or modify existing tools and equipment. Record specifications, production operations, and final dimensions of models for use in establishing operating standards and procedures. Rework or alter component model or parts as required to ensure that products meet standards. Wire and solder electrical and electronic connections and components. **SKILLS—Technology Design:** Generating or adapting equipment and technology to serve user needs. **Quality Control Analysis:** Conducting tests and inspections of products, services, or processes to evaluate quality or performance. **Operations Analysis:** Analyzing needs and product requirements to create a design. **Equipment Selection:** Determining the kind of tools and equipment needed to do a job. **Troubleshooting:** Determining causes of operating errors and deciding what to do about them. **Operation Monitoring:** Watching gauges, dials, or other indicators to make sure a machine is working properly. **Systems Analysis:** Determining how a system should work and how changes in conditions, operations, and the environment will affect outcomes. **Operation and Control:** Controlling operations of equipment or systems. **GOE—Interest Area:** 13. Manufacturing. **Work Group:** 13.05. Production Machining Technology. **Other Jobs in This Work Group:** Foundry Mold and Coremakers; Lay-Out Workers, Metal and Plastic; Machinists; Numerical Control Machine Tool Operators and Tenders, Metal and Plastic; Numerical Tool and Process Control Programmers; Patternmakers, Metal and Plastic; Tool and Die Makers; Tool Grinders, Filers, and Sharpeners. **PERSONALITY TYPE:** Realistic.

EDUCATION/TRAINING PROGRAM(S)—Sheet Metal Technology/Sheetworking. **RELATED KNOWLEDGE/COURSES—Mechanical Devices:** Knowledge of machines and tools, including their designs, uses, repair, and maintenance. **Design:** Knowledge of design techniques, tools, and principles involved in production of precision technical plans, blueprints, drawings, and models. **Building and Construction:** Knowledge of the materials, methods, and tools involved in the construction or repair of houses, buildings, or other structures such as highways and roads. **Engineering and Technology:** Knowledge of the practical application of engineering science and technology. This includes applying principles, techniques, procedures, and equipment to the design and production of various goods and services. **Computers and Electronics:** Knowledge of circuit boards, processors, chips, electronic equipment, and computer hardware and software, including applications and programming. **Telecommunications:** Knowledge of transmission, broadcasting, switching, control, and operation of telecommunications systems.

M

Motor Vehicle Inspectors

- ◎ Education/Training Required: Work experience in a related occupation
- ◎ Annual Earnings: $50,380
- ◎ Growth: 7.7%
- ◎ Annual Job Openings: 5,000
- ◎ Self-Employed: 0.4%
- ◎ Part-Time: 3.2%

Inspect automotive vehicles to ensure compliance with governmental regulations and safety standards. Inspects truck accessories, air lines, and electric circuits and reports needed repairs. Examines vehicles for damage and drives vehicle to detect malfunctions. Tests vehicle components for wear, damage, or improper adjustment, using mechanical or electrical devices. Applies inspection sticker to vehicles that pass inspection and rejection sticker to vehicles that fail. Prepares report on each vehicle for follow-up action by owner or police. Prepares and keeps record of vehicles delivered. Positions trailer and drives car onto truck trailer. Notifies authorities of owners having illegal equipment installed on vehicle. Services vehicles with fuel and water. **SKILLS—Science:** Using scientific rules and methods to solve problems. **Troubleshooting:** Determining causes of operating errors and deciding what to do about them. **Quality Control Analysis:** Conducting tests and inspections of products, services, or processes to evaluate quality or performance. **Operation Monitoring:** Watching gauges, dials, or other indicators to make sure a machine is working properly. **Technology Design:** Generating or adapting equipment and technology to serve user needs. **Systems Evaluation:** Identifying measures or indicators of system performance and the actions needed to improve or correct performance relative to the goals of the system. **Equipment Maintenance:** Performing routine maintenance on equipment and determining when and what kind of maintenance is needed. **GOE—Interest Area:** 07. Government and Public Administration. **Work Group:** 07.03. Regulations Enforcement. **Other Jobs in This Work Group:** Agricultural Inspectors; Aviation Inspectors; Child Support, Missing Persons, and Unemployment Insurance Fraud Investigators; Environmental Compliance Inspectors; Equal Opportunity Representatives and Officers; Financial Examiners; Fire Inspectors; Fish and Game Wardens; Forest Fire Inspectors and Prevention Specialists; Government Property Inspectors and Investigators; Immigration and Customs Inspectors; Licensing Examiners and Inspectors; Marine Cargo Inspectors; Mechanical Inspectors; Nuclear Monitoring Technicians; Occupational Health and Safety Specialists; Pressure Vessel Inspectors; Railroad Inspectors; Tax Examiners, Collectors, and Revenue Agents. **PERSONALITY TYPE:** Realistic.

EDUCATION/TRAINING PROGRAM(S)—No data available. **RELATED KNOWLEDGE/COURSES—Public Safety and Security:** Knowledge of relevant equipment, policies, procedures, and strategies to promote effective local, state, or national security operations for the protection of people, data, property, and institutions. **Mechanical Devices:** Knowledge of machines and tools, including their designs, uses, repair, and maintenance. **Computers and Electronics:** Knowledge of circuit boards, processors, chips, electronic equipment, and computer hardware and software, including applications and programming. **Engineering and Technology:** Knowledge of the practical application of engineering science and technology. This includes applying principles, techniques, procedures, and equipment to the design and production of various goods and services.

Multi-Media Artists and Animators

- ◎ Education/Training Required: Bachelor's degree
- ◎ Annual Earnings: $50,360
- ◎ Growth: 15.8%
- ◎ Annual Job Openings: 12,000
- ◎ Self-Employed: 53.5%
- ◎ Part-Time: 20.0%

Create special effects, animation, or other visual images, using film, video, computers, or other electronic tools and media, for use in products or creations such as computer games, movies, music videos, and commercials. Design complex graphics and animation, using independent judgment, creativity, and computer equipment. Create two-dimensional and three-dimensional images depicting objects in motion or illustrating a process, using computer animation or modeling programs. Make objects or characters appear lifelike by manipulating light, color, texture, shadow, and transparency and/or manipulating static images to give the illusion of motion. Assemble, typeset, scan, and produce digital camera-ready art or film negatives and printer's proofs. Apply story development, directing, cinematography, and editing to animation to create storyboards that show the flow of the animation and map out key scenes and characters. Script, plan, and create animated narrative sequences under tight deadlines, using computer software and hand-drawing techniques. Create basic designs, drawings, and illustrations for product labels, cartons, direct mail, or television. Create pen-and-paper images to be scanned, edited, colored, textured, or animated by computer. Develop briefings, brochures, multimedia presentations, Web pages, promotional products, technical illustrations, and computer artwork for use in products, technical manuals, literature, newsletters, and slide shows. **SKILLS—Operations Analysis:** Analyzing needs and product requirements to create a design. **Technology Design:** Generating or adapting equipment and technology to serve user needs. **Time Management:** Managing one's own time and the time of others. **Active Listening:** Giving full attention to what other people are saying, taking time to understand the points being made, asking questions as appropriate, and not interrupting at inappropriate times. **Persuasion:** Persuading others to change their minds or behavior. **Judgment and Decision Making:** Considering the relative costs and benefits of potential actions to choose the most appropriate one. **Reading Comprehension:** Understanding written sentences and paragraphs in work-related documents. **Learning Strategies:** Selecting and using training/instructional methods and procedures appropriate for the situation when learning or teaching new things. **GOE—Interest Area:** 03. Arts and Communication. **Work Group:** 03.09. Media Technology. **Other Jobs in This Work Group:** Audio and Video Equipment Technicians; Broadcast Technicians; Camera Operators, Television, Video, and Motion Picture; Film and Video Editors; Photographic Hand Developers; Photographic Reproduction Technicians; Photographic Retouchers and Restorers; Professional Photographers; Radio Operators; Sound Engineering Technicians. **PERSONALITY TYPE:** No data available.

EDUCATION/TRAINING PROGRAM(S)—Animation, Interactive Technology, Video Graphics, and Special Effects; Drawing; Graphic Design; Intermedia/Multimedia; Painting; Printmaking; Web Page, Digital/Multimedia, and Information Resources Design. **RELATED KNOWLEDGE/COURSES—Fine Arts:** Knowledge of the theory and techniques required to compose, produce, and perform works of music, dance, the visual arts, drama, and sculpture. **Design:** Knowledge of design techniques, tools, and principles involved in production of precision technical plans, blueprints, drawings, and models. **Computers and Electronics:** Knowledge of circuit boards, processors, chips, electronic equipment, and computer hardware and software, including applications and programming. **Communications and Media:** Knowledge of media production, communication, and dissemination techniques and methods. This includes alternative ways to inform and entertain via written, oral, and visual media. **English Language:** Knowledge of the structure and content of the English language, including the meaning and spelling of words, rules of composition, and grammar. **Clerical Practices:** Knowledge of administrative and clerical procedures and systems such as word processing, managing files and records, stenography and transcription, designing forms, and other office procedures and terminology.

Municipal Clerks

- Education/Training Required: Short-term on-the-job training
- Annual Earnings: $28,430
- Growth: 12.3%
- Annual Job Openings: 14,000
- Self-Employed: 2.6%
- Part-Time: 8.3%

Draft agendas and bylaws for town or city council, record minutes of council meetings, answer official correspondence, keep fiscal records and accounts, and prepare reports on civic needs. Participate in the administration of municipal elections, including preparation and distribution of ballots, appointment and training of election officers, and tabulation and certification of results. Record and edit the minutes of meetings and then distribute them to appropriate officials and staff members. Plan and direct the maintenance, filing, safekeeping, and computerization of all municipal documents. Issue public notification of all official activities and meetings. Maintain and update documents such as municipal codes and city charters. Prepare meeting agendas and packets of related information. Prepare ordinances, resolutions, and proclamations so that they can be executed, recorded, archived, and distributed. Respond to requests for information from the public, other municipalities, state officials, and state and federal legislative offices. Maintain fiscal records and accounts. Perform budgeting duties, including assisting in budget preparation, expenditure review, and budget administration. Perform general office duties such as taking and transcribing dictation, typing and proofreading correspondence, distributing and filing official forms, and scheduling appointments. Coordinate and maintain office-tracking systems for correspondence and follow-up actions. Research information in the municipal archives upon request of public officials and private citizens. Perform contract administration duties, assisting with bid openings and the awarding of contracts. Collaborate with other staff to assist in the development and implementation of goals, objectives, policies, and priorities. Represent municipalities at community events and serve as liaisons on community committees. Serve as a notary of the public. Issue various permits and licenses, including marriage, fishing, hunting, and dog licenses, and collect appropriate fees. Provide assistance to persons with disabilities in reaching less-accessible areas of municipal facilities. Process claims against the municipality, maintaining files and log of claims, and coordinate claim response and handling with municipal claims administrators. **SKILLS—Service Orientation:** Actively looking for ways to help people. **Social Perceptiveness:** Being aware of others' reactions and understanding why they react as they do. **Management of Financial Resources:** Determining how money will be spent to get the work done and accounting for these expenditures. **Active Listening:** Giving full attention to what other people are saying, taking time to understand the points being made, asking questions as appropriate, and not interrupting at inappropriate times. **Writing:** Communicating effectively in writing as appropriate for the needs of the audience. **Persuasion:** Persuading others to change their minds or behavior. **Time Management:** Managing one's own time and the time of others. **Management of Personnel Resources:** Motivating, developing, and directing people as they work, identifying the best people for the job. **GOE—Interest Area:** 07. Government and Public Administration. **Work Group:** 07.04. Public Administration Clerical Support. **Other Jobs in This Work Group:** Court Clerks; Court Reporters; License Clerks. **PERSONALITY TYPE:** Conventional.

EDUCATION/TRAINING PROGRAM(S)—General Office Occupations and Clerical Services. **RELATED KNOWLEDGE/COURSES—Clerical Practices:** Knowledge of administrative and clerical procedures and systems such as word processing, managing files and records, stenography and transcription, designing forms, and other office procedures and terminology. **Law and Government:** Knowledge of laws, legal codes, court procedures, precedents, government regulations, executive orders, agency rules, and the democratic political process. **English Language:** Knowledge of the structure and content of the English language, including the meaning and spelling of words, rules of composition, and grammar. **Customer and Personal Service:** Knowledge of principles and processes for providing customer and personal services. This includes customer needs assessment, meeting quality standards for services, and evaluation of customer satisfaction. **Personnel and Human Resources:** Knowledge of principles and procedures for personnel recruitment, selection, training, compensation and benefits, labor relations and negotiation, and personnel information systems. **Administration and Management:** Knowledge of business and management principles involved in strategic planning, resource allocation, human resources modeling, leadership technique, production methods, and coordination of people and resources.

Municipal Fire Fighters

- Education/Training Required: Long-term on-the-job training
- Annual Earnings: $38,330
- Growth: 20.7%
- Annual Job Openings: 29,000
- Self-Employed: 0%
- Part-Time: 1.1%

Control and extinguish municipal fires, protect life and property, and conduct rescue efforts. Administer first aid and cardiopulmonary resuscitation to injured persons. Rescue victims from burning buildings and accident sites. Search burning buildings to locate fire victims. Drive and operate firefighting vehicles and equipment. Dress with equipment such as fire-resistant clothing and breathing apparatus. Move toward the source of a fire, using knowledge of types of fires, construction design, building materials, and physical

Music Arrangers and Orchestrators

◉ Education/Training Required: Bachelor's degree
◉ Annual Earnings: $34,570
◉ Growth: 13.5%
◉ Annual Job Openings: 8,000
◉ Self-Employed: 39.3%
◉ Part-Time: 39.5%

Write and transcribe musical scores. Composes musical scores for orchestra, band, choral group, or individual instrumentalist or vocalist, using knowledge of music theory and instrumental and vocal capabilities. Transposes music from one voice or instrument to another to accommodate particular musician in musical group. Adapts musical composition for orchestra, band, choral group, or individual to style for which it was not originally written. Copies parts from score for individual performers. Determines voice, instrument, harmonic structure, rhythm, tempo, and tone balance to achieve desired effect. Transcribes musical parts from score written by arranger or orchestrator for each instrument or voice, using knowledge of music composition. **SKILLS—Coordination:** Adjusting actions in relation to others' actions. **Writing:** Communicating effectively in writing as appropriate for the needs of the audience. **Operations Analysis:** Analyzing needs and product requirements to create a design. **GOE— Interest Area:** 03. Arts and Communication. **Work Group:** 03.07. Music. **Other Jobs in This Work Group:** Composers; Music Directors; Musicians, Instrumental; Singers; Talent Directors. **PERSONALITY TYPE:** Artistic.

EDUCATION/TRAINING PROGRAM(S)—Conducting; Music Management and Merchandising; Music Performance, General; Music Theory and Composition; Music, Other; Musicology and Ethnomusicology; Religious/Sacred Music; Voice and Opera. **RELATED KNOWLEDGE/COURSES—Fine Arts:** Knowledge of the theory and techniques required to compose, produce, and perform works of music, dance, the visual arts, drama, and sculpture. **Administration and Management:** Knowledge of business and management principles involved in strategic planning, resource allocation, human resources modeling, leadership technique, production methods, and coordination of people and resources.

Music Directors

◉ Education/Training Required: Master's degree
◉ Annual Earnings: $34,570
◉ Growth: 13.5%
◉ Annual Job Openings: 8,000
◉ Self-Employed: 39.3%
◉ Part-Time: 39.5%

Direct and conduct instrumental or vocal performances by musical groups, such as orchestras or choirs. Assign and review staff work in such areas as scoring, arranging, and copying music and vocal coaching. Collaborate with music librarians to ensure availability of scores. Engage services of composers to write scores. Meet with composers to discuss interpretations of their work. Perform administrative tasks such as applying for grants, developing budgets, negotiating contracts, and designing and printing programs and other promotional materials. Transcribe musical compositions and melodic lines to adapt them to a particular group or to create a particular musical style. Confer with clergy to select music for church services. Coordinate and organize tours or hire touring companies to arrange concert dates, venues, accommodations, and transportation for longer tours. Plan and implement fundraising and promotional activities. Audition and select performers for musical presentations. Conduct guest soloists in addition to ensemble members. Consider such factors as ensemble size and abilities, availability of scores, and the need for musical variety in order to select music to be performed. Direct groups at rehearsals and live or recorded performances in order to achieve desired effects, such as tonal and harmonic balance dynamics, rhythm, and tempo. Meet with soloists and concertmasters to discuss and prepare for performances. Plan and schedule rehearsals and performances and arrange details such as locations, accompanists, and instrumentalists. Position members within groups to obtain balance among instrumental or vocal sections. Study scores to learn the music in detail and to develop interpretations. Use gestures to shape the music being played, communicating desired tempo, phrasing, tone, color, pitch, volume, and other performance aspects. **SKILLS—Management of Personnel Resources:** Motivating, developing, and directing people as they work, identifying the best people for the job. **Coordination:** Adjusting actions in relation to others' actions. **Instructing:** Teaching others how to do something. **Time Management:** Managing one's own time and the time of others. **Monitoring:** Monitoring or assessing your performance or that of other individuals or organizations to make improvements or take corrective action. **Learning Strategies:** Selecting and using training/instructional methods and procedures appropriate for the situation when learning or teaching new things. **Social Perceptiveness:** Being aware of others' reactions and understanding why they react as they do. **Operations Analysis:** Analyzing needs and product requirements to create a design. **GOE—Interest Area:** 03. Arts and Communication. **Work Group:** 03.07. Music. **Other Jobs in This Work Group:** Composers; Music Arrangers and Orchestrators; Musicians, Instrumental; Singers; Talent Directors. **PERSONALITY TYPE:** Artistic.

EDUCATION/TRAINING PROGRAM(S)—Conducting; Music Management and Merchandising; Music Performance, General; Music Theory and Composition; Music, Other; Musicology and Ethnomusicology; Religious/Sacred Music; Voice and Opera. **RELATED KNOWLEDGE/COURSES—Fine Arts:** Knowledge of the theory and techniques required to compose, produce, and perform works of music, dance, the visual arts, drama, and sculpture. **Personnel and Human Resources:** Knowledge of principles and procedures for personnel recruitment, selection, training, compensation and benefits, labor relations and negotiation, and personnel information systems. **Administration and Management:** Knowledge of business and management principles involved in strategic planning, resource allocation, human resources modeling, leadership technique, production methods, and coordination of people and resources. **Foreign Language:** Knowledge of the structure and content of a foreign (non-English) language, including the meaning and spelling of words, rules of composition and grammar, and pronunciation. **Transportation:** Knowledge of principles and methods for moving people or goods by air, rail, sea, or road, including the relative costs and benefits. **English Language:** Knowledge of the structure and content of the English language, including the meaning and spelling of words, rules of composition, and grammar.

Nannies

- ◎ Education/Training Required: Short-term on-the-job training
- ◎ Annual Earnings: $16,760
- ◎ Growth: 11.7%
- ◎ Annual Job Openings: 406,000
- ◎ Self-Employed: 43.4%
- ◎ Part-Time: 35.2%

Care for children in private households and provide support and expertise to parents in satisfying children's physical, emotional, intellectual, and social needs. Duties may include meal planning and preparation, laundry and clothing care, organization of play activities and outings, discipline, intellectual stimulation, language activities, and transportation. Perform first aid or CPR when required. Regulate children's rest periods and nap schedules. Meet regularly with parents to discuss children's activities and development. Help prepare and serve nutritionally balanced meals and snacks for children. Instruct children in safe behavior, such as seeking adult assistance when crossing the street and avoiding contact or play with unsafe objects. Organize and conduct age-appropriate recreational activities, such as games, arts and crafts, sports, walks, and play dates. Observe children's behavior for irregularities, take temperature, transport children to doctor, or administer medications as directed to maintain children's health. Model appropriate social behaviors and encourage concern for others to cultivate development of interpersonal relationships and communication skills. Work with parents to develop and implement discipline programs to promote desirable child behavior. Help develop and/or monitor family schedule. Supervise and assist with homework. Assign appropriate chores and praise targeted behaviors to encourage development of self-control, self-confidence, and responsibility. Transport children to schools, social outings, and medical appointments. Perform housekeeping and cleaning duties related to children's care. Instruct and assist children in the development of health and personal habits, such as eating, resting, and toilet behavior. Keep records of play, meal schedules, and bill payment. Teach and perform age-appropriate activities such as lap play, reading, and arts and crafts to encourage intellectual development of children. Remove hazards and develop appropriate boundaries and rules to create a safe environment for children. **SKILLS—Negotiation:** Bringing others together and trying to reconcile differences. **Social Perceptiveness:** Being aware of others' reactions and understanding why they react as they do. **Time Management:** Managing one's own time and the time of others. **Persuasion:** Persuading others to change their minds or behavior. **Instructing:** Teaching others how to do something. **Management of Financial Resources:** Determining how money will be spent to get the work done and accounting for these expenditures. **Speaking:** Talking to others to convey information effectively. **Active Listening:** Giving full attention to what other people are saying, taking time to understand the points being made, asking questions as appropriate, and not interrupting at inappropriate times. **Learning Strategies:** Selecting and using training/instructional methods and procedures appropriate for the situation when learning or teaching new things. **Service Orientation:** Actively looking for ways to help people. **GOE—Interest Area:** 10. Human Service. **Work Group:** 10.03. Child/Personal Care and Services. **Other Jobs in This Work Group:** Child Care Workers; Funeral Attendants; Personal and Home Care Aides. **PERSONALITY TYPE:** No data available.

EDUCATION/TRAINING PROGRAM(S)— Child Care Provider/Assistant. **RELATED KNOWLEDGE/COURSES—Philosophy and Theology:** Knowledge of different philosophical systems and religions. This includes their basic principles, values, ethics, ways of thinking, customs, and practices and their impact on human culture. **Medicine and Dentistry:** Knowledge of the information and techniques needed to diagnose and treat human injuries, diseases, and deformities. This includes symptoms, treatment alternatives, drug properties and interactions, and preventive health-care measures. **Psychology:** Knowledge of human behavior and performance; individual differences in ability, personality, and interests; learning and motivation; psychological research methods; and the assessment and treatment of behavioral and affective disorders. **Geography:** Knowledge of principles and methods for describing the features of land, sea, and air masses, including their physical characteristics; locations; interrelationships; and distribution of plant, animal, and human life. **Sociology and Anthropology:** Knowledge of group behavior and dynamics, societal trends and influences, human migrations, ethnicity, and cultures and their history and origins. **Therapy**

and Counseling: Knowledge of principles, methods, and procedures for diagnosis, treatment, and rehabilitation of physical and mental dysfunctions and for career counseling and guidance.

Natural Sciences Managers

- Education/Training Required: Work experience plus degree
- Annual Earnings: $88,660
- Growth: 11.3%
- Annual Job Openings: 5,000
- Self-Employed: 1.2%
- Part-Time: 0.9%

Plan, direct, or coordinate activities in such fields as life sciences, physical sciences, mathematics, statistics, and research and development in these fields. Confer with scientists, engineers, regulators, and others to plan and review projects and to provide technical assistance. Design and coordinate successive phases of problem analysis, solution proposals, and testing. Determine scientific and technical goals within broad outlines provided by top management and make detailed plans to accomplish these goals. Develop and implement policies, standards, and procedures for the architectural, scientific, and technical work performed to ensure regulatory compliance and operations enhancement. Plan and direct research, development, and production activities. Prepare project proposals. Advise and assist in obtaining patents or meeting other legal requirements. Conduct own research in field of expertise. Develop client relationships and communicate with clients to explain proposals, present research findings, establish specifications, or discuss project status. Develop innovative technology and train staff for its implementation. Hire, supervise, and evaluate engineers, technicians, researchers, and other staff. Prepare and administer budget, approve and review expenditures, and prepare financial reports. Recruit personnel and oversee the development and maintenance of staff competence. Review project activities and prepare and review research, testing, and operational reports. Make presentations at professional meetings to further knowledge in the field. Provide for stewardship of plant and animal resources and habitats, studying land use; monitoring animal populations; and/or providing shelter, resources, and medical treatment for animals. **SKILLS—Management of Material Resources:** Obtaining and seeing to the appropriate use of equipment, facilities, and materials needed to do certain work. **Science:** Using scientific rules and methods to solve problems. **Management of Financial Resources:** Determining how money will be spent to get the work done and accounting for these expenditures. **Management of Personnel Resources:** Motivating, developing, and directing people as they work, identifying the best people for the job. **Systems Analysis:** Determining how a system should work and how changes in conditions, operations, and the environment will affect outcomes. **Systems Evaluation:** Identifying measures or indicators of system performance and the actions needed to improve or correct performance relative to the goals of the system. **Coordination:** Adjusting actions in relation to others' actions. **Time Management:** Managing one's own time and the time of others. **GOE—Interest Area:** 15. Scientific Research, Engineering, and Mathematics. **Work Group:** 15.01. Managerial Work in Scientific Research, Engineering, and Mathematics. **Other Jobs in This Work Group:** Engineering Managers. **PERSONALITY TYPE:** Investigative.

EDUCATION/TRAINING PROGRAM(S)— Acoustics; Algebra and Number Theory; Analysis and Functional Analysis; Analytical Chemistry; Anatomy; Animal Genetics; Animal Physiology; Applied Mathematics; Applied Mathematics, Other; Astronomy; Astrophysics; Atmospheric Chemistry and Climatology; Atmospheric Physics and Dynamics; Atmospheric Sciences and Meteorology, General; Atmospheric Sciences and Meteorology, Other; Atomic/Molecular Physics; Biochemistry; Biological and Biomedical Sciences, Other; Biological and Physical Sciences; Biology/Biological Sciences, General; Biometry/Biometrics; Biophysics; Biopsychology; Biostatistics; Biotechnology; Botany/Plant Biology; Botany/Plant Biology, Other; Cell/Cellular Biology and Anatomical Sciences, Other; Cell/Cellular Biology and Histology; Chemical Physics; Chemistry, General; Chemistry, Other; Computational Mathematics; Ecology; Ecology, Evolution, Systematics, and Population Biology, Other; Elementary Particle Physics; Entomology; Evolutionary Biology; Geochemistry; Geochemistry and Petrology; Geological and Earth Sciences/Geosciences, Other; Geology/Earth Science, General; Geometry/Geomet-

ric Analysis; Geophysics and Seismology; Hydrology and Water Resources Science; Immunology; Inorganic Chemistry; Logic; Marine Biology and Biological Oceanography; Mathematics and Computer Science; Mathematics and Statistics, Other; Mathematics, General; Medical Microbiology and Bacteriology; Meteorology; Microbiology, General; Molecular Biology; Natural Sciences; Neuroscience; Nuclear Physics; Nutrition Sciences; Oceanography, Chemical and Physical; Operations Research; Optics/Optical Sciences; Organic Chemistry; Paleontology; Parasitology; Pathology/Experimental Pathology; Pharmacology; Physical and Theoretical Chemistry; Physical Sciences; Physical Sciences, Other; Physics, General; Physics, Other; Planetary Astronomy and Science; Plant Genetics; Plant Pathology/Phytopathology; Plant Physiology; Plasma and High-Temperature Physics; Polymer Chemistry; others. **RELATED KNOWLEDGE/COURSES—Chemistry:** Knowledge of the chemical composition, structure, and properties of substances and of the chemical processes and transformations that they undergo. This includes uses of chemicals and their danger signs, production techniques, and disposal methods. **Administration and Management:** Knowledge of business and management principles involved in strategic planning, resource allocation, human resources modeling, leadership technique, production methods, and coordination of people and resources. **Economics and Accounting:** Knowledge of economic and accounting principles and practices, the financial markets, banking, and the analysis and reporting of financial data. **Physics:** Knowledge and prediction of physical principles and laws and their interrelationships and applications to understanding fluid, material, and atmospheric dynamics and mechanical, electrical, atomic, and subatomic structures and processes. **Law and Government:** Knowledge of laws, legal codes, court procedures, precedents, government regulations, executive orders, agency rules, and the democratic political process. **Mathematics:** Knowledge of arithmetic, algebra, geometry, calculus, and statistics and their applications.

Network and Computer Systems Administrators

- Education/Training Required: Bachelor's degree
- Annual Earnings: $58,190
- Growth: 37.4%
- Annual Job Openings: 35,000
- Self-Employed: 0.5%
- Part-Time: 3.9%

Install, configure, and support an organization's local area network (LAN), wide area network (WAN), and Internet system or a segment of a network system. Maintain network hardware and software. Monitor network to ensure network availability to all system users and perform necessary maintenance to support network availability. May supervise other network support and client server specialists and plan, coordinate, and implement network security measures. Diagnose hardware and software problems and replace defective components. Perform data backups and disaster recovery operations. Maintain and administer computer networks and related computing environments, including computer hardware, systems software, applications software, and all configurations. Plan, coordinate, and implement network security measures in order to protect data, software, and hardware. Operate master consoles in order to monitor the performance of computer systems and networks and to coordinate computer network access and use. Perform routine network startup and shutdown procedures and maintain control records. Design, configure, and test computer hardware, networking software, and operating system software. Recommend changes to improve systems and network configurations and determine hardware or software requirements related to such changes. Confer with network users about how to solve existing system problems. Monitor network performance in order to determine whether adjustments need to be made and to determine where changes will need to be made in the future. Train people in computer system use. Load computer tapes and disks and install software and printer paper or forms. Gather data pertaining to customer needs and use the information to identify, predict, interpret, and evaluate system and network requirements. Analyze equipment performance records in order to determine the need for repair or replacement. Maintain logs related to network functions, as well as maintenance and repair records. Research new technology and implement it or recommend its implementation. Maintain an inventory of parts for emergency repairs. Coordinate with vendors and with company personnel in order to facilitate purchases. **SKILLS—Troubleshooting:** Determining causes of operating errors and deciding what to do about them. **Installation:** Installing equipment, machines, wiring, or programs to meet specifications. **Repairing:** Repairing machines or systems by using the needed tools. **Systems Evaluation:** Identifying measures or indicators of system performance and the actions needed to improve or correct performance relative to the goals of the system. **Systems Analysis:** Determining how a system should work and how changes in conditions, operations, and the environment will affect outcomes. **Service Orientation:** Actively looking for ways to help people. **Technology Design:** Generating or adapting equipment and technology to serve user needs. **Programming:** Writing computer programs for various purposes. **GOE—Interest Area:** 11. Information Technology. **Work Group:** 11.01. Managerial Work in Information Technology. **Other Jobs in This Work Group:** Computer and Information Systems Managers. **PERSONALITY TYPE:** No data available.

EDUCATION/TRAINING PROGRAM(S)—Computer and Information Sciences and Support Services, Other; Computer and Information Sciences, General; Computer and Information Systems Security; Computer Systems Analysis/Analyst; Computer Systems Networking and Telecommunications; Information Science/Studies; System Administration/Administrator; System, Networking, and LAN/WAN Management/Manager. **RELATED KNOWLEDGE/COURSES—Computers and Electronics:** Knowledge of circuit boards, processors, chips, electronic equipment, and computer hardware and software, including applications and programming. **Telecommunications:** Knowledge of transmission, broadcasting, switching, control, and operation of telecommunications systems. **Customer and Personal Service:** Knowledge of principles and processes for providing customer and personal services. This includes customer needs assessment, meeting quality standards for services, and evaluation of customer satisfaction. **Education and Training:** Knowledge of principles and methods for curriculum and training design, teaching and instruction for individuals and groups, and the measurement of training effects. **Engineering and Technology:** Knowledge of the practical application of engineering science and technology. This includes applying principles, techniques, procedures, and equipment to the design and production of various goods and services. **Administration and Management:** Knowledge of business and management principles involved in strategic planning, resource allocation, human resources modeling, leadership technique, production methods, and coordination of people and resources.

Network Systems and Data Communications Analysts

- ◎ Education/Training Required: Bachelor's degree
- ◎ Annual Earnings: $60,600
- ◎ Growth: 57.0%
- ◎ Annual Job Openings: 29,000
- ◎ Self-Employed: 23.6%
- ◎ Part-Time: 7.9%

Analyze, design, test, and evaluate network systems, such as local area networks (LAN); wide area networks (WAN); and Internet, intranet, and other data communications systems. Perform network modeling, analysis, and planning. Research and recommend network and data communications hardware and software. Includes telecommunications specialists who deal with the interfacing of computer and communications equipment. May supervise computer programmers. Maintain needed files by adding and deleting files on the network server and backing up files to guarantee their safety in the event of problems with the network. Monitor system performance and provide security measures, troubleshooting, and maintenance as needed. Assist users to diagnose and solve data communication problems. Set up user accounts, regulating and monitoring file access to ensure confidentiality and proper use. Design and implement network configurations, network architecture (including hardware and software technology, site locations, and integration of technologies), and systems. Maintain the peripherals, such as printers, that are connected to the network. Identify areas of operation that need upgraded equipment such as modems, fiber-optic cables, and telephone wires. Train users in use of

equipment. Develop and write procedures for installation, use, and troubleshooting of communications hardware and software. Adapt and modify existing software to meet specific needs. Work with other engineers, systems analysts, programmers, technicians, scientists, and top-level managers in the design, testing, and evaluation of systems. Test and evaluate hardware and software to determine efficiency, reliability, and compatibility with existing system and make purchase recommendations. Read technical manuals and brochures to determine which equipment meets establishment requirements. Consult customers, visit workplaces, or conduct surveys to determine present and future user needs. Visit vendors, attend conferences or training, and study technical journals to keep up with changes in technology. **SKILLS—Installation:** Installing equipment, machines, wiring, or programs to meet specifications. **Troubleshooting:** Determining causes of operating errors and deciding what to do about them. **Technology Design:** Generating or adapting equipment and technology to serve user needs. **Systems Analysis:** Determining how a system should work and how changes in conditions, operations, and the environment will affect outcomes. **Management of Material Resources:** Obtaining and seeing to the appropriate use of equipment, facilities, and materials needed to do certain work. **Systems Evaluation:** Identifying measures or indicators of system performance and the actions needed to improve or correct performance relative to the goals of the system. **Operations Analysis:** Analyzing needs and product requirements to create a design. **Programming:** Writing computer programs for various purposes. **Equipment Maintenance:** Performing routine maintenance on equipment and determining when and what kind of maintenance is needed. **GOE—Interest Area:** 11. Information Technology. **Work Group:** 11.02. Information Technology Specialties. **Other Jobs in This Work Group:** Computer Operators; Computer Programmers; Computer Security Specialists; Computer Software Engineers, Applications; Computer Software Engineers, Systems Software; Computer Support Specialists; Computer Systems Analysts; Database Administrators. **PERSONALITY TYPE:** Investigative.

EDUCATION/TRAINING PROGRAM(S)— Computer and Information Sciences, General; Computer and Information Systems Security; Computer Systems Analysis/Analyst; Computer Systems Networking and Telecommunications; Information Technology. **RELATED KNOWLEDGE/**

COURSES—Customer and Personal Service: Knowledge of principles and processes for providing customer and personal services. This includes customer needs assessment, meeting quality standards for services, and evaluation of customer satisfaction. **Computers and Electronics:** Knowledge of circuit boards, processors, chips, electronic equipment, and computer hardware and software, including applications and programming. **Telecommunications:** Knowledge of transmission, broadcasting, switching, control, and operation of telecommunications systems. **Education and Training:** Knowledge of principles and methods for curriculum and training design, teaching and instruction for individuals and groups, and the measurement of training effects. **Engineering and Technology:** Knowledge of the practical application of engineering science and technology. This includes applying principles, techniques, procedures, and equipment to the design and production of various goods and services. **Design:** Knowledge of design techniques, tools, and principles involved in production of precision technical plans, blueprints, drawings, and models.

New Accounts Clerks

- Education/Training Required: Work experience in a related occupation
- Annual Earnings: $26,860
- Growth: 11.2%
- Annual Job Openings: 24,000
- Self-Employed: 0%
- Part-Time: 14.8%

Interview persons desiring to open bank accounts. Explain banking services available to prospective customers and assist them in preparing application form. Answer customers' questions and explain available services such as deposit accounts, bonds, and securities. Compile information about new accounts, enter account information into computers, and file related forms or other documents. Refer customers to appropriate bank personnel in order to meet their financial needs. Interview customers in order to obtain information needed for opening accounts or renting safe-deposit boxes. Inform customers of procedures for applying for services such as ATM cards, direct deposit of checks, and certificates of deposit. Obtain credit

records from reporting agencies. Collect and record customer deposits and fees and issue receipts, using computers. Investigate and correct errors upon customers' request, according to customer and bank records. Perform teller duties as required. Execute wire transfers of funds. Duplicate records for distribution to branch offices. Issue initial and replacement safe-deposit keys to customers and admit customers to vaults. Perform foreign-currency transactions and sell traveler's checks. Schedule repairs for locks on safe-deposit boxes. **SKILLS—Service Orientation:** Actively looking for ways to help people. **Active Listening:** Giving full attention to what other people are saying, taking time to understand the points being made, asking questions as appropriate, and not interrupting at inappropriate times. **Social Perceptiveness:** Being aware of others' reactions and understanding why they react as they do. **Critical Thinking:** Using logic and reasoning to identify the strengths and weaknesses of alternative solutions, conclusions, or approaches to problems. **Writing:** Communicating effectively in writing as appropriate for the needs of the audience. **Speaking:** Talking to others to convey information effectively. **Judgment and Decision Making:** Considering the relative costs and benefits of potential actions to choose the most appropriate one. **Reading Comprehension:** Understanding written sentences and paragraphs in work-related documents. **GOE—Interest Area:** 06. Finance and Insurance. **Work Group:** 06.04. Finance/Insurance Customer Service. **Other Jobs in This Work Group:** Bill and Account Collectors; Loan Interviewers and Clerks; Tellers. **PERSONALITY TYPE:** Conventional.

EDUCATION/TRAINING PROGRAM(S)— Banking and Financial Support Services. **RELATED KNOWLEDGE/COURSES—Customer and Personal Service:** Knowledge of principles and processes for providing customer and personal services. This includes customer needs assessment, meeting quality standards for services, and evaluation of customer satisfaction. **Sales and Marketing:** Knowledge of principles and methods for showing, promoting, and selling products or services. This includes marketing strategy and tactics, product demonstrations, sales techniques, and sales control systems. **Economics and Accounting:** Knowledge of economic and accounting principles and practices, the financial markets, banking, and the analysis and reporting of financial data. **Mathematics:** Knowledge of arithmetic, algebra, geometry, calculus, and statistics and their applications. **Clerical Practices:**

Knowledge of administrative and clerical procedures and systems such as word processing, managing files and records, stenography and transcription, designing forms, and other office procedures and terminology. **Personnel and Human Resources:** Knowledge of principles and procedures for personnel recruitment, selection, training, compensation and benefits, labor relations and negotiation, and personnel information systems. **Law and Government:** Knowledge of laws, legal codes, court procedures, precedents, government regulations, executive orders, agency rules, and the democratic political process.

Nonfarm Animal Caretakers

◎ Education/Training Required: Short-term on-the-job training
◎ Annual Earnings: $17,460
◎ Growth: 22.2%
◎ Annual Job Openings: 32,000
◎ Self-Employed: 27.3%
◎ Part-Time: 31.7%

Feed, water, groom, bathe, exercise, or otherwise care for pets and other nonfarm animals, such as dogs, cats, ornamental fish or birds, zoo animals, and mice. Work in settings such as kennels, animal shelters, zoos, circuses, and aquariums. May keep records of feedings, treatments, and animals received or discharged. May clean, disinfect, and repair cages, pens, or fish tanks. Feed and water animals according to schedules and feeding instructions. Clean, organize, and disinfect animal quarters such as pens, stables, cages, and yards and animal equipment such as saddles and bridles. Answer telephones and schedule appointments. Examine and observe animals in order to detect signs of illness, disease, or injury. Respond to questions from patrons and provide information about animals, such as behavior, habitat, breeding habits, or facility activities. Provide treatment to sick or injured animals or contact veterinarians in order to secure treatment. Collect and record animal information such as weight, size, physical condition, treatments received, medications given, and food intake. Perform animal grooming duties such as washing, brushing, clipping, and trimming coats; cutting nails; and cleaning ears. Exercise animals in order to maintain their physical and

mental health. Order, unload, and store feed and supplies. Mix food, liquid formulas, medications, or food supplements according to instructions, prescriptions, and knowledge of animal species. Clean and disinfect surgical equipment. Discuss with clients their pets' grooming needs. Observe and caution children petting and feeding animals in designated areas in order to ensure the safety of humans and animals. Find homes for stray or unwanted animals. Adjust controls to regulate specified temperature and humidity of animal quarters, nurseries, or exhibit areas. Anesthetize and inoculate animals according to instructions. Transfer animals between enclosures in order to facilitate breeding, birthing, shipping, or rearrangement of exhibits. Install, maintain, and repair animal care facility equipment such as infrared lights, feeding devices, and cages. Train animals to perform certain tasks. Teach obedience classes. **SKILLS—Time Management:** Managing one's own time and the time of others. **Social Perceptiveness:** Being aware of others' reactions and understanding why they react as they do. **Persuasion:** Persuading others to change their minds or behavior. **Management of Financial Resources:** Determining how money will be spent to get the work done and accounting for these expenditures. **Instructing:** Teaching others how to do something. **Active Listening:** Giving full attention to what other people are saying, taking time to understand the points being made, asking questions as appropriate, and not interrupting at inappropriate times. **Coordination:** Adjusting actions in relation to others' actions. **Management of Material Resources:** Obtaining and seeing to the appropriate use of equipment, facilities, and materials needed to do certain work. **GOE—Interest Area:** 08. Health Science. **Work Group:** 08.05. Animal Care. **Other Jobs in This Work Group:** Animal Breeders; Animal Trainers; Veterinarians; Veterinary Assistants and Laboratory Animal Caretakers; Veterinary Technologists and Technicians. **PERSONALITY TYPE:** Realistic.

EDUCATION/TRAINING PROGRAM(S)—Agricultural/Farm Supplies Retailing and Wholesaling; Dog/Pet/Animal Grooming. **RELATED KNOWLEDGE/COURSES—Customer and Personal Service:** Knowledge of principles and processes for providing customer and personal services. This includes customer needs assessment, meeting quality standards for services, and evaluation of customer satisfaction. **Public Safety and Security:** Knowledge of relevant equipment, policies, procedures, and strategies to promote effective local, state, or national security operations for the protection of people, data, property, and institutions. **Sales and Marketing:** Knowledge of principles and methods for showing, promoting, and selling products or services. This includes marketing strategy and tactics, product demonstrations, sales techniques, and sales control systems. **Biology:** Knowledge of plant and animal organisms and their tissues, cells, functions, interdependencies, and interactions with each other and the environment. **Psychology:** Knowledge of human behavior and performance; individual differences in ability, personality, and interests; learning and motivation; psychological research methods; and the assessment and treatment of behavioral and affective disorders. **Medicine and Dentistry:** Knowledge of the information and techniques needed to diagnose and treat human injuries, diseases, and deformities. This includes symptoms, treatment alternatives, drug properties and interactions, and preventive health-care measures.

Nuclear Medicine Technologists

- ◎ Education/Training Required: Associate degree
- ◎ Annual Earnings: $56,450
- ◎ Growth: 23.6%
- ◎ Annual Job Openings: 2,000
- ◎ Self-Employed: 0.2%
- ◎ Part-Time: 17.5%

Prepare, administer, and measure radioactive isotopes in therapeutic, diagnostic, and tracer studies, utilizing a variety of radioisotope equipment. Prepare stock solutions of radioactive materials and calculate doses to be administered by radiologists. Subject patients to radiation. Execute blood volume, red cell survival, and fat absorption studies, following standard laboratory techniques. Calculate, measure and record radiation dosage or radiopharmaceuticals received, used, and disposed, using computer and following physician's prescription. Detect and map radiopharmaceuticals in patients' bodies, using a camera to produce photographic or computer images. Explain test procedures and safety precautions to patients and provide them with assistance during test procedures.

Administer radiopharmaceuticals or radiation to patients to detect or treat diseases, using radioisotope equipment, under direction of physician. Produce a computer-generated or film image for interpretation by a physician. Process cardiac function studies, using computer. Dispose of radioactive materials and store radiopharmaceuticals, following radiation safety procedures. Record and process results of procedures. Prepare stock radiopharmaceuticals, adhering to safety standards that minimize radiation exposure to workers and patients. Maintain and calibrate radioisotope and laboratory equipment. Gather information on patients' illnesses and medical history to guide the choice of diagnostic procedures for therapy. Measure glandular activity, blood volume, red-cell survival, and radioactivity of patient, using scanners, Geiger counters, scintillometers, and other laboratory equipment. Train and supervise student or subordinate nuclear medicine technologists. Position radiation fields, radiation beams, and patient to allow for most effective treatment of patient's disease, using computer. Add radioactive substances to biological specimens, such as blood, urine, and feces, to determine therapeutic drug or hormone levels. Develop treatment procedures for nuclear medicine treatment programs. **SKILLS—Science:** Using scientific rules and methods to solve problems. **Operation Monitoring:** Watching gauges, dials, or other indicators to make sure a machine is working properly. **Social Perceptiveness:** Being aware of others' reactions and understanding why they react as they do. **Service Orientation:** Actively looking for ways to help people. **Instructing:** Teaching others how to do something. **Operation and Control:** Controlling operations of equipment or systems. **Learning Strategies:** Selecting and using training/instructional methods and procedures appropriate for the situation when learning or teaching new things. **Active Learning:** Understanding the implications of new information for both current and future problem-solving and decision-making. **GOE—Interest Area:** 08. Health Science. **Work Group:** 08.06. Medical Technology. **Other Jobs in This Work Group:** Biological Technicians; Cardiovascular Technologists and Technicians; Diagnostic Medical Sonographers; Medical and Clinical Laboratory Technicians; Medical and Clinical Laboratory Technologists; Medical Equipment Preparers; Medical Records and Health Information Technicians; Opticians, Dispensing; Orthotists and Prosthetists; Radiologic Technicians; Radiologic Technologists. **PERSONALITY TYPE:** Investigative.

EDUCATION/TRAINING PROGRAM(S)— Nuclear Medical Technology/Technologist; Radiation Protection/Health Physics Technician. **RELATED KNOWLEDGE/COURSES—Medicine and Dentistry:** Knowledge of the information and techniques needed to diagnose and treat human injuries, diseases, and deformities. This includes symptoms, treatment alternatives, drug properties and interactions, and preventive health-care measures. **Customer and Personal Service:** Knowledge of principles and processes for providing customer and personal services. This includes customer needs assessment, meeting quality standards for services, and evaluation of customer satisfaction. **Biology:** Knowledge of plant and animal organisms and their tissues, cells, functions, interdependencies, and interactions with each other and the environment. **Physics:** Knowledge and prediction of physical principles and laws and their interrelationships and applications to understanding fluid, material, and atmospheric dynamics and mechanical, electrical, atomic, and subatomic structures and processes. **Chemistry:** Knowledge of the chemical composition, structure, and properties of substances and of the chemical processes and transformations that they undergo. This includes uses of chemicals and their danger signs, production techniques, and disposal methods. **Computers and Electronics:** Knowledge of circuit boards, processors, chips, electronic equipment, and computer hardware and software, including applications and programming.

Nursery and Greenhouse Managers

- ◎ Education/Training Required: Work experience in a related occupation
- ◎ Annual Earnings: $50,700
- ◎ Growth: 5.1%
- ◎ Annual Job Openings: 25,000
- ◎ Self-Employed: 0.9%
- ◎ Part-Time: 9.2%

Plan, organize, direct, control, and coordinate activities of workers engaged in propagating, cultivating, and harvesting horticultural specialties, such as trees, shrubs, flowers, mushrooms, and other plants. Confer with horticultural personnel in order to plan facility renovations or additions. Construct structures and accessories such as greenhouses and benches. Coordinate clerical, record-keeping, inventory, requisitioning, and marketing activities. Cut and prune trees, shrubs, flowers, and plants. Graft plants. Inspect facilities and equipment for signs of disrepair and perform necessary maintenance work. Negotiate contracts such as those for land leases or tree purchases. Assign work schedules and duties to nursery or greenhouse staff and supervise their work. Determine plant growing conditions, such as greenhouses, hydroponics, or natural settings, and set planting and care schedules. Determine types and quantities of horticultural plants to be grown, based on budgets, projected sales volumes, and/or executive directives. Explain and enforce safety regulations and policies. Hire employees and train them in gardening techniques. Identify plants as well as problems such as diseases, weeds, and insect pests. Manage nurseries that grow horticultural plants for sale to trade or retail customers, for display or exhibition, or for research. Select and purchase seeds, plant nutrients, disease control chemicals, and garden and lawn care equipment. Tour work areas to observe work being done, to inspect crops, and to evaluate plant and soil conditions. Apply pesticides and fertilizers to plants. Position and regulate plant irrigation systems and program environmental and irrigation control computers. Prepare soil for planting and plant or transplant seeds, bulbs, and cuttings. Provide information to customers on the care of trees, shrubs, flowers, plants, and lawns. **SKILLS— Management of Personnel Resources:** Motivating, developing, and directing people as they work, identifying the best people for the job. **Management of Financial Resources:** Determining how money will be spent to get the work done and accounting for these expenditures. **Management of Material Resources:** Obtaining and seeing to the appropriate use of equipment, facilities, and materials needed to do certain work. **Negotiation:** Bringing others together and trying to reconcile differences. **Systems Analysis:** Determining how a system should work and how changes in conditions, operations, and the environment will affect outcomes. **Systems Evaluation:** Identifying measures or indicators of system performance and the actions needed to improve or correct performance relative to the goals of the system. **Coordination:** Adjusting actions in relation to others' actions. **Operations Analysis:** Analyzing needs and product requirements to create a design. **Time Management:** Managing one's own time and the time of others. **GOE—Interest Area:** 01. Agriculture and Natural Resources. **Work**

Group: 01.01. Managerial Work in Agriculture and Natural Resources. **Other Jobs in This Work Group:** Agricultural Crop Farm Managers; Farmers and Ranchers; First-Line Supervisors and Manager/Supervisors—Agricultural Crop Workers; First-Line Supervisors and Manager/Supervisors—Animal Husbandry Workers; First-Line Supervisors and Manager/Supervisors—Extractive Workers; First-Line Supervisors and Manager/Supervisors—Fishery Workers; First-Line Supervisors and Manager/Supervisors—Horticultural Workers; First-Line Supervisors and Manager/Supervisors—Landscaping Workers; First-Line Supervisors and Manager/Supervisors—Logging Workers; Fish Hatchery Managers; Lawn Service Managers; Park Naturalists; Purchasing Agents and Buyers, Farm Products. **PERSONALITY TYPE:** Enterprising.

EDUCATION/TRAINING PROGRAM(S)— Agribusiness/Agricultural Business Operations; Agricultural Business and Management, General; Agricultural Business and Management, Other; Agricultural Production Operations, General; Agricultural Production Operations, Other; Agronomy and Crop Science; Crop Production; Farm/Farm and Ranch Management; Greenhouse Operations and Management; Horticultural Science; Ornamental Horticulture; Plant Nursery Operations and Management; Plant Protection and Integrated Pest Management; Plant Sciences, General; Range Science and Management. **RELATED KNOWLEDGE/COURSES— Biology:** Knowledge of plant and animal organisms and their tissues, cells, functions, interdependencies, and interactions with each other and the environment. **Administration and Management:** Knowledge of business and management principles involved in strategic planning, resource allocation, human resources modeling, leadership technique, production methods, and coordination of people and resources. **Personnel and Human Resources:** Knowledge of principles and procedures for personnel recruitment, selection, training, compensation and benefits, labor relations and negotiation, and personnel information systems. **Chemistry:** Knowledge of the chemical composition, structure, and properties of substances and of the chemical processes and transformations that they undergo. This includes uses of chemicals and their danger signs, production techniques, and disposal methods. **Food Production:** Knowledge of techniques and equipment for planting, growing, and harvesting food products (both plant and animal) for consumption, including storage/handling techniques. **Production and Processing:** Knowledge of raw materials, production processes, quality control, costs, and other techniques for maximizing the effective manufacture and distribution of goods.

Nursing Aides, Orderlies, and Attendants

- Education/Training Required: Short-term on-the-job training
- Annual Earnings: $20,980
- Growth: 24.9%
- Annual Job Openings: 302,000
- Self-Employed: 1.6%
- Part-Time: 21.9%

Provide basic patient care under direction of nursing staff. Perform duties such as feeding, bathing, dressing, grooming, or moving patients or changing linens. Turn and re-position bedridden patients, alone or with assistance, to prevent bedsores. Answer patients' call signals. Feed patients who are unable to feed themselves. Observe patients' conditions, measuring and recording food and liquid intake and output and vital signs, and report changes to professional staff. Provide patient care by supplying and emptying bedpans, applying dressings, and supervising exercise routines. Provide patients with help walking, exercising, and moving in and out of bed. Bathe, groom, shave, dress, and/or drape patients to prepare them for surgery, treatment, or examination. Collect specimens such as urine, feces, or sputum. Prepare, serve, and collect food trays. Clean rooms and change linens. Transport patients to treatment units, using a wheelchair or stretcher. Deliver messages, documents, and specimens. Answer phones and direct visitors. Administer medications and treatments, such as catheterizations, suppositories, irrigations, enemas, massages, and douches, as directed by a physician or nurse. Restrain patients if necessary. Maintain inventory by storing, preparing, sterilizing, and issuing supplies such as dressing packs and treatment trays. Explain medical instructions to patients and family members. Perform clerical duties such as processing documents and scheduling appointments. Work as part of a medical team that examines and treats clinic outpatients. Set up equipment such as oxygen tents, portable X-ray machines, and overhead irrigation bottles. **SKILLS—**

N

Social Perceptiveness: Being aware of others' reactions and understanding why they react as they do. **Time Management:** Managing one's own time and the time of others. **Instructing:** Teaching others how to do something. **Service Orientation:** Actively looking for ways to help people. **Monitoring:** Monitoring or assessing your performance or that of other individuals or organizations to make improvements or take corrective action. **Operation Monitoring:** Watching gauges, dials, or other indicators to make sure a machine is working properly. **Coordination:** Adjusting actions in relation to others' actions. **Persuasion:** Persuading others to change their minds or behavior. **GOE—Interest Area:** 08. Health Science. **Work Group:** 08.08. Patient Care and Assistance. **Other Jobs in This Work Group:** Home Health Aides; Licensed Practical and Licensed Vocational Nurses; Psychiatric Aides; Psychiatric Technicians. **PERSONALITY TYPE:** Social.

EDUCATION/TRAINING PROGRAM(S)— Health Aide; Nurse/Nursing Assistant/Aide and Patient Care Assistant. **RELATED KNOWLEDGE/COURSES—Psychology:** Knowledge of human behavior and performance; individual differences in ability, personality, and interests; learning and motivation; psychological research methods; and the assessment and treatment of behavioral and affective disorders. **Customer and Personal Service:** Knowledge of principles and processes for providing customer and personal services. This includes customer needs assessment, meeting quality standards for services, and evaluation of customer satisfaction. **Medicine and Dentistry:** Knowledge of the information and techniques needed to diagnose and treat human injuries, diseases, and deformities. This includes symptoms, treatment alternatives, drug properties and interactions, and preventive health-care measures. **Education and Training:** Knowledge of principles and methods for curriculum and training design, teaching and instruction for individuals and groups, and the measurement of training effects. **Foreign Language:** Knowledge of the structure and content of a foreign (non-English) language, including the meaning and spelling of words, rules of composition and grammar, and pronunciation. **English Language:** Knowledge of the structure and content of the English language, including the meaning and spelling of words, rules of composition, and grammar.

Nursing Instructors and Teachers, Postsecondary

- Education/Training Required: Master's degree
- Annual Earnings: $52,060
- Growth: 38.1%
- Annual Job Openings: 216,000
- Self-Employed: 0.3%
- Part-Time: 27.7%

Demonstrate and teach patient care in classroom and clinical units to nursing students. Includes both teachers primarily engaged in teaching and those who do a combination of both teaching and research. Initiate, facilitate, and moderate classroom discussions. Prepare and deliver lectures to undergraduate and/or graduate students on topics such as pharmacology, mental health nursing, and community health care practices. Keep abreast of developments in their field by reading current literature, talking with colleagues, and participating in professional conferences. Prepare course materials such as syllabi, homework assignments, and handouts. Supervise students' laboratory and clinical work. Evaluate and grade students' class work, laboratory and clinic work, assignments, and papers. Collaborate with colleagues to address teaching and research issues. Plan, evaluate, and revise curricula, course content, and course materials and methods of instruction. Assess clinical education needs, and patient and client teaching needs, utilizing a variety of methods. Compile, administer, and grade examinations or assign this work to others. Advise students on academic and vocational curricula and on career issues. Maintain student attendance records, grades, and other required records. Maintain regularly scheduled office hours in order to advise and assist students. Supervise undergraduate and/or graduate teaching, internship, and research work. Conduct research in a particular field of knowledge and publish findings in professional journals, books, and/or electronic media. Participate in student recruitment, registration, and placement activities. Serve on academic or administrative committees that deal with institutional policies, departmental matters, and academic issues. Coordinate training programs with area universities, clinics, hospitals, health agencies, and/or vocational schools. Compile bibliographies of specialized materials for outside reading assignments. Select and obtain materials and supplies such as textbooks and laboratory equipment. Participate in campus and community events. Write grant proposals to procure external research funding. Act as advisers to student organizations. Demonstrate patient care in clinical units of hospitals. Perform administrative duties such as serving as department head. **SKILLS—Instructing:** Teaching others how to do something. **Social Perceptiveness:** Being aware of others' reactions and understanding why they react as they do. **Science:** Using scientific rules and methods to solve problems. **Learning Strategies:** Selecting and using training/instructional methods and procedures appropriate for the situation when learning or teaching new things. **Writing:** Communicating effectively in writing as appropriate for the needs of the audience. **Service Orientation:** Actively looking for ways to help people. **Reading Comprehension:** Understanding written sentences and paragraphs in work-related documents. **Persuasion:** Persuading others to change their minds or behavior. **GOE—Interest Area:** 05. Education and Training. **Work Group:** 05.03. Postsecondary and Adult Teaching and Instructing. **Other Jobs in This Work Group:** Adult Literacy, Remedial Education, and GED Teachers and Instructors; Agricultural Sciences Teachers, Postsecondary; Anthropology and Archeology Teachers, Postsecondary; Architecture Teachers, Postsecondary; Area, Ethnic, and Cultural Studies Teachers, Postsecondary; Art, Drama, and Music Teachers, Postsecondary; Atmospheric, Earth, Marine, and Space Sciences Teachers, Postsecondary; Biological Science Teachers, Postsecondary; Business Teachers, Postsecondary; Chemistry Teachers, Postsecondary; Communications Teachers, Postsecondary; Computer Science Teachers, Postsecondary; Criminal Justice and Law Enforcement Teachers, Postsecondary; Economics Teachers, Postsecondary; Education Teachers, Postsecondary; Engineering Teachers, Postsecondary; English Language and Literature Teachers, Postsecondary; Environmental Science Teachers, Postsecondary; Farm and Home Management Advisors; Foreign Language and Literature Teachers, Postsecondary; Forestry and Conservation Science Teachers, Postsecondary; Geography Teachers, Postsecondary; Graduate Teaching Assistants; Health Specialties Teachers, Postsecondary; History Teachers, Postsecondary; Home Economics Teachers, Postsecondary; Law Teachers, Postsecondary; Library Science Teachers, Postsecondary; Mathematical Science Teachers, Postsecondary; Philosophy and Religion Teachers, Postsecondary; Physics Teachers, Postsecondary; Political Science Teachers, Postsecondary; Psychology Teachers, Postsecondary; Recreation and Fitness Studies Teachers, Postsecondary; Self-Enrichment Education Teachers; Social Work Teachers, Postsecondary; Sociology Teachers, Postsecondary; Vocational Education Teachers, Postsecondary. **PERSONALITY TYPE:** Social.

EDUCATION/TRAINING PROGRAM(S)—Adult Health Nurse/Nursing; Clinical Nurse Specialist; Family Practice Nurse/Nurse Practitioner; Maternal/Child Health and Neonatal Nurse/Nursing; Nurse Anesthetist; Nurse Midwife/Nursing Midwifery; Nursing—Registered Nurse Training (RN, ASN, BSN, MSN); Nursing Science (MS, PhD); Nursing, Other; Pediatric Nurse/Nursing; Perioperative/Operating Room and Surgical Nurse/Nursing; Pre-Nursing Studies; Psychiatric/Mental Health Nurse/Nursing; Public Health/Community Nurse/Nursing. **RELATED KNOWLEDGE/COURSES—Therapy and Counseling: Knowledge of principles, methods, and procedures for diagnosis, treatment, and rehabilitation of physical and mental dysfunctions and for career counseling and guidance. **Sociology and Anthropology:** Knowledge of group behavior and dynamics, societal trends and influences, human migrations, ethnicity, and cultures and their history and origins. **Education and Training:** Knowledge of principles and methods for curriculum and training design, teaching and instruction for individuals and groups, and the measurement of training effects. **Psychology:** Knowledge of human behavior and performance; individual differences in ability, personality, and interests; learning and motivation; psychological research methods; and the assessment and treatment of behavioral and affective disorders. **Medicine and Dentistry:** Knowledge of the information and techniques needed to diagnose and treat human injuries, diseases, and deformities. This includes symptoms, treatment alternatives, drug properties and interactions, and preventive health-care measures. **Biology:** Knowledge of plant and animal organisms and their tissues, cells, functions, interdependencies, and interactions with each other and the environment. **Philosophy and Theology:** Knowledge of different philosophical systems and religions. This includes their basic principles, values, ethics, ways of thinking, customs, and practices and their impact on human culture.

Obstetricians and Gynecologists

- Education/Training Required: First professional degree
- Annual Earnings: More than $145,600
- Growth: 19.5%
- Annual Job Openings: 38,000
- Self-Employed: 16.9%
- Part-Time: 8.1%

Diagnose, treat, and help prevent diseases of women, especially those affecting the reproductive system and the process of childbirth. Advise patients and community members concerning diet, activity, hygiene, and disease prevention. Analyze records, reports, test results, or examination information to diagnose medical condition of patient. Care for and treat women during prenatal, natal, and post-natal periods. Collect, record, and maintain patient information, such as medical histories, reports, and examination results. Explain procedures and discuss test results or prescribed treatments with patients. Monitor patients' condition and progress and re-evaluate treatments as necessary. Perform cesarean sections or other surgical procedures as needed to preserve patients' health and deliver babies safely. Prescribe or administer therapy, medication, and other specialized medical care to treat or prevent illness, disease, or injury. Refer patient to medical specialist or other practitioner when necessary. Treat diseases of female organs. Conduct research to develop or test medications, treatments, or procedures to prevent or control disease or injury. Consult with, or provide consulting services to, other physicians. Direct and coordinate activities of nurses, students, assistants, specialists, therapists, and other medical staff. Plan, implement, or administer health programs in hospitals, businesses, or communities for prevention and treatment of injuries or illnesses. Prepare government and organizational reports on birth, death, and disease statistics; workforce evaluations; or the medical status of individuals. **SKILLS—Science:** Using scientific rules and methods to solve problems. **Systems Evaluation:** Identifying measures or indicators of system performance and the actions needed to improve or correct performance relative to the goals of the system. **Reading Comprehension:** Understanding written sentences and paragraphs in work-related documents. **Active Learning:** Understanding the implications of new information for both current and future problem-solving and decision-making. **Judgment and Decision Making:** Considering the relative costs and benefits of potential actions to choose the most appropriate one. **Management of Personnel Resources:** Motivating, developing, and directing people as they work, identifying the best people for the job. **Systems Analysis:** Determining how a system should work and how changes in conditions, operations, and the environment will affect outcomes. **Social Perceptiveness:** Being aware of others' reactions and understanding why they react as they do. **GOE—Interest Area:** 08. Health Science. **Work Group:** 08.02. Medicine and Surgery. **Other Jobs in This Work Group:** Anesthesiologists; Family and General Practitioners; Internists, General; Medical Assistants; Medical Transcriptionists; Pediatricians, General; Pharmacists; Pharmacy Aides; Pharmacy Technicians; Physician Assistants; Psychiatrists; Registered Nurses; Surgeons; Surgical Technologists. **PERSONALITY TYPE:** Investigative.

EDUCATION/TRAINING PROGRAM(S)—Neonatal-Perinatal Medicine; Obstetrics and Gynecology. **RELATED KNOWLEDGE/COURSES—Medicine and Dentistry:** Knowledge of the information and techniques needed to diagnose and treat human injuries, diseases, and deformities. This includes symptoms, treatment alternatives, drug properties and interactions, and preventive health-care measures. **Biology:** Knowledge of plant and animal organisms and their tissues, cells, functions, interdependencies, and interactions with each other and the environment. **Therapy and Counseling:** Knowledge of principles, methods, and procedures for diagnosis, treatment, and rehabilitation of physical and mental dysfunctions and for career counseling and guidance. **Chemistry:** Knowledge of the chemical composition, structure, and properties of substances and of the chemical processes and transformations that they undergo. This includes uses of chemicals and their danger signs, production techniques, and disposal methods. **Administration and Management:** Knowledge of business and management principles involved in strategic planning, resource allocation, human resources modeling, leadership technique, production methods, and coordination of people and resources. **Physics:** Knowledge and prediction of physical principles and laws and their interrelationships and applications to understanding fluid, material, and atmospheric dynamics and mechanical, electrical, atomic, and subatomic structures and processes.

Occupational Health and Safety Specialists

- Education/Training Required: Master's degree
- Annual Earnings: $51,570
- Growth: 13.2%
- Annual Job Openings: 6,000
- Self-Employed: 2.4%
- Part-Time: 6.5%

Review, evaluate, and analyze work environments and design programs and procedures to control, eliminate, and prevent disease or injury caused by chemical, physical, and biological agents or ergonomic factors. May conduct inspections and enforce adherence to laws and regulations governing the health and safety of individuals. May be employed in the public or private sector. Collaborate with engineers and physicians to institute control and remedial measures for hazardous and potentially hazardous conditions or equipment. Collect samples of dust, gases, vapors, and other potentially toxic materials for analysis. Collect samples of hazardous materials or arrange for sample collection. Conduct audits at hazardous waste sites or industrial sites and participate in hazardous waste site investigations. Conduct safety training and education programs and demonstrate the use of safety equipment. Coordinate "right-to-know" programs regarding hazardous chemicals and other substances. Develop and maintain hygiene programs such as noise surveys, continuous atmosphere monitoring, ventilation surveys, and asbestos management plans. Develop and maintain medical monitoring programs for employees. Inspect and evaluate workplace environments, equipment, and practices in order to ensure compliance with safety standards and government regulations. Inspect specified areas to ensure the presence of fire prevention equipment, safety equipment, and first-aid supplies. Investigate accidents to identify causes and to determine how such accidents might be prevented in the future. Investigate health-related complaints and inspect facilities to ensure that they comply with public health legislation and regulations. Investigate the adequacy of ventilation, exhaust equipment, lighting, and other conditions that could affect employee health, comfort, or performance. Maintain and update emergency response plans and procedures. Maintain inventories of hazardous materials and hazardous wastes, using waste-tracking systems to ensure that materials are handled properly. Order suspension of activities that pose threats to workers' health and safety. Perform laboratory analyses and physical inspections of samples in order to detect disease or to assess purity or cleanliness. Prepare hazardous, radioactive, and mixed-waste samples for transportation and storage by treating, compacting, packaging, and labeling them. Provide new-employee health and safety orientations and develop materials for these presentations. **SKILLS—Science:** Using scientific rules and methods to solve problems. **Writing:** Communicating effectively in writing as appropriate for the needs of the audience. **Speaking:** Talking to others to convey information effectively. **Mathematics:** Using mathematics to solve problems. **Systems Analysis:** Determining how a system should work and how changes in conditions, operations, and the environment will affect outcomes. **Reading Comprehension:** Understanding written sentences and paragraphs in work-related documents. **Operation Monitoring:** Watching gauges, dials, or other indicators to make sure a machine is working properly. **Management of Financial Resources:** Determining how money will be spent to get the work done and accounting for these expenditures. **GOE—Interest Area:** 07. Government and Public Administration. **Work Group:** 07.03. Regulations Enforcement. **Other Jobs in This Work Group:** Agricultural Inspectors; Aviation Inspectors; Child Support, Missing Persons, and Unemployment Insurance Fraud Investigators; Environmental Compliance Inspectors; Equal Opportunity Representatives and Officers; Financial Examiners; Fire Inspectors; Fish and Game Wardens; Forest Fire Inspectors and Prevention Specialists; Government Property Inspectors and Investigators; Immigration and Customs Inspectors; Licensing Examiners and Inspectors; Marine Cargo Inspectors; Mechanical Inspectors; Motor Vehicle Inspectors; Nuclear Monitoring Technicians; Pressure Vessel Inspectors; Railroad Inspectors; Tax Examiners, Collectors, and Revenue Agents. **PERSONALITY TYPE:** Social.

EDUCATION/TRAINING PROGRAM(S)—Environmental Health; Industrial Safety Technology/Technician; Occupational Health and Industrial Hygiene; Occupational Safety and Health Technology/Technician; Quality Control and Safety Technologies/Technicians, Other. **RELATED KNOWLEDGE/COURSES—Public Safety and Security:** Knowledge of relevant equipment, policies, procedures, and strategies to promote effective local, state, or national security operations for the protection of people, data, property, and institutions. **Medicine and Dentistry:** Knowledge of the information and techniques needed to diagnose and treat human injuries, diseases, and deformities. This includes symptoms, treatment alternatives, drug properties and interactions, and preventive health-care measures. **Chemistry:** Knowledge of the chemical composition, structure, and properties of substances and of the chemical processes and transformations that they undergo. This includes uses of chemicals and their danger signs, production techniques, and disposal methods. **Physics:** Knowledge and prediction of physical principles and laws and their interrelationships and applications to understanding fluid, material, and atmospheric dynamics and mechanical, electrical, atomic, and subatomic structures and processes. **Law and Government:** Knowledge of laws, legal codes, court procedures, precedents, government regulations, executive orders, agency rules, and the democratic political process. **Economics and Accounting:** Knowledge of economic and accounting principles and practices, the financial markets, banking, and the analysis and reporting of financial data.

Occupational Therapist Assistants

- ◎ Education/Training Required: Associate degree
- ◎ Annual Earnings: $38,430
- ◎ Growth: 39.2%
- ◎ Annual Job Openings: 3,000
- ◎ Self-Employed: 2.9%
- ◎ Part-Time: 25.5%

Assist occupational therapists in providing occupational therapy treatments and procedures. May, in accordance with state laws, assist in development of treatment plans, carry out routine functions, direct activity programs, and document the progress of treatments. Generally requires formal training. Observe and record patients' progress, attitudes, and behavior and maintain this information in client records. Maintain and promote a positive attitude toward clients and their treatment programs. Monitor patients' performance in therapy activities, providing encouragement. Select therapy activities to fit patients' needs and capabilities. Instruct, or assist in instructing, patients and families in home programs, basic living skills, and the care and use of adaptive equipment. Evaluate the daily living skills and capacities of physically, developmentally, or emotionally disabled clients. Aid patients in dressing and grooming themselves. Implement, or assist occupational therapists with implementing, treatment plans designed to help clients function independently. Report to supervisors, verbally or in writing, on patients' progress, attitudes, and behavior. Alter treatment programs to obtain better results if treatment is not having the intended effect. Work under the direction of occupational therapists to plan, implement, and administer educational, vocational, and recreational programs that restore and enhance performance in individuals with functional impairments. Design, fabricate, and repair assistive devices and make adaptive changes to equipment and environments. Assemble, clean, and maintain equipment and materials for patient use. Teach patients how to deal constructively with their emotions. Perform clerical duties such as scheduling appointments, collecting data, and documenting health insurance billings. Transport patients to and from the occupational therapy work area. Demonstrate therapy techniques, such as manual and creative arts and games. Order any needed educational or treatment supplies. Assist educational specialists or clinical psychologists in administering situational or diagnostic tests to measure client's abilities or progress. **SKILLS—Social Perceptiveness:** Being aware of others' reactions and understanding why they react as they do. **Service Orientation:** Actively looking for ways to help people. **Instructing:** Teaching others how to do something. **Learning Strategies:** Selecting and using training/instructional methods and procedures appropriate for the situation when learning or teaching new things. **Persuasion:** Persuading others to change their minds or behavior. **Time Management:** Managing one's own time and the time of others. **Monitoring:** Monitoring or assessing your performance or that of other individuals or organizations to make improvements or take corrective action. **Active Listening:** Giving full attention to what other people are saying, taking time to understand the points being made, asking questions as appropriate, and not interrupting at inappropriate times. **GOE—Interest Area:** 08. Health Science. **Work Group:** 08.07. Medical Therapy. **Other Jobs in This Work Group:** Audiologists; Massage

Therapists; Occupational Therapist Aides; Occupational Therapists; Physical Therapist Aides; Physical Therapist Assistants; Physical Therapists; Radiation Therapists; Recreational Therapists; Respiratory Therapists; Respiratory Therapy Technicians; Speech-Language Pathologists. **PERSONALITY TYPE:** Social.

EDUCATION/TRAINING   PROGRAM(S)— Occupational Therapist Assistant. **RELATED KNOWLEDGE/COURSES—Psychology:** Knowledge of human behavior and performance; individual differences in ability, personality, and interests; learning and motivation; psychological research methods; and the assessment and treatment of behavioral and affective disorders. **Therapy and Counseling:** Knowledge of principles, methods, and procedures for diagnosis, treatment, and rehabilitation of physical and mental dysfunctions and for career counseling and guidance. **Sociology and Anthropology:** Knowledge of group behavior and dynamics, societal trends and influences, human migrations, ethnicity, and cultures and their history and origins. **Philosophy and Theology:** Knowledge of different philosophical systems and religions. This includes their basic principles, values, ethics, ways of thinking, customs, and practices and their impact on human culture. **Customer and Personal Service:** Knowledge of principles and processes for providing customer and personal services. This includes customer needs assessment, meeting quality standards for services, and evaluation of customer satisfaction. **Medicine and Dentistry:** Knowledge of the information and techniques needed to diagnose and treat human injuries, diseases, and deformities. This includes symptoms, treatment alternatives, drug properties and interactions, and preventive health-care measures.

Occupational Therapists

- ◎ Education/Training Required: Bachelor's degree
- ◎ Annual Earnings: $54,660
- ◎ Growth: 35.2%
- ◎ Annual Job Openings: 10,000
- ◎ Self-Employed: 4.0%
- ◎ Part-Time: 31.1%

Assess, plan, organize, and participate in rehabilitative programs that help restore vocational, home-

making, and daily living skills, as well as general independence, to disabled persons. Complete and maintain necessary records. Evaluate patients' progress and prepare reports that detail progress. Test and evaluate patients' physical and mental abilities and analyze medical data to determine realistic rehabilitation goals for patients. Select activities that will help individuals learn work and life-management skills within limits of their mental and physical capabilities. Plan, organize, and conduct occupational therapy programs in hospital, institutional, or community settings to help rehabilitate those impaired because of illness, injury, or psychological or developmental problems. Recommend changes in patients' work or living environments consistent with their needs and capabilities. Consult with rehabilitation team to select activity programs and coordinate occupational therapy with other therapeutic activities. Help clients improve decision-making, abstract reasoning, memory, sequencing, coordination, and perceptual skills, using computer programs. Develop and participate in health promotion programs, group activities, or discussions to promote client health, facilitate social adjustment, alleviate stress, and prevent physical or mental disability. Provide training and supervision in therapy techniques and objectives for students and nurses and other medical staff. Design and create or requisition special supplies and equipment, such as splints, braces, and computer-aided adaptive equipment. Plan and implement programs and social activities to help patients learn work and school skills and adjust to handicaps. Lay out materials such as puzzles, scissors, and eating utensils for use in therapy and clean and repair these tools after therapy sessions. Advise on health risks in the workplace and on health-related transition to retirement. Conduct research in occupational therapy. **SKILLS—Social Perceptiveness:** Being aware of others' reactions and understanding why they react as they do. **Service Orientation:** Actively looking for ways to help people. **Science:** Using scientific rules and methods to solve problems. **Technology Design:** Generating or adapting equipment and technology to serve user needs. **Instructing:** Teaching others how to do something. **Reading Comprehension:** Understanding written sentences and paragraphs in work-related documents. **Coordination:** Adjusting actions in relation to others' actions. **Learning Strategies:** Selecting and using training/instructional methods and procedures appropriate for the situation when learning or teaching new things. **Persuasion:** Persuading others to change their minds or behavior. **GOE—Interest Area:** 08. Health Science. **Work Group:** 08.07. Medical Therapy. **Other Jobs in This Work Group:** Audiologists; Massage Therapists; Occupational Therapist Aides; Occupational Therapist Assistants; Physical Therapist Aides; Physical Therapist Assistants; Physical Therapists; Radiation Therapists; Recreational Therapists; Respiratory Therapists; Respiratory Therapy Technicians; Speech-Language Pathologists. **PERSONALITY TYPE:** Social.

EDUCATION/TRAINING PROGRAM(S)— Occupational Therapy/Therapist. **RELATED KNOWLEDGE/COURSES—Therapy and Counseling:** Knowledge of principles, methods, and procedures for diagnosis, treatment, and rehabilitation of physical and mental dysfunctions and for career counseling and guidance. **Psychology:** Knowledge of human behavior and performance; individual differences in ability, personality, and interests; learning and motivation; psychological research methods; and the assessment and treatment of behavioral and affective disorders. **Customer and Personal Service:** Knowledge of principles and processes for providing customer and personal services. This includes customer needs assessment, meeting quality standards for services, and evaluation of customer satisfaction. **Medicine and Dentistry:** Knowledge of the information and techniques needed to diagnose and treat human injuries, diseases, and deformities. This includes symptoms, treatment alternatives, drug properties and interactions, and preventive health-care measures. **Education and Training:** Knowledge of principles and methods for curriculum and training design, teaching and instruction for individuals and groups, and the measurement of training effects. **Sociology and Anthropology:** Knowledge of group behavior and dynamics, societal trends and influences, human migrations, ethnicity, and cultures and their history and origins.

Office Clerks, General

- ◉ Education/Training Required: Short-term on-the-job training
- ◉ Annual Earnings: $22,770
- ◉ Growth: 10.4%
- ◉ Annual Job Openings: 550,000
- ◉ Self-Employed: 0.5%
- ◉ Part-Time: 25.7%

Perform duties too varied and diverse to be classified in any specific office clerical occupation and requiring limited knowledge of office management systems and procedures. Clerical duties may be assigned in accordance with the office procedures of individual establishments and may include a combination of answering telephones, bookkeeping, typing or word processing, stenography, office machine operation, and filing. Collect, count, and disburse money; do basic bookkeeping; and complete banking transactions. Communicate with customers, employees, and other individuals to answer questions, disseminate or explain information, take orders, and address complaints. Answer telephones, direct calls, and take messages. Compile, copy, sort, and file records of office activities, business transactions, and other activities. Complete and mail bills, contracts, policies, invoices, or checks. Operate office machines, such as photocopiers and scanners, facsimile machines, voice mail systems, and personal computers. Compute, record, and proofread data and other information, such as records or reports. Maintain and update filing, inventory, mailing, and database systems either manually or using a computer. Open, sort, and route incoming mail; answer correspondence; and prepare outgoing mail. Review files, records, and other documents to obtain information to respond to requests. Deliver messages and run errands. Inventory and order materials, supplies, and services. Complete work schedules, manage calendars, and arrange appointments. Process and prepare documents such as business or government forms and expense reports. Monitor and direct the work of lower-level clerks. Type, format, proofread, and edit correspondence and other documents from notes or dictating machines, using computers or typewriters. Count, weigh, measure, and/or organize materials. Train other staff members to perform work activities such as using computer applications. Prepare meeting agendas, attend meetings, and record and transcribe minutes. Troubleshoot problems involving office equipment, such as computer hardware and software. **SKILLS—Active Listening:** Giving full attention to what other people are saying, taking time to understand the points being made, asking questions as appropriate, and not interrupting at inappropriate times. **Reading Comprehension:** Understanding written sentences and paragraphs in work-related documents. **Social Perceptiveness:** Being aware of others' reactions and understanding why they react as they do. **Service Orientation:** Actively looking for ways to help people. **Writing:** Communicating effectively in writing as appropriate for the needs of the audience. **Speaking:** Talking to others to convey information effectively. **Learning Strategies:** Selecting and using training/instructional methods and procedures appropriate for the situation when learning or teaching new things. **GOE—Interest Area:** 04. Business and Administration. **Work Group:** 04.07. Records and Materials Processing. **Other Jobs in This Work Group:** Correspondence Clerks; File Clerks; Human Resources Assistants, Except Payroll and Timekeeping; Mail Clerks, Except Mail Machine Operators and Postal Service; Marking Clerks; Meter Readers, Utilities; Order Fillers, Wholesale and Retail Sales; Postal Service Clerks; Postal Service Mail Sorters, Processors, and Processing Machine Operators; Procurement Clerks; Production, Planning, and Expediting Clerks; Shipping, Receiving, and Traffic Clerks; Stock Clerks, Sales Floor; Stock Clerks—Stockroom, Warehouse, or Storage Yard; Weighers, Measurers, Checkers, and Samplers, Recordkeeping. **PERSONALITY TYPE:** Conventional.

EDUCATION/TRAINING PROGRAM(S)—General Office Occupations and Clerical Services. **RELATED KNOWLEDGE/COURSES—Clerical Practices:** Knowledge of administrative and clerical procedures and systems such as word processing, managing files and records, stenography and transcription, designing forms, and other office procedures and terminology. **Customer and Personal Service:** Knowledge of principles and processes for providing customer and personal services. This includes customer needs assessment, meeting quality standards for services, and evaluation of customer satisfaction. **Economics and Accounting:** Knowledge of economic and accounting principles and practices, the financial markets, banking, and the analysis and reporting of financial data. **Personnel and Human Resources:** Knowledge of principles and procedures for personnel recruitment, selection, training, compensation and benefits, labor relations and negotiation, and personnel information systems. **Computers and Electronics:** Knowledge of circuit boards, processors, chips, electronic equipment, and computer hardware and software, including applications and programming. **Mathematics:** Knowledge of arithmetic, algebra, geometry, calculus, and statistics and their applications. **English Language:** Knowledge of the structure and content of the English language, including the meaning and spelling of words, rules of composition, and grammar.

Office Machine and Cash Register Servicers

- Education/Training Required: Long-term on-the-job training
- Annual Earnings: $35,150
- Growth: 15.1%
- Annual Job Openings: 19,000
- Self-Employed: 12.2%
- Part-Time: 8.2%

Repair and service office machines, such as adding, accounting, calculating, duplicating, and typewriting machines. Includes the repair of manual, electrical, and electronic office machines. Tests machine to locate cause of electrical problems, using testing devices such as voltmeter, ohmmeter, and circuit test equipment. Disassembles machine and examines parts such as wires, gears, and bearings for wear and defects, using hand tools, power tools, and measuring devices. Operates machine such as typewriter, cash register, or adding machine to test functioning of parts and mechanisms. Assembles and installs machine according to specifications, using hand tools, power tools, and measuring devices. Cleans and oils mechanical parts to maintain machine. Reads specifications such as blueprints, charts, and schematics to determine machine settings and adjustments. Repairs, adjusts, or replaces electrical and mechanical components and parts, using hand tools, power tools, and soldering or welding equipment. Instructs operators and servicers in operation, maintenance, and repair of machine. **SKILLS— Installation:** Installing equipment, machines, wiring, or programs to meet specifications. **Repairing:** Repairing machines or systems by using the needed tools. **Equipment Maintenance:** Performing routine maintenance on equipment and determining when and what kind of maintenance is needed. **Instructing:** Teaching others how to do something. **Technology Design:** Generating or adapting equipment and technology to serve user needs. **Troubleshooting:** Determining causes of operating errors and deciding what to do about them. **Quality Control Analysis:** Conducting tests and inspections of products, services, or processes to evaluate quality or performance. **Science:** Using scientific rules and methods to solve problems. **Operation Monitoring:** Watching gauges, dials, or other indicators to make sure a machine is working properly. **GOE—**

Interest Area: 11. Information Technology. **Work Group:** 11.03. Digital Equipment Repair. **Other Jobs in This Work Group:** Automatic Teller Machine Servicers; Coin, Vending, and Amusement Machine Servicers and Repairers; Data Processing Equipment Repairers. **PERSONALITY TYPE:** Realistic.

EDUCATION/TRAINING PROGRAM(S)—Business Machine Repair; Computer Installation and Repair Technology/Technician. **RELATED KNOWLEDGE/COURSES—Computers and Electronics:** Knowledge of circuit boards, processors, chips, electronic equipment, and computer hardware and software, including applications and programming. **Mechanical Devices:** Knowledge of machines and tools, including their designs, uses, repair, and maintenance. **Engineering and Technology:** Knowledge of the practical application of engineering science and technology. This includes applying principles, techniques, procedures, and equipment to the design and production of various goods and services. **Design:** Knowledge of design techniques, tools, and principles involved in production of precision technical plans, blueprints, drawings, and models. **Telecommunications:** Knowledge of transmission, broadcasting, switching, control, and operation of telecommunications systems. **Education and Training:** Knowledge of principles and methods for curriculum and training design, teaching and instruction for individuals and groups, and the measurement of training effects.

Operating Engineers

- Education/Training Required: Moderate-term on-the-job training
- Annual Earnings: $35,360
- Growth: 10.4%
- Annual Job Openings: 45,000
- Self-Employed: 3.7%
- Part-Time: 2.6%

Operate several types of power construction equipment, such as compressors, pumps, hoists, derricks, cranes, shovels, tractors, scrapers, or motor graders, to excavate, move, and grade earth; erect structures; or pour concrete or other hard-surface pavement. May repair and maintain equipment in addition to other duties. Adjusts handwheels and depresses pedals to drive machines and control attachments, such as

blades, buckets, scrapers, and swing booms. Turns valves to control air and water output of compressors and pumps. Repairs and maintains equipment. **SKILLS—Repairing:** Repairing machines or systems by using the needed tools. **Operation and Control:** Controlling operations of equipment or systems. **Equipment Maintenance:** Performing routine maintenance on equipment and determining when and what kind of maintenance is needed. **Operation Monitoring:** Watching gauges, dials, or other indicators to make sure a machine is working properly. **Troubleshooting:** Determining causes of operating errors and deciding what to do about them. **GOE—Interest Area:** 02. Architecture and Construction. **Work Group:** 02.04. Construction Crafts. **Other Jobs in This Work Group:** Boat Builders and Shipwrights; Boilermakers; Brattice Builders; Brickmasons and Blockmasons; Carpet Installers; Ceiling Tile Installers; Cement Masons and Concrete Finishers; Commercial Divers; Construction Carpenters; Crane and Tower Operators; Dragline Operators; Drywall Installers; Electricians; Fence Erectors; Floor Layers, Except Carpet, Wood, and Hard Tiles; Floor Sanders and Finishers; Glaziers; Grader, Bulldozer, and Scraper Operators; Hazardous Materials Removal Workers; Insulation Workers, Floor, Ceiling, and Wall; Insulation Workers, Mechanical; Manufactured Building and Mobile Home Installers; Painters, Construction and Maintenance; Paperhangers; Paving, Surfacing, and Tamping Equipment Operators; Pile-Driver Operators; Pipe Fitters; Pipelayers; Pipelaying Fitters; Plasterers and Stucco Masons; Plumbers; Rail-Track Laying and Maintenance Equipment Operators; Refractory Materials Repairers, Except Brickmasons; Reinforcing Iron and Rebar Workers; Riggers; Roofers; Rough Carpenters; Security and Fire Alarm Systems Installers; Segmental Pavers; Sheet Metal Workers; Ship Carpenters and Joiners; Stone Cutters and Carvers; Stonemasons; Structural Iron and Steel Workers; Tapers; Terrazzo Workers and Finishers; Tile and Marble Setters. **PERSONALITY TYPE:** Realistic.

EDUCATION/TRAINING PROGRAM(S)—Construction/Heavy Equipment/Earthmoving Equipment Operation; Mobil Crane Operation/Operator. **RELATED KNOWLEDGE/COURSES—Mechanical Devices:** Knowledge of machines and tools, including their designs, uses, repair, and maintenance. **Building and Construction:** Knowledge of the materials, methods, and tools involved in the construction or repair of houses, buildings, or other structures such as highways and roads. **Sales and Marketing:** Knowledge of principles and methods for showing, promoting, and selling products or services. This includes marketing strategy and tactics, product demonstrations, sales techniques, and sales control systems. **Physics:** Knowledge and prediction of physical principles and laws and their interrelationships and applications to understanding fluid, material, and atmospheric dynamics and mechanical, electrical, atomic, and subatomic structures and processes. **Engineering and Technology:** Knowledge of the practical application of engineering science and technology. This includes applying principles, techniques, procedures, and equipment to the design and production of various goods and services. **Public Safety and Security:** Knowledge of relevant equipment, policies, procedures, and strategies to promote effective local, state, or national security operations for the protection of people, data, property, and institutions.

Operations Research Analysts

- Education/Training Required: Master's degree
- Annual Earnings: $60,190
- Growth: 6.2%
- Annual Job Openings: 6,000
- Self-Employed: 5.8%
- Part-Time: 2.7%

Formulate and apply mathematical modeling and other optimizing methods, using a computer to develop and interpret information that assists management with decision making, policy formulation, or other managerial functions. May develop related software, service, or products. Frequently concentrates on collecting and analyzing data and developing decision support software. May develop and supply optimal time, cost, or logistics networks for program evaluation, review, or implementation. Analyze information obtained from management in order to conceptualize and define operational problems. Break systems into their component parts, assign numerical values to each component, and examine the mathematical relationships between them. Collaborate with senior managers and decision-makers to identify and solve a variety of problems and to clarify manage-

ment objectives. Define data requirements; then gather and validate information, applying judgment and statistical tests. Design, conduct, and evaluate experimental operational models in cases where models cannot be developed from existing data. Formulate mathematical or simulation models of problems, relating constants and variables, restrictions, alternatives, conflicting objectives, and their numerical parameters. Observe the current system in operation and gather and analyze information about each of the parts of component problems, using a variety of sources. Perform validation and testing of models to ensure adequacy; reformulate models as necessary. Prepare management reports defining and evaluating problems and recommending solutions. Specify manipulative or computational methods to be applied to models. Study and analyze information about alternative courses of action in order to determine which plan will offer the best outcomes. Collaborate with others in the organization to ensure successful implementation of chosen problem solutions. Develop and apply time and cost networks in order to plan, control, and review large projects. Develop business methods and procedures, including accounting systems, file systems, office systems, logistics systems, and production schedules. **SKILLS—Systems Evaluation:** Identifying measures or indicators of system performance and the actions needed to improve or correct performance relative to the goals of the system. **Systems Analysis:** Determining how a system should work and how changes in conditions, operations, and the environment will affect outcomes. **Mathematics:** Using mathematics to solve problems. **Judgment and Decision Making:** Considering the relative costs and benefits of potential actions to choose the most appropriate one. **Science:** Using scientific rules and methods to solve problems. **Complex Problem Solving:** Identifying complex problems and reviewing related information to develop and evaluate options and implement solutions. **Monitoring:** Monitoring or assessing your performance or that of other individuals or organizations to make improvements or take corrective action. **Operations Analysis:** Analyzing needs and product requirements to create a design. **GOE—Interest Area:** 04. Business and Administration. **Work Group:** 04.05. Accounting, Auditing, and Analytical Support. **Other Jobs in This Work Group:** Accountants; Auditors; Budget Analysts; Industrial Engineering Technicians; Logisticians; Management Analysts. **PERSONALITY TYPE:** Investigative.

EDUCATION/TRAINING PROGRAM(S)—Management Science, General; Management Sciences and Quantitative Methods, Other; Operations Research. **RELATED KNOWLEDGE/COURSES—Mathematics:** Knowledge of arithmetic, algebra, geometry, calculus, and statistics and their applications. **Economics and Accounting:** Knowledge of economic and accounting principles and practices, the financial markets, banking, and the analysis and reporting of financial data. **Administration and Management:** Knowledge of business and management principles involved in strategic planning, resource allocation, human resources modeling, leadership technique, production methods, and coordination of people and resources. **Production and Processing:** Knowledge of raw materials, production processes, quality control, costs, and other techniques for maximizing the effective manufacture and distribution of goods. **Computers and Electronics:** Knowledge of circuit boards, processors, chips, electronic equipment, and computer hardware and software, including applications and programming. **Personnel and Human Resources:** Knowledge of principles and procedures for personnel recruitment, selection, training, compensation and benefits, labor relations and negotiation, and personnel information systems.

Opticians, Dispensing

- Education/Training Required: Long-term on-the-job training
- Annual Earnings: $27,950
- Growth: 18.2%
- Annual Job Openings: 10,000
- Self-Employed: 2.8%
- Part-Time: 19.9%

Design, measure, fit, and adapt lenses and frames for client according to written optical prescription or specification. Assist client with selecting frames. Measure customer for size of eyeglasses and coordinate frames with facial and eye measurements and optical prescription. Prepare work order for optical laboratory containing instructions for grinding and mounting lenses in frames. Verify exactness of finished lens spectacles. Adjust frame and lens position to fit client. May shape or reshape frames. Measure clients' bridge and eye size, temple length, vertex distance, pupillary distance, and optical centers of eyes, using measuring devices. Verify that finished lenses are ground to specifications. Prepare work orders and instructions for grinding lenses and fabricating eyeglasses. Assist clients in selecting frames according to style and color and ensure that frames are coordinated with facial and eye measurements and optical prescriptions. Maintain records of customer prescriptions, work orders, and payments. Perform administrative duties such as tracking inventory and sales, submitting patient insurance information, and performing simple bookkeeping. Recommend specific lenses, lens coatings, and frames to suit client needs. Sell goods such as contact lenses, spectacles, sunglasses, and other goods related to eyes in general. Heat, shape, or bend plastic or metal frames in order to adjust eyeglasses to fit clients, using pliers and hands. Evaluate prescriptions in conjunction with clients' vocational and avocational visual requirements. Instruct clients in how to wear and care for eyeglasses. Determine clients' current lens prescriptions, when necessary, using lensometers or lens analyzers and clients' eyeglasses. Show customers how to insert, remove, and care for their contact lenses. Repair damaged frames. Obtain a customer's previous record or verify a prescription with the examining optometrist or ophthalmologist. Arrange and maintain displays of optical merchandise. Fabricate lenses to meet prescription specifications. Grind lens edges or apply coatings to lenses. Assemble eyeglasses by cutting and edging lenses and then fitting the lenses into frames. Supervise the training of student opticians. **SKILLS—Persuasion:** Persuading others to change their minds or behavior. **Service Orientation:** Actively looking for ways to help people. **Technology Design:** Generating or adapting equipment and technology to serve user needs. **Speaking:** Talking to others to convey information effectively. **Social Perceptiveness:** Being aware of others' reactions and understanding why they react as they do. **Equipment Selection:** Determining the kind of tools and equipment needed to do a job. **Active Learning:** Understanding the implications of new information for both current and future problem-solving and decision-making. **Instructing:** Teaching others how to do something. **Management of Financial Resources:** Determining how money will be spent to get the work done and accounting for these expenditures. **GOE—Interest Area:** 08. Health Science. **Work Group:** 08.06. Medical Technology. **Other Jobs in This Work Group:** Biological Technicians; Cardiovascular Technologists and Technicians; Diagnostic

Medical Sonographers; Medical and Clinical Laboratory Technicians; Medical and Clinical Laboratory Technologists; Medical Equipment Preparers; Medical Records and Health Information Technicians; Nuclear Medicine Technologists; Orthotists and Prosthetists; Radiologic Technicians; Radiologic Technologists. **PERSONALITY TYPE:** Enterprising.

EDUCATION/TRAINING PROGRAM(S)—Opticianry/Ophthalmic Dispensing Optician. **RELATED KNOWLEDGE/COURSES—Sales and Marketing:** Knowledge of principles and methods for showing, promoting, and selling products or services. This includes marketing strategy and tactics, product demonstrations, sales techniques, and sales control systems. **Customer and Personal Service:** Knowledge of principles and processes for providing customer and personal services. This includes customer needs assessment, meeting quality standards for services, and evaluation of customer satisfaction. **Production and Processing:** Knowledge of raw materials, production processes, quality control, costs, and other techniques for maximizing the effective manufacture and distribution of goods. **Clerical Practices:** Knowledge of administrative and clerical procedures and systems such as word processing, managing files and records, stenography and transcription, designing forms, and other office procedures and terminology. **Psychology:** Knowledge of human behavior and performance; individual differences in ability, personality, and interests; learning and motivation; psychological research methods; and the assessment and treatment of behavioral and affective disorders. **Administration and Management:** Knowledge of business and management principles involved in strategic planning, resource allocation, human resources modeling, leadership technique, production methods, and coordination of people and resources.

Optometrists

- Education/Training Required: First professional degree
- Annual Earnings: $88,410
- Growth: 17.1%
- Annual Job Openings: 2,000
- Self-Employed: 29.2%
- Part-Time: 25.1%

Diagnose, manage, and treat conditions and diseases of the human eye and visual system. Examine eyes and visual system, diagnose problems or impairments, prescribe corrective lenses, and provide treatment. May prescribe therapeutic drugs to treat specific eye conditions. Examine eyes, using observation, instruments, and pharmaceutical agents, to determine visual acuity and perception, focus, and coordination and to diagnose diseases and other abnormalities such as glaucoma or color blindness. Analyze test results and develop a treatment plan. Prescribe, supply, fit, and adjust eyeglasses, contact lenses, and other vision aids. Prescribe medications to treat eye diseases if state laws permit. Educate and counsel patients on contact lens care, visual hygiene, lighting arrangements, and safety factors. Consult with and refer patients to ophthalmologist or other health care practitioner if additional medical treatment is determined necessary. Remove foreign bodies from the eye. Provide patients undergoing eye surgeries, such as cataract and laser vision correction, with pre- and postoperative care. Prescribe therapeutic procedures to correct or conserve vision. Provide vision therapy and low-vision rehabilitation. **SKILLS—Science:** Using scientific rules and methods to solve problems. **Judgment and Decision Making:** Considering the relative costs and benefits of potential actions to choose the most appropriate one. **Management of Personnel Resources:** Motivating, developing, and directing people as they work, identifying the best people for the job. **Active Listening:** Giving full attention to what other people are saying, taking time to understand the points being made, asking questions as appropriate, and not interrupting at inappropriate times. **Persuasion:** Persuading others to change their minds or behavior. **Service Orientation:** Actively looking for ways to help people. **Reading Comprehension:** Understanding written sentences and paragraphs in work-related documents. **Active Learning:** Understanding the implications of new information for both current and future problem-solving and decision-making. **Instructing:** Teaching others how to do something. **GOE—Interest Area:** 08. Health Science. **Work Group:** 08.04. Health Specialties. **Other Jobs in This Work Group:** Chiropractors; Podiatrists. **PERSONALITY TYPE:** Investigative.

EDUCATION/TRAINING PROGRAM(S)— Optometry (OD). **RELATED KNOWLEDGE/ COURSES—Medicine and Dentistry:** Knowledge of the information and techniques needed to diagnose and treat human injuries, diseases, and deformities. This includes symptoms, treatment alternatives, drug properties and interactions, and preventive health-care measures. **Biology:** Knowledge of plant and animal organisms and their tissues, cells, functions, interdependencies, and interactions with each other and the environment. **Psychology:** Knowledge of human behavior and performance; individual differences in ability, personality, and interests; learning and motivation; psychological research methods; and the assessment and treatment of behavioral and affective disorders. **Customer and Personal Service:** Knowledge of principles and processes for providing customer and personal services. This includes customer needs assessment, meeting quality standards for services, and evaluation of customer satisfaction. **Personnel and Human Resources:** Knowledge of principles and procedures for personnel recruitment, selection, training, compensation and benefits, labor relations and negotiation, and personnel information systems. **Sales and Marketing:** Knowledge of principles and methods for showing, promoting, and selling products or services. This includes marketing strategy and tactics, product demonstrations, sales techniques, and sales control systems.

Oral and Maxillofacial Surgeons

- Education/Training Required: First professional degree
- Annual Earnings: More than $145,600
- Growth: 4.1%
- Annual Job Openings: 7,000
- Self-Employed: 39.9%
- Part-Time: 22.3%

Perform surgery on mouth, jaws, and related head and neck structure to execute difficult and multiple extractions of teeth, to remove tumors and other abnormal growths, to correct abnormal jaw relations by mandibular or maxillary revision, to prepare mouth for insertion of dental prosthesis, or to treat fractured jaws. Administer general and local anesthetics. Collaborate with other professionals such as restorative dentists and orthodontists in order to plan treatment. Perform surgery on the mouth and jaws in order to treat conditions such as cleft lip and palate and jaw growth problems. Perform surgery to prepare the mouth for dental implants and to aid in the regeneration of deficient bone and gum tissues. Provide emergency treatment of facial injuries, including facial lacerations, intra-oral lacerations, and fractured facial bones. Remove impacted, damaged, and non-restorable teeth. Remove tumors and other abnormal growths of the oral and facial regions, using surgical instruments. Restore form and function by moving skin, bone, nerves, and other tissues from other parts of the body in order to reconstruct the jaws and face. Evaluate the position of the wisdom teeth in order to determine whether problems exist currently or might occur in the future. Perform minor cosmetic procedures, such as chin and cheek-bone enhancements, and minor facial rejuvenation procedures, including the use of Botox and laser technology. Treat infections of the oral cavity, salivary glands, jaws, and neck. Treat problems affecting the oral mucosa, such as mouth ulcers and infections. Treat snoring problems, using laser surgery. **SKILLS—Science:** Using scientific rules and methods to solve problems. **Reading Comprehension:** Understanding written sentences and paragraphs in work-related documents. **Judgment and Decision Making:** Considering the relative costs and benefits of potential actions to choose the most appropriate one. **Critical Thinking:** Using logic and reasoning to identify the strengths and weaknesses of alternative solutions, conclusions, or approaches to problems. **Learning Strategies:** Selecting and using training/instructional methods and procedures appropriate for the situation when learning or teaching new things. **Active Learning:** Understanding the implications of new information for both current and future problem-solving and decision-making. **Service Orientation:** Actively looking for ways to help people. **Speaking:** Talking to others to convey information effectively. **GOE—Interest Area:** 08. Health Science. **Work Group:** 08.03. Dentistry. **Other Jobs in This Work Group:** Dental Assistants; Dental Hygienists; Dentists, General; Orthodontists; Prosthodontists. **PERSONALITY TYPE:** Investigative.

EDUCATION/TRAINING PROGRAM(S)—Dental/Oral Surgery Specialty; Oral/Maxillofacial Surgery (Cert, MS, PhD). RELATED KNOWLEDGE/COURSES—Medicine and Dentistry: Knowledge of the information and techniques needed to diagnose and treat human injuries, diseases, and deformities. This includes symptoms, treatment alternatives, drug properties and interactions, and preventive health-care measures. **Chemistry:** Knowledge of the chemical composition, structure, and properties of substances and of the chemical processes and transformations that they undergo. This includes uses of chemicals and their danger signs, production techniques, and disposal methods. **Biology:** Knowledge of plant and animal organisms and their tissues, cells, functions, interdependencies, and interactions with each other and the environment. **Psychology:** Knowledge of human behavior and performance; individual differences in ability, personality, and interests; learning and motivation; psychological research methods; and the assessment and treatment of behavioral and affective disorders. **Therapy and Counseling:** Knowledge of principles, methods, and procedures for diagnosis, treatment, and rehabilitation of physical and mental dysfunctions and for career counseling and guidance. **English Language:** Knowledge of the structure and content of the English language, including the meaning and spelling of words, rules of composition, and grammar.

Orthodontists

◉ Education/Training Required: First professional degree
◉ Annual Earnings: More than $145,600
◉ Growth: 4.1%
◉ Annual Job Openings: 7,000
◉ Self-Employed: 39.9%
◉ Part-Time: 22.3%

Examine, diagnose, and treat dental malocclusions and oral cavity anomalies. Design and fabricate appliances to realign teeth and jaws to produce and maintain normal function and to improve appearance. Adjust dental appliances periodically in order to produce and maintain normal function. Coordinate orthodontic services with other dental and medical services. Design and fabricate appliances, such as space maintainers, retainers, and labial and lingual arch wires. Diagnose teeth and jaw or other dental-facial abnormalities. Examine patients in order to assess abnormalities of jaw development, tooth position, and other dental-facial structures. Fit dental appliances in patients' mouths in order to alter the position and relationship of teeth and jaws and to realign teeth. Prepare diagnostic and treatment records. Provide patients with proposed treatment plans and cost estimates. Study diagnostic records such as medical/dental histories, plaster models of the teeth, photos of a patient's face and teeth, and X rays in order to develop patient treatment plans. Instruct dental officers and technical assistants in orthodontic procedures and techniques. **SKILLS—Science:** Using scientific rules and methods to solve problems. **Technology Design:** Generating or adapting equipment and technology to serve user needs. **Reading Comprehension:** Understanding written sentences and paragraphs in work-related documents. **Active Learning:** Understanding the implications of new information for both current and future problem-solving and decision-making. **Operations Analysis:** Analyzing needs and product requirements to create a design. **Service Orientation:** Actively looking for ways to help people. **Critical Thinking:** Using logic and reasoning to identify the strengths and weaknesses of alternative solutions, conclusions, or approaches to problems. **Complex Problem Solving:** Identifying complex problems and reviewing related information to develop and evaluate options and implement solutions. **Equipment Selection:** Determining the kind of tools and equipment needed to do a job. **GOE—Interest Area:** 08. Health Science. **Work Group:** 08.03. Dentistry. **Other Jobs in This Work Group:** Dental Assistants; Dental Hygienists; Dentists, General; Oral and Maxillofacial Surgeons; Prosthodontists. **PERSONALITY TYPE:** Investigative.

EDUCATION/TRAINING PROGRAM(S)— Orthodontics Specialty; Orthodontics/Orthodontology (Cert, MS, PhD). **RELATED KNOWLEDGE/COURSES—Medicine and Dentistry:** Knowledge of the information and techniques needed to diagnose and treat human injuries, diseases, and deformities. This includes symptoms, treatment alternatives, drug properties and interactions, and preventive health-care measures. **Biology:** Knowledge of plant and animal organisms and their tissues, cells, functions, interdependencies, and interactions with each other and the environment. **Therapy and Counseling:** Knowledge of principles, methods, and procedures for diagnosis, treatment, and rehabilitation of physical and mental dysfunctions and for career counseling and guidance. **Chemistry:** Knowledge of the chemical composition, structure, and properties of substances and of the chemical processes and transformations that they undergo. This includes uses of chemicals and their danger signs, production techniques, and disposal methods. **Design:** Knowledge of design techniques, tools, and principles involved in production of precision technical plans, blueprints, drawings, and models. **Administration and Management:** Knowledge of business and management principles involved in strategic planning, resource allocation, human resources modeling, leadership technique, production methods, and coordination of people and resources.

Orthotists and Prosthetists

- ◎ Education/Training Required: Bachelor's degree
- ◎ Annual Earnings: $50,260
- ◎ Growth: 18.9%
- ◎ Annual Job Openings: 1,000
- ◎ Self-Employed: 2.1%
- ◎ Part-Time: 14.6%

Assist patients with disabling conditions of limbs and spine or with partial or total absence of limb by fitting and preparing orthopedic braces or prostheses. Design orthopedic and prosthetic devices based on physicians' prescriptions and examination and measurement of patients. Examine, interview, and measure patients in order to determine their appliance needs and to identify factors that could affect appliance fit. Fit, test, and evaluate devices on patients and make adjustments for proper fit, function, and comfort. Instruct patients in the use and care of orthoses and prostheses. Make and modify plaster casts of areas that will be fitted with prostheses or orthoses for use in the device construction process. Repair, rebuild, and modify prosthetic and orthopedic appliances. Select materials and components to be used based on device design. Maintain patients' records. Publish research findings and present them at conferences and seminars. Research new ways to construct and use orthopedic and prosthetic devices. Show and explain orthopedic and prosthetic appliances to health-care workers. Train and supervise orthopedic and prosthetic assistants and technicians and other support staff. Update skills and knowledge by attending conferences and seminars. Confer with physicians in order to formulate specifications and prescriptions for orthopedic and/or prosthetic devices. Construct and fabricate appliances or supervise others who are constructing the appliances. **SKILLS—Technology Design:** Generating or adapting equipment and technology to serve user needs. **Social Perceptiveness:** Being aware of others' reactions and understanding why they react as they do. **Speaking:** Talking to others to convey information effectively. **Science:** Using scientific rules and methods to solve problems. **Management of Personnel Resources:** Motivating, developing, and directing people as they work, identifying the best people for the job. **Instructing:** Teaching others how to do something. **Active Listening:** Giving full attention to what other people are saying, taking time to understand the points being made, asking questions as appropriate, and not interrupting at inappropriate times. **Quality Control Analysis:** Conducting tests and inspections of products, services, or processes to evaluate quality or performance. **GOE—Interest Area:** 08. Health Science. **Work Group:** 08.06. Medical Technology. **Other Jobs in This Work Group:** Biological Technicians; Cardiovascular Technologists and Technicians; Diagnostic Medical Sonographers; Medical and Clinical Laboratory Technicians; Medical and Clinical Laboratory Technologists; Medical Equipment Preparers; Medical Records and Health Information Technicians; Nuclear Medicine Technologists; Opticians, Dispensing; Radiologic Technicians; Radiologic Technologists. **PERSONALITY TYPE:** Social.

EDUCATION/TRAINING PROGRAM(S)—Assistive/Augmentative Technology and Rehabilitation Engineering; Orthotist/Prosthetist. **RELATED KNOWLEDGE/COURSES—Medicine and Dentistry:** Knowledge of the information and techniques needed to diagnose and treat human injuries, diseases, and deformities. This includes symptoms, treatment alternatives, drug properties and interactions, and preventive health-care measures. **Design:** Knowledge of design techniques, tools, and principles involved in production of precision technical plans, blueprints, drawings, and models. **Building and Construction:** Knowledge of the materials, methods, and tools involved in the construction or repair of houses, buildings, or other structures such as highways and roads. **Therapy and Counseling:** Knowledge of principles, methods, and procedures for diagnosis, treatment, and rehabilitation of physical and mental dysfunctions and for career counseling and guidance. **Engineering and Technology:** Knowledge of the practical application of engineering science and technology. This includes applying principles, techniques, procedures, and equipment to the design and production of various goods and services. **Physics:** Knowledge and prediction of physical principles and laws and their interrelationships and applications to understanding fluid, material, and atmospheric dynamics and mechanical, electrical, atomic, and subatomic structures and processes.

Packaging and Filling Machine Operators and Tenders

- Education/Training Required: Short-term on-the-job training
- Annual Earnings: $22,200
- Growth: 21.1%
- Annual Job Openings: 69,000
- Self-Employed: 0%
- Part-Time: 5.7%

Operate or tend machines to prepare industrial or consumer products for storage or shipment. Includes cannery workers who pack food products. Observe machine operations to ensure quality and conformity of filled or packaged products to standards. Adjust machine components and machine tension and pressure according to size or processing angle of product. Tend or operate machine that packages product. Remove finished packaged items from machine and separate rejected items. Regulate machine flow, speed, or temperature. Stop or reset machines when malfunctions occur, clear machine jams, and report malfunctions to a supervisor. Secure finished packaged items by hand-tying, sewing, gluing, stapling, or attaching fastener. Stock and sort product for packaging or filling machine operation and replenish packaging supplies such as wrapping paper, plastic sheet, boxes, cartons, glue, ink, or labels. Inspect and remove defective products and packaging material. Clean and remove damaged or otherwise inferior materials to prepare raw products for processing. Sort, grade, weigh, and inspect products, verifying and adjusting product weight or measurement to meet specifications. Clean, oil, and make minor adjustments or repairs to machinery and equipment, such as opening valves or setting guides. Monitor the production line, watching for problems such as pile-ups, jams, or glue that isn't sticking properly. Stack finished packaged items or wrap protective material around each item and pack the items in cartons or containers. Start machine by engaging controls. Count and record finished and rejected packaged items. Package the product in the form in which it will be sent out, for example, filling bags with flour from a chute or spout. Supply materials to spindles, conveyors, hoppers, or other feeding devices and unload packaged product. Attach identification labels to finished packaged items or cut stencils and stencil information on containers, such as lot numbers or shipping destinations. Clean packaging containers, line and pad crates, and/or assemble cartons to prepare for product packing. **SKILLS—Equipment Maintenance:** Performing routine maintenance on equipment and determining when and what kind of maintenance is needed. **Instructing:** Teaching others how to do something. **Quality Control Analysis:** Conducting tests and inspections of products, services, or processes to evaluate quality or performance. **Operation Monitoring:** Watching gauges, dials, or other indicators to make sure a machine is working properly. **Troubleshooting:** Determining causes of operating errors and deciding what to do about them. **Operation and Control:** Controlling operations of equipment or systems. **Coordination:** Adjusting actions in relation to others' actions. **Repairing:** Repairing machines or systems by using the needed tools. **GOE—Interest Area:** 13. Manufacturing. **Work Group:** 13.03. Production Work, Assorted Materials Processing. **Other Jobs in This Work Group:** Bakers, Manufacturing; Cementing and Gluing Machine Operators and Tenders; Chemical Equipment Controllers and Operators; Chemical Equipment Tenders; Cleaning, Washing, and Metal Pickling Equipment Operators and Tenders; Coating, Painting, and Spraying Machine Operators and Tenders; Combination Machine Tool Operators and Tenders, Metal and Plastic; Cooling and Freezing Equipment Operators and Tenders; Cutting and Slicing Machine Operators and Tenders; Electrolytic Plating and Coating Machine Operators and Tenders, Metal and Plastic; Extruding and Forming Machine Operators and Tenders, Synthetic or Glass Fibers; Extruding, Forming, Pressing, and Compacting Machine Operators and Tenders; Food and Tobacco Roasting, Baking, and Drying Machine Operators and Tenders; Food Batchmakers; Food Cooking Machine Operators and Tenders; Furnace, Kiln, Oven, Drier, and Kettle Operators and Tenders; Heat Treating, Annealing, and Tempering Machine Operators and Tenders, Metal and Plastic; Heaters, Metal and Plastic; Meat, Poultry, and Fish Cutters and Trimmers; Metal-Refining Furnace Operators and Tenders; Mixing and Blending Machine Setters, Operators, and Tenders; Nonelectrolytic Plating and Coating Machine Operators and Tenders, Metal and Plastic; Plastic Molding and Casting Machine Operators and Tenders; Pourers and Casters, Metal; Pressing Machine Operators and Tenders—Textile, Garment, and Related Materials; Production Helpers; Production Laborers; Sawing Machine Operators and Tenders; Separating, Filtering, Clarifying, Precipitating, and Still Machine Setters, Operators, and Tenders; Sewing Machine Operators, Garment; Sewing Machine Operators, Non-Garment; Shoe Machine Operators and Tenders; Slaughterers and Meat Packers; Stone Sawyers; Team Assemblers; Textile Bleaching and Dyeing Machine Operators and Tenders; Tire Builders; Woodworking Machine Operators and Tenders, Except Sawing. **PERSONALITY TYPE:** Realistic.

EDUCATION/TRAINING PROGRAM(S)—No data available. **RELATED KNOWLEDGE/COURSES—Production and Processing:** Knowledge of raw materials, production processes, quality control, costs, and other techniques for maximizing the effective manufacture and distribution of goods. **Mechanical Devices:** Knowledge of machines and tools, including their designs, uses, repair, and maintenance. **Psychology:** Knowledge of human behavior and performance; individual differences in ability, personality, and interests; learning and motivation; psychological research methods; and the assessment and treatment of behavioral and affective disorders. **Sociology and Anthropology:** Knowledge of group behavior and dynamics, societal trends and influences, human migrations, ethnicity, and cultures and their history and origins. **Public Safety and Security:** Knowledge of relevant equipment, policies, procedures, and strategies to promote effective local, state, or national security operations for the protection of people, data, property, and institutions. **Education and Training:** Knowledge of principles and methods for curriculum and training design, teaching and instruction for individuals and groups, and the measurement of training effects.

Packers and Packagers, Hand

- ◎ Education/Training Required: Short-term on-the-job training
- ◎ Annual Earnings: $17,150
- ◎ Growth: 14.4%
- ◎ Annual Job Openings: 198,000
- ◎ Self-Employed: 0.1%
- ◎ Part-Time: 15.3%

Pack or package by hand a wide variety of products and materials. Mark and label containers, container tags, or products, using marking tools. Measure, weigh, and count products and materials. Examine and inspect containers, materials, and products in order to ensure that packing specifications are met. Record product, packaging, and order information on specified forms and records. Remove completed or defective products or materials, placing them on moving equipment such as conveyors or in specified areas such as loading docks. Seal containers or materials, using glues, fasteners, nails, and hand tools. Load materials and products into package-processing equipment. Assemble, line, and pad cartons, crates, and containers, using hand tools. Clean containers, materials, supplies, or work areas, using cleaning solutions and hand tools. Transport packages to customers' vehicles. Place or pour products or materials into containers, using hand tools and equipment, or fill containers from spouts or chutes. Obtain, move, and sort products, materials, containers, and orders, using hand tools. **SKILLS—Persuasion:** Persuading others to change their minds or behavior. **Active Listening:** Giving full attention to what other people are saying, taking time to understand the points being made, asking questions as appropriate, and not interrupting at inappropriate times. **Management of Personnel Resources:** Motivating, developing, and directing people as they work, identifying the best people for the job. **Social Perceptiveness:** Being aware of others' reactions and understanding why they react as they do. **Learning Strategies:** Selecting and using training/instructional methods and procedures appropriate for the situation when learning or teaching new things. **Instructing:** Teaching others how to do something. **Coordination:** Adjusting actions in relation to others' actions. **Service Orientation:** Actively looking for ways to help people. **Quality Control Analysis:** Conducting tests and inspections of products, services, or processes to evaluate quality or performance. **GOE—Interest Area:** 13. Manufacturing. **Work Group:** 13.17. Loading, Moving, Hoisting, and Conveying. **Other Jobs in This Work Group:** Conveyor Operators and Tenders; Freight, Stock, and Material Movers, Hand; Hoist and Winch Operators; Industrial Truck and Tractor Operators; Irradiated-Fuel Handlers; Machine Feeders and Offbearers; Pump Operators, Except Wellhead Pumpers; Refuse and Recyclable Material Collectors; Tank Car, Truck, and Ship Loaders. **PERSONALITY TYPE:** Realistic.

EDUCATION/TRAINING PROGRAM(S)—No data available. **RELATED KNOWLEDGE/COURSES—Production and Processing:** Knowledge of raw materials, production processes, quality control, costs, and other techniques for maximizing the effective manufacture and distribution of goods. **Public Safety and Security:** Knowledge of relevant equipment, policies, procedures, and strategies to promote effective local, state, or national security operations for the protection of people, data, property, and institutions. **Food Production:** Knowledge of techniques and equipment for planting, growing, and harvesting food products (both plant and animal) for consumption, including storage/handling techniques. **Transportation:** Knowledge of principles and methods for moving people or goods by air, rail, sea, or road, including the relative costs and benefits. **Administration and Management:** Knowledge of business and management principles involved in strategic planning, resource allocation, human resources modeling, leadership technique, production methods, and coordination of people and resources. **Clerical Practices:** Knowledge of administrative and clerical procedures and systems such as word processing, managing files and records, stenography and transcription, designing forms, and other office procedures and terminology.

Painters and Illustrators

- Education/Training Required: Long-term on-the-job training
- Annual Earnings: $38,060
- Growth: 16.5%
- Annual Job Openings: 4,000
- Self-Employed: 55.5%
- Part-Time: 23.1%

Paint or draw subject material to produce original artwork or illustrations, using watercolors, oils, acrylics, tempera, or other paint mediums. Renders drawings, illustrations, and sketches of buildings, manufactured products, or models, working from sketches, blueprints, memory, or reference materials. Paints scenic backgrounds, murals, and portraiture for motion picture and television production sets, glass artworks, and exhibits. Etches, carves, paints, or draws artwork on material such as stone, glass, canvas, wood, and linoleum. Develops drawings, paintings, diagrams, and models of medical or biological subjects for use in publications, exhibits, consultations, research, and teaching. Studies style, techniques, colors, textures, and materials used by artist to maintain consistency in reconstruction or retouching procedures. Removes painting from frame or paint layer from canvas to restore artwork, following specified technique and equipment. Examines surfaces of paintings and proofs of artwork, using magnifying device, to determine method of restoration or needed corrections. Installs finished stained glass in window or door frame. Assembles, leads, and solders finished glass to fabricate stained glass article. Applies select solvents and cleaning agents to clean surface of painting and remove accretions, discolorations, and deteriorated varnish. Performs tests to determine factors such as age, structure, pigment stability, and probable reaction to various cleaning agents and solvents. Confers with professional personnel or client to discuss objectives of artwork and develop illustration ideas and theme to be portrayed. Brushes or sprays protective or decorative finish on completed background panels, informational legends, exhibit accessories, or finished painting. Integrates and develops visual elements, such as line, space, mass, color, and perspective to produce desired effect. **SKILLS—Operations Analysis:** Analyzing needs and product requirements to create a design. **Management of Material Resources:** Obtaining and seeing to the appropriate use of equipment, facilities, and materials needed to do certain work. **Installation:** Installing equipment, machines, wiring, or programs to meet specifications. **Quality Control Analysis:** Conducting tests and inspections of products, services, or processes to evaluate quality or performance. **Repairing:** Repairing machines or systems by using the needed tools. **GOE—Interest Area:** 03. Arts and Communication. **Work Group:** 03.04. Studio Art. **Other Jobs in This Work Group:** Cartoonists; Craft Artists; Potters; Sculptors; Sketch Artists. **PERSONALITY TYPE:** Artistic.

EDUCATION/TRAINING PROGRAM(S)—Art/Art Studies, General; Drawing; Fine Arts and Art Studies, Other; Fine/Studio Arts, General; Medical Illustration/Medical Illustrator; Painting; Visual and Performing Arts, General. **RELATED KNOWLEDGE/COURSES—Fine Arts:** Knowledge of the theory and techniques required to compose, produce, and perform works of music, dance, the visual arts, drama, and sculpture. **Design:** Knowledge of design techniques, tools, and principles involved in production of precision technical plans, blueprints, drawings, and models. **Chemistry:** Knowledge of the chemical composition, structure, and properties of substances and of the chemical processes and transformations that they undergo. This includes uses of chemicals and their danger signs, production techniques, and disposal methods. **History and Archeology:** Knowledge of historical events and their causes, indicators, and effects on civilizations and cultures. **Communications and Media:** Knowledge of media production, communication, and dissemination techniques and methods. This includes alternative ways to inform and entertain via written, oral, and visual media. **Engineering and Technology:** Knowledge of the practical application of engineering science and technology. This includes applying principles, techniques, procedures, and equipment to the design and production of various goods and services.

Painters, Construction and Maintenance

- Education/Training Required: Moderate-term on-the-job training
- Annual Earnings: $30,260
- Growth: 11.6%
- Annual Job Openings: 69,000
- Self-Employed: 41.7%
- Part-Time: 9.0%

Paint walls, equipment, buildings, bridges, and other structural surfaces, using brushes, rollers, and spray guns. May remove old paint to prepare surface prior to painting. May mix colors or oils to obtain desired color or consistency. Apply paint, stain, varnish, enamel, and other finishes to equipment, buildings, bridges, and/or other structures, using brushes, spray guns, or rollers. Apply primers or sealers to prepare new surfaces, such as bare wood or metal, for finish coats. Calculate amounts of required materials and estimate costs, based on surface measurements and/or work orders. Cover surfaces with dropcloths or masking tape and paper to protect surfaces during painting. Fill cracks, holes, and joints with caulk, putty, plaster, or other fillers, using caulking guns or putty knives. Mix and match colors of paint, stain, or varnish with oil and thinning and drying additives in order to obtain desired colors and consistencies. Polish final coats to specified finishes. Read work orders or receive instructions from supervisors or homeowners in order to determine work requirements. Remove fixtures such as pictures, doorknobs, lamps, and electric switch covers prior to painting. Remove old finishes by stripping, sanding, wire brushing, burning, or using water and/or abrasive blasting. Smooth surfaces, using sandpaper, scrapers, brushes, steel wool, and/or sanding machines. Wash and treat surfaces with oil, turpentine, mildew remover, or other preparations and sand rough spots to ensure that finishes will adhere properly. Bake finishes on painted and enameled articles, using baking ovens. Cut stencils and brush and spray lettering and decorations on surfaces. Erect scaffolding and swing gates or set up ladders to work above ground level. Select and purchase tools and finishes for surfaces to be covered, considering durability, ease of handling, methods of application, and customers' wishes. Spray or brush hot plastics or pitch onto surfaces. Use special finishing techniques such as sponging, ragging, layering, or faux finishing. Waterproof buildings, using waterproofers and caulking. **SKILLS—**None met the criteria. **GOE—Interest Area:** 02. Architecture and Construction. **Work Group:** 02.04. Construction Crafts. **Other Jobs in This Work Group:** Boat Builders and Shipwrights; Boilermakers; Brattice Builders; Brickmasons and Blockmasons; Carpet Installers; Ceiling Tile Installers; Cement Masons and Concrete Finishers; Commercial Divers; Construction Carpenters; Crane and Tower Operators; Dragline Operators; Drywall Installers; Electricians; Fence Erectors; Floor Layers, Except Carpet, Wood, and Hard Tiles; Floor Sanders and Finishers; Glaziers; Grader, Bulldozer, and Scraper Operators; Hazardous Materials Removal Workers; Insulation Workers, Floor, Ceiling, and Wall; Insulation Workers, Mechanical; Manufactured Building and Mobile Home Installers; Operating Engineers; Paperhangers; Paving, Surfacing, and Tamping Equipment Operators; Pile-Driver Operators; Pipe Fitters; Pipelayers; Pipelaying Fitters; Plasterers and Stucco

Masons; Plumbers; Rail-Track Laying and Maintenance Equipment Operators; Refractory Materials Repairers, Except Brickmasons; Reinforcing Iron and Rebar Workers; Riggers; Roofers; Rough Carpenters; Security and Fire Alarm Systems Installers; Segmental Pavers; Sheet Metal Workers; Ship Carpenters and Joiners; Stone Cutters and Carvers; Stonemasons; Structural Iron and Steel Workers; Tapers; Terrazzo Workers and Finishers; Tile and Marble Setters. **PERSONALITY TYPE:** Realistic.

EDUCATION/TRAINING PROGRAM(S)— Painting/Painter and Wall Coverer. **RELATED KNOWLEDGE/COURSES—Building and Construction:** Knowledge of the materials, methods, and tools involved in the construction or repair of houses, buildings, or other structures such as highways and roads. **Sales and Marketing:** Knowledge of principles and methods for showing, promoting, and selling products or services. This includes marketing strategy and tactics, product demonstrations, sales techniques, and sales control systems.

Painters, Transportation Equipment

- Education/Training Required: Moderate-term on-the-job training
- Annual Earnings: $35,120
- Growth: 17.5%
- Annual Job Openings: 9,000
- Self-Employed: 7.8%
- Part-Time: 4.5%

Operate or tend painting machines to paint surfaces of transportation equipment, such as automobiles, buses, trucks, trains, boats, and airplanes. Adjust controls on infrared ovens, heat lamps, portable ventilators, and exhaust units in order to speed the drying of vehicles between coats. Allow the sprayed product to dry and then touch up any spots that may have been missed. Apply designs, lettering, or other identifying or decorative items to finished products, using paint brushes or paint sprayers. Apply primer over any repairs made to vehicle surfaces. Apply rust-resistant undercoats and caulk and seal seams. Buff and wax the finished paintwork. Fill small dents and scratches with body fillers and smooth surfaces in order to prepare vehicles for painting. Lay out logos, symbols, or designs on painted surfaces according to blueprint specifications, using measuring instruments, stencils, and patterns. Mix paints to match color specifications or vehicles' original colors and then stir and thin the paints, using spatulas or power-mixing equipment. Monitor painting operations in order to identify flaws such as blisters and streaks so that their causes can be corrected. Operate lifting and moving devices in order to move equipment or materials so that areas to be painted are accessible. Paint by hand areas that cannot be reached with a spray gun or those that need retouching, using brushes. Pour paint into spray guns and adjust nozzles and paint mixes in order to get the proper paint flow and coating thickness. Remove accessories from vehicles, such as chrome or mirrors, and mask other surfaces with tape or paper in order to protect them from paint. Remove grease, dirt, paint, and rust from vehicle surfaces in preparation for paint application, using abrasives, solvents, brushes, blowtorches, washing tanks, or sandblasters. Sand the final finish and apply sealer once a vehicle has dried properly. Sand vehicle surfaces between coats of paint and/or primer in order to remove flaws and enhance adhesion for subsequent coats. Select paint according to company requirements and match colors of paint, following specified color charts. Select the correct spray gun system for the material being applied. Set up portable equipment such as ventilators, exhaust units, ladders, and scaffolding. **SKILLS—Operation and Control:** Controlling operations of equipment or systems. **GOE—Interest Area:** 13. Manufacturing. **Work Group:** 13.09. Hands-On Work, Assorted Materials. **Other Jobs in This Work Group:** Coil Winders, Tapers, and Finishers; Cutters and Trimmers, Hand; Fabric and Apparel Patternmakers; Glass Blowers, Molders, Benders, and Finishers; Grinding and Polishing Workers, Hand; Mold Makers, Hand; Molding and Casting Workers; Painting, Coating, and Decorating Workers; Sewers, Hand. **PERSONALITY TYPE:** Realistic.

EDUCATION/TRAINING PROGRAM(S)—Auto Body/Collision and Repair Technology/Technician. **RELATED KNOWLEDGE/COURSES—Design:** Knowledge of design techniques, tools, and principles involved in production of precision technical plans, blueprints, drawings, and models. **Mechanical Devices:** Knowledge of machines and tools, including their designs, uses, repair, and maintenance. **Fine Arts:** Knowledge of the theory and techniques required to compose, produce, and perform works of music, dance, the visual arts, drama, and sculpture. **Chemistry:** Knowledge of the chemical composition, structure, and properties of substances and of the chemical processes and transformations that they undergo. This includes uses of chemicals and their danger signs, production techniques, and disposal methods.

Paralegals and Legal Assistants

- Education/Training Required: Associate degree
- Annual Earnings: $39,130
- Growth: 28.7%
- Annual Job Openings: 29,000
- Self-Employed: 2.3%
- Part-Time: 10.8%

Assist lawyers by researching legal precedent, investigating facts, or preparing legal documents. Conduct research to support a legal proceeding, to formulate a defense, or to initiate legal action. Prepare legal documents, including briefs, pleadings, appeals, wills, contracts, and real estate closing statements. Prepare affidavits or other documents, maintain document file, and file pleadings with court clerk. Gather and analyze research data, such as statutes; decisions; and legal articles, codes, and documents. Investigate facts and law of cases to determine causes of action and to prepare cases. Call upon witnesses to testify at hearing. Direct and coordinate law office activity, including delivery of subpoenas. Arbitrate disputes between parties and assist in real estate closing process. Keep and monitor legal volumes to ensure that law library is up-to-date. Appraise and inventory real and personal property for estate planning. **SKILLS—Time Management:** Managing one's own time and the time of others. **Active Listening:** Giving full attention to what other people are saying, taking time to understand the points being made, asking questions as appropriate, and not interrupting at inappropriate times. **Writing:** Communicating effectively in writing as appropriate for the needs of the audience. **Instructing:** Teaching others how to do something. **Speaking:** Talking to others to convey information effectively. **Social Perceptiveness:** Being aware of others' reactions and understanding why they react as they do. **Reading Comprehension:**

Understanding written sentences and paragraphs in work-related documents. **Service Orientation:** Actively looking for ways to help people. **GOE—Interest Area:** 12. Law and Public Safety. **Work Group:** 12.03. Legal Support. **Other Jobs in This Work Group:** Law Clerks; Title Examiners and Abstractors; Title Searchers. **PERSONALITY TYPE:** Enterprising.

EDUCATION/TRAINING PROGRAM(S)—Legal Assistant/Paralegal. **RELATED KNOWLEDGE/ COURSES—Clerical Practices:** Knowledge of administrative and clerical procedures and systems such as word processing, managing files and records, stenography and transcription, designing forms, and other office procedures and terminology. **Law and Government:** Knowledge of laws, legal codes, court procedures, precedents, government regulations, executive orders, agency rules, and the democratic political process. **Customer and Personal Service:** Knowledge of principles and processes for providing customer and personal services. This includes customer needs assessment, meeting quality standards for services, and evaluation of customer satisfaction. **Computers and Electronics:** Knowledge of circuit boards, processors, chips, electronic equipment, and computer hardware and software, including applications and programming. **English Language:** Knowledge of the structure and content of the English language, including the meaning and spelling of words, rules of composition, and grammar. **Personnel and Human Resources:** Knowledge of principles and procedures for personnel recruitment, selection, training, compensation and benefits, labor relations and negotiation, and personnel information systems.

Parking Lot Attendants

- Education/Training Required: Short-term on-the-job training
- Annual Earnings: $16,800
- Growth: 19.2%
- Annual Job Openings: 19,000
- Self-Employed: 0.4%
- Part-Time: 31.6%

Park automobiles or issue tickets for customers in a parking lot or garage. May collect fee. Take numbered tags from customers, locate vehicles, and deliver vehicles or provide customers with instructions for locating vehicles. Keep parking areas clean and orderly to ensure that space usage is maximized. Direct motorists to parking areas or parking spaces, using hand signals or flashlights as necessary. Patrol parking areas in order to prevent vehicle damage and vehicle or property thefts. Park and retrieve automobiles for customers in parking lots, storage garages, or new car lots. Greet customers and open their car doors. Calculate parking charges and collect fees from customers. Issue ticket stubs or place numbered tags on windshields and give customers matching tags for locating parked vehicles. Lift, position, and remove barricades in order to open or close parking areas. Inspect vehicles in order to detect any damage. Review motorists' identification before allowing them to enter parking facilities. Escort customers to their vehicles in order to ensure their safety. Service vehicles with gas, oil, and water. **SKILLS— Service Orientation:** Actively looking for ways to help people. **Critical Thinking:** Using logic and reasoning to identify the strengths and weaknesses of alternative solutions, conclusions, or approaches to problems. **Systems Evaluation:** Identifying measures or indicators of system performance and the actions needed to improve or correct performance relative to the goals of the system. **Management of Personnel Resources:** Motivating, developing, and directing people as they work, identifying the best people for the job. **Learning Strategies:** Selecting and using training/instructional methods and procedures appropriate for the situation when learning or teaching new things. **Social Perceptiveness:** Being aware of others' reactions and understanding why they react as they do. **Coordination:** Adjusting actions in relation to others' actions. **Instructing:** Teaching others how to do something. **Time Management:** Managing one's own time and the time of others. **GOE—Interest Area:** 16. Transportation, Distribution, and Logistics. **Work Group:** 16.06. Other Services Requiring Driving. **Other Jobs in This Work Group:** Ambulance Drivers and Attendants, Except Emergency Medical Technicians; Bus Drivers, School; Bus Drivers, Transit and Intercity; Couriers and Messengers; Driver/Sales Workers; Postal Service Mail Carriers; Taxi Drivers and Chauffeurs. **PERSONALITY TYPE:** Realistic.

EDUCATION/TRAINING PROGRAM(S)—No data available. **RELATED KNOWLEDGE/COURSES—Customer and Personal Service:** Knowledge of principles and processes for providing customer and personal services. This includes customer needs assessment, meeting quality standards for services, and eval-

uation of customer satisfaction. **Public Safety and Security:** Knowledge of relevant equipment, policies, procedures, and strategies to promote effective local, state, or national security operations for the protection of people, data, property, and institutions. **Transportation:** Knowledge of principles and methods for moving people or goods by air, rail, sea, or road, including the relative costs and benefits. **Geography:** Knowledge of principles and methods for describing the features of land, sea, and air masses, including their physical characteristics; locations; interrelationships; and distribution of plant, animal, and human life. **Psychology:** Knowledge of human behavior and performance; individual differences in ability, personality, and interests; learning and motivation; psychological research methods; and the assessment and treatment of behavioral and affective disorders. **English Language:** Knowledge of the structure and content of the English language, including the meaning and spelling of words, rules of composition, and grammar.

Pediatricians, General

- Education/Training Required: First professional degree
- Annual Earnings: $135,730
- Growth: 19.5%
- Annual Job Openings: 38,000
- Self-Employed: 16.9%
- Part-Time: 8.1%

Diagnose, treat, and help prevent children's diseases and injuries. Advise patients, parents or guardians, and community members concerning diet, activity, hygiene, and disease prevention. Collect, record, and maintain patient information, such as medical history, reports, and examination results. Examine children regularly to assess their growth and development. Examine patients or order, perform, and interpret diagnostic tests to obtain information on medical condition and determine diagnosis. Explain procedures and discuss test results or prescribed treatments with patients and parents or guardians. Monitor patients' condition and progress and re-evaluate treatments as necessary. Plan and execute medical care programs to aid in the mental and physical growth and development of children and adolescents. Prescribe or administer treatment, therapy, medication, vaccination, and other specialized medical care to treat or prevent illness, disease, or injury in infants and children. Refer patient to medical specialist or other practitioner when necessary. Treat children who have minor illnesses, acute and chronic health problems, and growth and development concerns. Conduct research to study anatomy and develop or test medications, treatments, or procedures to prevent or control disease or injury. Direct and coordinate activities of nurses, students, assistants, specialists, therapists, and other medical staff. Operate on patients to remove, repair, or improve functioning of diseased or injured body parts and systems. Plan, implement, or administer health programs or standards in hospital, business, or community for information, prevention, or treatment of injury or illness. Provide consulting services to other physicians. Prepare reports for government or management of birth, death, and disease statistics; workforce evaluations; or medical status of individuals. **SKILLS—Science:** Using scientific rules and methods to solve problems. **Systems Evaluation:** Identifying measures or indicators of system performance and the actions needed to improve or correct performance relative to the goals of the system. **Reading Comprehension:** Understanding written sentences and paragraphs in work-related documents. **Active Learning:** Understanding the implications of new information for both current and future problem-solving and decision-making. **Judgment and Decision Making:** Considering the relative costs and benefits of potential actions to choose the most appropriate one. **Management of Personnel Resources:** Motivating, developing, and directing people as they work, identifying the best people for the job. **Systems Analysis:** Determining how a system should work and how changes in conditions, operations, and the environment will affect outcomes. **Social Perceptiveness:** Being aware of others' reactions and understanding why they react as they do. **GOE— Interest Area:** 08. Health Science. **Work Group:** 08.02. Medicine and Surgery. **Other Jobs in This Work Group:** Anesthesiologists; Family and General Practitioners; Internists, General; Medical Assistants; Medical Transcriptionists; Obstetricians and Gynecologists; Pharmacists; Pharmacy Aides; Pharmacy Technicians; Physician Assistants; Psychiatrists; Registered Nurses; Surgeons; Surgical Technologists. **PERSONALITY TYPE:** Investigative.

EDUCATION/TRAINING   PROGRAM(S)— Child/Pediatric Neurology; Family Medicine; Neonatal-Perinatal Medicine; Pediatric Cardiology; Pediatric Endocrinology; Pediatric Hemato-Oncology; Pediatric

Nephrology; Pediatric Orthopedics; Pediatric Surgery; Pediatrics. **RELATED KNOWLEDGE/COURSES—Medicine and Dentistry:** Knowledge of the information and techniques needed to diagnose and treat human injuries, diseases, and deformities. This includes symptoms, treatment alternatives, drug properties and interactions, and preventive health-care measures. **Biology:** Knowledge of plant and animal organisms and their tissues, cells, functions, interdependencies, and interactions with each other and the environment. **Therapy and Counseling:** Knowledge of principles, methods, and procedures for diagnosis, treatment, and rehabilitation of physical and mental dysfunctions and for career counseling and guidance. **Chemistry:** Knowledge of the chemical composition, structure, and properties of substances and of the chemical processes and transformations that they undergo. This includes uses of chemicals and their danger signs, production techniques, and disposal methods. **Administration and Management:** Knowledge of business and management principles involved in strategic planning, resource allocation, human resources modeling, leadership technique, production methods, and coordination of people and resources. **Physics:** Knowledge and prediction of physical principles and laws and their interrelationships and applications to understanding fluid, material, and atmospheric dynamics and mechanical, electrical, atomic, and subatomic structures and processes.

Personal and Home Care Aides

- Education/Training Required: Short-term on-the-job training
- Annual Earnings: $16,900
- Growth: 40.5%
- Annual Job Openings: 154,000
- Self-Employed: 7.1%
- Part-Time: 34.0%

Assist elderly or disabled adults with daily living activities at the person's home or in a daytime nonresidential facility. Duties performed at a place of residence may include keeping house (making beds, doing laundry, washing dishes) and preparing meals. May provide meals and supervised activities at nonresidential care facilities. May advise families, the eld-

erly, and disabled on such things as nutrition, cleanliness, and household utilities. Perform health-care related tasks, such as monitoring vital signs and medication, under the direction of registered nurses and physiotherapists. Administer bedside and personal care, such as ambulation and personal hygiene assistance. Prepare and maintain records of client progress and services performed, reporting changes in client condition to manager or supervisor. Perform housekeeping duties, such as cooking, cleaning, washing clothes and dishes, and running errands. Care for individuals and families during periods of incapacitation, family disruption, or convalescence, providing companionship, personal care, and help in adjusting to new lifestyles. Instruct and advise clients on issues such as household cleanliness, utilities, hygiene, nutrition, and infant care. Plan, shop for, and prepare meals, including special diets, and assist families in planning, shopping for, and preparing nutritious meals. Participate in case reviews, consulting with the team caring for the client, to evaluate the client's needs and plan for continuing services. Transport clients to locations outside the home, such as to physicians' offices or on outings, using a motor vehicle. Train family members to provide bedside care. Provide clients with communication assistance, typing their correspondence and obtaining information for them. SKILLS—Social Perceptiveness: Being aware of others' reactions and understanding why they react as they do. Persuasion: Persuading others to change their minds or behavior. Service Orientation: Actively looking for ways to help people. Learning Strategies: Selecting and using training/instructional methods and procedures appropriate for the situation when learning or teaching new things. Coordination: Adjusting actions in relation to others' actions. Active Listening: Giving full attention to what other people are saying, taking time to understand the points being made, asking questions as appropriate, and not interrupting at inappropriate times. Instructing: Teaching others how to do something. Critical Thinking: Using logic and reasoning to identify the strengths and weaknesses of alternative solutions, conclusions, or approaches to problems. GOE—Interest Area: 10. Human Service. Work Group: 10.03. Child/Personal Care and Services. Other Jobs in This Work Group: Child Care Workers; Funeral Attendants; Nannies. PERSONALITY TYPE: Social.

EDUCATION/TRAINING PROGRAM(S)—No data available. RELATED KNOWLEDGE/COURSES—Customer and Personal Service: Knowledge of principles and processes for providing customer and personal services. This includes customer needs assessment, meeting quality standards for services, and evaluation of customer satisfaction. Medicine and Dentistry: Knowledge of the information and techniques needed to diagnose and treat human injuries, diseases, and deformities. This includes symptoms, treatment alternatives, drug properties and interactions, and preventive health-care measures. Therapy and Counseling: Knowledge of principles, methods, and procedures for diagnosis, treatment, and rehabilitation of physical and mental dysfunctions and for career counseling and guidance.

Personal Financial Advisors

◉ Education/Training Required: Bachelor's degree
◉ Annual Earnings: $62,700
◉ Growth: 34.6%
◉ Annual Job Openings: 18,000
◉ Self-Employed: 37.7%
◉ Part-Time: 7.0%

Advise clients on financial plans, utilizing knowledge of tax and investment strategies, securities, insurance, pension plans, and real estate. Duties include assessing clients' assets, liabilities, cash flow, insurance coverage, tax status, and financial objectives to establish investment strategies. Analyze financial information obtained from clients to determine strategies for meeting clients' financial objectives. Answer clients' questions about the purposes and details of financial plans and strategies. Build and maintain client bases, keeping current client plans up-to-date and recruiting new clients on an ongoing basis. Contact clients periodically to determine if there have been changes in their financial status. Devise debt liquidation plans that include payoff priorities and timelines. Explain and document for clients the types of services that are to be provided and the responsibilities to be taken by the personal financial advisor. Explain to individuals and groups the details of financial assistance available to college and university students, such as loans, grants, and scholarships. Guide clients in the gathering of information such as bank account records, income tax returns, life and disability insurance records, pension plan information, and wills. Implement financial planning recommendations or refer clients to someone who can assist them with plan implementation. Interview clients to determine their current income, expenses, insurance coverage, tax status, financial objectives, risk tolerance, and other information needed to develop a financial plan. Monitor financial market trends to ensure that plans are effective and to identify any necessary updates. Prepare and interpret for clients information such as investment performance reports, financial document summaries, and income projections. Recommend strategies clients can use to achieve their financial goals and objectives, including specific recommendations in such areas as cash management, insurance coverage, and investment planning. Research and investigate available investment opportunities to determine whether they fit into financial plans. Review clients' accounts and plans regularly to determine whether life changes, economic changes, or financial performance indicate a need for plan reassessment. Sell financial products such as stocks, bonds, mutual funds, and insurance if licensed to do so. **SKILLS—Service Orientation:** Actively looking for ways to help people. **Speaking:** Talking to others to convey information effectively. **Management of Financial Resources:** Determining how money will be spent to get the work done and accounting for these expenditures. **Active Listening:** Giving full attention to what other people are saying, taking time to understand the points being made, asking questions as appropriate, and not interrupting at inappropriate times. **Judgment and Decision Making:** Considering the relative costs and benefits of potential actions to choose the most appropriate one. **Mathematics:** Using mathematics to solve problems. **Critical Thinking:** Using logic and reasoning to identify the strengths and weaknesses of alternative solutions, conclusions, or approaches to problems. **Reading Comprehension:** Understanding written sentences and paragraphs in work-related documents. **Writing:** Communicating effectively in writing as appropriate for the needs of the audience. **GOE—Interest Area:** 06. Finance and Insurance. **Work Group:** 06.05. Finance/Insurance Sales and Support. **Other Jobs in This Work Group:** Advertising Sales Agents; Insurance Sales Agents; Sales Agents, Financial Services; Sales Agents, Securities and Commodities. **PERSONALITY TYPE:** Social.

EDUCATION/TRAINING PROGRAM(S)— Finance, General; Financial Planning and Services. **RELATED KNOWLEDGE/COURSES—Econom-** ics and Accounting: Knowledge of economic and accounting principles and practices, the financial markets, banking, and the analysis and reporting of financial data. **Mathematics:** Knowledge of arithmetic, algebra, geometry, calculus, and statistics and their applications. **Administration and Management:** Knowledge of business and management principles involved in strategic planning, resource allocation, human resources modeling, leadership technique, production methods, and coordination of people and resources. **Law and Government:** Knowledge of laws, legal codes, court procedures, precedents, government regulations, executive orders, agency rules, and the democratic political process. **Therapy and Counseling:** Knowledge of principles, methods, and procedures for diagnosis, treatment, and rehabilitation of physical and mental dysfunctions and for career counseling and guidance. **Customer and Personal Service:** Knowledge of principles and processes for providing customer and personal services. This includes customer needs assessment, meeting quality standards for services, and evaluation of customer satisfaction.

Personnel Recruiters

- Education/Training Required: Bachelor's degree
- Annual Earnings: $41,190
- Growth: 27.3%
- Annual Job Openings: 29,000
- Self-Employed: 0.8%
- Part-Time: 7.7%

Seek out, interview, and screen applicants to fill existing and future job openings and promote career opportunities within an organization. Establish and maintain relationships with hiring managers to stay abreast of current and future hiring and business needs. Interview applicants to obtain information on work history, training, education, and job skills. Maintain current knowledge of Equal Employment Opportunity (EEO) and affirmative action guidelines and laws, such as the Americans with Disabilities Act. Perform searches for qualified candidates according to relevant job criteria, using computer databases, networking, Internet recruiting resources, cold calls, media, recruiting firms, and employee referrals. Prepare and maintain employment records. Contact applicants to inform them of employment possibilities, consideration, and selection. Inform potential applicants about facilities, operations, benefits, and job or career opportunities in organizations. Screen and refer applicants to hiring personnel in the organization, making hiring recommendations when appropriate. Arrange for interviews and provide travel arrangements as necessary. Advise managers and employees on staffing policies and procedures. Review and evaluate applicant qualifications or eligibility for specified licensing according to established guidelines and designated licensing codes. Hire applicants and authorize paperwork assigning them to positions. Conduct reference and background checks on applicants. Evaluate recruitment and selection criteria to ensure conformance to professional, statistical, and testing standards, recommending revision as needed. Recruit applicants for open positions, arranging job fairs with college campus representatives. Advise management on organizing, preparing, and implementing recruiting and retention programs. Supervise personnel clerks performing filing, typing and record-keeping duties. Project yearly recruitment expenditures for budgetary consideration and control. **SKILLS—Management of Personnel Resources:** Motivating, developing, and directing people as they work, identifying the best people for the job. **Negotiation:** Bringing others together and trying to reconcile differences. **Persuasion:** Persuading others to change their minds or behavior. **Service Orientation:** Actively looking for ways to help people. **Time Management:** Managing one's own time and the time of others. **Management of Financial Resources:** Determining how money will be spent to get the work done and accounting for these expenditures. **Social Perceptiveness:** Being aware of others' reactions and understanding why they react as they do. **Judgment and Decision Making:** Considering the relative costs and benefits of potential actions to choose the most appropriate one. **GOE—Interest Area:** 04. Business and Administration. **Work Group:** 04.03. Human Resources Support. **Other Jobs in This Work Group:** Compensation, Benefits, and Job Analysis Specialists; Employment Interviewers, Private or Public Employment Service; Training and Development Specialists. **PERSONALITY TYPE:** Enterprising.

EDUCATION/TRAINING PROGRAM(S)— Human Resources Management/Personnel Administration, General; Labor and Industrial Relations. **RELATED KNOWLEDGE/COURSES—Personnel and Human Resources:** Knowledge of principles and procedures for personnel recruitment, selection, training, compensation and benefits, labor relations and negotiation, and personnel information systems. **Clerical Practices:** Knowledge of administrative and clerical procedures and systems such as word processing, managing files and records, stenography and transcription, designing forms, and other office procedures and terminology. **Education and Training:** Knowledge of principles and methods for curriculum and training design, teaching and instruction for individuals and groups, and the measurement of training effects. **Sales and Marketing:** Knowledge of principles and methods for showing, promoting, and selling products or services. This includes marketing strategy and tactics, product demonstrations, sales techniques, and sales control systems. **Administration and Management:** Knowledge of business and management principles involved in strategic planning, resource allocation, human resources modeling, leadership technique, production methods, and coordination of people and resources. **Computers and Electronics:** Knowledge of circuit boards, processors, chips, electronic equipment, and computer hardware and software, including applications and programming.

Pest Control Workers

- Education/Training Required: Moderate-term on-the-job training
- Annual Earnings: $26,220
- Growth: 17.0%
- Annual Job Openings: 11,000
- Self-Employed: 9.1%
- Part-Time: 6.1%

Spray or release chemical solutions or toxic gases and set traps to kill pests and vermin, such as mice, termites, and roaches, that infest buildings and surrounding areas. Spray or dust chemical solutions, powders, or gases into rooms; onto clothing, furnishings, or wood; and over marshlands, ditches, and catch-basins. Set mechanical traps and place poisonous paste or bait in sewers, burrows, and ditches. Inspect premises to identify infestation source and extent of damage to property, wall and roof porosity, and access to infested locations. Cut or bore openings in building or surrounding concrete, access infested areas, insert nozzle, and inject pesticide to impregnate ground. Study preliminary reports and diagrams of infested area and determine treatment type required to eliminate and prevent recurrence of infestation. Direct and/or assist other workers in treatment and extermination processes to eliminate and control rodents, insects, and weeds. Measure area dimensions requiring treatment, using rule; calculate fumigant requirements; and estimate cost for service. Clean and remove blockages from infested areas to facilitate spraying procedure and provide drainage, using broom, mop, shovel, and rake. Position and fasten edges of tarpaulins over building and tape vents to ensure air-tight environment and check for leaks. Post warning signs and lock building doors to secure area to be fumigated. Drive truck equipped with power-spraying equipment. Record work activities performed. Clean work site after completion of job. Dig up and burnweeds or spray them with herbicides. **SKILLS—Mathematics:** Using mathematics to solve problems. **Operation and Control:** Controlling operations of equipment or systems. **Management of Personnel Resources:** Motivating, developing, and directing people as they work, identifying the best people for the job. **Operation Monitoring:** Watching gauges, dials, or other indicators to make sure a machine is working properly. **Judgment and Decision Making:** Considering the relative costs and benefits of potential actions to choose the most appropriate one. **GOE—Interest Area:** 01. Agriculture and Natural Resources. **Work Group:** 01.05. Nursery, Groundskeeping, and Pest Control. **Other Jobs in This Work Group:** Landscaping and Groundskeeping Workers; Nursery Workers; Pesticide Handlers, Sprayers, and Applicators, Vegetation; Tree Trimmers and Pruners. **PERSONALITY TYPE:** Realistic.

EDUCATION/TRAINING PROGRAM(S)—Agricultural/Farm Supplies Retailing and Wholesaling. **RELATED KNOWLEDGE/COURSES—Chemistry:** Knowledge of the chemical composition, structure, and properties of substances and of the chemical processes and transformations that they undergo. This includes uses of chemicals and their danger signs, production techniques, and disposal methods. **Mechanical Devices:** Knowledge of machines and tools, including their designs, uses, repair, and maintenance. **Biology:** Knowledge of plant and animal organisms and their tissues, cells, functions, interdependencies, and interactions with each other and the environment.

Pharmacists

- Education/Training Required: First professional degree
- Annual Earnings: $84,900
- Growth: 30.1%
- Annual Job Openings: 23,000
- Self-Employed: 3.4%
- Part-Time: 17.3%

Compound and dispense medications, following prescriptions issued by physicians, dentists, or other authorized medical practitioners. Review prescriptions to assure accuracy, to ascertain the needed ingredients, and to evaluate their suitability. Provide information and advice regarding drug interactions, side effects, dosage, and proper medication storage. Analyze prescribing trends to monitor patient compliance and to prevent excessive usage or harmful interactions. Order and purchase pharmaceutical supplies, medical supplies, and drugs, maintaining stock and storing and handling it properly. Maintain records, such as pharmacy files; patient profiles; charge system files; inventories; control records for radioactive nuclei; and registries of poisons, narcotics, and controlled drugs. Provide specialized services to help patients manage conditions such as diabetes, asthma, smoking cessation, or high blood pressure. Advise customers on the selection of medication brands, medical equipment, and health-care supplies. Collaborate with other health-care professionals to plan, monitor, review, and evaluate the quality and effectiveness of drugs and drug regimens, providing advice on drug applications and characteristics. Compound and dispense medications as prescribed by doctors and dentists by calculating, weighing, measuring, and mixing ingredients or oversee these activities. Offer health promotion and prevention activities, for example, training people to use devices such as blood pressure or diabetes monitors. Refer patients to other health professionals and agencies when appropriate. Prepare sterile solutions and infusions for use in surgical procedures, emergency rooms, or patients' homes. Plan, implement, and maintain procedures for mixing, packaging, and labeling pharmaceuticals according to policy and legal requirements to ensure quality, security, and proper disposal. Assay radiopharmaceuticals, verify rates of disintegration, and calculate the volume required to produce the desired results to ensure proper dosages.

Manage pharmacy operations, hiring and supervising staff, performing administrative duties, and buying and selling non-pharmaceutical merchandise. Work in hospitals or clinics or for HMOs, dispensing prescriptions, serving as a medical team consultant, or specializing in specific drug therapy areas such as oncology or nuclear pharmacotherapy. **SKILLS—Instructing:** Teaching others how to do something. **Social Perceptiveness:** Being aware of others' reactions and understanding why they react as they do. **Reading Comprehension:** Understanding written sentences and paragraphs in work-related documents. **Active Listening:** Giving full attention to what other people are saying, taking time to understand the points being made, asking questions as appropriate, and not interrupting at inappropriate times. **Science:** Using scientific rules and methods to solve problems. **Critical Thinking:** Using logic and reasoning to identify the strengths and weaknesses of alternative solutions, conclusions, or approaches to problems. **Speaking:** Talking to others to convey information effectively. **Active Learning:** Understanding the implications of new information for both current and future problem-solving and decision-making. **GOE—Interest Area:** 08. Health Science. **Work Group:** 08.02. Medicine and Surgery. **Other Jobs in This Work Group:** Anesthesiologists; Family and General Practitioners; Internists, General; Medical Assistants; Medical Transcriptionists; Obstetricians and Gynecologists; Pediatricians, General; Pharmacy Aides; Pharmacy Technicians; Physician Assistants; Psychiatrists; Registered Nurses; Surgeons; Surgical Technologists. **PERSONALITY TYPE:** Investigative.

EDUCATION/TRAINING PROGRAM(S)—Clinical and Industrial Drug Development (MS, PhD); Clinical, Hospital, and Managed Care Pharmacy (MS, PhD); Industrial and Physical Pharmacy and Cosmetic Sciences (MS, PhD); Medicinal and Pharmaceutical Chemistry (MS, PhD); Natural Products Chemistry and Pharmacognosy (MS, PhD); Pharmaceutics and Drug Design (MS, PhD); Pharmacoeconomics/Pharmaceutical Economics (MS, PhD); Pharmacy (PharmD [USA]; PharmD, BS/BPharm [Canada]); Pharmacy Administration and Pharmacy Policy and Regulatory Affairs (MS, PhD); Pharmacy, Pharmaceutical Sciences, and Administration, Other. **RELATED KNOWLEDGE/COURSES—Medicine and Dentistry:** Knowledge of the information and techniques needed to diagnose and treat human injuries, diseases, and deformities. This includes symptoms, treatment alternatives, drug properties and interactions, and preventive health-care measures. **Chemistry:** Knowledge of the chemical composition, structure, and properties of substances and of the chemical processes and transformations that they undergo. This includes uses of chemicals and their danger signs, production techniques, and disposal methods. **Customer and Personal Service:** Knowledge of principles and processes for providing customer and personal services. This includes customer needs assessment, meeting quality standards for services, and evaluation of customer satisfaction. **Psychology:** Knowledge of human behavior and performance; individual differences in ability, personality, and interests; learning and motivation; psychological research methods; and the assessment and treatment of behavioral and affective disorders. **Therapy and Counseling:** Knowledge of principles, methods, and procedures for diagnosis, treatment, and rehabilitation of physical and mental dysfunctions and for career counseling and guidance. **Mathematics:** Knowledge of arithmetic, algebra, geometry, calculus, and statistics and their applications.

Pharmacy Technicians

- Education/Training Required: Moderate-term on-the-job training
- Annual Earnings: $23,650
- Growth: 28.8%
- Annual Job Openings: 39,000
- Self-Employed: 0%
- Part-Time: 23.0%

Prepare medications under the direction of a pharmacist. May measure, mix, count out, label, and record amounts and dosages of medications. Receive written prescription or refill requests and verify that information is complete and accurate. Maintain proper storage and security conditions for drugs. Answer telephones, responding to questions or requests. Fill bottles with prescribed medications and type and affix labels. Assist customers by answering simple questions, locating items, or referring them to the pharmacist for medication information. Price and file prescriptions that have been filled. Clean and help maintain equipment and work areas and sterilize glassware according to prescribed methods. Establish and maintain patient profiles, including lists of medications taken by individual patients. Order, label, and count stock of medications, chemicals, and supplies and enter inventory data into computer. Receive and store incoming supplies, verify quantities against invoices, and inform supervisors of stock needs and shortages. Transfer medication from vials to the appropriate number of sterile, disposable syringes, using aseptic techniques. Add measured drugs or nutrients to intravenous solutions under sterile conditions to prepare intravenous (IV) packs under pharmacist supervision. Supply and monitor robotic machines that dispense medicine into containers and label the containers. Prepare and process medical insurance claim forms and records. Mix pharmaceutical preparations according to written prescriptions. Operate cash registers to accept payment from customers. Compute charges for medication and equipment dispensed to hospital patients and enter data in computer. Deliver medications and pharmaceutical supplies to patients, nursing stations, or surgery. Price stock and mark items for sale. Maintain and merchandise home health-care products and services. **SKILLS—Instructing:** Teaching others how to do something. **Service Orientation:** Actively looking for ways to help people. **Active Listening:** Giving full attention to what other people are saying, taking time to understand the points being made, asking questions as appropriate, and not interrupting at inappropriate times. **Active Learning:** Understanding the implications of new information for both current and future problem-solving and decision-making. **Speaking:** Talking to others to convey information effectively. **Critical Thinking:** Using logic and reasoning to identify the strengths and weaknesses of alternative solutions, conclusions, or approaches to problems. **Mathematics:** Using mathematics to solve problems. **Troubleshooting:** Determining causes of operating errors and deciding what to do about them. **GOE— Interest Area:** 08. Health Science. **Work Group:** 08.02. Medicine and Surgery. **Other Jobs in This Work Group:** Anesthesiologists; Family and General Practitioners; Internists, General; Medical Assistants; Medical Transcriptionists; Obstetricians and Gynecologists; Pediatricians, General; Pharmacists; Pharmacy Aides; Physician Assistants; Psychiatrists; Registered Nurses; Surgeons; Surgical Technologists. **PERSONALITY TYPE:** Conventional.

EDUCATION/TRAINING PROGRAM(S)—Pharmacy Technician/Assistant. **RELATED KNOWLEDGE/COURSES—Customer and Personal Service:** Knowledge of principles and processes for providing customer and personal services. This includes customer needs assessment, meeting quality standards for services, and evaluation of customer satisfaction. **Chemistry:** Knowledge of the chemical composition, structure, and properties of substances and of the chemical processes and transformations that they undergo. This includes uses of chemicals and their danger signs, production techniques, and disposal methods. **Medicine and Dentistry:** Knowledge of the information and techniques needed to diagnose and treat human injuries, diseases, and deformities. This includes symptoms, treatment alternatives, drug properties and interactions, and preventive health-care measures. **Mathematics:** Knowledge of arithmetic, algebra, geometry, calculus, and statistics and their applications. **Therapy and Counseling:** Knowledge of principles, methods, and procedures for diagnosis, treatment, and rehabilitation of physical and mental dysfunctions and for career counseling and guidance. **Clerical Practices:** Knowledge of administrative and clerical procedures and systems such as word processing, managing files and records, stenography and transcription, designing forms, and other office procedures and terminology.

Philosophy and Religion Teachers, Postsecondary

- Education/Training Required: Master's degree
- Annual Earnings: $51,800
- Growth: 38.1%
- Annual Job Openings: 216,000
- Self-Employed: 0.3%
- Part-Time: 27.7%

Teach courses in philosophy, religion, and theology. Evaluate and grade students' class work, assignments, and papers. Initiate, facilitate, and moderate classroom discussions. Prepare and deliver lectures to undergraduate and/or graduate students on topics such as ethics, logic, and contemporary religious thought. Prepare course materials such as syllabi, homework assignments, and handouts. Compile, administer, and grade examinations or assign this work to others. Keep abreast of developments in their field by reading current literature, talking with colleagues, and participating in professional conferences. Maintain student attendance records, grades, and other required records. Plan, evaluate, and revise curricula, course content, and course materials and methods of instruction. Maintain regularly scheduled office hours in order to advise and assist students. Select and obtain materials and supplies such as textbooks. Advise students on academic and vocational curricula and on career issues. Conduct research in a particular field of knowledge and publish findings in professional journals, books, and/or electronic media. Perform administrative duties such as serving as department head. Serve on academic or administrative committees that deal with institutional policies, departmental matters, and academic issues. Collaborate with colleagues to address teaching and research issues. Participate in campus and community events. Compile bibliographies of specialized materials for outside reading assignments. Participate in student recruitment, registration, and placement activities. Supervise undergraduate and/or graduate teaching, internship, and research work. **SKILLS— Instructing:** Teaching others how to do something. **Learning Strategies:** Selecting and using training/instructional methods and procedures appropriate for the situation when learning or teaching new things. **Writing:** Communicating effectively in writing as appropriate for the needs of the audience. **Critical Thinking:** Using logic and reasoning to identify the strengths and weaknesses of alternative solutions, conclusions, or approaches to problems. **Reading Comprehension:** Understanding written sentences and paragraphs in work-related documents. **Social Perceptiveness:** Being aware of others' reactions and understanding why they react as they do. **Speaking:** Talking to others to convey information effectively. **Persuasion:** Persuading others to change their minds or behavior. **GOE—Interest Area:** 05. Education and Training. **Work Group:** 05.03. Postsecondary and Adult Teaching and Instructing. **Other Jobs in This Work Group:** Adult Literacy, Remedial Education, and GED Teachers and Instructors; Agricultural Sciences Teachers, Postsecondary; Anthropology and Archeology Teachers, Postsecondary; Architecture Teachers, Postsecondary; Area, Ethnic, and Cultural Studies Teachers, Postsecondary; Art, Drama, and Music Teachers, Postsecondary; Atmospheric, Earth, Marine, and Space Sciences Teachers, Postsecondary; Biological Science Teachers, Postsecondary; Business Teachers, Postsecondary; Chemistry Teachers, Postsecondary; Communications Teachers, Postsecondary; Computer Science Teachers, Postsecondary; Criminal Justice and Law Enforcement Teachers, Postsecondary; Economics Teachers, Postsecondary; Education Teach-

ers, Postsecondary; Engineering Teachers, Postsecondary; English Language and Literature Teachers, Postsecondary; Environmental Science Teachers, Postsecondary; Farm and Home Management Advisors; Foreign Language and Literature Teachers, Postsecondary; Forestry and Conservation Science Teachers, Postsecondary; Geography Teachers, Postsecondary; Graduate Teaching Assistants; Health Specialties Teachers, Postsecondary; History Teachers, Postsecondary; Home Economics Teachers, Postsecondary; Law Teachers, Postsecondary; Library Science Teachers, Postsecondary; Mathematical Science Teachers, Postsecondary; Nursing Instructors and Teachers, Postsecondary; Physics Teachers, Postsecondary; Political Science Teachers, Postsecondary; Psychology Teachers, Postsecondary; Recreation and Fitness Studies Teachers, Postsecondary; Self-Enrichment Education Teachers, Postsecondary; Social Work Teachers, Postsecondary; Sociology Teachers, Postsecondary; Vocational Education Teachers, Postsecondary. **PERSONALITY TYPE:** No data available.

EDUCATION/TRAINING PROGRAM(S)— Bible/Biblical Studies; Buddhist Studies; Christian Studies; Divinity/Ministry (BD, MDiv.); Ethics; Hindu Studies; Missions/Missionary Studies and Missiology; Pastoral Counseling and Specialized Ministries, Other; Pastoral Studies/Counseling; Philosophy; Philosophy and Religious Studies, Other; Philosophy, Other; Pre-Theology/Pre-Ministerial Studies; Rabbinical Studies; Religion/Religious Studies; Religious Education; Religious/Sacred Music; Talmudic Studies; Theological and Ministerial Studies, Other; Theology and Religious Vocations, Other; Theology/Theological Studies. **RELATED KNOWLEDGE/COURSES—Philosophy and Theology:** Knowledge of different philosophical systems and religions. This includes their basic principles, values, ethics, ways of thinking, customs, and practices and their impact on human culture. **History and Archeology:** Knowledge of historical events and their causes, indicators, and effects on civilizations and cultures. **English Language:** Knowledge of the structure and content of the English language, including the meaning and spelling of words, rules of composition, and grammar. **Education and Training:** Knowledge of principles and methods for curriculum and training design, teaching and instruction for individuals and groups, and the measurement of training effects. **Sociology and Anthropology:** Knowledge of group behavior and dynamics, societal trends and influences, human migrations, ethnicity, and cultures and their history and origins. **Foreign Language:** Knowledge of the structure and content of a foreign (non-English) language, including the meaning and spelling of words, rules of composition and grammar, and pronunciation.

Photographers, Scientific

- ◎ Education/Training Required: Long-term on-the-job training
- ◎ Annual Earnings: $26,080
- ◎ Growth: 13.6%
- ◎ Annual Job Openings: 18,000
- ◎ Self-Employed: 52.5%
- ◎ Part-Time: 24.0%

Photograph variety of subject material to illustrate or record scientific/medical data or phenomena, utilizing knowledge of scientific procedures and photographic technology and techniques. Photographs variety of subject material to illustrate or record scientific or medical data or phenomena related to an area of interest. Sights and focuses camera to take picture of subject material to illustrate or record scientific or medical data or phenomena. Plans methods and procedures for photographing subject material and setup of required equipment. Observes and arranges subject material to desired position. Engages in research to develop new photographic procedures, materials, and scientific data. Sets up, mounts, or installs photographic equipment and cameras. Removes exposed film and develops film, using chemicals, touch-up tools, and equipment. **SKILLS—Science:** Using scientific rules and methods to solve problems. **Reading Comprehension:** Understanding written sentences and paragraphs in work-related documents. **Equipment Selection:** Determining the kind of tools and equipment needed to do a job. **Technology Design:** Generating or adapting equipment and technology to serve user needs. **Operation and Control:** Controlling operations of equipment or systems. **Management of Material Resources:** Obtaining and seeing to the appropriate use of equipment, facilities, and materials needed to do certain work. **Active Learning:** Understanding the implications of new information for both current and future problem-solving and decision-making. **Writing:** Communicating effectively in writing as appropriate for the needs of the audience. **GOE—Interest Area:** 15. Scientific Research, Engineering, and Mathematics. **Work Group:** 15.05. Physical Science Laboratory Technology. **Other Jobs in This Work Group:** Chemical Technicians; Nuclear Equipment Operation Technicians. **PERSONALITY TYPE:** Artistic.

EDUCATION/TRAINING PROGRAM(S)— Art/Art Studies, General; Commercial Photography; Film/Video and Photographic Arts, Other; Photography; Photojournalism; Visual and Performing Arts, General. **RELATED KNOWLEDGE/COURSES— Chemistry:** Knowledge of the chemical composition, structure, and properties of substances and of the chemical processes and transformations that they undergo. This includes uses of chemicals and their danger signs, production techniques, and disposal methods. **Fine Arts:** Knowledge of the theory and techniques required to compose, produce, and perform works of music, dance, the visual arts, drama, and sculpture. **Physics:** Knowledge and prediction of physical principles and laws and their interrelationships and applications to understanding fluid, material, and atmospheric dynamics and mechanical, electrical, atomic, and subatomic structures and processes. **Engineering and Technology:** Knowledge of the practical application of engineering science and technology. This includes applying principles, techniques, procedures, and equipment to the design and production of various goods and services. **Medicine and Dentistry:** Knowledge of the information and techniques needed to diagnose and treat human injuries, diseases, and deformities. This includes symptoms, treatment alternatives, drug properties and interactions, and preventive health-care measures. **Communications and Media:** Knowledge of media production, communication, and dissemination techniques and methods. This includes alternative ways to inform and entertain via written, oral, and visual media.

Physical Therapist Aides

◎ Education/Training Required: Associate degree

◎ Annual Earnings: $21,380

◎ Growth: 46.4%

◎ Annual Job Openings: 8,000

◎ Self-Employed: 0.4%

◎ Part-Time: 22.8%

Under close supervision of a physical therapist or physical therapy assistant, perform only delegated, selected, or routine tasks in specific situations. These duties include preparing the patient and the treatment area. Clean and organize work area and disinfect equipment after treatment. Observe patients during treatment to compile and evaluate data on patients' responses and progress and report to physical therapist. Instruct, motivate, safeguard, and assist patients practicing exercises and functional activities under direction of medical staff. Secure patients into or onto therapy equipment. Transport patients to and from treatment areas, using wheelchairs or providing standing support. Confer with physical therapy staff and others to discuss and evaluate patient information for planning, modifying, and coordinating treatment. Record treatment given and equipment used. Perform clerical duties, such as taking inventory, ordering supplies, answering telephone, taking messages, and filling out forms. Maintain equipment and furniture to keep it in good working condition, including performing the assembly and disassembly of equipment and accessories. Administer active and passive manual therapeutic exercises; therapeutic massage; and heat, light, sound, water, and electrical modality treatments, such as ultrasound. Change linens, such as bedsheets and pillowcases. Arrange treatment supplies to keep them in order. Assist patients in dressing, undressing, and putting on and removing supportive devices, such as braces, splints, and slings. Measure patient's range-of-joint motion, body parts, and vital signs to determine effects of treatments or for patient evaluations. Train patients to use orthopedic braces, prostheses, and supportive devices. Fit patients for orthopedic braces, prostheses, and supportive devices, adjusting fit as needed. Participate in patient care tasks, such as assisting with passing food trays, feeding residents, and bathing residents on bed rest. Administer traction to relieve neck and back pain, using intermittent and stat-ic traction equipment. **SKILLS—Social Perceptiveness:** Being aware of others' reactions and understanding why they react as they do. **Service Orientation:** Actively looking for ways to help people. **Learning Strategies:** Selecting and using training/instructional methods and procedures appropriate for the situation when learning or teaching new things. **Time Management:** Managing one's own time and the time of others. **Operation Monitoring:** Watching gauges, dials, or other indicators to make sure a machine is working properly. **Negotiation:** Bringing others together and trying to reconcile differences. **Persuasion:** Persuading others to change their minds or behavior. **Equipment Maintenance:** Performing routine maintenance on equipment and determining when and what kind of maintenance is needed. **GOE—Interest Area:** 08. Health Science. **Work Group:** 08.07. Medical Therapy. **Other Jobs in This Work Group:** Audiologists; Massage Therapists; Occupational Therapist Aides; Occupational Therapist Assistants; Occupational Therapists; Physical Therapist Assistants; Physical Therapists; Radiation Therapists; Recreational Therapists; Respiratory Therapists; Respiratory Therapy Technicians; Speech-Language Pathologists. **PERSONALITY TYPE:** Social.

EDUCATION/TRAINING PROGRAM(S)—Physical Therapist Assistant. **RELATED KNOWLEDGE/COURSES—Psychology:** Knowledge of human behavior and performance; individual differences in ability, personality, and interests; learning and motivation; psychological research methods; and the assessment and treatment of behavioral and affective disorders. **Customer and Personal Service:** Knowledge of principles and processes for providing customer and personal services. This includes customer needs assessment, meeting quality standards for services, and evaluation of customer satisfaction. **Medicine and Dentistry:** Knowledge of the information and techniques needed to diagnose and treat human injuries, diseases, and deformities. This includes symptoms, treatment alternatives, drug properties and interactions, and preventive health-care measures. **Therapy and Counseling:** Knowledge of principles, methods, and procedures for diagnosis, treatment, and rehabilitation of physical and mental dysfunctions and for career counseling and guidance. **Philosophy and Theology:** Knowledge of different philosophical systems and religions. This includes their basic principles, values, ethics, ways of thinking, customs, and practices and their impact on human culture. **Clerical Practices:**

Knowledge of administrative and clerical procedures and systems such as word processing, managing files and records, stenography and transcription, designing forms, and other office procedures and terminology.

Physical Therapist Assistants

- Education/Training Required: Associate degree
- Annual Earnings: $37,890
- Growth: 44.6%
- Annual Job Openings: 10,000
- Self-Employed: 0.4%
- Part-Time: 22.8%

Assist physical therapists in providing physical therapy treatments and procedures. May, in accordance with state laws, assist in the development of treatment plans, carry out routine functions, document the progress of treatment, and modify specific treatments in accordance with patient status and within the scope of treatment plans established by a physical therapist. Generally requires formal training. Instruct, motivate, safeguard, and assist patients as they practice exercises and functional activities. Confer with physical therapy staff and others to discuss and evaluate patient information for planning, modifying, and coordinating treatment. Administer active and passive manual therapeutic exercises; therapeutic massage; and heat, light, sound, water, and electrical modality treatments, such as ultrasound. Observe patients during treatments to compile and evaluate data on patients' responses and progress and report to physical therapist. Measure patients' range-of-joint motion, body parts, and vital signs to determine effects of treatments or for patient evaluations. Secure patients into or onto therapy equipment. Fit patients for orthopedic braces, prostheses, and supportive devices such as crutches. Train patients in the use of orthopedic braces, prostheses, and supportive devices. Transport patients to and from treatment areas, lifting and transferring them according to positioning requirements. Monitor operation of equipment and record use of equipment and administration of treatment. Clean work area and check and store equipment after treatment. Assist patients in dressing, undressing, and putting on and removing supportive devices, such

as braces, splints, and slings. Administer traction to relieve neck and back pain, using intermittent and static traction equipment. Perform clerical duties, such as taking inventory, ordering supplies, answering telephone, taking messages, and filling out forms. Prepare treatment areas and electrotherapy equipment for use by physiotherapists. Perform postural drainage, percussions, and vibrations and teach deep breathing exercises to treat respiratory conditions. **SKILLS—Social Perceptiveness:** Being aware of others' reactions and understanding why they react as they do. **Service Orientation:** Actively looking for ways to help people. **Instructing:** Teaching others how to do something. **Time Management:** Managing one's own time and the time of others. **Learning Strategies:** Selecting and using training/instructional methods and procedures appropriate for the situation when learning or teaching new things. **Writing:** Communicating effectively in writing as appropriate for the needs of the audience. **Speaking:** Talking to others to convey information effectively. **Active Learning:** Understanding the implications of new information for both current and future problem-solving and decision-making. **GOE—Interest Area:** 08. Health Science. **Work Group:** 08.07. Medical Therapy. **Other Jobs in This Work Group:** Audiologists; Massage Therapists; Occupational Therapist Aides; Occupational Therapist Assistants; Occupational Therapists; Physical Therapist Aides; Physical Therapists; Radiation Therapists; Recreational Therapists; Respiratory Therapists; Respiratory Therapy Technicians; Speech-Language Pathologists. **PERSONALITY TYPE:** Social.

EDUCATION/TRAINING PROGRAM(S)—Physical Therapist Assistant. **RELATED KNOWLEDGE/COURSES—Psychology:** Knowledge of human behavior and performance; individual differences in ability, personality, and interests; learning and motivation; psychological research methods; and the assessment and treatment of behavioral and affective disorders. **Therapy and Counseling:** Knowledge of principles, methods, and procedures for diagnosis, treatment, and rehabilitation of physical and mental dysfunctions and for career counseling and guidance. **Medicine and Dentistry:** Knowledge of the information and techniques needed to diagnose and treat human injuries, diseases, and deformities. This includes symptoms, treatment alternatives, drug properties and interactions, and preventive health-care measures. **Education and Training:** Knowledge of principles and methods for curriculum and training design, teaching and instruction for individuals and groups, and the measurement of training effects. **Customer and Personal Service:** Knowledge of principles and processes for providing customer and personal services. This includes customer needs assessment, meeting quality standards for services, and evaluation of customer satisfaction. **Sociology and Anthropology:** Knowledge of group behavior and dynamics, societal trends and influences, human migrations, ethnicity, and cultures and their history and origins.

Physical Therapists

- ⊚ Education/Training Required: Master's degree
- ⊚ Annual Earnings: $60,180
- ⊚ Growth: 35.3%
- ⊚ Annual Job Openings: 16,000
- ⊚ Self-Employed: 5.7%
- ⊚ Part-Time: 23.8%

Assess, plan, organize, and participate in rehabilitative programs that improve mobility, relieve pain, increase strength, and decrease or prevent deformity of patients suffering from disease or injury. Plan, prepare, and carry out individually designed programs of physical treatment to maintain, improve, or restore physical functioning; alleviate pain; and prevent physical dysfunction in patients. Perform and document an initial exam, evaluating the data to identify problems and determine a diagnosis prior to intervention. Evaluate effects of treatment at various stages and adjust treatments to achieve maximum benefit. Administer manual exercises, massage, and/or traction to help relieve pain, increase the patient's strength, and decrease or prevent deformity and crippling. Instruct patient and family in treatment procedures to be continued at home. Confer with the patient, medical practitioners, and appropriate others to plan, implement, and assess the intervention program. Review physician's referral and patient's medical records to help determine diagnosis and physical therapy treatment required. Record prognosis, treatment, response, and progress in patient's chart or enter information into computer. Obtain patients' informed consent to proposed interventions. Discharge patient from physical therapy when goals or projected outcomes have been attained and provide for appropriate followup care or referrals. Test and measure patient's strength, motor

development and function, sensory perception, functional capacity, and respiratory and circulatory efficiency and record data. Identify and document goals, anticipated progress, and plans for reevaluation. Provide information to the patient about the proposed intervention, its material risks and expected benefits, and any reasonable alternatives. Inform the patient when diagnosis reveals findings outside their scope and refer to an appropriate practitioner. Direct and supervise supportive personnel, assessing their competence, delegating specific tasks to them, and establishing channels of communication. Administer treatment involving application of physical agents, using equipment, moist packs, ultraviolet and infrared lamps, and ultrasound machines. Teach physical therapy students as well as those in other health professions. Evaluate, fit, and adjust prosthetic and orthotic devices and recommend modification to orthotist. **SKILLS— Instructing:** Teaching others how to do something. **Social Perceptiveness:** Being aware of others' reactions and understanding why they react as they do. **Reading Comprehension:** Understanding written sentences and paragraphs in work-related documents. **Learning Strategies:** Selecting and using training/instructional methods and procedures appropriate for the situation when learning or teaching new things. **Science:** Using scientific rules and methods to solve problems. **Service Orientation:** Actively looking for ways to help people. **Time Management:** Managing one's own time and the time of others. **Critical Thinking:** Using logic and reasoning to identify the strengths and weaknesses of alternative solutions, conclusions, or approaches to problems. **Coordination:** Adjusting actions in relation to others' actions. **GOE—Interest Area:** 08. Health Science. **Work Group:** 08.07. Medical Therapy. **Other Jobs in This Work Group:** Audiologists; Massage Therapists; Occupational Therapist Aides; Occupational Therapist Assistants; Occupational Therapists; Physical Therapist Aides; Physical Therapist Assistants; Radiation Therapists; Recreational Therapists; Respiratory Therapists; Respiratory Therapy Technicians; Speech-Language Pathologists. **PERSONALITY TYPE:** Social.

EDUCATION/TRAINING PROGRAM(S)—Kinesiotherapy/Kinesiotherapist; Physical Therapy/ Therapist. **RELATED KNOWLEDGE/ COURSES—Psychology:** Knowledge of human behavior and performance; individual differences in ability, personality, and interests; learning and motivation; psychological research methods; and the assessment and treatment of behavioral and affective disorders. **Therapy and Counseling:** Knowledge of principles, methods, and procedures for diagnosis, treatment, and rehabilitation of physical and mental dysfunctions and for career counseling and guidance. **Medicine and Dentistry:** Knowledge of the information and techniques needed to diagnose and treat human injuries, diseases, and deformities. This includes symptoms, treatment alternatives, drug properties and interactions, and preventive health-care measures. **Customer and Personal Service:** Knowledge of principles and processes for providing customer and personal services. This includes customer needs assessment, meeting quality standards for services, and evaluation of customer satisfaction. **Biology:** Knowledge of plant and animal organisms and their tissues, cells, functions, interdependencies, and interactions with each other and the environment. **Sociology and Anthropology:** Knowledge of group behavior and dynamics, societal trends and influences, human migrations, ethnicity, and cultures and their history and origins.

Physician Assistants

- ◎ Education/Training Required: Bachelor's degree
- ◎ Annual Earnings: $69,410
- ◎ Growth: 48.9%
- ◎ Annual Job Openings: 7,000
- ◎ Self-Employed: 0.8%
- ◎ Part-Time: 16.3%

Provide health-care services typically performed by a physician under the supervision of a physician. Conduct complete physicals, provide treatment, and counsel patients. May, in some cases, prescribe medication. Must graduate from an accredited educational program for physician assistants. Examine patients to obtain information about their physical condition. Interpret diagnostic test results for deviations from normal. Make tentative diagnoses and decisions about management and treatment of patients. Obtain, compile, and record patient medical data, including health history, progress notes, and results of physical examination. Administer or order diagnostic tests, such as X-ray, electrocardiogram, and laboratory tests. Prescribe therapy or medication with physician approval. Per-

form therapeutic procedures, such as injections, immunizations, suturing and wound care, and infection management. Instruct and counsel patients about prescribed therapeutic regimens, normal growth and development, family planning, emotional problems of daily living, and health maintenance. Provide physicians with assistance during surgery or complicated medical procedures. Supervise and coordinate activities of technicians and technical assistants. Visit and observe patients on hospital rounds or house calls, updating charts, ordering therapy, and reporting back to physician. **SKILLS—Social Perceptiveness:** Being aware of others' reactions and understanding why they react as they do. **Science:** Using scientific rules and methods to solve problems. **Instructing:** Teaching others how to do something. **Reading Comprehension:** Understanding written sentences and paragraphs in work-related documents. **Critical Thinking:** Using logic and reasoning to identify the strengths and weaknesses of alternative solutions, conclusions, or approaches to problems. **Active Listening:** Giving full attention to what other people are saying, taking time to understand the points being made, asking questions as appropriate, and not interrupting at inappropriate times. **Time Management:** Managing one's own time and the time of others. **Active Learning:** Understanding the implications of new information for both current and future problem-solving and decision-making. **GOE—Interest Area:** 08. Health Science. **Work Group:** 08.02. Medicine and Surgery. **Other Jobs in This Work Group:** Anesthesiologists; Family and General Practitioners; Internists, General; Medical Assistants; Medical Transcriptionists; Obstetricians and Gynecologists; Pediatricians, General; Pharmacists; Pharmacy Aides; Pharmacy Technicians; Psychiatrists; Registered Nurses; Surgeons; Surgical Technologists. **PERSONALITY TYPE:** Investigative.

EDUCATION/TRAINING PROGRAM(S)— Physician Assistant. **RELATED KNOWLEDGE/ COURSES—Medicine and Dentistry:** Knowledge of the information and techniques needed to diagnose and treat human injuries, diseases, and deformities. This includes symptoms, treatment alternatives, drug properties and interactions, and preventive health-care measures. **Biology:** Knowledge of plant and animal organisms and their tissues, cells, functions, interdependencies, and interactions with each other and the environment. **Therapy and Counseling:** Knowledge of principles, methods, and procedures for diagnosis, treatment, and rehabilitation of physical and mental dysfunctions and for career counseling and guidance. **Psychology:** Knowledge of human behavior and performance; individual differences in ability, personality, and interests; learning and motivation; psychological research methods; and the assessment and treatment of behavioral and affective disorders. **Customer and Personal Service:** Knowledge of principles and processes for providing customer and personal services. This includes customer needs assessment, meeting quality standards for services, and evaluation of customer satisfaction. **Chemistry:** Knowledge of the chemical composition, structure, and properties of substances and of the chemical processes and transformations that they undergo. This includes uses of chemicals and their danger signs, production techniques, and disposal methods.

Physicists

- Education/Training Required: Doctoral degree
- Annual Earnings: $87,450
- Growth: 6.9%
- Annual Job Openings: 1,000
- Self-Employed: 9.9%
- Part-Time: 2.4%

Conduct research into the phases of physical phenomena, develop theories and laws on the basis of observation and experiments, and devise methods to apply laws and theories to industry and other fields. Analyze data from research conducted to detect and measure physical phenomena. Describe and express observations and conclusions in mathematical terms. Design computer simulations to model physical data so that it can be better understood. Develop theories and laws on the basis of observation and experiments and apply these theories and laws to problems in areas such as nuclear energy, optics, and aerospace technology. Observe the structure and properties of matter and the transformation and propagation of energy, using equipment such as masers, lasers, and telescopes, in order to explore and identify the basic principles governing these phenomena. Perform complex calculations as part of the analysis and evaluation of data, using computers. Report experimental results by writing papers for scientific journals or by presenting information at scientific conferences. Collaborate with other scientists in the design, development, and testing of experimental, industrial, or medical equipment, instrumentation, and procedures. Conduct application evaluations and analyze results in order to determine commercial, industrial, scientific, medical, military, or other uses for electro-optical devices. Develop manufacturing, assembly, and fabrication processes of lasers, masers, infrared, and other light-emitting and light-sensitive devices. Provide support services for activities such as radiation therapy, diagnostic imaging, or seismology. Teach physics to students. Advise authorities of procedures to be followed in radiation incidents or hazards and assist in civil defense planning. Conduct research pertaining to potential environmental impacts of atomic energy–related industrial development in order to determine licensing qualifications. Develop standards of permissible concentrations of radioisotopes in liquids and gases. Direct testing and monitoring of contamination of radioactive equipment and recording of personnel and plant area radiation exposure data. **SKILLS—Science:** Using scientific rules and methods to solve problems. **Mathematics:** Using mathematics to solve problems. **Writing:** Communicating effectively in writing as appropriate for the needs of the audience. **Technology Design:** Generating or adapting equipment and technology to serve user needs. **Active Learning:** Understanding the implications of new information for both current and future problem-solving and decision-making. **Reading Comprehension:** Understanding written sentences and paragraphs in work-related documents. **Critical Thinking:** Using logic and reasoning to identify the strengths and weaknesses of alternative solutions, conclusions, or approaches to problems. **Operations Analysis:** Analyzing needs and product requirements to create a design. **Management of Personnel Resources:** Motivating, developing, and directing people as they work, identifying the best people for the job. **GOE—Interest Area:** 15. Scientific Research, Engineering, and Mathematics. **Work Group:** 15.02. Physical Sciences. **Other Jobs in This Work Group:** Astronomers; Atmospheric and Space Scientists; Chemists; Geographers; Geologists; Hydrologists; Materials Scientists. **PERSONALITY TYPE:** Investigative.

EDUCATION/TRAINING PROGRAM(S)— Acoustics; Astrophysics; Atomic/Molecular Physics; Elementary Particle Physics; Health/Medical Physics; Nuclear Physics; Optics/Optical Sciences; Physics, General; Physics, Other; Plasma and High-Temperature Physics; Solid State and Low-Temperature

Physics; Theoretical and Mathematical Physics. **RELATED KNOWLEDGE/COURSES—Physics:** Knowledge and prediction of physical principles and laws and their interrelationships and applications to understanding fluid, material, and atmospheric dynamics and mechanical, electrical, atomic, and subatomic structures and processes. **Mathematics:** Knowledge of arithmetic, algebra, geometry, calculus, and statistics and their applications. **Education and Training:** Knowledge of principles and methods for curriculum and training design, teaching and instruction for individuals and groups, and the measurement of training effects. **Engineering and Technology:** Knowledge of the practical application of engineering science and technology. This includes applying principles, techniques, procedures, and equipment to the design and production of various goods and services. **Design:** Knowledge of design techniques, tools, and principles involved in production of precision technical plans, blueprints, drawings, and models. **Production and Processing:** Knowledge of raw materials, production processes, quality control, costs, and other techniques for maximizing the effective manufacture and distribution of goods.

Physics Teachers, Postsecondary

- ◎ Education/Training Required: Master's degree
- ◎ Annual Earnings: $64,510
- ◎ Growth: 38.1%
- ◎ Annual Job Openings: 216,000
- ◎ Self-Employed: 0.3%
- ◎ Part-Time: 27.7%

Teach courses pertaining to the laws of matter and energy. Includes both teachers primarily engaged in teaching and those who do a combination of both teaching and research. Evaluate and grade students' class work, laboratory work, assignments, and papers. Prepare and deliver lectures to undergraduate and/or graduate students on topics such as quantum mechanics, particle physics, and optics. Compile, administer, and grade examinations or assign this work to others. Maintain student attendance records, grades, and other required records. Supervise students' laboratory work. Prepare course materials such as syllabi, homework assignments, and handouts. Maintain regularly

scheduled office hours in order to advise and assist students. Supervise undergraduate and/or graduate teaching, internship, and research work. Keep abreast of developments in their field by reading current literature, talking with colleagues, and participating in professional conferences. Plan, evaluate, and revise curricula, course content, and course materials and methods of instruction. Initiate, facilitate, and moderate classroom discussions. Conduct research in a particular field of knowledge and publish findings in professional journals, books, and/or electronic media. Advise students on academic and vocational curricula and on career issues. Select and obtain materials and supplies such as textbooks and laboratory equipment. Collaborate with colleagues to address teaching and research issues. Participate in student recruitment, registration, and placement activities. Serve on academic or administrative committees that deal with institutional policies, departmental matters, and academic issues. Write grant proposals to procure external research funding. Perform administrative duties such as serving as department head. **SKILLS—Science:** Using scientific rules and methods to solve problems. **Instructing:** Teaching others how to do something. **Learning Strategies:** Selecting and using training/instructional methods and procedures appropriate for the situation when learning or teaching new things. **Mathematics:** Using mathematics to solve problems. **Programming:** Writing computer programs for various purposes. **Critical Thinking:** Using logic and reasoning to identify the strengths and weaknesses of alternative solutions, conclusions, or approaches to problems. **Active Learning:** Understanding the implications of new information for both current and future problem-solving and decision-making. **Reading Comprehension:** Understanding written sentences and paragraphs in work-related documents. **GOE—Interest Area:** 05. Education and Training. **Work Group:** 05.03. Postsecondary and Adult Teaching and Instructing. **Other Jobs in This Work Group:** Adult Literacy, Remedial Education, and GED Teachers and Instructors; Agricultural Sciences Teachers, Postsecondary; Anthropology and Archeology Teachers, Postsecondary; Architecture Teachers, Postsecondary; Area, Ethnic, and Cultural Studies Teachers, Postsecondary; Art, Drama, and Music Teachers, Postsecondary; Atmospheric, Earth, Marine, and Space Sciences Teachers, Postsecondary; Biological Science Teachers, Postsecondary; Business Teachers, Postsecondary; Chemistry Teachers, Postsecondary; Communications

Teachers, Postsecondary; Computer Science Teachers, Postsecondary; Criminal Justice and Law Enforcement Teachers, Postsecondary; Economics Teachers, Postsecondary; Education Teachers, Postsecondary; Engineering Teachers, Postsecondary; English Language and Literature Teachers, Postsecondary; Environmental Science Teachers, Postsecondary; Farm and Home Management Advisors; Foreign Language and Literature Teachers, Postsecondary; Forestry and Conservation Science Teachers, Postsecondary; Geography Teachers, Postsecondary; Graduate Teaching Assistants; Health Specialties Teachers, Postsecondary; History Teachers, Postsecondary; Home Economics Teachers, Postsecondary; Law Teachers, Postsecondary; Library Science Teachers, Postsecondary; Mathematical Science Teachers, Postsecondary; Nursing Instructors and Teachers, Postsecondary; Philosophy and Religion Teachers, Postsecondary; Political Science Teachers, Postsecondary; Psychology Teachers, Postsecondary; Recreation and Fitness Studies Teachers, Postsecondary; Self-Enrichment Education Teachers; Social Work Teachers, Postsecondary; Sociology Teachers, Postsecondary; Vocational Education Teachers, Postsecondary. **PERSONALITY TYPE:** Investigative.

EDUCATION/TRAINING PROGRAM(S)— Acoustics; Atomic/Molecular Physics; Elementary Particle Physics; Nuclear Physics; Optics/Optical Sciences; Physics, General; Physics, Other; Plasma and High-Temperature Physics; Solid State and Low-Temperature Physics; Theoretical and Mathematical Physics. **RELATED KNOWLEDGE/COURSES— Physics:** Knowledge and prediction of physical principles and laws and their interrelationships and applications to understanding fluid, material, and atmospheric dynamics and mechanical, electrical, atomic, and subatomic structures and processes. **Mathematics:** Knowledge of arithmetic, algebra, geometry, calculus, and statistics and their applications. **Education and Training:** Knowledge of principles and methods for curriculum and training design, teaching and instruction for individuals and groups, and the measurement of training effects. **Computers and Electronics:** Knowledge of circuit boards, processors, chips, electronic equipment, and computer hardware and software, including applications and programming. **Engineering and Technology:** Knowledge of the practical application of engineering science and technology. This includes applying principles, techniques, procedures, and equipment to the design and production of various goods and services. **Chem-**

istry: Knowledge of the chemical composition, structure, and properties of substances and of the chemical processes and transformations that they undergo. This includes uses of chemicals and their danger signs, production techniques, and disposal methods.

Pipe Fitters

- Education/Training Required: Long-term on-the-job training
- Annual Earnings: $41,290
- Growth: 18.7%
- Annual Job Openings: 56,000
- Self-Employed: 10.3%
- Part-Time: 3.4%

Lay out, assemble, install, and maintain pipe systems, pipe supports, and related hydraulic and pneumatic equipment for steam, hot water, heating, cooling, lubricating, sprinkling, and industrial production and processing systems. Cut, thread, and hammer pipe to specifications, using tools such as saws, cutting torches, and pipe threaders and benders. Assemble and secure pipes, tubes, fittings, and related equipment according to specifications by welding, brazing, cementing, soldering, and threading joints. Attach pipes to walls, structures, and fixtures, such as radiators or tanks, using brackets, clamps, tools, or welding equipment. Inspect, examine, and test installed systems and pipe lines, using pressure gauge, hydrostatic testing, observation, or other methods. Measure and mark pipes for cutting and threading. Lay out full-scale drawings of pipe systems, supports, and related equipment, following blueprints. Plan pipe system layout, installation, or repair according to specifications. Select pipe sizes and types and related materials, such as supports, hangers, and hydraulic cylinders, according to specifications. Cut and bore holes in structures, such as bulkheads, decks, walls, and mains, prior to pipe installation, using hand and power tools. Modify, clean, and maintain pipe systems, units, fittings, and related machines and equipment, following specifications and using hand and power tools. Install automatic controls used to regulate pipe systems. Turn valves to shut off steam, water, or other gases or liquids from pipe sections, using valve keys or wrenches. Remove and replace worn components. Prepare cost estimates for clients. Inspect work sites for obstructions and to ensure that holes will not cause structural weakness. Operate motorized pumps to remove water from flooded manholes, basements, or facility floors. **SKILLS—Installation:** Installing equipment, machines, wiring, or programs to meet specifications. **Repairing:** Repairing machines or systems by using the needed tools. **Management of Personnel Resources:** Motivating, developing, and directing people as they work, identifying the best people for the job. **Coordination:** Adjusting actions in relation to others' actions. **Systems Analysis:** Determining how a system should work and how changes in conditions, operations, and the environment will affect outcomes. **Persuasion:** Persuading others to change their minds or behavior. **Service Orientation:** Actively looking for ways to help people. **Equipment Maintenance:** Performing routine maintenance on equipment and determining when and what kind of maintenance is needed. **GOE— Interest Area:** 02. Architecture and Construction. **Work Group:** 02.04. Construction Crafts. **Other Jobs in This Work Group:** Boat Builders and Shipwrights; Boilermakers; Brattice Builders; Brickmasons and Blockmasons; Carpet Installers; Ceiling Tile Installers; Cement Masons and Concrete Finishers; Commercial Divers; Construction Carpenters; Crane and Tower Operators; Dragline Operators; Drywall Installers; Electricians; Fence Erectors; Floor Layers, Except Carpet, Wood, and Hard Tiles; Floor Sanders and Finishers; Glaziers; Grader, Bulldozer, and Scraper Operators; Hazardous Materials Removal Workers; Insulation Workers, Floor, Ceiling, and Wall; Insulation Workers, Mechanical; Manufactured Building and Mobile Home Installers; Operating Engineers; Painters, Construction and Maintenance; Paperhangers; Paving, Surfacing, and Tamping Equipment Operators; Pile-Driver Operators; Pipelayers; Pipelaying Fitters; Plasterers and Stucco Masons; Plumbers; Rail-Track Laying and Maintenance Equipment Operators; Refractory Materials Repairers, Except Brickmasons; Reinforcing Iron and Rebar Workers; Riggers; Roofers; Rough Carpenters; Security and Fire Alarm Systems Installers; Segmental Pavers; Sheet Metal Workers; Ship Carpenters and Joiners; Stone Cutters and Carvers; Stonemasons; Structural Iron and Steel Workers; Tapers; Terrazzo Workers and Finishers; Tile and Marble Setters. **PERSONALITY TYPE:** Realistic.

EDUCATION/TRAINING PROGRAM(S)—Pipefitting/Pipefitter and Sprinkler Fitter; Plumbing and Related Water Supply Services, Other; Plumbing Technology/Plumber. **RELATED KNOWLEDGE/**

COURSES—Building and Construction: Knowledge of the materials, methods, and tools involved in the construction or repair of houses, buildings, or other structures such as highways and roads. **Design:** Knowledge of design techniques, tools, and principles involved in production of precision technical plans, blueprints, drawings, and models. **Engineering and Technology:** Knowledge of the practical application of engineering science and technology. This includes applying principles, techniques, procedures, and equipment to the design and production of various goods and services. **Mechanical Devices:** Knowledge of machines and tools, including their designs, uses, repair, and maintenance. **Economics and Accounting:** Knowledge of economic and accounting principles and practices, the financial markets, banking, and the analysis and reporting of financial data. **Transportation:** Knowledge of principles and methods for moving people or goods by air, rail, sea, or road, including the relative costs and benefits.

Pipelaying Fitters

- Education/Training Required: Moderate-term on-the-job training
- Annual Earnings: $41,290
- Growth: 18.7%
- Annual Job Openings: 56,000
- Self-Employed: 10.3%
- Part-Time: 3.4%

Align pipeline section in preparation of welding. Signal tractor driver for placement of pipeline sections in proper alignment. Insert steel spacer. Correct misalignments of pipe, using a sledgehammer. Guide pipe into trench and signal hoist operator to move pipe until alignment is achieved so that pipes can be welded together. Insert spacers between pipe ends. Inspect joints to ensure uniform spacing and proper alignment of pipe surfaces. **SKILLS—Installation:** Installing equipment, machines, wiring, or programs to meet specifications. **Equipment Maintenance:** Performing routine maintenance on equipment and determining when and what kind of maintenance is needed. **Repairing:** Repairing machines or systems by using the needed tools. **GOE—Interest Area:** 02. Architecture and Construction. **Work Group:** 02.04. Construction Crafts. **Other Jobs in This Work Group:** Boat

Builders and Shipwrights; Boilermakers; Brattice Builders; Brickmasons and Blockmasons; Carpet Installers; Ceiling Tile Installers; Cement Masons and Concrete Finishers; Commercial Divers; Construction Carpenters; Crane and Tower Operators; Dragline Operators; Drywall Installers; Electricians; Fence Erectors; Floor Layers, Except Carpet, Wood, and Hard Tiles; Floor Sanders and Finishers; Glaziers; Grader, Bulldozer, and Scraper Operators; Hazardous Materials Removal Workers; Insulation Workers, Floor, Ceiling, and Wall; Insulation Workers, Mechanical; Manufactured Building and Mobile Home Installers; Operating Engineers; Painters, Construction and Maintenance; Paperhangers; Paving, Surfacing, and Tamping Equipment Operators; Pile-Driver Operators; Pipe Fitters; Pipelayers; Plasterers and Stucco Masons; Plumbers; Rail-Track Laying and Maintenance Equipment Operators; Refractory Materials Repairers, Except Brickmasons; Reinforcing Iron and Rebar Workers; Riggers; Roofers; Rough Carpenters; Security and Fire Alarm Systems Installers; Segmental Pavers; Sheet Metal Workers; Ship Carpenters and Joiners; Stone Cutters and Carvers; Stonemasons; Structural Iron and Steel Workers; Tapers; Terrazzo Workers and Finishers; Tile and Marble Setters. **PERSONALITY TYPE:** Realistic.

EDUCATION/TRAINING PROGRAM(S)— Pipefitting/Pipefitter and Sprinkler Fitter; Plumbing and Related Water Supply Services, Other; Plumbing Technology/Plumber. **RELATED KNOWLEDGE/ COURSES—Mechanical Devices:** Knowledge of machines and tools, including their designs, uses, repair, and maintenance. **Building and Construction:** Knowledge of the materials, methods, and tools involved in the construction or repair of houses, buildings, or other structures such as highways and roads.

Plant Scientists

- Education/Training Required: Bachelor's degree
- Annual Earnings: $51,200
- Growth: 9.1%
- Annual Job Openings: 2,000
- Self-Employed: 8.9%
- Part-Time: 7.0%

Conduct research in breeding, production, and yield of plants or crops and control of pests. Conducts research to determine best methods of planting, spraying, cultivating, and harvesting horticultural products. Studies crop production to discover effects of various climatic and soil conditions on crops. Conducts experiments and investigations to determine methods of storing, processing, and transporting horticultural products. Aids in control and elimination of agricultural, structural, and forest pests by developing new and improved pesticides. Identifies and classifies species of insects and allied forms, such as mites and spiders. Improves bee strains, utilizing selective breeding by artificial insemination. Conducts experiments regarding causes of bee diseases and factors affecting yields of nectar pollen on various plants visited by bees. Studies insect distribution and habitat and recommends methods to prevent importation and spread of injurious species. Develops methods for control of noxious weeds, crop diseases, and insect pests. Experiments to develop new or improved varieties of products having specific features, such as higher yield, resistance to disease, size, or maturity. **SKILLS—Science:** Using scientific rules and methods to solve problems. **Writing:** Communicating effectively in writing as appropriate for the needs of the audience. **Critical Thinking:** Using logic and reasoning to identify the strengths and weaknesses of alternative solutions, conclusions, or approaches to problems. **Active Learning:** Understanding the implications of new information for both current and future problem-solving and decision-making. **Quality Control Analysis:** Conducting tests and inspections of products, services, or processes to evaluate quality or performance. **Reading Comprehension:** Understanding written sentences and paragraphs in work-related documents. **Complex Problem Solving:** Identifying complex problems and reviewing related information to develop and evaluate options and implement solutions. **Operations Analysis:** Analyzing needs and product requirements to create a design. **GOE—Interest Area:** 01. Agriculture and Natural Resources. **Work Group:** 01.02. Resource Science/Engineering for Plants, Animals, and the Environment. **Other Jobs in This Work Group:** Agricultural Engineers; Animal Scientists; Environmental Engineers; Foresters; Mining and Geological Engineers, Including Mining Safety Engineers; Petroleum Engineers; Range Managers; Soil Conservationists; Soil Scientists; Zoologists and Wildlife Biologists. **PERSONALITY TYPE:** Investigative.

EDUCATION/TRAINING PROGRAM(S)—Agricultural and Horticultural Plant Breeding; Agriculture, General; Agronomy and Crop Science; Horticultural Science; Plant Protection and Integrated Pest Management; Plant Sciences, General; Plant Sciences, Other; Range Science and Management; Soil Chemistry and Physics; Soil Microbiology; Soil Science and Agronomy, General. **RELATED KNOWLEDGE/COURSES—Food Production:** Knowledge of techniques and equipment for planting, growing, and harvesting food products (both plant and animal) for consumption, including storage/handling techniques. **Biology:** Knowledge of plant and animal organisms and their tissues, cells, functions, interdependencies, and interactions with each other and the environment. **Chemistry:** Knowledge of the chemical composition, structure, and properties of substances and of the chemical processes and transformations that they undergo. This includes uses of chemicals and their danger signs, production techniques, and disposal methods. **English Language:** Knowledge of the structure and content of the English language, including the meaning and spelling of words, rules of composition, and grammar. **Communications and Media:** Knowledge of media production, communication, and dissemination techniques and methods. This includes alternative ways to inform and entertain via written, oral, and visual media. **Education and Training:** Knowledge of principles and methods for curriculum and training design, teaching and instruction for individuals and groups, and the measurement of training effects.

Plasterers and Stucco Masons

- Education/Training Required: Long-term on-the-job training
- Annual Earnings: $32,440
- Growth: 13.5%
- Annual Job Openings: 8,000
- Self-Employed: 9.6%
- Part-Time: 7.2%

Apply interior or exterior plaster, cement, stucco, or similar materials. May also set ornamental plaster. Apply coats of plaster or stucco to walls, ceilings, or partitions of buildings, using trowels, brushes, or spray guns. Apply weatherproof decorative coverings to exterior surfaces of buildings, such as troweling or spraying on coats of stucco. Clean and prepare surfaces for applications of plaster, cement, stucco, or similar materials, such as by drywall taping. Cure freshly plastered surfaces. Install guidewires on exterior surfaces of buildings to indicate thickness of plaster or stucco and nail wire mesh, lath, or similar materials to the outside surface to hold stucco in place. Mix mortar and plaster to desired consistency or direct workers who perform mixing. Mold and install ornamental plaster pieces, panels, and trim. Rough the undercoat surface with a scratcher so the finish coat will adhere. Spray acoustic materials or texture finish over walls and ceilings. Apply insulation to building exteriors by installing prefabricated insulation systems over existing walls or by covering the outer wall with insulation board, reinforcing mesh, and a base coat. Create decorative textures in finish coat, using brushes or trowels, sand, pebbles, or stones. **SKILLS—Coordination:** Adjusting actions in relation to others' actions. **Installation:** Installing equipment, machines, wiring, or programs to meet specifications. **Management of Personnel Resources:** Motivating, developing, and directing people as they work, identifying the best people for the job. **GOE—Interest Area:** 02. Architecture and Construction. **Work Group:** 02.04. Construction Crafts. **Other Jobs in This Work Group:** Boat Builders and Shipwrights; Boilermakers; Brattice Builders; Brickmasons and Blockmasons; Carpet Installers; Ceiling Tile Installers; Cement Masons and Concrete Finishers; Commercial Divers; Construction Carpenters; Crane and Tower Operators; Dragline Operators; Drywall Installers; Electricians; Fence Erectors; Floor Layers, Except Carpet, Wood, and Hard Tiles; Floor Sanders and Finishers; Glaziers; Grader, Bulldozer, and Scraper Operators; Hazardous Materials Removal Workers; Insulation Workers, Floor, Ceiling, and Wall; Insulation Workers, Mechanical; Manufactured Building and Mobile Home Installers; Operating Engineers; Painters, Construction and Maintenance; Paperhangers; Paving, Surfacing, and Tamping Equipment Operators; Pile-Driver Operators; Pipe Fitters; Pipelayers; Pipelaying Fitters; Plumbers; Rail-Track Laying and Maintenance Equipment Operators; Refractory Materials Repairers, Except Brickmasons; Reinforcing Iron and Rebar Workers; Riggers; Roofers; Rough Carpenters; Security and Fire Alarm Systems Installers; Segmental Pavers; Sheet Metal Workers; Ship Carpenters and Joiners; Stone Cutters and Carvers; Stonemasons;

Structural Iron and Steel Workers; Tapers; Terrazzo Workers and Finishers; Tile and Marble Setters. **PERSONALITY TYPE:** Realistic.

EDUCATION/TRAINING PROGRAM(S)—Construction Trades, Other. **RELATED KNOWLEDGE/COURSES—Building and Construction:** Knowledge of the materials, methods, and tools involved in the construction or repair of houses, buildings, or other structures such as highways and roads. **Design:** Knowledge of design techniques, tools, and principles involved in production of precision technical plans, blueprints, drawings, and models. **Engineering and Technology:** Knowledge of the practical application of engineering science and technology. This includes applying principles, techniques, procedures, and equipment to the design and production of various goods and services.

Plumbers

- ◎ Education/Training Required: Long-term on-the-job training
- ◎ Annual Earnings: $41,290
- ◎ Growth: 18.7%
- ◎ Annual Job Openings: 56,000
- ◎ Self-Employed: 10.3%
- ◎ Part-Time: 3.4%

Assemble, install, and repair pipes, fittings, and fixtures of heating, water, and drainage systems according to specifications and plumbing codes. Assemble pipe sections, tubing, and fittings, using couplings; clamps; screws; bolts; cement; plastic solvent; caulking; or soldering, brazing, and welding equipment. Fill pipes or plumbing fixtures with water or air and observe pressure gauges to detect and locate leaks. Review blueprints and building codes and specifications to determine work details and procedures. Prepare written work cost estimates and negotiate contracts. Study building plans and inspect structures to assess material and equipment needs, to establish the sequence of pipe installations, and to plan installation around obstructions such as electrical wiring. Keep records of assignments and produce detailed work reports. Perform complex calculations and planning for special or very large jobs. Locate and mark the position of pipe installations, connections, passage holes, and fixtures in structures, using measuring instruments such as rulers and levels. Measure, cut, thread, and bend pipe to required angle, using hand and power tools or machines such as pipe cutters, pipe-threading machines, and pipe-bending machines. Install pipe assemblies, fittings, valves, appliances such as dishwashers and water heaters, and fixtures such as sinks and toilets, using hand and power tools. Cut openings in structures to accommodate pipes and pipe fittings, using hand and power tools. Hang steel supports from ceiling joists to hold pipes in place. Repair and maintain plumbing, replacing defective washers, replacing or mending broken pipes, and opening clogged drains. Direct workers engaged in pipe cutting and preassembly and installation of plumbing systems and components. Install underground storm, sanitary, and water piping systems and extend piping to connect fixtures and plumbing to these systems. Clear away debris in a renovation. Install oxygen and medical gas in hospitals. Use specialized techniques, equipment, or materials, such as performing computer-assisted welding of small pipes or working with the special piping used in microchip fabrication. **SKILLS—Installation:** Installing equipment, machines, wiring, or programs to meet specifications. **Repairing:** Repairing machines or systems by using the needed tools. **Troubleshooting:** Determining causes of operating errors and deciding what to do about them. **Management of Material Resources:** Obtaining and seeing to the appropriate use of equipment, facilities, and materials needed to do certain work. **Equipment Selection:** Determining the kind of tools and equipment needed to do a job. **Management of Financial Resources:** Determining how money will be spent to get the work done and accounting for these expenditures. **Coordination:** Adjusting actions in relation to others' actions. **Management of Personnel Resources:** Motivating, developing, and directing people as they work, identifying the best people for the job. **GOE—Interest Area:** 02. Architecture and Construction. **Work Group:** 02.04. Construction Crafts. **Other Jobs in This Work Group:** Boat Builders and Shipwrights; Boilermakers; Brattice Builders; Brickmasons and Blockmasons; Carpet Installers; Ceiling Tile Installers; Cement Masons and Concrete Finishers; Commercial Divers; Construction Carpenters; Crane and Tower Operators; Dragline Operators; Drywall Installers; Electricians; Fence Erectors; Floor Layers, Except Carpet, Wood, and Hard Tiles; Floor Sanders and Finishers; Glaziers; Grader, Bulldozer, and Scraper Operators; Hazardous Materials Removal Workers; Insulation Workers, Floor, Ceiling, and Wall; Insulation Workers, Mechanical; Manufactured Building and Mobile Home Installers; Operating Engineers; Painters, Construction and Maintenance; Paperhangers; Paving, Surfacing, and Tamping Equipment Operators; Pile-Driver Operators; Pipe Fitters; Pipelayers; Pipelaying Fitters; Plasterers and Stucco Masons; Rail-Track Laying and Maintenance Equipment Operators; Refractory Materials Repairers, Except Brickmasons; Reinforcing Iron and Rebar Workers; Riggers; Roofers; Rough Carpenters; Security and Fire Alarm Systems Installers; Segmental Pavers; Sheet Metal Workers; Ship Carpenters and Joiners; Stone Cutters and Carvers; Stonemasons; Structural Iron and Steel Workers; Tapers; Terrazzo Workers and Finishers; Tile and Marble Setters. **PERSONALITY TYPE: Realistic.**

EDUCATION/TRAINING PROGRAM(S)—Pipefitting/Pipefitter and Sprinkler Fitter; Plumbing and Related Water Supply Services, Other; Plumbing Technology/Plumber. **RELATED KNOWLEDGE/ COURSES—Physics:** Knowledge and prediction of physical principles and laws and their interrelationships and applications to understanding fluid, material, and atmospheric dynamics and mechanical, electrical, atomic, and subatomic structures and processes. **Building and Construction:** Knowledge of the materials, methods, and tools involved in the construction or repair of houses, buildings, or other structures such as highways and roads. **Mechanical Devices:** Knowledge of machines and tools, including their designs, uses, repair, and maintenance. **Chemistry:** Knowledge of the chemical composition, structure, and properties of substances and of the chemical processes and transformations that they undergo. This includes uses of chemicals and their danger signs, production techniques, and disposal methods. **Design:** Knowledge of design techniques, tools, and principles involved in production of precision technical plans, blueprints, drawings, and models. **Sales and Marketing:** Knowledge of principles and methods for showing, promoting, and selling products or services. This includes marketing strategy and tactics, product demonstrations, sales techniques, and sales control systems.

Podiatrists

- ◉ Education/Training Required: First professional degree
- ◉ Annual Earnings: $94,400
- ◉ Growth: 15.0%
- ◉ Annual Job Openings: 1,000
- ◉ Self-Employed: 44.4%
- ◉ Part-Time: 15.6%

Diagnose and treat diseases and deformities of the human foot. Advise patients about treatments and foot care techniques necessary for prevention of future problems. Correct deformities by means of plaster casts and strapping. Diagnose diseases and deformities of the foot, using medical histories, physical examinations, X rays, and laboratory test results. Make and fit prosthetic appliances. Prescribe medications, corrective devices, physical therapy, or surgery. Refer patients to physicians when symptoms indicative of systemic disorders, such as arthritis or diabetes, are observed in feet and legs. Treat bone, muscle, and joint disorders affecting the feet. Treat conditions such as corns, calluses, ingrown nails, tumors, shortened tendons, bunions, cysts, and abscesses by surgical methods. Treat deformities, using mechanical methods such as whirlpool or paraffin baths and electrical methods such as shortwave and low-voltage currents. Educate the public about the benefits of foot care through techniques such as speaking engagements, advertising, and other forums. Perform administrative duties such as hiring employees, ordering supplies, and keeping records. **SKILLS—Active Learning:** Understanding the implications of new information for both current and future problem-solving and decision-making. **Reading Comprehension:** Understanding written sentences and paragraphs in work-related documents. **Technology Design:** Generating or adapting equipment and technology to serve user needs. **Judgment and Decision Making:** Considering the relative costs and benefits of potential actions to choose the most appropriate one. **Equipment Selection:** Determining the kind of tools and equipment needed to do a job. **Systems Evaluation:** Identifying measures or indicators of system performance and the actions needed to improve or correct performance relative to the goals of the system. **Active Listening:** Giving full attention to what other people are saying, taking time to understand the points being made, asking questions as appropriate, and not interrupting at inappropriate times. **Service Orientation:** Actively looking for ways to help people. **Complex Problem Solving**: Identifying complex problems and reviewing related information to develop and evaluate options and implement solutions. **GOE—Interest Area:** 08. Health Science. **Work Group:** 08.04. Health Specialties. **Other Jobs in This Work Group:** Chiropractors; Optometrists. **PERSONALITY TYPE:** Social.

EDUCATION/TRAINING PROGRAM(S)—Podiatric Medicine/Podiatry (DPM). **RELATED KNOWLEDGE/COURSES—Medicine and Dentistry:** Knowledge of the information and techniques needed to diagnose and treat human injuries, diseases, and deformities. This includes symptoms, treatment alternatives, drug properties and interactions, and preventive health-care measures. **Biology:** Knowledge of plant and animal organisms and their tissues, cells, functions, interdependencies, and interactions with each other and the environment. **Chemistry:** Knowledge of the chemical composition, structure, and properties of substances and of the chemical processes and transformations that they undergo. This includes uses of chemicals and their danger signs, production techniques, and disposal methods. **Therapy and Counseling:** Knowledge of principles, methods, and procedures for diagnosis, treatment, and rehabilitation of physical and mental dysfunctions and for career counseling and guidance. **Physics:** Knowledge and prediction of physical principles and laws and their interrelationships and applications to understanding fluid, material, and atmospheric dynamics and mechanical, electrical, atomic, and subatomic structures and processes. **English Language:** Knowledge of the structure and content of the English language, including the meaning and spelling of words, rules of composition, and grammar.

Poets and Lyricists

- Education/Training Required: Bachelor's degree
- Annual Earnings: $44,350
- Growth: 16.1%
- Annual Job Openings: 23,000
- Self-Employed: 67.9%
- Part-Time: 24.2%

Write poetry or song lyrics for publication or performance. Writes words to fit musical compositions, including lyrics for operas, musical plays, and choral works. Chooses subject matter and suitable form to express personal feeling and experience or ideas or to narrate story or event. Adapts text to accommodate musical requirements of composer and singer. Writes narrative, dramatic, lyric, or other types of poetry for publication. **SKILLS—Writing:** Communicating effectively in writing as appropriate for the needs of the audience. **Reading Comprehension:** Understanding written sentences and paragraphs in work-related documents. **GOE—Interest Area:** 03. Arts and Communication. **Work Group:** 03.02. Writing and Editing. **Other Jobs in This Work Group:** Copy Writers; Creative Writers; Editors; Technical Writers. **PERSONALITY TYPE:** Artistic.

EDUCATION/TRAINING PROGRAM(S)—Broadcast Journalism; Business/Corporate Communications; Communication Studies/Speech Communication and Rhetoric; Communication, Journalism, and Related Programs, Other; Creative Writing; English Composition; Family and Consumer Sciences/Human Sciences Communication; Journalism; Mass Communication/Media Studies; Playwriting and Screenwriting; Technical and Business Writing. **RELATED KNOWLEDGE/COURSES—Fine Arts:** Knowledge of the theory and techniques required to compose, produce, and perform works of music, dance, the visual arts, drama, and sculpture. **Communications and Media:** Knowledge of media production, communication, and dissemination techniques and methods. This includes alternative ways to inform and entertain via written, oral, and visual media. **English Language:** Knowledge of the structure and content of the English language, including the meaning and spelling of words, rules of composition, and grammar.

Police Detectives

- Education/Training Required: Work experience in a related occupation
- Annual Earnings: $53,990
- Growth: 22.4%
- Annual Job Openings: 11,000
- Self-Employed: 0%
- Part-Time: 0.5%

Conduct investigations to prevent crimes or solve criminal cases. Examine crime scenes to obtain clues and evidence, such as loose hairs, fibers, clothing, or weapons. Secure deceased body and obtain evidence from it, preventing bystanders from tampering with it prior to medical examiner's arrival. Obtain evidence from suspects. Provide testimony as a witness in court. Analyze completed police reports to determine what additional information and investigative work is needed. Prepare charges, responses to charges, or information for court cases according to formalized procedures. Note, mark, and photograph location of objects found, such as footprints, tire tracks, bullets, and bloodstains, and take measurements of the scene. Obtain facts or statements from complainants, witnesses, and accused persons and record interviews, using recording device. Obtain summary of incident from officer in charge at crime scene, taking care to avoid disturbing evidence. Examine records and governmental agency files to find identifying data about suspects. Prepare and serve search and arrest warrants. Block or rope off scene and check perimeter to ensure that entire scene is secured. Summon medical help for injured individuals and alert medical personnel to take statements from them. Provide information to lab personnel concerning the source of an item of evidence and tests to be performed. Monitor conditions of victims who are unconscious so that arrangements can be made to take statements if consciousness is regained. Secure persons at scene, keeping witnesses from conversing or leaving the scene before investigators arrive. Preserve, process, and analyze items of evidence obtained from crime scenes and suspects, placing them in proper containers and destroying evidence no longer needed. Record progress of investigation, maintain informational files on suspects, and submit reports to commanding officer or magistrate to authorize warrants. Take photographs from all angles of relevant parts of a crime scene, including entrance and exit routes and streets and intersections. Organize scene search, assigning specific tasks and areas of search to individual officers and obtaining adequate lighting as necessary. **SKILLS—Persuasion:** Persuading others to change their minds or behavior. **Negotiation:** Bringing others together and trying to reconcile differences. **Social Perceptiveness:** Being aware of others' reactions and understanding why they react as they do. **Coordination:** Adjusting actions in relation to others' actions. **Service Orientation:** Actively looking for ways to help people. **Active Listening:** Giving full attention to what other people are saying, taking time to understand the points being made, asking questions as appropriate, and not interrupting at inappropriate times. **Speaking:** Talking to others to convey information effectively. **Critical Thinking:** Using logic and reasoning to identify the strengths and weaknesses of alternative solutions, conclusions, or approaches to problems. **Learning Strategies:** Selecting and using training/instructional methods and procedures appropriate for the situation when learning or teaching new things. **Time Management:** Managing one's own time and the time of others. **GOE—Interest Area:** 12. Law and Public Safety. **Work Group:** 12.04. Law Enforcement and Public Safety. **Other Jobs in This Work Group:** Bailiffs; Correctional Officers and Jailers; Criminal Investigators and Special Agents; Fire Investigators; Forensic Science Technicians; Highway Patrol Pilots; Parking Enforcement Workers; Police Identification and Records Officers; Police Patrol Officers; Sheriffs and Deputy Sheriffs; Transit and Railroad Police. **PERSONALITY TYPE:** Enterprising.

EDUCATION/TRAINING PROGRAM(S)— Criminal Justice/Police Science; Criminalistics and Criminal Science. **RELATED KNOWLEDGE/ COURSES—Public Safety and Security:** Knowledge of relevant equipment, policies, procedures, and strategies to promote effective local, state, or national security operations for the protection of people, data, property, and institutions. **Law and Government:** Knowledge of laws, legal codes, court procedures, precedents, government regulations, executive orders, agency rules, and the democratic political process. **Psychology:** Knowledge of human behavior and performance; individual differences in ability, personality, and interests; learning and motivation; psychological research methods; and the assessment and treatment of behavioral and affective disorders. **Customer and Personal Service:** Knowledge of principles and processes for providing customer and personal services. This includes customer needs assessment, meeting quality standards for services, and evaluation of customer satisfaction. **Education and Training:** Knowledge of principles and methods for curriculum and training design, teaching and instruction for individuals and groups, and the measurement of training effects. **Therapy and Counseling:** Knowledge of principles, methods, and procedures for diagnosis, treatment, and rehabilitation of physical and mental dysfunctions and for career counseling and guidance.

Police Identification and Records Officers

- Education/Training Required: Work experience in a related occupation
- Annual Earnings: $53,990
- Growth: 22.4%
- Annual Job Openings: 11,000
- Self-Employed: 0%
- Part-Time: 0.5%

Collect evidence at crime scene, classify and identify fingerprints, and photograph evidence for use in criminal and civil cases. Photograph crime or accident scenes for evidence records. Testify in court and present evidence. Dust selected areas of crime scene and lift latent fingerprints, adhering to proper preservation procedures. Look for trace evidence, such as fingerprints, hairs, fibers, or shoe impressions, using alternative light sources when necessary. Analyze and process evidence at crime scenes and in the laboratory, wearing protective equipment and using powders and chemicals. Package, store, and retrieve evidence. Serve as technical advisor and coordinate with other law enforcement workers to exchange information on crime-scene collection activities. Perform emergency work during off-hours. Submit evidence to supervisors. Process film and prints from crime or accident scenes. Identify, classify, and file fingerprints, using systems such as the Henry Classification system. **SKILLS—Persuasion:** Persuading others to change their minds or behavior. **Negotiation:** Bringing others together and trying to reconcile differences. **Service Orientation:** Actively looking for ways to help people. **Judgment and Decision Making:** Considering the relative costs and benefits of potential actions to choose the most appropriate one. **Social Perceptiveness:** Being aware of others' reactions and understanding why they react as they do. **Critical Thinking:** Using logic and reasoning to identify the strengths and weaknesses of alternative solutions, conclusions, or approaches to problems. **Time Management:** Managing one's own time and the time of others. **Learning Strategies:** Selecting and using training/instructional methods and procedures appropriate for the situation when learning or teaching new things. **GOE—Interest Area:** 12. Law and Public Safety. **Work Group:** 12.04. Law Enforcement and Public Safety. **Other Jobs in This Work Group:** Bailiffs; Correctional Officers and Jail-

ers; Criminal Investigators and Special Agents; Fire Investigators; Forensic Science Technicians; Highway Patrol Pilots; Parking Enforcement Workers; Police Detectives; Police Patrol Officers; Sheriffs and Deputy Sheriffs; Transit and Railroad Police. **PERSONALITY TYPE:** Conventional.

EDUCATION/TRAINING PROGRAM(S)— Criminal Justice/Police Science; Criminalistics and Criminal Science. **RELATED KNOWLEDGE/ COURSES—Law and Government:** Knowledge of laws, legal codes, court procedures, precedents, government regulations, executive orders, agency rules, and the democratic political process. **Customer and Personal Service:** Knowledge of principles and processes for providing customer and personal services. This includes customer needs assessment, meeting quality standards for services, and evaluation of customer satisfaction. **Public Safety and Security:** Knowledge of relevant equipment, policies, procedures, and strategies to promote effective local, state, or national security operations for the protection of people, data, property, and institutions. **Telecommunications:** Knowledge of transmission, broadcasting, switching, control, and operation of telecommunications systems. **Psychology:** Knowledge of human behavior and performance; individual differences in ability, personality, and interests; learning and motivation; psychological research methods; and the assessment and treatment of behavioral and affective disorders. **Computers and Electronics:** Knowledge of circuit boards, processors, chips, electronic equipment, and computer hardware and software, including applications and programming.

Police Patrol Officers

- Education/Training Required: Long-term on-the-job training
- Annual Earnings: $45,210
- Growth: 24.7%
- Annual Job Openings: 67,000
- Self-Employed: 0%
- Part-Time: 1.4%

Patrol assigned area to enforce laws and ordinances, regulate traffic, control crowds, prevent crime, and arrest violators. Provide for public safety by maintaining order, responding to emergencies, protecting people and property, enforcing motor vehicle and criminal laws, and promoting good community relations. Identify, pursue, and arrest suspects and perpetrators of criminal acts. Record facts to prepare reports that document incidents and activities. Review facts of incidents to determine if criminal act or statute violation was involved. Render aid to accident victims and other persons requiring first aid for physical injuries. Testify in court to present evidence or act as witness in traffic and criminal cases. Evaluate complaint and emergency-request information to determine response requirements. Patrol specific area on foot, horseback, or motorized conveyance, responding promptly to calls for assistance. Monitor, note, report, and investigate suspicious persons and situations, safety hazards, and unusual or illegal activity in patrol area. Investigate traffic accidents and other accidents to determine causes and to determine whether a crime has been committed. Photograph or draw diagrams of crime or accident scenes and interview principals and eyewitnesses. Monitor traffic to ensure motorists observe traffic regulations and exhibit safe driving procedures. Relay complaint and emergency-request information to appropriate agency dispatchers. Issue citations or warnings to violators of motor vehicle ordinances. Direct traffic flow and reroute traffic in case of emergencies. Inform citizens of community services and recommend options to facilitate longer-term problem resolution. Provide road information to assist motorists. Process prisoners and prepare and maintain records of prisoner bookings and prisoner status during booking and pre-trial process. **SKILLS—Negotiation:** Bringing others together and trying to reconcile differences. **Persuasion:** Persuading others to change their minds or behavior. **Social Perceptiveness:** Being aware of others' reactions and understanding why they react as they do. **Judgment and Decision Making:** Considering the relative costs and benefits of potential actions to choose the most appropriate one. **Service Orientation:** Actively looking for ways to help people. **Active Listening:** Giving full attention to what other people are saying, taking time to understand the points being made, asking questions as appropriate, and not interrupting at inappropriate times. **Critical Thinking:** Using logic and reasoning to identify the strengths and weaknesses of alternative solutions, conclusions, or approaches to problems. **Coordination:** Adjusting actions in relation to others' actions. **GOE—Interest Area:** 12. Law and Public Safety. **Work Group:** 12.04. Law Enforcement and Public Safety. **Other Jobs in This Work Group:** Bailiffs; Correctional Officers and

Jailers; Criminal Investigators and Special Agents; Fire Investigators; Forensic Science Technicians; Highway Patrol Pilots; Parking Enforcement Workers; Police Detectives; Police Identification and Records Officers; Sheriffs and Deputy Sheriffs; Transit and Railroad Police. **PERSONALITY TYPE:** Social.

EDUCATION/TRAINING PROGRAM(S)—Criminal Justice/Police Science; Criminalistics and Criminal Science. **RELATED KNOWLEDGE/COURSES—Public Safety and Security:** Knowledge of relevant equipment, policies, procedures, and strategies to promote effective local, state, or national security operations for the protection of people, data, property, and institutions. **Law and Government:** Knowledge of laws, legal codes, court procedures, precedents, government regulations, executive orders, agency rules, and the democratic political process. **Customer and Personal Service:** Knowledge of principles and processes for providing customer and personal services. This includes customer needs assessment, meeting quality standards for services, and evaluation of customer satisfaction. **Psychology:** Knowledge of human behavior and performance; individual differences in ability, personality, and interests; learning and motivation; psychological research methods; and the assessment and treatment of behavioral and affective disorders. **Telecommunications:** Knowledge of transmission, broadcasting, switching, control, and operation of telecommunications systems. **Sociology and Anthropology:** Knowledge of group behavior and dynamics, societal trends and influences, human migrations, ethnicity, and cultures and their history and origins. **Therapy and Counseling:** Knowledge of principles, methods, and procedures for diagnosis, treatment, and rehabilitation of physical and mental dysfunctions and for career counseling and guidance.

Police, Fire, and Ambulance Dispatchers

- Education/Training Required: Moderate-term on-the-job training
- Annual Earnings: $28,930
- Growth: 12.7%
- Annual Job Openings: 15,000
- Self-Employed: 0.6%
- Part-Time: 8.5%

Receive complaints from public concerning crimes and police emergencies. Broadcast orders to police patrol units in vicinity of complaint to investigate. Operate radio, telephone, or computer equipment to receive reports of fires and medical emergencies and relay information or orders to proper officials. Determine response requirements and relative priorities of situations and dispatch units in accordance with established procedures. Record details of calls, dispatches, and messages. Question callers to determine their locations and the nature of their problems in order to determine type of response needed. Enter, update, and retrieve information from teletype networks and computerized data systems regarding such things as wanted persons, stolen property, vehicle registration, and stolen vehicles. Scan status charts and computer screens and contact emergency response field units in order to determine emergency units available for dispatch. Relay information and messages to and from emergency sites, to law enforcement agencies, and to all other individuals or groups requiring notification. Receive incoming telephone or alarm system calls regarding emergency and non-emergency police and fire service, emergency ambulance service, information, and after-hours calls for departments within a city. Maintain access to and security of highly sensitive materials. Observe alarm registers and scan maps in order to determine whether a specific emergency is in the dispatch service area. Maintain files of information relating to emergency calls such as personnel rosters and emergency call-out and pager files. Monitor various radio frequencies such as those used by public works departments, school security, and civil defense in order to keep apprised of developing situations. Learn material and pass required tests for certification. Read and effectively interpret small-scale maps and information from a computer screen in order to determine locations and provide directions. Answer routine inquiries and refer calls not requiring dispatches to appropriate departments and agencies. Provide emergency medical instructions to callers. Monitor alarm systems to detect emergencies such as fires and illegal entry into establishments. Test and adjust communication and alarm systems and report malfunctions to maintenance units. Operate and maintain mobile dispatch vehicles and equipment. **SKILLS—Active Listening:** Giving full attention to what other people are saying, taking time to understand the points being made, asking questions as appropriate, and not interrupting at inappropriate times. **Speaking:** Talking to others to convey information effectively. **Social Perceptiveness:** Being aware of others' reactions and understanding why they react as they do. **Critical Thinking:** Using logic and reasoning to identify the strengths and weaknesses of alternative solutions, conclusions, or approaches to problems. **Judgment and Decision Making:** Considering the relative costs and benefits of potential actions to choose the most appropriate one. **Service Orientation:** Actively looking for ways to help people. **Active Learning:** Understanding the implications of new information for both current and future problem-solving and decision-making. **Learning Strategies:** Selecting and using training/instructional methods and procedures appropriate for the situation when learning or teaching new things. **Coordination:** Adjusting actions in relation to others' actions. **GOE—Interest Area:** 03. Arts and Communication. **Work Group:** 03.10. Communications Technology. **Other Jobs in This Work Group:** Air Traffic Controllers; Airfield Operations Specialists; Central Office Operators; Directory Assistance Operators; Dispatchers, Except Police, Fire, and Ambulance. **PERSONALITY TYPE:** Social.

EDUCATION/TRAINING PROGRAM(S)—No data available. **RELATED KNOWLEDGE/COURSES—Customer and Personal Service:** Knowledge of principles and processes for providing customer and personal services. This includes customer needs assessment, meeting quality standards for services, and evaluation of customer satisfaction. **Telecommunications:** Knowledge of transmission, broadcasting, switching, control, and operation of telecommunications systems. **Clerical Practices:** Knowledge of administrative and clerical procedures and systems such as word processing, managing files and records, stenography and transcription, designing forms, and other office procedures and terminology. **Public Safety and Security:** Knowledge of relevant equipment, policies, procedures, and strategies to promote effective local, state, or national security operations for the protection of people, data, property, and institutions. **Law and Government:** Knowledge of laws, legal codes, court procedures, precedents, government regulations, executive orders, agency rules, and the democratic political process. **Computers and Electronics:** Knowledge of circuit boards, processors, chips, electronic equipment, and computer hardware and software, including applications and programming.

Political Science Teachers, Postsecondary

◉ Education/Training Required: Master's degree
◉ Annual Earnings: $58,980
◉ Growth: 38.1%
◉ Annual Job Openings: 216,000
◉ Self-Employed: 0.3%
◉ Part-Time: 27.7%

Teach courses in political science, international affairs, and international relations. Initiate, facilitate, and moderate classroom discussions. Prepare and deliver lectures to undergraduate and/or graduate students on topics such as classical political thought, international relations, and democracy and citizenship. Evaluate and grade students' class work, assignments, and papers. Compile, administer, and grade examinations or assign this work to others. Prepare course materials such as syllabi, homework assignments, and handouts. Keep abreast of developments in their field by reading current literature, talking with colleagues, and participating in professional conferences. Plan, evaluate, and revise curricula, course content, and course materials and methods of instruction. Maintain student attendance records, grades, and other required records. Maintain regularly scheduled office hours in order to advise and assist students. Advise students on academic and vocational curricula and on career issues. Select and obtain materials and supplies such as textbooks. Conduct research in a particular field of knowledge and publish findings in professional journals, books, and/or electronic media. Supervise undergraduate and/or graduate teaching, internship, and research work. Collaborate with colleagues to address teaching and research issues. Serve on academic or administrative committees that deal with institutional policies, departmental matters, and academic issues. Participate in campus and community events. Participate in student recruitment, registration, and placement activities. Compile bibliographies of specialized materials for outside reading assignments. Act as advisers to student organizations. Perform administrative duties such as serving as department head. **SKILLS—Instructing:** Teaching others how to do something. **Learning Strategies:** Selecting and using training/instructional methods and procedures appropriate for the situation when learning or teaching new things. **Persuasion:** Persuading others to change their minds or behavior. **Writing:** Communicating effectively in writing as appropriate for the needs of the audience. **Critical Thinking:** Using logic and reasoning to identify the strengths and weaknesses of alternative solutions, conclusions, or approaches to problems. **Reading Comprehension:** Understanding written sentences and paragraphs in work-related documents. **Speaking:** Talking to others to convey information effectively. **Active Learning:** Understanding the implications of new information for both current and future problem-solving and decision-making. **GOE—Interest Area:** 05. Education and Training. **Work Group:** 05.03. Postsecondary and Adult Teaching and Instructing. **Other Jobs in This Work Group:** Adult Literacy, Remedial Education, and GED Teachers and Instructors; Agricultural Sciences Teachers, Postsecondary; Anthropology and Archeology Teachers, Postsecondary; Architecture Teachers, Postsecondary; Area, Ethnic, and Cultural Studies Teachers, Postsecondary; Art, Drama, and Music Teachers, Postsecondary; Atmospheric, Earth, Marine, and Space Sciences Teachers, Postsecondary; Biological Science Teachers, Postsecondary; Business Teachers, Postsecondary; Chemistry Teachers, Postsecondary; Communications Teachers, Postsecondary; Computer Science Teachers, Postsecondary; Criminal Justice and Law Enforcement Teachers, Postsecondary; Economics Teachers, Postsecondary; Education Teachers, Postsecondary; Engineering Teachers, Postsecondary; English Language and Literature Teachers, Postsecondary; Environmental Science Teachers, Postsecondary; Farm and Home Management Advisors; Foreign Language and Literature Teachers, Postsecondary; Forestry and Conservation Science Teachers, Postsecondary; Geography Teachers, Postsecondary; Graduate Teaching Assistants; Health Specialties Teachers, Postsecondary; History Teachers, Postsecondary; Home Economics Teachers, Postsecondary; Law Teachers, Postsecondary; Library Science Teachers, Postsecondary; Mathematical Science Teachers, Postsecondary; Nursing Instructors and Teachers, Postsecondary; Philosophy and Religion Teachers, Postsecondary; Physics Teachers, Postsecondary; Psychology Teachers, Postsecondary; Recreation and Fitness Studies Teachers, Postsecondary; Self-Enrichment Education Teachers; Social Work Teachers, Postsecondary; Sociology Teachers, Postsecondary; Vocational Education Teachers, Postsecondary. **PERSONALITY TYPE:** Social.

EDUCATION/TRAINING PROGRAM(S)— American Government and Politics (United States); Political Science and Government, General; Political Science and Government, Other; Social Science Teacher Education. **RELATED KNOWLEDGE/ COURSES—Philosophy and Theology:** Knowledge of different philosophical systems and religions. This includes their basic principles, values, ethics, ways of thinking, customs, and practices and their impact on human culture. **History and Archeology:** Knowledge of historical events and their causes, indicators, and effects on civilizations and cultures. **Sociology and Anthropology:** Knowledge of group behavior and dynamics, societal trends and influences, human migrations, ethnicity, and cultures and their history and origins. **Geography:** Knowledge of principles and methods for describing the features of land, sea, and air masses, including their physical characteristics; locations; interrelationships; and distribution of plant, animal, and human life. **Law and Government:** Knowledge of laws, legal codes, court procedures, precedents, government regulations, executive orders, agency rules, and the democratic political process. **Education and Training:** Knowledge of principles and methods for curriculum and training design, teaching and instruction for individuals and groups, and the measurement of training effects.

Postal Service Mail Carriers

- Education/Training Required: Short-term on-the-job training
- Annual Earnings: $44,450
- Growth: –0.5%
- Annual Job Openings: 20,000
- Self-Employed: 0%
- Part-Time: 6.5%

Sort mail for delivery. Deliver mail on established route by vehicle or on foot. Bundle mail in preparation for delivery or transportation to relay boxes. Deliver mail to residences and business establishments along specified routes by walking and/or driving, using a combination of satchels, carts, cars, and small trucks. Enter change-of-address orders into computers that process forwarding-address stickers. Hold mail for customers who are away from delivery locations. Leave notices telling patrons where to collect mail that could not be delivered. Maintain accurate records of deliveries. Meet schedules for the collection and return of mail. Record address changes and redirect mail for those addresses. Return incorrectly addressed mail to senders. Return to the post office with mail collected from homes, businesses, and public mailboxes. Sign for cash-on-delivery and registered mail before leaving the post office. Sort mail for delivery, arranging it in delivery sequence. Travel to post offices to pick up the mail for routes and/or pick up mail from postal relay boxes. Turn in money and receipts collected along mail routes. Answer customers' questions about postal services and regulations. Complete forms that notify publishers of address changes. Obtain signed receipts for registered, certified, and insured mail; collect associated charges; and complete any necessary paperwork. Provide customers with change-of-address cards and other forms. Register, certify, and insure parcels and letters. Report any unusual circumstances concerning mail delivery, including the condition of street letter boxes. Sell stamps and money orders. **SKILLS—**None met the criteria. **GOE—Interest Area:** 16. Transportation, Distribution, and Logistics. **Work Group:** 16.06. Other Services Requiring Driving. **Other Jobs in This Work Group:** Ambulance Drivers and Attendants, Except Emergency Medical Technicians; Bus Drivers, School; Bus Drivers, Transit and Intercity; Couriers and Messengers; Driver/Sales Workers; Parking Lot Attendants; Taxi Drivers and Chauffeurs. **PERSONALITY TYPE:** Conventional.

EDUCATION/TRAINING PROGRAM(S)—General Office Occupations and Clerical Services. **RELATED KNOWLEDGE/COURSES—Transportation:** Knowledge of principles and methods for moving people or goods by air, rail, sea, or road, including the relative costs and benefits. **Geography:** Knowledge of principles and methods for describing the features of land, sea, and air masses, including their physical characteristics; locations; interrelationships; and distribution of plant, animal, and human life.

Precision Devices Inspectors and Testers

- ◎ Education/Training Required: Moderate-term on-the-job training
- ◎ Annual Earnings: $28,410
- ◎ Growth: 4.7%
- ◎ Annual Job Openings: 87,000
- ◎ Self-Employed: 1.2%
- ◎ Part-Time: 5.0%

Verify accuracy of and adjust precision devices, such as meters and gauges, testing instruments, and clock and watch mechanisms, to ensure operation of device is in accordance with design specifications. Inspects materials, products, and work in progress for conformance to specifications and adjusts process or assembly equipment to meet standards. Reads dials and meters to verify functioning of equipment according to specifications. Tests and measures finished products, components, or assemblies for functioning, operation, accuracy, or assembly to verify adherence to functional specifications. Marks items for acceptance or rejection, records test results and inspection data, and compares findings with specifications to ensure conformance to standards. Completes necessary procedures to satisfy licensing requirements. Computes and/or calculates data and other information. Confers with vendors and others regarding inspection results and recommends corrective procedures. Disassembles defective parts and components. Estimates operational data to meet acceptable standards. Operates or tends machinery and equipment and uses hand tools. Discards or rejects products, materials, and equipment not meeting specifications. Analyzes and interprets blueprints, sample data, and other materials to determine, change, or measure specifications or inspection and testing procedures. Fabricates, installs, positions, or connects components, parts, finished products, or instruments for testing or operational purposes. Cleans and maintains test equipment and instruments and certifies that precision instruments meet standards. **SKILLS—Quality Control Analysis:** Conducting tests and inspections of products, services, or processes to evaluate quality or performance. **Operation Monitoring:** Watching gauges, dials, or other indicators to make sure a machine is working properly. **Technology Design:** Generating or adapting equipment and technology to serve user needs. **Installation:** Installing equipment, machines, wiring, or programs to meet specifications. **Science:** Using scientific rules and methods to solve problems. **Troubleshooting:** Determining causes of operating errors and deciding what to do about them. **Equipment Maintenance:** Performing routine maintenance on equipment and determining when and what kind of maintenance is needed. **Operation and Control:** Controlling operations of equipment or systems. **GOE—Interest Area:** 13. Manufacturing. **Work Group:** 13.07. Production Quality Control. **Other Jobs in This Work Group:** Electrical and Electronic Inspectors and Testers; Graders and Sorters, Agricultural Products; Materials Inspectors; Production Inspectors, Testers, Graders, Sorters, Samplers, Weighers. **PERSONALITY TYPE:** Realistic.

EDUCATION/TRAINING PROGRAM(S)— Quality Control Technology/Technician. **RELATED KNOWLEDGE/COURSES—Design:** Knowledge of design techniques, tools, and principles involved in production of precision technical plans, blueprints, drawings, and models. **Mechanical Devices:** Knowledge of machines and tools, including their designs, uses, repair, and maintenance. **Production and Processing:** Knowledge of raw materials, production processes, quality control, costs, and other techniques for maximizing the effective manufacture and distribution of goods. **Mathematics:** Knowledge of arithmetic, algebra, geometry, calculus, and statistics and their applications. **Engineering and Technology:** Knowledge of the practical application of engineering science and technology. This includes applying principles, techniques, procedures, and equipment to the design and production of various goods and services. **Physics:** Knowledge and prediction of physical principles and laws and their interrelationships and applications to understanding fluid, material, and atmospheric dynamics and mechanical, electrical, atomic, and subatomic structures and processes.

Precision Dyers

- ◎ Education/Training Required: Postsecondary vocational training
- ◎ Annual Earnings: $17,220
- ◎ Growth: 12.3%
- ◎ Annual Job Openings: 47,000
- ◎ Self-Employed: 6.8%
- ◎ Part-Time: 16.9%

Change or restore the color of articles, such as garments, drapes, and slipcovers, by means of dyes. Work requires knowledge of the composition of the textiles being dyed or restored and the chemical properties of bleaches and dyes and their effects upon such textiles. Matches sample color, applying knowledge of bleaching agent and dye properties and type, construction, condition, and color of article. Immerses article in bleaching bath to strip colors. Immerses article in dye solution and stirs with stick or dyes article in rotary-drum or paddle-dyeing machine. Rinses article in water and acetic acid solution to remove excess dye and to fix colors. Dissolves dye or bleaching chemicals in water. Operates or directs operation of extractor and drier. Sprays or brushes article with prepared solution to remove stains. Measures and mixes amounts of bleaches, dyes, oils, and acids, following formulas. Applies dye to article, using spray gun, electrically rotated brush, or hand brush. Examines article to identify fabric and original dye by sight, by touch, or by testing sample with fire or chemical reagent. Tests dye on swatch of fabric to ensure color match. **SKILLS— Science:** Using scientific rules and methods to solve problems. **GOE—Interest Area:** 13. Manufacturing. **Work Group:** 13.11. Apparel, Shoes, Leather, and Fabric Care. **Other Jobs in This Work Group:** Custom Tailors; Fabric Menders, Except Garment; Laundry and Drycleaning Machine Operators and Tenders, Except Pressing; Pressers, Delicate Fabrics; Pressers, Hand; Shoe and Leather Workers and Repairers; Shop and Alteration Tailors; Spotters, Dry Cleaning; Upholsterers. **PERSONALITY TYPE:** Realistic.

EDUCATION/TRAINING PROGRAM(S)—No data available. **RELATED KNOWLEDGE/COURSES—Chemistry:** Knowledge of the chemical composition, structure, and properties of substances and of the chemical processes and transformations that they undergo. This includes uses of chemicals and their danger signs, production techniques, and disposal methods. **Production and Processing:** Knowledge of raw materials, production processes, quality control, costs, and other techniques for maximizing the effective manufacture and distribution of goods.

Preschool Teachers, Except Special Education

- Education/Training Required: Bachelor's degree
- Annual Earnings: $20,980
- Growth: 36.2%
- Annual Job Openings: 88,000
- Self-Employed: 2.2%
- Part-Time: 24.9%

Instruct children (normally up to 5 years of age) in activities designed to promote social, physical, and intellectual growth needed for primary school in preschool, day care center, or other child development facility. May be required to hold state certification. Provide a variety of materials and resources for children to explore, manipulate, and use, both in learning activities and in imaginative play. Attend to children's basic needs by feeding them, dressing them, and changing their diapers. Teach basic skills such as color, shape, number, and letter recognition; personal hygiene; and social skills. Establish and enforce rules for behavior and procedures for maintaining order. Read books to entire classes or to small groups. Organize and lead activities designed to promote physical, mental, and social development, such as games, arts and crafts, music, storytelling, and field trips. Observe and evaluate children's performance, behavior, social development, and physical health. Identify children showing signs of emotional, developmental, or health-related problems and discuss them with supervisors, parents or guardians, and child development specialists. Meet with parents and guardians to discuss their children's progress and needs, determine their priorities for their children, and suggest ways that they can promote learning and development. Enforce all administration policies and rules governing students. Prepare materials and classrooms for class activities. Teach proper eating habits and personal hygiene. Serve meals and snacks in accordance with nutritional guidelines. Assimilate arriving children to the school environment by greeting them, helping them remove outerwear, and selecting activities of interest to them. Adapt teaching methods and instructional materials to meet students' varying needs and interests. Establish clear objectives for all lessons, units, and projects and communicate those objectives to children. Demonstrate activities to children. Arrange indoor and outdoor space to facilitate creative play, motor-skill activities, and safety. Maintain accurate and complete student records as required by laws, district policies, and administrative regulations. Prepare reports on students and activities as required by administration. Plan and conduct activities for a balanced program of instruction, demonstration, and work time that provides students with opportunities to observe, question, and investigate. **SKILLS—Learning Strategies:** Selecting and using training/instructional methods and procedures appropriate for the situation when learning or teaching new things. **Social Perceptiveness:** Being aware of others' reactions and understanding why they react as they do. **Instructing:** Teaching others how to do something. **Negotiation:** Bringing others together and trying to reconcile differences. **Service Orientation:** Actively looking for ways to help people. **Writing:** Communicating effectively in writing as appropriate for the needs of the audience. **Monitoring:** Monitoring or assessing your performance or that of other individuals or organizations to make improvements or take corrective action. **Persuasion:** Persuading others to change their minds or behavior. **Time Management:** Managing one's own time and the time of others. **GOE— Interest Area:** 05. Education and Training. **Work Group:** 05.02. Preschool, Elementary, and Secondary Teaching and Instructing. **Other Jobs in This Work Group:** Elementary School Teachers, Except Special Education; Kindergarten Teachers, Except Special Education; Middle School Teachers, Except Special and Vocational Education; Secondary School Teachers, Except Special and Vocational Education; Special Education Teachers, Middle School; Special Education Teachers, Preschool, Kindergarten, and Elementary School; Special Education Teachers, Secondary School; Teacher Assistants; Vocational Education Teachers, Middle School; Vocational Education Teachers, Secondary School. **PERSONALITY TYPE:** Social.

EDUCATION/TRAINING PROGRAM(S)— Child Care and Support Services Management; Early Childhood Education and Teaching; Kindergarten/ Preschool Education and Teaching. **RELATED KNOWLEDGE/COURSES—Customer and Personal Service:** Knowledge of principles and processes for providing customer and personal services. This includes customer needs assessment, meeting quality standards for services, and evaluation of customer satisfaction. **Philosophy and Theology:** Knowledge of different philosophical systems and religions. This

includes their basic principles, values, ethics, ways of thinking, customs, and practices and their impact on human culture. **Psychology:** Knowledge of human behavior and performance; individual differences in ability, personality, and interests; learning and motivation; psychological research methods; and the assessment and treatment of behavioral and affective disorders. **Education and Training:** Knowledge of principles and methods for curriculum and training design, teaching and instruction for individuals and groups, and the measurement of training effects. **Sociology and Anthropology:** Knowledge of group behavior and dynamics, societal trends and influences, human migrations, ethnicity, and cultures and their history and origins. **Medicine and Dentistry:** Knowledge of the information and techniques needed to diagnose and treat human injuries, diseases, and deformities. This includes symptoms, treatment alternatives, drug properties and interactions, and preventive health-care measures.

Pressure Vessel Inspectors

- ◉ Education/Training Required: Long-term on-the-job training
- ◉ Annual Earnings: $47,390
- ◉ Growth: 9.8%
- ◉ Annual Job Openings: 20,000
- ◉ Self-Employed: 0.9%
- ◉ Part-Time: 5.3%

Inspect pressure vessel equipment for conformance with safety laws and standards regulating their design, fabrication, installation, repair, and operation. Inspects drawings, designs, and specifications for piping, boilers, and other vessels. Performs standard tests to verify condition of equipment and calibration of meters and gauges, using test equipment and hand tools. Inspects gas mains to determine that rate of flow, pressure, location, construction, or installation conform to standards. Evaluates factors such as materials used, safety devices, regulators, construction quality, riveting, welding, pitting, corrosion, cracking, and safety valve operation. Calculates allowable limits of pressure, strength, and stresses. Examines permits and inspection records to determine that inspection schedule and remedial actions conform to procedures and regulations. Keeps records and prepares reports of inspections and investigations for administrative or legal authorities. Investigates accidents to determine causes and to develop methods of preventing recurrences. Confers with engineers, manufacturers, contractors, owners, and operators concerning problems in construction, operation, and repair. Witnesses acceptance and installation tests. Recommends or orders actions to correct violations of legal requirements or to eliminate unsafe conditions. **SKILLS— Quality Control Analysis:** Conducting tests and inspections of products, services, or processes to evaluate quality or performance. **Operation Monitoring:** Watching gauges, dials, or other indicators to make sure a machine is working properly. **Mathematics:** Using mathematics to solve problems. **Science:** Using scientific rules and methods to solve problems. **Operations Analysis:** Analyzing needs and product requirements to create a design. **Systems Evaluation:** Identifying measures or indicators of system performance and the actions needed to improve or correct performance relative to the goals of the system. **Writing:** Communicating effectively in writing as appropriate for the needs of the audience. **Systems Analysis:** Determining how a system should work and how changes in conditions, operations, and the environment will affect outcomes. **GOE—Interest Area:** 07. Government and Public Administration. **Work Group:** 07.03. Regulations Enforcement. **Other Jobs in This Work Group:** Agricultural Inspectors; Aviation Inspectors; Child Support, Missing Persons, and Unemployment Insurance Fraud Investigators; Environmental Compliance Inspectors; Equal Opportunity Representatives and Officers; Financial Examiners; Fire Inspectors; Fish and Game Wardens; Forest Fire Inspectors and Prevention Specialists; Government Property Inspectors and Investigators; Immigration and Customs Inspectors; Licensing Examiners and Inspectors; Marine Cargo Inspectors; Mechanical Inspectors; Motor Vehicle Inspectors; Nuclear Monitoring Technicians; Occupational Health and Safety Specialists; Railroad Inspectors; Tax Examiners, Collectors, and Revenue Agents. **PERSONALITY TYPE:** Realistic.

EDUCATION/TRAINING PROGRAM(S)—No data available. **RELATED KNOWLEDGE/COURSES—Physics:** Knowledge and prediction of physical principles and laws and their interrelationships and applications to understanding fluid, material, and atmospheric dynamics and mechanical, electrical, atomic, and subatomic structures and processes. **Public Safety and Security:** Knowledge of relevant equipment, policies, procedures, and strategies to promote effective local, state, or national security operations for the protection of people, data, property, and institutions. **Mechanical Devices:** Knowledge of machines and tools, including their designs, uses, repair, and maintenance. **Engineering and Technology:** Knowledge of the practical application of engineering science and technology. This includes applying principles, techniques, procedures, and equipment to the design and production of various goods and services. **Law and Government:** Knowledge of laws, legal codes, court procedures, precedents, government regulations, executive orders, agency rules, and the democratic political process. **Design:** Knowledge of design techniques, tools, and principles involved in production of precision technical plans, blueprints, drawings, and models.

Private Detectives and Investigators

- Education/Training Required: Work experience in a related occupation
- Annual Earnings: $32,110
- Growth: 25.3%
- Annual Job Openings: 9,000
- Self-Employed: 34.7%
- Part-Time: 7.8%

Detect occurrences of unlawful acts or infractions of rules in private establishment or seek, examine, and compile information for client. Apprehend suspects and release them to law enforcement authorities or security personnel. Conduct background investigations of individuals, such as pre-employment checks, to obtain information about an individual's character, financial status, or personal history. Conduct private investigations on a paid basis. Confer with establishment officials, security departments, police, or postal officials to identify problems, provide information, and receive instructions. Monitor industrial or commercial properties to enforce conformance to establishment rules and to protect people or property. Observe and document activities of individuals in order to detect unlawful acts or to obtain evidence for cases, using binoculars and still or video cameras. Obtain and analyze information on suspects, crimes, and disturbances in order to solve cases, to identify criminal activity, and to gather information for court cases. Perform undercover operations such as evaluating the performance and honesty of employees by posing as customers or employees. Question persons to obtain evidence for cases of divorce, child custody, or missing persons or information about individuals' character or financial status. Search computer databases, credit reports, public records, tax and legal filings, and other resources in order to locate persons or to compile information for investigations. Write reports and case summaries to document investigations. Alert appropriate personnel to suspects' locations. Count cash and review transactions, sales checks, and register tapes in order to verify amounts and to identify shortages. Expose fraudulent insurance claims or stolen funds. Investigate companies' financial standings or locate funds stolen by embezzlers, using accounting skills. Testify at hearings and court trials to present evidence. Warn troublemakers causing problems on establishment premises and eject them from premises when necessary. **SKILLS—Systems Evaluation:** Identifying measures or indicators of system performance and the actions needed to improve or correct performance relative to the goals of the system. **Persuasion:** Persuading others to change their minds or behavior. **Systems Analysis:** Determining how a system should work and how changes in conditions, operations, and the environment will affect outcomes. **Active Listening:** Giving full attention to what other people are saying, taking time to understand the points being made, asking questions as appropriate, and not interrupting at inappropriate times. **Critical Thinking:** Using logic and reasoning to identify the strengths and weaknesses of alternative solutions, conclusions, or approaches to problems. **Social Perceptiveness:** Being aware of others' reactions and understanding why they react as they do. **Writing:** Communicating effectively in writing as appropriate for the needs of the audience. **Speaking:** Talking to others to convey information effectively. **GOE—Interest Area:** 12. Law and Public Safety. **Work Group:** 12.05. Safety and Security. **Other Jobs in This Work Group:** Animal Control Workers; Crossing Guards; Gaming Surveillance Officers and Gaming Investigators; Lifeguards, Ski Patrol, and Other Recreational Protective Service Workers; Security Guards. **PERSONALITY TYPE:** Enterprising.

EDUCATION/TRAINING PROGRAM(S)— Criminal Justice/Police Science. **RELATED KNOWLEDGE/COURSES—Public Safety and Security:** Knowledge of relevant equipment, policies, procedures, and strategies to promote effective local, state, or national security operations for the protection of people, data, property, and institutions. **Psychology:** Knowledge of human behavior and performance; individual differences in ability, personality, and interests; learning and motivation; psychological research methods; and the assessment and treatment of behavioral and affective disorders. **Telecommunications:** Knowledge of transmission, broadcasting, switching, control, and operation of telecommunications systems. **Law and Government:** Knowledge of laws, legal codes, court procedures, precedents, government regulations, executive orders, agency rules, and the democratic political process. **Medicine and Dentistry:** Knowledge of the information and techniques needed to diagnose and treat human injuries, diseases, and deformities. This includes symptoms, treatment alternatives, drug properties and interactions, and preventive health-care measures. **Therapy and Counseling:** Knowledge of principles, methods, and procedures for diagnosis, treatment, and rehabilitation of physical and mental dysfunctions and for career counseling and guidance.

Private Sector Executives

- ◉ Education/Training Required: Work experience plus degree
- ◉ Annual Earnings: $140,350
- ◉ Growth: 16.7%
- ◉ Annual Job Openings: 63,000
- ◉ Self-Employed: 14.6%
- ◉ Part-Time: 5.3%

Determine and formulate policies and business strategies and provide overall direction of private sector organizations. Plan, direct, and coordinate operational activities at the highest level of management with the help of subordinate managers. Directs, plans, and implements policies and objectives of organization or business in accordance with charter and board of directors. Directs activities of organization to plan procedures, establish responsibilities, and coordinate functions among departments and sites. Analyzes operations to evaluate performance of company and staff and to determine areas of cost reduction and program improvement. Confers with board members, organization officials, and staff members to establish policies and formulate plans. Reviews financial statements and sales and activity reports to ensure that organization's objectives are achieved. Assigns or delegates responsibilities to subordinates. Directs and coordinates activities of business involved with buying and selling investment products and financial services. Establishes internal control procedures. Presides over or serves on board of directors, management committees, or other governing boards. Directs inservice training of staff. Administers program for selection of sites, construction of buildings, and provision of equipment and supplies. Screens, selects, hires, transfers, and discharges employees. Promotes objectives of institution or business before associations, public, government agencies, or community groups. Negotiates or approves contracts with suppliers and distributors and with maintenance, janitorial, and security providers. Prepares reports and budgets. Directs non-merchandising departments of business, such as advertising, purchasing, credit, and accounting. Directs and coordinates activities of business or department concerned with production, pricing, sales, and/or distribution of products. Directs and coordinates organization's financial and budget activities to fund operations, maximize investments, and increase efficiency. **SKILLS—Management of Financial Resources:** Determining how money will be spent to get the work done and accounting for these expenditures. **Systems Analysis:** Determining how a system should work and how changes in conditions, operations, and the environment will affect outcomes. **Systems Evaluation:** Identifying measures or indicators of system performance and the actions needed to improve or correct performance relative to the goals of the system. **Management of Personnel Resources:** Motivating, developing, and directing people as they work, identifying the best people for the job. **Judgment and Decision Making:** Considering the relative costs and benefits of potential actions to choose the most appropriate one. **Coordination:** Adjusting actions in relation to others' actions. **Management of Material Resources:** Obtaining and seeing to the appropriate use of equipment, facilities, and materials needed to do certain work. **Negotiation:** Bringing others together and trying to reconcile differences. **GOE—Interest Area:** 04. Business and Administration. **Work Group:** 04.01. Managerial Work in General Business. **Other Jobs in This Work Group:** Chief Executives; Compensation and Benefits Managers; General and Operations Managers; Human Resources Managers; Training and Development Managers. **PERSONALITY TYPE:** Enterprising.

EDUCATION/TRAINING PROGRAM(S)—Business Administration and Management, General;

Business/Commerce, General; Entrepreneurship/Entrepreneurial Studies; International Business/Trade/Commerce; Public Administration; Public Administration and Social Service Professions, Other; Public Policy Analysis. **RELATED KNOWLEDGE/COURSES—Economics and Accounting:** Knowledge of economic and accounting principles and practices, the financial markets, banking, and the analysis and reporting of financial data. **Production and Processing:** Knowledge of raw materials, production processes, quality control, costs, and other techniques for maximizing the effective manufacture and distribution of goods. **Administration and Management:** Knowledge of business and management principles involved in strategic planning, resource allocation, human resources modeling, leadership technique, production methods, and coordination of people and resources. **Sales and Marketing:** Knowledge of principles and methods for showing, promoting, and selling products or services. This includes marketing strategy and tactics, product demonstrations, sales techniques, and sales control systems. **Personnel and Human Resources:** Knowledge of principles and procedures for personnel recruitment, selection, training, compensation and benefits, labor relations and negotiation, and personnel information systems. **Building and Construction:** Knowledge of the materials, methods, and tools involved in the construction or repair of houses, buildings, or other structures such as highways and roads. **Psychology:** Knowledge of human behavior and performance; individual differences in ability, personality, and interests; learning and motivation; psychological research methods; and the assessment and treatment of behavioral and affective disorders.

Probation Officers and Correctional Treatment Specialists

- Education/Training Required: Bachelor's degree
- Annual Earnings: $39,600
- Growth: 14.7%
- Annual Job Openings: 15,000
- Self-Employed: 0.2%
- Part-Time: 10.6%

Provide social services to assist in rehabilitation of law offenders in custody or on probation or parole. Make recommendations for actions involving formulation of rehabilitation plan and treatment of offender, including conditional release and education and employment stipulations. Prepare and maintain case folder for each assigned inmate or offender. Write reports describing offenders' progress. Inform offenders or inmates of requirements of conditional release, such as office visits, restitution payments, or educational and employment stipulations. Discuss with offenders how such issues as drug and alcohol abuse and anger management problems might have played roles in their criminal behavior. Gather information about offenders' backgrounds by talking to offenders, their families and friends, and other people who have relevant information. Develop rehabilitation programs for assigned offenders or inmates, establishing rules of conduct, goals, and objectives. Develop liaisons and networks with other parole officers, community agencies, staff in correctional institutions, psychiatric facilities, and after-care agencies in order to make plans for helping offenders with life adjustments. Arrange for medical, mental health, or substance abuse treatment services according to individual needs and/or court orders. Provide offenders or inmates with assistance in matters concerning detainers, sentences in other jurisdictions, writs, and applications for social assistance. Arrange for post-release services such as employment, housing, counseling, education, and social activities. Recommend remedial action or initiate court action when terms of probation or parole are not complied with. Interview probationers and parolees regularly to evaluate their progress in accomplishing goals and maintaining the terms specified in their probation contracts and rehabilitation plans. Supervise people on community-based sentences, including people on electronically monitored home detention. Assess the suitability of penitentiary inmates for release under parole and statutory release programs and submit recommendations to parole boards. Investigate alleged parole violations, using interviews, surveillance, and search and seizure. Conduct prehearing and presentencing investigations and testify in court regarding offenders' backgrounds and recommended sentences and sentencing conditions. **SKILLS—Social Perceptiveness:** Being aware of others' reactions and understanding why they react as they do. **Persuasion:** Persuading others to change their minds or behavior. **Time Management:** Managing one's own time and the time of others.

Negotiation: Bringing others together and trying to reconcile differences. **Learning Strategies:** Selecting and using training/instructional methods and procedures appropriate for the situation when learning or teaching new things. **Management of Personnel Resources:** Motivating, developing, and directing people as they work, identifying the best people for the job. **Coordination:** Adjusting actions in relation to others' actions. **Instructing:** Teaching others how to do something. **GOE—Interest Area:** 10. Human Service. **Work Group:** 10.01. Counseling and Social Work. **Other Jobs in This Work Group:** Child, Family, and School Social Workers; Clinical Psychologists; Counseling Psychologists; Marriage and Family Therapists; Medical and Public Health Social Workers; Mental Health and Substance Abuse Social Workers; Mental Health Counselors; Rehabilitation Counselors; Residential Advisors; Social and Human Service Assistants; Substance Abuse and Behavioral Disorder Counselors. **PERSONALITY TYPE:** Social.

EDUCATION/TRAINING PROGRAM(S)— Social Work. **RELATED KNOWLEDGE/COURSES—Therapy and Counseling:** Knowledge of principles, methods, and procedures for diagnosis, treatment, and rehabilitation of physical and mental dysfunctions and for career counseling and guidance. **Psychology:** Knowledge of human behavior and performance; individual differences in ability, personality, and interests; learning and motivation; psychological research methods; and the assessment and treatment of behavioral and affective disorders. **Sociology and Anthropology:** Knowledge of group behavior and dynamics, societal trends and influences, human migrations, ethnicity, and cultures and their history and origins. **Public Safety and Security:** Knowledge of relevant equipment, policies, procedures, and strategies to promote effective local, state, or national security operations for the protection of people, data, property, and institutions. **Law and Government:** Knowledge of laws, legal codes, court procedures, precedents, government regulations, executive orders, agency rules, and the democratic political process. **Philosophy and Theology:** Knowledge of different philosophical systems and religions. This includes their basic principles, values, ethics, ways of thinking, customs, and practices and their impact on human culture.

Producers

- ☺ Education/Training Required: Work experience plus degree
- ☺ Annual Earnings: $52,840
- ☺ Growth: 18.3%
- ☺ Annual Job Openings: 10,000
- ☺ Self-Employed: 32.8%
- ☺ Part-Time: 9.1%

Plan and coordinate various aspects of radio, television, stage, or motion picture production, such as selecting script; coordinating writing, directing, and editing; and arranging financing. Coordinate the activities of writers, directors, managers, and other personnel throughout the production process. Monitor post-production processes in order to ensure accurate completion of all details. Perform management activities such as budgeting, scheduling, planning, and marketing. Determine production size, content, and budget, establishing details such as production schedules and management policies. Compose and edit scripts or provide screenwriters with story outlines from which scripts can be written. Conduct meetings with staff to discuss production progress and to ensure production objectives are attained. Resolve personnel problems that arise during the production process by acting as liaisons between dissenting parties when necessary. Produce shows for special occasions, such as holidays or testimonials. Edit and write news stories from information collected by reporters. Write and submit proposals to bid on contracts for projects. Hire directors, principal cast members, and key production staff members. Arrange financing for productions. Select plays, scripts, books, or ideas to be produced. Review film, recordings, or rehearsals to ensure conformance to production and broadcast standards. Perform administrative duties such as preparing operational reports, distributing rehearsal call sheets and script copies, and arranging for rehearsal quarters. Obtain and distribute costumes, props, music, and studio equipment needed to complete productions. Negotiate contracts with artistic personnel, often in accordance with collective bargaining agreements. Maintain knowledge of minimum wages and working conditions established by unions and/or associations of actors and technicians. Plan and coordinate the production of musical recordings, selecting music and directing performers. Negotiate with parties, including independent producers and the distributors and broadcasters who will be handling completed productions. Develop marketing plans for finished products, collaborating with sales associates to supervise product distribution. Determine and direct the content of radio programming. **SKILLS—Negotiation:** Bringing others together and trying to reconcile differences. **Coordination:** Adjusting actions in relation to others' actions. **Management of Personnel Resources:** Motivating, developing, and directing people as they work, identifying the best people for the job. **Monitoring:** Monitoring or assessing your performance or that of other individuals or organizations to make improvements or take corrective action. **Writing:** Communicating effectively in writing as appropriate for the needs of the audience. **Social Perceptiveness:** Being aware of others' reactions and understanding why they react as they do. **Time Management:** Managing one's own time and the time of others. **Speaking:** Talking to others to convey information effectively. **Management of Financial Resources:** Determining how money will be spent to get the work done and accounting for these expenditures. **GOE—Interest Area:** 03. Arts and Communication. **Work Group:** 03.01. Managerial Work in Arts and Communication. **Other Jobs in This Work Group:** Agents and Business Managers of Artists, Performers, and Athletes; Art Directors; Program Directors; Public Relations Managers; Technical Directors/Managers. **PERSONALITY TYPE:** Artistic.

EDUCATION/TRAINING PROGRAM(S)—Cinematography and Film/Video Production; Directing and Theatrical Production; Drama and Dramatics/Theatre Arts, General; Dramatic/Theatre Arts and Stagecraft, Other; Film/Cinema Studies; Radio and Television; Theatre/Theatre Arts Management. **RELATED KNOWLEDGE/COURSES— Communications and Media:** Knowledge of media production, communication, and dissemination techniques and methods. This includes alternative ways to inform and entertain via written, oral, and visual media. **Clerical Practices:** Knowledge of administrative and clerical procedures and systems such as word processing, managing files and records, stenography and transcription, designing forms, and other office procedures and terminology. **Administration and Management:** Knowledge of business and management principles involved in strategic planning, resource allocation, human resources modeling, leadership technique, production methods, and coordination of people and resources. **English Language:**

Knowledge of the structure and content of the English language, including the meaning and spelling of words, rules of composition, and grammar. **Fine Arts:** Knowledge of the theory and techniques required to compose, produce, and perform works of music, dance, the visual arts, drama, and sculpture. **Sales and Marketing:** Knowledge of principles and methods for showing, promoting, and selling products or services. This includes marketing strategy and tactics, product demonstrations, sales techniques, and sales control systems.

Product Safety Engineers

- Education/Training Required: Bachelor's degree
- Annual Earnings: $63,730
- Growth: 7.9%
- Annual Job Openings: 4,000
- Self-Employed: 1.6%
- Part-Time: 1.5%

Develop and conduct tests to evaluate product safety levels and recommend measures to reduce or eliminate hazards. Conduct research to evaluate safety levels for products. Evaluate potential health hazards or damage that could occur from product misuse. Investigate causes of accidents, injuries, or illnesses related to product usage in order to develop solutions to minimize or prevent recurrence. Participate in preparation of product usage and precautionary label instructions. Recommend procedures for detection, prevention, and elimination of physical, chemical, or other product hazards. Report accident investigation findings. **SKILLS—Quality Control Analysis:** Conducting tests and inspections of products, services, or processes to evaluate quality or performance. **Operations Analysis:** Analyzing needs and product requirements to create a design. **Science:** Using scientific rules and methods to solve problems. **Technology Design:** Generating or adapting equipment and technology to serve user needs. **Mathematics:** Using mathematics to solve problems. **Writing:** Communicating effectively in writing as appropriate for the needs of the audience. **Active Learning:** Understanding the implications of new information for both current and future problem-solving and decision-making. **Troubleshooting:** Determining causes of operating errors and deciding what to do about them. **GOE—Interest Area:** 15. Scientific

Research, Engineering, and Mathematics. **Work Group:** 15.08. Industrial and Safety Engineering. **Other Jobs in This Work Group:** Fire-Prevention and Protection Engineers; Industrial Engineers; Industrial Safety and Health Engineers. **PERSONALITY TYPE:** Investigative.

EDUCATION/TRAINING PROGRAM(S)—Environmental/Environmental Health Engineering. **RELATED KNOWLEDGE/COURSES—Chemistry:** Knowledge of the chemical composition, structure, and properties of substances and of the chemical processes and transformations that they undergo. This includes uses of chemicals and their danger signs, production techniques, and disposal methods. **Engineering and Technology:** Knowledge of the practical application of engineering science and technology. This includes applying principles, techniques, procedures, and equipment to the design and production of various goods and services. **Physics:** Knowledge and prediction of physical principles and laws and their interrelationships and applications to understanding fluid, material, and atmospheric dynamics and mechanical, electrical, atomic, and subatomic structures and processes. **Public Safety and Security:** Knowledge of relevant equipment, policies, procedures, and strategies to promote effective local, state, or national security operations for the protection of people, data, property, and institutions. **Production and Processing:** Knowledge of raw materials, production processes, quality control, costs, and other techniques for maximizing the effective manufacture and distribution of goods. **Biology:** Knowledge of plant and animal organisms and their tissues, cells, functions, interdependencies, and interactions with each other and the environment.

Production Inspectors, Testers, Graders, Sorters, Samplers, Weighers

- Education/Training Required: Short-term on-the-job training
- Annual Earnings: $28,410
- Growth: 4.7%
- Annual Job Openings: 87,000
- Self-Employed: 1.2%
- Part-Time: 5.0%

Inspect, test, grade, sort, sample, or weigh nonagricultural raw materials or processed, machined, fabricated, or assembled parts or products. Work may be performed before, during, or after processing. Grades, classifies, and sorts products according to size, weight, color, or other specifications. Marks, affixes, or stamps product or container to identify defects or denote grade or size information. Records inspection or test data, such as weight, temperature, grade, or moisture content and number inspected or graded. Collects or selects samples for testing or for use as model. Discards or routes defective products or contaminants for rework or reuse. Notifies supervisor or specified personnel of deviations from specifications, machine malfunctions, or need for equipment maintenance. Reads work order to determine inspection criteria and to verify identification numbers and product type. Uses or operates product to test functional performance. Computes percentages or averages, using formulas and calculator, and prepares reports of inspection or test findings. Sets controls, starts machine, and observes machine that automatically sorts or inspects products. Counts number of product tested or inspected and stacks or arranges for further processing, shipping, or packing. Cleans, trims, makes adjustments, or repairs product or processing equipment to correct defects found during inspection. Transports inspected or tested products to other work stations, using handtruck or lift truck. Wraps and packages product for shipment or delivery. Weighs materials, products, containers, or samples to verify packaging weight, to determine percentage of each ingredient, or to determine sorting. Compares color, shape, texture, or grade of product or material with color chart, template, or sample to verify conformance to standards. Tests samples, materials, or products, using test equipment such as thermometer, voltmeter, moisture meter, or tensiometer, for conformance to specifications. Measures dimensions of product, using measuring instruments, such as rulers, calipers, gauges, or micrometers, to verify conformance to specifications. Examines product or monitors processing of product, using any or all of five senses, to determine defects or grade. **SKILLS—Quality Control Analysis:** Conducting tests and inspections of products, services, or processes to evaluate quality or performance. **Operation Monitoring:** Watching gauges, dials, or other indicators to make sure a machine is working properly. **Operation and Control:** Controlling operations of equipment or systems. **Repairing:** Repairing machines or systems by using the needed tools. **Management of Material Resources:** Obtaining and seeing to the appropriate use of equipment, facilities, and materials needed to do certain work. **Troubleshooting:** Determining causes of operating errors and deciding what to do about them. **Equipment Maintenance:** Performing routine maintenance on equipment and determining when and what kind of maintenance is needed. **GOE—Interest Area:** 13. Manufacturing. **Work Group:** 13.07. Production Quality Control. **Other Jobs in This Work Group:** Electrical and Electronic Inspectors and Testers; Graders and Sorters, Agricultural Products; Materials Inspectors; Precision Devices Inspectors and Testers. **PERSONALITY TYPE:** Realistic.

EDUCATION/TRAINING PROGRAM(S)— Quality Control Technology/Technician. **RELATED KNOWLEDGE/COURSES—Production and Processing:** Knowledge of raw materials, production processes, quality control, costs, and other techniques for maximizing the effective manufacture and distribution of goods. **Engineering and Technology:** Knowledge of the practical application of engineering science and technology. This includes applying principles, techniques, procedures, and equipment to the design and production of various goods and services. **Mechanical Devices:** Knowledge of machines and tools, including their designs, uses, repair, and maintenance.

Production Laborers

- ◎ Education/Training Required: Short-term on-the-job training
- ◎ Annual Earnings: $20,180
- ◎ Growth: 11.3%
- ◎ Annual Job Openings: 67,000
- ◎ Self-Employed: 0.8%
- ◎ Part-Time: 5.5%

Perform variety of routine tasks to assist in production activities. Carries or handtrucks supplies to work stations. Records information such as number of product tested, meter readings, and date and time product placed in oven. Examines product to verify conformance to company standards. Mixes ingredients according to formula. Feeds item into processing machine. Inserts parts into partial assembly during various stages of assembly to complete product. Counts finished product to determine completion of production order. Washes machines; equipment; vehicles; and products such as prints, rugs, and table linens. Folds parts of product and final product during processing. Separates product according to weight, grade, size, and composition of material used to produce product. Cuts or breaks flashing from materials or products. Places product in equipment or on work surface for further processing, inspecting, or wrapping. Positions spout or chute of storage bin to fill containers during processing. Breaks up defective products for reprocessing. Attaches slings, ropes, cables, or identification tags to objects such as pipes, hoses, and bundles. Weighs raw materials for distribution. Threads ends of items such as thread, cloth, and lace through needles, rollers, and around takeup tube. Ties product in bundles for further processing or shipment, following prescribed procedure. Lifts raw materials, final products, and items packed for shipment manually or by using hoist. Loads and unloads items from machines, conveyors, and conveyance. **SKILLS—Installation:** Installing equipment, machines, wiring, or programs to meet specifications. **Repairing:** Repairing machines or systems by using the needed tools. **GOE—Interest Area:** 13. Manufacturing. **Work Group:** 13.03. Production Work, Assorted Materials Processing. **Other Jobs in This Work Group:** Bakers, Manufacturing; Cementing and Gluing Machine Operators and Tenders; Chemical Equipment Controllers and Operators; Chemical Equipment Tenders; Cleaning, Washing, and Metal Pickling Equipment Operators and Tenders; Coating, Painting, and Spraying Machine Operators and Tenders; Combination Machine Tool Operators and Tenders, Metal and Plastic; Cooling and Freezing Equipment Operators and Tenders; Cutting and Slicing Machine Operators and Tenders; Electrolytic Plating and Coating Machine Operators and Tenders, Metal and Plastic; Extruding and Forming Machine Operators and Tenders, Synthetic or Glass Fibers; Extruding, Forming, Pressing, and Compacting Machine Operators and Tenders; Food and Tobacco Roasting, Baking, and Drying Machine Operators and Tenders; Food Batchmakers; Food Cooking Machine Operators and Tenders; Furnace, Kiln, Oven, Drier, and Kettle Operators and Tenders; Heat Treating, Annealing, and Tempering Machine Operators and Tenders, Metal and Plastic; Heaters, Metal and Plastic; Meat, Poultry, and Fish Cutters and Trimmers; Metal-Refining Furnace Operators and Tenders; Mixing and Blending Machine Setters, Operators, and

Tenders; Nonelectrolytic Plating and Coating Machine Operators and Tenders, Metal and Plastic; Packaging and Filling Machine Operators and Tenders; Plastic Molding and Casting Machine Operators and Tenders; Pourers and Casters, Metal; Pressing Machine Operators and Tenders—Textile, Garment, and Related Materials; Production Helpers; Sawing Machine Operators and Tenders; Separating, Filtering, Clarifying, Precipitating, and Still Machine Setters, Operators, and Tenders; Sewing Machine Operators, Garment; Sewing Machine Operators, Non-Garment; Shoe Machine Operators and Tenders; Slaughterers and Meat Packers; Stone Sawyers; Team Assemblers; Textile Bleaching and Dyeing Machine Operators and Tenders; Tire Builders; Woodworking Machine Operators and Tenders, Except Sawing. **PERSONALITY TYPE:** Realistic.

EDUCATION/TRAINING PROGRAM(S)—No data available. **RELATED KNOWLEDGE/COURSES—Production and Processing:** Knowledge of raw materials, production processes, quality control, costs, and other techniques for maximizing the effective manufacture and distribution of goods. **Administration and Management:** Knowledge of business and management principles involved in strategic planning, resource allocation, human resources modeling, leadership technique, production methods, and coordination of people and resources.

Production, Planning, and Expediting Clerks

- Education/Training Required: Short-term on-the-job training
- Annual Earnings: $36,340
- Growth: 14.1%
- Annual Job Openings: 51,000
- Self-Employed: 0.4%
- Part-Time: 9.3%

Coordinate and expedite the flow of work and materials within or between departments of an establishment according to production schedule. Duties include reviewing and distributing production, work, and shipment schedules; conferring with department supervisors to determine progress of work and completion dates; and compiling reports on progress of work, inventory levels, costs, and production problems. Arrange for delivery, assembly, and distribution of supplies and parts in order to expedite flow of materials and meet production schedules. Calculate figures such as required amounts of labor and materials, manufacturing costs, and wages, using pricing schedules, adding machines, calculators, or computers. Compile and prepare documentation related to production sequences; transportation; personnel schedules; and purchase, maintenance, and repair orders. Compile information such as production rates and progress, materials inventories, materials used, and customer information so that status reports can be completed. Confer with establishment personnel, vendors, and customers to coordinate production and shipping activities and to resolve complaints or eliminate delays. Contact suppliers to verify shipment details. Examine documents, materials, and products and monitor work processes in order to assess completeness, accuracy, and conformance to standards and specifications. Requisition and maintain inventories of materials and supplies necessary to meet production demands. Review documents such as production schedules, work orders, and staffing tables to determine personnel and materials requirements and material priorities. Revise production schedules when required due to design changes, labor or material shortages, backlogs, or other interruptions, collaborating with management, marketing, sales, production, and engineering. Confer with department supervisors and other personnel to assess progress and discuss needed changes. Distribute production schedules and work orders to departments. Establish and prepare product construction directions and locations and information on required tools, materials, and equipment, numbers of workers needed, and cost projections. Maintain files such as maintenance records, bills of lading, and cost reports. Plan production commitments and timetables for business units, specific programs, and/or jobs, using sales forecasts. Provide documentation and information to account for delays, difficulties, and changes to cost estimates. Record production data, including volume produced, consumption of raw materials, and quality control measures. **SKILLS—Management of Material Resources:** Obtaining and seeing to the appropriate use of equipment, facilities, and materials needed to do certain work. **Management of Personnel Resources:** Motivating, developing, and directing people as they work, identifying the best people for the job. **Systems Analysis:** Determining how a system should work and how changes in conditions, operations, and the environment will affect outcomes. **Management of Financial Resources:** Determining how money will be spent to get the work done and accounting for these expenditures. **Systems Evaluation:** Identifying measures or indicators of system performance and the actions needed to improve or correct performance relative to the goals of the system. **Time Management:** Managing one's own time and the time of others. **Service Orientation:** Actively looking for ways to help people. **Writing:** Communicating effectively in writing as appropriate for the needs of the audience. **GOE—Interest Area:** 04. Business and Administration. **Work Group:** 04.07. Records and Materials Processing. **Other Jobs in This Work Group:** Correspondence Clerks; File Clerks; Human Resources Assistants, Except Payroll and Timekeeping; Mail Clerks, Except Mail Machine Operators and Postal Service; Marking Clerks; Meter Readers, Utilities; Office Clerks, General; Order Fillers, Wholesale and Retail Sales; Postal Service Clerks; Postal Service Mail Sorters, Processors, and Processing Machine Operators; Procurement Clerks; Shipping, Receiving, and Traffic Clerks; Stock Clerks, Sales Floor; Stock Clerks—Stockroom, Warehouse, or Storage Yard; Weighers, Measurers, Checkers, and Samplers, Recordkeeping. **PERSONALITY TYPE:** Conventional.

EDUCATION/TRAINING PROGRAM(S)—Parts, Warehousing, and Inventory Management Operations. **RELATED KNOWLEDGE/COURSES—Clerical Practices:** Knowledge of administrative and clerical procedures and systems such as word processing, managing files and records, stenography and transcription, designing forms, and other office procedures and terminology. **Production and Processing:** Knowledge of raw materials, production processes, quality control, costs, and other techniques for maximizing the effective manufacture and distribution of goods. **Economics and Accounting:** Knowledge of economic and accounting principles and practices, the financial markets, banking, and the analysis and reporting of financial data. **Mathematics:** Knowledge of arithmetic, algebra, geometry, calculus, and statistics and their applications. **Computers and Electronics:** Knowledge of circuit boards, processors, chips, electronic equipment, and computer hardware and software, including applications and programming. **Administration and Management:** Knowledge of business and management principles involved in strategic planning, resource allocation, human resources modeling, leadership technique, production methods, and coordination of people and resources.

Professional Photographers

- ◉ Education/Training Required: Long-term on-the-job training
- ◉ Annual Earnings: $26,080
- ◉ Growth: 13.6%
- ◉ Annual Job Openings: 18,000
- ◉ Self-Employed: 52.5%
- ◉ Part-Time: 24.0%

Photograph subjects or newsworthy events, using still cameras, color or black-and-white film, and variety of photographic accessories. Frames subject matter and background in lens to capture desired image. Focuses camera and adjusts settings based on lighting, subject material, distance, and film speed. Selects and assembles equipment and required background properties according to subject, materials, and conditions. Directs activities of workers assisting in setting up photograph. Arranges subject material in desired position. Estimates or measures light level, distance, and number of exposures needed, using measuring devices and formulas. **SKILLS—Equipment Selection:** Determining the kind of tools and equipment needed to do a job. **Management of Material Resources:** Obtaining and seeing to the appropriate use of equipment, facilities, and materials needed to do certain work. **Technology Design:** Generating or adapting equipment and technology to serve user needs. **Operation and Control:** Controlling operations of equipment or systems. **Systems Analysis:** Determining how a system should work and how changes in conditions, operations, and the environment will affect outcomes. **Management of Personnel Resources:** Motivating, developing, and directing people as they work, identifying the best people for the job. **Social Perceptiveness:** Being aware of others' reactions and understanding why they react as they do. **GOE—Interest Area:** 03. Arts and Communication. **Work Group:** 03.09. Media Technology. **Other Jobs in This Work Group:** Audio and Video Equipment Technicians; Broadcast Technicians; Camera Operators, Television, Video, and Motion Picture; Film and Video Editors; Multi-Media Artists and Animators; Photographic Hand Developers; Photographic Reproduction Technicians; Photographic Retouchers and Restorers; Radio Operators; Sound Engineering Technicians. **PERSONALITY TYPE:** Artistic.

EDUCATION/TRAINING PROGRAM(S)— Art/Art Studies, General; Commercial Photography; Film/Video and Photographic Arts, Other; Photography; Photojournalism; Visual and Performing Arts, General. **RELATED KNOWLEDGE/COURSES— Fine Arts:** Knowledge of the theory and techniques required to compose, produce, and perform works of music, dance, the visual arts, drama, and sculpture. **Communications and Media:** Knowledge of media production, communication, and dissemination techniques and methods. This includes alternative ways to inform and entertain via written, oral, and visual media. **Chemistry:** Knowledge of the chemical composition, structure, and properties of substances and of the chemical processes and transformations that they undergo. This includes uses of chemicals and their danger signs, production techniques, and disposal methods. **Geography:** Knowledge of principles and methods for describing the features of land, sea, and air masses, including their physical characteristics; locations; interrelationships; and distribution of plant, animal, and human life. **Physics:** Knowledge and prediction of physical principles and laws and their interrelationships and applications to understanding fluid, material, and atmospheric dynamics and mechanical, electrical, atomic, and subatomic structures and processes. **Transportation:** Knowledge of principles and methods for moving people or goods by air, rail, sea, or road, including the relative costs and benefits.

Program Directors

- ◉ Education/Training Required: Work experience plus degree
- ◉ Annual Earnings: $52,840
- ◉ Growth: 18.3%
- ◉ Annual Job Openings: 10,000
- ◉ Self-Employed: 32.8%
- ◉ Part-Time: 9.1%

Direct and coordinate activities of personnel engaged in preparation of radio or television station program schedules and programs, such as sports or news.

Check completed program logs for accuracy and conformance with FCC rules and regulations and resolve program log inaccuracies. Confer with directors and production staff to discuss issues such as production and casting problems, budgets, policies, and news coverage. Coordinate activities between departments such as news and programming. Cue announcers, actors, performers, and guests. Develop promotions for current programs and specials. Direct and coordinate activities of personnel engaged in broadcast news, sports, or programming. Establish work schedules and assign work to staff members. Evaluate new and existing programming for suitability and in order to assess the need for changes, using information such as audience surveys and feedback. Monitor and review programming in order to ensure that schedules are met, guidelines are adhered to, and performances are of adequate quality. Monitor network transmissions for advisories concerning daily program schedules, program content, special feeds, and/or program changes. Perform personnel duties such as hiring staff and evaluating work performance. Plan and schedule programming and event coverage based on broadcast length, time availability, and other factors such as community needs, ratings data, and viewer demographics. Act as a liaison between talent and directors, providing information that performers/guests need to prepare for appearances and communicating relevant information from guests, performers, or staff to directors. Conduct interviews for broadcasts. Develop budgets for programming and broadcasting activities and monitor expenditures to ensure that they remain within budgetary limits. Develop ideas for programs and features that a station could produce. Operate and maintain on-air and production audio equipment. Prepare copy and edit tape so that material is ready for broadcasting. Read news, read and/or record public service and promotional announcements, and otherwise participate as a member of an on-air shift as required. Review information about programs and schedules in order to ensure accuracy and provide such information to local media outlets as necessary. **SKILLS—Management of Personnel Resources:** Motivating, developing, and directing people as they work, identifying the best people for the job. **Coordination:** Adjusting actions in relation to others' actions. **Management of Financial Resources:** Determining how money will be spent to get the work done and accounting for these expenditures. **Management of Material Resources:** Obtaining and seeing to the appropriate use of equipment, facilities, and materials needed to do certain work. **Writing:** Communicating effectively in writing as appropriate for the needs of the audience. **Time Management:** Managing one's own time and the time of others. **Systems Analysis:** Determining how a system should work and how changes in conditions, operations, and the environment will affect outcomes. **Reading Comprehension:** Understanding written sentences and paragraphs in work-related documents. **GOE—Interest Area:** 03. Arts and Communication. **Work Group:** 03.01. Managerial Work in Arts and Communication. **Other Jobs in This Work Group:** Agents and Business Managers of Artists, Performers, and Athletes; Art Directors; Producers; Public Relations Managers; Technical Directors/Managers. **PERSONALITY TYPE:** Enterprising.

EDUCATION/TRAINING PROGRAM(S)—Cinematography and Film/Video Production; Directing and Theatrical Production; Drama and Dramatics/Theatre Arts, General; Dramatic/Theatre Arts and Stagecraft, Other; Film/Cinema Studies; Radio and Television; Theatre/Theatre Arts Management. **RELATED KNOWLEDGE/COURSES**—**Communications and Media:** Knowledge of media production, communication, and dissemination techniques and methods. This includes alternative ways to inform and entertain via written, oral, and visual media. **Administration and Management:** Knowledge of business and management principles involved in strategic planning, resource allocation, human resources modeling, leadership technique, production methods, and coordination of people and resources. **Personnel and Human Resources:** Knowledge of principles and procedures for personnel recruitment, selection, training, compensation and benefits, labor relations and negotiation, and personnel information systems. **Economics and Accounting:** Knowledge of economic and accounting principles and practices, the financial markets, banking, and the analysis and reporting of financial data. **Telecommunications:** Knowledge of transmission, broadcasting, switching, control, and operation of telecommunications systems. **English Language:** Knowledge of the structure and content of the English language, including the meaning and spelling of words, rules of composition, and grammar.

Property, Real Estate, and Community Association Managers

- ◎ Education/Training Required: Bachelor's degree
- ◎ Annual Earnings: $39,980
- ◎ Growth: 12.8%
- ◎ Annual Job Openings: 35,000
- ◎ Self-Employed: 46.0%
- ◎ Part-Time: 15.3%

Plan, direct, or coordinate selling, buying, leasing, or governance activities of commercial, industrial, or residential real estate properties. Act as liaisons between on-site managers or tenants and owners. Confer regularly with community association members to ensure their needs are being met. Determine and certify the eligibility of prospective tenants, following government regulations. Direct and coordinate the activities of staff and contract personnel and evaluate their performance. Direct collection of monthly assessments; rental fees; and deposits and payment of insurance premiums, mortgage, taxes, and incurred operating expenses. Inspect grounds, facilities, and equipment routinely to determine necessity of repairs or maintenance. Investigate complaints, disturbances, and violations and resolve problems, following management rules and regulations. Maintain records of sales, rental or usage activity, special permits issued, maintenance and operating costs, or property availability. Manage and oversee operations, maintenance, administration, and improvement of commercial, industrial, or residential properties. Market vacant space to prospective tenants through leasing agents, advertising, or other methods. Meet with prospective tenants to show properties, explain terms of occupancy, and provide information about local areas. Negotiate the sale, lease, or development of property and complete or review appropriate documents and forms. Plan, schedule, and coordinate general maintenance, major repairs, and remodeling or construction projects for commercial or residential properties. Prepare and administer contracts for provision of property services such as cleaning, maintenance, and security services. Prepare detailed budgets and financial reports for properties. Purchase building and maintenance sup-plies, equipment, or furniture. Analyze information on property values, taxes, zoning, population growth, and traffic volume and patterns in order to determine if properties should be acquired. Clean common areas, change light bulbs, and make minor property repairs. Confer with legal authorities to ensure that renting and advertising practices are not discriminatory and that properties comply with state and federal regulations. **SKILLS—Management of Financial Resources:** Determining how money will be spent to get the work done and accounting for these expenditures. **Management of Personnel Resources:** Motivating, developing, and directing people as they work, identifying the best people for the job. **Negotiation:** Bringing others together and trying to reconcile differences. **Management of Material Resources:** Obtaining and seeing to the appropriate use of equipment, facilities, and materials needed to do certain work. **Systems Evaluation:** Identifying measures or indicators of system performance and the actions needed to improve or correct performance relative to the goals of the system. **Coordination:** Adjusting actions in relation to others' actions. **Systems Analysis:** Determining how a system should work and how changes in conditions, operations, and the environment will affect outcomes. **Judgment and Decision Making:** Considering the relative costs and benefits of potential actions to choose the most appropriate one. **GOE—Interest Area:** 14. Retail and Wholesale Sales and Service. **Work Group:** 14.01. Managerial Work in Retail/Wholesale Sales and Service. **Other Jobs in This Work Group:** Advertising and Promotions Managers; First-Line Supervisors/Managers of Non-Retail Sales Workers; First-Line Supervisors/Managers of Retail Sales Workers; Funeral Directors; Marketing Managers; Purchasing Managers; Sales Managers. **PERSONALITY TYPE:** Enterprising.

EDUCATION/TRAINING PROGRAM(S)—Real Estate. RELATED KNOWLEDGE/COURSES— Administration and Management: Knowledge of business and management principles involved in strategic planning, resource allocation, human resources modeling, leadership technique, production methods, and coordination of people and resources. **Law and Government:** Knowledge of laws, legal codes, court procedures, precedents, government regulations, executive orders, agency rules, and the democratic political process. **Sales and Marketing:** Knowledge of principles and methods for showing, promoting, and selling products or services. This includes marketing strategy and tactics, product demonstrations, sales techniques, and sales control systems. **Economics and Accounting:** Knowledge of economic and accounting principles and practices, the financial markets, banking, and the analysis and reporting of financial data. **Personnel and Human Resources:** Knowledge of principles and procedures for personnel recruitment, selection, training, compensation and benefits, labor relations and negotiation, and personnel information systems. **Building and Construction:** Knowledge of the materials, methods, and tools involved in the construction or repair of houses, buildings, or other structures such as highways and roads.

Prosthodontists

- Education/Training Required: First professional degree
- Annual Earnings: More than $145,600
- Growth: 4.1%
- Annual Job Openings: 7,000
- Self-Employed: 39.9%
- Part-Time: 22.3%

Construct oral prostheses to replace missing teeth and other oral structures to correct natural and acquired deformation of mouth and jaws; to restore and maintain oral function, such as chewing and speaking; and to improve appearance. Collaborate with general dentists, specialists, and other health professionals in order to develop solutions to dental and oral health concerns. Design and fabricate dental prostheses or supervise dental technicians and laboratory bench workers who construct the devices. Fit prostheses to patients, making any necessary adjustments and modifications. Measure and take impressions of patients' jaws and teeth in order to determine the shape and size of dental prostheses, using face bows, dental articulators, recording devices, and other materials. Replace missing teeth and associated oral structures with permanent fixtures, such as crowns and bridges, or removable fixtures, such as dentures. Restore function and aesthetics to traumatic injury victims or to individuals with diseases or birth defects. Bleach discolored teeth in order to brighten and whiten them. Place veneers onto teeth in order to con-

ceal defects. Repair, reline, and/or rebase dentures. Treat facial pain and jaw joint problems. Use bonding technology on the surface of the teeth in order to change tooth shape or to close gaps. **SKILLS—Science:** Using scientific rules and methods to solve problems. **Technology Design:** Generating or adapting equipment and technology to serve user needs. **Reading Comprehension:** Understanding written sentences and paragraphs in work-related documents. **Judgment and Decision Making:** Considering the relative costs and benefits of potential actions to choose the most appropriate one. **Critical Thinking:** Using logic and reasoning to identify the strengths and weaknesses of alternative solutions, conclusions, or approaches to problems. **Service Orientation:** Actively looking for ways to help people. **Equipment Selection:** Determining the kind of tools and equipment needed to do a job. **Mathematics:** Using mathematics to solve problems. **Operations Analysis:** Analyzing needs and product requirements to create a design. **GOE—Interest Area:** 08. Health Science. **Work Group:** 08.03. Dentistry. **Other Jobs in This Work Group:** Dental Assistants; Dental Hygienists; Dentists, General; Oral and Maxillofacial Surgeons; Orthodontists. **PERSONALITY TYPE:** Investigative.

EDUCATION/TRAINING PROGRAM(S)— Prosthodontics Specialty; Prosthodontics/Prosthodontology (Cert, MS, PhD). **RELATED KNOWLEDGE/COURSES—Medicine and Dentistry:** Knowledge of the information and techniques needed to diagnose and treat human injuries, diseases, and deformities. This includes symptoms, treatment alternatives, drug properties and interactions, and preventive health-care measures. **Chemistry:** Knowledge of the chemical composition, structure, and properties of substances and of the chemical processes and transformations that they undergo. This includes uses of chemicals and their danger signs, production techniques, and disposal methods. **Biology:** Knowledge of plant and animal organisms and their tissues, cells, functions, interdependencies, and interactions with each other and the environment. **Design:** Knowledge of design techniques, tools, and principles involved in production of precision technical plans, blueprints, drawings, and models. **English Language:** Knowledge of the structure and content of the English language, including the meaning and spelling of words, rules of composition, and grammar.

Psychiatrists

- ◉ Education/Training Required: First professional degree
- ◉ Annual Earnings: More than $145,600
- ◉ Growth: 19.5%
- ◉ Annual Job Openings: 38,000
- ◉ Self-Employed: 16.9%
- ◉ Part-Time: 8.1%

Diagnose, treat, and help prevent disorders of the mind. Analyze and evaluate patient data and test or examination findings to diagnose nature and extent of mental disorder. Prescribe, direct, and administer psychotherapeutic treatments or medications to treat mental, emotional, or behavioral disorders. Collaborate with physicians, psychologists, social workers, psychiatric nurses, or other professionals to discuss treatment plans and progress. Gather and maintain patient information and records, including social and medical history obtained from patients, relatives, and other professionals. Counsel outpatients and other patients during office visits. Design individualized care plans, using a variety of treatments. Examine or conduct laboratory or diagnostic tests on patient to provide information on general physical condition and mental disorder. Advise and inform guardians, relatives, and significant others of patients' conditions and treatment. Review and evaluate treatment procedures and outcomes of other psychiatrists and medical professionals. Teach, conduct research, and publish findings to increase understanding of mental, emotional, and behavioral states and disorders. Prepare and submit case reports and summaries to government and mental health agencies. Serve on committees to promote and maintain community mental health services and delivery systems. **SKILLS—Social Perceptiveness:** Being aware of others' reactions and understanding why they react as they do. **Persuasion:** Persuading others to change their minds or behavior. **Active Learning:** Understanding the implications of new information for both current and future problem-solving and decision-making. **Science:** Using scientific rules and methods to solve problems. **Active Listening:** Giving full attention to what other people are saying, taking time to understand the points being made, asking questions as appropriate, and not interrupting at inappropriate times. **Negotiation:** Bringing others together and trying to reconcile differences. **Systems Analysis:** Determining how a system should work and how changes in conditions, operations, and the environment will affect outcomes. **Learning Strategies:** Selecting and using training/instructional methods and procedures appropriate for the situation when learning or teaching new things. **Complex Problem Solving:** Identifying complex problems and reviewing related information to develop and evaluate options and implement solutions. **GOE—Interest Area:** 08. Health Science. **Work Group:** 08.02. Medicine and Surgery. **Other Jobs in This Work Group:** Anesthesiologists; Family and General Practitioners; Internists, General; Medical Assistants; Medical Transcriptionists; Obstetricians and Gynecologists; Pediatricians, General; Pharmacists; Pharmacy Aides; Pharmacy Technicians; Physician Assistants; Registered Nurses; Surgeons; Surgical Technologists. **PERSONALITY TYPE:** Investigative.

EDUCATION/TRAINING PROGRAM(S)— Child Psychiatry; Physical Medical and Rehabilitation/Psychiatry; Psychiatry. **RELATED KNOWLEDGE/COURSES—Therapy and Counseling:** Knowledge of principles, methods, and procedures for diagnosis, treatment, and rehabilitation of physical and mental dysfunctions and for career counseling and guidance. **Medicine and Dentistry:** Knowledge of the information and techniques needed to diagnose and treat human injuries, diseases, and deformities. This includes symptoms, treatment alternatives, drug properties and interactions, and preventive health-care measures. **Psychology:** Knowledge of human behavior and performance; individual differences in ability, personality, and interests; learning and motivation; psychological research methods; and the assessment and treatment of behavioral and affective disorders. **Biology:** Knowledge of plant and animal organisms and their tissues, cells, functions, interdependencies, and interactions with each other and the environment. **Philosophy and Theology:** Knowledge of different philosophical systems and religions. This includes their basic principles, values, ethics, ways of thinking, customs, and practices and their impact on human culture. **Sociology and Anthropology:** Knowledge of group behavior and dynamics, societal trends and influences, human migrations, ethnicity, and cultures and their history and origins.

Psychology Teachers, Postsecondary

◎ Education/Training Required: Master's degree
◎ Annual Earnings: $55,600
◎ Growth: 38.1%
◎ Annual Job Openings: 216,000
◎ Self-Employed: 0.3%
◎ Part-Time: 27.7%

Teach courses in psychology, such as child, clinical, and developmental psychology and psychological counseling. Prepare and deliver lectures to undergraduate and/or graduate students on topics such as abnormal psychology, cognitive processes, and work motivation. Evaluate and grade students' class work, laboratory work, assignments, and papers. Initiate, facilitate, and moderate classroom discussions. Compile, administer, and grade examinations or assign this work to others. Keep abreast of developments in their field by reading current literature, talking with colleagues, and participating in professional conferences. Prepare course materials such as syllabi, homework assignments, and handouts. Plan, evaluate, and revise curricula, course content, and course materials and methods of instruction. Maintain student attendance records, grades, and other required records. Supervise undergraduate and/or graduate teaching, internship, and research work. Maintain regularly scheduled office hours in order to advise and assist students. Conduct research in a particular field of knowledge and publish findings in professional journals, books, and/or electronic media. Advise students on academic and vocational curricula and on career issues. Select and obtain materials and supplies such as textbooks. Collaborate with colleagues to address teaching and research issues. Serve on academic or administrative committees that deal with institutional policies, departmental matters, and academic issues. Compile bibliographies of specialized materials for outside reading assignments. Participate in student recruitment, registration, and placement activities. Supervise students' laboratory work. Perform administrative duties such as serving as department head. Act as advisers to student organizations. Write grant proposals to procure external research funding. **SKILLS—Instructing:** Teaching others how to do something. **Learning Strategies:** Selecting and using training/instructional methods and procedures appropriate for the situation when learning or teaching new things. **Social Perceptiveness:** Being aware of others' reactions and understanding why they react as they do. **Active Learning:** Understanding the implications of new information for both current and future problem-solving and decision-making. **Science:** Using scientific rules and methods to solve problems. **Critical Thinking:** Using logic and reasoning to identify the strengths and weaknesses of alternative solutions, conclusions, or approaches to problems. **Persuasion:** Persuading others to change their minds or behavior. **Writing:** Communicating effectively in writing as appropriate for the needs of the audience. **GOE—Interest Area:** 05. Education and Training. **Work Group:** 05.03. Postsecondary and Adult Teaching and Instructing. **Other Jobs in This Work Group:** Adult Literacy, Remedial Education, and GED Teachers and Instructors; Agricultural Sciences Teachers, Postsecondary; Anthropology and Archeology Teachers, Postsecondary; Architecture Teachers, Postsecondary; Area, Ethnic, and Cultural Studies Teachers, Postsecondary; Art, Drama, and Music Teachers, Postsecondary; Atmospheric, Earth, Marine, and Space Sciences Teachers, Postsecondary; Biological Science Teachers, Postsecondary; Business Teachers, Postsecondary; Chemistry Teachers, Postsecondary; Communications Teachers, Postsecondary; Computer Science Teachers, Postsecondary; Criminal Justice and Law Enforcement Teachers, Postsecondary; Economics Teachers, Postsecondary; Education Teachers, Postsecondary; Engineering Teachers, Postsecondary; English Language and Literature Teachers, Postsecondary; Environmental Science Teachers, Postsecondary; Farm and Home Management Advisors; Foreign Language and Literature Teachers, Postsecondary; Forestry and Conservation Science Teachers, Postsecondary; Geography Teachers, Postsecondary; Graduate Teaching Assistants; Health Specialties Teachers, Postsecondary; History Teachers, Postsecondary; Home Economics Teachers, Postsecondary; Law Teachers, Postsecondary; Library Science Teachers, Postsecondary; Mathematical Science Teachers, Postsecondary; Nursing Instructors and Teachers, Postsecondary; Philosophy and Religion Teachers, Postsecondary; Physics Teachers, Postsecondary; Political Science Teachers, Postsecondary; Recreation and Fitness Studies Teachers, Postsecondary; Self-Enrichment Education Teachers; Social Work Teachers, Postsecondary; Sociology Teachers, Postsecondary; Vocational Education Teachers, Postsecondary. **PERSONALITY TYPE:** Social.

EDUCATION/TRAINING PROGRAM(S)—Clinical Psychology; Cognitive Psychology and Psycholinguistics; Community Psychology; Comparative Psychology; Counseling Psychology; Developmental and Child Psychology; Educational Psychology; Experimental Psychology; Industrial and Organizational Psychology; Marriage and Family Therapy/Counseling; Personality Psychology; Physiological Psychology/Psychobiology; Psychology Teacher Education; Psychology, General; Psychology, Other; Psychometrics and Quantitative Psychology; School Psychology; Social Psychology; Social Science Teacher Education. **RELATED KNOWLEDGE/COURSES—Psychology:** Knowledge of human behavior and performance; individual differences in ability, personality, and interests; learning and motivation; psychological research methods; and the assessment and treatment of behavioral and affective disorders. **Therapy and Counseling:** Knowledge of principles, methods, and procedures for diagnosis, treatment, and rehabilitation of physical and mental dysfunctions and for career counseling and guidance. **Education and Training:** Knowledge of principles and methods for curriculum and training design, teaching and instruction for individuals and groups, and the measurement of training effects. **Sociology and Anthropology:** Knowledge of group behavior and dynamics, societal trends and influences, human migrations, ethnicity, and cultures and their history and origins. **Philosophy and Theology:** Knowledge of different philosophical systems and religions. This includes their basic principles, values, ethics, ways of thinking, customs, and practices and their impact on human culture. **English Language:** Knowledge of the structure and content of the English language, including the meaning and spelling of words, rules of composition, and grammar.

Public Relations Managers

◎ Education/Training Required: Work experience plus degree
◎ Annual Earnings: $70,000
◎ Growth: 23.4%
◎ Annual Job Openings: 10,000
◎ Self-Employed: 0.9%
◎ Part-Time: 4.8%

Plan and direct public relations programs designed to create and maintain a favorable public image for employer or client or, if engaged in fundraising, plan and direct activities to solicit and maintain funds for special projects and nonprofit organizations. Identify main client groups and audiences and determine the best way to communicate publicity information to them. Write interesting and effective press releases, prepare information for media kits, and develop and maintain company Internet or intranet Web pages. Develop and maintain the company's corporate image and identity, which includes the use of logos and signage. Manage communications budgets. Manage special events such as sponsorship of races, parties introducing new products, or other activities the firm supports in order to gain public attention through the media without advertising directly. Draft speeches for company executives and arrange interviews and other forms of contact for them. Assign, supervise, and review the activities of public relations staff. Evaluate advertising and promotion programs for compatibility with public relations efforts. Establish and maintain effective working relationships with local and municipal government officials and media representatives. Confer with labor relations managers to develop internal communications that keep employees informed of company activities. Direct activities of external agencies, establishments, and departments that develop and implement communication strategies and information programs. Formulate policies and procedures related to public information programs, working with public relations executives. Respond to requests for information about employers' activities or status. Establish goals for soliciting funds, develop policies for collection and safeguarding of contributions, and coordinate disbursement of funds. Facilitate consumer relations or the relationship between parts of the company such as the managers and employees or different branch offices. Maintain company archives. Manage in-house communication courses. Produce films and other video products, regulate their distribution, and operate film library. **SKILLS—Social Perceptiveness:** Being aware of others' reactions and understanding why they react as they do. **Management of Financial Resources:** Determining how money will be spent to get the work done and accounting for these expenditures. **Service Orientation:** Actively looking for ways to help people. **Monitoring:** Monitoring or assessing your performance or that of other individuals or organizations to make improvements or take corrective action. **Persuasion:** Persuading others to change their minds or behavior. **Coordination:** Adjusting actions in relation to others' actions. **Negotiation:** Bringing others together and trying to reconcile differences. **Time Management:** Managing one's own time and the time of others. **GOE—Interest Area:** 03. Arts and Communication. **Work Group:** 03.01. Managerial Work in Arts and Communication. **Other Jobs in This Work Group:** Agents and Business Managers of Artists, Performers, and Athletes; Art Directors; Producers; Program Directors; Technical Directors/Managers. **PERSONALITY TYPE:** No data available.

EDUCATION/TRAINING PROGRAM(S)—Public Relations/Image Management. **RELATED KNOWLEDGE/COURSES—Sales and Marketing:** Knowledge of principles and methods for showing, promoting, and selling products or services. This includes marketing strategy and tactics, product demonstrations, sales techniques, and sales control systems. **Economics and Accounting:** Knowledge of economic and accounting principles and practices, the financial markets, banking, and the analysis and reporting of financial data. **Education and Training:** Knowledge of principles and methods for curriculum and training design, teaching and instruction for individuals and groups, and the measurement of training effects. **Law and Government:** Knowledge of laws, legal codes, court procedures, precedents, government regulations, executive orders, agency rules, and the democratic political process. **Customer and Personal Service:** Knowledge of principles and processes for providing customer and personal services. This includes customer needs assessment, meeting quality standards for services, and evaluation of customer satisfaction. **Foreign Language:** Knowledge of the structure and content of a foreign (non-English) language, including the meaning and spelling of words, rules of composition and grammar, and pronunciation.

Public Relations Specialists

- Education/Training Required: Bachelor's degree
- Annual Earnings: $43,830
- Growth: 32.9%
- Annual Job Openings: 28,000
- Self-Employed: 6.1%
- Part-Time: 12.5%

Engage in promoting or creating good will for individuals, groups, or organizations by writing or selecting favorable publicity material and releasing it through various communications media. May prepare and arrange displays and make speeches. Prepare or edit organizational publications for internal and external audiences, including employee newsletters and stockholders' reports. Respond to requests for information from the media or designate another appropriate spokesperson or information source. Establish and maintain cooperative relationships with representatives of community, consumer, employee, and public interest groups. Plan and direct development and communication of informational programs to maintain favorable public and stockholder perceptions of an organization's accomplishments and agenda. Confer with production and support personnel to produce or coordinate production of advertisements and promotions. Arrange public appearances, lectures, contests, or exhibits for clients to increase product and service awareness and to promote goodwill. Study the objectives, promotional policies, and needs of organizations to develop public relations strategies that will influence public opinion or promote ideas, products, and services. Confer with other managers to identify trends and key group interests and concerns or to provide advice on business decisions. Consult with advertising agencies or staff to arrange promotional campaigns in all types of media for products, organizations, or individuals. Coach client representatives in effective communication with the public and with employees. Prepare and deliver speeches to further public relations objectives. Purchase advertising space and time as required to promote client's product or agenda. Plan and conduct market and public opinion research to test products or determine potential for product success, communicating results to client or management. **SKILLS—Persuasion:** Persuading others to change their minds or behavior. **Service Orientation:** Actively looking for ways to help people. **Negotiation:** Bringing others together and trying to reconcile differences. **Social Perceptiveness:** Being aware of others' reactions and understanding why they react as they do. **Coordination:** Adjusting actions in relation to others' actions. **Management of Financial Resources:** Determining how money will be spent to get the work done and accounting for these expenditures. **Writing:** Communicating effectively in writing as appropriate for the needs of the audience. **Monitoring:** Monitoring or assessing your performance or that of other individuals or organizations to make improvements or take corrective action. **GOE—Interest Area:** 03. Arts and Communication. **Work Group:** 03.03. News, Broadcasting, and Public Relations. **Other Jobs in This Work Group:** Broadcast News Analysts; Caption Writers; Interpreters and Translators; Reporters and Correspondents. **PERSONALITY TYPE:** Enterprising.

EDUCATION/TRAINING PROGRAM(S)— Communication Studies/Speech Communication and Rhetoric; Family and Consumer Sciences/Human Sciences Communication; Health Communication; Political Communication; Public Relations/Image Management. **RELATED KNOWLEDGE/COURSES—Sales and Marketing:** Knowledge of principles and methods for showing, promoting, and selling products or services. This includes marketing strategy and tactics, product demonstrations, sales techniques, and sales control systems. **Customer and Personal Service:** Knowledge of principles and processes for providing customer and personal services. This includes customer needs assessment, meeting quality standards for services, and evaluation of customer satisfaction. **Communications and Media:** Knowledge of media production, communication, and dissemination techniques and methods. This includes alternative ways to inform and entertain via written, oral, and visual media. **Administration and Management:** Knowledge of business and management principles involved in strategic planning, resource allocation, human resources modeling, leadership technique, production methods, and coordination of people and resources. **Clerical Practices:** Knowledge of administrative and clerical procedures and systems such as word processing, managing files and records, stenography and transcription, designing forms, and other office procedures and terminology. **English Language:** Knowledge of the structure and content of the English language, including the meaning and spelling of words, rules of composition, and grammar.

Public Transportation Inspectors

- Education/Training Required: Work experience in a related occupation
- Annual Earnings: $50,380
- Growth: 7.7%
- Annual Job Openings: 5,000
- Self-Employed: 0.4%
- Part-Time: 3.2%

Monitor operation of public transportation systems to ensure good service and compliance with regulations. Investigate accidents, equipment failures, and complaints. Observes employees performing assigned duties to note their deportment, treatment of passengers, and adherence to company regulations and schedules. Observes and records time required to load and unload passengers or freight volume of traffic on vehicle and at stops. Investigates schedule delays, accidents, and complaints. Inspects company vehicles and other property for evidence of abuse, damage, and mechanical malfunction and directs repair. Determines need for changes in service, such as additional vehicles, route changes, and revised schedules to improve service and efficiency. Drives automobile along route to detect conditions hazardous to equipment and passengers and negotiates with local governments to eliminate hazards. Submits written reports to management with recommendations for improving service. Reports disruptions to service. Assists in dispatching equipment when necessary. Recommends promotions and disciplinary actions involving transportation personnel. **SKILLS—Operations Analysis:** Analyzing needs and product requirements to create a design. **Writing:** Communicating effectively in writing as appropriate for the needs of the audience. **Systems Evaluation:** Identifying measures or indicators of system performance and the actions needed to improve or correct performance relative to the goals of the system. **Management of Personnel Resources:** Motivating, developing, and directing people as they work, identifying the best people for the job. **Monitoring:** Monitoring or assessing your performance or that of other individuals or organizations to make improvements or take corrective action. **Speaking:** Talking to others to convey information effectively. **Systems Analysis:** Determining how a system should work and how changes in conditions, operations, and the environment will affect outcomes. **Negotiation:** Bringing others together and trying to reconcile differences. **GOE—Interest Area:** 16. Transportation, Distribution, and Logistics. **Work Group:** 16.07. Transportation Support Work. **Other Jobs in This Work Group:** Bridge and Lock Tenders; Cargo and Freight Agents; Cleaners of Vehicles and Equipment; Freight Inspectors; Railroad Yard Workers; Stevedores, Except Equipment Operators; Traffic Technicians; Train Crew Members. **PERSONALITY TYPE:** Enterprising.

EDUCATION/TRAINING PROGRAM(S)—No data available. **RELATED KNOWLEDGE/COURSES—Transportation:** Knowledge of principles and methods for moving people or goods by air, rail, sea, or road, including the relative costs and benefits. **Personnel and Human Resources:** Knowledge of principles and procedures for personnel recruitment, selection, training, compensation and benefits, labor relations and negotiation, and personnel information systems. **Public Safety and Security:** Knowledge of relevant equipment, policies, procedures, and strategies to promote effective local, state, or national security operations for the protection of people, data, property, and institutions. **Law and Government:** Knowledge of laws, legal codes, court procedures, precedents, government regulations, executive orders, agency rules, and the democratic political process. **Geography:** Knowledge of principles and methods for describing the features of land, sea, and air masses, including their physical characteristics; locations; interrelationships; and distribution of plant, animal, and human life. **Administration and Management:** Knowledge of business and management principles involved in strategic planning, resource allocation, human resources modeling, leadership technique, production methods, and coordination of people and resources.

Purchasing Agents, Except Wholesale, Retail, and Farm Products

- Education/Training Required: Bachelor's degree
- Annual Earnings: $47,680
- Growth: 11.2%
- Annual Job Openings: 29,000
- Self-Employed: 1.3%
- Part-Time: 5.5%

Purchase machinery, equipment, tools, parts, supplies, or services necessary for the operation of an establishment. Purchase raw or semi-finished materials for manufacturing. Purchase the highest quality merchandise at the lowest possible price and in correct amounts. Prepare purchase orders, solicit bid proposals, and review requisitions for goods and services. Research and evaluate suppliers based on price, quality, selection, service, support, availability, reliability, production and distribution capabilities, and the supplier's reputation and history. Analyze price proposals, financial reports, and other data and information to determine reasonable prices. Monitor and follow applicable laws and regulations. Negotiate or renegotiate and administer contracts with suppliers, vendors, and other representatives. Monitor shipments to ensure that goods come in on time and, in the event of problems, trace shipments and follow up undelivered goods. Confer with staff, users, and vendors to discuss defective or unacceptable goods or services and determine corrective action. Evaluate and monitor contract performance to ensure compliance with contractual obligations and to determine need for changes. Maintain and review computerized or manual records of items purchased, costs, delivery, product performance, and inventories. Review catalogs, industry periodicals, directories, trade journals, and Internet sites and consult with other department personnel to locate necessary goods and services. Study sales records and inventory levels of current stock to develop strategic purchasing programs that facilitate employee access to supplies. Interview vendors and visit suppliers' plants and distribution centers to examine and learn about products, services, and prices. Arrange the payment of duty and freight charges. Hire, train, and/or supervise purchasing clerks, buyers, and expediters. Write and review product specifications, maintaining a working technical knowledge of the goods or services to be purchased. Monitor changes affecting supply and demand, tracking market conditions, price trends, or futures markets. Formulate policies and procedures for bid proposals and procurement of goods and services. **SKILLS—Time Management:** Managing one's own time and the time of others. **Management of Personnel Resources:** Motivating, developing, and directing people as they work, identifying the best people for the job. **Negotiation:** Bringing others together and trying to reconcile differences. **Persuasion:** Persuading others to change their minds or behavior. **Coordination:** Adjusting actions in relation to others' actions. **Speaking:** Talking to others to convey information effectively. **Learning Strategies:** Selecting and using training/instructional methods and procedures appropriate for the situation when learning or teaching new things. **Management of Material Resources:** Obtaining and seeing to the appropriate use of equipment, facilities, and materials needed to do certain work. **GOE—Interest Area:** 14. Retail and Wholesale Sales and Service. **Work Group:** 14.05. Purchasing. **Other Jobs in This Work Group:** Wholesale and Retail Buyers, Except Farm Products. **PERSONALITY TYPE:** Enterprising.

EDUCATION/TRAINING PROGRAM(S)—Sales, Distribution, and Marketing Operations, General. **RELATED KNOWLEDGE/COURSES—Clerical Practices:** Knowledge of administrative and clerical procedures and systems such as word processing, managing files and records, stenography and transcription, designing forms, and other office procedures and terminology. **Economics and Accounting:** Knowledge of economic and accounting principles and practices, the financial markets, banking, and the analysis and reporting of financial data. **Production and Processing:** Knowledge of raw materials, production processes, quality control, costs, and other techniques for maximizing the effective manufacture and distribution of goods. **Administration and Management:** Knowledge of business and management principles involved in strategic planning, resource allocation, human resources modeling, leadership technique, production methods, and coordination of people and resources. **Computers and Electronics:** Knowledge of circuit boards, processors, chips, electronic equipment, and computer hardware and software, including applications and programming. **Mathematics:** Knowledge of arithmetic, algebra, geometry, calculus, and statistics and their applications.

Purchasing Managers

- Education/Training Required: Work experience plus degree
- Annual Earnings: $72,450
- Growth: 4.8%
- Annual Job Openings: 9,000
- Self-Employed: 0.2%
- Part-Time: 2.6%

Plan, direct, or coordinate the activities of buyers, purchasing officers, and related workers involved in purchasing materials, products, and services. Maintain records of goods ordered and received. Locate vendors of materials, equipment, or supplies and interview them in order to determine product availability and terms of sales. Prepare and process requisitions and purchase orders for supplies and equipment. Control purchasing department budgets. Interview and hire staff and oversee staff training. Review purchase order claims and contracts for conformance to company policy. Analyze market and delivery systems in order to assess present and future material availability. Develop and implement purchasing and contract management instructions, policies, and procedures. Participate in the development of specifications for equipment, products, or substitute materials. Resolve vendor or contractor grievances and claims against suppliers. Represent companies in negotiating contracts and formulating policies with suppliers. Review, evaluate, and approve specifications for issuing and awarding bids. Direct and coordinate activities of personnel engaged in buying, selling, and distributing materials, equipment, machinery, and supplies. Prepare bid awards requiring board approval. Prepare reports regarding market conditions and merchandise costs. Administer online purchasing systems. **SKILLS—Negotiation:** Bringing others together and trying to reconcile differences. **Management of Material Resources:** Obtaining and seeing to the appropriate use of equipment, facilities, and materials needed to do certain work. **Management of Financial Resources:** Determining how money will be spent to get the work done and accounting for these expenditures. **Operations Analysis:** Analyzing needs and product requirements to create a design. **Persuasion:** Persuading others to change their minds or behavior. **Time Management:** Managing one's own time and the time of others. **Active Learning:** Understanding the implications of new information for both current and future problem-solving and decision-making. **Coordination:** Adjusting actions in relation to others' actions. **GOE—Interest Area:** 14. Retail and Wholesale Sales and Service. **Work Group:** 14.01. Managerial Work in Retail/Wholesale Sales and Service. **Other Jobs in This Work Group:** Advertising and Promotions Managers; First-Line Supervisors/Managers of Non-Retail Sales Workers; First-Line Supervisors/Managers of Retail Sales Workers; Funeral Directors; Marketing Managers; Property, Real Estate, and Community Association Managers; Sales Managers. **PERSONALITY TYPE:** Enterprising.

EDUCATION/TRAINING PROGRAM(S)—Purchasing, Procurement/Acquisitions, and Contracts Management. **RELATED KNOWLEDGE/COURSES—Personnel and Human Resources:** Knowledge of principles and procedures for personnel recruitment, selection, training, compensation and benefits, labor relations and negotiation, and personnel information systems. **Economics and Accounting:** Knowledge of economic and accounting principles and practices, the financial markets, banking, and the analysis and reporting of financial data. **Production and Processing:** Knowledge of raw materials, production processes, quality control, costs, and other techniques for maximizing the effective manufacture and distribution of goods. **Administration and Management:** Knowledge of business and management principles involved in strategic planning, resource allocation, human resources modeling, leadership technique, production methods, and coordination of people and resources. **Education and Training:** Knowledge of principles and methods for curriculum and training design, teaching and instruction for individuals and groups, and the measurement of training effects. **Mathematics:** Knowledge of arithmetic, algebra, geometry, calculus, and statistics and their applications.

Radiation Therapists

- ◉ Education/Training Required: Associate degree
- ◉ Annual Earnings: $57,700
- ◉ Growth: 31.6%
- ◉ Annual Job Openings: 1,000
- ◉ Self-Employed: 0%
- ◉ Part-Time: 14.2%

Provide radiation therapy to patients as prescribed by a radiologist according to established practices and standards. Duties may include reviewing prescription and diagnosis; acting as liaison with physician and supportive care personnel; preparing equipment such as immobilization, treatment, and protection devices; and maintaining records, reports, and files. May assist in dosimetry procedures and tumor localization. Administer prescribed doses of radiation to specific body parts, using radiation therapy equipment according to established practices and standards. Position patients for treatment with accuracy according to prescription. Enter data into computer and set controls to operate and adjust equipment and regulate dosage. Follow principles of radiation protection for patient, self, and others. Maintain records, reports, and files as required, including such information as radiation dosages, equipment settings, and patients' reactions. Review prescription, diagnosis, patient chart, and identification. Conduct most treatment sessions independently in accordance with the long-term treatment plan and under the general direction of the patient's physician. Check radiation therapy equipment to ensure proper operation. Observe and reassure patients during treatment and report unusual reactions to physician or turn equipment off if unexpected adverse reactions occur. Check for side effects such as skin irritation, nausea, and hair loss to assess patients' reaction to treatment. Educate, prepare, and reassure patients and their families by answering questions, providing physical assistance, and reinforcing physicians' advice regarding treatment reactions and post-treatment care. Calculate actual treatment dosages delivered during each session. Prepare and construct equipment, such as immobilization, treatment, and protection devices. Photograph treated area of patient and process film. Help physicians, radiation oncologists, and clinical physicists to prepare physical and technical aspects of radiation treatment plans, using information about patient condition and anatomy. Train and supervise student or subordinate radiotherapy technologists. Act as liaison with physicist and supportive-care personnel. Provide assistance to other health-care personnel during dosimetry procedures and tumor localization. Implement appropriate follow-up care plans. Store, sterilize, or prepare the special applicators containing the radioactive substance implanted by the physician. Assist in the preparation of sealed radioactive materials, such as cobalt, radium, cesium, and isotopes, for use in radiation treatments. **SKILLS—Operation**

Monitoring: Watching gauges, dials, or other indicators to make sure a machine is working properly. **Technology Design:** Generating or adapting equipment and technology to serve user needs. **Operation and Control:** Controlling operations of equipment or systems. **Time Management:** Managing one's own time and the time of others. **Management of Personnel Resources:** Motivating, developing, and directing people as they work, identifying the best people for the job. **Instructing:** Teaching others how to do something. **Service Orientation:** Actively looking for ways to help people. **Social Perceptiveness:** Being aware of others' reactions and understanding why they react as they do. **GOE—Interest Area:** 08. Health Science. **Work Group:** 08.07. Medical Therapy. **Other Jobs in This Work Group:** Audiologists; Massage Therapists; Occupational Therapist Aides; Occupational Therapist Assistants; Occupational Therapists; Physical Therapist Aides; Physical Therapist Assistants; Physical Therapists; Recreational Therapists; Respiratory Therapists; Respiratory Therapy Technicians; Speech-Language Pathologists. **PERSONALITY TYPE:** Social.

EDUCATION/TRAINING PROGRAM(S)—Medical Radiologic Technology/Science—Radiation Therapist. **RELATED KNOWLEDGE/COURSES—Medicine and Dentistry:** Knowledge of the information and techniques needed to diagnose and treat human injuries, diseases, and deformities. This includes symptoms, treatment alternatives, drug properties and interactions, and preventive health-care measures. **Customer and Personal Service:** Knowledge of principles and processes for providing customer and personal services. This includes customer needs assessment, meeting quality standards for services, and evaluation of customer satisfaction. **Psychology:** Knowledge of human behavior and performance; individual differences in ability, personality, and interests; learning and motivation; psychological research methods; and the assessment and treatment of behavioral and affective disorders. **Biology:** Knowledge of plant and animal organisms and their tissues, cells, functions, interdependencies, and interactions with each other and the environment. **Physics:** Knowledge and prediction of physical principles and laws and their interrelationships and applications to understanding fluid, material, and atmospheric dynamics and mechanical, electrical, atomic, and subatomic structures and processes. **Therapy and Counseling:** Knowledge of principles, methods, and procedures for diagnosis, treatment, and rehabilitation of physical and mental dysfunctions and for career counseling and guidance.

Radiologic Technicians

◎ Education/Training Required: Associate degree
◎ Annual Earnings: $43,350
◎ Growth: 22.9%
◎ Annual Job Openings: 21,000
◎ Self-Employed: 0.2%
◎ Part-Time: 17.5%

Maintain and use equipment and supplies necessary to demonstrate portions of the human body on X-ray film or fluoroscopic screen for diagnostic purposes. Use beam-restrictive devices and patient-shielding techniques to minimize radiation exposure to patient and staff. Position X-ray equipment and adjust controls to set exposure factors, such as time and distance. Position patient on examining table and set up and adjust equipment to obtain optimum view of specific body area as requested by physician. Determine patients' X-ray needs by reading requests or instructions from physicians. Make exposures necessary for the requested procedures, rejecting and repeating work that does not meet established standards. Process exposed radiographs, using film processors or computer-generated methods. Explain procedures to patients to reduce anxieties and obtain cooperation. Perform procedures such as linear tomography; mammography; sonograms; joint and cyst aspirations; routine contrast studies; routine fluoroscopy; and examinations of the head, trunk, and extremities under supervision of physician. Prepare and set up X-ray room for patient. Assure that sterile supplies, contrast materials, catheters, and other required equipment are present and in working order, requisitioning materials as necessary. Maintain records of patients examined, examinations performed, views taken, and technical factors used. Provide assistance to physicians or other technologists in the performance of more-complex procedures. Monitor equipment operation and report malfunctioning equipment to supervisor. Provide students and other technologists with suggestions of additional views, alternate positioning, or improved techniques to ensure that the images produced are of the highest quality. Coordinate work of other technicians or technologists when procedures require more than one person. Assist with on-the-job training of new employees and students and provide input to supervisors regarding training performance. Maintain a current file of examination protocols. Operate mobile X-ray equipment in operating room, in emergency room, or at patient's bedside. Provide assistance in radiopharmaceutical administration, monitoring patients' vital signs and notifying the radiologist of any relevant changes. **SKILLS—Service Orientation:** Actively looking for ways to help people. **Science:** Using scientific rules and methods to solve problems. **Negotiation:** Bringing others together and trying to reconcile differences. **Instructing:** Teaching others how to do something. **Active Listening:** Giving full attention to what other people are saying, taking time to understand the points being made, asking questions as appropriate, and not interrupting at inappropriate times. **Social Perceptiveness:** Being aware of others' reactions and understanding why they react as they do. **Equipment Selection:** Determining the kind of tools and equipment needed to do a job. **Operation Monitoring:** Watching gauges, dials, or other indicators to make sure a machine is working properly. **GOE—Interest Area:** 08. Health Science. **Work Group:** 08.06. Medical Technology. **Other Jobs in This Work Group:** Biological Technicians; Cardiovascular Technologists and Technicians; Diagnostic Medical Sonographers; Medical and Clinical Laboratory Technicians; Medical and Clinical Laboratory Technologists; Medical Equipment Preparers; Medical Records and Health Information Technicians; Nuclear Medicine Technologists; Opticians, Dispensing; Orthotists and Prosthetists; Radiologic Technologists. **PERSONALITY TYPE:** Realistic.

EDUCATION/TRAINING PROGRAM(S)— Allied Health Diagnostic, Intervention, and Treatment Professions, Other; Medical Radiologic Technology/ Science—Radiation Therapist; Radiologic Technology/Science—Radiographer. **RELATED KNOWLEDGE/COURSES—Clerical Practices:** Knowledge of administrative and clerical procedures and systems such as word processing, managing files and records, stenography and transcription, designing forms, and other office procedures and terminology. **Psychology:** Knowledge of human behavior and performance; individual differences in ability, personality, and interests; learning and motivation; psychological research methods; and the assessment and treatment of behavioral

and affective disorders. **Medicine and Dentistry:** Knowledge of the information and techniques needed to diagnose and treat human injuries, diseases, and deformities. This includes symptoms, treatment alternatives, drug properties and interactions, and preventive health-care measures. **Customer and Personal Service:** Knowledge of principles and processes for providing customer and personal services. This includes customer needs assessment, meeting quality standards for services, and evaluation of customer satisfaction. **Physics:** Knowledge and prediction of physical principles and laws and their interrelationships and applications to understanding fluid, material, and atmospheric dynamics and mechanical, electrical, atomic, and subatomic structures and processes. **English Language:** Knowledge of the structure and content of the English language, including the meaning and spelling of words, rules of composition, and grammar.

Radiologic Technologists

- Education/Training Required: Associate degree
- Annual Earnings: $43,350
- Growth: 22.9%
- Annual Job Openings: 21,000
- Self-Employed: 0.2%
- Part-Time: 17.5%

Take X rays and CAT scans or administer nonradioactive materials into patient's bloodstream for diagnostic purposes. Includes technologists who specialize in other modalities, such as computed tomography, ultrasound, and magnetic resonance. Review and evaluate developed X rays, videotape, or computergenerated information to determine if images are satisfactory for diagnostic purposes. Use radiation safety measures and protection devices to comply with government regulations and to ensure safety of patients and staff. Explain procedures and observe patients to ensure safety and comfort during scan. Operate or oversee operation of radiologic and magnetic imaging equipment to produce images of the body for diagnostic purposes. Position and immobilize patient on examining table. Position imaging equipment and adjust controls to set exposure time and distance, according to specification of examination. Key commands and data into computer to document and specify scan sequences, adjust transmitters and receivers, or photograph certain images. Monitor video display of area being scanned and adjust density or contrast to improve picture quality. Monitor patients' conditions and reactions, reporting abnormal signs to physician. Set up examination rooms, ensuring that all necessary equipment is ready. Prepare and administer oral or injected contrast media to patients. Take thorough and accurate patient medical histories. Remove and process film. Record, process, and maintain patient data and treatment records and prepare reports. Coordinate work with clerical personnel and other technologists. Demonstrate new equipment, procedures, and techniques to staff and provide technical assistance. Provide assistance with such tasks as dressing and changing to seriously ill, injured, or disabled patients. Move ultrasound scanner over patient's body and watch pattern produced on video screen. Measure thickness of section to be radiographed, using instruments similar to measuring tapes. Operate fluoroscope to aid physician to view and guide wire or catheter through blood vessels to area of interest. Assign duties to radiologic staff to maintain patient flows and achieve production goals. Collaborate with other medical team members, such as physicians and nurses, to conduct angiography or special vascular procedures. Perform administrative duties such as developing departmental operating budget, coordinating purchases of supplies and equipment, and preparing work schedules. **SKILLS—Instructing:** Teaching others how to do something. **Social Perceptiveness:** Being aware of others' reactions and understanding why they react as they do. **Service Orientation:** Actively looking for ways to help people. **Reading Comprehension:** Understanding written sentences and paragraphs in work-related documents. **Operation Monitoring:** Watching gauges, dials, or other indicators to make sure a machine is working properly. **Active Listening:** Giving full attention to what other people are saying, taking time to understand the points being made, asking questions as appropriate, and not interrupting at inappropriate times. **Speaking:** Talking to others to convey information effectively. **Critical Thinking:** Using logic and reasoning to identify the strengths and weaknesses of alternative solutions, conclusions, or approaches to problems. **Learning Strategies:** Selecting and using training/instructional methods and procedures appropriate for the situation when learning or teaching new things. **Coordination:** Adjusting actions

in relation to others' actions. **GOE—Interest Area:** 08. Health Science. **Work Group:** 08.06. Medical Technology. **Other Jobs in This Work Group:** Biological Technicians; Cardiovascular Technologists and Technicians; Diagnostic Medical Sonographers; Medical and Clinical Laboratory Technicians; Medical and Clinical Laboratory Technologists; Medical Equipment Preparers; Medical Records and Health Information Technicians; Nuclear Medicine Technologists; Opticians, Dispensing; Orthotists and Prosthetists; Radiologic Technicians. **PERSONALITY TYPE:** Realistic.

EDUCATION/TRAINING PROGRAM(S)— Allied Health Diagnostic, Intervention, and Treatment Professions, Other; Medical Radiologic Technology/Science—Radiation Therapist; Radiologic Technology/Science—Radiographer. **RELATED KNOWLEDGE/COURSES—Medicine and Dentistry:** Knowledge of the information and techniques needed to diagnose and treat human injuries, diseases, and deformities. This includes symptoms, treatment alternatives, drug properties and interactions, and preventive health-care measures. **Customer and Personal Service:** Knowledge of principles and processes for providing customer and personal services. This includes customer needs assessment, meeting quality standards for services, and evaluation of customer satisfaction. **Psychology:** Knowledge of human behavior and performance; individual differences in ability, personality, and interests; learning and motivation; psychological research methods; and the assessment and treatment of behavioral and affective disorders. **Physics:** Knowledge and prediction of physical principles and laws and their interrelationships and applications to understanding fluid, material, and atmospheric dynamics and mechanical, electrical, atomic, and subatomic structures and processes. **Biology:** Knowledge of plant and animal organisms and their tissues, cells, functions, interdependencies, and interactions with each other and the environment. **Chemistry:** Knowledge of the chemical composition, structure, and properties of substances and of the chemical processes and transformations that they undergo. This includes uses of chemicals and their danger signs, production techniques, and disposal methods.

Railroad Inspectors

- Education/Training Required: Work experience in a related occupation
- Annual Earnings: $50,380
- Growth: 7.7%
- Annual Job Openings: 5,000
- Self-Employed: 0.4%
- Part-Time: 3.2%

Inspect railroad equipment, roadbed, and track to ensure safe transport of people or cargo. Fills paint container on rail-detector car used to mark section of defective rail with paint. Directs crews to repair or replace defective equipment or to re-ballast roadbed. Places lanterns or flags in front and rear of train to signal that inspection is being performed. Seals leaks found during inspection that can be sealed with caulking compound. Replaces defective brake rod pins and tightens safety appliances. Notifies train dispatcher of railcar to be moved to shop for repair. Makes minor repairs. Packs brake bearings with grease. Inspects signals and track wiring to determine continuity of electrical connections. Examines roadbed, switches, fishplates, rails, and ties to detect damage or wear. Examines locomotives and cars to detect damage or structural defects. Inspects and tests completed work. Operates switches to determine working conditions. Tests and synchronizes rail-flaw-detection machine, using circuit tester and hand tools, and reloads machine with paper and ink. Starts machine and signals worker to operate rail-detector car. Prepares reports on repairs made and equipment, railcars, or roadbed needing repairs. Tags railcars needing immediate repair. **SKILLS—Repairing:** Repairing machines or systems by using the needed tools. **Troubleshooting:** Determining causes of operating errors and deciding what to do about them. **Operation Monitoring:** Watching gauges, dials, or other indicators to make sure a machine is working properly. **Equipment Maintenance:** Performing routine maintenance on equipment and determining when and what kind of maintenance is needed. **Quality Control Analysis:** Conducting tests and inspections of products, services, or processes to evaluate quality or performance. **Management of Personnel Resources:** Motivating, developing, and directing people as they work, identifying the best people for the job. **Systems Analysis:** Determining how a system should work and how changes in conditions, operations, and the environment will affect outcomes. **Science:** Using scientific rules and methods to solve problems. **Time Management:** Managing one's own time and the time of others. **GOE—Interest Area:** 07. Government and Public Administration. **Work Group:** 07.03. Regulations Enforcement. **Other Jobs in This Work Group:** Agricultural Inspectors; Aviation Inspectors; Child Support, Missing Persons, and Unemployment Insurance Fraud Investigators; Environmental Compliance Inspectors; Equal Opportunity Representatives and Officers; Financial Examiners; Fire Inspectors; Fish and Game Wardens; Forest Fire Inspectors and Prevention Specialists; Government Property Inspectors and Investigators; Immigration and Customs Inspectors; Licensing Examiners and Inspectors; Marine Cargo Inspectors; Mechanical Inspectors; Motor Vehicle Inspectors; Nuclear Monitoring Technicians; Occupational Health and Safety Specialists; Pressure Vessel Inspectors; Tax Examiners, Collectors, and Revenue Agents. **PERSONALITY TYPE:** Realistic.

EDUCATION/TRAINING PROGRAM(S)—No data available. **RELATED KNOWLEDGE/COURSES—Transportation:** Knowledge of principles and methods for moving people or goods by air, rail, sea, or road, including the relative costs and benefits. **Public Safety and Security:** Knowledge of relevant equipment, policies, procedures, and strategies to promote effective local, state, or national security operations for the protection of people, data, property, and institutions. **Mechanical Devices:** Knowledge of machines and tools, including their designs, uses, repair, and maintenance. **Engineering and Technology:** Knowledge of the practical application of engineering science and technology. This includes applying principles, techniques, procedures, and equipment to the design and production of various goods and services. **Building and Construction:** Knowledge of the materials, methods, and tools involved in the construction or repair of houses, buildings, or other structures such as highways and roads. **Geography:** Knowledge of principles and methods for describing the features of land, sea, and air masses, including their physical characteristics; locations; interrelationships; and distribution of plant, animal, and human life.

Real Estate Brokers

- ◎ Education/Training Required: Work experience in a related occupation
- ◎ Annual Earnings: $58,720
- ◎ Growth: 2.4%
- ◎ Annual Job Openings: 11,000
- ◎ Self-Employed: 59.1%
- ◎ Part-Time: 14.8%

Operate real estate office or work for commercial real estate firm, overseeing real estate transactions. Other duties usually include selling real estate or renting properties and arranging loans. Sell, for a fee, real estate owned by others. Obtain agreements from property owners to place properties for sale with real estate firms. Monitor fulfillment of purchase contract terms to ensure that they are handled in a timely manner. Compare a property with similar properties that have recently sold in order to determine its competitive market price. Act as an intermediary in negotiations between buyers and sellers over property prices and settlement details and during the closing of sales. Generate lists of properties for sale, their locations and descriptions, and available financing options, using computers. Maintain knowledge of real estate law; local economies; fair housing laws; and types of available mortgages, financing options, and government programs. Check work completed by loan officers, attorneys, and other professionals to ensure that it is performed properly. Arrange for financing of property purchases. Appraise property values, assessing income potential when relevant. Maintain awareness of current income tax regulations, local zoning, building and tax laws, and growth possibilities of the area where a property is located. Manage and operate real estate offices, handling associated business details. Supervise agents who handle real estate transactions. Rent properties or manage rental properties. Arrange for title searches of properties being sold. Give buyers virtual tours of properties in which they are interested, using computers. Review property details to ensure that environmental regulations are met. Develop, sell, or lease property used for industry or manufacturing. **SKILLS—Negotiation:** Bringing others together and trying to reconcile differences. **Management of Financial Resources:** Determining how money will be spent to get the work done and accounting for these expenditures. **Persuasion:** Persuading others to change their minds or behavior. **Service Orientation:** Actively looking for ways to help people. **Active Listening:** Giving full attention to what other people are saying, taking time to understand the points being made, asking questions as appropriate, and not interrupting at inappropriate times. **Judgment and Decision Making:** Considering the relative costs and benefits of potential actions to choose the most appropriate one. **Mathematics:** Using mathematics to solve problems. **Complex Problem Solving:** Identifying complex problems and reviewing related information to develop and evaluate options and implement solutions. **GOE—Interest Area:** 14. Retail and Wholesale Sales and Service. **Work Group:** 14.03. General Sales. **Other Jobs in This Work Group:** Parts Salespersons; Real Estate Sales Agents; Retail Salespersons; Sales Representatives, Wholesale and Manufacturing, Except Technical and Scientific Products; Service Station Attendants. **PERSONALITY TYPE:** No data available.

EDUCATION/TRAINING PROGRAM(S)—Real Estate. **RELATED KNOWLEDGE/COURSES—Sales and Marketing:** Knowledge of principles and methods for showing, promoting, and selling products or services. This includes marketing strategy and tactics, product demonstrations, sales techniques, and sales control systems. **Customer and Personal Service:** Knowledge of principles and processes for providing customer and personal services. This includes customer needs assessment, meeting quality standards for services, and evaluation of customer satisfaction. **Law and Government:** Knowledge of laws, legal codes, court procedures, precedents, government regulations, executive orders, agency rules, and the democratic political process. **Personnel and Human Resources:** Knowledge of principles and procedures for personnel recruitment, selection, training, compensation and benefits, labor relations and negotiation, and personnel information systems. **Building and Construction:** Knowledge of the materials, methods, and tools involved in the construction or repair of houses, buildings, or other structures such as highways and roads. **Administration and Management:** Knowledge of business and management principles involved in strategic planning, resource allocation, human resources modeling, leadership technique, production methods, and coordination of people and resources.

Real Estate Sales Agents

- Education/Training Required: Postsecondary vocational training
- Annual Earnings: $35,670
- Growth: 5.7%
- Annual Job Openings: 34,000
- Self-Employed: 59.0%
- Part-Time: 14.8%

Rent, buy, or sell property for clients. Perform duties such as studying property listings, interviewing prospective clients, accompanying clients to property site, discussing conditions of sale, and drawing up real estate contracts. Includes agents who represent buyer. Present purchase offers to sellers for consideration. Confer with escrow companies, lenders, home inspectors, and pest control operators to ensure that terms and conditions of purchase agreements are met before closing dates. Interview clients to determine what kinds of properties they are seeking. Prepare documents such as representation contracts, purchase agreements, closing statements, deeds, and leases. Coordinate property closings, overseeing signing of documents and disbursement of funds. Act as an intermediary in negotiations between buyers and sellers, generally representing one or the other. Promote sales of properties through advertisements, open houses, and participation in multiple listing services. Compare a property with similar properties that have recently sold in order to determine its competitive market price. Coordinate appointments to show homes to prospective buyers. Generate lists of properties that are compatible with buyers' needs and financial resources. Display commercial, industrial, agricultural, and residential properties to clients and explain their features. Arrange for title searches to determine whether clients have clear property titles. Review plans for new construction with clients, enumerating and recommending available options and features. Answer clients' questions regarding construction work, financing, maintenance, repairs, and appraisals. Inspect condition of premises and arrange for necessary maintenance or notify owners of maintenance needs. Accompany buyers during visits to and inspections of property, advising them on the suitability and value of the homes they are visiting. Advise sellers on how to make homes more appealing to potential buyers. Arrange meetings between buyers and sellers when details of transactions need to be negotiated. Advise clients on market conditions, prices, mortgages, legal requirements, and related matters. Evaluate mortgage options to help clients obtain financing at the best prevailing rates and terms. Review property listings, trade journals, and relevant literature and attend conventions, seminars, and staff and association meetings in order to remain knowledgeable about real estate markets. **SKILLS—Negotiation:** Bringing others together and trying to reconcile differences. **Coordination:** Adjusting actions in relation to others' actions. **Service Orientation:** Actively looking for ways to help people. **Time Management:** Managing one's own time and the time of others. **Social Perceptiveness:** Being aware of others' reactions and understanding why they react as they do. **Speaking:** Talking to others to convey information effectively. **Active Listening:** Giving full attention to what other people are saying, taking time to understand the points being made, asking questions as appropriate, and not interrupting at inappropriate times. **Writing:** Communicating effectively in writing as appropriate for the needs of the audience. **Management of Financial Resources:** Determining how money will be spent to get the work done and accounting for these expenditures. **GOE—Interest Area:** 14. Retail and Wholesale Sales and Service. **Work Group:** 14.03. General Sales. **Other Jobs in This Work Group:** Parts Salespersons; Real Estate Brokers; Retail Salespersons; Sales Representatives, Wholesale and Manufacturing, Except Technical and Scientific Products; Service Station Attendants. **PERSONALITY TYPE:** Enterprising.

EDUCATION/TRAINING PROGRAM(S)—Real Estate. **RELATED KNOWLEDGE/COURSES—Sales and Marketing:** Knowledge of principles and methods for showing, promoting, and selling products or services. This includes marketing strategy and tactics, product demonstrations, sales techniques, and sales control systems. **Customer and Personal Service:** Knowledge of principles and processes for providing customer and personal services. This includes customer needs assessment, meeting quality standards for services, and evaluation of customer satisfaction. **Clerical Practices:** Knowledge of administrative and clerical procedures and systems such as word processing, managing files and records, stenography and transcription, designing forms, and other office procedures and terminology. **Law and Government:** Knowledge of laws, legal codes, court procedures, precedents, government regulations, executive orders, agency rules,

R

and the democratic political process. **Economics and Accounting:** Knowledge of economic and accounting principles and practices, the financial markets, banking, and the analysis and reporting of financial data. **Administration and Management:** Knowledge of business and management principles involved in strategic planning, resource allocation, human resources modeling, leadership technique, production methods, and coordination of people and resources.

Receptionists and Information Clerks

- Education/Training Required: Short-term on-the-job training
- Annual Earnings: $21,830
- Growth: 29.5%
- Annual Job Openings: 296,000
- Self-Employed: 1.2%
- Part-Time: 31.5%

Answer inquiries and obtain information for general public, customers, visitors, and other interested parties. Provide information regarding activities conducted at establishment and location of departments, offices, and employees within organization. Operate telephone switchboard to answer, screen, and forward calls, providing information, taking messages, and scheduling appointments. Receive payment and record receipts for services. Perform administrative support tasks such as proofreading, transcribing handwritten information, and operating calculators or computers to work with pay records, invoices, balance sheets, and other documents. Greet persons entering establishment, determine nature and purpose of visit, and direct or escort them to specific destinations. Hear and resolve complaints from customers and public. File and maintain records. Transmit information or documents to customers, using computer, mail, or facsimile machine. Schedule appointments and maintain and update appointment calendars. Analyze data to determine answers to questions from customers or members of the public. Provide information about establishment such as location of departments or offices, employees within the organization, or services provided. Keep a current record of staff members' whereabouts and availability. Collect, sort, distribute, and prepare mail, messages, and courier deliveries. Calcu-

late and quote rates for tours, stocks, insurance policies, and other products and services. Take orders for merchandise or materials and send them to the proper departments to be filled. Process and prepare memos, correspondence, travel vouchers, or other documents. Schedule space and equipment for special programs and prepare lists of participants. Enroll individuals to participate in programs and notify them of their acceptance. **SKILLS—Service Orientation:** Actively looking for ways to help people. **Social Perceptiveness:** Being aware of others' reactions and understanding why they react as they do. **Active Listening:** Giving full attention to what other people are saying, taking time to understand the points being made, asking questions as appropriate, and not interrupting at inappropriate times. **Writing:** Communicating effectively in writing as appropriate for the needs of the audience. **Reading Comprehension:** Understanding written sentences and paragraphs in work-related documents. **Speaking:** Talking to others to convey information effectively. **Critical Thinking:** Using logic and reasoning to identify the strengths and weaknesses of alternative solutions, conclusions, or approaches to problems. **Learning Strategies:** Selecting and using training/instructional methods and procedures appropriate for the situation when learning or teaching new things. **GOE—Interest Area:** 14. Retail and Wholesale Sales and Service. **Work Group:** 14.06. Customer Service. **Other Jobs in This Work Group:** Adjustment Clerks; Cashiers; Counter and Rental Clerks; Customer Service Representatives, Utilities; Gaming Change Persons and Booth Cashiers; Order Clerks. **PERSONALITY TYPE:** Conventional.

EDUCATION/TRAINING PROGRAM(S)—General Office Occupations and Clerical Services; Health Unit Coordinator/Ward Clerk; Medical Reception/Receptionist; Receptionist. **RELATED KNOWLEDGE/COURSES—Customer and Personal Service:** Knowledge of principles and processes for providing customer and personal services. This includes customer needs assessment, meeting quality standards for services, and evaluation of customer satisfaction. **Clerical Practices:** Knowledge of administrative and clerical procedures and systems such as word processing, managing files and records, stenography and transcription, designing forms, and other office procedures and terminology. **Computers and Electronics:** Knowledge of circuit boards, processors, chips, electronic equipment, and computer hardware and software, including applications and programming.

Transportation: Knowledge of principles and methods for moving people or goods by air, rail, sea, or road, including the relative costs and benefits. **Administration and Management:** Knowledge of business and management principles involved in strategic planning, resource allocation, human resources modeling, leadership technique, production methods, and coordination of people and resources. **English Language:** Knowledge of the structure and content of the English language, including the meaning and spelling of words, rules of composition, and grammar.

Recreation and Fitness Studies Teachers, Postsecondary

- Education/Training Required: Master's degree
- Annual Earnings: $44,320
- Growth: 38.1%
- Annual Job Openings: 216,000
- Self-Employed: 0.3%
- Part-Time: 27.7%

Teach courses pertaining to recreation, leisure, and fitness studies, including exercise physiology and facilities management. Evaluate and grade students' class work, assignments, and papers. Maintain student attendance records, grades, and other required records. Prepare and deliver lectures to undergraduate and/or graduate students on topics such as anatomy, therapeutic recreation, and conditioning theory. Prepare course materials such as syllabi, homework assignments, and handouts. Compile, administer, and grade examinations or assign this work to others. Maintain regularly scheduled office hours in order to advise and assist students. Plan, evaluate, and revise curricula, course content, and course materials and methods of instruction. Initiate, facilitate, and moderate classroom discussions. Keep abreast of developments in their field by reading current literature, talking with colleagues, and participating in professional conferences. Advise students on academic and vocational curricula and on career issues. Participate in student recruitment, registration, and placement activities. Collaborate with colleagues to address teaching and research issues. Select and obtain materials and supplies such as textbooks.

Participate in campus and community events. Serve on academic or administrative committees that deal with institutional policies, departmental matters, and academic issues. Compile bibliographies of specialized materials for outside reading assignments. Supervise undergraduate and/or graduate teaching, internship, and research work. Perform administrative duties such as serving as department heads. Prepare students to act as sports coaches. Conduct research in a particular field of knowledge and publish findings in professional journals, books, and/or electronic media. Act as advisers to student organizations. **SKILLS—Instructing:** Teaching others how to do something. **Learning Strategies:** Selecting and using training/instructional methods and procedures appropriate for the situation when learning or teaching new things. **Social Perceptiveness:** Being aware of others' reactions and understanding why they react as they do. **Persuasion:** Persuading others to change their minds or behavior. **Time Management:** Managing one's own time and the time of others. **Service Orientation:** Actively looking for ways to help people. **Negotiation:** Bringing others together and trying to reconcile differences. **Active Learning:** Understanding the implications of new information for both current and future problem-solving and decision-making. **Monitoring:** Monitoring or assessing your performance or that of other individuals or organizations to make improvements or take corrective action. **GOE—Interest Area:** 05. Education and Training. **Work Group:** 05.03. Postsecondary and Adult Teaching and Instructing. **Other Jobs in This Work Group:** Adult Literacy, Remedial Education, and GED Teachers and Instructors; Agricultural Sciences Teachers, Postsecondary; Anthropology and Archeology Teachers, Postsecondary; Architecture Teachers, Postsecondary; Area, Ethnic, and Cultural Studies Teachers, Postsecondary; Art, Drama, and Music Teachers, Postsecondary; Atmospheric, Earth, Marine, and Space Sciences Teachers, Postsecondary; Biological Science Teachers, Postsecondary; Business Teachers, Postsecondary; Chemistry Teachers, Postsecondary; Communications Teachers, Postsecondary; Computer Science Teachers, Postsecondary; Criminal Justice and Law Enforcement Teachers, Postsecondary; Economics Teachers, Postsecondary; Education Teachers, Postsecondary; Engineering Teachers, Postsecondary; English Language and Literature Teachers, Postsecondary; Environmental Science Teachers, Postsecondary; Farm and Home Management Advisors; Foreign Language and Literature Teachers, Postsecondary; Forestry and Conservation Science Teachers, Postsecondary; Geography Teachers, Postsecondary; Graduate Teaching Assistants; Health Specialties Teachers, Postsecondary; History Teachers, Postsecondary; Home Economics Teachers, Postsecondary; Law Teachers, Postsecondary; Library Science Teachers, Postsecondary; Mathematical Science Teachers, Postsecondary; Nursing Instructors and Teachers, Postsecondary; Philosophy and Religion Teachers, Postsecondary; Physics Teachers, Postsecondary; Political Science Teachers, Postsecondary; Psychology Teachers, Postsecondary; Self-Enrichment Education Teachers; Social Work Teachers, Postsecondary; Sociology Teachers, Postsecondary; Vocational Education Teachers, Postsecondary. **PERSONALITY TYPE:** No data available.

EDUCATION/TRAINING PROGRAM(S)— Health and Physical Education, General; Parks, Recreation and Leisure Studies; Sport and Fitness Administration/Management. **RELATED KNOWLEDGE/COURSES—Education and Training:** Knowledge of principles and methods for curriculum and training design, teaching and instruction for individuals and groups, and the measurement of training effects. **Psychology:** Knowledge of human behavior and performance; individual differences in ability, personality, and interests; learning and motivation; psychological research methods; and the assessment and treatment of behavioral and affective disorders. **English Language:** Knowledge of the structure and content of the English language, including the meaning and spelling of words, rules of composition, and grammar. **Personnel and Human Resources:** Knowledge of principles and procedures for personnel recruitment, selection, training, compensation and benefits, labor relations and negotiation, and personnel information systems. **Customer and Personal Service:** Knowledge of principles and processes for providing customer and personal services. This includes customer needs assessment, meeting quality standards for services, and evaluation of customer satisfaction. **Philosophy and Theology:** Knowledge of different philosophical systems and religions. This includes their basic principles, values, ethics, ways of thinking, customs, and practices and their impact on human culture.

Recreation Workers

- Education/Training Required: Bachelor's degree
- Annual Earnings: $19,320
- Growth: 20.5%
- Annual Job Openings: 56,000
- Self-Employed: 5.7%
- Part-Time: 35.6%

Conduct recreation activities with groups in public, private, or volunteer agencies or recreation facilities. Organize and promote activities such as arts and crafts, sports, games, music, dramatics, social recreation, camping, and hobbies, taking into account the needs and interests of individual members. Enforce rules and regulations of recreational facilities in order to maintain discipline and ensure safety. Organize, lead, and promote interest in recreational activities such as arts, crafts, sports, games, camping, and hobbies. Manage the daily operations of recreational facilities. Administer first aid according to prescribed procedures and notify emergency medical personnel when necessary. Ascertain and interpret group interests, evaluate equipment and facilities, and adapt activities to meet participant needs. Greet new arrivals to activities, introducing them to other participants, explaining facility rules, and encouraging their participation. Explain principles, techniques, and safety procedures to participants in recreational activities and demonstrate use of materials and equipment. Evaluate recreation areas, facilities, and services in order to determine if they are producing desired results. Complete and maintain time and attendance forms and inventory lists. Confer with management in order to discuss and resolve participant complaints. Supervise and coordinate the work activities of personnel, such as training staff members and assigning work duties. Meet and collaborate with agency personnel, community organizations, and other professional personnel to plan balanced recreational programs for participants. Schedule maintenance and use of facilities. Direct special activities or events such as aquatics, gymnastics, or performing arts. Meet with staff to discuss rules, regulations, and work-related problems. Provide for entertainment and set up related decorations and equipment. Encourage participants to develop their own activities and leadership skills through group discussions. Serve as liaison between park or recreation administrators and activity instructors. Evaluate staff performance, recording evaluations on appropriate forms. Oversee the purchase, planning, design, construction, and upkeep of recreation facilities and areas. **SKILLS—Management of Personnel Resources:** Motivating, developing, and directing people as they work, identifying the best people for the job. **Service Orientation:** Actively looking for ways to help people. **Management of Financial Resources:** Determining how money will be spent to get the work done and accounting for these expenditures. **Social Perceptiveness:** Being aware of others' reactions and understanding why they react as they do. **Management of Material Resources:** Obtaining and seeing to the appropriate use of equipment, facilities, and materials needed to do certain work. **Time Management:** Managing one's own time and the time of others. **Instructing:** Teaching others how to do something. **Coordination:** Adjusting actions in relation to others' actions. **GOE—Interest Area:** 09. Hospitality, Tourism, and Recreation. **Work Group:** 09.02. Recreational Services. **Other Jobs in This Work Group:** Amusement and Recreation Attendants; Gaming and Sports Book Writers and Runners; Gaming Dealers; Locker Room, Coatroom, and Dressing Room Attendants; Motion Picture Projectionists; Slot Key Persons; Ushers, Lobby Attendants, and Ticket Takers. **PERSONALITY TYPE:** Social.

EDUCATION/TRAINING PROGRAM(S)— Health and Physical Education/Fitness, Other; Parks, Recreation, and Leisure Facilities Management; Parks, Recreation, and Leisure Studies; Parks, Recreation, Leisure, and Fitness Studies, Other; Sport and Fitness Administration/Management. **RELATED KNOWLEDGE/COURSES—Customer and Personal Service:** Knowledge of principles and processes for providing customer and personal services. This includes customer needs assessment, meeting quality standards for services, and evaluation of customer satisfaction. **Psychology:** Knowledge of human behavior and performance; individual differences in ability, personality, and interests; learning and motivation; psychological research methods; and the assessment and treatment of behavioral and affective disorders. **Clerical Practices:** Knowledge of administrative and clerical procedures and systems such as word processing, managing files and records, stenography and transcription, designing forms, and other office procedures and terminology. **Education and Training:** Knowledge of principles and methods for curriculum and training

design, teaching and instruction for individuals and groups, and the measurement of training effects. **Therapy and Counseling:** Knowledge of principles, methods, and procedures for diagnosis, treatment, and rehabilitation of physical and mental dysfunctions and for career counseling and guidance. **Sales and Marketing:** Knowledge of principles and methods for showing, promoting, and selling products or services. This includes marketing strategy and tactics, product demonstrations, sales techniques, and sales control systems.

Recreational Vehicle Service Technicians

- ◎ Education/Training Required: Long-term on-the-job training
- ◎ Annual Earnings: $28,980
- ◎ Growth: 21.8%
- ◎ Annual Job Openings: 4,000
- ◎ Self-Employed: 1.2%
- ◎ Part-Time: 14.2%

Diagnose, inspect, adjust, repair, or overhaul recreational vehicles, including travel trailers. May specialize in maintaining gas, electrical, hydraulic, plumbing, or chassis/towing systems as well as repairing generators, appliances, and interior components. Confer with customers, read work orders, and examine vehicles needing repair in order to determine the nature and extent of damage. Connect electrical systems to outside power sources and activate switches to test the operation of appliances and light fixtures. Connect water hoses to inlet pipes of plumbing systems and test operation of toilets and sinks. Examine or test operation of parts or systems that have been repaired to ensure completeness of repairs. Inspect recreational vehicles to diagnose problems and then perform necessary adjustment, repair, or overhaul. List parts needed, estimate costs, and plan work procedures, using parts lists, technical manuals, and diagrams. Locate and repair frayed wiring, broken connections, or incorrect wiring, using ohmmeters, soldering irons, tape, and hand tools. Remove damaged exterior panels and repair and replace structural frame members. Repair leaks with caulking compound or replace pipes, using pipe wrenches. Repair plumbing and propane gas lines, using caulking compounds and plastic or copper pipe. Open and close doors, windows, and drawers to test their operation, trimming edges to fit as necessary. Refinish wood surfaces on cabinets, doors, moldings, and floors, using power sanders, putty, spray equipment, brushes, paints, or varnishes. Reset hardware, using chisels, mallets, and screwdrivers. Seal open sides of modular units to prepare them for shipment, using polyethylene sheets, nails, and hammers. **SKILLS—Installation:** Installing equipment, machines, wiring, or programs to meet specifications. **Repairing:** Repairing machines or systems by using the needed tools. **Troubleshooting:** Determining causes of operating errors and deciding what to do about them. **Equipment Maintenance:** Performing routine maintenance on equipment and determining when and what kind of maintenance is needed. **Quality Control Analysis:** Conducting tests and inspections of products, services, or processes to evaluate quality or performance. **Systems Evaluation:** Identifying measures or indicators of system performance and the actions needed to improve or correct performance relative to the goals of the system. **Equipment Selection:** Determining the kind of tools and equipment needed to do a job. **Technology Design:** Generating or adapting equipment and technology to serve user needs. **Management of Material Resources:** Obtaining and seeing to the appropriate use of equipment, facilities, and materials needed to do certain work. **GOE—Interest Area:** 13. Manufacturing. **Work Group:** 13.14. Vehicle and Facility Mechanical Work. **Other Jobs in This Work Group:** Aircraft Body and Bonded Structure Repairers; Aircraft Engine Specialists; Aircraft Rigging Assemblers; Aircraft Structure Assemblers, Precision; Aircraft Systems Assemblers, Precision; Airframe-and-Power-Plant Mechanics; Automotive Body and Related Repairers; Automotive Glass Installers and Repairers; Automotive Master Mechanics; Automotive Specialty Technicians; Bus and Truck Mechanics and Diesel Engine Specialists; Farm Equipment Mechanics; Fiberglass Laminators and Fabricators; Mobile Heavy Equipment Mechanics, Except Engines; Motorboat Mechanics; Motorcycle Mechanics; Outdoor Power Equipment and Other Small Engine Mechanics; Rail Car Repairers; Tire Repairers and Changers. **PERSONALITY TYPE:** Realistic.

EDUCATION/TRAINING PROGRAM(S)—Vehicle Maintenance and Repair Technologies, Other. **RELATED KNOWLEDGE/COURSES—Building and Construction:** Knowledge of the materials, methods, and tools involved in the construction or repair of houses, buildings, or other structures such as highways and roads. **Mechanical Devices:** Knowledge of machines and tools, including their designs, uses, repair, and maintenance. **Design:** Knowledge of design techniques, tools, and principles involved in production of precision technical plans, blueprints, drawings, and models. **Engineering and Technology:** Knowledge of the practical application of engineering science and technology. This includes applying principles, techniques, procedures, and equipment to the design and production of various goods and services. **Physics:** Knowledge and prediction of physical principles and laws and their interrelationships and applications to understanding fluid, material, and atmospheric dynamics and mechanical, electrical, atomic, and subatomic structures and processes.

Refractory Materials Repairers, Except Brickmasons

- ◉ Education/Training Required: Short-term on-the-job training
- ◉ Annual Earnings: $37,640
- ◉ Growth: 16.3%
- ◉ Annual Job Openings: 155,000
- ◉ Self-Employed: 6.1%
- ◉ Part-Time: 2.1%

Build or repair furnaces, kilns, cupolas, boilers, converters, ladles, soaking pits, ovens, etc., using refractory materials. Bolt sections of wooden molds together, using wrenches, and line molds with paper to prevent clay from sticking to molds. Chip slag from linings of ladles or remove linings when beyond repair, using hammers and chisels. Disassemble molds and cut, chip, and smooth clay structures such as floaters, drawbars, and L-blocks. Drill holes in furnace walls, bolt overlapping layers of plastic to walls, and hammer surfaces to compress layers into solid sheets. Dry and bake new linings by placing inverted linings over burners, by building fires in ladles, or by using blowtorches. Dump and tamp clay in molds, using tamping tools. Fasten stopper heads to rods with metal pins to assemble refractory stoppers used to plug pouring nozzles of steel ladles. Install clay structures in melting tanks and drawing kilns to control the flow and temperature of molten glass, using hoists and hand tools. Measure furnace walls to determine dimensions and then cut required number of sheets from plastic block, using saws. Mix specified amounts of sand, clay, mortar powder, and water to form refractory clay or mortar, using shovels or mixing machines. Reline or repair ladles and pouring spouts with refractory clay, using trowels. Remove worn or damaged plastic block refractory linings of furnaces, using hand tools. Spread mortar on stopper heads and rods, using trowels, and slide brick sleeves over rods to form refractory jackets. Tighten locknuts holding refractory stopper assemblies together, spread mortar on jackets to seal sleeve joints, and dry mortar in ovens. Climb scaffolding, carrying hoses, and spray surfaces of cupolas with refractory mixtures, using spray equipment. Install preformed metal scaffolding in interiors of cupolas, using hand tools. Transfer clay structures to curing ovens, melting tanks, and drawing kilns, using forklifts. **SKILLS— Repairing:** Repairing machines or systems by using the needed tools. **Installation:** Installing equipment, machines, wiring, or programs to meet specifications. **Operation and Control:** Controlling operations of equipment or systems. **Equipment Maintenance:** Performing routine maintenance on equipment and determining when and what kind of maintenance is needed. **Troubleshooting:** Determining causes of operating errors and deciding what to do about them. **Science:** Using scientific rules and methods to solve problems. **Equipment Selection:** Determining the kind of tools and equipment needed to do a job. **Operation Monitoring:** Watching gauges, dials, or other indicators to make sure a machine is working properly. **GOE—Interest Area:** 02. Architecture and Construction. **Work Group:** 02.04. Construction Crafts. **Other Jobs in This Work Group:** Boat Builders and Shipwrights; Boilermakers; Brattice Builders; Brickmasons and Blockmasons; Carpet Installers; Ceiling Tile Installers; Cement Masons and Concrete Finishers; Commercial Divers; Construction Carpenters; Crane and Tower Operators; Dragline Operators; Drywall Installers; Electricians; Fence Erectors; Floor Layers, Except Carpet, Wood, and Hard Tiles; Floor Sanders and Finishers; Glaziers; Grader, Bulldozer, and Scraper Operators; Hazardous Materials Removal Workers; Insulation Workers, Floor, Ceiling, and Wall; Insulation Workers, Mechanical; Manufactured Building and Mobile Home Installers; Operating Engineers; Painters, Construction and Maintenance; Paperhang-ers; Paving, Surfacing, and Tamping Equipment Operators; Pile-Driver Operators; Pipe Fitters; Pipelayers; Pipelaying Fitters; Plasterers and Stucco Masons; Plumbers; Rail-Track Laying and Maintenance Equipment Operators; Reinforcing Iron and Rebar Workers; Riggers; Roofers; Rough Carpenters; Security and Fire Alarm Systems Installers; Segmental Pavers; Sheet Metal Workers; Ship Carpenters and Joiners; Stone Cutters and Carvers; Stonemasons; Structural Iron and Steel Workers; Tapers; Terrazzo Workers and Finishers; Tile and Marble Setters. **PERSONALITY TYPE:** Realistic.

EDUCATION/TRAINING PROGRAM(S)— Industrial Mechanics and Maintenance Technology. **RELATED KNOWLEDGE/COURSES—Building and Construction:** Knowledge of the materials, methods, and tools involved in the construction or repair of houses, buildings, or other structures such as highways and roads. **Mechanical Devices:** Knowledge of machines and tools, including their designs, uses, repair, and maintenance. **Production and Processing:** Knowledge of raw materials, production processes, quality control, costs, and other techniques for maximizing the effective manufacture and distribution of goods. **Engineering and Technology:** Knowledge of the practical application of engineering science and technology. This includes applying principles, techniques, procedures, and equipment to the design and production of various goods and services. **Chemistry:** Knowledge of the chemical composition, structure, and properties of substances and of the chemical processes and transformations that they undergo. This includes uses of chemicals and their danger signs, production techniques, and disposal methods. **Fine Arts:** Knowledge of the theory and techniques required to compose, produce, and perform works of music, dance, the visual arts, drama, and sculpture.

Refrigeration Mechanics

- ◎ Education/Training Required: Long-term on-the-job training
- ◎ Annual Earnings: $36,260
- ◎ Growth: 31.8%
- ◎ Annual Job Openings: 35,000
- ◎ Self-Employed: 15.4%
- ◎ Part-Time: 3.1%

Install and repair industrial and commercial refrigerating systems. Braze or solder parts to repair defective joints and leaks. Observe and test system operation, using gauges and instruments. Test lines, components, and connections for leaks. Dismantle malfunctioning systems and test components, using electrical, mechanical, and pneumatic testing equipment. Adjust or replace worn or defective mechanisms and parts, and reassemble repaired systems. Read blueprints to determine location, size, capacity, and type of components needed to build refrigeration system. Supervise and instruct assistants. Install wiring to connect components to an electric power source. Perform mechanical overhauls and refrigerant reclaiming. Cut, bend, thread, and connect pipe to functional components and water, power, or refrigeration system. Adjust valves according to specifications and charge system with proper type of refrigerant by pumping the specified gas or fluid into the system. Estimate, order, pick up, deliver, and install materials and supplies needed to maintain equipment in good working condition. Install expansion and control valves, using acetylene torches and wrenches. Mount compressor, condenser, and other components in specified locations on frames, using hand tools and acetylene welding equipment. Keep records of repairs and replacements made and causes of malfunctions. Lay out reference points for installation of structural and functional components, using measuring instruments. Schedule work with customers and initiate work orders, house requisitions, and orders from stock. Fabricate and assemble structural and functional components of refrigeration system, using hand tools, power tools, and welding equipment. Lift and align components into position, using hoist or block and tackle. Drill holes and install mounting brackets and hangers into floor and walls of building. Insulate shells and cabinets of systems. **SKILLS—Installation:** Installing equipment, machines, wiring, or programs to meet specifications. **Repairing:** Repairing machines or systems by using the needed tools. **Equipment Maintenance:** Performing routine maintenance on equipment and determining when and what kind of maintenance is needed. **Operation Monitoring:** Watching gauges, dials, or other indicators to make sure a machine is working properly. **Troubleshooting:** Determining causes of operating errors and deciding what to do about them. **Systems Analysis:** Determining how a system should work and how changes in conditions, operations, and the environment will affect outcomes. **Systems Evaluation:** Identifying measures or indicators of system performance and the actions needed to improve or correct performance relative to the goals of the system. **Science:** Using scientific rules and methods to solve problems. **GOE—Interest Area:** 02. Architecture and Construction. **Work Group:** 02.05. Systems and Equipment Installation, Maintenance, and Repair. **Other Jobs in This Work Group:** Central Office and PBX Installers and Repairers; Communication Equipment Mechanics, Installers, and Repairers; Electric Meter Installers and Repairers; Electrical and Electronics Repairers, Powerhouse, Substation, and Relay; Electrical Power-Line Installers and Repairers; Elevator Installers and Repairers; Frame Wirers, Central Office; Heating and Air Conditioning Mechanics; Home Appliance Installers; Maintenance and Repair Workers, General; Meter Mechanics; Station Installers and Repairers, Telephone; Telecommunications Facility Examiners; Telecommunications Line Installers and Repairers. **PERSONALITY TYPE:** Realistic.

EDUCATION/TRAINING PROGRAM(S)— Heating, Air Conditioning, and Refrigeration Technology/Technician (ACH/ACR/ACHR/HRAC/HVAC/AC Technology); Heating, Air Conditioning, Ventilation, and Refrigeration Maintenance Technology/Technician (HAC, HACR, HVAC, HVACR); Solar Energy Technology/Technician. **RELATED KNOWLEDGE/COURSES—Building and Construction:** Knowledge of the materials, methods, and tools involved in the construction or repair of houses, buildings, or other structures such as highways and roads. **Mechanical Devices:** Knowledge of machines and tools, including their designs, uses, repair, and maintenance. **Engineering and Technology:** Knowledge of the practical application of engineering science and technology. This includes applying principles, techniques, procedures, and equipment to the design and production of various goods and services. **Customer and Personal Service:** Knowledge of principles and processes for providing customer and personal services. This includes customer needs assessment, meeting quality standards for services, and evaluation of customer satisfaction. **Physics:** Knowledge and prediction of physical principles and laws and their interrelationships and applications to understanding fluid, material, and atmospheric dynamics and mechanical, electrical, atomic, and subatomic structures and processes. **Design:** Knowledge of design techniques, tools, and principles involved in production of precision technical plans, blueprints, drawings, and models.

Refuse and Recyclable Material Collectors

- Education/Training Required: Short-term on-the-job training
- Annual Earnings: $25,760
- Growth: 17.6%
- Annual Job Openings: 42,000
- Self-Employed: 1.8%
- Part-Time: 12.1%

Collect and dump refuse or recyclable materials from containers into truck. May drive truck. Inspect trucks prior to beginning routes to ensure safe operating condition. Refuel trucks and add other necessary fluids, such as oil. Fill out any needed reports for defective equipment. Drive to disposal sites to empty trucks that have been filled. Drive trucks along established routes through residential streets and alleys or through business and industrial areas. Operate equipment that compresses the collected refuse. Operate automated or semi-automated hoisting devices that raise refuse bins and dump contents into openings in truck bodies. Dismount garbage trucks to collect garbage and remount trucks to ride to the next collection point. Communicate with dispatchers concerning delays, unsafe sites, accidents, equipment breakdowns, and other maintenance problems. Keep informed of road and weather conditions to determine how routes will be affected. Tag garbage or recycling containers to inform customers of problems such as excess garbage or inclusion of items that are not permitted. Clean trucks and compactor bodies after routes have been completed. Sort items set out for recycling and throw materials into designated truck compartments. Organize schedules for refuse collection. **SKILLS—Equipment Maintenance:** Performing routine maintenance on equipment and determining when and what kind of maintenance is needed. **Operation Monitoring:** Watching gauges, dials, or other indicators to make sure a machine is working properly. **Operation and Control:** Controlling operations of equipment or systems. **Social Perceptiveness:** Being aware of others' reactions and understanding why they react as they do. **Coordination:** Adjusting actions in relation to others' actions. **Repairing:** Repairing machines or systems by using the needed tools. **Troubleshooting:** Determining causes of operating errors and deciding what to do

about them. **Learning Strategies:** Selecting and using training/instructional methods and procedures appropriate for the situation when learning or teaching new things. **GOE—Interest Area:** 13. Manufacturing. **Work Group:** 13.17. Loading, Moving, Hoisting, and Conveying. **Other Jobs in This Work Group:** Conveyor Operators and Tenders; Freight, Stock, and Material Movers, Hand; Hoist and Winch Operators; Industrial Truck and Tractor Operators; Irradiated-Fuel Handlers; Machine Feeders and Offbearers; Packers and Packagers, Hand; Pump Operators, Except Wellhead Pumpers; Tank Car, Truck, and Ship Loaders. **PERSONALITY TYPE:** Realistic.

EDUCATION/TRAINING PROGRAM(S)—No data available. **RELATED KNOWLEDGE/COURSES—Transportation:** Knowledge of principles and methods for moving people or goods by air, rail, sea, or road, including the relative costs and benefits. **Customer and Personal Service:** Knowledge of principles and processes for providing customer and personal services. This includes customer needs assessment, meeting quality standards for services, and evaluation of customer satisfaction. **Public Safety and Security:** Knowledge of relevant equipment, policies, procedures, and strategies to promote effective local, state, or national security operations for the protection of people, data, property, and institutions. **Education and Training:** Knowledge of principles and methods for curriculum and training design, teaching and instruction for individuals and groups, and the measurement of training effects. **Production and Processing:** Knowledge of raw materials, production processes, quality control, costs, and other techniques for maximizing the effective manufacture and distribution of goods. **Mechanical Devices:** Knowledge of machines and tools, including their designs, uses, repair, and maintenance.

Registered Nurses

- Education/Training Required: Associate degree
- Annual Earnings: $52,330
- Growth: 27.3%
- Annual Job Openings: 215,000
- Self-Employed: 1.2%
- Part-Time: 22.0%

Assess patient health problems and needs, develop and implement nursing care plans, and maintain medical records. Administer nursing care to ill, injured, convalescent, or disabled patients. May advise patients on health maintenance and disease prevention or provide case management. Licensing or registration required. Includes advance practice nurses such as nurse practitioners, clinical nurse specialists, certified nurse midwives, and certified registered nurse anesthetists. Advanced practice nursing is practiced by RNs who have specialized formal, post-basic education and who function in highly autonomous and specialized roles. Maintain accurate, detailed reports and records. Monitor, record, and report symptoms and changes in patients' conditions. Record patients' medical information and vital signs. Modify patient treatment plans as indicated by patients' responses and conditions. Consult and coordinate with health-care team members to assess, plan, implement, and evaluate patient care plans. Order, interpret, and evaluate diagnostic tests to identify and assess patient's condition. Monitor all aspects of patient care, including diet and physical activity. Direct and supervise less-skilled nursing/health-care personnel or supervise a particular unit on one shift. Prepare patients for, and assist with, examinations and treatments. Observe nurses and visit patients to ensure that proper nursing care is provided. Assess the needs of individuals, families, and/or communities, including assessment of individuals' home and/or work environments, to identify potential health or safety problems. Instruct individuals, families, and other groups on topics such as health education, disease prevention, and childbirth and develop health improvement programs. Prepare rooms, sterile instruments, equipment, and supplies, and ensure that stock of supplies is maintained. Inform physician of patient's condition during anesthesia. Deliver infants and provide prenatal and postpartum care and treatment under obstetrician's supervision. Administer local, inhalation, intravenous, and other anesthetics. Provide health care, first aid, immunizations, and assistance in convalescence and rehabilitation in locations such as schools, hospitals, and industry. Perform physical examinations, make tentative diagnoses, and treat patients en route to hospitals or at disaster site triage centers. Conduct specified laboratory tests. Hand items to surgeons during operations. Prescribe or recommend drugs, medical devices, or other forms of treatment, such as physical therapy, inhalation therapy, or related therapeutic procedures.

Direct and coordinate infection control programs, advising and consulting with specified personnel about necessary precautions. **SKILLS—Social Perceptiveness:** Being aware of others' reactions and understanding why they react as they do. **Service Orientation:** Actively looking for ways to help people. **Instructing:** Teaching others how to do something. **Time Management:** Managing one's own time and the time of others. **Learning Strategies:** Selecting and using training/instructional methods and procedures appropriate for the situation when learning or teaching new things. **Critical Thinking:** Using logic and reasoning to identify the strengths and weaknesses of alternative solutions, conclusions, or approaches to problems. **Coordination:** Adjusting actions in relation to others' actions. **Active Learning:** Understanding the implications of new information for both current and future problem-solving and decision-making. **Monitoring:** Monitoring or assessing your performance or that of other individuals or organizations to make improvements or take corrective action. **Negotiation:** Bringing others together and trying to reconcile differences. **GOE—Interest Area:** 08. Health Science. **Work Group:** 08.02. Medicine and Surgery. **Other Jobs in This Work Group:** Anesthesiologists; Family and General Practitioners; Internists, General; Medical Assistants; Medical Transcriptionists; Obstetricians and Gynecologists; Pediatricians, General; Pharmacists; Pharmacy Aides; Pharmacy Technicians; Physician Assistants; Psychiatrists; Surgeons; Surgical Technologists. **PERSONALITY TYPE:** Social.

EDUCATION/TRAINING PROGRAM(S)—Adult Health Nurse/Nursing; Clinical Nurse Specialist; Critical Care Nursing; Family Practice Nurse/Nurse Practitioner; Maternal/Child Health and Neonatal Nurse/Nursing; Nurse Anesthetist; Nurse Midwife/Nursing Midwifery; Nursing—Registered Nurse Training (RN, ASN, BSN, MSN); Nursing Science (MS, PhD); Nursing, Other; Occupational and Environmental Health Nursing; Pediatric Nurse/Nursing; Perioperative/Operating Room and Surgical Nurse/Nursing; Psychiatric/Mental Health Nurse/Nursing; Public Health/Community Nurse/Nursing. **RELATED KNOWLEDGE/COURSES—Psychology:** Knowledge of human behavior and performance; individual differences in ability, personality, and interests; learning and motivation; psychological research methods; and the assessment and treatment of behavioral and affective disorders. **Medicine and Dentistry:** Knowledge of the information and techniques needed to diagnose and treat human injuries, diseases, and deformities. This includes symptoms, treatment alternatives, drug properties and interactions, and preventive health-care measures. **Customer and Personal Service:** Knowledge of principles and processes for providing customer and personal services. This includes customer needs assessment, meeting quality standards for services, and evaluation of customer satisfaction. **Therapy and Counseling:** Knowledge of principles, methods, and procedures for diagnosis, treatment, and rehabilitation of physical and mental dysfunctions and for career counseling and guidance. **Sociology and Anthropology:** Knowledge of group behavior and dynamics, societal trends and influences, human migrations, ethnicity, and cultures and their history and origins. **Biology:** Knowledge of plant and animal organisms and their tissues, cells, functions, interdependencies, and interactions with each other and the environment.

Rehabilitation Counselors

- Education/Training Required: Bachelor's degree
- Annual Earnings: $27,870
- Growth: 33.8%
- Annual Job Openings: 19,000
- Self-Employed: 4.4%
- Part-Time: 14.6%

Counsel individuals to maximize the independence and employability of persons coping with personal, social, and vocational difficulties that result from birth defects, illness, disease, accidents, or the stress of daily life. Coordinate activities for residents of care and treatment facilities. Assess client needs and design and implement rehabilitation programs that may include personal and vocational counseling, training, and job placement. Analyze information from interviews, educational and medical records, consultation with other professionals, and diagnostic evaluations in order to assess clients' abilities, needs, and eligibility for services. Arrange for physical, mental, academic, vocational, and other evaluations to obtain information for assessing clients' needs and developing rehabilitation plans. Collaborate with clients' families to implement rehabilitation plans that include behavioral, residential, social, and/or employment goals.

Confer with clients to discuss their options and goals so that rehabilitation programs and plans for accessing needed services can be developed. Confer with physicians, psychologists, occupational therapists, and other professionals in order to develop and implement client rehabilitation programs. Develop and maintain relationships with community referral sources such as schools and community groups. Develop rehabilitation plans that fit clients' aptitudes, education levels, physical abilities, and career goals. Direct case service allocations, authorizing expenditures and payments. Maintain close contact with clients during job training and placements in order to resolve problems and evaluate placement adequacy. Monitor and record clients' progress in order to ensure that goals and objectives are met. Prepare and maintain records and case files, including documentation such as clients' personal and eligibility information, services provided, narratives of client contacts, and relevant correspondence. Arrange for on-site job coaching or assistive devices such as specially equipped wheelchairs in order to help clients adapt to work or school environments. Collaborate with community agencies to establish facilities and programs to assist persons with disabilities. Develop diagnostic procedures for determining clients' needs. Locate barriers to client employment, such as inaccessible work sites, inflexible schedules, and transportation problems, and work with clients to develop strategies for overcoming these barriers. Participate in job development and placement programs, contacting prospective employers, placing clients in jobs, and evaluating the success of placements. **SKILLS**—No data available. **GOE—Interest Area:** 10. Human Service. **Work Group:** 10.01. Counseling and Social Work. **Other Jobs in This Work Group:** Child, Family, and School Social Workers; Clinical Psychologists; Counseling Psychologists; Marriage and Family Therapists; Medical and Public Health Social Workers; Mental Health and Substance Abuse Social Workers; Mental Health Counselors; Probation Officers and Correctional Treatment Specialists; Residential Advisors; Social and Human Service Assistants; Substance Abuse and Behavioral Disorder Counselors. **PERSONALITY TYPE:** No data available.

EDUCATION/TRAINING PROGRAM(S)—Assistive/Augmentative Technology and Rehabilitation Engineering; Vocational Rehabilitation Counseling/Counselor. **RELATED KNOWLEDGE/COURSES**—No data available.

Reinforcing Iron and Rebar Workers

- Education/Training Required: Long-term on-the-job training
- Annual Earnings: $35,160
- Growth: 16.7%
- Annual Job Openings: 2,000
- Self-Employed: 0%
- Part-Time: 3.8%

Position and secure steel bars or mesh in concrete forms in order to reinforce concrete. Use a variety of fasteners, rod-bending machines, blowtorches, and hand tools. Cut and fit wire mesh or fabric, using hooked rods, and position fabric or mesh in concrete to reinforce concrete. Cut rods to required lengths, using metal shears, hacksaws, bar cutters, or acetylene torches. Bend steel rods with hand tools and rodbending machines and weld them with arc-welding equipment. Determine quantities, sizes, shapes, and locations of reinforcing rods from blueprints, sketches, or oral instructions. Position and secure steel bars, rods, cables, or mesh in concrete forms, using fasteners, rod-bending machines, blowtorches, and hand tools. Space and fasten together rods in forms according to blueprints, using wire and pliers. Place blocks under rebar to hold the bars off the deck when reinforcing floors. **SKILLS**—None met the criteria. **GOE—Interest Area:** 02. Architecture and Construction. **Work Group:** 02.04. Construction Crafts. **Other Jobs in This Work Group:** Boat Builders and Shipwrights; Boilermakers; Brattice Builders; Brickmasons and Blockmasons; Carpet Installers; Ceiling Tile Installers; Cement Masons and Concrete Finishers; Commercial Divers; Construction Carpenters; Crane and Tower Operators; Dragline Operators; Drywall Installers; Electricians; Fence Erectors; Floor Layers, Except Carpet, Wood, and Hard Tiles; Floor Sanders and Finishers; Glaziers; Grader, Bulldozer, and Scraper Operators; Hazardous Materials Removal Workers; Insulation Workers, Floor, Ceiling, and Wall; Insulation Workers, Mechanical; Manufactured Building and Mobile Home Installers; Operating Engineers; Painters, Construction and Maintenance; Paperhangers; Paving, Surfacing, and Tamping Equipment Operators; Pile-Driver Operators; Pipe Fitters; Pipelayers; Pipelaying Fitters; Plasterers and Stucco Masons; Plumbers; Rail-Track Laying and Maintenance Equipment Operators; Refractory Materials Repairers, Except Brickmasons; Riggers; Roofers; Rough Carpenters; Security and Fire Alarm Systems Installers; Segmental Pavers; Sheet Metal Workers; Ship Carpenters and Joiners; Stone Cutters and Carvers; Stonemasons; Structural Iron and Steel Workers; Tapers; Terrazzo Workers and Finishers; Tile and Marble Setters. **PERSONALITY TYPE: Realistic.**

EDUCATION/TRAINING PROGRAM(S)—Construction Trades, Other. **RELATED KNOWLEDGE/COURSES—Building and Construction:** Knowledge of the materials, methods, and tools involved in the construction or repair of houses, buildings, or other structures such as highways and roads. **Physics:** Knowledge and prediction of physical principles and laws and their interrelationships and applications to understanding fluid, material, and atmospheric dynamics and mechanical, electrical, atomic, and subatomic structures and processes. **Design:** Knowledge of design techniques, tools, and principles involved in production of precision technical plans, blueprints, drawings, and models. **Engineering and Technology:** Knowledge of the practical application of engineering science and technology. This includes applying principles, techniques, procedures, and equipment to the design and production of various goods and services.

Reservation and Transportation Ticket Agents

- Education/Training Required: Short-term on-the-job training
- Annual Earnings: $27,750
- Growth: 12.2%
- Annual Job Openings: 35,000
- Self-Employed: 1.1%
- Part-Time: 15.7%

Make and confirm reservations for passengers and sell tickets for transportation agencies such as airlines, bus companies, railroads, and steamship lines. May check baggage and direct passengers to designated concourse, pier, or track. Arranges reservations and routing for passengers at request of ticket agent. Examines passenger ticket or pass to direct passenger to specified area for loading. Plans route and computes ticket cost, using schedules, rate books, and computer. Reads coded data on tickets to ascertain destination, marks tickets, and assigns boarding pass. Assists passengers requiring special assistance to board or depart conveyance. Informs travel agents in other locations of space reserved or available. Sells travel insurance. Announces arrival and departure information, using public-address system. Telephones customer or ticket agent to advise of changes with travel conveyance or to confirm reservation. Sells and assembles tickets for transmittal or mailing to customers. Answers inquiries made to travel agencies or transportation firms, such as airlines, bus companies, railroad companies, and steamship lines. Checks baggage and directs passenger to designated location for loading. Assigns specified space to customers and maintains computerized inventory of passenger space available. Determines whether space is available on travel dates requested by customer. **SKILLS—Service Orientation:** Actively looking for ways to help people. **Active Listening:** Giving full attention to what other people are saying, taking time to understand the points being made, asking questions as appropriate, and not interrupting at inappropriate times. **Speaking:** Talking to others to convey information effectively. **GOE—Interest Area:** 09. Hospitality, Tourism, and Recreation. **Work Group:** 09.03. Hospitality and Travel Services. **Other Jobs in This Work Group:** Baggage Porters and Bellhops; Concierges; Flight Attendants; Hotel, Motel, and Resort Desk Clerks; Janitors and Cleaners, Except Maids and Housekeeping Cleaners; Maids and Housekeeping Cleaners; Tour Guides and Escorts; Transportation Attendants, Except Flight Attendants and Baggage Porters; Travel Agents; Travel Clerks; Travel Guides. **PERSONALITY TYPE:** Conventional.

EDUCATION/TRAINING PROGRAM(S)—Selling Skills and Sales Operations; Tourism and Travel Services Marketing Operations; Tourism Promotion Operations. **RELATED KNOWLEDGE/COURSES—Geography:** Knowledge of principles and methods for describing the features of land, sea, and air masses, including their physical characteristics; locations; interrelationships; and distribution of plant, animal, and human life. **Transportation:** Knowledge of principles and methods for moving people or goods by air, rail, sea, or road, including the relative costs and benefits. **Clerical Practices:** Knowledge of administra-

tive and clerical procedures and systems such as word processing, managing files and records, stenography and transcription, designing forms, and other office procedures and terminology. **Sales and Marketing:** Knowledge of principles and methods for showing, promoting, and selling products or services. This includes marketing strategy and tactics, product demonstrations, sales techniques, and sales control systems. **Computers and Electronics:** Knowledge of circuit boards, processors, chips, electronic equipment, and computer hardware and software, including applications and programming. **Telecommunications:** Knowledge of transmission, broadcasting, switching, control, and operation of telecommunications systems.

Residential Advisors

- Education/Training Required: Moderate-term on-the-job training
- Annual Earnings: $21,430
- Growth: 33.6%
- Annual Job Openings: 12,000
- Self-Employed: 0.7%
- Part-Time: 22.0%

Coordinate activities for residents of boarding schools, college fraternities or sororities, college dormitories, or similar establishments. Order supplies and determine need for maintenance, repairs, and furnishings. May maintain household records and assign rooms. May refer residents to counseling resources if needed. Enforce rules and regulations to ensure the smooth and orderly operation of dormitory programs. Provide emergency first aid and summon medical assistance when necessary. Mediate interpersonal problems between residents. Administer, coordinate, or recommend disciplinary and corrective actions. Communicate with other staff to resolve problems with individual students. Counsel students in the handling of issues such as family, financial, and educational problems. Make regular rounds to ensure that residents and areas are safe and secure. Observe students in order to detect and report unusual behavior. Determine the need for facility maintenance and repair; notify appropriate personnel. Collaborate with counselors to develop counseling programs that address the needs of individual students. Develop program plans for individuals or assist in plan development. Hold regular meetings with each assigned unit. Direct and participate in on- and off-campus recreational activities for residents of institutions, boarding schools, fraternities or sororities, children's homes, or similar establishments. Assign rooms to students. Provide requested information on students' progress and the development of case plans. Confer with medical personnel to better understand the backgrounds and needs of individual residents. Answer telephones and route calls or deliver messages. Supervise participants in work-study programs. Process contract cancellations for students who are unable to follow residence hall policies and procedures. Sort and distribute mail. Supervise the activities of housekeeping personnel. Order supplies for facilities. Supervise students' housekeeping work to ensure that it is done properly. **SKILLS—Social Perceptiveness:** Being aware of others' reactions and understanding why they react as they do. **Monitoring:** Monitoring or assessing your performance or that of other individuals or organizations to make improvements or take corrective action. **Management of Personnel Resources:** Motivating, developing, and directing people as they work, identifying the best people for the job. **Service Orientation:** Actively looking for ways to help people. **Persuasion:** Persuading others to change their minds or behavior. **Time Management:** Managing one's own time and the time of others. **Negotiation:** Bringing others together and trying to reconcile differences. **Active Listening:** Giving full attention to what other people are saying, taking time to understand the points being made, asking questions as appropriate, and not interrupting at inappropriate times. **Learning Strategies:** Selecting and using training/instructional methods and procedures appropriate for the situation when learning or teaching new things. **GOE—Interest Area:** 10. Human Service. **Work Group:** 10.01. Counseling and Social Work. **Other Jobs in This Work Group:** Child, Family, and School Social Workers; Clinical Psychologists; Counseling Psychologists; Marriage and Family Therapists; Medical and Public Health Social Workers; Mental Health and Substance Abuse Social Workers; Mental Health Counselors; Probation Officers and Correctional Treatment Specialists; Rehabilitation Counselors; Social and Human Service Assistants; Substance Abuse and Behavioral Disorder Counselors. **PERSONALITY TYPE:** Social.

EDUCATION/TRAINING PROGRAM(S)— Hotel/Motel Administration/Management. **RELATED KNOWLEDGE/COURSES—Therapy and**

Counseling: Knowledge of principles, methods, and procedures for diagnosis, treatment, and rehabilitation of physical and mental dysfunctions and for career counseling and guidance. **Psychology:** Knowledge of human behavior and performance; individual differences in ability, personality, and interests; learning and motivation; psychological research methods; and the assessment and treatment of behavioral and affective disorders. **Philosophy and Theology:** Knowledge of different philosophical systems and religions. This includes their basic principles, values, ethics, ways of thinking, customs, and practices and their impact on human culture. **Sociology and Anthropology:** Knowledge of group behavior and dynamics, societal trends and influences, human migrations, ethnicity, and cultures and their history and origins. **Customer and Personal Service:** Knowledge of principles and processes for providing customer and personal services. This includes customer needs assessment, meeting quality standards for services, and evaluation of customer satisfaction. **Personnel and Human Resources:** Knowledge of principles and procedures for personnel recruitment, selection, training, compensation and benefits, labor relations and negotiation, and personnel information systems.

Respiratory Therapists

- Education/Training Required: Associate degree
- Annual Earnings: $43,140
- Growth: 34.8%
- Annual Job Openings: 10,000
- Self-Employed: 0%
- Part-Time: 15.5%

Assess, treat, and care for patients with breathing disorders. Assume primary responsibility for all respiratory care modalities, including the supervision of respiratory therapy technicians. Initiate and conduct therapeutic procedures; maintain patient records; and select, assemble, check, and operate equipment. Set up and operate devices such as mechanical ventilators, therapeutic gas administration apparatus, environmental control systems, and aerosol generators, following specified parameters of treatment. Provide emergency care, including artificial respiration, external cardiac massage, and assistance with cardiopulmonary resuscitation. Determine requirements for treatment, such as type, method and duration of therapy; precautions to be taken; and medication and dosages, compatible with physicians' orders. Monitor patient's physiological responses to therapy, such as vital signs, arterial blood gases, and blood chemistry changes, and consult with physician if adverse reactions occur. Read prescription, measure arterial blood gases, and review patient information to assess patient condition. Work as part of a team of physicians, nurses, and other health-care professionals to manage patient care. Enforce safety rules and ensure careful adherence to physicians' orders. Maintain charts that contain patients' pertinent identification and therapy information. Inspect, clean, test, and maintain respiratory therapy equipment to ensure equipment is functioning safely and efficiently, ordering repairs when necessary. Educate patients and their families about their conditions and teach appropriate disease management techniques, such as breathing exercises and the use of medications and respiratory equipment. Explain treatment procedures to patients to gain cooperation and allay fears. Relay blood analysis results to a physician. Perform pulmonary function and adjust equipment to obtain optimum results in therapy. Perform bronchopulmonary drainage and assist or instruct patients in performance of breathing exercises. Demonstrate respiratory care procedures to trainees and other health-care personnel. Teach, train, supervise, and utilize the assistance of students, respiratory therapy technicians, and assistants. Use a variety of testing techniques to assist doctors in cardiac and pulmonary research and to diagnose disorders. Make emergency visits to resolve equipment problems. Conduct tests such as electrocardiograms, stress testing, and lung capacity tests to evaluate patients' cardiopulmonary functions. **SKILLS—Instructing:** Teaching others how to do something. **Science:** Using scientific rules and methods to solve problems. **Active Learning:** Understanding the implications of new information for both current and future problem-solving and decision-making. **Service Orientation:** Actively looking for ways to help people. **Reading Comprehension:** Understanding written sentences and paragraphs in work-related documents. **Time Management:** Managing one's own time and the time of others. **Troubleshooting:** Determining causes of operating errors and deciding what to do about them. **Mathematics:** Using mathematics to solve problems. **GOE—Interest Area:** 08. Health Science. **Work Group:** 08.07. Medical Therapy. **Other Jobs in This Work Group:** Audi-

ologists; Massage Therapists; Occupational Therapist Aides; Occupational Therapist Assistants; Occupational Therapists; Physical Therapist Aides; Physical Therapist Assistants; Physical Therapists; Radiation Therapists; Recreational Therapists; Respiratory Therapy Technicians; Speech-Language Pathologists. **PERSONALITY TYPE:** Investigative.

EDUCATION/TRAINING PROGRAM(S)—Respiratory Care Therapy/Therapist. **RELATED KNOWLEDGE/COURSES—Medicine and Dentistry:** Knowledge of the information and techniques needed to diagnose and treat human injuries, diseases, and deformities. This includes symptoms, treatment alternatives, drug properties and interactions, and preventive health-care measures. **Customer and Personal Service:** Knowledge of principles and processes for providing customer and personal services. This includes customer needs assessment, meeting quality standards for services, and evaluation of customer satisfaction. **Psychology:** Knowledge of human behavior and performance; individual differences in ability, personality, and interests; learning and motivation; psychological research methods; and the assessment and treatment of behavioral and affective disorders. **Biology:** Knowledge of plant and animal organisms and their tissues, cells, functions, interdependencies, and interactions with each other and the environment. **Education and Training:** Knowledge of principles and methods for curriculum and training design, teaching and instruction for individuals and groups, and the measurement of training effects. **Chemistry:** Knowledge of the chemical composition, structure, and properties of substances and of the chemical processes and transformations that they undergo. This includes uses of chemicals and their danger signs, production techniques, and disposal methods.

Respiratory Therapy Technicians

- Education/Training Required: Postsecondary vocational training
- Annual Earnings: $36,740
- Growth: 34.2%
- Annual Job Openings: 5,000
- Self-Employed: 0%
- Part-Time: 23.0%

Provide specific, well-defined respiratory care procedures under the direction of respiratory therapists and physicians. Use ventilators and various oxygen devices and aerosol and breathing treatments in the provision of respiratory therapy. Work with patients in areas such as the emergency room, neonatal/pediatric intensive care, and surgical intensive care, treating conditions including emphysema, chronic bronchitis, asthma, cystic fibrosis, and pneumonia. Read and evaluate physicians' orders and patients' chart information to determine patients' condition and treatment protocols. Keep records of patients' therapy, completing all necessary forms. Set equipment controls to regulate the flow of oxygen, gases, mists, or aerosols. Provide respiratory care involving the application of well-defined therapeutic techniques under the supervision of a respiratory therapist and a physician. Assess patients' response to treatments and modify treatments according to protocol if necessary. Prepare and test devices such as mechanical ventilators, therapeutic gas administration apparatus, environmental control systems, aerosol generators, and EKG machines. Monitor patients during treatment and report any unusual reactions to the respiratory therapist. Explain treatment procedures to patients. Clean, sterilize, check, and maintain respiratory therapy equipment. Perform diagnostic procedures to assess the severity of respiratory dysfunction in patients. Follow and enforce safety rules applying to equipment. Administer breathing and oxygen procedures such as intermittent positive pressure breathing treatments, ultrasonic nebulizer treatments, and incentive spirometer treatments. Recommend and review bedside procedures, X rays, and laboratory tests. Interview and examine patients to collect clinical data. Teach patients how to use respiratory equipment at home. Teach or oversee other workers who provide respiratory care services. **SKILLS—Troubleshooting:** Determining causes of operating errors and deciding what to do about them. **Operation Monitoring:** Watching gauges, dials, or other indicators to make sure a machine is working properly. **Time Management:** Managing one's own time and the time of others. **Social Perceptiveness:** Being aware of others' reactions and understanding why they react as they do. **Operation and Control:** Controlling operations of equipment or systems. **Learning Strategies:** Selecting and using training/instructional methods and procedures appropriate for the situation when learning or teaching new things. **Instructing:** Teaching others how to do something. **Equipment Maintenance:** Performing routine maintenance on equipment and determining when and what kind of maintenance is needed. **GOE—Interest Area:** 08. Health Science. **Work Group:** 08.07. Medical Therapy. **Other Jobs in This Work Group:** Audiologists; Massage Therapists; Occupational Therapist Aides; Occupational Therapist Assistants; Occupational Therapists; Physical Therapist Aides; Physical Therapist Assistants; Physical Therapists; Radiation Therapists; Recreational Therapists; Respiratory Therapists; Speech-Language Pathologists. **PERSONALITY TYPE:** No data available.

EDUCATION/TRAINING PROGRAM(S)—Respiratory Care Therapy/Therapist; Respiratory Therapy Technician/Assistant. **RELATED KNOWLEDGE/COURSES—Medicine and Dentistry:** Knowledge of the information and techniques needed to diagnose and treat human injuries, diseases, and deformities. This includes symptoms, treatment alternatives, drug properties and interactions, and preventive health-care measures. **Psychology:** Knowledge of human behavior and performance; individual differences in ability, personality, and interests; learning and motivation; psychological research methods; and the assessment and treatment of behavioral and affective disorders. **Customer and Personal Service:** Knowledge of principles and processes for providing customer and personal services. This includes customer needs assessment, meeting quality standards for services, and evaluation of customer satisfaction. **Chemistry:** Knowledge of the chemical composition, structure, and properties of substances and of the chemical processes and transformations that they undergo. This includes uses of chemicals and their danger signs, production techniques, and disposal methods. **Physics:** Knowledge and prediction of physical principles and laws and their interrelationships and applications to understanding fluid, material, and atmospheric dynamics and mechanical, electrical, atomic, and subatomic structures and processes. **Biology:** Knowledge of plant and animal organisms and their tissues, cells, functions, interdependencies, and interactions with each other and the environment.

Retail Salespersons

- Education/Training Required: Short-term on-the-job training
- Annual Earnings: $18,680
- Growth: 14.6%
- Annual Job Openings: 1,014,000
- Self-Employed: 4.3%
- Part-Time: 32.6%

Sell merchandise such as furniture, motor vehicles, appliances, or apparel in a retail establishment. Greet customers and ascertain what each customer wants or needs. Open and close cash registers, performing tasks such as counting money; separating charge slips, coupons, and vouchers; balancing cash drawers; and making deposits. Maintain knowledge of current sales and promotions, policies regarding payment and exchanges, and security practices. Compute sales prices and total purchases and receive and process cash or credit payment. Maintain records related to sales. Watch for and recognize security risks and thefts and know how to prevent or handle these situations. Recommend, select, and help locate or obtain merchandise based on customer needs and desires. Answer questions regarding the store and its merchandise. Describe merchandise and explain use, operation, and care of merchandise to customers. Ticket, arrange, and display merchandise to promote sales. Prepare sales slips or sales contracts. Place special orders or call other stores to find desired items. Demonstrate use or operation of merchandise. Clean shelves, counters, and tables. Exchange merchandise for customers and accept returns. Bag or package purchases and wrap gifts. Help customers try on or fit merchandise. Inventory stock and requisition new stock. Prepare merchandise for purchase or rental. Sell or arrange for delivery, insurance, financing, or service contracts for merchandise. Estimate and quote trade-in allowances. **SKILLS—Social Perceptiveness:** Being aware of others' reactions and understanding why they react as they do. **Writing:** Communicating effectively in writing as appropriate for the needs of the audience. **Speaking:** Talking to others to convey information effectively. **Critical Thinking:** Using logic and reasoning to identify the strengths and weaknesses of alternative solutions, conclusions, or approaches to problems. **Negotiation:** Bringing others together and trying to reconcile differences. **Instructing:** Teaching others how to do something. **Management of Personnel Resources:** Motivating, developing, and directing people as they work, identifying the best people for the job. **GOE—Interest Area:** 14. Retail and Wholesale Sales and Service. **Work Group:** 14.03. General Sales. **Other Jobs in This Work Group:** Parts Salespersons; Real Estate Brokers; Real Estate Sales Agents; Sales Representatives, Wholesale and Manufacturing, Except Technical and Scientific Products; Service Station Attendants. **PERSONALITY TYPE:** Enterprising.

EDUCATION/TRAINING PROGRAM(S)—Floriculture/Floristry Operations and Management; Retailing and Retail Operations; Sales, Distribution, and Marketing Operations, General; Selling Skills and Sales Operations. **RELATED KNOWLEDGE/COURSES—Sales and Marketing:** Knowledge of principles and methods for showing, promoting, and selling products or services. This includes marketing strategy and tactics, product demonstrations, sales techniques, and sales control systems. **Customer and Personal Service:** Knowledge of principles and processes for providing customer and personal services. This includes customer needs assessment, meeting quality standards for services, and evaluation of customer satisfaction. **Administration and Management:** Knowledge of business and management principles involved in strategic planning, resource allocation, human resources modeling, leadership technique, production methods, and coordination of people and resources. **Education and Training:** Knowledge of principles and methods for curriculum and training design, teaching and instruction for individuals and groups, and the measurement of training effects. **Personnel and Human Resources:** Knowledge of principles and procedures for personnel recruitment, selection, training, compensation and benefits, labor relations and negotiation, and personnel information systems. **Clerical Practices:** Knowledge of administrative and clerical procedures and systems such as word processing, managing files and records, stenography and transcription, designing forms, and other office procedures and terminology.

R

Roofers

- ◎ Education/Training Required: Moderate-term on-the-job training
- ◎ Annual Earnings: $30,840
- ◎ Growth: 18.6%
- ◎ Annual Job Openings: 38,000
- ◎ Self-Employed: 31.9%
- ◎ Part-Time: 10.0%

Cover roofs of structures with shingles, slate, asphalt, aluminum, wood, and related materials. May spray roofs, sidings, and walls with material to bind, seal, insulate, or soundproof sections of structures. Align roofing materials with edges of roofs. Apply alternate layers of hot asphalt or tar and roofing paper to roofs, according to specification. Apply gravel or pebbles over top layers of roofs, using rakes or stiff-bristled brooms. Apply plastic coatings and membranes, fiberglass, or felt over sloped roofs before applying shingles. Cement or nail flashing-strips of metal or shingle over joints to make them watertight. Cover exposed nailheads with roofing cement or caulking to prevent water leakage and rust. Cover roofs and exterior walls of structures with slate, asphalt, aluminum, wood, gravel, gypsum, and/or related materials, using brushes, knives, punches, hammers, and other tools. Cut felt, shingles, and strips of flashing and fit them into angles formed by walls, vents, and intersecting roof surfaces. Cut roofing paper to size, using knives, and nail or staple roofing paper to roofs in overlapping strips to form bases for other materials. Glaze top layers to make a smooth finish or embed gravel in the bitumen for rough surfaces. Inspect problem roofs to determine the best procedures for repairing them. Install partially overlapping layers of material over roof insulation surfaces, determining distance of roofing material overlap by using chalklines, gauges on shingling hatchets, or lines on shingles. Install vapor barriers and/or layers of insulation on the roof decks of flat roofs and seal the seams. Install, repair, or replace single-ply roofing systems, using waterproof sheet materials such as modified plastics, elastomeric, or other asphaltic compositions. Mop or pour hot asphalt or tar onto roof bases. Clean and maintain equipment. Hammer and chisel away rough spots or remove them with rubbing bricks to prepare surfaces for waterproofing. Punch holes in slate, tile, terra cotta, or wooden shingles, using punches and hammers. Remove snow, water, or debris from roofs prior to applying roofing materials. Set up scaffolding to provide safe access to roofs. Spray roofs, sidings, and walls with material to bind, seal, insulate, or soundproof sections of structures, using spray guns, air compressors, and heaters. **SKILLS—Repairing:** Repairing machines or systems by using the needed tools. **Installation:** Installing equipment, machines, wiring, or programs to meet specifications. **Coordination:** Adjusting actions in relation to others' actions. **Equipment Selection:** Determining the kind of tools and equipment needed to do a job. **Operation and Control:** Controlling operations of equipment or systems. **GOE—Interest Area:** 02. Architecture and Construction. **Work Group:** 02.04. Construction Crafts. **Other Jobs in This Work Group:** Boat Builders and Shipwrights; Boilermakers; Brattice Builders; Brickmasons and Blockmasons; Carpet Installers; Ceiling Tile Installers; Cement Masons and Concrete Finishers; Commercial Divers; Construction Carpenters; Crane and Tower Operators; Dragline Operators; Drywall Installers; Electricians; Fence Erectors; Floor Layers, Except Carpet, Wood, and Hard Tiles; Floor Sanders and Finishers; Glaziers; Grader, Bulldozer, and Scraper Operators; Hazardous Materials Removal Workers; Insulation Workers, Floor, Ceiling, and Wall; Insulation Workers, Mechanical; Manufactured Building and Mobile Home Installers; Operating Engineers; Painters, Construction and Maintenance; Paperhangers; Paving, Surfacing, and Tamping Equipment Operators; Pile-Driver Operators; Pipe Fitters; Pipelayers; Pipelaying Fitters; Plasterers and Stucco Masons; Plumbers; Rail-Track Laying and Maintenance Equipment Operators; Refractory Materials Repairers, Except Brickmasons; Reinforcing Iron and Rebar Workers; Riggers; Rough Carpenters; Security and Fire Alarm Systems Installers; Segmental Pavers; Sheet Metal Workers; Ship Carpenters and Joiners; Stone Cutters and Carvers; Stonemasons; Structural Iron and Steel Workers; Tapers; Terrazzo Workers and Finishers; Tile and Marble Setters. **PERSONALITY TYPE:** Realistic.

EDUCATION/TRAINING PROGRAM(S)— Roofer. **RELATED KNOWLEDGE/COURSES—Building and Construction:** Knowledge of the materials, methods, and tools involved in the construction or repair of houses, buildings, or other structures such as highways and roads. **Mechanical Devices:** Knowledge of machines and tools, including their designs, uses, repair, and maintenance.

Rough Carpenters

- Education/Training Required: Moderate-term on-the-job training
- Annual Earnings: $34,900
- Growth: 10.1%
- Annual Job Openings: 193,000
- Self-Employed: 29.7%
- Part-Time: 5.3%

Build rough wooden structures, such as concrete forms; scaffolds; tunnel, bridge, or sewer supports; billboard signs; and temporary frame shelters according to sketches, blueprints, or oral instructions. Study blueprints and diagrams to determine dimensions of structure or form to be constructed. Measure materials or distances, using square, measuring tape, or rule to lay out work. Cut or saw boards, timbers, or plywood to required size, using handsaw, power saw, or woodworking machine. Assemble and fasten material together to construct wood or metal framework of structure, using bolts, nails, or screws. Anchor and brace forms and other structures in place, using nails, bolts, anchor rods, steel cables, planks, wedges, and timbers. Mark cutting lines on materials, using pencil and scriber. Erect forms, framework, scaffolds, hoists, roof supports, or chutes, using hand tools, plumb rule, and level. Install rough door and window frames, subflooring, fixtures, or temporary supports in structures undergoing construction or repair. Examine structural timbers and supports to detect decay and replace timbers as required, using hand tools, nuts, and bolts. Bore boltholes in timber, masonry, or concrete walls, using power drill. Fabricate parts, using woodworking and metalworking machines. **SKILLS—Repairing:** Repairing machines or systems by using the needed tools. **Installation:** Installing equipment, machines, wiring, or programs to meet specifications. **Management of Personnel Resources:** Motivating, developing, and directing people as they work, identifying the best people for the job. **Equipment Selection:** Determining the kind of tools and equipment needed to do a job. **Mathematics:** Using mathematics to solve problems. **Coordination:** Adjusting actions in relation to others' actions. **Technology Design:** Generating or adapting equipment and technology to serve user needs. **Equipment Maintenance:** Performing routine maintenance on equipment and determining when and what kind of maintenance is needed. **GOE—Interest Area:** 02.

Architecture and Construction. **Work Group:** 02.04. Construction Crafts. **Other Jobs in This Work Group:** Boat Builders and Shipwrights; Boilermakers; Brattice Builders; Brickmasons and Blockmasons; Carpet Installers; Ceiling Tile Installers; Cement Masons and Concrete Finishers; Commercial Divers; Construction Carpenters; Crane and Tower Operators; Dragline Operators; Drywall Installers; Electricians; Fence Erectors; Floor Layers, Except Carpet, Wood, and Hard Tiles; Floor Sanders and Finishers; Glaziers; Grader, Bulldozer, and Scraper Operators; Hazardous Materials Removal Workers; Insulation Workers, Floor, Ceiling, and Wall; Insulation Workers, Mechanical; Manufactured Building and Mobile Home Installers; Operating Engineers; Painters, Construction and Maintenance; Paperhangers; Paving, Surfacing, and Tamping Equipment Operators; Pile-Driver Operators; Pipe Fitters; Pipelayers; Pipelaying Fitters; Plasterers and Stucco Masons; Plumbers; Rail-Track Laying and Maintenance Equipment Operators; Refractory Materials Repairers, Except Brickmasons; Reinforcing Iron and Rebar Workers; Riggers; Roofers; Security and Fire Alarm Systems Installers; Segmental Pavers; Sheet Metal Workers; Ship Carpenters and Joiners; Stone Cutters and Carvers; Stonemasons; Structural Iron and Steel Workers; Tapers; Terrazzo Workers and Finishers; Tile and Marble Setters. **PERSONALITY TYPE:** Realistic.

EDUCATION/TRAINING PROGRAM(S)—Carpentry/Carpenter. **RELATED KNOWLEDGE/COURSES—Building and Construction:** Knowledge of the materials, methods, and tools involved in the construction or repair of houses, buildings, or other structures such as highways and roads. **Design:** Knowledge of design techniques, tools, and principles involved in production of precision technical plans, blueprints, drawings, and models. **Engineering and Technology:** Knowledge of the practical application of engineering science and technology. This includes applying principles, techniques, procedures, and equipment to the design and production of various goods and services. **Mechanical Devices:** Knowledge of machines and tools, including their designs, uses, repair, and maintenance. **Production and Processing:** Knowledge of raw materials, production processes, quality control, costs, and other techniques for maximizing the effective manufacture and distribution of goods. **Public Safety and Security:** Knowledge of relevant equipment, policies, procedures, and strategies to promote effective local, state, or national security operations for the protection of people, data, property, and institutions.

Sales Agents, Financial Services

- ◎ Education/Training Required: Bachelor's degree
- ◎ Annual Earnings: $69,200
- ◎ Growth: 13.0%
- ◎ Annual Job Openings: 39,000
- ◎ Self-Employed: 12.8%
- ◎ Part-Time: 6.0%

Sell financial services such as loan, tax, and securities counseling to customers of financial institutions and business establishments. Contact prospective customers in order to present information and explain available services. Determine customers' financial services needs and prepare proposals to sell services that address these needs. Develop prospects from current commercial customers, referral leads, and sales and trade meetings. Prepare forms or agreements to complete sales. Sell services and equipment, such as trusts, investments, and check processing services. Evaluate costs and revenue of agreements in order to determine continued profitability. Make presentations on financial services to groups in order to attract new clients. Review business trends in order to advise customers regarding expected fluctuations. **SKILLS—Persuasion:** Persuading others to change their minds or behavior. **Systems Analysis:** Determining how a system should work and how changes in conditions, operations, and the environment will affect outcomes. **Management of Financial Resources:** Determining how money will be spent to get the work done and accounting for these expenditures. **Service Orientation:** Actively looking for ways to help people. **Systems Evaluation:** Identifying measures or indicators of system performance and the actions needed to improve or correct performance relative to the goals of the system. **Negotiation:** Bringing others together and trying to reconcile differences. **Active Learning:** Understanding the implications of new information for both current and future problem-solving and decision-making. **Monitoring:** Monitoring or assessing your performance or that of other individuals or organizations to make improvements or take corrective action. **GOE—**

Interest Area: 06. Finance and Insurance. **Work Group:** 06.05. Finance/Insurance Sales and Support. **Other Jobs in This Work Group:** Advertising Sales Agents; Insurance Sales Agents; Personal Financial Advisors; Sales Agents, Securities and Commodities. **PERSONALITY TYPE:** Enterprising.

EDUCATION/TRAINING PROGRAM(S)—Business and Personal/Financial Services Marketing Operations; Financial Planning and Services; Investments and Securities. **RELATED KNOWLEDGE/ COURSES—Economics and Accounting:** Knowledge of economic and accounting principles and practices, the financial markets, banking, and the analysis and reporting of financial data. **Sales and Marketing:** Knowledge of principles and methods for showing, promoting, and selling products or services. This includes marketing strategy and tactics, product demonstrations, sales techniques, and sales control systems. **Computers and Electronics:** Knowledge of circuit boards, processors, chips, electronic equipment, and computer hardware and software, including applications and programming. **Mathematics:** Knowledge of arithmetic, algebra, geometry, calculus, and statistics and their applications. **Law and Government:** Knowledge of laws, legal codes, court procedures, precedents, government regulations, executive orders, agency rules, and the democratic political process. **Communications and Media:** Knowledge of media production, communication, and dissemination techniques and methods. This includes alternative ways to inform and entertain via written, oral, and visual media.

Sales Agents, Securities and Commodities

- ◎ Education/Training Required: Bachelor's degree
- ◎ Annual Earnings: $69,200
- ◎ Growth: 13.0%
- ◎ Annual Job Openings: 39,000
- ◎ Self-Employed: 12.8%
- ◎ Part-Time: 6.0%

Buy and sell securities in investment and trading firms and develop and implement financial plans for individuals, businesses, and organizations. Develop financial plans based on analysis of clients' financial status and discuss financial options with clients. Relay buy or sell orders to securities exchanges or to firm trading departments. Record transactions accurately and keep clients informed about transactions. Analyze market conditions in order to determine optimum times to execute securities transactions. Review financial periodicals, stock and bond reports, business publications, and other material in order to identify potential investments for clients and to keep abreast of trends affecting market conditions. Read corporate reports and calculate ratios to determine best prospects for profit on stock purchases and to monitor client accounts. Interview clients to determine clients' assets, liabilities, cash flow, insurance coverage, tax status, and financial objectives. Review all securities transactions to ensure accuracy of information and that trades conform to regulations of governing agencies. Prepare documents needed to implement plans selected by clients. Complete sales order tickets and submit for processing of client-requested transactions. Inform and advise concerned parties regarding fluctuations and securities transactions affecting plans or accounts. Prepare financial reports to monitor client or corporate finances. Identify potential clients, using advertising campaigns, mailing lists, and personal contacts. Contact prospective customers to determine customer needs, present information, and explain available services. Explain stock market terms and trading practices to clients. Offer advice on the purchase or sale of particular securities. Supply the latest price quotes on any security, as well as information on the activities and financial positions of the corporations issuing these securities. Calculate costs for billings and commissions purposes. **SKILLS—Management of Financial Resources:** Determining how money will be spent to get the work done and accounting for these expenditures. **Systems Analysis:** Determining how a system should work and how changes in conditions, operations, and the environment will affect outcomes. **Systems Evaluation:** Identifying measures or indicators of system performance and the actions needed to improve or correct performance relative to the goals of the system. **Persuasion:** Persuading others to change their minds or behavior. **Service Orientation:** Actively looking for ways to help people. **Negotiation:** Bringing others together and trying to reconcile differences. **Active Learning:** Understanding the implications of new information for both current and future problem-solving and decision-making. **Judgment and Decision Making:** Considering the relative costs and benefits of

potential actions to choose the most appropriate one. **GOE—Interest Area:** 06. Finance and Insurance. **Work Group:** 06.05. Finance/Insurance Sales and Support. **Other Jobs in This Work Group:** Advertising Sales Agents; Insurance Sales Agents; Personal Financial Advisors; Sales Agents, Financial Services. **PERSONALITY TYPE:** Enterprising.

EDUCATION/TRAINING PROGRAM(S)—Business and Personal/Financial Services Marketing Operations; Financial Planning and Services; Investments and Securities. **RELATED KNOWLEDGE/ COURSES—Economics and Accounting:** Knowledge of economic and accounting principles and practices, the financial markets, banking, and the analysis and reporting of financial data. **Sales and Marketing:** Knowledge of principles and methods for showing, promoting, and selling products or services. This includes marketing strategy and tactics, product demonstrations, sales techniques, and sales control systems. **Mathematics:** Knowledge of arithmetic, algebra, geometry, calculus, and statistics and their applications. **Computers and Electronics:** Knowledge of circuit boards, processors, chips, electronic equipment, and computer hardware and software, including applications and programming. **Customer and Personal Service:** Knowledge of principles and processes for providing customer and personal services. This includes customer needs assessment, meeting quality standards for services, and evaluation of customer satisfaction. **Personnel and Human Resources:** Knowledge of principles and procedures for personnel recruitment, selection, training, compensation and benefits, labor relations and negotiation, and personnel information systems.

Sales Engineers

- Education/Training Required: Bachelor's degree
- Annual Earnings: $70,620
- Growth: 19.9%
- Annual Job Openings: 7,000
- Self-Employed: 0.6%
- Part-Time: 0.8%

Sell business goods or services for which selling requires a technical background equivalent to a baccalaureate degree in engineering. Arrange for demonstrations or trial installations of equipment. Attend company training seminars to become familiar with product lines. Collaborate with sales teams to understand customer requirements, to promote the sale of company products, and to provide sales support. Confer with customers and engineers to assess equipment needs and to determine system requirements. Create sales or service contracts for products or services. Develop sales plans to introduce products in new markets. Develop, present, or respond to proposals for specific customer requirements, including request for proposal responses and industry-specific solutions. Identify resale opportunities and support them to achieve sales plans. Keep informed on industry news and trends; products; services; competitors; relevant information about legacy, existing, and emerging technologies; and the latest product-line developments. Plan and modify product configurations to meet customer needs. Prepare and deliver technical presentations that explain products or services to customers and prospective customers. Recommend improved materials or machinery to customers, documenting how such changes will lower costs or increase production. Research and identify potential customers for products or services. Secure and renew orders and arrange delivery. Sell products requiring extensive technical expertise and support for installation and use, such as material handling equipment, numerical-control machinery, and computer systems. Visit prospective buyers at commercial, industrial, or other establishments to show samples or catalogs and to inform them about product pricing, availability, and advantages. Attend trade shows and seminars to promote products or to learn about industry developments. Diagnose problems with installed equipment. Document account activities, generate reports, and keep records of business transactions with customers and suppliers. Maintain sales forecasting reports. Provide information needed for the development of custom-made machinery. Provide technical and non-technical support and services to clients or other staff members regarding the use, operation, and maintenance of equipment. SKILLS—Technology Design: Generating or adapting equipment and technology to serve user needs. Troubleshooting: Determining causes of operating errors and deciding what to do about them. Operations Analysis: Analyzing needs and product requirements to create a design. Negotiation:

Bringing others together and trying to reconcile differences. Persuasion: Persuading others to change their minds or behavior. Management of Material Resources: Obtaining and seeing to the appropriate use of equipment, facilities, and materials needed to do certain work. Service Orientation: Actively looking for ways to help people. Speaking: Talking to others to convey information effectively. GOE—Interest Area: 14. Retail and Wholesale Sales and Service. Work Group: 14.02. Technical Sales. Other Jobs in This Work Group: Sales Representatives, Agricultural; Sales Representatives, Chemical and Pharmaceutical; Sales Representatives, Electrical/Electronic; Sales Representatives, Instruments; Sales Representatives, Mechanical Equipment and Supplies; Sales Representatives, Medical. PERSONALITY TYPE: Enterprising.

EDUCATION/TRAINING PROGRAM(S)—Selling Skills and Sales Operations. RELATED KNOWLEDGE/COURSES—Sales and Marketing: Knowledge of principles and methods for showing, promoting, and selling products or services. This includes marketing strategy and tactics, product demonstrations, sales techniques, and sales control systems. Design: Knowledge of design techniques, tools, and principles involved in production of precision technical plans, blueprints, drawings, and models. Engineering and Technology: Knowledge of the practical application of engineering science and technology. This includes applying principles, techniques, procedures, and equipment to the design and production of various goods and services. Production and Processing: Knowledge of raw materials, production processes, quality control, costs, and other techniques for maximizing the effective manufacture and distribution of goods. Physics: Knowledge and prediction of physical principles and laws and their interrelationships and applications to understanding fluid, material, and atmospheric dynamics and mechanical, electrical, atomic, and subatomic structures and processes. Economics and Accounting: Knowledge of economic and accounting principles and practices, the financial markets, banking, and the analysis and reporting of financial data.

Sales Managers

- ◎ Education/Training Required: Work experience plus degree
- ◎ Annual Earnings: $84,220
- ◎ Growth: 30.5%
- ◎ Annual Job Openings: 54,000
- ◎ Self-Employed: 3.0%
- ◎ Part-Time: 4.7%

Direct the actual distribution or movement of a product or service to the customer. Coordinate sales distribution by establishing sales territories, quotas, and goals and establish training programs for sales representatives. Analyze sales statistics gathered by staff to determine sales potential and inventory requirements and monitor the preferences of customers. Resolve customer complaints regarding sales and service. Represent company at trade association meetings to promote products. Plan and direct staffing, training, and performance evaluations to develop and control sales and service programs. Visit franchised dealers to stimulate interest in establishment or expansion of leasing programs. Confer with potential customers regarding equipment needs and advise customers on types of equipment to purchase. Oversee regional and local sales managers and their staffs. Direct clerical staff to keep records of export correspondence, bid requests, and credit collections and to maintain current information on tariffs, licenses, and restrictions. Direct foreign sales and service outlets of an organization. Monitor customer preferences to determine focus of sales efforts. Direct and coordinate activities involving sales of manufactured products, services, commodities, real estate, or other subjects of sale. Determine price schedules and discount rates. Review operational records and reports to project sales and determine profitability. Direct, coordinate, and review activities in sales and service accounting and record-keeping and in receiving and shipping operations. Confer or consult with department heads to plan advertising services and to secure information on equipment and customer specifications. Advise dealers and distributors on policies and operating procedures to ensure functional effectiveness of business. Prepare budgets and approve budget expenditures. **SKILLS—Negotiation:** Bringing others together and trying to reconcile differences. **Service Orientation:** Actively looking for ways to help people. **Management of Personnel Resources:** Motivating, developing, and directing people as they work, identifying the best people for the job. **Persuasion:** Persuading others to change their minds or behavior. **Time Management:** Managing one's own time and the time of others. **Monitoring:** Monitoring or assessing your performance or that of other individuals or organizations to make improvements or take corrective action. **Instructing:** Teaching others how to do something. **Social Perceptiveness:** Being aware of others' reactions and understanding why they react as they do. **GOE—Interest Area:** 14. Retail and Wholesale Sales and Service. **Work Group:** 14.01. Managerial Work in Retail/Wholesale Sales and Service. **Other Jobs in This Work Group:** Advertising and Promotions Managers; First-Line Supervisors/Managers of Non-Retail Sales Workers; First-Line Supervisors/Managers of Retail Sales Workers; Funeral Directors; Marketing Managers; Property, Real Estate, and Community Association Managers; Purchasing Managers. **PERSONALITY TYPE:** Enterprising.

EDUCATION/TRAINING PROGRAM(S)—Business Administration and Management, General; Business/Commerce, General; Consumer Merchandising/Retailing Management; Marketing, Other; Marketing/Marketing Management, General. **RELATED KNOWLEDGE/COURSES—Sales and Marketing:** Knowledge of principles and methods for showing, promoting, and selling products or services. This includes marketing strategy and tactics, product demonstrations, sales techniques, and sales control systems. **Computers and Electronics:** Knowledge of circuit boards, processors, chips, electronic equipment, and computer hardware and software, including applications and programming. **Mathematics:** Knowledge of arithmetic, algebra, geometry, calculus, and statistics and their applications. **Customer and Personal Service:** Knowledge of principles and processes for providing customer and personal services. This includes customer needs assessment, meeting quality standards for services, and evaluation of customer satisfaction. **Administration and Management:** Knowledge of business and management principles involved in strategic planning, resource allocation, human resources modeling, leadership technique, production methods, and coordination of people and resources. **Law and Government:** Knowledge of laws, legal codes, court procedures, precedents, government regulations, executive orders, agency rules, and the democratic political process.

Sales Representatives, Agricultural

- Education/Training Required: Moderate-term on-the-job training
- Annual Earnings: $58,580
- Growth: 19.3%
- Annual Job Openings: 44,000
- Self-Employed: 4.6%
- Part-Time: 8.1%

Sell agricultural products and services, such as animal feeds; farm and garden equipment; and dairy, poultry, and veterinarian supplies. Solicits orders from customers in person or by phone. Demonstrates use of agricultural equipment or machines. Recommends changes in customer use of agricultural products to improve production. Prepares reports of business transactions. Informs customer of estimated delivery schedule, service contracts, warranty, or other information pertaining to purchased products. Displays or shows customer agricultural-related products. Compiles lists of prospective customers for use as sales leads. Prepares sales contracts for orders obtained. Consults with customer regarding installation, setup, or layout of agricultural equipment and machines. Quotes prices and credit terms. **SKILLS—Persuasion:** Persuading others to change their minds or behavior. **Negotiation:** Bringing others together and trying to reconcile differences. **Speaking:** Talking to others to convey information effectively. **Active Listening:** Giving full attention to what other people are saying, taking time to understand the points being made, asking questions as appropriate, and not interrupting at inappropriate times. **Writing:** Communicating effectively in writing as appropriate for the needs of the audience. **Mathematics:** Using mathematics to solve problems. **Instructing:** Teaching others how to do something. **GOE—Interest Area:** 14. Retail and Wholesale Sales and Service. **Work Group:** 14.02. Technical Sales. **Other Jobs in This Work Group:** Sales Engineers; Sales Representatives, Chemical and Pharmaceutical; Sales Representatives, Electrical/Electronic; Sales Representatives, Instruments; Sales Representatives, Mechanical Equipment and Supplies; Sales Representatives, Medical. **PERSONALITY TYPE:** Enterprising.

EDUCATION/TRAINING PROGRAM(S)—Business, Management, Marketing, and Related Support Services, Other; Selling Skills and Sales Operations. **RELATED KNOWLEDGE/COURSES—Sales and Marketing:** Knowledge of principles and methods for showing, promoting, and selling products or services. This includes marketing strategy and tactics, product demonstrations, sales techniques, and sales control systems. **Economics and Accounting:** Knowledge of economic and accounting principles and practices, the financial markets, banking, and the analysis and reporting of financial data. **Mathematics:** Knowledge of arithmetic, algebra, geometry, calculus, and statistics and their applications. **Food Production:** Knowledge of techniques and equipment for planting, growing, and harvesting food products (both plant and animal) for consumption, including storage/handling techniques. **Telecommunications:** Knowledge of transmission, broadcasting, switching, control, and operation of telecommunications systems. **Communications and Media:** Knowledge of media production, communication, and dissemination techniques and methods. This includes alternative ways to inform and entertain via written, oral, and visual media.

Sales Representatives, Chemical and Pharmaceutical

- Education/Training Required: Moderate-term on-the-job training
- Annual Earnings: $58,580
- Growth: 19.3%
- Annual Job Openings: 44,000
- Self-Employed: 4.6%
- Part-Time: 8.1%

Sell chemical or pharmaceutical products or services, such as acids, industrial chemicals, agricultural chemicals, medicines, drugs, and water treatment supplies. Promotes and sells pharmaceutical and chemical products to potential customers. Explains water-treatment package benefits to customer and sells chemicals to treat and resolve water process problems. Estimates and advises customer of service costs to correct water-treatment process problems. Discusses characteristics and clinical studies pertaining to pharmaceutical products with physicians, dentists, hospitals, and retail/wholesale establishments. Distributes drug samples to customer and takes orders for pharmaceutical supply items from customer. Inspects, tests, and observes chemical changes in water system equipment, utilizing test kit, reference manual, and knowledge of chemical treatment. **SKILLS—Science:** Using scientific rules and methods to solve problems. **Persuasion:** Persuading others to change their minds or behavior. **Speaking:** Talking to others to convey information effectively. **Social Perceptiveness:** Being aware of others' reactions and understanding why they react as they do. **Active Listening:** Giving full attention to what other people are saying, taking time to understand the points being made, asking questions as appropriate, and not interrupting at inappropriate times. **Negotiation:** Bringing others together and trying to reconcile differences. **GOE—Interest Area:** 14. Retail and Wholesale Sales and Service. **Work Group:** 14.02. Technical Sales. **Other Jobs in This Work Group:** Sales Engineers; Sales Representatives, Agricultural; Sales Representatives, Electrical/Electronic; Sales Representatives, Instruments; Sales Representatives, Mechanical Equipment and Supplies; Sales Representatives, Medical. **PERSONALITY TYPE:** Enterprising.

EDUCATION/TRAINING PROGRAM(S)—Business, Management, Marketing, and Related Support Services, Other; Selling Skills and Sales Operations. **RELATED KNOWLEDGE/COURSES—Sales and Marketing:** Knowledge of principles and methods for showing, promoting, and selling products or services. This includes marketing strategy and tactics, product demonstrations, sales techniques, and sales control systems. **Chemistry:** Knowledge of the chemical composition, structure, and properties of substances and of the chemical processes and transformations that they undergo. This includes uses of chemicals and their danger signs, production techniques, and disposal methods. **Biology:** Knowledge of plant and animal organisms and their tissues, cells, functions, interdependencies, and interactions with each other and the environment. **Medicine and Dentistry:** Knowledge of the information and techniques needed to diagnose and treat human injuries, diseases, and deformities. This includes symptoms, treatment alternatives, drug properties and interactions, and preventive health-care measures. **Mathematics:** Knowledge of arithmetic, algebra, geometry, calculus, and statistics and their applications. **Economics and Accounting:** Knowledge of economic and accounting principles and practices, the financial markets, banking, and the analysis and reporting of financial data.

Sales Representatives, Electrical/Electronic

- Education/Training Required: Moderate-term on-the-job training
- Annual Earnings: $58,580
- Growth: 19.3%
- Annual Job Openings: 44,000
- Self-Employed: 4.6%
- Part-Time: 8.1%

Sell electrical, electronic, or related products or services, such as communication equipment, radiographic-inspection equipment and services, ultrasonic equipment, electronics parts, computers, and EDP systems. Analyzes communication needs of customer and consults with staff engineers regarding technical problems. Trains establishment personnel in equipment use, utilizing knowledge of electronics and product sold. Recommends equipment to meet customer requirements, considering salable features such as flexibility, cost, capacity, and economy of operation. Negotiates terms of sale and services with customer. Sells electrical or electronic equipment such as computers, data-processing, and radiographic equipment to businesses and industrial establishments. **SKILLS—Persuasion:** Persuading others to change their minds or behavior. **Negotiation:** Bringing others together and trying to reconcile differences. **Instructing:** Teaching others how to do something. **Operations Analysis:** Analyzing needs and product requirements to create a design. **Active Listening:** Giving full attention to what other people are saying, taking time to understand the points being made, asking questions as appropriate, and not interrupting at inappropriate times. **Equipment Selection:** Determining the kind of tools and equipment needed to do a job. **Speaking:** Talking to others to convey information effectively. **Technology Design:** Generating or adapting equipment and technology to serve user needs. **GOE—Interest Area:** 14. Retail and Wholesale Sales and Service. **Work Group:** 14.02. Technical Sales. **Other Jobs in This Work Group:** Sales Engineers; Sales Representatives, Agricul-

S

tural; Sales Representatives, Chemical and Pharmaceutical; Sales Representatives, Instruments; Sales Representatives, Mechanical Equipment and Supplies; Sales Representatives, Medical. **PERSONALITY TYPE:** Enterprising.

EDUCATION/TRAINING PROGRAM(S)—Business, Management, Marketing, and Related Support Services, Other; Selling Skills and Sales Operations. **RELATED KNOWLEDGE/COURSES—Sales and Marketing:** Knowledge of principles and methods for showing, promoting, and selling products or services. This includes marketing strategy and tactics, product demonstrations, sales techniques, and sales control systems. **Computers and Electronics:** Knowledge of circuit boards, processors, chips, electronic equipment, and computer hardware and software, including applications and programming. **Economics and Accounting:** Knowledge of economic and accounting principles and practices, the financial markets, banking, and the analysis and reporting of financial data. **Education and Training:** Knowledge of principles and methods for curriculum and training design, teaching and instruction for individuals and groups, and the measurement of training effects. **Telecommunications:** Knowledge of transmission, broadcasting, switching, control, and operation of telecommunications systems. **Mathematics:** Knowledge of arithmetic, algebra, geometry, calculus, and statistics and their applications.

Sales Representatives, Instruments

- ◉ Education/Training Required: Moderate-term on-the-job training
- ◉ Annual Earnings: $58,580
- ◉ Growth: 19.3%
- ◉ Annual Job Openings: 44,000
- ◉ Self-Employed: 4.6%
- ◉ Part-Time: 8.1%

Sell precision instruments, such as dynamometers; spring scales; and laboratory, navigation, and surveying instruments. Assists customer with product selection, utilizing knowledge of engineering specifications and catalog resources. Evaluates customer needs and emphasizes product features based on technical knowl-

edge of product capabilities and limitations. Sells weighing and other precision instruments, such as spring scales; dynamometers; and laboratory, navigational, and surveying instruments to customer. **SKILLS—Persuasion:** Persuading others to change their minds or behavior. **Active Listening:** Giving full attention to what other people are saying, taking time to understand the points being made, asking questions as appropriate, and not interrupting at inappropriate times. **Service Orientation:** Actively looking for ways to help people. **Speaking:** Talking to others to convey information effectively. **GOE—Interest Area:** 14. Retail and Wholesale Sales and Service. **Work Group:** 14.02. Technical Sales. **Other Jobs in This Work Group:** Sales Engineers; Sales Representatives, Agricultural; Sales Representatives, Chemical and Pharmaceutical; Sales Representatives, Electrical/Electronic; Sales Representatives, Mechanical Equipment and Supplies; Sales Representatives, Medical. **PERSONALITY TYPE:** Enterprising.

EDUCATION/TRAINING PROGRAM(S)—Business, Management, Marketing, and Related Support Services, Other; Selling Skills and Sales Operations. **RELATED KNOWLEDGE/COURSES—Sales and Marketing:** Knowledge of principles and methods for showing, promoting, and selling products or services. This includes marketing strategy and tactics, product demonstrations, sales techniques, and sales control systems. **Engineering and Technology:** Knowledge of the practical application of engineering science and technology. This includes applying principles, techniques, procedures, and equipment to the design and production of various goods and services.

Sales Representatives, Mechanical Equipment and Supplies

- ◉ Education/Training Required: Moderate-term on-the-job training
- ◉ Annual Earnings: $58,580
- ◉ Growth: 19.3%
- ◉ Annual Job Openings: 44,000
- ◉ Self-Employed: 4.6%
- ◉ Part-Time: 8.1%

Sell mechanical equipment, machinery, materials, and supplies, such as aircraft and railroad equipment and parts, construction machinery, material-handling equipment, industrial machinery, and welding equipment. Recommends and sells textile, industrial, construction, railroad, and oil field machinery, equipment, materials, supplies, and services, utilizing knowledge of machine operations. Computes installation or production costs, estimates savings, and prepares and submits bid specifications to customer for review and approval. Submits orders for product and follows up on order to verify that material list is accurate and delivery schedule meets project deadline. Appraises equipment and verifies customer credit rating to establish trade-in value and contract terms. Reviews existing machinery/equipment placement and diagrams proposal to illustrate efficient space utilization, using standard measuring devices and templates. Attends sales and trade meetings and reads related publications to obtain current market condition information, business trends, and industry developments. Inspects establishment premises to verify installation feasibility and obtains building blueprints and elevator specifications to submit to engineering department for bid. Demonstrates and explains use of installed equipment and production processes. Arranges for installation and test-operation of machinery and recommends solutions to product-related problems. Contacts current and potential customers, visits establishments to evaluate needs, and promotes sale of products and services. **SKILLS—Operations Analysis:** Analyzing needs and product requirements to create a design. **Persuasion:** Persuading others to change their minds or behavior. **Negotiation:** Bringing others together and trying to reconcile differences. **Equipment Selection:** Determining the kind of tools and equipment needed to do a job. **Active Listening:** Giving full attention to what other people are saying, taking time to understand the points being made, asking questions as appropriate, and not interrupting at inappropriate times. **Instructing:** Teaching others how to do something. **Speaking:** Talking to others to convey information effectively. **Reading Comprehension:** Understanding written sentences and paragraphs in work-related documents. **GOE—Interest Area:** 14. Retail and Wholesale Sales and Service. **Work Group:** 14.02. Technical Sales. **Other Jobs in This Work Group:** Sales Engineers; Sales Representatives, Agricultural; Sales Representatives, Chemical and Pharmaceutical; Sales Representatives, Electrical/Electronic; Sales Representatives,

Instruments; Sales Representatives, Medical. **PERSONALITY TYPE:** Enterprising.

EDUCATION/TRAINING PROGRAM(S)—Business, Management, Marketing, and Related Support Services, Other; Selling Skills and Sales Operations. **RELATED KNOWLEDGE/COURSES—Sales and Marketing:** Knowledge of principles and methods for showing, promoting, and selling products or services. This includes marketing strategy and tactics, product demonstrations, sales techniques, and sales control systems. **Mathematics:** Knowledge of arithmetic, algebra, geometry, calculus, and statistics and their applications. **Economics and Accounting:** Knowledge of economic and accounting principles and practices, the financial markets, banking, and the analysis and reporting of financial data. **Design:** Knowledge of design techniques, tools, and principles involved in production of precision technical plans, blueprints, drawings, and models. **Telecommunications:** Knowledge of transmission, broadcasting, switching, control, and operation of telecommunications systems. **Engineering and Technology:** Knowledge of the practical application of engineering science and technology. This includes applying principles, techniques, procedures, and equipment to the design and production of various goods and services.

Sales Representatives, Medical

- Education/Training Required: Moderate-term on-the-job training
- Annual Earnings: $58,580
- Growth: 19.3%
- Annual Job Openings: 44,000
- Self-Employed: 4.6%
- Part-Time: 8.1%

Sell medical equipment, products, and services. Does not include pharmaceutical sales representatives. Promotes sale of medical and dental equipment, supplies, and services to doctors, dentists, hospitals, medical schools, and retail establishments. Writes specifications to order custom-made surgical appliances, using customer measurements and physician prescriptions. Advises customer regarding office layout, legal and insurance regulations, cost analysis, and collection methods. Designs and fabricates custom-made medical appliances. Selects surgical appliances from stock and fits and sells appliance to customer. Studies data describing new products to accurately recommend purchase of equipment and supplies. **SKILLS—Technology Design:** Generating or adapting equipment and technology to serve user needs. **Persuasion:** Persuading others to change their minds or behavior. **Negotiation:** Bringing others together and trying to reconcile differences. **Operations Analysis:** Analyzing needs and product requirements to create a design. **Active Listening:** Giving full attention to what other people are saying, taking time to understand the points being made, asking questions as appropriate, and not interrupting at inappropriate times. **Writing:** Communicating effectively in writing as appropriate for the needs of the audience. **Speaking:** Talking to others to convey information effectively. **Service Orientation:** Actively looking for ways to help people. **Equipment Selection:** Determining the kind of tools and equipment needed to do a job. **GOE—Interest Area:** 14. Retail and Wholesale Sales and Service. **Work Group:** 14.02. Technical Sales. **Other Jobs in This Work Group:** Sales Engineers; Sales Representatives, Agricultural; Sales Representatives, Chemical and Pharmaceutical; Sales Representatives, Electrical/Electronic; Sales Representatives, Instruments; Sales Representatives, Mechanical Equipment and Supplies. **PERSONALITY TYPE:** Enterprising.

EDUCATION/TRAINING PROGRAM(S)—Business, Management, Marketing, and Related Support Services, Other; Selling Skills and Sales Operations. **RELATED KNOWLEDGE/COURSES—Sales and Marketing:** Knowledge of principles and methods for showing, promoting, and selling products or services. This includes marketing strategy and tactics, product demonstrations, sales techniques, and sales control systems. **Design:** Knowledge of design techniques, tools, and principles involved in production of precision technical plans, blueprints, drawings, and models. **Mathematics:** Knowledge of arithmetic, algebra, geometry, calculus, and statistics and their applications. **Economics and Accounting:** Knowledge of economic and accounting principles and practices, the financial markets, banking, and the analysis and reporting of financial data. **Engineering and Technology:** Knowledge of the practical application of engineering science and technology. This includes applying principles, techniques, procedures, and equipment to the design and production of various goods and services. **Medicine and Dentistry:** Knowledge of the information and techniques needed to diagnose and treat human injuries, diseases, and deformities. This includes symptoms, treatment alternatives, drug properties and interactions, and preventive health-care measures.

Sales Representatives, Wholesale and Manufacturing, Except Technical and Scientific Products

- ◉ Education/Training Required: Moderate-term on-the-job training
- ◉ Annual Earnings: $45,400
- ◉ Growth: 19.1%
- ◉ Annual Job Openings: 160,000
- ◉ Self-Employed: 4.6%
- ◉ Part-Time: 8.1%

Sell goods for wholesalers or manufacturers to businesses or groups of individuals. Work requires substantial knowledge of items sold. Answer customers' questions about products, prices, availability, product uses, and credit terms. Arrange and direct delivery and installation of products and equipment. Contact regular and prospective customers to demonstrate products, explain product features, and solicit orders. Estimate or quote prices, credit or contract terms, warranties, and delivery dates. Forward orders to manufacturers. Identify prospective customers by using business directories, following leads from existing clients, participating in organizations and clubs, and attending trade shows and conferences. Monitor market conditions; product innovations; and competitors' products, prices, and sales. Negotiate details of contracts and payments and prepare sales contracts and order forms. Prepare drawings, estimates, and bids that meet specific customer needs. Provide customers with product samples and catalogs. Recommend products to customers based on customers' needs and interests. Buy products from manufacturers or brokerage firms and distribute them to wholesale and retail clients. Check stock levels and reorder merchandise as neces-

ساير. Consult with clients after sales or contract signings in order to resolve problems and to provide ongoing support. Negotiate with retail merchants to improve product exposure such as shelf positioning and advertising. Obtain credit information about prospective customers. Perform administrative duties, such as preparing sales budgets and reports, keeping sales records, and filing expense account reports. Plan, assemble, and stock product displays in retail stores or make recommendations to retailers regarding product displays, promotional programs, and advertising. Train customers' employees to operate and maintain new equipment. **SKILLS—Management of Material Resources:** Obtaining and seeing to the appropriate use of equipment, facilities, and materials needed to do certain work. **Negotiation:** Bringing others together and trying to reconcile differences. **Persuasion:** Persuading others to change their minds or behavior. **Service Orientation:** Actively looking for ways to help people. **Speaking:** Talking to others to convey information effectively. **Social Perceptiveness:** Being aware of others' reactions and understanding why they react as they do. **Writing:** Communicating effectively in writing as appropriate for the needs of the audience. **Instructing:** Teaching others how to do something. **Operations Analysis:** Analyzing needs and product requirements to create a design. **Systems Evaluation:** Identifying measures or indicators of system performance and the actions needed to improve or correct performance relative to the goals of the system. **GOE—Interest Area:** 14. Retail and Wholesale Sales and Service. **Work Group:** 14.03. General Sales. **Other Jobs in This Work Group:** Parts Salespersons; Real Estate Brokers; Real Estate Sales Agents; Retail Salespersons; Service Station Attendants. **PERSONALITY TYPE:** Enterprising.

EDUCATION/TRAINING PROGRAM(S)— Apparel and Accessories Marketing Operations; Business, Management, Marketing, and Related Support Services, Other; Fashion Merchandising; General Merchandising, Sales, and Related Marketing Operations, Other; Sales, Distribution, and Marketing Operations, General; Special Products Marketing Operations; Specialized Merchandising, Sales, and Related Marketing Operations, Other. **RELATED KNOWLEDGE/ COURSES—Sales and Marketing:** Knowledge of principles and methods for showing, promoting, and selling products or services. This includes marketing strategy and tactics, product demonstrations, sales techniques, and sales control systems. **Communica-**

tions and Media: Knowledge of media production, communication, and dissemination techniques and methods. This includes alternative ways to inform and entertain via written, oral, and visual media. **Customer and Personal Service:** Knowledge of principles and processes for providing customer and personal services. This includes customer needs assessment, meeting quality standards for services, and evaluation of customer satisfaction. **Transportation:** Knowledge of principles and methods for moving people or goods by air, rail, sea, or road, including the relative costs and benefits. **Economics and Accounting:** Knowledge of economic and accounting principles and practices, the financial markets, banking, and the analysis and reporting of financial data. **Psychology:** Knowledge of human behavior and performance; individual differences in ability, personality, and interests; learning and motivation; psychological research methods; and the assessment and treatment of behavioral and affective disorders.

School Psychologists

- Education/Training Required: Master's degree
- Annual Earnings: $54,950
- Growth: 24.4%
- Annual Job Openings: 17,000
- Self-Employed: 25.4%
- Part-Time: 27.2%

Investigate processes of learning and teaching and develop psychological principles and techniques applicable to educational problems. Compile and interpret students' test results, along with information from teachers and parents, in order to diagnose conditions and to help assess eligibility for special services. Report any pertinent information to the proper authorities in cases of child endangerment, neglect, or abuse. Assess an individual child's needs, limitations, and potential, using observation, review of school records, and consultation with parents and school personnel. Select, administer, and score psychological tests. Provide consultation to parents, teachers, administrators, and others on topics such as learning styles and behavior modification techniques. Promote an understanding of child development and its relationship to learning and behavior. Collaborate with other educational professionals to develop teaching strategies

School Psychologists

S

S

S

and school programs. Counsel children and families to help solve conflicts and problems in learning and adjustment. Develop individualized educational plans in collaboration with teachers and other staff members. Maintain student records, including special education reports, confidential records, records of services provided, and behavioral data. Serve as a resource to help families and schools deal with crises, such as separation and loss. Attend workshops, seminars, and/or professional meetings in order to remain informed of new developments in school psychology. Design classes and programs to meet the needs of special students. Refer students and their families to appropriate community agencies for medical, vocational, or social services. Initiate and direct efforts to foster tolerance, understanding, and appreciation of diversity in school communities. Collect and analyze data to evaluate the effectiveness of academic programs and other services, such as behavioral management systems. Provide educational programs on topics such as classroom management, teaching strategies, or parenting skills. Conduct research to generate new knowledge that can be used to address learning and behavior issues. **SKILLS—Social Perceptiveness:** Being aware of others' reactions and understanding why they react as they do. **Learning Strategies:** Selecting and using training/instructional methods and procedures appropriate for the situation when learning or teaching new things. **Negotiation:** Bringing others together and trying to reconcile differences. **Persuasion:** Persuading others to change their minds or behavior. **Service Orientation:** Actively looking for ways to help people. **Writing:** Communicating effectively in writing as appropriate for the needs of the audience. **Active Learning:** Understanding the implications of new information for both current and future problem-solving and decision-making. **Active Listening:** Giving full attention to what other people are saying, taking time to understand the points being made, asking questions as appropriate, and not interrupting at inappropriate times. **Coordination:** Adjusting actions in relation to others' actions. **GOE—Interest Area:** 15. Scientific Research, Engineering, and Mathematics. **Work Group:** 15.04. Social Sciences. **Other Jobs in This Work Group:** Anthropologists; Archeologists; Economists; Historians; Industrial-Organizational Psychologists; Political Scientists; Sociologists. **PERSONALITY TYPE:** Investigative.

EDUCATION/TRAINING PROGRAM(S)—Clinical Child Psychology; Clinical Psychology; Counseling Psychology; Developmental and Child Psychology; Psychoanalysis and Psychotherapy; Psychology, General; School Psychology. **RELATED KNOWLEDGE/COURSES—Therapy and Counseling:** Knowledge of principles, methods, and procedures for diagnosis, treatment, and rehabilitation of physical and mental dysfunctions and for career counseling and guidance. **Psychology:** Knowledge of human behavior and performance; individual differences in ability, personality, and interests; learning and motivation; psychological research methods; and the assessment and treatment of behavioral and affective disorders. **Sociology and Anthropology:** Knowledge of group behavior and dynamics, societal trends and influences, human migrations, ethnicity, and cultures and their history and origins. **Education and Training:** Knowledge of principles and methods for curriculum and training design, teaching and instruction for individuals and groups, and the measurement of training effects. **Philosophy and Theology:** Knowledge of different philosophical systems and religions. This includes their basic principles, values, ethics, ways of thinking, customs, and practices and their impact on human culture. **Customer and Personal Service:** Knowledge of principles and processes for providing customer and personal services. This includes customer needs assessment, meeting quality standards for services, and evaluation of customer satisfaction.

Sculptors

- Education/Training Required: Long-term on-the-job training
- Annual Earnings: $38,060
- Growth: 16.5%
- Annual Job Openings: 4,000
- Self-Employed: 55.5%
- Part-Time: 23.1%

Design and construct three-dimensional art works, using materials such as stone, wood, plaster, and metal and employing various manual and tool techniques. Carves objects from stone, concrete, plaster, wood, or other material, using abrasives and tools such as chisels, gouges, and mall. Models substances such as clay or wax, using fingers and small hand tools to form objects. Cuts, bends, laminates, arranges, and fastens individual or mixed raw and manufactured materials and products to form works of art. Constructs artistic forms from metal or stone, using metalworking, welding, or masonry tools and equipment. **SKILLS—** None met the criteria. **GOE—Interest Area:** 03. Arts and Communication. **Work Group:** 03.04. Studio Art. **Other Jobs in This Work Group:** Cartoonists; Craft Artists; Painters and Illustrators; Potters; Sketch Artists. **PERSONALITY TYPE:** Artistic.

EDUCATION/TRAINING PROGRAM(S)— Art/Art Studies, General; Ceramic Arts and Ceramics; Fine Arts and Art Studies, Other; Fine/Studio Arts, General; Sculpture; Visual and Performing Arts, General. **RELATED KNOWLEDGE/COURSES—Fine Arts:** Knowledge of the theory and techniques required to compose, produce, and perform works of music, dance, the visual arts, drama, and sculpture. **Design:** Knowledge of design techniques, tools, and principles involved in production of precision technical plans, blueprints, drawings, and models. **Engineering and Technology:** Knowledge of the practical application of engineering science and technology. This includes applying principles, techniques, procedures, and equipment to the design and production of various goods and services. **Building and Construction:** Knowledge of the materials, methods, and tools involved in the construction or repair of houses, buildings, or other structures such as highways and roads.

Secondary School Teachers, Except Special and Vocational Education

- ◎ Education/Training Required: Bachelor's degree
- ◎ Annual Earnings: $45,650
- ◎ Growth: 18.2%
- ◎ Annual Job Openings: 118,000
- ◎ Self-Employed: 0%
- ◎ Part-Time: 8.8%

Instruct students in secondary public or private schools in one or more subjects at the secondary level, such as English, mathematics, or social studies. May be designated according to subject matter specialty, such as typing instructors, commercial teachers, or English teachers. Establish and enforce rules for behavior and procedures for maintaining order among the students for whom they are responsible. Instruct through lectures, discussions, and demonstrations in one or more subjects, such as English, mathematics, or social studies. Establish clear objectives for all lessons, units, and projects and communicate those objectives to students. Prepare, administer, and grade tests and assignments to evaluate students' progress. Prepare materials and classrooms for class activities. Adapt teaching methods and instructional materials to meet students' varying needs and interests. Maintain accurate and complete student records as required by laws, district policies, and administrative regulations. Assign and grade class work and homework. Observe and evaluate students' performance, behavior, social development, and physical health. Enforce all administration policies and rules governing students. Plan and conduct activities for a balanced program of instruction, demonstration, and work time that provides students with opportunities to observe, question, and investigate. Prepare students for later grades by encouraging them to explore learning opportunities and to persevere with challenging tasks. Guide and counsel students with adjustment and/or academic problems or special academic interests. Instruct and monitor students in the use and care of equipment and materials in order to prevent injuries and damage. Prepare for assigned classes and show written evidence of preparation upon request of immediate supervisors. Use computers, audiovisual aids, and other equipment and materials to supplement presentations. Meet with parents and guardians to discuss their children's progress and to determine their priorities for their children and their resource needs. Confer with parents or guardians, other teachers, counselors, and administrators in order to resolve students' behavioral and academic problems. Prepare objectives and outlines for courses of study, following curriculum guidelines or requirements of states and schools. Meet with other professionals to discuss individual students' needs and progress. **SKILLS—Learning Strategies:** Selecting and using training/instructional methods and procedures appropriate for the situation when learning or teaching new things. **Instructing:** Teaching others how to do something. **Social Perceptiveness:** Being aware of others' reactions and understanding why they react as they do. **Persuasion:** Persuading others to change their minds or behavior. **Time Management:** Managing one's own time and the time of others. **Monitoring:** Monitoring or assessing your performance or that of other individuals or organizations to make improvements or take corrective action. **Service Orientation:** Actively looking for ways to help people. **Negotiation:** Bringing others together and trying to reconcile differences. **GOE—Interest Area:** 05. Education and Training. **Work Group:** 05.02. Preschool, Elementary, and Secondary Teaching and Instructing. **Other Jobs in This Work Group:** Elementary School Teachers, Except Special Education; Kindergarten Teachers, Except Special Education; Middle School Teachers, Except Special and Vocational Education; Preschool Teachers, Except Special Education; Special Education Teachers, Middle School; Special Education Teachers, Preschool, Kindergarten, and Elementary School; Special Education Teachers, Secondary School; Teacher Assistants; Vocational Education Teachers, Middle School; Vocational Education Teachers, Secondary School. **PERSONALITY TYPE:** Social.

EDUCATION/TRAINING PROGRAM(S)—Agricultural Teacher Education; Art Teacher Education; Biology Teacher Education; Business Teacher Education; Chemistry Teacher Education; Computer Teacher Education; Drama and Dance Teacher Education; Driver and Safety Teacher Education; English/Language Arts Teacher Education; Family and Consumer Sciences/Home Economics Teacher Education; Foreign Language Teacher Education; French Language Teacher Education; Geography Teacher Education; German Language Teacher Education; Health Occupations Teacher Education; Health Teacher Education; History Teacher Education; Junior High/Intermediate/Middle School Education and Teaching; Latin Teacher Education; Mathematics Teacher Education; Music Teacher Education; Physical Education Teaching and Coaching; Physics Teacher Education; Reading Teacher Education; Sales and Marketing Operations/Marketing and Distribution Teacher Education; Science Teacher Education/General Science Teacher Education; Secondary Education and Teaching; Social Science Teacher Education; Social Studies Teacher Education; Spanish Language Teacher Education; Speech Teacher Education; Teacher Education and Professional Development, Specific Subject Areas, Other; Teacher Education, Multiple Levels; Technology Teacher Education/Industrial Arts Teacher Education. **RELATED KNOWLEDGE/COURSES—Education and Training:** Knowledge of principles and methods for curriculum and training design, teaching and instruction for individuals and groups, and the measurement of training effects. **Sociology and Anthropology:** Knowledge of group behavior and

dynamics, societal trends and influences, human migrations, ethnicity, and cultures and their history and origins. **Philosophy and Theology:** Knowledge of different philosophical systems and religions. This includes their basic principles, values, ethics, ways of thinking, customs, and practices and their impact on human culture. **History and Archeology:** Knowledge of historical events and their causes, indicators, and effects on civilizations and cultures. **Geography:** Knowledge of principles and methods for describing the features of land, sea, and air masses, including their physical characteristics; locations; interrelationships; and distribution of plant, animal, and human life. **Psychology:** Knowledge of human behavior and performance; individual differences in ability, personality, and interests; learning and motivation; psychological research methods; and the assessment and treatment of behavioral and affective disorders.

Security and Fire Alarm Systems Installers

- ◉ Education/Training Required: Postsecondary vocational training
- ◉ Annual Earnings: $33,410
- ◉ Growth: 30.2%
- ◉ Annual Job Openings: 5,000
- ◉ Self-Employed: 6.8%
- ◉ Part-Time: 2.8%

Install, program, maintain, and repair security and fire alarm wiring and equipment. Ensure that work is in accordance with relevant codes. Adjust sensitivity of units based on room structures and manufacturers' recommendations, using programming keypads. Consult with clients to assess risks and to determine security requirements. Drill holes for wiring in wall studs, joists, ceilings, and floors. Examine systems to locate problems such as loose connections or broken insulation. Feed cables through access holes, roof spaces, and cavity walls to reach fixture outlets; then position and terminate cables, wires, and strapping. Inspect installation sites and study work orders, building plans, and installation manuals in order to determine materials requirements and installation procedures. Install, maintain, or repair security systems, alarm devices, and related equipment, following blueprints of electrical layouts and building plans. Mount and fasten control panels, door and window contacts, sensors, and video cameras and attach electrical and telephone wiring in order to connect components. Mount raceways and conduits and fasten wires to wood framing, using staplers. Test and repair circuits and sensors, following wiring and system specifications. Test backup batteries, keypad programming, sirens, and all security features in order to ensure proper functioning and to diagnose malfunctions. Demonstrate systems for customers and explain details such as the causes and consequences of false alarms. Keep informed of new products and developments. Order replacement parts. Prepare documents such as invoices and warranties. Provide customers with cost estimates for equipment installation. **SKILLS**—No data available. **GOE—Interest Area:** 02. Architecture and Construction. **Work Group:** 02.04. Construction Crafts. **Other Jobs in This Work Group:** Boat Builders and Shipwrights; Boilermakers; Brattice Builders; Brickmasons and Blockmasons; Carpet Installers; Ceiling Tile Installers; Cement Masons and Concrete Finishers; Commercial Divers; Construction Carpenters; Crane and Tower Operators; Dragline Operators; Drywall Installers; Electricians; Fence Erectors; Floor Layers, Except Carpet, Wood, and Hard Tiles; Floor Sanders and Finishers; Glaziers; Grader, Bulldozer, and Scraper Operators; Hazardous Materials Removal Workers; Insulation Workers, Floor, Ceiling, and Wall; Insulation Workers, Mechanical; Manufactured Building and Mobile Home Installers; Operating Engineers; Painters, Construction and Maintenance; Paperhangers; Paving, Surfacing, and Tamping Equipment Operators; Pile-Driver Operators; Pipe Fitters; Pipelayers; Pipelaying Fitters; Plasterers and Stucco Masons; Plumbers; Rail-Track Laying and Maintenance Equipment Operators; Refractory Materials Repairers, Except Brickmasons; Reinforcing Iron and Rebar Workers; Riggers; Roofers; Rough Carpenters; Segmental Pavers; Sheet Metal Workers; Ship Carpenters and Joiners; Stone Cutters and Carvers; Stonemasons; Structural Iron and Steel Workers; Tapers; Terrazzo Workers and Finishers; Tile and Marble Setters. **PERSONALITY TYPE:** No data available.

EDUCATION/TRAINING PROGRAM(S)—Electrician; Security System Installation, Repair, and Inspection Technology/Technician. **RELATED KNOWLEDGE/COURSES**—No data available.

Security Guards

◎ Education/Training Required: Short-term on-the-job training
◎ Annual Earnings: $20,320
◎ Growth: 31.9%
◎ Annual Job Openings: 228,000
◎ Self-Employed: 0.9%
◎ Part-Time: 15.1%

Guard, patrol, or monitor premises to prevent theft, violence, or infractions of rules. Patrol industrial and commercial premises to prevent and detect signs of intrusion and ensure security of doors, windows, and gates. Answer alarms and investigate disturbances. Monitor and authorize entrance and departure of employees, visitors, and other persons to guard against theft and maintain security of premises. Write reports of daily activities and irregularities, such as equipment or property damage, theft, presence of unauthorized persons, or unusual occurrences. Call police or fire departments in cases of emergency, such as fire or presence of unauthorized persons. Circulate among visitors, patrons, and employees to preserve order and protect property. Answer telephone calls to take messages, answer questions, and provide information during non- business hours or when switchboard is closed. Warn persons of rule infractions or violations and apprehend or evict violators from premises, using force when necessary. Operate detecting devices to screen individuals and prevent passage of prohibited articles into restricted areas. Escort or drive motor vehicle to transport individuals to specified locations and to provide personal protection. Inspect and adjust security systems, equipment, and machinery to ensure operational use and to detect evidence of tampering. Drive and guard armored vehicle to transport money and valuables to prevent theft and ensure safe delivery. **SKILLS—Social Perceptiveness:** Being aware of others' reactions and understanding why they react as they do. **Negotiation:** Bringing others together and trying to reconcile differences. **Learning Strategies:** Selecting and using training/instructional methods and procedures appropriate for the situation when learning or teaching new things. **Speaking:** Talking to others to convey information effectively. **Active Listening:** Giving full attention to what other people are saying, taking time to understand the points being made, asking questions as appropriate, and not interrupting at inappropriate times. **Time Management:** Managing one's own time and the time of others. **Writing:** Communicating effectively in writing as appropriate for the needs of the audience. **Monitoring:** Monitoring or assessing your performance or that of other individuals or organizations to make improvements or take corrective action. **GOE—Interest Area:** 12. Law and Public Safety. **Work Group:** 12.05. Safety and Security. **Other Jobs in This Work Group:** Animal Control Workers; Crossing Guards; Gaming Surveillance Officers and Gaming Investigators; Lifeguards, Ski Patrol, and Other Recreational Protective Service Workers; Private Detectives and Investigators. **PERSONALITY TYPE:** Social.

EDUCATION/TRAINING PROGRAM(S)—Securities Services Administration/Management; Security and Loss Prevention Services. **RELATED KNOWLEDGE/COURSES—Public Safety and Security:** Knowledge of relevant equipment, policies, procedures, and strategies to promote effective local, state, or national security operations for the protection of people, data, property, and institutions. **Customer and Personal Service:** Knowledge of principles and processes for providing customer and personal services. This includes customer needs assessment, meeting quality standards for services, and evaluation of customer satisfaction. **Law and Government:** Knowledge of laws, legal codes, court procedures, precedents, government regulations, executive orders, agency rules, and the democratic political process. **Clerical Practices:** Knowledge of administrative and clerical procedures and systems such as word processing, managing files and records, stenography and transcription, designing forms, and other office procedures and terminology. **Telecommunications:** Knowledge of transmission, broadcasting, switching, control, and operation of telecommunications systems. **Transportation:** Knowledge of principles and methods for moving people or goods by air, rail, sea, or road, including the relative costs and benefits.

Self-Enrichment Education Teachers

- ◎ Education/Training Required: Work experience in a related occupation
- ◎ Annual Earnings: $30,880
- ◎ Growth: 40.1%
- ◎ Annual Job Openings: 39,000
- ◎ Self-Employed: 19.9%
- ◎ Part-Time: 41.0%

Teach or instruct courses other than those that normally lead to an occupational objective or degree. Courses may include self-improvement, nonvocational, and nonacademic subjects. Teaching may or may not take place in a traditional educational institution. Conduct classes, workshops, and demonstrations and provide individual instruction to teach topics and skills such as cooking, dancing, writing, physical fitness, photography, personal finance, and flying. Instruct students individually and in groups, using various teaching methods such as lectures, discussions, and demonstrations. Adapt teaching methods and instructional materials to meet students' varying needs and interests. Assign and grade class work and homework. Confer with other teachers and professionals to plan and schedule lessons promoting learning and development. Enforce policies and rules governing students. Establish clear objectives for all lessons, units, and projects and communicate those objectives to students. Instruct and monitor students in use and care of equipment and materials in order to prevent injury and damage. Maintain accurate and complete student records as required by administrative policy. Meet with other instructors to discuss individual students and their progress. Monitor students' performance in order to make suggestions for improvement and to ensure that they satisfy course standards, training requirements, and objectives. Observe students to determine qualifications, limitations, abilities, interests, and other individual characteristics. Plan and conduct activities for a balanced program of instruction, demonstration, and work time that provides students with opportunities to observe, question, and investigate. Plan and supervise class projects, field trips, visits by guest speakers, contests, or other experiential activities and guide students in learning from those activities. Prepare and administer written, oral, and performance tests and issue grades in accordance with performance. Prepare and implement remedial programs for students requiring extra help. Prepare instructional program objectives, outlines, and lesson plans. Prepare materials and classrooms for class activities. Prepare students for further development by encouraging them to explore learning opportunities and to persevere with challenging tasks. Review instructional content, methods, and student evaluations in order to assess strengths and weaknesses and to develop recommendations for course revision, development, or elimination. **SKILLS—Instructing:** Teaching others how to do something. **Writing:** Communicating effectively in writing as appropriate for the needs of the audience. **Speaking:** Talking to others to convey information effectively. **Learning Strategies:** Selecting and using training/instructional methods and procedures appropriate for the situation when learning or teaching new things. **Service Orientation:** Actively looking for ways to help people. **Systems Evaluation:** Identifying measures or indicators of system performance and the actions needed to improve or correct performance relative to the goals of the system. **Reading Comprehension:** Understanding written sentences and paragraphs in work-related documents. **Active Listening:** Giving full attention to what other people are saying, taking time to understand the points being made, asking questions as appropriate, and not interrupting at inappropriate times. **GOE—Interest Area:** 05. Education and Training. **Work Group:** 05.03. Postsecondary and Adult Teaching and Instructing. **Other Jobs in This Work Group:** Adult Literacy, Remedial Education, and GED Teachers and Instructors; Agricultural Sciences Teachers, Postsecondary; Anthropology and Archeology Teachers, Postsecondary; Architecture Teachers, Postsecondary; Area, Ethnic, and Cultural Studies Teachers, Postsecondary; Art, Drama, and Music Teachers, Postsecondary; Atmospheric, Earth, Marine, and Space Sciences Teachers, Postsecondary; Biological Science Teachers, Postsecondary; Business Teachers, Postsecondary; Chemistry Teachers, Postsecondary; Communications Teachers, Postsecondary; Computer Science Teachers, Postsecondary; Criminal Justice and Law Enforcement Teachers, Postsecondary; Economics Teachers, Postsecondary; Education Teachers, Postsecondary; Engineering Teachers, Postsecondary; English Language and Literature Teachers, Postsecondary; Environmental Science Teachers, Postsecondary; Farm and Home Management Advisors; Foreign Language and Literature Teachers, Postsecondary; Forestry and Conservation Science Teachers, Postsecondary; Geography Teachers, Postsecondary; Graduate Teaching Assistants; Health Specialties

Teachers, Postsecondary; History Teachers, Postsecondary; Home Economics Teachers, Postsecondary; Law Teachers, Postsecondary; Library Science Teachers, Postsecondary; Mathematical Science Teachers, Postsecondary; Nursing Instructors and Teachers, Postsecondary; Philosophy and Religion Teachers, Postsecondary; Physics Teachers, Postsecondary; Political Science Teachers, Postsecondary; Psychology Teachers, Postsecondary; Recreation and Fitness Studies Teachers, Postsecondary; Social Work Teachers, Postsecondary; Sociology Teachers, Postsecondary; Vocational Education Teachers, Postsecondary. **PERSONALITY TYPE:** Social.

EDUCATION/TRAINING PROGRAM(S)—Adult and Continuing Education and Teaching. **RELATED KNOWLEDGE/COURSES—Education and Training:** Knowledge of principles and methods for curriculum and training design, teaching and instruction for individuals and groups, and the measurement of training effects. **English Language:** Knowledge of the structure and content of the English language, including the meaning and spelling of words, rules of composition, and grammar. **Economics and Accounting:** Knowledge of economic and accounting principles and practices, the financial markets, banking, and the analysis and reporting of financial data. **History and Archeology:** Knowledge of historical events and their causes, indicators, and effects on civilizations and cultures. **Philosophy and Theology:** Knowledge of different philosophical systems and religions. This includes their basic principles, values, ethics, ways of thinking, customs, and practices and their impact on human culture. **Sociology and Anthropology:** Knowledge of group behavior and dynamics, societal trends and influences, human migrations, ethnicity, and cultures and their history and origins.

Septic Tank Servicers and Sewer Pipe Cleaners

- Education/Training Required: Moderate-term on-the-job training
- Annual Earnings: $28,870
- Growth: 21.2%
- Annual Job Openings: 3,000
- Self-Employed: 13.9%
- Part-Time: 4.5%

Clean and repair septic tanks, sewer lines, or drains. May patch walls and partitions of tank, replace damaged drain tile, or repair breaks in underground piping. Ensure that repaired sewer line joints are tightly sealed before backfilling begins. Clean and repair septic tanks; sewer lines; or related structures such as manholes, culverts, and catch basins. Cover repaired pipes with dirt and pack backfilled excavations, using air and gasoline tampers. Cut damaged sections of pipe with cutters, remove broken sections from ditches, and replace pipe sections, using pipe sleeves. Inspect manholes to locate sewer line stoppages. Install rotary knives on flexible cables mounted on machine reels according to the diameters of pipes to be cleaned. Locate problems, using specially designed equipment, and mark where digging must occur to reach damaged tanks or pipes. Measure excavation sites, using plumbers' snakes, tapelines, or lengths of cutting heads within sewers, and mark areas for digging. Operate sewer-cleaning equipment, including power rodders, high-velocity water jets, sewer flushers, bucket machines, wayne balls, and vac-alls. Rotate cleaning rods manually, using turning pins. Start machines to feed revolving cables or rods into openings, stopping machines and changing knives to conform to pipe sizes. Withdraw cables from pipes and examine them for evidence of mud, roots, grease, and other deposits indicating broken or clogged sewer lines. Break asphalt and other pavement so that pipes can be accessed, using airhammers, picks, and shovels. Communicate with supervisors and other workers, using equipment such as wireless phones, pagers, or radio telephones. Dig out sewer lines manually, using shovels. Drive trucks to transport crews, materials, and equipment. Prepare and keep records of actions taken, including maintenance and repair work. Requisition or order tools and equipment. Service, adjust, and make minor repairs to equipment, machines, and attachments. Tap mainline sewers to install sewer saddles. Update sewer maps and manhole charts. Clean and disinfect domestic basements and other areas flooded by sewer stoppages. **SKILLS—Installation:** Installing equipment, machines, wiring, or programs to meet specifications. **Repairing:** Repairing machines or systems by using the needed tools. **Operation and Control:** Controlling operations of equipment or systems. **Management of Material Resources:** Obtaining and seeing to the appropriate use of equipment, facilities, and materials needed to do certain work. **Equipment Maintenance:** Performing routine maintenance on equipment and

determining when and what kind of maintenance is needed. **Equipment Selection:** Determining the kind of tools and equipment needed to do a job. **Mathematics:** Using mathematics to solve problems. **Troubleshooting:** Determining causes of operating errors and deciding what to do about them. **GOE—Interest Area:** 02. Architecture and Construction. **Work Group:** 02.06. Construction Support/Labor. **Other Jobs in This Work Group:** Carpenter Assemblers and Repairers; Construction Laborers; Grips and Set-Up Workers, Motion Picture Sets, Studios, and Stages; Helpers—Brickmasons, Blockmasons, Stonemasons, and Tile and Marble Setters; Helpers—Carpenters; Helpers—Electricians; Helpers—Installation, Maintenance, and Repair Workers; Helpers—Painters, Paperhangers, Plasterers, and Stucco Masons; Helpers—Pipelayers, Plumbers, Pipefitters, and Steamfitters; Highway Maintenance Workers. **PERSONALITY TYPE:** Realistic.

EDUCATION/TRAINING PROGRAM(S)— Plumbing Technology/Plumber. **RELATED KNOWLEDGE/COURSES—Mechanical Devices:** Knowledge of machines and tools, including their designs, uses, repair, and maintenance. **Building and Construction:** Knowledge of the materials, methods, and tools involved in the construction or repair of houses, buildings, or other structures such as highways and roads. **Engineering and Technology:** Knowledge of the practical application of engineering science and technology. This includes applying principles, techniques, procedures, and equipment to the design and production of various goods and services. **Economics and Accounting:** Knowledge of economic and accounting principles and practices, the financial markets, banking, and the analysis and reporting of financial data. **Transportation:** Knowledge of principles and methods for moving people or goods by air, rail, sea, or road, including the relative costs and benefits. **Design:** Knowledge of design techniques, tools, and principles involved in production of precision technical plans, blueprints, drawings, and models. **Geography:** Knowledge of principles and methods for describing the features of land, sea, and air masses, including their physical characteristics; locations; interrelationships; and distribution of plant, animal, and human life.

Set Designers

- ◎ Education/Training Required: Bachelor's degree
- ◎ Annual Earnings: $35,800
- ◎ Growth: 20.9%
- ◎ Annual Job Openings: 2,000
- ◎ Self-Employed: 32.2%
- ◎ Part-Time: 16.5%

Design sets for theatrical, motion picture, and television productions. Integrates requirements, including script, research, budget, and available locations to develop design. Presents drawings for approval and makes changes and corrections as directed. Selects furniture, draperies, pictures, lamps, and rugs for decorative quality and appearance. Confers with heads of production and direction to establish budget and schedules and discuss design ideas. Directs and coordinates set construction, erection, or decoration activities to ensure conformance to design, budget, and schedule requirements. Assigns staff to complete design ideas and prepare sketches, illustrations, and detailed drawings of sets or graphics and animation. Examines dressed set to ensure props and scenery do not interfere with movements of cast or view of camera. Reads script to determine location, set, or decoration requirements. Estimates costs of design materials and construction or rental of location or props. Researches and consults experts to determine architectural and furnishing styles to depict given periods or locations. Designs and builds scale models of set design or miniature sets used in filming backgrounds or special effects. Prepares rough draft and scale working drawings of sets, including floor plans, scenery, and properties to be constructed. **SKILLS—Management of Financial Resources:** Determining how money will be spent to get the work done and accounting for these expenditures. **Management of Material Resources:** Obtaining and seeing to the appropriate use of equipment, facilities, and materials needed to do certain work. **Management of Personnel Resources:** Motivating, developing, and directing people as they work, identifying the best people for the job. **Systems Evaluation:** Identifying measures or indicators of system performance and the actions needed to improve or correct performance relative to the goals of the system. **Persuasion:** Persuading others to change their minds or behavior. **Operations Analysis:** Analyzing needs and product requirements to create a design. **Negotiation:** Bringing others together and trying to reconcile differences. **Systems Analysis:** Determining how a system should work and how changes in conditions, operations, and the environment will affect outcomes. **GOE—Interest Area:** 03. Arts and Communication. **Work Group:** 03.05. Design. **Other Jobs in This Work Group:** Commercial and Industrial Designers; Exhibit Designers; Fashion Designers; Floral Designers; Graphic Designers; Interior Designers; Merchandise Displayers and Window Trimmers. **PERSONALITY TYPE:** Artistic.

EDUCATION/TRAINING PROGRAM(S)—Design and Applied Arts, Other; Design and Visual Communications, General; Illustration; Technical Theatre/Theatre Design and Technology. **RELATED KNOWLEDGE/COURSES—Fine Arts:** Knowledge of the theory and techniques required to compose, produce, and perform works of music, dance, the visual arts, drama, and sculpture. **Design:** Knowledge of design techniques, tools, and principles involved in production of precision technical plans, blueprints, drawings, and models. **Building and Construction:** Knowledge of the materials, methods, and tools involved in the construction or repair of houses, buildings, or other structures such as highways and roads. **Engineering and Technology:** Knowledge of the practical application of engineering science and technology. This includes applying principles, techniques, procedures, and equipment to the design and production of various goods and services. **Communications and Media:** Knowledge of media production, communication, and dissemination techniques and methods. This includes alternative ways to inform and entertain via written, oral, and visual media. **History and Archeology:** Knowledge of historical events and their causes, indicators, and effects on civilizations and cultures.

Sheet Metal Workers

- ◎ Education/Training Required: Moderate-term on-the-job training
- ◎ Annual Earnings: $35,560
- ◎ Growth: 19.8%
- ◎ Annual Job Openings: 30,000
- ◎ Self-Employed: 3.1%
- ◎ Part-Time: 2.7%

Fabricate, assemble, install, and repair sheet metal products and equipment, such as ducts, control boxes, drainpipes, and furnace casings. Work may involve any of the following: setting up and operating fabricating machines to cut, bend, and straighten sheet metal; shaping metal over anvils, blocks, or forms, using hammer; operating soldering and welding equipment to join sheet metal parts; and inspecting, assembling, and smoothing seams and joints of burred surfaces. Determine project requirements, including scope, assembly sequences, and required methods and materials, according to blueprints, drawings, and written or verbal instructions. Lay out, measure, and mark dimensions and reference lines on material such as roofing panels according to drawings or templates, using calculators, scribes, dividers, squares, and rulers. Maneuver completed units into position for installation and anchor the units. Convert blueprints into shop drawings to be followed in the construction and assembly of sheet metal products. Install assemblies such as flashing, pipes, tubes, heating and air conditioning ducts, furnace casings, rain gutters, and downspouts in supportive frameworks. Select gauges and types of sheet metal or non-metallic material according to product specifications. Drill and punch holes in metal for screws, bolts, and rivets. Fasten seams and joints together with welds, bolts, cement, rivets, solder, caulks, metal drive clips, and bonds in order to assemble components into products or to repair sheet metal items. Fabricate or alter parts at construction sites, using shears, hammers, punches, and drills. Trim, file, grind, deburr, buff, and smooth surfaces, seams, and joints of assembled parts, using hand tools and portable power tools. Finish parts, using hacksaws and hand, rotary, or squaring shears. Maintain equipment, making repairs and modifications when necessary. Shape metal material over anvils, blocks, or other forms, using hand tools. Transport prefabricated parts to construction sites for assembly and installation. Develop and lay out patterns that use materials most efficiently, using computerized metalworking equipment to experiment with different layouts. Inspect individual parts, assemblies, and installations for conformance to specifications and building codes, using measuring instruments such as calipers, scales, and micrometers. Secure metal roof panels in place and then interlock and fasten grooved panel edges. **SKILLS—Installation:** Installing equipment, machines, wiring, or programs to meet specifications. **Equipment Maintenance:** Performing routine maintenance on equipment and determining when and what kind of maintenance is needed. **Repairing:** Repairing machines or systems by using the needed tools. **Coordination:** Adjusting actions in relation to others' actions. **Mathematics:** Using mathematics to solve problems. **Technology Design:** Generating or adapting equipment and technology to serve user needs. **Troubleshooting:** Determining causes of operating errors and deciding what to do about them. **Instructing:** Teaching others how to do something. **GOE—Interest Area:** 02. Architecture and Construction. **Work Group:** 02.04. Construction Crafts. **Other Jobs in This Work Group:** Boat Builders and Shipwrights; Boilermakers; Brattice Builders; Brickmasons and Blockmasons; Carpet Installers; Ceiling Tile Installers; Cement Masons and Concrete Finishers; Commercial Divers; Construction Carpenters; Crane and Tower Operators; Dragline Operators; Drywall Installers; Electricians; Fence Erectors; Floor Layers, Except Carpet, Wood, and Hard Tiles; Floor Sanders and Finishers; Glaziers; Grader, Bulldozer, and Scraper Operators; Hazardous Materials Removal Workers; Insulation Workers, Floor, Ceiling, and Wall; Insulation Workers, Mechanical; Manufactured Building and Mobile Home Installers; Operating Engineers; Painters, Construction and Maintenance; Paperhangers; Paving, Surfacing, and Tamping Equipment Operators; Pile-Driver Operators; Pipe Fitters; Pipelayers; Pipelaying Fitters; Plasterers and Stucco Masons; Plumbers; Rail-Track Laying and Maintenance Equipment Operators; Refractory Materials Repairers, Except Brickmasons; Reinforcing Iron and Rebar Workers; Riggers; Roofers; Rough Carpenters; Security and Fire Alarm Systems Installers; Segmental Pavers; Ship Carpenters and Joiners; Stone Cutters and Carvers; Stonemasons; Structural Iron and Steel Workers; Tapers; Terrazzo Workers and Finishers; Tile and Marble Setters. **PERSONALITY TYPE:** Realistic.

EDUCATION/TRAINING PROGRAM(S)—Sheet Metal Technology/Sheetworking. **RELATED KNOWLEDGE/COURSES—Building and Construction:** Knowledge of the materials, methods, and tools involved in the construction or repair of houses, buildings, or other structures such as highways and roads. **Mechanical Devices:** Knowledge of machines and tools, including their designs, uses, repair, and maintenance. **Design:** Knowledge of design techniques, tools, and principles involved in production of precision technical plans, blueprints, drawings, and models. **Production and Processing:** Knowledge of raw materials, production processes, quality control, costs, and other techniques for maximizing the effective manufacture and distribution of goods. **Physics:** Knowledge and prediction of physical principles and laws and their interrelationships and applications to understanding fluid, material, and atmospheric dynamics and mechanical, electrical, atomic, and subatomic structures and processes. **Mathematics:** Knowledge of arithmetic, algebra, geometry, calculus, and statistics and their applications.

Sheriffs and Deputy Sheriffs

◎ Education/Training Required: Long-term on-the-job training

◎ Annual Earnings: $45,210

◎ Growth: 24.7%

◎ Annual Job Openings: 67,000

◎ Self-Employed: 0%

◎ Part-Time: 1.4%

Enforce law and order in rural or unincorporated districts or serve legal processes of courts. May patrol courthouse, guard court or grand jury, or escort defendants. Drive vehicles or patrol specific areas to detect law violators, issue citations, and make arrests. Execute arrest warrants, locating and taking persons into custody. Investigate illegal or suspicious activities. Notify patrol units to take violators into custody or to provide needed assistance or medical aid. Question individuals entering secured areas to determine their business, directing and rerouting individuals as necessary. Record daily activities and submit logs and other related reports and paperwork to appropriate authorities. Serve statements of claims, subpoenas, summonses, jury summonses, orders to pay alimony, and other court orders. Take control of accident scenes to maintain traffic flow, to assist accident victims, and to investigate causes. Verify that the proper legal charges have been made against law offenders. Patrol and guard courthouses, grand jury rooms, or assigned areas in order to provide security, enforce laws, maintain order, and arrest violators. Locate and confiscate real or personal property as directed by court order. Manage jail operations and tend to jail inmates. Place people in protective custody. Transport or escort prisoners and defendants en route to courtrooms, prisons or jails,

attorneys' offices, or medical facilities. **SKILLS— Social Perceptiveness:** Being aware of others' reactions and understanding why they react as they do. **Service Orientation:** Actively looking for ways to help people. **Active Listening:** Giving full attention to what other people are saying, taking time to understand the points being made, asking questions as appropriate, and not interrupting at inappropriate times. **Speaking:** Talking to others to convey information effectively. **Judgment and Decision Making:** Considering the relative costs and benefits of potential actions to choose the most appropriate one. **Coordination:** Adjusting actions in relation to others' actions. **Writing:** Communicating effectively in writing as appropriate for the needs of the audience. **Critical Thinking:** Using logic and reasoning to identify the strengths and weaknesses of alternative solutions, conclusions, or approaches to problems. **GOE—Interest Area:** 12. Law and Public Safety. **Work Group:** 12.04. Law Enforcement and Public Safety. **Other Jobs in This Work Group:** Bailiffs; Correctional Officers and Jailers; Criminal Investigators and Special Agents; Fire Investigators; Forensic Science Technicians; Highway Patrol Pilots; Parking Enforcement Workers; Police Detectives; Police Identification and Records Officers; Police Patrol Officers; Transit and Railroad Police. **PERSONALITY TYPE:** Social.

EDUCATION/TRAINING PROGRAM(S)— Criminal Justice/Police Science; Criminalistics and Criminal Science. **RELATED KNOWLEDGE/ COURSES—Public Safety and Security:** Knowledge of relevant equipment, policies, procedures, and strategies to promote effective local, state, or national security operations for the protection of people, data, property, and institutions. **Law and Government:** Knowledge of laws, legal codes, court procedures, precedents, government regulations, executive orders, agency rules, and the democratic political process. **Psychology:** Knowledge of human behavior and performance; individual differences in ability, personality, and interests; learning and motivation; psychological research methods; and the assessment and treatment of behavioral and affective disorders. **Geography:** Knowledge of principles and methods for describing the features of land, sea, and air masses, including their physical characteristics; locations; interrelationships; and distribution of plant, animal, and human life. **Sociology and Anthropology:** Knowledge of group behavior and dynamics, societal trends and influences, human migrations, ethnicity, and cultures and their history and origins. **Clerical Practices:** Knowledge of

S

administrative and clerical procedures and systems such as word processing, managing files and records, stenography and transcription, designing forms, and other office procedures and terminology. **Telecommunications:** Knowledge of transmission, broadcasting, switching, control, and operation of telecommunications systems.

Ship Carpenters and Joiners

- ◉ Education/Training Required: Moderate-term on-the-job training
- ◉ Annual Earnings: $34,900
- ◉ Growth: 10.1%
- ◉ Annual Job Openings: 193,000
- ◉ Self-Employed: 29.7%
- ◉ Part-Time: 5.3%

Fabricate, assemble, install, or repair wooden furnishings in ships or boats. Reads blueprints to determine dimensions of furnishings in ships or boats. Shapes and laminates wood to form parts of ship, using steam chambers, clamps, glue, and jigs. Repairs structural woodwork and replaces defective parts and equipment, using hand tools and power tools. Shapes irregular parts and trims excess material from bulkhead and furnishings to ensure fit meets specifications. Constructs floors, doors, and partitions, using woodworking machines, hand tools, and power tools. Cuts wood or glass to specified dimensions, using hand tools and power tools. Assembles and installs hardware, gaskets, floors, furnishings, or insulation, using adhesive, hand tools, and power tools. Transfers dimensions or measurements of wood parts or bulkhead on plywood, using measuring instruments and marking devices. Greases gears and other moving parts of machines on ship. **SKILLS—Installation:** Installing equipment, machines, wiring, or programs to meet specifications. **Repairing:** Repairing machines or systems by using the needed tools. **Equipment Maintenance:** Performing routine maintenance on equipment and determining when and what kind of maintenance is needed. **Operations Analysis:** Analyzing needs and product requirements to create a design. **Systems Analysis:** Determining how a system should work and how changes in conditions, operations, and the environment will affect outcomes. **GOE—Interest Area:** 02.

Architecture and Construction. **Work Group:** 02.04. Construction Crafts. **Other Jobs in This Work Group:** Boat Builders and Shipwrights; Boilermakers; Brattice Builders; Brickmasons and Blockmasons; Carpet Installers; Ceiling Tile Installers; Cement Masons and Concrete Finishers; Commercial Divers; Construction Carpenters; Crane and Tower Operators; Dragline Operators; Drywall Installers; Electricians; Fence Erectors; Floor Layers, Except Carpet, Wood, and Hard Tiles; Floor Sanders and Finishers; Glaziers; Grader, Bulldozer, and Scraper Operators; Hazardous Materials Removal Workers; Insulation Workers, Floor, Ceiling, and Wall; Insulation Workers, Mechanical; Manufactured Building and Mobile Home Installers; Operating Engineers; Painters, Construction and Maintenance; Paperhangers; Paving, Surfacing, and Tamping Equipment Operators; Pile-Driver Operators; Pipe Fitters; Pipelayers; Pipelaying Fitters; Plasterers and Stucco Masons; Plumbers; Rail-Track Laying and Maintenance Equipment Operators; Refractory Materials Repairers, Except Brickmasons; Reinforcing Iron and Rebar Workers; Riggers; Roofers; Rough Carpenters; Security and Fire Alarm Systems Installers; Segmental Pavers; Sheet Metal Workers; Stone Cutters and Carvers; Stonemasons; Structural Iron and Steel Workers; Tapers; Terrazzo Workers and Finishers; Tile and Marble Setters. **PERSONALITY TYPE:** Realistic.

EDUCATION/TRAINING PROGRAM(S)—Carpentry/Carpenter. **RELATED KNOWLEDGE/ COURSES—Building and Construction:** Knowledge of the materials, methods, and tools involved in the construction or repair of houses, buildings, or other structures such as highways and roads. **Design:** Knowledge of design techniques, tools, and principles involved in production of precision technical plans, blueprints, drawings, and models. **Engineering and Technology:** Knowledge of the practical application of engineering science and technology. This includes applying principles, techniques, procedures, and equipment to the design and production of various goods and services. **Mechanical Devices:** Knowledge of machines and tools, including their designs, uses, repair, and maintenance.

Sketch Artists

- Education/Training Required: Long-term on-the-job training
- Annual Earnings: $38,060
- Growth: 16.5%
- Annual Job Openings: 4,000
- Self-Employed: 55.5%
- Part-Time: 23.1%

Sketch likenesses of subjects according to observation or descriptions either to assist law enforcement agencies in identifying suspects, to depict courtroom scenes, or for entertainment purposes of patrons, using mediums such as pencil, charcoal, and pastels. Draws sketch, profile, or likeness of posed subject or photograph, using pencil, charcoal, pastels, or other medium. Assembles and arranges outlines of features to form composite image according to information provided by witness or victim. Alters copy of composite image until witness or victim is satisfied that composite is best possible representation of suspect. Poses subject to accentuate most pleasing features or profile. Classifies and codes components of image, using established system, to help identify suspect. Prepares series of simple line drawings conforming to description of suspect and presents drawings to informant for selection of sketch. Interviews crime victims and witnesses to obtain descriptive information concerning physical build, sex, nationality, and facial features of unidentified suspect. Measures distances and develops sketches of crime scene from photograph and measurements. Searches police photograph records, using classification and coding system to determine if existing photograph of suspects is available. Operates photocopy or similar machine to reproduce composite image. **SKILLS—Active Listening:** Giving full attention to what other people are saying, taking time to understand the points being made, asking questions as appropriate, and not interrupting at inappropriate times. **Social Perceptiveness:** Being aware of others' reactions and understanding why they react as they do. **Speaking:** Talking to others to convey information effectively. **GOE—Interest Area:** 03. Arts and Communication. **Work Group:** 03.04. Studio Art. **Other Jobs in This Work Group:** Cartoonists; Craft Artists; Painters and Illustrators; Potters; Sculptors. **PERSONALITY TYPE:** Artistic.

EDUCATION/TRAINING PROGRAM(S)— Art/Art Studies, General; Drawing; Fine Arts and Art Studies, Other; Fine/Studio Arts, General; Medical Illustration/Medical Illustrator; Visual and Performing Arts, General. **RELATED KNOWLEDGE/COURSES—Fine Arts:** Knowledge of the theory and techniques required to compose, produce, and perform works of music, dance, the visual arts, drama, and sculpture. **Design:** Knowledge of design techniques, tools, and principles involved in production of precision technical plans, blueprints, drawings, and models.

Slaughterers and Meat Packers

- Education/Training Required: Moderate-term on-the-job training
- Annual Earnings: $20,860
- Growth: 18.1%
- Annual Job Openings: 23,000
- Self-Employed: 1.0%
- Part-Time: 7.0%

Work in slaughtering, meat-packing, or wholesale establishments performing precision functions involving the preparation of meat. Work may include specialized slaughtering tasks, cutting standard or premium cuts of meat for marketing, making sausage, or wrapping meats. Cut, trim, skin, sort, and wash viscera of slaughtered animals to separate edible portions from offal. Grind meat into hamburger and into trimmings used to prepare sausages, luncheon meats, and other meat products. Remove bones and cut meat into standard cuts in preparation for marketing. Saw, split, or scribe carcasses into smaller portions to facilitate handling. Sever jugular veins to drain blood and facilitate slaughtering. Shackle hind legs of animals to raise them for slaughtering or skinning. Shave or singe and defeather carcasses and wash them in preparation for further processing or packaging. Skin sections of animals or whole animals. Slit open, eviscerate, and trim carcasses of slaughtered animals. Stun animals prior to slaughtering. Trim head meat and sever or remove parts of animals' heads or skulls. Trim, clean, and/or cure animal hides. Wrap dressed carcasses and/or meat cuts. Tend assembly lines, performing a few of the many cuts needed to process a carcass. Slaughter animals in accordance with religious law and determine that carcasses meet specified religious standards. **SKILLS**—None met the criteria. **GOE—Interest Area:** 13. Manufacturing. **Work Group:** 13.03. Production Work, Assorted Materials Processing. **Other Jobs in This Work Group:** Bakers, Manufacturing; Cementing and Gluing Machine Operators and Tenders; Chemical Equipment Controllers and Operators; Chemical Equipment Tenders; Cleaning, Washing, and Metal Pickling Equipment Operators and Tenders; Coating, Painting, and Spraying Machine Operators and Tenders; Combination Machine Tool Operators and Tenders, Metal and Plastic; Cooling and Freezing Equipment Operators and Tenders; Cutting and Slicing Machine Operators and Tenders; Electrolytic Plating and Coating Machine Operators and Tenders, Metal and Plastic; Extruding and Forming Machine Operators and Tenders, Synthetic or Glass Fibers; Extruding, Forming, Pressing, and Compacting Machine Operators and Tenders; Food and Tobacco Roasting, Baking, and Drying Machine Operators and Tenders; Food Batchmakers; Food Cooking Machine Operators and Tenders; Furnace, Kiln, Oven, Drier, and Kettle Operators and Tenders; Heat Treating, Annealing, and Tempering Machine Operators and Tenders, Metal and Plastic; Heaters, Metal and Plastic; Meat, Poultry, and Fish Cutters and Trimmers; Metal-Refining Furnace Operators and Tenders; Mixing and Blending Machine Setters, Operators, and Tenders; Nonelectrolytic Plating and Coating Machine Operators and Tenders, Metal and Plastic; Packaging and Filling Machine Operators and Tenders; Plastic Molding and Casting Machine Operators and Tenders; Pourers and Casters, Metal; Pressing Machine Operators and Tenders—Textile, Garment, and Related Materials; Production Helpers; Production Laborers; Sawing Machine Operators and Tenders; Separating, Filtering, Clarifying, Precipitating, and Still Machine Setters, Operators, and Tenders; Sewing Machine Operators, Garment; Sewing Machine Operators, Non-Garment; Shoe Machine Operators and Tenders; Stone Sawyers; Team Assemblers; Textile Bleaching and Dyeing Machine Operators and Tenders; Tire Builders; Woodworking Machine Operators and Tenders, Except Sawing. **PERSONALITY TYPE:** Realistic.

EDUCATION/TRAINING PROGRAM(S)—Meat Cutting/Meat Cutter. RELATED KNOWLEDGE/ COURSES—Food Production: Knowledge of techniques and equipment for planting, growing, and harvesting food products (both plant and animal) for consumption, including storage/handling techniques. **Biology:** Knowledge of plant and animal organisms and their tissues, cells, functions, interdependencies, and interactions with each other and the environment. **Philosophy and Theology:** Knowledge of different philosophical systems and religions. This includes their basic principles, values, ethics, ways of thinking, customs, and practices and their impact on human culture. **Public Safety and Security:** Knowledge of relevant equipment, policies, procedures, and strategies to promote effective local, state, or national security operations for the protection of people, data, property, and institutions. **Production and Processing:** Knowledge of raw materials, production processes, quality control, costs, and other techniques for maximizing the effective manufacture and distribution of goods. **Law and Government:** Knowledge of laws, legal codes, court procedures, precedents, government regulations, executive orders, agency rules, and the democratic political process.

Social and Community Service Managers

◎ Education/Training Required: Bachelor's degree
◎ Annual Earnings: $46,810
◎ Growth: 27.7%
◎ Annual Job Openings: 19,000
◎ Self-Employed: 6.6%
◎ Part-Time: 10.7%

Plan, organize, or coordinate the activities of a social service program or community outreach organization. Oversee the program or organization's budget and policies regarding participant involvement, program requirements, and benefits. Work may involve directing social workers, counselors, or probation officers. Establish and maintain relationships with other agencies and organizations in community in order to meet community needs and to ensure that services are not duplicated. Prepare and maintain records and reports such as budgets, personnel records, or training manuals. Direct activities of professional and technical staff members and volunteers. Evaluate the work of staff and volunteers in order to ensure that programs are of appropriate quality and that resources are used effectively. Establish and oversee administrative procedures to meet objectives set by boards of directors or senior management. Participate in the determination of organizational policies regarding such issues as participant eligibility, program requirements, and program benefits. Research and analyze member or community needs in order to determine program directions and goals. Speak to community groups to explain and interpret agency purposes, programs, and policies. Recruit, interview, and hire or sign up volunteers and staff. Represent organizations in relations with governmental and media institutions. Plan and administer budgets for programs, equipment, and support services. Analyze proposed legislation, regulations, or rule changes in order to determine how agency services could be impacted. Act as consultants to agency staff and other community programs regarding the interpretation of program-related federal, state, and county regulations and policies. Implement and evaluate staff training programs. Direct fundraising activities and the preparation of public relations materials. **SKILLS—Social Perceptiveness:** Being aware of others' reactions and understanding why they react as they do. **Management of Personnel Resources:** Motivating, developing, and directing people as they work, identifying the best people for the job. **Service Orientation:** Actively looking for ways to help people. **Negotiation:** Bringing others together and trying to reconcile differences. **Persuasion:** Persuading others to change their minds or behavior. **Instructing:** Teaching others how to do something. **Monitoring:** Monitoring or assessing your performance or that of other individuals or organizations to make improvements or take corrective action. **Learning Strategies:** Selecting and using training/instructional methods and procedures appropriate for the situation when learning or teaching new things. **GOE—Interest Area:** 07. Government and Public Administration. **Work Group:** 07.01. Managerial Work in Government and Public Administration. **Other Jobs in This Work Group:** Government Service Executives. **PERSONALITY TYPE:** Social.

EDUCATION/TRAINING PROGRAM(S)—Business Administration and Management, General; Business, Management, Marketing, and Related Support Services, Other; Business/Commerce, General; Community Organization and Advocacy; Entrepreneurship/Entrepreneurial Studies; Human Services, General; Non-Profit/Public/Organizational Management; Public Administration. **RELATED KNOWLEDGE/COURSES—Psychology:** Knowledge of human behavior and performance; individual differences in ability, personality, and interests; learning and motivation; psychological research methods; and the assessment and treatment of behavioral and affective disorders. **Customer and Personal Service:** Knowledge of principles and processes for providing customer and personal services. This includes customer needs assessment, meeting quality standards for services, and evaluation of customer satisfaction. **Sociology and Anthropology:** Knowledge of group behavior and dynamics, societal trends and influences, human migrations, ethnicity, and cultures and their history and origins. **Education and Training:** Knowledge of principles and methods for curriculum and training design, teaching and instruction for individuals and groups, and the measurement of training effects. **Therapy and Counseling:** Knowledge of principles, methods, and procedures for diagnosis, treatment, and rehabilitation of physical and mental dysfunctions and for career counseling and guidance. **Clerical Practices:** Knowledge of administrative and clerical procedures and systems such as word processing, managing files and records, stenography and transcription, designing forms, and other office procedures and terminology.

Social and Human Service Assistants

- Education/Training Required: Moderate-term on-the-job training
- Annual Earnings: $24,270
- Growth: 48.7%
- Annual Job Openings: 63,000
- Self-Employed: 0.2%
- Part-Time: 10.6%

Assist professionals from a wide variety of fields, such as psychology, rehabilitation, or social work, to provide client services, as well as support for families. May assist clients in identifying available benefits and social and community services and help clients obtain them. May assist social workers with developing, organizing, and conducting programs to prevent and resolve problems relevant to substance abuse, human relationships, rehabilitation, or adult day care. Provide information on and refer individuals to public or private agencies and community services for assistance. Keep records and prepare reports for owner or management concerning visits with clients. Visit individuals in homes or attend group meetings to provide information on agency services, requirements, and procedures. Advise clients regarding food stamps, child care, food, money management, sanitation, and housekeeping. Submit to and review reports and problems with superior. Oversee day-to-day group activities of residents in institution. Interview individuals and family members to compile information on social, educational, criminal, institutional, or drug history. Meet with youth groups to acquaint them with consequences of delinquent acts. Transport and accompany clients to shopping area and to appointments, using automobile. Explain rules established by owner or management, such as sanitation and maintenance requirements and parking regulations. Observe and discuss meal preparation and suggest alternate methods of food preparation. Demonstrate use and care of equipment for tenant use. Consult with supervisor concerning programs for individual families. Monitor free, supplementary meal program to ensure cleanliness of facility and that eligibility guidelines are met for persons receiving meals. Observe clients' food selections and recommend alternate economical and nutritional food choices. Inform tenants of facilities such as laundries and playgrounds. Care for children in client's home during client's appointments. Assist in locating housing for displaced individuals. Assist clients with preparation of forms, such as tax or rent forms. Assist in planning of food budget, utilizing charts and sample budgets. **SKILLS—Social Perceptiveness:** Being aware of others' reactions and understanding why they react as they do. **Service Orientation:** Actively looking for ways to help people. **Management of Financial Resources:** Determining how money will be spent to get the work done and accounting for these expenditures. **Learning Strategies:** Selecting and using training/instructional methods and procedures appropriate for the situation when learning or teaching new things. **Time Management:** Managing one's own time and the time of others. **Instructing:** Teaching others how to do something. **Active Listening:** Giving full attention to what other people are saying, taking time to understand the points being made, asking questions as appropriate, and not interrupting at inappropriate times. **Speaking:** Talking to others to convey information effectively. **GOE—Interest Area:** 10. Human Service. **Work Group:** 10.01. Counseling and Social Work. **Other Jobs in This Work Group:** Child, Family, and School Social Workers; Clinical Psychologists; Counseling Psychologists; Marriage and Family Therapists; Medical and Public Health Social Workers; Mental Health and Substance Abuse Social Workers; Mental Health Counselors; Probation Officers and Correctional Treatment Specialists; Rehabilitation Counselors; Residential Advisors; Substance Abuse and Behavioral Disorder Counselors. **PERSONALITY TYPE:** Social.

EDUCATION/TRAINING PROGRAM(S)—Mental and Social Health Services and Allied Professions, Other. **RELATED KNOWLEDGE/COURSES**—**Therapy and Counseling:** Knowledge of principles, methods, and procedures for diagnosis, treatment, and rehabilitation of physical and mental dysfunctions and for career counseling and guidance. **Psychology:** Knowledge of human behavior and performance; individual differences in ability, personality, and interests; learning and motivation; psychological research methods; and the assessment and treatment of behavioral and affective disorders. **Customer and Personal Service:** Knowledge of principles and processes for providing customer and personal services. This includes customer needs assessment, meeting quality standards for services, and evaluation of customer satisfaction. **Clerical Practices:** Knowledge of administrative and clerical procedures and systems such as word processing, managing files and records, stenography and transcription, designing forms, and other office procedures and terminology. **Sociology and Anthropology:** Knowledge of group behavior and dynamics, societal trends and influences, human migrations, ethnicity, and cultures and their history and origins. **Philosophy and Theology:** Knowledge of different philosophical systems and religions. This includes their basic principles, values, ethics, ways of thinking, customs, and practices and their impact on human culture.

Social Science Research Assistants

- Education/Training Required: Associate degree
- Annual Earnings: $34,360
- Growth: 17.5%
- Annual Job Openings: 18,000
- Self-Employed: 1.1%
- Part-Time: 20.2%

Assist social scientists in laboratory, survey, and other social research. May perform publication activities, laboratory analysis, quality control, or data management. Normally these individuals work under the direct supervision of a social scientist and assist in those activities which are more routine. Perform descriptive and multivariate statistical analyses of data, using computer software. Recruit and schedule research participants. Administer standardized tests to research subjects and/or interview them in order to collect research data. Code data in preparation for computer entry. Conduct Internet-based and library research. Develop and implement research quality control procedures. Edit and submit protocols and other required research documentation. Obtain informed consent of research subjects and/or their guardians. Prepare tables, graphs, fact sheets, and written reports summarizing research results. Prepare, manipulate, and manage extensive databases. Provide assistance in the design of survey instruments such as questionnaires. Screen potential subjects in order to determine their suitability as study participants. Track research participants and perform any necessary follow-up tasks. Verify the accuracy and validity of data entered in databases; correct any errors. Allocate and manage laboratory space and resources. Design and create special programs for tasks such as statistical analysis and data entry and cleaning. Perform data entry and other clerical work as required for project completion. Perform needs assessments and/or consult with clients in order to determine the types of research and information that are required. Present research findings to groups of people. Provide assistance with the preparation of project-related reports, manuscripts, and presentations. Supervise the work of survey interviewers. Track laboratory supplies and expenses such as participant reimbursement. Collect specimens such as blood samples as required by research projects. **SKILLS**—No data available. **GOE—Interest Area:** 15. Scientific Research, Engineering, and Mathematics. **Work Group:** 15.06. Mathematics and Data Analysis. **Other Jobs in This Work Group:** Actuaries; Mathematical Technicians; Mathematicians; Statistical Assistants; Statisticians. **PERSONALITY TYPE:** No data available.

EDUCATION/TRAINING PROGRAM(S)— Social Sciences, General. **RELATED KNOWLEDGE/COURSES**—No data available.

Social Work Teachers, Postsecondary

◎ Education/Training Required: Master's degree
◎ Annual Earnings: $51,960
◎ Growth: 38.1%
◎ Annual Job Openings: 216,000
◎ Self-Employed: 0.3%
◎ Part-Time: 27.7%

Teach courses in social work. Initiate, facilitate, and moderate classroom discussions. Evaluate and grade students' class work, assignments, and papers. Prepare and deliver lectures to undergraduate and/or graduate students on topics such as family behavior, child and adolescent mental health, and social intervention evaluation. Keep abreast of developments in their field by reading current literature, talking with colleagues, and participating in professional conferences. Conduct research in a particular field of knowledge and publish findings in professional journals, books, and/or electronic media. Supervise students' laboratory and field work. Prepare course materials such as syllabi, homework assignments, and handouts. Supervise undergraduate and/or graduate teaching, internship, and research work. Maintain regularly scheduled office hours in order to advise and assist students. Plan, evaluate, and revise curricula, course content, and course materials and methods of instruction. Collaborate with colleagues and with community agencies in order to address teaching and research issues. Compile, administer, and grade examinations or assign this work to others. Advise students on academic and vocational curricula and on career issues. Maintain student attendance records, grades, and other required records. Write grant proposals to procure external research funding. Serve on academic or administrative committees that deal with institutional policies, departmental matters, and academic issues. Perform administrative duties such as serving as department head. Compile bibliographies of specialized materials for outside reading assignments. Select and obtain materials and supplies such as textbooks and laboratory equipment. Participate in student recruitment, registration, and placement activities. Participate in campus and community events. Provide professional consulting services to government and/or industry. Act as advisers to student organizations. **SKILLS—Social Perceptive-**

ness: Being aware of others' reactions and understanding why they react as they do. **Instructing:** Teaching others how to do something. **Service Orientation:** Actively looking for ways to help people. **Learning Strategies:** Selecting and using training/instructional methods and procedures appropriate for the situation when learning or teaching new things. **Negotiation:** Bringing others together and trying to reconcile differences. **Critical Thinking:** Using logic and reasoning to identify the strengths and weaknesses of alternative solutions, conclusions, or approaches to problems. **Writing:** Communicating effectively in writing as appropriate for the needs of the audience. **Active Learning:** Understanding the implications of new information for both current and future problem-solving and decision-making. **GOE—Interest Area:** 05. Education and Training. **Work Group:** 05.03. Postsecondary and Adult Teaching and Instructing. **Other Jobs in This Work Group:** Adult Literacy, Remedial Education, and GED Teachers and Instructors; Agricultural Sciences Teachers, Postsecondary; Anthropology and Archeology Teachers, Postsecondary; Architecture Teachers, Postsecondary; Area, Ethnic, and Cultural Studies Teachers, Postsecondary; Art, Drama, and Music Teachers, Postsecondary; Atmospheric, Earth, Marine, and Space Sciences Teachers, Postsecondary; Biological Science Teachers, Postsecondary; Business Teachers, Postsecondary; Chemistry Teachers, Postsecondary; Communications Teachers, Postsecondary; Computer Science Teachers, Postsecondary; Criminal Justice and Law Enforcement Teachers, Postsecondary; Economics Teachers, Postsecondary; Education Teachers, Postsecondary; Engineering Teachers, Postsecondary; English Language and Literature Teachers, Postsecondary; Environmental Science Teachers, Postsecondary; Farm and Home Management Advisors; Foreign Language and Literature Teachers, Postsecondary; Forestry and Conservation Science Teachers, Postsecondary; Geography Teachers, Postsecondary; Graduate Teaching Assistants; Health Specialties Teachers, Postsecondary; History Teachers, Postsecondary; Home Economics Teachers, Postsecondary; Law Teachers, Postsecondary; Library Science Teachers, Postsecondary; Mathematical Science Teachers, Postsecondary; Nursing Instructors and Teachers, Postsecondary; Philosophy and Religion Teachers, Postsecondary; Physics Teachers, Postsecondary; Political Science Teachers, Postsecondary; Psychology Teachers, Postsecondary; Recreation and Fitness Studies Teachers, Postsecondary;

Self-Enrichment Education Teachers; Sociology Teachers, Postsecondary; Vocational Education Teachers, Postsecondary. **PERSONALITY TYPE:** No data available.

EDUCATION/TRAINING PROGRAM(S)—Clinical/Medical Social Work; Social Work; Teacher Education and Professional Development, Specific Subject Areas, Other. **RELATED KNOWLEDGE/COURSES—Sociology and Anthropology:** Knowledge of group behavior and dynamics, societal trends and influences, human migrations, ethnicity, and cultures and their history and origins. **Therapy and Counseling:** Knowledge of principles, methods, and procedures for diagnosis, treatment, and rehabilitation of physical and mental dysfunctions and for career counseling and guidance. **Psychology:** Knowledge of human behavior and performance; individual differences in ability, personality, and interests; learning and motivation; psychological research methods; and the assessment and treatment of behavioral and affective disorders. **Education and Training:** Knowledge of principles and methods for curriculum and training design, teaching and instruction for individuals and groups, and the measurement of training effects. **Philosophy and Theology:** Knowledge of different philosophical systems and religions. This includes their basic principles, values, ethics, ways of thinking, customs, and practices and their impact on human culture. **English Language:** Knowledge of the structure and content of the English language, including the meaning and spelling of words, rules of composition, and grammar.

Sociologists

- Education/Training Required: Master's degree
- Annual Earnings: $57,870
- Growth: 13.4%
- Annual Job Openings: Fewer than 500
- Self-Employed: 0%
- Part-Time: 8.6%

Study human society and social behavior by examining the groups and social institutions that people form, as well as various social, religious, political, and business organizations. May study the behavior and interaction of groups, trace their origin and growth, and analyze the influence of group activities on indi-

vidual members. Prepare publications and reports containing research findings. Analyze and interpret data in order to increase the understanding of human social behavior. Plan and conduct research to develop and test theories about societal issues such as crime, group relations, poverty, and aging. Collect data about the attitudes, values, and behaviors of people in groups, using observation, interviews, and review of documents. Develop, implement, and evaluate methods of data collection, such as questionnaires or interviews. Teach sociology. Direct work of statistical clerks, statisticians, and others who compile and evaluate research data. Consult with and advise individuals such as administrators, social workers, and legislators regarding social issues and policies, as well as the implications of research findings. Collaborate with research workers in other disciplines. Develop approaches to the solution of groups' problems, based on research findings in sociology and related disciplines. Observe group interactions and role affiliations to collect data, identify problems, evaluate progress, and determine the need for additional change. Develop problem intervention procedures, utilizing techniques such as interviews, consultations, role playing, and participant observation of group interactions. **SKILLS—Science:** Using scientific rules and methods to solve problems. **Writing:** Communicating effectively in writing as appropriate for the needs of the audience. **Management of Financial Resources:** Determining how money will be spent to get the work done and accounting for these expenditures. **Critical Thinking:** Using logic and reasoning to identify the strengths and weaknesses of alternative solutions, conclusions, or approaches to problems. **Reading Comprehension:** Understanding written sentences and paragraphs in work-related documents. **Active Learning:** Understanding the implications of new information for both current and future problem-solving and decision-making. **Complex Problem Solving:** Identifying complex problems and reviewing related information to develop and evaluate options and implement solutions. **Management of Personnel Resources:** Motivating, developing, and directing people as they work, identifying the best people for the job. **GOE—Interest Area:** 15. Scientific Research, Engineering, and Mathematics. **Work Group:** 15.04. Social Sciences. **Other Jobs in This Work Group:** Anthropologists; Archeologists; Economists; Educational Psychologists; Historians; Industrial-Organizational Psychologists; Political Scientists. **PERSONALITY TYPE:** Investigative.

EDUCATION/TRAINING PROGRAM(S)— Criminology; Demography and Population Studies; Sociology; Urban Studies/Affairs. **RELATED KNOWLEDGE/COURSES—Sociology and Anthropology:** Knowledge of group behavior and dynamics, societal trends and influences, human migrations, ethnicity, and cultures and their history and origins. **Philosophy and Theology:** Knowledge of different philosophical systems and religions. This includes their basic principles, values, ethics, ways of thinking, customs, and practices and their impact on human culture. **Psychology:** Knowledge of human behavior and performance; individual differences in ability, personality, and interests; learning and motivation; psychological research methods; and the assessment and treatment of behavioral and affective disorders. **English Language:** Knowledge of the structure and content of the English language, including the meaning and spelling of words, rules of composition, and grammar. **History and Archeology:** Knowledge of historical events and their causes, indicators, and effects on civilizations and cultures. **Mathematics:** Knowledge of arithmetic, algebra, geometry, calculus, and statistics and their applications.

Sociology Teachers, Postsecondary

- Education/Training Required: Master's degree
- Annual Earnings: $54,860
- Growth: 38.1%
- Annual Job Openings: 216,000
- Self-Employed: 0.3%
- Part-Time: 27.7%

Teach courses in sociology. Evaluate and grade students' class work, assignments, and papers. Prepare and deliver lectures to undergraduate and/or graduate students on topics such as race and ethnic relations, measurement and data collection, and workplace social relations. Initiate, facilitate, and moderate classroom discussions. Compile, administer, and grade examinations or assign this work to others. Prepare course materials such as syllabi, homework assignments, and handouts. Keep abreast of developments in their field by reading current literature, talking with colleagues, and participating in professional conferences. Maintain student attendance records, grades, and other required records. Maintain regularly scheduled office hours in order to advise and assist students. Plan, evaluate, and revise curricula, course content, and course materials and methods of instruction. Advise students on academic and vocational curricula and on career issues. Collaborate with colleagues to address teaching and research issues. Conduct research in a particular field of knowledge and publish findings in professional journals, books, and/or electronic media. Select and obtain materials and supplies such as textbooks and laboratory equipment. Supervise undergraduate and/or graduate teaching, internship, and research work. Serve on academic or administrative committees that deal with institutional policies, departmental matters, and academic issues. Participate in student recruitment, registration, and placement activities. Perform administrative duties such as serving as department head. Supervise students' laboratory and field work. Write grant proposals to procure external research funding. Act as advisers to student organizations. **SKILLS—Instructing:** Teaching others how to do something. **Learning Strategies:** Selecting and using training/instructional methods and procedures appropriate for the situation when learning or teaching new things. **Social Perceptiveness:** Being aware of others' reactions and understanding why they react as they do. **Writing:** Communicating effectively in writing as appropriate for the needs of the audience. **Critical Thinking:** Using logic and reasoning to identify the strengths and weaknesses of alternative solutions, conclusions, or approaches to problems. **Active Learning:** Understanding the implications of new information for both current and future problem-solving and decision-making. **Persuasion:** Persuading others to change their minds or behavior. **Speaking:** Talking to others to convey information effectively. **GOE—Interest Area:** 05. Education and Training. **Work Group:** 05.03. Postsecondary and Adult Teaching and Instructing. **Other Jobs in This Work Group:** Adult Literacy, Remedial Education, and GED Teachers and Instructors; Agricultural Sciences Teachers, Postsecondary; Anthropology and Archeology Teachers, Postsecondary; Architecture Teachers, Postsecondary; Area, Ethnic, and Cultural Studies Teachers, Postsecondary; Art, Drama, and Music Teachers, Postsecondary; Atmospheric, Earth, Marine, and Space Sciences Teachers, Postsecondary; Biological Science Teachers, Postsecondary; Business Teachers, Postsecondary; Chemistry Teachers, Postsecondary; Communications Teachers, Postsecondary; Computer Science Teachers, Postsecondary; Criminal Justice and Law Enforcement Teachers, Postsecondary; Economics Teachers, Postsecondary; Education Teachers, Postsecondary; Engineering Teachers, Postsecondary; English Language and Literature Teachers, Postsecondary; Environmental Science Teachers, Postsecondary; Farm and Home Management Advisors; Foreign Language and Literature Teachers, Postsecondary; Forestry and Conservation Science Teachers, Postsecondary; Geography Teachers, Postsecondary; Graduate Teaching Assistants; Health Specialties Teachers, Postsecondary; History Teachers, Postsecondary; Home Economics Teachers, Postsecondary; Law Teachers, Postsecondary; Library Science Teachers, Postsecondary; Mathematical Science Teachers, Postsecondary; Nursing Instructors and Teachers, Postsecondary; Philosophy and Religion Teachers, Postsecondary; Physics Teachers, Postsecondary; Political Science Teachers, Postsecondary; Psychology Teachers, Postsecondary; Recreation and Fitness Studies Teachers, Postsecondary; Self-Enrichment Education Teachers; Social Work Teachers, Postsecondary; Vocational Education Teachers, Postsecondary. **PERSONALITY TYPE:** Social.

EDUCATION/TRAINING PROGRAM(S)— Social Science Teacher Education; Sociology. **RELATED KNOWLEDGE/COURSES—Sociology and Anthropology:** Knowledge of group behavior and dynamics, societal trends and influences, human migrations, ethnicity, and cultures and their history and origins. **Education and Training:** Knowledge of principles and methods for curriculum and training design, teaching and instruction for individuals and groups, and the measurement of training effects. **Philosophy and Theology:** Knowledge of different philosophical systems and religions. This includes their basic principles, values, ethics, ways of thinking, customs, and practices and their impact on human culture. **History and Archeology:** Knowledge of historical events and their causes, indicators, and effects on civilizations and cultures. **English Language:** Knowledge of the structure and content of the English language, including the meaning and spelling of words, rules of composition, and grammar. **Psychology:** Knowledge of human behavior and performance; individual differences in ability, personality, and interests; learning and motivation; psychological research methods; and the assessment and treatment of behavioral and affective disorders.

Soil Scientists

- Education/Training Required: Bachelor's degree
- Annual Earnings: $51,200
- Growth: 9.1%
- Annual Job Openings: 2,000
- Self-Employed: 8.9%
- Part-Time: 7.0%

Research or study soil characteristics, map soil types, and investigate responses of soils to known management practices to determine use capabilities of soils and effects of alternative practices on soil productivity. Studies soil characteristics and classifies soils according to standard types. Provides advice on rural or urban land use. Performs chemical analysis on microorganism content of soil to determine microbial reactions and chemical mineralogical relationship to plant growth. Investigates responses of specific soil types to soil management practices, such as fertilization, crop rotation, and industrial waste control. Conducts experiments on farms or experimental stations to determine best soil types for different plants. **SKILLS—Science:** Using scientific rules and methods to solve problems. **Operations Analysis:** Analyzing needs and product requirements to create a design. **Reading Comprehension:** Understanding written sentences and paragraphs in work-related documents. **Writing:** Communicating effectively in writing as appropriate for the needs of the audience. **Active Learning:** Understanding the implications of new information for both current and future problem-solving and decision-making. **Critical Thinking:** Using logic and reasoning to identify the strengths and weaknesses of alternative solutions, conclusions, or approaches to problems. **Systems Evaluation:** Identifying measures or indicators of system performance and the actions needed to improve or correct performance relative to the goals of the system. **Mathematics:** Using mathematics to solve problems. **GOE—Interest Area:** 01. Agriculture and Natural Resources. **Work Group:** 01.02. Resource Science/Engineering for Plants, Animals, and the Environment. **Other Jobs in This Work Group:** Agricultural Engineers; Animal Scientists; Environmental Engineers; Foresters; Mining and Geological Engineers, Including Mining Safety Engineers; Petroleum Engineers; Plant Scientists; Range Managers; Soil Conservationists; Zoologists and Wildlife Biologists.

PERSONALITY TYPE: Investigative.

EDUCATION/TRAINING PROGRAM(S)—Agricultural and Horticultural Plant Breeding; Agriculture, General; Agronomy and Crop Science; Horticultural Science; Plant Protection and Integrated Pest Management; Plant Sciences, General; Plant Sciences, Other; Range Science and Management; Soil Chemistry and Physics; Soil Microbiology; Soil Science and Agronomy, General. **RELATED KNOWLEDGE/COURSES—Food Production:** Knowledge of techniques and equipment for planting, growing, and harvesting food products (both plant and animal) for consumption, including storage/handling techniques. **Chemistry:** Knowledge of the chemical composition, structure, and properties of substances and of the chemical processes and transformations that they undergo. This includes uses of chemicals and their danger signs, production techniques, and disposal methods. **Biology:** Knowledge of plant and animal organisms and their tissues, cells, functions, interdependencies, and interactions with each other and the environment. **Geography:** Knowledge of principles and methods for describing the features of land, sea, and air masses, including their physical characteristics; locations; interrelationships; and distribution of plant, animal, and human life. **Mathematics:** Knowledge of arithmetic, algebra, geometry, calculus, and statistics and their applications. **Physics:** Knowledge and prediction of physical principles and laws and their interrelationships and applications to understanding fluid, material, and atmospheric dynamics and mechanical, electrical, atomic, and subatomic structures and processes.

Solderers

- Education/Training Required: Short-term on-the-job training
- Annual Earnings: $30,620
- Growth: 17.0%
- Annual Job Openings: 71,000
- Self-Employed: 5.6%
- Part-Time: 2.1%

Solder together components to assemble fabricated metal products, using soldering iron. Melts and applies solder along adjoining edges of workpieces to solder joints, using soldering iron, gas torch, or electric-ultrasonic equipment. Grinds, cuts, buffs, or bends edges of workpieces to be joined to ensure snug fit, using power grinder and hand tools. Removes workpieces from molten solder and holds parts together until color indicates that solder has set. Cleans workpieces, using chemical solution, file, wire brush, or grinder. Cleans tip of soldering iron, using chemical solution or cleaning compound. Melts and separates soldered joints to repair misaligned or damaged assemblies, using soldering equipment. Applies flux to workpiece surfaces in preparation for soldering. Heats soldering iron or workpiece to specified temperature for soldering, using gas flame or electric current. Dips workpieces into molten solder or places solder strip between seams and heats seam with iron to band items together. Aligns and clamps workpieces together, using rule, square, or hand tools, or positions items in fixtures, jigs, or vise. Melts and applies solder to fill holes, indentations, and seams of fabricated metal products, using soldering equipment. **SKILLS—Operation and Control:** Controlling operations of equipment or systems. **Equipment Maintenance:** Performing routine maintenance on equipment and determining when and what kind of maintenance is needed. **Equipment Selection:** Determining the kind of tools and equipment needed to do a job. **Installation:** Installing equipment, machines, wiring, or programs to meet specifications. **Operation Monitoring:** Watching gauges, dials, or other indicators to make sure a machine is working properly. **Repairing:** Repairing machines or systems by using the needed tools. **GOE—Interest Area:** 13. Manufacturing. **Work Group:** 13.04. Welding, Brazing, and Soldering. **Other Jobs in This Work Group:** Brazers; Fitters, Structural Metal—Precision; Metal Fabricators, Structural Metal Products; Soldering and Brazing Machine Operators and Tenders; Welder-Fitters; Welders and Cutters; Welders, Production; Welding Machine Operators and Tenders; Welding Machine Setters and Set-Up Operators. **PERSONALITY TYPE:** Realistic.

EDUCATION/TRAINING PROGRAM(S)— Welding Technology/Welder. **RELATED KNOWLEDGE/COURSES—Building and Construction:** Knowledge of the materials, methods, and tools involved in the construction or repair of houses, buildings, or other structures such as highways and roads. **Mechanical Devices:** Knowledge of machines and tools, including their designs, uses, repair, and maintenance. **Production and Processing:** Knowledge of raw materials, production processes, quality control, costs,

and other techniques for maximizing the effective manufacture and distribution of goods.

Sound Engineering Technicians

- Education/Training Required: Postsecondary vocational training
- Annual Earnings: $38,110
- Growth: 25.5%
- Annual Job Openings: 2,000
- Self-Employed: 8.6%
- Part-Time: 12.5%

Operate machines and equipment to record, synchronize, mix, or reproduce music, voices, or sound effects in sporting arenas, theater productions, recording studios, or movie and video productions. Confer with producers, performers, and others in order to determine and achieve the desired sound for a production such as a musical recording or a film. Mix and edit voices, music, and taped sound effects for live performances and for prerecorded events, using sound mixing boards. Record speech, music, and other sounds on recording media, using recording equipment. Regulate volume level and sound quality during recording sessions, using control consoles. Reproduce and duplicate sound recordings from original recording media, using sound editing and duplication equipment. Separate instruments, vocals, and other sounds and then combine sounds later during the mixing or post-production stage. Set up, test, and adjust recording equipment for recording sessions and live performances; tear down equipment after event completion. Synchronize and equalize prerecorded dialogue, music, and sound effects with visual action of motion pictures or television productions, using control consoles. Create musical instrument digital interface programs for music projects, commercials, or film post-production. Keep logs of recordings. Prepare for recording sessions by performing activities such as selecting and setting up microphones. Report equipment problems and ensure that required repairs are made. **SKILLS— Operation and Control:** Controlling operations of equipment or systems. **Operation Monitoring:** Watching gauges, dials, or other indicators to make sure a machine is working properly. **Equipment Maintenance:** Performing routine maintenance on equipment and determining when and what kind of maintenance is needed. **Management of Personnel Resources:** Motivating, developing, and directing people as they work, identifying the best people for the job. **Equipment Selection:** Determining the kind of tools and equipment needed to do a job. **Troubleshooting:** Determining causes of operating errors and deciding what to do about them. **Management of Material Resources:** Obtaining and seeing to the appropriate use of equipment, facilities, and materials needed to do certain work. **Quality Control Analysis:** Conducting tests and inspections of products, services, or processes to evaluate quality or performance. **GOE—Interest Area:** 03. Arts and Communication. **Work Group:** 03.09. Media Technology. **Other Jobs in This Work Group:** Audio and Video Equipment Technicians; Broadcast Technicians; Camera Operators, Television, Video, and Motion Picture; Film and Video Editors; Multi-Media Artists and Animators; Photographic Hand Developers; Photographic Reproduction Technicians; Photographic Retouchers and Restorers; Professional Photographers; Radio Operators. **PERSONALITY TYPE:** Realistic.

EDUCATION/TRAINING   PROGRAM(S)— Communications Technology/Technician; Recording Arts Technology/Technician. **RELATED KNOWLEDGE/COURSES—Computers and Electronics:** Knowledge of circuit boards, processors, chips, electronic equipment, and computer hardware and software, including applications and programming. **Engineering and Technology:** Knowledge of the practical application of engineering science and technology. This includes applying principles, techniques, procedures, and equipment to the design and production of various goods and services. **Telecommunications:** Knowledge of transmission, broadcasting, switching, control, and operation of telecommunications systems. **Communications and Media:** Knowledge of media production, communication, and dissemination techniques and methods. This includes alternative ways to inform and entertain via written, oral, and visual media. **Administration and Management:** Knowledge of business and management principles involved in strategic planning, resource allocation, human resources modeling, leadership technique, production methods, and coordination of people and resources. **Fine Arts:** Knowledge of the theory and techniques required to compose, produce, and perform works of music, dance, the visual arts, drama, and sculpture.

Special Education Teachers, Middle School

◉ Education/Training Required: Bachelor's degree
◉ Annual Earnings: $44,160
◉ Growth: 30.0%
◉ Annual Job Openings: 59,000
◉ Self-Employed: 0.3%
◉ Part-Time: 9.3%

Teach middle school subjects to educationally and physically handicapped students. Includes teachers who specialize and work with audibly and visually handicapped students and those who teach basic academic and life processes skills to the mentally impaired. Establish and enforce rules for behavior and policies and procedures to maintain order among students. Maintain accurate and complete student records and prepare reports on children and activities, as required by laws, district policies, and administrative regulations. Prepare materials and classrooms for class activities. Confer with parents, administrators, testing specialists, social workers, and professionals to develop individual educational plans designed to promote students' educational, physical, and social development. Develop and implement strategies to meet the needs of students with a variety of handicapping conditions. Teach socially acceptable behavior, employing techniques such as behavior modification and positive reinforcement. Modify the general education curriculum for special-needs students based upon a variety of instructional techniques and instructional technology. Employ special educational strategies and techniques during instruction to improve the development of sensory- and perceptual-motor skills, language, cognition, and memory. Confer with parents or guardians, other teachers, counselors, and administrators in order to resolve students' behavioral and academic problems. Instruct through lectures, discussions, and demonstrations in one or more subjects, such as English, mathematics, or social studies. Coordinate placement of students with special needs into mainstream classes. Meet with parents and guardians to discuss their children's progress and to determine their priorities for their children and their resource needs. Prepare, administer, and grade tests and assignments to evaluate students' progress. Guide and counsel students with

S

adjustment and/or academic problems or special academic interests. Observe and evaluate students' performance, behavior, social development, and physical health. Establish clear objectives for all lessons, units, and projects and communicate those objectives to students. Teach students personal development skills such as goal setting, independence, and self-advocacy. Plan and conduct activities for a balanced program of instruction, demonstration, and work time that provides students with opportunities to observe, question, and investigate. **SKILLS—Learning Strategies:** Selecting and using training/instructional methods and procedures appropriate for the situation when learning or teaching new things. **Instructing:** Teaching others how to do something. **Social Perceptiveness:** Being aware of others' reactions and understanding why they react as they do. **Persuasion:** Persuading others to change their minds or behavior. **Negotiation:** Bringing others together and trying to reconcile differences. **Time Management:** Managing one's own time and the time of others. **Monitoring:** Monitoring or assessing your performance or that of other individuals or organizations to make improvements or take corrective action. **Service Orientation:** Actively looking for ways to help people. **GOE—Interest Area:** 05. Education and Training. **Work Group:** 05.02. Preschool, Elementary, and Secondary Teaching and Instructing. **Other Jobs in This Work Group:** Elementary School Teachers, Except Special Education; Kindergarten Teachers, Except Special Education; Middle School Teachers, Except Special and Vocational Education; Preschool Teachers, Except Special Education; Secondary School Teachers, Except Special and Vocational Education; Special Education Teachers, Preschool, Kindergarten, and Elementary School; Special Education Teachers, Secondary School; Teacher Assistants; Vocational Education Teachers, Middle School; Vocational Education Teachers, Secondary School. **PERSONALITY TYPE:** Social.

EDUCATION/TRAINING PROGRAM(S)—Special Education and Teaching, General. **RELATED KNOWLEDGE/COURSES—Psychology:** Knowledge of human behavior and performance; individual differences in ability, personality, and interests; learning and motivation; psychological research methods; and the assessment and treatment of behavioral and affective disorders. **Geography:** Knowledge of principles and methods for describing the features of land, sea, and air masses, including their physical characteristics; locations; interrelationships; and distribution of

plant, animal, and human life. **History and Archeology:** Knowledge of historical events and their causes, indicators, and effects on civilizations and cultures. **Education and Training:** Knowledge of principles and methods for curriculum and training design, teaching and instruction for individuals and groups, and the measurement of training effects. **Therapy and Counseling:** Knowledge of principles, methods, and procedures for diagnosis, treatment, and rehabilitation of physical and mental dysfunctions and for career counseling and guidance. **Sociology and Anthropology:** Knowledge of group behavior and dynamics, societal trends and influences, human migrations, ethnicity, and cultures and their history and origins.

Special Education Teachers, Preschool, Kindergarten, and Elementary School

- ◎ Education/Training Required: Bachelor's degree
- ◎ Annual Earnings: $43,570
- ◎ Growth: 30.0%
- ◎ Annual Job Openings: 59,000
- ◎ Self-Employed: 0.3%
- ◎ Part-Time: 9.3%

Teach elementary and preschool school subjects to educationally and physically handicapped students. Includes teachers who specialize and work with audibly and visually handicapped students and those who teach basic academic and life-processes skills to the mentally impaired. Instruct students in academic subjects, using a variety of techniques such as phonetics, multisensory learning, and repetition, in order to reinforce learning and to meet students' varying needs and interests. Employ special educational strategies and techniques during instruction to improve the development of sensory- and perceptual-motor skills, language, cognition, and memory. Teach socially acceptable behavior, employing techniques such as behavior modification and positive reinforcement. Modify the general education curriculum for special-needs students based upon a variety of instructional techniques and technologies. Meet with parents and guardians to discuss their children's progress and to determine their priorities for their children and their resource needs. Plan and conduct activities for a balanced program of instruction, demonstration, and work time that provides students with opportunities to observe, question, and investigate. Establish and enforce rules for behavior and policies and procedures to maintain order among the students for whom they are responsible. Confer with parents, administrators, testing specialists, social workers, and professionals to develop individual educational plans designed to promote students' educational, physical, and social development. Maintain accurate and complete student records and prepare reports on children and activities as required by laws, district policies, and administrative regulations. Establish clear objectives for all lessons, units, and projects and communicate those objectives to students. Develop and implement strategies to meet the needs of students with a variety of handicapping conditions. Prepare classrooms for class activities and provide a variety of materials and resources for children to explore, manipulate, and use, both in learning activities and imaginative play. Confer with parents or guardians, teachers, counselors, and administrators in order to resolve students' behavioral and academic problems. Observe and evaluate students' performance, behavior, social development, and physical health. Teach students personal development skills such as goal setting, independence, and self-advocacy. **SKILLS—Instructing:** Teaching others how to do something. **Learning Strategies:** Selecting and using training/instructional methods and procedures appropriate for the situation when learning or teaching new things. **Social Perceptiveness:** Being aware of others' reactions and understanding why they react as they do. **Time Management:** Managing one's own time and the time of others. **Monitoring:** Monitoring or assessing your performance or that of other individuals or organizations to make improvements or take corrective action. **Negotiation:** Bringing others together and trying to reconcile differences. **Coordination:** Adjusting actions in relation to others' actions. **Service Orientation:** Actively looking for ways to help people. **GOE—Interest Area:** 05. Education and Training. **Work Group:** 05.02. Preschool, Elementary, and Secondary Teaching and Instructing. **Other Jobs in This Work Group:** Elementary School Teachers, Except Special Education; Kindergarten Teachers, Except Special Education; Middle School Teachers, Except Special and Vocational Education; Preschool Teachers, Except Special Education; Secondary School Teachers, Except Special and Vocational Education; Special Education Teachers, Middle School; Special Education Teachers, Secondary School; Teacher Assistants; Vocational Education Teachers, Middle School; Vocational Education Teachers, Secondary School. **PERSONALITY TYPE:** Social.

EDUCATION/TRAINING PROGRAM(S)—Education/Teaching of Individuals with Autism; Education/Teaching of Individuals with Emotional Disturbances; Education/Teaching of Individuals with Hearing Impairments, Including Deafness; Education/Teaching of Individuals with Mental Retardation; Education/Teaching of Individuals with Multiple Disabilities; Education/Teaching of Individuals with Orthopedic and Other Physical Health Impairments; Education/Teaching of Individuals with Specific Learning Disabilities; Education/Teaching of Individuals with Speech or Language Impairments; Education/Teaching of Individuals with Traumatic Brain Injuries; Education/Teaching of Individuals with Vision Impairments, Including Blindness; Special Education and Teaching, General; Special Education and Teaching, Other. **RELATED KNOWLEDGE/COURSES—Psychology:** Knowledge of human behavior and performance; individual differences in ability, personality, and interests; learning and motivation; psychological research methods; and the assessment and treatment of behavioral and affective disorders. **Education and Training:** Knowledge of principles and methods for curriculum and training design, teaching and instruction for individuals and groups, and the measurement of training effects. **Geography:** Knowledge of principles and methods for describing the features of land, sea, and air masses, including their physical characteristics; locations; interrelationships; and distribution of plant, animal, and human life. **History and Archeology:** Knowledge of historical events and their causes, indicators, and effects on civilizations and cultures. **Sociology and Anthropology:** Knowledge of group behavior and dynamics, societal trends and influences, human migrations, ethnicity, and cultures and their history and origins. **Therapy and Counseling:** Knowledge of principles, methods, and procedures for diagnosis, treatment, and rehabilitation of physical and mental dysfunctions and for career counseling and guidance.

S

Special Education Teachers, Secondary School

- ◎ Education/Training Required: Bachelor's degree
- ◎ Annual Earnings: $45,700
- ◎ Growth: 30.0%
- ◎ Annual Job Openings: 59,000
- ◎ Self-Employed: 0.3%
- ◎ Part-Time: 9.3%

Teach secondary school subjects to educationally and physically handicapped students. Includes teachers who specialize and work with audibly and visually handicapped students and those who teach basic academic and life processes skills to the mentally impaired. Maintain accurate and complete student records and prepare reports on children and activities as required by laws, district policies, and administrative regulations. Teach socially acceptable behavior, employing techniques such as behavior modification and positive reinforcement. Prepare materials and classrooms for class activities. Establish and enforce rules for behavior and policies and procedures to maintain order among students. Confer with parents, administrators, testing specialists, social workers, and professionals to develop individual educational plans designed to promote students' educational, physical, and social development. Instruct through lectures, discussions, and demonstrations in one or more subjects such as English, mathematics, or social studies. Employ special educational strategies and techniques during instruction to improve the development of sensory- and perceptual-motor skills, language, cognition, and memory. Plan and conduct activities for a balanced program of instruction, demonstration, and work time that provides students with opportunities to observe, question, and investigate. Teach personal development skills such as goal setting, independence, and self-advocacy. Prepare students for later grades by encouraging them to explore learning opportunities and to persevere with challenging tasks. Establish clear objectives for all lessons, units, and projects and communicate those objectives to students. Develop and implement strategies to meet the needs of students with a variety of handicapping conditions. Modify the general education curriculum for special-needs stu-

dents, based upon a variety of instructional techniques and technologies. Meet with other professionals to discuss individual students' needs and progress. Confer with parents or guardians, other teachers, counselors, and administrators in order to resolve students' behavioral and academic problems. Meet with parents and guardians to discuss their children's progress and to determine their priorities for their children and their resource needs. Guide and counsel students with adjustment and/or academic problems or special academic interests. **SKILLS—Learning Strategies:** Selecting and using training/instructional methods and procedures appropriate for the situation when learning or teaching new things. **Social Perceptiveness:** Being aware of others' reactions and understanding why they react as they do. **Instructing:** Teaching others how to do something. **Negotiation:** Bringing others together and trying to reconcile differences. **Service Orientation:** Actively looking for ways to help people. **Persuasion:** Persuading others to change their minds or behavior. **Time Management:** Managing one's own time and the time of others. **Coordination:** Adjusting actions in relation to others' actions. **GOE—Interest Area:** 05. Education and Training. **Work Group:** 05.02. Preschool, Elementary, and Secondary Teaching and Instructing. **Other Jobs in This Work Group:** Elementary School Teachers, Except Special Education; Kindergarten Teachers, Except Special Education; Middle School Teachers, Except Special and Vocational Education; Preschool Teachers, Except Special Education; Secondary School Teachers, Except Special and Vocational Education; Special Education Teachers, Middle School; Special Education Teachers, Preschool, Kindergarten, and Elementary School; Teacher Assistants; Vocational Education Teachers, Middle School; Vocational Education Teachers, Secondary School. **PERSONALITY TYPE:** Social.

EDUCATION/TRAINING PROGRAM(S)—Special Education and Teaching, General. **RELATED KNOWLEDGE/COURSES—Therapy and Counseling:** Knowledge of principles, methods, and procedures for diagnosis, treatment, and rehabilitation of physical and mental dysfunctions and for career counseling and guidance. **Psychology:** Knowledge of human behavior and performance; individual differences in ability, personality, and interests; learning and motivation; psychological research methods; and the assessment and treatment of behavioral and affective disorders. **Geography:** Knowledge of principles and methods for describing the features of land, sea, and air masses, including their physical characteristics; locations; interrelationships; and distribution of plant, animal, and human life. **History and Archeology:** Knowledge of historical events and their causes, indicators, and effects on civilizations and cultures. **Education and Training:** Knowledge of principles and methods for curriculum and training design, teaching and instruction for individuals and groups, and the measurement of training effects. **Philosophy and Theology:** Knowledge of different philosophical systems and religions. This includes their basic principles, values, ethics, ways of thinking, customs, and practices and their impact on human culture.

Speech-Language Pathologists

- ◉ Education/Training Required: Master's degree
- ◉ Annual Earnings: $52,410
- ◉ Growth: 27.2%
- ◉ Annual Job Openings: 10,000
- ◉ Self-Employed: 8.2%
- ◉ Part-Time: 28.1%

Assess and treat persons with speech, language, voice, and fluency disorders. May select alternative communication systems and teach their use. May perform research related to speech and language problems. Monitor patients' progress and adjust treatments accordingly. Evaluate hearing and speech/language test results and medical or background information to diagnose and plan treatment for speech, language, fluency, voice, and swallowing disorders. Administer hearing or speech/language evaluations, tests, or examinations to patients to collect information on type and degree of impairments, using written and oral tests and special instruments. Record information on the initial evaluation, treatment, progress, and discharge of clients. Develop and implement treatment plans for problems such as stuttering, delayed language, swallowing disorders, and inappropriate pitch or harsh voice problems, based on own assessments and recommendations of physicians, psychologists, and social workers. Develop individual or group programs in schools to deal with speech or language problems. Instruct clients in techniques for more effective communication, including sign language, lip reading, and voice improvement. Teach clients to control or

strengthen tongue, jaw, face muscles, and breathing mechanisms. Develop speech exercise programs to reduce disabilities. Consult with and advise educators or medical staff on speech or hearing topics such as communication strategies and speech and language stimulation. Instruct patients and family members in strategies to cope with or avoid communication-related misunderstandings. Design, develop, and employ alternative diagnostic or communication devices and strategies. Conduct lessons and direct educational or therapeutic games to assist teachers dealing with speech problems. Refer clients to additional medical or educational services if needed. Participate in conferences or training or publish research results to share knowledge of new hearing or speech disorder treatment methods or technologies. Communicate with non-speaking students, using sign language or computer technology. Provide communication instruction to dialect speakers or students with limited English proficiency. Use computer applications to identify and assist with communication disabilities. **SKILLS— Instructing:** Teaching others how to do something. **Learning Strategies:** Selecting and using training/instructional methods and procedures appropriate for the situation when learning or teaching new things. **Social Perceptiveness:** Being aware of others' reactions and understanding why they react as they do. **Service Orientation:** Actively looking for ways to help people. **Time Management:** Managing one's own time and the time of others. **Speaking:** Talking to others to convey information effectively. **Active Learning:** Understanding the implications of new information for both current and future problem-solving and decision-making. **Coordination:** Adjusting actions in relation to others' actions. **GOE—Interest Area:** 08. Health Science. **Work Group:** 08.07. Medical Therapy. **Other Jobs in This Work Group:** Audiologists; Massage Therapists; Occupational Therapist Aides; Occupational Therapist Assistants; Occupational Therapists; Physical Therapist Aides; Physical Therapist Assistants; Physical Therapists; Radiation Therapists; Recreational Therapists; Respiratory Therapists; Respiratory Therapy Technicians. **PERSONALITY TYPE:** Social.

EDUCATION/TRAINING PROGRAM(S)—Audiology/Audiologist and Speech-Language Pathology/Pathologist; Communication Disorders Sciences and Services, Other; Communication Disorders, General; Speech-Language Pathology/Pathologist. **RELATED KNOWLEDGE/COURSES—Therapy and Coun-**

S

seling: Knowledge of principles, methods, and procedures for diagnosis, treatment, and rehabilitation of physical and mental dysfunctions and for career counseling and guidance. **Psychology:** Knowledge of human behavior and performance; individual differences in ability, personality, and interests; learning and motivation; psychological research methods; and the assessment and treatment of behavioral and affective disorders. **Education and Training:** Knowledge of principles and methods for curriculum and training design, teaching and instruction for individuals and groups, and the measurement of training effects. **English Language:** Knowledge of the structure and content of the English language, including the meaning and spelling of words, rules of composition, and grammar. **Sociology and Anthropology:** Knowledge of group behavior and dynamics, societal trends and influences, human migrations, ethnicity, and cultures and their history and origins. **Medicine and Dentistry:** Knowledge of the information and techniques needed to diagnose and treat human injuries, diseases, and deformities. This includes symptoms, treatment alternatives, drug properties and interactions, and preventive health-care measures.

Spotters, Dry Cleaning

- ◎ Education/Training Required: Short-term on-the-job training
- ◎ Annual Earnings: $17,220
- ◎ Growth: 12.3%
- ◎ Annual Job Openings: 47,000
- ◎ Self-Employed: 6.8%
- ◎ Part-Time: 16.9%

Identify stains in wool, synthetic, and silk garments and household fabrics and apply chemical solutions to remove stain. Determine spotting procedures on basis of type of fabric and nature of stain. Sprays steam, water, or air over spot to flush out chemicals, dry material, raise nap, or brighten color. Cleans fabric, using vacuum or airhose. Spreads article on worktable and positions stain over vacuum head or on marble slab. Mixes bleaching agent with hot water in vats and soaks material until it is bleached. Applies bleaching powder to spot and sprays with steam to remove stains from certain fabrics which do not respond to other cleaning solvents. Sprinkles chemical solvents over stain and pats area with brush or sponge until stain is removed. Inspects spots to ascertain composition and select solvent. Operates dry-cleaning machine. Applies chemicals to neutralize effect of solvents. **SKILLS—Operation Monitoring:** Watching gauges, dials, or other indicators to make sure a machine is working properly. **GOE—Interest Area:** 13. Manufacturing. **Work Group:** 13.11. Apparel, Shoes, Leather, and Fabric Care. **Other Jobs in This Work Group:** Custom Tailors; Fabric Menders, Except Garment; Laundry and Drycleaning Machine Operators and Tenders, Except Pressing; Precision Dyers; Pressers, Delicate Fabrics; Pressers, Hand; Shoe and Leather Workers and Repairers; Shop and Alteration Tailors; Upholsterers. **PERSONALITY TYPE:** Realistic.

EDUCATION/TRAINING PROGRAM(S)—No data available. **RELATED KNOWLEDGE/COURSES—Chemistry:** Knowledge of the chemical composition, structure, and properties of substances and of the chemical processes and transformations that they undergo. This includes uses of chemicals and their danger signs, production techniques, and disposal methods. **Food Production:** Knowledge of techniques and equipment for planting, growing, and harvesting food products (both plant and animal) for consumption, including storage/handling techniques.

Statement Clerks

- ◎ Education/Training Required: Short-term on-the-job training
- ◎ Annual Earnings: $27,040
- ◎ Growth: 7.9%
- ◎ Annual Job Openings: 78,000
- ◎ Self-Employed: 2.2%
- ◎ Part-Time: 16.1%

Prepare and distribute bank statements to customers, answer inquiries, and reconcile discrepancies in records and accounts. Compare previously prepared bank statements with canceled checks and reconcile discrepancies. Encode and cancel checks, using bank machines. Load machines with statements, cancelled checks, and envelopes in order to prepare statements for distribution to customers or stuff envelopes by hand. Maintain files of canceled checks and customers' signatures. Match statements with batches of canceled checks by account numbers. Monitor equipment in order to ensure proper operation. Retrieve checks returned to customers in error, adjusting customer accounts and answering inquiries about errors as necessary. Route statements for mailing or over-the-counter delivery to customers. Verify signatures and required information on checks. Weigh envelopes containing statements in order to determine correct postage and affix postage, using stamps or metering equipment. Fix minor problems, such as equipment jams, and notify repair personnel of major equipment problems. Post stop-payment notices in order to prevent payment of protested checks. Take orders for imprinted checks. **SKILLS—Active Listening:** Giving full attention to what other people are saying, taking time to understand the points being made, asking questions as appropriate, and not interrupting at inappropriate times. **Reading Comprehension:** Understanding written sentences and paragraphs in work-related documents. **GOE—Interest Area:** 04. Business and Administration. **Work Group:** 04.06. Mathematical Clerical Support. **Other Jobs in This Work Group:** Billing, Cost, and Rate Clerks; Bookkeeping, Accounting, and Auditing Clerks; Brokerage Clerks; Payroll and Timekeeping Clerks; Tax Preparers. **PERSONALITY TYPE:** Conventional.

EDUCATION/TRAINING PROGRAM(S)— Accounting Technology/Technician and Bookkeeping. **RELATED KNOWLEDGE/COURSES—Clerical Practices:** Knowledge of administrative and clerical procedures and systems such as word processing, managing files and records, stenography and transcription, designing forms, and other office procedures and terminology. **Economics and Accounting:** Knowledge of economic and accounting principles and practices, the financial markets, banking, and the analysis and reporting of financial data. **Computers and Electronics:** Knowledge of circuit boards, processors, chips, electronic equipment, and computer hardware and software, including applications and programming. **Telecommunications:** Knowledge of transmission, broadcasting, switching, control, and operation of telecommunications systems.

Station Installers and Repairers, Telephone

- Education/Training Required: Postsecondary vocational training
- Annual Earnings: $49,840
- Growth: –0.6%
- Annual Job Openings: 23,000
- Self-Employed: 4.6%
- Part-Time: 1.7%

Install and repair telephone station equipment, such as telephones, coin collectors, telephone booths, and switching-key equipment. Installs communication equipment, such as intercommunication systems and related apparatus, using schematic diagrams, testing devices, and hand tools. Assembles telephone equipment, mounts brackets, and connects wire leads, using hand tools and following installation diagrams or work order. Analyzes equipment operation, using testing devices to locate and diagnose nature of malfunction and ascertain needed repairs. Operates and tests equipment to ensure elimination of malfunction. Climbs poles to install or repair outside service lines. Disassembles components and replaces, cleans, adjusts, and repairs parts, wires, switches, relays, circuits, or signaling units, using hand tools. Repairs cables, lays out plans for new equipment, and estimates material required. **SKILLS—Troubleshooting:** Determining causes of operating errors and deciding what to do about them. **Installation:** Installing equipment, machines, wiring, or programs to meet specifications. **Repairing:** Repairing machines or systems by using the needed tools. **Equipment Maintenance:** Performing routine maintenance on equipment and determining when and what kind of maintenance is needed. **Quality Control Analysis:** Conducting tests and inspections of products, services, or processes to evaluate quality or performance. **Operation Monitoring:** Watching gauges, dials, or other indicators to make sure a machine is working properly. **Operation and Control:** Controlling operations of equipment or systems. **Technology Design:** Generating or adapting equipment and technology to serve user needs. **GOE—Interest Area:** 02. Architecture and Construction. **Work Group:** 02.05. Systems and Equipment Installation, Maintenance, and Repair. **Other Jobs in This Work Group:** Central Office and PBX Installers and Repairers; Communication Equipment Mechanics, Installers, and Repairers; Electric Meter Installers and Repairers; Electrical and Electronics Repairers, Powerhouse, Substation, and Relay; Electrical Power-Line Installers and Repairers; Elevator Installers and Repairers; Frame Wirers, Central Office; Heating and Air Conditioning Mechanics; Home Appliance Installers; Maintenance and Repair Workers, General; Meter Mechanics; Refrigeration Mechanics; Telecommunications Facility Examiners; Telecommunications Line Installers and Repairers. **PERSONALITY TYPE:** Realistic.

EDUCATION/TRAINING PROGRAM(S)— Communications Systems Installation and Repair Technology. **RELATED KNOWLEDGE/COURSES—Telecommunications:** Knowledge of transmission, broadcasting, switching, control, and operation of telecommunications systems. **Computers and Electronics:** Knowledge of circuit boards, processors, chips, electronic equipment, and computer hardware and software, including applications and programming. **Mechanical Devices:** Knowledge of machines and tools, including their designs, uses, repair, and maintenance. **Engineering and Technology:** Knowledge of the practical application of engineering science and technology. This includes applying principles, techniques, procedures, and equipment to the design and production of various goods and services. **Design:** Knowledge of design techniques, tools, and principles involved in production of precision technical plans, blueprints, drawings, and models. **Geography:** Knowledge of principles and methods for describing the features of land, sea, and air masses, including their physical characteristics; locations; interrelationships; and distribution of plant, animal, and human life.

Stevedores, Except Equipment Operators

- Education/Training Required: Short-term on-the-job training
- Annual Earnings: $20,120
- Growth: 6.6%
- Annual Job Openings: 525,000
- Self-Employed: 0.8%
- Part-Time: 21.0%

Manually load and unload ship cargo. Stack cargo in transit shed or in hold of ship, using pallet or cargo board. Attach and move slings to lift cargo. Guide load lift. Carries or moves cargo by handtruck to wharf and stacks cargo on pallets to facilitate transfer to and from ship. Stacks cargo in transit shed or in hold of ship as directed. Attaches and moves slings used to lift cargo. Guides load being lifted to prevent swinging. Shores cargo in ship's hold to prevent shifting during voyage. **SKILLS—**None met the criteria. **GOE— Interest Area:** 16. Transportation, Distribution, and Logistics. **Work Group:** 16.07. Transportation Support Work. **Other Jobs in This Work Group:** Bridge and Lock Tenders; Cargo and Freight Agents; Cleaners of Vehicles and Equipment; Freight Inspectors; Public Transportation Inspectors; Railroad Yard Workers; Traffic Technicians; Train Crew Members. **PERSONALITY TYPE:** Realistic.

EDUCATION/TRAINING PROGRAM(S)—No data available. **RELATED KNOWLEDGE/COURSES—Transportation:** Knowledge of principles and methods for moving people or goods by air, rail, sea, or road, including the relative costs and benefits. **Production and Processing:** Knowledge of raw materials, production processes, quality control, costs, and other techniques for maximizing the effective manufacture and distribution of goods. **Physics:** Knowledge and prediction of physical principles and laws and their interrelationships and applications to understanding fluid, material, and atmospheric dynamics and mechanical, electrical, atomic, and subatomic structures and processes.

Storage and Distribution Managers

- Education/Training Required: Work experience in a related occupation
- Annual Earnings: $66,600
- Growth: 19.7%
- Annual Job Openings: 13,000
- Self-Employed: 1.1%
- Part-Time: 2.4%

Plan, direct, and coordinate the storage and distribution operations within an organization or the activities of organizations that are engaged in storing and

distributing materials and products. Supervise the activities of workers engaged in receiving, storing, testing, and shipping products or materials. Plan, develop, and implement warehouse safety and security programs and activities. Review invoices, work orders, consumption reports, and demand forecasts in order to estimate peak delivery periods and to issue work assignments. Schedule and monitor air or surface pickup, delivery, or distribution of products or materials. Interview, select, and train warehouse and supervisory personnel. Confer with department heads to coordinate warehouse activities, such as production, sales, records control, and purchasing. Respond to customers' or shippers' questions and complaints regarding storage and distribution services. Inspect physical conditions of warehouses, vehicle fleets, and equipment and order testing, maintenance, repair, or replacement as necessary. Develop and document standard and emergency operating procedures for receiving, handling, storing, shipping, or salvaging products or materials. Examine products or materials in order to estimate quantities or weight and type of container required for storage or transport. Negotiate with carriers, warehouse operators, and insurance company representatives for services and preferential rates. Issue shipping instructions and provide routing information to ensure that delivery times and locations are coordinated. Examine invoices and shipping manifests for conformity to tariff and customs regulations. Prepare and manage departmental budgets. Prepare or direct preparation of correspondence; reports; and operations, maintenance, and safety manuals. Arrange for necessary shipping documentation and contact customs officials in order to effect release of shipments. Advise sales and billing departments of transportation charges for customers' accounts. Evaluate freight costs and the inventory costs associated with transit times in order to ensure that costs are appropriate. Participate in setting transportation and service rates. Track and trace goods while they are en route to their destinations, expediting orders when necessary. **SKILLS—Management of Personnel Resources:** Motivating, developing, and directing people as they work, identifying the best people for the job. **Operations Analysis:** Analyzing needs and product requirements to create a design. **Monitoring:** Monitoring or assessing your performance or that of other individuals or organizations to make improvements or take corrective action. **Management of Material Resources:** Obtaining and seeing to the appropriate use of equipment, facilities, and materials needed to do certain work. **Persuasion:** Persuading others to change their minds or behavior. **Service Orientation:** Actively looking for ways to help people. **Social Perceptiveness:** Being aware of others' reactions and understanding why they react as they do. **Systems Analysis:** Determining how a system should work and how changes in conditions, operations, and the environment will affect outcomes. **GOE—Interest Area:** 16. Transportation, Distribution, and Logistics. **Work Group:** 16.01. Managerial Work in Transportation. **Other Jobs in This Work Group:** Aircraft Cargo Handling Supervisors; First-Line Supervisors/Managers of Transportation and Material-Moving Machine and Vehicle Operators; Postmasters and Mail Superintendents; Railroad Conductors and Yardmasters; Transportation Managers. **PERSONALITY TYPE:** Enterprising.

EDUCATION/TRAINING PROGRAM(S)—Aeronautics/Aviation/Aerospace Science and Technology, General; Aviation/Airway Management and Operations; Business Administration and Management, General; Business/Commerce, General; Logistics and Materials Management; Public Administration. **RELATED KNOWLEDGE/COURSES—Customer and Personal Service:** Knowledge of principles and processes for providing customer and personal services. This includes customer needs assessment, meeting quality standards for services, and evaluation of customer satisfaction. **Administration and Management:** Knowledge of business and management principles involved in strategic planning, resource allocation, human resources modeling, leadership technique, production methods, and coordination of people and resources. **Sales and Marketing:** Knowledge of principles and methods for showing, promoting, and selling products or services. This includes marketing strategy and tactics, product demonstrations, sales techniques, and sales control systems. **Personnel and Human Resources:** Knowledge of principles and procedures for personnel recruitment, selection, training, compensation and benefits, labor relations and negotiation, and personnel information systems. **Education and Training:** Knowledge of principles and methods for curriculum and training design, teaching and instruction for individuals and groups, and the measurement of training effects. **Production and Processing:** Knowledge of raw materials, production processes, quality control, costs, and other techniques for maximizing the effective manufacture and distribution of goods.

Structural Iron and Steel Workers

- ◎ Education/Training Required: Long-term on-the-job training
- ◎ Annual Earnings: $42,430
- ◎ Growth: 15.9%
- ◎ Annual Job Openings: 9,000
- ◎ Self-Employed: 6.2%
- ◎ Part-Time: 1.8%

Raise, place, and unite iron or steel girders, columns, and other structural members to form completed structures or structural frameworks. May erect metal storage tanks and assemble prefabricated metal buildings. Assemble hoisting equipment and rigging, such as cables, pulleys, and hooks, to move heavy equipment and materials. Bolt aligned structural-steel members in position for permanent riveting, bolting, or welding into place. Connect columns, beams, and girders with bolts, following blueprints and instructions from supervisors. Drive drift pins through rivet holes in order to align rivet holes in structural-steel members with corresponding holes in previously placed members. Erect metal and precast concrete components for structures such as buildings, bridges, dams, towers, storage tanks, fences, and highway guardrails. Fasten structural-steel members to hoist cables, using chains, cables, or rope. Force structural-steel members into final positions, using turnbuckles, crowbars, jacks, and hand tools. Hoist steel beams, girders, and columns into place, using cranes, or signal hoisting equipment operators to lift and position structural-steel members. Pull, push, or pry structural-steel members into approximate positions for bolting into place. Ride on girders or other structural-steel members to position them or use rope to guide them into position. Unload and position prefabricated steel units for hoisting as needed. Verify vertical and horizontal alignment of structural-steel members, using plumb bobs, laser equipment, transits, and/or levels. Catch hot rivets in buckets and insert rivets in holes, using tongs. Cut, bend, and weld steel pieces, using metal shears, torches, and welding equipment. Dismantle structures and equipment. Fabricate metal parts such as steel frames, columns, beams, and girders, according to blueprints or instructions from supervisors. Hold rivets while riveters use air hammers to form heads on rivets. Insert sealing strips, wiring, insulating material, ladders, flanges, gauges, and valves, depending on types of structures being assembled. Place blocks under reinforcing bars used to reinforce floors. Read specifications and blueprints to determine the locations, quantities, and sizes of materials required. **SKILLS—Installation:** Installing equipment, machines, wiring, or programs to meet specifications. **Repairing:** Repairing machines or systems by using the needed tools. **Coordination:** Adjusting actions in relation to others' actions. **Management of Material Resources:** Obtaining and seeing to the appropriate use of equipment, facilities, and materials needed to do certain work. **Equipment Selection:** Determining the kind of tools and equipment needed to do a job. **Operation and Control:** Controlling operations of equipment or systems. **Technology Design:** Generating or adapting equipment and technology to serve user needs. **GOE—Interest Area:** 02. Architecture and Construction. **Work Group:** 02.04. Construction Crafts. **Other Jobs in This Work Group:** Boat Builders and Shipwrights; Boilermakers; Brattice Builders; Brickmasons and Blockmasons; Carpet Installers; Ceiling Tile Installers; Cement Masons and Concrete Finishers; Commercial Divers; Construction Carpenters; Crane and Tower Operators; Dragline Operators; Drywall Installers; Electricians; Fence Erectors; Floor Layers, Except Carpet, Wood, and Hard Tiles; Floor Sanders and Finishers; Glaziers; Grader, Bulldozer, and Scraper Operators; Hazardous Materials Removal Workers; Insulation Workers, Floor, Ceiling, and Wall; Insulation Workers, Mechanical; Manufactured Building and Mobile Home Installers; Operating Engineers; Painters, Construction and Maintenance; Paperhangers; Paving, Surfacing, and Tamping Equipment Operators; Pile-Driver Operators; Pipe Fitters; Pipelayers; Pipelaying Fitters; Plasterers and Stucco Masons; Plumbers; Rail-Track Laying and Maintenance Equipment Operators; Refractory Materials Repairers, Except Brickmasons; Reinforcing Iron and Rebar Workers; Riggers; Roofers; Rough Carpenters; Security and Fire Alarm Systems Installers; Segmental Pavers; Sheet Metal Workers; Ship Carpenters and Joiners; Stone Cutters and Carvers; Stonemasons; Tapers; Terrazzo Workers and Finishers; Tile and Marble Setters. **PERSONALITY TYPE:** Realistic.

EDUCATION/TRAINING PROGRAM(S)—Construction Trades, Other; Metal Building Assembly/Assembler. **RELATED KNOWLEDGE/**

COURSES—**Building and Construction:** Knowledge of the materials, methods, and tools involved in the construction or repair of houses, buildings, or other structures such as highways and roads. **Mechanical Devices:** Knowledge of machines and tools, including their designs, uses, repair, and maintenance. **Public Safety and Security:** Knowledge of relevant equipment, policies, procedures, and strategies to promote effective local, state, or national security operations for the protection of people, data, property, and institutions. **Engineering and Technology:** Knowledge of the practical application of engineering science and technology. This includes applying principles, techniques, procedures, and equipment to the design and production of various goods and services. **Physics:** Knowledge and prediction of physical principles and laws and their interrelationships and applications to understanding fluid, material, and atmospheric dynamics and mechanical, electrical, atomic, and subatomic structures and processes. **Design:** Knowledge of design techniques, tools, and principles involved in production of precision technical plans, blueprints, drawings, and models.

Substance Abuse and Behavioral Disorder Counselors

- Education/Training Required: Master's degree
- Annual Earnings: $32,130
- Growth: 23.3%
- Annual Job Openings: 10,000
- Self-Employed: 4.5%
- Part-Time: 14.6%

Counsel and advise individuals with alcohol, tobacco, drug, or other problems, such as gambling and eating disorders. May counsel individuals, families, or groups or engage in prevention programs. Counsel clients and patients, individually and in group sessions, to assist in overcoming dependencies, adjusting to life, and making changes. Complete and maintain accurate records and reports regarding the patients' histories and progress, services provided, and other required information. Develop client treatment plans based on research, clinical experience, and client histories. Review and evaluate clients' progress in relation to

measurable goals described in treatment and care plans. Interview clients, review records, and confer with other professionals in order to evaluate individuals' mental and physical condition and to determine their suitability for participation in a specific program. Intervene as advocate for clients or patients in order to resolve emergency problems in crisis situations. Provide clients or family members with information about addiction issues and about available services and programs, making appropriate referrals when necessary. Modify treatment plans to comply with changes in client status. Coordinate counseling efforts with mental health professionals and other health professionals such as doctors, nurses, and social workers. Attend training sessions in order to increase knowledge and skills. Plan and implement follow-up and aftercare programs for clients to be discharged from treatment programs. Conduct chemical dependency program orientation sessions. Counsel family members to assist them in understanding, dealing with, and supporting clients or patients. Participate in case conferences and staff meetings. Act as liaisons between clients and medical staff. Coordinate activities with courts, probation officers, community services, and other post-treatment agencies. Confer with family members or others close to clients in order to keep them informed of treatment planning and progress. Instruct others in program methods, procedures, and functions. Follow progress of discharged patients in order to determine effectiveness of treatments. Develop, implement, and evaluate public education, prevention, and health promotion programs, working in collaboration with organizations, institutions, and communities. SKILLS—**Social Perceptiveness:** Being aware of others' reactions and understanding why they react as they do. **Persuasion:** Persuading others to change their minds or behavior. **Service Orientation:** Actively looking for ways to help people. **Negotiation:** Bringing others together and trying to reconcile differences. **Learning Strategies:** Selecting and using training/instructional methods and procedures appropriate for the situation when learning or teaching new things. **Instructing:** Teaching others how to do something. **Active Listening:** Giving full attention to what other people are saying, taking time to understand the points being made, asking questions as appropriate, and not interrupting at inappropriate times. **Time Management:** Managing one's own time and the time of others. GOE—**Interest Area:** 10. Human Service. **Work Group:** 10.01. Counseling and Social Work. **Other Jobs in This Work**

Group: Child, Family, and School Social Workers; Clinical Psychologists; Counseling Psychologists; Marriage and Family Therapists; Medical and Public Health Social Workers; Mental Health and Substance Abuse Social Workers; Mental Health Counselors; Probation Officers and Correctional Treatment Specialists; Rehabilitation Counselors; Residential Advisors; Social and Human Service Assistants. **PERSONALITY TYPE:** Social.

EDUCATION/TRAINING PROGRAM(S)—Clinical/Medical Social Work; Mental and Social Health Services and Allied Professions, Other; Substance Abuse/Addiction Counseling. **RELATED KNOWLEDGE/COURSES—Therapy and Counseling:** Knowledge of principles, methods, and procedures for diagnosis, treatment, and rehabilitation of physical and mental dysfunctions and for career counseling and guidance. **Psychology:** Knowledge of human behavior and performance; individual differences in ability, personality, and interests; learning and motivation; psychological research methods; and the assessment and treatment of behavioral and affective disorders. **Sociology and Anthropology:** Knowledge of group behavior and dynamics, societal trends and influences, human migrations, ethnicity, and cultures and their history and origins. **Philosophy and Theology:** Knowledge of different philosophical systems and religions. This includes their basic principles, values, ethics, ways of thinking, customs, and practices and their impact on human culture. **Customer and Personal Service:** Knowledge of principles and processes for providing customer and personal services. This includes customer needs assessment, meeting quality standards for services, and evaluation of customer satisfaction. **Education and Training:** Knowledge of principles and methods for curriculum and training design, teaching and instruction for individuals and groups, and the measurement of training effects.

Subway and Streetcar Operators

- Education/Training Required: Moderate-term on-the-job training
- Annual Earnings: $49,290
- Growth: 13.2%
- Annual Job Openings: 2,000
- Self-Employed: 0%
- Part-Time: 8.8%

Operate subway or elevated suburban train with no separate locomotive or electric-powered streetcar to transport passengers. May handle fares. Drive and control rail-guided public transportation, such as subways; elevated trains; and electric-powered streetcars, trams, or trolleys, in order to transport passengers. Make announcements to passengers, such as notifications of upcoming stops or schedule delays. Operate controls to open and close transit vehicle doors. Regulate vehicle speed and the time spent at each stop in order to maintain schedules. Report delays, mechanical problems, and emergencies to supervisors or dispatchers, using radios. Monitor lights indicating obstructions or other trains ahead and watch for car and truck traffic at crossings to stay alert to potential hazards. Attend meetings on driver and passenger safety in order to learn ways in which job performance might be affected. Collect fares from passengers and issue change and transfers. Complete reports, including shift summaries and incident or accident reports. Direct emergency evacuation procedures. Greet passengers; provide information; and answer questions concerning fares, schedules, transfers, and routings. Record transactions and coin receptor readings in order to verify the amount of money collected. **SKILLS—Operation and Control:** Controlling operations of equipment or systems. **Operation Monitoring:** Watching gauges, dials, or other indicators to make sure a machine is working properly. **GOE— Interest Area:** 16. Transportation, Distribution, and Logistics. **Work Group:** 16.04. Rail Vehicle Operation. **Other Jobs in This Work Group:** Locomotive Engineers; Locomotive Firers; Rail Yard Engineers, Dinkey Operators, and Hostlers. **PERSONALITY TYPE:** Realistic.

EDUCATION/TRAINING PROGRAM(S)— Truck and Bus Driver/Commercial Vehicle Operation.

RELATED KNOWLEDGE/COURSES—**Transportation:** Knowledge of principles and methods for moving people or goods by air, rail, sea, or road, including the relative costs and benefits. **Geography:** Knowledge of principles and methods for describing the features of land, sea, and air masses, including their physical characteristics; locations; interrelationships; and distribution of plant, animal, and human life. **Clerical Practices:** Knowledge of administrative and clerical procedures and systems such as word processing, managing files and records, stenography and transcription, designing forms, and other office procedures and terminology. **Customer and Personal Service:** Knowledge of principles and processes for providing customer and personal services. This includes customer needs assessment, meeting quality standards for services, and evaluation of customer satisfaction. **Telecommunications:** Knowledge of transmission, broadcasting, switching, control, and operation of telecommunications systems.

Surgeons

- Education/Training Required: First professional degree
- Annual Earnings: More than $145,600
- Growth: 19.5%
- Annual Job Openings: 38,000
- Self-Employed: 16.9%
- Part-Time: 8.1%

Treat diseases, injuries, and deformities by invasive methods, such as manual manipulation or by using instruments and appliances. Analyze patient's medical history, medication allergies, physical condition, and examination results to verify operation's necessity and to determine best procedure. Prescribe preoperative and postoperative treatments and procedures, such as sedatives, diets, antibiotics, and preparation and treatment of the patient's operative area. Direct and coordinate activities of nurses, assistants, specialists, residents, and other medical staff. Examine patient to provide information on medical condition and surgical risk. Follow established surgical techniques during the operation. Operate on patients to correct deformities, repair injuries, prevent and treat diseases, or improve or restore patients' functions. Refer patient to medical specialist or other practitioners when necessary. Conduct research to develop and test surgical techniques that can improve operating procedures and outcomes. Examine instruments, equipment, and operating room to ensure sterility. Manage surgery services, including planning, scheduling and coordination, determination of procedures, and procurement of supplies and equipment. Prepare case histories. Provide consultation and surgical assistance to other physicians and surgeons. Diagnose bodily disorders and orthopedic conditions and provide treatments such as medicines and surgeries in clinics, hospital wards, and operating rooms. **SKILLS—Science:** Using scientific rules and methods to solve problems. **Systems Evaluation:** Identifying measures or indicators of system performance and the actions needed to improve or correct performance relative to the goals of the system. **Management of Personnel Resources:** Motivating, developing, and directing people as they work, identifying the best people for the job. **Judgment and Decision Making:** Considering the relative costs and benefits of potential actions to choose the most appropriate one. **Systems Analysis:** Determining how a system should work and how changes in conditions, operations, and the environment will affect outcomes. **Operation and Control:** Controlling operations of equipment or systems. **Reading Comprehension:** Understanding written sentences and paragraphs in work-related documents. **Coordination:** Adjusting actions in relation to others' actions. **GOE—Interest Area:** 08. Health Science. **Work Group:** 08.02. Medicine and Surgery. **Other Jobs in This Work Group:** Anesthesiologists; Family and General Practitioners; Internists, General; Medical Assistants; Medical Transcriptionists; Obstetricians and Gynecologists; Pediatricians, General; Pharmacists; Pharmacy Aides; Pharmacy Technicians; Physician Assistants; Psychiatrists; Registered Nurses; Surgical Technologists. **PERSONALITY TYPE:** Investigative.

EDUCATION/TRAINING PROGRAM(S)—Adult Reconstructive Orthopedics (Orthopedic Surgery); Colon and Rectal Surgery; Critical Care Surgery; General Surgery; Hand Surgery; Neurological Surgery/Neurosurgery; Orthopedic Surgery of the Spine; Orthopedics/Orthopedic Surgery; Otolaryngology; Pediatric Orthopedics; Pediatric Surgery; Plastic Surgery; Sports Medicine; Thoracic Surgery; Urology; Vascular Surgery. **RELATED KNOWLEDGE/COURSES—Medicine and Dentistry:** Knowledge of the information and techniques needed to diagnose and treat human injuries, diseases, and deformities.

This includes symptoms, treatment alternatives, drug properties and interactions, and preventive health-care measures. **Biology:** Knowledge of plant and animal organisms and their tissues, cells, functions, interdependencies, and interactions with each other and the environment. **Chemistry:** Knowledge of the chemical composition, structure, and properties of substances and of the chemical processes and transformations that they undergo. This includes uses of chemicals and their danger signs, production techniques, and disposal methods. **Administration and Management:** Knowledge of business and management principles involved in strategic planning, resource allocation, human resources modeling, leadership technique, production methods, and coordination of people and resources. **Therapy and Counseling:** Knowledge of principles, methods, and procedures for diagnosis, treatment, and rehabilitation of physical and mental dysfunctions and for career counseling and guidance. **Physics:** Knowledge and prediction of physical principles and laws and their interrelationships and applications to understanding fluid, material, and atmospheric dynamics and mechanical, electrical, atomic, and subatomic structures and processes.

Surgical Technologists

- Education/Training Required: Postsecondary vocational training
- Annual Earnings: $34,010
- Growth: 27.9%
- Annual Job Openings: 13,000
- Self-Employed: 0%
- Part-Time: 23.0%

Assist in operations under the supervision of surgeons, registered nurses, or other surgical personnel. May help set up operating room; prepare and transport patients for surgery; adjust lights and equipment; pass instruments and other supplies to surgeons and surgeon's assistants; hold retractors; cut sutures; and help count sponges, needles, supplies, and instruments. Count sponges, needles, and instruments before and after operation. Hand instruments and supplies to surgeons and surgeons' assistants, hold retractors and cut sutures, and perform other tasks as directed by surgeon during operation. Scrub arms and hands and assist the surgical team to scrub and put on gloves, masks, and surgical clothing. Position patients on the operating table and cover them with sterile surgical drapes to prevent exposure. Provide technical assistance to surgeons, surgical nurses, and anesthesiologists. Wash and sterilize equipment, using germicides and sterilizers. Prepare, care for, and dispose of tissue specimens taken for laboratory analysis. Clean and restock the operating room, placing equipment and supplies and arranging instruments according to instruction. Prepare dressings or bandages and apply or assist with their application following surgery. Operate, assemble, adjust, or monitor sterilizers, lights, suction machines, and diagnostic equipment to ensure proper operation. Monitor and continually assess operating room conditions, including patient and surgical team needs. Observe patients' vital signs to assess physical condition. Maintain supply of fluids, such as plasma, saline, blood, and glucose, for use during operations. Maintain files and records of surgical procedures. **SKILLS—Instructing:** Teaching others how to do something. **Troubleshooting:** Determining causes of operating errors and deciding what to do about them. **Learning Strategies:** Selecting and using training/instructional methods and procedures appropriate for the situation when learning or teaching new things. **Equipment Selection:** Determining the kind of tools and equipment needed to do a job. **Social Perceptiveness:** Being aware of others' reactions and understanding why they react as they do. **Reading Comprehension:** Understanding written sentences and paragraphs in work-related documents. **Active Learning:** Understanding the implications of new information for both current and future problem-solving and decision-making. **Coordination:** Adjusting actions in relation to others' actions. **Service Orientation:** Actively looking for ways to help people. **Operation Monitoring:** Watching gauges, dials, or other indicators to make sure a machine is working properly. **GOE—Interest Area:** 08. Health Science. **Work Group:** 08.02. Medicine and Surgery. **Other Jobs in This Work Group:** Anesthesiologists; Family and General Practitioners; Internists, General; Medical Assistants; Medical Transcriptionists; Obstetricians and Gynecologists; Pediatricians, General; Pharmacists; Pharmacy Aides; Pharmacy Technicians; Physician Assistants; Psychiatrists; Registered Nurses; Surgeons. **PERSONALITY TYPE:** Realistic.

EDUCATION/TRAINING PROGRAM(S)— Pathology/Pathologist Assistant; Surgical Technology/Technologist. **RELATED KNOWLEDGE/ COURSES—Medicine and Dentistry:** Knowledge of the information and techniques needed to diagnose and treat human injuries, diseases, and deformities. This includes symptoms, treatment alternatives, drug properties and interactions, and preventive health-care measures. **Customer and Personal Service:** Knowledge of principles and processes for providing customer and personal services. This includes customer needs assessment, meeting quality standards for services, and evaluation of customer satisfaction. **Chemistry:** Knowledge of the chemical composition, structure, and properties of substances and of the chemical processes and transformations that they undergo. This includes uses of chemicals and their danger signs, production techniques, and disposal methods. **Psychology:** Knowledge of human behavior and performance; individual differences in ability, personality, and interests; learning and motivation; psychological research methods; and the assessment and treatment of behavioral and affective disorders. **Philosophy and Theology:** Knowledge of different philosophical systems and religions. This includes their basic principles, values, ethics, ways of thinking, customs, and practices and their impact on human culture. **Education and Training:** Knowledge of principles and methods for curriculum and training design, teaching and instruction for individuals and groups, and the measurement of training effects.

Survey Researchers

◎ Education/Training Required: Bachelor's degree
◎ Annual Earnings: $26,490
◎ Growth: 33.6%
◎ Annual Job Openings: 3,000
◎ Self-Employed: 9.3%
◎ Part-Time: 11.7%

Design or conduct surveys. May supervise interviewers who conduct the survey in person or over the telephone. May present survey results to client. Collaborate with other researchers in the planning, implementation, and evaluation of surveys. Conduct surveys and collect data, using methods such as interviews, questionnaires, focus groups, market analysis surveys, public opinion polls, literature reviews, and file reviews. Consult with clients in order to identify survey needs and any specific requirements, such as special samples. Determine and specify details of sur-

vey projects, including sources of information, procedures to be used, and the design of survey instruments and materials. Direct and review the work of staff members, including survey support staff and interviewers who gather survey data. Direct updates and changes in survey implementation and methods. Monitor and evaluate survey progress and performance, using sample disposition reports and response rate calculations. Prepare and present summaries and analyses of survey data, including tables, graphs, and fact sheets that describe survey techniques and results. Produce documentation of the questionnaire development process, data collection methods, sampling designs, and decisions related to sample statistical weighting. Support, plan, and coordinate operations for single or multiple surveys. Analyze data from surveys, old records, and/or case studies, using statistical software programs. Conduct research in order to gather information about survey topics. Hire and train recruiters and data collectors. Review, classify, and record survey data in preparation for computer analysis. Write training manuals to be used by survey interviewers. **SKILLS**—No data available. **GOE—Interest Area:** 06. Finance and Insurance. **Work Group:** 06.02. Finance/Insurance Investigation and Analysis. **Other Jobs in This Work Group:** Appraisers, Real Estate; Assessors; Claims Examiners, Property and Casualty Insurance; Cost Estimators; Credit Analysts; Financial Analysts; Insurance Adjusters, Examiners, and Investigators; Insurance Appraisers, Auto Damage; Insurance Underwriters; Loan Counselors; Loan Officers; Market Research Analysts. **PERSONALITY TYPE:** No data available.

EDUCATION/TRAINING PROGRAM(S)— Applied Economics; Business/Managerial Economics; Economics, General; Marketing Research. **RELATED KNOWLEDGE/COURSES**—No data available.

Surveying Technicians

◎ Education/Training Required: Long-term on-the-job training
◎ Annual Earnings: $30,380
◎ Growth: 23.1%
◎ Annual Job Openings: 10,000
◎ Self-Employed: 5.5%
◎ Part-Time: 7.0%

Adjust and operate surveying instruments, such as the theodolite and electronic distance-measuring equipment, and compile notes, make sketches, and enter data into computers. Adjust and operate surveying instruments such as prisms, theodolites, and electronic distance-measuring equipment. Compile information necessary to stake projects for construction, using engineering plans. Run rods for benches and cross-section elevations. Position and hold the vertical rods, or targets, that theodolite operators use for sighting in order to measure angles, distances, and elevations. Record survey measurements and descriptive data, using notes, drawings, sketches, and inked tracings. Perform calculations to determine earth curvature corrections, atmospheric impacts on measurements, traverse closures and adjustments, azimuths, level runs, and placement of markers. Conduct surveys to ascertain the locations of natural features and human-made structures on the Earth's surface, underground, and under water, using electronic distance-measuring equipment and other surveying instruments. Search for section corners, property irons, and survey points. Operate and manage land-information computer systems, performing tasks such as storing data, making inquiries, and producing plots and reports. Direct and supervise work of subordinate members of surveying parties. Set out and recover stakes, marks, and other monumentation. Lay out grids and determine horizontal and vertical controls. Compare survey computations with applicable standards in order to determine adequacy of data. Collect information needed to carry out new surveys, using source maps, previous survey data, photographs, computer records, and other relevant information. Prepare topographic and contour maps of land surveyed, including site features and other relevant information such as charts, drawings, and survey notes. Maintain equipment and vehicles used by surveying crews. Place and hold measuring tapes when electronic distance-measuring equipment is not used. Provide assistance in the development of methods and procedures for conducting field surveys. Perform manual labor, such as cutting brush for lines; carrying stakes, rebar, and other heavy items; and stacking rods. **SKILLS—Mathematics:** Using mathematics to solve problems. **Coordination:** Adjusting actions in relation to others' actions. **Troubleshooting:** Determining causes of operating errors and deciding what to do about them. **Instructing:** Teaching others how to do something. **Time Management:** Managing one's own time and the time of others. **Active Learning:** Understanding the implications of new information for both current and future problem-solving and decision-making. **Equipment Selection:** Determining the kind of tools and equipment needed to do a job. **Equipment Maintenance:** Performing routine maintenance on equipment and determining when and what kind of maintenance is needed. **GOE—Interest Area:** 15. Scientific Research, Engineering, and Mathematics. **Work Group:** 15.09. Engineering Technology. **Other Jobs in This Work Group:** Aerospace Engineering and Operations Technicians; Calibration and Instrumentation Technicians; Cartographers and Photogrammetrists; Civil Engineering Technicians; Electrical Engineering Technicians; Electro-Mechanical Technicians; Electronic Drafters; Electronics Engineering Technicians; Environmental Engineering Technicians; Mapping Technicians; Mechanical Drafters; Mechanical Engineering Technicians. **PERSONALITY TYPE:** Realistic.

EDUCATION/TRAINING PROGRAM(S)—Cartography; Surveying Technology/Surveying. **RELATED KNOWLEDGE/COURSES—Building and Construction:** Knowledge of the materials, methods, and tools involved in the construction or repair of houses, buildings, or other structures such as highways and roads. **Design:** Knowledge of design techniques, tools, and principles involved in production of precision technical plans, blueprints, drawings, and models. **Geography:** Knowledge of principles and methods for describing the features of land, sea, and air masses, including their physical characteristics; locations; interrelationships; and distribution of plant, animal, and human life. **Engineering and Technology:** Knowledge of the practical application of engineering science and technology. This includes applying principles, techniques, procedures, and equipment to the design and production of various goods and services. **Mathematics:** Knowledge of arithmetic, algebra, geometry, calculus, and statistics and their applications. **Computers and Electronics:** Knowledge of circuit boards, processors, chips, electronic equipment, and computer hardware and software, including applications and programming.

Talent Directors

- Education/Training Required: Long-term on-the-job training
- Annual Earnings: $52,840
- Growth: 18.3%
- Annual Job Openings: 10,000
- Self-Employed: 32.8%
- Part-Time: 9.1%

Audition and interview performers to select most appropriate talent for parts in stage, television, radio, or motion picture productions. Arrange for and/or design screen tests or auditions for prospective performers. Attend or view productions in order to maintain knowledge of available actors. Audition and interview performers in order to match their attributes to specific roles or to increase the pool of available acting talent. Contact agents and actors in order to provide notification of audition and performance opportunities and to set up audition times. Locate performers or extras for crowd and background scenes and stand-ins or photo doubles for actors by direct contact or through agents. Maintain talent files that include information such as performers' specialties, past performances, and availability. Negotiate contract agreements with performers, with agents, or between performers and agents or production companies. Prepare actors for auditions by providing scripts and information about roles and casting requirements. Read scripts and confer with producers in order to determine the types and numbers of performers required for a given production. Review performer information such as photos, resumes, voice tapes, videos, and union membership in order to decide whom to audition for parts. Select performers for roles or submit lists of suitable performers to producers or directors for final selection. Hire and supervise workers who help locate people with specified attributes and talents. Serve as liaisons between directors, actors, and agents. **SKILLS—Negotiation:** Bringing others together and trying to reconcile differences. **Management of Personnel Resources:** Motivating, developing, and directing people as they work, identifying the best people for the job. **Speaking:** Talking to others to convey information effectively. **Social Perceptiveness:** Being aware of others' reactions and understanding why they react as they do. **Persuasion:** Persuading others to change their minds or behavior. **Active Listening:** Giving full attention to what other people are saying, taking time to understand the points being made, asking questions as appropriate, and not interrupting at inappropriate times. **Writing:** Communicating effectively in writing as appropriate for the needs of the audience. **Reading Comprehension:** Understanding written sentences and paragraphs in work-related documents. **GOE—Interest Area:** 03. Arts and Communication. **Work Group:** 03.07. Music. **Other Jobs in This Work Group:** Composers; Music Arrangers and Orchestrators; Music Directors; Musicians, Instrumental; Singers. **PERSONALITY TYPE:** Artistic.

EDUCATION/TRAINING PROGRAM(S)—Cinematography and Film/Video Production; Directing and Theatrical Production; Drama and Dramatics/Theatre Arts, General; Dramatic/Theatre Arts and Stagecraft, Other; Film/Cinema Studies; Radio and Television; Theatre/Theatre Arts Management. **RELATED KNOWLEDGE/COURSES—Fine Arts:** Knowledge of the theory and techniques required to compose, produce, and perform works of music, dance, the visual arts, drama, and sculpture. **Sales and Marketing:** Knowledge of principles and methods for showing, promoting, and selling products or services. This includes marketing strategy and tactics, product demonstrations, sales techniques, and sales control systems. **Administration and Management:** Knowledge of business and management principles involved in strategic planning, resource allocation, human resources modeling, leadership technique, production methods, and coordination of people and resources. **Personnel and Human Resources:** Knowledge of principles and procedures for personnel recruitment, selection, training, compensation and benefits, labor relations and negotiation, and personnel information systems. **Communications and Media:** Knowledge of media production, communication, and dissemination techniques and methods. This includes alternative ways to inform and entertain via written, oral, and visual media. **Economics and Accounting:** Knowledge of economic and accounting principles and practices, the financial markets, banking, and the analysis and reporting of financial data.

Tapers

- Education/Training Required: Moderate-term on-the-job training
- Annual Earnings: $39,070
- Growth: 20.8%
- Annual Job Openings: 5,000
- Self-Employed: 19.1%
- Part-Time: 5.9%

Seal joints between plasterboard or other wallboard to prepare wall surface for painting or papering. Apply texturizing compounds and primers to walls and ceilings before final finishing, using trowels, brushes, rollers, or spray guns. Check adhesives to ensure that they will work and will remain durable. Countersink nails or screws below surfaces of walls before applying sealing compounds, using hammers or screwdrivers. Install metal molding at wall corners to secure wallboard. Mix sealing compounds by hand or with portable electric mixers. Press paper tape over joints to embed tape into sealing compound and to seal joints. Remove extra compound after surfaces have been covered sufficiently. Sand rough spots of dried cement between applications of compounds. Seal joints between plasterboard or other wallboard in order to prepare wall surfaces for painting or papering. Select the correct sealing compound or tape. Spread and smooth cementing material over tape, using trowels or floating machines to blend joints with wall surfaces. Spread sealing compound between boards or panels and over cracks, holes, and nail and screw heads, using trowels, broadknives, or spatulas. Use mechanical applicators that spread compounds and embed tape in one operation. Apply additional coats to fill in holes and make surfaces smooth. Sand or patch nicks or cracks in plasterboard or wallboard. **SKILLS**—None met the criteria. **GOE—Interest Area:** 02. Architecture and Construction. **Work Group:** 02.04. Construction Crafts. **Other Jobs in This Work Group:** Boat Builders and Shipwrights; Boilermakers; Brattice Builders; Brickmasons and Blockmasons; Carpet Installers; Ceiling Tile Installers; Cement Masons and Concrete Finishers; Commercial Divers; Construction Carpenters; Crane and Tower Operators; Dragline Operators; Drywall Installers; Electricians; Fence Erectors; Floor Layers, Except Carpet, Wood, and Hard Tiles; Floor Sanders and Finishers; Glaziers; Grader, Bulldozer, and Scraper Operators; Hazardous Materials Removal Workers; Insulation Workers, Floor, Ceiling, and Wall; Insulation Workers, Mechanical; Manufactured Building and Mobile Home Installers; Operating Engineers; Painters, Construction and Maintenance; Paperhangers; Paving, Surfacing, and Tamping Equipment Operators; Pile-Driver Operators; Pipe Fitters; Pipelayers; Pipelaying Fitters; Plasterers and Stucco Masons; Plumbers; Rail-Track Laying and Maintenance Equipment Operators; Refractory Materials Repairers, Except Brickmasons; Reinforcing Iron and Rebar Workers; Riggers; Roofers; Rough Carpenters; Security and Fire Alarm Systems Installers; Segmental Pavers; Sheet Metal Workers; Ship Carpenters and Joiners; Stone Cutters and Carvers; Stonemasons; Structural Iron and Steel Workers; Terrazzo Workers and Finishers; Tile and Marble Setters. **PERSONALITY TYPE:** Realistic.

EDUCATION/TRAINING PROGRAM(S)—Construction Trades, Other. **RELATED KNOWLEDGE/COURSES—Building and Construction:** Knowledge of the materials, methods, and tools involved in the construction or repair of houses, buildings, or other structures such as highways and roads. **Sales and Marketing:** Knowledge of principles and methods for showing, promoting, and selling products or services. This includes marketing strategy and tactics, product demonstrations, sales techniques, and sales control systems.

Tax Examiners, Collectors, and Revenue Agents

- Education/Training Required: Bachelor's degree
- Annual Earnings: $43,490
- Growth: 5.0%
- Annual Job Openings: 9,000
- Self-Employed: 0%
- Part-Time: 5.4%

Determine tax liability or collect taxes from individuals or business firms according to prescribed laws and regulations. Collect taxes from individuals or businesses according to prescribed laws and regulations. Maintain knowledge of tax code changes and of accounting procedures and theory in order to properly evaluate financial information. Maintain records for each case, including contacts, telephone numbers, and actions taken. Confer with taxpayers or their representatives in order to discuss the issues, laws, and regulations involved in returns and to resolve problems with returns. Contact taxpayers by mail or telephone in order to address discrepancies and to request supporting documentation. Send notices to taxpayers when accounts are delinquent. Notify taxpayers of any overpayment or underpayment and either issue a refund or request further payment. Conduct independent field audits and investigations of income tax returns in order to verify information and/or to amend tax liabilities. Review filed tax returns in order to determine whether claimed tax credits and deductions are allowed by law. Review selected tax returns in order to determine the nature and extent of audits to be performed on them. Enter tax return information into computers for processing. Examine accounting systems and records in order to determine whether accounting methods used were appropriate and in compliance with statutory provisions. Process individual and corporate income tax returns and sales and excise tax returns. Impose payment deadlines on delinquent taxpayers and monitor payments in order to ensure that deadlines are met. Check tax forms in order to verify that names and taxpayer identification numbers are correct, that computations have been performed correctly, and that amounts match those on supporting documentation. Examine and analyze tax assets and liabilities in order to determine resolution of delinquent tax problems. Recommend criminal prosecutions and/or civil penalties. Determine appropriate methods of debt settlement, such as offers of compromise, wage garnishment, or seizure and sale of property. Secure a taxpayer's agreement to discharge a tax assessment or submit contested determinations to other administrative or judicial conferees for appeals hearings. **SKILLS—Service Orientation:** Actively looking for ways to help people. **Active Learning:** Understanding the implications of new information for both current and future problem-solving and decision-making. **Instructing:** Teaching others how to do something. **Speaking:** Talking to others to convey information effectively. **Mathematics:** Using mathematics to solve problems. **Complex Problem Solving:** Identifying complex problems and reviewing related information to develop and evaluate options and implement solutions. **Active Listening:** Giving full attention to what other people are saying, taking time to understand the points being made, asking questions as appropriate, and not interrupting at inappropriate times. **Learning Strategies:** Selecting and using training/instructional methods and procedures appropriate for the situation when learning or teaching new things. **GOE—Interest Area:** 07. Government and Public Administration. **Work Group:** 07.03. Regulations Enforcement. **Other Jobs in This Work Group:** Agricultural Inspectors; Aviation Inspectors; Child Support, Missing Persons, and Unemployment Insurance Fraud Investigators; Environmental Compliance Inspectors; Equal Opportunity Representatives and Officers; Financial Examiners; Fire Inspectors; Fish and Game Wardens; Forest Fire Inspectors and Prevention Specialists; Government Property Inspectors and Investigators; Immigration and Customs Inspectors; Licensing Examiners and Inspectors; Marine Cargo Inspectors; Mechanical Inspectors; Motor Vehicle Inspectors; Nuclear Monitoring Technicians; Occupational Health and Safety Specialists; Pressure Vessel Inspectors; Railroad Inspectors. **PERSONALITY TYPE:** Conventional.

EDUCATION/TRAINING PROGRAM(S)— Accounting; Taxation. **RELATED KNOWLEDGE/COURSES—Customer and Personal Service:** Knowledge of principles and processes for providing customer and personal services. This includes customer needs assessment, meeting quality standards for services, and evaluation of customer satisfaction. **Law and Government:** Knowledge of laws, legal codes, court procedures, precedents, government regulations, executive orders, agency rules, and the democratic political process. **Computers and Electronics:** Knowledge of circuit boards, processors, chips, electronic equipment, and computer hardware and software, including applications and programming. **Economics and Accounting:** Knowledge of economic and accounting principles and practices, the financial markets, banking, and the analysis and reporting of financial data. **Clerical Practices:** Knowledge of administrative and clerical procedures and systems such as word processing, managing files and records, stenography and transcription, designing forms, and other office procedures and terminology. **Psychology:** Knowledge of human behavior and performance; individual differences in ability, personality, and interests; learning and motivation; psychological research methods; and the assessment and treatment of behavioral and affective disorders.

Tax Preparers

- ◎ Education/Training Required: Moderate-term on-the-job training
- ◎ Annual Earnings: $27,730
- ◎ Growth: 23.2%
- ◎ Annual Job Openings: 11,000
- ◎ Self-Employed: 26.2%
- ◎ Part-Time: 20.3%

Prepare tax returns for individuals or small businesses, but do not have the background or responsibilities of an accredited or certified public accountant. Check data input or verify totals on forms prepared by others to detect errors in arithmetic, data entry, or procedures. Compute taxes owed or overpaid, using adding machines or personal computers, and complete entries on forms, following tax form instructions and tax tables. Interview clients to obtain additional information on taxable income and deductible expenses and allowances. Prepare or assist in preparing simple to complex tax returns for individuals or small businesses. Review financial records such as income statements and documentation of expenditures in order to determine forms needed to prepare tax returns. Use all appropriate adjustments, deductions, and credits to keep clients' taxes to a minimum. Calculate form preparation fees according to return complexity and processing time required. Consult tax law handbooks or bulletins in order to determine procedures for preparation of atypical returns. Furnish taxpayers with sufficient information and advice in order to ensure correct tax form completion. **SKILLS—Mathematics:** Using mathematics to solve problems. **Reading Comprehension:** Understanding written sentences and paragraphs in work-related documents. **Active Listening:** Giving full attention to what other people are saying, taking time to understand the points being made, asking questions as appropriate, and not interrupting at inappropriate times. **Speaking:** Talking to others to convey information effectively. **Active Learning:** Understanding the implications of new information for both current and future problem-solving and decision-making. **Judgment and Decision Making:** Considering the relative costs and benefits of potential actions to choose the most appropriate one. **Monitoring:** Monitoring or assessing your performance or that of other individuals or organizations to make improvements or take corrective action. **GOE—Interest Area:**

04. Business and Administration. **Work Group:** 04.06. Mathematical Clerical Support. **Other Jobs in This Work Group:** Billing, Cost, and Rate Clerks; Bookkeeping, Accounting, and Auditing Clerks; Brokerage Clerks; Payroll and Timekeeping Clerks; Statement Clerks. **PERSONALITY TYPE:** Conventional.

EDUCATION/TRAINING PROGRAM(S)— Accounting Technology/Technician and Bookkeeping; Taxation. **RELATED KNOWLEDGE/COURSES— Economics and Accounting:** Knowledge of economic and accounting principles and practices, the financial markets, banking, and the analysis and reporting of financial data. **Law and Government:** Knowledge of laws, legal codes, court procedures, precedents, government regulations, executive orders, agency rules, and the democratic political process. **Clerical Practices:** Knowledge of administrative and clerical procedures and systems such as word processing, managing files and records, stenography and transcription, designing forms, and other office procedures and terminology. **Mathematics:** Knowledge of arithmetic, algebra, geometry, calculus, and statistics and their applications.

Taxi Drivers and Chauffeurs

- ◎ Education/Training Required: Short-term on-the-job training
- ◎ Annual Earnings: $19,570
- ◎ Growth: 21.7%
- ◎ Annual Job Openings: 28,000
- ◎ Self-Employed: 4.8%
- ◎ Part-Time: 17.3%

Drive automobiles, vans, or limousines to transport passengers. May occasionally carry cargo. Test vehicle equipment such as lights, brakes, horns, and windshield wipers in order to ensure proper operation. Notify dispatchers or company mechanics of vehicle problems. Drive taxicabs, limousines, company cars, or privately owned vehicles in order to transport passengers. Follow regulations governing taxi operation and ensure that passengers follow safety regulations. Pick up passengers at prearranged locations, at taxi stands, or by cruising streets in high-traffic areas. Perform routine vehicle maintenance, such as regulating tire pressure and adding gasoline, oil, and water. Communicate with dispatchers by radio, telephone, or computer in order to exchange information and receive requests for passenger service. Record name, date, and taxi identification information on trip sheets, along with trip information such as time and place of pickup and drop-off and total fee. Complete accident reports when necessary. Provide passengers with assistance entering and exiting vehicles and help them with any luggage. Arrange to pick up particular customers or groups on a regular schedule. Vacuum and clean interiors and wash and polish exteriors of automobiles. Pick up or meet employers according to requests, appointments, or schedules. Operate vans with special equipment such as wheelchair lifts to transport people with special needs. Collect fares or vouchers from passengers and make change and/or issue receipts, as necessary. Determine fares based on trip distances and times, using taximeters and fee schedules, and announce fares to passengers. Perform minor vehicle repairs such as cleaning spark plugs or take vehicles to mechanics for servicing. Turn the taximeter on when passengers enter the cab and turn it off when they reach the final destination. Report to taxicab services or garages in order to receive vehicle assignments. Perform errands for customers or employers, such as delivering or picking up mail and packages. Provide passengers with information about the local area and points of interest and/or give advice on hotels and restaurants. **SKILLS—Service Orientation:** Actively looking for ways to help people. **Operation and Control:** Controlling operations of equipment or systems. **Installation:** Installing equipment, machines, wiring, or programs to meet specifications. **Equipment Maintenance:** Performing routine maintenance on equipment and determining when and what kind of maintenance is needed. **Social Perceptiveness:** Being aware of others' reactions and understanding why they react as they do. **Learning Strategies:** Selecting and using training/instructional methods and procedures appropriate for the situation when learning or teaching new things. **Negotiation:** Bringing others together and trying to reconcile differences. **Coordination:** Adjusting actions in relation to others' actions. **Instructing:** Teaching others how to do something. **GOE—Interest Area:** 16. Transportation, Distribution, and Logistics. **Work Group:** 16.06. Other Services Requiring Driving. **Other Jobs in This Work Group:** Ambulance Drivers and Attendants, Except Emergency Medical Technicians; Bus Drivers, School; Bus Drivers, Transit and Intercity; Couriers and Messengers; Driver/Sales

Workers; Parking Lot Attendants; Postal Service Mail Carriers. **PERSONALITY TYPE:** Realistic.

EDUCATION/TRAINING PROGRAM(S)— Truck and Bus Driver/Commercial Vehicle Operation. **RELATED KNOWLEDGE/COURSES—Transportation:** Knowledge of principles and methods for moving people or goods by air, rail, sea, or road, including the relative costs and benefits. **Economics and Accounting:** Knowledge of economic and accounting principles and practices, the financial markets, banking, and the analysis and reporting of financial data. **English Language:** Knowledge of the structure and content of the English language, including the meaning and spelling of words, rules of composition, and grammar. **Clerical Practices:** Knowledge of administrative and clerical procedures and systems such as word processing, managing files and records, stenography and transcription, designing forms, and other office procedures and terminology.

Teacher Assistants

- ◎ Education/Training Required: Short-term on-the-job training
- ◎ Annual Earnings: $19,410
- ◎ Growth: 23.0%
- ◎ Annual Job Openings: 259,000
- ◎ Self-Employed: 0.3%
- ◎ Part-Time: 41.1%

Perform duties that are instructional in nature or deliver direct services to students or parents. Serve in a position for which a teacher or another professional has ultimate responsibility for the design and implementation of educational programs and services. Discuss assigned duties with classroom teachers in order to coordinate instructional efforts. Prepare lesson materials, bulletin board displays, exhibits, equipment, and demonstrations. Present subject matter to students under the direction and guidance of teachers, using lectures, discussions, or supervised role-playing methods. Tutor and assist children individually or in small groups in order to help them master assignments and to reinforce learning concepts presented by teachers. Supervise students in classrooms, halls, cafeterias, school yards, and gymnasiums or on field trips. Conduct demonstrations to teach such skills as sports, dancing, and handicrafts. Distribute teaching materials such as textbooks, workbooks, papers, and pencils to students. Distribute tests and homework assignments and collect them when they are completed. Enforce administration policies and rules governing students. Grade homework and tests and compute and record results, using answer sheets or electronic marking devices. Instruct and monitor students in the use and care of equipment and materials in order to prevent injuries and damage. Observe students' performance and record relevant data to assess progress. Organize and label materials and display students' work in a manner appropriate for their eye levels and perceptual skills. Organize and supervise games and other recreational activities to promote physical, mental, and social development. Participate in teacher-parent conferences regarding students' progress or problems. Plan, prepare, and develop various teaching aids such as bibliographies, charts, and graphs. Prepare lesson outlines and plans in assigned subject areas and submit outlines to teachers for review. Provide extra assistance to students with special needs, such as non-English-speaking students or those with physical and mental disabilities. Take class attendance and maintain attendance records. Assist in bus loading and unloading. Assist librarians in school libraries. Attend staff meetings and serve on committees as required. Carry out therapeutic regimens such as behavior modification and personal development programs under the supervision of special education instructors, psychologists, or speech-language pathologists. **SKILLS— Learning Strategies:** Selecting and using training/instructional methods and procedures appropriate for the situation when learning or teaching new things. **Instructing:** Teaching others how to do something. **Service Orientation:** Actively looking for ways to help people. **Speaking:** Talking to others to convey information effectively. **Active Listening:** Giving full attention to what other people are saying, taking time to understand the points being made, asking questions as appropriate, and not interrupting at inappropriate times. **Social Perceptiveness:** Being aware of others' reactions and understanding why they react as they do. **Reading Comprehension:** Understanding written sentences and paragraphs in work-related documents. **Writing:** Communicating effectively in writing as appropriate for the needs of the audience. **GOE— Interest Area:** 05. Education and Training. **Work Group:** 05.02. Preschool, Elementary, and Secondary Teaching and Instructing. **Other Jobs in This Work Group:** Elementary School Teachers, Except Special Education; Kindergarten Teachers, Except Special

Education; Middle School Teachers, Except Special and Vocational Education; Preschool Teachers, Except Special Education; Secondary School Teachers, Except Special and Vocational Education; Special Education Teachers, Middle School; Special Education Teachers, Preschool, Kindergarten, and Elementary School; Special Education Teachers, Secondary School; Vocational Education Teachers, Middle School; Vocational Education Teachers, Secondary School. **PERSONALITY TYPE:** Social.

EDUCATION/TRAINING PROGRAM(S)— Teacher Assistant/Aide; Teaching Assistants/Aides, Other. **RELATED KNOWLEDGE/COURSES— Education and Training:** Knowledge of principles and methods for curriculum and training design, teaching and instruction for individuals and groups, and the measurement of training effects. **English Language:** Knowledge of the structure and content of the English language, including the meaning and spelling of words, rules of composition, and grammar. **History and Archeology:** Knowledge of historical events and their causes, indicators, and effects on civilizations and cultures. **Psychology:** Knowledge of human behavior and performance; individual differences in ability, personality, and interests; learning and motivation; psychological research methods; and the assessment and treatment of behavioral and affective disorders. **Sociology and Anthropology:** Knowledge of group behavior and dynamics, societal trends and influences, human migrations, ethnicity, and cultures and their history and origins. **Clerical Practices:** Knowledge of administrative and clerical procedures and systems such as word processing, managing files and records, stenography and transcription, designing forms, and other office procedures and terminology.

Technical Directors/Managers

- Education/Training Required: Long-term on-the-job training
- Annual Earnings: $52,840
- Growth: 18.3%
- Annual Job Openings: 10,000
- Self-Employed: 32.8%
- Part-Time: 9.1%

Coordinate activities of technical departments, such as taping, editing, engineering, and maintenance, to produce radio or television programs. Direct technical aspects of newscasts and other productions, checking and switching between video sources and taking responsibility for the on-air product, including camera shots and graphics. Test equipment in order to ensure proper operation. Monitor broadcasts in order to ensure that programs conform to station or network policies and regulations. Observe pictures through monitors and direct camera and video staff concerning shading and composition. Act as liaisons between engineering and production departments. Supervise and assign duties to workers engaged in technical control and production of radio and television programs. Schedule use of studio and editing facilities for producers and engineering and maintenance staff. Confer with operations directors in order to formulate and maintain fair and attainable technical policies for programs. Operate equipment to produce programs or broadcast live programs from remote locations. Train workers in use of equipment such as switchers, cameras, monitors, microphones, and lights. Switch between video sources in a studio or on multi-camera remotes, using equipment such as switchers, video slide projectors, and video effects generators. Set up and execute video transitions and special effects such as fades, dissolves, cuts, keys, and supers, using computers to manipulate pictures as necessary. Collaborate with promotions directors to produce on-air station promotions. Discuss filter options, lens choices, and the visual effects of objects being filmed with photography directors and video operators. Follow instructions from production managers and directors during productions, such as commands for camera cuts, effects, graphics, and takes. **SKILLS—Operation Monitoring:** Watching gauges, dials, or other indicators to make sure a machine is working properly. **Time Management:** Managing one's own time and the time of others. **Operation and Control:** Controlling operations of equipment or systems. **Monitoring:** Monitoring or assessing your performance or that of other individuals or organizations to make improvements or take corrective action. **Coordination:** Adjusting actions in relation to others' actions. **Management of Personnel Resources:** Motivating, developing, and directing people as they work, identifying the best people for the job. **Troubleshooting:** Determining causes of operating errors and deciding what to do about them. **Instructing:** Teaching others how to do some-

thing. **Systems Analysis:** Determining how a system should work and how changes in conditions, operations, and the environment will affect outcomes. **GOE—Interest Area:** 03. Arts and Communication. **Work Group:** 03.01. Managerial Work in Arts and Communication. **Other Jobs in This Work Group:** Agents and Business Managers of Artists, Performers, and Athletes; Art Directors; Producers; Program Directors; Public Relations Managers. **PERSONALITY TYPE:** Realistic.

EDUCATION/TRAINING PROGRAM(S)—Cinematography and Film/Video Production; Directing and Theatrical Production; Drama and Dramatics/Theatre Arts, General; Dramatic/Theatre Arts and Stagecraft, Other; Film/Cinema Studies; Radio and Television; Theatre/Theatre Arts Management. **RELATED KNOWLEDGE/COURSES**—**Communications and Media:** Knowledge of media production, communication, and dissemination techniques and methods. This includes alternative ways to inform and entertain via written, oral, and visual media. **Telecommunications:** Knowledge of transmission, broadcasting, switching, control, and operation of telecommunications systems. **Computers and Electronics:** Knowledge of circuit boards, processors, chips, electronic equipment, and computer hardware and software, including applications and programming. **Engineering and Technology:** Knowledge of the practical application of engineering science and technology. This includes applying principles, techniques, procedures, and equipment to the design and production of various goods and services. **Philosophy and Theology:** Knowledge of different philosophical systems and religions. This includes their basic principles, values, ethics, ways of thinking, customs, and practices and their impact on human culture. **Sales and Marketing:** Knowledge of principles and methods for showing, promoting, and selling products or services. This includes marketing strategy and tactics, product demonstrations, sales techniques, and sales control systems.

Technical Writers

- Education/Training Required: Bachelor's degree
- Annual Earnings: $53,490
- Growth: 27.1%
- Annual Job Openings: 6,000
- Self-Employed: 7.3%
- Part-Time: 5.5%

Write technical materials, such as equipment manuals, appendices, or operating and maintenance instructions. May assist in layout work. Organize material and complete writing assignment according to set standards regarding order, clarity, conciseness, style, and terminology. Maintain records and files of work and revisions. Edit, standardize, or make changes to material prepared by other writers or establishment personnel. Confer with customer representatives, vendors, plant executives, or publisher to establish technical specifications and to determine subject material to be developed for publication. Review published materials and recommend revisions or changes in scope, format, content, and methods of reproduction and binding. Select photographs, drawings, sketches, diagrams, and charts to illustrate material. Study drawings, specifications, mockups, and product samples to integrate and delineate technology, operating procedure, and production sequence and detail. Interview production and engineering personnel and read journals and other material to become familiar with product technologies and production methods. Observe production, developmental, and experimental activities to determine operating procedure and detail. Arrange for typing, duplication, and distribution of material. Assist in laying out material for publication. Analyze developments in specific field to determine need for revisions in previously published materials and development of new material. Review manufacturer's and trade catalogs, drawings, and other data relative to operation, maintenance, and service of equipment. Draw sketches to illustrate specified materials or assembly sequence. **SKILLS—Writing:** Communicating effectively in writing as appropriate for the needs of the audience. **Coordination:** Adjusting actions in relation to others' actions. **Active Listening:** Giving full attention to what other people are saying, taking time to understand the points being made, asking questions as appropriate, and not interrupting at inappropriate times. **Active Learning:** Understanding the implications of new information for both current and future problem-solving and decision-making. **Technology Design:** Generating or adapting equipment and technology to serve user needs. **Reading Comprehension:** Understanding written sentences and paragraphs in work-related documents. **Learning Strategies:** Selecting and using training/instructional methods and procedures appropriate for the situation when learning or teaching new things. **Service Orientation:** Actively looking for ways to help people. **GOE—Interest Area:** 03. Arts and Communication. **Work Group:** 03.02. Writing and Editing. **Other Jobs in This Work Group:** Copy Writers; Creative Writers; Editors; Poets and Lyricists. **PERSONALITY TYPE:** Artistic.

EDUCATION/TRAINING PROGRAM(S)—Business/Corporate Communications; Family and Consumer Sciences/Human Sciences Communication; Technical and Business Writing. **RELATED KNOWLEDGE/COURSES—Clerical Practices:** Knowledge of administrative and clerical procedures and systems such as word processing, managing files and records, stenography and transcription, designing forms, and other office procedures and terminology. **English Language:** Knowledge of the structure and content of the English language, including the meaning and spelling of words, rules of composition, and grammar. **Communications and Media:** Knowledge of media production, communication, and dissemination techniques and methods. This includes alternative ways to inform and entertain via written, oral, and visual media. **Computers and Electronics:** Knowledge of circuit boards, processors, chips, electronic equipment, and computer hardware and software, including applications and programming. **Education and Training:** Knowledge of principles and methods for curriculum and training design, teaching and instruction for individuals and groups, and the measurement of training effects. **Engineering and Technology:** Knowledge of the practical application of engineering science and technology. This includes applying principles, techniques, procedures, and equipment to the design and production of various goods and services.

Telecommunications Facility Examiners

- Education/Training Required: Long-term on-the-job training
- Annual Earnings: $49,840
- Growth: −0.6%
- Annual Job Openings: 23,000
- Self-Employed: 4.6%
- Part-Time: 1.7%

Examine telephone transmission facilities to determine equipment requirements for providing subscribers with new or additional telephone services. Examines telephone transmission facilities to determine requirements for new or additional telephone services. Visits subscribers' premises to arrange for new installations, such as telephone booths and telephone poles. Designates cables available for use. Climbs telephone poles or stands on truck-mounted boom to examine terminal boxes for available connections. **SKILLS—Technology Design:** Generating or adapting equipment and technology to serve user needs. **Installation:** Installing equipment, machines, wiring, or programs to meet specifications. **GOE—Interest Area:** 02. Architecture and Construction. **Work Group:** 02.05. Systems and Equipment Installation, Maintenance, and Repair. **Other Jobs in This Work Group:** Central Office and PBX Installers and Repairers; Communication Equipment Mechanics, Installers, and Repairers; Electric Meter Installers and Repairers; Electrical and Electronics Repairers, Powerhouse, Substation, and Relay; Electrical Power-Line Installers and Repairers; Elevator Installers and Repairers; Frame Wirers, Central Office; Heating and Air Conditioning Mechanics; Home Appliance Installers; Maintenance and Repair Workers, General; Meter Mechanics; Refrigeration Mechanics; Station Installers and Repairers, Telephone; Telecommunications Line Installers and Repairers. **PERSONALITY TYPE:** Realistic.

EDUCATION/TRAINING PROGRAM(S)— Communications Systems Installation and Repair Technology. **RELATED KNOWLEDGE/COURSES—Telecommunications:** Knowledge of transmission, broadcasting, switching, control, and operation of telecommunications systems. **Computers and Electronics:** Knowledge of circuit boards, processors, chips, electronic equipment, and computer hardware and software, including applications and programming. **Engineering and Technology:** Knowledge of the practical application of engineering science and technology. This includes applying principles, techniques, procedures, and equipment to the design and production of various goods and services. **Geography:** Knowledge of principles and methods for describing the features of land, sea, and air masses, including their physical characteristics; locations; interrelationships; and distribution of plant, animal, and human life.

Telecommunications Line Installers and Repairers

- Education/Training Required: Long-term on-the-job training
- Annual Earnings: $40,330
- Growth: 18.8%
- Annual Job Openings: 13,000
- Self-Employed: 3.7%
- Part-Time: 1.4%

String and repair telephone and television cable, including fiber optics and other equipment for transmitting messages or television programming. Access specific areas to string lines and install terminal boxes, auxiliary equipment, and appliances, using bucket trucks or by climbing poles and ladders or entering tunnels, trenches, or crawl spaces. Inspect and test lines and cables, recording and analyzing test results to assess transmission characteristics and locate faults and malfunctions. Install equipment such as amplifiers and repeaters in order to maintain the strength of communications transmissions. Lay underground cable directly in trenches or string it through conduits running through trenches. Measure signal strength at utility poles, using electronic test equipment. Place insulation over conductors and seal splices with moisture-proof covering. Pull up cable by hand from large reels mounted on trucks; then pull lines through ducts by hand or with winches. Set up service for customers, installing, connecting, testing, and adjusting equipment. Splice cables, using hand tools, epoxy, or mechanical equipment. String cables between structures and lines from poles, towers, or trenches and pull lines to proper tension. Travel to customers' premises to install, maintain, and repair audio and visual electronic reception equipment and accessories. Use a variety of construction equipment to complete installations, including digger derricks, trenchers, and cable plows. Clean and maintain tools and test equipment. Compute impedance of wires from poles to houses in order to determine additional resistance needed for reducing signals to desired levels. Dig holes for power poles, using power augers or shovels; set poles in place with cranes; and hoist poles upright, using winches. Dig trenches for underground wires and cables. Explain cable service to subscribers after installation and collect any installation fees that are due. Fill and tamp holes, using cement, earth, and tamping devices. Participate in the construction and removal of telecommunication towers and associated support structures. **SKILLS—Installation:** Installing equipment, machines, wiring, or programs to meet specifications. **Repairing:** Repairing machines or systems by using the needed tools. **Troubleshooting:** Determining causes of operating errors and deciding what to do about them. **Equipment Maintenance:** Performing routine maintenance on equipment and determining when and what kind of maintenance is needed. **Operation Monitoring:** Watching gauges, dials, or other indicators to make sure a machine is working properly. **Systems Evaluation:** Identifying measures or indicators of system performance and the actions needed to improve or correct performance relative to the goals of the system. **Operation and Control:** Controlling operations of equipment or systems. **Mathematics:** Using mathematics to solve problems. **GOE—Interest Area:** 02. Architecture and Construction. **Work Group:** 02.05. Systems and Equipment Installation, Maintenance, and Repair. **Other Jobs in This Work Group:** Central Office and PBX Installers and Repairers; Communication Equipment Mechanics, Installers, and Repairers; Electric Meter Installers and Repairers; Electrical and Electronics Repairers, Powerhouse, Substation, and Relay; Electrical Power-Line Installers and Repairers; Elevator Installers and Repairers; Frame Wirers, Central Office; Heating and Air Conditioning Mechanics; Home Appliance Installers; Maintenance and Repair Workers, General; Meter Mechanics; Refrigeration Mechanics; Station Installers and Repairers, Telephone; Telecommunications Facility Examiners. **PERSONALITY TYPE:** Realistic.

EDUCATION/TRAINING PROGRAM(S)— Communications Systems Installation and Repair Technology. **RELATED KNOWLEDGE/COURSES—Telecommunications:** Knowledge of transmis-

sion, broadcasting, switching, control, and operation of telecommunications systems. **Computers and Electronics:** Knowledge of circuit boards, processors, chips, electronic equipment, and computer hardware and software, including applications and programming. **Mechanical Devices:** Knowledge of machines and tools, including their designs, uses, repair, and maintenance. **Physics:** Knowledge and prediction of physical principles and laws and their interrelationships and applications to understanding fluid, material, and atmospheric dynamics and mechanical, electrical, atomic, and subatomic structures and processes. **Sales and Marketing:** Knowledge of principles and methods for showing, promoting, and selling products or services. This includes marketing strategy and tactics, product demonstrations, sales techniques, and sales control systems. **Engineering and Technology:** Knowledge of the practical application of engineering science and technology. This includes applying principles, techniques, procedures, and equipment to the design and production of various goods and services.

Tellers

- ◎ Education/Training Required: Short-term on-the-job training
- ◎ Annual Earnings: $21,120
- ◎ Growth: 9.4%
- ◎ Annual Job Openings: 127,000
- ◎ Self-Employed: 0.2%
- ◎ Part-Time: 30.9%

Receive and pay out money. Keep records of money and negotiable instruments involved in a financial institution's various transactions. Balance currency, coin, and checks in cash drawers at ends of shifts and calculate daily transactions, using computers, calculators, or adding machines. Cash checks and pay out money after verifying that signatures are correct, that written and numerical amounts agree, and that accounts have sufficient funds. Receive checks and cash for deposit, verify amounts, and check accuracy of deposit slips. Examine checks for endorsements and to verify other information such as dates, bank names, identification of the persons receiving payments, and the legality of the documents. Enter customers' transactions into computers in order to record transactions and issue computer-generated receipts. Count currency, coins, and checks received, by hand or using currency-counting machine, in order to prepare them for deposit or shipment to branch banks or the Federal Reserve Bank. Identify transaction mistakes when debits and credits do not balance. Prepare and verify cashier's checks. Arrange monies received in cash boxes and coin dispensers according to denomination. Process transactions such as term deposits, retirement savings plan contributions, automated teller transactions, night deposits, and mail deposits. Receive mortgage, loan, or public utility bill payments, verifying payment dates and amounts due. Resolve problems or discrepancies concerning customers' accounts. Explain, promote, or sell products or services such as travelers' checks, savings bonds, money orders, and cashier's checks, using computerized information about customers to tailor recommendations. Perform clerical tasks such as typing, filing, and microfilm photography. Monitor bank vaults to ensure cash balances are correct. Order a supply of cash to meet daily needs. Sort and file deposit slips and checks. Receive and count daily inventories of cash, drafts, and travelers' checks. Process and maintain records of customer loans. Count, verify, and post armored-car deposits. Carry out special services for customers, such as ordering bank cards and checks. Compute financial fees, interest, and service charges. Obtain and process information required for the provision of services, such as opening accounts, savings plans, and purchasing bonds. **SKILLS—Service Orientation:** Actively looking for ways to help people. **Active Learning:** Understanding the implications of new information for both current and future problem-solving and decision-making. **Active Listening:** Giving full attention to what other people are saying, taking time to understand the points being made, asking questions as appropriate, and not interrupting at inappropriate times. **Social Perceptiveness:** Being aware of others' reactions and understanding why they react as they do. **Mathematics:** Using mathematics to solve problems. **Instructing:** Teaching others how to do something. **Time Management:** Managing one's own time and the time of others. **Learning Strategies:** Selecting and using training/instructional methods and procedures appropriate for the situation when learning or teaching new things. **GOE—Interest Area:** 06. Finance and Insurance. **Work Group:** 06.04. Finance/Insurance Customer Service. **Other Jobs in This Work Group:** Bill and Account Collectors; Loan Interviewers and Clerks; New Accounts Clerks. **PERSONALITY TYPE:** Conventional.

EDUCATION/TRAINING PROGRAM(S)— Banking and Financial Support Services. **RELATED KNOWLEDGE/COURSES—Customer and Personal Service:** Knowledge of principles and processes for providing customer and personal services. This includes customer needs assessment, meeting quality standards for services, and evaluation of customer satisfaction. **Sales and Marketing:** Knowledge of principles and methods for showing, promoting, and selling products or services. This includes marketing strategy and tactics, product demonstrations, sales techniques, and sales control systems. **English Language:** Knowledge of the structure and content of the English language, including the meaning and spelling of words, rules of composition, and grammar. **Clerical Practices:** Knowledge of administrative and clerical procedures and systems such as word processing, managing files and records, stenography and transcription, designing forms, and other office procedures and terminology. **Public Safety and Security:** Knowledge of relevant equipment, policies, procedures, and strategies to promote effective local, state, or national security operations for the protection of people, data, property, and institutions. **Economics and Accounting:** Knowledge of economic and accounting principles and practices, the financial markets, banking, and the analysis and reporting of financial data.

Tile and Marble Setters

◎ Education/Training Required: Long-term on-the-job training
◎ Annual Earnings: $35,410
◎ Growth: 26.5%
◎ Annual Job Openings: 4,000
◎ Self-Employed: 0%
◎ Part-Time: 5.0%

Apply hard tile, marble, and wood tile to walls, floors, ceilings, and roof decks. Align and straighten tile, using levels, squares, and straightedges. Determine and implement the best layout to achieve a desired pattern. Cut and shape tile to fit around obstacles and into odd spaces and corners, using hand and power cutting tools. Finish and dress the joints and wipe excess grout from between tiles, using damp sponge. Apply mortar to tile back, position the tile, and press or tap with trowel handle to affix tile to base. Mix, apply, and spread plaster, concrete, mortar, cement, mastic, glue, or other adhesives to form a bed for the tiles, using brush, trowel, and screed. Prepare cost and labor estimates based on calculations of time and materials needed for project. Measure and mark surfaces to be tiled, following blueprints. Level concrete and allow to dry. Build underbeds and install anchor bolts, wires, and brackets. Prepare surfaces for tiling by attaching lath or waterproof paper or by applying a cement mortar coat onto a metal screen. Study blueprints and examine surface to be covered to determine amount of material needed. Cut, surface, polish, and install marble and granite and/or install pre-cast terrazzo, granite, or marble units. Install and anchor fixtures in designated positions, using hand tools. Cut tile backing to required size, using shears. Remove any old tile, grout, and adhesive, using chisels and scrapers, and clean the surface carefully. Lay and set mosaic tiles to create decorative wall, mural, and floor designs. Assist customers in selection of tile and grout. Remove and replace cracked or damaged tile. Measure and cut metal lath to size for walls and ceilings, using tin snips. Select and order tile and other items to be installed, such as bathroom accessories, walls, panels, and cabinets, according to specifications. Mix and apply mortar or cement to edges and ends of drain tiles to seal halves and joints. Spread mastic or other adhesive base on roof deck to form base for promenade tile, using serrated spreader. **SKILLS—Installation:** Installing equipment, machines, wiring, or programs to meet specifications. **Social Perceptiveness:** Being aware of others' reactions and understanding why they react as they do. **Management of Financial Resources:** Determining how money will be spent to get the work done and accounting for these expenditures. **Mathematics:** Using mathematics to solve problems. **Instructing:** Teaching others how to do something. **Coordination:** Adjusting actions in relation to others' actions. **Critical Thinking:** Using logic and reasoning to identify the strengths and weaknesses of alternative solutions, conclusions, or approaches to problems. **Complex Problem Solving:** Identifying complex problems and reviewing related information to develop and evaluate options and implement solutions. **GOE—Interest Area:** 02. Architecture and Construction. **Work Group:** 02.04. Construction Crafts. **Other Jobs in This Work Group:** Boat Builders and Shipwrights; Boilermakers; Brattice Builders; Brickmasons and Blockmasons; Carpet Installers; Ceiling Tile Installers; Cement Masons and Concrete Finishers; Commercial Divers; Construction Carpenters; Crane and Tower Operators; Dragline Operators; Drywall Installers; Electricians; Fence Erectors; Floor Layers, Except Carpet, Wood, and Hard Tiles; Floor Sanders and Finishers; Glaziers; Grader, Bulldozer, and Scraper Operators; Hazardous Materials Removal Workers; Insulation Workers, Floor, Ceiling, and Wall; Insulation Workers, Mechanical; Manufactured Building and Mobile Home Installers; Operating Engineers; Painters, Construction and Maintenance; Paperhangers; Paving, Surfacing, and Tamping Equipment Operators; Pile-Driver Operators; Pipe Fitters; Pipelayers; Pipelaying Fitters; Plasterers and Stucco Masons; Plumbers; Rail-Track Laying and Maintenance Equipment Operators; Refractory Materials Repairers, Except Brickmasons; Reinforcing Iron and Rebar Workers; Riggers; Roofers; Rough Carpenters; Security and Fire Alarm Systems Installers; Segmental Pavers; Sheet Metal Workers; Ship Carpenters and Joiners; Stone Cutters and Carvers; Stonemasons; Structural Iron and Steel Workers; Tapers; Terrazzo Workers and Finishers. **PERSONALITY TYPE:** Realistic.

EDUCATION/TRAINING PROGRAM(S)— Building/Construction Finishing, Management, and Inspection, Other. **RELATED KNOWLEDGE/ COURSES—Building and Construction:** Knowledge of the materials, methods, and tools involved in the construction or repair of houses, buildings, or other structures such as highways and roads. **Design:** Knowledge of design techniques, tools, and principles involved in production of precision technical plans, blueprints, drawings, and models. **Production and Processing:** Knowledge of raw materials, production processes, quality control, costs, and other techniques for maximizing the effective manufacture and distribution of goods. **Administration and Management:** Knowledge of business and management principles involved in strategic planning, resource allocation, human resources modeling, leadership technique, production methods, and coordination of people and resources. **Economics and Accounting:** Knowledge of economic and accounting principles and practices, the financial markets, banking, and the analysis and reporting of financial data. **Transportation:** Knowledge of principles and methods for moving people or goods by air, rail, sea, or road, including the relative costs and benefits.

Tractor-Trailer Truck Drivers

- ◎ Education/Training Required: Moderate-term on-the-job training
- ◎ Annual Earnings: $33,520
- ◎ Growth: 19.0%
- ◎ Annual Job Openings: 299,000
- ◎ Self-Employed: 13.1%
- ◎ Part-Time: 7.7%

Drive tractor-trailer truck to transport products, livestock, or materials to specified destinations. Drives tractor-trailer combination, applying knowledge of commercial driving regulations, to transport and deliver products, livestock, or materials, usually over long distance. Maneuvers truck into loading or unloading position, following signals from loading crew as needed. Drives truck to weigh station before and after loading and along route to document weight and conform to state regulations. Maintains driver log according to I.C.C. regulations. Inspects truck before and after trips and submits report indicating truck condition. Reads bill of lading to determine assignment. Fastens chain or binders to secure load on trailer during transit. Loads or unloads or assists in loading and unloading truck. Works as member of two-person team driving tractor with sleeper bunk behind cab. Services truck with oil, fuel, and radiator fluid to maintain tractor-trailer. Obtains customer's signature or collects payment for services. Inventories and inspects goods to be moved. Wraps goods, using pads, packing paper, and containers, and secures load to trailer wall, using straps. Gives directions to helper in packing and moving goods to trailer. **SKILLS—Operation and Control:** Controlling operations of equipment or systems. **Equipment Maintenance:** Performing routine maintenance on equipment and determining when and what kind of maintenance is needed. **Repairing:** Repairing machines or systems by using the needed tools. **Management of Material Resources:** Obtaining and seeing to the appropriate use of equipment, facilities, and materials needed to do certain work. **Troubleshooting:** Determining causes of operating errors and deciding what to do about them. **Operation Monitoring:** Watching gauges, dials, or other indicators to make sure a machine is working properly. **GOE—Interest Area:** 16. Transportation, Distribution, and Logistics.

Work Group: 16.03. Truck Driving. **Other Jobs in This Work Group:** Truck Drivers, Heavy; Truck Drivers, Light or Delivery Services. **PERSONALITY TYPE:** Realistic.

EDUCATION/TRAINING PROGRAM(S)— Truck and Bus Driver/Commercial Vehicle Operation. **RELATED KNOWLEDGE/COURSES—Transportation:** Knowledge of principles and methods for moving people or goods by air, rail, sea, or road, including the relative costs and benefits. **Geography:** Knowledge of principles and methods for describing the features of land, sea, and air masses, including their physical characteristics; locations; interrelationships; and distribution of plant, animal, and human life. **Mechanical Devices:** Knowledge of machines and tools, including their designs, uses, repair, and maintenance. **Law and Government:** Knowledge of laws, legal codes, court procedures, precedents, government regulations, executive orders, agency rules, and the democratic political process. **Public Safety and Security:** Knowledge of relevant equipment, policies, procedures, and strategies to promote effective local, state, or national security operations for the protection of people, data, property, and institutions. **Telecommunications:** Knowledge of transmission, broadcasting, switching, control, and operation of telecommunications systems.

Training and Development Managers

- ◎ Education/Training Required: Work experience plus degree
- ◎ Annual Earnings: $67,460
- ◎ Growth: 19.4%
- ◎ Annual Job Openings: 21,000
- ◎ Self-Employed: 0%
- ◎ Part-Time: 3.7%

Plan, direct, or coordinate the training and development activities and staff of an organization. Conduct orientation sessions and arrange on-the-job training for new hires. Evaluate instructor performance and the effectiveness of training programs, providing recommendations for improvement. Develop testing and evaluation procedures. Conduct or arrange for ongoing technical training and personal development classes for staff members. Confer with management and conduct surveys to identify training needs based on projected production processes, changes, and other factors. Develop and organize training manuals, multimedia visual aids, and other educational materials. Plan, develop, and provide training and staff development programs, using knowledge of the effectiveness of methods such as classroom training, demonstrations, on-the-job training, meetings, conferences, and workshops. Analyze training needs to develop new training programs or modify and improve existing programs. Review and evaluate training and apprenticeship programs for compliance with government standards. Train instructors and supervisors in techniques and skills for training and dealing with employees. Coordinate established courses with technical and professional courses provided by community schools and designate training procedures. Prepare training budget for department or organization. **SKILLS— Management of Personnel Resources:** Motivating, developing, and directing people as they work, identifying the best people for the job. **Learning Strategies:** Selecting and using training/instructional methods and procedures appropriate for the situation when learning or teaching new things. **Management of Financial Resources:** Determining how money will be spent to get the work done and accounting for these expenditures. **Negotiation:** Bringing others together and trying to reconcile differences. **Service Orientation:** Actively looking for ways to help people. **Instructing:** Teaching others how to do something. **Social Perceptiveness:** Being aware of others' reactions and understanding why they react as they do. **Persuasion:** Persuading others to change their minds or behavior. **GOE—Interest Area:** 04. Business and Administration. **Work Group:** 04.01. Managerial Work in General Business. **Other Jobs in This Work Group:** Chief Executives; Compensation and Benefits Managers; General and Operations Managers; Human Resources Managers; Private Sector Executives. **PERSONALITY TYPE:** Enterprising.

EDUCATION/TRAINING PROGRAM(S)— Human Resources Development; Human Resources Management/Personnel Administration, General. **RELATED KNOWLEDGE/COURSES—Clerical Practices:** Knowledge of administrative and clerical procedures and systems such as word processing, managing files and records, stenography and transcription, designing forms, and other office procedures and terminology. **Personnel and Human Resources:** Knowl-

edge of principles and procedures for personnel recruitment, selection, training, compensation and benefits, labor relations and negotiation, and personnel information systems. **Administration and Management:** Knowledge of business and management principles involved in strategic planning, resource allocation, human resources modeling, leadership technique, production methods, and coordination of people and resources. **Education and Training:** Knowledge of principles and methods for curriculum and training design, teaching and instruction for individuals and groups, and the measurement of training effects. **Psychology:** Knowledge of human behavior and performance; individual differences in ability, personality, and interests; learning and motivation; psychological research methods; and the assessment and treatment of behavioral and affective disorders. **Computers and Electronics:** Knowledge of circuit boards, processors, chips, electronic equipment, and computer hardware and software, including applications and programming.

Training and Development Specialists

- Education/Training Required: Bachelor's degree
- Annual Earnings: $44,570
- Growth: 27.9%
- Annual Job Openings: 35,000
- Self-Employed: 0.8%
- Part-Time: 7.7%

Conduct training and development programs for employees. Coordinate recruitment and placement of training program participants. Evaluate training materials prepared by instructors, such as outlines, text, and handouts. Develop alternative training methods if expected improvements are not seen. Assess training needs through surveys; interviews with employees; focus groups; and/or consultation with managers, instructors, or customer representatives. Screen, hire, and assign workers to positions based on qualifications. Select and assign instructors to conduct training. Devise programs to develop executive potential among employees in lower-level positions. Design, plan, organize, and direct orientation and training for employees or customers of industrial or commercial establishment. Negotiate contracts with clients, including desired training outcomes, fees, and expenses. Supervise instructors, evaluate instructor performance, and refer instructors to classes for skill development. Monitor training costs to ensure budget is not exceeded and prepare budget reports to justify expenditures. Refer trainees to employer relations representatives, to locations offering job placement assistance, or to appropriate social services agencies if warranted. Keep up with developments in area of expertise by reading current journals, books, and magazine articles. Present information, using a variety of instructional techniques and formats such as role-playing, simulations, team exercises, group discussions, videos, and lectures. Schedule classes based on availability of classrooms, equipment, and instructors. Organize and develop or obtain training procedure manuals and guides and course materials such as handouts and visual materials. Offer specific training programs to help workers maintain or improve job skills. Monitor, evaluate, and record training activities and program effectiveness. Attend meetings and seminars to obtain information for use in training programs or to inform management of training program status. **SKILLS—Service Orientation:** Actively looking for ways to help people. **Instructing:** Teaching others how to do something. **Social Perceptiveness:** Being aware of others' reactions and understanding why they react as they do. **Writing:** Communicating effectively in writing as appropriate for the needs of the audience. **Speaking:** Talking to others to convey information effectively. **Persuasion:** Persuading others to change their minds or behavior. **Active Learning:** Understanding the implications of new information for both current and future problem-solving and decision-making. **Learning Strategies:** Selecting and using training/instructional methods and procedures appropriate for the situation when learning or teaching new things. **Time Management:** Managing one's own time and the time of others. **GOE—Interest Area:** 04. Business and Administration. **Work Group:** 04.03. Human Resources Support. **Other Jobs in This Work Group:** Compensation, Benefits, and Job Analysis Specialists; Employment Interviewers, Private or Public Employment Service; Personnel Recruiters. **PERSONALITY TYPE:** Social.

EDUCATION/TRAINING PROGRAM(S)— Human Resources Management/Personnel Administration, General; Organizational Behavior Studies. **RELATED KNOWLEDGE/COURSES—Customer and Personal Service:** Knowledge of principles and processes for providing customer and personal services. This includes customer needs assessment, meeting quality standards for services, and evaluation of customer satisfaction. **Psychology:** Knowledge of human behavior and performance; individual differences in ability, personality, and interests; learning and motivation; psychological research methods; and the assessment and treatment of behavioral and affective disorders. **Sociology and Anthropology:** Knowledge of group behavior and dynamics, societal trends and influences, human migrations, ethnicity, and cultures and their history and origins. **Personnel and Human Resources:** Knowledge of principles and procedures for personnel recruitment, selection, training, compensation and benefits, labor relations and negotiation, and personnel information systems. **Education and Training:** Knowledge of principles and methods for curriculum and training design, teaching and instruction for individuals and groups, and the measurement of training effects. **Public Safety and Security:** Knowledge of relevant equipment, policies, procedures, and strategies to promote effective local, state, or national security operations for the protection of people, data, property, and institutions.

Transit and Railroad Police

- Education/Training Required: Long-term on-the-job training
- Annual Earnings: $45,430
- Growth: 15.9%
- Annual Job Openings: 1,000
- Self-Employed: 0%
- Part-Time: 1.4%

Protect and police railroad and transit property, employees, or passengers. Apprehend or remove trespassers or thieves from railroad property or coordinate with law enforcement agencies in apprehensions and removals. Direct and coordinate the daily activities and training of security staff. Direct security activities at derailments, fires, floods, and strikes involving railroad property. Examine credentials of unauthorized persons attempting to enter secured areas. Investigate or direct investigations of freight theft, suspicious damage or loss of passengers' valuables, and other crimes on railroad property. Patrol railroad yards, cars, stations, and other facilities in order to protect company property and shipments and to maintain order. Plan and implement special safety and preventive programs, such as fire and accident prevention. Prepare reports documenting investigation activities and results. Record and verify seal numbers from boxcars containing frequently pilfered items, such as cigarettes and liquor, in order to detect tampering. Seal empty boxcars by twisting nails in door hasps, using nail twisters. Interview neighbors, associates, and former employers of job applicants in order to verify personal references and to obtain work history data. **SKILLS—Management of Personnel Resources:** Motivating, developing, and directing people as they work, identifying the best people for the job. **Active Listening:** Giving full attention to what other people are saying, taking time to understand the points being made, asking questions as appropriate, and not interrupting at inappropriate times. **Speaking:** Talking to others to convey information effectively. **Social Perceptiveness:** Being aware of others' reactions and understanding why they react as they do. **Coordination:** Adjusting actions in relation to others' actions. **Writing:** Communicating effectively in writing as appropriate for the needs of the audience. **Systems Analysis:** Determining how a system should work and how changes in conditions, operations, and the environment will affect outcomes. **Learning Strategies:** Selecting and using training/instructional methods and procedures appropriate for the situation when learning or teaching new things. **GOE—Interest Area:** 12. Law and Public Safety. **Work Group:** 12.04. Law Enforcement and Public Safety. **Other Jobs in This Work Group:** Bailiffs; Correctional Officers and Jailers; Criminal Investigators and Special Agents; Fire Investigators; Forensic Science Technicians; Highway Patrol Pilots; Parking Enforcement Workers; Police Detectives; Police Identification and Records Officers; Police Patrol Officers; Sheriffs and Deputy Sheriffs. **PERSONALITY TYPE:** Enterprising.

EDUCATION/TRAINING PROGRAM(S)— Security and Loss Prevention Services; Security and Protective Services, Other. **RELATED KNOWLEDGE/COURSES—Public Safety and Security:** Knowledge of relevant equipment, policies, procedures, and strategies to promote effective local, state, or national security operations for the protection of people, data, property, and institutions. **Law and Government:** Knowledge of laws, legal codes, court procedures, precedents, government regulations, exec-

utive orders, agency rules, and the democratic political process. **Transportation:** Knowledge of principles and methods for moving people or goods by air, rail, sea, or road, including the relative costs and benefits. **Administration and Management:** Knowledge of business and management principles involved in strategic planning, resource allocation, human resources modeling, leadership technique, production methods, and coordination of people and resources. **Personnel and Human Resources:** Knowledge of principles and procedures for personnel recruitment, selection, training, compensation and benefits, labor relations and negotiation, and personnel information systems. **Sociology and Anthropology:** Knowledge of group behavior and dynamics, societal trends and influences, human migrations, ethnicity, and cultures and their history and origins.

Transportation Managers

- ◉ Education/Training Required: Work experience in a related occupation
- ◉ Annual Earnings: $66,600
- ◉ Growth: 19.7%
- ◉ Annual Job Openings: 13,000
- ◉ Self-Employed: 1.1%
- ◉ Part-Time: 2.4%

Plan, direct, and coordinate the transportation operations within an organization or the activities of organizations that provide transportation services. Direct activities related to dispatching, routing, and tracking transportation vehicles, such as aircraft and railroad cars. Plan, organize, and manage the work of subordinate staff to ensure that the work is accomplished in a manner consistent with organizational requirements. Direct investigations to verify and resolve customer or shipper complaints. Serve as contact persons for all workers within assigned territories. Implement schedule and policy changes. Collaborate with other managers and staff members in order to formulate and implement policies, procedures, goals, and objectives. Monitor operations to ensure that staff members comply with administrative policies and procedures, safety rules, union contracts, and government regulations. Promote safe work activities by conducting safety audits, attending company safety meetings, and meeting with individual staff members. Develop criteria, application instructions, procedural manuals, and contracts for federal and state public transportation programs. Monitor spending to ensure that expenses are consistent with approved budgets. Direct and coordinate, through subordinates, activities of operations department in order to obtain use of equipment, facilities, and human resources. Direct activities of staff performing repairs and maintenance to equipment, vehicles, and facilities. Conduct investigations in cooperation with government agencies to determine causes of transportation accidents and to improve safety procedures. Analyze expenditures and other financial information in order to develop plans, policies, and budgets for increasing profits and improving services. Negotiate and authorize contracts with equipment and materials suppliers and monitor contract fulfillment. Supervise workers assigning tariff classifications and preparing billing. Set operations policies and standards, including determination of safety procedures for the handling of dangerous goods. Recommend or authorize capital expenditures for acquisition of new equipment or property in order to increase efficiency and services of operations department. Prepare management recommendations, such as proposed fee and tariff increases or schedule changes. **SKILLS—Negotiation:** Bringing others together and trying to reconcile differences. **Time Management:** Managing one's own time and the time of others. **Coordination:** Adjusting actions in relation to others' actions. **Instructing:** Teaching others how to do something. **Monitoring:** Monitoring or assessing your performance or that of other individuals or organizations to make improvements or take corrective action. **Critical Thinking:** Using logic and reasoning to identify the strengths and weaknesses of alternative solutions, conclusions, or approaches to problems. **Management of Financial Resources:** Determining how money will be spent to get the work done and accounting for these expenditures. **Active Learning:** Understanding the implications of new information for both current and future problem-solving and decision-making. **GOE—Interest Area:** 16. Transportation, Distribution, and Logistics. **Work Group:** 16.01. Managerial Work in Transportation. **Other Jobs in This Work Group:** Aircraft Cargo Handling Supervisors; First-Line Supervisors/Managers of Transportation and Material-Moving Machine and Vehicle Operators; Postmasters and Mail Superintendents; Railroad Conductors and Yardmasters; Storage and Distribution Managers. **PERSONALITY TYPE:** Enterprising.

EDUCATION/TRAINING PROGRAM(S)—Aeronautics/Aviation/Aerospace Science and Technology, General; Aviation/Airway Management and Operations; Business Administration and Management, General; Business/Commerce, General; Logistics and Materials Management; Public Administration. RELATED KNOWLEDGE/COURSES—Transportation: Knowledge of principles and methods for moving people or goods by air, rail, sea, or road, including the relative costs and benefits. **Customer and Personal Service:** Knowledge of principles and processes for providing customer and personal services. This includes customer needs assessment, meeting quality standards for services, and evaluation of customer satisfaction. **Clerical Practices:** Knowledge of administrative and clerical procedures and systems such as word processing, managing files and records, stenography and transcription, designing forms, and other office procedures and terminology. **Administration and Management:** Knowledge of business and management principles involved in strategic planning, resource allocation, human resources modeling, leadership technique, production methods, and coordination of people and resources. **Sales and Marketing:** Knowledge of principles and methods for showing, promoting, and selling products or services. This includes marketing strategy and tactics, product demonstrations, sales techniques, and sales control systems. **Psychology:** Knowledge of human behavior and performance; individual differences in ability, personality, and interests; learning and motivation; psychological research methods; and the assessment and treatment of behavioral and affective disorders.

Travel Clerks

- Education/Training Required: Short-term on-the-job training
- Annual Earnings: $27,750
- Growth: 12.2%
- Annual Job Openings: 35,000
- Self-Employed: 1.1%
- Part-Time: 15.7%

Provide tourists with travel information, such as points of interest, restaurants, rates, and emergency service. Duties include answering inquiries; offering suggestions; and providing literature pertaining to

trips, excursions, sporting events, concerts, and plays. **May make reservations, deliver tickets, arrange for visas, or contact individuals and groups to inform them of package tours.** Provides customers with travel suggestions and information such as guides, directories, brochures, and maps. Contacts motel, hotel, resort, and travel operators by mail or telephone to obtain advertising literature. Studies maps, directories, routes, and rate tables to determine travel route and cost and availability of accommodations. Calculates estimated travel rates and expenses, using items such as rate tables and calculators. Informs client of travel dates, times, connections, baggage limits, medical and visa requirements, and emergency information. Obtains reservations for air, train, or car travel and hotel or other housing accommodations. Confirms travel arrangements and reservations. Assists client in preparing required documents and forms for travel, such as visas. Plans itinerary for travel and accommodations, using knowledge of routes, types of carriers, and regulations. Provides information concerning fares, availability of travel, and accommodations, either orally or by using guides, brochures, and maps. Confers with customers by telephone, writing, or in person to answer questions regarding services and determine travel preferences. **SKILLS—Service Orientation:** Actively looking for ways to help people. **Active Listening:** Giving full attention to what other people are saying, taking time to understand the points being made, asking questions as appropriate, and not interrupting at inappropriate times. **Speaking:** Talking to others to convey information effectively. **Social Perceptiveness:** Being aware of others' reactions and understanding why they react as they do. **GOE— Interest Area:** 09. Hospitality, Tourism, and Recreation. **Work Group:** 09.03. Hospitality and Travel Services. **Other Jobs in This Work Group:** Baggage Porters and Bellhops; Concierges; Flight Attendants; Hotel, Motel, and Resort Desk Clerks; Janitors and Cleaners, Except Maids and Housekeeping Cleaners; Maids and Housekeeping Cleaners; Reservation and Transportation Ticket Agents; Tour Guides and Escorts; Transportation Attendants, Except Flight Attendants and Baggage Porters; Travel Agents; Travel Guides. **PERSONALITY TYPE:** Conventional.

EDUCATION/TRAINING PROGRAM(S)—Selling Skills and Sales Operations; Tourism and Travel Services Marketing Operations; Tourism Promotion Operations. **RELATED KNOWLEDGE/COURSES—Geography:** Knowledge of principles and methods for describing the features of land, sea, and air masses, including their physical characteristics; locations; interrelationships; and distribution of plant, animal, and human life. **Transportation:** Knowledge of principles and methods for moving people or goods by air, rail, sea, or road, including the relative costs and benefits. **Customer and Personal Service:** Knowledge of principles and processes for providing customer and personal services. This includes customer needs assessment, meeting quality standards for services, and evaluation of customer satisfaction. **Telecommunications:** Knowledge of transmission, broadcasting, switching, control, and operation of telecommunications systems.

Treasurers, Controllers, and Chief Financial Officers

- Education/Training Required: Work experience plus degree
- Annual Earnings: $81,880
- Growth: 18.3%
- Annual Job Openings: 71,000
- Self-Employed: 3.1%
- Part-Time: 4.8%

Plan, direct, and coordinate the financial activities of an organization at the highest level of management. Includes financial reserve officers. Coordinate and direct the financial planning, budgeting, procurement, or investment activities of all or part of an organization. Develop internal control policies, guidelines, and procedures for activities such as budget administration, cash and credit management, and accounting. Prepare or direct preparation of financial statements, business activity reports, financial position forecasts, annual budgets, and/or reports required by regulatory agencies. Advise management on short-term and long-term financial objectives, policies, and actions. Analyze the financial details of past, present, and expected operations in order to identify development opportunities and areas where improvement is needed. Delegate authority for the receipt, disbursement, banking, protection, and custody of funds, securities, and financial instruments. Evaluate needs for procurement of funds and investment of surpluses and make appropriate recommendations. Lead staff training and development in budgeting and financial management areas. Maintain current knowledge of organizational policies and procedures, federal and state policies and directives, and current accounting standards. Supervise employees performing financial reporting, accounting, billing, collections, payroll, and budgeting duties. Conduct or coordinate audits of company accounts and financial transactions to ensure compliance with state and federal requirements and statutes. Develop and maintain relationships with banking, insurance, and non-organizational accounting personnel in order to facilitate financial activities. Monitor and evaluate the performance of accounting and other financial staff; recommend and implement personnel actions such as promotions and dismissals. Monitor financial activities and details such as reserve levels to ensure that all legal and regulatory requirements are met. Perform tax planning work. Provide direction and assistance to other organizational units regarding accounting and budgeting policies and procedures and efficient control and utilization of financial resources. Receive and record requests for disbursements; authorize disbursements in accordance with policies and procedures. **SKILLS—Management of Financial Resources:** Determining how money will be spent to get the work done and accounting for these expenditures. **Systems Analysis:** Determining how a system should work and how changes in conditions, operations, and the environment will affect outcomes. **Systems Evaluation:** Identifying measures or indicators of system performance and the actions needed to improve or correct performance relative to the goals of the system. **Judgment and Decision Making:** Considering the relative costs and benefits of potential actions to choose the most appropriate one. **Complex Problem Solving:** Identifying complex problems and reviewing related information to develop and evaluate options and implement solutions. **Mathematics:** Using mathematics to solve problems. **Management of Personnel Resources:** Motivating, developing, and directing people as they work, identifying the best people for the job. **Critical Thinking:** Using logic and reasoning to identify the strengths and weaknesses of alternative solutions, conclusions, or approaches to problems. **Operations Analysis:** Analyzing needs and product requirements to create a design. **GOE—Interest Area:** 06. Finance and Insurance. **Work Group:** 06.01. Managerial Work in Finance and Insurance. **Other Jobs in This Work Group:** Financial Managers, Branch or Department. **PERSONALITY TYPE:** Enterprising.

EDUCATION/TRAINING PROGRAM(S)— Accounting and Business/Management; Accounting and Finance; Credit Management; Finance and Financial Management Services, Other; Finance, General; International Finance; Public Finance. **RELATED KNOWLEDGE/COURSES—Economics and Accounting:** Knowledge of economic and accounting principles and practices, the financial markets, banking, and the analysis and reporting of financial data. **Administration and Management:** Knowledge of business and management principles involved in strategic planning, resource allocation, human resources modeling, leadership technique, production methods, and coordination of people and resources. **Law and Government:** Knowledge of laws, legal codes, court procedures, precedents, government regulations, executive orders, agency rules, and the democratic political process. **Mathematics:** Knowledge of arithmetic, algebra, geometry, calculus, and statistics and their applications. **English Language:** Knowledge of the structure and content of the English language, including the meaning and spelling of words, rules of composition, and grammar. **Personnel and Human Resources:** Knowledge of principles and procedures for personnel recruitment, selection, training, compensation and benefits, labor relations and negotiation, and personnel information systems.

Tree Trimmers and Pruners

- Education/Training Required: Short-term on-the-job training
- Annual Earnings: $26,150
- Growth: 18.6%
- Annual Job Openings: 11,000
- Self-Employed: 25.6%
- Part-Time: 15.3%

Cut away dead or excess branches from trees or shrubs to maintain right-of-way for roads, sidewalks, or utilities or to improve appearance, health, and value of tree. Prune or treat trees or shrubs, using handsaws, pruning hooks, shears, and clippers. May use truck-mounted lifts and power pruners. May fill cavities in trees to promote healing and prevent deterioration. Cable, brace, tie, bolt, stake, and guy trees and branches to provide support. Clean, sharpen, and lubricate tools and equipment. Clear sites, streets, and grounds of woody and herbaceous materials, such as tree stumps and fallen trees and limbs. Climb trees, using climbing hooks and belts, or climb ladders to gain access to work areas. Collect debris and refuse from tree trimming and removal operations into piles, using shovels, rakes, or other tools. Cut away dead and excess branches from trees or clear branches around power lines, using climbing equipment or buckets of extended truck booms and/or chainsaws, hooks, handsaws, shears, and clippers. Inspect trees to determine if they have diseases or pest problems. Load debris and refuse onto trucks and haul it away for disposal. Operate shredding and chipping equipment and feed limbs and brush into the machines. Spray trees to treat diseased or unhealthy trees, including mixing chemicals and calibrating spray equipment. Prune, cut down, fertilize, and spray trees as directed by tree surgeons. Remove broken limbs from wires, using hooked extension poles. Trim jagged stumps, using saws or pruning shears. Trim, top, and reshape trees to achieve attractive shapes or to remove low-hanging branches. Water, root-feed, and fertilize trees. Apply tar or other protective substances to cut surfaces to seal surfaces and to protect them from fungi and insects. Harvest tanbark by cutting rings and slits in bark and stripping bark from trees, using spuds or axes. Hoist tools and equipment to tree trimmers and lower branches with ropes or block and tackle. Install lightning protection on trees. Plan and develop budgets for tree work and estimate the monetary value of trees. Provide information to the public regarding trees, such as advice on tree care. Scrape decayed matter from cavities in trees and fill holes with cement to promote healing and to prevent further deterioration. Split logs or wooden blocks into bolts, pickets, posts, or stakes, using hand tools such as ax wedges, sledgehammers, and mallets. Supervise others engaged in tree-trimming work and train lower-level employees. **SKILLS—Operation and Control:** Controlling operations of equipment or systems. **GOE—Interest Area:** 01. Agriculture and Natural Resources. **Work Group:** 01.05. Nursery, Groundskeeping, and Pest Control. **Other Jobs in This Work Group:** Landscaping and Groundskeeping Workers; Nursery Workers; Pest Control Workers; Pesticide Handlers, Sprayers, and Applicators, Vegetation. **PERSONALITY TYPE: Realistic.**

EDUCATION/TRAINING PROGRAM(S)— Applied Horticulture/Horticultural Business Services, Other. **RELATED KNOWLEDGE/COURSES— Chemistry:** Knowledge of the chemical composition, structure, and properties of substances and of the chemical processes and transformations that they undergo. This includes uses of chemicals and their danger signs, production techniques, and disposal methods. **Biology:** Knowledge of plant and animal organisms and their tissues, cells, functions, interdependencies, and interactions with each other and the environment. **Mechanical Devices:** Knowledge of machines and tools, including their designs, uses, repair, and maintenance.

Truck Drivers, Heavy

- ◉ Education/Training Required: Short-term on-the-job training
- ◉ Annual Earnings: $33,520
- ◉ Growth: 19.0%
- ◉ Annual Job Openings: 299,000
- ◉ Self-Employed: 13.1%
- ◉ Part-Time: 7.7%

Drive truck with capacity of more than three tons to transport materials to specified destinations. Drives truck with capacity of more than three tons to transport and deliver cargo, materials, or damaged vehicle. Maintains radio or telephone contact with base or supervisor to receive instructions or be dispatched to new location. Maintains truck log according to state and federal regulations. Keeps record of materials and products transported. Position blocks and ties rope around items to secure cargo for transport. Cleans, inspects, and services vehicle. Operates equipment on vehicle to load, unload, or disperse cargo or materials. Obtains customer signature or collects payment for goods delivered and delivery charges. Assists in loading and unloading truck manually. **SKILLS—Equipment Maintenance:** Performing routine maintenance on equipment and determining when and what kind of maintenance is needed. **Repairing:** Repairing machines or systems by using the needed tools. **Operation Monitoring:** Watching gauges, dials, or other indicators to make sure a machine is working properly. **Operation and Control:** Controlling operations of equipment or systems. **GOE—Interest Area:** 16. Transportation, Distribution, and Logistics. **Work Group:** 16.03. Truck Driving. **Other Jobs in This Work Group:** Tractor-Trailer Truck Drivers; Truck Drivers, Light or Delivery Services. **PERSONALITY TYPE: Realistic.**

EDUCATION/TRAINING PROGRAM(S)— Truck and Bus Driver/Commercial Vehicle Operation. **RELATED KNOWLEDGE/COURSES—Transportation:** Knowledge of principles and methods for moving people or goods by air, rail, sea, or road, including the relative costs and benefits. **Geography:** Knowledge of principles and methods for describing the features of land, sea, and air masses, including their physical characteristics; locations; interrelationships; and distribution of plant, animal, and human life. **Telecommunications:** Knowledge of transmission, broadcasting, switching, control, and operation of telecommunications systems. **Mechanical Devices:** Knowledge of machines and tools, including their designs, uses, repair, and maintenance. **Public Safety and Security:** Knowledge of relevant equipment, policies, procedures, and strategies to promote effective local, state, or national security operations for the protection of people, data, property, and institutions. **Law and Government:** Knowledge of laws, legal codes, court procedures, precedents, government regulations, executive orders, agency rules, and the democratic political process.

Truck Drivers, Light or Delivery Services

- ◎ Education/Training Required: Short-term on-the-job training
- ◎ Annual Earnings: $24,540
- ◎ Growth: 23.2%
- ◎ Annual Job Openings: 219,000
- ◎ Self-Employed: 4.7%
- ◎ Part-Time: 17.3%

Drive a truck or van with a capacity of under 26,000 GVW, primarily to deliver or pick up merchandise or to deliver packages within a specified area. May require use of automatic routing or location software. May load and unload truck. Drive vehicles with capacities under three tons in order to transport materials to and from specified destinations such as railroad stations, plants, residences, and offices or within industrial yards. Inspect and maintain vehicle supplies and equipment, such as gas, oil, water, tires, lights, and brakes, in order to ensure that vehicles are in proper working condition. Load and unload trucks, vans, or automobiles. Obey traffic laws and follow established traffic and transportation procedures. Read maps and follow written and verbal geographic directions. Verify the contents of inventory loads against shipping papers. Maintain records such as vehicle logs, records of cargo, or billing statements in accordance with regulations. Perform emergency repairs such as changing tires or installing light bulbs, fuses, tire chains, and spark plugs. Present bills and receipts and collect payments for goods delivered or loaded. Report any mechanical problems encountered with vehicles. Report delays, accidents, or other traffic and transportation situations to bases or other vehicles, using telephones or mobile two-way radios. Turn in receipts and money received from deliveries. Drive trucks equipped with public address systems through city streets in order to broadcast announcements for advertising or publicity purposes. Sell and keep records of sales for products from truck inventory. Use and maintain the tools and equipment found on commercial vehicles, such as weighing and measuring devices. **SKILLS—Repairing:** Repairing machines or systems by using the needed tools. **Equipment Maintenance:** Performing routine maintenance on equipment and determining when and what kind of maintenance is needed. **Operation Monitoring:** Watching gauges, dials, or other indicators to make sure a machine is working properly. **Operation and Control:** Controlling operations of equipment or systems. **Troubleshooting:** Determining causes of operating errors and deciding what to do about them. **GOE—Interest Area:** 16. Transportation, Distribution, and Logistics. **Work Group:** 16.03. Truck Driving. **Other Jobs in This Work Group:** Tractor-Trailer Truck Drivers; Truck Drivers, Heavy. **PERSONALITY TYPE:** Realistic.

EDUCATION/TRAINING PROGRAM(S)— Truck and Bus Driver/Commercial Vehicle Operation. **RELATED KNOWLEDGE/COURSES—Transportation:** Knowledge of principles and methods for moving people or goods by air, rail, sea, or road, including the relative costs and benefits. **Telecommunications:** Knowledge of transmission, broadcasting, switching, control, and operation of telecommunications systems. **Geography:** Knowledge of principles and methods for describing the features of land, sea, and air masses, including their physical characteristics; locations; interrelationships; and distribution of plant, animal, and human life. **Mechanical Devices:** Knowledge of machines and tools, including their designs, uses, repair, and maintenance. **Law and Government:** Knowledge of laws, legal codes, court procedures, precedents, government regulations, executive orders, agency rules, and the democratic political process. **Public Safety and Security:** Knowledge of relevant equipment, policies, procedures, and strategies to promote effective local, state, or national security operations for the protection of people, data, property, and institutions.

Urban and Regional Planners

- ◎ Education/Training Required: Master's degree
- ◎ Annual Earnings: $53,450
- ◎ Growth: 10.7%
- ◎ Annual Job Openings: 5,000
- ◎ Self-Employed: 2.6%
- ◎ Part-Time: 10.1%

Develop comprehensive plans and programs for use of land and physical facilities of local jurisdictions, such as towns, cities, counties, and metropolitan areas. Design, promote, and administer government plans and policies affecting land use, zoning, public utilities, community facilities, housing, and transportation. Hold public meetings and confer with government, social scientists, lawyers, developers, the public, and special interest groups to formulate and develop land use or community plans. Recommend approval, denial, or conditional approval of proposals. Determine the effects of regulatory limitations on projects. Assess the feasibility of proposals and identify necessary changes. Create, prepare, or requisition graphic and narrative reports on land use data, including land area maps overlaid with geographic variables such as population density. Advise planning officials on project feasibility, cost-effectiveness, regulatory conformance, and possible alternatives. Conduct field investigations, surveys, impact studies, or other research in order to compile and analyze data on economic, social, regulatory, and physical factors affecting land use. Discuss with planning officials the purpose of land use projects such as transportation, conservation, residential, commercial, industrial, and community use. Keep informed about economic and legal issues involved in zoning codes, building codes, and environ-

mental regulations. Mediate community disputes and assist in developing alternative plans and recommendations for programs or projects. Coordinate work with economic consultants and architects during the formulation of plans and the design of large pieces of infrastructure. Review and evaluate environmental impact reports pertaining to private and public planning projects and programs. Supervise and coordinate the work of urban planning technicians and technologists. Investigate property availability. **SKILLS—Persuasion:** Persuading others to change their minds or behavior. **Coordination:** Adjusting actions in relation to others' actions. **Complex Problem Solving:** Identifying complex problems and reviewing related information to develop and evaluate options and implement solutions. **Service Orientation:** Actively looking for ways to help people. **Social Perceptiveness:** Being aware of others' reactions and understanding why they react as they do. **Time Management:** Managing one's own time and the time of others. **Writing:** Communicating effectively in writing as appropriate for the needs of the audience. **Speaking:** Talking to others to convey information effectively. **GOE—Interest Area:** 07. Government and Public Administration. **Work Group:** 07.02. Public Planning. **Other Jobs in This Work Group:** City Planning Aides. **PERSONALITY TYPE:** Investigative.

EDUCATION/TRAINING PROGRAM(S)— City/Urban, Community, and Regional Planning. **RELATED KNOWLEDGE/COURSES—Design:** Knowledge of design techniques, tools, and principles involved in production of precision technical plans, blueprints, drawings, and models. **Geography:** Knowledge of principles and methods for describing the features of land, sea, and air masses, including their physical characteristics; locations; interrelationships; and distribution of plant, animal, and human life. **Building and Construction:** Knowledge of the materials, methods, and tools involved in the construction or repair of houses, buildings, or other structures such as highways and roads. **Customer and Personal Service:** Knowledge of principles and processes for providing customer and personal services. This includes customer needs assessment, meeting quality standards for services, and evaluation of customer satisfaction. **Law and Government:** Knowledge of laws, legal codes, court procedures, precedents, government regulations, executive orders, agency rules, and the democratic political process. **Clerical Practices:** Knowledge of administrative and clerical procedures and systems such as word processing, managing files and records, stenography and transcription, designing forms, and other office procedures and terminology.

Valve and Regulator Repairers

- ◎ Education/Training Required: Moderate-term on-the-job training
- ◎ Annual Earnings: $43,710
- ◎ Growth: 12.0%
- ◎ Annual Job Openings: 5,000
- ◎ Self-Employed: 0.7%
- ◎ Part-Time: 2.0%

Test, repair, and adjust mechanical regulators and valves. Replaces, repairs, or adjusts defective valve or regulator parts and tightens attachments, using hand tools, power tools, and welder. Tests valves and regulators for leaks, temperature, and pressure settings, using precision testing equipment. Examines valves or mechanical control device parts for defects, dents, or loose attachments. Measures salvageable parts removed from mechanical control devices for conformance to standards or specifications, using gauges, micrometers, and calipers. Dips valves and regulators in molten lead to prevent leakage and paints valves, fittings, and other devices, using spray gun. Advises customers on proper installation of valves or regulators and related equipment. Records repair work, inventories parts, and orders new parts. Correlates testing data, performs technical calculations, and writes test reports to record data. Cleans corrosives and other deposits from serviceable parts, using solvents, wire brushes, or sandblaster. Lubricates wearing surfaces of mechanical parts, using oils or other lubricants. Disassembles mechanical control devices or valves, such as regulators, thermostats, or hydrants, using power tools, hand tools, and cutting torch. **SKILLS—Repairing:** Repairing machines or systems by using the needed tools. **Equipment Maintenance:** Performing routine maintenance on equipment and determining when and what kind of maintenance is needed. **Installation:** Installing equipment, machines, wiring, or programs to meet specifications. **Quality Control Analysis:** Conducting tests and inspections of products, services, or processes to evaluate quality or performance. **Troubleshooting:**

Determining causes of operating errors and deciding what to do about them. **Mathematics:** Using mathematics to solve problems. **Writing:** Communicating effectively in writing as appropriate for the needs of the audience. **Science:** Using scientific rules and methods to solve problems. **Operation and Control:** Controlling operations of equipment or systems. **GOE—Interest Area:** 13. Manufacturing. **Work Group:** 13.13. Machinery Repair. **Other Jobs in This Work Group:** Bicycle Repairers; Gas Appliance Repairers; Hand and Portable Power Tool Repairers; Industrial Machinery Mechanics; Locksmiths and Safe Repairers; Maintenance Workers, Machinery; Mechanical Door Repairers; Millwrights; Signal and Track Switch Repairers. **PERSONALITY TYPE:** Realistic.

EDUCATION/TRAINING PROGRAM(S)— Electromechanical and Instrumentation and Maintenance Technologies/Technicians, Other. **RELATED KNOWLEDGE/COURSES—Mechanical Devices:** Knowledge of machines and tools, including their designs, uses, repair, and maintenance. **Physics:** Knowledge and prediction of physical principles and laws and their interrelationships and applications to understanding fluid, material, and atmospheric dynamics and mechanical, electrical, atomic, and subatomic structures and processes. **Engineering and Technology:** Knowledge of the practical application of engineering science and technology. This includes applying principles, techniques, procedures, and equipment to the design and production of various goods and services. **Mathematics:** Knowledge of arithmetic, algebra, geometry, calculus, and statistics and their applications. **Chemistry:** Knowledge of the chemical composition, structure, and properties of substances and of the chemical processes and transformations that they undergo. This includes uses of chemicals and their danger signs, production techniques, and disposal methods. **Building and Construction:** Knowledge of the materials, methods, and tools involved in the construction or repair of houses, buildings, or other structures such as highways and roads.

Veterinarians

◎ Education/Training Required: First professional degree

◎ Annual Earnings: $66,590

◎ Growth: 25.1%

◎ Annual Job Openings: 4,000

◎ Self-Employed: 27.7%

◎ Part-Time: 10.6%

Diagnose and treat diseases and dysfunctions of animals. May engage in a particular function, such as research and development, consultation, administration, technical writing, sale or production of commercial products, or rendering of technical services to commercial firms or other organizations. Includes veterinarians who inspect livestock. Examine animals to detect and determine the nature of diseases or injuries. Treat sick or injured animals by prescribing medication, setting bones, dressing wounds, or performing surgery. Inoculate animals against various diseases such as rabies and distemper. Collect body tissue, feces, blood, urine, or other body fluids for examination and analysis. Operate diagnostic equipment such as radiographic and ultrasound equipment and interpret the resulting images. Advise animal owners regarding sanitary measures, feeding, and general care necessary to promote health of animals. Educate the public about diseases that can be spread from animals to humans. Train and supervise workers who handle and care for animals. Provide care to a wide range of animals or specialize in a particular species, such as horses or exotic birds. Euthanize animals. Establish and conduct quarantine and testing procedures that prevent the spread of diseases to other animals or to humans and that comply with applicable government regulations. Conduct postmortem studies and analyses to determine the causes of animals' deaths. Perform administrative duties such as scheduling appointments, accepting payments from clients, and maintaining business records. Direct the overall operations of animal hospitals, clinics, or mobile services to farms. Drive mobile clinic vans to farms so that health problems can be treated and/or prevented. Specialize in a particular type of treatment such as dentistry, pathology, nutrition, surgery, microbiology, or internal medicine. Inspect and test horses, sheep, poultry, and other animals to detect the presence of communicable diseases. Plan and execute animal nutrition and repro-

duction programs. Research diseases to which animals could be susceptible. Inspect animal housing facilities to determine their cleanliness and adequacy. Determine the effects of drug therapies, antibiotics, or new surgical techniques by testing them on animals. **SKILLS—Science:** Using scientific rules and methods to solve problems. **Instructing:** Teaching others how to do something. **Management of Financial Resources:** Determining how money will be spent to get the work done and accounting for these expenditures. **Reading Comprehension:** Understanding written sentences and paragraphs in work-related documents. **Service Orientation:** Actively looking for ways to help people. **Complex Problem Solving:** Identifying complex problems and reviewing related information to develop and evaluate options and implement solutions. **Management of Personnel Resources:** Motivating, developing, and directing people as they work, identifying the best people for the job. **Active Learning:** Understanding the implications of new information for both current and future problem-solving and decision-making. **Judgment and Decision Making:** Considering the relative costs and benefits of potential actions to choose the most appropriate one. **GOE—Interest Area:** 08. Health Science. **Work Group:** 08.05. Animal Care. **Other Jobs in This Work Group:** Animal Breeders; Animal Trainers; Nonfarm Animal Caretakers; Veterinary Assistants and Laboratory Animal Caretakers; Veterinary Technologists and Technicians. **PERSONALITY TYPE:** Investigative.

EDUCATION/TRAINING PROGRAM(S)— Comparative and Laboratory Animal Medicine (Cert, MS, PhD); Laboratory Animal Medicine; Large Animal/Food Animal and Equine Surgery and Medicine (Cert, MS, PhD); Small/Companion Animal Surgery and Medicine (Cert, MS, PhD); Theriogenology; Veterinary Anatomy (Cert, MS, PhD); Veterinary Anesthesiology; Veterinary Biomedical and Clinical Sciences, Other (Cert, MS. PhD); Veterinary Dentistry; Veterinary Dermatology; Veterinary Emergency and Critical Care Medicine; Veterinary Infectious Diseases (Cert, MS, PhD); Veterinary Internal Medicine; Veterinary Medicine (DVM); Veterinary Microbiology; Veterinary Microbiology and Immunobiology (Cert, MS, PhD); Veterinary Nutrition; Veterinary Ophthalmology; Veterinary Pathology; Veterinary Pathology and Pathobiology (Cert, MS, PhD); Veterinary Physiology (Cert, MS, PhD); Veterinary Practice; Veterinary Preventive Medicine; Veterinary Preventive Medicine Epidemiology and Public Health (Cert, MS,

PhD); Veterinary Radiology; Veterinary Residency Programs, Other; Veterinary Sciences/Veterinary Clinical Sciences, General (Cert, MS, PhD); Veterinary Surgery; Veterinary Toxicology; Veterinary Toxicology and Pharmacology (Cert, MS, PhD); Zoological Medicine. **RELATED KNOWLEDGE/COURSES— Medicine and Dentistry:** Knowledge of the information and techniques needed to diagnose and treat human injuries, diseases, and deformities. This includes symptoms, treatment alternatives, drug properties and interactions, and preventive health-care measures. **Biology:** Knowledge of plant and animal organisms and their tissues, cells, functions, interdependencies, and interactions with each other and the environment. **Chemistry:** Knowledge of the chemical composition, structure, and properties of substances and of the chemical processes and transformations that they undergo. This includes uses of chemicals and their danger signs, production techniques, and disposal methods. **Customer and Personal Service:** Knowledge of principles and processes for providing customer and personal services. This includes customer needs assessment, meeting quality standards for services, and evaluation of customer satisfaction. **Sales and Marketing:** Knowledge of principles and methods for showing, promoting, and selling products or services. This includes marketing strategy and tactics, product demonstrations, sales techniques, and sales control systems. **Education and Training:** Knowledge of principles and methods for curriculum and training design, teaching and instruction for individuals and groups, and the measurement of training effects.

Veterinary Assistants and Laboratory Animal Caretakers

- Education/Training Required: Short-term on-the-job training
- Annual Earnings: $18,660
- Growth: 26.2%
- Annual Job Openings: 11,000
- Self-Employed: 2.1%
- Part-Time: 25.3%

Feed, water, and examine pets and other nonfarm animals for signs of illness, disease, or injury in labo- ratories and animal hospitals and clinics. Clean and disinfect cages and work areas and sterilize laboratory and surgical equipment. May provide routine post-operative care, administer medication orally or topically, or prepare samples for laboratory examination under the supervision of veterinary or laboratory animal technologists or technicians, veterinarians, or scientists. Monitor animals recovering from surgery and notify veterinarians of any unusual changes or symptoms. Administer anesthetics during surgery and monitor the effects on animals. Clean, maintain, and sterilize instruments and equipment. Administer medication, immunizations, and blood plasma to animals as prescribed by veterinarians. Provide emergency first aid to sick or injured animals. Clean and maintain kennels, animal holding areas, examination and operating rooms, and animal loading/unloading facilities to control the spread of disease. Hold or restrain animals during veterinary procedures. Perform routine laboratory tests or diagnostic tests such as taking and developing X rays. Fill medication prescriptions. Collect laboratory specimens such as blood, urine, and feces for testing. Examine animals to detect behavioral changes or clinical symptoms that could indicate illness or injury. Assist veterinarians in examining animals to determine the nature of illnesses or injuries. Prepare surgical equipment and pass instruments and materials to veterinarians during surgical procedures. Perform enemas, catheterization, ear flushes, intravenous feedings, and gavages. Prepare feed for animals according to specific instructions such as diet lists and schedules. Exercise animals and provide them with companionship. Record information relating to animal genealogy, feeding schedules, appearance, behavior, and breeding. Educate and advise clients on animal health care, nutrition, and behavior problems. Perform hygiene-related duties such as clipping animals' claws and cleaning and polishing teeth. Prepare examination or treatment rooms by stocking them with appropriate supplies. Provide assistance with euthanasia of animals and disposal of corpses. Perform office reception duties such as scheduling appointments and helping customers. Dust, spray, or bathe animals to control insect pests. Write reports, maintain research information, and perform clerical duties. Perform accounting duties, including bookkeeping, billing customers for services, and maintaining inventories. Assist professional personnel with research projects in commercial, public health, or research laboratories. **SKILLS— Instructing:** Teaching others how to do something.

Science: Using scientific rules and methods to solve problems. **Active Listening:** Giving full attention to what other people are saying, taking time to understand the points being made, asking questions as appropriate, and not interrupting at inappropriate times. **Social Perceptiveness:** Being aware of others' reactions and understanding why they react as they do. **Service Orientation:** Actively looking for ways to help people. **Reading Comprehension:** Understanding written sentences and paragraphs in work-related documents. **Learning Strategies:** Selecting and using training/instructional methods and procedures appropriate for the situation when learning or teaching new things. **Operation Monitoring:** Watching gauges, dials, or other indicators to make sure a machine is working properly. **Troubleshooting:** Determining causes of operating errors and deciding what to do about them. **GOE—Interest Area:** 08. Health Science. **Work Group:** 08.05. Animal Care. **Other Jobs in This Work Group:** Animal Breeders; Animal Trainers; Nonfarm Animal Caretakers; Veterinarians; Veterinary Technologists and Technicians. **PERSONALITY TYPE:** Realistic.

EDUCATION/TRAINING PROGRAM(S)—Veterinary/Animal Health Technology/Technician and Veterinary Assistant. **RELATED KNOWLEDGE/ COURSES—Medicine and Dentistry:** Knowledge of the information and techniques needed to diagnose and treat human injuries, diseases, and deformities. This includes symptoms, treatment alternatives, drug properties and interactions, and preventive health-care measures. **Chemistry:** Knowledge of the chemical composition, structure, and properties of substances and of the chemical processes and transformations that they undergo. This includes uses of chemicals and their danger signs, production techniques, and disposal methods. **Biology:** Knowledge of plant and animal organisms and their tissues, cells, functions, interdependencies, and interactions with each other and the environment. **Clerical Practices:** Knowledge of administrative and clerical procedures and systems such as word processing, managing files and records, stenography and transcription, designing forms, and other office procedures and terminology. **Customer and Personal Service:** Knowledge of principles and processes for providing customer and personal services. This includes customer needs assessment, meeting quality standards for services, and evaluation of customer satisfaction. **Sales and Marketing:** Knowledge of principles and methods for showing, promoting, and selling products or services. This includes marketing strategy and tactics, product demonstrations, sales techniques, and sales control systems.

Veterinary Technologists and Technicians

- ◎ Education/Training Required: Associate degree
- ◎ Annual Earnings: $24,940
- ◎ Growth: 44.1%
- ◎ Annual Job Openings: 11,000
- ◎ Self-Employed: 0%
- ◎ Part-Time: 23.0%

Perform medical tests in a laboratory environment for use in the treatment and diagnosis of diseases in animals. Prepare vaccines and serums for prevention of diseases. Prepare tissue samples, take blood samples, and execute laboratory tests such as urinalysis and blood counts. Clean and sterilize instruments and materials and maintain equipment and machines. Administer anesthesia to animals, under the direction of a veterinarian, and monitor animals' responses to anesthetics so that dosages can be adjusted. Care for and monitor the condition of animals recovering from surgery. Prepare and administer medications, vaccines, serums, and treatments as prescribed by veterinarians. Perform laboratory tests on blood, urine, and feces, such as urinalyses and blood counts, to assist in the diagnosis and treatment of animal health problems. Administer emergency first aid, such as performing emergency resuscitation or other lifesaving procedures. Collect, prepare, and label samples for laboratory testing, culture, or microscopic examination. Clean and sterilize instruments, equipment, and materials. Provide veterinarians with the correct equipment and instruments as needed. Fill prescriptions, measuring medications and labeling containers. Prepare animals for surgery, performing such tasks as shaving surgical areas. Take animals into treatment areas and assist with physical examinations by performing such duties as obtaining temperature, pulse, and respiration data. Observe the behavior and condition of animals and monitor their clinical symptoms. Take and develop diagnostic radiographs, using X-ray equipment. Maintain laboratory, research, and treatment records, as well as inventories of pharmaceuticals, equipment, and supplies. Give enemas and perform catheterizations, ear flushes, intravenous feedings, and gavages. Prepare treatment rooms for surgery. Maintain instruments, equipment, and machinery to ensure proper working condition. Perform dental work such as cleaning, polishing, and extracting teeth. Clean kennels, animal holding areas, surgery suites, examination rooms, and animal loading/unloading facilities to control the spread of disease. Provide information and counseling regarding issues such as animal health care, behavior problems, and nutrition. Provide assistance with animal euthanasia and the disposal of remains. Dress and suture wounds and apply splints and other protective devices. Perform a variety of office, clerical, and accounting duties, such as reception, billing, bookkeeping, and/or selling products. **SKILLS— Instructing:** Teaching others how to do something. **Social Perceptiveness:** Being aware of others' reactions and understanding why they react as they do. **Science:** Using scientific rules and methods to solve problems. **Operation Monitoring:** Watching gauges, dials, or other indicators to make sure a machine is working properly. **Active Learning:** Understanding the implications of new information for both current and future problem-solving and decision-making. **Time Management:** Managing one's own time and the time of others. **Reading Comprehension:** Understanding written sentences and paragraphs in work-related documents. **Active Listening:** Giving full attention to what other people are saying, taking time to understand the points being made, asking questions as appropriate, and not interrupting at inappropriate times. **Equipment Maintenance:** Performing routine maintenance on equipment and determining when and what kind of maintenance is needed. **GOE—Interest Area:** 08. Health Science. **Work Group:** 08.05. Animal Care. **Other Jobs in This Work Group:** Animal Breeders; Animal Trainers; Nonfarm Animal Caretakers; Veterinarians; Veterinary Assistants and Laboratory Animal Caretakers. **PERSONALITY TYPE:** No data available.

EDUCATION/TRAINING PROGRAM(S)—Veterinary/Animal Health Technology/Technician and Veterinary Assistant. **RELATED KNOWLEDGE/ COURSES—Biology:** Knowledge of plant and animal organisms and their tissues, cells, functions, interdependencies, and interactions with each other and the environment. **Customer and Personal Service:** Knowledge of principles and processes for providing customer and personal services. This includes customer

needs assessment, meeting quality standards for services, and evaluation of customer satisfaction. **Medicine and Dentistry:** Knowledge of the information and techniques needed to diagnose and treat human injuries, diseases, and deformities. This includes symptoms, treatment alternatives, drug properties and interactions, and preventive health-care measures. **Chemistry:** Knowledge of the chemical composition, structure, and properties of substances and of the chemical processes and transformations that they undergo. This includes uses of chemicals and their danger signs, production techniques, and disposal methods. **Sales and Marketing:** Knowledge of principles and methods for showing, promoting, and selling products or services. This includes marketing strategy and tactics, product demonstrations, sales techniques, and sales control systems. **Mathematics:** Knowledge of arithmetic, algebra, geometry, calculus, and statistics and their applications.

Vocational Education Teachers, Postsecondary

- ◎ Education/Training Required: Work experience in a related occupation
- ◎ Annual Earnings: $40,740
- ◎ Growth: 38.1%
- ◎ Annual Job Openings: 216,000
- ◎ Self-Employed: 0.3%
- ◎ Part-Time: 27.7%

Teach or instruct vocational or occupational subjects at the postsecondary level (but at less than the baccalaureate) to students who have graduated or left high school. Includes correspondence school instructors; industrial, commercial, and government training instructors; and adult education teachers and instructors who prepare persons to operate industrial machinery and equipment and transportation and communications equipment. Teaching may take place in public or private schools whose primary business is education or in a school associated with an organization whose primary business is other than education. Supervise and monitor students' use of tools and equipment. Observe and evaluate students' work to determine progress, provide feedback, and make suggestions for improvement. Present lectures and conduct discussions to increase students' knowledge and competence, using visual aids such as graphs, charts, videotapes, and slides. Administer oral, written, or performance tests in order to measure progress and to evaluate training effectiveness. Prepare reports and maintain records such as student grades, attendance rolls, and training activity details. Supervise independent or group projects, field placements, laboratory work, or other training. Determine training needs of students or workers. Provide individualized instruction and tutorial and/or remedial instruction. Conduct on-the-job training, classes, or training sessions to teach and demonstrate principles, techniques, procedures, and/or methods of designated subjects. Develop curricula and plan course content and methods of instruction. Prepare outlines of instructional programs and training schedules and establish course goals. Integrate academic and vocational curricula so that students can obtain a variety of skills. Develop teaching aids such as instructional software, multimedia visual aids, or study materials. Select and assemble books, materials, supplies, and equipment for training, courses, or projects. Advise students on course selection, career decisions, and other academic and vocational concerns. Participate in conferences, seminars, and training sessions to keep abreast of developments in the field and integrate relevant information into training programs. Serve on faculty and school committees concerned with budgeting, curriculum revision, and course and diploma requirements. Review enrollment applications and correspond with applicants to obtain additional information. Arrange for lectures by experts in designated fields. **SKILLS—Instructing:** Teaching others how to do something. **Learning Strategies:** Selecting and using training/instructional methods and procedures appropriate for the situation when learning or teaching new things. **Social Perceptiveness:** Being aware of others' reactions and understanding why they react as they do. **Service Orientation:** Actively looking for ways to help people. **Time Management:** Managing one's own time and the time of others. **Persuasion:** Persuading others to change their minds or behavior. **Speaking:** Talking to others to convey information effectively. **Negotiation:** Bringing others together and trying to reconcile differences. **GOE—Interest Area:** 05. Education and Training. **Work Group:** 05.03. Postsecondary and Adult Teaching and Instructing. **Other Jobs in This Work Group:** Adult Literacy, Remedial Education, and GED Teachers and Instructors; Agricultural Sciences Teachers, Postsecondary; Anthropology and Archeology Teachers, Postsecondary; Architecture Teachers, Postsecondary; Area, Ethnic, and Cultural Studies Teachers, Postsecondary; Art, Drama, and Music Teachers, Postsecondary; Atmospheric, Earth, Marine, and Space Sciences Teachers, Postsecondary; Biological Science Teachers, Postsecondary; Business Teachers, Postsecondary; Chemistry Teachers, Postsecondary; Communications Teachers, Postsecondary; Computer Science Teachers, Postsecondary; Criminal Justice and Law Enforcement Teachers, Postsecondary; Economics Teachers, Postsecondary; Education Teachers, Postsecondary; Engineering Teachers, Postsecondary; English Language and Literature Teachers, Postsecondary; Environmental Science Teachers, Postsecondary; Farm and Home Management Advisors; Foreign Language and Literature Teachers, Postsecondary; Forestry and Conservation Science Teachers, Postsecondary; Geography Teachers, Postsecondary; Graduate Teaching Assistants; Health Specialties Teachers, Postsecondary; History Teachers, Postsecondary; Home Economics Teachers, Postsecondary; Law Teachers, Postsecondary; Library Science Teachers, Postsecondary; Mathematical Science Teachers, Postsecondary; Nursing Instructors and Teachers, Postsecondary; Philosophy and Religion Teachers, Postsecondary; Physics Teachers, Postsecondary; Political Science Teachers, Postsecondary; Psychology Teachers, Postsecondary; Recreation and Fitness Studies Teachers, Postsecondary; Self-Enrichment Education Teachers; Social Work Teachers, Postsecondary; Sociology Teachers, Postsecondary. **PERSONALITY TYPE:** Social.

EDUCATION/TRAINING PROGRAM(S)—Agricultural Teacher Education; Business Teacher Education; Health Occupations Teacher Education; Sales and Marketing Operations/Marketing and Distribution Teacher Education; Teacher Education and Professional Development, Specific Subject Areas, Other; Technical Teacher Education; Technology Teacher Education/Industrial Arts Teacher Education; Trade and Industrial Teacher Education. **RELATED KNOWLEDGE/COURSES—Education and Training:** Knowledge of principles and methods for curriculum and training design, teaching and instruction for individuals and groups, and the measurement of training effects. **Psychology:** Knowledge of human behavior and performance; individual differences in ability, personality, and interests; learning and motivation; psychological research methods; and the assessment and treatment of behavioral and affective disorders. **Computers and Electronics:** Knowledge of circuit boards, processors, chips, electronic equipment, and computer hardware and software, including applications and programming. **Customer and Personal Service:** Knowledge of principles and processes for providing customer and personal services. This includes customer needs assessment, meeting quality standards for services, and evaluation of customer satisfaction. **Clerical Practices:** Knowledge of administrative and clerical procedures and systems such as word processing, managing files and records, stenography and transcription, designing forms, and other office procedures and terminology. **Sales and Marketing:** Knowledge of principles and methods for showing, promoting, and selling products or services. This includes marketing strategy and tactics, product demonstrations, sales techniques, and sales control systems.

Vocational Education Teachers, Secondary School

◎ Education/Training Required: Bachelor's degree

◎ Annual Earnings: $45,920

◎ Growth: 9.0%

◎ Annual Job Openings: 12,000

◎ Self-Employed: 0%

◎ Part-Time: 8.8%

Teach or instruct vocational or occupational subjects at the secondary school level. Prepare materials and classroom for class activities. Maintain accurate and complete student records as required by law, district policy, and administrative regulations. Instruct students individually and in groups, using various teaching methods such as lectures, discussions, and demonstrations. Establish and enforce rules for behavior and procedures for maintaining order among the students for whom they are responsible. Observe and evaluate students' performance, behavior, social development, and physical health. Instruct and monitor students in the use and care of equipment and materials in order to prevent injury and damage. Plan and conduct activities for a balanced program of instruction, demonstration, and work time that provides students with opportunities to observe, question, and investigate. Prepare, administer, and grade tests and assignments in order to evaluate students' progress. Enforce all administration policies and rules governing students. Assign and grade class work and homework. Instruct students in the knowledge and skills required in a specific occupation or occupational field, using a systematic plan of lectures; discussions; audiovisual presentations; and laboratory, shop, and field studies. Establish clear objectives for all lessons, units, and projects and communicate those objectives to students. Use computers, audiovisual aids, and other equipment and materials to supplement presentations. Plan and supervise work-experience programs in businesses, industrial shops, and school laboratories. Prepare students for later grades by encouraging them to explore learning opportunities and to persevere with challenging tasks. Confer with parents or guardians, other teachers, counselors, and administrators in order to resolve students' behavioral and academic problems. Prepare objectives and outlines for courses of study, following curriculum guidelines or requirements of states and schools. Guide and counsel students with adjustment and/or academic problems or special academic interests. Select, order, store, issue, and inventory classroom equipment, materials, and supplies. **SKILLS—Instructing:** Teaching others how to do something. **Learning Strategies:** Selecting and using training/instructional methods and procedures appropriate for the situation when learning or teaching new things. **Social Perceptiveness:** Being aware of others' reactions and understanding why they react as they do. **Management of Financial Resources:** Determining how money will be spent to get the work done and accounting for these expenditures. **Persuasion:** Persuading others to change their minds or behavior. **Service Orientation:** Actively looking for ways to help people. **Time Management:** Managing one's own time and the time of others. **Management of Personnel Resources:** Motivating, developing, and directing people as they work, identifying the best people for the job. **GOE—Interest Area:** 05. Education and Training. **Work Group:** 05.02. Preschool, Elementary, and Secondary Teaching and Instructing. **Other Jobs in This Work Group:** Elementary School Teachers, Except Special Education; Kindergarten Teachers, Except Special Education; Middle School Teachers, Except Special and Vocational Education; Preschool Teachers, Except Special Education; Secondary School Teachers, Except Special and Vocational Education; Special Education Teachers, Middle School; Special

Education Teachers, Preschool, Kindergarten, and Elementary School; Special Education Teachers, Secondary School; Teacher Assistants; Vocational Education Teachers, Middle School. **PERSONALITY TYPE:** Social.

EDUCATION/TRAINING PROGRAM(S)—Technology Teacher Education/Industrial Arts Teacher Education. **RELATED KNOWLEDGE/COURSES**—**Education and Training:** Knowledge of principles and methods for curriculum and training design, teaching and instruction for individuals and groups, and the measurement of training effects. **Psychology:** Knowledge of human behavior and performance; individual differences in ability, personality, and interests; learning and motivation; psychological research methods; and the assessment and treatment of behavioral and affective disorders. **Clerical Practices:** Knowledge of administrative and clerical procedures and systems such as word processing, managing files and records, stenography and transcription, designing forms, and other office procedures and terminology. **Customer and Personal Service:** Knowledge of principles and processes for providing customer and personal services. This includes customer needs assessment, meeting quality standards for services, and evaluation of customer satisfaction. **Computers and Electronics:** Knowledge of circuit boards, processors, chips, electronic equipment, and computer hardware and software, including applications and programming. **Sociology and Anthropology:** Knowledge of group behavior and dynamics, societal trends and influences, human migrations, ethnicity, and cultures and their history and origins. **Therapy and Counseling:** Knowledge of principles, methods, and procedures for diagnosis, treatment, and rehabilitation of physical and mental dysfunctions and for career counseling and guidance.

Waiters and Waitresses

- ◎ Education/Training Required: Short-term on-the-job training
- ◎ Annual Earnings: $14,050
- ◎ Growth: 17.5%
- ◎ Annual Job Openings: 721,000
- ◎ Self-Employed: 0.3%
- ◎ Part-Time: 49.9%

Take orders and serve food and beverages to patrons at tables in dining establishment. Check patrons' identification in order to ensure that they meet minimum age requirements for consumption of alcoholic beverages. Collect payments from customers. Write patrons' food orders on order slips, memorize orders, or enter orders into computers for transmittal to kitchen staff. Take orders from patrons for food or beverages. Check with customers to ensure that they are enjoying their meals and take action to correct any problems. Serve food and/or beverages to patrons; prepare and serve specialty dishes at tables as required. Prepare checks that itemize and total meal costs and sales taxes. Remove dishes and glasses from tables or counters and take them to kitchen for cleaning. Present menus to patrons and answer questions about menu items, making recommendations upon request. Inform customers of daily specials. Clean tables and/or counters after patrons have finished dining. Prepare hot, cold, and mixed drinks for patrons and chill bottles of wine. Explain how various menu items are prepared, describing ingredients and cooking methods. Prepare tables for meals, including setting up items such as linens, silverware, and glassware. Perform food preparation duties such as preparing salads, appetizers, and cold dishes; portioning desserts; and brewing coffee. Stock service areas with supplies such as coffee, food, tableware, and linens. Garnish and decorate dishes in preparation for serving. Fill salt, pepper, sugar, cream, condiment, and napkin containers. Escort customers to their tables. Describe and recommend wines to customers. Bring wine selections to tables with appropriate glasses and pour the wines for customers. **SKILLS**—**Service Orientation:** Actively looking for ways to help people. **Persuasion:** Persuading others to change their minds or behavior. **Instructing:** Teaching others how to do something. **Social Perceptiveness:** Being aware of others' reactions and understanding why they react as they do. **Learning Strategies:** Selecting and using training/instructional methods and procedures appropriate for the situation when learning or teaching new things. **Negotiation:** Bringing others together and trying to reconcile differences. **Coordination:** Adjusting actions in relation to others' actions. **Speaking:** Talking to others to convey information effectively. **GOE—Interest Area:** 09. Hospitality, Tourism, and Recreation. **Work Group:** 09.05. Food and Beverage Service. **Other Jobs in This Work Group:** Bartenders; Combined Food Preparation and Serving Workers, Including Fast Food;

Counter Attendants, Cafeteria, Food Concession, and Coffee Shop; Dining Room and Cafeteria Attendants and Bartender Helpers; Food Servers, Nonrestaurant; Hosts and Hostesses, Restaurant, Lounge, and Coffee Shop. **PERSONALITY TYPE:** Social.

EDUCATION/TRAINING PROGRAM(S)—Food Service, Waiter/Waitress, and Dining Room Management/Manager. **RELATED KNOWLEDGE/ COURSES—Customer and Personal Service:** Knowledge of principles and processes for providing customer and personal services. This includes customer needs assessment, meeting quality standards for services, and evaluation of customer satisfaction. **Food Production:** Knowledge of techniques and equipment for planting, growing, and harvesting food products (both plant and animal) for consumption, including storage/handling techniques. **Sales and Marketing:** Knowledge of principles and methods for showing, promoting, and selling products or services. This includes marketing strategy and tactics, product demonstrations, sales techniques, and sales control systems. **Psychology:** Knowledge of human behavior and performance; individual differences in ability, personality, and interests; learning and motivation; psychological research methods; and the assessment and treatment of behavioral and affective disorders. **Education and Training:** Knowledge of principles and methods for curriculum and training design, teaching and instruction for individuals and groups, and the measurement of training effects. **Public Safety and Security:** Knowledge of relevant equipment, policies, procedures, and strategies to promote effective local, state, or national security operations for the protection of people, data, property, and institutions.

Water and Liquid Waste Treatment Plant and System Operators

◎ Education/Training Required: Long-term on-the-job training

◎ Annual Earnings: $34,960

◎ Growth: 16.0%

◎ Annual Job Openings: 9,000

◎ Self-Employed: 0%

◎ Part-Time: 1.2%

Operate or control an entire process or system of machines, often through the use of control boards, to transfer or treat water or liquid waste. Add chemicals, such as ammonia, chlorine, and lime, to disinfect and deodorize water and other liquids. Operate and adjust controls on equipment to purify and clarify water, process or dispose of sewage, and generate power. Inspect equipment and monitor operating conditions, meters, and gauges to determine load requirements and detect malfunctions. Collect and test water and sewage samples, using test equipment and color analysis standards. Record operational data, personnel attendance, and meter and gauge readings on specified forms. Maintain, repair, and lubricate equipment, using hand tools and power tools. Clean and maintain tanks and filter beds, using hand tools and power tools. Direct and coordinate plant workers engaged in routine operations and maintenance activities. **SKILLS— Operation Monitoring:** Watching gauges, dials, or other indicators to make sure a machine is working properly. **Installation:** Installing equipment, machines, wiring, or programs to meet specifications. **Operation and Control:** Controlling operations of equipment or systems. **Troubleshooting:** Determining causes of operating errors and deciding what to do about them. **Management of Material Resources:** Obtaining and seeing to the appropriate use of equipment, facilities, and materials needed to do certain work. **Management of Personnel Resources:** Motivating, developing, and directing people as they work, identifying the best people for the job. **Operations Analysis:** Analyzing needs and product requirements to create a design. **Equipment Maintenance:** Performing routine maintenance on equipment and determining when and what kind of maintenance is needed. **GOE—Interest Area:** 13. Manufacturing. **Work Group:** 13.16. Utility Operation and Energy Distribution. **Other Jobs in This Work Group:** Auxiliary Equipment Operators, Power; Boiler Operators and Tenders, Low Pressure; Chemical Plant and System Operators; Gas Compressor Operators; Gas Distribution Plant Operators; Gas Processing Plant Operators; Gas Pumping Station Operators; Gaugers; Nuclear Power Reactor Operators; Petroleum Pump System Operators; Petroleum Refinery and Control Panel Operators; Power Distributors and Dispatchers; Power Generating Plant Operators, Except Auxiliary Equipment Operators; Ship Engineers; Stationary Engineers. **PERSONALITY TYPE:** Realistic.

EDUCATION/TRAINING PROGRAM(S)— Water Quality and Wastewater Treatment Management and Recycling Technology/Technician. **RELAT-ED KNOWLEDGE/COURSES—Biology:** Knowledge of plant and animal organisms and their tissues, cells, functions, interdependencies, and interactions with each other and the environment. **Chemistry:** Knowledge of the chemical composition, structure, and properties of substances and of the chemical processes and transformations that they undergo. This includes uses of chemicals and their danger signs, production techniques, and disposal methods. **Physics:** Knowledge and prediction of physical principles and laws and their interrelationships and applications to understanding fluid, material, and atmospheric dynamics and mechanical, electrical, atomic, and sub-atomic structures and processes. **Public Safety and Security:** Knowledge of relevant equipment, policies, procedures, and strategies to promote effective local, state, or national security operations for the protection of people, data, property, and institutions. **Mathematics:** Knowledge of arithmetic, algebra, geometry, calculus, and statistics and their applications. **Law and Government:** Knowledge of laws, legal codes, court procedures, precedents, government regulations, executive orders, agency rules, and the democratic political process.

Weighers, Measurers, Checkers, and Samplers, Recordkeeping

- ◎ Education/Training Required: Short-term on-the-job training
- ◎ Annual Earnings: $24,570
- ◎ Growth: 14.6%
- ◎ Annual Job Openings: 16,000
- ◎ Self-Employed: 2.0%
- ◎ Part-Time: 12.9%

Weigh, measure, and check materials, supplies, and equipment for the purpose of keeping relevant records. Duties are primarily clerical by nature. Collect or prepare measurement, weight, or identification labels and attach them to products. Collect product samples and prepare them for laboratory analysis or testing. Compare product labels, tags, or tickets; shipping manifests; purchase orders; and bills of lading to verify accuracy of shipment contents, quality specifica-

tions, and/or weights. Count or estimate quantities of materials, parts, or products received or shipped. Document quantity, quality, type, weight, test result data, and value of materials or products in order to maintain shipping, receiving, and production records and files. Examine products or materials, parts, subassemblies, and packaging for damage, defects, or shortages, using specification sheets, gauges, and standards charts. Inspect products and examination records to determine the number of defects per worker and the reasons for examiners' rejections. Maintain financial records, such as accounts of daily collections and billings and records of receipts issued. Operate scalehouse computers to obtain weight information about incoming shipments such as those from waste haulers. Remove from stock products or loads not meeting quality standards and notify supervisors or appropriate departments of discrepancies or shortages. Weigh or measure materials, equipment, or products to maintain relevant records, using volume meters, scales, rules, and/or calipers. Communicate with customers and vendors to exchange information regarding products, materials, and services. Compute product totals and charges for shipments. Examine or prepare plans, layouts, or drawings of facilities or finished products to identify storage locations or to verify parts assemblies. Maintain, monitor, and clean work areas, such as recycling collection sites, drop boxes, counters and windows, and areas around scale houses. Prepare measurement tables and conversion charts, using standard formulas. Signal or instruct other workers to weigh, move, or check products. Sort products or materials into predetermined sequences or groupings for display, packing, shipping, or storage. Store samples of finished products in labeled cartons and record their location. **SKILLS—Operation and Control:** Controlling operations of equipment or systems. **Operation Monitoring:** Watching gauges, dials, or other indicators to make sure a machine is working properly. **GOE— Interest Area:** 04. Business and Administration. **Work Group:** 04.07. Records and Materials Processing. **Other Jobs in This Work Group:** Correspondence Clerks; File Clerks; Human Resources Assistants, Except Payroll and Timekeeping; Mail Clerks, Except Mail Machine Operators and Postal Service; Marking Clerks; Meter Readers, Utilities; Office Clerks, General; Order Fillers, Wholesale and Retail Sales; Postal Service Clerks; Postal Service Mail Sorters, Processors, and Processing Machine Operators; Procurement Clerks; Production, Planning, and Expediting Clerks;

Shipping, Receiving, and Traffic Clerks; Stock Clerks, Sales Floor; Stock Clerks—Stockroom, Warehouse, or Storage Yard. **PERSONALITY TYPE:** Conventional.

EDUCATION/TRAINING PROGRAM(S)—General Office Occupations and Clerical Services. **RELATED KNOWLEDGE/COURSES—Clerical Practices:** Knowledge of administrative and clerical procedures and systems such as word processing, managing files and records, stenography and transcription, designing forms, and other office procedures and terminology. **Design:** Knowledge of design techniques, tools, and principles involved in production of precision technical plans, blueprints, drawings, and models. **Transportation:** Knowledge of principles and methods for moving people or goods by air, rail, sea, or road, including the relative costs and benefits. **Production and Processing:** Knowledge of raw materials, production processes, quality control, costs, and other techniques for maximizing the effective manufacture and distribution of goods.

Welder-Fitters

- Education/Training Required: Long-term on-the-job training
- Annual Earnings: $30,620
- Growth: 17.0%
- Annual Job Openings: 71,000
- Self-Employed: 5.6%
- Part-Time: 2.1%

Lay out, fit, and fabricate metal components to assemble structural forms such as machinery frames, bridge parts, and pressure vessels, using knowledge of welding techniques, metallurgy, and engineering requirements. Includes experimental welders who analyze engineering drawings and specifications to plan welding operations where procedural information is unavailable. Lays out, positions, and secures parts and assemblies according to specifications, using straightedge, combination square, calipers, and ruler. Tack-welds or welds components and assemblies, using electric, gas, arc, or other welding equipment. Cuts workpiece, using powered saws, hand shears, or chipping knife. Melts lead bar, wire, or scrap to add lead to joint or to extrude melted scrap into reusable form. Installs or repairs equipment such as lead pipes, valves, floors, and tank linings. Observes tests on welded sur-faces, such as hydrostatic, X-ray, and dimension tolerance, to evaluate weld quality and conformance to specifications. Inspects grooves, angles, or gap allowances, using micrometer, caliper, and precision measuring instruments. Removes rough spots from workpiece, using portable grinder, hand file, or scraper. Welds components in flat, vertical, or overhead positions. Heats, forms, and dresses metal parts, using hand tools, torch, or arc-welding equipment. Ignites torch and adjusts valves, amperage, or voltage to obtain desired flame or arc. Analyzes engineering drawings and specifications to plan layout, assembly, and welding operations. Develops templates and other work aids to hold and align parts. Determines required equipment and welding method, applying knowledge of metallurgy, geometry, and welding techniques. **SKILLS—Repairing:** Repairing machines or systems by using the needed tools. **Installation:** Installing equipment, machines, wiring, or programs to meet specifications. **Equipment Maintenance:** Performing routine maintenance on equipment and determining when and what kind of maintenance is needed. **Equipment Selection:** Determining the kind of tools and equipment needed to do a job. **Quality Control Analysis:** Conducting tests and inspections of products, services, or processes to evaluate quality or performance. **Mathematics:** Using mathematics to solve problems. **Operation Monitoring:** Watching gauges, dials, or other indicators to make sure a machine is working properly. **GOE—Interest Area:** 13. Manufacturing. **Work Group:** 13.04. Welding, Brazing, and Soldering. **Other Jobs in This Work Group:** Brazers; Fitters, Structural Metal—Precision; Metal Fabricators, Structural Metal Products; Solderers; Soldering and Brazing Machine Operators and Tenders; Welders and Cutters; Welders, Production; Welding Machine Operators and Tenders; Welding Machine Setters and Set-Up Operators. **PERSONALITY TYPE:** Realistic.

EDUCATION/TRAINING PROGRAM(S)—Welding Technology/Welder. **RELATED KNOWLEDGE/COURSES—Design:** Knowledge of design techniques, tools, and principles involved in production of precision technical plans, blueprints, drawings, and models. **Building and Construction:** Knowledge of the materials, methods, and tools involved in the construction or repair of houses, buildings, or other structures such as highways and roads. **Mechanical Devices:** Knowledge of machines and tools, including their designs, uses, repair, and maintenance. **Production and Processing:** Knowledge of raw materials, production processes, quality control, costs, and other techniques for maximizing the effective manufacture and distribution of goods. **Engineering and Technology:** Knowledge of the practical application of engineering science and technology. This includes applying principles, techniques, procedures, and equipment to the design and production of various goods and services. **Physics:** Knowledge and prediction of physical principles and laws and their interrelationships and applications to understanding fluid, material, and atmospheric dynamics and mechanical, electrical, atomic, and subatomic structures and processes.

Welders and Cutters

- ◎ Education/Training Required: Long-term on-the-job training
- ◎ Annual Earnings: $30,620
- ◎ Growth: 17.0%
- ◎ Annual Job Openings: 71,000
- ◎ Self-Employed: 5.6%
- ◎ Part-Time: 2.1%

Use hand-welding and flame-cutting equipment to weld together metal components and parts or to cut, trim, or scarf metal objects to dimensions as specified by layouts, work orders, or blueprints. Welds metal parts or components together, using brazing, gas, or arc-welding equipment. Repairs broken or cracked parts, fills holes, and increases size of metal parts, using welding equipment. Welds in flat, horizontal, vertical, or overhead position. Cleans or degreases parts, using wire brush, portable grinder, or chemical bath. Inspects finished workpiece for conformance to specifications. Chips or grinds off excess weld, slag, or spatter, using hand scraper or power chipper, portable grinder, or arc-cutting equipment. Positions workpieces and clamps together or assembles in jigs or fixtures. Preheats workpiece, using hand torch or heating furnace. Ignites torch or starts power supply and strikes arc. Reviews layouts, blueprints, diagrams, or work orders in preparation for welding or cutting metal components. Selects and inserts electrode or gas nozzle into holder and connects hoses and cables to obtain gas or specified amperage, voltage, or polarity. Connects and turns regulator valves to activate and adjust gas flow and pressure to obtain desired flame. Selects and installs torch, torch tip, filler rod, and flux according to

welding chart specifications or type and thickness of metal. Guides electrodes or torch along weld line at specified speed and angle to weld, melt, cut, or trim metal. **SKILLS—Operation Monitoring:** Watching gauges, dials, or other indicators to make sure a machine is working properly. **Repairing:** Repairing machines or systems by using the needed tools. **Operation and Control:** Controlling operations of equipment or systems. **Equipment Maintenance:** Performing routine maintenance on equipment and determining when and what kind of maintenance is needed. **Installation:** Installing equipment, machines, wiring, or programs to meet specifications. **Quality Control Analysis:** Conducting tests and inspections of products, services, or processes to evaluate quality or performance. **GOE—Interest Area:** 13. Manufacturing. **Work Group:** 13.04. Welding, Brazing, and Soldering. **Other Jobs in This Work Group:** Brazers; Fitters, Structural Metal—Precision; Metal Fabricators, Structural Metal Products; Solderers; Soldering and Brazing Machine Operators and Tenders; Welder-Fitters; Welders, Production; Welding Machine Operators and Tenders; Welding Machine Setters and Set-Up Operators. **PERSONALITY TYPE:** Realistic.

EDUCATION/TRAINING PROGRAM(S)— Welding Technology/Welder. **RELATED KNOWLEDGE/COURSES—Building and Construction:** Knowledge of the materials, methods, and tools involved in the construction or repair of houses, buildings, or other structures such as highways and roads. **Mechanical Devices:** Knowledge of machines and tools, including their designs, uses, repair, and maintenance. **Design:** Knowledge of design techniques, tools, and principles involved in production of precision technical plans, blueprints, drawings, and models. **Production and Processing:** Knowledge of raw materials, production processes, quality control, costs, and other techniques for maximizing the effective manufacture and distribution of goods. **Physics:** Knowledge and prediction of physical principles and laws and their interrelationships and applications to understanding fluid, material, and atmospheric dynamics and mechanical, electrical, atomic, and subatomic structures and processes. **Chemistry:** Knowledge of the chemical composition, structure, and properties of substances and of the chemical processes and transformations that they undergo. This includes uses of chemicals and their danger signs, production techniques, and disposal methods.

Welders, Production

- Education/Training Required: Short-term on-the-job training
- Annual Earnings: $30,620
- Growth: 17.0%
- Annual Job Openings: 71,000
- Self-Employed: 5.6%
- Part-Time: 2.1%

Assemble and weld metal parts on production line, using welding equipment requiring only a limited knowledge of welding techniques. Welds or tack-welds metal parts together, using spot-welding gun or hand, electric, or gas welding equipment. Connects hoses from torch to tanks of oxygen and fuel gas and turns valves to release mixture. Ignites torch and regulates flow of gas and air to obtain desired temperature, size, and color of flame. Preheats workpieces preparatory to welding or bending, using torch. Fills cavities or corrects malformation in lead parts and hammers out bulges and bends in metal workpieces. Examines workpiece for defects and measures workpiece with straightedge or template to ensure conformance with specifications. Climbs ladders or works on scaffolds to disassemble structures. Signals crane operator to move large workpieces. Dismantles metal assemblies or cuts scrap metal, using thermal-cutting equipment such as flame-cutting torch or plasma-arc equipment. Positions and secures workpiece, using hoist, crane, wire and banding machine, or hand tools. Selects, positions, and secures torch, cutting tips, or welding rod according to type, thickness, area, and desired temperature of metal. Guides and directs flame or electrodes on or across workpiece to straighten, bend, melt, or build up metal. Fuses parts together, seals tension points, and adds metal to build up parts. **SKILLS—Operation Monitoring:** Watching gauges, dials, or other indicators to make sure a machine is working properly. **Operation and Control:** Controlling operations of equipment or systems. **Equipment Maintenance:** Performing routine maintenance on equipment and determining when and what kind of maintenance is needed. **Repairing:** Repairing machines or systems by using the needed tools. **Troubleshooting:** Determining causes of operating errors and deciding what to do about them. **Installation:** Installing equipment, machines, wiring, or programs to meet specifications. **Quality Control Analysis:** Conducting tests and inspections of products, services, or processes to evaluate quality or performance. **GOE—Interest Area:** 13. Manufacturing. **Work Group:** 13.04. Welding, Brazing, and Soldering. **Other Jobs in This Work Group:** Brazers; Fitters, Structural Metal—Precision; Metal Fabricators, Structural Metal Products; Solderers; Soldering and Brazing Machine Operators and Tenders; Welder-Fitters; Welders and Cutters; Welding Machine Operators and Tenders; Welding Machine Setters and Set-Up Operators. **PERSONALITY TYPE:** Realistic.

EDUCATION/TRAINING PROGRAM(S)— Welding Technology/Welder. **RELATED KNOWLEDGE/COURSES—Mechanical Devices:** Knowledge of machines and tools, including their designs, uses, repair, and maintenance. **Production and Processing:** Knowledge of raw materials, production processes, quality control, costs, and other techniques for maximizing the effective manufacture and distribution of goods. **Building and Construction:** Knowledge of the materials, methods, and tools involved in the construction or repair of houses, buildings, or other structures such as highways and roads. **Physics:** Knowledge and prediction of physical principles and laws and their interrelationships and applications to understanding fluid, material, and atmospheric dynamics and mechanical, electrical, atomic, and subatomic structures and processes.

Wholesale and Retail Buyers, Except Farm Products

- Education/Training Required: Bachelor's degree
- Annual Earnings: $42,230
- Growth: 4.3%
- Annual Job Openings: 24,000
- Self-Employed: 9.9%
- Part-Time: 18.1%

Buy merchandise or commodities, other than farm products, for resale to consumers at the wholesale or retail level, including both durable and nondurable goods. Analyze past buying trends, sales records, price, and quality of merchandise to determine value

and yield. Select, order, and authorize payment for merchandise according to contractual agreements. May conduct meetings with sales personnel and introduce new products. Examine, select, order, and purchase at the most favorable price merchandise consistent with quality, quantity, specification requirements, and other factors. Negotiate prices, discount terms, and transportation arrangements for merchandise. Analyze and monitor sales records, trends, and economic conditions to anticipate consumer buying patterns and determine what the company will sell and how much inventory is needed. Interview and work closely with vendors to obtain and develop desired products. Authorize payment of invoices or return of merchandise. Inspect merchandise or products to determine value or yield. Set or recommend mark-up rates, mark-down rates, and selling prices for merchandise. Confer with sales and purchasing personnel to obtain information about customer needs and preferences. Consult with store or merchandise managers about budget and goods to be purchased. Conduct staff meetings with sales personnel to introduce new merchandise. Manage the department for which they buy. Use computers to organize and locate inventory and operate spreadsheet and word-processing software. Train and supervise sales and clerical staff. Provide clerks with information to print on price tags, such as price, mark-ups or mark-downs, manufacturer number, season code, and style number. Determine which products should be featured in advertising, the advertising medium to be used, and when the ads should be run. Monitor competitors' sales activities by following their advertisements in newspapers and other media. **SKILLS—Management of Financial Resources:** Determining how money will be spent to get the work done and accounting for these expenditures. **Management of Material Resources:** Obtaining and seeing to the appropriate use of equipment, facilities, and materials needed to do certain work. **Negotiation:** Bringing others together and trying to reconcile differences. **Service Orientation:** Actively looking for ways to help people. **Management of Personnel Resources:** Motivating, developing, and directing people as they work, identifying the best people for the job. **Learning Strategies:** Selecting and using training/instructional methods and procedures appropriate for the situation when learning or teaching new things. **Instructing:** Teaching others how to do something. **Operations Analysis:** Analyzing needs and product requirements to create a design. **GOE—Interest Area:** 14. Retail and Wholesale Sales and Service. **Work Group:** 14.05. Purchasing. **Other Jobs in This Work Group:** Purchasing Agents, Except Wholesale, Retail, and Farm Products. **PERSONALITY TYPE:** Enterprising.

EDUCATION/TRAINING PROGRAM(S)— Apparel and Accessories Marketing Operations; Apparel and Textile Marketing Management; Fashion Merchandising; Merchandising and Buying Operations; Sales, Distribution, and Marketing Operations, General. **RELATED KNOWLEDGE/COURSES— Sales and Marketing:** Knowledge of principles and methods for showing, promoting, and selling products or services. This includes marketing strategy and tactics, product demonstrations, sales techniques, and sales control systems. **Customer and Personal Service:** Knowledge of principles and processes for providing customer and personal services. This includes customer needs assessment, meeting quality standards for services, and evaluation of customer satisfaction. **Clerical Practices:** Knowledge of administrative and clerical procedures and systems such as word processing, managing files and records, stenography and transcription, designing forms, and other office procedures and terminology. **Economics and Accounting:** Knowledge of economic and accounting principles and practices, the financial markets, banking, and the analysis and reporting of financial data. **Administration and Management:** Knowledge of business and management principles involved in strategic planning, resource allocation, human resources modeling, leadership technique, production methods, and coordination of people and resources. **Mathematics:** Knowledge of arithmetic, algebra, geometry, calculus, and statistics and their applications.

Index

D

J–K

L

M

N

O

R

S

T

U–V

W–Z